Professional Java E-Commerce

Subrahmanyam Allamaraju
Ronald Ashri
Chád Darby
Robert Flenner
Tracie Karsjens
Mark Kerzner
Alex Krotov
Alex Linde
Jim MacIntosh
James McGovern
Thor Mirchandani
Bryan Plaster
Don Reamy
Dr P G Sarang
Dave Writz

Wrox Press Ltd. ®

Professional Java E-Commerce

© 2001 Wrox Press

All rights reserved. No part of this book may be reproduced, stored in a retrieval system, or transmitted in any form or by any means, without the prior written permission of the publisher, except in the case of brief quotations embodied in critical articles or reviews.

The author and publisher have made every effort in the preparation of this book to ensure the accuracy of the information. However, the information contained in this book is sold without warranty, either express or implied. Neither the authors, Wrox Press nor its dealers or distributors will be held liable for any damages caused or alleged to be caused either directly or indirectly by this book.

First Printed February, 2001

Published by Wrox Press Ltd,
Arden House, 1102 Warwick Road, Acocks Green,
Birmingham, B27 6BH, UK
Printed in Canada
ISBN 1-861004-81-8

Trademark Acknowledgements

Wrox has endeavored to provide trademark information about all the companies and products mentioned in this book by the appropriate use of capitals. However, Wrox cannot guarantee the accuracy of this information.

Credits

Authors
Subrahmanyam Allamaraju
Ronald Ashri
Chád Darby
Robert Flenner
Tracie Karsjens
Mark Kerzner
Alex Krotov
Alex Linde
Jim MacIntosh
James McGovern
Thor Mirchandani
Bryan Plaster
Don Reamy
Dr P G Sarang
Dave Writz

Specification
Andrew Longshaw

Category Manager
Paul Cooper

Technical Architect
Ian Blackham

Technical Editors
Helen Callaghan
Allan Jones
Robert FE Shaw
Andrew Tracey
Mark Waterhouse

Author Agent
Emma Batch

Project Manager
Chandima Nethisinghe

Proofreader
Fiona Berryman

Technical Reviewers
Danny Ayers
Craig A. Berry
Jaeda Goodman
Rahul Gupta
Andrew Harbourne-Thomas
Norman Hensley
David Hudson
Dan Kirkpatrick
Meeraj Kunnumpurath
Hang Lau
Edward Lee
Alex Linde
Jim MacIntosh
Glenn Mitchell
Stephan Osmont
Steve Parker
David Schultz
Keyur Shah
Mike Shakesheave
Graham Tilbury
Tommy Wan
Andrew Watt
John Zukowski

Production Project Coordinator
Pip Wonson

Cover Design
Shelley Frazier

Production Manager
Simon Hardware

Figures
Shabnam Hussain

Additional Figures
Pip Wonson

Index
Adrian Axinte

About the Authors

Subrahmanyam Allamaraju

Subrahmanyam is a Senior Engineer with BEA Systems. His interest in modeling led him from his Ph.D. in Electrical Engineering to object-oriented programming, and then to distributed computing and software architecture. In this process, he drifted from his one-time home - the Indian Institute of Technology, to Computervision, and Wipro Infotech, and later to BEA Systems. You can find more about his current activities at his home http://www.Subrahmanyam.com.

Subrahmanyam would like to thank Varaa for her hand in code samples (in the face of tight deadlines), and sharing his frustration as well as exhilaration.

Ronald Ashri

Ronald Ashri is a postgraduate researcher at the University of Southampton, working in the "Intelligence, Agents and Multimedia" group that is part of the Department of Electronics and Computer Science. His research is focused on infrastructures for agents in heterogeneous network environments, which range from the typical PC to Palm-style devices and mobile phones. This work is jointly funded by British Telecom and the University of Southampton. Other interests include the use of Jini network technology for the support of agent-based systems.

Earlier, Ronald worked for a short period at Adastral Park, BT's research center, focusing on security issues for mobile agents. He graduated from Warwick University with a First Class Honours degree in Computer Systems Engineering.

Many thanks to the great Wrox team for all the hard work they've put into making this book a reality. Special thanks to Katia, Andreas, Photini, Daniel, Carla, and Titta.

Chád Darby

Chád Darby is the founder of J9 Consulting, a Java consulting firm. He has experience developing n-tier web applications for Fortune 500 companies and the Department of Defense. Chád has published articles in Java Report, Java Developer's Journal, and Web Techniques. He has also been an invited speaker at conferences including SD West 99, XML DevCon 2000, and JavaCon 2000.

Chád recently gave a presentation on WAP and XML in Sydney, Australia. In between consulting and writing projects, he teaches Java courses for Learning Tree International. Chád is a Sun certified Java developer and holds a B.S. in Computer Science from Carnegie Mellon University.

Robert Flenner

Robert Flenner is an active author, independent contractor, and software developer. He has been involved in defining and designing E-Commerce systems for large enterprises. He has successfully coordinated application architecture strategies and led projects utilizing local and well as geographically dispersed development teams. He has extensive experience consulting with global companies on both strategic and tactical IT development and deployment. His technical consulting experience includes Web, CORBA, distributed object modeling, workflow, and high availability transaction processing. He is currently promoting and developing a framework for distributed development and collaboration. He can be contacted at rflenner@metronet.com.

Tracie Karsjens

Tracie Karsjens is a Minneapolis-based consultant working primarily in web based applications. She has been working with Java since 1996 and her experience covers every tier of enterprise Java applications. Tracie is a strong advocate for lightweight methodologies and techniques such as refactoring and unit testing.

Tracie wishes to thank the colleagues who have provided valuable lessons helpful while working on this book, particularly Jim, Brian and Mike. As always, Tracie also wishes to express her appreciation to her parents and her husband Timothy without whom the work on this book would not have been possible.

Mark Kerzner

Mark Kerzner has degrees in Math and in Computer Science, and 20 years of software development experience. He likes taking all available exams, so by now he has Microsoft, Java, and Weblogic certifications. He loves learning languages, both computer and human. He can be reached at kerzner@shmsoft.com.

Alex Krotov

Alex Krotov just defended his PhD at the University of Sheffield, UK in Computational Linguistics. He now lives in Portland, Oregon and works for the Center for Human-Computer Communication at Oregon Graduate Institute. His research interests include Natural Language Processing, and, in particular, language parsing and statistical NLP.

He was involved in developing CONVERSE, a 'talking computer', which won the Loebner Contest in New York in 1997.

Alex is also interested in Eastern Philosophy, and is actively practicing yoga and Zen Buddhism.

Alex Linde

Alex has been worked as a consultant and professional developer in the Internet field for over 5 years. His experience ranges from designing large-scale Internet hosting solutions, to lead developer for the Psion Series 3 Internet browser. Initially a C/C++ programmer, he moved to CGI and ISAPI, then on to COM and ASP as the technology advanced. He has been working with Java since 1996, and recently architected a major portal system using J2EE.

Alex is currently responsible for strategy at magic4 (http://www.magic4.com) who have developed an embedded multimedia client for mobile messaging.

Alex lives in the north of England with wife Christina and two boys Peter & Diarmuid. In his meagre free time, he enjoys playing bass guitar badly.

Jim MacIntosh

For 30 years Jim MacIntosh worked as a journalist, primarily as a radio reporter and newscast lineup editor. Workplace cutbacks sent him back to school, to become a Sun Certified Java Programmer, and to whet his appetite for all things IT. He created his own consulting company, MacIntosh Technical, and spent most of the past year working as a writer, reviewer and instructor of Java related technologies. He lives in the suburban town of Quispamsis, New Brunswick (Canada, not New Jersey!) with his wife Judy (love ya, Gorgeous) and two grown-up brats.

James McGovern

James McGovern is an industry recognized technologist focused on strategy and architecture for high-profile e-Business web sites. He has worked on sites such as wingspanbank.com, lowestloan.com and Carbonek Financial Services. He serves as a member of the board of advisors for several emerging dot-coms.

He would like to thank his wife Sherry, James & Mattie McGovern, Sylvester James, and Soogia Rattan for their support and encouragement.

His interests include mountain biking, paintball, lasertag, and watching martial arts movies. He attended Charter Oak State College. He is a frequent speaker at key technology forums and conferences throughout the United States. He holds industry certifications from Sun, Microsoft, and Cisco. He can be reached at mcgovern@cyberservices.com.

Thor Mirchandani

Thor grew up in Sweden, where he studied medicine, electronic engineering, programming, and philosophy at the University of Uppsala. After graduation, he embarked on a short career in surgery, then returned to his first love, computers, switching careers to software development. Thor specializes in distributed and multi-tier architectures for commerce and manufacturing, preferably using Java and C/C++. He has about fifteen years experience in the field, mostly as a consultant. Thor is presently working as Director of E-Commerce and Emerging Technologies for Technisource, Inc., a Fort Lauderdale, and Florida based consulting and outsourcing company. He lives in Winston-Salem, North Carolina, where he raises four boys (and their numerous pets). Thor's interests include literature, classical music, and reviving old, dilapidated Italian sports cars.

For Viktor, Indy, Patrick and Seth – my VIPS

Bryan Plaster

Bryan is an avid developer and software enthusiast who thrives on new technologies and engineering feats, whatever they may be. He also enjoys writing regularly for private and on-line publications. Bryan currently resides in McKinney, Texas with his lovely wife Jeanie.

Don Reamy

Don Reamy is the Chief Technology Officer at ibexONE (www.ibexone.com). He has been developing commercial software for 15 years and developing in Java since 1996. Don has also been working on a open source Java compiler he plans to release in the near future. His other interested include being an avid musician and playing his Paul Reed Smith guitar. Don can be reached at don@reamey.com or dreamey@ibexone.com.

I would like to thank my wife Julie for being a great stay at home mom for my son Jordan.

Dr P G Sarang

A contractor to Sun Microsystems, Dr. Poornachandra Sarang trains Sun's corporate clients on various courses from their official curriculum. He also conducts "Train The Trainers" program and "Instructor Authorization Tests" on behalf of Sun. As CEO of ABCOM Information Systems Pvt. Ltd., Dr. Sarang specializes in training and project development on the Java/CORBA platform. With almost 20 years of industry experience, Dr. Sarang has developed a number of products and successfully completed various industry projects. He is a regular speaker in national and international conferences and regularly contributes technical articles to reputed international journals and magazines.

Dave Writz

Dave Writz is a principal and co-founder of Cornerstone Consulting, a Milwaukee, Wisconsin based service organization specializing in building distributed applications. Dave is responsible for the management of the consulting staff and their projects. Under his guidance Cornerstone has recently been named to Milwaukee's Future 50. This prestigious award recognizes entrepreneurial companies poised for success in the Milwaukee area.

Throughout his career, Dave has concentrated building software solutions using object-oriented analysis, design, and programming techniques. He has lead teams responsible for defining Internet and Intranet strategies, then evaluating, selecting, and introducing new technologies including Java, XML/XSL, CORBA, EJB, and other advanced technologies. While serving as a mentor, architect, and developer Dave has been able to help Fortune 1000 as well as emerging companies utilize information technology as a competitive advantage.

Dave would like to thank the Cornerstone team for their hard work and dedication and "daddy's girls" Katie, Rachel, and Julie whose love and support inspire and motivate everything he does.

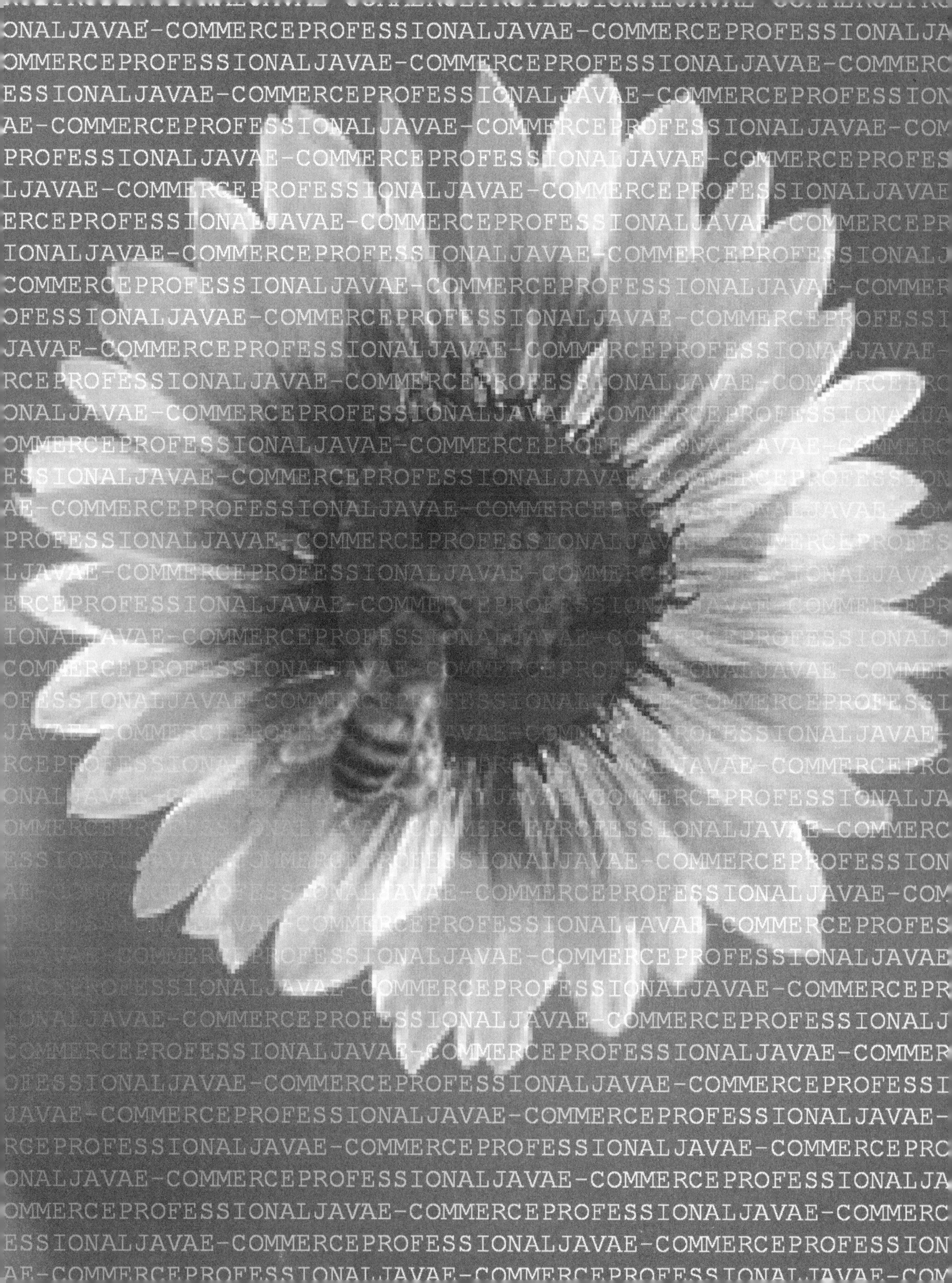

Table of Contents

Table of Contents

Table of Contents

Table of Contents

Table of Contents

Table of Contents

Table of Contents

Table of Contents

Table of Contents

Introduction

The explosion in the use of the Internet has made participation in e-commerce a reality for individuals, and small organizations, as well as revolutionizing the manner in which larger organizations (who have been involved with electronic transactions for much longer) can conduct their business.

The phrase e-commerce encompasses a multitude of different transactions or business interactions. Some individuals may see e-commerce as a simple business to consumer relationship where physical goods are purchased from the desktop. Others may see the potential of buying services (such as information feeds) and selling to other individuals, while organizations can use the ubiquity of the Web to work with each other to build more efficient, low cost integrated supply chains. Of course device development means that e-commerce isn't restricted to desk bound monitors – televisions, mobile phones, hand-held devices, and even smart cards, are beginning to offer methods of taking part in commercial transactions, wherever you are physically.

This aim of this book is to show how the Java platform and Java technologies can be leveraged to build solutions that will address the diversity of interactions that fall within the one general domain. Our approach has been to break the topic down into discrete sections that deal with:

- ❑ The business landscape surrounding e-commerce
- ❑ The underlying principles of designing effective Java based e-commerce solutions
- ❑ Developing e-commerce sites that involve the individual consumer
- ❑ Developing e-commerce solutions that enable businesses to work together
- ❑ Utilizing the latest technologies in solutions that will enable the consumer on the move to take part in e-commerce

Within this framework, we illustrate how to build your own solutions using code samples contained within the book and available for download from www.wrox.com. Additionally, there are a number of *In the Marketplace* chapters where developers pass on their hints, tips, and experiences of building real world solutions.

Who is this Book For?

This book is aimed at providing professional Java developers and programmers with the information required to make decisions about what approach to take in the development of e-commerce solutions, and how to implement those decisions.

As the book is specifically focused on delivering material to address issues in the problem domain of e-commerce, we are not setting out to teach particular aspects of technology, but to show how Java technologies can be applied. Thus, the book is positioned above *Professional Java Server Programming – J2EE Edition (ISBN 1-861004-65-6)* in the Wrox Java tree, and readers are expected to have a good grasp of both the core Java language and APIs, and J2EE technologies.

What's Covered in this Book

Our first section – **The E-Commerce Landscape** – contains **Chapters 1 to 3** by Tracie Karsjens, that start by providing a business context for e-commerce and introducing some general concepts. They move on to looking at the requirements that successful e-commerce solutions need to meet, before finishing with a discussion of the project planning aspects of application development.

The second section – **Architecting Java Based E-Commerce Systems** – looks at the types of technological issues that need to be addressed in this problem domain and the Java technologies we can employ. Three chapters by Subrahmanyam Allamaraju investigate various aspects of designing and utilizing Java e-commerce applications: **Chapter 4** discusses the application and technical requirements for e-commerce systems, **Chapter 5** provides an overview of the attributes of the Java platform, and more specifically J2EE technology, and **Chapter 6** looks at the different architectural styles that can be used to address the needs of various applications.

From there we move on to Chád Darby's **Chapter 7** on data transfer and transformation, where XML and XSLT are highlighted (for those not familiar with the topics Jim MacIntosh has written a couple of primers on XML and XSLT in **Appendices A** and **B** respectively). To finish the section, in **Chapter 8** Don Reamey writes about Java security and security in an e-commerce setting.

After these first scene-setting blocks, we set to work and start building solutions. **B2C E-Commerce Solutions** is a section dealing with the most publicly well known (and hyped) aspect of e-commerce, where individual consumers conduct transactions with trading organizations. In **Chapters 9 to 12**, Dr. Poornachandra Sarang takes us all the way through building a simple B2C site that allows a customer to buy a configured computer on-line. Starting with the basic functionality of a site – a home page, catalog, shopping cart, and checkout – these chapters build and refine the site until in the fourth chapter we look at using EJBs to enable the site to scale.

Following on from this we have our first *In the Marketplace* chapter (**Chapter 13**) where Mark Kerzner and Alex Krotov describe the trials and tribulations of developing a B2C site for a retailer of luxury goods, using BEA WebLogic and TheoryCenter components. Our next two chapters look at the topic of portal sites; in **Chapter 14**, Bryan Plaster reviews the basic principles of such sites illustrating it with sample code, while in **Chapter 15**, in the second of our *In the Marketplace* chapters, Alex Linde talks about the customizable portal architecture he's been involved in building for magic4.

Bob Flenner opens up the fourth section, on **B2B E-Commerce Solutions**, with three chapters on developing a general approach and an illustrative application to integrating business applications. **Chapter 16** reviews the basic issues of developing B2B applications , while in **Chapter 17** we look at integrating supply chains. In **Chapter 18** we look at effectively using XSL in the supply chain, and we round off the example in **Chapter 19** when the issues of mass integration are discussed. The supply chain theme is picked up in **Chapter 20**, where Dave Writz uses an *In the Marketplace* chapter to describe an intriguing real-world example of the huge labor savings that can be made by using XML and XSLT. This is followed by a couple of chapters by Bryan Plaster – application service providers are discussed in **Chapter 21** with an illustration of integrating workflow being provided in **Chapter 22**. In our final visit to the *Marketplace* in **Chapter 23**, Thor Mirchandani takes us into the world of corporate purchasing and advances some personal experiences of problem solving and e-commerce project methodology.

Our last section, on **M-Commerce**, has two chapters looking at aspects of mobile e-commerce. In **Chapter 24** Ronald Ashri gives an extensive overview of developing technologies with the aim of giving readers a head start in this area, while in **Chapter 25** Bryan Plaster gives us a quick insight into Java technology in the pocket, when he describes how to program smart cards.

What You Need to Use this Book

Clear details of the software needed for a particular sample application are included in each chapter, but you will basically need the Java 2 Platform, Standard Edition SDK (JDK 1.3) and the Java 2 Platform, Enterprise Edition SDK 1.2.1 Reference Implementation to use the book.

The following additional software also plays a major role in the book (note this list isn't exhaustive as many other items of software are alluded to at various points):

Web Container for B2B application

- ❏ Allaire's JRun 3.0, http://commerce.allaire.com/download/

Database for B2C application

- ❏ Cloudscape (an in-process version comes with the J2EE RI), http://www.cloudscape.com

Additional Software

- ❏ The Java API for XML Parsing (JAXP) 1.1 early access, http://java.sun.com/xml/
- ❏ Xalan XSLT Processor and Xerces XML Parser, http://xml.apache.org
- ❏ Java Secure Sockets Extension (JSSE), 1.0.1, http://java.sun.com/products/jsse/
- ❏ Sun's J2ME Wireless Toolkit, http://www.java.sun.com/products/j2mewtoolkit/

The code in the book will work on a single machine, provided it is networked (that is, it can see http://localhost through the local browser).

The complete source code from the book is available for download from:

http://www.wrox.com

Conventions

To help you get the most from the text and keep track of what's happening, we've used a number of conventions throughout the book.

For instance:

> **These boxes hold important, not-to-be forgotten information which is directly relevant to the surrounding text.**

While the background style is used for asides to the current discussion.

As for styles in the text:

- ❑ When we introduce them, we **highlight** important words.
- ❑ We show keyboard strokes like this: *Ctrl-A*.
- ❑ We show filenames and code within the text like so: doGet().
- ❑ Text on user interfaces and URLs are shown as: Menu.

We present code in three different ways. Definitions of methods and properties are shown as follows:

```
protected void doGet(HttpServletRequest req, HttpServletResponse resp)
                throws ServletException, IOException
```

Example code is shown:

```
In our code examples, the code foreground style shows new, important,
    pertinent code
while code background shows code that's less important in the present context,
    or has been seen before.
```

Customer Support

We want to know what you think about this book: what you liked, what you didn't like, and what you think we can do better next time. You can send your comments, either by returning the reply card in the back of the book, or by e-mail (to feedback@wrox.com). Please be sure to mention the book title in your message.

Errata

We've made every effort to make sure that there are no errors in the text or the code. However, to err is human, and as such we recognize the need to keep you informed of any mistakes as they're spotted and corrected. Errata sheets are available for all our books at www.wrox.com. If you find an error that hasn't already been reported, please let us know.

E-mail Support

If you wish to directly query a problem in the book page with an expert who knows the book in detail then e-mail support@wrox.com, with the title of the book and the last four numbers of the ISBN in the subject field of the e-mail. A typical e-mail should include the following things:

- ❏ The **name, last four digits of the ISBN** and **page number** of the problem in the Subject field.

- ❏ Your **name**, **contact info** and the **problem** in the body of the message.

We *won't* send you junk mail. We need the details to save your time and ours. When you send an e-mail it will go through the following chain of support:

- ❏ Customer Support – Your message is delivered to one of our customer support staff who are the first people to read it. They have files on most frequently asked questions and will answer anything general immediately. They answer general questions about the book and the web site.

- ❏ Editorial – Deeper queries are forwarded to the technical editor responsible for that book. They have experience with the programming language or particular product and are able to answer detailed technical questions on the subject. Once an issue has been resolved, the editor can post the errata to the web site.

- ❏ The Authors – Finally, in the unlikely event that the editor can't answer your problem, they will forward the request to the author. We try to protect the author from any distractions from writing. However, we are quite happy to forward specific requests to them. All Wrox authors help with the support on their books. They'll mail the customer and the editor with their response, and again all readers should benefit.

P2P.WROX.COM

For author and peer support join the Java mailing lists. Our unique system provides **programmer to programmer™ support** on mailing lists, forums and newsgroups, all *in addition* to our one-to-one e-mail system. Be confident that your query is not just being examined by a support professional, but by the many Wrox authors and other industry experts present on our mailing lists. At p2p.wrox.com you'll find a number of different lists aimed at Java developers that will support you, not only while you read this book, but also as you develop your own applications. Particularly appropriate to this book is the Java E-Commerce list, but there are many other relevant ones covering topics like servlets, EJBs, and JSPs.

To enroll for support just follow this four-step system:

1. Go to p2p.wrox.com.

2. Click on the Java button.

3. Click on the mailing list you wish to join.

4. Fill in your e-mail address and password (of at least 4 digits) and e-mail it to us.

Why this System Offers the Best Support

You can choose to join the mailing lists or you can receive them as a weekly digest. If you don't have the time, or facility, to receive the mailing list, then you can search our online archives. Junk and spam mails are deleted, and your own e-mail address is protected by the unique Lyris system. Any queries about joining or leaving lists, or any other queries about the list, should be sent to listsupport@p2p.wrox.com.

PROFESSIONALJAVAE-COMMERCE

Section 1

The E-Commerce Landscape

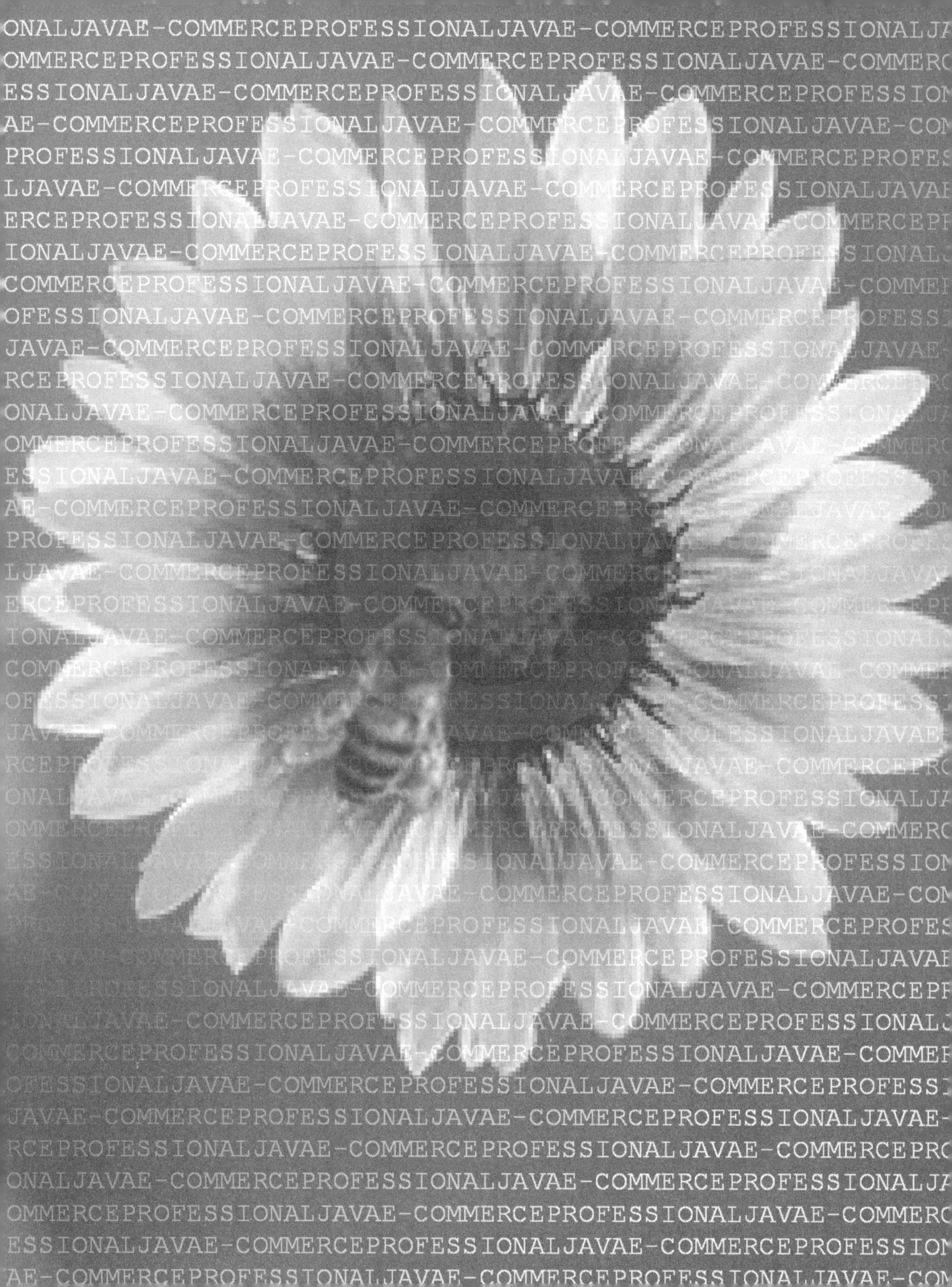

1

Defining E-Commerce

The evolution of the Internet is one of the most exciting technological advances in recent history. One of the most interesting aspects of this evolution is the emergence of electronic commerce (**e-commerce**) as a mainstream and viable alternative to more traditional methods of commerce. Commerce itself is a part of human civilization that dates back to the beginning of human production. It should be no surprise that, as the rapid rise of e-commerce shakes the very basic assumptions we hold about commerce, a great many people find themselves a little overwhelmed.

The challenges for technologists in the realm of e-commerce are particularly intriguing. Not only are we faced with changing technologies, but we are also faced with changes to the business models we have come to expect. Companies on the cutting edge of e-commerce are setting new trends and breaking new ground in creating new business models and using technology in increasingly innovative ways.

In this chapter, we'll discuss some of the fundamentals of e-commerce. It's important for all of the players in an e-commerce project to have a good idea of what e-commerce is about and how to approach some of the core concepts. As such, this chapter (and the other chapters in this section) will discuss:

- ❑ Where e-commerce comes from
- ❑ Where e-commerce is now and where it is going
- ❑ The fundamentals of developing appropriate strategies for this business environment
- ❑ The different manifestations of e-commerce and their unique characteristics
- ❑ How to gather the necessary requirements for an e-commerce application
- ❑ How to manage and plan an e-commerce initiative
- ❑ The role that Java plays in e-commerce applications
- ❑ Specific technologies, techniques and approaches that are useful when attempting an e-commerce initiative

However, before jumping deeply into the specifics of e-commerce implementation, it is still very important to understand the basic concepts of e-commerce and its role in the electronic business (**e-business**) landscape. By building on these core definitions, we will be better placed to understand the specific details of e-commerce applications.

Defining E-Commerce in the Shadow of E-Business

The definition of e-commerce is impossible without first discussing the concept of e-business.

> **E-business is defined as the process of using electronic technology to do business.**

Since e-business occurs anytime a company uses electronic technology in the course of conducting business, e-business can be anything from a sales pitch on a website to an electronic exchange of data.

Before we can begin e-business, we must realize that utilizing electronic technology effectively requires a fundamental re-examination of the way in which we do business. Many companies have chosen to embrace e-commerce because they feel that it is a way to improve efficiency, offer new and innovative services, and increase the quality of their business. While a lot of companies find success in e-business, many others find themselves ill prepared for the realities of e-business. In large part, companies that are successful in e-business recognize that this is a fundamentally different way of doing business, instead of being just a new tool to fit to old methods.

For example, if a carpenter has used a hand-held manual saw for many years, he would probably find a great increase in productivity if he were to toss aside his manual saw and purchase an electric power saw instead. However, if he did not recognize that this new tool requires a new way of using it, he would have little success. Imagine this carpenter trying to use an electric saw without plugging it in, but instead simply sawing manually back and forth as was his custom. This sounds ridiculous, but is a good example of the way many companies try to use the new tools of e-business using their old methods.

Just as the carpenter tried to use his new tool without learning a new technique, many companies try to bypass the important exercise of re-evaluating their business and instead jump directly into e-business initiatives. A successful e-business strategy must be integrated into all facets of an organization with ample discussion and thought given to planning for the future of the company in the face of e-business.

> **E-commerce can be defined as a subset of e-business, and is the subset of e-business that focuses specifically on commerce.**

Commerce is the exchange of goods and services for other goods and services or for some other form of payment. E-commerce is simply a company conducting commerce using electronic technology. Since commerce is a type of business and e-commerce is about conducting that business electronically, e-commerce is clearly a type of e-business. This implies that all the same keys to success for e-business also apply for e-commerce.

Success in the e-commerce arena requires a focus on e-business across the company as a whole. E-commerce can't be done in a vacuum in any sense of the word. In addition to requiring a comprehensive e-business strategy, e-commerce also requires input from a large portion of the company in order to be successful.

Developing an E-Business Strategy

Since successful e-commerce requires an e-business strategy, it is important to consider what that means. For some companies, particularly those formed in the wake of the Internet economy, there is little distinction between a business strategy and an e-business strategy. While the success of such Internet-focused companies has varied widely, there is something to be learned from this concept.

If a company has decided that the Internet and other types of electronic technology are a critical component to the success of the business, there should be little difference between a business strategy and an e-business strategy simply because e-business becomes the company's business. However, even if a company does not base their success or failure on e-business, there is still a necessity for a company determined to launch an e-business initiative to consider and plan their strategy for success in the e-business arena.

While the exact details of an e-business strategy are generally different from industry to industry and from company to company, there are a few very general questions every company should ask in framing an e-business strategy. These are important for the management of a company to understand, but it is also important for developers to understand these issues. If a company approaches a team, internal or external, with a request for an e-business solution, these questions must be addressed. If they are not addressed prior to the formation of a project team, the task of asking these questions falls to the team and perhaps even to the developers. In an ideal world, a team would not proceed until the basic strategy for e-business was in place.

Some important questions to consider are:

- ❏ What is our business strategy as a whole?
- ❏ Why do we want to do business electronically?
- ❏ What is the overall measure of success for this company?
- ❏ What are the results we want?
- ❏ How will we know that we have been successful?
- ❏ What parts of our business are best suited for the electronic world?
- ❏ What parts of our business are least suited for the electronic world?
- ❏ What new aspects of our business do we expect or hope to develop using this technology?

Obviously there is a lot more to a comprehensive e-business strategy than these few questions, but any company that cannot easily answer these questions is not prepared to attempt an e-commerce initiative. At times, this is an acceptable outcome. A company should not proceed with an e-business initiative simply because e-business is popular. Some companies simply do not have a business model that makes sense to include e-business.

If the company really does feel that e-business is the right move for their business, but is still unable to address the questions posed above, the company needs to re-evaluate their positions. The questions listed here are extremely high-level indicators of whether a company is aware of the reasons and goals of their e-business initiatives. A company that cannot answer these questions is not ready to provide the clear direction that an e-business initiative requires in order to be successful.

The Basics of E-Commerce

As previously defined, e-commerce is fundamentally about conducting commerce utilizing electronic technology. While that might sound like an obvious statement, in reality few people understand the true scope of e-commerce. We tend to think about e-commerce as limited to the Internet, and more specifically to the World Wide Web (often simply called the web). This type of thinking limits the scope of possibilities for what e-commerce is and can become. E-commerce can mean conducting commerce over the Internet, but it can also mean other forms of electronic communications.

In reality, the roots of e-commerce lie not in the Internet, but in other forms of electronic communication. Technologies like **Electronic Data Interchange** (**EDI**) and **Electronic Funds Transfer** (**EFT**) predate the emergence of e-commerce on the Internet. These older, high-powered technologies form the roots of the e-commerce we see today. For example, if credit card companies had not long ago effectively used technology to process the many transactions that they receive, we would not be able to have the proliferation of websites selling goods and services.

However, the important distinction between these older technologies and the emerging Internet-based e-commerce applications is that these older technologies were only designed to connect one business to one other business. In fact, the protocols themselves were biased toward point-to-point communication. The more recent advances in e-commerce tend to be more akin to e-markets and are based around a network-to-network model. This approach allows for a one-to-many or many-to-many approach to e-commerce, greatly expanding the potential reach of any single business.

It's ironic, considering the roots of e-commerce, that we tend to think of it as all about the Internet. Conducting commerce electronically may mean a web site selling books to consumers, but it can also mean a book distributor sending his order for books to the publisher using EDI. This book will discuss some of the more traditional uses of the Internet for e-commerce, as well as some of the still-emerging ways to conduct e-commerce (such as wireless communications).

The other core issue in understanding e-commerce is that e-commerce is not merely a focus on the electronic aspect of conducting commerce electronically. E-commerce, like e-business, requires a re-examination of the ways in which we use this new tool. What's interesting and exciting about commerce in the e-commerce age is that as the landscape (the platforms, the medium, and the bandwidth) changes, we will also see a dramatic change in the way in which we approach commerce, and the expectations that we have about it. This change in expectations occurs for both businesses and consumers, and thus we see a redefinition in the approach both parties have in entering an e-commerce exchange.

The Growth of E-Commerce

Jumping into the world of e-commerce, it's important to consider this recent trend in the context of the overall evolution of the Internet. Of course most developers are aware of the origins of the Internet in the 1960's in the form of the ARPANET, the original United States government sponsored network that eventually became the Internet. What is important to the understanding of e-commerce is not the evolution of the hardware or underlying network but the evolution of the usage of the Internet, and the role that it plays in the lives of users. Clearly as bandwidth increases and higher speed network access reaches consumers, these factors play a role in consumer adoption of e-commerce. As the technology becomes more convenient and more accessible, it is easier for people to use it. However, there remains a disparity between a user having the ability to access the Internet and a user actually logging on and making e-commerce a part of their daily lives.

There is a great deal of money available to people who are able to understand and harness the factors that make people spend their money and time on a particular product or service. Further, if the product becomes a part of everyday life, there is even more money to be made. Ideally the creator of something new wants a lot of people to buy it and use it. But if the excitement is fleeting and the product is merely a fad, the revenue stream quickly fades. For e-commerce to be successful and beneficial to companies, it must survive to be more than a fad and become a part of the way people live their lives.

The first step in the adoption of a new thing is to make it accessible. Clearly, e-commerce companies have tried very hard to do that, and the advances in hardware and software have made it easier and cheaper to reach consumers and other business. However, as we previously mentioned, people don't always use that which is available. Fundamentally, for something to stick, it must make lives better in such a way that the benefit is greater than the cost. This is what e-commerce companies are trying to do with advertising and marketing. For example, e-commerce ads often talk of the ease of avoiding crowds at stores as one part of the e-commerce business proposition.

Making e-commerce a part of our cultures and a part of our lives may be an excellent way to increase revenues for companies. While many companies do see an increase in sales, profit margin, and other critical factors, there are also companies that have seen a marked decrease in revenues from physical stores, so there is clearly a balance to be struck. However, as more companies strive for the perceived benefits of e-commerce it is important to consider the advances in the Internet over the last few years as they relate to the ultimate experience of the user.

Which Came First – the Technology or the Uses?

One of the interesting features of the Internet is that it seems that we invented the technology first with one purpose in mind, and then invented new uses for it. The early web pages were text and were really no more than a way to put content – static text – on the web, and that was really what the web was designed for. HTTP is clearly a request/response protocol and intended to be used as a way to display the static data of these early web pages. It was not intended, by its very nature, to be a protocol of interactivity.

As we discovered how exciting the web was, we invested a lot of time busily inventing a variety of new uses for it. As we thought of new ways to use HTTP to make it more interactive, we quickly developed ways to maximize the usage of the web. As an example, using HTTP to download an applet or a QuickTime movie to the client is a way of exploiting the request/response nature of HTTP to make it more interactive.

Once web pages started to gain a foothold on the Internet, we quickly saw users trying to use the web not for posting static content – but for the purposes of interaction. By staying aware of this trend, we saw the creation of JavaScript, Java applets, and the fully-fledged applications we use today. Did the users' desire create the new advances, or did the users simply react to new advances as they arrived? While there is no decisive answer, it is clear that monitoring the way consumers interact with technology is an excellent way to predict and anticipate future trends.

What is interesting about this phenomenon is not that we maximized on a technological innovation – that happens all the time. The interesting thing is that this has the same implications for applications that we develop today. Some of the technologies we are using are as cutting edge as HTTP was several years ago. Likewise, we should expect that as we use these technologies as they are intended, we will also see an evolution occur. The technologies that today seem obvious to use for e-commerce might, in the near future, provide completely different services to users. In addition, it is critical for developers to be on the lookout for new uses for the technologies we have today. It is through re-evaluation and vigilant examination that any technology is able to advance.

An Aside – The Clothing Service

An interesting example of the phenomenon of inventing the technology and then discovering the uses is a story recounted by Nicholas Negroponte, director of the Media Laboratory of the Massachusetts Institute of Technology, founder of Wired Magazine and the keynote speaker at Electronic Commerce World 1998. Mr. Negroponte often travels for six or seven days straight. Rather than take clothing for each day, he uses Federal Express to send four shirts to wherever he is staying the third night. Upon receiving the package, he removes the clean shirts, replaces them with the dirty shirts, and Fed Ex's the package back to his home.

Clearly Fed Ex never intended to be a company providing clothing service to travelers. They intended to provide a service to deliver packages in a cost effective manner. And it wasn't Fed Ex that did anything different. They simply carried out their existing business plan – delivering packages for consumers. However, when you are successful in a venture (and by all accounts Fed Ex *is* successful – currently delivering five millions shipments every business day) you have the opportunity for your users to develop their own uses.

This story is an example of a technology that takes on a life of its own. It becomes something more than was intended by its creator based on the usage pattern of an individual. That's what's really exciting about the technologies we work with; a technology that was created by one person to perform a specific task (ship packages) can be used by a creative individual in a completely different way (transport laundry).

This type of **user-centric** evolution can be served by companies that are aware of the uses of their technology, be it delivering packages or conducting commerce on the Internet. The next question is if it is profitable to market the business in such a way as to exploit these ideas. For Fed Ex, adding laundry services might not be the best decision.

However, say for example you are a seller of books and you created your site to sell new books to consumers. If you see that people tend to use your site to locate used books, you can take one of two approaches. You can decide that the intent of the technology was to sell new books and refuse to consider other uses. Or, you can capitalize on the way your technology evolved through usage, and add a used book search. This is a case where recognizing the ways in which people use the technology and then catering to these uses is an excellent idea.

Understanding the Audience

As companies develop new approaches for e-commerce and new ways to reach partners and consumers it is critical that these approaches are weighed against the audience. What are people looking for from the Internet in general and e-commerce specifically? And more importantly, what can we predict about what people will be expecting in the future? This is the type of information that is important to understand when considering new ventures in e-commerce.

There are a plethora of materials on the topic of knowing your audience, as this has been a critical marketing issue since well before the Internet. What's unique about the Internet is that, for the first time, we have the ability to really know the audience. We can see and log everything they do as they interact with an application. A smart e-commerce venture knows how to gather and use this information to make sure that the current and future functionality of the application is reaching the audience in the intended manner.

Usability is also a huge issue in understanding the audience. A successful e-commerce initiative will take a hard look at usability since this is one of the critical factors in success. It makes sense for this to be such an important issue as a customer must be able to use the site in order to spend money there. Conducting consumer focus groups and usability testing is an excellent way to approach this issue.

Fundamentally though, it is important for all aspects of a project to consider the end user of the technology. One of the ways in which this can be achieved is through understanding the ways in which people interact with the technology around them.

Considering the Six Webs

Bill Joy, Chief Scientist of Sun Microsystems, often speaks about a concept he calls the **Six Webs**. Essentially what Joy is discussing is the idea of considering the unique ways in which users interact with information. These different webs use different software and different modes of communication, but all intersect on some level. Joy defines the six webs as the **Near** web, the **Far** web, the **Here** web, the **Voice** web, the **E-commerce** web and the **Device** web.

Let's examine these in turn:

❑ The *Near* web is the way we interact with the Internet today in the most traditional sense – a user sitting at a desktop computer.

❑ The *Far* web is for entertainment, accessed by lying on your couch through a remote control. This isn't web pages available over a cable modem, but is instead a new and little explored form of interactive entertainment.

❑ The *Here* web is the way in which we use mobile devices to access the web, such as a mobile phone or PDA.

❑ The *Voice* web is another emerging web that uses voice recognition to drive your access to the information.

These four webs outline Bill Joy's vision of the four major ways users interact with technology to get information. The two remaining webs are really less user oriented and more business oriented:

❑ The *E-commerce* web is about systems working behind the scenes to automate things such as inventory, billing, and shipping.

❑ The *Device* web is a web that involves devices that can recognize each other and react accordingly.

Joy's webs have been criticized for being too limited as many people consider there to be more than just six webs. Regardless, these six webs do outline some very critical areas for developers to consider. It is not sufficient to think about an application in the context of one client. We no longer develop client/server applications or purely HTML applications. Instead we must consider all the possible "webs" or ways for users to approach the application (the *Near, Far, Here* and *Voice* webs). We must also consider all the possible interaction between the application we are developing and other systems (the *E-commerce* and *Device* webs).

Since four of these webs involve the way a user interacts with information and the other two involve the ways systems act, it is very possible to consider the existence of an application that can be a part of more than one web. For example, a traditional e-commerce application is a part of the near web, as the user interacts with it in the traditional way. However, it is also a part of the e-commerce web as it clearly performs automated e-commerce functions.

It is the intersection of the webs in cases like this that is so important for developers to consider. An application that is developed primarily for one venue, or web, can easily be expected to move into another venue within the life of the application. The architecture of the application should consider the evolution of the web to date as well as the possible directions of the future. This is often easier said than done, but any consideration that can be given to the evolution of the different webs will help to extend the lifetime of the application.

Joy's six webs are examples of different uses of very similar technologies, and are important because a successful e-commerce initiative must understand the different webs (uses of technology). In addition, a successful e-commerce initiative will use this understanding of the different webs to focus their business initiatives.

The Future of E-Commerce

While anyone who can predict the exact future of the Internet stands to make an astounding amount of money, there are several indicators of possible future progress available to us. Specifically, we are concerned with the Internet in its role as one medium of e-commerce and the future of e-commerce as a whole.

Joy has outlined four ways (the first four webs) that he sees users interacting with technology now and in the future. Using his approach, we can probably determine a variety of different interfaces for how we could get such information. Any interface between a human and the information they want is a valid prediction of something we might see in the future. Certainly there is a lot of room to add a variety of "webs" and create new ways to get the information that consumers need to them.

There is another factor to consider in the future of e-commerce – the system itself. We have such a wide variety of e-commerce applications today, but they tend to mirror more traditional methods of commerce. For example, an e-commerce site often carries through the notion of a shopping cart because that is what we might use in a traditional store. We have seen and can expect to continue to see new commerce models emerging that could only be done using technology and would never be possible or profitable without the technology.

One other important consideration is that the struggle to utilize the technologies and ideas we have today is an ongoing one. As we learn more about what we want and need, we will continue to adapt the technologies to follow suit. A good example of this phenomenon is the recent so-called "dot-com revolution". As the technology of the web became very mainstream, there were a multitude of companies that sprung up to try to take advantage of this technology and the perceived new market. A very small number of these companies were successful and whilst some of them failed for other reasons, some simply failed because their particular use of new technologies was simply not one that was wanted or needed. On the other hand, those that were able to understand the needs of the market and could adapt the technology to meet those needs were often successful.

Realization of E-Commerce

The emergence of e-commerce has lead to the creation of many different applications that are typically grouped into several categories of e-commerce. While these types of categorizations represent the typical approach to e-commerce, there is nothing that dictates that a company must stick to one type of application, or keep different types of applications segregated. In fact, some successful e-commerce applications provide a variety of services spanning several of the following types of e-commerce applications.

Business to Consumer (B2C)

> **Business to Consumer (B2C)** applications are applications that provide an interface from businesses directly to their consumers.

The most common example of a B2C application is a retail web site featuring the business's products or services that can be directly purchased by the consumer.

The importance of B2C varies dramatically from company to company. For some companies, reaching consumers is and has always been the critical aspect of their business. For a company that runs a chain of retail stores, B2C should be one of the most important pieces of their Internet strategy. On the other hand, a manufacturing company that already has third parties who distribute, market, and sell their products is probably less concerned about B2C, as it is not their core focus. That doesn't mean, however, that upon a re-examination of their priorities they won't decide to bypass the middleman and sell directly to the consumer.

This is an interesting dilemma for anyone involved in an e-commerce project. Retail is a difficult business that is now easily accessible to anyone. It is clearly much more cost efficient to open a B2C site than to open your own physical store. This brings forth a host of issues for a new B2C company to answer.

The issues involved in exploring a new B2C opportunity range from the minute to the more overwhelming. Many companies that have never sold directly to consumers are beginning to explore that option. These companies have to deal with large issues such as organization restructuring and exploring new marketing. Often, in addition to these large overarching issues, there are small issues that also need to be addressed. For example, some companies don't even sell directly to consumers – they only sell to distributors in large quantities. Opening a B2C e-commerce site means addressing a large number of small issues such as the ability to accept and process credit cards and to ship in small quantities. In general, companies moving into B2C markets have a wide range of issues to consider.

B2C applications are (and will continue to be) among the most visible on the Internet as they appeal to the masses. Common examples of B2C applications include selling goods such as books or movies on the Internet direct to consumers, or selling services (such as a credit check) on the Internet direct to consumers.

Success Factors

B2C applications have a couple of areas that are particularly critical to success. First, there is the issue of the bottom line. Businesses obviously make no money when a user browses but does not buy. The desire to convert a browser to a buyer is expressed in order conversion rates. These rates express the number of orders in a given period divided by the total number of visits. An August 2000 survey by Boston Consulting Group and Shop.org showed that order conversion rates in the second quarter 2000 were 1.9 percent. This is an improvement over the 1.8 percent of 1999, but not nearly the percentages online retailers would like to see.

Another hot topic in B2C applications is personalization. Allowing a user to indicate preferences and offering content based on the user's previous purchases make conversion rates much higher according to an October 1999 report by Nielsen/NetRatings. The trend toward personalization is likely to remain a hot topic as it increases customer loyalty.

We'll be looking at B2C applications specifically in Section 3.

Business to Business (B2B)

Forging new relationships between businesses is becoming critical for businesses to survive and flourish in this increasingly fast paced world. **Business to Business** or **B2B** applications provide new opportunities for businesses to leverage emerging technologies to build their businesses.

B2B applications are one of the hidden success stories of the last year. There is dramatically more money to be made (or saved) in B2B applications than in B2C. According to Forrester Research, online revenue from B2B will reach US$4.6 trillion in the next three years while B2C only hopes to reach US$108 billion. To be fair, there is an economic benefit that is harder to track in B2C as existing retailers gain exposure and increase customer loyalty. However, it is hard to argue with numbers that show such an overwhelming amount of money being grabbed by B2B applications.

Interestingly enough, B2B seems to be the biggest factor in the United States. According to the Boston Consulting Group, one fourth of all B2B purchasing in the United States will be done online by 2003. Additionally, while US$2.8 trillion will come out of B2B e-commerce in North America, the rest of the world will reach only US$1.8 trillion.

Examples of B2B applications include facilitating transactions for goods/services between companies, selling goods/services on the Internet to businesses, and supply chain integration. Another example is online procurement of goods from one company to another.

Legacy integration is a huge issue in B2B applications as it can be both detrimental and beneficial. If existing applications such as EDI or EFT are extended to help the B2B process, then the existing legacy applications can be a big help in moving forward. On the other hand, if two companies want to trade data, but have dramatically different legacy systems, legacy integration can be a challenge to overcome.

Other important issues in B2B applications are security, speed, and flexibility. Anything that improves the process of interaction between companies will serve to enhance the B2B market.

We'll look at B2B applications in Section 4 of the book.

Business to Business to Consumer (B2B2C)

Business to Business to Consumer is one of the least well-defined pieces of the e-commerce spectrum. **B2B2C** is basically defined as using B2B to help support and rejuvenate companies attempting B2C. This essentially capitalizes on the fact that B2B has been an overwhelming financial success, while B2C hasn't performed anywhere near as well. B2B2C has the potential to be a very hot market area as it capitalizes the success of B2B and the potential demand of B2C.

B2B provides a way for B2C companies to reduce costs and improve their B2C services. This is essentially the value proposition behind B2B2C initiatives. An example of B2B2C is developing products to help B2C companies increase profit by integrating inventory from the manufacturer to the distributor. An application that links one online catalog to another would be considered a B2B2C application as it capitalizes on both B2B and B2C.

Consumer to Consumer and Consumer to Business to Consumer (C2C AND C2B2C)

Consumer to Consumer, or **C2C**, is an interesting relatively new piece of the e-commerce world. C2C applications involve consumers conducting commerce directly with other consumers. This obviously means that the company facilitating the transaction must find some non-traditional revenue stream. This could be a small cut of the transaction, a service fee, advertising, or some combination of these.

C2C applications have played a role in the explosion of consumers using the Internet. EBay, for example, is an excellent example of a C2C application that is extremely popular with consumers. Probably one of the most obscure acronyms, **Consumer to Business to Consumer**, or **C2B2C** involves consumers conducting transactions with other consumers using a business as an intermediary.

The exact difference between this model and a consumer-centric auction site like EBay is not completely clear-cut. However, an example of a C2B2C site is autotrader.com. This site facilitates the transactions of selling used cars between consumers, but also contains an inventory of used cars to sell to the consumer. The important consideration of these two classifications is that we now have to consider business models that do not even begin to resemble the types of business models that traditional physical companies have dealt with. It also shows that there are some new and innovative models to make money in the new e-commerce environment.

Mobile Commerce (M-Commerce)

Mobile Commerce or **M-commerce** involves conducting commerce utilizing mobile devices. This is interesting because unlike the other categorizations of e-commerce it is defined not by who the actors are but by the technology itself. An m-commerce application can be B2B, B2C or any other of the classifications. It is simply considered to be m-commerce if it is done using mobile devices.

Wireless solutions have traditionally been a larger force in Europe and Japan than other parts of the world, but studies show the US is catching up. In August 2000, a study by DataMonitor predicted that the market for wireless e-commerce solutions in the United States would grow 1,000 percent by the year 2005. This would put the market at approximately $1.2 billion (US$) annually. Clearly wireless is an area where there is worldwide demand for this type of communication.

M-commerce is a unique member of Joy's webs, as it is defined by a unique interface with the system. One of the biggest pitfalls of m-commerce applications is treating it like a web site. Mobile computing is a different world from the Internet in ways ranging from the business model to the user interface. It is critical to success to treat m-commerce as different from a web site, in part because m-commerce applications differ from traditional web based applications in the amount and type of information that can and should be conveyed to the user.

Examples of m-commerce are making the purchase of goods/services available to consumers using wireless devices, and facilitating transactions between companies using wireless devices.

M-commerce technologies are discussed in Section 5.

Benefits of E-Commerce

There are some benefits of e-commerce that span the categorizations of sites. Clearly, automation of business has been a cost saving measure dating back to the invention of the assembly line. Automation of business processes is valuable not only because it frees valuable labor from menial tasks, but also because it allows those individuals to pursue new and ideally beneficial initiatives that they would not have been able to previously.

In addition to automation, e-commerce benefits companies because it forces them to take a long hard look at the way they do business. Innovation is the only thing that forces companies to re-examine and potentially update outdated policies and procedures. In addition, the relatively low overhead of e-commerce reduces some of the barriers to entry in the more traditional commerce arena. The other benefits of e-commerce are classified according to the type of e-commerce being pursued by a particular organization.

B2C

B2C applications are beneficial to existing retail companies because they allow them to increase their customer base and in some cases reach entire demographics that they might not be able to reach in a physical or "bricks and mortar" store. For example, stores that cater to teenagers will typically market to an older audience in a B2C application because they need to market e-commerce to individuals who are old enough to have credit cards.

While this might seem like the company is reducing their demographics, what is really happening is that they are being forced to re-examine their focus. They will need to consider if they should market to an older crowd in the physical stores and they will consider marketing to this older crowd such as parents and grandparents online. This type of strategy is helpful to a company because it gives them new opportunities (a parent might be more likely to go to a teen-focused store online than in person) and forces them to reconsider the opportunities they have.

B2C allows companies to extend their existing services to consumers as well. Being able to special order an item and have it delivered to a store for pickup is a handy service that increases customer loyalty and is only available because of the B2C initiative.

B2C is beneficial for consumers because it gives them access to a world of stores instead of the stores in their local town. It also provides a more competitive market giving consumers access to a wide variety of choices and lower prices. Some B2C sites have even explored new pricing models, such as Priceline.com, which allows customers to name their own prices for a variety of goods and services. These types of innovations are only available in an e-commerce setting.

Finally, B2C applications open up a new world for companies that are not already well known throughout their country or world. The extended visibility that the Internet provides can allow local or regional businesses to reach out to markets they never would have been able to reach in the physical world.

B2B

B2B is beneficial to businesses because it has the potential to dramatically lower costs. In few other types of applications is the impact so directly towards the bottom line. By making communication easier and faster, using new technologies and standards such as XML, the quicker the inventory can move, the more efficient the process.

In addition, B2B applications help automate communication between companies. As well as streamlining the process, this also helps reduce the potential for errors and helps provide better goods and services.

B2B2C

The biggest benefit of B2B2C is to help B2C companies raise profits. By leveraging the benefits of B2B to streamline and improve business, B2C companies have the ability to make more money by growing revenue and cutting costs. Many of the benefits of crossing over from one type of e-commerce into another are still speculative. Ideally, a company that is successful in one area of e-commerce can capitalize on this success by leveraging that skill in other areas of their e-commerce strategy. This is not always something easy to capitalize on, but the lessons learned in successful B2B applications have the potential to be carried into the B2C arena.

C2C and C2B2C

Consumer centric business models would not even exist without the Internet, so clearly the benefit of this model is the fact that it exists at all. By allowing consumers to interact, businesses have a fairly easy revenue stream and consumers have access to an entirely new way to purchase and sell goods and services.

M-Commerce

M-commerce is one of the more unique models for bringing benefit to business. In some aspects, m-commerce is defined by the delivery mechanism as opposed to the type of application. Given this, an m-commerce application has the potential to have all the benefits of a B2B or B2C application.

In addition, m-commerce, although not fully mature, has the potential to make it more convenient for consumers to spend money and purchase goods and services. Since wireless devices travel with the consumer, the ability or perhaps temptation to purchase goods and services is always present. This is clearly a technique that can be used to raise revenue.

In the B2B arena, m-commerce can make it easier for companies to collaborate by utilizing the standards of the wireless world. Of course, these new technologies do not only present us with benefits, but also with several pitfalls that need to be taken into account.

Pitfalls of E-Commerce

Why do so many e-commerce projects and entire e-commerce businesses end in failure? This is a difficult and challenging question to answer but there are some overall things that tend to lead directly to failure in e-commerce. Certainly, this is not an all-encompassing list, but does bring to light some issues to consider:

- ❏ **Adopting the wrong business model** – Many companies fail because of the fundamental issue of an unworkable business model. In the explosion of the Internet the basic economic principles of business models have often been ignored. A quick survey of failing internet companies will show that many neglect to do things as simple as selling a product for more than it costs to make and ship.

- ❏ **Poor technology choices** – Technology choices are critical to success in many ways. In choosing the technology to use, there are often many right choices. However, getting the right people to implement the technology, making good decisions about when to integrate other products, and making decisions about technology at the right times are all critical factors that are often neglected leading to failure.

- ❏ **Ignorance of user base** – Ignoring or neglecting the needs of users is one of the biggest pitfalls in e-commerce, particularly B2C applications. It is very important to conduct user analysis and make sure you are meeting and exceeding customer expectations. In a B2C site, having a good customer service department is critical and is an area in which many initiatives fail.

- ❏ **Poor management** – Management is an easy scapegoat, but there is clearly a need for good management in a successful e-commerce initiative. Not having a knowledgeable strong management is a pitfall to be avoided.

❑ **Unreasonable expectations** – Expectations must be managed on a variety of fronts to avoid failure. Certainly, the expectations of the customer must be managed in a B2C site, but there are other factors to consider. For example, effectively managing the expectations about the still young area of mobile devices is important as well as managing the expectations about other technology.

These are just a few of the pitfalls to be avoided in e-commerce initiatives, and clearly there are more – many of which will be very specific to the organization. Communication and flexibility continue to be important to e-commerce initiatives like they are in any project.

Java's role in the E-Commerce World

The Java programming language is a good choice for development of e-commerce applications as Java has many feature sets that allow it to be an effective platform for e-commerce. In addition, Sun has a strong understanding of the critical business issues necessary to consider for e-business. There are several features of Java that make it a good choice for e-commerce development:

❑ **Java is platform independent** – There are cases in which the platform independence of Java can be leveraged to be an asset to e-commerce development. Clearly, most developers are slightly skeptical of write once, run anywhere, but in the wireless world especially, this promise has some potential.

❑ **Java is multi-threaded** – This feature is critical to building effective server-side applications and is a true advantage Java has over many other languages and platforms.

❑ **Java is network aware** – The core Java language has always had the capability to interact with networks and includes APIs to support common network protocols. This makes e-commerce easier since the basic structure is available with the language.

❑ **Java tends towards faster development cycles** – In this world of "Internet time" the faster an application can be delivered, the happier a business is. Java is structured in such a way to allow for this rapid development.

❑ **Java is object-oriented** – Object-oriented development is an excellent choice for e-commerce applications because it allows for well-componentized applications.

❑ **Java has new APIs Available** – APIs such as the **Java 2 Enterprise Edition (J2EE)**, **Java 2 Micro Edition (J2ME)**, and the APIs for XML parsing, to name a few are constantly being developed and refined to better suit emerging standards and technologies.

❑ **Java has a relatively fast learning curve** – Although there are differences of opinion on the matter, many people feel that Java has a relatively low learning curve making it quick to adopt in an environment that needs a new technology for e-commerce.

Java is not the only technology for e-commerce development nor is it always the best. Certainly, there is a legitimate decision to be made. However, the reasons explained in this section are some of the things that weigh in Java's favor in making this decision. These reasons are also some of the reasons that Java is typically chosen in e-commerce applications.

Another reason that Java is often chosen for e-commerce development is the support for Java in a variety of application servers. Servers such as BEA WebLogic, ATG Dynamo and IBM WebSphere each lend their own compelling reasons for using Java technology. These various servers are often chosen for their various features and Java is thus implicitly chosen as the development tool.

While there are clearly other benefits of the Java language of which most Java developers are aware, the features listed here are a few key features that make it especially beneficial for e-commerce development. One of the Java technologies that has revolutionized the e-commerce arena the most is Java 2 Enterprise Edition (J2EE).

Java 2 Enterprise Edition

Java 2 Enterprise Edition (J2EE) is a leader among technologies geared towards e-commerce and is, as Sun refers to it "a key piece of the end-to-end Java solution: the technology engine for end-to-end e-commerce". Java already had a presence in web-based applications when Sun announced J2EE, and the move to J2EE only solidified it. J2EE presents a solid solution for building strong server side applications that include the critical pieces needed. In addition, the inclusion of technologies such as Java Server Pages (JSP) creates a flexible user interface layer that can cleanly tie into this strong server side layer.

J2EE makes the Java language an even better player in the e-commerce arena because of some key features:

❏ J2EE makes Java a fully-fledged server-side development platform

❏ J2EE has a solid infrastructure that provides a well tested implementation of many common application needs such as security and messaging

❏ J2EE standardizes development making it easier for companies to commit to J2EE and share third party code

❏ J2EE handles many critical tasks of e-commerce such as transaction management and database access

❏ J2EE provides a solid backend for wireless applications and many wireless companies use J2EE on the server for this purpose

There are several J2EE technologies that stand out in their ability to support the benefits of Java as an e-commerce development tool. You will learn more about the role of these technologies in e-commerce throughout this book:

❏ Enterprise JavaBeans (EJBs) provide a robust framework for creating component based applications

❏ Java Server Pages (JSPs) bring flexibility to the user interface layer

❏ Java Servlets work with JSPs to provide interaction between the user interface layer and the backend application

❏ Java Naming Directory Interface (JNDI) provides connectivity from Java to other naming and directory spaces

❏ Java Database Connectivity (JDBC) provides an interface for access to relational databases

❏ Java Message Service (JMS) provides a messaging API for communication between services

❏ Java Transaction API (JTA) and Java Transaction Service (JTS) provide transaction services

❏ Java Mail provides e-mail capability to J2EE applications

Clearly these are just a few key reasons that J2EE is such a big player in the e-commerce world. So much of web development is being done in Java and J2EE is now the standard for server-side Java development. It seems clear that J2EE is and will continue to be a huge piece of e-commerce technology.

XML

E-commerce requires many different types of communications and an unprecedented amount of data changes hands. The many different platforms and systems interacting require a platform neutral standard for data exchange. One of the technologies that can fill this niche is XML, the extensible markup language established as a standard by the **World Wide Web Consortium** (**W3C**).

While XML is not a Java or a Sun technology, it is an important technology for e-commerce. It is unclear if XML plays such a big role in e-commerce because it is inherently well suited to the task or because there is such good support available for it in languages like Java. Regardless, XML is an important part of a large amount of e-commerce development

By being standardized and platform neutral, XML provides an excellent framework for exchanging data. While there are some limitations and some developers do have some frustrations with XML, it remains one of the robust solutions for e-commerce data exchange available today.

Critical to the adoptions of a data standard are the tools for manipulating the data. XML has support for both the **Simple API for XML** (**SAX**) and **Document Object Model** (**DOM**) implementations available in Java as well as other languages, which only enhances the ability of XML to be a factor in e-commerce applications.

We'll highlight Java programming details as related to XML in Chapter 7, while Appendices A and B contain more introductory information on XML and the related technology XSLT.

Summary

We've spent a great deal of time in this chapter attempting to understand what e-commerce is and what that means to business and to developers. There are several important points to summarize:

- ❑ E-commerce is growing. It is reasonable to expect continued growth in all aspects of e-commerce. The trend is clearly not over.

- ❑ E-business strategy is a critical predecessor to e-commerce initiatives.

- ❑ Understanding the ways a user interacts with an e-business / e-commerce application is important to be successful.

- ❑ It is important to try to predict and anticipate new trends in e-commerce. This can often be achieved by looking at the new ways that users use applications.

In general, e-commerce is a huge market that still needs to be explored to its fullest. A recent study by A.T. Kearney shows that "e-retailers are missing out on more than $6.1 billion in lost sales today, or 13 % of the total worldwide revenue." A.T. Kearney attributes this loss of revenue to the fact that consumers can't do what they want online. What they want to do is hard to define, but what is clear is that consumers' needs are not being met by websites. This is exactly why it is so important to consider the users and understand the overall approach to e-business. When money is available and is not being capitalized on, businesses need to stand up and take notice. It is by understanding and exploring e-commerce that companies can realize the full potential of the Internet.

The next important step in building an e-commerce site is to begin to gather the requirements for the e-commerce system you are going to build. In the next chapter, we will expand on what we have discussed in this chapter by exploring various techniques for gathering requirements. We will also discuss some items to consider when gathering requirements.

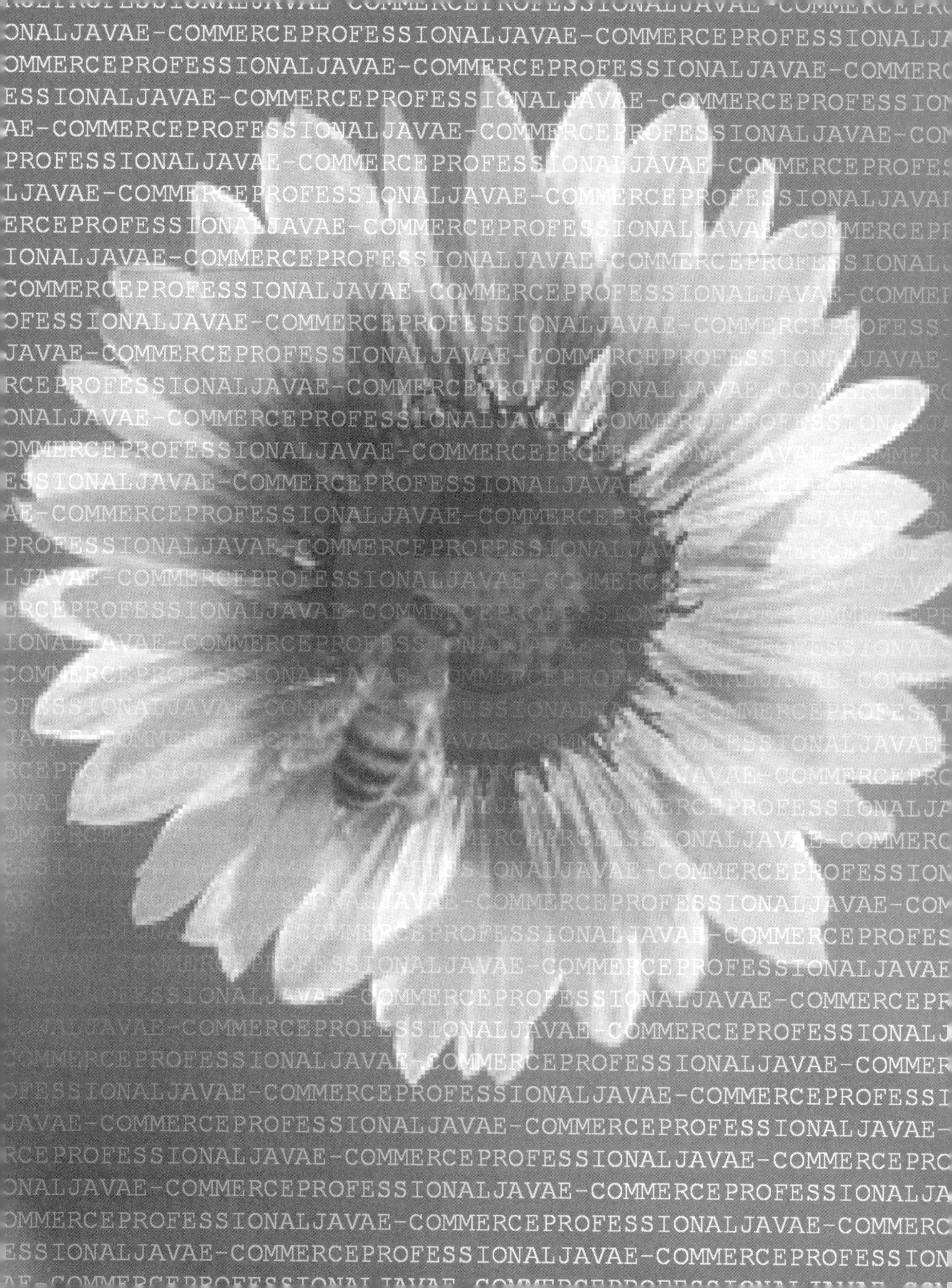
PROFESSIONALJAVAE-COMMERCE

2

Requirements for E-Commerce Systems

Gathering requirements is an absolutely *critical* part of the process of building an e-commerce system. As obvious as that is, many companies fail (or waste large amounts of money) because they are not effective in defining what it is they really hope to gain from their e-commerce system and more importantly how they expect to achieve this gain.

There are two important points that need to be addressed before beginning our discussion on gathering requirements for e-commerce systems. First, it is important to note that gathering the requirements for a system is something that typically occurs within the context of an appropriate methodology and project lifecycle. In this chapter, we'll discuss the specifics of gathering requirements, and then move on in Chapter 3 to better frame the requirements gathering process within the context of the project lifecycle.

The other important point to note is that most of the information in this chapter could equally be applied to a project that *isn't* an e-commerce project. Most software projects have core similarities regardless of the type of application being developed. These types of considerations are contained in this chapter as well as those concerns that are more specific to e-commerce applications.

Given these two points, we can now discuss the aspects of gathering requirements for e-commerce applications. In this chapter, we will look at some general issues surrounding requirements gathering such as:

❑   The different roles people play in gathering requirements

❑   Differences between e-commerce systems and other applications

❑   Business requirements – setting and meeting goals

Once we have established this basic understanding of requirements gathering, we will discuss some of the specific considerations in gathering requirements. We'll talk about some of the issues, both technical and non-technical, that need to be considered during the requirements gathering process.

The People Involved in the Process of Gathering Requirements

Before we begin to discuss the process itself, we'll need to understand and identify the different groups of people involved and their responsibilities during the process. Note that at this point we are simply identifying the people involved, and not implying any sort of hierarchy or process.

Developers

One of the groups of people involved in the development of an e-commerce application is obviously the **developers**. It is both naïve and incorrect to assume that developers are only technical and have no input in the requirements gathering process. For this discussion you will see a focus on developers as the technical experts, as that is the role that they most commonly play. However, this does not imply that developers may not also play additional roles, such as business analyst, or even project manage.

Business Users

In addition to the developers, there are the **business users**. For the purposes of this discussion, business users are defined as those users *inside* the company that is building the system. These are the people who will use and maintain the system. For example, the people responsible for keeping the product catalogue up to date in a B2C application would be considered business users. In a B2B system, the business users are the people who interact with and use the information from the system. Business users are also the individuals who have a working knowledge of the business as it stands today. Because of this, the business users make many of the decisions and provide a great deal of the requirements.

Quality Assurance

Another important group to consider is the **quality assurance group**. Although different methodologies vary the amount of interaction the QA staff has in the requirements gathering process, there is clearly a need for some involvement. At the end of the day, the QA team is responsible for making sure that the application meets the requirements. It makes sense, then, that the more involved they can be with the requirements gathering process, the more likely they are to be successful in their evaluation of the application.

Users

Users are an important part of the requirements gathering process, too. Clearly users of an e-commerce system might exist either internally or externally to the company building the application. For example, with a B2C system, users are obviously the people from outside the company who interact with the system to purchase goods and services. For a B2B application, however, the users of the system could be people inside the company as well as people outside the company. As we have already identified the concept of business users, who are the individuals *inside* the company who will use the application, we will refer to users as people *outside* the company who will use the application. Given this definition, not all e-commerce applications may have a clearly distinct user, but many times there is someone outside the company using the system, and they are the users.

The Requirements Gatherer

Of course, there is someone in charge of gathering and documenting the requirements for the system. Their job is slightly different, as they must interact with all of the other groups to gather the requirements. The actual person who performs this task can be anyone from the project manager to a business analyst to the developers themselves. For the purpose of this discussion, we will simply refer to this person as the **requirements gatherer**.

There is absolutely no intent in this discussion to segregate or pigeonhole anyone involved in the process of defining requirements for an e-commerce project. Clearly everyone involved has a variety of skills and may even play a variety of roles. These groups of people we have defined – developers, business users, users, and the requirements gatherer – serve more as roles for people to play than as definitions of jobs.

In fact, all of these people are critical to the process of gathering requirements. Every person involved in the process of gathering requirements has a different background, skill set and point of reference. These different points of view help give the most well rounded view of the requirements and expectations of the system as possible. Because each group we have discussed has a very unique perspective, the chances of the application succeeding are dramatically reduced if any one of these groups is absent from the process.

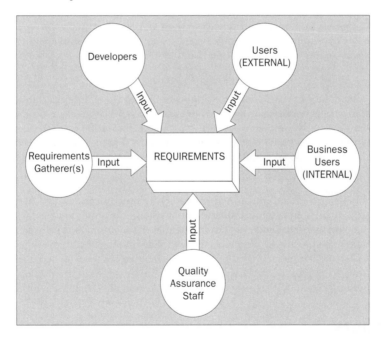

Differences Between E-Commerce Systems and Other Applications

Even for individuals that are very used to building large systems and gathering requirements, there are a variety of things that are different when approaching an e-commerce application. Clearly, there are a lot of technical and business differences between different platforms and systems. A mainframe application is very different from a web application. However, in Chapter 1 when we discussed what an e-commerce application is, we talked about how e-commerce is defined more by function than by technology or platform. Thus, when we talk about the difference between e-commerce applications and other types of applications, we are not really talking about the technology issues.

Instead, what we are really talking about are some of the trends one tends to see in e-commerce applications. For example, an application that displays human resource information to employees could be a web application. In many ways, it is similar to a typical B2C e-commerce site. They both are web based and serve dynamic information to the user, probably from a database. The differences lie in some of the basic things that e-commerce applications tend to deal with. For example, since e-commerce applications deal with money by definition, this is a consideration that is often unique to e-commerce applications and differentiates the B2C application from the HR application.

Another common theme in e-commerce applications is the audience base. In many cases, the way a company makes money is by drawing customers to their web site to buy products. This is of course primarily a factor for consumer-focused applications. Given this, e-commerce applications tend to focus on maximizing the customer base, which bring issues like internationalisation, security, and scalability to the forefront.

There are other considerations in e-commerce applications that we will discuss later in this section. These considerations are generalizations, as any application could have just as stringent requirements for issues like security as an e-commerce application. What is important to understand is that there are some general differences in building e-commerce applications that need to be considered during the requirements gathering process. Whether they are applicable or not the specific application being built is an issue for the project team to decide.

Each group of people involved in the requirements gathering process must be prepared for the general considerations that may be unique to e-commerce applications. It is important for each group of people to be prepared for the particular challenges that await them in the requirements gathering process, since it is so important that once the process is under way the complete involvement of every person not be hindered in anyway. For example, if a developer was unprepared for the wide technology challenges and the business users were unprepared for how large a challenge e-commerce applications are, the chance that they would both be able to fully concentrate on the task at hand – defining requirements – is lowered.

For Developers

E-commerce applications often combine many different standards and technologies, and these are often more diverse than most other types of applications. Developers need to understand that, unlike some other types of applications, e-commerce applications need a great deal of thought and planning in a variety of technical areas. Security, scalability, user interface design, performance, maintenance, speed of development, and integration with multiple external systems are concerns in any application, but in developing e-commerce systems there is no room for compromise in any of these areas. All of these concerns must be fully addressed, in detail, from the start. In addition, an e-commerce application often includes multiple user interfaces, such as one interface for users and a different one for business users.

Because of the complexity of integration often involved, e-commerce applications demand that thought be given upfront to the architecture. Certainly, there are other types of applications like this, but for developers who have built more internal applications or more traditional Internet applications and work in very low-key, informal environments, this can be a big difference when moving on to e-commerce applications.

The Effects of Testing

Any application that deals with transactions (especially with monetary transactions) requires even more thorough testing than an application that is not transactional in nature. In addition, an application that is exposed to a large number of untrained users requires more testing than an application that is accessed by fewer trained users. This is because trained users are less likely to veer from the intended use of the application (the area that a lot of testing focuses on) while an untrained user is more likely to interact with the application in almost any way possible. It should be noted that although a good testing department will test all the areas of the application, considerations like deadlines and lack of resources often limit testing to the intended use of the application.

An application that is intended to provide a service to users only gets one chance to inspire customer loyalty. An application that exchanges sensitive data between organizations cannot afford even one mistake or loss of data. In addition, an application that must handle large loads requires even more comprehensive volume and load testing than other types of applications.

These reasons all show that an e-commerce application requires even more comprehensive testing than other types of applications. Developers must be aware of the need for testing and assist in the process to ensure an effective application.

Dealing with the Requirements Gathering Process

The last important difference for developers in e-commerce applications is people. As we discussed in Chapter 1, e-commerce applications are best done by first establishing an effective e-business strategy. Because of this, there is often a need for businesses to do a lot of work to understand what they want to build into an e-commerce application. This can be a frustrating process for developers, as the clients (either internal or external) simply can't make up their minds. It is important for developers to understand that the process of requirements gathering is critical to their day-to-day work, and even more difficult in the e-commerce arena.

Developers must be an integral part of the requirements gathering process. In many ways, determining the requirements is really a melding of the business process and the technology – business users represent the business process, while developers represent the technology. The developers, therefore, are every bit as critical to the requirements gathering process as the business users and must be a part of the requirements gathering process from the very beginning. This is something that comes naturally to some developers based on their temperament or previous experience. For other developers this can be a challenge they must overcome.

For Business Users

Business users are valuable because they know the business, and therefore know exactly what the application needs to be able to do. However, an e-commerce initiative often challenges how a company does business. Chapter 1 discussed how the way a company conducts business outside of technology might not be a perfect fit for doing business electronically. Thus, all business processes – and potentially even the business model – need to be re-examined and reconsidered.

What business users need to understand is that change is not necessarily a threat to those who are willing to be creative and adapt. Unless there are overall reasons for cutbacks at the company, if individuals are willing to adapt they have nothing to fear from a new system. If the overall success of the company is the business users' overriding goal (as it should be) then they should understand that change is necessary for a company to survive.

The Challenge of Planning

In addition to the perceived threat of change, business users also face a tremendous task in undertaking an e-commerce project. In many ways, an e-commerce application needs to be planned more thoroughly than an internal application or a static site, and be tightly integrated with all aspects of the business.

This is a significant investment of time and effort. It is critical that the managers of the organization make sure that their people are available. As is often the case in organizations, the people who have the most knowledge are often the ones who have the least free time. Because of the support needed for the initiative by the business it is important that the appropriate people be made available even if it means a temporary shift of responsibilities.

Establishing the New System

In many ways, the success or failure of the system from a political standpoint falls to the business users. No matter how wonderful the application may be, if it is not used, it is not a success. If the business users can meet the challenge of adapting their work patterns to the new system, it will be a success. This is, of course, true of any application, but the increased complexity of e-commerce applications can increase this challenge and add the need for user training and initiatives to help the support of the application grow.

Business users may also have to help establish new systems that have nothing to do with technology. For example, if a company has never had a B2C application, they need to put into place a way to fulfill orders as well as some sort of customer service. Overall, business users need to be dedicated to the project, in tune with the business, and open to (and prepared for) change. They must also be aggressive advocates for their needs and not intimidated by technology. Business users must be willing to be an advocate for the business just as strongly as the developers are advocates for the technology.

For Users

Although users are not necessarily involved directly in the process of building the application, their input is critical to the success of the project. A well-built e-commerce application needs to have an intuitive user interface that is understandable to and usable by the users. This is best done by understanding what the users want and need. In order to get this type of information, the information gatherer may hold user focus groups, may conduct surveys, and may do market research. There are also many resources available that discuss the issues of user interface design and information architecture.

As the application is designed, users must be constantly considered. Will it make their lives or their jobs easier? In a B2B application, the application must give users an independence from the group of people responsible for building and maintaining systems within a company (usually the IT department), rather than making them more reliant upon them. Users need to feel empowered to do their jobs rather than rely on other groups. If an application is well-made, it will allow users to do their jobs as much as possible. For example, in a B2C application, the business people who determine what products the company sells will ideally also be able to update the product catalog on the e-commerce site.

In many ways, the users are the hardest group to extract information from. As they may be potentially anyone with a computer, it is hard to find out exactly what they want. The best way to find out the users' reaction to the application is to have them interact with the application itself. Since the application doesn't exist until something has been built, the process of gathering user requirements often continues even after the initial release of the application has launched. In fact, some kinds of information can only be gained after the application is launched (such as user logs and typical user behavior patterns).

For the Requirements Gatherer

The requirements gatherer has the hardest job during the process of gathering requirements, as they are the focal point of the process. It is important to note that the requirements gatherer is often more than one person. If this is the case, the team must be aware that communication is important to consolidating all requirements. In many ways, the requirements gatherer plays the role of peacemaker or therapist to the people involved in the process during the requirements gathering phase. They are a problem solver and must face all the challenges of an e-commerce project, but there are some challenges unique to the requirements gatherer as well.

An e-commerce project requires a great deal of creativity on the part of the requirements gatherer to ask the right questions to drive the process. In addition, the requirements gatherer needs to understand a very wide view of the business, and regardless of how well their questions are phrased this is a difficult task. They must be very organized and prepared to handle a large volume of information.

In addition, the requirement, gatherer must often serve as a bridge between different groups of people. Often, they are the bridge between the business users and the developers, but they may also have to help interaction between other groups. It is important for the requirements gatherer to understand the motivations of all involved groups and to have a high level understanding of their issues in order to be able to help facilitate communication.

The rest of this chapter discusses some of the things that must be considered in an e-commerce application. In many ways these items constitute a list of the challenges for a requirements gatherer. However, in addition to being challenging, the role of the requirements gatherer is also incredibly critical to the success of the project.

Business Requirements

There are some steps that can be taken in order to gather requirements in a more effective manner. This is by no means a directive of the only way to gather requirements. Instead, it is a helpful list of some considerations.

Setting Goals for an E-Commerce Initiative

A successful e-commerce application must have a goal. This sounds so obvious, until you consider that this goal must be one that is shared by everyone on the project and that the goal must be well publicized. One of the first things that the requirements gatherer should do is determine the goal (or goals) for the project. If there is more than one goal then the goals should be prioritized. The goals decided on need to be agreed upon by everyone involved in the project, especially the project stakeholders. The goals should then be made very clear to everyone involved in the project, perhaps even posted in a prominent place.

The reason for placing such a priority on goals for the project is that the project must have a framework for all decisions. Some examples of goals for e-commerce projects are improving the customer conversion rate (B2C) or cutting costs of procurement (B2B). The goals established for an e-commerce site must be reasonable and well researched. A site can say it wants to be the next Yahoo! but this must be backed up with market research and common sense. The goals must be reasonably achievable within the time frame allotted to the project and must be agreed to by everyone from the CEO all the way down to the individual members of the project team.

Once the goals are in place, it is easier to determine the requirements because a solid goal gives a framework for making decisions, and having a list of goals for a project sets a more objective standard for making decisions. Clearly this is not an entirely objective process as one person might feel that the goal is better served by a particular decision than another person does, but it ensures that the discussions are grounded in the same basic assumptions.

It also ensures an objective way to evaluate the success of the project upon its completion. How well the goals were met is an excellent way to evaluate everything about the project from the technology to the process. To some degree, the methodology used will dictate the way in which the goals are used, but regardless of the specifics of the methodology, the goals are clear objectives that can be used throughout the project to measure success.

Meeting Stated Goals: The Process of Gathering Requirements

Once the goals have been established, the next step is to determine what the project will be. Clearly things like determining the scope of the project and other steps might occur before or during requirements gathering. However, since these types of things tend to be reliant on the methodology being used, in this section we will examine the basic idea of requirements gathering. In the next chapter, we will discuss how and where requirements gathering falls into the larger methodology.

It might be tempting for developers to discount the actual process of requirements gathering, and focus on the end results instead. Certainly, in many traditional methodologies the tasks of facilitating the requirements gathering falls to the project manager or business analyst. However, in some methodologies, the developers themselves are actually responsible for getting the needed requirements from the appropriate people. However, even if the developers do not have the formal responsibility for gathering the requirements, in many cases they are responsible for refining and following up on the requirements when they do not have all the needed information. Given this, it is important for developers to understand different ways to gather information and some ways to do this effectively.

The Mechanics of Gathering Requirements

When gathering requirements from people who are readily available, the most common way of gathering requirements is to hold meetings. This often means a series of very long meetings. The moderator for these is usually the requirements gatherer, but the requirements gatherer could ask a business user to lead a certain part of the discussion if appropriate. Some areas of the process might be best served by a discussion, others by brainstorming or by reviewing existing documentation.

Although meetings are often the norm, there are other ways to gather information. A requirements gatherer can shadow certain people for a day to learn more about their job and their part of the business process. Looking at existing documentation is also helpful as well as having the appropriate technical people examine existing systems or interview the original developers.

There are cases when the people who need to be talked to are not readily available. As we discussed earlier, this often happens when an application is being developed for use by a set of users outside of the company. For example, a B2C application doesn't have an easily accessible set of users. This is the case in which we need to rely on techniques like user interviews, surveys, and if possible feedback from the existing site in order to understand the desires of the users.

It is important to avoid the risks and pitfalls of poor communication by making sure that there are as few steps as possible between the person giving the requirement and the person implementing it. There should not be a "throw it over the wall" mentality, where each group or person works independently on his or her part and then hands it to the next person with no communication. The team should instead have a spirit of integration between the various team members regardless of individual roles.

The Difficulties of Compromise

Companies need to balance various concerns in order to best meet their goals for a project, but this is often difficult. A project will often have a whole list of things that are important. Consider the following sample list of things to include in a B2C application. In this example the customer has an existing B2C site that they are looking to revise.

- ❑ The company wants to get new content available on the site such as product reviews and detailed descriptions.

- ❑ The company has several new catalogs of products with unique data sets that they want on the site.

- ❑ There are some new features the company wants added to the site, such as the ability to look up products by manufacturer.

- ❑ The company is very concerned with adding new customers and has ideas on how to add customers by doing promotions that encourage people to register with the site.

- ❑ Maximizing the conversion rate of new customers is a very high priority and to facilitate this the company wants to focus on the way pages are designed and linked together.

- ❑ The company wants to change the way they have done customer service and expand the capabilities of the customer service representatives.

There is a lot of work here to do that would require a lot of time. If the company is willing to be patient, then everything can be accomplished. But if, like many companies, the company has a deadline by which they want this phase of the project to be complete there are some compromises to make.

Sometimes a fear of the expense or inconvenience of programming causes companies to try to do too much in one release. A bad experience with the IT department or with a consulting organization leads to the belief that there won't be a phase two so everything must be done right away. It is important for companies to try to put aside this fear and make good decisions. It is also important for the team to look for and handle this type of response. Many methodologies ask the business to rank features of the site based on their importance. If a company prioritizes every feature of the project as a "number one priority", this is a sign that they are scared to save some items for later as they fear there might not be a later. In this case, they need to be reassured that there will be ongoing work. One way to reassure the business users is to actually shrink the size of the iterations. Once the first iteration has been completed and the second has begun, the users will be reassured to see that there is more than one iteration.

There is another area in which compromise is important. Ideally, an e-commerce site will be designed in such a way that it is completely controlled by business users and rids them of their dependence on the IT department. In reality, trying to put too much control in the hands of the business users to save money and hassle from the IT department can cost more than it's worth. It is important to make some difficult compromises here. Give business users control and flexibility where it is appropriate and beneficial for them, but let the IT department control what would be too difficult to pass to business users.

Making it an Iterative Process

One of the things that can be done to make requirements gathering easier is to make the process iterative. To some degree this is dictated by the methodology being followed, but within the constraints of the methodology it is helpful to make the requirements iterative. Much of an e-commerce initiative is tied to responding to the needs of users. Rather than attempt to make every decision in a vacuum, it is often helpful to do it in stages, addressing the high priority items in phase one, getting it up and running, and using subsequent phases to enhance the project.

This approach does two things. Firstly, it allows the business users to make decisions being more informed about the response of the users, and secondly it allows the business users to see the functionality in place. Getting data on how users are interacting with the system is, as we previously mentioned, the best way to know how they actually feel about a system. Getting something available quickly can prevent a company from wasting time and money guessing at what the user wants.

Giving the business users something to work with is in itself a huge argument for gathering requirements in phases. It is very hard for anyone to imagine how a system will function. The earlier an actual application can be in front of the business users, the more concrete and helpful their input will become. The requirements become a set of enhancements to a baseline, instead of requirements determined without a baseline at all.

Arguments Against the Iterative Process

Some typical resistance to gathering the requirements and developing in iterations is that the code that is built in each iteration might not be as high quality, as it might be a quick fix or a retrofit rather than a solid design. While these are valid concerns, a short iteration (or any other technique for that matter) is not an excuse for developing poorly designed or written code. Just because things are done differently doesn't mean that the code can't be of high quality. In the next chapter, we'll discuss some methodologies that lean towards short iterations and see some of the techniques used to produce high quality code.

There is also the argument that the benefits of getting something to the users early can be achieved by simply building a prototype. While the benefits are the same, it is better from a cost issue if the code that is produced can be reused. Often prototypes are not reused, and are produced as a tool rather than a real part of the application. There is a time and a place for both prototypes and the methodologies that support them, as we will discuss in the next chapter.

Convincing businesses to gather requirements in an iterative manner can be difficult. It requires a great deal of trust between the business and the project team. However, this trust should already be in place or it will have an effect on all aspects of the process. Again, shrinking the size of iterations is a good way to build trust. It shows business that the developers are serious about what they say, and that they can indeed deliver the small high quality pieces they promise.

Important Considerations

There are some important issues that must be considered when gathering requirements for an e-commerce system that may not emerge in other types of applications. These issues are:

- ❑ Privacy and Security.
- ❑ Bridging the Gaps Between Countries.
- ❑ Payment Considerations.
- ❑ Customer Service.

What is interesting about these considerations is that they require input on both a business and a technological level, requiring a high level of cooperation and communication between team members. We shall now take a look at each of these in turn.

Privacy and Security

Privacy is one of the hottest topics on the Internet today, and e-commerce is really the reason that this is such an important issue. Conducting a commerce transaction is one of the few times when the actual identity of an individual and his personal information are an integral part of the process. While it is simple to participate in an online chat with only an alias, a user must disclose their name, address and credit card numbers in order to complete a B2C e-commerce transaction.

Tracking users and their browsing habits and storing and using this data is an important issue to consider. This is a particularly timely topic as users are expressing more concern over this type of data. Users are also concerned with being identified through the use of cookies. These types of issues must be addressed as a part of the requirements gathering process.

This level of information being passed to an e-commerce site brings new concerns to the table. It is also an issue for businesses in B2B applications as businesses are even more concerned about protecting access to the proprietary information in their systems. Information important enough to trade with another business is probably more likely to be something a company does not want shared outside of that interaction.

In m-commerce security is also an important consideration, and is a much more volatile subject considering the lack of clearly defined standards, especially in the United States. When a device is wireless, it does not require physical access to a network. This opens the door for a potential security leak without ever actually being in contact with the network. This is a legitimate and relevant concern.

Dealing with Payments

When dealing with payments, there must be security in place. In a B2C Internet application, this is commonly done using Secure Socket Layer (SSL). Business users must decide what pages contain information sensitive enough to require SSL encryption. In addition, the security must extend past the HTTP layer. It doesn't make sense to use SSL for the request and then write the numbers to an easily hacked database. We look at SSL in more detail in Chapter 8.

Critical information must be continuously secure regardless of the type of application. For B2B, security must be a mutual decision for each company involved in the transaction. These are business decisions that can only be resolved with the input and help of developers.

In addition to the privacy and security issues that companies are highly motivated to address, there are also legal restrictions to consider. While issues regarding who has the right to police the Internet, (if anyone), remain unresolved, companies are bound by certain laws that, depending on the locale, may require them to take special precautions with the identities of their customers. In almost any locale, a business that is negligent with security can have a liability to the companies they do business with.

Bridging the Gaps Between Countries

One large decision to be considered in the process of gathering requirements is how to address other countries within the application. Making the application usable in different countries, or **internationalization**, is a very important topic for e-commerce applications. As new markets open up so do new concerns, and one of the largest of these is the handling of multiple languages.

Language is a huge issue to tackle and is not one to be entered into lightly. There are also issues between supporting languages that share an alphabet versus supporting multiple alphabets. In addition to the consideration of language, each new location brings forward other concerns such as the ways dates and numbers are represented. For example, 01/10/00 could be January 10th or October 1st depending on the locale.

How (or if) multiple languages are to be handled is something that must be considered early in the process so that the system can consider and handle the decision. Again, a company must balance the desire to reach new markets with the cost of creating a multi-lingual solution. The cost of maintaining multiple languages for the application must be considered along with the cost of building that piece of the application. The company must also consider the costs of bringing in the people to do jobs such as translation or other tasks to support each locale.

Multiple Languages

Many companies choose to address multi-lingual issues as a part of a future release that may or may not come to fruition. However, if there is any reason to believe that the company might be interested in supporting many languages and countries, this should be identified early on so that the architecture is not closed to such a decision in the future.

In addition to the language issue, there is also the question of export restrictions. Assuming that the application is selling goods as opposed to services, they must consider what is or is not allowed as far as exporting of their product is concerned. An excellent example of this is selling DVDs, which are encoded for specific regions and are prohibited from being sold outside of the specific region. This is something that must be considered and weighed as a part of the requirements gathering process.

Payment Considerations

Payment is a huge consideration as it directly affects the bottom line. An application must consider the payment methods that will be allowed in the application. In a B2B application, a comprehensive strategy for determining the exchange of money must be determined. In a B2C application, the company must decide what payment options to accept. In any e-commerce application, issues like handling different currencies and the conversion between them must be considered if the application is to be used in more than one locale.

Credit cards are the standard for payment on B2C sites. Accepting credit cards might be new to an organization that, at a corporate level, has never sold anything to consumers. This is something that must be considered both technically and in terms of business process. There are additional payment options for B2C sites, largely because some shoppers still prefer to not give out credit cards numbers. Sites often react to this by allowing the user to call in their credit card numbers or pay by check. A company must weigh the comfort level of the user with credit cards against the cost of building additional functionality to support those users who are not comfortable.

Digital Payment Schemes

An application might also want to consider new types of digital payment such as PayPal or something similar. PayPal is a service that allows businesses or individuals to send payments to other businesses or individuals. Essentially, partnering with a site like PayPal (or another site like it) makes its customers more comfortable since they know they are dealing with a reputable site that specializes in payments. In addition, it can take some of the responsibility off of an e-commerce site. These options add more flexibility for users, but might not pay off in the time and money necessary to add the feature if very few users are interested in that type of functionality.

Taxes and shipping costs must also be considered in the issue of payment. These issues are clouded by the geographical scope of the web site. For example, a site that serves many countries has a more complex model for calculating shipping costs than a company that only sells products domestically. Taxes must also be considered, and the rules for application vary by locale. These must be considered and factored into the requirements gathering process.

Customer Service

One thing to consider when launching an e-commerce initiative is the need for customer service. Customer service largely relates to B2C applications, but it is extremely important. A September 1998 study by Jupiter Communications showed that 47% of people are more likely to buy online if the site has real-time customer interaction. Sites that include interaction with real people such as live chat using text or voice are also more profitable because a live person is more effective at encouraging customers to purchase more.

As we discussed earlier, a company might not already have an established method of customer service if e-commerce is new to them. They then must decide if this is something that they want to outsource or handle in-house. Outsourcing is often cheaper and provides an already established solution. On the other hand, many companies want the control afforded by keeping this process in house. Regardless of whether the process is in-house or outsourced there is some technological integration that must occur between the site and the application used by the customer service representatives.

There are also some issues to consider about the capabilities of the customer service representative. What information should they be able to access about a person or an order? Certainly they should be able to see that an order has been placed, but should they be able to see credit card information? They should be able to see the total price of an order, but should they be able to change the total of an order? Should they be able to apply discounts and modify shipping information? There is clearly a balance to consider between giving them too much access and making them ineffective.

Tracking Customer Behaviour

Customer service is also an area that many companies focus on for tracking customer behaviour. The interaction between the staff and the customers (as well as the interaction between the customers and the site) is an important area to track because it allows a site to monitor the concerns of the customer and presents an opportunity to fix them. For example, if a customer has ordered three things, and they have all been delayed, the company know they have a problem to address with fulfillment. In addition, they have the opportunity to offer the customer a free gift or discount to make them happier with the site.

In general, customer service is extremely important for the health of a B2C site. Many failed B2C sites can attribute some of their failure to poor customer service. It is important then to consider the goals and strategies for customer service during the requirements phase of the e-commerce application.

Technology Decisions

There are a lot of decisions to consider in the requirements gathering process as far as technology is concerned. What is important about these items is that the technical staff must be involved in presenting options and helping make decisions on these issues. These decisions are easier if project goals have been set and prioritized as discussed earlier in the Chapter.

The technology decisions are also affected by whether or not there is an existing site. One of the first decisions is whether or not the existing site should be updated or replaced. This depends a lot on what is there currently, and a re-examination of the reasons for it being present in the first place. It often becomes a cost issue as to whether it is cheaper to adapt the existing site or to start over. It is also important to keep in mind that you should adopt the most suitable and effective technology for your business model rather than chasing the most sophisticated.

Regardless of whether there is an existing site or not, the following items all need to be considered with decisions made during the requirements gathering process:

- Scalability
- Fault tolerance
- Integration
- User interface design

Scalability

An application is considered to be scalable if it can support an increasingly large number of concurrent users without degradation in performance. Certainly, this is a very abstract statement. There is definitely an upper limit to the need for scalability for each application. An application, in addition to being scalable, should balance this with the ability to support equally as well a small number of users. The issue of degradation in performance is really an issue of what level of degradation is acceptable to the user base. The system need not have the same response time for one user as it does for 500 concurrent users if, in both cases, the response time is acceptable to the user.

Scalability is particularly important for e-commerce applications, which in many cases are only successful if they have an increasingly large number of concurrent users. While the strategy for scalability is a part of the architectural process, the requirements for scalability are something that must be determined by the business and the technical staff during the requirements gathering process.

The Projected Load

The team must determine a projected maximum load for the application within whatever time period is determined to be reasonable. This projected load must be a reasonable estimate based on all known information about the system and user base and must not be a guess, or a number representing the desired number of users. The time period should reflect the reasonable amount of time the system should be expected to provide the desired scalability without upgrades or changes to the system. If the projected load is larger than the actual load, the company will spend more money than is necessary. This may or may not be a huge issue depending on the company. Some companies may not have the money to spare while others might be more comfortable investing in the solution with the knowledge that the user base will continue to increase.

The danger area is not when the actual load is lower than the projected load, but when the actual load is higher than the projected load. Zona Research recently conducted a survey that indicated that $4.35 billion ($US) in e-commerce sales is lost each year in the US due to unacceptable download speeds. When download speeds are unacceptable, users are more likely to leave the site, and this explains the loss in revenue. As a rule, Zona Research found that the average user would wait only eight seconds for a page to load. However, a small change can make a big difference. On one website Zona Research observed that trimming the initial page size from 40 KB to 34 KB cut off about one second of the download time. However, this small change made the rate of users who don't wait for the page to load drop about 20 percent.

Determining Scalability Requirements

The question then becomes how to determine the requirements for scalability. A research analyst from Doculabs was recently quoted as recommending that a website should be capable of scaling for 5,000 or more concurrent users without degrading. This is probably a fair number for large applications, but only addresses Internet applications, and completely ignores m-commerce sites and other media. The reality is that there is no magic number. An evaluation of the market for the application is more likely to be successful in choosing a number for maximum load.

In addition, there are some scalability concerns that vary based on the type of application. For example, an application that is computationally intensive (such as a trading application) has different scalability concerns than an application that is memory intensive (such as a bookstore) with a large number of user objects in the session objects. These types of concerns must be weighed when determining what is needed to achieve the desired scalability.

There are some tradeoffs with scalability as with all other decisions. Adding hardware adds more than simply the cost of the hardware; it also adds more floor space, more money for maintenance, and increases the complexity of the system. The more complex the system, the more points of failure there are within the application.

Fault Tolerance

Fault tolerance is the ability for a system to withstand power outages, hardware and software failures, and network failures. Essentially, the less fault tolerant an application is, the more likely it is to be unavailable for users. A study conducted by Oracle suggested that every minute a site is down costs a company $1400 ($US). This number was calculated from a survey of 400 large companies, and numbers would be lower for companies that make less money per minute.

The major reason to consider the requirements for fault tolerance is that people have very little patience for an application that doesn't respond. It is very easy for an application to lose users forever if the application is unavailable. Thus, an important business decision is how fault tolerant the site must be, while the technical discussion could center upon the optimal server clustering arrangement to provide fall-over support.

In addition to simply staying up and running, the site must also seamlessly re-route users when a portion of the site goes down. Ideally, the user will have no idea that anything has happened to the site. When there is a failure, the business must decide how much effort is put into making sure that the system can come back up on its own when possible. This is an important trade-off to be made by weighing the cost of building this feature into the system versus staffing the application with additional system administrators.

As with the case of scalability, the developers must help the business users decide what makes sense for their business needs. The developers are better equipped to understand the implications of the fault tolerance decisions, but the business users most often make the ultimate decision. The tradeoffs are clear – cost of lost sales versus cost of additional hardware and development costs. This is a decision the company has to make based on the needs and goals for the business.

Integration

Integration is an important consideration for e-commerce applications. First, there is the issue of existing applications. There may already be an inventory system, or a payment processing system, for example. These systems need to be integrated with the new e-commerce application and must be considered early on in the process. In fact in many cases, the success of an e-commerce initiative depends very much on how successful the integration with legacy systems is.

There is also the issue of consideration of integration with an existing database schema. This is especially true if you are implementing a package solution rather than building the e-commerce application from scratch. If you are building, for example, a B2C application, and the company already has their product data in a database with a particular schema, you will need to consider the best way to utilize that schema very early on. This is as much a part of integration as integrating with a mainframe, but issues like database schema integration between a product and existing data are more likely to be left until later in the process.

The final piece of integration to consider is integration between tool sets. For example, suppose you are building an e-commerce application using an application server, but the company has also invested in a content management system. You need to consider very early on the points of integration between the two products and the custom code you are creating.

For the most part, integration is a part of the architectural process rather than a part of the requirements gathering process. However, these items cannot be ignored during the requirements gathering process. The systems that must be integrated and the points of integration must be identified during the requirements gathering process. If they are not identified here and stated as requirements, there is no objective way to evaluate the success of the integration.

User Interface Design

Although user interface design is important to the success of the application, there is often little interaction between the user interface designers and the developers. The user interface designers might talk directly to the business users to determine what the application should look like. This process is often independent from requirements gathering when in reality these processes should be closely integrated.

Often, the user interface is developed (for example in HTML) and is extremely difficult to integrate with the backend systems. It is to alleviate this risk that the user interface designers must be involved in the process with the developers. Early communication and identification of user interface requirements in parallel with technical or business requirements are very important to ensure success later on in the process. However, the main purpose of early communication between developers and UI developers is that the hooks between the frontend UI and backend are planned for from the earliest stage, allowing optimal decisions.

The process of gathering requirements must also consider some items critical to user interface design. Determining the supported platforms and clients is a very important step. In a web application, the browser types and version supported as well as the platforms they are supported on must be determined. In an m-commerce application, the mobile devices supported must also be discussed and determined.

Business Considerations

In addition to the technology considerations, there are some business considerations, which are specific to e-commerce applications. As was discussed in Chapter 1, e-commerce is part of e-business and an e-commerce site must reflect and support the way the organization does business. However, these business processes may need to be re-evaluated in light of new opportunities with technology.

Considering the Package

In the case where the e-commerce site is implementing a package rather than writing all the code from scratch, there are some interesting considerations. One mistake often made is the selection of a software package that not only has the necessary requirements, but some other features that may obscure some of the other requirements that have been initially gathered when they are implemented. This is unfair to business and development as it makes it more difficult for both of them to do their job.

Business needs to make good decisions that are cost effective. If they know what the tool already provides, they have the option of accepting that feature as appropriate for the application, thus saving money. Technology also benefits from considering the package, as it is easier to use built-in functionality of a package than it is to try to customize behavior into a package.

Thus, when an e-commerce application is implementing a package solution for any aspect of the application, it is important that the requirements gatherer relies on the developers to explain the existing functionality of the package to business so that business can make well-informed decisions. The requirements really become a set of small changes from the baseline of the package rather than a completely independent list of requirements.

Reporting

Reporting is something that is sometimes overlooked in an e-commerce application. Good reporting of what is actually happening in the application is very important to motivate and inform business. Business must decide early on in the process what types of information they want to gather about the site and how they want this information reported.

Sometimes, a company will decide that they want to log and report on everything. When a company is requesting a log of every action every user performs on the site, this is often a sign that they are unsure of what they really want. In this case, they need to understand that logging everything comes with an overhead, and that they should spend more time considering what it is that they actually need to make good decisions about the site.

Summary

The process of gathering requirements is by no means easy. It is challenging for any application and even more challenging for e-commerce applications. There are many ways to be effective in gathering requirements, but some of the most important steps that we have discussed in this section are:

- ❑ Understand that there are a variety of distinct groups involved in requirements gathering: developers, business users, users, QA staff and the requirements gatherer(s).
- ❑ Understand the differences between e-commerce systems and other applications and how these differences affect the different people involved.
- ❑ Gather business requirements by *first* setting goals and *then* gathering requirements to help meet them.
- ❑ Gather requirements effectively using techniques to facilitate rather than hinder the process.
- ❑ Understand that compromise is an important part of gathering requirements.
- ❑ Consider making the requirements gathering process an iterative process.
- ❑ Consider important topics like privacy, security, internationalization, payment and customer service.
- ❑ Consider important technology decisions like scalability, fault tolerance, integration, and user interface design.
- ❑ Consider important business decisions like implementing a package solution and reporting.

These steps can help make the process of gathering requirements easier, but it is only by intense communication and cooperation from all involved parties that the process, and thus the project, has a chance for success.

The process of gathering requirements is also influenced by the methodology of the project or by how the project will be run. In the next chapter, we will discuss different options for planning and running e-commerce projects.

3

Planning the Project

In the previous chapter we talked about gathering requirements, but in this section we will discuss the topics of planning the project and getting started building it. Planning the project is a distinct exercise from gathering requirements because while the requirements gathering process addresses the what, planning the project addresses the how. These tasks are not necessarily sequential, but are both extremely important. This chapter assumes that you are undertaking the process of gathering requirements since skipping that step increases your risk of project failure dramatically.

The planning step of the process is the step where the roles each person will play in creating the system are better defined. It is where concrete deadlines are set and phases determined. It is also where the project plan, whether formal or informal, is determined. This is, of course, a very important phase of the project. It is also a process that varies greatly from project to project depending on the project methodologies or corporate cultures.

In this chapter we will discuss the following topics as they relate to planning the project:

- ❏   First we will discuss the different players in the process, what they need to do their jobs, and the issues they need to understand.

- ❏   Next we will discuss the issue of project ownership, and the tradeoffs of doing it yourself or outsourcing.

- ❏   Then we will discuss some of the different methodologies available – specifically the waterfall methodology, the Rational Unified Process, and Extreme Programming.

- ❏   Once we have discussed methodologies, we will take a look at other concerns for planning such as tools, hosting options, and other considerations.

- ❏   We will conclude with a summary of this chapter and a look back at the previous two chapters to see at how we can tie together these topics.

Understanding the Players

One of the first things to consider in planning the project is the people involved. When planning the project, we can consider people in the same roles as we did in gathering requirements. There are developers, business users, and users. We need to also consider the project manager, the managers, the CEO and board, and the quality assurance team. These individual groups all have certain things that should be guaranteed to them in order to treat them fairly. There are also things that each group needs to understand in order to be more effective team members. An e-commerce project, like any other initiative, is a team effort and as such each team member needs to be prepared to deal with the rest of the team appropriately.

Developers

Developers are a very important part of the process of planning a project, as developers are often the ones called upon to estimate how long various requirements will take to build. As the planning phase is left behind and development begins, developers become the critical piece of the puzzle in getting the application built and deployed. Given this, there are certain things that developers need in order to ensure that they are able and willing to do their best and produce at 100 %. There are also things developers need to consider, and need to be willing to compromise on.

Their Needs

- ❑ Developers need to receive detailed requirements – they should never have to guess what was meant or build pieces of the system that have not been defined.

- ❑ Developers need to receive timely clarification from the appropriate people when the requirements are unclear or when questions arise.

- ❑ Developers need to have their estimates respected.

- ❑ Developers need to work reasonable hours and have reasonable, and achievable, deadlines.

- ❑ Developers need the proper tools and environments, both hardware and software, to do their job effectively.

These things might seem like the appropriate way to treat professionals. Unfortunately, almost anyone who has worked as a developer has suffered through unclear requirements and unreasonable schedules, amongst other things. As a developer, you have a responsibility to speak up when any of your needs, such as the ones mentioned here, are not being met. In a perfect world, other team members would provide for all your needs, but in the real world you have just as much responsibility to provide for your needs as anyone else on the team.

What they Need to Understand

Just as developers need certain things provided for them, they also need to give on certain items. It can be difficult to be patient when waiting for requirements and sitting through meetings. Developers need to consider the following items when frustrated or impatient with the planning process:

- ❑ Developers need to understand the criticality of the system to the business.

- ❑ Developers need to understand that they are creating an entirely new area of the business, so they need to understand that changes in requirements will and should occur as the application evolves.

- ❑ Developers need to understand that the business users won't know what they want up front, and need to be proactive to help get them there.

❏ Developers need to facilitate as much communication and feedback with business as possible (remembering to balance technical and non-technical language).

❏ Developers need to be watchful of emerging technologies and standards to best serve the goals of the company.

❏ Developers need to resist the temptation to always build it themselves, and take the time to explore third-party solutions – it's important to look for ways that can help save time and money.

Not all developers have the same weaknesses and strengths. Some developers find walking the line between the business goals and the technology simple, while others struggle with it. Regardless of how easy things come, it is always good to review the process to help the communication and flow within the project.

Other Team Members' Needs and Responsibilities

Although there are a great many issues regarding project planning and the role of different groups of people, in this section we will focus on some of the important issues that developers need to be aware of in their interactions with other team members. It is important for all groups to be mindful of their interactions within the project.

Project Manager

❏ Project managers need accurate and timely feedback from all members of the team, and need to be informed of roadblocks as quickly as possible so that they can act accordingly.

❏ Project managers need to have help making decisions as the project varies from the schedule.

Managers, Board and CEO

❏ The managers at all levels need to have a solid value proposition and see it executed.

❏ The managers at all levels need to have realistic budgets that are actually adhered to.

All Business Users

❏ All business users need to have their requests understood and taken seriously.

❏ All business users need to be involved in the development process – they won't be writing code, but should get to see the results as they are created and get to understand what is happening at all parts of development.

❏ All business users need to receive feedback as quickly as possible regarding the return on investment – basically they need to see what they are getting for their money.

❏ Business users need to be prepared to make strategic decisions as they are needed. In many cases, it is the developers who are best poised to give the business users the information they need to make these critical decisions.

❏ Business users need to manage the expectations of the organization and keep them realistic.

Users

❏ Users need an easy to understand application, or training to make the application easy to understand so they can gain value from the application. Unless the application is very simple, training and documentation should be mandatory.

❑   Users need to have feedback from the system and be able to see the results of their requests. Once the application is available to the users, they need a way to make comments and suggestions on the way they want to interact with the system.

❑   Users need to feel valued as a part of the process. Whether the users are in a partner company or members of the general public they need to be made part of the process. Soliciting information through user surveys and focus groups is an excellent way to do this.

❑   Users need to understand that the perfect product isn't often produced after the first iteration. In today's world of fast releases, it doesn't hurt for everyone to have a little more patience with the evolution of software. There is obviously a balance between an unusable application and an application with a few bugs, so developers need to be mindful of this difference and help users accept the small bugs.

Quality Assurance / Testing

❑   The quality assurance team is a very important part of the process – testers need to be involved at all steps of the process in order to understand the requirements and the deadlines, and then to test the application as it is available.

❑   Primarily, testers need cooperation from everyone on the project to help to make sure the software is as free of bugs as possible.

Project Ownership

One of the important steps in planning the project is to determine who is responsible for the actual work. There are a variety of options a company can choose from ranging from, doing the project in-house to outsourcing the project. In addition to deciding who is responsible for building the application, companies may choose to outsource the requirements gathering process and the project management. It should be noted that different parts of the project can be handled in different ways and even if they are handled in the same way different people or groups can handle them. For example, a company could choose to do the requirements gathering themselves, but outsource the project management to one company and the technology to another company.

Do it Yourself

Do it yourself implies that the work is handled by the company initiating and taking ownership of the application. This means that the company's IT department is responsible for the technology and various people from different business departments handle the other roles. This seems to be something that companies often prefer to do, but they are often unable to do so because of staffing shortages or other limitations. For example, a recent study by Forrester Research found two-thirds of companies worldwide experience delays or problems with projects due to staffing shortages. Delays of a year or more are experienced by 27 % of companies.

Risks

There are some additional risks to consider before deciding to handle a project in-house:

❑   You might not have the right skill-set in place amongst your staff to be able complete the project. Consulting organizations have an advantage in that they often have experts in a variety of areas. If you choose in do it yourself, you have to be certain not only that you have enough people to do the work, but that you have the right people for each job.

❑ Consider employee turnover. If the company has exactly the right number of people with the right skills, a company must also be sure those people aren't going anywhere. A consulting company usually has backups and can bring in additional people to fill a vacancy. A company doing the work in-house doesn't have that luxury, and has to go through the entire hiring cycle to replace employees who leave.

❑ Make sure the team can be responsive to the industry. Within a company there tends to be a somewhat isolated environment. Unless the company has historically embraced a wide variety of technologies, the developers are probably familiar with a few product sets, which may or may not be applicable to the e-commerce project at hand. The isolated environment that often exists within a company may mean that the team is not aware of or responsive to e-commerce trends.

❑ Consider all technologies. Another risk of doing it yourself comes when you have a group of people in your organization that are experts in a particular technology. If all the development in an organization has traditionally been done using that particular technology, there is a risk that the natural tendency would be to use that technology for all e-commerce initiatives. While this technology might be totally appropriate, there is still a risk in that the company simply doesn't have the experience to know about other technologies. Having a wide breadth of knowledge about various tools is something that consulting services organizations can afford to do but is very expensive for companies.

❑ In order to alleviate some of the other risks, you might choose to retrain your staff in the newest technologies. This is expensive, and is not always successful, but can be a good idea.

Benefits

There are some wonderful benefits to be gained from doing it yourself that make it very attractive. Here are some of the big reasons companies choose to do it themselves.

❑ You get to keep all the knowledge in-house. Rather than paying someone else to build it and then paying them to teach your people how to support it, or even outsourcing the support, you simply have your people build it from the ground up and have intimate knowledge of the system. The knowledge one gains by building a system can never be equaled by a training course or a knowledge transfer session.

❑ Having a knowledge of the system makes it easier to maintain and expand the system as your needs grow and change. You also have the benefit of first hand knowledge when training new employees or employees who weren't involved with the process.

❑ Doing it yourself also allows a company to keep all the control in-house. You are free to set your own standards for coding, your own standards for design, and even your own methodologies.

Outsource

Outsourcing has become a very popular trend in e-commerce development largely because of the lack of availability of resources to complete the work. A recent report by Forrester found that U.S. companies would outsource nearly $20 billion ($US) this year for building e-commerce sites. This number includes money spent on both design and technical services. To meet the demand for outsourcing, there are a variety of different types of consulting services available, from using independent contractors to augment a project, all the way up to a full service consulting firm. Typically, a company goes through a process of shopping for the individual or organization that most clearly matches their desired level of service.

Risks

There are a lot of risks in outsourcing the projects for your company. Some of the major risks include.

❑ The consulting organization doesn't necessarily share the same risk as your company. If the project is critical to your success or your e-commerce strategy, it is not likely to have the same importance to the company you contract with.

❑ Knowledge transfer is difficult. Just as do it yourself gives you the benefit of controlling the knowledge in-house, outsourcing carries the risk of losing knowledge. In addition to simply not controlling the knowledge of the system, there is also the risk that the knowledge won't or can't be transferred successfully.

❑ You can lose control of the project. When the employees don't belong to the company and may not even be on site, there is less control for the company that owns the project over the code, the implementations, the process and the day-to-day operations of the project. Loss of control also brings a risk of rising costs and lack of quality to the project.

Benefits

There are some benefits of outsourcing, and these are many of the reasons that companies tend towards outsourcing as an option for their e-commerce applications.

❑ A consulting organization is more likely to have people with the right skill sets needed to actually complete the work. In addition to being able to staff the project, consulting organizations also have a wide array of knowledge.

❑ When you hire a consulting organization, you are hiring not only the individuals you work with, but also the knowledge of all the individuals within that organization. You're effecetively hiring the sum total of knowledge of every project every person in the company has worked on.

❑ You gain perspective on the industry, in this case e-commerce. A consulting organization that is selling e-commerce services has worked on e-commerce before and should have a good understanding of the issues involved in both the business side and the technological side of e-commerce.

❑ Outsourcing is useful because you are required to explain your business process to the individuals who are becoming involved in the process. Often, explaining a process is an excellent way to examine the process as you attempt to see it through the eyes of others.

Spin Off a Separate Division or Company

One of the options that a company may pursue in starting an e-commerce application is to take some of their employees and spin off a new division or even a new company. This can be a great approach for larger initiatives as it clearly makes the statement that the company is committed to the initiative and that they are willing to make it as high a priority as all other initiatives. This can be helpful in getting respect for a new project from the other more established projects within the company, but like all approaches it has some pluses and some minuses.

Risks

❑ The new entity is isolated by artificial boundaries from the parent business. This has wide implications depending on how nimble the organization is. For example, figuring out who is responsible for ordering supplies is a problem that must be addressed, but one which distracts the new entity from the task at hand.

❑ Another risk is that a new entity is likely to include some new employees or at the very least a new organization for existing employees. For any group of people, there is a learning curve for the new structure and for the teams in the new entity to adjust. Suddenly, there is time that needs to be spent adjusting to the new surroundings rather than digging into the task.

Benefits

❑ It isolates the company from some risk stemming from the e-commerce initiative. This is especially true if the company chooses to spin off a subsidiary rather than just a separate division.

❑ As a separate entity, it is easier to track the expenditures and income of the new company and thus easier to see whether the project is a financial success or failure.

❑ If the project does have failures, the new structure provides some protection to the parent company.

❑ Rather than having a team of people distracted by their other duties, a new entity ensures that the team is made up of employees dedicated only to the success of their division or company, which in this case is the project itself. This prevents situations where developers are maintaining existing sites while trying to create the new application.

❑ A new entity can do it themselves within the company or outsource and get all risks and benefits of either option. There is a lot of flexibility as far as how the new entity chooses to conduct the project, and how the entity chooses to run the project can easily be left up to the entity.

Making the Ultimate Decision

Making the ultimate decision about who does the work is difficult and requires input from all parties as well as an unbiased evaluation of the state of the company. This can be a difficult task and requires some thought and the investment of time. It is also important to keep in mind that there is no reason why a combination of the approaches addressed here or even different approaches for different phases of the project can't be an acceptable solution as well. Whatever the ultimate decision, it is important to periodically review the decision to make sure it still makes sense in light of new developments in the project or in the marketplace.

Methodologies

Another important step in planning the project is to choose the methodology for the project. The methodology chosen for the project often has a great deal to do with when and how the requirements are gathered, and it is therefore not commonly recommended to choose the methodology after gathering the requirements.

Choosing a methodology is important. The methodology chosen must be compatible with the culture of the company and well suited to the temperaments of all the people involved. Given this, the process of choosing a methodology is one that must involve a representative sampling of people involved in the project. Furthermore, it must be constantly re-evaluated as the company learns more about how the methodology works for them.

Traditional Methodologies

If the corporate culture is more traditional, or if the people involved are more comfortable with these types of methodologies, then using these is probably the better option. Traditional methodologies often have the most written about them and it is easy to find people with a great deal of experience using them.

On the other hand, traditional methodologies often have a history of many failures as well as their successes. They are less likely to be adaptive to the latest trends in management and in general are less nimble since they are clearly defined. They are also often less and less relevant to the new business models evolving in "Internet Time".

Example – Waterfall

An example of a traditional methodology is the waterfall methodology. There are many variations on the waterfall methodology, but the basic idea is that the analysis is done up front, followed by the design, the implementation, the testing and, finally, the deployment. This is called the waterfall methodology because each phase flows into the next like a series of waterfalls.

The waterfall methodology is in many ways the epitome of the traditional methodology, as many more traditional methodologies contain echoes of this one.

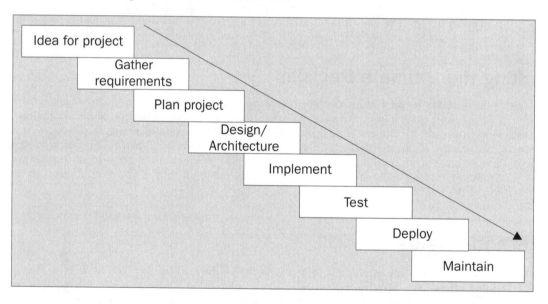

Strengths

There are some strong benefits of the waterfall methodology and they also apply to traditional methodologies in general. For example:

- ❑ The waterfall methodology simply asks the team to think, then plan, then execute, then ensure that you executed as intended. This is very much like other types of engineering methodologies.

- ❑ The waterfall methodology is very structured and easy to follow. This makes the process predictable and repeatable.

❑ The waterfall methodology, like many traditional methodologies, enforces discipline. If it is followed, it ensures that nothing will be done without all the steps before it. Thus, the team is fully prepared for each step of the process. The developers will never be asked to code until the project is scoped and planned, for example.

Traditional methodologies in general (and specifically waterfall) tend to force a well thought out process before action is taken in actually building the system. This eliminates the need to rework code that was built without giving enough thought to what was being built.

Weaknesses

The waterfall methodology has all these strengths, but it is not lacking in weaknesses as well. Some of the weaknesses of the waterfall methodology are as follows:

❑ The waterfall methodology, like many traditional methodologies, requires the analysis phase to address all issues and details so that they can be thrown over the fence to the planning and then on to the development teams.

❑ There is nothing built-in to the process to address mistakes or oversights. There is also no input from development as to the cost of each requirement and options to make the process less expensive.

❑ The waterfall methodology can also add significant time to the development process. By forcing each team to wait until the previous team is finished, the timeline is delayed.

❑ There is no room for feedback from business or for building quick solutions. There is also nothing in the process that requires or encourages communication between the teams responsible for each phase of the process.

The waterfall methodology is not always used directly as-is, but there are elements of the waterfall methodology in many others. By understanding the strengths and weaknesses of the waterfall methodology, you are better equipped to understand the strengths and weaknesses in other similar methodologies.

Example – Rational Unified Process

The **Rational Unified Process** (**RUP**) is a methodology created and owned by the Rational Company. This process differs from the waterfall methodology in that it creates a very clear set of deliverables for each phase of the process. In many ways, RUP is one of the most detailed methodologies available, and helps the team through every step of the way.

Another major difference between waterfall and RUP is that RUP builds in small iterations and allows for a great deal of feedback, which is often missing from the waterfall methodology. RUP is also tightly integrated with other products and services offered by Rational. Some of the key ideas of RUP are as follows:

❑ **Gathering requirements** – One of the key concepts of RUP is having an overall vision of the requirement workflow. This piece of the process contains answers to many of the basic questions we posed in the previous chapter such as identifying the problem to solve and defining requirements.

❑ **Having a Plan** – Another key step in RUP is developing the Software Development Plan. This plan contains all the information needed to plan and manage the project and addresses issues such as Project Organization, Schedule (Project Plan, Iteration Plan, Resources, Tools), Requirements Management Plan, Configuration Management Plan, Problem Resolution Plan, QA Plan, Test Plan, Test Cases, Evaluation Plan, and Product Acceptance Plan.

❑ **Identify and Mitigate Risks** – RUP asks the team to identify the highest risk items early in the project and address them early. In addition to identifying each risk, a mitigation strategy should also be included for each risk.

❑ **Assigning and Tracking Issues** – RUP requires regular status meetings to address issues and follow up on them. This process is the key to handling project issues effectively.

❑ **The Business Case** – The business case is created to assess the return on investment (ROI) from a project and justify the expenditures being made.

❑ **Architecture** – In RUP, the system is architected in a very methodical way. This area of the process uses Rational tools such as Rational Rose and includes a detailed process for choosing, defining and refining the architecture. A software architecture document is created to reflect the final architecture.

❑ **Build and Test the System** – Building the system in RUP is focused on iterations, which are each built and tested and deliver a release.

❑ **Regular Evaluation** – RUP calls for continuous re-evaluation of the process after each iteration. This approach allows the process to be continually optimized.

❑ **Manage and Control Change** – RUP calls for each requested change to the requirements to be communicated in the form of a change request. These requests are then managed through a process to ensure consistent results.

❑ **Considering Users** – RUP calls for clear documentation focused around the user such as a user guide, installation guide, release notes or additional materials.

These are some of the basic ideas of the Rational Unified Process, but clearly not all aspects as it is a detailed and complex methodology. It is important to weigh some of the strengths and weaknesses of the methodology in order to better understand it.

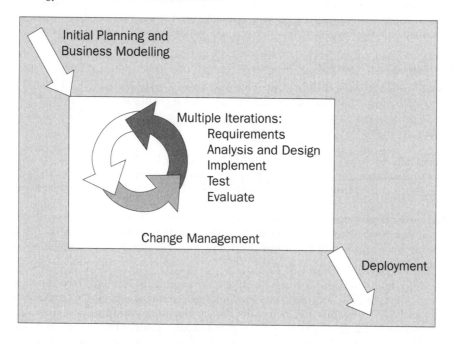

Initial Planning and Business Modelling

Multiple Iterations:
Requirements
Analysis and Design
Implement
Test
Evaluate

Change Management

Deployment

Strengths

RUP is a very popular methodology and is chosen by many organizations because of its many strengths. Some of these strengths are as follows:

❑ RUP is well defined yet flexible, making it easy to adopt even when unfamiliar with the process.

❑ A great deal of documentation is generated as a part of RUP, making the methodology very comfortable to organizations that prefer a lot of documentation.

❑ RUP is designed and structured around the web, making it a good choice for web applications.

❑ Because it is a good blend of traditional methodologies updated for current trends, RUP is a good process to use in traditional organizations that want to use web technologies.

❑ Rational provides many tools and a great deal of support to help people adopt RUP. In addition, many large consulting organizations have adopted RUP, making it a well-known methodology. Because of this, it is easy to find experts (even outside of Rational) who have expertise using RUP.

Weaknesses

❑ RUP is complex and many people find it overwhelming to use regardless of the support available.

❑ Because RUP is owned by Rational, there are costs associated with adopting the methodology. In addition, the many tools recommended by the project increase the cost of the project.

❑ The heavy documentation generated by RUP is often so overwhelming that it does not get updated to reflect changes in the system. This is not so much a fault of the methodology (which does call for updates) but instead is a practical risk of any methodology with a great deal of documentation.

❑ As compared to some non-traditional methodologies, which we will discuss next, RUP tends to make communication very formal and can make some communication between team members less spontaneous. This is arguably a strength of the methodology depending on the project and organization, but for small projects this formalization can be limiting.

The biggest issue surrounding traditional methodologies is that they do not handle change well and are not necessarily nimble enough to always respond appropriately to the e-commerce landscape. While this is definitely less true of RUP than of waterfall, there is still a difference between these traditional methodologies and the less traditional methodologies we will discuss in the next section. On the other hand, traditional methodologies are tried and true and have lead to success for a great many companies.

Non-Traditional Methodologies

If the business is more nimble and flexible with a rapidly evolving e-business strategy, there is room to consider less traditional methodologies. These methodologies tend to have evolved in the last few years and are often a direct result of the Internet revolution. While they tend to be more flexible, they also have less written about them and less people with experience using and managing these types of projects. Depending on the schedule of the project, a less traditional methodology might be the best way to achieve the project goals within the allotted time.

Example – Extreme Programming

Extreme Programming (**XP**) is a relatively new methodology that prefers to be called a "lightweight discipline." Rather than dictate the exact flow of the process, extreme programming focuses around a core set of values: namely simplicity, communication, feedback and courage. These four values are seen in almost every aspect of XP. In addition to these values, XP also focuses on people – both the users and the developers have critical roles that are emphasized by the methodology.

The name *Extreme Programming* comes from the idea that there are certain practices in development that we know are good. XP makes them extreme by saying that if a little is good, a lot is better. For example, we know that code reviews are a good thing. XP takes this to an extreme by saying that if code reviews are good then *all* code should be reviewed *all* the time as it is written. This practice is implemented using pair programming where two developers work on one workstation.

Pair programming is one practice of XP, and XP focuses on this and other core practices to help uphold the core values. Some of these practices include:

- ❏ **The Planning Game** – Instead of more conventional approaches to estimating a project and planning for a release, XP follows a different model. Essentially, development tells business how fast things can get done and business chooses a set of task cards by fixing the date or fixing the functionality. This allows business control of the schedule or the scope, but allows development to control the estimates.

- ❏ **Pair Programming** – Extreme programming believes so strongly in communication and feedback that it actually places two developers at each computer working together. As we mentioned previously, this approach is intended to maximize communication and learning and to provide for continuous code reviews by peers.

- ❏ **Focus on Testing** – Unit testing is required of developers and functional testing is required of business at a more intimate level than most other methodologies. Again, since testing is a good process, XP takes it to an extreme and places a great deal of focus on unit and functional testing. All code that is written is accompanied by a unit test to make sure it works and continues to work. These unit tests are often written before the code itself is written.

- ❏ **Refactoring** – Having a framework of tests allows developers to be flexible and to change the code without fear of breaking it. Refactoring is the idea that when a developer goes to implement a new feature, he or she first asks how he could change the system so that it would be simplest to implement the new feature. Then, he or she refactors, or changes, the system in the way that they identified. The framework of tests allows them to do this with confidence and the fact that in XP there is collective code ownership allows them to do this without waiting for someone else to change their code.

- ❏ **Do the Simplest Thing That Could Possibly Work** – Simplicity is the key in extreme programming and any feature that isn't needed immediately isn't implemented. In addition, those that are implemented are done in the simplest, clearest way possible. A simple system is less prone to bugs and promotes extensibility and re-work.

Essentially, extreme programming embraces the idea that business will change its mind. This leads the process to accept and even encourage changes as the system grows. This is a dramatic change from the traditional methodologies, which attempt to manage change rather than accept it as an important input to the system.

Like all methodologies, extreme programming has some good and bad points that should be weighed before choosing or rejecting it as a methodology.

Strengths

- ❑ Since XP is focused around clients and developers, it fosters excellent communication and can often lead to the finished product being closer to what the client really wants.

- ❑ If the team is ready for XP, it can be a faster process since it is structured to be a fast development process.

- ❑ By maximizing common sense practices, XP often generates very high quality code that is easy to maintain and extend.

- ❑ XP is empowering for developers and clients. If both parties are able to accept this power, the process can lead to great feeling about the process.

- ❑ Because change is expected and embraced, XP allows for changes to be made throughout the process without raising cost.

Weaknesses

- ❑ XP is not geared for project teams larger than 10 – 15 people, so it is unsuited for large projects.

- ❑ XP generates almost no documentation outside of the code and the unit tests. While these can serve as excellent documentation when the XP processes are followed, many organizations are simply not comfortable with this lack of documentation.

- ❑ The processes in XP around development such as pair programming and unit testing can be very hard for some developers to accept. It requires the development team to work very much as a team all the time and leaves little room for developers who like to work solo. This can be a real adjustment for a team and can be hard to accept.

XP and other non-traditional, flexible methodologies have evolved in response to the Internet and are often geared towards very small teams with very involved business people. If either of these conditions cannot be met, then a more traditional methodology is probably a better choice for the project.

Learn from Experience

Whatever methodology you choose, it is important to always re-examine the methodology with all parties throughout project. For example, you might ask the developers, "Is the documentation really helpful?" or you might ask business, "Was the prototype worth the cost?" As you make these types of assessments, you have a better idea of how successful the methodology is in the context of your particular project.

These types of questions can be asked at two points in the process to be most effective. First, they can be asked continually (although this tends to be less formal). Second, they can be asked formally at project milestones in order to solicit the best information possible.

The other important thing to do as you continually evaluate the methodology is to adapt the methodology to best suit the company. Communicate the costs of the methodology to the decision makers so that they can make informed decisions about the deliverables and their worth, and measure objectively how much the project phases are meeting planned project goals. Don't create a deliverable just because it shows up on a schedule. Continually making sure that the process is valuable is one of the responsibilities of all the interested parties.

Creating the Plan for the Project

Creating the plan for the project is largely structured according to what the methodology calls for. In a more traditional methodology, this may mean that the project manager inputs the tasks and estimates into a project management tool and begins to assign resources. In a less traditional methodology, such as extreme programming, this means beginning the planning game for the first iteration. Regardless of the mechanics of the methodology, there must be some sort of plan for how the project is to proceed.

Typically the project manager is responsible for creating the schedule and plan for the project or the current iteration of the project. There are several items that he must consider in planning the project and in tracking progress against the plan.

Managing Requirements

Managing requirements is an important part of the process of setting up the plan for the project. This is a difficult balancing act because while you want some clarity and stability of requirements so you can proceed, you also want to give the client the flexibility to create a system that embodies what they actually want to do.

It is important to remember that there are four basic pieces to a project: resources, quality, scope and time. It is important to understand that the client, defined as the person or persons commissioning the work, can control only three of the four pieces. A project is created from the following equation:

Resources x Quality x Scope x Time = The Project

Each of these four pieces has an effect on the others. For example, if the client demands a particular amount of work be done in a particular amount of time using only the people assigned to the task, the variable is quality and it will vary depending on how reasonable the constraints are on the other three pieces. Likewise if a client demands quality, controls scope, and controls the number of resources, the variable they cannot control is the deadline by which the project will be completed.

It is important to manage the detailed requirements, but also to manage the overarching requirements regarding resources, quality, scope and time. If a company wants to control all four of these variables, the project team must make it clear that it is impossible to control all four. Understanding that one variable must be left free to grow or shrink as the others are controlled is important to remember as the project team and the project manager manage requirements.

Using Tools

The tools being used have an impact on the project plan and must be considered as a part of the planning process. First, there are tools used in the analysis and design phase. These tools include applications that allow developers to create diagrams in Unified Modeling Language (UML), database schemas and other diagrams. Examples of these tools include:

- Rational Rose
- Platinum ERWin
- Microsoft Visio

These tools need to be purchased early on in the process because of their early involvement in the project. As with all tools mentioned here, time needs to be budgeted to configure these tools and to learn how to use them. Time for training must also be included in project plans and budget estimates.

A second grouping of tools that needs to be considered is tools that facilitate development such as development environments. Some examples of integrated development environments (IDEs) for Java include:

❑   IBM's Visual Age for Java

❑   Borland's JBuilder

❑   WebGain's Visual Cafe

These tools should help the development process, but if this is a new tool the team will need time to become familiar with the tool, and perhaps even to attend training. Once they are familiar with the packages themselves, they will also need to take some time to develop a usage pattern and best practices for the company. All of these costs, including development environment procurement, installation and training, should be factored into the cost of the project.

Yet another type of tool to consider is tools that the application will run on or with, such as an application server. These tools take time to install and configure and learn just like the development tools, but they also require time to architect a solution that utilizes the tools. The more tools involved the more integration time must be budgeted and the more testing time must be budgeted to ensure that the tool has been used correctly. Some examples of application servers include:

❑   ATG's Dynamo

❑   IBM's WebSphere

❑   BEA's WebLogic

There are other types of tools that need to be considered that vary slightly by the application. Some thought should be given to the following types of tools. These must all be considered and given time in the project plan. Some things to consider include:

❑   **The Java Virtual Machine (JVM) being used** – It is important to make sure that all tools will work with whatever version of the JVM you have decided on for your project. In addition, it is important to configure the JVM properly and budget time for tweaking the settings.

❑   **Databases and database servers** – While typically the job of a database administrator, the activity of setting up the database and configuring the database server(s) needs to be budgeted into the plan. In addition, time for activities such as making sure the database is functioning correctly and that the JDBC drivers are working needs to be included as well.

❑   **Other applications or APIs to other applications** – If the system is going to communicate with different applications, there must be time budgeted to make sure that the tools are in place. For example, if the system is going to talk to the mainframe through some kind of Java API, the team needs time to make sure that API is installed and working correctly.

❑   **Testing tools** – If the system is going to be tested using automated testing tools such as unit testing frameworks, load testers or tools that run scripts, time needs to be budgeted to set these tools up. If there are scripts to be written to facilitate automated testing, time needs to be budgeted for this as well.

❑   **Build Scripts** – Regardless of whether an automated tool is used to build the application and deploy it from one environment to another, there needs to be time budgeted to consider the build process. The build process is the way in which all elements of a project (code, properties files, etc.) are bundled together into one entity that can be deployed to a server. If an automated tool is used, for example ANT from the Jakarta project, time must be budgeted to configure the tool and write the build scripts.

In estimating all the time needed by tools, the team must consider the ease of use as well as the amount of explicit and implicit time the tool will take from the project. In addition to the time the tool will take, it is also appropriate to consider the value of the tool and the time it will save for the project. All these figures should be included in the final estimates of tasks involving or related to the tools that were selected for the project.

Hosting Options

The strategy for hosting the application is also a consideration in planning the project. There are a couple of basic options for a company as far as hosting is concerned. Essentially, they can either host the application internally or outsource the hosting to another company. This decision essentially depends on the infrastructure of the company and their capability to handle hosting an application.

Housing the Application Internally

If the application is to be housed internally, the plan for the project must consider the time taken to configure the hosting environment and to deploy the application. This most likely includes interaction between the developers and the systems administration staff and time must be budgeted for that. If the company has never hosted an e-commerce application, the setup could be fairly involved – for example, if a company has never hosted an application with SSL, they need to purchase the appropriate certificates and configure the servers to handle it.

Hosting internally is a good choice for companies that have the infrastructure, both people and hardware, to handle it. It provides the most control and the most access to the machines when problems occur. It also minimizes monthly costs over the life of the application.

One the other hand, hosting internally has higher upfront costs and requires the most ongoing work from the company. With increased access and control comes increased responsibility.

Outsourcing Hosting

If the application is hosted externally, there must still be time budgeted to interact with the company that is hosting the site. This still involves time to document and explain the requirements for the application and to hand it over to the hosting company. This time is difficult to estimate but must be considered.

In addition to hosting the application, there is also time to consider for configuring items such as the database. There is always some involvement with systems administration even if it is simply making sure developers have access to the necessary items on the network. These things should always be considered as a part of planning the project.

General Hosting Concerns

Regardless of whether the application is hosted internally or externally, some concerns must be addressed during the planning phase of the project:

❏ **What platform is the application to be deployed on?** If this is a different platform development one, thorough testing must be built into the process. For example, if the developers use Windows NT, but the application will be deployed on Unix, the application must be tested in Unix before deployment.

❏ **What are the restrictions of the network?** Even if the application is deployed in the same environment as it was developed in, there are always differences between one box on a network and others. Testing must be done as early as possible to alleviate these issues. For example, if the server is on a different subnet from the development machines, you need to test to make sure the application can still access the network resources it needs.

❏ **What is the deployment process?** Getting the various artifacts of a build of the systems from the developers' machines, version control system, or build machine to the production machines is a complicated process. Which needs to be defined and put in place early in the deployment process, particularly if this involves interaction with an outside hosting company.

❏ **What are the security requirements?** These issues are very important to communicate to the hosting site, internal or external. Does the application require SSL? Is there a need for a VPN or other network based security? Should this application be separated from other applications through some type of security? All these issues need to be addressed and communicated.

❏ **What are the system requirements?** Determining and communicating the needs for uptime, redundancy, and performance are all critical pieces of the process of planning hosting. These issues as well as sizing of the needed hardware need to be addressed as soon as possible in the process.

❏ **What are the Java specific issues?** The issues that arise when looking specifically at Java relate to the issues we discussed in the section on tools. One of the biggest issues is the JVM and communicating the configuration needs for it. Other issues specific to the tools must be considered as well.

In addition to these issues, the overall technical architecture of the system needs to be communicated to the hosting organization. It is also the responsibility of the project team to determine if the hosting organization is capable of meeting the requirements of the system. For example, if the system will handle a large number of users, the team needs to determine if the hosting organization can handle this load. In an external hosting situation, such needs can be communicated and agreed to in a service agreement, but internally it is important to determine if needs can be met as well.

The key to success in hosting is to make sure that all pertinent information is determined early in the process and is effectively communicated to the hosting service. Any failure or delay in this process can lead to problems with hosting when it comes time for deployment.

Other Considerations

There are other considerations that have been discussed in the process of gathering requirements and planning the project, but which now need to be considered in terms of their effect on the project plan.

Customer Service

Customer service is an item that was discussed as a part of B2C applications. Since it is such a critical piece of the application, it must be considered as a part of the project plan. The time to explore options and set up an alternative in this area must be considered as a part of the planning project.

Another item to consider is the need for applications to support the customer service process. If the customer service representatives need access to the same data as the customer can view on the site, it may or may not be necessary to build them a separate application to access and manipulate this data. If there is already an existing means for customer service to access information or if there is no difference between what a customer service representative and customer can do on the site, you might not need such an application. However, if there is a clear difference between what customers can do and what customer service representatives need to do and there is no existing tool, then planning and building one should be considered in the project plan.

Disaster Recovery

Another item that should be considered in the project plan is disaster recovery. The scenario for how the company plans to handle a large-scale emergency such as a natural disaster should be considered. Smaller disasters such as a fire in the server room need also be considered. Even if the decision is to hope there is no disaster until there is more time to consider the matter, the time to consider disaster recovery should be part of planning the project.

Application Support

Lastly, there is the procedural item of supporting the application. The need for applications support basically falls out into two basic categories. First, there is the need to consider the support of the hardware – keeping the database and the servers running and on the network. Second, there is the idea of supporting the actual application such as what happens when an error appears in the logs.

Time should also be budgeted to consider who will handle errors in the application and how they will be handled. These discussions should focus around different types of errors such as expected errors (a product is unavailable) to unexpected errors (a page cannot be displayed). Procedures must be set up to address how each type of error is handled from both a technical and procedural standpoint.

Now What? Getting Started

Once the project requirements are gathered and the project is planned, the next step is to actually get started building it. There are some steps that can be taken throughout the process to make development easier and more productive.

- ❑ **Take small steps** – Companies that try to accomplish too much right away are setting themselves up for failure. As with anything, inching towards the goal is better than missing the goal altogether.

- ❑ **Encourage feedback and communication** – The better the team, the better the product of their efforts. One thing that is valuable in helping a team become better is to encourage the type of communication and feedback that help individuals do their jobs better.

- ❑ **Continuously re-evaluate** – Don't be afraid to change horses midstream if there is no way to win the race on your current horse. In other words, re-evaluating the process and the people is critical to success.

- ❑ **Increase motivation by having realistic time goals** – Nothing motivates a team like achieving a goal. It is important to make it possible to achieve reasonable goals that have meaning and value.

- ❑ **Address problems head-on and as early as possible** – Avoidance of a problem is often a human failure. It is also one of the biggest reasons e-commerce initiatives fail. Don't be afraid to handle problems.

❑ **Be prepared for changing requirements as everyone learns more about the effort** –Don't penalize the people involved for being creative. Encourage change and flexibility and be prepared for requirements changes.

In addition, it is important to remember that no amount of requirements gathering or planning can prepare a team for every eventuality. It is important to learn from each project to find the best way for your organization to run an e-commerce application. Each step in this process of learning should make it easier and easier to produce quality e-commerce applications that meet their stated goals and bring value to the company.

Summary

This chapter along with the previous two chapters have discussed the idea of e-commerce and what this means to business. We have also discussed the issues to be considered for gathering requirements and planning the project. Some of the important issues we have talked about include:

❑ E-commerce is a subset of e-business which requires a comprehensive business strategy. This strategy may differ from existing strategies and should permeate the process from conception to realization.

❑ Putting a strong emphasis on the people involved in the process of creating an e-business application is critical to success. This includes an emphasis on the people building the application and the people using it.

❑ Java, specifically J2EE, is an important piece of e-commerce and can be used to build high quality, flexible e-commerce applications. The following chapters of this book will devote a great deal more time to exploring the uses of Java in the e-commerce arena.

❑ Setting goals for an e-commerce application helps guide and evaluate the process. These goals should be set as early as possible and followed through in the requirements phase and the planning phase.

❑ E-commerce lends itself well to an iterative process to emphasize feedback and communication. There are a variety of methodologies to help with this process.

❑ There are a variety of issues that need to be considered in the process such as hosting, tools, privacy, security, and a host of others. These issues are all-important and should be considered from both a technological and business perspective.

Choosing the right methodology for your organization and project is very important for success. In general, developing e-commerce applications is a process of learning. This learning occurs in all aspects of the process from developers learning about technology to business users learning about their business. This process of learning should be embraced and accepted as an important part of developing applications.

As the following chapters discuss technical decisions and issues of architecture, keep in mind the issues discussed in these introductory chapters. Framing all decisions about the application in the methodology and processes used is important for a project to be cohesive and effective in its goals.

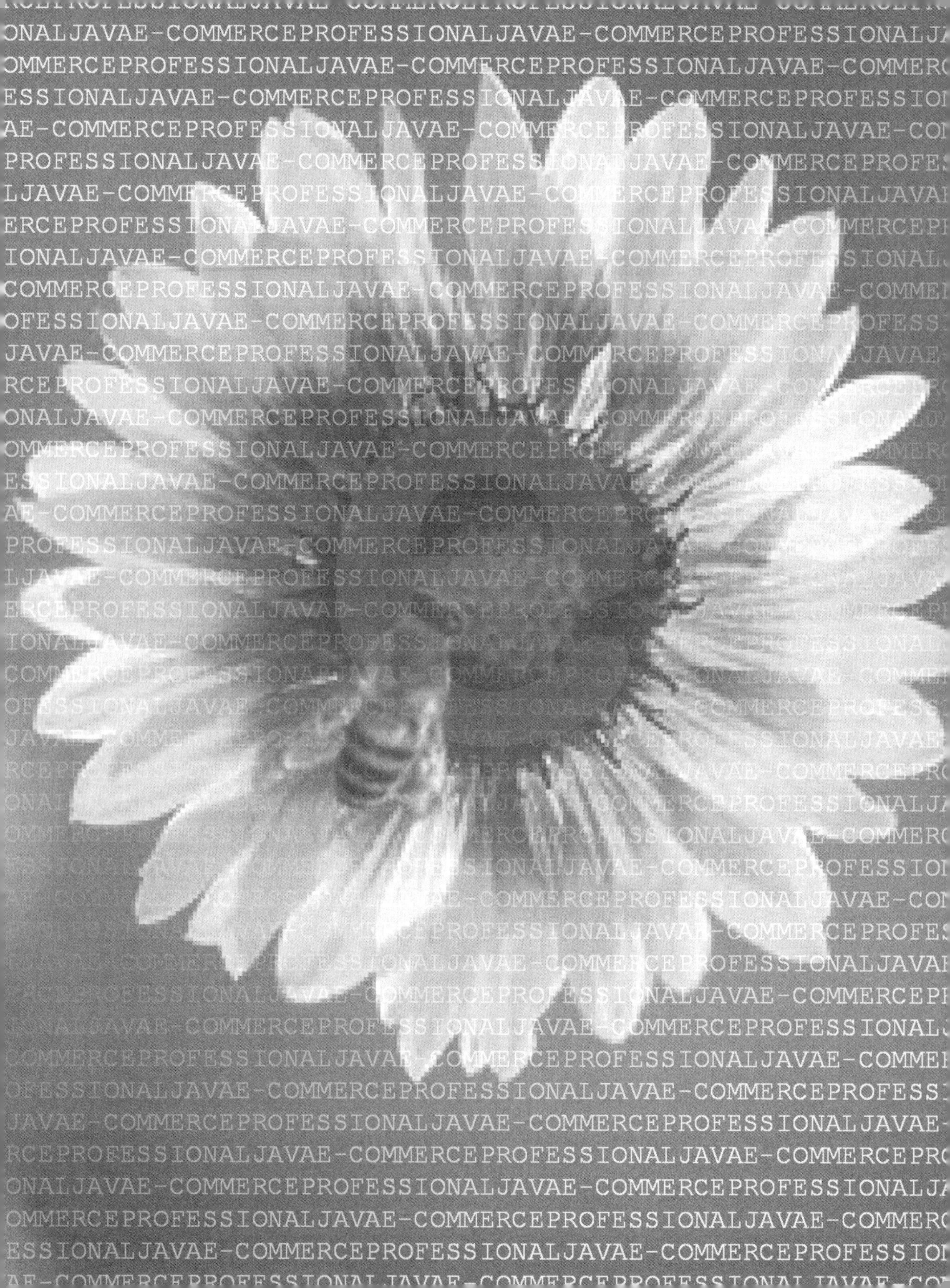
PROFESSIONALJAVAE-COMMERCE

Section 2

Architecting Java Based E-Commerce Systems

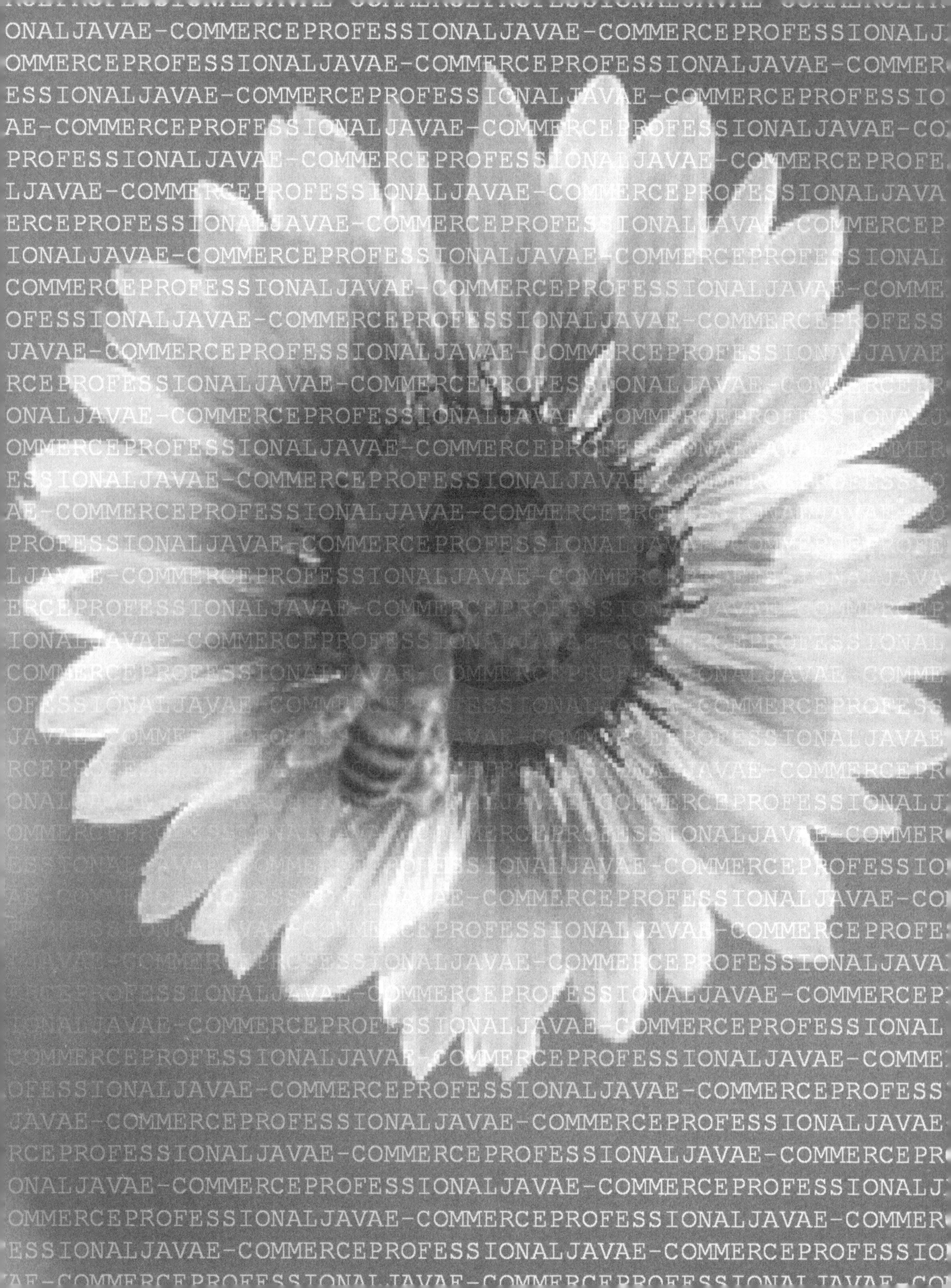

4

Architecting E-Commerce Applications

The purpose of e-commerce is to bring together buyers and sellers and provide the infrastructure for them to sell/exchange goods, services, and information electronically. As far as the underlying technology is concerned, an e-commerce system is essentially an infrastructure and a set of applications that facilitate electronic information access and transactions.

This section of the book aims to identify the technical requirements of e-commerce systems and introduce the core Java (and associated) technologies that provide the basis for these systems. Subsequent sections of the book will illustrate how these architectures and technologies can be utilized for e-commerce.

It is a common assumption that the Internet is what is fuelling today's e-commerce systems. Although this is in fact the case, this same assumption typically extends to include the World Wide Web as the primary medium for electronic commerce. As discussed in Section 1, such a view limits the possibilities for various types of e-commerce. In reality, the magnitude and complexity of e-commerce applications is far greater than that which takes place across web browsers and other internet-enabled electronic and mobile devices.

It is therefore necessary to analyse the broad nature of e-commerce applications, and, depending on specific application requirements, to identify the technologies applicable for building particular e-commerce applications. This is true with any type of application, not just for e-commerce applications. However, due to the high visibility of the Web, the underlying complexity of e-commerce applications is often perceptible. Therefore, the basic theme of this chapter will be to emphasize the complexity that is not typically visible over web browsers and the Internet.

In this chapter we will cover:

❑ What factors help to make an e-commerce application successful

❑ How these lead us to choose specific technologies and architectures

❑ How the technology requirements for e-commerce applications have evolved

In the next chapter, we will continue the discussion by looking at how the Java 2 Enterprise Edition (J2EE) provides the core infrastructure for building web-centric enterprise applications that support e-commerce.

> *As with the rest of this book we assume a certain familiarity with server-side Java technologies – more detailed tutorial type coverage of many of these topics may be found in Professional Java Server Programming, J2EE Edition, ISBN 1-861004065-6, also from Wrox Press.*

Successful E-Commerce Applications

Before we identify the key requirements for e-commerce applications, let us study what makes an e-commerce application successful. The answer varies widely with what one perceives an e-commerce application is. For many, an e-commerce application is a web site with a catalogue, a shopping cart, and facilities to capture credit card information and commit orders in a database. However, individuals participating in e-commerce may not hold the same perception.

For instance, for an on-line shopper, e-commerce applications should have easy access to information on-line (whether from a web browser or from a PDA), let them conduct transactions on-line, and guarantee security during these processes. For an executive of a new e-commerce company, flexibility is the key, as it allows quicker business adaptation. Similarly, for a similar executive of a bricks-and-mortar business house wanting to conduct commerce electronically, the ability to integrate seamlessly with the existing enterprise applications as well as user interfaces is a key requirement.

As you see from the above examples, it is not one or the other feature/attribute that makes an e-commerce application successful – it is in-fact a combination of the factors involved.

This section attempts to identify certain key attributes that contribute to successful e-commerce applications. These are:

❑ Flexibility

❑ Multi-channel interfaces

❑ Security

❑ Integration

In the following subsections, we will discuss how and why each of these factors is relevant.

Before we consider why these attributes are the key to successful e-commerce applications, note that these attributes are qualitative (we can't say that a given system is 100 percent flexible, or 100 percent secure, or 100 percent integration capable) and for a given e-commerce system, these attributes can be achieved (as well as compromised) in many ways. Furthermore, various strategies to achieve these attributes may contradict one another – for instance, a high-performance architecture may not allow for flexibility, and vice versa. Apart from this complex association between these attributes, these attributes mostly require different solutions in software and hardware. In the following sections, we are concerned about achieving these attributes by using software means only.

These attributes are not new to the software industry. However, in the e-commerce area, what is new is the fact that these attributes are just as important as the business processes. Without an architecture possessing these attributes, it is difficult to achieve the goals of e-commerce.

Also, note that there are other requirements such as performance, scalability and suchlike that are common to most of the applications. We will not discuss these requirements in this chapter because these are the basic requirements for any application, not just e-commerce applications.

Flexibility

Change is the order of the day in e-commerce systems. E-commerce systems are subject to frequent structural changes due to changes in products, services, and business processes. Apart from the fact that e-commerce offers global reach for businesses, e-commerce has considerable advantages over other types of business in that it can offer more flexibility in terms of offering new products, services, and business models. Therefore, flexibility to adapt to changes is a *key* requirement for e-commerce systems.

Traditionally, change is considered to be a disturbing input in the process of architecting and building software. Accordingly, traditional software systems build to meet specific business processes and other use cases, and flexibility is not always an immediate consideration. In order to gain the true benefits of e-commerce, the application should be built to be flexible, so that it can continue to offer the value as the e-commerce system of a business evolves.

In the e-commerce systems, changes occur in several ways. The following list gives a range of changes that frequently occur:

- ❑ **Updates to information and presentation format** – Most of the consumer oriented e-commerce systems should be built to allow frequent updates to information content, and sometimes to the format of presentation. In fact, today, this flexibility is usually expected of any e-commerce application.

- ❑ **New products, services, and updates** – E-commerce systems are required to be more dynamic than their traditional counterparts in offering new products, services, and updates to products and services as dictated by market conditions.

- ❑ **Changing business processes** – Several factors contribute to changes in business processes. Examples include new products and services, trade agreements with partners, promotions, campaigns and so on. Each of these may dictate changes to the underlying execution logic for various business processes. Consider, for instance, the case of product pricing. Trade agreements, campaigns, promotions, and so on dictate the way that pricing is calculated.

Although these types of changes are not entirely new, the relevance of these changes has gained more importance in the e-commerce area.

Multi-Channel Interfaces

Traditionally, customers could interact and transact with businesses via two channels – bricks-and-mortar offices (either personally or via catalogue mail orders) and telephones. In most cases customer interaction remained manual, although the internal business operations were automated with mainframes or client-server applications. Similarly, before the current advances in B2B technologies, the only channel that existed between businesses (apart from paper-based communication) was electronic data interchange (EDI). With EDI, partners could exchange business data over private networks. However, the usage was limited to large corporations managing their supply-chains via EDI.

Today, the scene is very diverse. Connectivity and transparent business processes are the key factors that drive business systems, and the traditional notion that an application is meant to serve a single kind of interface (whether human or application) is no longer valid. Today buyers and sellers can reach each other through several different channels.

With the proliferation of the Internet and associated technologies, and advances in Internet-enabled mobile devices, customers have more options that range from web browsers and Web TVs to WAP (Wireless Application Protocol) phones and PDAs. Although some of the business processes are customized for different access channels, the core processes generally remain the same for all such channels. For instance, in order to place a trade at E*Trade, a trader can use the E*Trade web site, or an Internet enabled mobile phone, or a PDA, or a regular telephone using E*Trade's interactive voice recognition system.

As well as this, more and more businesses are opening up their business processes to partners. Irrespective of whether a business belongs to B2C or B2B category, e-commerce applications need to be accessible for trusted partners or partner networks. Considering a moderately complex e-commerce system, the following figure shows the typical interface requirements for e-commerce applications:

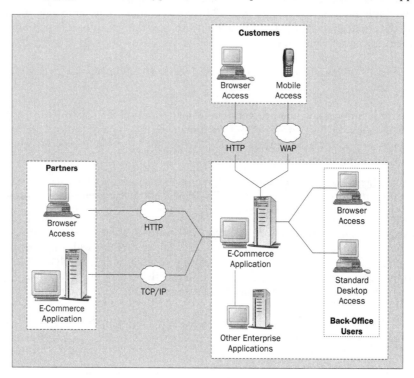

This figure shows two types of interfaces – human interfaces and application interfaces.

Human Interfaces

Our figure illustrates five different types of interaction between humans and the application:

❑ **Individual buyers/sellers accessing the e-commerce application via the Internet** – This is the most common and widely used form of interface.

❑ **Individual buyers/sellers accessing the e-commerce application via Internet enabled mobile phones, PDAs and other similar means** – Although this form of access is recent when compared to the desktop-based browser access, this form of access is expected to increase exponentially over the next few years.

❑ **Back-office access via web browsers over internal/private network** – This form of access is slowly replacing the native desktop client interfaces that were omnipresent during the client-server era.

❑ **Back-office access via standard desktop applications** – Although web browsers are slowly replacing these interfaces, native desktop interfaces are well suited for certain types of data access. Reasons for this include quick navigation, richer graphical interfaces and so on.

❑ **Employees of partner organizations accessing the e-commerce application via a secure network** – This pattern is becoming increasingly predominant with a drive to offer more transparent business processes.

Application Interfaces

In addition to the human interfaces we have a couple of application interfaces:

❑ **Back-office applications participating in business processes** – As we shall discuss in a latter section in this chapter, e-commerce applications are often required to integrate with other back-office applications in order to provide an end-to-end business process application.

❑ **Partner applications exchanging information and conducting transactions electronically** – This is the basic pattern in B2B commerce systems. However, most businesses today participate in both B2C and B2B scenarios. For instance, an online electronics vendor participates in B2C commerce with online consumers, and may participate in B2B transactions with manufacturers/suppliers.

On the surface, these interface requirements sound highly typical. However, let us dig into this a little further:

Usage Patterns across Different Interface Channels

Different types of users have very different usage patterns. For instance, a trader conducting a stock trade using a WAP-enabled mobile phone requires a very lean user interface with a trade achievable within a few clicks. On the other hand, the same user would like to have more information and more options available when conducting a similar stock trade on a web browser. Although the user is participating in the same business process (to buy/sell stocks), the user interface and the information exchanged could be different. Similarly, consider back-office users accessing the same e-commerce application using web browsers. Such users participate in a different (and possibly more elaborate and complex) use cases, with access to more privileged information.

Application Security for Different Types of Access

This varies across the range of users and application interfaces considered above. We shall discuss more details of this later.

Application Performance

While it is commonly agreed that high performance is always required, the same level of performance and responsiveness need not be provided for all classes of users/interfaces. For instance, back-office users may tolerate higher response times as a side effect of having more elaborate user interfaces. Similarly, in the case of B2C systems, the number of users of the application could vary very widely while the number of back-office users remains constant, and performance and responsiveness requirements for these user types may vary widely. The same can be said of batch processing applications.

From these points, it is clear that the nature of the e-commerce application, and the types of users and applications that access the application, dictate the architecture of e-commerce applications.

Security

In a networked e-commerce system, security is a prime concern to all participants for several reasons:

❑ The majority of transactions happen automatically without human intervention and verification. In such an automated process where there are no manual checkpoints there are always concerns regarding trust associated with the participants in business processes. Even before an attempt is made to trust a party, how are we to establish the identity of the party? Once a transaction takes place, how are we to establish that the transaction has really taken place between the transacting parties? Mere records in a database do not necessarily establish this fact.

❑ Confidential data is transmitted across public networks. In such a scenario, how can we guarantee that the data has not been modified while in transit (integrity), or that the data was not read while in transit (confidentiality)?

❑ Transacting parties have no identity other than the digital identity provided by the underlying e-commerce application.

These concerns manifest into concepts such as authentication, authorization, non-repudiation, data security and so on. We will discuss more about these requirements in Chapter 8

Integration

Integration is yet another requirement for e-commerce systems. In fact, lack of integration in an enterprise could be fatal for one of today's e-commerce systems. The following factors illustrate why integration is an important requirement for e-commerce systems:

❑ No application can be built to offer all imaginable business functionality. Even those off-the-shelf e-commerce products that claim to provide end-to-end commerce functionality quickly lose the end-to-end proposition with changes to market conditions and business models. Market conditions may require the e-commerce system to open more channels for business transactions than those that such e-commerce products offer. Similarly, changes in business models may require addition of other systems to fulfill the missing links of business processes. Both of these cases raise a need for integration with existing or new enterprise applications.

❑ As mentioned in Chapter 2, most e-commerce applications are built on top of existing enterprise applications. This is a common situation with traditional bricks-and-mortar companies expanding their business models to conduct business electronically. In these cases, the new e-commerce application provides the Internet enabled B2C or B2B interfaces while existing applications handle most of the core business processes. The new e-commerce application merely extends the business processes and opens them up to customers and partners. This approach requires a tight integration between the new e-commerce application and the existing enterprise applications.

❑ Certain types of e-commerce applications exist solely to connect multiple businesses with new end-to-end business processes. For instance, some of the trade portals (such as shopping sites with Yahoo, MSN, and so on) today follow this model. These portals offer common business processes such a shopping cart, catalogue search, checkout and so on, and leave order fulfillment to merchants participating in the portal. The level of sophistication of such applications depends on the sophistication of connectivity across different merchants and the portal.

In all of these cases, it is necessary to make different applications talk to one another. It is possible that such applications are across different platforms implemented in different programming languages. In order to illustrate the problem, let us consider a B2C commerce site selling books over the Internet. Such a B2C site should at least include functionality to browse the catalogue, select books and put them into the shopping cart, submit billing and shipping information, and to submit the order. However, what happens when a customer fills in a shopping cart, hits the checkout button, and submits the order?

Several business processes need to happen in order to fulfill this order. These business processes typically span inventory management, sales, accounting, shipping and so on. Since each of these back-end business processes is complex, it is likely that different (and disparate) applications implement parts of the order fulfillment process. The following figure illustrates this scenario. The application on the left is the B2C web site. The applications to the right are the backend enterprise applications that fulfill different parts of the sales process.

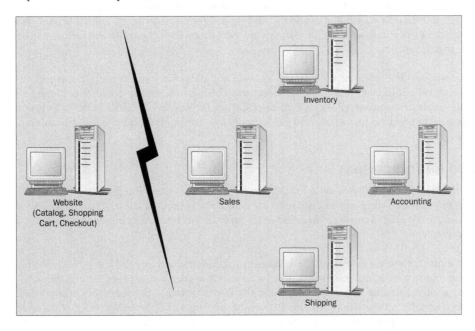

What happens if these applications do not communicate with each other? In order to fulfill a business process in such an enterprise there must be manual interventions (including data entry and verification), batch imports and exports of data (across applications) and so on, as shown in the figure below:

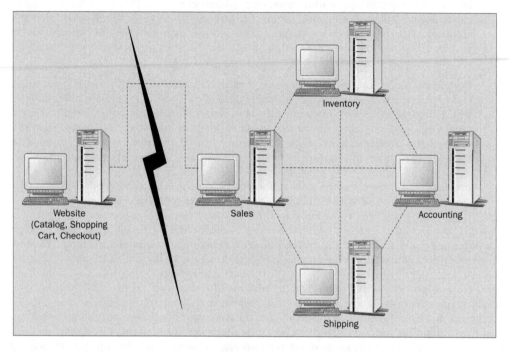

In this figure, each broken line represents a potential break in the overall business process, and requires manual or batch integration. This effectively means that the infrastructure supporting e-commerce is not integrated, and therefore cannot execute the end-to-end purchase process. Such a broken process results in increased cost per transaction, and even increased processing time. Both the factors are detrimental to e-commerce systems.

Note that the problem of integration is well known, and dates back to the early client-server era. However, the effect of lack of application integration becomes prominent with e-commerce as it directly affects the goals of e-commerce – that is to provide the application infrastructure for buyers and sellers to participate in business processes, and the benefits of e-commerce viz., cost per transaction and processing time.

The Need for Integration

The above scenario describes a need for intra-enterprise application integration – that is, to integrate various applications within the enterprise to provide a seamless execution of business processes end-to-end. This is particularly important in another scenario that is becoming increasingly predominant with B2B commerce.

In B2B commerce systems, some of the business processes extend beyond the boundaries of a given enterprise and two or more enterprises may be required to participate in a given business process. Consider a virtual on-line bookstore where the site is connected to the inventory systems of different publishers, and the online store provides a common interface and shopping facilities for purchasing books directly from publishers. In this case, order, inventory, and shipping functions span across multiple enterprises with real-time information exchange.

Although this scenario looks very similar to application integration within an enterprise, it is more technically complex as the applications across organizations tend to be disparate. Apart from technical disparity, the meaning and context of a business transaction may be significantly different across different enterprises. A technical infrastructure that considers both the above e-commerce integration scenarios is very crucial to a successful e-commerce system.

Now that we've looked at some of the scenarios that are prevalent in the current e-commerce arena, let us take a look and see how they can be realized.

Technical Requirements and Approaches

So far, in this chapter, we have discussed four basic qualifiers of successful e-commerce applications: flexibility, multi-channel interfaces, security and integration. How do these qualifiers translate into technical requirements, and what are the technologies that meet these requirements?

Today, there is a wide range of technologies that can be used to build e-commerce applications. These technologies range from web technologies such as HTML, ASP and CGI to Enterprise Java technologies such as JSP pages, Enterprise JavaBeans (EJB), Java Messaging Service, and so on.

Due to the specialized nature of each of these technologies, it is outside the scope of this chapter to discuss all of these technologies. Instead of discussing each of them in detail, we will instead focus on how these technologies, at a generic level, relate to the current problem – how to build successful e-commerce applications.

Our discussion will be broken down into the following topics:

- ❑ Dynamic, personalized user interfaces
- ❑ Channel specific user interfaces
- ❑ Layered implmentations of business processes
- ❑ Application Integration
- ❑ Transactions

However, in order to facilitate the discussion, this section briefly introduces the principles behind various technologies as and when required. Secondly, this section does not particularly emphasize Java based technologies. A more comprehensive overview of Enterprise Java technologies for building e-commerce applications will be provided in the next chapter.

Dynamic, Personalized User Interfaces

For e-commerce applications (particularly for users accessing the application via web browsers) one of the basic requirements is to be able to generate pages with dynamic user interfaces as opposed to static web pages. In other words, based on who the user is, and the functionality that the user is allowed access to, the e-commerce application should be able to generate a user-specific interface.

With e-commerce applications, it is very common to have different types of users accessing the same application at the same time. Sometimes, such users may participate in the same or related business processes. In such cases, it is complex to maintain separate sets of user interface pages for each type of user, particularly when there are parts of interfaces common to several types of users. **Dynamic user interfaces** allow the application to handle the complexity of dealing with these cases, and grants them the ability to tailor the user interface based on user identity.

In addition, particularly with information rich applications (such as B2C sites selling millions of products), personalized content is also required. **Personalization** is the ability to provide a user interface based on users' patterns of information access, profile, information preferences, and so on. As the content available at the site grows, personalization is necessary to retain the focus of the user by generating content specifically targeted towards the user.

Channel Specific User Interfaces

As we discussed in the previous section, many e-commerce applications need to support access from multiple channels. Although you may not build all such channels initially, you should make sure that the underlying infrastructure allows their support for later additions. As we discuss in the following section, a layered implementation of business processes allows for channel specific user interfaces.

Layered Implementation of Business Processes

In this section we move our focus onto the architectural aspects of application development starting by describing two-tier architectures before discussing multi-tier architectures and showing a couple of examples of that approach. We conclude this sub-section by looking at the key features of the architecture and the technical requirements needed to support it.

Two-Tier Architecture

The basic idea behind a **two-tier architecture** is to centralize the data access while distributing the business logic and user interfaces to client machines. In this approach, the logic to implement business processes is embedded within user interfaces and data access (such as database stored procedures and other database vendor specific programming techniques). The most commonly mentioned limitations of this architecture are that the client machines bear the processing load, and that performance suffers due to excessive network traffic. As we shall see below, another important reason why this architecture is inappropriate is due to its lack of abstraction for business logic.

This approach is being replaced with the **three-tier architecture**. However, be aware that the two-tier approach is still predominant in many e-commerce applications today. Several tool/product vendors and even books on Internet technologies suggest this approach for building e-commerce applications.

What is the impact of such architecture for e-commerce applications? To answer this, let us consider one such architecture for web applications. The following figure represents an e-commerce application implemented using the two-tier architecture:

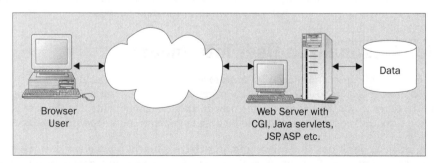

In this figure, the web server hosts applications written using CGI, Java servlets, Java Server Pages, ASP, and so on. These applications implement the business processes on receipt of HTTP requests, and manage the user interface navigation accordingly.

The most interesting aspect of this architecture is its simplicity. This architecture requires neither elaborate design nor complex infrastructure. However, this architecture is unsuitable for e-commerce applications. The fundamental limitation with this architecture is that it is flat and does not include any layer of abstraction for implementing business processes. But why is it necessary to have such a layer of abstraction?

As discussed in the previous section, e-commerce applications are expected to be accessed through a variety of channels by users as well as by applications. Each of these channels may require different considerations for designing human/application interfaces. In addition, all such human/application interfaces may invoke the same set of business processes.

However, the two-tier architecture does not allow multiple channels directly. As a result, you would end up developing separate sets of user interfaces for different types of user interfaces with the business logic spread across all such user interfaces. For instance, the logic built into the web server tier cannot be used for an application interface or for a non-web client. Such an approach is not maintainable.

Multi-Tier Architecture and Layering

It is therefore clear that the decoupling of the business process implementation from both user interfaces and database access logic is necessary. The three-tier architecture has provision for such decoupling. The three-tier architecture introduces an intermediate tier between user interface and data access tiers. This additional tier is meant for deploying business process logic. Note that the notion of a separate tier for business process logic also allows a physical abstraction layer. We may depict the three-tier architecture for web applications as follows:

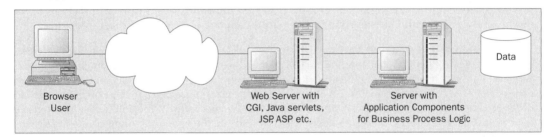

Browser
User

Web Server with
CGI, Java servlets,
JSP, ASP etc.

Server with
Application Components
for Business Process Logic

Data

Although the above shows the middle-tier on a single machine, with the help of distributed component technologies it is possible to distribute this tier across additional machines based on logical grouping of application logic. Such an architecture is also known as a **multi-tier architecture**.

How are we to architect the middle-tier so that it meets the goals of flexibility, multi-channel access, and integration? One possible solution is to build additional **layers** within the middle-tier. Layering allows logical separation between different parts of an application. In a layered architecture, application programs/modules/components in upper layers depend on application programs/modules/components in lower layers. Layering thus introduces a logical uni-directional dependency among different parts of an application. Layering need not involve physical separation across different processes or machines, however. Depending on the specific application and deployment requirements, these layers could easily be developed to be distributed.

Let us now consider a possible layered architecture for building e-commerce applications.

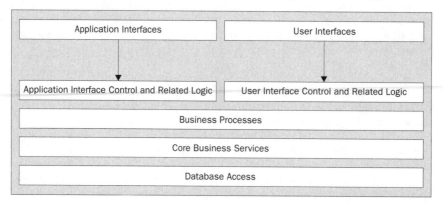

Before we study the details of this architecture let's just reiterate the point that the various layers in this architecture do not necessarily imply a physical separation. Although, depending on specific deployment requirements, you may split these layers across physically separate tiers.

At the bottom of this architecture lies the database access layer. The purpose of this layer is to provide the services related to accessing data. Depending on implementation, this layer may include the logic to connect to databases and access/manipulate data held within databases.

The layer above the database access layer is the core business service layer. In this architecture, a service is different from a process. Business processes are implementations of specific use cases. The business service layer provides functionality (services) common to several use cases (processes).

Why is this separation required? This separation of use case implementation from business services guarantees that use case implementation can be changed without having to reimplement common services. For instance, consider application logic to process payment instruments such as credit cards, checks and so on. This functionality could be common to several use cases such as order processing, order amendment, order cancellation and so on. Given the possibility of reusing the payment processing logic across these use cases, it is more appropriate to separate the commonly used payment service into the core business service layer.

Note that both the business process layer and core business services layer are independent of user/application interfaces. The layers on top of the business process layer are meant to drive the application and user interfaces respectively. The exact nature and purpose of these layers depends on the type of the user/application interface. Let us consider two cases of user/application interfaces:

Example A – An Interface for Mobile Devices and Internet Browsers

Let us consider an e-commerce application providing browser as well as mobile device access to certain e-commerce business processes.

As you will see in Chapter 24, **Wireless Application Protocol** (**WAP**) is the standard protocol used for developing web-based applications for mobile phones and other mobile devices. WAP does for mobile devices what HTTP and TCP/IP do for web browsers and servers. When compared to the standard World Wide Web, mobile networks have certain limitations such as low bandwidth, high latency, and possibly unpredictable availability. Similarly, when compared to standard web browsers, mobile devices have limited CPU, memory and battery life, and require a simpler user interface due to limitations placed upon the content that they can display. In order to deal with these limitations, **Wireless Markup Language** (**WML**) is used as the language for developing user interfaces. WML is analogous to HTML for standard web browsers.

Since the e-commerce application has to deal with two separate types of user interfaces – an HTML based interface for web browsers, and a WML based interface for mobile devices – it is appropriate to consider XML to develop a single user interface. This suits the current purpose as we can develop the interface without forcing ourselves to use any specific styling. This XML can then be converted into HTML and WML respectively using the **Extensible Stylesheet Language** (**XSL**) transformations. The application of XML and XSL to e-commerce solutions is discussed in Chapter 7.

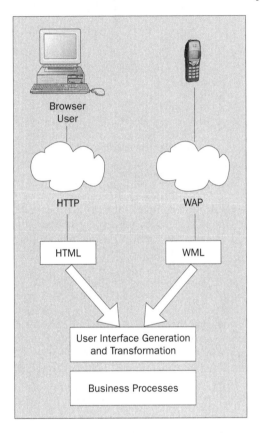

In this case, the user interface control layer can implement the generation of XML and transformation of XML into HTML and WML as shown in the figure above.

Example B – An Asynchronous Application Interface

Let us now consider a B2B transaction between a buyer organization and a seller organization. A typical transaction is the buyer sending purchase orders to the seller. Let us assume that the buyer-side e-commerce application sends purchase orders as XML documents to the seller-side e-commerce application asynchronously.

Asynchronous communication between applications can be achieved using message brokers. With message brokers, the sender of a message need not wait for the recipient to receive and respond to a message. As the name implies, the message broker technology facilitates information exchange between applications, insulating both the sending and receiving application from both platform disparity and availability. Vendors such as IBM and TIBCO originally popularized this technology. The most commonly used message broker implementation is based on message queues. In a queue-based system, sender applications send messages to a queue, while the recipient receives messages from the queue.

The following figure shows the e-commerce application receiving purchase orders asynchronously. The arrow between the sender and the recipient denotes that the communication is asynchronous.

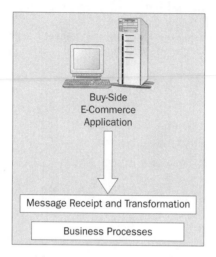

In this scenario, the buy-side application composes purchase order requests as an XML document and sends it to a queue without having to rely on the immediate availability of the sell-side application. The message broker takes care of delivering the message as and when the buy-side application is available to access messages.

Application components on the sell-side e-commerce application receive the purchase order request (still in XML format) from the queue. The top rectangle shows these responsibilities. Before invoking the business process responsible for processing the incoming purchase orders, the incoming messages should be converted into a format that the business processes can understand. For instance, in a Java implementation, the business processes would be methods on certain objects, and executing the business process would involve calling these methods. The arguments to such methods could be a `PurchaseOrder` object with all the information for creating a purchase order encapsulated. In this case, the incoming purchase order request (as an XML document) should be transformed into a `PurchaseOrder` object and sent as an argument to the business process methods.

In this case, the application interface layer is responsible for receiving the messages, validating the messages, and transforming the XML data into Java objects. Note that this example is somewhat simplified. In reality, a more elaborate message routing system could replace the simple message queue.

The Key Features

In both of the above cases, the business process and the core service layers remain independent of human/application interfaces. The key features of this architecture are:

❑ **Flexibility** – This is an elaborate architecture with multiple layers with each layer responsible for a set of functionality built on top of layers below. This architecture allows flexible user interfaces, changes to business processes, and changes to core services.

❑ **Multi-channel access** – The two example scenarios we discussed above illustrate how this architecture can support multiple channels of access.

Now that we have discussed an architecture capable of handling multiple channels of access, what are the technical requirements for implementing such an architecture?

A Distributed Component Programming Model

A multi-layered architecture can be implemented either with plain Java objects, or with distributed components. However, a simple object-based implementation does not allow for physical separation of layers to allow for distribution. Since plain objects cannot be invoked by objects in another process, the various layers of objects cannot be separated physically.

A physical separation of layers has the advantage that each physical layer can be administered and monitored separately. Moreover, depending on processing and memory requirements, constituents of physical layers can be deployed on different machines in a network, thereby allowing for both scalability and redundancy. In addition, a distributed component based implementation has the advantage that distributed components can be built to be coarse-grained. This is a typical requirement for building the business process and service layers.

In a Java environment, there are at least three component models for building distributed components:

❏ Java RMI (Remote Method Invocation)

❏ CORBA (Common Object Request Broker Architecture)

❏ EJB (Enterprise JavaBeans)

All of these technologies provide a basic programming model for specifying, developing, and deploying distributed components. For instance, the Java RMI technology specifies base interfaces for specifying a component, a compiler for generating proxies and stubs for client access and server development respectively, an RMI registry for making server objects (or, loosely speaking, components) available over network to client applications, and a set of infrastructure classes that support remote method invocation. Similarly, CORBA and EJB (overviewed in the next chapter) also provide programming models and other facilities for building distributed components.

A Deployment Platform

When developing e-commerce applications, we are no longer dealing with simple Java applications, or custom built servers. In order to support rapid development and maintenance, distributed component based applications require a platform that simplifies most of the distributed component programming and deployment issues.

Such a deployment platform should support the basic runtime infrastructure, and access to other enterprise services such as database access, transactions, naming (or object location) services, security and so on. The infrastructure should support creation of the proxy/stub objects, object creation and lifecycle management, multi-threading, and suchlike.

These facilities are essential for developing e-commerce applications, as most of the e-commerce infrastructure is server-side, with a potentially large number of different types of clients accessing the distributed components. Instead of the application developer having to deal with managing these basic resources, the deployment platform should provide built-in support for this. Application servers supporting J2EE provide **containers** that serve as deployment platform for deploying and managing distributed components.

Support for Communication Protocols

As we discussed above, e-commerce applications require basic support for TCP/IP and HTTP communication protocols. TCP (Transmission Control Protocol) over IP (Internet Protocol) is the most widely used communications protocol and the entire gamut of Internet technologies is built over

TCP/IP. The IP protocol makes sure that data reaches the intended receiver when sent by one of two parties communicating over the Internet. In IP, data is sent in multiple packets for efficiency reasons. The TCP keeps track of all these packets and makes sure that these packets are assembled in the same order they were dispatched and are error free. TCP and IP work together to move data around the Internet.

HTTP (Hypertext Transfer Protocol) is a generic, stateless, application-level protocol that works on a request/response basis. With HTTP, a client sends a request to a server in the form of a request method, a URI (Uniform Resource Identifier), the protocol version, followed by a MIME-like message containing request modifiers, client information, and any body content over a connection with the server. The server in turn responds with a status-line followed by a MIME-like message containing server information, metadata describing the content, and body content (depending on the type of the request).

Application Integration

Capability for integrating e-commerce applications with other enterprise applications is a key requirement for implementing end-to-end business processes spanning various systems in the enterprise. Being a key requirement, application integration is also complex because many enterprises will have several types of proprietary and legacy systems and commercial enterprise applications in operation.

The complexity of your specific application integration task largely depends on the technical nature of these enterprise applications. These applications range from **ERP (Enterprise Resource Planning)** systems from vendors such as SAP, Baan, Oracle, and so on, or commercial off-the-shelf systems for different enterprise tasks, mainframe applications, or even home-grown client-server or distributed applications. There is no single technology or approach that can be used to integrate all such systems developed using possibly disparate technologies. Some of these applications may not even allow any form of integration.

Depending on the need for integration, you can apply different approaches for application integration:

- ❏ **Integrating the User Interfaces** – This approach involves building a new user interface layer that integrates all user interfaces of enterprise applications. This approach is commonly used when most of the functionality of these applications is user driven. However, this approach does not completely integrate the underlying business processes, it can only integrate user-interface driven business processes.

- ❏ **Integrating the Services** – This is the most desirable approach for application integration. This approach is also known as application interface level integration. The basic idea behind this approach is to expose the services of each enterprise application through programmatic interfaces, and to build code that can invoke these interfaces from other applications. In essence, this approach lets you integrate the core business processes or services. Note that this approach relies neither on the user interfaces nor on the databases. Provided you are able to find appropriate glue (middleware) technologies that can integrate applications at the service/process level, you have the best possible solution to integrate your e-commerce application with the rest of the enterprise.

- ❏ **Integrating the Databases** – This approach relies on integrating applications by sharing (directly or indirectly) the data that various applications rely on. This approach involves extracting data from database of one application, and storing the data in the database of another application. This process may involve transforming the data if the applications do not share the same data definition for different business entities. In some legacy situations, applications may store data in files, and in such cases, files may be exchanged between different applications.

For gaining the advantage of seamless and automatic business process execution, the second approach is the most appropriate. User-interface level integration is suitable only when these processes involve human intervention. On the other hand, database level integration is the only possibly means of integration when there are several client-server applications that need integration. Although integrating the services is the best possible approach, it may not always be possible to integrate applications at the system level. In such cases, you may devise additional semi-automatic integration channels using database level integration.

Service Level Integration

However, how do you achieve process or service level integration between your e-commerce application and the rest of the enterprise? There are essentially two approaches for achieving this:

❑ **Distributed Object Technologies** – Distributed object technologies such as CORBA, COM, and RMI enable objects across different processes to communicate with each other – hence the name distributed objects. Distributed object technologies can be used both for building distributed applications, and for building component layers that can be used to integrate applications. In the case of application integration, distributed object technologies supply the infrastructure that can be used to build component layers on top of existing applications. In some cases, application vendors expose core services of their applications as distributed object interfaces. For instance, SAP provides COM/DCOM/CORBA interfaces for SAP business objects. These interfaces can be invoked from other non-SAP applications to invoke the business processes implemented within SAP.

❑ **Message Brokers** – This is another widely used technology for connecting application via asynchronous message channels. Unlike distributed object technology, where applications interact with each other in real-time, message brokers provide asynchronous communication between applications. As discussed in the previous section, an e-commerce application can send a purchase order request to an order-processing system without having to rely on its immediate availability. In this technology, the messages can include both data and any other requests. This technology is relevant for both intra-enterprise integration and for connecting businesses in the case of B2B. In the emerging networked B2B world, message broker technology plays a very dominant role. In fact, at the lowest level, most of the today's B2B products act as business message routers between applications across businesses.

Both these technologies are traditionally grouped into what is known as **middleware**. The purpose of middleware is to supply the communication infrastructure required for applications to communicate with each other.

Facilitating Integration

Therefore, in order to support application integration, the e-commerce infrastructure should support both distributed object technologies and messaging:

❑ **Support for Distributed Protocols** – To support interface-centric application integration, e-commerce applications need to be accessible through certain distributed protocols such as IIOP, RMI, RMI-IIOP and so on.

IIOP (Internet Inter-ORB Protocol) is the protocol used by CORBA for communication between clients and server objects. Specified by the OMG (Object Management Group), IIOP is actually a TCP/IP version of a more generic OMG-defined protocol called GIOP (General Inter-ORB Protocol). All CORBA/2.0 compliant ORBs (Object Request Brokers) support object communication via IIOP.

RMI (Remote Method Invocation) is one of the primary mechanisms for communication between Java clients and servers. RMI allows interfaces to specify remote objects. Clients can call methods on these remote objects as though these objects were local. The exact wire-level transportation is implementation specific. Sun uses Java Remote Method Protocol (JRMP) over TCP/IP for wire-level transportation. However, other protocols are possible. Note that RMI is strictly meant for Java-to-Java communication.

RMI-IIOP is an extension of RMI, but over IIOP, which allows you to define a remote interface to any object that can be implemented in any language that supports OMG's CORBA language mappings and an ORB. RMI-IIOP allows programmers to use RMI for specifying remote objects, and IIOP for wire-level communication, thus providing wire-level interoperability with CORBA.

However, why do we need support for these distributed protocols for building e-commerce applications? Although it is possible to build e-commerce applications entirely in Java and J2EE, there will be cases where you need to integrate Java e-commerce applications with legacy enterprise applications developed using non-Java technologies, or ERP systems, or even mainframes. For instance, consider the case of integrating an e-commerce application with an ERP. The above distributed protocols can be used to bridge Java e-commerce applications with such enterprise systems.

❏ **Support for Message Brokers** – In addition to distributed protocols, the e-commerce infrastructure should include support for message brokers. Note that, unlike distributed object technology, before the advent of Java messaging service, there was no standard set for message brokers. Although message broker products such as IBM's MQSeries and TIBCO's Rendezvous support similar features in their products, there was no standard API defined for message brokers.

Transactions

The most fundamental core asset of any enterprise is information. In the most primitive form, data is information. E-commerce applications are typically distributed, and therefore there are several components that act on shared data. In addition, in an integrated enterprise, several applications participate in integrated business processes that manipulate shared data.

Shared access to data could be destructive if applications perform conflicting operations on data. Secondly, applications manipulate the data as the business process execution continues. However, if a business process aborts in the middle due to some failure, the data in the database may remain in an inconsistent or corrupted state. The concepts of a **transaction** and a **transaction manager** (or a **transaction processing service**) guarantee that as applications create and manipulate the data, integrity of the data is maintained.

Since e-commerce applications have to deal with such inconsistencies, transaction processing is an important aspect of e-commerce applications. A **transaction** is a unit of work that has the properties of **atomicity**, **consistency**, **isolation**, and **durability** (so called ACID properties).

Atomicity

A transaction is a series of steps that succeeds or fails as a unit. If any one step should fail, all other associated steps shoulds fail, and the data is returned to its pre-transaction state. For instance, consider a business process consists of three steps, with each step modifying data in some tables. Although these are independent steps from the database point of view, all such steps constitute a single business transaction. The notion of "atomicity" preserves this.

Consistency

A transaction should transform the system from one consistent state to another. In the case of relational databases, a consistent transaction should preserve all the integrity constraints defined for the data.

Isolation

Each transaction should appear to execute independently of other transactions that may be executing concurrently in the same environment. The effect of executing a set of transactions serially should be the same as that of running them concurrently. This requires two things:

❏   During the course of a transaction, the intermediate (possibly inconsistent) state of the data should not be exposed to any other transactions.

❏   Two concurrent transactions should not be able to operate on the same data. Database management systems usually implement this feature using locking.

Ideally, the state of the database can be maintained consistently as long as business processes execute one after the other sequentially. However, this is not feasible as there could be several processes executing concurrently. In such cases, the notion of "isolation" makes it appear that these processes are executing sequentially, since changes from other processes do not affect a given business process.

Durability

The effects of a completed transaction should always be persistent. That is, the database should reflect the results of execution of a transaction.

These properties, guarantee that a transaction is never incomplete, the data is never inconsistent, concurrent transactions are independent, and the effects of a transaction are persistent.

Since distributed transactions could involve several applications and databases, preserving transactions across such disparate systems has always been a challenge. Distributed transaction processing involves a protocol and a coordination mechanism to deal with different applications and databases. In the distributed transaction-processing domain, **X/Open DTP** (**Distributed Transaction Processing**) is the most widely adopted model for building transactional applications. This model specifies certain interfaces and a protocol (called the two-phase commit and recovery protocol). Almost all vendors developing products related to transaction processing, relational databases, and message queuing support the interfaces defined in the DTP model.

This model defines three components:

❏   Application programs

❏   Resource managers

❏   A transaction manager

The resource managers are those that manage persistent data (such as database management systems). The transaction manager is the one that coordinates various database operations occurring in a transaction. The DTP model also specifies functional interfaces between application programs and the transaction manager (known as the TX interface), and between the transaction manager and the resource managers (the XA interface). With products complying with these interfaces, one can implement transactions with the two-phase commit and recovery protocol to comply with the requirements for transactions. The two-phase commit and recovery protocol involves two steps. In the first step, the transaction manager queries each resource manager if operations performed with that resource manager could be committed. If so, the transaction manager then requests each of the resource managers to commit those operations permanently to the database.

The Object Transaction Service

OTS (Object Transaction Service) is another distributed transaction processing model specified by the OMG (Object Management Group). The OTS specification can be found at ftp://ftp.omg.org/pub/docs/formal/00-06-28.pdf. This model is based on the X/Open DTP model, and replaces the functional TX and XA interfaces with CORBA IDL interfaces. In this model, the various objects communicate via CORBA method calls over IIOP. However, the OTS model is interoperable with the X/Open DTP model. An application using transactional objects could use the TX interface with the transaction manager for transaction demarcation. However, the OTS is not as widely adopted as the X/Open model and later technologies such as MTS (Microsoft Transaction Service) and J2EE transactions. One of the main reasons is the complexity of development.

Within the J2EE architecture, the JDBC 2.0 standard extension API, and the Java Transaction API provide interfaces for implementing distributed transactions. In addition, the Java Transaction Service (JTS) specifies a Java mapping of the OTS. In the next chapter, we shall briefly review these facilities.

Summary of Technical Requirements

We have now identified the following technical needs for building e-commerce applications:

- ❑ Ability to build dynamic, personalized web user interfaces
- ❑ Ability to support multi-channel user interfaces
- ❑ Ability to support application interfaces
- ❑ A programming model to specify and build distributed components
- ❑ A deployment platform to support distributed components
- ❑ Support for distributed transactions
- ❑ Support for asynchronous message driven communication
- ❑ Security

The Evolution of Technology Requirements

The above requirements may be summarized into the following architecture:

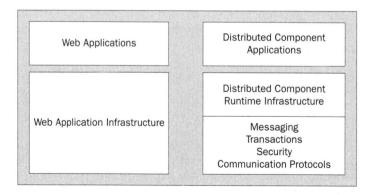

In this figure, the above requirements are classified into two categories – web technologies and middleware technologies. In this section, we will briefly discuss the evolution of these technologies.

Web Technologies

The boxes on the left represent what are traditionally called web technologies. Some of the most commonly used technologies in this category include the CGI (Common Gateway Interface) using Perl, Shell Scripts, C and so on, Web server APIs such NSAPI (from the erstwhile Netscape), and ISAPI (from Microsoft), PHP (initially stood for Personal Home Pages, now stands for PHP: Hypertext Pre-processor). Note that, before these technologies, there was no notion of web applications. The content was completely static, and the only purpose of web technology was to publish static information.

These technologies introduce programmable logic within the HTTP request-response model. Upon receipt of an HTTP request, these technologies allow you to invoke native language (typically C) programs or interpreted programs such as Perl shell scripts. These programs can parse HTTP requests (such as form submissions), execute business logic, and generate HTML programmatically. This approach gives the basic flexibility of generating dynamic content. From basic web servers capable of static HTML, the ability to generate content programmatically is a significant evolutionary change. In order to facilitate database access, these programs can rely on either vendor-specific or third party native language database drivers.

> The ability to process HTTP requests programmatically and generate custom responses is a major leap from a static web to an interactive web. This is one of the fundamental evolutionary changes that have led to today's e-commerce world. These technologies have led to the evolution of the first generation of e-commerce applications, most of which are still popular and actively serving their purposes.

However, these technologies are limited in their ability. The most notable issues with these technologies are their lack of support for statefulness, and the need to generate content programmatically. Note that HTTP is a stateless protocol, and the protocol does not support managing conversational state on either the web server or the client browser. Although cookies and other related session management techniques give the ability to track user sessions, the ability to store information against a session is crucial for any conversation to happen via the web. A more critical limitation is the need for programming to generate content. With some of these technologies, dynamic content requires programming.

Web Application Servers

These limitations have motivated the evolution of web application servers such as the Netscape Application Server (now called iPlanet Application Server), NetDynamics (now merged into the iPlanet Application Server), and a host of other vendors including Oracle, Apple, BlueStone, and so on. These application servers introduced the notion of web applications with capabilities to execute application logic written in programming languages such as C++ and Java, and generate content using templates.

In its simple form, a template is a parameterized HTML page – that is, a template consists of certain proprietary markers along with HTML code. The exact syntax and approach varies from vendor to vendor. Therefore, instead of writing programs to generate content, one can use HTML editors to author templates. The underlying application server processes these templates at run time, and thereby generates HTML.

The major goal of these technologies is to make web application development easier. The second-generation of e-commerce applications were built using these technologies. Apart from providing programmability and page templates, these products also focused on rapid development, clustering, and load-balancing for performance and fail-over purposes. These products, for the first time, provided enterprise-level web architecture for building e-commerce applications. Most of these products provided a significant amount of infrastructure support in their programming models for web applications.

As you will see later in this section, the advent of J2EE has changed this scenario significantly.

Middleware Technologies

The boxes on the right side of the figure shown earlier represent the distributed component and messaging technologies with other technical requirements such as transactions and security. This second category is traditionally called middleware technologies. Although the evolution of these technologies dates back to the RPC (Remote Procedure Call) era (1980s), the basic motivation behind these technologies is to allow applications (whether on the same machine or on different machines) to communicate with each other. As we discussed previously in this chapter, there are essentially two approaches to make applications communicate with each other:

- ❏ Distributed components
- ❏ Message brokers

The most notable distributed component technologies are CORBA, and COM/DCOM. Although both these technologies evolved from the notion of RPC, CORBA is meant for allowing applications written in disparate languages for different operating platforms to communicate with each other using interfaces. On the other hand, COM/DCOM is meant for developing distributed component applications on Microsoft Windows platforms. Another application of CORBA is to use the CORBA infrastructure to build distributed component applications. In fact, this has been the only cross-platform distributed component technology for building distributed applications.

Although CORBA provides the basic infrastructure for distributed components to communicate with each other, one of the major complexities of CORBA occurs when you consider other enterprise requirements such as transactions and security. While the OMG has specifications (and implementations of them) to deal with these requirements (the Object Transaction Service, and the Security Service), it is still complex for developers to integrate these technologies and rapidly build distributed applications. Moreover, the infrastructure provided by CORBA is not adequate in most of the cases. The developer will have to deal with code generation for proxies and stubs, developing the stubs, and even creating server objects. These technologies also leave a number of details to be configured in the network.

The second category of middleware technology is message broker technologies. Two vendors originally pioneered this technology – IBM with MQSeries for message queuing, and TIBCO with their TIB/Rendezvous for publish-and-subscribe. Of these, the notion of message queuing allowed enterprises to integrate their systems in a loosely coupled manner.

Integrated Paradigm

Until recently, these technologies remained independent. Although it was possible to build end-to-end applications using web and middleware technologies together, there were no technologies that provided an integrated platform. It has been up to the developers to integrate these technologies. Due to this limitation, such integration was not wide spread. Accordingly, most of the early e-commerce applications were built predominantly using e-commerce applications, while managing the integration with middleware-centric applications on a case-by-case basis.

However, this situation has changed over the past couple of years with the emergence of two competing technologies, namely **J2EE** from Sun Microsystems (with support from several other vendors such as IBM, BEA, Oracle, and so on), and the **Windows DNA** platform (also part of the .NET strategy) from Microsoft. While J2EE is the specification of a platform, the DNA is a suite of products/APIs/tools from Microsoft, which include ASP/ASP+, COM+, MTS, MSMQ, MS SQL Server, and so on.

Until the advent of these technologies, the web and middleware technologies evolved on their own. While the web technologies enabled enterprises to build web-based commerce systems, the middleware technologies allowed enterprises to build distributed applications, and to integrate existing enterprise applications. As businesses tried to integrate their web initiatives with their enterprise applications, the need for an integration of web infrastructure with enterprise infrastructure became critical. It has been a challenge to integrate these two paradigms and provide end-to-end business processes across these vendor-driven proprietary technologies.

J2EE is a result of integration of these two technologies. J2EE combines the best practices in both paradigms, and provides a comprehensive infrastructure by considering web applications, distributed component applications, application integration, and an infrastructure that shields developers from most of the complex issues related to web and middleware applications. In the next chapter, we shall see more details of this technology.

Summary

In this chapter, we have discussed the critical success factors for e-commerce applications, and how these factors relate to enabling technologies. We have also briefly discussed the evolution of the enabling technologies into J2EE.

The basic theme of this chapter is to emphasize the fact the e-commerce does not start with browsers and end with web servers and web applications. Today, e-commerce requires end-to-end information access and business process execution across the enterprise, and across enterprises, allowing multiple channels to access the information and participate in business processes. Considering various scenarios that contribute to successful e-commerce applications, we have identified four factors:

- ❑ Flexibility, such that e-commerce applications can be adapted to ever-changing business requirements

- ❑ Multi-channel interfaces, such that e-commerce applications can be accessed via multiple channels ranging from regular browser-based interfaces to mobile devices to applications from the same or other enterprises

- ❑ Security, such that e-commerce transactions can be conducted with trust, confidentiality and data integrity

- ❑ Integration, such that end-to-end business processes can be implemented seamlessly across the enterprise and across enterprises

In order to build e-commerce applications to conform to the above, e-commerce application development involves:

- ❑ Component based technologies for building layered implementation of business processes and services

- ❑ Web technologies for building varieties of user interfaces

❑ Integration technologies such as message brokers and XML such that applications can be integrated for both B2C and B2B domains

❑ Security across the above

If you draw a blueprint of your e-commerce system based on the discussion in this chapter, you will find that a significant amount of time and effort will have to be spent on component development and integration.

It is ironic that many e-commerce projects tend to postpone some of the above requirements and focus only on building web sites with functionality related web-based customer access, catalogues, shopping carts and so on. As shown in this chapter, such a myopic view of e-commerce will not succeed in utilizing the true potential of the current e-commerce business models as well as what can be achieved with the current e-commerce technologies.

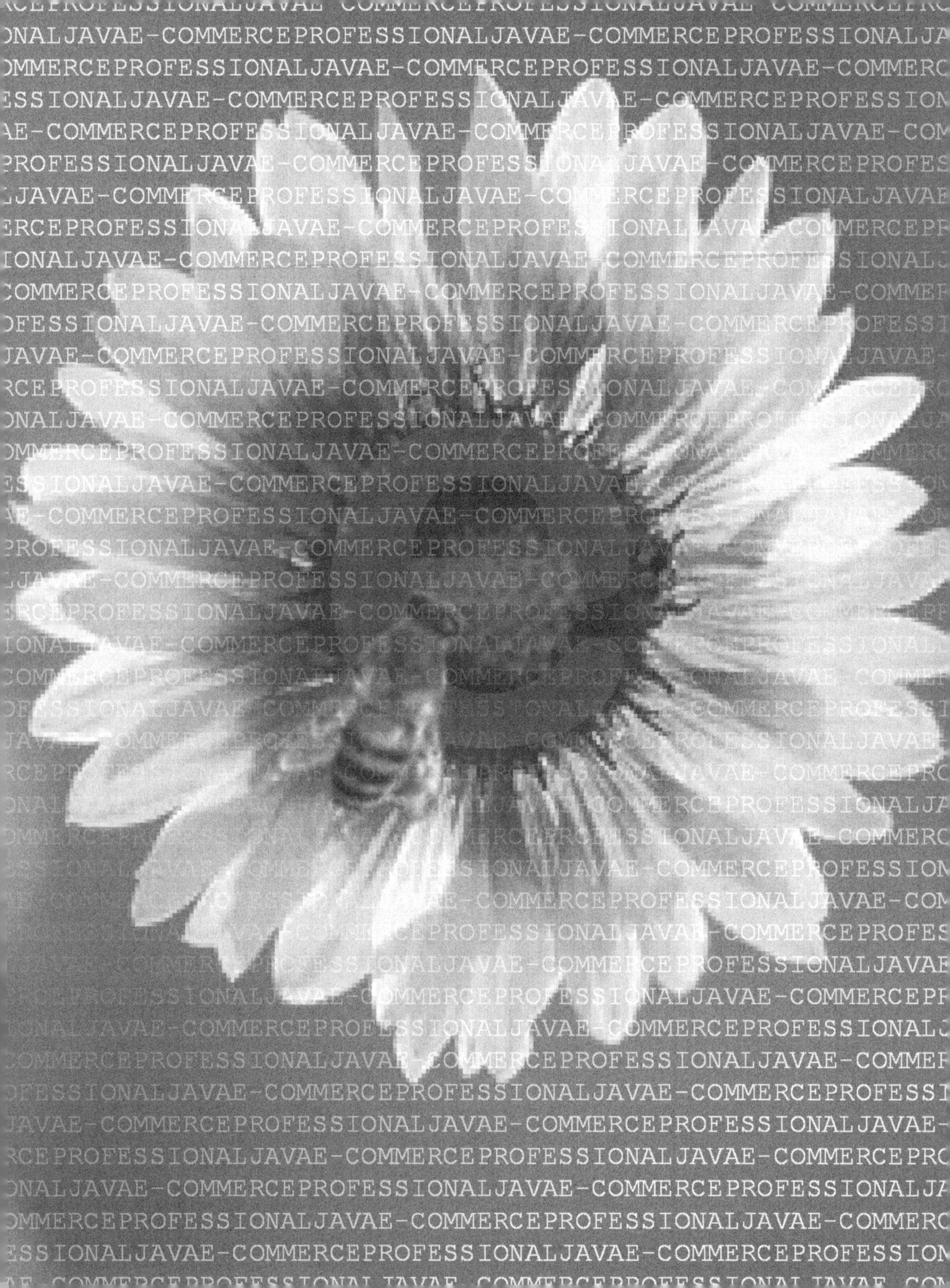
PROFESSIONALJAVAE-COMMERCE

5

J2EE for E-Commerce Applications

The J2EE (Java 2 Enterprise Edition) has now been around for about two years. Over these years, it has replaced several proprietary and non-standard technologies as the choice for building e-commerce and other internet-centric enterprise applications. Considering the multitude and complexity of technical infrastructure requirements for e-commerce applications, you will find out in this chapter how J2EE suits such requirements by providing a comprehensive infrastructure. Today, J2EE is the de-facto standard for building e-commerce applications.

However, what is J2EE? Before we attempt to answer this question, let us go back to the previous chapter where we identified an infrastructure-centric technical architecture for building e-commerce applications. To recap, this architecture consists of the following:

- ❑ A core infrastructure supporting communication protocols, distributed invocation protocols, messaging and transaction processing services, and security

- ❑ A distributed component runtime infrastructure

- ❑ A web application runtime infrastructure

- ❑ A programming model to develop distributed components

- ❑ A programming model to develop web applications capable of dynamic interfaces

As we discussed in the previous chapter, you can create this infrastructure intensive architecture by integrating traditional web and middleware technologies. However, with J2EE, it is not necessary to do so. J2EE specifies a more elaborate infrastructure and more complex component programming models.

J2EE is a specification developed by Sun along with other leading vendors working on Internet and middleware-related technologies. Sun released the first version of J2EE in early 1999. Over the past two years, J2EE has been revised to include better infrastructure support and more mature programming models. J2EE now stands at version 1.2, and you can access J2EE documents at http://java.sun.com/j2ee. At the time of writing this chapter, version 1.3 of the J2EE specification is in the final draft stage, and is likely to be finalized by the time you read this book.

J2EE is a specification that includes the following:

❑ Programming models and associated APIs for developing distributed components and web applications.

❑ A set of enterprise APIs that provides various services such as transactions, naming, messaging, database access, and so on.

❑ The responsibilities of a J2EE runtime. The runtime can host J2EE applications, and provides access to implementations of the enterprise APIs.

Several vendors offer application servers compatible with J2EE. Some of the notable vendors include BEA (WebLogic Application Server), IBM (WebSphere Application Server), and the Sun-AOL alliance – iPlanet (iPlanet Application Server), Borland (Borland Application Server, formerly Inprise Application Server), Iona (iPortal Application Server). A complete list of products, with their feature support, can be found at http://www.flashline.com/components/appservermatrix.jsp. Apart from providing the core J2EE platform, these products also include development, deployment, and administration tools.

For the rest of this chapter, let us use the term J2EE platform to refer to an application server complying with the J2EE specification.

The purpose of this chapter is essentially to present an overview of J2EE. We will cover the following topics in this chapter:

❑ J2EE architecture

❑ J2EE application components

❑ J2EE services

❑ Packaging and deploying J2EE applications

> Note that a complete description of each of these services is beyond the scope of this chapter – our aim here is merely to provide an overview as a foundation for the rest of the book. For more details, including programming exercises, you should refer to *Professional Java Server Programming, J2EE Edition*, ISBN 1-861004-65-6, also by Wrox Press.

J2EE Architecture

The following figure shows the various constituents of the J2EE platform.

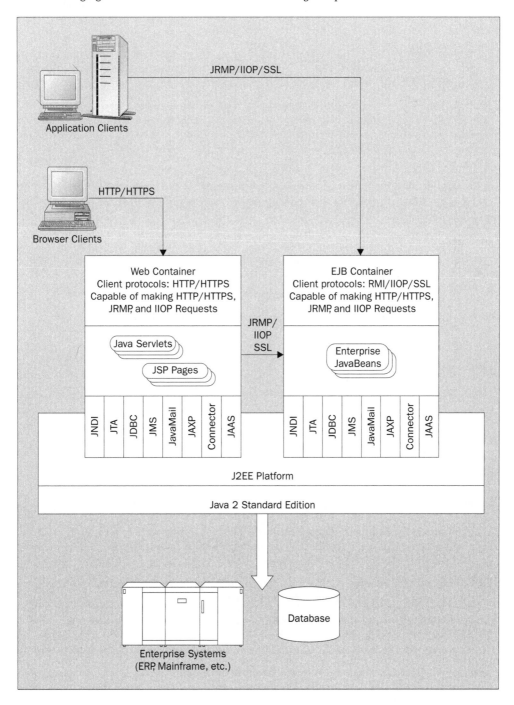

This figure also shows how web and application clients can access the J2EE platform. Let us now consider the details of this architecture:

❑ **J2SE:** – At the bottom of this architecture is the J2SE runtime environment, which provides all the standard Java facilities to the J2EE platform and the applications deployed thereon. The J2SE runtime is an integral part of the J2EE platform.

❑ **J2EE Containers** – This architecture shows two types of containers each providing runtime support specific to J2EE applications. These containers implement the respective container-specific APIs. We will shortly see what J2EE applications are and the role of these containers.

❑ **J2EE Services** – The vertical blocks at the bottom of each container represent the J2EE service APIs. These APIs provide several facilities that J2EE applications require. As we shall see later in this chapter, some of these facilities correspond to traditional middleware (such as naming, transactions, messaging, security, etc.). Other services include database access, access to legacy, systems etc.

❑ **J2EE Application Components** – The rounded rectangles in the previous figure are what are called application components. These components are what a developer develops and deploys on J2EE containers.

Note that the above architecture also shows the protocols between clients and application components. For instance, web browsers use HTTP and HTTPS to communicate with application components deployed on web containers. Similarly, components deployed on the EJB container can be invoked using the JRMP or IIOP with or without SSL.

In the following subsections, let us discuss this architecture in more detail by looking at:

❑ The J2EE Runtime

❑ J2EE Applications and Components

❑ J2EE Services

❑ J2EE Clients

❑ Declarative Services

The J2EE Runtime

The J2EE platform consists of one or more containers. The J2EE specifies four types of containers.

❑ **Web containers for running web applications** – The web container provides support for running web applications. In J2EE, you can build web applications with dynamic interface capabilities using Java servlets and JSP pages.

❑ **EJB Containers for running EJBs** – The EJB container provides support for Enterprise JavaBeans, which are J2EE's distributed components.

❑ **Applet containers for running applets:** – The applet container supports a runtime environment for running applets in web browsers. Although applets once occupied an important segment of Java development, in the enterprise world, the role of applets is limited.

❑ **Application client containers for running standard Java application clients** – Although web clients are the most common form of clients, there are cases where application clients play an important role. These are:

❑ **Graphical User Interface applications developed using AWT (Abstract Windowing Toolkit) or Swing** – Such clients may be developed for back-office users and administrators.

❑ **Other J2EE or non-J2EE Java applications invoking J2EE components** – Such application clients can be used for integration purposes.

Of these four types of containers, the web and EJB containers are of importance for developing e-commerce applications. However, there may be situations where you would rather develop applet or application clients.

The best way to understand the J2EE architecture is to understand its runtime. The J2EE is specified in such a manner that the developer gets the following advantages:

❑ **Management of application components** – Since J2EE applications are server-side applications, you need a process to host these applications. The basic purpose of the J2EE container runtime is to create instances of J2EE application components. The runtime saves the developer from having to explicitly create instances of various application components. Instead, based on the type of an application component, and based on certain configuration information, J2EE containers determine how and when to create instances, and how to recycle instances once the instances serve their requests. These tasks are nontrivial for a developer to deal with in every possible application. Moreover, such tasks are common to server side applications in general.

❑ **Access to application components** – J2EE applications are distributed and remote to clients. Therefore, you need the communication and protocol support for the clients to connect to the J2EE application components. The container runtime also supports the required protocols for client access. For instance, the web container supports the HTTP and HTTPS protocols so that browsers can send HTTP/HTTPS requests to web application components. This is the same for the EJB container. Secondly, the application components deployed on these containers need not deal with the actual protocols that clients use to connect. In the case of web containers, web application components such as Java servlets and JSP pages need to directly deal with HTTP. Instead, the container provides a higher-level API to access the request information. Similarly, EJB components need not understand how the communication between them and clients is handled. J2EE runtime also manages threads such that, depending on the type of application component, instances of J2EE application components can be accessed in a thread-safe manner. In most of the cases, the runtime eliminates the need for developers to explicitly program for multi-threaded access.

❑ **Access to enterprise service APIs** – As you can see, J2EE integrates a variety of APIs that have been in existence (in various forms) for quite some time. For instance, the notion of transactions, messaging, database access, and naming are not new. Although some of the service APIs (such as the APIs for XML support, and connector) are new, J2EE standardizes the programming API for these services. The obvious advantage of this standardization is that application components need not depend on the implementation details. In some cases, it is quite possible to plug-in third-party implementations for a given service. Apart from this, in order to allow flexibility of various implementations, and to eliminate proprietary configuration procedures, J2EE also specifies how application components should access these services. For instance, J2EE specifies how to obtain a database connection in a driver independent manner. The same is true for mail, messaging, transactions, and so on. As long as the service implementations conform to the standard, an administrator of the J2EE platform can make the services available to applications in a standardized manner. In this way, the J2EE runtime acts as a gateway to all the enterprise services.

101

What does it mean to the developer? J2EE specifies a clear demarcation between application components and the runtime, such that most of the commonly required facilities are abstracted within the runtime. Moreover, since the runtime eliminates dependency on proprietary APIs and procedures, J2EE applications can ideally be deployed on any J2EE compliant container runtime.

Note that J2EE does not specify the nature and structure of the runtime. By specifying how the application components and the services behave, the specification implies certain behavior for containers. It's up to the container vendor to provide this behavior.

J2EE Applications and Components

The J2EE specifies two kinds of components for application development – Web components and EJB components. The use of these collectively gives rise to applications.

Web components

Java servlets and **JavaServer Pages (JSP)** are the J2EE web components. Unlike traditional components, which are defined by custom interfaces, these components have their interfaces defined by the Java servlet API.

Java servlets are small application programs that can process HTTP requests and generate HTTP responses programmatically. JSP are also based on Java servlets; however, JSP follow the notion of pages (content) as opposed to programs. JSP are similar to HTML/XML documents with additional **scriptlets** and JSP tags to generate parts of the content dynamically.

In J2EE, web components are packaged and deployed as web applications. A web application is a collection of Java servlets, JSP, other helper classes and class libraries, and static resources such as HTML, XHTML, or XML documents and images.

J2EE web containers host web application components. The web container is essentially a Java runtime providing an implementation of the Java servlet API, and an infrastructure for compiling and executing JSP's. The web container is responsible for initializing, invoking, and managing the life cycle of Java servlets and Java Server Pages.

J2EE also specifies a packaging structure, and a **deployment descriptor** for web applications. The packaging structure specifies locations for various web components, class files, and other static content. Web applications can be customized by modifying the deployment descriptor before deployment. A deployment descriptor is an XML file with several configuration options for web applications.

EJB Components

Enterprise Java Beans are the distributed components of J2EE. The development of distributed components (for example using RMI or CORBA) involves several steps that are usually complex. Unlike these technologies, EJB components are simpler to develop, and the EJB container handles most of the steps associated with distributed component development. There are three types of EJBs – **session beans, entity beans**, and **message driven beans**.

An EJB is essentially a remote object. The EJB API specifies certain base interfaces for implementing EJBs. Apart from being remote objects, EJBs are transactional. You can configure methods on EJBs to be executed within transactions. Apart from this, you can also protect methods on EJBs, so that only users with specific roles can execute methods on EJBs. Such configuration activities can be done at deployment time, by configuring a deployment descriptor.

In J2EE, EJBs are usually packaged into `.JAR` files with an additional deployment descriptor file. Similar to the web application deployment descriptor, the EJB deployment descriptor is also an XML file.

Enterprise Applications

J2EE introduces the notion of **enterprise applications**. An enterprise application is essentially a collection of web and EJB modules, with each module consisting of one or more `.WAR` (for web applications) or `.JAR` (for EJBs) files. Enterprise applications are packaged into Enterprise Archive (`.EAR`) files. Each `.EAR` file also includes a deployment descriptor that can be used to bundle and configure various modules.

J2EE Services

In a given J2EE platform, the containers will either implement the J2EE services directly, or provide hooks to other implementations, such that application components can access these services without having to deal with third-party implementations directly. The following APIs compose the J2EE services:

- ❑ **JNDI (Java Naming and Directory Interface)** – The role of the Java Naming and Directory Interface (JNDI) API in the J2EE platform is two-fold. Firstly, it provides a unified interface to deal with multiple naming and directory services such as LDAP, Novell Directory Services, Netscape Directory Services, amongst others. Secondly, a J2EE application utilizes JNDI to look up interfaces used to create EJBs and JDBC connections, amongst other things.

- ❑ **JTA (Java Transaction API)** –The JTA is a means for working with transactions and especially distributed transactions. Under the J2EE platform, distributed transactions can be implemented either programmatically or declaratively. The JTA allows for programmatic control of transactions in J2EE applications.

- ❑ **JDBC (Java Database Connectivity)** – In addition to the standard JDBC API (the `java.sql` package of J2SE), the J2EE introduces an extension. This extended API is optimized for the J2EE platform, providing a more sophisticated means of creating database connections and dealing with certain advanced features of database connections. This extension also specifies an architecture for dealing with connection pooling and transactions transparently.

- ❑ **JMS (Java Messaging Service)** – The JMS provides enterprise-messaging facilities to J2EE. The JMS specifies certain messaging facilities, using applications that can exchange business data as messages asynchronously.

- ❑ **JavaMail** – The Java Mail API provides a platform and protocol-independent API for electronic mail. JavaMail supports the most widely used Internet mail protocols such as IMAP4, POP3, and SMTP.

- ❑ **JAXP (Java API for XML Parsing)** – This API introduces support for parsing and manipulating XML documents independent of the underlying parser technology. This API has been added to J2EE version 1.3.

- ❑ **Connector** – The connector architecture introduces a standard architecture for connecting to heterogeneous enterprise information systems such as ERP systems, transaction processing systems on mainframes, and database systems.

- ❑ **JAAS (Java Authentication and Authorization Service)** – J2EE version 1.3 now includes support for the JAAS. The JAAS package allows access control to be imposed on parts of code, based on the identity of the user running the code.

We will consider more details of these APIs later in this chapter.

J2EE Clients

As shown in the J2EE architecture, there are primarily two types of clients in the J2EE architecture:

❑ **Web clients** – Web clients are meant for browser based access. The user interface is generated on the server-side as HTML or XML for the clients; the browser then downloads and renders it. HTTP and/or HTTPS are the protocols used by the clients to communicate with web containers. Web containers include application components such as Java servlets and JSP pages, which implement the web client's functionality. With the help of the application components, these web containers accept requests and generate responses from web clients.

❑ **EJB clients** – These are applications that access EJB components in EJB containers. There are two kinds of EJB clients – the first are J2EE or non-J2EE Java applications that use the RMI-IIOP protocol to access the EJB components. The second category of EJB clients is web container components, such as Java servlets and JSP pages. These components can also access the EJB components through the RMI-IIOP protocol in much the same way as the application clients can.

In both cases, application components are accessed by clients through their container. Through the web container, web clients access JSP pages and Java servlets and EJB clients access the EJB components via the EJB container.

Declarative Services

J2EE architecture is able to dynamically create services for application components, and it does this through **declarations** that are specified outside your application components. The declarations are specified through the simple means of **deployment descriptors**. Deployment descriptors are XML files. You can use either vendor-provided tools or other XML/text editors to configure deployment descriptor files.

The deployment descriptor is a definition of the contract between the container and component. A deployment descriptor must be specified for each group of application components. For instance, a set of EJB components can be described together in a single deployment descriptor file. In the instance of web containers, each group of web application components is also required to have a specified deployment descriptor.

Certain types of services (such as transactions, or security, amongst others), depending on the type of the component, can be specified in the deployment descriptor. A declarative service is a service or action that is performed by the container on the application's behalf. This approach is intended to reduce the amount of application programming required to use these services.

In J2EE, the container is the one that receives client requests and delegates the requests to various components. Thus, the container acts as an intermediary between clients and application components. Due to this interception, the container can interpose declarative services based on deployment-time configuration. The associated flexibility allows you to postpone certain decisions to deployment time as opposed to compile time. The container can thus selectively enhance your components based on the deployment descriptor.

The declarative services for EJB containers, including transactions and security, can be specified in deployment descriptors. In the case of web containers, you can specify the required security roles for accessing components within web applications.

J2EE Components

Now we've got an overview of the overall architecture, let's look at the various units in more detail starting with the J2EE components – servlets, JavaServer pages, and EJBs.

Java Servlets

For web applications, browsers, or other internet-enabled devices are the clients. Browsers and web servers use HTTP for communication. When a browser makes an HTTP request, based on the type and contents of the request, the web server is required to generate an appropriate response. This is the basic model for web applications.

Java servlets allow you to embed application logic in the HTTP request-response process. Java servlets are specified in the Java Servlet API Specification 2.2 available at http://java.sun.com/products/servlet.

> *Note that, the next version of the servlet specification (2.3) is in the final stages and is likely to be finalized by the time you read this book.*

Java servlets are server-side programs that programmatically extend the functionality of the web server by generating custom responses to HTTP requests. Java servlets are deployed as part of web applications on web containers. A web container works in tandem with web servers to handle requests for specified dynamic content.

Web containers invoke Java servlets triggered by incoming HTTP requests. In order to facilitate this, servlets are registered with the container via the deployment descriptor. This process involves specifying a URI pattern corresponding to a servlet. Based on the HTTP request URI, the container can therefore identify a servlet. When the container invokes a servlet, the web container exchanges the incoming request information with the servlet, such that the servlet can analyze the incoming request and generate responses dynamically. The web container in turn interfaces with the web server by accepting requests for servlets, and transmitting responses back to the web server.

The servlet framework provides a better abstraction of the HTTP request-response paradigm by specifying a programming API for encapsulating requests, responses, and sessions when compared to the CGI and proprietary server extensions such as NSAPI or ISAPI. Additionally, servlets have all the advantages of the Java programming language, including platform independence.

The Java Servlet API

The Java servlet API is specified in two Java extension packages: `javax.servlet` and `javax.servlet.http`. Of these, in the `javax.servlet` package contains protocol independent classes and interfaces, while the second package `javax.servlet.http` contains classes and interfaces that are specific to HTTP. In general, you'll need to use both these packages to develop servlets.

The Java servlet API provides for two types of servlets:

❑ **Multi-threaded servlets:** This is the most commonly used type of servlet. You can extend the `javax.servlet.http.HttpServlet` class to implement your servlets that can handle multiple requests within a given servlet instance. In this model, the web container maintains a single instance of the servlet, and directs all requests to the same instance in multiple threads. As long as your servlet instance is thread-independent without synchronized blocks and thread-unsafe code, this model offers the best possible throughput.

❑ **Single-thread servlets**: This model is meant for servlets that are thread-sensitive. Servlets of this type implement the `javax.servlet.SingleThreadModel` interface. This is a marker interface and does not specify any methods. When a servlet implements this interface, the web container makes sure that a given instance of this servlet handles one request at a time.

One of the common requirements for web applications is the ability to maintain client state across multiple requests. This is required, as the HTTP is a stateless protocol, and browsers can carry forward any state. In order to manage client state, the Java servlet API has the notion of session. An HTTP session (represented by the `javax.servlet.http.HttpSession` interface) is essentially an object associated with a given HTTP request. Servlets can store named objects in HTTP session objects, and retrieve them when required. However, how can we maintain a session across multiple HTTP requests? Web containers use either cookies or URL rewriting to maintain sessions. The default mechanism is via cookies, and when client browsers do not accept cookies, web containers rely on URL rewriting.

In addition to maintaining client-specific state, you can also maintain state common to all servlets in a given application, using the servlet context. The `javax.servlet.ServletContext` interface represents the context. Servlet context is common to all servlets (and JSP pages too) within a web application running on a JVM. Apart from the ability to maintain application state, servlet context can also be used to perform certain common tasks such as logging, and accessing application initialization parameters, amongst others.

JavaServer Pages

There are two ways to achieving dynamic content generation: programmatic content generation, and template-based content generation. Java servlets fall into the first category, while **JavaServer Pages (JSP)** belong to the second category. JSP pages are specified in the JavaServer Pages 1.1 Specification, available at http://java.sun.com/products/jsp.

The JSP technology is an extension of the Java servlet technology. However, when compared to servlets, which are pure Java programs, JSP pages are text-based documents. A JSP page contains the following:

❑ HTML or XML for the static content

❑ JSP **scriptlets** to embed regular Java language statements

❑ Custom JSP **tags** to extend HTML/XML tags

A JSP page acts like a template for producing content, because JSP pages provide a general representation of content that can produce multiple views depending on the results of JSP tags and scriptlets.

A template is basically an HTML/XML page with special placeholders (JSP tags and scriptlets) embedded. Special processing information is contained in these placeholders for the underlying template processor (or content generator). The usual HTML/XML tags allow you to define the static structure and content of a JSP page. You can include programming logic to be executed during page generation using the additional JSP tags and scriptlets that are embedded in the page.

The ability to keep the content design and development activities loosely coupled with the design and development of the application logic is the key advantage of this technology. On the other hand, if you choose to develop the content purely with Java servlets, content development and application logic will be strongly coupled. This is undesirable because such lumped applications do not lend themselves to easy maintenance. For instance, application logic typically includes input validation, EJB access, associated exception handling, etc., while content development includes generating formatted HTML/XML. Since each of these tasks require different skills, it is appropriate not to couple these tasks.

JSP technology is based on page compilation. In this technology, the web container converts JSP pages into servlet classes, and compiles them. The generated servlet class, when invoked, will produce the static content (HTML/XML) as specified in the JSP page while executing embedded scriptlets and custom tags. This process typically happens when the web container invokes a JSP page for the first time in response to a request or at container startup. Web containers also allow you to pre-compile JSPs into servlets. Most of the containers available today repeat this process whenever the page is modified. As mentioned above, you can also use scriptlets or tags for dynamic content in JSPs.

A scriptlet is essentially a set of regular Java statements embedded within special markers mixed within HTML/XML content. The JSP container executes these statements while executing the compiled JSP. However, this approach has the limitation that a page with scriptlets is difficult to maintain due to Java code mixed with HTML/XML.

JSP Tags

A better alternative to scriptlets is to use custom JSP tags. JSP tag extensions let you enhance the markup tags specified by HTML/XML/JSP. Similar to normal HTML/XML tags, custom JSP tags can accept attributes. The JSP API includes certain interfaces for implementing the logic behind each tag. Using special descriptor files (with extension .tld), you can register custom tags with web containers. Based on this information, the web container invokes the underlying tag implementation classes when a tag is encountered in a JSP page.

JSP tags offer a very flexible extension mechanism for extending the functionality of JSP pages. Although you can develop JSP tags to include complex business logic, it is preferable to limit tags for user interface related logic, and not business logic. As discussed in the previous chapter, considering multiple channels of interfaces, it is better to maintain most of the business logic within EJBs deployed on EJB containers.

Enterprise JavaBeans

Enterprise JavaBeans (EJB) is a comprehensive technology that provides the infrastructure for building enterprise level server-side distributed Java components. The EJB technology provides a distributed component architecture that integrates several enterprise-level requirements such as distribution, transactions, security, messaging, persistence, and connectivity to mainframes and ERP systems etc.

When compared to other distributed component technologies such as CORBA and RMI, the EJB architecture hides most of the underlying system-level semantics that are typical of distributed component applications, such as instance management, object pooling, multiple-threading, and connection pooling. Secondly, unlike other component models, EJB technology provides us with different types of components for business logic, persistence, and enterprise messages. Note that the long-overdue **CORBA Component Model** (**CCM**) also includes similar categories of beans and system-level abstractions.

What is an EJB? An EJB is essentially a remote object with semantics specified for creation, invocation, and deletion. Transparent to the client using an EJB, the EJB container manages all the system-level issues mentioned above. Just the way a web container provides the runtime to execute servlets and JSP pages, the EJB container provides a runtime for EJB instances.

When dealing with any distributed component technology, the following questions become pertinent:

❑	How do we create the client-side and server-side proxy objects? A client-side proxy represents the server-side object on the client-side. As far as the client is concerned, the client-side proxy is equivalent to the server-side object. On the other hand, the purpose of the server-side proxy is to provide the basic infrastructure to receive client requests and delegate these request to the actual implementation object.

❑ How can a client obtain a reference to client-side proxy object? In order to communicate with the server-side object, the client needs to obtain a reference to the proxy.

❑ How do we inform the distributed component system that a specific component is no longer in use by the client?

In order to deal with these, the EJB architecture specifies two kinds of interfaces for each bean – these are the home interface, and the remote interface. These are regular Java interfaces extending the `javax.ejb.EJBHome` and `javax.ejb.EJBObject` interfaces respectively. These interfaces specify the bean contract to the clients. However, as a bean developer, you need not provide implementation for these interfaces. On the home interface, you can specify methods that can be used to create remote objects. The remote interface should include business methods for client access.

You can consider using the home interface to specify a remote object capable of creating objects conforming to the remote interface. This may sound indirect – but the home interface is analogous to a factory of remote objects. This level of indirection does not exist in other distributed component techniques.

How do we provide implementation for these two interfaces? As mentioned previously, the EJB architecture specifies three types of beans – session beans, entity beans, and message-driven beans. We shall shortly see what these three types mean. For each of these types of beans, the EJB API specifies interfaces. Apart from specifying the home and remote interfaces, as the bean developer, you are also responsible for implementing one of these bean interfaces (depending on the type of the bean). For instance, for session beans, the bean developer should implement the `javax.ejb.SessionBean` interface. The EJB architecture requires you to implement the methods specified in the bean interface, and also the methods specified in the home and remote interfaces. Note that there is no inheritance relationship between the home and remote interfaces, and the bean implementation class. The EJB container relies on specific method names, and uses delegation for invoking methods on bean instances. During the deployment time, you should specify the home and remote interfaces and bean implementation class to define a bean.

Let us now get back to the three questions posed above:

❑ **Proxy Objects** – In the EJB architecture, the container (or container-specific tools) generates the proxy objects for all beans. The exact procedure is up to the container vendor. In most of the container implementations, this step is transparent to the developer.

❑ **Reference to Proxy** – The EJB container for each bean publishes a proxy object implementation to the home interface in the JNDI implementation of the J2EE platform. You can use JNDI to look for this and obtain a reference. Since this object implements the home interface, you can use one of the creation methods of the home object to obtain a proxy to the remote interface. When you invoke a creation method on the home proxy object, the container makes sure that a bean instance is created on the EJB container runtime, and its proxy is returned to the client. Once the proxy for the remote interface is obtained, the client can use the proxy just like any remote object.

❑ **Bean Lifetime** – Once the client decides that it no longer requires the bean, it can inform the EJB container by calling a remove method on the bean. This disassociates the bean instance from the proxy such that the client can no longer use the proxy to invoke the bean.

This is the basic architecture of EJBs. Note that, in this process, you need not deal with how instances are created and managed on the server-side. This is the responsibility of the EJB container.

Types of EJBs

The EJB architecture is based on the premise that, in an enterprise architecture, database persistence-related logic should be independent of the business logic that relies on the data. This is a very useful abstraction for separating business logic concerns from database concerns. With such an abstraction in place, the implementation of business logic can deal with business data without depending on how the data is stored in a relational database.

Accordingly, the EJB architecture (version 1.1) specifies two basic types of beans:

- ❑ Session beans
- ❑ Entity beans

These two types of beans are meant for synchronous invocation. When a client invokes a method on a bean of one of the above types, the client thread will be blocked until the EJB container completes executing the method on the bean instance. Secondly, such beans can respond to synchronous requests only. This mechanism does not leave scope for beans to respond to messages that arrive asynchronously over a messaging service such as JMS. In order to allow this, the EJB architecture (version 2.0, currently in the final stages) has introduced a third type of bean called a message-driven bean.

Let us now briefly discuss each of these three types of beans.

Session Beans

Session beans are plain remote objects meant for abstracting business logic. For instance, in the layered architecture we discussed in the previous chapter, session beans can be used to implement the core business services as well as the business processes.

Session beans are *transaction-aware*. In a distributed component environment, managing transactions across several components (possibly distributed) mandates distributed transaction processing. This is a complex task. Although it is possible for you control the transaction boundaries programmatically, the EJB architecture allows the container to manage transactions declaratively. This mechanism lets you specify transactions across bean methods – that is, you can specify whether the code with-in a bean method should execute within a transaction or not. We shall discuss declarative transactions in more detail in a later section in this chapter.

Secondly, session beans are *client-specific*. That is, session bean instances (on the server side) are specific to the client that created them (on the client side). This eliminates the need for the developer to deal with multiple threading and concurrency.

The EJB architecture allows beans to retain state across multiple method invocations. For instance, a bean can store some state in private variables during one method call, and a subsequent method call can rely on this state. That is, a bean can maintain conversational state. This type of bean is called a **stateful** session bean. You can specify whether a bean is stateful or not in the bean's deployment descriptor.

> *However, be aware that stateful beans are resource intensive – for each active client, the EJB container will be required to maintain a separate instance. Secondly, stateful beans are not persistent. That is, containers do not maintain the state across server shutdown and start up.*

Entity Beans

Entity beans are meant to represent persistent business entities. For instance, in a B2B application, a purchase order is a business identity and requires persistence in a persistent store such as a relational database. The various purchase order attributes can be defined as the attributes of an entity bean.

Since database operations involve create, update, load, delete and find operations, the EJB architecture requires entity beans to implement these operations. Entity beans should implement the `javax.ejb.EntityBean` interface that specifies the load and delete operations among others. In addition, the bean developer should specify the appropriate create and find methods on the home interface, and provide their implementation in an entity bean.

Unlike session beans, entity beans have a *client-independent* identity. This is because an entity bean encapsulates persistent data. The EJB architecture lets you register a primary key class to encapsulate the minimal set of attributes required to represent the identity of an entity bean. Clients can use these primary key objects to create, locate, or delete entity beans.

Since entity beans represent persistent state, entity beans can be shared across different clients.

Similar to session beans, entity beans are also transactional, except for the fact that bean instances are not allowed to programmatically control transactions.

But, how do we manage persistence-related logic using entity beans? The EJB architecture has two approaches for managing persistence:

Bean-Managed Persistence (BMP)

In this approach, the bean is responsible for managing its state by embedding database persistence logic (for instance, JDBC code) within the methods for create, load, store, delete, and find operations. This is a straightforward approach and the bean developer can implement the persistence logic in any manner required.

Container-Managed Persistence (CMP)

This is a more sophisticated approach whereby the container manages the persistence logic. In this approach, the bean developer does not implement the persistence logic. Instead, the bean developer relies on the deployment descriptor to specify attributes whose persistence should be managed by the container. However, the EJB architecture does not specify how these attributes should be mapped to the database. Most of the container-managed persistence (CMP) implementations rely on additional vendor-specific deployment descriptors to specify this mapping information. Using this mapping information, the container manages the persistence.

> The 2.0 version of the EJB specification enhances this model by introducing facilities to manage associations between entities, and between entities and their dependent objects. Secondly, it also introduces a query language for specifying the find operations on entity beans.

Message-Driven Beans

Message-driven beans are a recent addition to the EJB architecture (version 2.0). A message-driven bean is a bean instance that can listen to messages from the JMS. Unlike other types of beans, a message-driven bean is a local (not remote) object without home and remote interfaces. In a J2EE platform, message-driven beans are registered against JMS destinations. When a JMS message receives a destination, the EJB container invokes the associated message-driven bean.

In short, message-driven beans do not require home and remote interfaces as instances of these beans are created based on receipt of JMS messages. This is an asynchronous activity and does not involve clients directly.

The main purpose of message-driven beans is to implement business logic in response to JMS messages. For instance, consider a B2B e-commerce application receiving a purchase order via a JMS message as an XML document. On receipt of such a message, in order to persist this data and perform any business logic, you can implement a message-driven bean and associate it with the corresponding JMS destination. Note that message-driven beans are completely decoupled from the clients that send messages.

J2EE Services

In the previous section, we have seen an overview of the two types of components that can be developed within a J2EE platform. In this section, let us consider an overview of the various J2EE service APIs.

JNDI

The purpose of the Java Naming and Directory Interface (JNDI) is to simplify access to **naming** and **directory** services. A naming service is a service that provides for the creation of a standard name for a given set of data. In a naming service, names exist in **context**. A context is a name that is used to make it easier to manage entries in the naming service and to allow the reuse of common names. A context provides a hierarchical structure to the set of names. A naming service itself does not provide any search capabilities. A directory service is a naming service that includes meta-data describing the object referenced by that name. Using this metadata, you can search the directory service to find objects without knowing its name. A directory service always includes the naming service. Typically, these two services are used together.

Traditionally, there are different APIs to deal with different directory services. Some of the most commonly used directory services include Novell Directory Services (NDS), Network Information Services (NIS/NIS+), Windows NT Domains, and Active Directory Services (ADS), and several implementations of the LDAP (Lightweight Directory Access Protocol). JNDI simplifies access to these services by providing a common API and an **SPI** (**Service Provider Interface**). The API is what applications use to access a naming and directory service. The SPI is what binds an API with a specific implementation of the JNDI API. Using this approach, it is possible to isolate the applications with the specific semantics of underlying naming and directory services.

For e-commerce applications, JNDI is relevant for two reasons:

❑ JNDI is the mechanism used by J2EE to publish several types of objects. For instance, when you deploy a bean on the EJB container of a J2EE platform, the EJB container binds the home proxy object with the specified name in the underlying JNDI implementation of the J2EE platform. Other examples include environment variables used by beans, JDBC data sources, JMS topics and queues.

❑ JNDI can be used to access directory services existing within the enterprise

JTA

The role of the Java Transaction API in J2EE is to provide programmatic transaction demarcation support. In simple terms, transaction demarcation means to indicate the underlying transaction processing infrastructure; the start and end points of a transaction. For instance, the JDBC 2.1 Core API has methods in the `java.sql.Connection` interface, by using these you can start, and end local transactions by disabling auto-commit and invoking either `commit()` or `rollback()` methods at the end of the transaction. However, these are local transactions as the transaction scope is limited to a single connection from a single JDBC client. However, this JDBC-centric API is not suitable for programmatically controlling the transaction demarcation in distributed applications.

As far as J2EE is concerned, the only interface that developers should be concerned about is the `javax.transaction.UserTransaction` interface. This interface has methods to start, commit, and rollback distributed transactions.

In J2EE, the JTA interface is implemented by the J2EE platform provider. At server start up, a J2EE platform creates an object implementing this interface, and publishes it within JNDI. Application components (servlets, JSPs, and EJBs) can retrieve this object, and begin, commit, and rollback transactions using this object.

Note that, as we shall discuss later in this chapter, it is generally not required to programmatically demarcate transactions using this API. As long as your transactional logic is implemented within EJBs, you can configure the EJBs to declaratively control transaction demarcation.

JDBC

Relational databases are the primary enterprise resources in most of the e-commerce applications today. The JDBC 2.1 Core API of the Java 2 Standard Edition provides the basic infrastructure for executing SQL statements and extracting the results. However, the basic JDBC 2.1 architecture is meant primarily for clients for applications based on the client-server architecture. Although the core API has the necessary abstractions for use with e-commerce application components on the server-side, this API has the following limitations:

- ❑ Applications using the JDBC 2.1 API rely on static class initializers and property files to load JDBC driver classes, and applications are not isolated from driver package names.

- ❑ Secondly, the JDBC 2.1 API does not use connection pooling. Connection pooling is an important requirement on the server side, as the numbers of clients typically exceed the number of database connections available.

- ❑ Thirdly, the JDBC 2.1 API does not consider distributed transactions. The only possibility with JDBC 2.1 API is to implement local transactions using the commit and rollback methods on JDBC connection objects.

The JDBC 2.0 Optional Package API addresses these limitations. J2EE applications are required to use this API to obtain database connections. After obtaining a connection, applications can use the JDBC 2.1 Core API for database programming.

The JDBC 2.0 Optional Package API provides the following facilities:

- ❑ **JNDI based lookup for accessing databases via their logical names** – Instead of each client trying to load the driver classes in their respective local virtual machines, using JNDI based lookup allows us to access the database resources using logical names assigned to these resources.

❑ **Connection pooling** – The JDBC Optional Package API specifies an additional intermediate layer for implementing connection pooling. That allows the responsibility for connection pooling to be shifted from application developers to driver and application server vendors.

❑ **Distributed transactions** – JDBC driver/application server vendors can support distributed transactions transparently of JDBC applications. The default `java.sql.Connection` object can not participate in distributed transactions, as it does not support the XA interface. The XA interface allows distributed transaction managers to coordinate the two-phase commit and recovery protocol. With the Optional Package API, J2EE platform administrators can plug-in an implementation of the `java.sql.Connection` interface that supports the XA interface.

❑ **Rowsets** – `Rowset` is a JavaBeans compliant object that encapsulates database resultsets and access information. A rowset may be connected or disconnected. Note that, in the JDBC 2.1 API, `ResultSets` are connected. That is, the connection is open while the object exists. However, rowsets allow us to encapsulate a set of rows, without necessarily maintaining a connection. Rowsets also allow us to update the data, and propagate the changes back to the underlying database.

Unlike the standard JDBC 2.1 API, the JDBC 2.0 Optional Package API specifies a pluggable architecture whereby J2EE platform vendors, database vendors, and independent driver vendors can provide implementations providing transaction and connection pooling support.

JMS

The Java Messaging Service provides the message-oriented middleware abstraction for J2EE. The purpose of JMS is to abstract most commonly used enterprise messaging concepts, so that enterprise Java applications need not deal with the underlying implementations, including the platform/network level details such as protocols or configuration. Instead, enterprise Java applications can use the JMS API to deal with messaging, while a J2EE platform administrator can set up the J2EE platform for JMS-based messaging.

The JMS provides two models for messaging – publish/subscribe, and point-to-point. These are the most commonly used enterprise messaging models popularized by TIBCO's TIB/Rendezvous, and IBM's MQSeries.

❑ **Publish/subscribe** – This is a one-to-many publishing model whereby a client application can publish messages to topics. Clients interested in these topics register with the JMS. Based on this information, all subscribed clients receive those messages.

❑ **Point-to-point model** – In this model, a client application sends messages, through a queue, to normally one client that is setup to receive messages from the queue. They will receive the messages sent to them from the queue in sequence. The JMS maintains the message queues, so that once the message is sent, the client is decoupled from the queue. A JMS message queue represents the destination for a message sender and a data source for a message receiver.

In order to send or receive messages, clients open JMS sessions. These JMS sessions are transactional, and therefore both senders and recipients act under a transaction while sending or receiving messages. The JMS specification also allows clients to send acknowledgements upon receipt of a message.

JavaMail

The JavaMail API provides a collection of abstract classes that define classes and interfaces common across general mail systems. While it seems simple to send and receive electronic mails using desktop mail clients, sending and receiving mails programmatically is a complex task involving several mail protocols (such as SMTP, IMAP, POP3, etc.), which are commonly available today. The JavaMail also supports MIME messages.

The JavaMail API provides a generic abstraction of mail systems. The JavaMail API can be implemented for a given mail server system. Using a JavaMail provider (an implementation), enterprise applications can send and receive electronic mails without having to deal with the underlying protocol details.

JavaMail providers implement two types of protocols. The first protocol is called transport, and is for sending messages to their destinations. The most commonly used transport type is SMTP transport. The second protocol is a store that can be used to retrieve messages. For this, the most commonly used stores are POP3 and IMAP.

The main usage of the JavaMail API in J2EE is the ability to send and receive electronic mails, and not necessarily to provide a JavaMail store within a J2EE platform. The most common application of this API is to send electronic mails based on business events.

JAXP

Although there are numerous applications for XML technology, the basic XML infrastructure requirements are limited to SAX parsers and DOM builders, and also XSLT transformation engines. However, as the XML technology itself is evolving, there are several parsers and transformation engines available today both commercially as well as from open-source software initiatives such as the parsers from Apache. These parsers support different features, based on specific application requirements; it has been the responsibility of application developers to choose the right parser for a given application.

The JAXP (Java API for XML Parsing) simplifies this scenario by providing a pluggable framework for dealing with SAX parsers, DOM builders, and XSLT transformation engines. This API specifies two packages: `javax.xml.parsers` and `javax.xml.transform` to abstract parsers and transformation engines respectively. Note that the support for transformation has been added in the JAXP 1.1 specification (currently under final review).

In the JAXP framework, SAX/DOM parsers can be created using implementations of `javax.xml.parsers.SAXParserFactory` or `javax.xml.parsers.DocumentBuilderFactory` classes. Using the configuration mechanisms specified by the JAXP framework, you can configure the JAXP to use a specific implementation of these factories.

In addition to creating SAX parser and DOM builder classes, the factory classes can selectively create specific instances based on the features required. Some of the features include name space support, validation, schema support, and more. Applications can set these features on the factory classes, and based on the parsers available in a given environment, the factory can return an appropriate SAX parser of DOM builder class.

Connector

Although most of the time e-commerce applications deal with relational databases as the sole means of information storage, this is not always the case. Many enterprises maintain their data and business processes in other enterprise information systems such as transactional applications on mainframes, and Enterprise Resource Planning (ERP) systems. Traditionally, application server vendors used to provide proprietary APIs so that applications could interface with Enterprise Information Systems (EIS). However, due to the diverse nature of these enterprise information systems, very often developers are required to deal with a variety of APIs. In addition, there is no mechanism for applications to connect to EISs.

The Java connector architecture fills this gap by specifying a standard architecture for integrating J2EE platforms with enterprise information systems.

The connector architecture consists of two parts:

❑ **Common Client Interface (CCI)** – The API that J2EE application components use to connect to EISs, and access their resources. The CCI is specified in the `javax.resource.cci` package.

❑ **Service Provider Interface (SPI)** – This API specifies an adapter for a given EIS. For instance, an ERP vendor can implement this interface. This API is specified in `javax.resource.spi` and `javax.resource.spi.security` packages.

In this architecture, the J2EE platform vendor need not be concerned with implementing the SPI for different types of EISs. Instead, a J2EE platform vendor can implement a custom J2EE platform-side adapter so that any SPI implementation can be plugged in at deployment time.

This approach has two advantages:

❑ It eliminates the need for a J2EE platform to support multiple adapters for each type of EIS.

❑ It also eliminates the need for applications to deal with proprietary APIs. Instead, applications rely on the CCI to communicate with enterprise information systems.

Note that this approach is similar to the way different JDBC implementations can be plugged in a J2EE platform. Neither the J2EE platform nor applications deal directly with any specific JDBC driver implementation.

At the time of writing this chapter, the connector specification is still to be finalized. However, in future, we should expect adapters from vendors of enterprise information systems. For the current connection specification, refer to http://java.sun.com/j2ee/connector/. At the time of writing this chapter, Sun is working on Version 3.0 of the JDBC API. This API specifies a service provider interface for JDBC such that one can provide a JDBC resource adapter for the connector API.

JAAS

In the standard Java security framework, the Java runtime grants or denies permission to execute a given part of Java code based on the source of the code, and who signed the code. This mechanism is suitable for avoiding executing untrusted code, and is applicable where code is downloaded from various sources. However, in enterprise applications, a more important requirement is to protect code from unauthorized execution – that is to deny rights to execute a given part of code based on who is executing the code. The Java Authentication and Authorization Service (JAAS) provides this support to the Java platform. The JAAS support in the J2EE platform extends authorization to all Java resources. Note that, without this support, the only protectable resources are J2EE application components (including web resources).

The requirement for JAAS support is being added to J2EE 1.3. This support adds two important facilities (which were up till now incomplete) for enterprise applications:

❑ **Authentication** – The JAAS provides an authentication approach whereby the J2EE platform can reliably establish the identity of a client irrespective of how the client is connecting to the platform. The JAAS specifies a pluggable authentication module that can be plugged into a J2EE platform such that the authentication technology can be enhanced without changes to J2EE applications. Before JAAS, J2EE did not specify any mechanism whereby the server could establish the identity of the client. Note that the declarative form-based login for web applications (discussed shortly later) only specifies a means of collecting HTTP client credentials, but does not specify how to authenticate an HTTP client. The JAAS support fills this gap.

❑ **Authorization** – As you will find in Chapter 8, authorization is the process of allowing or denying access to certain resources based on user identity. Two forms of authorization are provided in the J2EE platform – caller authorization, and code authorization.

Java servlets, JSP pages (and other web resources), and methods in EJBs can be made to require caller authorization. Caller authorization allows access to clients with a specified role, and denies access to all such clients that do not have the correct role. This is a role based authorization approach, whereby an identity (say, a user) can have one or more roles. Caller authorization does not depend on JAAS.

The second form of authorization is code authorization. Using the code authorization support provided by JAAS, a J2EE platform may restrict the use of certain Java classes and methods. This support extends the same facilities that exist for the J2SE to the J2EE environment.

Declarative Services

Here we discuss declarative security for firstly Web applications, and secondly EJBs.

Declarative Security for Web Applications

One of the most common requirements for e-commerce applications is to protect access to certain parts of web applications. For instance, in a typical shopping cart application, you may not allow unregistered customers to place orders. Therefore, for a customer to be able to place an order, they must be able to identify themselves to the web site. In order to implement such facilities, the following are required:

❑ The ability to identify the user, and verify if the user can access a given page (or more generally, any web application resource, including servlets, JSP pages, static HTML pages, images or other) – this is known as **authorization**.

❑ The ability to query the user for their identity, and verify that the user-supplied credentials agree with those for the predefined set of users – this is known as **authentication**.

The J2EE has a built-in declarative security mechanism to enable both of these abilities. This approach is declarative because there is no need for you to implement these features programmatically in the code for your web applications.

This approach is based upon identifying users through their **roles**. In J2EE, a user can have one or more roles, and resources can be protected, so that they require a user to have a specific role. Once the web container identifies a resource for a request URI, it checks if the requesting user (identified via session cookie or session ID embedded in the URI) has the role required to access the resource. If not, the web container initiates a login mechanism to get the user credentials. The most commonly used mechanism for login is via a login page. A login page can be a static HTML page or a JSP page. The J2EE specifies how this page should be developed. This login page should include an HTML form to collect the user name and password. The web container uses this data to check the role of the user. If the role matches the required role, the container sends the requested resource to the user. In this manner, web resource authorization is linked to user authentication.

This is a very flexible mechanism and can be entirely configured via the web application deployment descriptor. The login mechanism works seamlessly with the flow of HTTP requests, and is invoked only on demand. Apart from the form-based approach discussed above, J2EE also allows for HTTP basic and digest authentication as well.

Note that J2EE does not specify how to create and manage users and their roles. It also does not specify the underlying security implementation. Some of the J2EE platform vendors specify APIs for creating and managing users. These APIs also allow you to implement custom authentication based on user data stored in relational databases or LDAP servers.

Declarative Security for EJBs

Similar to web resources, EJBs can also be protected against unauthorized access.

Unlike web containers, EJB containers do not deal with authentication. EJB containers expect that EJB clients (such as web applications) establish user identity and pass the user identity to the EJB container along with each request to execute EJB methods. Based on the role of the user making the request, the container determines if the user can invoke a method. If the role is incorrect, the EJB container throws security exceptions indicating to the client that the requested method cannot be executed with the given identity.

As we discussed in the previous chapter, e-commerce applications can be accessed from non-web as well as web channels. Given this scenario, it is important to protect both web applications as well as EJBs. As a part of your e-commerce application design process, make sure to consider security, and to the greatest extent possible, rely on declarative security. Declarative security is container-implemented, and therefore you need not incur rigorous testing, as you would do with custom security solutions.

Declarative Transactions for EJBs

A transaction can be specified by what is known as **transaction demarcation**. Transaction demarcation enables work done by distributed components to be bound by a global transaction. It is a way of marking groups of operations to constitute a transaction.

As discussed previously, one way to control demarcation is to use the `javax.transaction.UserTransaction` interface. However, J2EE specifies a more flexible mechanism known as declarative demarcation for EJBs. In this technique, EJBs are marked as transactional at deployment time.

This has two implications:

❑ The responsibility of demarcation shifts from the application to the EJB container. For this reason, the technique is also known as **container-managed demarcation**.

❑ The demarcation is postponed from application build time (static) to the component deployment time (dynamic).

The EJB architecture specifies six identifiers (Not Supported, Supports, Requires New, Required, Mandatory, and Never) for container-managed transactions. You can specify one of these identifiers for each bean method. Depending on the type of identifier, the EJB container will either start a new transaction, or allow the method to execute in the current transaction, if it exists.

J2EE Applications, Packaging, and Deployment

We have discussed in the previous sections that J2EE applications consist of Java servlets, JSP pages, and EJB components. In addition, typical J2EE application development involves developing several auxiliary Java classes, JSP tag libraries, third-party Java libraries, etc. While it is one task to identify these classes during the application design phase, it is another task to make sure that these classes are deployed on a J2EE platform. A typical deployment involves bundling all these classes, and providing deployment descriptors. A successful deployment should make sure that all the required classes are made available to the J2EE runtime and all deployment descriptors are configured such that the platform can invoke the J2EE application components.

In order to simplify the deployment process, J2EE specifies an elaborate application model in terms of Enterprise Applications. In J2EE, an enterprise application is a collection of modules, with each module consisting of one or more components of a given type.

In this chapter, we've talked about web components, EJB components, and application clients. In the J2EE application model, each of these can be packaged into respective modules – such as web modules, EJB modules, and application client modules.

For instance, consider an e-commerce application consisting of several EJBs, JSP pages, servlets, and several static HTML pages and images. All these can be grouped into the following modules:

❑ A web module consisting of all JSP pages, servlet classes, static HTML pages, and images

❑ An EJB module consisting of EJB classes

In J2EE, web modules can be packaged into web archive (WAR) files with a deployment descriptor (web.xml). Similarly, EJB modules can be packaged in regular JAR files with a deployment descriptor (ejb-jar.xml). In addition, if your application includes Java application clients, you may package those client classes into a JAR file with a deployment descriptor (application-client.xml).

Once you package individual application components and clients into the above types of modules, you can compose such modules into enterprise applications. Similar to each of these modules, enterprise applications also have a deployment descriptor (application.xml). Enterprise applications can be packaged into Enterprise Archive (EAR) files.

The following figure shows the J2EE application model.

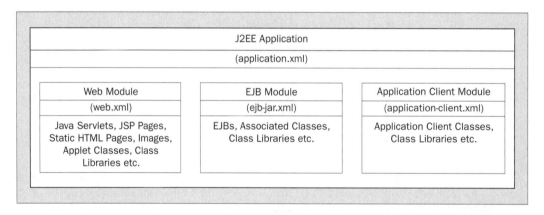

In all the above cases, using the deployment descriptors you can not only describe the contents of various modules/applications, but also configure these prior to deployment. Some of the features that can be configured at deployment time include transactions for EJBs, security for EJBs and web applications, etc.

In this model, J2EE application development involves the following steps:

❑ **Develop application components** – This step includes developing JSP pages, servlets, EJBs, and other associated Java classes. This step may also involve development of any application clients.

❏ **Compose application components into modules** – This step involves packaging application components and application clients into respective JAR or WAR files. Note that this step also involves writing respective deployment descriptors for each of these modules.

❏ **Composition of modules into applications** – Once the various modules are ready, the next step is to assemble these modules into J2EE applications.

❏ **Application deployment** – This is the last stage. The actual deployment process depends on the specific platform you are using. Typically, this process involves specifying the location of the EAR file to the J2EE platform.

You may notice that this is a bottom-up procedure. You start with individual application components and related classes, and compose them into modules and then the modules into applications. There are certain benefits with this approach:

❏ You can group your development artifacts into related groups. In a given e-commerce development team, there may be small teams responsible for developing different parts of the architecture. For instance, one of the teams may be responsible for developing catalog and shopping cart functionality, while another team may be responsible for developing the entire order management functionality. In order to maintain this separation, you may consider separate modules for components developed by each of these teams.

❏ A packaged module can be reused in multiple applications. In this sense, the notion of a module serves as a means of coarse-grained reuse.

In addition to specifying the above application packaging model, J2EE also describes the roles of persons responsible for each of the above tasks:

❏ **Application Component Provider** – The application developer that creates the application components. The responsibility of an application component provider does not extend beyond packaging various application components into modules.

❏ **Application Assembler** – An application assembler takes the application modules and assembles them into applications.

❏ **Deployer** – The deployer takes the packaged application, installs, and configures it for the particular J2EE platform.

❏ **System Administrator** – Responsible for maintaining and administering the application once it has been deployed.

The people responsible for each of these roles will be required to customize the deployment descriptors at various levels. For instance, in order to use a datasource, for database connection, the application component provider merely specifies the logical name of the datasource in the deployment descriptor. The application assembler may map this name to another logical name that is appropriate for that module. The deployer finally maps this name to a datasource created for the specific J2EE platform and the database meant for the application. In this fashion, this model attempts to isolate various packaging and deployment concerns at various levels.

Summary

This chapter has attempted the almost impossible task of presenting a brief overview of J2EE in a single chapter. The purpose of this is just to cover all the essential aspects of J2EE very briefly; to draw a snapshot of all associated technologies and concepts and provide a basis for later chapters.

All of these chapters are covered in considerably more depth, in a volume dedicated to this technology (*Professional Java Server Programming, J2EE Edition, ISBN 1-861004-65-6, also by Wrox Press*).

As you recall, in the previous chapter, we have discussed certain technical requirements for e-commerce applications. Let us now map those requirements to appropriate J2EE technologies:

- ❑ **Dynamic, personalized user interfaces** – Java servlets and JSP pages are the building blocks for developing dynamic, personalized web user interfaces.

- ❑ **Multi-channel user interfaces** – Java servlets and JSP pages, coupled with XML and associated technologies let you serve multi-channel interfaces.

- ❑ **Application interfaces** – EJBs as well as Java application clients can be used for developing application interfaces.

- ❑ **Programming model for distributed components** – EJBs are the distributed components in J2EE, while the JNDI provides the infrastructure for transparent look for EJBs.

- ❑ **Distributed transactions** – As we have seen in this chapter, transactions can be implemented declaratively or programmatically using the deployment descriptors or the JTA. In addition, the JDBC Optional Package API allows EJBs to participate in distributed transactions.

- ❑ **Asynchronous messaging** – The JMS and message-driven beans allow for asynchronous messaging.

- ❑ **Security** – You can declaratively protect J2EE application components against unauthorized access.

As you can see from this list, J2EE is mature enough to satisfy most of the e-commerce application development requirements, including a programming model, and a set of services. The J2EE specification is still evolving. Sun conducts most of these enhancements via a community process. If you are interested in further developments in J2EE and Java in general, refer to the Java Community Process web site at http://java.sun.com/aboutJava/communityprocess/.

In the next chapter, we shall examine some of the architectural styles for building e-commerce applications using J2EE.

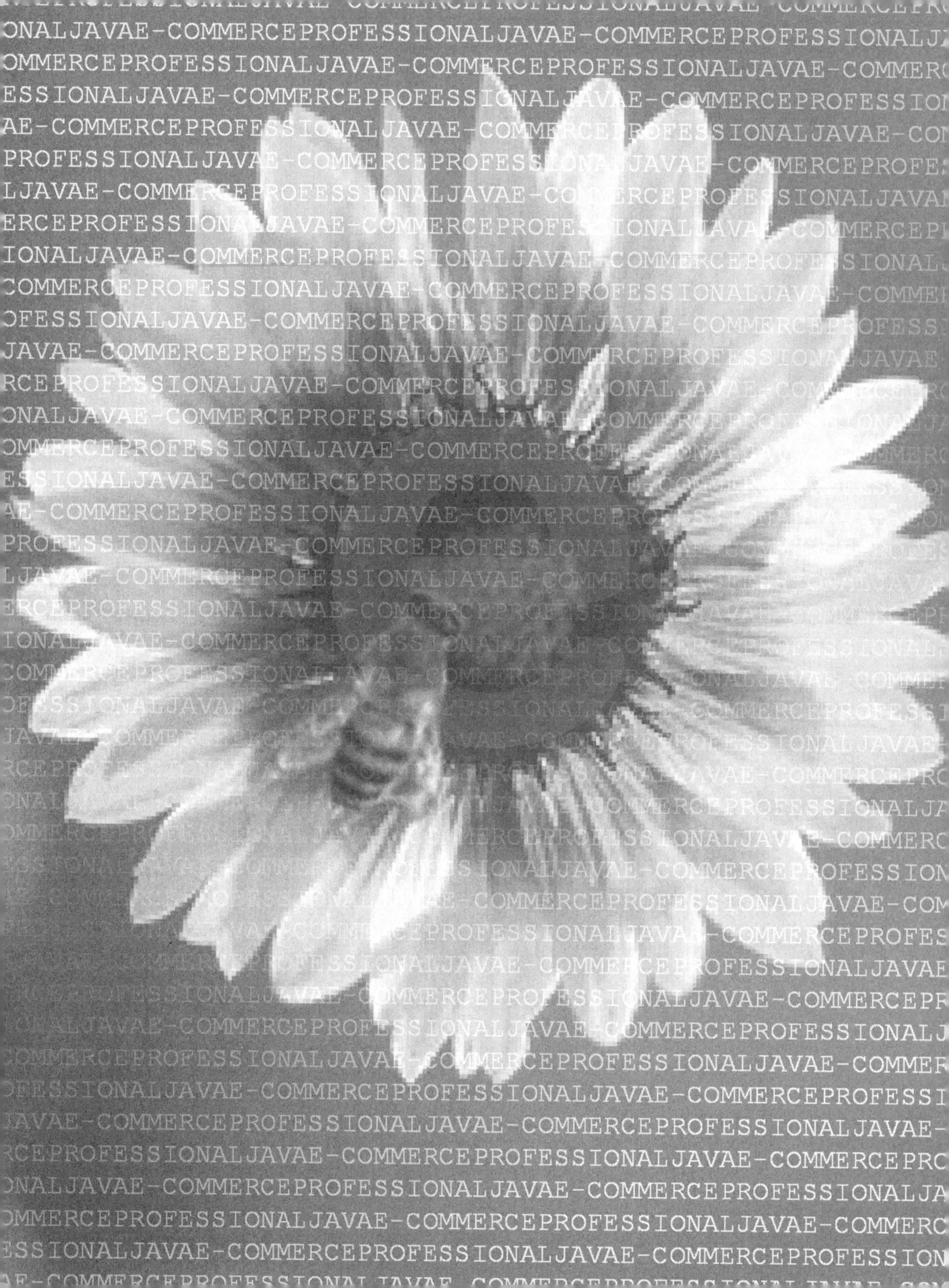
PROFESSIONALJAVAE-COMMERCE

6

Approaches for E-Commerce Architectures

There are no silver bullets for the perils of architecting software systems, at least not for e-commerce applications. J2EE won't address *all* the design and architecture needs for you, but does this imply that J2EE is not adequate for typical e-commerce application development?

In order to answer this question, let us consider the goals of J2EE. The principal goal of J2EE is to specify a platform – one that can be used to build distributed, object-oriented, enterprise applications. As we discussed in the previous chapter, what J2EE provides is a component model, and a core infrastructure. Its programming model includes Java servlets, JSP pages, beans and tags to address web application development needs, and EJBs to address distributed component development needs. The infrastructure includes several APIs such as JTA, JNDI, JMS, JDBC and so on, which are well integrated within the platform. The platform also provides the runtime support through web and EJB containers for deploying and managing J2EE applications.

Does J2EE specify any architecture for enterprise applications? Although the term "architecture" is used to refer to "the structure" or "structural views" of software, an architecture is (in simple terms) what tells you how to structure or organize various programs (whether JSP pages, or EJBs or other classes) of an application in order to implement the business use cases and other facilities. Several proponents and adapters of J2EE imply that J2EE does specify architecture for applications. However, that is not the case. J2EE does not go beyond specifying the programming model, the infrastructure, and the runtime. This leaves the application developer, as always, to make the important decisions about architecture, based on their specific business and technical requirements.

In this chapter, we shall address certain issues that affect the architecture of an e-commerce application whether it's a stand-alone application or one involving integration. Note that we will not try to develop various architectures in this chapter; instead, our focus will be on identifying certain styles applicable under different scenarios. Depending on specific application needs, you might find that your requirements can be addressed by one of the styles discussed in this chapter, or you may construct your own by extending the styles suggested in this chapter.

The following topics will be covered in this chapter:

❑ Component granularity

❑ Component interfaces

❑ Transactions in e-commerce applications

❑ Modes of connectivity

In this chapter, the phrase "distributed component" is used to mean an EJB in J2EE, and a generic term "client application" to mean all types of clients – from web clients (such as servlets and JSP pages), to stand-alone GUI-driven clients, to external applications. Although it is possible to use other relevant non-Java/non-J2EE technologies here, such technologies are excluded from this particular discussion since you'll be using Java and J2EE based technologies in the rest of this book.

Component Granularity

With component developers in the J2EE world, **granularity** is one of first design questions. Granularity is how clients perceive components. In the case of components representing data (such as entity beans), granularity relates to whether clients see the data as large chunks or as simple attributes. In the case of components representing business logic (such as session beans), do clients see moderately complex business processes, or simple operations? In both cases, if your answer points to large data or complex logic, you can classify such a component to be **coarse-grained**. If the client only sees small data or simple logic, it is said to be **fine-grained**.

There are several questions related to granularity. Should you develop a single bean for the entire order management system, or should you develop it into four beans, or just a simple object for the order management? What are the guidelines? Are there any tradeoffs? The answers to such questions cannot be definitive. Perhaps, in some of the applications, these questions may not matter at all. In certain other systems, the answers to such questions may greatly affect the overall application complexity, maintainability and performance. Nonetheless, it is important to consider the question of granularity during the design time.

Abstraction

Unlike other distributed technologies such as CORBA, J2EE and EJBs provide a very high-level of abstraction of the underlying distributed technology. This is true for both clients and bean developers alike. The abstraction is so strong that the difference between an object that can be referenced locally and a distributed component (an EJB) is very marginal.

The aim of shielding the developers from the underlying distribution and other system-level issues has been one of the goals of J2EE.

When compared to CORBA, EJB development is simpler due to this level of abstraction. In fact, one of the criticisms of CORBA has been that it does not isolate the developers from the perils of distributed component development. For instance, dealing with security and transactions (using the security and transaction services respectively) is not a trivial task. It requires a thorough understanding of both distributed transactions and security. In most cases, the developers will be required to understand the underlying concepts for these technologies. This is one of the main reasons that the adaptation of CORBA has been slow for building distributed component applications. On the other hand, dealing with transactions within J2EE is a relatively simple task.

The abstractions provided by J2EE are essential in dealing with the complex and fast-paced development tasks of e-commerce and other enterprise applications. Without the shielding that J2EE offers developers from the underlying technology, it would be a monumental task to develop, debug, and maintain these applications.

Client Development

As mentioned above, with EJB, the distinction between an object and a bean is marginal. Let us first consider a client invoking methods on a local (non-EJB) object:

```
// Create the object
OrderService orderService = new OrderService();

// Invoke a method
try
{
    orderService.placeOrder(order);
}
catch(SomeException se)
{
    // Catch a business exception
}
```

In this example, the order management functionality of an e-commerce application is developed as a plain object. Therefore, the client creates the object first, and then invokes a method, and catches any exception thrown by the object during the method execution.

Let us now consider the same functionality developed as an EJB:

```
// Obtain the home
OrderServiceHome orderServiceHome = //  JNDI lookup

// Create the service
OrderService orderService = orderServiceHome.create();

// Invoke a method
try
{
    orderService.placeOrder(order);
}
catch(SomeException se)
{
    // Catch a business exception
}
```

To keep the discussion simple, I have intentionally omitted the exceptions related to JNDI lookup, bean creation, and remote method invocation.

As you see from these two code snippets, there are two differences between these approaches – object creation, and exception handling. In the first case, an instance of the `OrderService` class is created using the Java `new` operator. In the second case, the same reference is created using a method on the bean's remote interface. The exception handling also differs as the client is dealing with JNDI and remote methods in the second case. Apart from these, from the client's perspective, there are no differences between these two implementations.

However, there is one side effect to such an abstraction provided by J2EE and EJB – that is, developers often miss the fact that they are dealing with distributed components and not plain objects. In reality, there are several differences:

❑ **Network traffic** – Client calls travel via the network to the distributed component.

❑ **Instance management** – Containers hold instances of components, while clients see proxy objects. A proxy is not a real object, but represents the server-side component on the client-side.

❑ **Container interception for transactions, and security** – Containers receive client-requests and hand-off to instances, and while doing so, manage declarative transactions and security.

However, these details are abstracted within the container and other infrastructure.

Bean Development

The same holds true for the bean developer. With an EJB, instead of developing just one class, the developer specifies two interfaces (the home and remote respectively), and develops an implementation class. Although the implementation class will have certain additional methods for the home interface, it is largely EJB-independent.

As far as the bean developer is concerned, they are developing a class conforming to a framework. To extend this argument further, it is easy to see the developer need not even be aware of what a transaction is to develop EJBs. In the majority of cases, the container-provided defaults for transactions might do the job. One of the immediate victims of this view is component granularity, and component distribution drives granularity decisions.

The key point here is that higher-level abstractions such as EJB and J2EE are like double-edged swords. Being high-level abstractions, their goal is to shield the developers from the issues of distributed technology, such that distributed component development is as close to normal object development as possible – for both the client applications and component developers. Because of this, developers miss the fact that they are dealing with distributed components that are transaction/security aware, and that their components communicate over the wire.

However, what is a distributed component?

> *A distributed component is one that can be invoked across process boundaries via an interface for its services.*

Although both CORBA and EJB support this notion, there are fundamental differences in their evolution.

CORBA and EJB

CORBA was originally developed to make applications communicate with each other (using interfaces), with the **Interface Definition Language (IDL)** to support the development of interfaces, and with the ORB providing the infrastructure to facilitate the network-level communication. This is essentially an integration problem. Let us consider two different applications, one written in C and deployed on a Unix machine, and the other developed in COBOL running on a mainframe. CORBA allows interface wrappers on top of these applications. The purpose is to make these applications communicate with each other without any dependency on the programming language or the operating platform of these applications.

You can also use CORBA to develop distributed component applications. In this case, we are not concerned about making applications communicate. The goal is instead to build applications as a set of distributed components. Although reusability is cited as one of the reasons for such an approach, the main advantage is the ability to develop loosely coupled applications. Distributed components can be easily distributed to suit specific deployment and processing needs, without ever affecting the client applications. Secondly, since distributed components are interface-centric, interfaces remain independent of implementations, and implementations can be changed without affecting the client applications.

On the other hand, the primary goal of EJB is not application integration. The basic EJB technology is *not* meant for building interoperable interfaces for applications developed on disparate platforms using disparate programming languages. Instead, the purpose is to provide a distributed component framework for building applications as a set of distributed components. So, although CORBA meets both these requirements, EJB is concerned only with the latter requirement – that is to build distributed applications. The following figure illustrates these differences:

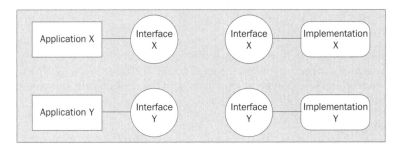

The blocks on the left show how applications can be wrapped using CORBA. The rectangular blocks are the applications, and with the help of CORBA, these applications can expose language/platform independent interfaces to client applications/components. Here the purpose of the interface is to expose certain services.

Traditionally CORBA interfaces are coarse-grained, as they evolved from interfaces to applications, and applications typically provide a number of (often complex) services.

A *coarse-grained interface* is one that abstracts coarse concepts. For instance, a Person interface with name and address is *fine-grained* whereas a Customer interface with not only name and address, but also abstracting the customer relation, history, account status etc. is a *coarse-grained* interface.

The blocks on the right show the EJB approach. With EJBs, you design and specify a set of interfaces, and provide implementations. The rounded rectangles are objects that implement the interfaces. While traditional object modelling practices focus on abstraction and encapsulation of domain data/logic, such abstractions tend to remain fine-grained. In this case, domain concepts such as Order, Customer, Placing an Order etc. get translated into objects encapsulating respective details, and the remote interfaces (the circles in the above figure) merely expose access to these objects.

The EJB model does not imply fine-grained or coarse-grained interfaces. Neither does CORBA. However, evolution of these models, and how these technologies are discussed and used, leads to fine-grained or coarse-grained interfaces.

The Effect of Evolution on Granularity

As we've just said, in many cases CORBA applications are built as a set of services – services, by nature, are coarse-grained – so CORBA interfaces are generally designed to be coarse-grained. An object-view of a service is not the norm with CORBA applications. On the other hand, EJBs are instance-centric, not application-centric. In reality, using the EJB technology, we are wrapping certain objects with remote interfaces. Therefore, the common practice is to take an object-view with EJBs.

While it is not always necessary to maintain these application interfaces as coarse-grained, there are certain advantages of adhering to coarse-grained interfaces. These are **decoupling** and **performance**.

Decoupling

As an e-commerce application evolves, its size increases. There will be more and more components added to the system with more and more functionality. When you start developing a new e-commerce application from ground-up, there will be relatively limited functionality to encapsulate to begin with. As the application evolves, you will add more features to the same system, often by adding new components.

This results in a muddle of interfaces that your applications have to deal with. That is, various parts of your application become **highly coupled** making maintenance highly difficult. However, by keeping the interfaces coarse, you will be able to limit the number of interfaces, and thus reduce the coupling.

Performance

The second benefit is to do with performance. With a number of fine-grained interfaces, clients (external clients or components internal to the application) will have to deal with a number of remote interfaces. Depending on the deployment model, most of the method calls on these interfaces involve the following tasks:

❑   Network traffic

❑   **Marshaling** and **unmarshaling** of Java types for method arguments, return types, and exceptions

❑   Container interception for transactions, security, instance management, threading, and so on

Each of these tasks is performance intensive, and consumes both CPU and network resources. You can reduce this by getting the functionality executed in larger chunks – that is, maintain coarse interfaces.

The design trick is to remember that we are dealing with distributed components and not objects. That is, to consider the fact that a client method reaches the bean via a proxy on the server, reaches another proxy (or an adapter) object on the server side, and then finally the bean instance. In this journey, the data gets packed into formats suitable for network transfer (marshaling), and gets unpacked (unmarshaling) into Java types on the server side. In addition, the container intervenes to check whether it has to start transactions or make the method call participate in existing method calls, or if the caller has the required role to invoke the method, and if so, takes appropriate actions.

Note that many J2EE platforms optimise remote calls when the beans/clients are co-located. For instance, when bean A makes a call to bean B, and when instances of both beans are within the same runtime (JVM), the container can make direct method calls on bean B. However, even in such cases, all the above steps (except marshaling, unmarshaling, and the network access) happen. Although this considerably improves performance, there will still be an overhead, as the container will have to interpose its services for transactions and security.

Although an object view of distributed applications helps you to abstract the business domain concepts well, a rigorous application of object-oriented view would lead to several fine-grained abstractions, leading to fine-grained interfaces. In order not to be trapped into this, for implementing business processes and services, it is necessary to focus on procedural abstractions.

Component Interfaces

An important consideration related to component granularity is the size or type of an interface. In any distributed component technology, the contract between a client and the component's implementations is specified through an interface. An interface is nothing but a collection of methods – in other words, the interface is similar to a tag associated with a set of methods. We invoke the methods with respect to a reference to the tag.

For instance, consider the `OrderService` bean discussed in the previous section. What are the typical services expected of this bean? These services include placing orders, searching for orders, updating orders etc. Your design might include several other business-specific methods in this interface. The remote interface for this `OrderService` would include methods such as `placeOrder()`, `findOrder()`, `updateOrder()`, `updateStatus()` etc. as listed below:

```
public OrderService extends javax.ejb.EJBObject
{
    public void placeOrder(...);
    public Collection findOrder(...) throws NotFoundException;
    public void updateOrder(...);
    public void updateStatus(...) throws InvalidStatusException;
    ...
}
```

Let's have a look at the implications of defining such an interface.

Client Contract

The fundamental requirement is that the client be aware of this interface. This knowledge is not limited to the name of the remote interface and its methods. The client should be aware of the following:

❑   Methods supported by the interface

❑   Data types of arguments of methods

❑   Data types of return types of methods

❑   Exceptions thrown by methods and the meaning of such exceptions

Knowledge of Context

In addition to the semantics of the interface, the client should be aware of how and when to invoke an interface and needs to know the:

❑ Pre-conditions to invoke a method (under what conditions can the client invoke a method in the interface)

❑ Pre-conditions on argument types (how to construct valid arguments for methods)

❑ Post-conditions on argument types (what the state of the arguments will be after the method completes execution)

❑ Post-conditions on return types (what will be the state of the return types)

Although the distributed component is what provides the interface, both the component and client are bound by this interface. The contract between the client and the component is not completely uni-directional. Although not semantically, this is a bi-directional contract in implementation.

Clients and Interfaces

While the component can abstract its contract in the form of an interface, the client has no such luxury. The client cannot abstract its knowledge of the interface (the methods as well as the context) in any form, other than the code in the client that uses the interface. In a majority of cases, this knowledge will be spread across dozens of lines of code across several classes and methods.

This is not a limitation of interfaces. Interfaces are just meant to provide uni-directional abstractions. However, the objective of this discussion is to point out the fact that, the interface designer should be responsible enough to consider the fact that the client is aware of not only the methods specified in the contract, but also the context under which to invoke the interface. When not designed carefully, the client will be forced to make assumptions of how the interface is implemented. This defeats the purpose of the interface altogether – the purpose is to isolate the client from making such assumptions, not to force it.

Layers and Interfaces

There is another side effect to do with separation of concerns in a layered architecture. One of the means of developing layers is to expose a layer with a set of interfaces to the layers on top. The rationale behind this approach is to make sure that the layers above do not depend on the implementation details of the layers below. This allows the separation of various business/application concerns into a set of layers with well-abstracted interfaces. However, this model will break when increasingly more contextual knowledge is exposed outside the interface. This couples the clients very tightly with the components.

Despite this side effect, the notion of a typed interface is very crucial for developing distributed e-commerce applications. The interface designer is responsible for making sure that the context knowledge required by clients (especially user interfaces and application interfaces) is minimized.

Let us now extend this discussion, and consider a business process that includes several sub-processes and tasks, with each sub-process implemented as a distributed component. Here is how the client interacts with the components to execute the business process:

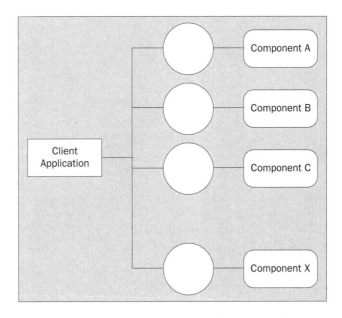

In this figure, the circles connected to rounded rectangles (components) represent their interfaces. In this architecture, in order to deal with the business process, the client has to deal with all of these components. The client's knowledge of these components is embedded within the client code. Moreover, only the client has the overall knowledge of the business process. The client has the knowledge of each of these sub-processes, the order in which these sub-processes should be invoked, the exception handling, transaction boundaries, and so on. While this may be acceptable when the sub-processes involved are limited in number, this approach will be difficult to maintain as the number of components involved increases. This also translates to inter-dependencies between teams involved in developing these components.

Also, consider the fact that business processes involve not just data manipulation, but also decision making logic, and other business rules. For example, the state of a domain object (such as a purchase order) may dictate execution of alternative business processes. In the above example, this situation makes the client code more complex – as it will be forced to deal with such decision-making, and execute appropriate alternative flows of business logic. The result is that, a large portion of the business logic knowledge will leak through the interface to the client side.

The Façade Pattern

You might immediately suggest that introducing an additional layer between the client and the components in the above figure can solve this problem. The new layer can now include another component abstracting all other components on the right hand side of this figure. This is a well-known design pattern known as the **façade pattern**. For basic details of this pattern (although not in the context of distributed components), refer to *Design Patterns, Erich Gamma et al (ISBN 0-201-63361-2)*.

The following shows the same set of components with a new façade component introduced between the client and the rest of the components. Instead of dealing with several interfaces, the client now deals with a single interface.

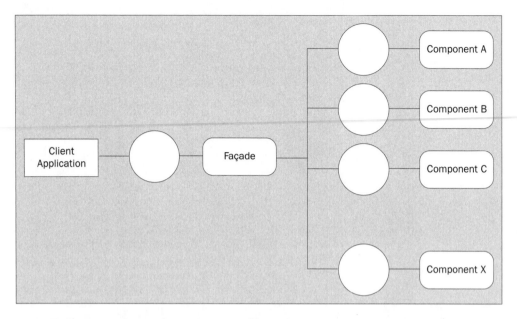

An immediate implication of this design is that it lets you build islands of components as subsystems, with each subsystem exposed with a single interface, and each subsystem implementing related business tasks. In the above figure, the façade represents a subsystem consisting of the rest of the components. With such façade components, your application can be refactored into a set of subsystems. The individual components to the right of the façade need not be exposed outside the subsystem. As the size of the application increases, this design scales well enough to be maintainable.

Another implication is that this approach reduces cross-subsystem complexity. In a given software application, complexity manifests in different forms – complex associations, complexity of business process logic, algorithmic complexity, and so on. Of all these forms, the most common form of complexity that occurs in most of the applications is one due to numerous **associations** between different parts of applications.

Associations

What is an association? In raw terms, an association is a reference to an object. Without a façade, the number of interfaces that a client will have to deal with increases, and thus also the number of object references (and their JNDI lookup, and their interfaces) it has to deal with. This increases coupling and affects maintainability of the overall application. The façade therefore limits the complexity, as there are fewer interfaces for the client to deal with.

Now that we have seen the benefits of having a façade for each subsystem, how should the façade interface be designed? There are two alternatives, depending on the specific business processes that your subsystem is required to represent, and the types of data to be exchanged (method arguments, return types, and exceptions) between the client and the subsystem.

The first solution involves two steps:

❑   To develop the façade interface as a union of all interfaces between clients and the components within the subsystem.

❑ To move the contextual knowledge of individual component interfaces and usage to the façade implementation.

In other words, the façade interface must be specified as a set of methods such that these methods represent the responsibilities of all components and the client knowledge within the subsystem. Such an interface is not difficult to specify – it involves refactoring the client applications and moving all the knowledge related to the individual components to the façade. For instance, if the client has to deal with different components for creating an order, processing the payment, and updating the inventory in order to implement a checkout process, all such tasks can be combined into a façade component with a single method to perform the checkout. In this case, instead of invoking three separate components, the client invokes a single component – the façade.

Although this approach is useful to limit the number of dependencies and exposing the subsystem with a single interface, there is still one issue to deal with. Depending on what is being implemented within these components behind the façade, there is a possibility that your façade interface will have several methods with several types of arguments, return types and exceptions. As long as this interface can be specified and documented unambiguously, and as long as the client is not required to make assumptions about the internal implementation, the façade serves the purpose. However, if you found that the façade were too complex to specify, further refactoring would be necessary to make the façade interface less typed and less specific. This is the second approach.

Note that, in a typical interface, the data does not carry much context. For instance, consider the `OrderService` interface discussed before. This has a method called `updateStatus()`, which possibly takes some primary key information, and the new status. In this case, the data does not express any business context. The context is expressed (partially) by the method name. However, what happens if there are dozens of such methods on the interface? You can avoid this by making the interface less generic, and by letting the data carry the context. In the case of the `OrderService`, this involves having a generic method that can update order data, and takes the data (primary keys, status etc.) in the form of a more general object (say, a `Hashmap`, or even an XML document). The arguments will now contain the context (in this case, what to do with the data), metadata (what data is being sent), and the data itself.

In order to understand this better, consider the case of a servlet.

Servlets

A servlet has a very generic interface. Keeping aside the methods to manage the lifecycle (the `init()` and `destroy()` methods), the servlet interface consists of the service method that takes generic `request` and `response` objects (for HTTP `requests` and HTTP `responses` respectively). The details of what the servlet is supposed to do can be represented in two ways. The first approach is to have different servlets for different tasks, so that the name of the servlet expresses what it does.

Let us instead consider a more generic servlet that can do several related tasks. Based on the data contained in the request, the servlet can decide what to do, and perform the job on the data in the request. This is a typeless interface, where the data expresses the context and what the client wants to be done.

You can adopt a similar design for façade interfaces in certain cases. However, you might find this counter-intuitive, counter-OO and typeless. This approach is typeless because the arguments are generic types, and not specific types representing business domain entities. While these remarks are true for fine-grained objects, these arguments do not necessarily hold good for coarse-grained components representing subsystems.

This typeless interface pattern is suitable for application integration as well as integrating with B2B systems. However, note that by making the interface **typeless**, you may lose some of the compile-time flexibility associated with strongly typed interfaces. Typeless interfaces are not preferable if the clients and the components are tightly coupled.

In both the cases, the façade represents a gateway into the system (or subsystem). The typeless interface helps to maintain a very low coupling between your e-commerce application and other interfacing applications. Although you can specify the arguments as certain Java types, a better alternative could be to use XML documents to represent the arguments. In fact, defining the argument type as an XML document reduces the coupling further as the calling client/application need not depend on the argument types used by the subsystem internally.

Transactions in E-Commerce Applications

As discussed in Chapter 4, transactions are an important requirement to preserve the ACID properties of business operations on persistent business data. In this section, let us consider the nature of transactions.

Transaction Duration

Whether programmatic (bean-managed) or declarative (container-managed), J2EE transactions are short-lived in most scenarios. Short transactions offer better scalability.

Consider, for instance, web driven clients invoking methods on layers of EJBs. Irrespective of whether you use programmatic or declarative transactions, the duration of a transaction cannot be more than that of the HTTP request-response process. This is to do with the general method of implementing transactions. J2EE containers manage transactions by associating the current service thread with the transaction context. A service thread is the thread started by the web or EJB container on the receipt of a request from a client outside the J2EE platform (such as an HTTP request from a browser, or a request from a remote client application).

In the case of web-based invocation of EJBs, the service thread starts when the container receives the HTTP request. This HTTP request ends with completely sending a response back to the client (browser) making the HTTP request. Since the service thread does not exist after this stage (the container might recycle the thread), the transaction context cannot be managed by the container. As a result, transactions cannot span across multiple HTTP requests.

This implies that you cannot maintain transactions across business processes that involve multiple requests and responses from the client. The following figure illustrates how J2EE transactions are implemented:

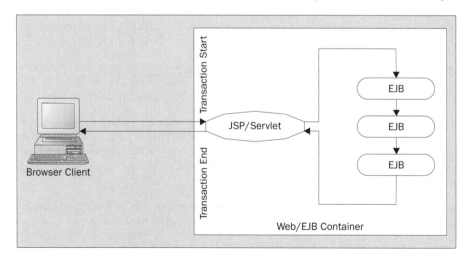

This figure shows a typical model and illustrates a service thread involving a servlet/JSP and a few EJBs. In this figure, the arrows indicate the execution of a service thread. The points with labels "Transaction Start" and "Transaction End" are the maximum possible boundaries for the duration of a transaction.

The Advantages of Short Transactions

The main advantage of keeping transactions short is to reduce database contention. With short transactions, data is locked for very short intervals of time, and the database is not required to maintain the transaction logs/buffers for long intervals.

Secondly, with web-based interaction, long transactions are disastrous, as there is no guarantee that the client would ever make the next step in a given business process. Holding the database locks even for a minute could affect the performance drastically. With short transactions, you will have to design your applications such that the integrity of the business processes is maintained.

For instance, consider a business process requiring the user to perform four steps in four separate HTTP requests. Since we're dealing with short transactions, you can start a transaction at the beginning of the first request and end it at the end of the last request. You can either have one transaction during the fourth request to commit all the data collected/processed during the first three requests, or four transactions with each transaction committing parts of data in the database. This decision raises two issues:

❑ If you consider a single transaction during the fourth request, in order to manage the data collected during the first three steps, you need to rely on in-memory storage (using HTTP sessions, or stateful session beans), or store the data in temporary tables. In either case, or when the user never makes the fourth request, you need to clean up the data at the end of the transaction, or at the end of some timeout interval (for instance on HTTP session timeout).

❑ Depending on the specific use case, and depending on your implementation, you may be required to implement logic to undo the modifications made during the first three steps. However, this is not a trivial task, and the best solution is to avoid such pitfalls altogether.

In order to avoid both of the above problems, consider implementing the business process such that the data committed to the database does not depend on the following HTTP requests during the course of any HTTP request-to-response. This guarantees the following:

❑ **Scalability** – you avoid in-memory as well as temporary storage

❑ **Consistency** – you need not deal with inconsistency due to aborted business processes

There is another side effect of short-transactions with web-based interaction. A typical use case involves reading data from a database, presenting the data via a JSP page, and when the user updates the data, update the database with modified data. In this case, you can bracket both the read and update operations with transactions. However, you cannot include both operations within a single transaction as these two operations happen across two different client requests.

Protection Against Stale States

The net result is that, during the time the data is first read, and latter updated, another application or component might have updated or deleted the same data. This is possible because there is no transaction protecting the data during this interval. This leaves the application and user with **stale state** that may not correspond to the data in the database. Once your application commits such stale state, the database integrity will be compromised because your application did not preserve the updates made by another application.

Although the database is consistent from the database point of view, from the point of view of the applications using the data, this is not the case. In case your application is susceptible to this, you will have to devise custom solutions to make sure that you alert the user that the data has been updated in the database.

Note that this problem is common to all applications that rely on information in memory, either via long-term or short-term caching.

In the specific case that we're discussing, caching is implicit as the client-tier maintains the state for a short while. One simple solution is to make a copy of the original data in memory, and just before the update, check to see if this in-memory copy matches the data in the database. Note that there are performance implications with any such approach – but at least the data will not be modified inadvertently and inconsistently. Currently, this is an issue that developers will have to deal with.

You might argue that application clients can maintain long transactions by programmatically starting and ending transactions using the `javax.transaction.UserTransaction` object. Typically, application clients connect to server-side components for longer intervals involving several requests to components. However, J2EE platform implementations are not required to provide transaction support for application clients. In other words, application clients cannot start and end transactions. Although application clients can maintain long client threads, these threads do not translate to long transactions. In this case, transaction duration will be limited to that of the outer-most request (made by the client).

Transaction Distribution

In J2EE, transactions are often distributed, and distributed transactions have their overheads. Distributed transactions occur in the following two scenarios:

❑ **Multiple databases** – Consider a case where, during a single transaction, your components access two different database systems. Because there are two physical databases, the same database connection cannot be used for accessing both the databases. Your components will therefore use two different database connections from two different connections pools maintained by the J2EE platform. In order to guarantee ACID properties, the J2EE platform will maintain a transaction across the various operations conducted using these two connection objects. This is a distributed transaction.

❑ **Distributed container** – Almost all J2EE platforms support clustering, which means that the container includes more than one JVM executing on one or more physical machines. In a clustered environment (depending on the deployment strategy provided by the container) it is possible that a single service thread spans across multiple JVMs (processes). Since multiple processes cannot share the same connection object (unless the container vendor offers remotable connections), the service thread would involve more than one database connection. As far as the database is concerned, there are two separate connections modifying the data. In order to deal with this, the J2EE platform must implement a distributed transaction spanning both the connection objects.

The commit operation for such a distributed transaction would involve the two-phase commit protocol, supported by some J2EE platforms. In order to coordinate the actions performed by several database connections or databases, the two-phase commit protocol allows a transaction manager to query all database transactions involved if each of these actions can be committed permanently, and if so, to request for commit. In other words, this is a means of coordinating several otherwise independent transactions (performed across each single connection) into a single transaction. Note that the two-phase commit operation is expensive to do often, as it would involve polling across different resource managers before committing the transaction.

Of the above two scenarios, the first scenario can be avoided completely by not accessing multiple database systems within a single service thread. However, the second scenario may not be avoidable. In general, any good container implementation would attempt to avoid this.

Modes of Connectivity

There are two modes of connectivity possible with distributed systems – **synchronous**, and **asynchronous**. The most commonly used mode of connectivity in e-commerce applications is the synchronous mode.

In the synchronous mode, when the client invokes a method on a component the client thread waits until the component returns from executing the method. In this mode, the client expects the component to exist and be available for service at the time of making the request, and during the request. This communication model guarantees ordered execution of business tasks – the tasks get executed in the order the methods are invoked, and the client can detect any failure immediately.

However, there are cases where an asynchronous mode of communication is more suitable. In this mode, a client can invoke a method on a component when a component is unavailable. This method call is stored until such time as the component is free to act upon it. The client does not expect the component to exist at the time of making the request. This obviously leaves open the problem of failed transactions, because the failure may not be reported until much later.

In this section, we will walk through three case studies (corresponding to issues with availability, responsiveness, and resource constraints) to identify technical requirements that mandate asynchronous mode of communication in your e-commerce applications. Note that the scenarios we are going to discuss in the following subsections do not illustrate concrete implementations, they are just to highlight certain common technical issues you might notice with synchronous mode of communication.

Scenario 1 – Availability

Consider a simple retail merchant conducting business electronically. A typical e-commerce application would allow customers to browse the catalogue, select items into a shopping cart, and place the order using a web browser. Let us assume that the merchant has a separate in-house order fulfillment system that processes orders.

Depending on the technology of implementation of the fulfillment system, you may build a database level or process level integration with the order fulfillment system. With such integration in place, the following is a possible implementation of the shopping cart checkout process:

❑ Prepare the order

❑ Commit the order in the local database (for the e-commerce application)

❑ Interface with the fulfillment system and communicate the order for fulfillment

❑ If integration is at the database level, this step would involve transferring the data to the database of the fulfillment system after any data transformation

❑ If integration is at the process level, this step would involve invoking a method with the order data on a service component of the fulfillment system

❑ Return order confirmation information

At the end of this process, the customer will have the order confirmed. The following figure represents this process.

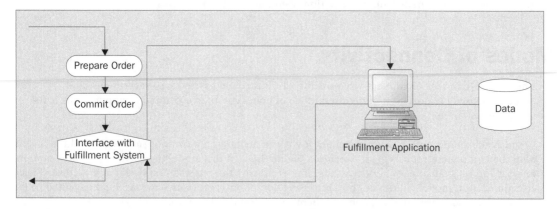

In this figure, the hexagonal box represents a component responsible for interfacing with the fulfillment application.

Now, let us pose a constraint on the fulfillment system. For whatever business/technical reasons, let us assume that the fulfillment system remains out of service for a few hours at the end of each day. Some of the possible reasons include day-end batch processing, even system maintenance, or updates to the application.

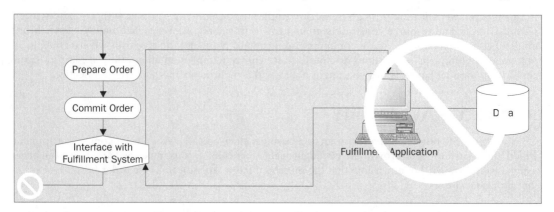

During such periods, the e-commerce application cannot capture orders when implemented in the above manner. This is a typical situation whenever there are dependencies with other systems that are not available around the clock. A system with less availability would force the same level of (un)availability on all other systems communicating with it synchronously.

What is the solution? Would you shut down the e-commerce application when the fulfillment application is not available, or modify the fulfillment application such that it is available round-the-clock? The first solution would be very unacceptable for any e-commerce application. The second solution may require expensive reengineering. The only feasible (and less destructive) solution is to decouple these systems such that the availability of other relevant enterprise systems is taken into consideration.

Scenario 2 – Responsiveness

Let us now consider the same business process as in the previous scenario, but with one slight difference. Let us now include a credit card payment process as part of the checkout process. Here is a sample flow diagram:

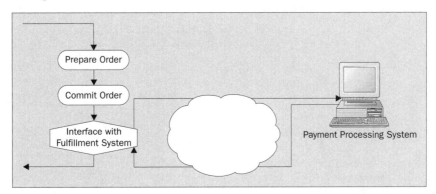

In this scenario, the implementation of the checkout process includes a component that interfaces with an online third-party payment processing system that can process credit card payments. There are several such payment processing solutions available today, the most popular being the solutions from CyberCash and CyberSource. These solutions let you process the payments synchronously such that you can fulfill the orders immediately with the assurance that the payment has been processed. This is a common deployment scenario for many online retail e-commerce systems.

In this scenario, we have introduced three potential issues that could lead to frozen browsers with customers waiting for an order confirmation from the e-commerce system:

❑ **Quality of connectivity** – The above process involves an additional HTTP request (over SSL) to connect to the payment processing system. This communication typically happens across the public Internet. Due to this additional round-trip, the quality of connectivity cannot be guaranteed. A slow connection between these systems leads to a delay in response for the end user.

❑ **Failed network connections** – A failure in the network connection with the payment processing system would make the above business process fail.

❑ **Non-availability** – The above process would fail if the payment processing system were out of service. Irrespective of the quality of service contracts with such payment processing systems, there is still a possibility that this could affect the availability of your e-commerce system.

The following figure lists the potential failure spots:

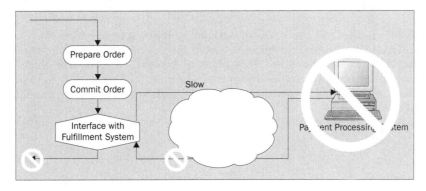

139

Scenario 3 – Resource Constraints

Let us look at the fulfillment system again, and consider a scenario where the fulfillment system is a typical client-server system originally developed for capturing and processing orders (including fulfillment) using a call center. Let us also assume that this system was designed for a couple of hundred representatives who connect to the database and place orders using desktop client applications.

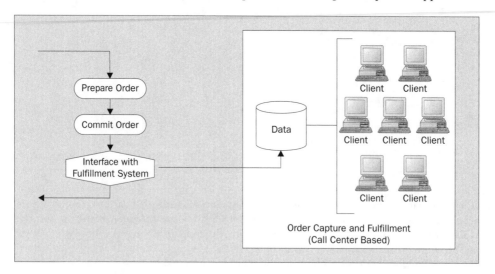

Such client-server applications are typically implemented with database-stored procedures, and SQL calls from the client-side. Databases in such systems will have certain stringent constraints as far as connectivity is concerned. Since it is a database-centric client-server application, there will be frequent and significant database roundtrips and business logic execution on the database server. Moreover, process loads and network traffic on such systems remain fairly constant. Note that such systems are generally designed for a reasonably fixed process and connection loads.

The above implementation introduces an online e-commerce application. Since most of the processing and fulfillment logic is already developed within the database, it is reasonable to attempt to reuse the same logic for the e-commerce application. Therefore, for every order placed over the Internet, the e-commerce application connects to the database, and executes whatever logic is applicable.

Let us analyse the outcome. Internet traffic is quite unpredictable. At any given time, there is a likelihood that there are a large number of customers attempting to place orders using the Internet. For each order placed (concurrently), the e-commerce application requires a database connection such that it can connect to the fulfillment database.

However, additional database connections to the fulfillment database may affect the overall performance. Firstly, the database may get overloaded and the e-commerce application may not be able to obtain new database connections. Secondly, even when a connection could be obtained, a large number of such connections would affect the overall performance. Therefore, both the Internet users and call-center personnel would experience deteriorated performance due to increased traffic as well as database contention.

Asynchronous Communication

In the previous subsections, we considered three different scenarios representing three different technical issues:

❑ **Availability** – When the e-commerce application depends on subsystems or external applications that are not guaranteed to be available round-the-clock, the availability of the e-commerce application would be limited to the availability of the least available application.

❑ **Responsiveness** – As the thread of execution gets longer, clients would experience deteriorated response time, or failed (timed-out) connections.

❑ **Resource constraints** – This situation arises when your e-commerce application attempts to synchronously connect to another system designed with reasonably fixed capacity.

Although we have considered three fictitious cases to factor out these technical issues, you may be able to identify several such scenarios in your e-commerce applications. But before we attempt to devise a solution to the above, there are some business questions to be considered: Can the business process in question be partly done with the remaining tasks delayed? If so, are there business issues involved? Can such business issues be adequately compensated in case of partial execution?

Whether your e-commerce system allows an affirmative answer or not depends on various business constraints. There may also be trade-offs associated with an affirmative answer. Nonetheless, considering that your business requirements allow certain tasks to be delayed, there are two approaches that can aid in solving this problem:

❑ Batch processing
❑ Asynchronous messaging

Let us now take a look at each of these in turn.

Batch Processing

Batch processing is a common strategy adopted frequently in many enterprise applications. In batch processing systems, the data is captured in the database as the data is entered from various channels. At designated intervals, the batch processing application loads the data in memory either in bulk or a single row/record, performs whatever operations are required, and updates the database. For instance, in the case of payment processing (*Scenario 2*), the batch processing application might load the data, connect and send the data to the online payment processing system, and based on the response, update the database tables.

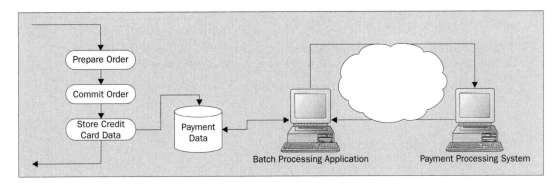

The above figure shows a possible batch implementation of credit card processing. Note, however, that this implementation affects the way that business is conducted. With batch processing in place, credit cards are now being processed *after* checkout and not *during* checkout. However, with this implementation, the responsiveness of the e-commerce application is not dependent on the payment processing system.

Depending on the specific business process under consideration, batch processing may or may not be preferable. For instance, consider that price information is available in a separate inventory system. Depending on how frequently the prices change, you may or may not wish to use batch processing – for instance, if the price changes very frequently, batch processing will be unreliable.

Asynchronous Messaging

The other solution is to rely on J2EE's support for messaging via the JMS. The following figure illustrates the case of the third scenario with a JMS layer introduced to execute fulfillment asynchronously.

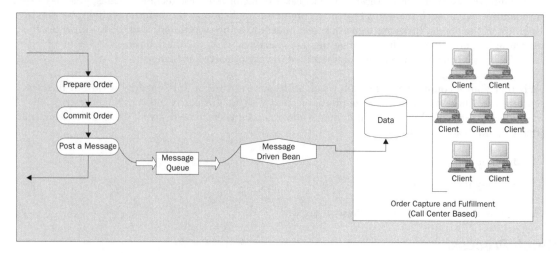

This implementation lets you process the orders asynchronously. However, to ensure that no message is lost due to a server-crash or restart, you should consider a JMS implementation that provides message persistence and guaranteed delivery.

However, the JMS based solution would not deal with availability completely. What happens if the other database is not available when the message bean receives the message? The bean cannot write to the database. Therefore, as long as the other system cannot be modified to add JMS support to receive messages asynchronously, the above architecture does not, by itself, solve this. In such cases, you may have to use a combination of batch and message oriented approaches.

> *Note that we have not discussed all possible cases that lead to asynchronous solutions here. Other cases for asynchronous connectivity include mainframe integration, integration with B2B systems, and so on.*

Summary

Most of the J2EE based e-commerce application development exercises include JSP pages and EJBs preceded by analysis and design phases to help identify the various components. However, as e-commerce applications evolve, and more and more functionality is sought from e-commerce applications, the technical demands on e-commerce applications increase. Such demands require more complex solutions.

In this chapter, we have dealt with certain architecture styles concerning component granularity, interface granularity and typeless interfaces, transaction scoping and distribution, and asynchronous communication. We have also covered:

❑   How the use of J2EE and EJBs can aid the process of abstraction

❑   How coarse-grained components can help improve both decoupling and performance

❑   Clients and interfaces, and how to get the maximum benefit from their interaction

❑   Separation of concerns in a layered architecture in order to ensure that the layers above do not depend on the implementation details of the layers below

❑   Using façades to simplify the client-component interface requirements

❑   The reasons why short transactions are better in the e-commerce landscape

The purpose of these discussions is to highlight some of the often-neglected technical issues and design styles. However, the set of topics discussed here is not comprehensive enough to cover all possible scenarios. As you start to develop different types of e-commerce applications later in this book, you'll discover more scenarios and architectural styles.

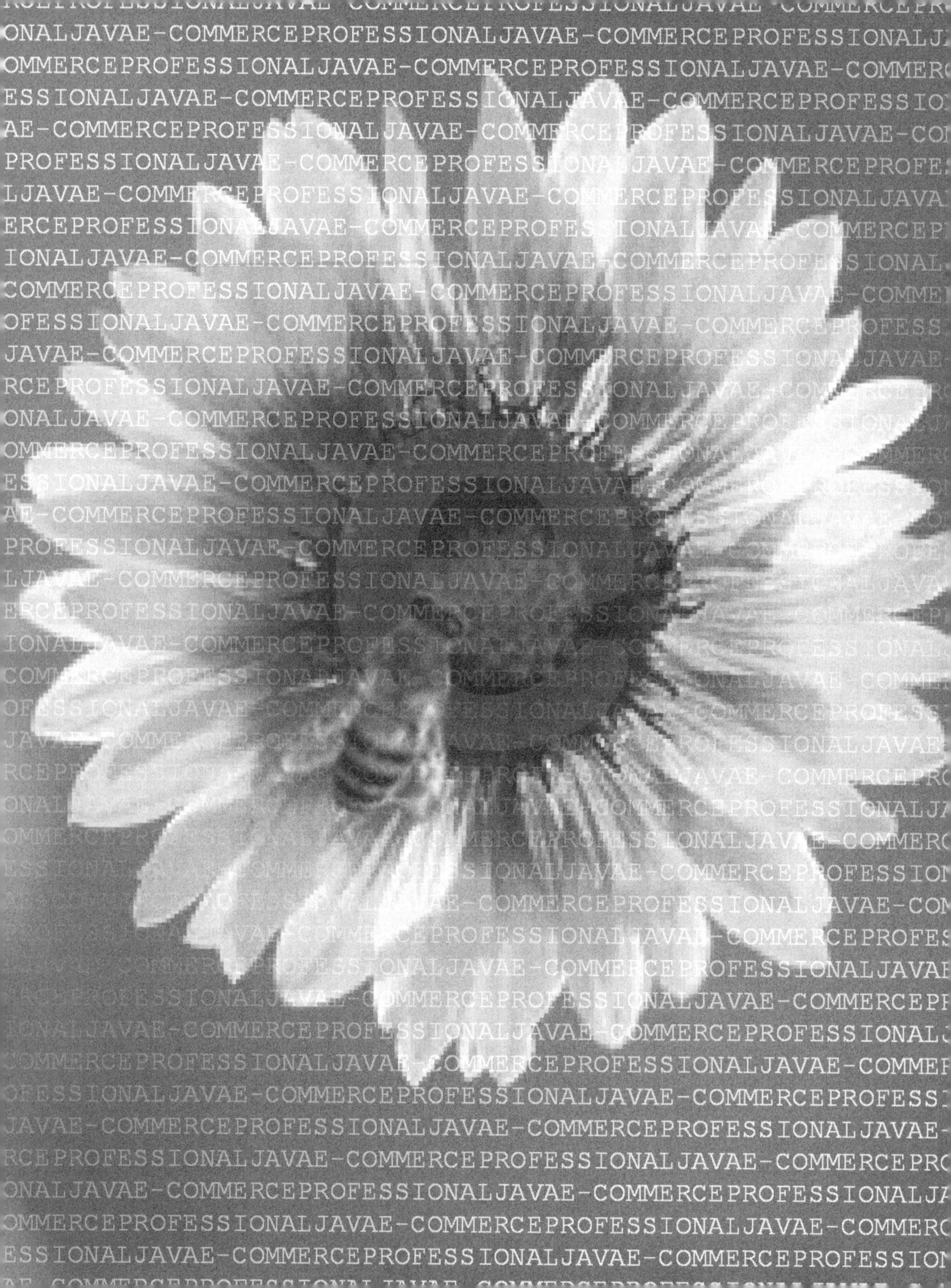

7

Delivering Data and Data Transformation – XML/XSLT

This chapter covers the Java programming details for processing XML documents. As we show, in the first section of the chapter, and in the subsequent B2C and B2B related chapters, XML and related technologies have a huge part to play in facilitating the growth of e-commerce. Indeed Chapter 20 illustrates the great benefit that using XML and XSLT brought to a financial services company.

If you're unfamiliar with XML and XSLT there are primers on each of these subjects in Appendix A and Appendix B respectively.

Our route through the chapter is as follows:

❑   An introduction to **Commerce XML (cXML)**

❑   A look at the Java XML APIs

❑   Using the **Simple API for XML (SAX)** to process XML documents

❑   Processing XML documents with the **Document Object Model (DOM)**

❑   Coverage of the **Java API for XML Parsing (JAXP)**

❑   Generating XML with JSP and servlets

❑   Using XSLT to transform XML data

Within the section on the SAX API we examine the methods required to implement a SAX content handler for processing the parser events and cover the steps required to register the content handler with the parser. Examples are included that integrate the SAX API with the JavaMail API to send XML-driven e-mail messages. Then as we move onto the DOM API, the role of DOM in XML applications is discussed with a comparison to the SAX API. This section contains coding examples where DOM objects are created based on an existing XML input source and examples where a DOM object is created from scratch, and details on how to validate XML documents with DOM.

When we look at generating XML content with JDBC, JSP, and servlets we'll look at a coding example where a company's product inventory is stored in a relational database and a servlet uses JDBC to access the database. The servlet then works in conjunction with a JSP page to dynamically generate a cXML document. Finally when we discuss data transformation with XSLT, coding examples are presented on how to convert XML data to HTML content with an XSLT processor and JSP (allowing the creation of browser independent XML based applications).

> Unlike the previous chapters in the book we're now moving from discussing theory to getting our hands dirty with code. While there is plenty of code presented over the next pages, working code samples can be downloaded from the Wrox website (**www.wrox.com**). We'll often refer to a directory structure for these files – this is the structure these files have been archived in, and all the code examples assume that you save the files in these directories.

Most of the XML documents used in the chapter adhere to the **Commerce XML** specification (**cXML**), so our starting point is to overview the cXML formats and discuss the various cXML documents for describing a product inventory and a purchase order.

Commerce XML

Commerce XML (cXML) is a collection of industry standard **document type definitions** (**DTD**) for business-to-business commerce. Ariba spearheaded the cXML standardization process and over 30 companies joined in the effort. cXML allows various buyers, sellers, and suppliers to communicate using a standard meta-language and includes DTDs to describe inventory, purchase orders, shipping notifications, and payment transactions. cXML documents are normally transmitted over HTTP and cXML has support for sending asynchronous messages.

> *The following sections are just a brief overview of cXML. The complete cXML specification, and detailed information on cXML, can be found at www.cxml.org.*

In this chapter, we will discuss two types of cXML documents:

❑ Catalogs

❑ Purchase Orders

Catalogs

Catalogs describe product inventory and the description includes product IDs, prices and shipping details such as lead-time. The catalog information can be stored as a static file or it can be dynamically generated at request time. A Java servlet or JavaServer Page (JSP) can generate the catalog based on the client's request and information stored in the inventory database (we'll see the actual programming techniques later in the chapter).

Once a catalog is created then it is normally imported into a buyer's procurement system (as shown). Depending on the application requirements, the buyer could update its procurement system at preset intervals, such as a daily or weekly update. The procurement system may also make a request from the supplier's catalog for each client request; however, this approach may produce erratic response times due to network delays.

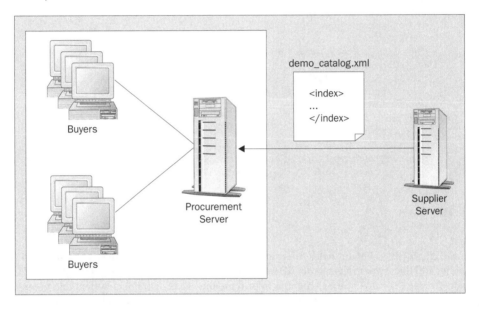

A cXML catalog describing inventory entries for two automobiles may look like this:

```xml
<?xml version="1.0" ?>
<!DOCTYPE Index SYSTEM "http://xml.cXML.org/schemas/cXML/1.1.009/cXML.dtd">

<Index>
  <SupplierID domain="DUNS">12-123-1234</SupplierID>
  <IndexItem>
    <IndexItemAdd>
      <ItemID>
        <SupplierPartID>auto-98765</SupplierPartID>
      </ItemID>
      <ItemDetail>
        <UnitPrice>
          <Money currency="USD">8000</Money>
        </UnitPrice>
        <Description xml:lang="en">Honda Civic del Sol</Description>
        <UnitOfMeasure/>
        <Classification domain="cdc">2dr</Classification>
```

```
            <ManufacturerPartID>honda-12345</ManufacturerPartID>
            <ManufacturerName>Honda</ManufacturerName>
          </ItemDetail>
          <IndexItemDetail>
            <LeadTime>7</LeadTime>
            <ExpirationDate>2001-09-01</ExpirationDate>
            <EffectiveDate>2001-01-01</EffectiveDate>
          </IndexItemDetail>
        </IndexItemAdd>
        <IndexItemAdd>
          <ItemID>
            <SupplierPartID>auto-54321</SupplierPartID>
          </ItemID>
          <ItemDetail>
            <UnitPrice>
               <Money currency="USD">19000</Money>
            </UnitPrice>
            <Description xml:lang="en">Honda Accord</Description>
            <UnitOfMeasure/>
            <Classification domain="cdc">4dr</Classification>
            <ManufacturerPartID>honda-98765</ManufacturerPartID>
            <ManufacturerName>Honda</ManufacturerName>
          </ItemDetail>
          <IndexItemDetail>
            <LeadTime>7</LeadTime>
            <ExpirationDate>2001-09-01</ExpirationDate>
            <EffectiveDate>2001-01-01</EffectiveDate>
          </IndexItemDetail>
        </IndexItemAdd>
      </IndexItem>
    </Index>
```

The `<IndexItemAdd>` element states this is a new inventory item and the buyer's procurement system should either add this entry to their procurement database or perform an update. The cXML DTD also defines an `<IndexItemDelete>` element to inform the buyer's procurement system that the item has been removed from the supplier's inventory. In this chapter, we will develop servlets that dynamically generate cXML catalogs based on information stored in a database.

Purchase Orders

In a typical B2B interaction, a buying organization will purchase products from a supplier. A purchase order describes the items to purchase along with the terms and recipients for the purchase. cXML defines:

- ❑ A purchase order document that is sent by the buying organization
- ❑ A purchase acknowledgement document for use by a supplier

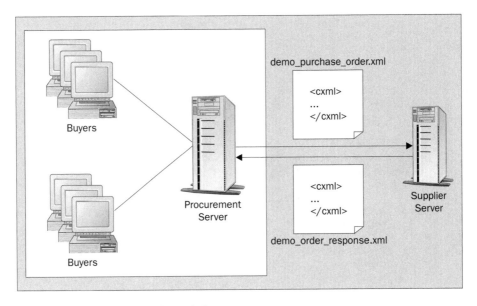

A sample cXML purchase order is shown below:

```
<?xml version="1.0" encoding="UTF-8"?>
<!DOCTYPE cXML SYSTEM "http://xml.cXML.org/schemas/cXML/1.1.009/cXML.dtd">
<cXML payloadID="454545@cxml.buyer.com" xml:lang="en-US"
      timestamp="2001-02-14T16:32:43-06:00">
    <Header>
        <From>
         ...
        </From>
        <To>
         ...
        </To>
        <Sender>
         ...
        </Sender>
    </Header>
    <Request deploymentMode="test">
        <OrderRequest>
            <OrderRequestHeader ...>
                <Total>
                    <Money currency="USD">912.54</Money>
                </Total>
                <ShipTo>
                    <Address>
                     ...
                    </Address>
                </ShipTo>
                <BillTo>
                    <Address>
                     ...
                    </Address>
                </BillTo>
                <Shipping trackingDomain="FedEx" trackingId="987654321">
```

```
            <Money currency="USD">9.99</Money>
            <Description xml:lang="en-us">FedEx 2-day</Description>
        </Shipping>
        <Tax>
            <Money currency="USD">4.54</Money>
            <Description xml:lang="en">local</Description>
        </Tax>
        <Payment>
            <PCard number="890126" expiration="2002-08-16"/>
        </Payment>
    </OrderRequestHeader>
    <ItemOut quantity="2" requestedDeliveryDate="2001-11-13">
        <ItemID>
            <SupplierPartID>14542</SupplierPartID>
        </ItemID>
        <ItemDetail>
            ...
        </ItemDetail>
        <ShipTo>
            <Address>
                ...
            </Address>
        </ShipTo>
        ...
        ...
    </ItemOut>
    </OrderRequest>
    </Request>
</cXML>
```

For each purchase order that is generated, the <cxml> element contains a payload identifier attribute. This unique identifier is used for message acknowledgement. As you can see, a cXML purchase order is composed of a header and the actual request. The header identifies the sender and recipients of the purchase order. The actual order request describes the items to purchase along with the purchasing details such as credit card number, and also the shipping details. Purchase orders can also be generated dynamically by a servlet or a JSP based on HTML form data.

When the supplier receives a purchase order request, they can respond using a purchase order acknowledgement. This is typically the case in a synchronous messaging system such as HTTP. However, for an asynchronous messaging model, the supplier may send responses in some other fashion. A sample order request response document may have the form:

```
<?xml version="1.0" encoding="UTF-8"?>
<!DOCTYPE cXML SYSTEM "http://xml.cXML.org/schemas/cXML/1.1.009/cXML.dtd">
<cXML payloadID="454545@cxml.buyer.com" xml:lang="en-US"
    timestamp="2001-02-14T16:34:43-06:00">
    <Response>
        <Status code="200" text="OK"/>
    </Response>
</cXML>
```

Notice, that the cXML tag in the response has a payload identifier that matches the initial purchase order request. The cXML response codes are modeled after the HTTP status codes so, in this case, a status code of 200 means the purchase order was received satisfactorily.

Now we've got a grasp of what cXML is, we'll move on to see how we can process cXML documents using the Java XML APIs.

Java XML APIs

During the development of XML enabled applications, our application will need to process the contents of an XML document. In a B2B scenario, the XML document may contain a catalog of products from your supplier. As a developer, we need an API that will allow us to analyze the contents of the document and perform some operation.

A number of APIs are available for processing XML documents. The two that that will be discussed in this chapter are:

❑ The **Simple API for XML (SAX)** – SAX is an event driven API that was developed by the readers of the xml-dev mailing list. David Megginson headed the project and he maintains the current API documentation at his site, http://www.megginson.com.

❑ The **Document Object Model (DOM)** – The DOM API is a tree-structured API that is based on the W3C recommendation. The current API documentation is available at http://www.w3c.org. Using DOM, an XML document is represented as a tree object in memory. Methods are available for traversing the document in a tree-like fashion and also modifying the contents of a document.

Before we discuss the SAX and DOM APIs we need to quickly mention XML parsers.

XML Parsers

During the development of XML applications, you will use an XML parser. The parser is responsible for dissecting the document into smaller elements or tokens. There are a number of XML parsers available for the various programming language such as C++ and Visual Basic. As you may have guessed, Java-based XML parsers are also available. The Java-based XML parsers provide a Java API for accessing and processing the contents of an XML document. Java-based XML parsers that implement the SAX and DOM API are available at http://www.w3c.org/xml.

> In this chapter, we will use the Apache Xerces Parser. Xerces is an open source development project that is freely downloadable from http://xml.apache.org. The code examples in this chapter have been run using Xerces Java Parser version 1.2.2.

Another nice feature of the Xerces parser is that it provides the latest support for SAX Level 2 and DOM Level 2.

Processing XML Documents with SAX 2.0

SAX is an event-driven API. During the processing of an XML document, SAX events are generated. For example, if we had the following XML document:

```
<?xml version="1.0" ?>
    <customer>
```

151

```
        <customer_name>Larry Ro</customer_name>
        <customer_email>larryro@fiction.wrox.com</customer_email>
    </customer>
```

The parser would generate the following SAX events:

```
start document
start element:    customer
start element:    customer_name
characters:    Larry Ro
end element:    customer_name
start element:    customer_email
characters:    larryro@fiction.wrox.com
end element:    customer_email
end element:    customer
end document
```

Notice that the parser processes the document in a top-down fashion.

The Role of SAX

Since SAX is an event-driven API, it is good for linear document processing. It is also a lightweight API since it only reads the XML document as a stream. Once an element is parsed it is purged. The XML document is not stored in memory, which makes the SAX API very efficient in terms of memory resources.

SAX is useful for processing very large documents. In a B2B scenario, it is possible that our application will access an XML document exceeding 1MB. Instead of attempting to load the entire document into memory, we simply read the data stream. The parser will generate SAX events that can be processed by a handler.

However, you should be aware of the weak points of the SAX API. Firstly, the API is read-only, so there is no way to modify the contents of the XML document. Also, it is a challenge to manage parent-child relationships during the processing of a document. Finally, if after processing the document with SAX you realise you need to extract additional information, then the document would have to be processed again to retrieve this extra data.

> *Remember, the entire document is not held in memory – if you want to keep track of information, then you will need to set up your own state management.*

SAX API and the Xerces Parser

During the processing of an XML document, the parser will generate events. The SAX model is somewhat analogous to the Java AWT event model. Once a parser is created then you register a handler with the parser. The parser will send events to all registered handlers. This is similar to adding a listener to a GUI component.

The program below demonstrates how to use the Xerces parser. `EzSaxParse` is a command-line program that will process an XML file by calling methods in the registered handler. The program can also process an XML document using a URL. The usage of the program is:

```
java EzSaxParse xmlfile
```

Here's the source code:

```java
import org.apache.xerces.parsers.SAXParser;

import org.xml.sax.SAXException;
import org.xml.sax.XMLReader;

import java.io.IOException;

public class EzSaxParse {

    public static void main(String[] args) {

        // check usage
        if (args.length != 1) {
            System.out.println("Usage: java EzSaxParse <file or URL>");
            System.exit(1);
        }

        // get the name of the XML file or URL
        String theXmlRef = args[0];

        try {
            // Step 1:  create an instance of Xerces SAX Parser
            XMLReader myXmlReader = new SAXParser();

            // Step 2:  Set the content handler
            myXmlReader.setContentHandler(new EchoContentHandler());

            // Step 3:  Parse the XML document
            myXmlReader.parse(theXmlRef);
        }
        catch (IOException exc) {
            exc.printStackTrace();
        }
        catch (SAXException exc) {
            exc.printStackTrace();
        }
    }
}
```

Notice the reference to the Xerces SAX parser with the statement:

```java
import org.apache.xerces.parsers.SAXParser;
```

Inside of the `main()` method, the XML file or URL is retrieved from the command-line. Then we create an instance of the Xerces SAX parser using the code:

```java
XMLReader myXmlReader = new SAXParser();
```

The Xerces SAX parser actually implements the standard interface `org.xml.sax.XMLReader`. The `XMLReader` provides methods for registering event listeners/handlers and parsing an XML document. Next, we register a handler with the parser. This handler will be notified of events regarding the content of the XML document.

153

```
myXmlReader.setContentHandler(new EchoContentHandler());
```

This method creates an instance of the class `EchoContentHandler`. This is a custom class that is discussed below – for now it is sufficient to understand that a handler is being registered with the parser.

The actual parsing of the document is initiated by calling the parse method as shown below:

```
myXmlReader.parse(theXmlRef);
```

The `XMLReader` also provides a method for processing a `java.io.InputStream`. This is useful if you are developing a custom networked application and need to process an XML document being sent over a socket connection.

Handling SAX Events

In order for your program to be informed of the SAX events, you must implement a handler. The SAX 2.0 API defines the following handler interfaces:

Interface	Description
org.xml.sax.ContentHandler	Receives notification of document contents
org.xml.sax.DTDHandler	Receives notification of DTD related events
org.xml.sax.ErrorHandler	Receives notifications for customized error handling

Most applications will commonly implement the `ContentHandler` interface. This interface defines methods for handling events of the document content. The methods of the `ContentHandler` interface are shown below:

```
package org.xml.sax;
public interface ContentHandler {

    /**
     *  Called at the beginning of the document
     */

    public void startDocument() throws SAXException;

    /**
     *  Called at the end of the document
     */

    public void endDocument() throws SAXException;

    /**
     *  Called at the beginning of an element
     */

    public void startElement(String namespaceURI, String localName,
```

```
                          String qualifiedName, Attributes attribs)
                throws SAXException;

/**
 *  Called at the end of an element
 */
public void endElement(String namespaceURI,
                       String localName,
                       String qualifiedName)
                throws SAXException;

/**
 *  Called when processing body content or CDATA
 */

public void characters(char[] ch, int start, int length)
                throws SAXException;

/**
 *  For validating parsers, sends ignorable white space such
 *  as tabs, carriage returns, etc…
 */

public void ignorableWhitespace(char[] ch, int start, int length)
                throws SAXException;

  /**
   *  Called when processing instructions are encountered.
   */

public void processingInstruction(String target, String data)
                throws SAXException;

/**
 *  Called at the beginning of a prefix mapping.
 *  A prefix mapping is an element that uses the xmlns
 *  attribute to declare a namespace for an associated prefix.
 */

public void setDocumentLocator(Locator locator)
                throws SAXException;

/**
 *  Non-validating parsers may skip over an entity.
 *  The entity name is passed into this method
 */

public void skippedEntity(String name)
                throws SAXException;

/**
 *  Called at the beginning of a prefix mapping.
 *  A prefix mapping is an element that uses the xmlns
 *  attribute to declare a namespace for an associated prefix.
 */
```

```
    public void startPrefixMapping(String prefix, String uri)
            throws SAXException;

    /**
      * Called at the end of a prefix mapping.  A prefix mapping
      * is an element that uses the xmlns attribute to declare a
      * namespace for an associated prefix.
      */

    public void endPrefixMapping(String prefix)
            throws SAXException;
}
```

During application development, a handler will normally have to implement all of the methods listed in the ContentHandler interface. The SAX API also provides the adapter class, org.xml.sax.helpers.DefaultHandler. The DefaultHandler provides a default implementation of the following interfaces: EntityResolver, DTDHandler, ContentHandler, ErrorHandler. Our application can simply subclass the DefaultHandler and override the methods of interest.

Echoing the Contents of an XML Document

In the following example, we'll process an XML document using the SAX API. This example will simply echo the contents of the file to the standard output. This example is actually composed of two classes:

❑   EchoContentHandler.java – This handler listens for the startDocument() and endDocument(), startElement() and endElement(), and characters() events.

❑   EzSaxParse.java – This serves as the driver for the program.

As the EzSaxParse.java class was discussed in the previous section let's focus on EchoContentHandler.java:

```
import org.xml.sax.helpers.DefaultHandler;

import org.xml.sax.Attributes;
import org.xml.sax.SAXException;

import java.io.IOException;

public class EchoContentHandler extends DefaultHandler {
```

As you can see, our custom class, EchoContentHandler, extends org.xml.sax.helpers.DefaultHandler. Recall that the DefaultHandler provides a default implementation for the following interfaces: EntityResolver, DTDHandler, ContentHandler, ErrorHandler.

In the EchoContentHandler class we simply overrode the methods that we were interested in. Let's discuss the methods of this class beginning with startElement():

```
    public void startElement(String nameSpace, String localName,
                         String rawName, Attributes attributes) {
```

```
        // display the start element tag name
        System.out.print("<" + localName);

        // check to see if we have attributes
        int attributesLength = attributes.getLength();
        if (attributesLength > 0) {
            // display the name-value pair for each attribute
            for (int i=0; i < attributesLength; i++) {
                System.out.print(" " + attributes.getLocalName(i) + "=" +
                                  "\"" + attributes.getValue(i) + "\"" );
            }
        }          // close the start element tag
        System.out.println(">");
    };
```

The parser calls the `startElement` method at the beginning of an element. The `localName` parameter is the actual name of the element tag. The parser also passes in the list of attributes for this element. The `for` loop processes the attributes by retrieving the name and value of each attribute.

```
    public void characters(char[] data, int start, int  length) {
        System.out.println(new String(data, start, length));
    }
```

When the parser processes text body content for an element, it then calls the `characters()` method. In our method, we simply convert the `char` array to `String` and display the contents.

```
    public void endElement(String nameSpace, String localName,
                           String rawName) {
        // Display the end element w/ tag name
        System.out.println("</" + localName + ">");
    };
```

For the ending of each element, we simply display the end tag with its associated name.

```
    public void startDocument() throws SAXException {
        System.out.println("Start Document");
    };

    public void endDocument() throws SAXException {
        System.out.println("End Document");
    };
}
```

For informational purposes, we also display a message when the parser processes the start/end of the document.

Running the Example

Before we can compile and execute the examples, we need to properly configure the development environment.

❑ The first step is to download and install the Xerces Java Parser (available from http://xml.apache.org) – we used version 1.2.2 – and the support code for the chapter from the Wrox website at (www.wrox.com). In the following steps we use xerces_install_dir to reference the root installation directory for Xerces and to set the classpath environment variable to point to the Xerces JAR file, use the command line instruction:

```
set classpath=.;xerces_install_dir\xerces.jar
```

❑   Extract the downloaded code archive to an appropriate directory (the code for this example is in the download file with the path `ProJavaEcomm\ch07\sax_demo_1`). Then compile the Java code in that directory and test the program by using the instruction:

```
java EzSaxParse catalog_1.xml
```

The program will display the contents of the sample cXML file provided as part of the code download and also in Appendix C, `catalog_1.xml`. The `EzSaxParse` program can accept any XML file or URL since it only echoes the contents of the file.

Integrating SAX and JavaMail

The previous example was fairly straightforward – read a document and display the contents. However, XML enabled Java applications will need to process the data as it is parsed. In this section, we'll develop a Java application that sends e-mail, and stores e-mail addresses in an XML file. This program could be used in an e-commerce application to notify customers of new products, or it could be used to send notifications to business partners.

All the files we're going to create now should be saved in a directory such as `c:\ProJavaEcomm\ch07\sax_demo_2`. If you choose to download the files, they are in the code download bundle in a directory with this name.

The customer's e-mail information is stored in the following XML file:

```
<?xml version="1.0" ?>
<customer_mail_list>
    <customer>
        <customer_name>Larry Ro</customer_name>
        <customer_email>larryro@fiction.wrox.com</customer_email>
    </customer>

    <customer>
        <customer_name>Traci Lee</customer_name>
        <customer_email>tracilee@fiction.wrox.com</customer_email>
    </customer>

    <customer>
        <customer_name>Sarah Well</customer_name>
        <customer_email>sarahwell@fiction.wrox.com</customer_email>
    </customer>
</customer_mail_list>
```

Our application will use the SAX parser to retrieve the customer names and e-mail addresses. We'll also use the JavaMail API to compose and send the e-mail message. This example is composed of two classes: `EzMailParse` and `EzMailHandler`.

EzMailParse

This serves as the main driver. It reads in the name of the XML file and creates the parser instance. It also registers the `EzMailHandler` with the parser and processes the document.

Let's start with `EzMailParse`:

```java
import java.io.IOException;
import org.apache.xerces.parsers.SAXParser;
import org.xml.sax.SAXException;
import org.xml.sax.XMLReader;

public class EzMailParse {

    public static void main(String[] args) {

        // Check usage
        if (args.length != 1) {
            System.out.println("Usage: java EzMailParse <xml file>");
            System.exit(1);
        }

        // Get the name of the customer xml file
        String theXmlRef = args[0];

        try {
            // Step 1:  create an instance of Xerces SAX Parser
            XMLReader myXmlReader = new SAXParser();

            // Step 2:  Set the content handler
            myXmlReader.setContentHandler(new EzMailHandler());

            // Step 3:  Parse the XML document
            myXmlReader.parse(theXmlRef);
        }
        catch (IOException exc) {
            exc.printStackTrace();
        }
        catch (SAXException exc) {
            exc.printStackTrace();
        }
    }
}
```

This code is very similar to the `EzSaxParse` from the previous section. The only difference is step 2 where we set the content handler. In this example, the content handler is `EzMailHandler`.

EzMailHandler

This program handles the SAX events that are generated by the parser. It retrieves the customer's name and e-mail address by overriding the `startElement()`, `endElement()`, and `characters()` methods.

The source code for `EzMailHandler` is shown below:

```java
import org.xml.sax.Attributes;
import org.xml.sax.helpers.DefaultHandler;
import org.xml.sax.Locator;
import org.xml.sax.SAXException;
```

```
import java.io.IOException;
import javax.mail.internet.InternetAddress;
import javax.mail.internet.MimeMessage;
import javax.mail.Message;
import javax.mail.MessagingException;
import javax.mail.Session;
import javax.mail.Transport;

public class EzMailHandler extends DefaultHandler {

    private boolean customerNameFlag;
    private boolean customerEmailFlag;

    private String customerName;
    private String customerEmail;

    /**
     *  Constructor to explicitly set the flags to false;
     */
    public EzMailHandler() {
        customerNameFlag = false;
        customerEmailFlag = false;
    }

    /**
     *  Checks the names of the element.  Sets the appropriate flag.
     *  The flag is used later by the characters(...) method.
     */
    public void startElement(String nameSpace, String localName,
                                  String rawName, Attributes attributes)
        throws SAXException {

        if (localName.equals("customer_name")) {
            customerNameFlag = true;
        }
        else if (localName.equals("customer_email")) {
            customerEmailFlag = true;
        }
    };

    /**
     *  Check the flag.  Assign the value to the appropriate String data
     *  member.
     */
    public void characters(char[] data, int start, int  length)
        throws SAXException {

        if (customerNameFlag) {
            customerName = new String(data, start, length);
            customerNameFlag = false;
        }
        else if (customerEmailFlag) {
            customerEmail = new String(data, start, length);
            customerEmailFlag = false;
        }
    }
```

The `EzMailHandler` overrides the `startElement()` method and checks for the tag name. If the tag name is `customer_name` then it sets a boolean flag to true. Next, the parser calls the `characters()` method and passes in the content. Based on the boolean flag that was set in the `startElement()` method, then we'll assign the data to either the customer name or customer e-mail. Notice that when you are using the SAX parser, you need to define your own boolean variables to keep track of state between different elements.

```
/**
 *  If we are at the end of a customer element then
 *  send an e-mail message to the customer.
 */
public void endElement(String nameSpace, String localName,
                          String rawName)
    throws SAXException {

    try {
        if (localName.equals("customer")) {
            // send the e-mail for this customer
            sendMailTo(customerName, customerEmail);
        }
    }
    catch (MessagingException exc) {
        exc.printStackTrace();
        throw new SAXException(exc);
    }
}
```

In the `endElement()` method, we check to see if we are at the end of the customer element. If so, then we know that we've already processed the elements for `customer_name` and `customer_email`. We can use this information to send an e-mail message:

```
/**
 *  Helper method for sending e-mail.  Uses the JavaMail API.  <p>
 *
 *  For testing:
 *  <ol>
 *  <li>  You must set properties for your SMTP mail host. </li>
 *  <li>  Set the address of the sender.  </li>
 *  <li>  Update the xml document with real e-mail addresses. </li>
 *  </ol>
 */
private void sendMailTo(String customerName, String customerEmail)
    throws MessagingException {

    // setup a mail session for the smtp host
    String myMailHost = "smtp.fiction.wrox.com";

    java.util.Properties  props = new java.util.Properties();
    props.put("mail.smtp.host", myMailHost);
    Session mailSession = Session.getDefaultInstance(props, null);

    // construct the email message
    InternetAddress fromAddress = new
                          InternetAddress("admin@mydot.com");
    InternetAddress toAddress = new InternetAddress(customerEmail);
```

```
        MimeMessage theMessage = new MimeMessage(mailSession);
        theMessage.setFrom(fromAddress);
        theMessage.addRecipient(Message.RecipientType.TO, toAddress);
        theMessage.setSentDate(new java.util.Date());
        theMessage.setSubject("Our cXML Catalog is available");
        theMessage.setText("Hi " + customerName +
                    ",  Our cXML Catalog is available at our website!");

        // now let's send the message
        Transport.send(theMessage);
        System.out.println("Sent message to: " + customerEmail);
    }
}
```

The `sendMailTo()` method uses the JavaMail API for message composition and transmission. The first major step of sending e-mail is the configuration of the mail session. The mail session needs the name of the SMTP host to send out the message. For testing in your environment you should use the name of the SMTP host at your Internet Service Provider or corporate network. Once the mail session is configured, then the e-mail message is constructed. Finally, to send the message, make a call to the static method `send()` defined in the `Transport` class.

Running the Example

This example relies on the JavaMail API. You can download it from http://java.sun.com/products/javamail. The JavaMail API also depends on the JavaBeans Activation Framework (JAF). I've found it easier to simply download and install the J2EE Reference Implementation from http://java.sun.com/j2ee. The `j2ee.jar` file includes the JavaMail API and JavaBeans Activation Framework and many others. So, one simple download and you are ready to go.

❑   Download and extract the J2EE Reference Implementation

In the following steps, we use *j2ee_install_dir* to reference your root installation directory for the J2EE Reference Implementation, and *xerces_install_dir* to reference the root installation directory for Xerces. We'll be running this example from the directory where we've saved the files, `c:\ProJavaEcomm\ch07\sax_demo_2`.

❑   Set the classpath environment variable to point to the Xerces JAR file and `j2ee.jar`:

set classpath=.;xerces_install_dir\xerces.jar;j2ee_install_dir\lib\j2ee.jar

❑   Modify the `EzMailHandler.java` file to point to your SMTP mail host
❑   Modify the `customer_mail_list.xml` file with valid e-mail addresses
❑   Compile the code, and then run it by typing:

java EzMailParse customer_mail_list.xml

The program will process the XML file (`customer_mail_list.xml`) and send out e-mail messages. Feel free to customize this example with your own messages.

Processing XML Documents with DOM

The Document Object Model (DOM) API represents an XML document as an in-memory tree object. The DOM tree can be constructed from an existing XML document or we can create an XML document from scratch using the DOM APIs.

In the previous section, we used an XML file for a list of customer e-mail addresses, as shown below:

```
<?xml version="1.0" ?>
<customer_mail_list>
    <customer>
        <customer_name>Larry Ro</customer_name>
        <customer_email>larryro@fiction.wrox.com</customer_email>
    </customer>
    ... ...
</customer_mail_list>
```

When using the DOM API, this document is loaded into memory and is modeled as a tree:

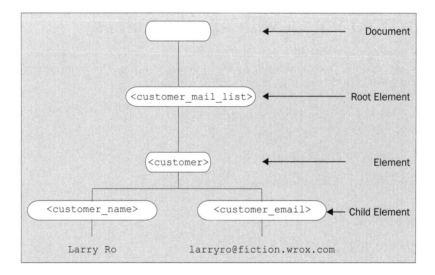

The Role of DOM

DOM is good for creating well-formed XML documents that can also be validated. DOM is also useful for reading in an existing XML document and performing multiple queries again the document contents. The technique of querying the document means traversing the tree and accessing the element values.

Please be aware that by using the DOM API, the application will potentially consume large amounts of memory, depending upon the size of the document. Even for very large XML documents, the DOM API will attempt to read the entire document into memory. In this scenario, DOM may not be the desired choice. Only use the DOM API for reading XML documents if you need to make multiple queries on the document. A better approach may be to use the SAX API and simply store the information that you will need to repeatedly access.

Exploring the DOM API

The DOM API is defined in the package org.w3c.dom. The API is composed of a collection of interfaces for describing the tree structure. A complete list of DOM interfaces can be found in the on-line documentation. Below is a list of the commonly used interfaces defined in org.w3c.dom:

Interfaces	Description
Node	Primary datatype representing a single node in the document
Document	The entire XML document
Element	An element node and any contained nodes
Text	Text string
NodeList	List of child nodes for a given element
NamedNodeMap	Used to retrieve nodes by name

Creating a DOM Parser with Apache Xerces

The challenge in using the DOM API is that there isn't a standard way of building the initial DOM tree. The coding techniques are different depending on the DOM implementation. The following code examples illustrate how to create a DOM tree using the Apache Xerces parser:

```
import org.apache.xerces.parsers.DOMParser;
import org.w3c.dom.Document;

public class BuildTree {

    public static void main(String[] args) {

        // check for correct usage
        if (args.length != 1) {
            System.out.println("Usage: java BuildTree <xml file>");
            System.exit(1);
        }

        // reference to the XML resource
        String theXmlRef = args[0];

        try {
            // setup the parser and parse the document
            System.out.println("Creating the parser");
            DOMParser parser = new DOMParser();

            // build a DOM tree for the XML
            parser.parse(theXmlRef);

            // now get a reference to the document
            Document doc = parser.getDocument();
```

```
            //  … … process on the tree
        }
        catch (Exception exc) {
            exc.printStackTrace();
        }
    }
}
```

In the program, BuildTree, we use the DOMParser class defined in org.apache.xerces.parsers. In the main() method, we create an instance of the parser. Next, we build the DOM document tree in memory by calling the parser.parse() method. Finally, to obtain a handle to the document tree, we call parser.getDocument(). Once we have a reference to the document tree then we can process it accordingly.

Some examples of processing include:

❑   Traversing the tree and simply displaying its contents

❑   Performing multiple queries / searches on the document based on user requests

❑   Modifying the contents of the document

❑   Adding additional nodes to the document

❑   Writing the XML document to a file

Traversing the DOM Tree

In this section, we will discuss techniques for traversing a tree. As we traverse a tree, we will visit the various nodes. The Node interface provides the following methods for retrieving metadata for a given node in the tree:

Method	Description
int getNodeType()	Returns an integer that represents the node type
String getNodeName()	Returns the name of the node depending on the node type (see table below)
String getNodeValue()	Returns the value of the node depending on the node type (see table below)

The following table displays a list of commonly used node types. See the DOM API for a complete list of node types:

DOM Interface	getNodeType()	getNodeName()	getNodeValue()
Element	Node.ELEMENT_NODE	Name of element	null
Text	Node.TEXT_NODE	#text	Context of the text node
Attr	Node.ATTRIBUTE_NODE	Attribute name	Attribute value

In a tree-based structure, a given node may also have child nodes. The `Node` interface provides a method that retrieves a list of child nodes. We can use a recursive algorithm to process the child nodes. This technique is illustrated in the `EzDomEcho` program. `EzDomEcho` will display the contents of an XML document. The first part of `EzDomEcho` is shown below:

```java
import org.apache.xerces.parsers.DOMParser;
import org.w3c.dom.Document;
import org.w3c.dom.Node;
import org.w3c.dom.NodeList;
import org.w3c.dom.NamedNodeMap;

public class EzDomEcho {

    public static void main(String[] args) {

        // check for correct usage
        if (args.length != 1) {
            System.out.println("Usage: java EzDomEcho <xml file>");
            System.exit(1);
        }

        // reference to the XML resource
        String theXmlRef = args[0];

        try {
            // setup the parser and parse the document
            System.out.println("Creating the parser");
            DOMParser parser = new DOMParser();

            System.out.println("Building DOM object for file: " +
                                                theXmlRef);
            parser.parse(theXmlRef);
            System.out.println("...finished\n");

            // now get a reference to the document
            Document doc = parser.getDocument();
            Node root = doc.getDocumentElement();

            System.out.println("Displaying document");
            EzDomEcho echo = new EzDomEcho();
            echo.traverseTree(root);
        }
        catch (Exception exc) {
            exc.printStackTrace();
        }
    }
```

In the `main()` method, we create an instance of the DOM parser and retrieve a reference to the `Document` object. Then we access the root element by calling `doc.getDocumentElement()` method. Next, we create an instance of the `EzDomEcho` class and pass the root node. The `traverseTree()` method will recursively process the elements for the root node.

The `traverseTree()` method is shown below. This method accepts a `Node` element and determines the node type. If it is an element node then we display the node and its attributes. If the node is a text node of CDATA section, then we simply display the node value.

```java
public void traverseTree(Node theNode) {

    int nodeType = theNode.getNodeType();
    switch (nodeType) {
        case Node.ELEMENT_NODE:
            displayNodeAndAttributes(theNode);
            break;

        case Node.CDATA_SECTION_NODE:
        case Node.TEXT_NODE:
                System.out.println(theNode.getNodeValue());
            break;
    }
}
```

The `displayNodeAndAttributes()` method is shown below. This method displays the node name and then checks to see if it has attributes. If attributes are available, then we print the name/value pairs for each one. Next, we check to see if the node has any children – if so, then we call the `traverseTree()` method for each child node:

```java
public void displayNodeAndAttributes(Node theNode) {
    // display the node name and attributes
    String nodeName = theNode.getNodeName();
    System.out.print("<" + nodeName);

    // do attribute work
    NamedNodeMap attributes = theNode.getAttributes();
    Node tempAttrib;
    for (int i=0; i < attributes.getLength(); i++) {
        tempAttrib = attributes.item(i);
        System.out.print(" " + tempAttrib.getNodeName() + "=" +
                    "\"" + tempAttrib.getNodeValue()  + "\"" );
    }
    System.out.println(">");

    // now perform the recursion for each child node
    if (theNode.hasChildNodes())      {
        NodeList children = theNode.getChildNodes();
        int childCount = children.getLength();
        for (int i=0; i < childCount; i++) {
            traverseTree(children.item(i));
        }
    }
    // print out the end tag
    System.out.println("</" +nodeName + ">");
}
```

Running the Example

In a similar manner to the previous example, we're running this from the directory containing the files we've just created (or downloaded), which we'll assume will be c:\ProJavaEcomm\ch07\dom_demo_1.

❑   Set the classpath environment variable to point to the Xerces JAR file:

```
set classpath=.;xerces_install_dir\xerces.jar
```

❑   Compile the code, and test the program by typing:

```
java EzDomEcho customer_mail_list.xml
```

The program will display the contents of the XML file.

Validating with DOM

The DOM parser can also validate the XML document. A document is considered valid if it follows the grammar rules of the Document Type Definition (DTD). See Appendix A for a discussion of defining a DTD.

DTDs are very useful in B2B scenarios; when your application receives an XML document from another application, you can validate the document to verify that it follows the grammar rules defined in the DTD. Also, before your application sends an XML document to another application, you can validate it.

The following code snippet shows how to validate with the Xerces DOM parser:

```
...
DOMParser parser = new DOMParser();

// set up validation
parser.setFeature("http://xml.org/sax/features/validation", true);

parser.parse(theXmlRef);
...
```

When the XML document is processed, the content is compared against the DTD. If the document doesn't follow the grammar rules defined in the DTD then an exception is thrown. You can also customize the error handling for DTD errors. Simply create an implementation of the org.xml.sax.ErrorHandler interface. This interface defines methods to handle errors, fatal errors, and warnings. In your implementation, provide handler code for the appropriate errors. An implementation of the ErrorHandler interface is shown below. This implementation simply displays the exception:

```
import org.xml.sax.ErrorHandler;
import org.xml.sax.SAXException;
import org.xml.sax.SAXParseException;

public class EzDomErrorHandler implements ErrorHandler {

    public void error(SAXParseException exception) {
        System.out.println(exception);
    }

    public void fatalError(SAXParseException exception)  {
        System.out.println(exception);
    }

    public void warning(SAXParseException exception) {
        System.out.println(exception);
    }
}
```

Once the `ErrorHandler` implementation is developed, register it with the parser as shown in the code segment below:

```
...
DOMParser parser = new DOMParser();

// register error handler
parser.setErrorHandler(new EzDomErrorHandler());

parser.setFeature("http://xml.org/sax/features/validation", true);

parser.parse(theXmlRef);
...
```

Running the Example

Again, we're running this example from it's own directory , which we'll be calling
`c:\ProJavaEcomm\ch07\dom_demo_2`.

❑   Make sure that the classpath is still set as for the previous example

❑   Make the following modifications to the file: `EzDomEcho.java`

```
...
DOMParser parser = new DOMParser();

// register error handler
parser.setErrorHandler(new EzDomErrorHandler());

parser.setFeature("http://xml.org/sax/features/validation", true);

System.out.println("Building DOM object for file: "  + theXmlRef);
parser.parse(theXmlRef);
...
```

❑   Compile the new code, and test it by typing:

```
java EzDomEcho catalog_1.xml
```

The document `catalog_1.xml` is a cXML document that adheres to the cXML DTD. If all is well, then the program will display the contents of the file. To test the validation features, make a modification to the file `catalog_1.xml` such as deleting the line:

```
<SupplierID domain="DUNS">12-123-1234</SupplierID>
```

Save the file and test the program again. It should generate errors and pass them to the error handler.

Creating New XML Documents Using DOM

The DOM API has a collection of methods for programmatically creating XML documents. The ability to create XML documents from scratch is good for the following tasks: building an XML document based on HTML form input, ensuring the document is well-formed, also for validating the new document against a DTD.

Interestingly enough, the DOM API does not provide a standard way of creating an instance of the `Document` interface. Currently, it is up to the providers of the DOM implementation. In the Apache Xerces parser, you can create an empty XML document using the following code:

```
import org.w3c.dom.Document;
import org.apache.xerces.dom.DocumentImpl;

...

theDocument = new DocumentImpl();
...
```

The Xerces parser provides an implementation of the `Document` interface.

Here is a list of commonly used methods for creating XML documents. The return types for these methods are defined in the package `org.w3c.dom`. These methods are defined in the `org.w3c.dom.Document` interface:

org.w3c.dom.Document Methods	Description
`Attr createAttribute(String name)`	Creates an attribute with the given name
`Attr createAttributeNS(String namespaceURI, String qualifiedName)`	Creates an attribute with the given qualified name and namespace URI
`CDATASection createCDATASection(String data)`	Creates a CDATA section with the given data
`Comment createComment(String data)`	Creates a comment with the given data
`Element createElement(String tagName)`	Creates an element of the type specified.
`Element createElementNS(String namespaceURI, String qualifiedName)`	Creates an element of the given qualified name and namespace URI
`EntityReference createEntityReference(String name)`	Creates an `EntityReference` object
`ProcessingInstruction createProcessingInstruction(String target, String data)`	Creates a `ProcessingInstruction` node given the specified name and data strings
`Text createTextNode(String data)`	Creates a `Text` node with the given data

The development approach is similar to developing GUIs. In the GUI world, we would create a container and then add components to that container. Using DOM, we create a document and then add elements to it.

Earlier in the section, we presented an XML document that contained customer e-mail addresses as shown below:

```
<?xml version="1.0" ?>
<customer_mail_list>
    <customer>
        <customer_name>Larry Ro</customer_name>
        <customer_email>larryro@fiction.wrox.com</customer_email>
    </customer>
```

```
    </customer_mail_list>
```

The following code fragment creates the XML document using the DOM API:

```
import org.w3c.dom.Document;
import org.w3c.dom.Element;
import org.w3c.dom.TextNode;
import org.apache.xerces.dom.DocumentImpl;

....
theDocument = new DocumentImpl();

Element root = theDocument.createElement("customer_mail_list");
theDocument.appendChild(root);

Element customer = theDocument.createElement("customer");
root.appendChild(customer);

Element name = theDocument.createElement("customer_name");
name.appendChild(theDocument.createTextNode("Larry Ro"));
customer.appendChild(name);

Element email = theDocument.createElement("customer_email");
email.appendChild(theDocument.createTextNode
    ("larryro@fiction.wrox.com"));
customer.appendChild(email);
...
```

In the code above, the elements are created and added as child nodes to the appropriate element. For elements that contain body content, a text node is created and added to the element. Notice how we simply give the element name without the angled brackets. Also, notice that there was no requirement to specify the end tags for an element. The DOM API handles those low-level structural details.

For a given element, we can also set attributes. In the example below, we are adding an attribute to the e-mail element to describe whether this is a home or work e-mail address:

```
email.setAttribute("location", "home");
```

If the element requires additional attributes, simply call the setAttribute() method as needed.

The next example will cover the programming details for creating a cXML Order Request document. The cXML document is shown below:

```
<?xml version="1.0" encoding="UTF-8"?>
<cXML payloadID="666555444@redbook.com"
    timestamp="2001-11-13T14:33:22-08:00" xml:lang="en-US">
  <Header>
      <From>
          <Credential domain="RedBooks">
              <Identity>admin@p2p.com</Identity>
          </Credential>
      </From>
      <To>
```

```
                <Credential domain="DUNS">
                    <Identity>999666333</Identity>
                </Credential>
        </To>
        <Sender>
            <Credential domain="RedBooks">
                <Identity>admin@acme.com</Identity>
                <SharedSecret>programmer2programmer</SharedSecret>
            </Credential>
            <UserAgent>RedBook Network V2.0</UserAgent>
        </Sender>
    </Header>
    <Request>
        <OrderRequest>
        <OrderRequestHeader orderID="DO9876" orderDate="2001-11-02" type="new">
            <Total>
                <Money currency="USD">79.99</Money>
                </Total>
                <BillTo>
                    <Address>
                        <Name xml:lang="en">Belbay Associates</Name>
                            <PostalAddress name="foo">
                            <Street>7658 Belbay</Street>
                            <City>Houston</City>
                            <State>TX</State>
                            <PostalCode>77033</PostalCode>
                            <Country isoCountryCode="US">United States</Country>
                                </PostalAddress>
                        </Address>
                    </BillTo>
                    <Shipping trackingDomain="FedEx" trackingId="9876543210">
                        <Money currency="USD">7.50</Money>
                        <Description xml:lang="en-us">FedEx 2-day</Description>
                    </Shipping>
                    <Payment>
                        <PCard number="98765430232" expiration="2002-12-12"/>
                    </Payment>
            </OrderRequestHeader>
            <ItemOut quantity="2" requestedDeliveryDate="2001-11-20">
                <ItemID>
                    <SupplierPartID>455455</SupplierPartID>
                </ItemID>
            </ItemOut>
        </OrderRequest>
    </Request>
</cXML>
```

The following program is OrderRequest.java. It includes a main routine that constructs a cXML order request using the DOM API. Let's examine this coding example, which we'll save in c:\ProJavaEcomm\ch07\dom_demo_2:

```java
import org.apache.xerces.dom.DocumentImpl;

import org.w3c.dom.Document;
```

```java
import org.w3c.dom.Element;
import org.w3c.dom.Node;

public class OrderRequest {

    private Document theDocument;

    public OrderRequest() {
        theDocument = new DocumentImpl();

        Element root = theDocument.createElement("cXML");
        theDocument.appendChild(root);

        root.setAttribute("payloadID", "666555444@redbook.com");
        root.setAttribute("timestamp", "2001-11-13T14:33:22-08:00");
        root.setAttribute("xml:lang", "en-US");

        buildHeader(root);
        buildBody(root);
    }
```

The code above serves as the constructor for `OrderRequest`. It creates an instance of the Apache Xerces `DocumentImpl` class, labeled `theDocument`. The instance is used to create a root element for cXML. Then, the attributes for `payloadID`, `timestamp` and `xml:lang` are set accordingly for the root element.

```java
protected void buildHeader(Node root) {
    Element header = theDocument.createElement("Header");
    root.appendChild(header);

    /**
     *   <From>
     *       <Credential domain="RedBooks">
     *           <Identity>admin@p2p.com</Identity>
     *       </Credential>
     *   </From>
     */
    Element from = theDocument.createElement("From");
    header.appendChild(from);
    buildCredential(from, "RedBooks", "admin@p2p.com");

    /**
     *   <To>
     *       <Credential domain="DUNS">
     *           <Identity>999666333</Identity>
     *       </Credential>
     *   </To>
     */
    Element to = theDocument.createElement("To");
    header.appendChild(to);
    buildCredential(to, "DUNS", "999666333");

    /**
     *   <Sender>
     *       <Credential domain="RedBooks">
```

```
 *                <Identity>admin@acme.com</Identity>
 *                <SharedSecret>programmer2programmer</SharedSecret>
 *         </Credential>
 *         <UserAgent>RedBook Network V2.0</UserAgent>
 *    </Sender>
 */
Element sender = theDocument.createElement("Sender");
header.appendChild(sender);
buildCredential(sender, "RedBooks", "admin@acme.com",
    "programmer2programmer");

Element userAgent = theDocument.createElement("UserAgent");
sender.appendChild(userAgent);
userAgent.appendChild(theDocument.createTextNode("RedBook
    Network V2.0"));
}
```

The builderHeader() method is responsible for building the cXML header for an OrderRequest. During construction of the header, we repeatedly need to build the credentials for the sender and reciever. This functionality is factored out in the method below, buildCredential():

```
/**
 *  Helper method for building credentials
 */
protected void buildCredential(Node theElement, String theDomain,
        String theText, String theSecretText) {

    Element credential = theDocument.createElement("Credential");
    credential.setAttribute("domain", theDomain);
    theElement.appendChild(credential);

    Element identity = theDocument.createElement("Identity");
    credential.appendChild(identity);
    identity.appendChild(theDocument.createTextNode(theText));

    if (theSecretText != null) {
        Element sharedSecret =
                theDocument.createElement("SharedSecret");
        credential.appendChild(sharedSecret);

      sharedSecret.appendChild(
              theDocument.createTextNode(theSecretText));
    }
}

/**
 *  Helper method for building credentials
 */
protected void buildCredential(Node theElement, String theDomain,
                        String theText) {

    String theSecretText = null;
    buildCredential(theElement, theDomain, theText, theSecretText);
}
```

The main body of the cXML document is constructed using the `buildBody()` method shown below. It uses the DOM API to add the appropriate sub-elements to the document body. This is a long code listing that is supported by in-line comments to describe the different sections being built:

```java
/**
 *  Helper method for building the order request
 */
protected void buildBody(Node root) {

    Element request = theDocument.createElement("Request");
    root.appendChild(request);

    Element orderRequest = theDocument.createElement("OrderRequest");
    request.appendChild(orderRequest);

    Element orderRequestHeader =
                        theDocument.createElement("OrderRequestHeader");
    orderRequestHeader.setAttribute("orderID", "D09876");
    orderRequestHeader.setAttribute("orderDate", "2001-11-02");
    orderRequestHeader.setAttribute("type", "new");
    orderRequest.appendChild(orderRequestHeader);

    /**
     *   <Total>
     *       <Money currency="USD">79.99</Money>
     *   </Total>
     */
    Element total = theDocument.createElement("Total");
    orderRequestHeader.appendChild(total);

    Element money  = theDocument.createElement("Money");
    money.setAttribute("currency", "USD");
    money.appendChild(theDocument.createTextNode("79.99"));
    total.appendChild(money);

    /**
     *   <BillTo>
     *       <Address>
     *           <Name xml:lang="en">Belbay Associates</Name>
     *           <PostalAddress name="foo">
     *               <Street>7658 Belbay</Street>
     *               <City>Houston</City>
     *               <State>TX</State>
     *               <PostalCode>77033</PostalCode>
     *               <Country isoCountryCode="US">United States</Country>
     *           </PostalAddress>
     *       </Address>
     *   </BillTo>
     */
    Element billTo = theDocument.createElement("BillTo");
    orderRequestHeader.appendChild(billTo);

    Element address = theDocument.createElement("Address");
    billTo.appendChild(address);

    Element addrName = theDocument.createElement("Name");
```

```
addrName.setAttribute("xml:lang", "en");
addrName.appendChild(theDocument.createTextNode("Belbay Associates"));
address.appendChild(addrName);

Element postal = theDocument.createElement("PostalAddress");
postal.setAttribute("name", "foo");
address.appendChild(postal);          // crazy child ;-)

buildPostalAddress(postal, "Street", "7658 Belbay");
buildPostalAddress(postal, "City", "Houston");
buildPostalAddress(postal, "State", "TX");
buildPostalAddress(postal, "PostalCode", "77033");

Element country = theDocument.createElement("Country");
country.setAttribute("isoCountryCode", "US");
country.appendChild(theDocument.createTextNode("United States"));
postal.appendChild(country);

/**
 *    <Shipping trackingDomain="FedEx" trackingId="9876543210">
 *        <Money currency="USD">7.50</Money>
 *        <Description xml:lang="en-us">FedEx 2-day</Description>
 *    </Shipping>
 */
Element shipping = theDocument.createElement("Shipping");
shipping.setAttribute("trackingDomain", "FedEx");
shipping.setAttribute("trackingId", "9876543210");
orderRequestHeader.appendChild(shipping);

Element shipMoney = theDocument.createElement("Money");
shipMoney.setAttribute("currency", "USD");
shipMoney.appendChild(theDocument.createTextNode("7.50"));
shipping.appendChild(shipMoney);

Element shipDesc = theDocument.createElement("Description");
shipDesc.setAttribute("xml:lang", "en-us");
shipDesc.appendChild(theDocument.createTextNode("FedEx 2-day"));
shipping.appendChild(shipDesc);

/**
 *    <Payment>
 *        <PCard number="98765430232" expiration="2002-12-12"/>
 *    </Payment>
 */
Element payment = theDocument.createElement("Payment");
orderRequestHeader.appendChild(payment);

Element pcard = theDocument.createElement("PCard");
pcard.setAttribute("number", "98765430232");
pcard.setAttribute("expiration", "2002-12-12");
payment.appendChild(pcard);

// end order request header

/**
```

```
 *     <ItemOut quantity="2" requestedDeliveryDate="2001-11-20">
 *        <ItemID>
 *            <SupplierPartID>455455</SupplierPartID>
 *        </ItemID>
 *     </ItemOut>
 */
    Element itemOut = theDocument.createElement("ItemOut");
    itemOut.setAttribute("quantity", "2");
    itemOut.setAttribute("requestedDeliveryDate", "2001-11-20");
    orderRequest.appendChild(itemOut);

    Element itemId = theDocument.createElement("ItemID");
    itemOut.appendChild(itemId);

    Element supplierPartId =
              theDocument.createElement("SupplierPartId");
    supplierPartId.appendChild(theDocument.createTextNode("455455"));
    itemId.appendChild(supplierPartId);

}

/**
 * Helper method for building the postal address
 */
protected void buildPostalAddress(Node postal, String name, String text) {

    Element theInfo = theDocument.createElement(name);
    theInfo.appendChild(theDocument.createTextNode(text));
    postal.appendChild(theInfo);
}

public Document getDocument() {
    return theDocument;
}
```

Finally, the main driver of the application is shown below. The `main()` method constructs an `OrderRequest` object and retrieves a reference to the root element. The `EzDomEcho` class is reused to display the actual document. This is accomplished by calling the `traverse()` method on the `EzDomEcho` instance and passing in a reference to the root element:

```
public static void main(String[] args) {

    try {
        // constuct an order request
        OrderRequest sampleOrderRequest = new OrderRequest();

        // get a reference to the document
        Document doc = sampleOrderRequest.getDocument();
        Node root = doc.getDocumentElement();

        // display the newly constructed document
        EzDomEcho echo = new EzDomEcho();
        echo.traverseTree(root);
    }
    catch (Exception exc) {
```

```
                    exc.printStackTrace();
            }
        }
    }
```

Running the Example

As usual, we're running this example from a directory of its own, which we mentioned earlier:
`c:\ProJavaEcomm\ch07\dom_demo_2`.

❑ Set the classpath environment variable to point to the Xerces JAR file as for the previous examples.

❑ Compile the code, and test the program by typing:

java OrderRequest

The program will construct a cXML Order Request document and display it.

Java API for XML Parsing (JAXP)

So far in this chapter, we have used the Apache Xerces parser. If we wanted to change to another XML parser implementation, then it would require modifications to our source code. It would be nice if we could develop source code that was independent of the low-level parser implementation. Sun Microsystems identified this problem and provided a solution: JAXP. JAXP is available as a free download from http://java.sun.com/xml.

> The code examples in this chapter use JAXP 1.1 Early Access, which supports DOM Level 2 and SAX 2.0.

JAXP provides an additional layer of abstraction for XML parser implementations. In particular, it provides a standard interface for creating an instance of the parser using a factory mechanism. Also, JAXP provides a standard mechanism for parsing the document with a given input source. This concept is very similar to the JDBC Driver API. Different database vendors implement the standard JDBC driver API. Application developers can then develop JDBC in a database independent fashion.

When we use JAXP, the XML parser implementation is not explicitly imported into the application. Instead, passing in a system property identifies the XML parser. To use a SAX based parser, we assign a value to the system property `javax.xml.parsers.SAXParserFactory`. Likewise, for a DOM based parser, we use the system property `javax.xml.parsers.DocumentBuilderFactory`. If a property value is not provided, then JAXP will use the default parser implementation provided by Sun Microsystems code named Crimson.

In order to take advantage of JAXP, an XML parser vendor implements the appropriate classes defined in JAXP. JAXP is defined in the package `javax.xml.parsers`. This package contains four abstract classes that are listed below:

Classes defined in `javax.xml.parsers`	Description
`SAXParserFactory`	Defines a factory API for configuring and obtaining a SAX parser
`SAXParser`	Defines an API for parsing XML documents; encapsulates `org.xml.sax.XMLReader`
`DocumentBuilderFactory`	Defines a factory API for configuring and obtaining a DOM parser
`DocumentBuilder`	Defines an API for parsing XML documents into a DOM object tree

Using SAX with JAXP

We can modify our existing SAX examples to use JAXP. The difference occurs when we create an instance of the SAX parser and actually perform the processing. The code snippet below shows how to create an instance of the parser using JAXP:

```
// Step 1:  create an instance of the SAX Parser Factory
SAXParserFactory factory = SAXParserFactory.newInstance();

// Step 2:  create an instance of the SAX Parser
SAXParser saxParser = factory.newSAXParser();

// Step 3:  Parse the XML document with the given content handler
saxParser.parse(theXmlRef, new EchoContentHandler());
```

First create an instance of the `SAXParserFactory`. The `SAXParserFactory` can create instances of a `SAXParser` based on the system property `javax.xml.parsers.SAXParserFactory`.

The `SAXParserFactory` is used to configure the `SAXParser`. For example, we can specify that the parser instances should perform validation by calling the `setValidating(true)` method on the `SAXParserFactory`.

Once we have a `SAXParserFactory` instance, we use it to create an instance of the `SAXParser`. The `SAXParser` class encapsulates the `org.xml.sax.XMLReader` class. The `SAXParser` instance actually parses the document. This is accomplished by calling the `parse()` method and passing in the XML document reference and the content handler. Remember that JAXP standardizes the way SAX parsers are created so no changes are required to the source code for the content handler.

The source code below is a revised example of the `EzSaxParse.java` that now uses JAXP:

```
import javax.xml.parsers.SAXParserFactory;
import javax.xml.parsers.SAXParser;
import javax.xml.parsers.ParserConfigurationException;
import org.xml.sax.SAXException;
import org.xml.sax.XMLReader;
```

179

```java
import java.io.IOException;

public class EzSaxParse {

    public static void main(String[] args) {

        // check usage
        if (args.length != 1) {
            System.out.println("Usage: java EzSaxParse <file or URL>");
            System.exit(1);
        }

        // get the name of the XML file or URL
        String theXmlRef = args[0];

        try {
            // Step 1:  create an instance of the SAX Parser Factory
            SAXParserFactory factory = SAXParserFactory.newInstance();

            // Step 2:  create an instance of the SAX Parser
            SAXParser saxParser = factory.newSAXParser();

            // Step 3:  Parse the XML document with the given handler
            saxParser.parse(theXmlRef, new EchoContentHandler());
        }
        catch (IOException exc) {
            exc.printStackTrace();
        }
        catch (SAXException exc) {
            exc.printStackTrace();
        }
        catch (ParserConfigurationException exc) {
            exc.printStackTrace();
        }
    }
}
```

Running the Example

Before we can compile and execute the examples, we need to properly configure the development environment.

❑ Download JAXP from http://java.sun.com/xml

❑ Extract the download

In the following steps, we use *jaxp_install_dir* to reference your root installation directory for JAXP. We're also assuming that the code has been saved in the directory `c:\ProJavaEcomm\ch07\jaxp_sax_demo`, from which we will run the example.

❑ Set the classpath environment variable to point to the following JAR files with the following one line command:

```
set classpath=.;jaxp_install_dir\jaxp.jar;jaxp_install_dir\crimson.jar;
    jaxp_install_dir\xalan.jar
```

❏   Compile the code, and then test it by typing:

```
java EzSaxParse catalog_1.xml
```

The program will execute as before, by displaying the contents of the sample cXML file, `catalog_1.xml`.

Using DOM with JAXP

We can also modify the DOM examples to use JAXP. As was the case with the SAX modifications, the DOM changes occur when we get an instance of the DOM parser. The snippet below shows the basic process:

```
// Step 1:  Create the factory
DocumentBuilderFactory factory = DocumentBuilderFactory.newInstance();

// Step 2:  Create the document builder
DocumentBuilder builder = factory.newDocumentBuilder();

// Step 3:  Parse the document
Document doc = builder.parse(theXmlRef);
```

We first get an instance of the `DocumentBuilderFactory`. The factory is used to create a new instance of a `DocumentBuilder` object. The `DocumentBuilder` object allows us to parse an XML input source and build a DOM object tree. Once the XML is parsed, the builder returns a `Document` object as defined in the `org.w3c.dom` package.

The source code below is a modified version of the `EzDomEcho.java` example. Please note that we are no longer importing the Apache Xerces parser, instead we are making use of JAXP. We can plug in a different DOM implementation by simply setting the system property `javax.xml.parsers.DocumentBuilderFactory`.

```
import javax.xml.parsers.DocumentBuilderFactory;
import javax.xml.parsers.DocumentBuilder;
import org.w3c.dom.Document;
import org.w3c.dom.Node;
import org.w3c.dom.NodeList;
import org.w3c.dom.NamedNodeMap;

public class EzDomEcho {

    public static void main(String[] args) {

        // check for correct usage
        if (args.length != 1) {
            System.out.println("Usage: java EzDomEcho <xml file>");
            System.exit(1);
        }

        // reference to the XML resource
        String theXmlRef = args[0];
```

```
    try {
        // Step 1:  Create the factory
        DocumentBuilderFactory factory =
                            DocumentBuilderFactory.newInstance();

        // Step 2:  Create the document builder
        DocumentBuilder builder = factory.newDocumentBuilder();

        // Step 3:  Parse the document
        Document doc = builder.parse(theXmlRef);

        // Retrieve the root node
        Node root = doc.getDocumentElement();
        root.normalize();

        EzDomEcho echo = new EzDomEcho();
        echo.traverseTree(root);
    }
    catch (Exception exc) {
        exc.printStackTrace();
    }
}

public void traverseTree(Node theNode) {
    // same code as the previous example
}

public void displayNodeAndAttributes(Node theNode) {
    // same code as the previous example
}
}
```

Running the Example

This sample runs very much like the previous sample, with the only difference being the command given to run it:

```
java EzDomEcho customer_mail_list.xml
```

Generating XML with JSP and Servlets

So far, we have discussed the programming requirements for parsing XML documents. The XML documents were already developed for us and saved as static files on the file system. However, data-driven XML applications are commonly based on information stored in a database. For enterprise applications the XML data may reside on a remote computer. For example, in a B2B application, Company A may need to retrieve customer information from Company B as an XML document. Another example is that Company A may need to retrieve an inventory list from Company B as an XML document.

There are a number of techniques for exchanging the XML data. We can transmit the XML data using low-level TCP/IP socket connections. This will require Company A and Company B to agree upon a custom low-level socket protocol. This will also require custom coding by the developers of the client and server programmers. Currently, the most common technique is to use HTTP to transmit XML documents. HTTP is a proven standards-based protocol that supports the desired request-response interaction.

On the server machine, we need a process that will handle the request and actually generate the XML document. This task can easily be accomplished using JSPs or servlets. JSPs and servlets are commonly used to generate HTML content. However, they are not limited to HTML. We can easily generate XML documents by simply setting the response content type to text/xml. Once the content type is set, the JSP/servlet generates the appropriate XML tags and data. If the incoming request depends on information stored in an enterprise information system such as a relational database, then the JSP/servlet submits an SQL query to the database. The JSP/servlet processes the result set and builds the desired XML document. The XML document is then returned to the client as part of the HTTP response. The application interaction is shown below:

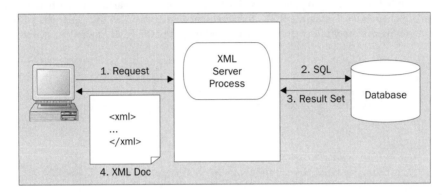

The architecture shown above uses the data access design pattern. The purpose of this is to provide an object, called a *data accessor*. The data accessor encapsulates the JDBC and SQL code. Clients simply access the data accessor through a standard interface to retrieve data. The clients are shielded from the details of the data source connections, database schema and database implementation. In fact, this approach simplifies application maintenance. If the backend databases are modified, then we simply have to update the data accessor and the clients will remain unchanged. This reinforces the concepts of abstraction and encapsulation.

Commercial products are available for generating XML documents based on database information. These products are labeled XML data servers. Database vendors have also taken notice of XML and are adding native XML support to their respective database servers. Below is a list of database vendors that provide XML data servers. Note that this list is just a snapshot; by the time you read this, the list may have doubled/tripled in size. Get the latest info at http://www.xml.com.

Product	Company	Website
SQL Server 2000	Microsoft	http://www.microsoft.com/xml
Oracle	Oracle	http://www.oracle.com/xml
DB2	IBM	http://www.ibm.com
others	*others*	http://www.xml.com

If your favorite database isn't on the list above, then you can use a third-party XML data server. These third-party products provide adapters that connect to many databases. Check out these products for more information:

Product	Company	Website
webMethod	webMethods	http://www.webmethods.com
excelon	Excelon Corp	http://www.exceloncorp.com

Simple JSP Example

Let's create a simple JSP example to generate XML. In this example, the actual data is defined in the JSP page; later in the chapter we'll integrate JDBC for accessing a database. The JSP generates an XML document containing customer information. The desired output of the XML document is shown below:

```
<customer_list>
    <customer>
        <customer_name> Larry Ro </customer_name>
        <customer_email> larryro@fiction.wrox.com</customer_email>
    </customer>

    <customer>
        <customer_name> Traci Lee </customer_name>
        <customer_email> tracilee@fiction.wrox.com </customer_email>
    </customer>

    <customer>
        <customer_name> Bub Franklin </customer_name>
        <customer_email> bub@fiction.wrox.com </customer_email>
    </customer>

    <customer>
        <customer_name> Sarah Powell </customer_name>
        <customer_email> sarahpowell@fiction.wrox.com </customer_email>
    </customer>
</customer_list>
```

The XML data is generated with the following JSP file, `customer_list.jsp`:

```
<%@ page contentType="text/xml" %>

<%
    String[][] data = {{"Larry Ro", "larryro@fiction.wrox.com"},
                       {"Traci Lee",  "tracilee@fiction.wrox.com"},
                       {"Bub Franklin", "bub@fiction.wrox.com"},
                       {"Sarah Powell", "sarahpowell@fiction.wrox.com"}};
%>

<customer_list>

<% for (int i=0; i < data.length; i++) { %>
    <customer>
        <customer_name> <%= data[i][0] %> </customer_name>
        <customer_email> <%= data[i][1] %> </customer_email>
    </customer>
<% } %>

</customer_list>
```

The most important line of the code example is:

```
<%@ page contentType="text/xml" %>
```

By default, JSP will send back the data as text/html. However, we are explicitly setting the context type to text/xml.

Next, the JSP page defines the customer data using a scriptlet. The data is defined as a two-dimensional array of strings. Later in the chapter, we'll use JDBC to access a database. For now, let's focus on the mechanics of generating XML.

The JSP page contains the XML template tags and scripting elements to generate the body content for the XML tags. The root element for the customer information is defined using the <customer_list> element. The JSP page then uses a for loop to process the data. For each data element, we build a <customer> element. This is accomplished with the code below:

```
<customer_list>

<% for (int i=0; i < data.length; i++) { %>
    <customer>
        <customer_name> <%= data[i][0] %> </customer_name>
        <customer_email> <%= data[i][1] %> </customer_email>
    </customer>
<%  }  %>

</customer_list>
```

We can access the JSP page with an XML-enabled web browser. For example, Microsoft Internet Explorer 5.x has support for viewing XML documents.

Microsoft Internet Explorer 5.x can easily render XML data. It uses a default style sheet to display the contents of the XML document. Older versions of Netscape Navigator (4.x) do not have client-side support for XML. However, the new version of Netscape Navigator version 6 provides XML support. For now, don't worry about the browser support for XML. Later in this chapter, we'll implement a server-side design pattern for processing XML data on the server. Also, we'll learn how to use another XML technology called XSL to convert the XML data to HTML.

Running the Example

A JSP/servlet container is required to test the JSP and servlet demos in this section. The servlet container should support JSP 1.1 and Servlet 2.2. In this section, we will use the Tomcat server available from http://jakarta.apache.org. This is a good choice since Tomcat is the official reference implementation for the JSP and Servlet specification.

The following directions assume that you have already downloaded and installed Tomcat. I'll refer to the Tomcat installation directory as *tomcat_install_dir*.

❑   Assuming you've downloaded the code from www.wrox.com, make sure you have the following files (the second one can be found in Appendix C):

```
c:\ProJavaEcomm\ch07\webapp\customer_list.jsp
```

```
c:\ProJavaEcomm\ch07\webapp\WEB-INF\web.xml
```

❏   Edit the Tomcat specific file located at:

```
tomcat_install_dir\conf\server.xml
```

❏   Near the bottom of the file, add the following entry:

```
<Context path="/ch07demo" docBase="c:\ProJavaEcomm\ch07\webapp"
                debug="0" reloadable="true" >
</Context>
```

This defines a named web application for these demos. When you access your web server, simply give http://localhost:8080/ch07demo.

❏   Restart the Tomcat server

❏   Start up your web browser and open the following URL:

http://localhost:8080/ch07demo/customer_list.jsp

The browser should resemble the screen shot below:

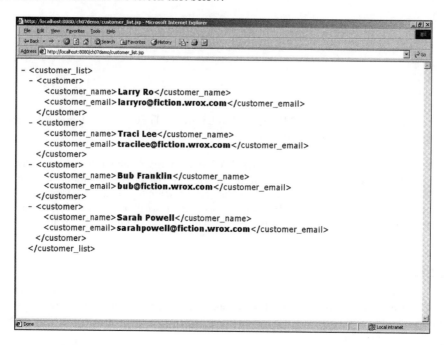

Generating cXML with Servlets, JSP and JDBC

In this section, we'll generate a cXML document using servlets, JSP and JDBC. We'll generate a cXML catalog document. Recall from our earlier discussion that cXML catalogs describe the product inventory. This description includes product ids, prices, and shipping details such as lead-time. A sample cXML document is shown below:

```
<?xml version="1.0" ?>
<!DOCTYPE Index SYSTEM "http://xml.cXML.org/schemas/cXML/1.1.009/cXML.dtd">
```

```
<Index>
  <SupplierID domain="DUNS">12-123-1234</SupplierID>
  <IndexItem>
    <IndexItemAdd>
      <ItemID>
        <SupplierPartID>auto-98765</SupplierPartID>
      </ItemID>
      <ItemDetail>
        <UnitPrice>
          <Money currency="USD">8000</Money>
        </UnitPrice>
        <Description xml:lang="en">Honda Civic del Sol</Description>
        <UnitOfMeasure/>
        <Classification domain="year">1993</Classification>
        <ManufacturerPartID>honda-12345</ManufacturerPartID>
        <ManufacturerName>Honda</ManufacturerName>
      </ItemDetail>
      <IndexItemDetail>
        <LeadTime>7</LeadTime>
        <ExpirationDate>2001-09-01</ExpirationDate>
        <EffectiveDate>2001-01-01</EffectiveDate>
      </IndexItemDetail>
    </IndexItemAdd>
  </IndexItem>
</Index>
```

The cXML catalog will be generated dynamically by a servlet. The servlet will accept the initial request and submit an SQL query to the database using JDBC. The servlet will then process the result set and pass the data to a JSP. The JSP will retrieve the data passed by the servlet and generate a cXML catalog document. The application interaction is shown below:

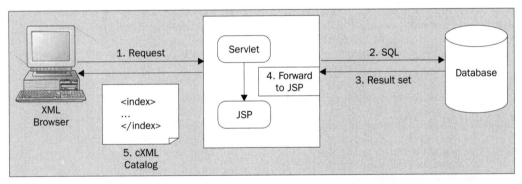

Our database table contains the product information. The table has the following database schema:

Table Name: Cars	
Column Name	**Type**
id	INTEGER
supplier_id	VARCHAR2 / TEXT

table continued on following page

Table Name: Cars	
supplier_part_id	VARCHAR2 / TEXT
price	INTEGER
description	VARCHAR2 / TEXT
year	INTEGER
manufacturer_part_id	VARCHAR2 / TEXT
manufacturer_name	VARCHAR2 / TEXT

You can create this table using your favorite database engine. However, in this chapter, we'll use an MS-Access database. The MS-Access database is available in the downloaded archive from www.wrox.com. It is installed in the directory c:\ProJavaEcomm\ch07\data\cars.mdb.

The application is composed of the following files:

File	Description
IndexItem.java	Value object that represents the data for an item.
CarsCatalogServlet.java	Handles the initial request and submits the SQL to the database. Converts the result set into an ArrayList of IndexItem objects. Then forwards the ArrayList to build_catalog.jsp.
build_catalog_data.jsp	Handles the construction of the cXML catalog.

Let's examine the source code for IndexItem.java. The IndexItem class serves as a data structure for a given IndexItem in the catalog. Recall that an IndexItem is basically an item in our inventory.

```java
package nature;

/**
 *  This class represents an IndexItem for a cXML catalog
 */
public class IndexItem implements java.io.Serializable {

    private String supplierId;
    private String supplierPartId;
    private double price;
    private String description;
    private int year;
    private String manufacturerPartId;
    private String manufacturerName;

    public IndexItem() {

    }
```

```
    public IndexItem(String theSupplierId, String theSupplierPartId,
                     double thePrice, String theDescription,
                     int theYear, String theManufacturerPartId,
                     String theManufacturerName)  {

        supplierId = theSupplierId;
        supplierPartId = theSupplierPartId;
        price = thePrice;
        description = theDescription;
        year = theYear;
        manufacturerPartId = theManufacturerPartId;
        manufacturerName = theManufacturerName;
    }

    public String getSupplierId() {
        return supplierId;
    }

    public String getSupplierPartId() {
        return supplierPartId;
    }

    public double getPrice() {
        return price;
    }

    public String getDescription() {
        return description;
    }

    public int getYear() {
        return year;
    }

    public String getManufacturerPartId() {
        return manufacturerPartId;
    }

    public String getManufacturerName() {
        return manufacturerName;
    }
}
```

We will use a servlet to generate the cars catalog by connecting to a database. Before we discuss the source code for the servlet, let's examine database configuration information. Servlet parameters are used to configure the database configuration. The parameters are actually stored in the application deployment descriptor file located at c:\ProJavaEcomm\ch07\webapp\WEB-INF\web.xml. The deployment descriptor contains the following parameters:

```
<web-app>
...
    <servlet>
        <servlet-name>CarsCatalogServlet</servlet-name>
        <servlet-class>nature.CarsCatalogServlet</servlet-class>
        <init-param>
```

```
            <param-name>dbUrl</param-name>
            <param-value>jdbc:odbc:CarsDSN</param-value>
            <description>JDBC database URL</description>
        </init-param>
        <init-param>
            <param-name>dbDriver</param-name>
            <param-value>sun.jdbc.odbc.JdbcOdbcDriver</param-value>
            <description>JDBC Driver name</description>
        </init-param>
        <init-param>
            <param-name>user</param-name>
            <param-value>test</param-value>
            <description>User ID for database</description>
        </init-param>
        <init-param>
            <param-name>pass</param-name>
            <param-value>test</param-value>
            <description>Password for database</description>
        </init-param>
    </servlet>

    <servlet-mapping>
        <servlet-name>CarsCatalogServlet</servlet-name>
        <url-pattern>/cars_catalog</url-pattern>
    </servlet-mapping>
</web-app>
```

If you are using a different database engine then you will need to update the parameters accordingly.

The CarsCatalogServlet performs the following actions:

❑ Submits the SQL to the database using JDBC

❑ Processes the result set and creates an ArrayList of IndexItem objects

❑ Forwards the ArrayList to build_catalog_data.jsp

```
package nature;

import java.io.*;
import java.sql.*;
import java.util.ArrayList;
import javax.servlet.*;
import javax.servlet.http.*;

public class CarsCatalogServlet extends HttpServlet {

    private Connection myConn;

    public void init() throws ServletException {

        String dbUrl = getInitParameter("dbUrl");
        String dbDriver = getInitParameter("dbDriver");
        String user = getInitParameter("user");
```

```
        String pass = getInitParameter("pass");

        try {
            // Load the driver
            log("Loading driver: " + dbDriver);
            Class.forName(dbDriver);

            // Get a connection
            log("Getting connection to: " + dbUrl);
            log("User id = " + user);
            myConn  = DriverManager.getConnection(dbUrl, user, pass);

            log("Connection successful!");

        }
        catch (Exception exc) {
            log(exc.toString());
            throw new ServletException(exc.getMessage());
        }
    }
```

In the `init()` method, the servlet retrieves the parameters for the database configuration. As mentioned earlier, the database configuration is stored as servlet parameters in the `web.xml` file. Using this information, the servlet loads the JDBC driver and makes a connection to the database.

In the `doGet()` method below, the servlet builds a query based on the request parameter: `manufacturer_name`. Once the servlet retrieves the result set it then creates an `ArrayList` of `IndexItem` objects. It then sets attributes on the request object. This will allow the JSP page to retrieve the data from the request object. The servlet then sends data to `build_catalog_data.jsp`.

Let's examine this process, step-by-step...

The code below builds the SQL statement based on HTML form. The basic SQL is:

```
SELECT * from cars
```

If the HTML form field for `manufacturer_name` is provided, then it is used in the WHERE clause for the query, such as:

```
SELECT * from cars WHERE manufacturer_name = '…'
```

The SQL is then executed and the results are returned:

```
    public void doGet (HttpServletRequest request,
                        HttpServletResponse response)
        throws ServletException, IOException {

        try {
            //  Build the SQL query
            String searchByName =
                        request.getParameter("manufacturer_name");
            String carSql = "SELECT * from cars";
            if ((searchByName != null) &&
```

```
                        !(searchByName.equals("All"))) {
              carSql += " WHERE manufacturer_name = '"
                    + searchByName + "'";
    }

    // Execute SQL query
    Statement myStmt = myConn.createStatement();
    ResultSet myRs = myStmt.executeQuery(carSql);
```

The next block of code processes the result set. The result set is used to build an `ArrayList` of `IndexItem` objects:

```
    String supplierId = null;
    String supplierPartId = null;
             String description = null;
             String manufacturerPartId = null;
    String manufacturerName = null;
    double price;
    int year;

    IndexItem temp;
    ArrayList carList = new ArrayList();

    // Build an ArrayList of IndexItem objects
    while (myRs.next()) {
        // Retrieve data from the result set
        supplierId = myRs.getString("supplier_id");
        supplierPartId =
               myRs.getString("supplier_part_id");
        price = myRs.getDouble("price");
        description = myRs.getString("description");
        year = myRs.getInt("year");
        manufacturerPartId =
            myRs.getString("manufacturer_part_id");
        manufacturerName =
            myRs.getString("manufacturer_name");

        // Create an IndexItem object
        temp = new IndexItem(supplierId, supplierPartId,
                price, description, year,
                manufacturerPartId, manufacturerName);

        // Add the IndexObject to the ArrayList
        carList.add(temp);
    }

    myRs.close();
    myStmt.close();
```

Next, the servlet code performs the required steps to pass the data to the JSP. This is accomplished by setting attributes in the `request` object for the actual car list data and the supplier id. Then, a request dispatcher is retrieved from the `ServletContext`. Finally, the dispatcher is used to forward the `request` and `response` objects over to the `build_catalog_data.jsp`:

```
                // Set attributes for the JSP to access
                request.setAttribute("data", carList);
                request.setAttribute("supplierId", supplierId);

                // Get a request dispatcher and forward to JSP
                ServletContext context = getServletContext();
                RequestDispatcher dispatcher =
                context.getRequestDispatcher("/build_catalog_data.jsp");
                dispatcher.forward(request, response);
        }
        catch (Exception exc) {
                log("Oops, an error occurred: " + exc.toString());
        }
    }
}
```

The code for `build_catalog_data.jsp` is shown below. This JSP retrieves data from the `request` object and constructs a cXML catalog. The JSP contains the basic template for a cXML catalog and it uses JSP scripting elements to populate the template with dynamic data.

```
<%@ page contentType="text/xml" %>
<%@ page import="java.util.*,nature.*" %>

<?xml version="1.0" ?>
<!DOCTYPE Index SYSTEM "http://xml.cXML.org/schemas/cXML/1.1.009/cXML.dtd">

<%
    ArrayList data = (ArrayList) request.getAttribute("data");
    String supplierId = (String) request.getAttribute("supplierId");
    Iterator myIterator = data.iterator();
%>

<Index>
  <SupplierID domain="DUNS"> <%= supplierId %> </SupplierID>
  <IndexItem>

<%
    IndexItem tempItem = null;
    while (myIterator.hasNext()) {
        tempItem = (IndexItem) myIterator.next();
%>
    <IndexItemAdd>
        <ItemID>
            <SupplierPartID>
                <%= tempItem.getSupplierPartId() %>
            </SupplierPartID>
        </ItemID>
        <ItemDetail>
            <UnitPrice>
                <Money currency="USD">
                    <%= tempItem.getPrice() %>
                </Money>
            </UnitPrice>
            <Description xml:lang="en">
                <%= tempItem.getDescription() %>
            </Description>
            <UnitOfMeasure/>
            <Classification domain="year">
                <%= tempItem.getYear() %>
            </Classification>
```

```
            <ManufacturerPartID>
                <%= tempItem.getManufacturerPartId() %>
            </ManufacturerPartID>
            <ManufacturerName>
                <%= tempItem.getManufacturerName() %>
            </ManufacturerName>
        </ItemDetail>
        <IndexItemDetail>
            <LeadTime>7</LeadTime>
            <ExpirationDate>2001-09-01</ExpirationDate>
            <EffectiveDate>2001-01-01</EffectiveDate>
        </IndexItemDetail>
    </IndexItemAdd>

<%
    }    // end while loop
%>
  </IndexItem>
</Index>
```

Running The Example

This example requires a database. An MS-Access database is available in the download archive from www.wrox.com. It is installed in the directory c:\ProJavaEcomm\ch07\data\cars.mdb. You will need to set up an ODBC DSN called CarsDSN. If you choose to use a different ODBC DSN then you will need to make the appropriate changes to the web.xml and restart the Tomcat server.

If you are not using MS-Access, then create a table using the database schema presented earlier in this section. You will need to make the appropriate changes to web.xml for database configuration.

❑   Start the MS Internet Explorer browser.

❑   Visit the URL http://localhost:8080/ch07demo/test_form.html.

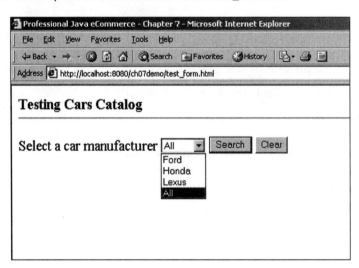

❑   Select a manufacturer and press the Search button. You should receive a cXML catalog similar to the one below:

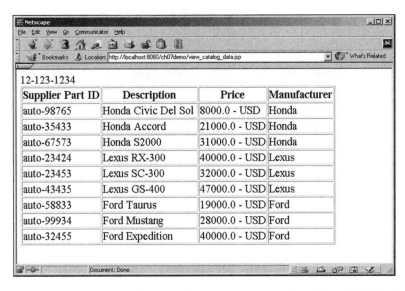

As you can see, we can generate cXML catalog documents using servlets, JSP and JDBC. The servlet accessed the database and retrieved the data. The JSP page was responsible for constructing the cXML catalog with the data provided by the servlet.

In the next section, we'll learn how to convert XML data to HTML.

Transforming XML Data with XSLT

XSL is the extensible style sheet language that is composed of two independent languages:

❑ Formatting Object Language (XSL-FO)

❑ Transformation Language (XSLT)

The Formatting Object language describes how content should be rendered. XSL-FO is a sophisticated version of Cascading Style Sheets (CSS). Using XSL-FO, we can define the formatting style for element tags such as `<H1>`, `<font>`, and `<p>`. XSL-FO APIs are also available that can convert an XML document to a PDF file. For more information on the PDF conversion check out the Apache project XSL-FOP at http://xml.apache.org.

The Transformation language (XSLT) is growing in popularity among XML developers. XSLT defines constructs for converting/transforming XML documents into other text-based formats. We can convert an XML document that follows a specific DTD to another XML document schema. In this section, we'll use XSLT to convert XML documents to HTML.

If you need a general introduction to XSLT then see Appendix B at the back of the book or, for more in-depth coverage, see XSLT Programmer's Reference (ISBN 1-861003-12-9).

The XSLT transformation is composed of three key players:

❑ Source XML Document

- ❏ XSLT Style Sheet
- ❏ XSLT Processor

The XSLT style sheet contains a template and XSL conversion rules. The XML document and XSLT style sheet are passed into an XSLT processor. The processor applies the XSLT style sheet to the XML document and outputs the result. The application interaction is shown below:

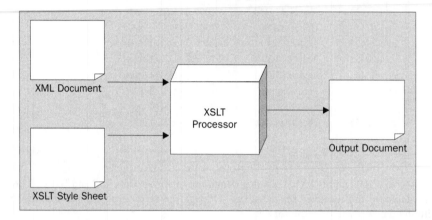

In our example, we want to convert the cXML catalog for cars into an HTML table as shown below:

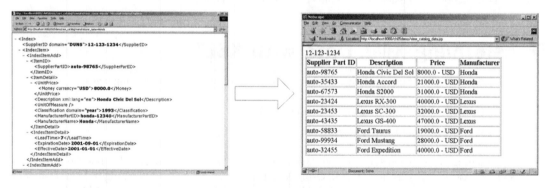

To accomplish our task, we have to first define an XSLT style sheet. The style sheet contains the HTML template code for the table and the conversion rules to retrieve the data. The desired stylesheet, `cars_list.xsl`, is shown below:

```xml
<?xml version="1.0"?>
<xsl:stylesheet xmlns:xsl="http://www.w3.org/1999/XSL/Transform"
                version="1.0">

<xsl:output method="html"/>

<xsl:template match="/Index/IndexItem">

<html><body>

<table border="1">
    <tr>
```

```
            <th>Supplier Part ID</th>
            <th>Description</th>
            <th>Price</th>
            <th>Manufacturer</th>
        </tr>

    <xsl:for-each select="IndexItemAdd">
        <tr>
            <td>
                <xsl:value-of select="ItemID/SupplierPartID"/>
            </td>
            <td>
                <xsl:value-of select="ItemDetail/Description"/>
            </td>
            <td>
                <xsl:value-of select="ItemDetail/UnitPrice/Money"/> -
                <xsl:value-of
                    select="ItemDetail/UnitPrice/Money/@currency"/>
            </td>
            <td>
                <xsl:value-of select="ItemDetail/ManufacturerName"/>
            </td>
        </tr>
    </xsl:for-each>

</table>

</body></html>

</xsl:template>
</xsl:stylesheet>
```

In this style sheet, we define the HTML template code for the table. The style sheet uses an XSL construct for looping over each `IndexItemAdd` element.

```
<xsl:for-each select="IndexItemAdd">
    ... ...
</xsl:for-each>
```

As we process each `IndexItemAdd` element, we need to retrieve data nested inside of the element. This is accomplished by using an XPath query of the form:

```
<xsl:value-of select="ItemID/SupplierPartID"/>
```

This fragment will retrieve the `SupplierPartID`, which is a sub-element of `ItemID`. In the stylesheet, we repeat the use of the `<xsl:value-of select=.../>` construct for the additional elements.

Now that we have the XSL style sheet defined, we need an XSLT processor to perform the transformation.

> **We'll use the Apache Xalan XSLT processor that is available at http://xml.apache.org. This code example uses Apache Xalan version 1.1.**

197

In this example, we will implement a server-side design pattern for transformation. We'll develop a JSP page that will retrieve the XML data and style sheet. The JSP page will then create an instance of the Apache Xalan XSLT processor. The application interaction is shown below:

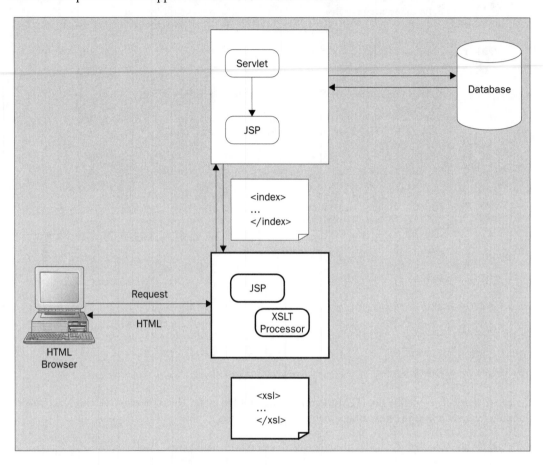

The code for `view_catalog_data.jsp` is shown below:

```
<%@ page import="org.apache.xalan.xslt.*" errorPage="oops.jsp" %>

<%
    // Step 1.  Determine the manufacturer name
    String manufacturerName =
request.getParameter("manufacturer_name");

    if (manufacturerName == null) {
        manufacturerName = "All";
    }

    // Step 2.  Create the processor
    XSLTProcessor myProcessor = XSLTProcessorFactory.getProcessor();

    // Step 3.  Setup the XML input and the XSL input
    XSLTInputSource xmlSource = new
```

```
         XSLTInputSource("http://localhost:8080/ch07demo/cars_catalog?" +
                 "manufacturer_name=" + manufacturerName);

         XSLTInputSource xslStylesheet = new
             XSLTInputSource("http://localhost:8080/ch07demo/cars_list.xsl");

         // Step 4.  Setup the target...let's use the "out" object to send it
         //               back to client
         XSLTResultTarget xmlOutput = new XSLTResultTarget(out);

         // Step 5.  Now let's process the files
         myProcessor.process(xmlSource, xslStylesheet, xmlOutput);
%>
```

Since the JSP page is using the Apache Xalan XSLT processor, an `import` statement is used at the beginning.

The first step is to determine if the manufacturer name was passed with the HTTP request. If not, then the manufacturer name is set to "All" to retrieve a list of all cars.

In the second step, we get an instance of the Apache Xalan XSLT processor.

Next, we set up the XML input source. The input source could be a static XML document. However, in this example, we will connect to the `CarsCatalogServlet` that we created earlier. Recall this servlet has the URL mapping of `cars_catalog` as defined in the `web.xml` file. The servlet accesses the database and retrieves a cXML catalog containing the cars for the given manufacturer name. We also set up a reference to the XSL style sheet that we created, `cars_list.xsl`.

In the fourth step, we create an output source for the XSL transformation. We'll use the JSP predefined object, `out`.

In the final step, we call the process method on the XSLT processor instance. The process method accepts the parameters for the XML input source, XSL style sheet and the XML output. The XSLT processor will send the converted data to the `out` object, which will return the data to the web browser.

The important feature of this example is that the result of the transformation is an HTML document. The HTML document can be viewed in either Internet Explorer or Netscape. Remember earlier in the chapter, the examples required an XML compliant web browser. By performing the XML conversion on the server side, we've created an application that is browser independent.

Running the Example

This example requires the Apache Xalan classes. Xalan can be downloaded from http://xml.apache.org/xalan/index.html. Once downloaded, extract to your file system.

❑   Add the Apache Xalan classes to Tomcat's class path. Edit the file `tomcat_install_dir\bin\tomcat.bat`. Add the following entries:

   `set CLASSPATH=%CLASSPATH%;xalan_install_dir\lib\xerces.jar`

   `set CLASSPATH=%CLASSPATH%;xalan_install_dir\lib\xalan.jar`

   Replace `xalan_install_dir` with the directory where you installed Xalan.

- ❏ Restart the Tomcat server
- ❏ Open any web browser: MS Internet Explorer or Netscape Communicator
- ❏ Visit the URL: http://localhost:8080/ch07demo/view_catalog_data.jsp

Your browser should resemble the screen shot below:

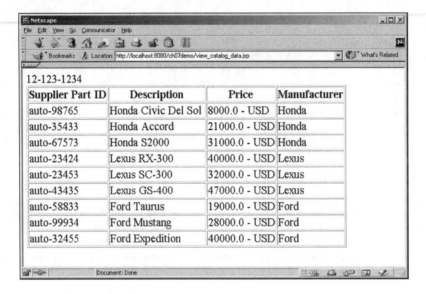

Summary

This chapter covered the Java programming details for processing XML documents using the SAX API. The chapter integrated the SAX and JavaMail APIs to send e-mail messages based on an XML data file.

We explored the use of the DOM API, including coding examples where DOM objects are created based on existing XML input sources. Examples were also shown where a DOM object was created from scratch and validated.

The chapter also discussed the process for generating XML content with JDBC, JSP and servlets. The coding examples created a cXML catalog for a company based on information stored in a relational database. Servlets used JDBC in conjunction with JSP to dynamically generate the cXML document.

The final section of the chapter discussed data transformation with XSLT. Coding examples were presented on how to convert XML data to HTML content.

PROFESSIONALJAVAE-COMMERCE

8

Security

This chapter is intended to provide a basic introduction into the many possible aspects of securing an e-commerce system operating on the Java platform. The goal is not to provide an exhaustive discussion of all topics, but to give a good overview of the basic concepts and terminology of the area. Remember, security should not be an after-thought in a project; it must be part of the design from the beginning to the end, at every layer and every tier.

Security is a vast and specialized topic. To fully understand the security implications of hosting an e-commerce application, the limitations of the language, the data transmission methods being used, and the issues surrounding the software (the application, the application server, and the operating system on which the system runs) must all be taken into account. Of course, we mustn't forget that the most robust software security available won't keep an e-commerce site up and running if the servers themselves aren't physically secure from vandals or thieves.

Here, we're going to restrict ourselves to just looking at application aspects of security – the basic Java security model, basic cryptographic principles extending into a discussion of authentication and secure data transmission, and finally some server-side security topics.

So, our path through the chapter is as follows:

❑ An introduction to security concepts – how systems can be compromised and basic approaches to securing them

❑ A brief overview of cryptography and its application within the computing world

❑ The underlying Java security model and the available extensions to it

❑ Coverage of the business protocol **Secure Electronic Transactions** (**SET**)

❑ A look at authentication and authorization outside SSL and SET

❑ Server side security issues such as data security, EJB security, and site security

❑ A brief overview of firewalls and how they can be used to provide security features

In this chapter we'll be making use of the **Java Secure Socket Extension (JSSE)**, **Java Authentication and Authorization Service (JAAS)**, and the **Java Cryptography Extension (JCE)** as well as the J2SE and J2EE all of which are available from http://java.sun.com.

Considering Security Concepts

To put the technical details of the chapter in context let's start by looking at the different ways in which computer systems can be compromised by remote (software) attack. Such attacks can result in a loss or slowdown of network services, a loss of data (or data integrity), a loss of confidentiality, and, in the worst instance, an inability to trade. Indeed, a well-publicized breach of security will undermine customer confidence and reduce business. Following on from this, we'll look at various standard approaches to making successful attacks more difficult to achieve.

Security Attacks

A breach of security is obviously something that you need to prevent in order to do business. However, there are many people out there who will attempt to hack their way into your systems either for profit or even for fun in some cases. We will refer to these persons as **adversaries**. These adversaries can attack your system in a number of ways. In this section we'll look at:

❑ Replay attacks

❑ Man in the middle (MITM) attacks

❑ Denial of Service (DoS) attacks

❑ Viruses

We'll take a look at each of these in turn, before we start to discuss some methods of defending against them.

Replay Attacks

This type of attack occurs when a user submits data to a remote computer and an adversary attempts to record the conversation to be replayed at a later date. For example, if a user logs on to an Internet bank account using their user ID and password combination, the adversary could attempt to record the request/response transaction. At a later date, the authentication transaction could be replayed back to the server and the adversary could gain access to the user's bank account. While the replay attack will not allow the adversary to perform arbitrary operations, they can still cause serious problems.

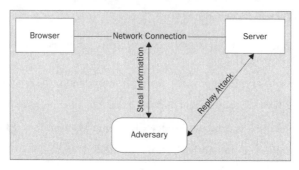

Man in the Middle (MITM)

MITM attacks predate the digital era – for instance, unscrupulous restaurant waiters have long been able to overcharge customers, pay the appropriate amount into the till, and keep the extra for themselves. This logic extends to the Web. Imagine browsing an online site and, at checkout time, submitting your credit card details. If these details end up going to a compromised server, which returns a fake confirmation response, you may find your credit card debited for the purchase while the genuine store won't have a record of the purchase.

So how can this occur? Normally, the user communicates via their browser with the site using a valid proxy server. In an MITM attack a malicious server will take this information from the user instead. This server then has all of the information that the authentic server would have received – personal details, credit card authorization details and suchlike.

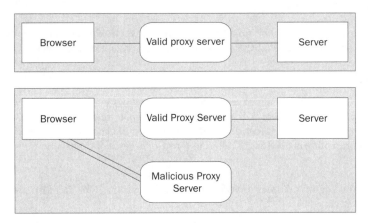

Denial of Service (DoS)

DoS attacks are aimed at devices and networks. The goal is to cripple a device or network so that external users no longer have access to your network resources. Without hacking password files or stealing sensitive data, a denial-of-service hacker simply starts a process that will generate enough traffic to your site that it denies service to the site's legitimate users. Here, of course, there is a physical angle to the problem – unplugging the network connection from a computer achieves a simple DoS attack.

DoS attacks are not always as simple as generating too much traffic or creating a physical DoS attack. Exploiting known problems in vendors' TCP/IP implementations can also cause them.

If you are working on operating systems such as Linux where the source code is available. You may find yourself constantly updating software and reconfiguring hardware more often because the hackers will have access to the same source code that you do.

Take a look at http://www.doshelp.com/ for more information on DoS attacks.

Viruses

Finally, one of the most well known forms of computer attacks is the multitude of viruses that exist in the digital universe. Some of the most recent viruses use the ever-present e-mail systems to spread their infestation to other systems. One of the most publicized viruses was the "I love you" virus, which used Microsoft's popular VB script language to bring systems to their knees. It is recommended that an anti virus software package is installed. Although anti virus software can't guard against all viruses, it is a good start.

Now that we're aware of some of the various types of attack, what types of approaches may be taken to frustrate them?

Defending Against Attacks

In this section we will attempt to create a guide for how to approach security. We'll begin by considering the basic ways in which security can be implemented, and move from this into a more theoretical discussion of the techniques. To begin with, we'll look at three main areas:

❑   Access control

❑   Authentication

❑   Privacy and data integrity

These three are the basic solutions behind all security problems. Looking at them one-by-one, we'll see that they can be used to help prevent all of the attacks mentioned above if used correctly.

Access Control

The first and most fundamental area is access control, which allows you to determine who has (and who shouldn't have) access to your system. For example, if you are planning on having a user login, with content restricted to certain users, you need to understand each method of access control and decide which works best in your situation. Following is a list of different forms of access controls techniques and where they are normally used:

❑   **Anonymous Logon** – Allows anyone to access the system. This can also apply to FTP and HTTP servers.

❑   **Basic Authentication** – Requires a user ID and password. This method is not very secure because the data, username and passwords are sent across the wire as clear text or base 64 encoded (which we'll discuss later). However, this form of authentication is still useful for some sites, such as those that might only require users to login in order to count the number of registered users.

❑   **Digest Authentication** – Similar to Basic authentication, but the password is not sent over the wire. Instead a hashed version of the password is created and sent to the server. Hashing is a technique for converting an input into an approximate random number. This means that for each input every output should be equally likely.

❑   **TCP/IP Addresses**– This allows you to restrict users based upon the IP address or domain from where the request originated. However, if your users are using a proxy server, all requests will originate from the same IP address. Also, if a dynamic host configuration protocol (DCHP) server is being used, a user may get a different IP address each time a user connects to the network, so this method may not be very reliable in determining who the user is.

❑   **Authorization Methods Specific to the J2EE Environment** – We will discuss these later on in the chapter when we talk about the Java-specific security implementations.

At the highest-level, access control is fairly simple. The server takes a request, goes through a series of checks, and then denies or grants access based on the results. If verification fails at any point along the way, access is immediately denied.

One example of such an access control method is useful for avoiding replay attacks. The basic principle is for each message to include a random non-repeating number, called a **random nonce**. Each party in the communication keeps a list of all the nonces that have been used, and rejects transactions with duplicate nonces. While effective, this method is expensive to implement, since it requires an unbounded amount of storage on both the server, as well as an unbounded amount of time to search the previous-nonce list for each request.

Authentication and Authorization

Authentication is needed to ensure that the parties involved in a communication process are who they say they are. Authorization deals with what those parties are permitted to do. We will discuss authentication and authorization in more detail in the sections dealing with JAAS and J2EE.

For example, a remote process connects to a server and says: "I am Bob and I want to delete the file `allAccounts.xls`." The server must answer two important questions prior to giving Bob the ability to carry out the request:

❑ Is this process actually controlled by Bob (so can we authenticate Bob?)?

❑ Is Bob allowed to delete the file `allAccounts.xls` (is Bob authorized to do this?)?

Only after both questions have been positively answered can the action of allowing Bob to delete the file take place. In this scenario, the most important question is whether or not this is really Bob. If it is Bob, then it will be a simple matter of looking up what Bob is allowed to do in an **access control list** (**ACL**). We will have a more in-depth discussion about access control a little later in the chapter.

Over the course of the chapter we'll look at several different aspects of authentication:

❑ **Client Certificates** – When we look at cryptography and **Public Key Encryption (PKE)** we'll encounter the use of digital certificates for authentication.

❑ **Public Key Infrastructure (PKI)** – We'll also cover the question of confirming that your keys have been issued by the body that you believe to have issued them during our discussion of certificates.

❑ **HTTP Authentication** – During the discussion of web servers we will talk more about relying on them to verify the users.

❑ **J2EE Authentication** – The various J2EE authentication techniques will also be discussed later in this chapter when we talk about EJBs and servlets.

Privacy and Data Integrity

Privacy techniques ensure that nobody else has access to your secure communication. Data integrity methods help to ensure that the data you send is the data your user receives. Financial transactions are an area illustrating the risks of corrupted data or malicious alteration. If you purchase something, you want to make sure that the amount hasn't been altered, either maliciously or through an error caused by a system going down before the transaction was completed. Some of the more common techniques used for this are:

❑ **Encryption** – Encryption is the general term used for setting up a secure channel. To set up a secure channel, you generally need a valid server certificate. You can either make your own or request one through a third-party certificate authority. You can also encrypt the data stored in the database using various tools such as the Java Cryptography Architecture.

❏ **Secure Sockets Layer (SSL)** – This is a specific protocol used to provide a secure channel between two endpoints. SSL has the ability to protect data in transit and to identify the machine that is being communicated with.

❏ **Private Communication Technology (PCT)** – This has very good security properties and was backward compatible with SSLv2.

❏ **Transport Layer Security (TLS)** – TLS is a protocol used primarily in messaging applications using Simple Mail Transfer Protocol (SMTP). The Internet Engineering Task Force (IETF) created this protocol in 1996. The goal was to bring together approaches created by Microsoft and Netscape.

This brings us onto the topic of **non-repudiation**.

Non-repudiation

Before we talk more about security, we need to understand some terminology. You have undoubtedly heard the term **non-repudiation** quite frequently in discussions of security. What this means is:

❏ The ability to determine if the data has been altered. This can be accomplished through a service that provides proof of the veracity and origin of data. This integrity needs to be seen as an unforgeable bond, which can be verified by any third party at any time.

❏ An authentication that assures it is genuine, and that cannot subsequently be denied.

When we talk about non-repudiation we must also talk about **digital signatures.** The term is sometimes used incorrectly. The term actually means using your **private key** to sign a message. As we'll discuss in the next section on cryptography, the receiver would need to use your **public key** to decrypt the message. This in itself is a form of non-repudiation, so long as your private key has not been compromised.

In short, security needs to be fundamental to whatever system you're designing and needs, in a distributed environment, to be end-to-end. Over the course of this chapter we'll be spending a lot of time looking at how we can control who has access to an application, how much access they have, how they can communicate with the application securely and how to defend our application against attack. First, however we'll start by having a look at cryptography and how it works.

Basic Cryptographic Concepts

Cryptography is the science (or art in some cases) of writing and solving **ciphers.** A cipher is an algorithm that can be used to convert **plaintext** (readable text) into an encoded (or encrypted) form usually referred to as **ciphertext**.

Cryptography can be of great help to us in building a secure private system, so that even if the system is compromised the data cannot be easily accessed. For example disguising the data in an e-mail message, or data packet, will make it harder to read even if intercepted on its passage across a network. Similarly encrypting data on a hard disk will render it hard to analyze even if stolen and the files accessed.

We're going to start this section by looking at what a cipher is, different types of cipher, and certificates before seeing how these techniques can be used in authentication.

Ciphers

Using a very simple cipher (the Caesar cipher) we can encrypt the readable text (the plaintext):

Mary had a little lamb

into the more unreadable ciphertext:

Nbsz ibe b mjuumf mbnc

Quite obviously the encryption routine is simply based on mapping one letter of the alphabet onto another letter – in the Caesar cipher two alphabets are lined up alongside each other, but offset, and the **key** to the cipher is the degree to which the alphabets are offset. Here the key could be thought of as a shift of 1 – *a* maps to *b*, *b* maps to *c*, and on until you get to *z* in the plaintext which maps to *a* in the ciphertext.

So, simplistically the cryptographic algorithm used here is the mapping of letters to each other. The key to encryption is a shift of 1 and to decrypt the message the key is –1.

Now this was a very simple example – more useful cryptography is based on heavy-duty mathematics – but, we can categorize the two principle approaches to encryption under the headings of **symmetric ciphers** and **asymmetric ciphers**.

Symmetric Ciphers

In this type of routine the same key is used for encrypting and decrypting the data on both ends of the algorithm as the following diagram illustrates:

Since the same private key is used to encrypt and decrypt the data this system is at risk from *man in the middle* attacks, due to the need to transport the private key from one location to another. If the key falls into the wrong hands, that adversary not only has the ability to read the communications, but also to change the content of the data.

Such symmetric algorithms are also termed **secret key** or **private key** algorithms.

Asymmetric Ciphers

The use of asymmetric (or **public key**) algorithms addresses the inherent security weakness of the symmetric key approach. In this approach, without delving into the mathematics, a user has a public and a private key that work together (a **key pair**) – the public key can be widely distributed to anyone who wants to send a message to the user, while the private key is retained by the user and is not transmitted anywhere.

There are two ways in which this combination can be used. In the first of these (illustrated below), the public key is used to encrypt the data. This data can then only be decrypted with the private key, and therefore can only be read by the owner of the private key. In this situation, the data can be intercepted and the malicious user can even own the public key, but the only way that the data can be decrypted is with the private key.

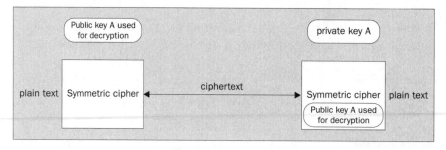

The other way to use this combination is if the private key is used to encrypt the plaintext. The public key can decrypt it, and because the public key can only decrypt messages that were encrypted with the private key, this means that it must have been encrypted with the private key. We therefore have a method of establishing the identity of the person sending the message, as only that one person would have a copy of the private key.

The Size of the Key

The terms 128-bit encryption or 64-bit encryption refer to the size of the key that is used during the encryption process. Normally the longer the key the more difficult it is to break (since the longer the key the more possible combinations can be produced), remember however that the longer the key is the more time it will take to encrypt the data. A long key is known as a **strong** key.

Asymmetric ciphers, as described above, use variable size keys, which the developer may determine. Symmetric ciphers, on the other hand, can use variable and fixed length keys.

There are a number of standard algorithms that are commonly used:

❑ **Secure Hash Algorithm 1 (SHA-1)** – This National Institute of Standards and Technology (NIST) developed algorithm creates a 160-bit message digest, which, as mentioned previously diminishes the chance of cracking the key.

❑ **Message Digest #5 (MD5)** – Developed by Ronald Rivest of RSA Data Security Inc; it produces fixed length keys of 128-bit message digest.

❑ **Data Encryption Standard (DES)** – A symmetric cipher created by IBM and partially from the National Security Agency (NSA). DES only uses a 56-bit key size, which makes it somewhat susceptible to attacks. Can be used in more advanced ways (such as Triple-DES) to reduce the security risk.

❑ **Digital Signature Algorithm (DSA)** – An asymmetric algorithm developed by the NSA and released by NIST. It allows variable key size ranging from 512-bits to 1024-bit.

The Legality of Ciphers

A complex web of national and international laws regulate the use of cryptography. In some countries, such as the United States, it is legal to use strong cryptography but software that implements it may not be exported under some circumstances. In other countries, such as France, it is illegal to use strong cryptography at all.

However, these laws are changing rapidly. Recently, 33 countries in the Wassenaar Arrangement (http://www.wassenaar.org) have agreed to establish the same cryptography export controls as the United States. Currently free software is exempted from these restrictions. Recently the United States loosened the export restrictions slightly, allowing web browsers to be used for strong encryption when communicating with financial institutions or when an American-owned company overseas needs to browse its home office's web site.

Of course, the encryption techniques we've just talked about are all well and good for providing increased security of data transmission between trusted parties, but what happens when we want to communicate with parties that we don't know so well – in short, how can we establish identity on the Internet? That's where **certificates** come in.

Certificates

Digital certificates are simply blocks of data that contain information that identifies an entity. In their simplest form, certificates contain a public key and a name, but may also contain an expiration date, the name of the **Certificate Authority** (**CA**) that issued the certificate, a serial number, and perhaps other information. Most importantly, it contains the digital signature of the certificate issuer. As certificates provide a means of identifying an entity they become an appropriate way of disseminating public keys and thus we start to build a **Public Key Infrastructure** (**PKI**).

Since anyone can create and issue a certificate (the specifications for certificates are widely available) the role of the Certificate Authority is crucial to maintaining the viability of certificates. CAs are trusted third parties who are generally recognized within the Internet community as being able to reliably confirm that a public key is being issued by the name on the certificate.

Examples of such CAs are VeriSign (http://www.verisign.com), Thawte (http://www.thawte.com) and Entrust (http://www.entrust.net) but there are many more. Some of them even offer free test certificates for use when developing a site. CAs will charge a fee for providing a certificate, and for that fee will research a company (or individual) to confirm the applicant's credentials.

Without going into too much further detail, there are eventualities where you may want to issue your own certificates, yet to validate them those certificates will have to be linked to a trusted entity. One can see this will eventually create a chain of certificates, each one certifying the previous one until the parties involved are confident of the identity in question. Thus hierarchies of trust are developed.

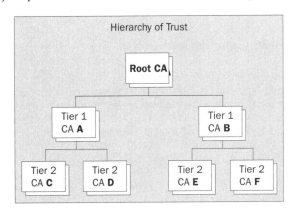

Obtaining Certificates

In order to use certificates with your server, you need to obtain one from a Certificate Authority. Normally this is accomplished by submitting a **Certificate Signature Request** (**CSR**), and other identifying information, as requested, to the CA.

The first step is to generate a key, which can be done by using the Java 2 based keytool (which can be found in `%JAVA_HOME%\bin` directory). The Java 2 documentation states the following about keytool.

> "Keytool is a key and certificate management utility. It enables users to administer their own public/private key pairs and associated certificates for use in self-authentication (where the user authenticates himself/herself to other users/services) or data integrity and authentication services, using digital signatures. It also allows users to cache the public keys (in the form of certificates) of their communicating peers."

Initially the keystore (the place where keys are located) should have zero entries. This can be verified by running the keytool with the `-list` switch. This option returns the number of entries and the default keystore provider.

```
keytool -list
```

The following syntax allows you to create a key pair under the default alias *mykey*,

```
keytool -genkey
```

During this process, the user will be prompted for such input as is necessary by the program (e.g. passwords and suchlike). When it has finished running, there is one key with the default alias of *mykey*. This key is stored in the keystore as follows; obviously you will have a different timestamp and fingerprint.

```
mykey, Sun Dec 10 23:05:10 EST 2000, keyEntry,
Certificate fingerprint (MD5): AB:53:DC:B7:F9:A7:1A:F4:42:D6:7B:E1:81:85:24:22
```

Once you have created an entry, you can then request a signed certificate from a Certificate Authority. The certificate request is generated by using the `-certreq` switch as follows:

```
keytool -certreq
```

This command will create the following certificate request.

```
-----BEGIN NEW CERTIFICATE REQUEST-----
MIIBRTCB8AIBADCBijELMAkGA1UEBhMCVVMxFzAVBgNVBAgTDk5vcnRoIENhcm9saW5hMRIw
EAYDVQQHEwljaGFybG90dGUxDDAKBgNVBAoTA1JURzEMMAoGA1UECxMDU1RHMRMwEQYDVQQD
EwpkYW1hZ2UtaW5jMR0wGwYJKoZIhvcNAQkBFg5kb25AcmVhbWV5LmNvbTBcMA0GCSqGSIb3
DQEBAQUAA0sAMEgCQQDJe3gKOgU+YN74t+xWOeaj9ZWAtcF4v2E9kmyRUE8DGcJLsfK6vy3u
KEMYNIJ4Uv/JvqD2peWoxn9eHF/bwcwlAgMBAAGgADANBgkqhkiG9w0BAQQFAANBACFq3kfO
8GidzhLOVqP57T7RH6vSz+hj9ksV3uTdxos3vhxkTNMBFjX3mo8IvKkgZ94ixMFpyYOzIa5j
uR6rZqs=
-----END NEW CERTIFICATE REQUEST-----
```

Once you have the certificate request, you need to follow your CA's guidelines for submitting and purchasing the certificate. If you choose VeriSign, they offer several options such as *Global Site Services*, which features strong 128-bit encryption for domestic and export web browsers, and *Secure Site Services*, which offers 128-bit encryption for domestic United States web browsers and 40-bit encryption for export web browsers.

Once you have completed the procedure for obtaining your certificate, you can use keytool to import the certificate into the keystore.

```
keytool -import -file newcert.cer
```

But what if we don't want to have ourselves certificated? We're still left with the problem that we need to find some way to exchange data over the open channels that make up the Internet without compromising our security. As we are about to see, keys can be used to make this possible.

Shared Key Authentication

Shared key authentication is based upon the principle of exchanging a secret key then encrypting a message with that key for transmission. In this scenario we establish two users Jordan and Bob, and assume they already share a secret key, K_{jb} that has already been established in a secure manner. This protocol is based upon a **challenge-response** protocol, which means one user sends a random number to the other user, who then transforms it, and sends it back. In this protocol we will define the following notation.

❑   *J, B* are the principals in the system, Jordan and Bob

❑ R_i is the challenge and the subscript identifies the challenger of the response

❑ K_i is the key and the subscript indicates the owner

The following illustration describes a simple shared key challenge response transaction:

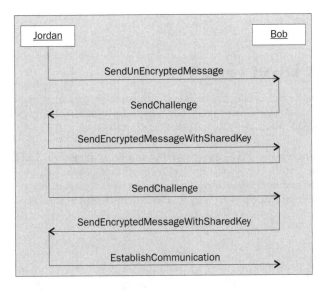

1. Jordan sends his identity as an unencrypted message J to Bob.

2. Bob sends a challenge to Jordan in the form of a large random number R_b.

3. Jordan then sends the challenge back to Bob using the shared secret key $K_{jb}(R_b)$.

4. Jordan then sends a challenge to Bob in the form of a large random number R_j.

5. Bob now sends the challenge back to Jordan using the shared secret key $K_{jb}(R_j)$.

6. Now they have established the authenticity of the users involved in the transactions and they can establish secure communication.

The Diffie-Hellman Key Exchange

We've assumed that our fictional users, Jordan and Bob had a shared key. What if they don't? How do we establish one using an unsecured medium like the Internet?

The protocol that allows the exchange of shared keys is known as the Diffie-Hellman key exchange. The protocol is based upon modular arithmetic and prime numbers. Each principal would select a large prime number, n and g such that $(n-1)/2$ is also a prime number. As mentioned, these numbers can be exchanged in a public environment because they don't play a role in ensuring the privacy of the algorithm. At this point Jordan and Bob need to pick a large number, $(x$ and $y)$, that is kept secret and not exchanged to anyone.

In our scenario, Jordan will initiate the exchange by sending a message containing $(n\ g,\ g^x \bmod n)$. Bob then sends a message containing $(g^y \bmod n)$. Jordan is now responsible for computing the secret key by raising it to the power of x as follows $(g^y \bmod n)^x$. Bob must also perform the same calculation to generate the secret key. The beauty of this calculation is that both return the same result $g^{xy} \bmod n$. What this means is, even if someone attempted a replay attack, they would need to know the value of the secret key, x, in order to decode the data.

What other methods can we use to achieve this end?

Secure Socket Layer (SSL)

SSL endeavors to solve the end-to-end secure data transmission predicament by providing authentication of both server and client and full data encryption. The only draw back is that one, or both, of the entities involved in the connection must have a digital certificate installed.

SSL uses **Public Key Encryption (PKE)** for encrypting and decrypting data. The **SSL Handshake Protocol** supports server and client authentication. It is a connection-based protocol that uses encryption to offer authentication, integrity, and non-repudiation. SSL is a type of sockets communication and it resides between TCP/IP and upper layer applications, requiring no changes to the application layer

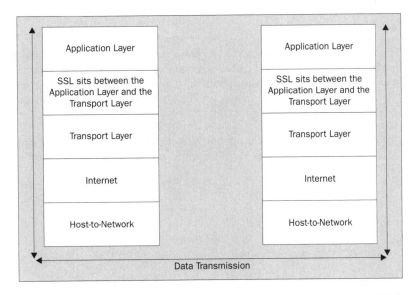

The SSL protocol is application independent, allowing protocols like HTTP, FTP, and Telnet to be placed transparently on top of it. The protocol is able to handle encryption keys as well as ensuring the server is authenticated before the client exchanges data. SSL maintains the security and integrity of the transmission channel by using encryption, authentication and message authentication codes.

Authentication is carried out using the SSL Handshake Protocol. This consists of two parts: server authentication and an optional client authentication. The server sends its certificate (public key) to the client, when the client makes a request. The client then generates a master key, which it encrypts with the server's public key, and then transmits the encrypted master key back to the server. The server is then responsible for retrieving the master key and authenticating itself to the client by using the master key as the source of authentication. Subsequent data is then encrypted and authenticated with keys resulting from this master key. The optional client authentication phase is based upon a challenge/response approach. The server sends a challenge to the client, then the client authenticates itself to the server by returning the client's digital signature on the challenge, as well as its public-key certificate.

There are some downsides to using SSL as part of your transport protocol, but the most important of these is performance. Since information going back and forth between the client and server is being put through an encryption and decryption process instead of being sent as clear text, there will be a noticeable performance degradation. The speed difference may not be noticeable on a single page, but if all a website's pages were encrypted, performance could be significantly reduced.

Now we've talked about SSL and how it works, we'll see how to put it into action using the **Java Secure Socket Extension (JSSE)** later on in the chapter.

Now let's take a look at the ways in which the Java platform supports security.

Security in Java

In this section, we'll be examining how Java deals with security. We'll begin with a look at the evolution of security features, and move into a discussion of the current standing in terms of both the built-in features, and the expansions to the core security features that are available: **Java Secure Socket Extension (JSSE)**, **Java Authentication and Authorization Service (JAAS)**, and the **Java Cryptography Extension (JCE)**.

The Sandbox

The original approach to Java security used a model known as the **Sandbox Model**. It was implemented by Java enabled web browsers that ran applets embedded in web pages, but is not only limited to browsers as it can also be implemented in stand-alone Java applications. The model defines the scope that the application has in terms of local and remote access to resources. Within this section we are thinking about the security provided by the Java platform for systems executing Java code.

In the instance of downloaded code, such as applets, they are considered not trusted and are not allowed access to the local system. Downloaded code, for the most part, is only able to access the server from which it originated.

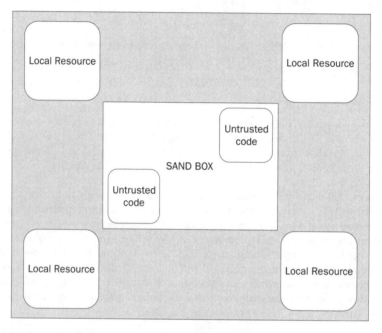

In this illustration, the un-trusted code in the sandbox does not have any access to the local resources outside of the sandbox. This is an oversimplified diagram; however, it clearly depicts how un-trusted code is partitioned from the local computer resources. A security manager enforces these restrictions by monitoring the code in the executing Java classes ensuring that the file system and other local resources are not tampered with and that external communication is limited to the originating server.

As previously mentioned, when executing an applet in a browser, the browser is responsible for determining the security policy of the applet. However, you must remember that the vendor of the browser is responsible for determining what that security policy is. Even though all browsers are not written in Java they still take on the responsibility of the security manager to enforce security policies.

There were problems with the original model, such as preventing applets from performing tasks on the local system. This severely limits what can be done with applets. JDK 1.1 solved this issue by creating **signed applets**. A signed applet is considered trusted by the Sandbox Model and therefore has access to the same resources that local code is privileged to. Requiring the user to confirm those privileges further ensures security.

It must also be noted that if your business is based upon the use of this applet, it is ultimately the user's choice if they choose to accept it or not. This can be detrimental to a company if a large percentage of the users decide they do not want to download the code. In this situation it would be advisable to provide other alternatives to the users. This could include an HTML version of the same applet. Obviously the HTML version may not be able to mimic the exact functionality of the applet, but it could provide a good alternative.

Core Java Security

Let's now have a look at the fundamental parts of the Java security architecture:

- ❏ The byte code verifier
- ❏ The class loader
- ❏ The security manager
- ❏ The access controller

In this section, we'll take a look at the above framework, before exploring the extensions to the environment.

Following is a diagram that illustrates how the different parts of the Java security model fit together:

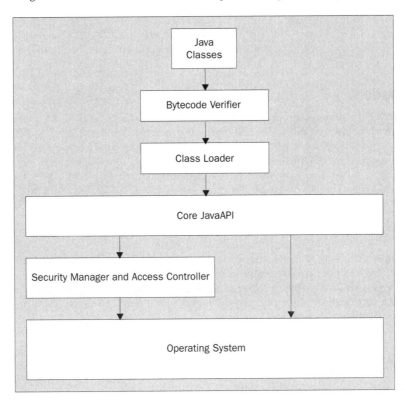

The Byte Code Verifier

When a .java file is compiled, it produces a .class file, which consists of byte code that is loaded into the virtual machine (VM). The job of the byte code verifier is to ensure that what the VM receives is legitimate code and is called by the virtual machine when a class's byte codes are being converted into class objects. This verifier is not accessible to the programmer because it is part of the VM and there is no interface to it.

The verifier checks or proves the following:

❑ The class is in the correct format by checking that the class is of the correct byte length, and that the magic number (a 0xCAFEBABE byte stream) is correct and found in the right places.

❑ Every class has only one super class.

❑ There are no illegal data conversions, for instance converting an object into an array of bytes.

❑ Final classes are not sub classed.

❑ No stack overflows or underflows. This is important because a common practice for hackers is to force stack errors with C/C++. By forcing these errors, it is possible to determine function locations in memory. Once the memory location is known, it is possible to corrupt the memory and gain access to the system.

The byte code verifier is very useful in determining if a class has been tampered with prior to execution. Classes that are loaded from the CLASSPATH are considered trusted, and therefore are not subject to being verified. Classes that are not loaded from the CLASSPATH are considered not trusted and must be verified. It is also possible to force the byte code verifier to check all classes by using the -verify switch.

The Class Loader

The class loader's main purpose is to find the specified class and load it into the VM. The class loader must work with the security manager and the access controller (see below) to determine if the class that is being loaded meets the security policy that is being enforced. This is necessary if a rogue class attempts to do something that is not allowed. One scenario would be the use of an applet that tries to delete files on the local system. In this situation the security manager would determine if the applet has that privilege. The class loader assists with enforcing security because it knows where a class originated and if it was a signed class and trusted by the user.

The Security Manager

At the simplest level the security manager is the object responsible for enforcing the sandbox's security on executing code. The security manager performs runtime permission checking of sensitive operations, which can include opening network sockets, reading or writing local files, or creating new SecurityManagers. For example, if a Java program attempts to open a socket connection the security manager will determine if that operation is legal for that code.

The security manager's job is also to throw security exceptions if an application or applet tries to access something outside of the sandbox without permission. All applets and applications in Java must be granted explicit permissions to access local system resources, apart from read access to the directory (and subdirectories) where the program is invoked.

By default, Java applications do not have security managers unless the developer provides one. However, with the advent of Java 2 there is a default security manager that should make life a little easier. The default manager, `java.lang.SecurityManager`, is set with no express permissions. To allow permissions outside the sandbox, you would normally create a subclass of security manager, and then override the permissions that you wished to use. However, Java applets have an extremely strict security manager to prevent them from operating outside the sandbox.

The `SecurityManager` is an abstract class that provides the following operations:

```
public class java.lang.SecurityManager extends java.lang.Object {
    protected boolean inCheck;
    static java.lang.Class class$java$lang$SecurityManager;
    static {};
    public java.lang.SecurityManager();
    public void checkAccept(java.lang.String, int);
    public void checkAccess(java.lang.Thread);
    public void checkAccess(java.lang.ThreadGroup);
    public void checkAwtEventQueueAccess();
    public void checkConnect(java.lang.String, int);
    public void checkConnect(java.lang.String, int, java.lang.Object);
    public void checkCreateClassLoader();
    public void checkDelete(java.lang.String);
    public void checkExec(java.lang.String);
    public void checkExit(int);
    public void checkLink(java.lang.String);
    public void checkListen(int);
    public void checkMemberAccess(java.lang.Class, int);
    public void checkMulticast(java.net.InetAddress);
    public void checkMulticast(java.net.InetAddress, byte);
    public void checkPackageAccess(java.lang.String);
    public void checkPackageDefinition(java.lang.String);
    public void checkPermission(java.security.Permission);
    public void checkPermission(java.security.Permission, java.lang.Object);
    public void checkPrintJobAccess();
    public void checkPropertiesAccess();
    public void checkPropertyAccess(java.lang.String);
    public void checkRead(java.io.FileDescriptor);
    public void checkRead(java.lang.String);
    public void checkRead(java.lang.String, java.lang.Object);
    public void checkSecurityAccess(java.lang.String);
    public void checkSetFactory();
    public void checkSystemClipboardAccess();
    public boolean checkTopLevelWindow(java.lang.Object);
    public void checkWrite(java.io.FileDescriptor);
    public void checkWrite(java.lang.String);
    static java.lang.Class class$(java.lang.String);
    protected native int classDepth(java.lang.String);
    protected int classLoaderDepth();
    protected java.lang.ClassLoader currentClassLoader();
    protected java.lang.Class currentLoadedClass();
    protected native java.lang.Class getClassContext()[];
    public boolean getInCheck();
    public java.lang.Object getSecurityContext();
    public java.lang.ThreadGroup getThreadGroup();
    protected boolean inClass(java.lang.String);
    protected boolean inClassLoader();
}
```

If you decide to implement you own security manager you need to determine which methods you need to override and provide a concrete method for them. Following is a small code example of how you might implement this for a file deletion, with the implementation left out for simplicity:

```
public class MySecurityManager extends SecurityManager{
    public void checkDelete(String str) {
        // Determine if the file can be deleted by the current thread
            // If it cannot be deleted
                throw new SecurityException("checkDelete");
    }
}
```

For more information on writing a `SecurityManager`, please take a look at the following link:

http://developer.java.sun.com/developer/onlineTraining/Security/Fundamentals/magercises/Security Manager/

The Access Controller

The job of the access controller is to allow or deny access from the Java Core API to the operating system. The access controller is made up of one class with a private constructor. The class has several static methods that can be called to decide if an operation should succeed or fail. The access controller differs from the security manager, because prior to Java 2 the security manager was the only entity that was responsible for access to the sandbox. However, with Java 2 the access controller is capable of allowing or preventing most access to the operating system. Also in Java 2 the security manager uses the access controller for the majority of its access decisions.

The e-commerce we're concerning ourselves with in this book is conducted over the Internet. Since data can be easily intercepted as it moves around the Internet, for it to be kept private it will need to be disguised, bringing us neatly on to the topic of the Java implementations of cryptography.

The Java Cryptography Architecture (JCA) and Java Cryptography Extension (JCE)

The **Java Cryptography Architecture** (**JCA**) provides a framework for carrying out cryptography using the Java platform. The JCA allows extensibility through specific design patterns, which allow for the definition of cryptographic models and algorithms. The basic design of the JCA follows a Model-View-Controller (MVC) pattern, by separating the concepts from the implementation. A cryptographic provider provides the implementation. If you are using Java 2, you have a default implementation named SUN, but others can be purchased or you can even write one yourself.

The JCE is basically a cryptographic provider and it goes by the name SunJCE. The JCE is, however, considered to be an extension to the JCA. Since the JCE is an extension, it is not part of the core JDK. The default JCA only provides the concept or interface. In order to use the JCA you need to have a provider, someone who actually implements the concepts classes.

You can plug in new providers by modifying the `java.security` file which can be found in `%java_home%/jre/lib/security`. You need to set the following value:

```
security.provider.n=providerclassname
```

Where n is the number of the current provider that is provided by the user. This means that when you configure your system, you are responsible for assigning the correct number to the provider. The JCA ships with several classes that represent the cryptographic concepts.

Concept Classes

As mentioned earlier the JCA follows the MVC pattern. The concept classes can be thought of as the view, and the actual algorithms defined by the specific provider can be considered as the model. This means that if a different provider is plugged in to your environment the only thing that will change is the algorithm. The interface into the class will not be changed. These classes are outlined as follows:

Class or Interface	Description
`java.security.cert.Certificate`	Cryptographic certificate
`javax.crypto.Cipher`	Cipher
`java.security.Key`	A key used for signing
`javax.crypto.KeyAgreement`	A key exchange protocol
`java.security.KeyFactory`	Translates keys from one format to another
`javax.crypto.KeyGenerator`	Creates symmetric ciphers
`java.security.KeyPairGenerator`	Creates pairs of keys
`javax.crypto.Mac`	Message authentication code
`java.security.MessageDigest`	A hash function
`javax.crypto.SecretKeyFactory`	Translates keys
`java.security.SecureRandom`	A strong random number generator
`java.security.SignatureGenerator`	A digital signature

The next step in this discussion will be to talk about the JSSE, and how it can be used to implement SSL.

Java Secure Socket Extension

Normally when you talk about SSL, it is commonly assumed that a browser is being used to communicate with a server process. However, there are many instances where it may be necessary to create a GUI client that talks to a homegrown process or a servlet using SSL, which is one of many locations where the JSSE can be used.

The JSSE has the following features:

- ❑ Pure Java implementation
- ❑ Exportable outside of the United States
- ❑ Secure Sockets Layer (SSL) v3 support
- ❑ Transport Layer Security (TLS) 1.0 support
- ❑ Utilities for key and certificate management

- ❏ SSLSocket and SSLServerSocket classes
- ❏ Cipher Suite negotiation to initiate or verify secure communications
- ❏ Client and server authentication, as a part of the normal SSL handshaking
- ❏ HTTPS support
- ❏ Server Session Management to manage the cache of sessions
- ❏ RSA cryptography algorithms

Setting up JSSE

To install the JSSE follow the steps outlined below (for more details see
http://www.javasoft.com/products/jsse).

- ❏ Firstly download JSSE 1.0.2 and save it on your local disk. Note that this requires Java 2 SDK v 1.2.1 or greater, or Java 2 Runtime Environment v 1.2.1 or greater to be already installed.

- ❏ Uncompress and extract the downloaded file to give a jsse1.0.2 directory with two subdirectories – doc and lib. This latter subdirectory contains the extension files jsse.jar, jcert.jar, and jnet.jar.

- ❏ Install the JSSE JAR files either in the JDK/JRE ("installed extension") or bundle them with your applet or application ("bundled extension"). If you wish to install them as an installed extension, place them in the <java-home>/lib/ext directory.

An example program that shows how to use the JSSE to connect to an SSL site is shown below. The program assumes:

- ❏ You have a valid server that you can connect to using SSL.
- ❏ An index.html file is present in the document root of your web server.
- ❏ You are running an SSL enabled site on your local computer.
- ❏ The local loop-back address is available. The code references port 443 since most servers default to 443 as the SSL port. You will need to check your documentation to ensure the correct port is configured.

Once these prerequisites have been met, running this code will stream back the content of the page, index.html.

```
import java.io.*;
import java.security.*;
import java.net.*;
import javax.net.ssl.*;

public class JSSExample
{

    public static void main(String[] args)
    throws java.lang.Exception
    {
        JSSExample example = new JSSExample();
        example.HTTPGet("127.0.0.1","/index.html",443);
    }
```

The code only requires creating your SSL socket from the `SSLSocketFactory` as follows:

```
public void HTTPGet(String host,String URI, int port)
throws java.lang.Exception
{
    /*
    * Create an SSLSocketFactory object
    */
    SSLSocketFactory factory =
(SSLSocketFactory)SSLSocketFactory.getDefault();

    SSLSocket sslSocket = null;
    PrintWriter ostream = null;
    BufferedReader istream = null;

    try
    {

        /*
        * Get the SSL Socket from the factory
        * Then use it as normal
        */
        sslSocket = (SSLSocket)factory.createSocket(host,port);

        ostream = new PrintWriter(sslSocket.getOutputStream());
        istream = new BufferedReader(new
InputStreamReader(sslSocket.getInputStream() ));

    }
    catch(java.lang.Exception e)
    {
        e.printStackTrace();
    }
```

All of the work of connecting to an SSL enabled server is abstracted from the user just by creating your socket using the JSSE. The following section of code creates an HTTP GET request and sends it to the server using the secure socket connection.

```
    try
    {
        StringBuffer httpStringBuffer = new StringBuffer();

        /*
        * Create an HTTP GET Request
        */
        httpStringBuffer.append("GET "+URI+" HTTP/1.1\r\n");
        httpStringBuffer.append("Accept-Language: en-us\r\n");
        httpStringBuffer.append("Host: "+host+":"+port+"\r\n");
        httpStringBuffer.append("Connection: Keep-Alive\r\n\r\n");

        /*
        * Send request to server using the SSL output stream
        */
        ostream.print(httpStringBuffer.toString());
        ostream.flush();
```

```
        /*
         * Read and print the data.
         */
        int intValue = istream.read();
        while(  intValue > 0 )
        {
            char ch = (char)intValue;
            System.out.print(ch);

            intValue=istream.read();
        }

        sslSocket.close();
    }
    catch(java.lang.Exception e)
    {
        e.printStackTrace();
    }
}
}
```

Although, HTTP is used in this example you could use this socket connection for any type of protocol you develop to transport your data in a secure fashion. Along with creating secure socket connections, the JSSE ships with Java classes for:

❑   Networking applications

❑   Secure socket optional package

❑   Public key certificates

As we have already seen, information transmitted using the HTTP protocol, the default protocol for data access over the Internet, is very easy to read. All someone needs is a network analyzer (sniffer) and they can view every request and response transmitted over a socket. This is possible because the HTTP protocol is an open protocol and data is sent as clear text, (when not encrypted); this includes sensitive, private data, such as credit card numbers and the like. So as you can see SSL is very important for protocols such as HTTP. You can find more information about the SSL Specification at http://home.netscape.com/eng/security/.

Java Authentication and Authorization Service

The **Java Authentication and Authorization Service (JAAS)** is an extension to Java 2 and, whereas the core Java 2 security model allows us to enforce security based upon where the code came from and who digitally signed the code, JAAS provides the ability to enforce user-based security – in other words, depending upon the user running the code.

The JAAS architecture is divided into two parts – authentication and authorization. The authentication portion of the service allows the ability to determine who is running the code. The code can be a Java application, servlet, applet or bean, and the authorization component of the JAAS basically supplements the existing authorization of Java 2, adding the ability to authorize code based upon who was authenticated to run it.

The authentication component of the JAAS is designed to be **pluggable**. This means that the developer can write to the JAAS authentication service and different authentication schemes can be plugged into the application. The benefit of this is that you only have to write to one interface and as long as the application uses a pluggable security scheme, the application code will never change.

Within the authentication and authorization components of JAAS, there is another separation into the core classes of the system.

Core Classes of JAAS

The different category of classes and interfaces of JAAS are as follows.

❑   **Common Classes** (classes that are part of both the authentication and the authorization components) – `Subject`, `Principal`, `Credential`. Please be advised that JAAS uses the existing Java 2 `java.security.Principal` class.

❑   **Authentication Classes** – `LoginContext`, `LoginModule`, `CallbackHandler`, `Callback`

❑   **Authorization Classes** – `Policy`, `AuthPermission`, `PrivateCredentialPermission`

Let's have a look at each of them in more detail.

Common Classes

The `Subject` class is responsible for distinguishing an entity such as a person. The `Subject` may have multiple **principals** all bound to it by different names. For instance if the `Subject` is a person, it may have a principal bound to it by name and it may also have a social security number bound to it by name. Each of the aforementioned items is a unique principal but they are bound to the same `Subject`.

According to the Java documentation, a principal is anything that can have an identity. This can be a user name or a group of users identified by a particular name. We can also substitute the name **realm** for principal. We'll look at realms when we look at access control lists.

The `credential` class is not part of the JAAS, which means that the developer has the ability to use any Java class as a `credential` object. This means that you can use a user-defined class as a `credential` and bind that to a `Subject`.

Authentication Classes

The `LoginContext` class is used for authenticating subjects and allows the ability to write application independent code. This is made possible by the use of a `Configuration` class. The `Configuration` class determines which `LoginModules` are to be used by which application.

The `LoginModule` is the actual interface that allows developers to write the application independent code. This is accomplished because a vendor must implement the `LoginModule` to perform a specific task. For instance, one implementation of the `LoginModule` might have the ability to authenticate a user against an LDAP (Lightweight Directory Access Protocol – we'll talk about this in more detail in the later section on Security Management in Enterprise JavaBeans) server, and another implementation may talk directly to hardware and perform a retinal scan.

The `CallbackHandler` interface is used to gather information from a user. For instance, if an application needs to get information for specific bank accounts once a user has logged in, the `CallbackHandler` can be implemented to perform such a task.

The `Callback` interface can be used to pass several different callbacks to the `CallbackHandler` interface. This allows for several types of callbacks to be used within one application.

Authorization Classes

The `Policy` class is an abstract class that is used for representing JAAS access control.

The `AuthPermission` class is used to determine what permissions the current subject has. However, it does not have the ability to act upon the permission.

The `PrivateCredentialPermission` class is used to gain access to the private credential stored in the `Subject` class.

Now that we've covered Java Security, let's take a look at a protocol used for the secure handling of financial transactions.

Secure Electronic Transactions

Secure Electronic Transactions (**SET**) is an Internet protocol developed by a consortium led by MasterCard, Visa and others. The protocol was designed specifically for financial transactions and supports 56-bit security encryption. One of the key benefits behind the development of SET is rather than encrypting the entire flow of communications (as in SSL/TLS) SET only encrypts the financial transaction information. One challenge to global SET adoption is the requirement for client-side certificates. As we have already discussed, certificates are going to be important on client-side applications such as browsers, applets and stand alone applications. The infrastructure and process for issuing these credentials is not well established for consumers. Consequently, it is likely that SET will be first adopted by procurement card-based purchases between businesses.

SET was designed to support the following business requirements:

❑   Provide confidential payment and order information – The specification must ensure that the data that is transmitted is protected during transmission. Also it is necessary to provide the assurance to cardholders that their payment is safe and can only be accessed by the anticipated addressee.

❑   Ensure the integrity of all data transmitted – Guarantees that if the data is altered during the transmission, the transaction will not be processed. This eliminates man in the middle attacks.

❑   Ensure best of breed design and security practices to protect all parties involved.

❑   Create a protocol that can exist with any transport mechanism – This means SET should be able to run on top of TCP/IP, IIOP, HTTP etc.

❑   Encourage the cooperation of software and network providers – By having multiple vendors working together, the specification is able to become a standard for financial transactions.

❑   Provide authentication to cardholders – Specifies that the cardholder is truly the owner of the card.

❑   Provide authentication that a merchant can accept branded payment cards – Lets cardholders know that the merchant they are attempting to do business with can conduct secure transactions using SET, and lets cardholders know that the merchant has an affiliation with a financial institution.

This is accomplished through the use of digital signatures and merchant certificates.

Cryptography in SET

We have already discussed the differences in symmetric and asymmetric key encryption and the pros and cons of both. SET uses a combination of both to create the **digital envelopes** and the **dual signatures** of SET messages.

Digital Envelopes

A digital envelop in SET is when a message is encrypted using a symmetric key. Once the message is encrypted using the symmetric key the key is then encrypted using the public key of the message addressee. Both the encrypted message and key are sent to the recipient, thus you have the digital envelope.

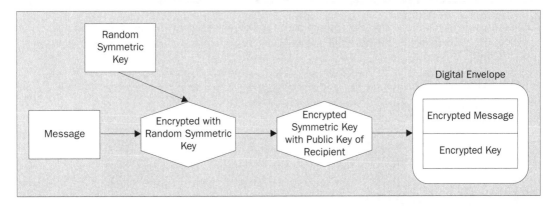

Once the recipient receives the message, they will use their private key to decrypt the symmetric key then decrypt the actual message.

The SET specification states the following about created random symmetric keys:

"To provide the highest degree of protection, it is essential that the programming methods and random number generation algorithms generate keys in a way that ensures that the keys cannot be easily reproduced using information about either the algorithm used or the environment in which the keys are generated."

Dual Signatures

Dual signatures are a distinct public/private key pair. This means that each set message will contain two asymmetric key pairs. Dual signatures are basically a concatenation of two separate messages as the following diagram depicts:

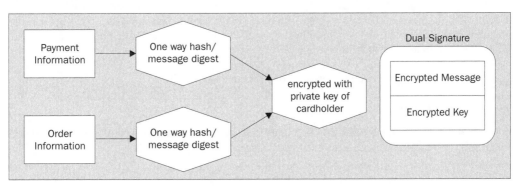

Dual Signatures can be very important when a cardholder sends a transaction. Normally an electronic transaction will need information about the order and payment information. Obviously, the financial institution will need the financial information and the merchant will need the order information. Dual signatures allow us to send this transaction as one unit and protect each sub transaction from the other party. In other words, the bank will not be able to view the order information, and more importantly the merchant will not be able to view the financial transaction information.

You can obtain more information about SET at http://setco.org.

More Authentication and Authorization

Obviously, we can't hope to cover the entire breadth and depth of security in one chapter. In this section, we'll outline some of the other options that are available. In particular, we'll look at four different areas associated with this topic:

❑ HTTP authentication for JSPs and servlets

❑ Kerberos authentication

❑ Cookies

Let's look at each of these in turn.

HTTP Authentication

The simplest way to make JSPs and servlets secure is to use **HTTP authentication**. HTTP authentication is based upon a username/password and challenge/response framework. This type of authentication is normally based upon the web server or application server, maintaining some type of repository of users and groups and their corresponding passwords. When a user requests a secure resource, the server prompts the user to enter a username and password for the requested resource. Normally the browser will display a dialog to allow the user to enter the username and password that will be sent to the server. On successful authentication of the user, the web server resource will be accessed.

There is a problem with HTTP Authentication, however: it does not provide any type of integrity or confidentiality. The information is transmitted using **Base64 encryption**, sometimes known as **ASCII armor**, which can be easily decrypted (we'll discuss the specifics of this later). By default, most servers such as Apache or WebLogic store their usernames and passwords in clear text on the file system. This means that your passwords are only as secure as the server they are on. Anyone hacking into the file system can easily access the supposedly secure information. However, it is possible to place HTTP authentication information in an RDBMS or Lightweight Directory Access Protocol (LDAP) storage system (this topic is beyond the scope of this chapter, and you should consult with your documentation to determine how to connect your HTTP authentication to some other source).

One simple method to implement this feature is to use Access Control Lists.

Access Control Lists

As mentioned earlier, access control is any technique that selectively grants or denies users access to system resources. This can include files, directories, networks, services, and functionality.

The process of associating users and groups of users with specific rights is also known as an access control list (ACL). If a user has the correct rights, he or she can perform the given operation or if the user belongs to a group that has been granted the correct rights the operation may be performed. We will see later in this chapter how EJB containers perform security in a transparent fashion using ACLs as the main source for authorization.

The following diagram displays how groups and users logically may appear:

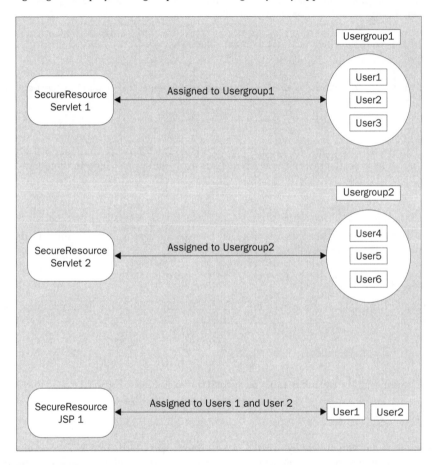

This diagram graphically shows how users are associated with specific resources. In this situation Usergroup1 includes User1, User2 and User3, and they are allowed to access the secure resource Servlet 1. However they cannot access secure resource Servlet 2. The third example shows that User1 and User2 are allowed to access secure resource JSP 1. This is a form of access control list, because in all three examples there is a list of authorized users for each resource.

Since every server handles setting up users and passwords differently, you will need to check the documentation provided with your server. We'll use Sun's J2EE reference implementation as an example of how to set up users, groups and perform HTTP authentication. The creation of users and groups is specific to Sun's J2EE; however we will deploy the servlet using a web archive (.WAR file) which is portable across multiple servers and containers.

Realms

A realm is a collection of users that are controlled by the same authentication policy. Most servers allow you to set up users in specific realms; this could be LDAP, RDBMS, NT domain or Unix. In this section we will focus on the `realmtool` supplied by Sun's Java 2 Enterprise Edition reference implementation.

The `realmtool` utility is a command-line program that allows you to add and remove users in the default and certificate realms. The information that is added is stored in the `%J2EE_HOME%\config\realms\keyfile` and the `%J2EE_HOME%\config\realms\privileges` file.

The `keyfile` is used for storing users and their associated passwords; the `privileges` file is used for storing groups.

To display all users in the default realm, use the command (please remember that the switches are case sensitive):

```
realmtool -list default
```

To add a user to the default realm you specify the `-add` flag. The following command will add a user named Jordan that is protected by the password mypassword , and will include Jordan in the admin and nurse groups:

```
realmtool -add jordan mypassword admin,nurse
```

To remove a user you specify the `-remove` flag. For example, to remove a user named Jordan from the default realm, you would type the following command:

```
realmtool -remove default jordan
```

To add a group to the default realm specify the `-addGroup` flag. The following command adds the specialist group:

```
realmtool -addGroup specialist
```

To remove a group from the default realm, you specify the `-removeGroup` flag.

```
realmtool -removeGroup specialist
```

In order to use the users and groups we created, we need to create a web archive file. Security in a web application is configured using three elements. The `<login-config>` element specifies how the user is prompted to login and the location of the security realm. If this element is present, the user must be authenticated in order to access any resource in the web application. A `<security-constraint>` is used to define the access privileges to a collection of resources via their URL mapping. A `<security-role>` element represents a group or user in the security realm. This security role name is used in the `<security-constraint>` element and can be linked to an alternative role name used in servlet code via the `<security-role-ref>` element The role-name tag defines the name of the security role or principal that is used in the servlet code.

```
<servlet>
    <servlet-name>LoginServlet</servlet-name>
    <servlet-class>com.login.Base64</servlet-class>
    <security-role>
        <role-name>specialist</role-name>
```

```
    </security-role>
    <security-constraint>
       <auth-constraint>
          <role-name>specialist</role-name>
       </auth-constraint>
       <user-data-constraint>
          <transport-guarantee>NONE</transport-guarantee>
       </user-data-constraint>
    </security-constraint>
</servlet>
```

As you can see the role name is the same name that was used previously to create our user group. Each server is going to allow you to create your users and groups differently; however, as long as they are J2EE compliant, you should be able to use a .WAR file to deploy your servlets.

Base64 Encoding

In Base64 format, groups of 24 bits are broken into four 6-bit units, with each 6-bit unit being sent as a legal ASCII character. "A" represents 0, "B" represents 1 and so on to the end of the alphabet, and this is followed by the 10 numeric digits 0-9. Finally + and / are represented by 62 and 63 respectively.

Base64 uses == and = to denote that the last group contained only 8 or 16 bits respectively. In this format carriage returns and line feeds are ignored, and binary text can be sent safely without encoding.

A very simplistic example of how you can use HTTP authentication and create your own custom authorization is shown below where we have servlet code for decoding Base64 authentication. Please be advised that this example does use the non supported sun.misc.* package. You can also use the classes provided by the W3C for handling Base64. These classes can be found at http://www.w3.org/PICS/refcode/Parser/ under the w3c.tools.codec Encoder/Decoder for Base64 link.

```
package com.login;

import java.io.*;
import javax.servlet.*;
import javax.servlet.http.*;

public class Base64 extends HttpServlet {
    public void service(HttpServletRequest req, HttpServletResponse resp)
              throws ServletException, IOException {
```

The code for the service() method starts by setting the content type to text/html. It then obtains a PrintWriter from the HttpServletResponse object:

```
        resp.setContentType("text/html");
        PrintWriter out = new PrintWriter(resp.getOutputStream());
        resp.getOutputStream().println("<HTML>");
        resp.getOutpuStream().println("<body>");
```

In order to get the Base64 encoded text we need to pull the information from the request stream using the getHeader() method of the HttpServletRequest object.

The "Authorization" header contains the user name and password collected from the client, if any. A null indicates none were given and must be handled accordingly. We can now control entry to the servlet by checking for valid user name and passwords before allowing processing to continue with the remainder of the servlet:

```
String header = req.getHeader("Authorization");
   System.out.println(header);
     String decode = header.substring(6);

        sun.misc.Base64Decoder dec = new sun.misc.Base64Decoder();
        String usernamePassword  = new String(dec.decodeBuffer(decode));

        int colon = usernamePassword .indexOf(":");
        String username = usernamePassword .substring(0,colon);
        String password = usernamePassword .substring(colon ,
                                               header.length());
   resp.getOutputStream().println("</BODY>");
   resp.getOutputStream().println("</HTML>");


  }
 }
```

The encoded data stored in the variable upd appears as follows:

```
Basic SlAxOlBBU1NXT1JE
```

In order to remove the word Basic from the data we need to do a String.substring() on the data and remove the first 6 characters. The user name and password sent to the browser are stored in the following format, once they have been decoded:

```
username:password
```

The Base64 decoder provided by Sun is used to decode the user name password into a human readable format.

```
sun.misc.Base64Decoder dec = new sun.misc.BASE64Decoder();
String header = new String(dec.decodeBuffer(decode));
```

HTTP authentication is a great tool for protecting access to web server resources using ACL. However, it does have its downsides:

❑ Knowing how Base64 works, we can easily sniff the information and decode it using any Base64 decoder. That is why HTTP authentication is only recommended in low security situations or in conjunction with other secure protocols.

❑ The method described above only protects access to the web environment from the web server itself. It still does not provide any type of security from the local directory. This means that if someone is able to telnet or FTP to the file system, HTTP authentication will be of no value.

❑ Most web servers do not have any type of lock out mechanism, so someone could attempt a brute force attack. The malicious user then has the ability to try multiple times to break into your system. One option is to utilize HTTP logging that most web servers supply. This may give you the ability to see if unauthorized users are attempting to access the system.

Let's now take a brief look at Kerberos authentication, and follow this up with a brief look at cookies, before we move onto server-side security issues.

Kerberos Authentication

Kerberos authentication is based upon the synchronization of three servers. The servers involved are:

❑ **Authentication Server** – The authentication server is responsible for validating the user and sending an encrypted ticket back to the user.

❑ **Ticket or Credential Server** – Once the user has the ticket, it is encrypted using the user's secret key and sent to the ticket server. The ticket server will then attempt to ask the user to supply a password. With this information the ticket server will return a session key back to the user.

Inside the ticket there can be various pieces of information, but one important piece of data is the timestamp. The timestamp can be used similarly to the random nonce we spoke of earlier. By using the timestamp, we can determine when a user connected to the system and try to prevent replay attacks by checking the timestamp. This also means that the servers need to be synchronized by the timestamp.

❑ **Business Server** – The session key returned from the ticket server is then used to access secure servers within the environment. It's also a common practice to have the business server contact the ticket server to validate the ticket and the session.

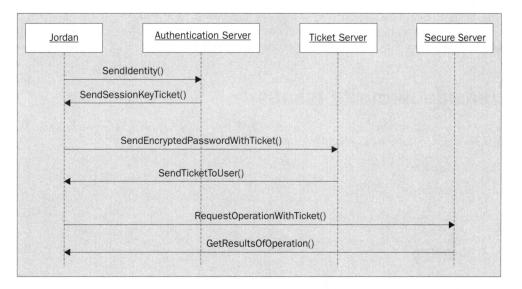

Cookies

Although cookies are not considered a security tool, many sites use them to determine what a user is authorized to do. This is considered a *very* simple form of security, and is not recommended for high security sites.

Cookies are sent to the browser through the Set-Cookie header in the following format:

```
HTTP/1.1 200 OK
Date: Mon, 13 Nov 2000 19:12:56 GMT
Content-type: text/html
Set-Cookie: NAME=VALUE; Comment=COMMENT; Domain=DOMAINNAME; Max-Age=SECONDS;
Path=PATH
Location:
```

The highlighted section in the previous HTTP header represents the cookie that is being sent back to the client machine. As the cookie information is sent back as clear text as part of the HTTP header, this means that not only can this information be sniffed going across the wire, but it can also be subject to an MOTM attack.

Many sites enforce restricted content access and other security concerns through the use of a login process. However, since users tend to find logging in inconvenient, cookies can be useful in low security situations. Assuming that the browser supports cookies and that the user has enabled cookies, we can save user information on the local machine in such a way that allows us to recognize them the next time they come to the site using the same machine. Together with session tracking, this is the most common use for cookies.

This in itself causes huge security issues. Some versions of Internet Explorer made it possible for malicious users to build a special URL that would make Internet Explore reveal all the cookies that it had stored for a specific domain. What this means is that if a site relies on cookies, your information stored in the cookies would be available to the malicious user. Please see http://www.peacefire.org/ for more information.

There have been numerous rumors that state that some sites use cookies to track user movements across the Internet and then sell that data or abuse that data. Some rumors even state that cookies are being used to scan hard drives and gather information from the local file system. Fortunately, this is not currently possible. Cookies are small bits of data that are not in an executable format. The good thing is that most web browsers allow the user to turn cookies off, so this should quell most of these fears. However, if a site relies on cookies for personalization, you may not be able to access the site correctly if you do this.

Server-side Security Issues

Now that we've discussed the problems on the client-side, let's take a look at the server-side issues. In this section, we'll look at three main areas in this sphere:

- ❑ Data security
- ❑ EJB security

Let us begin by looking at data security.

Data Security

In recent years, we have seen the number of databases and data warehouses holding mission-critical data growing into terabytes in size, and sometimes supporting thousands of users. This means that it is crucial that data security precautions are taken to ensure the overall functioning and competitive advantage of the enterprise. Businesses, such as banks, insurance firms, and credit-card companies that routinely deal with large amounts of sensitive data cannot afford to have malicious users gaining access to their database systems.

At a fundamental level, the entire security system of any database (outside of the connection to the database) depends upon passwords. Some database systems allow administrators to explicitly perform account locking, define password-complexity parameters, and specify password-aging and expiration parameters for user profiles. These new features extend the functionality of the database and use profiles to convey higher security levels.

Some of the key elements of database security that need to be considered are:

- ❑ **System Security** – As we have already mentioned, the operating system security is the first step in having a secure database running on it.

- ❑ **Data Security** – Ensuring only the correct users can access and/or alter the data that they are authorized to see.

- ❑ **User Security** – User security concerns the strategies and methodologies used to implement security for different groups of users (authorization). User groups or classes for a typical data schema would include end users, data administrators, security administrators, application developers, and application administrators.

- ❑ **Password Management** – Setting password strength and locking out users after several failed login attempts, aging and expiring passwords, tracking history, and verifying complexity.

- ❑ **System Auditing** – Tracking actions within the database such as INSERT, UPDATE and DELETE operations.

We have talked about how we can make your connection secure going from the browser to the web server and from the web server to the application server. However, how do we ensure the connection from the application server to the database is secure?

Database Connections

Normally when you connect to a database in Java, you use JDBC. This means that you have to have a driver that supports your database. Some databases such as Oracle 8i now support connecting to the database using SSL. This is very important in three tier models where the database may reside on a different computer or network from the application server.

Systems like Microsoft's SQL Server rely on the underlying operating system to help with authentication and database connections. However, the documentation states the following in reference to connections to SQL Server across the Internet: "*Though this connection is less secure than Microsoft Proxy Server, using a firewall or an encrypted connection will help keep sensitive data secure.*"

If you plan to use SQL Server, it would be prudent to investigate how to create a secure connection using standards like SSL. Currently SQL Server states that the TCP/IP Sockets Net-Library can be integrated with Microsoft Proxy Server to implement secure Internet and intranet communications.

Security Management in Enterprise JavaBeans

In this section we will discuss the following items for security management in the Enterprise JavaBean (EJB) architecture that are provided for you.

- ❑ The need for secure EJBs
- ❑ Roles and principals
- ❑ Authentication
- ❑ Authorization
- ❑ How the security mechanism is portable over multiple application servers

Let's take a look at each of these in turn.

The Need for Secure EJBs

The first thing we need to understand is why there is a need to apply security policies to Enterprise JavaBeans. Consider the following scenario: A bean provider has just created an EJB that is sold as part of their e-commerce suite for the medical community. The bean is used by medical personnel (doctors, nurses and admin staff) to create confidential patient reports, and then to send the reports to other physicians. In this scenario, only certain personnel can perform specific tasks. One such example are the doctors who need to create the reports (who will obviously need to be able to insert records into the database). These doctors should also have the ability to delete the same records.

Other actors in this system will have different rights based upon the role they play in this system. For instance, there will be administrative, technical, and nursing staff, and a host of other actors who will be interacting with the system. What this means to the bean provider is that there cannot be hard coded security policies built into the system based upon physical user names. This is where the EJB architecture comes into play – it allows bean providers to concentrate on the specific task at hand, and then allows the application assembler to concentrate on creating roles and mapping principals to roles.

Before we discuss how the bean provider creates a bean without any knowledge of how it is used from a security perspective, let's talk about principals and what they mean to EJB.

Roles and Principals

Security roles should be logical roles or actors, which represent specific types of users that will have the same access to the system. As previously mentioned the actors in our fictional system are grouped logically depending upon the role they play – for instance, the nursing role may not have the same rights as the doctor role. So, how are these roles created?

The bean developer needs to be able to give the bean to the application assembler and allow it to be configured at deployment time. This is accomplished using the deployment descriptor. We know that the deployment descriptor is used to tell the container information about the bean. The deployment descriptor is also used to define the security policy for the bean. An example of a deployment descriptor defining security roles is as follows:

```
<assembly-descriptor>
      <security-role>
      <role-name>nurse</role-name>
   </security-role>
      <security-role>
      <role-name>doctor</role-name>
   </security-role>
</assembly-descriptor>
```

The `security-role` element contains the definition of a security role. The definition consists of an optional description of the security role, and the security role name. In this example two roles were created the nurse and the doctor role.

Now that the understanding of roles has been discussed, we need to define what a principal is and how it is created. As we specified earlier, a principal is anything that can have an identity. The EJB 1.1 specification states the following information about principals and mapping them to roles defined in the deployment descriptor:

"If the security infrastructure performs principal mapping, the `getCallerPrincipal()` method returns the principal that is the result of the mapping, not the original caller principal. The management of the security infrastructure, such as principal mapping, is performed by the System Administrator role; it is beyond the scope of the EJB specification."

What this means is that each application server that supports the EJB 1.1 specification can map application level principals to roles however they deem appropriate, as long as the `getCallerPrincipal()` method returns the correct information. We will explore the `realmtool` provided by the J2EE reference implementation for adding users/principals to the Sun J2EE EJB container later. You will need to check the documentation for your application server to determine how to add users/principals to the system.

Authentication

Once the roles and principals have been created, we must authenticate the principals against a source that was defined by the EJB container. The EJB container must be able to provide the means to authenticate the users along with ensuring that the security policies that are in the deployment descriptor are enforced. However, the EJB 1.1 specification does not state how this authentication takes place. What this means, unfortunately, is that every vendor can implement the authentication process differently.

The J2EE reference implementation has a relatively weak authentication system. By default, when a client connects to the J2EE server, a dialog box is displayed that asks for the username and password. This username and password are checked against the default realm.

The default realm is used for all clients except web clients that use HTTPS protocol and certificates. The authentication from a web client takes place when a user attempts to access a protected resource, such as a servlet. When the servlet is invoked the container prompts the user with a dialog box to enter the username and password. This username and password are checked against the default realm and the authentication service verifies that they exist and the password is valid.

The following diagram illustrates the authorization procedure:

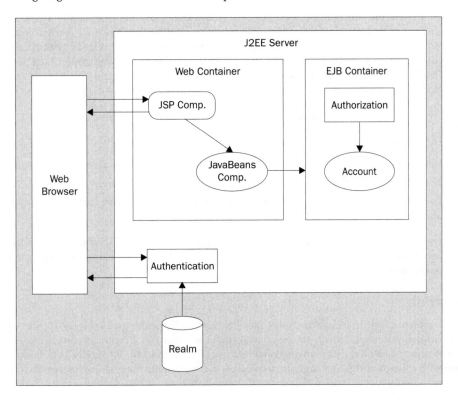

This example is specific to the J2EE reference implementation, so you will need to check your server documentation for authentication instructions.

Declarative security is security managed by the EJB container. As developers, we need only declare that a method or bean should be secured and the rest is done automatically. Declarative security is very simple: we create the deployment descriptor and put the correct principals and groups within it, and leave the rest to the container. The container will then be responsible for throwing exceptions based upon different security violations.

Without the feature of declarative security, you would need to use complex APIs to handle the authentication and authorization process within the EJB code. Ideally we should try to avoid this altogether; a full treatment of this subject is outside the scope of the chapter and so will not be covered. You can visit http://java.sun.com/products/ejb/training.html for more information.

Let's take a look at implementing security in an EJB. Currently, the username and passwords are stored as clear text in the `auth.properties` file if you are using the Java 2 SDK Enterprise Edition reference implementation. This is not something that should be used except in very low security environments, and even then we may require the use of SSL.

One possible alternative is the use of directory services for authentication, such as:

❑   Lightweight Directory Access Protocol (LDAP)

❑   Active Directory Service (ADS)

❑   Novell Directory Services (NDS)

❑   Windows NT Domains

All of these systems allow user information to be stored at the individual level and at a group level. It is also possible to use these services for authenticating users. Lightweight Directory Access Protocol (LDAP) was created at the University of Michigan to adapt a complex enterprise directory system named X.500 to the Internet. LDAP runs directly over TCP, and can be used to access a standalone LDAP directory service. The LDAP service could be directly accessed using Java Naming and Directory Interface (JNDI), which would allow you to find a user and authenticate that user against a secure source.

LDAP is very helpful for performing authentication for the following reasons:

❑   LDAP is extremely fast and optimized for reads

❑   Most application servers allow the ability to plug into LDAP as one of the realms that can be used for authentication

❑   Users and groups can be defined within a secure directory service instead of a plain text file on the file system

As mentioned previously, the LDAP server can be accessed using JNDI within your Java object; however, some application servers such as WebLogic allow the authentication process in different realms appear to be seamless.

Authorization

As well as authenticating users, we can also control access to EJBs at the method level. By specifying policies at the deployment descriptor level, we can control what each user can do within their profile. Access control can ensure only that certain users can access specific methods of the EJB. If we refer back to our medical example where we created doctor and nurse roles, we can now apply method level access to those roles.

The following illustration describes how ACLs are associated with specific methods in an EJB:

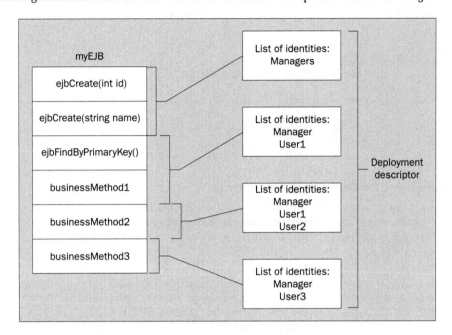

In this diagram you can clearly see that only specific users are associated with a specific method of the bean. This is considered authorization, because only the users who are associated with the specific method can invoke that method. In EJB 1.1 ACLs can be associated with specific methods by using an XML deployment descriptor. Method level permissions are specified using the <method-permission> element. Each element may include a list of one or more security roles and a list of one or more methods. There are three legal formats for creating a method permission element:

Format 1

This format refers to all methods in the EJB:

```
<method>
    <ejb-name>YOUR_EJB_NAME</ejb-name>
    <method-name>*</method-name>
</method>
```

Format 2

This format is used to refer to a specified method or multiple overloaded method names:

```
<method>
    <ejb-name> YOUR_EJB_NAME </ejb-name>
    <method-name>YOUR_METHOD_NAME</method-name>
</method>
```

Format 3

This format is used to refer to one method in a set of overloaded method names:

```
<method>
    <ejb-name> YOUR_EJB_NAME </ejb-name>
    <method-name>YOUR_METHOD_NAME</method-name>
    <method-params>
        <method-param>PARAMETER 1</method-param>
        ...
        <method-param>PARAMETER N</method-param>
    </method-params>
</method>
```

Assigning Roles Using the Deployment Descriptor

This section will discuss some of the necessary tags that are needed to map users to methods within your enterprise bean. Knowing how to format the deployment descriptor is the first step, but now it is necessary to assign security roles to method permissions. The following example shows the deployment descriptor for our session bean:

```
<?xml version="1.0"?>
<!DOCTYPE ejb-jar PUBLIC '-//Sun Microsystems, Inc.//DTD Enterprise
    JavaBeans 1.1//EN' 'http://java.sun.com/j2ee/dtds/ejb-jar_1_1.dtd'>
<ejb-jar>
    <enterprise-beans>
        <session>
            <ejb-name>sessionbean</ejb-name>
            <home>com.login.sessionbeanHome</home>
            <remote>com.login.sessionbean</remote>
            <ejb-class>com.login.sessionbeanEJB</ejb-class>
            <session-type>Stateless</session-type>
            <transaction-type>Container</transaction-type>
        </session>
    </enterprise-beans>

    <assembly-descriptor>
        <security-role>
            <description>The users in user group1</description>
            <role-name>usergroup1</role-name>
        </security-role>

        <security-role>
            <description>The users in user group2</description>
            <role-name>usergroup2</role-name>
        </security-role>

        <security-role>
            <description>The users in user group3</description>
            <role-name>usergroup3</role-name>
        </security-role>
```

The next section of the code illustrates the creation of three roles or groups:

- ❑ Usergroup1
- ❑ Usergroup2
- ❑ Usergroup3

These roles then have methods assigned to them using the `<method-permission>` tag as follows:

- ❑ Usergroup1 has access to the `create()` and `ejbMethodOne()` methods
- ❑ Usergroup2 has access to the `create()` and `ejbMethodTwo()` methods
- ❑ Usergroup3 has access to the `create()` and `ejbMethodThree()` methods

This means that only users who are part of the specified roles will be able to access the methods in the EJB.

```
<method-permission>
   <role-name>usergroup1</role-name>
   <method>
      <ejb-name>sessionbean</ejb-name>
      <method-name>create</method-name>
   </method>
   <method>
      <ejb-name>sessionbean</ejb-name>
      <method-name>ejbMethodOne</method-name>
   </method>
</method-permission>

<method-permission>
   <role-name>usergroup2</role-name>
   <method>
      <ejb-name>sessionbean</ejb-name>
      <method-name>create</method-name>
   </method>
   <method>
      <ejb-name>sessionbean</ejb-name>
      <method-name>ejbMethodTwo</method-name>
   </method>
</method-permission>

<method-permission>
   <role-name>usergroup3</role-name>
   <method>
      <ejb-name>sessionbean</ejb-name>
      <method-name>create</method-name>
   </method>
   <method>
      <ejb-name>sessionbean</ejb-name>
      <method-name>ejbMethodThree</method-name>
   </method>
</method-permission>

<container-transaction>
   <method>
      <ejb-name>sessionbean</ejb-name>
```

```
            <method-name>*</method-name>
        </method>
        <trans-attribute>Required</trans-attribute>
    </container-transaction>
  </assembly-descriptor>
</ejb-jar>
```

The bean provider can also use the `security-role-ref` element. This element is used to declare a security role reference in the EJB code. The `security-role-ref` element may also contain an optional `role-link` element to link to a defined security role. This allows the application assembler or deployer to link the names of the security roles used in the code to the security roles defined for an assembled application.

From a declarative perspective, our job is basically done. The container will handle the security for us and it will throw an exception when a user who does not have the correct permissions tries to access a secure method.

Now that we have seen the XML for creating the users, let's go back and do it the easy way using the tools provided for us with the J2EE SDK. We have already discussed how the `realmtool` utility works; now let's put it into action by creating the three fictional user groups discussed earlier and add some users to those groups.

First let's create some user groups as follows:

```
realmtool -addGroup usergroup1
realmtool -addGroup usergroup2
realmtool -addGroup usergroup3
```

These commands created three groups usergroup1, usergroup2 and usergroup3. Now let's add some users to the groups:

```
realmtool -add drsmith password usergroup1
realmtool -add drbrown password usergroup2
realmtool -add drdolittle password usergroup3
```

Now that we have created users and groups, we need to associate them with our EJB and assign users to principals to specific methods within the bean. That is accomplished using the deployment tool supplied by Sun. In order to complete this example please make sure you have downloaded Sun's Java 2 Enterprise Edition and read the documentation on deploying beans. This section is only going to focus on the security aspects not initial aspects of configuring the bean.

You can run the deployment tool using the following command on a Windows based system:

```
%J2EE_HOME%\bin\deploytool.bat
```

Make sure you are on the Security tab of the deployment tool. This picture shows the roles already created; however we will go through the steps to create them for the bean.

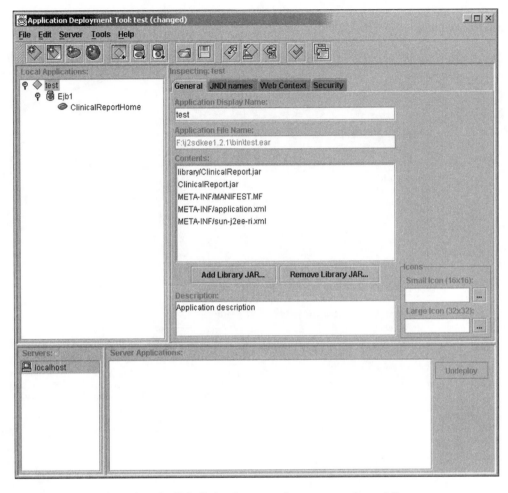

From this tab we need to select the **Edit Roles** button and create our roles as follows:

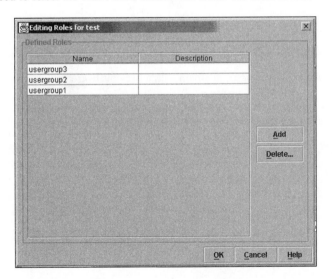

We can click on the Add button to add new roles, and Delete to remove roles that we no longer require. When we have assigned the roles, simply click on the OK button to return to the previous screen:

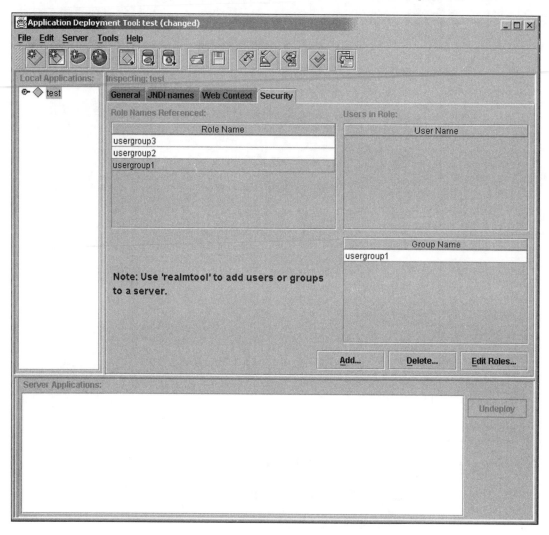

Once the roles are created, we can associate them with a previously created group name as seen above.

If you want to obtain more control, you can use the programmatic solution. This is accomplished by using the `javax.ejb.EJBContext`. The interface appears as follows:

```
public interface javax.ejb.EJBContext
{
    public abstract Principal getCallerPrincipal();
    public abstract EJBHome getEJBHome();
    public abstract Properties getEnvironment();
    public abstract boolean getRollbackOnly()
        throws IllegalStateException;
```

```
        public abstract UserTransaction getUserTransaction()
            throws IllegalStateException;
        public abstract boolean isCallerInRole(String s);
        public abstract void setRollbackOnly()
            throws IllegalStateException;
    }
```

The EJBContext can be used to gather information about the bean's home object, information about the current transaction state, environment properties, and in our situation, obtaining security information. A bean can query its environment to determine if the caller is part of the current role and is able to perform the specific operations. The two methods we are going to concentrate on are getCallerPrincipal() and isCallerInRole(String roleName).

Let's discuss the getCallerPrincipal() method. This method is used to return the name of the current user, the principal who invoked the bean. You're probably asking, "Why do I need to do this when the container handles security for me?" Well, picture the scenario where you may need to instantiate an entity bean based upon the current principal. In this situation, you would need to have a technique for getting that user. The code for doing this may look as follows:

```
public void businessMethod3()
    {
        java.security.Principal p = ctx.getCallerPrincipal();
        //lookup an entity bean and get home interface
            .
            .
            .
        String name = (String)p.getName();
        myEntityBean.findByPrimaryKey(name);

        // do something with the data
    }
```

If you want to determine if the current principal is in a specific group, you can use isCallerInRole() to determine this. Unfortunately, the problem with this method is that you need to provide it with an actual group name. Most developers will hard code this value to save time. However, you could use JNDI to store the name or read it from the deployment descriptor:

```
public void businessMethod1()
{
    //for demonstration only, the name of the group is hardcoded.
    private static final String USERGROUP1 = "usergroup1"
    boolean isInRole = isCallerInRole(USERGROUP1);
    if(!isInGroup){
        throw new java.lang.SecurityException("Unauthorized access");
    }
    //lookup entity bean and perform some operations
}
```

At runtime, a client will be allowed to invoke a method only if the principal associated with the client has been assigned in the deployment descriptor, to have at least one security role allowed to invoke the method. As you can see, it is very straight forward to use isCallerInRole() and getCallerPrincipal() to determine security information about your runtime environment of the bean. Now that we've dealt with EJB security, let's take a look at another important element in the security process.

245

Firewalls

While not a networking administration book, we shouldn't let the chapter end without a few words on one of the more general aspects of Web site security. Firewalls restrict the network traffic to and from computers. The restrictions can be based upon several different factors, such as:

❑ The origin or destination of the traffic

❑ The type of protocol

❑ The applications in use

For J2EE applications, specifically EJB, and for CORBA based applications, firewalls present a few problems. A normal scenario is when a server-side application (such as an EJB container or CORBA server implementation) is protected by a server-side firewall and clients are behind a client-side firewall. The problem is that most firewalls allow only specific traffic on specific ports. This could be HTTP protocol on port 80, for example. Most EJB applications are using some type of variant of RMI or RMI/IIOP and most CORBA based applications use IIOP or some other proprietary protocol.

What does this mean to end-users? It means that they will not be able to access the system because of the constraints placed upon the system by means of the firewall configuration. Let's dig into this further by looking at the different types of firewalls and then at client-side and server-side firewalls.

Firewall Types

Most firewalls operate using different mechanisms. Some of the most common utilize filtering. This can be based upon the origin and destination of the packets, application specific filtering or protocol based filtering. We will talk about each of these filtering types and how they impact your application.

Origin and Destination Firewalls

Firewalls that filter packets based upon the origin and or destination are closely tied to routers. This is accomplished by setting policies on the router to restrict specific information. The origin and destination is determined by the IP and subnet or IP address and port, for example: 192.168.0.1:7001. This is normally referred to as a **filtering firewall**. In a J2EE or CORBA environment it will be necessary to set the port that the server runs on in order to allow network traffic to reach the server. Obviously you will need to check your documentation to set the port for your specific server; however, the J2EE implementation sets the port in the ejb.properties file using the http.port=9191 key. This file can be found in %J2EE_HOME%\config directory of your J2EE installation.

The following diagram describes a typical scenario where specific IP addresses are filtered based upon the from and to IP address.

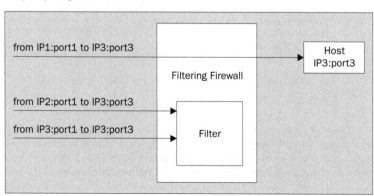

Gateway Firewalls

Gateway firewalls, typically, are **dual homed** or **bastion host**. This means a computer that has two network cards. One network card is exposed to the Internet, and the other is exposed to the internal network. Using this configuration, it is possible to block access to the internal network because the network cards can be configured to be on different subnets. However, this does not prevent someone from opening a telnet session to the bastion host and trying to gain access to the internal network. This can be accomplished if the administrator allows malicious users to open connections to computers within the intranet from the bastion host. Obviously, the attacker would need a userid and password to make this work.

In this situation, a gateway would need to be implemented to allow traffic to access the internal network. The gateways can be generic (that is, allow all traffic), protocol specific or application specific.

The following diagram shows an incoming connection from the Internet and how the networks (internal and external) can be separated by using a gateway. This can work for companies that want to keep their internal networks separated and it can also work for home users who are sharing a network connection with multiple computers.

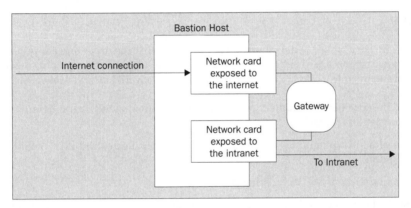

Client-side Firewalls

Client-side firewalls can commonly be seen in corporate environments where access to specific sites is restricted from the employees and to also protect the company from outside attacks. You may also see firewalls on ISP sites when you are restricted to certain protocols such as HTTP or NNTP.

Some of the problems you may see with client-side firewalls occur when an applet or application is distributed over the Internet and the client does not have control of the firewall. This means that if your application/applet talks something other than HTTP (IIOP, RMI/IIOP or some other protocol) the traffic may be blocked by the client-side firewall.

A normal scenario in this instance is something called HTTP tunneling. This means that non HTTP requests are bundled up and sent in an HTTP wrapper over the standard port which is port 80. This allows EJB/CORBA applications to run as normal without having a specific port opened on the firewall. However, using tunneling may result in poor performance, a price that may be too great to pay for some applications.

Server-side Firewalls

In some instances you may see multiple server-side firewalls. This is typically done when you need to protect the server farm from both internal and external traffic. This is sometimes called a **Demilitarized Zone (DMZ)**, because the logical view resembles a military DMZ as seen below.

This diagram represents Internet traffic entering the web farm through one firewall and then entering the network through a second firewall:

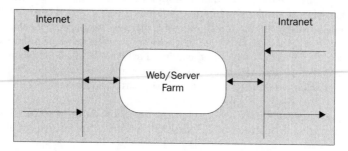

This type of configuration allows network administrators to create a secure environment for running corporate applications that can be accessed by both internal and external customers.

Summary

In this chapter, we have looked at the different types of attacks that can occur on your system and why security is necessary in this age of electronic commerce. We then covered briefly, some aspects of the Java security model and the role it plays in e-commerce. We've also covered the following areas:

❑　The difference between authentication and authorization along with different types of authentication schemes.

❑　The basics of cryptography, the use of ciphers and certificates and PKE (Public Key Encryption).

❑　The importance of SSL in securing sites.

❑　How the Java Security framework has grown, and the current extensions to this technology – JCA (Java Cryptography Architecture), JCE (Java Cryptography Extension), JAAS (Java Authentication and Authorization Service), and JSSE (Java Secure Socket Extension).

❑　Secure Electronic Transactions (SET) and how it is used for transactions with particular reference to Dual Envelopes and Dual signatures.

❑　HTTP Authentication, Access Control Lists (ACLs), Base 64 Encoding, and the use of cookies in authentication processes.

❑　How having a securing connection does not mean that you have a secure site – you also need to have a secure application.

❑　Finally, we saw how to apply a firewall to help keep unwanted persons from interfering with your network.

As we said at the head of the chapter, security is a diverse and complicated topic – hopefully this chapter has given you a grounding in the types of security issues you are likely to come across when developing an e-commerce application.

Now after this section's overview of technologies and approaches that enable us to build e-commerce applications, let's move onto to the implementation sections of the book.

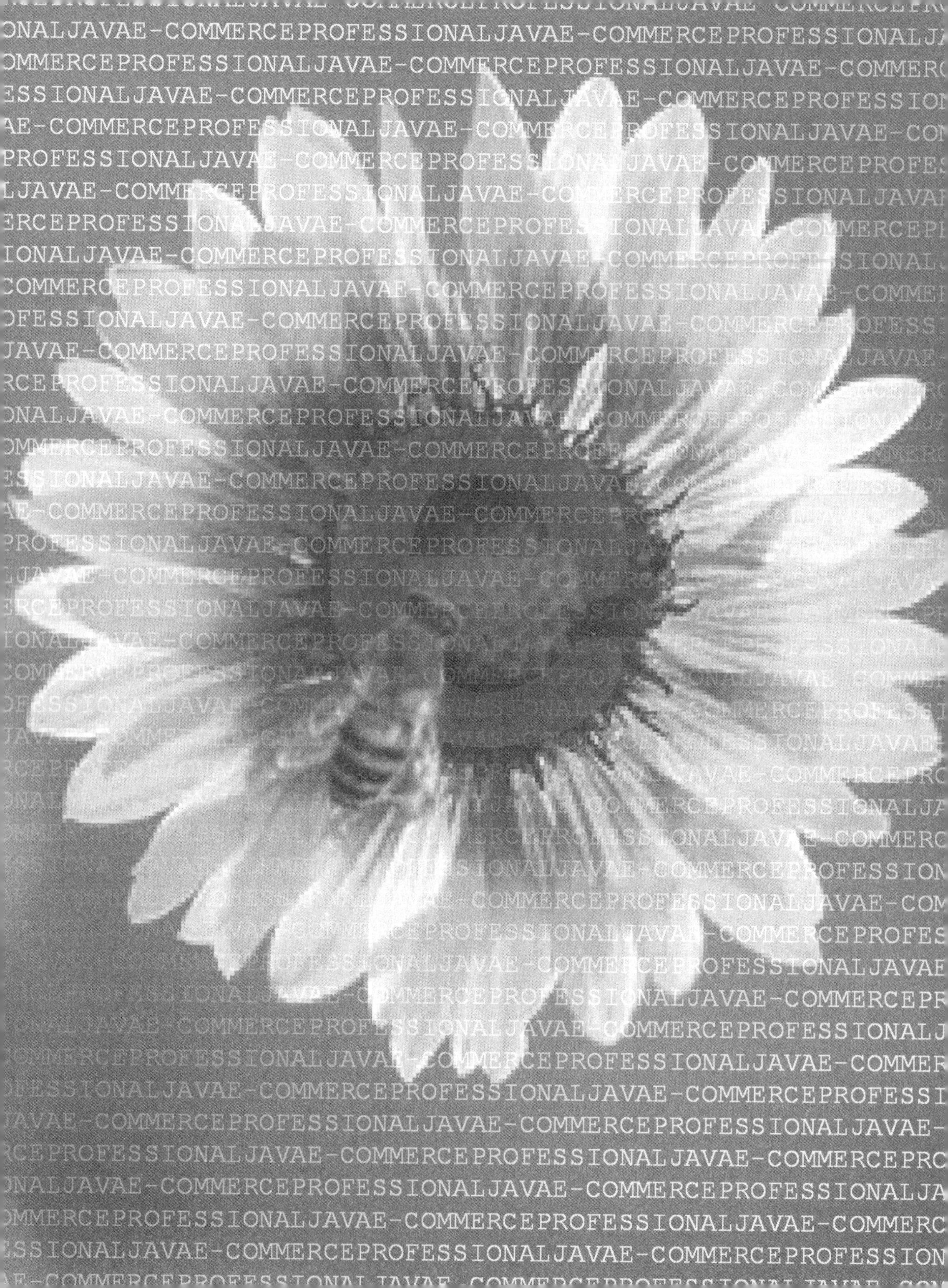
PROFESSIONALJAVAE-COMMERCE

Section 3

B2C E-Commerce Solutions

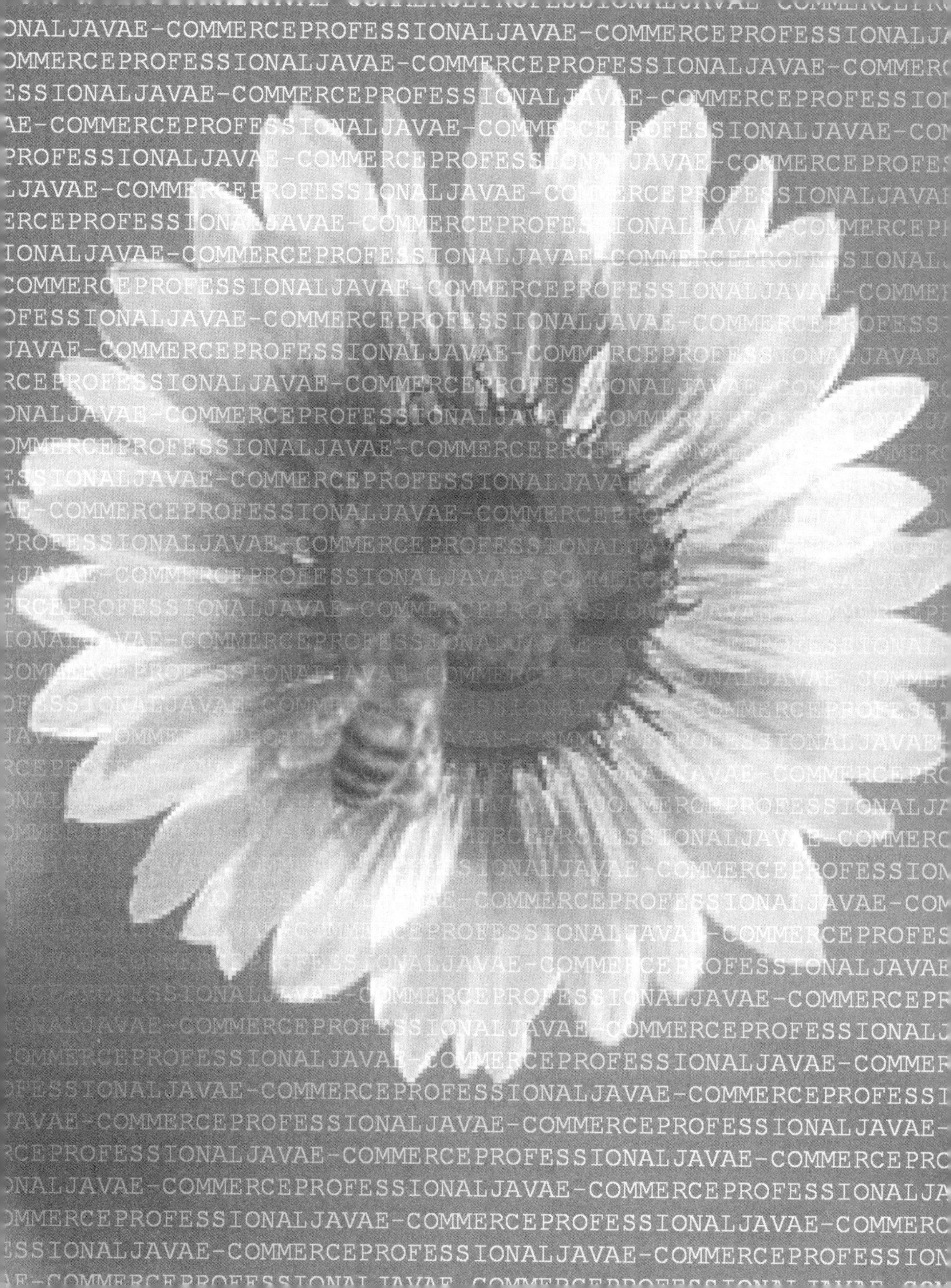
PROFESSIONALJAVAE-COMMERCE

B2C E-Commerce: Simple Site to Sell Goods Online

9

Web based sales have become an ever-growing source of revenue for many businesses that have previously been selling their goods entirely through traditional retail channels. Not only is the cost of selling their goods on the Web lower, but it also increases their customer market to a global scale. Many businesses have found new market segments on the Web of which they wouldn't have previously dreamt. Thus, the Web has opened many new marketing opportunities to the businesses. Such web sites may provide a wide variety of services depending on the nature of the business. A simple online store may sell its products to the customers through its web site, while a stock-trading house may supply a real-time feed of the stock prices to its customers, accept trading online and execute such trading on the stock exchange on behalf of the customer.

In this section, we'll study the creation of a simple site that sells its products online. Over the course of this chapter we'll look at:

- ❑ Site requirements
- ❑ Security
- ❑ Application architecture
- ❑ Coding the site
- ❑ Creating and deploying the application

Requirements for an Online Store

Any good software project first starts with the requirement study (as was discussed in Chapter 2). We shall look at the requirements of an online web store.

When you build a "bricks-and-mortar" store, you display your products on the shelves. A customer, visiting the store, looks through the products displayed on the shelves, finds a product they are interested in and puts the product in their shopping basket. If the customer does not find the desired product on the shelf, they may request help from a sales assistant; then find the shelf where the product is placed and add it to their shopping basket. This process is iterative until the time the customer has finished selecting products for purchase. The customer now proceeds to the checkout and pays for their purchases by credit/debit card, check, or cash. After the purchases have been completed, the customer carries out the goods by themselves or may request the store to dispatch the goods to the desired address.

The Online Shopping Experience

The procedures for setting up the online store and operating it are analogous to the above scenario. When you create a web site for your store, you will need to display the products on your web site. The web site may carry the picture of each product along with the details/specifications for the product that will help the customer in making their purchasing decisions. When the customer finds a desired product, they will add the product to their shopping basket.

You will need to provide an interface similar to a shopping basket; the term **shopping cart** is commonly used on the web. The customer continues choosing additional products, adding them to the cart until they have finished their selections. At this stage, the customer may review the shopping cart and evaluate the total cost of all the purchases. As compared to the traditional in-store purchases, the web store offers this additional benefit of evaluating the total cost of the purchases at any time before proceeding to the checkout. Once the customer is satisfied with the purchases and the total cost (that may include the shipping cost too), the customer proceeds to the **checkout**.

The customer now receives payment options. If the customer decides to pay by credit card, the online web store will validate such a purchase with the customer's bank with the help of a credit bureau in real time. Once the customer's credit has been approved, the store forwards the list of purchases to its shipping department, which ships the goods to the customer's location. For the benefit of the customers, you may like to store the customer shipping information in your database. Therefore, if the customer re-visits your store for additional purchases they will not be required to re-enter the shipping address on every purchase. You may also retain the customer's credit card information in your database so that the customer does not have to enter this information on every purchase. You may also want to track the customer's preferences and offer personalized services for those regular customers.

Your task as a developer is to provide this functionality for the web store. In this chapter and those following, you will learn several techniques used in the development of a web store.

Security

The issue of security is dealt with thoroughly in Chapter 8, but we'll provide a brief recap over the next couple of pages.

For any Internet business, security poses a major threat for business success. When we talk about security, it comes at various levels and it's important that all the loose ends must be tied properly to ensure that the entire system is fully secured. Remember, a single weak link in the chain makes the whole chain weak. The most important part of any secured system is the people who are using it. A highly secured system can easily become unsecured if the user does not take enough precautions on securing his/her password. For this, we must ensure that each password must have a minimum length and the user is forced to change the password periodically. The user must also ensure that he/she does not use a password that is easy to guess.

The general architecture of a web-based e-commerce application is shown below. While implementing security, we must consider security at different tiers and within the data transmission network between tiers. First, we will discuss the security issues at the server level and then we will consider the security issues for data transmission.

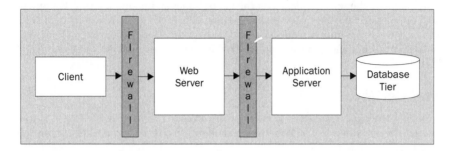

Server Security – Firewalls

As illustrated in the previous diagram, your entire architecture may consist of several servers. Access to these servers must be properly controlled. For this, we introduce firewalls at different positions. The firewall provides IP filtering. Thus, you can control who has access to your servers. The first firewall is put between the client and your web server. You can reject the access to your web server by providing IP filtering through this firewall. In addition, the firewall may be configured to pass only certain protocols to the web tier.

Once a client gains an access to the web tier, a second firewall may do further filtering before access is granted to your corporate server containing the business logic and backend database. In some highly secured systems, you may deploy another web server behind the second firewall. The first web server will expose only limited functionality to the customer. The second web server will call your business logic embedded in servlets and EJBs. It is advisable to use two firewalls from two different vendors. Thus, even if a hacker is able to penetrate the first firewall, he or she will not be able to penetrate the second firewall by using similar techniques.

The database server is the most crucial part of any organization's storage. The database may contain sensitive company information and must be protected from unwanted eyes. The database engine provides several methods for controlling the access to the various database tables. The security in a database is provided at several levels. The user is typically authenticated to gain access to the database. You may control the access to each table and each column in your table. The permissions may be granted for read, write or read/write. Not only that, each record may be encrypted. Thus, any illegal access to the database will not reveal the contents to the hacker. The data encryption obviously slows down the database access and should be used with care. Sensitive information such as credit card numbers, social security numbers, and the like may be encrypted. The database administrator is responsible for implementing this kind of security on your database. The administrator defines the roles for users of your database and grants the appropriate permissions on various database objects, depending on the role under which the user is logged in.

By taking the above measures, you can secure the sensitive data from the remote users. However, a theft of the physical server cannot be ruled out and you should impose adequate security measures to protect the server from physical theft. The server containing the sensitive data should be kept in a secured room where the entry to the room is granted only to the authorized personnel. The log of all persons entering the secured area should be maintained for audit purposes.

Data Transmission Security

In the case of our online selling site, where the consumers place an order with the store using their credit cards, the secured transmission of the sensitive data over the net becomes an important factor. For any Business to Consumer (B2C) online sales site, the customer is sometimes concerned about revealing their credit card details on the Internet. Your web store must provide a secured path for this kind of information flow so that the consumer feels confident while shopping at your store online. This is usually achieved using digital certificates and secured sockets.

PKI – Digital Certificates

One way of securing the data contents is to encrypt the contents using a key before it is transmitted. At the other end, you use the same key to decrypt the data and retrieve the original contents. This is called symmetric cryptography. The problem with this technique is if the key is stolen, somebody can access your sensitive data and impersonate you while sending documents. To overcome this problem, the key used for encryption/decryption is now split into two portions – public and private. The public portion of the key is freely distributed and private portion is truly kept a secret. This is called asymmetric cryptography.

In general, we have two situations where the public and private keys may be used for secured data transmission. Consider a situation where the customer receives an invoice from the online store electronically. In this case, the customer would be interested in establishing the authenticity of the document by ascertaining that the sender of the document really is who they claim to be, and the document has not been tampered with on its way. In the second scenario, a customer may submit their credit card information to a web store. Such information must be protected from the hackers. We will see how the public key infrastructure (PKI) helps in both these situations.

Establishing Authenticity

In the first situation, whenever the business sends an invoice to the customer electronically, the invoice is digitally signed using its private key. The invoice, along with the signature, is then dispatched to the customer. The public key of the sender is provided to the customer. Using this public key the customer verifies the signature on the received document. If the signature is verified, the customer can trust the source of document and the fact that the document has not been tampered with on its way. Since the public keys are openly distributed and one can create the public/private keys easily, using the tools provided in JDK, it is easy for somebody to impersonate a supplier. Thus, it is necessary to establish the authenticity of the public key itself. Someone else vouching for its authenticity accomplishes this. This external authority is known as a **Certificate Authority** (**CA**) which serves as an independent auditor.

The CA issues a digital certificate signed using their private key. The certificate contains the public key of the company seeking the certification and other relevant information about the company. Anyone who can impersonate you can easily impersonate even a CA by creating bogus public and private keys for the CA. The public key of the CA may now be authenticated by another CA who issues a digital certificate to this effect. Such digital certificates issued by different certification authorities may be chained to reduce the possibility of impersonating each party involved in the chain. However, you must trust the CA at the root of the chain. This is usually accomplished by making the public key of the root known truly publicly and may be published by different parties. For example, when you install Windows or JDK on your machine, the certificates of the well known CAs get installed on your machine. If you are still in doubt, you may print the public key of the CA and fax it to the CA for verification. .

Secure Data Transmission

In the second situation, when the customer sends the credit card details to a web store online, it is necessary to encrypt the data so that even if somebody hacks the data transmission line, the data itself may not become meaningful to the hacker. To achieve this, the supplier initially sends their public key to the consumer. Using this public key, the consumer encrypts the data and sends it to the supplier. Now, only the supplier who has a valid private key will be able to decrypt the data. In some situations, the consumer may also be interested in receiving the encrypted data from the server, which they alone should be able to decrypt. In such a situation, the process is identical to the earlier one. The consumer supplies their public key to the supplier; the supplier encrypts the document using this public key and sends the document to the original consumer. The consumer now decrypts the document using their private key. This technique is used in Secure Sockets Layer that is discussed in the next section.

Note that the data encryption is computationally expensive. The encryption may be provided in either software or dedicated hardware. The hardware encryption is recommended for sites with heavy volume, as it is much faster as compared to software encryption. Another important point to note is that the credit card information submitted by a customer may be decrypted only by the credit card company and the vendor may not be able to gain access to this information. This way, the entire transaction becomes more secure than buying goods in a shop where the shop employees can easily gain access to your credit card information.

Secure Sockets Layer

Secure Sockets Layer, popularly known as SSL, provides a protocol between low level TCP/IP and high level HTTP. SSL, originally developed by Netscape, allows the secured transmission of data between the two remote machines.

If your web page is deployed on a secured server, the client makes contact with the server using the HTTPS protocol. The server then sends a certificate to the client that contains its public key. The client verifies the validity and authenticity of the certificate from a list of trusted CA certificates that it possesses. The certificates of all the trusted parties must be pre-installed on the client machine. The certificates are stored in the registry and keystores. You will also need to set the security policy for the client machine. Once the certificate is authenticated, the client generates a pre-master secret (essentially some binary or character data). The client then encrypts this pre-master secret using the public key supplied by the server, and sends it to the server. The server now decrypts this pre-master secret and generates a master secret (another binary or character key). Similarly, the client generates a master secret from its pre-master secret. Note that both the pre-master secret and master secret are different from the public and private keys of the server or the client. The two secrets are known only to the client and the server involved in the communication. The pre-master secret is discarded by both as soon as the final master secret is created Both the parties now use this master secret for encryption/decryption while sending data between the two machines.

To use this feature, your server must support SSL. You can enable HTTPS protocol on your server by installing the certificate on your server. You will need to generate your private and public keys for this.

Web Store Application Architecture

A web store application typically consists of multiple tiers. The middle-tier consists of a web store that hosts your web pages and also contains the business logic implemented in servlets, JSPs, and JavaBeans. The database tier holds the inventory of your products and the front end provides the user interface. The architecture is illustrated below. In this chapter, we will use a very simple architecture for our web store application. The later chapters will expand on this and add more functionality to our web store application.

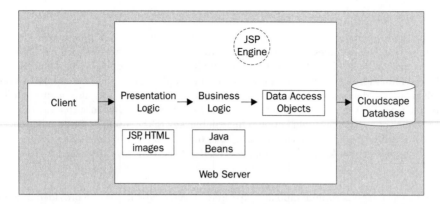

In our first version of the application, the back-end database holds the inventory of products. When you expand your application, you will use the back-end database to store other information such as product information in addition to the personalization information for each customer, etc. The servlet, JSP page, or JavaBean running on the middle tier accesses this database and generates a catalog of your products to display to the customer. The customer sees the product catalog as an HTML page. The catalog describes the features of each product that may be viewed by a customer. The front-end also allows user interaction where the customer makes their selections and adds the selected products to the shopping cart.

When the purchases are confirmed, you must ensure that you update the inventory in the warehouse database. You may also incorporate some back-end business logic that monitors the level of each product sold and places an online order to the supplier when the stocks fall below the pre-determined threshold. The back-end logic can also be helpful in determining which products are selling well and which are dead stock. This kind of reporting will help you manage your resources more efficiently.

The back-end logic can also be used for tracking the preferences of the customers visiting the store frequently. For example, a customer typically buys a 2% fat-free milk and bread every week. In a web store, it is easy to track the customer's preferences and provide a personalized service to each customer by offering such regularly purchased items to the customer whenever they visit your store. The personalization techniques and benefits are discussed in Chapter 10.

The Sample Store

In this section, we will develop a web store that sells computers online. The store provides a standard PC configuration and allows the customer to configure the computer to meet their individual needs. The selections made by the customer are added to the shopping cart maintained in the Session Context on the server. The server maintains a unique session context for each client.

The customer can configure more than one desktop model. The customer is then requested to enter the quantity of each selected model. Once the customer is satisfied with the selection, they are presented with several shipping options. The customer selects the desired shipping mode.

The system now presents an order form to the customer detailing all their purchases and the total shipping cost. The customer is then requested to select the payment mode; the customer may pay by check or credit card. In case of credit card payments, the customer is requested to enter the credit card information. The business logic at the middle tier verifies the credit purchases with the credit bureau and after obtaining the online authorization from the customer's bank, proceeds with the order confirmation.

A confirmation slip with a "Thank You" note is then e-mailed to the customer and the confirmed order is dispatched to the warehouse. The back-end logic now updates the product quantity in the warehouse and keeps track of the inventory. The warehouse will then ship the goods to the customer.

The application flow is illustrated below.

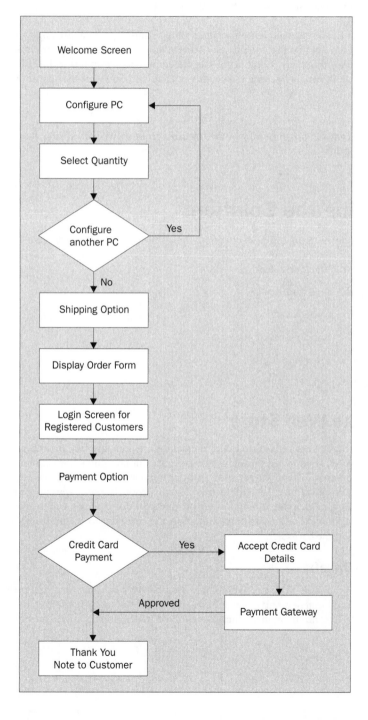

Software Used

We will build the entire web store application using JSPs and JavaBeans. For testing, we will deploy it on the reference implementation (RI) of J2EE. In practical situations, you will use a commercial application server or a web server that supports the JSP engine. We will use Cloudscape (see www.cloudscape.com for software download and setup information) as the database for this project.

Though, we've used J2EE reference implementation and the Cloudscape database engine for the current project, these don't have to be used – if you prefer using any other commercial server of your choice, you should be able to deploy the entire code without any modifications as the entire code complies with J2EE standards. We decided to use J2EE implementation simply because it is readily available to everyone as a part of the J2EE SDK installation.

> Note, all the code for the store may be downloaded from the Wrox web site at www.wrox.com.

Implementing the Solution:

In this section we'll get down to the business of coding the application and the topics we'll consider are:

- ❑ Setting up the back end database
- ❑ Creating the store home page
- ❑ Creating the product catalog
- ❑ Building the shopping cart
- ❑ Setting up membership login
- ❑ Coding the checkout

Setting up the Web Store

The first step in setting up our web store is to build the warehouse database for our web store. The warehouse stocks the products that you want to sell through your store. As our computer store contains the standard configuration for a bare-bones PC and the separate add-ons to create the complete system, we will create a table in our database to store this inventory. We will then add some products to our warehouse by adding data in these tables. The next step is to generate the catalog for our products. In this case, we will display a standard configuration for our desktop PC to the customer and allow the customer to customize it. We will use JSP pages to display these options to the customer.

Setting up the Database

Cloudscape comes with the J2EE SDK installation; it is used here for building our web store database. The listing below gives the SQL used for generating our database. I have tried to keep the entire application as simple as possible so that we can concentrate on the principles involved in developing a B2C e-commerce site.

```
DROP TABLE CONFIGURATION;

CREATE TABLE CONFIGURATION (
    CONFIGID VARCHAR(15) NOT NULL,
    CPU VARCHAR(15) NOT NULL,
    MOTHER VARCHAR(25) NOT NULL,
    HDD VARCHAR(10) NOT NULL,
    RAM VARCHAR(10) NOT NULL,
    MONITOR VARCHAR(10) NOT NULL,
    VIDEO VARCHAR(10) NOT NULL,
    CDROM VARCHAR(10) NOT NULL,
    NETWORK VARCHAR(10) NOT NULL
);

ALTER TABLE CONFIGURATION
    DROP CONSTRAINT CONFIGKEY;

ALTER TABLE CONFIGURATION
    ADD CONSTRAINT CONFIGKEY Primary Key (CONFIGID);

DROP TABLE CUSTOMER;

CREATE TABLE CUSTOMER (
    EMAIL VARCHAR(50) NOT NULL,
    NAME VARCHAR(50) NOT NULL,
    ADDRESS VARCHAR(255) NOT NULL,
    CITY VARCHAR(20) NOT NULL,
    PIN VARCHAR(10) NOT NULL,
    PHONE VARCHAR(15) NOT NULL,
    COMPANY VARCHAR(50),
    PASSWORD VARCHAR(15),
    FAX VARCHAR(15),
    BIRTH_MONTH INT,
    STATE VARCHAR(20),
    COUNTRY VARCHAR(20)
);

ALTER TABLE CUSTOMER
    DROP CONSTRAINT EMAILKEY;

ALTER TABLE CUSTOMER
    ADD CONSTRAINT EMAILKEY Primary Key (EMAIL);

DROP TABLE INVENTORY;

CREATE TABLE INVENTORY (
    PRODUCT_ID VARCHAR(15) NOT NULL,
    DESCRIPTION VARCHAR(50),
    QUANTITY INT NOT NULL,
    UNIT_PRICE DOUBLE PRECISION NOT NULL,
    NAME VARCHAR(25)
);

ALTER TABLE INVENTORY
    DROP CONSTRAINT PRODUCT;
```

```
ALTER TABLE INVENTORY
    ADD CONSTRAINT PRODUCT Primary Key (PRODUCT_ID);

DROP TABLE ORDERS;

CREATE TABLE ORDERS (
    ORDERID VARCHAR(15) NOT NULL,
    CUSTOMERID VARCHAR(15) NOT NULL,
    CONFIGID VARCHAR(15) NOT NULL,
    QTY INT NOT NULL,
    AMOUNT DOUBLE PRECISION NOT NULL
);

ALTER TABLE ORDERS
    DROP CONSTRAINT ORDERCONFIGKEY;

ALTER TABLE ORDERS
    ADD CONSTRAINT ORDERCONFIGKEY Primary Key (ORDERID,CONFIGID);
```

Save the above SQL code in `createTab.sql` file and create the database by running the following batch file. This batch file is provided in your J2EE installation and is called `CreateCloudTable.bat`. Note that you will need to set the `J2EE_HOME` variable to point to your J2EE installation folder. The datasource name used is `OnlinePCDB`. This is the name used by J2EE RI to refer to the database. Our JSP pages and EJBs in later chapters use this name to obtain a reference to the database.

```
set J2EE_HOME=c:\j2sdkee1.2.1

set
classpath=%J2EE_HOME%\lib\cloudscape\client.jar;%J2EE_HOME%\lib\cloudscape\tools.j
ar;%J2EE_HOME%\lib\cloudscape\cloudscape.jar;%J2EE_HOME%\lib\cloudscape\RmiJdbc.ja
r;%J2EE_HOME%\lib\cloudscape\license.jar

%JAVA_HOME%\bin\java -
Dij.connection.OnlinePCDB=jdbc:cloudscape:OnlinePCDB\;create=true -
Dcloudscape.system.home=%J2EE_HOME%\cloudscape -ms16m -mx32m
COM.cloudscape.tools.ij createTab.sql
```

The database structure is shown in the diagram below:

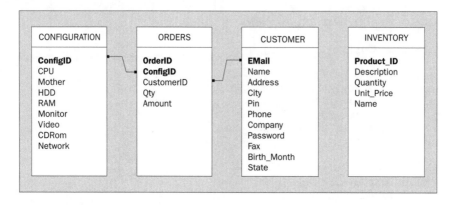

Our database contains only four tables:

❑ The CONFIGURATION table contains information about the custom configuration for each selected PC. It contains a unique ID and several fields detailing the parts requested by the customer.

❑ The ORDERS table stores the confirmed orders received from our customers. Each Order entry consists of a unique OrderID, a CustomerID, ConfigurationID, quantity, and the amount. The CustomerID field denotes the customer to whom the order belongs. The ConfigurationID links to the CONFIGURATION table that stores the custom configuration selected by the customer. The quantity denotes the quantity requested by the customer and the amount field contains the total amount for this item.

❑ The CUSTOMER table contains the customer's e-mail ID as the primary key along with the other relevant customer information. The Pin field represents the ZIP/Postcode information.

❑ The INVENTORY table maintains our parts inventory. Each part has an ID, name, unit price, quantity, and description.

Once you create the database, you may populate it with the sample data supplied in the SampleData.txt file. To upload the data in your database, use the following batch file:

```
set J2EE_HOME=c:\j2sdkee1.2.1

set
classpath=%J2EE_HOME%\lib\cloudscape\client.jar;%J2EE_HOME%\lib\cloudscape\tools.j
ar;%J2EE_HOME%\lib\cloudscape\cloudscape.jar;%J2EE_HOME%\lib\cloudscape\RmiJdbc.ja
r;%J2EE_HOME%\lib\cloudscape\license.jar

%JAVA_HOME%\bin\java -
Dij.connection.OnlinePCDB=jdbc:cloudscape:OnlinePCDB\;create=true -
Dcloudscape.system.home=%J2EE_HOME%\cloudscape -ms16m -mx32m
COM.cloudscape.tools.ij SampleData.sql
```

The SQL required while running the above batch file is given in file SampleData.sql:

```
INSERT INTO INVENTORY
SELECT * from NEW FileImport('SampleData.txt') AS myExternalData;
```

Database Access

Having created the database, the next step is to develop a utility class for database access. This is called ConnectionManager:

```
/* ConnectionManager.java */
import java.sql.*;

/** ConnectionManager class loads the jdbc driver and provides methods for
connecting and disconnecting to the database */
public class ConnectionManager {
    protected Connection con;
    protected String driver = "COM.cloudscape.core.RmiJdbcDriver";
    protected String url = "jdbc:cloudscape:rmi:OnlinePCDB";

/** Load the driver and make connection to the database */
    public Connection logOn() {
        try {
```

```
            Class.forName( driver ).newInstance();
            con = DriverManager.getConnection( url, "", "" );
        } catch(Exception ex) {
            ex.printStackTrace();
        }
        return con;
    }

    /** Close the database connection */
    public void logOff(){
        try {
            con.close();
        } catch(Exception ex) {
            ex.printStackTrace();
        }
    }
}
```

The `ConnectionManager` has two methods, `logOn()` and `logOff()`. The `logOn()` method loads the JDBC driver and establishes the connection to our database. The `logOff()` method closes the database connection. Note that though I am loading the JDBC driver explicitly in the above code, it will not be necessary to do so if you are using an application server. An application server will provide you with a datasource to which you can connect. Such datasources are pooled and shared between the concurrent users, resulting in the more efficient use of resources.

Having built the database, we now proceed to the site development. We begin our development with the home page for our site.

Web Store Home Page

When the customer logs on to our site, they will see the home page of our online PC store.

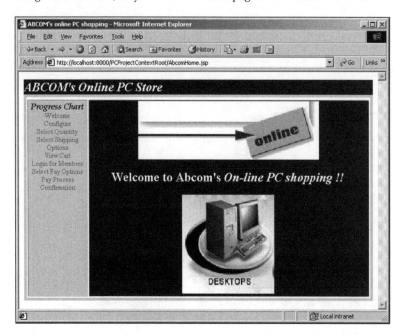

All subsequent pages of our web site will look similar to this home page. We use the format shown below for all our pages. At the top of the page, a banner is displayed; on the left-hand side, a progress chart is displayed and the rest of the screen is used for customer interaction.

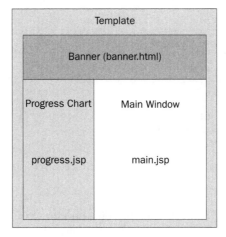

The home page is stored in the AbcomHome.jsp file and contains a banner at the top that displays our store name. This is common on all the subsequent pages of our site. We use a JSP include directive to include the banner file on all subsequent pages. Any changes made in the banner will then be reflected on all the pages.

On the left hand side, a progress chart is displayed that displays the status of the customer's progress of the shopping. The shopping process involves several stages; these are listed in this left hand side column. As the customer moves ahead through the various stages of shopping, this display is updated to show the current status. The customer follows several steps for each purchase. These involve configuring the PC, selecting quantity, selecting shipping options, viewing cart contents, logging in as an existing customer or creating a new customer profile, selecting payment options and finally making payment to complete the transaction.

As the customer moves through each step, the progress chart is updated to show the completed steps in a different color. Thus, the customer can easily identify the current status of his/her shopping progress at any step.

I could have used client side JavaScript code to update this display. However, I avoided using JavaScript and fully developed the site using Java alone. Thus, the progress bar is another JSP page. The center of the page shows the welcome message to the user. The subsequent pages will provide user interface in this area. The code for our home page is given here:

```
<%-- AbcomHome.jsp --%>
<%-- Displays the home page to the user, follows the template with Banner
at the top and Progress chart on the left --%>
<HTML>
<%@ page language="java"  import="java.util.*" %>

<jsp:useBean id="GlobalBean" scope="session" class="GlobalVarBean" />
<jsp:setProperty name="GlobalBean" property="level" value="1" />

<HTML>
<HEAD>
```

```
        <TITLE>ABCOM's online PC shopping</TITLE>
    </HEAD>

    <BODY>

    <TABLE BORDER="5" WIDTH="100%" STYLE="border-style: solid" HEIGHT="336">
    <TR BGCOLOR="#0000FF" TEXT="#FFFFFF" COLSPAN="2" VALIGN="middle">
            <%@ include file="Banner.html" %>
    </TR>
    <TR>
        <TD WIDTH="18%" HEIGHT="262" BGCOLOR="#66FFFF" VALIGN="top">
            <jsp:include page="ProgressChart.jsp" flush="true" />
            </TD>
            <TD WIDTH="82%" height="262" bgcolor="#0000FF">
            <%@ include file="Main.html" %>
            </TD>
    </TR>
    </TABLE>
    </BODY>
    </HTML>
```

Note that we use `<%@ include ... >` directive for including `Banner.html` and `Main.html` files. However, to include `ProgressChart.jsp` we use the `<jsp:include >` tag. This is because `ProgressChart.jsp` regenerates the page as the user progresses through the shopping process. The `Banner.html` and `Main.html` are static web pages.

The home page declares a `GlobalVarBean` and includes the two files `ProgressChart.jsp` and `Main.html`.

The home page instantiates a JavaBean called `GlobalBean` which is declared to have the scope of the client session. The bean instances created in your JSP page may have different scopes. In some of our examples, we will create bean instances with the page scope. Such a bean instance will be available only within the scope of the current page and is recreated every time the page is loaded.

```
<jsp:useBean id="GlobalBean" scope="session" class="GlobalVarBean" />
```

An HTML table is created to include the banner, progress chart, and the main screen. The `Banner.html` file simply contains the company logo.

```
<!-- Banner.html -->
<HTML>

<HEAD>
<BASE TARGET="contents">
</HEAD>

<BODY>
<I><B><FONT SIZE="5" COLOR="#FFFFFF">
ABCOM's Online PC Store</FONT></B></I>
</BODY>

</HTML>
```

The `Main.html` file contains two images and the link to the next page.

```
<!-- Main.html -->
<HTML>
<BODY>
```

```
<P ALIGN="center">
    <IMG BORDER="0" SRC="onlineLOGO.jpg" WIDTH="350" HEIGHT="110"></P>
<P ALIGN="center">
    <B><FONT FACE="Arabia" SIZE="5" COLOR="#FFFFFF">Welcome to Abcom's
    <I> Online PC shopping !!
    </I></FONT></B>
</P>
<P ALIGN="center">
    <A HREF="Level2.jsp" TARGET="_self">
    <IMG BORDER="0" SRC="desktop.gif" WIDTH="178" HEIGHT="186"></A>
</P>
</BODY>
</HTML>
```

The `GlobalVarBean` class declares two properties. These are called `cart` and `ProgressLevel`. The `cart` property serves the purpose of storing the customer's purchases and the `ProgressLevel` variable is used for tracking the customer's shopping progress.

```
/* GlobalVarBean.java */
import java.beans.*;
import java.util.*;

/**     The GlobalVarBean declares two variables - ProgressLevel that tracks the
level of shopping progress for the customer and cart Vector that is used for
storing shopping contents */

public class GlobalVarBean {
    private int ProgressLevel;
    private Vector cart = new Vector();

    public void setLevel(int level) {
        ProgressLevel = level;
    }

    public int getLevel() {
        return ProgressLevel;
    }

    public Vector getCart() {
        return cart;
    }

    /** Add the configured PC item to the cart */

    public void addToCart(OrderItemBean OrderItem) {
        cart.addElement(OrderItem);
    }
}
```

The bean defines a method called `addToCart()` that receives an `OrderItem` object to be added to the cart. The `OrderItemBean` defines the structure for each item added to the cart. I will discuss the `OrderItemBean` class later.

I will now discuss the `ProgressChart.jsp` file before moving to the next screen of our application.

```
<%-- ProgressChart.jsp --%>
<%-- Displays the current status of the shopping to the user --%>
<HTML>
```

```
<jsp:useBean id="GlobalBean" scope="session" class="GlobalVarBean" />

<BODY>

<P ALIGN="center" STYLE="margin-top: 0; margin-bottom: 0">
   <b><I><FONT FACE="Book Antiqua" SIZE="3" COLOR="#0000FF">Progress
Chart</FONT></I></B>
</P>

<%-- The level variable in GlobalBean maintains the current shopping level. The
program retrieves this variable and sets the colors for the
shopping items according to the level reached so far --%>

   <%
       int level = GlobalBean.getLevel();
       String str1 = "<P ALIGN=\"center\" STYLE=\"margin-top: 0;
          margin-bottom: 0\">
       <font face=Book Antiqua size=2 color=";
       String str2 = "</FONT></P>";
       String[] items = {
          "Welcome",
          "Configure",
          "Select Quantity",
          "Select Shipping Options",
          "View Cart",
          "Login for Members",
          "Select Pay Options",
          "Pay Process",
          "Confirmation"
       };

       for (int i=0; i < items.length; i++) {
          String colorStr = "#FF3300";
          if (i < level){ colorStr = "#009933";}
          out.write(str1 + colorStr + ">" + items[i] + str2);
       }
   %>

</BODY>
</HTML>
```

The `ProgressChart.jsp` file creates a `String` array that is used for storing the various shopping levels. The variable that tracks the shopping level is stored in the `GlobalVarBean` class instance. The scriptlet code accesses this variable.

```
int level = GlobalBean.getLevel();
```

The program now sets up a loop for displaying the various shopping levels. The color of the shopping level is decided by the value in the `ProgressLevel` variable `colorStr`.

```
for (int i=0; i < items.length; i++) {
   String colorStr = "#FF3300";
   if (i < level) {
      colorStr = "#009933";
   }
   out.write(str1 + colorStr + ">" + items[i] + str2);
}
```

As the user progresses with their shopping, the ProgressLevel variable is modified and the ProgressChart.jsp file is updated to display the changes. The steps completed are shown in a different color. By looking at the progress chart, the customer knows exactly how far he/she has moved in the shopping process and how many more steps are required to complete the current transaction. Note that the progress chart is a display of the shopping status to the customer. The customer cannot jump the steps by using this chart.

The next step of our application is to display a catalog of products from our warehouse and allow the customer to customize the PC of their choice.

Creating the Catalog

The store catalog typically consists of several pages detailing each product that the store sells. A catalog is created from the warehouse database and may be stored as static HTML pages. Alternatively, you may generate the catalog dynamically using JSP pages.

The advantage of a static HTML catalog is that the customer sees a very fast response. The disadvantage is that you have to update the catalog periodically and the displayed catalog may not always show all the products that you sell through your store. Creating catalog contents dynamically certainly takes some time to process and the customer may encounter a slow response on your site. However, a newly added product to the warehouse is immediately shown in the catalog.

In our sample application, I will use the dynamic catalog creation approach since the number of products is very limited. Thus, loading the catalog may not take too much time. To reduce the database access time further, we can cache the data. This is explained in subsequent chapters. Now, let us look at the next screen of our application.

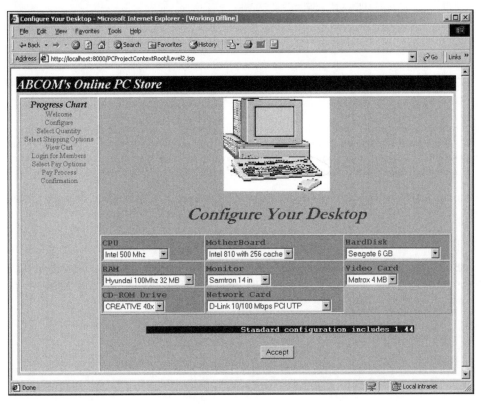

The configuration screen is generated by Level2.jsp file. The JSP file uses the instance of GlobalVarBean and sets the ProgressLevel variable to 2.

```
<jsp:useBean id="GlobalBean" scope="session" class="GlobalVarBean" />
<jsp:setProperty name="GlobalBean" property="level" value="2" />
```

Likewise, the entire application contains a Leveln.jsp file between every two screens. Each such JSP file accesses the ProgressLevel variable and sets it to the appropriate level. Each such Level JSP file also adheres to our template and replaces the main screen area with the appropriate screen of the application. In this case, the Assemble.jsp file generates our main screen area that offers customization of the PC.

```
<%-- Level2.jsp --%>
<%@ page language="java" %>

<HTML>

<jsp:useBean id="GlobalBean" scope="session" class="GlobalVarBean" />
<jsp:setProperty name="GlobalBean" property="level" value="2" />

<BODY>

<TABLE BORDER="5" WIDTH="100%" STYLE="border-style: solid" HEIGHT="336">
    <TR BGCOLOR="#0000FF" TEXT="#FFFFFF">
        <%@ include file="Banner.html" %>
    </TR>
    <TR>
        <TD WIDTH="18%" HEIGHT="262" BGCOLOR="#66FFFF" VALIGN="top">
            <jsp:include page="ProgressChart.jsp" flush="true" />
        </TD>
        <TD WIDTH="82%" HEIGHT="262" BGCOLOR="#C0C0C0">
            <jsp:include page="Assemble.jsp" flush="true" />
        </TD>
    </TR>
</TABLE>
</BODY>
</HTML>
```

The configuration screen contains several list boxes offering a choice of selection for each item required by the desktop PC. These choice boxes are populated directly from the underlying database. Therefore, in future, if you stock a new motherboard, the choice will be immediately available to the customer as soon as the warehouse database is updated. I shall now discuss the Assemble.jsp file.

The Assemble.jsp file creates an instance of the AssembleBean class. The bean is declared to have page scope.

```
<jsp:useBean id="abean" scope="page" class="AssembleBean" />
```

The AssembleBean class is used for fetching the data for each list box from the warehouse database. I shall discuss this class shortly. Our Assemble.jsp file after instantiating the bean uses a Scriptlet to connect to the database:

```
<%
    abean.connect();
    Vector v;
    Iterator it;
%>
```

The scriptlet also declares two variables of type `Vector` and `Iterator`.

The `AssembleBean` provides a method called `getItemData()` that returns a list of items in a vector. The item type is passed as a string argument to the `getItemData()` method:

```
<% v = abean.getItemData("cpu"); %>
```

The program then iterates through the elements of the vector and adds these to the list box:

```
<%
    it = v.iterator();
    while (it.hasNext()) {
        String itnew = (String)it.next();
%>
<option> <%= itnew %></option> <% } %>
```

Likewise, the `getItemData()` method is called several times to fetch the data for each inventory item. The data is displayed in the corresponding list box using code similar to the one shown above. The code listing for `Assemble.jsp` is given here for easy reference:

```
<%-- Assemble.jsp --%>
<%-- Displays the various items from the inventory database to the user. Each item
is displayed in a drop-down list box --%>
<html>

<%@ page language="java" import="java.util.*,java.sql.*" %>
<jsp:useBean id="abean" scope="page" class="AssembleBean" />

<%-- Connect to the database and declare variables --%>
<%
    abean.connect();
    Vector v;
    Iterator it;
%>

<html>
<head>
    <title>Configure Your Desktop</title>
</head>

<body bgcolor="#FFFFFF">

    <p align="center">
        <img border="0" src="desktop.gif" width="198" height="168">
    </p>
    <p align="center"><b><i><font face="Garamond" size="6"
color="#3333CC">Configure Your Desktop</font></i></b>
    </p>

    <form method=POST action="Level3.jsp" target="_self">

<%-- Create an HTML table to display the various component options --%>
<table border="1" cellspacing="1" width="100%">
    <tr bgcolor="#9999FF">
```

```
        <td><font color="#3333CC">
           <font face="Courier New"><b>CPU</b></font>
<%-- The getItemData method returns a vector containing the different CPU types in
our inventory --%>
           <%
              v = abean.getItemData("cpu");
           %>

<%-- Create an Iterator on the vector and add the retrieved items to the drop down
list box --%>
           <p style="margin-top: 0; margin-bottom: 0">
           <select name="speed" size="1" style="color: #000080">
           <%
              it = v.iterator();
              while (it.hasNext()) {
                   String itnew = (String)it.next(); %>
                   <option> <%= itnew %></option>
           <% } %>
           </select></font></p>
        </td>

        <td><font color="#3333CC">
<%-- Retrieve and add the mother board types to the list box --%>
           <font face="Courier New"><b>MotherBoard</b></font>
           <%
              v = abean.getItemData("mother");
           %>
           <p style="margin-top: 0; margin-bottom: 0">
           <select name="mother" size="1" style="color: #000080">
           <%
              it =v.iterator();
              while(it.hasNext()){
                String itnew = (String)it.next(); %>
                <option> <%= itnew %></option>
            <% } %>
           </select></font></p>
        </td>

        <td><font color="#3333CC">
<%-- Retrieve and add the hard drive types to the list box --%>
           <font face="Courier New"><b>HardDisk</b></font>
           <%
             v=abean.getItemData("hard");
           %>
           <p style="margin-top: 0; margin-bottom: 0">
           <select name="hard" size="1" style="color: #000080">
           <%
             it =v.iterator();
             while(it.hasNext()){
                String itnew = (String)it.next(); %>
                 <option> <%= itnew %></option>
           <% } %>
             </select></font></p>
        </td>
     </tr>
```

```
    <tr bgcolor="#9999FF">
<%-- Retrieve and add the RAM types to the list box --%>
    <td><font color="#3333CC">
        <font face="Courier New"><b>RAM</b></font>
        <%
          v=abean.getItemData("ram");
        %>
          <p style="margin-top: 0; margin-bottom: 0">
          <select size="1" name="ram" style="color: #000080">
        <%
          it =v.iterator();
          while(it.hasNext()){
            String itnew = (String)it.next(); %>
              <option> <%= itnew %></option>
        <% } %>
          </select></font></p>

    </td>

    <td><font color="#3333CC">
<%-- Retrieve and add the monitor types to the list box --%>
        <font face="Courier New"><b>Monitor</b></font>
        <%
          v=abean.getItemData("monitor");
        %>
        <p style="margin-top: 0; margin-bottom: 0">
        <select name="monitor" size="1" style="color: #000080">
        <%
          it =v.iterator();
          while(it.hasNext()){
            String itnew = (String)it.next(); %>
              <option> <%= itnew %></option>
        <% } %>
          </select></font></p>
    </td>

    <td><font color="#3333CC">
<%-- Retrieve and add the video board types to the list box --%>
        <font face="Courier New"><b>Video Card</b></font>
        <%
          v=abean.getItemData("video");
        %>
        <p style="margin-top: 0; margin-bottom: 0">
        <select size="1" name="video" style="color: #000080">
        <%
          it =v.iterator();
          while(it.hasNext()){
            String itnew = (String)it.next(); %>
              <option> <%= itnew %></option>
        <% } %>
          </select></font></p>
    </td>
  </tr>

  <tr bgcolor="#9999FF">
```

273

```
<%-- Retrieve and add the CD-ROM types to the list box --%>
    <td><font color="#3333CC">
        <font face="Courier New"><b>CD-ROM Drive</b></font>
        <%
            v=abean.getItemData("cdrom");
        %>
        <p style="margin-top: 0; margin-bottom: 0">
        <select size="1" name="cd" style="color: #000080">
        <%
            it =v.iterator();
            while(it.hasNext()){
                String itnew = (String)it.next(); %>
                    <option> <%= itnew %></option>
        <% } %>
        </select></font></p>
    </td>

    <td><font color="#3333CC">
<%-- Retrieve and add the network card types to the list box --%>
        <font face="Courier New"><b>Network Card</b></font>
        <%
            v=abean.getItemData("network");
        %>
        <p style="margin-top: 0; margin-bottom: 0">
        <select size="1" name="card" style="color: #000080">
        <%
            it =v.iterator();
            while(it.hasNext()){
                String itnew = (String)it.next(); %>
                    <option> <%= itnew %></option>
        <% } %>
        </select></font></p>
    </td>
   </tr>
   </table>

<%-- Display a scrolling text message to the user --%>
        <p align="center"> <font face="Courier" size="1"><b>
            <marquee style="color: #FFFFFF" bgcolor="#0000FF" width="500"
                height="13">Standard configuration includes 1.44MB FDD, 104
                Key Keyboard, Mouse, SMPS, Cabinet. </marquee></b></font>
        </p>

        <p align="center"><font color="#0000FF"><input type="submit"
value="Accept" name="submit">
        </font></p>

   </form>

<%-- Close the database connection --%>
    <%
        abean.disconnect();
    %>

</body>
</html>
```

At the end, the program code disconnects from the database by calling the `disconnect()` method on the `AssembleBean` instance. This closes the database connection. When the user accepts the configuration, the selections in each list box are sent to the next page with the help of the **Submit** button.

I shall now discuss the `AssembleBean.java` file.

```java
/* AssembleBean.java */
import java.io.*;
import java.util.*;
import java.beans.*;
import java.sql.*;

/** AssembleBean retrieves the Item description from INVENTORY table. The caller
    calls getItemData method to retrieve the item description in a Vector */

public class AssembleBean {
    private Connection con;
    private ConnectionManager conMan = new ConnectionManager();
    private Statement stmt;
    private ResultSet rs;
    private Vector v;

    /** Connect to the database */
    public void connect() {
        try {
            con = conMan.logOn();
        } catch(Exception ex) {
            ex.printStackTrace();
        }
    }

    /** Disconnect from the database */
    public void disconnect() {
        try {
            conMan.logOff();
        } catch(Exception ex) {
            ex.printStackTrace();
        }
    }

    /** Retrieve description of the item from the inventory table and return to the
    caller in a vector */

    public Vector getItemData(String Item) {
        String SQL;
        try {
            SQL = "SELECT DESCRIPTION FROM INVENTORY WHERE NAME = '" + Item +
                "'";
            v = new Vector();
            stmt = con.createStatement();
            rs = stmt.executeQuery(SQL);
            if(rs != null) {
                while(rs.next()) {
                    String str = rs.getString(1);
                    v.addElement(str);
                }
            }
        } catch(Exception ex) {
```

```
            ex.printStackTrace();
        }
        return v;
    }
}
```

The `AssembleBean` creates an instance of `ConnectionManager` class to obtain a connection to the warehouse database.

```
private ConnectionManager conMan = new ConnectionManager();
```

The `connect()` and `disconnect()` methods use this connection object. The `getItemData()` method also uses this connection object for executing a query on the database. The `getItemData()` method receives a string parameter describing the item to be fetched. An SQL SELECT statement is constructed based on this parameter.

```
SQL = "SELECT DESCRIPTION FROM INVENTORY WHERE NAME = '" + Item + "'";
```

The program then creates the `Statement` object and executes the query on the database.

```
stmt = con.createStatement();
rs = stmt.executeQuery(SQL);
```

Instead of using `createStatement`, you may use `PreparedStatement` so that the SQL is not compiled on every call. The use of `PreparedStatement` will improve the performance. Alternatively, you may use stored procedures in your database. However, the use of stored procedures will tie down your program to a particular database and the application may not be ported easily to another database engine in future. The vector is then populated from the result set and returned to the caller.

```
if(rs != null) {
    while(rs.next()) {
        String str = rs.getString(1);
        v.addElement(str);
    }
}
```

Having seen the code for the home page, we will now move to the next screen of our application.

The Shopping Cart

When the user shops at your web store, you need to provide them with an electronic shopping cart. A user may surf through the various pages of your site during their visit and add the purchases to the shopping cart. The state of the shopping cart must be maintained throughout the client's session until the time the user finally confirms the orders in the cart by making payment. If the user does not confirm the order and closes the browser or is timed out by the server due to a long period of inactivity, the cart contents will be lost.

Maintaining State

As HTTP is a stateless protocol, maintaining the state across multiple pages is not possible unless some other technique for storing state is employed. The state may be maintained on the client machine with the help of cookies. However, not all browsers support cookies; sometimes the user may turn off the cookie support on the browser or it may be a corporate policy on your office PC not to allow the cookies. A state may be maintained across several pages by using the technique of URL rewriting. Another option is to maintain the state of the cart on the server. For this, you may use servlets or JSP pages. A servlet can maintain the client state in an `HttpSession` object. A JSP page that is compiled into a servlet can use this session object. In the case of a JSP page, a JavaBean class may be instantiated on the home page and made available throughout the client session.

Holding State on the Server

When you maintain the client state on the server in a servlet or JSP page, your application does not become truly scalable, as a separate instance of the servlet or JSP page must be maintained on a per client basis. The situation may be overcome by using Enterprise JavaBeans (EJBs). There are two types of EJBs – session and entity beans. The session beans can be stateless or stateful. A stateless session bean does not maintain the client state, while a stateful session bean maintains the client state in its instance variables. The EJB container supports component pooling for both stateless and stateful beans. Thus, if you create the shopping cart in a stateful session bean, the application scalability can be easily achieved.

There is also a down side to maintaining the client state on the server. In the real world, any web application is deployed with the clustering and load balancing support on the server. One may even take care of situations like failover where the client is automatically moved to another server if the server to which they are logged on to fails for some reasons. All these can cause a major concern as far as the client state management is concerned. In case of servlets, the `HttpSession` is valid only for the server process under which the servlet is running. Therefore, if you move the client to a different machine, a different `HttpSession` is created. The EJBs solve this problem by maintaining the client state in the bean itself. Therefore, even if the client's bean is moved to another machine, the client's state is still maintained.

> *In our web store example, we will create a JavaBean that is available for the entire scope of the client session. We will create the shopping cart in this JavaBean class.*

Displaying the Cart

We now move to the next screen of our application. Once the customer configures the computer with their choice of components, they proceeds to the next screen where the customer can select the quantity for the configured computer and proceed to the shipping options. The customer may wish to buy more than one kind of PC and can go back to the earlier configuration screen for customizing another PC. When the customer moves to the next screen, all the selections will be added to the shopping cart.

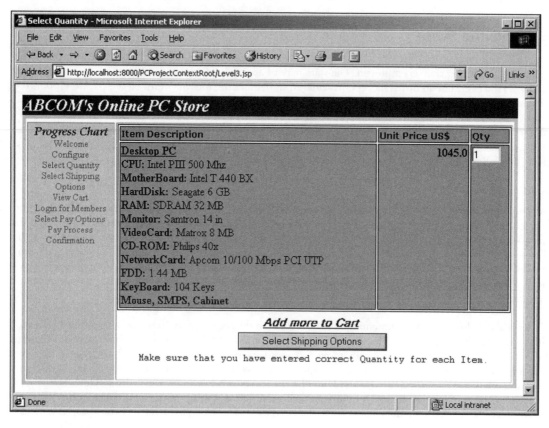

Level3.jsp generates the above page.

```
<%-- Level3.jsp --%>
<%@ page language="java" %>

<html>

<jsp:useBean id="GlobalBean" scope="session" class="GlobalVarBean" />
<jsp:setProperty name="GlobalBean" property="level" value="3" />

<body>

<table border="5" width="100%" style="border-style: solid" height="336">
   <tr bgcolor="#0000FF" text="#FFFFFF">
      <%@ include file="Banner.html" %>
   </tr>
   <tr>
      <td width="18%" height="262" bgcolor="#66FFFF" valign="top">
          <jsp:include page="ProgressChart.jsp" flush="true" />
      </td>
      <td width="82%" height="262" bgcolor="#FFFFFF">
          <jsp:include page="CartItems.jsp" flush="true" />
      </td>
   </tr>
</table>
</body>
</html>
```

Before we go much further, it is worth discussing `leveln.jsp` files – one accompanies each of our code-bearing `.jsp` files after our home page file. As we saw earlier, the level property is incremented by one each time we move through a step in our web application. The value of this increment is then used to decide which of the `Leveln.jsp` files should be used. What the "level" pages do is redraw the background of the pages displaying our functional `.jsp` files, which they then include. In the example above, we can see that `Level3.jsp` differs from `Level2.jsp` in that it now includes `CartItems.jsp`, whereas `Level2.jsp` specified the `Assemble.jsp` inclusion. `Level4.jsp` includes the `ShippingOptions.jsp`, and so on.

The level property is managed by `GlobalBean` in the class `GlobalVarBean`. All the "level" pages are also available for review by downloading the code from the Wrox site (www.wrox.com).

The main screen display area uses the `CartItems.jsp` file to display the configuration selected by the customer. The `CartItems` page uses two beans – the `GlobalVarBean` instance created on our home page and the `OrderItemBean` instance that stores the configuration details for each order item.

```
<jsp:useBean id="ordItem" scope="page" class="OrderItemBean" />
<jsp:useBean id="GlobalBean" scope="session" class="GlobalVarBean" />
```

As seen earlier, the `GlobalVarBean` instance contains a `cart` vector that is used for storing each cart item. Each cart item is an instance of `OrderItemBean`. This class is instantiated on this page and is available only in the page scope. Thus, each invocation of the page creates another instance of this Bean. The `OrderItemBean` represents the configuration information for the PC that is required for display on the current page. We will convert this bean to an entity bean in Chapter 12. I shall discuss the `OrderItemBean` class after describing the `CartItems.jsp` file fully.

The `CartItems.jsp` file retrieves the user's selections from the previous page by using the request object. The full file (and all the other files associated with this example) are available for download at www.wrox.com.

```
String speed=request.getParameter("speed");
String mother=request.getParameter("mother");
String hard=request.getParameter("hard");
...
```

Once all the parameters are retrieved, these are stored in the instance of `OrderItemBean`:

```
ordItem.setSpeed(speed);
ordItem.setMother(mother);
ordItem.setHD(hard);
...
```

The program then calls the `calcPCPrice()` method on the bean to compute the price for the selected configuration. The computed price is stored in the instance variable of the current object:

```
ordItem.calcPCPrice();
```

The order item is still not ready for adding to the cart. The default quantity for each item is one. The user may change this quantity before moving to the next screen. The program calls the `addToCart()` method of the `GlobalVarBean` class to add the item object to the cart:

```
        GlobalBean.addToCart(ordItem);
```

The next part of the JSP page is to display the current contents to the user and allow the user to add more contents to the cart. To display the current contents of the cart, we need to first obtain the reference to our cart object. The program then creates an iterator to iterate through the cart contents. Each item in the cart is of type OrderItemBean. The following code segment shows how each item is retrieved from the cart:

```
<%
    cart = GlobalBean.getCart();
    Iterator it = cart.iterator();
    while (it.hasNext()) {
        ordItem = (OrderItemBean)it.next();
%>
```

For each cart item, we then describe the individual parts of each configured PC by calling the appropriate get methods of the OrderItemBean class. The getPrice() method retrieves the unit price for each configured PC that is displayed in a separate column of the HTML table:

```
<B>CPU: </b><%= ordItem.getSpeed() %> <BR>
<B>MotherBoard: </b><%= ordItem.getMother() %> <BR>
<B>HardDisk: </b><%= ordItem.getHD() %> <BR>
...
<TD VALIGN="top" align="right"><B> <%= ordItem.getPrice() %> </B></TD>
```

The getQty() method retrieves the unit quantity and displays it in an edit control. The user can modify the contents of this edit control to select the desired quantity. The quantity for each item is copied into the cart when the user moves to the next screen:

```
<TD VALIGN="top"><B>
    <INPUT TYPE="text" NAME="Qty" VALUE=<%= ordItem.getQty() %> SIZE="3"> </B></TD>
```

The user is then presented with two options, either to move to the next screen to select shipping options or to configure another PC for purchase. If the user decides to configure another PC, the user is re-directed to the earlier screen for the selection of the PC configuration. The full code for CartItems.jsp is as follows:

```
<%-- CartItems.jsp --%>
<%-- Displays the current contents of the cart to the user and allows
the user to select the quantity for each configured PC --%>
<html>
<head>
    <title>Select Quantity</title>
</head>

<%@ page language="java" import="java.util.*" %>

<%-- OrderItemBean stores the configuration details of the PC --%>
<jsp:useBean id="ordItem" scope="page" class="OrderItemBean" />
<%-- GlobalVarBean maintains the shopping cart --%>
<jsp:useBean id="GlobalBean" scope="session" class="GlobalVarBean" />
```

```
<%-- Get the PC configuration details from the parameters and store
    them in the OrderItemBean class instance. Add the OrderItemBean
    object to the shopping cart maintained in GlobalVarBean object --%>
<%
   Vector cart = new Vector();

   String speed=request.getParameter("speed");
   String mother=request.getParameter("mother");
   String hard=request.getParameter("hard");
   String ram=request.getParameter("ram");
   String monitor=request.getParameter("monitor");
   String video=request.getParameter("video");
   String cd=request.getParameter("cd");
   String card=request.getParameter("card");

   ordItem.setSpeed(speed);
   ordItem.setMother(mother);
   ordItem.setHD(hard);
   ordItem.setRAM(ram);
   ordItem.setMonitor(monitor);
   ordItem.setVideo(video);
   ordItem.setCD(cd);
   ordItem.setCard(card);
   ordItem.setQty(1);
       ordItem.calcPCPrice();
   GlobalBean.addToCart(ordItem);
%>

<body bgcolor="#FFFFFF">

<form method="post" action="Level4.jsp" target="_self">

<%-- Create an HTML table for displaying the list of selectd PC's to the user --%>
<table width="100%" border="1" bordercolor="#000000">
   <tr bgcolor="#9999FF">
      <td><b><font face="Verdana, Arial, Helvetica, sans-serif" size="2">Item
Description</font></b></td>
      <td><b><font face="Verdana, Arial, Helvetica, sans-serif" size="2">Unit
Price US$</font></b></td>
      <td><b><font face="Verdana, Arial, Helvetica, sans-serif"
size="2">Qty</font></b></td>
   </tr>

   <%-- Retrieve the cart and get each PC configuration from the cart --%>
   <%
      cart = GlobalBean.getCart();
      Iterator it = cart.iterator();
      while (it.hasNext()) {
          ordItem = (OrderItemBean)it.next();
   %>

   <%-- For each PC configuration display the configuration in HTML table --%>
   <tr bgcolor="#9999FF"><font face="Verdana" size="2">
      <td><b><u> Desktop PC </b></u><br>
         <b>CPU: </b><%= ordItem.getSpeed() %> <br>
         <b>MotherBoard: </b><%= ordItem.getMother() %> <br>
         <b>HardDisk: </b><%= ordItem.getHD() %> <br>
         <b>RAM: </b><%= ordItem.getRAM() %> <br>
         <b>Monitor: </b><%= ordItem.getMonitor() %><br>
         <b>VideoCard: </b><%= ordItem.getVideo() %> <br>
         <b>CD-ROM: </b><%= ordItem.getCD() %> <br>
```

281

```
        <b>NetworkCard: </b><%= ordItem.getCard() %> <br>
        <b>FDD: </b>1.44 MB<br>
        <b>KeyBoard: </b>104 Keys<br>
        <b>Mouse, SMPS, Cabinet<br></b></td>
    <td valign="top" align="right"><b> <%= ordItem.getPrice() %> </b></td>
    <td valign="top"><b>
        <input type="text" name="Qty" value=<%= ordItem.getQty() %> size="3">
</b></td>
        </font>
    </tr>

<% } %>
</table>

<table border="0" width="100%" cellspacing="5" cellpadding="0">
    <tr>
        <td width="100%">
            <p align="center"><a href="Level2.jsp" target="_self"><b><i>
            <font face="Microsoft Sans Serif" size="3" color="#0000FF">Add
            more to Cart</font></i></b></a></td>
    </tr>
    <tr>
        <td width="100%">
            <p align="center">
            <input type="submit" value="Select Shipping Options" name="submit"></td>
    </tr>
    <tr>
        <td width="100%">
            <p align="center"><font face="Courier" size="1" color="#0000FF">
            Make sure that you have entered correct Quantity for each Item.
            </font></td>
    </tr>
</table>
</form>
</body>
</html>
```

I shall now discuss the `OrderItemBean` class. The `OrderItemBean` class declares several instance variables that hold the description for each type of item selected by the customer while configuring the PC. The class also declares an `ItemPrice` variable for holding the price of this item. A business method called `calcPCPrice` computes the price for the selected configuration and stores it in this variable. The instance variable `Qty` holds the quantity for the current item:

```
String Speed, Mother, Monitor, HD, CD, Video, RAM, Card;
double ItemPrice=0;
int Qty=1;
```

The instance method `calcPCPrice()` uses the `OrderUtil` class to connect and disconnect to the database. For each item in the order, the `calcPrice()` method on the `OrderUtil` class is called to retrieve the price for the currently selected item. The total price of the PC is computed by calling `calcPrice()` method on each component and is stored in the instance variable – `ItemPrice`:

```
public void calcPCPrice() {
    ordUtil = new OrderUtil();
```

```
      ordUtil.connect();
      ItemPrice = ordUtil.calcPrice(Speed);
      ItemPrice += ordUtil.calcPrice(MotherBoard);
      … rest of the calcPrice method calls
      ordUtil.disconnect();
}
```

In addition to the above instance method, the `OrderItemBean` class declares several `get`/`set` methods to access/modify the various instance variables. The complete code for `OrderItemBean` class can be found below:

```java
/* OrderItemBean.java */
import java.beans.*;
import java.io.*;
import java.sql.*;
import java.util.*;
import java.util.Date;

/** OrderItemBean declares variables for storing order details for each
    ordered PC. The class provides a utility method called calcPCPrice that
    computes the item price based on the selections */

public class OrderItemBean {
    private String Speed, MotherBoard, Monitor, HD, CD, Video, RAM, Card ;
    private OrderUtil ordUtil;
    private double ItemPrice=0;
    private int Qty=1;

    /** Computes the price for the current configuration */
    public void calcPCPrice() {
        ordUtil = new OrderUtil();
        ordUtil.connect();
        ItemPrice = ordUtil.calcPrice(Speed);
        ItemPrice += ordUtil.calcPrice(MotherBoard);
        ItemPrice += ordUtil.calcPrice(HD);
        ItemPrice += ordUtil.calcPrice(RAM);
        ItemPrice += ordUtil.calcPrice(Monitor);
        ItemPrice += ordUtil.calcPrice(Video);
        ItemPrice += ordUtil.calcPrice(CD);
        ItemPrice += ordUtil.calcPrice(Card);

        ordUtil.disconnect();

    }
    public int getQty() {
        return Qty;
    }
    public void setQty(int Qty) {
        this.Qty = Qty;
    }
    public double getPrice() {
        return ItemPrice;
    }
    public String getSpeed() {
        return Speed;
```

```
        }
        public void setSpeed(String Speed) {
            this.Speed = Speed;
        }
        public String getMother() {
            return MotherBoard;
        }
        public void setMother(String MotherBoard) {
            this.MotherBoard = MotherBoard;
        }
        public String getHD() {
            return HD;
        }
        public void setHD(String HD) {
            this.HD = HD;
        }
        public String getRAM() {
            return RAM;
        }
        public void setRAM(String RAM) {
            this.RAM = RAM;
        }
        public String getMonitor() {
            return Monitor;
        }
        public void setMonitor(String Monitor) {
            this.Monitor = Monitor;
        }
        public String getVideo() {
            return Video;
        }
        public void setVideo(String Video) {
            this.Video = Video;
        }
        public String getCD() {
            return CD;
        }
        public void setCD(String CD) {
            this.CD = CD;
        }
        public String getCard() {
            return Card;
        }
        public void setCard(String Card) {
            this.Card = Card;
        }
    }
```

I shall now discuss the `OrderUtil` class. This class provides a method called `calcPrice()` that receives the item name for which the price is to be determined and returns the price to the caller. The `OrderUtil` class declares a connection object and uses the `ConnectionManager` class to connect and disconnect to the warehouse database. The `calcPrice()` method constructs an SQL string for fetching the unit price for the selected item from the database.

```
String sql = "Select UNIT_PRICE from INVENTORY where DESCRIPTION = '" + Item +
"'";
```

The program constructs a `Statement` object and executes the query using the above constructed SQL string. The unit price is then retrieved from the `ResultSet` and returned to the caller.

```
Statement stmt = con.createStatement();
ResultSet rs = stmt.executeQuery(sql);
rs.next();
String Price = rs.getString(1);
UnitPrice = Double.parseDouble(Price);
```

The complete listing for the `OrderUtil` class is given below.

```java
/* OrderUtil.java */
import java.sql.*;

/** OrderUtil class is an utility class that provides a method called calcPrice
    which returns the price for the selected Item */

public class OrderUtil {
    private Connection con;
    private ConnectionManager conMan;

    /** Connect to the database */

    public void connect() {
        try {
            conMan = new ConnectionManager();
            con = conMan.logOn();
        } catch(Exception ex){
            ex.printStackTrace();
        }
    }

    /** Disconnect from the database */
    public void disconnect() {
        try {
            conMan.logOff();
        } catch(Exception ex){
            ex.printStackTrace();
        }
    }

    /** Determines the price of the item from the inventory database and returns to
    the caller */
    public double calcPrice(String Item){
        double UnitPrice=0;
        try {
```

```
            String sql = "Select UNIT_PRICE from INVENTORY where DESCRIPTION = '" +
    Item + "'";
            Statement stmt = con.createStatement();
            ResultSet rs = stmt.executeQuery(sql);
            rs.next();
            String Price = rs.getString(1);
            UnitPrice = Double.parseDouble(Price);
        } catch(Exception e){
            System.out.println("Exception in totalPrice(): " +e.getMessage());
        }
        return UnitPrice;
    }
}
```

Displaying the Shipping Options

After selecting the quantity for each configured PC, the customer proceeds to the shipping options page. This is shown below.

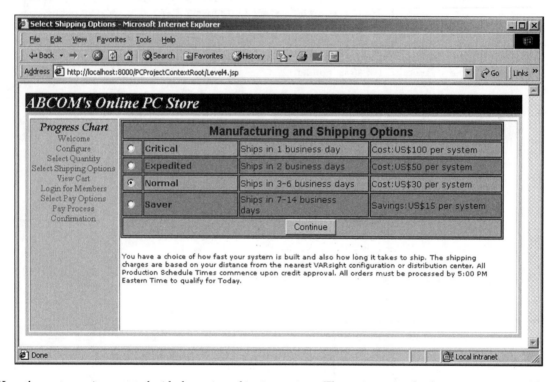

Here the customer is presented with the various shipping options. The main screen display area is generated by ShippingOptions.jsp file.

Here, the program first retrieves the quantity selections for each configured PC by calling the getParameterValues() method on the request object:

```
String[] QtyValues = request.getParameterValues("Qty");
```

Note that we do not attempt to save the quantity on the earlier screen as it would probably require the use of some scripting language on the client side. When the customer submits the page, the program retrieves the quantity selections from the request object and adds it to our cart contents. As the number of PC configurations is variable and decided by the customer while shopping, we need to use the `getParameterValues()` method that retrieves all the parameter values for the parameter name `Qty`. This method returns an array of `String` values. The length of the array determines the number of PC configurations selected by the user.

The program then obtains the reference to our global cart object and creates an `Iterator` on it to iterate through all the items in the cart:

```
Vector cart = GlobalBean.getCart();
Iterator it = cart.iterator();
```

For each cart item, the `setQty()` method is called to set the quantity in the `OrderItemBean` instance:

```
OrderItemBean ordItem = (OrderItemBean)it.next();
int Qty = Integer.parseInt(QtyValues[i]);
ordItem.setQty(Qty);
```

`ShippingOptions.jsp` is shown in its entirety below:

```
<%-- ShippingOptions.jsp --%>
<%-- Displays the various pre-defined shipping options to the user and
    requests user to select one for the current order --%>
<html>
<head>
    <title>Select Shipping Options</title>
</head>

<%@ page language="java" import="java.util.*" %>

<jsp:useBean id="GlobalBean" scope="session" class="GlobalVarBean" />

<body>

<%-- Sets the quantity for each configured PC in the shopping cart --%>
    <%
        String[] QtyValues = request.getParameterValues("Qty");
        Vector cart = GlobalBean.getCart();
        Iterator it = cart.iterator();
        for(int i=0; i<QtyValues.length; i++) {
            OrderItemBean ordItem = (OrderItemBean)it.next();
            int Qty = Integer.parseInt(QtyValues[i]);
            ordItem.setQty(Qty);
        }
    %>
```

```
<form method="POST" action="Level5.jsp" align="left" target="_self">

<table border="1" bgcolor="#9999FF" bordercolor="#000000">
   <tr>
      <td width="590" align="center" colspan="4" valign="top">
         <font face="Arial" size="4" color="#004080"><strong>
            Manufacturing and Shipping Options</strong></font></td>
   </tr>
   <tr>
      <td width="25" align="left" bgcolor="#C0C0C0" valign="middle">
         <input type="radio" value="100" name="Schedule">
      </td>
      <td width="130" align="left" valign="middle" bgcolor="#C0C0C0">
         <font face="Verdana" size="2" color="#004080">
         <strong>Critical</strong></font>
      </td>
      <td width="177" align="left" valign="middle" bgcolor="#C0C0C0">
         <font face="Verdana" size="2" color="#0000FF">Ships in 1 business
day</font>
      </td>
      <td width="180" align="left" valign="middle" bgcolor="#C0C0C0">
         <font face="Verdana" size="2" color="#0000FF">Cost:US$100 per system
</font>
      </td>
   </tr>
   <tr>
      <td width="25" align="left" valign="middle">
         <input type="radio" value="50" name="Schedule">
      </td>
      <td width="130" align="left" valign="middle">
         <font face="Verdana" size="2" color="#004080"><strong>
Expedited</strong></font>
      </td>
      <td width="177" align="left" valign="middle">
         <font face="Verdana" size="2" color="#0000FF">Ships in 2 business
days</font>
      </td>
      <td width="180" align="left" valign="middle">
         <font face="Verdana" size="2" color="#0000FF">Cost:US$50 per
system</font>
      </td>
   </tr>
   <tr>
      <td width="25" align="left" bgcolor="#C0C0C0" valign="middle">
         <input type="radio" value="30" checked name="Schedule">
      </td>
      <td width="130" align="left" valign="middle" bgcolor="#C0C0C0">
         <font face="Verdana" size="2"
color="#004080"><strong>Normal</strong></font>
      </td>
```

```
            <td width="177" align="left" valign="middle" bgcolor="#C0C0C0">
                <font face="Verdana" size="2" color="#0000FF">Ships in 3-6 business
days</font>
            </td>
            <td width="180" align="left" valign="middle" bgcolor="#C0C0C0">
                <font face="Verdana" size="2" color="#0000FF">Cost:US$30 per
system</font>
            </td>
        </tr>
        <tr>
            <td width="25" align="left" valign="middle">
                <input type="radio" value="15" name="Schedule">
            </td>
            <td width="130" align="left" valign="middle">
                <font face="Verdana" size="2"
color="#004080"><strong>Saver</strong></font>
            </td>
            <td width="177" align="left" valign="middle">
                <font face="Verdana" size="2" color="#0000FF">Ships in 7-14 business
days</font>
            </td>
            <td width="180" align="left" valign="middle">
                <font face="Verdana" size="2" color="#0000FF">Savings:US$15 per
system</font>
            </td>
        </tr>
        <tr>
            <td width="590" align="center" colspan="4" valign="middle"
bgcolor="#C0C0C0">
                <font face="Arial" size="2" color="#004080"><strong>
                <input type="submit" name="submit" value="Continue">
                </strong></font>
            </td>
             </td>
        </tr>
</table>
</form>

<table border="0" cellpadding="0" width="610">
    <tr>
        <td valign="top" align="left" width="589">
        <p align="left"><font face="Verdana" size="1" color="#0000FF">You have a
choice about how fast your system is built and also how long it takes to ship. The
shipping charges are based on your distance from the nearest VARsight
configuration or distribution center.  All Production Schedule Times commence upon
credit approval. All orders must be processed by 5:00 PM Eastern Time to qualify
for Today.</font></p>
        </td>
    </tr>
</table>
</body>
</html>
```

Displaying the Order Form

Once the customer is done with the selection of the shipping options, they proceed to the next screen where the final order form is presented. This is shown below.

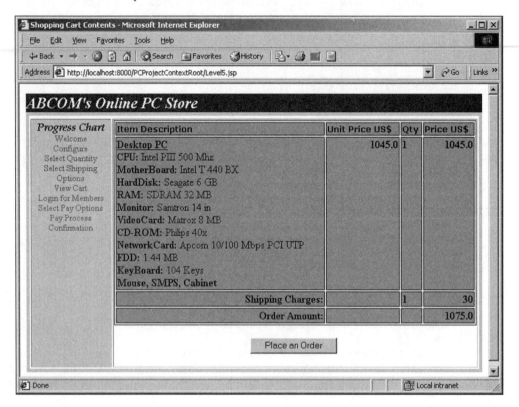

The order form lists all the user selections along with the unit price for each configured PC, the quantity for each PC and the total price for each selected item. At the bottom, we display the total shipping charges and the final order amount. The order form is generated by ShoppingCartContents.jsp file:

```
<%-- ShoppingCartContents.jsp --%>
<%-- Displays the complete order form to the user along with the quantity, price
of each configured PC and the total order value --%>
<html>
<head>
    <title>Shopping Cart Contents</title>
</head>

<%@ page language="java" import="java.util.*" %>

<jsp:useBean id="GlobalBean" scope="session" class="GlobalVarBean" />

    <%
        double TotalAmount = 0;
        double TotalPrice = 0;
```

```
              int TotalShipCharge = 0;
              int TotalQty = 0;
              String Charge = request.getParameter("Schedule");
              int ShipCharge = Integer.parseInt(Charge);
     %>

<body bgcolor="#FFFFFF">

<form method="post" action="Level6.jsp" target="_self">

<table width="100%" border="1" bordercolor="#000000">
     <tr bgcolor="#9999FF">
        <td><b><font face="Verdana" size="2">Item Description</font></b></td>
        <td><b><font face="Verdana" size="2">Unit Price US$</font></b></td>
        <td><b><font face="Verdana" size="2">Qty</font></b></td>
        <td><b><font face="Verdana" size="2">Price US$</font></b></td>
     </tr>

     <%
        Vector cart = GlobalBean.getCart();
        Iterator it = cart.iterator();
        while (it.hasNext()) {
           OrderItemBean ordItem = (OrderItemBean)it.next();
           double Price = ordItem.getPrice();
           int Qty = ordItem.getQty();
            TotalQty += Qty;
            double ItemPrice = Price * Qty;
            TotalPrice += ItemPrice;
            TotalShipCharge += ShipCharge * Qty;
     %>

        <tr bgcolor="#9999FF"><font face="Verdana" size="2">
           <td><b><u> Desktop PC </b></u><br>
           <b>CPU: </b><%= ordItem.getSpeed() %> <br>
           <b>MotherBoard: </b><%= ordItem.getMother() %> <br>
           <b>HardDisk: </b><%= ordItem.getHD() %> <br>
           <b>RAM: </b><%= ordItem.getRAM() %> <br>
           <b>Monitor: </b><%= ordItem.getMonitor() %><br>
           <b>VideoCard: </b><%= ordItem.getVideo() %> <br>
           <b>CD-ROM: </b><%= ordItem.getCD() %> <br>
           <b>NetworkCard: </b><%= ordItem.getCard() %> <br>
           <b>FDD: </b>1.44 MB<br>
           <b>KeyBoard: </b>104 Keys<br>
           <b>Mouse, SMPS, Cabinet<br></b></td>
              <td valign="top" align="right"><b> <%= ordItem.getPrice()
%> </b></td>
              <td valign="top"><b> <%= ordItem.getQty() %> </b></td>
              <td valign="top" align="right"><b> <%= ItemPrice %> </b>
</td>
        </tr>

     <%
        }
        TotalAmount = TotalPrice + TotalShipCharge;
     %>
```

```
    <tr bgcolor="#9999FF"><font face="Verdana" size="2">
        <td valign="top" align="right"><b>Shipping Charges:</b></td>
        <td valign="top">    </td>
        <td valign="top"><b> <%= TotalQty %> </b></td>
        <td valign="top" align="right"><b> <%= TotalShipCharge %> </b></td>
    </tr>

    <tr bgcolor="#9999FF"><font face="Verdana" size="2">
        <td valign="top" align="right"><b>Order Amount:</b></td>
        <td valign="top">    </td>
        <td valign="top">    </td>
        <td valign="top" align="right"><b> <%= TotalAmount %> </b></td>
    </tr>
</table>

<p align="center">
<input type="submit" value="Place an Order" name="submit">

</form>
</body>
</html>
```

This JSP file is similar to our CartItems.jsp file, except one more column is added to the right hand side to display the total price for each configured PC and two rows are added to the bottom that display the shipping charges and the total order amount. The program first obtains the shipping option from the request object and sets the ShipCharge variable:

```
String Charge = request.getParameter("Schedule");
int ShipCharge = Integer.parseInt(Charge);
```

Note that the values for shipping charges are hard-coded in HTML. In real-life situations, you may create a database table and read the values from the table at the runtime. This will allow you to reset the shipping charges any time such a change is desired. As in the case of CartItems.jsp file, the program obtains a reference to the global cart object and retrieves each cart item. The total order price is then computed using the UnitPrice and the Qty for each item to which the total shipping charge is added:

```
<%
    Vector cart = GlobalBean.getCart();
    Iterator it = cart.iterator();
    while (it.hasNext()) {
        OrderItemBean ordItem = (OrderItemBean)it.next();
        double Price = ordItem.getPrice();
        int Qty = ordItem.getQty();
        TotalQty += Qty;
        double ItemPrice = Price * Qty;
        TotalPrice += ItemPrice;
        TotalShipCharge += ShipCharge * Qty;
%>
```

The rest of the code in the ShoppingCartContents.jsp file is essentially the HTML code that displays the complete order form to the user.

At this stage, the customer is done with their order selection. The next step is to request the customer to login for the final order confirmation.

Member Login

Once the customer has shopped at our store, we should present the payment options to the customer and proceed to the order confirmation. Why do we ask customer to login as a member? There could be several valid reasons for registering the customer as a member. You can maintain the list of registered customers in your member database that stores the various kind of information related to the customer. Such information can contain, for example, a mailing address for the customer so that the customer does not have to type in the mailing address every time they shop at your store. You may also store the credit card information entered by the customer during their first purchase. If you decide to store this information in your database, you must assure the customer about the security of such sensitive information. The member login may also be used for personalization where you may offer a personalized service to the customer by tracking their habits during every visit made by the customer. Such login ID can also be used for storing the partial orders to the database. This is an added service to the customer who even if he/she abandons the shopping can retrieve the earlier shopping cart contents from the database.

In our web store application, we will ask the customer to login using their e-mail ID. Our customer database uses this field as the primary key for uniquely determining our registered customers. When the customer logs in with the e-mail ID, we will present the shipping address details to the customer for their confirmation.

I shall discuss the membership in more detail in the next chapter where I will discuss the code for creating new members and allowing the existing customers to modify their records.

The Login Screen

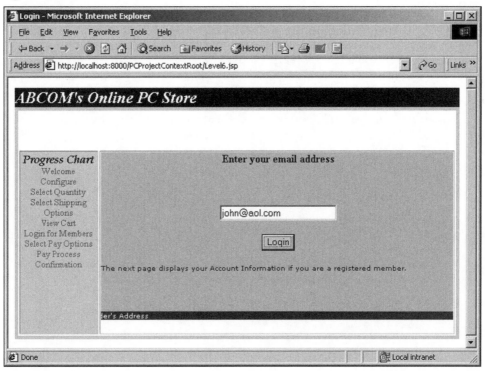

The main display area of our template in the above screen is generated by `LoginScreen.jsp` file. This file is essentially only HTML code that creates an edit control for the customer to enter the e-mail ID and a submit button that submits the information to the next page. Once the customer enters the valid e-mail ID, the information from our database pertaining to this ID is displayed to the customer. The complete code listing for `LoginScreen.jsp` file is given below.

```
<%-- LoginScreen.jsp --%>
<%-- Accepts the login information from the user --%>
<HTML>
<HEAD>
<TITLE>Login</TITLE>
</HEAD>

<BODY>

<FORM action="Level7.jsp" method=post name=theForm target=_self align="left">

<TABLE border=0 cellPadding=0 cellSpacing=0 bgcolor="#C0C0C0" width="100%">
    <TBODY>
        <TR>
        <TD align=left vAlign=top >
            <p align="center"><STRONG>
                <font face="Times New Roman" size="3" color="#0000FF">Enter your email
address</font></STRONG></p>
            <BR><BR>
            <p align="center"><INPUT type="text" maxLength=50 name="email"
size=25></p>
            <p align="center"><INPUT type="submit" name="submit" value="Login"></p>
                <p style="margin: 0" align="left"><FONT color=#0000FF
face=Verdana size=1>The next page displays your Account Information if you
are a registered member.</FONT></p>
            <BR><BR><BR>
                <font face="Verdana" size="1" color="#808080">
<marquee bgcolor="#004080" style="color: #FFFFFF"  height="12">Credit Card
Purchases will only be shipped to the Cardholder's Address</marquee>
</font>
        </TD>
        </TR>
    </TBODY>
</TABLE>
</FORM>
</BODY>
</HTML>
```

Displaying Customer Information

The customer information from the database is displayed on the Customer Information form shown below.

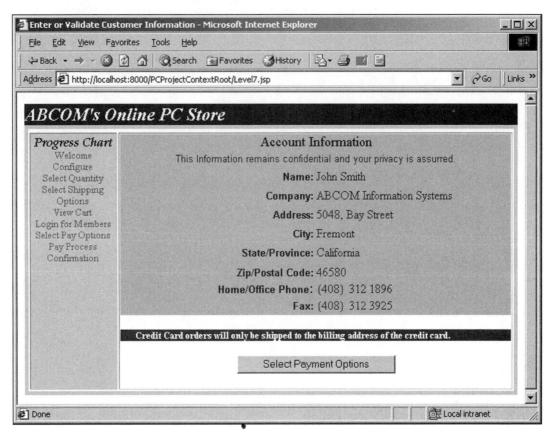

This page is generated by `AccountInfo.jsp` file. The `AccountInfo` page instantiates `AccountInfoBean` class with page scope:

```
<jsp:useBean id="AccountBean" scope="page" class="AccountInfoBean" />
```

The `AccountInfoBean` class retrieves the customer information for the given e-mail ID. This class is discussed later.

The program after creating `AccountInfoBean` instance, calls the `connect()` method on it to connect to the customer database. The program then calls the `displayInfo()` method on this `Bean` object to retrieve the customer information. The customer information is stored in the several instance variables of the `Bean` class. The program finally calls the `disconnect()` method on the bean to disconnect from the database:

```
<%-- AccountInfo.jsp --%>
<%-- Displays the account information of the user specified by the e-mail
parameter --%>
<html>
```

```
<%@ page language="java" %>

<jsp:useBean id="AccountBean" scope="page" class="AccountInfoBean" />

<%-- Connect to the database, retrieve the account information for the
user selected by e-mail parameter and disconnect from the database --%>
<%
    AccountBean.connect();
    String email = request.getParameter("email");
    AccountBean.displayInfo(email);
    AccountBean.disconnect();
%>
<html>
<head>
    <title>Enter or Validate Customer Information</title>
</head>

<body>
<form method="POST" action = "Level8.jsp" target="_self">

<%-- Create an HTML table to display the account information --%>
<table border="0"  cellspacing="0" cellpadding="0" bgcolor="#C0C0C0" width="100%">
<tr>
    <td valign="top" align="center" height="24">
    <p align="center"><font size="4" color="#0000FF">Account Information</font>
    </td>
</tr>
<tr>
    <td valign="top" align="left" height="19">
        <p align="center"><font color="#0000FF" face="Arial"><small>
This Information remains confidential and your privacy is assured.
    </small></font>
    </td>
</tr>
</table>

<%-- In each table row, display the title and the corresponding field value by
calling the getXXX method on the AccountBean. --%>

<table border="0" cellpadding="0" cellspacing="0" bgcolor="#C0C0C0" width="100%">
```

The program then displays the customer information on the form by calling the get methods of the bean to retrieve the individual fields. The output is formatted in an HTML table:

```
<tr>
    <td align="right" height="25" width="50%"><small><strong>
    <font color="#0000FF" face="Arial">Name: </font></strong></small>
    </td>
        <td height="25" align="left" width="50%"><font color="#0000FF">
        <%= AccountBean.getName() %>
        </td>
</tr>
<tr>
    <td align="right"  height="25" width="50%"><small><strong>
        <font color="#0000FF"face="Arial">Company: </font></strong></small>
```

```
        </td>
        <td height="25" align="left" width="50%"><font color="#0000FF">
        <%= AccountBean.getCompany() %>
        </td>
</tr>
<tr>
    <td align="right" height="25" width="50%"><small><strong>
        <font color="#0000FF" face="Arial">Address: </font></strong>
      </small>
    </td>
    <td height="25" align="left" width="50%"><font color="#0000FF">
        <%= AccountBean.getAddress() %>
    </td>
</tr>
<tr>
    <td align="right"  height="25" width="50%"><strong><small>
        <font color="#0000FF" face="Arial">City: </font></small>
      </strong>
    </td>
    <td  height="25" align="left" width="50%"><font color="#0000FF">
        <%= AccountBean.getCity() %>
    </td>
</tr>
<tr>
    <td align="right"  height="26" width="50%"><strong><small>
      <font color="#0000FF"face="Arial">State/Province: </font>
      </small></strong>
    </td>
    <td height="26" align="left" width="50%"><font color="#0000FF">
        <%= AccountBean.getState() %>
    </td>
</tr>
<tr>
    <td align="right" height="25" width="50%"><strong><small>
    <font color="#0000FF" face="Arial">Zip/Postal Code: </font>
        </small></strong>
    </td>
    <td height="25" align="left" width="50%"><font color="#0000FF">
        <%= AccountBean.getPin() %>
    </td>
</tr>
<tr>
    <td align="right" height="16" width="50%"><strong><small>
    <font color="#0000FF" face="Arial">Home/Office</font></small>
    <font color="#0000FF"face="Arial"><small>Phone</small>: 
        <br></font></strong>
    </td>
    <td height="16" align="left" width="50%"><font color="#0000FF">
        <%= AccountBean.getPhone() %>
    </td>
</tr>
<tr>
    <td align="right" height="25" width="50%"><small><strong>
    <font color="#0000FF" face="Arial">Fax: </font></strong></small>
    </td>
```

```
      <td height="25" align="left" width="50%"><font color="#0000FF">
         <%= AccountBean.getFax() %>
      </td>
   </tr>
   </table>

   <%-- Display a scrolling text message to the user --%>
      <p align="center"><strong><font color="#004080"><small><marquee
   bgcolor="#004080" style="color: #FFFFFF">Credit Card orders will only beshipped to
   the billing address of the credit card.</marquee></small>
   </font></strong>
      <p align="center"><input type="submit" value="Select Payment Options"
   name="B1">
   </form>
   </body>
   </html>
```

I shall now discuss the `AccountInfoBean` class. This class declares several instance variables that map to the database fields of our customer table.

```
/* AccountInfoBean.java */

import java.beans.*;
import java.io.*;
import java.sql.*;
import java.util.*;

/** AccountInfoBean class retrieves the customer information from the customer
    table. The customer is selected by the e-mail ID */

public class AccountInfoBean {
    private Connection con;
    private ConnectionManager conMan;
    private String sql;
    private Statement stmt;
    private ResultSet rs;
    private String Name, Company, Address, City, State, Pin, Phone, Fax;
```

The class provides connect and disconnect methods, which are used for making and breaking the connection to the database. The code uses an instance of `ConnectionManager` class for database access.

The `AccountInfoBean` class has an instance method called `displayInfo` that takes a `String` argument. The argument specifies the e-mail ID; this is the key field in the customer table. The method retrieves the customer record and initializes the instance variables with the retrieved record.

```
    /** Obtain a connection to the database */
    public Connection connect() {
        try {
            conMan = new ConnectionManager();
            con = conMan.logOn();
        } catch(Exception ex) {
            ex.printStackTrace();
        }
```

```
        return con;
    }

    /** Disconnect from the database */
    public void disconnect() {
        try {
            conMan.logOff();
        } catch(Exception ex){
            ex.printStackTrace();
        }
    }
```

The code generates an SQL statement that uses the e-mail ID entered by the user:

```
    /** Retrieve the customer information from the CUSTOMER table */
    public void displayInfo(String Email) {
        try {
            String sql = "Select NAME, COMPANY, ADDRESS, CITY, STATE, PIN, PHONE, FAX
" + "From CUSTOMER Where EMAIL = '" + Email + "'";
            System.out.println("sql = " + sql);
```

The program then constructs a `Statement` object and fires the query on the database. If the record is found, it is used for initializing the appropriate instance variables:

```
        stmt = con.createStatement();
        rs = stmt.executeQuery(sql);
        if(rs != null) {
            rs.next();
            Name = rs.getString(1);
            Company = rs.getString(2);
            Address = rs.getString(3);
            City = rs.getString(4);
            State = rs.getString(5);
            Pin = rs.getString(6);
            Phone = rs.getString(7);
            Fax = rs.getString(8);
        }
        disconnect();
    } catch(Exception ex){
        ex.printStackTrace();
    }
}

public String getName() {
    System.out.println("name= " + Name);
    return Name;
}
public String getAddress() {
    return Address;
}
public String getCity() {
    return City;
```

```
    }
    public String getState() {
        return State;
    }
    public String getPin() {
        return Pin;
    }
    public String getPhone() {
        return Phone;
    }
    public String getFax() {
        return Fax;
    }
    public String getCompany() {
        return Company;
    }
}
```

Once the customer confirms the valid shipping address, they proceed to the checkout.

The Checkout

When they reach the checkout, the customer is requested to select the mode of payment. In our web store, we will accept the payment either by credit card or by check. If the customer decides to pay by check, they will have to mail the check to our store. In case of credit card payments, we will collect the credit card information from the customer. Such information must be collected using a secured server.

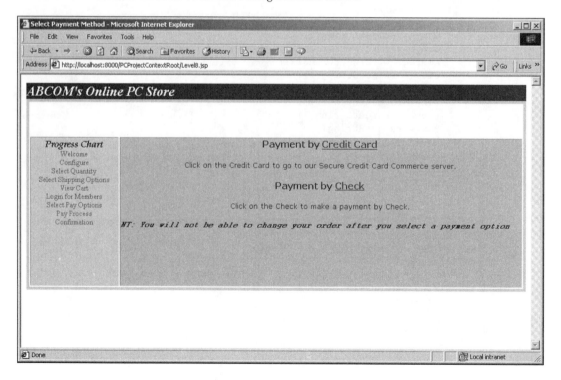

The above page is generated by the `SelectPaymentMethod.jsp` file that essentially contains only HTML code. The user is given a choice to pay by Check or Credit Card. The code for the `SelectPaymentMethod.jsp` file is given here.

```
<%-- SelectPaymentMethod.jsp --%>
<%-- Requests the user to select the credit card or check payment options --%>
<html>

<head>
    <title>Select Payment Method</title>
</head>

<body>

<p align="center">
    <font size="3"><strong>
    <font face="Verdana" color="#0000FF">Payment by</font>
    <font face="Verdana" color="#004080">
    <a href="Level9.jsp" target="_self">Credit Card</a></font></strong></font></p>

<p align="center"><font face="Verdana" color="#0000FF" size="2">Click on the
    Credit Card to go to our Secure Credit Card Commerce server.</font></p>

<p align="center">
    <font size="3"><strong>
    <font face="Verdana" color="#0000FF">Payment by </font>
    <font face="Verdana" color="#004080">
    <a href="Level10.jsp" target="_self">Check</a></font></strong></font></p>

<p align="center"><font face="Verdana" color="#0000FF" size="2">Click on the
    Check to make a payment by Check.</font></p>

<p align="center"><font face="Courier" color="#0000FF" size="2">
    <marquee><i><strong><b>IMPORTANT: </b>You will not
    be able to change your order after you select a payment option</strong>
    </i></marquee></font></blink></p>
</body>
</html>
```

If the customer decides to pay by credit card, the program requests the user to enter the credit card information. This is shown overleaf.

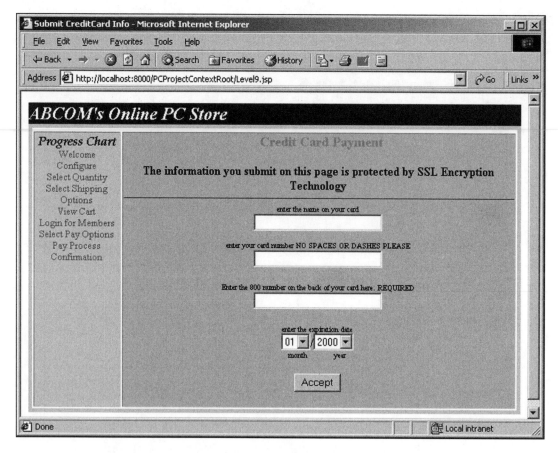

The above screen is generated by the `CreditCard.jsp` file that is once again a pure HTML code. The complete code listing for the `CreditCard.jsp` file is given below.

```
<%-- CreditCard.jsp --%>
<%-- Accept the credit card details from the user --%>
<HTML>
<HEAD>
   <TITLE>Submit CreditCard Info</TITLE>
</HEAD>

<BODY>

<FORM action="Level10.jsp" method=post target="_self">

<TABLE border=0 borderColorDark=#ffffff cellPadding=0 cellSpacing=0 width="100%">
   <TBODY>
    <TR>
       <TD align=center vAlign=top>
          <P><STRONG><FONT color=#004080 size=3></FONT><FONT color=#ff8000
size=4>  Credit Card Payment</FONT></STRONG></P>
             <CENTER><B><STRONG>The information you submit on this page is
protected by SSL Encryption Technology</B></STRONG></CENTER>
          <HR color=#004080 SIZE=1>
```

```
            </TD>
        </TR>
        <TR>
            <TD align=middle >
                <FONT face="Times New Roman" size=1>enter the name on your card </FONT>
                <BR>
                <FONT face="Times New Roman" size=1><INPUT name=CardName
size=25><BR><BR>enter your card number NO SPACES OR DASHES PLEASE</FONT>
                <BR>
                <INPUT name=CardNumber size=25><BR><BR><FONT face="Times New Roman"
size=1>Enter the 800 number on the back of your card here.
REQUIRED</FONT>
                <BR>
                <INPUT name=Card800Num size=25><BR><BR><FONT face="Times New Roman"
size=1>enter the expiration date</FONT>
                <BR>
            <SELECT name=expmonth size=1>
                <OPTION selected value=01>01</OPTION>
                <OPTION value=02>02</OPTION>
                <OPTION value=03>03</OPTION>
                <OPTION value=04>04</OPTION>
                <OPTION value=05>05</OPTION>
                <OPTION value=06>06</OPTION>
                <OPTION value=07>07</OPTION>
                <OPTION value=08>08</OPTION>
                <OPTION value=09>09</OPTION>
                <OPTION value=10>10</OPTION>
                <OPTION value=11>11</OPTION>
                <OPTION value=12>12</OPTION>

            </SELECT>/<SELECT name=expyear size=1>
                <OPTION selected value=00>2000</OPTION>
                <OPTION value=01>2001</OPTION>
                <OPTION value=02>2002</OPTION>
                <OPTION value=03>2003</OPTION>
                <OPTION value=04>2004</OPTION>
                <OPTION value=05>2005</OPTION>
                <OPTION value=06>2006</OPTION>
                <OPTION value=07>2007</OPTION>
                <OPTION value=08>2008</OPTION>
            </SELECT><BR><FONT face="Times New Roman" size=1>month
         
year</FONT><BR><BR>
                <INPUT type=submit name=submit value="Accept">
            </TD>
        </TR>
    </TBODY>
    </TABLE>
    </FORM>
    </BODY>
    </HTML>
```

This page must be stored on a secured web server.

Once the program captures this information, the credit approval may be done in real time. The customer is sent a "Thank You" note after the credit approval is received.

Confirming the Order

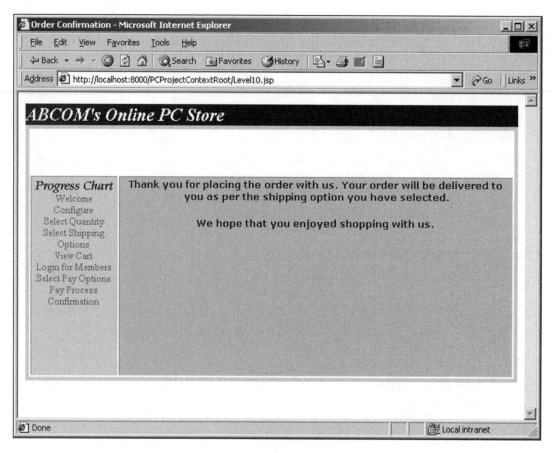

The above page is generated by using `Confirmation.jsp` file, the listing for which is given below. We use the same confirmation page for both check and credit card payments. In a real system, you will need to provide additional functionality in both cases (we won't be doing that in this simple example).

```
<%-- Confirmation.jsp --%>
<%-- Displays an order confirmation note to the user --%>
<html>

<head>
    <title>Order Confirmation</title>
</head>

<body>
    <p align="center"><font face="Verdana" size="2" color="#0000FF">
    <b>Thank you for placing the order with us. Your order will be delivered to you
as per the shipping option you have selected. </b></font></p>
    <p align="center"><font face="Verdana" size="2" color="#0000FF"><b>We hope that
you have enjoyed shopping with us.</b></font></p>
</body>

</html>
```

Credit Card Authorization

Our web store may provide a freephone line for accepting the credit card information from the customer. However, an online credit card approval system is always preferred as compared to the manual system. In the first place, as a business, you will need to obtain a commercial account from your bank so you will be able to accept credit card payments from your customers.

A credit card authorization process involves swiping the customer's credit card so that the credit authorization request goes to your bank. Your bank in turn sends a request to the customer's bank. If the customer's bank authorizes the payment, your bank is informed and ultimately you will receive the credit authorization from your bank. All these things happen in real time over a secured network.

To implement credit card payments in your web store, you will need to link with a credit card authorization company who specializes in such matters. This company will provide a URL that runs a CGI script on their server. The script accepts a few parameters such as credit card number, expiration date, requested amount, etc. The company's server will then acquire authorization from the customer's bank and inform you of the result by calling a URL specified by you at the time of request.

All the credit card requests should be transmitted using SSL. This has been accepted as a worldwide standard for secured transactions. This will require you to have your own secured server. Even if you have your own secured server, you will like to deploy all the other web pages on a non-secured server. The secured server has a communication overhead and thus normal pages that do not transmit sensitive information over the Internet should not be put on a secured server. On a secured server, the data that flows between the client and the server is encypted/decrypted at both ends. Thus, the communication is much slower as compared to HTTP. The web page that gathers the sensitive information from the customer should be put on a secured server. If you do not have your own secured server, you may contract a company that provides such services. In this case, you may have to generate the order ID for every request you send to the credit authorization company. Thus, when you receive the feedback from the company, you can distinguish between the multiple approvals/denials by checking the order ID associated with each reply.

Creating and Deploying the Application

The code discussed in this chapter was tested using the Reference Implementation of J2EE. If you have downloaded the code from the WROX web site, you will find all the required files for this project in the `.zip` file. The structure of this folder along with the various files it contains is given here.

Don't worry about the `.jsp` files `Level4.jsp` through `Level10.jsp` for now, as they will become relevant in the next chapter.

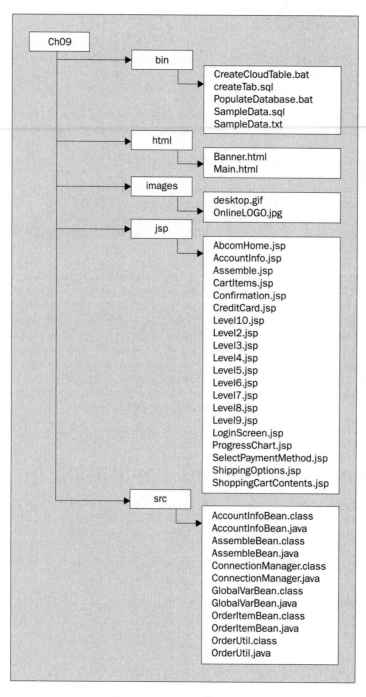

To compile and deploy the code yourself, you will first need to compile all the `.java` files. Make sure that your JAVA_HOME and J2EE_HOME environment variables are set correctly to point to your appropriate installation directories. Open up a command prompt and compile all the `.java` files by navigating to the downloaded `/ch09/src` folder (the drive being whichever one you have downloaded the code to on your machine) and using the following command:

```
javac *.java
```

This compiles all the `.java` files and places the generated code in the same folder. If you get errors during compilation, check your environment settings.

Next, you will create an application and deploy it on the application server. I assume that by this time you have successfully created the database as explained in the earlier section. If not, do this now, by opening a command prompt and navigating to the folder `bin`. Run `CreateCloudTable.bat` and `PopulateDatabase.bat` from here. If this throws up an error, type the provided code from the book directly into the command prompt. Your machine should be able to find the auxiliary files needed to create the database.

With the database created, restart the Cloudscape engine by typing the following command on the cmd prompt.

```
Cloudscape -start
```

The start command opens a new command window and Cloudscape starts running in it. To shut down the Cloudscape engine, you use the `cloudscape -stop` command.

Once the Cloudscape engine is running, open another command prompt window and start the J2EE application server, by typing the following command on the command window.

```
start j2ee -verbose
```

Next, start the deployment tool by typing the following command line in another new command window.

```
start deploytool
```

This opens the deployment tool in a new window.

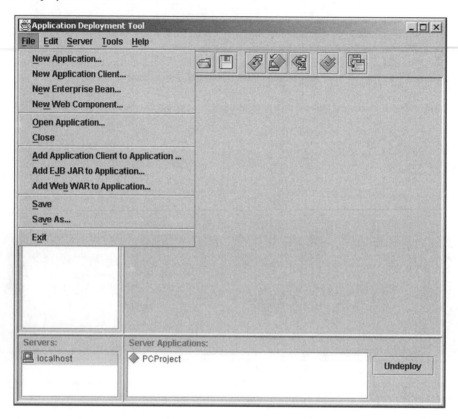

Under the File menu option, select New Application. Click on the Browse button to navigate to your ch09 folder. Type in the name of the application as PCProject.ear. This also sets the default application name to the same as the project file name. Click on OK to create the project.

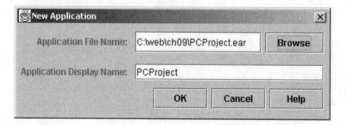

Now, you will need to create a .WAR file to which you can add the various WEB components. Go to the File menu again, and select the New Web Component menu option (alternatively, click on the world icon on the toolbar). This opens a wizard that guides you through the various stages of creating the .WAR file. On the first Introduction screen, simply select Next to move to the next screen. You will use this new screen to add the various components in your .WAR file.

In the WAR Display Name field, type PCProjectWAR as the name of your .WAR file. Click on the Add button to add the various components. A new window should open up, resembling the adjacent window:

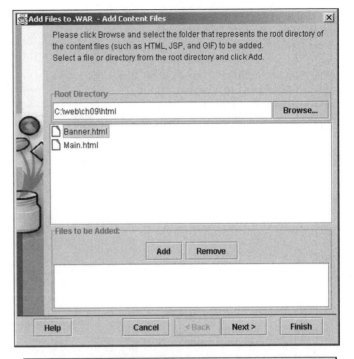

Browse through to your ch09 folder if it is not displayed. Click on the html folder in your ch09 directory, or you could also type in the root directory for the HTML files. Note that you will need to type the full qualifying path for your folder.

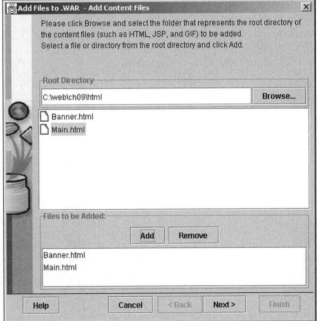

Click on Banner.html, and once it is highlighted, click on Add. The selected file should now appear in the Files to be Added pane at the bottom of the window. Repeat this for Main.html as well. Don't hit the Next button just yet, though!

Now, type in the full qualifying path of your
jsp folder in the **Root Directory** field (it
should be in your ch09 folder in the same
way html was). This should display all the
.jsp files in the folder. Select all of the files
one by one and add them to the .WAR by
clicking on the **Add** button.

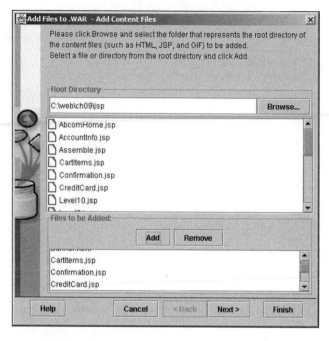

Likewise, select and add the files from the images folder. This completes the addition of all the HTML, JSP and
graphic images to our project – we have defined our content, the next thing to do is to define our code.

Click on the **Next** button, to add the
.class files to our .WAR. Click on the
src folder and add in all .class files.

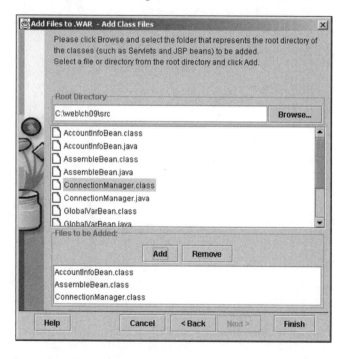

Click on the Finish button to complete the addition of components. Now, a screen will appear listing the files associated with your application. Click on the Next button to move to the next screen of the wizard. Here you will be required to select the web component type. Select JSP by clicking on the JSP radio button. Now click Next.

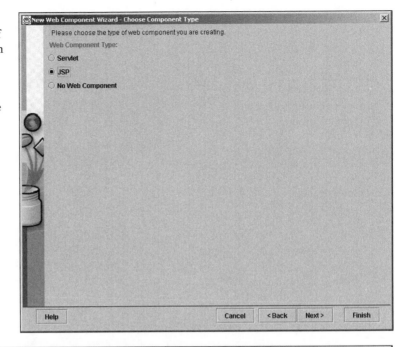

On the next screen, you can select the General properties for your component. In the drop-down menu of JSP Filename select AbcomHome.jsp. In the Web Component Display Name field, type PCProjectWEB. Leave the rest of the options to their default values and click Finish.

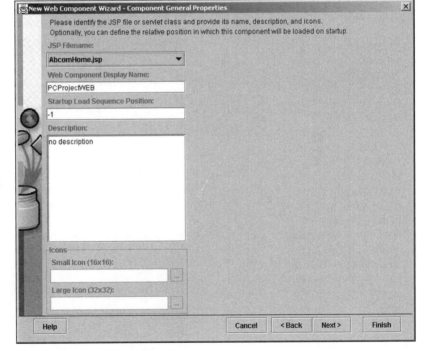

This returns you to the first screen of your deployment tool. Notice that a .WAR file with the name PCProjectWAR is added to your project. This completes the project creation process. Now, you will deploy this project on the server. Select the Deploy Application option under the Tools menu.

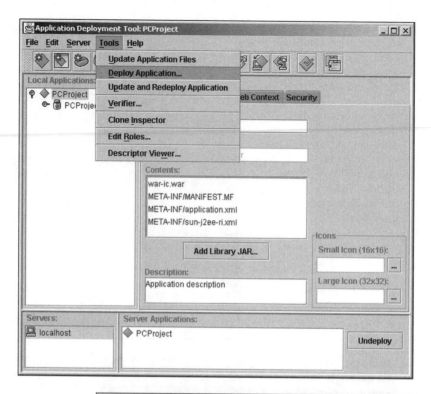

This opens another wizard that guides you through the deployment process. On the first screen select the Target Server where you would like to deploy the application. If you are running the server locally, select the default localhost option and click on the Next button to move to the next screen. We do not need a Client Jar file for this application so leave the check box unchecked.

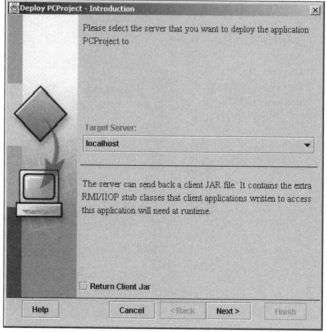

On the next screen, type the name of the **Context Root** as `PCProjectContextRoot` and press **Next**.

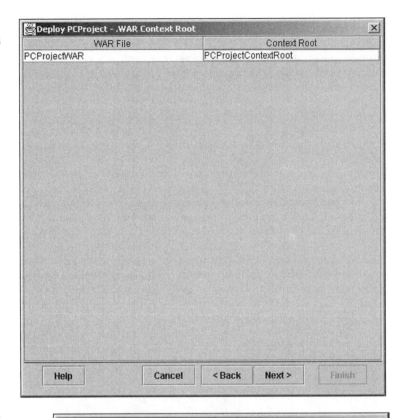

This is the final screen and it tells you your project is about to be deployed, so click on the **Finish** button to start the deployment process. During this process, the application server generates the various classes such as stubs and skeletons required by your project. It also creates a `PCProjectContextRoot` folder in the `public_html` folder of your J2EE installation folder and copies the required files into this folder. When the progress pane shows that this process is complete, click on **OK** to exit the wizard.

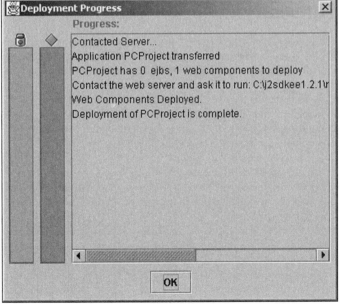

At this stage, your application is deployed and ready for testing.

Testing

Testing is one of the most important phases of any software development project. When you develop and deploy your application, you will first need to test the application for functionality and ensure that the application behaves as you would expect.

To run the application, open the browser and type in the following URL:

```
http://localhost:8000/PCProjectContextRoot/AbcomHome.jsp
```

This loads the first page of our application. Click on the "Desktops" image to move to the next screen. Move through the various shopping stages as described in the earlier section. Note that since you do not have a registered user created in your database at this stage, you will see the Account Information screen displaying all null values. You will learn how to create a user account for your site in Chapter 10 when we discuss site membership.

The next phase you may like to do is to test for scalability. The application typically works for a single user environment or for a limited number of users. However, when there are many concurrent users for your application, the performance may be severely degraded. You may wish to simulate such a scenario to do stress-testing of your application by writing a few test scripts or using third party tools. One such stress test tool is available from RSW software (www.rswsoftware.com).

The site developed so far only uses JSP and HTML pages. JSP technology may not really scale up when the site load increases. We will discuss these scalability issues further in Chapter 12, where I will show the use of EJBs to make the application more scalable.

Summary

In this chapter, you have learned the techniques of developing a B2C e-commerce site based on JSP technology. We discussed the design of a simple web-store that sells personal computers on-line, where the customer can configure the personal computer to his/her choice.

First, we created a database for storing the inventory of the components in the store. The user is presented with the choice of components from this inventory. The use of JSP pages for such data access was discussed. After configuring the PC, the user selects the quantity and proceeds to checkout. The design of the shopping cart and how to maintain the client selections throughout the client session was discussed.

At the time of checkout the user selects the shipping option. Here, the importance of member registration was emphasized. The user then selects the payment option to conclude the shopping process. The application illustrates the use of JSP pages in the design of an B2C e-commerce site.

In the next few chapters, we will add some more functionality to this site and look into various aspects of improving the performance and scalability of our e-commerce site. In this chapter, we assumed that the user is already registered with us a member. In the next chapter, we will discuss how to create a membership database. We will also discuss how to create re-usable code for the site development, the importance of JSP taglibs, and we will learn the importance of internationalization in your site design.

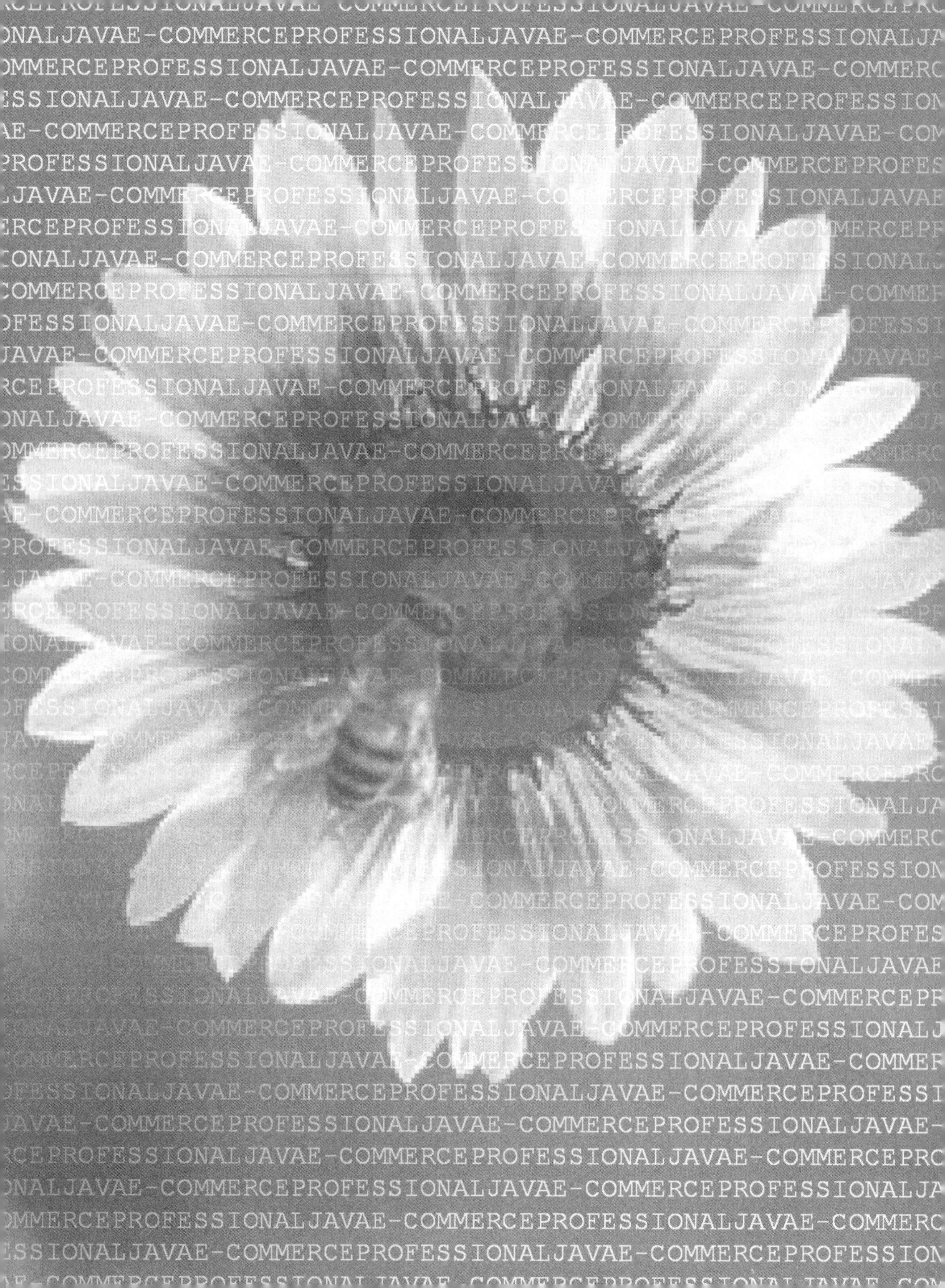
PROFESSIONALJAVAE-COMMERCE

B2C E-Commerce: Site Usability

In the previous chapter, we studied the development of a simple web store for selling goods online. A real web store would require a more sophisticated design than the one discussed in Chapter 9. You must provide additional functionality to the site to ensure that clients are satisfied doing business with you.

There are a wide variety of factors affecting how effective an online store is, and in this chapter we're going to have a look at implementing a number of features that enhance both the maintainability of the site, and its effectiveness in the customer's eyes.

So in this chapter we'll look at:

- ❏ General features desired by customers
- ❏ JSP taglibs for re-usability of code
- ❏ Search facilities
- ❏ Feedback mechanisms
- ❏ Membership schemes
- ❏ Internationalization

Our emphasis in this chapter is to show how to implement these features without too much complication. As such, the code for each of these chapters can be run separately without any reliance on code from the previous chapter. Again though, all the code is available from www.wrox.com.

Customer Friendly Sites

In this section we'll quickly review a number of factors that should be considered when designing and implementing a B2C site.

The very first thing to ensure is that customers can actually get to your site – this means your site must be fast. If your home page takes too long to load, it is likely that the customer will give up trying to access your site and try one of your competitors (some people will give up on a web page if it takes more than eight seconds to load). Therefore, a good intuitive user interface that loads quickly even on the slowest connection is a necessity.

Improving Speed

There are a number of options for improving the performance of a site but not all of them may be realistic options.

You can probably provide better performance by improving the server hardware and/or the network bandwidth. If you are hosting your web store on somebody else's server, these things will be beyond your control and the only way to improve the response time of your site will be to design it for efficiency or switch over to another company that provides wider bandwidth.

To reduce the response time to the user, one needs to analyze the bottlenecks in the entire site design. The primary reason for poor response time in loading pages could be due to the heavy use of graphics on the page.

Avoid using large images on the page, but, if such images are required, provide a thumbnail of the image. The user may then click on this thumbnail to retrieve a fully blown up high-resolution image. If your web page is a JSP, note that the first time use of this page requires a longer time to load as the page is compiled into a servlet. Thus users may see a very slow response from your site when it's under peak load.

Another issue with hosting an online web store is the accessibility and the availability of the site.

Accessibility and Availability

Remember, a conventional retail shop may remain open for just 12 hours a day. However, for a web store, it should remain open 24 hours a day, 7 days a week. With an online store, you will find people shopping at the store at all times of the day and night.

To make the system accessible and available globally, you must ensure 100 percent uptime for the server. This seems difficult, but can be achieved by providing multiple servers in the cluster with failover and mirroring support. This is also called high availability (HA) clustering. You should also plan your scheduled backups during off-peak hours. Such hosting and networking issues lie outside the scope of this book.

Organization

Your online web store must be simple enough for even the least knowledgeable customers to use – too complicated a design for the web site can put customers off. The web store should provide easy access to the items the customers are searching for. Just imagine that you walk into a grocery store and cannot locate the common items such as milk, cereal, etc. This will be quite frustrating and you may not visit this store a second time. The grocery store organizes the items by categories and displays big readable signs to guide you through the store. In the absence of this categorization and signs, you could be totally lost in the store searching for each item.

The same applies to the design of an online store. Your web store must guide the customer with proper links to ensure that the customer quickly finds whatever they desire. Thus, the customer will re-visit your site only if you keep usability in mind while designing it.

Sometimes, despite the best efforts of shop designers, some, often more obscure, items are still hard to find. In such circumstances talking to a store representative will often solve the problem. The same principles apply in the design of an online store. You should provide a search facility to the customer who types in the desired item in the search dialog that searches the entire site and returns the result to the customer.

Relating to the Customer

To become an effective business, customer feedback is extremely important and that is why you will find those "Tell us how are we doing" kind of forms in all the stores. Similarly, your online store should supply feedback forms or at the least provide an e-mail address where customers can send you appreciations, suggestions, and complaints.

Another important aspect of effective selling is providing a membership option to your regular customers. This saves customers valuable time while shopping in your store. You may maintain the customer database with the shipping info, credit card details, etc. You may also track the customer's purchasing habits and provide a personalized service to each of your members. For example, many e-commerce sites inform customers of their current specials and also send out coupons. This helps to ensure a long-term relationship with the customer, and the chances of losing the customer to the competition are minimized.

Of course when you start out on a business venture you're unlikely to get it right first time. Improvements will always have to be made, and building a site that is maintainable and flexible is key to being able to continually add functionality and respond to customer feedback. Let's start by looking at a technique to improve the maintainability of the site.

JSP Taglibs

If the code behind your site isn't re-usable, it could slow down both development and implementation, of the original site and any new functionality you might want to add at a later date. Here we'll discuss the use of **tag libraries** in JSP code whereby you can use the re-usable code that can be shared between several page designers and several web pages of your site.

As you have seen in the earlier chapters, Java code can easily clutter JSP pages and sometimes it makes it difficult for designers to modify these pages. Also, there is a great risk that the designers may unknowingly modify the Java code embedded in these pages. JSP allows you to define **custom tags** that allow a clear separation between the Java code and the HTML. Of course, JSP **taglibs** are not the only way to achieve this separation of presentation and functionality; you can also use JavaBeans to encapsulate the business logic. However, many people feel that JSP taglibs provide a more elegant solution.

To illustrate the use of JSP custom tags, we will construct a custom tag called `userinfo` that fetches the user record from the database (see *Setting up the Database* in Chapter 9) based on the e-mail address and displays it on our `RegistrationForm.jsp` page described in the last chapter. The site which we have built so far is simple and primitive that helps in understanding the principles of e-commerce site design. Thus, there isn't much code so far developed which could be converted in custom tags. I have selected the case of fetching user information from the database for our custom tag. Typically, database access may be done through JavaBeans called through JSP.

Rather than modifying the code from the earlier chapter, we will develop and test the custom tag independently. The code may then be incorporated in the existing project more easily. We'll first start with the HTML page that calls our custom tag and later on explain the construction of the custom tag itself.

The HTML page accepts the e-mail address from the user in an edit control. The HTML code (InputEmail.jsp) is given below:

```
<%-- InputEmail.jsp --%>
<HTML>
<HEAD></HEAD>
<BODY BGCOLOR="#C0C0C0" TEXT="#000000">

<FORM METHOD="POST" ACTION="AccountInfo.jsp">

<P ALIGN="left"><B>Enter your email</B>
    <INPUT TYPE="text" NAME="email" SIZE="20"></P>
<P><INPUT TYPE="submit" VALUE="Submit" NAME="B1"></P>
</FORM>

</BODY>
</HTML>
```

After entering the e-mail address, the user clicks on the Submit button to submit the request to the AccountInfo.jsp file:

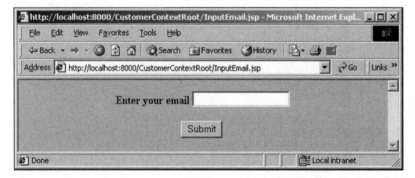

Let's look at what the AccountInfo.jsp does with the information it is passed (note that here we're just going through the basic operation; the topic of validation is covered in depth in the next chapter). Much of the code is identical to the RegistrationForm discussed in the last chapter. The user information is printed in an HTML table, with each field displayed in a cell in the HTML table as shown in the following screenshot:

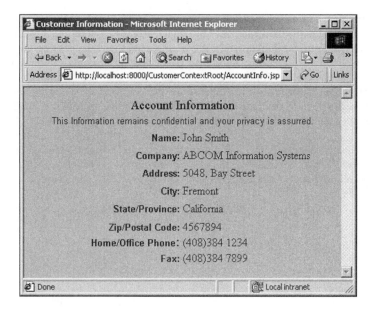

The complete code for `AccountInfo.jsp` file is given below:

```
<%-- AccountInfo.jsp --%>
<html>
<head>
   <title>Customer Information</title>
</head>

<body bgcolor="#C0C0C0">

<%@ page language="java" import="java.util.*" %>
```

Firstly, it uses the `getParameter()` method on the request object to read the value of the input parameter:

```
<%-- read the input parameter from request object --%>

<% String mail = request.getParameter("email"); %>
```

The program then declares the use of the custom library (which contains our custom tags) with the prefix `pcpro` by calling the following statement:

```
<%-- declare the use of custom library with the prefix pcpro --%>

<%@ taglib uri="taglib.tld" prefix="pcpro" %>
```

The call to the `userinfo` custom tag is made in the following statement:

```
<%-- Use the custom tag userinfo, pass email as parameter --%>

<pcpro:userinfo email= "<%=mail%>" ></pcpro:userinfo>
```

Note that our `userinfo` custom tag uses `pcpro` as a prefix and takes an attribute called `email`. The value of the attribute is specified in the mail variable. One can clearly see from this example that the use of custom tags hides the Java code from the web designer. We simply need to tell the designer to use the `userinfo` tag from our custom tag library called `pcpro` to retrieve the customer information. We also specify that the designer needs to input the e-mail address of the customer whose information is desired. To pass the e-mail address parameter to our custom tag, we use the scriptlet tags `<%=` and `%>`. The scriptlet tags indicate that the contents of `mail` should be used as an attribute value rather than the literal string "mail". You may include any valid Java expression in this scriptlet code that evaluates to a `String` variable.

The custom tag reads the customer information from the database, populates the vector with the fields of the customer record, and returns a `HashMap` to the caller in the parameter called `DBData`. The JSP reads the returned value by calling `getAttribute()` method on the `pageContext` object:

```
<%-- Copy the data received from custom tag into a HashMap --%>

<%
    String ErrorMsg;
    HashMap MapData = null;
    MapData = (HashMap)pageContext.getAttribute("DBData");
```

If the returned `HashMap` is empty, the program displays an appropriate message to the user:

```
    if(MapData.isEmpty()){
%>

<%-- The customer record does not exist --%>

<p align="center"><font size="4" color="#0000FF">No record found</font>
<%
}
    else {
%>

<%-- Display the customer record --%>

<table border="0"  cellspacing="0" cellpadding="0" bgcolor="#C0C0C0"
    width="100%">
<tr>
    <td valign="top" align="center" height="24">
        <p align="center"><font size="4" color="#0000FF">Account
            Information</font>
    </td>
</tr>
<tr>
    <td valign="top" align="left" height="19">
        <p align="center"><font color="#0000FF" face="Arial"><small>
        This Information remains confidential and your privacy is assurred.
        </small> </font>
    </td>
</tr>
</table>
```

If the record is found, it is returned by our custom tag `userinfo` in the `DBData` attribute. The program gets the each key value from the `DBData` HashMap and displays it to the user by repeating an HTML code block shown here.

```
<%-- For each customer record column, get the value of HashMap and display in HTML
table --%>

<table border="0" cellpadding="0" cellspacing="0" bgcolor="#C0C0C0"
   width="100%">
   <tr>
      <td align="right" height="25" width="50%"><small><strong>
         <font color="#0000FF" face="Arial">Name: </font></strong></small>
      </td>
      <td height="25" align="left" width="50%"><font color="#0000FF">
         <%= (String)MapData.get("NAME") %>
      </td>
   </tr>
   <tr>
      <td align="right" height="25" width="50%"><small><strong>
         <font color="#0000FF" face="Arial"> Company:  </font>
            </strong></small>
      </td>
      <td height="25" align="left" width="50%"><font color="#0000FF">
         <%= (String)MapData.get("COMPANY") %>
      </td>
   </tr>
   <tr>
      <td align="right" height="25" width="50%"><small><strong>
         <font color="#0000FF" face="Arial">Address: </font>
            </strong></small>
      </td>
      <td height="25" align="left" width="50%"><font color="#0000FF">
         <%= (String)MapData.get("Address") %>
      </td>
   </tr>
   <tr>
      <td align="right" height="25" width="50%"><strong><small>
         <font color="#0000FF" face="Arial">City: </font>
            </small></strong>
      </td>
      <td  height="25" align="left" width="50%"><font color="#0000FF">
         <%= (String)MapData.get("City") %>
      </td>
   </tr>
   <tr>
      <td align="right" height="26" width="50%"><strong><small>
         <font color="#0000FF" face="Arial">State: </font>
            </small></strong>
      </td>
      <td height="26" align="left" width="50%"><font color="#0000FF">
         <%= (String)MapData.get("STATE") %>
      </td>
   </tr>
   <tr>
      <td align="right" height="25" width="50%"><strong><small>
         <font color="#0000FF" face="Arial">Zip Code: </font>
            </small></strong>
         </td>
         <td height="25" align="left" width="50%"><font color="#0000FF">
         <%= (String)MapData.get("PIN") %>
```

```
            </td>
        </tr>
        <tr>
            <td align="right" height="25" width="50%"><strong><small>
                <font color="#0000FF" face="Arial">Country: </font>
                    </small></strong>
                </td>
                <td height="25" align="left" width="50%"><font color="#0000FF">
                <%= (String)MapData.get("COUNTRY") %>
            </td>
        </tr>
        <tr>
            <td align="right" height="16" width="50%"><strong><small>
                <font color="#0000FF" face="Arial">Phone</small>: <br>
                    </font></strong>
                </td>
                <td height="16" align="left" width="50%"><font color="#0000FF">
                <%= (String)MapData.get("PHONE") %>
            </td>
        </tr>
        <tr>
            <td align="right" height="25" width="50%"><small><strong>
                <font color="#0000FF" face="Arial">Fax: </font></strong></small>
            </td>
            <td height="25" align="left" width="50%"><font color="#0000FF">
                <%= (String)MapData.get("FAX") %>
            </td>
        </tr>
    </table>
    <% } %>
    </body>
    </html>
```

We populated the Customer table in our Cloudscape database using the data file (SampleUserData.txt). The file is shown below:

```
"jsmith@abcom.com","John Smith","5048, Bay Street","Fremont","4567894","(408)384
1234","ABCOM Information Systems","pass","(408)384 7899","1","California","USA"
"allanj@wrox.com","Allan Jones","1102, Warwick Road","Birmingham","B27
6BH","(0121)6874999","Wrox Press Ltd","pass","(0121)687 4101","2","West
Midlands","UK"
"roberts@wrox.com","Robert Shaw","29 S. LaSalle St, Suite
520","Chicago","60603","(0121)6874157","Wrox Press Inc","pass","(0121)687
4101","11","Illinois","USA"
"ianb@wrox.com","Ian Blackham","30, Lincoln Road","Birmingham","B27
6PA","(0121)6874998","Wrox Press Ltd","pass","(0121)687 4101","5","West
Midlands","UK"
```

The script PopulateUserDatabase.bat is used to run the SQL (SampleUserData.sql) file. The code for SampleUserData.sql is shown below:

```
INSERT INTO CUSTOMER
SELECT * from NEW FileImport(
    'SampleUserData.txt') AS myExternalData;
```

CustomerInfoTag.java

We now look at the development of the `CustomerInfo` tag itself. The complete code for `CustomerInfoTag.java` is presented below:

```
/** CustomerInfoTag.java */
import javax.servlet.jsp.*;
import javax.servlet.jsp.tagext.*;
import java.util.*;
import java.sql.*;
```

To create the custom tag, a public class called `CustomerInfoTag` is created that extends `BodyTagSupport`. The `BodyTagSupport` provides a `doInitBody` method that we override in our subclass. This method is called at the tag start whenever the JSP page encounters our custom tag. We will override this method to fetch the data from the CUSTOMER table.

```
/** CustomerInfo tag makes a database connection and retrieves the
customer record for a given e-mail ID. The result is returned in a
HashMap to the caller */

public class CustomerInfoTag extends BodyTagSupport {
    private String email = null;
    protected Connection con;
    protected String driver = "COM.cloudscape.core.RmiJdbcDriver";
    protected String url = "jdbc:cloudscape:rmi:OnlinePCDB";
    Statement stmt;
    ResultSet rs;
    Vector dataVec;

    public void setEmail(String email){
        this.email = email;
    }

    /** Load the database driver, make connection to the default database and
    fetch the customer record. If found, add the contents in a HashMap and return
    to the caller by setting the attribute called DBData */
    public void doInitBody(){
        try {
            Class.forName( driver ).newInstance();
            con = DriverManager.getConnection( url, "", "" );
```

The `CustomerInfoTag` defines the `setEmail()` method that accepts a `String` parameter. This method is called when the custom tag is encountered in the JSP tag. The `doInitBody()` method is at the tag start. This method loads the database driver and makes the connection to the database. The program then creates a `Statement`, formats SQL for fetching the customer record and executes the query on the database.

```
        stmt = con.createStatement();
        String query = "SELECT NAME, COMPANY, ADDRESS, CITY, STATE, PIN, " +
            "PHONE, FAX, COUNTRY FROM CUSTOMER WHERE EMAIL='" +email+ "'" ;
        rs = stmt.executeQuery(query);
```

The retrieved fields are then added to the HashMap:

```
            HashMap MapData = new HashMap();
            if(rs.next()){
                MapData.put ("NAME", rs.getString ("NAME"));
                MapData.put ("COMPANY", rs.getString ("COMPANY"));
                MapData.put ("ADDRESS", rs.getString ("ADDRESS"));
                MapData.put ("CITY", rs.getString ("CITY"));
                MapData.put ("STATE", rs.getString ("STATE"));
                MapData.put ("PIN", rs.getString ("PIN"));
                MapData.put ("PHONE", rs.getString ("PHONE"));
                MapData.put ("FAX", rs.getString ("FAX"));
                MapData.put ("COUNTRY", rs.getString ("COUNTRY"));
            }
```

In case of a null record, the program returns an empty `HashMap` to the caller. The program then sets the "`DBData`" attribute equal to the `HashMap` and closes the database connection:

```
            pageContext.setAttribute("DBData", MapData);
        }
        catch (SQLException e) {
            System.out.println (e.getMessage());
        }
        catch(Exception ex){
            System.out.println("Exception " +ex);
        }
        finally {
            try {
                con.close();
            }
            catch (SQLException ee) {}
        }
    }
}
```

The next step in the development of a custom tag is to develop a `CustomerInfoTagExtraInfo` class that is shown below. This class defines one method called `getVariableInfo()` that returns an array of `VariableInfo`. The `VariableInfo` array contains the `DBData` element of HashMap type.

```
/** CustomerInfoExtraInfo.java */
import javax.servlet.jsp.*;
import javax.servlet.jsp.tagext.*;
import java.util.Vector;

/** Declare a variable called DBData of type HashMap */
public class CustomerInfoTagExtraInfo extends TagExtraInfo {
    public VariableInfo[] getVariableInfo(TagData data)
    {
        return new VariableInfo[] {
            new VariableInfo("DBData","java.util.HashMap",true,
                VariableInfo.AT_END),
        };
    }
}
```

The final requirement of the custom tag development is to write the tag library descriptor in a `.tld` file that is shown below:

```
<!-taglib.tld -->
<?xml version="1.0" encoding="ISO-8859-1" ?>
<!DOCTYPE taglib
    PUBLIC "-//Sun Microsystems, Inc.//DTD JSP Tag Library 1.1//EN"
    "http://java.sun.com/j2ee/dtds/web-jsptaglibrary_1_1.dtd">

<!-- a tab library descriptor -->

<taglib>
    <tlibversion>1.0</tlibversion>
    <jspversion>1.1</jspversion>
    <urn></urn>
    <info>
        Tag library for Online PC Project
    </Info>

    <tag>
        <name>userinfo</name>
        <tagclass>CustomerInfoTag</tagclass>
        <teiclass>CustomerInfoTagExtraInfo</teiclass>
        <bodycontent>JSP</Bodycontent>
        <info>
            This is a Mail tag for getting the Record from DataBase
        </Info>
        <attribute>
        <name>email</name>
        <required>true</required>
        <rtexprvalue>true</rtexprvalue>
        <type>String</type>
        </attribute>
    </tag>
</taglib>
```

Once all the files are created, add them into your J2EE project and deploy the project. Do not forget to add the above .tld file in the project. The only files you will require for this section are:

❏   InputEmail.jsp

❏   taglib.tld

❏   AccountInfo.jsp

❏   CustomerInfoTagExtraInfo.class

❏   CustomerInfoTag.class

A call to the pcpro:userinfo tag in your HTML code will display the user record on the screen. The e-mail ID of the user is set as an attribute to the userinfo tag. This achieves the clear separation between the Java code and the HTML.

Now let's return to the topic of improving the site usability for the customer and show how we can implement a simple search functionality.

Searching

The web store described in Chapter 9 does not carry many products. If the customer is interested in a particular make of product (and may even know the exact part number for that product), how do they search our store to locate the product? Trawling through a large inventory may not always be easy, nor is it a particularly attractive option.

Searching may involve a text search on your site to find out every occurrence of the specified keyword or may involve searching the underlying database. If you have created a static catalog for your web store, a text search for the product keyword would be required. This can be achieved easily if you have an Index Server that can quickly carry out the search on all your web pages and return the results to the user. However, if you were generating the catalog dynamically, a search on a product would require a database search and that must be programmed. We will add a search facility to our web store where the user can select the type of item and request information for all such product items in our stock.

The `Search.jsp` opens the search page to the user:

The drop down list box contains the types of items that our web store stocks. The user selects the item from this list. The code for `Search.jsp` is given below, which is simply an HTML form.

```
<%-- Search.jsp --%>
<HTML>
<HEAD>
<TITLE>SEARCH..</TITLE>
</HEAD>

<BODY BGCOLOR="#C0C0C0" text="#000000">

<FORM METHOD="POST" ACTION="SearchInfo.jsp">

   <P ALIGN="center">
   <FONT COLOR="#808000"><FONT SIZE="6"><B><I>Online SEARCH...</I></B>
      </FONT></FONT></P>
```

```
<P ALIGN="center">
<FONT COLOR="#808000"><STRONG>Search on following Items:</STRONG></FONT></P>
<P ALIGN="center">
    <SELECT SIZE="1" NAME="item">
        <OPTION>cpu</OPTION>
        <OPTION>motherboards</OPTION>
        <OPTION>hard disks</OPTION>
        <OPTION>ram</OPTION>
        <OPTION>monitor</OPTION>
        <OPTION>video</OPTION>
        <OPTION>cdrom</OPTION>
        <OPTION>network</OPTION>
    </SELECT></P>
<P ALIGN="center">
<INPUT TYPE="submit" VALUE="Search" NAME="B1">

</FORM>
</BODY>
</HTML>
```

The output result of a search is shown here:

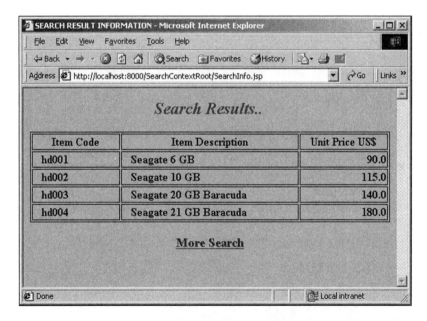

On submitting the request, the program calls `SearchInfo.jsp` file, the code for which is given below:

```
<%-- SearchInfo.jsp --%>
<HTML>

<%@ page language="java" import="java.util.*,java.sql.*" %>
```

The `SearchInfo.jsp` obtains the user-selected parameter from the request object:

```
<% String item = request.getParameter("item"); %>
```

The page instantiates the `SearchInfo` bean with page scope. The catalog search is done in this bean. The code for this bean is discussed after we've finished with the JSP:

```
<jsp:useBean id="Search" scope="page" class="SearchInfo" />

<%
    Vector OuterVec;
    Vector InnerVec;
%>

<HEAD>
<TITLE>SEARCH RESULT INFORMATION</TITLE>
</HEAD>

<BODY BGCOLOR="#C0C0C0">

<FORM METHOD="POST" ACTION = "SearchInfo.jsp" >

<P ALIGN="center">
<FONT FACE="Times New Roman" SIZE="5" COLOR="#008000"><B><I>Search
    Results..</I></B></FONT></P>

<TABLE WIDTH="100%" BORDER="1" BORDERCOLOR="#000000" ALIGN="center"
    BGCOLOR="#FFFFFF">

<TR>
<TD ALIGN="center" WIDTH="15%"><FONT FACE="Verdana" SIZE="2" COLOR="#0000FF">
    <B>Item Code</B></FONT></TD>
<TD ALIGN="center" WIDTH="30%"><FONT FACE="Verdana" SIZE="2" COLOR="#0000FF">
    <B>Item Description</B></FONT></TD>
<TD ALIGN="center" WIDTH="15%"><FONT FACE="Verdana" SIZE="2" COLOR="#0000FF">
    <B>Unit Price US$</B></FONT></TD>
</TR>
```

The scriptlet code calls `getSearchInfo()` method on the Search bean. The method returns a list of items in a vector. Each item contains the item number, description, and the unit price. Each item is also returned in the vector form. Thus, the program creates two iterators, one for traversing the list of items and the second for traversing the individual entries in an item.

```
<%
    OuterVec = Search.getSearchInfo(item);
    Iterator it1 = OuterVec.iterator();
    while (it1.hasNext()) {
        InnerVec = (Vector)it1.next();
        Iterator it2 = InnerVec.iterator();
        while (it2.hasNext()) {
%>
```

For each retrieved entry, the program displays the entry by calling the `next()` method on the iterator:

```
<TR>
<TD><FONT FACE="Verdana" SIZE="2" COLOR="#0000FF">
    <B>   <%= it2.next() %></B></FONT></TD>
<TD><FONT FACE="Verdana" SIZE="2" COLOR="#0000FF">
    <B>   <%= it2.next() %></B></FONT></TD>
```

```
<TD ALIGN=right><FONT FACE="Verdana" SIZE="2" COLOR="#0000FF">
    <B><%= it2.next() %></B></FONT></TD>
</TR>
    <% }
    }
%>
</table>

<P ALIGN="center"><B><FONT FACE="Times New Roman" SIZE="4">
    <a href="Search.jsp">More Search</a></FONT></B></P>
</form>
</Body>
</HTML>
```

The SearchInfo Bean

We're now going to discuss the code for the `SearchInfo` bean. The complete code for `SearchInfo.java` is given below:

```java
/* SearchInfo.java */
import java.beans.*;
import java.io.*;
import java.sql.*;
import java.util.*;

public class SearchInfo {
    private String SQL;
    private Vector SearchResult;
    private Vector SQLResult;
    private Connection con;
    private ConnectionManager conMan;
    private Statement stmt;
    private ResultSet rs;

    public Vector getSearchInfo(String item) {
        try {
```

The `SearchInfo` bean uses the `ConnectionManager` object to make a connection to the database:

```java
        conMan = new ConnectionManager();
        con = conMan.logOn();
```

The code then generates an SQL statement for retrieving the values for a selected item type:

```java
        SQL = "SELECT PRODUCT_ID, DESCRIPTION, UNIT_PRICE FROM
            INVENTORY WHERE NAME = '" +item+ "'";
        stmt = con.createStatement();
        rs = stmt.executeQuery(SQL);
```

The code then creates a `SearchResult` vector for storing information about each selected item and iterates through the recordset to add the elements to the vector:

```
            SearchResult = new Vector();
            while(rs.next()) {
```

Each item itself consists of three fields: product ID, description, and unit price. Thus the program creates another vector, reads the fields from the recordset, creates the SQLResult vector and adds it to the outer vector:

```
            SQLResult = new Vector();
            SQLResult.addElement(rs.getString(1));
            SQLResult.addElement(rs.getString(2));
            Double temp = new Double(rs.getDouble(3));
            SQLResult.addElement(temp);
            SearchResult.addElement(SQLResult);
        }
```

The program then closes the database connection and returns the constructed vector to the caller:

```
        rs.close();
        stmt.close();
        conMan.logOff();
        } catch(Exception e) {
            System.out.println("sql error in this block");
            e.printStackTrace ();
        }
        return SearchResult;
    }
}
```

Our next topic is to address the issue of how to provide some information to the customer about how their order is being handled – such as the internal order number.

Providing Feedback

In our web store application, a "Thank You" note was displayed to the customer after the payment authorization was received. If the customer wishes to follow up this order (say the delivery doesn't arrive on time) they will need more information. Remember a crucial part of commerce is delivering the products to the customer – the best site in the world won't help your business if goods never reach the customer. In this section we'll look at how you can e-mail customers with information, for example, order details for their reference (for security reasons remember not to include credit card details in such a note).

J2EE supports the JavaMail API, and this API provides an interface for composing and sending e-mail messages through your program code. To demonstrate this concept, the code below composes a simple "Thank You" note and sends it to the customer:

```
/* Mailer.java */
import javax.activation.*;
import javax.mail.*;
import javax.mail.internet.*;
import javax.naming.*;
```

```
public class Mailer {
   public void sendMail(String recipient) {
      try {
         Context initial = new InitialContext();
         Session session =
            (Session) initial.lookup("java:comp/env/TheMailSession");
         Message msg = new MimeMessage(session);
         msg.setFrom();
         msg.setRecipients(Message.RecipientType.TO,
            InternetAddress.parse(recipient, false));
         msg.setSubject("Order Confirmation");
         msg.setText("Thank you for your order.");
         Transport.send(msg);
      } catch(Exception e) {
         e.printStackTrace();
      }
   }
}
```

The sendMail() method of the Mailer class accepts the e-mail address of the recipient as a String parameter. The program obtains the JNDI context and looks up the TheMailSession environment variable. This is the mail session set up on your J2EE installation. A new mail message is created by constructing an instance of MimeMessage class. The program then sets the various parameters of the mail message by calling its several methods. The body of the message is set using setText() method. You may compose your entire order form in the message body. The message is dispatched to the recipient by calling the Transport.send() method. You will need to call this method in your JSP page.

You'll probably have noticed the lack of an order ID being passed in for the e-mail. This is because, for this simple site, we are assuming that each customer has only one pending order that is deleted after dispatch. It is crude, but this is only an example.

Custom Tag For Mail Message

The above functionality could be coded in the JSP custom tag very easily. The use of the custom tag illustrates how to hide the program code from the page designer. We'll create a custom tag called mail that receives the e-mail ID of the recipient as the attribute and dispatches mail to the recipient. For testing of this custom tag, we'll use a simple JSP page (EnterEmail.jsp) that accepts the e-mail ID from the user and calls a JSP page that uses our custom tag:

```
<%-- EnterEmail.jsp --%>
<HTML>
<BODY BGCOLOR="#C0C0C0" text="#000000">
<FORM METHOD="POST" ACTION="MailMessage.jsp">
   <P ALIGN="left"><B>Enter your email</B>
      <INPUT TYPE="text" NAME="email" SIZE="20"></P>
   <P><INPUT TYPE="submit" VALUE="Submit" NAME="B1"></P>
</FORM>
</BODY>
</HTML>
```

EnterEmail.jsp is essentially an HTML page that accepts the e-mail address in an edit control, and on form submission calls another JSP called MailMessage.jsp. The complete code listing for MailMessage.jsp is given here:

```
<%-- MailMessage.jsp --%>
<HTML>
<BODY>
<BODY BGCOLOR="#C0C0C0" TEXT="#000000">

<%@ page language="java" import="java.util.*" %>
```

`MailMessage.jsp` uses our custom library with the prefix set to `pcpro`:

```
<%@ taglib uri="taglib.tld" prefix="pcpro" %>
```

The JSP obtains the input e-mail address by calling the `getParameter()` method on the `request` object:

```
<%
    String eml = request.getParameter("email");
%>
```

The program then uses the mail tag to send e-mail to the requested address. The details of sending mail are totally hidden from the page designer in this custom tag. The tag takes one attribute of `String` type. The attribute is used in the tag body to retrieve the e-mail address for the recipient:

```
<Pcpro:mail
    email="<%= eml %>" >
</Pcpro:mail>
```

The mail tag returns a response to the caller. The program reads this response by calling the `getAttribute()` method on the `pageContext` object. The response is displayed to the user by the JSP:

```
<%
    String message = (String)pageContext.getAttribute("Message");
%>

    <P><B><FONT SIZE="5"><%= message %>
</FONT></B></P>
</BODY>
</HTML>
```

Let us now discuss the code for the custom tag itself. Our `SendMailTag` class extends `BodyTagSupport` and defines a `setEmail()` method that accepts a `String` parameter. The attribute defined in our custom tag calls this method and sends the attribute value to this method. The `sendMail()` method is the same as the one defined in our `Mailer` class. Thus, this entire code will be hidden from the page designer who has to simply use the mail tag to send a confirmation note to the customer.

The complete listing for `SendMailTag.java` is given here:

```
/* SendMailTag.java */
import java.io.IOException;
import java.io.Serializable;
import java.rmi.RemoteException;
```

```
import java.text.*;
import java.util.*;
import javax.activation.*;
import javax.mail.*;
import javax.mail.internet.*;
import javax.naming.*;
import javax.servlet.jsp.*;
import javax.servlet.jsp.tagext.*;

public class SendMailTag extends BodyTagSupport {

    private static final String mailer = "JavaMailer";
    String recipient;
    String str;

    public void setEmail(String email) {
        recipient = email;
    }

    public void doInitBody() throws JspException {
        try {
            System.out.println("recipient " +recipient);
```

The `doInitBody()` method calls the `sendMail()` method, then creates the confirmation note to the user and calls the `setAttribute()` method on `pageContext` to send a response to the caller:

```
            sendMail(recipient);
            str = "Your Order Confirmation has been mailed to " +recipient;
            pageContext.setAttribute("Message",str);
        } catch(Exception ex) {
            throw new JspTagException(ex.toString());
        }
    }

    public void sendMail(String recipient) {
        try {
            Context initial = new InitialContext();
            Session session =
                (Session) initial.lookup("java:comp/env/TheMailSession");
            Message msg = new MimeMessage(session);
            msg.setFrom("info@mystore.com");
            msg.setRecipients(Message.RecipientType.TO,
                InternetAddress.parse(recipient, false));
            msg.setSubject("Order Confirmation");
            msg.setText("Thank you for your order.");
            Transport.send(msg);
        } catch(Exception e) {
            e.printStackTrace();
        }
    }
}
```

Our custom tag accepts the e-mail ID of the recipient. However, the code can be easily modified to add extra attributes to the tag. For example, you may like the message body to be composed by the page designer and sent as a parameter to the custom tag.

We then write the `SendMailTagExtraInfo` class that extends `TagExtraInfo`. The class defines a `getVariableInfo()` method that returns a `VariableInfo` array. We set the return value for our tag as a first element in this array:

```
/* SendMailTagExtraInfo.java */
import java.util.Vector;
import javax.servlet.jsp.*;
import javax.servlet.jsp.tagext.*;

public class SendMailTagExtraInfo extends TagExtraInfo {
    public VariableInfo[] getVariableInfo(TagData data) {
        System.out.println("getVariableInfo()");
        return new VariableInfo[] {
            new VariableInfo("Message","String",true, variableInfo.AT_END),
        };
    }
}
```

Finally, to add the custom tag to our library, you will need to modify the `taglib.tld` file to incorporate the mail tag. Make the following modification to our `taglib.tld` file to include the new tag – note that all our custom tags must be declared in the same descriptor file.

```
<!-- taglib.tld -->
<?xml version="1.0" encoding="ISO-8859-1" ?>
<!DOCTYPE taglib
        PUBLIC "-//Sun Microsystems, Inc.//DTD JSP Tag Library 1.1//EN"
                "http://java.sun.com/j2ee/dtds/web-jsptaglibrary_1_1.dtd">

<!-- a tab library descriptor -->

<taglib>
  <tlibversion>1.0</tlibversion>
  <jspversion>1.1</jspversion>
  <urn></urn>
  <info>
     Tag library for Online PC Project
  </Info>

  <tag>
    <name>userinfo</name>
    <tagclass>CustomerInfoTag</tagclass>
    <teiclass>CustomerInfoTagExtraInfo</teiclass>
    <bodycontent>JSP</Bodycontent>
    <info>
       This is a Mail tag for getting the Record from DataBase
    </Info>
    <attribute>
      <name>email</name>
      <required>true</required>
        <rtexprvalue>true</rtexprvalue>
      <type>String</type>
    </attribute>
  </tag>

  <tag>
```

```
<name>mail</name>
<tagclass>SendMailTag</tagclass>
<teiclass>SendMailTagExtraInfo</teiclass>
<bodycontent>JSP</Bodycontent>
<info>
    This is a Mail tag for sending Order Confirmation
</Info>
<attribute>
  <name>email</name>
  <required>true</required>
      <rtexprvalue>true</rtexprvalue>
  <type>String</type>
</attribute>
</tag>
```

```
</taglib>
```

Once the tag library is modified, make the necessary changes in the J2EE application, or create a new application, adding the required files to the application and then re-deploy the application. The designer can now call the mail custom tag as shown below in the HTML code to send a "Thank you" note to the customer specified by the e-mail attribute of the tag:

```
<Pcpro:mail
    email="<%= eml %>" >
</Pcpro:mail>
```

In the last chapter, we discussed membership benefits. Now, we're going to go through the implementation.

Membership

We can ask the customer to create a login membership to our store. When the customer signs up as a new member, we collect the information from the customer such as shipping address, credit card number, etc. so that the customer does not have to enter this information every time they shop at our store.

Note that we'll need to use a secured connection (HTTPS) while accepting such information – for this, you'll have to look at chapters 8 and 9. The membership may also be used for personalization, whereby we may offer personalized services to the regular customers. If we are collecting user information, we'll need to assure the customer about the privacy of such information. This will give confidence to the user when they re-visit our site.

The membership module described below is developed independently and may be easily integrated into our web store application at a later time. For the existing customers, the program asks for their e-mail address and password; if the user is validated, the record will be fetched from the database and displayed to the user. The customer can now modify the information, including the password, and save the changes to the database. If the user has forgotten their password and they ask the site for a reminder, the program asks for something that the user entered while signing up, in this case, it asks for the month of their birth. The program validates the month and if found correct, e-mails the password to the customer. If the customer is signing up for the first time, the program collects all this information from the customer and updates the database.

We're using e-mail as a login ID for the membership. Many sites prefer this as users find this easy to remember. Also, since the e-mail address is unique, this avoids the duplication of records while providing personalization using data mining techniques. The downside of using e-mail addresses as a login may be that the customer feels you are intruding on their privacy by asking for their e-mail address. The customer may be reluctant to give their e-mail address, fearing that it could be misused for marketing other services.

Displaying Member Records

The program starts with the login screen shown in the next screenshot.

> Note that you should deploy this page on a secured server to ensure that the customer's login ID and password do not travel the net unprotected:

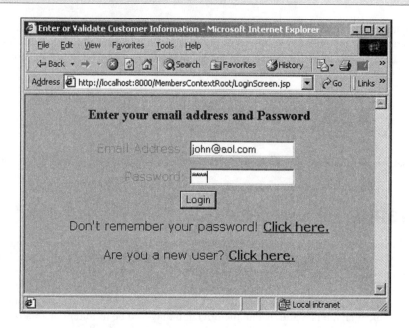

This new login screen is generated by `LoginScreen.jsp` file that is essentially HTML code. The screen sets up two text boxes for accepting e-mail address and the password from the customer. The complete code for the `LoginScreen.jsp` file is given here:

```
<%-- LoginScreen.jsp --%>
<%-- Provides user inferface for customer log in.
A link is provided to retrieve the password in case if customer has forgotten the
password. For the new customers, a separate link is provided. --%>

<HTML>
<HEAD>
    <TITLE>Enter or Validate Customer Information</TITLE>
</HEAD>

<BODY bgcolor="#C0C0C0">
```

On pressing **Login**, the program calls `UpdateInfo.jsp`.

```
<FORM action=UpdateInfo.jsp method=post name=theForm target=_self align="left">

<TABLE border=0 cellPadding=0 cellSpacing=0 width="100%" align="center">
    <TBODY>
        <TR>
            <TD align=center vAlign=top height="37" colspan="2">
                <p align="center"><STRONG><font face="Times New Roman" size="4"
                    color="#0000FF"><b>Enter your email address and Password</b>
                    </font></STRONG></p>
            </td>
        </tr>
        <tr>
            <TD align=right vAlign=middle >
                <p align="right"><FONT color=#8080FF face=Verdana size=3>Email
                    Address: </FONT></p>
            </td>
            <TD align=left vAlign=middle  height="37">
                <p align="left"><input type="text" name="email" size="20">
            </td>
        </tr>
        <tr>
            <td align=right valign=middle >
                <p align="right"><FONT color=#8080FF face=Verdana
                    size=3>Password: </FONT></p>
            </td>
            <td align=center valign=middle  height="37">
                <p align="left"><input type="password" name="password" size="20">
            </td>
        </tr>
        <tr>
            <TD align=center vAlign=top  height="38" colspan="2">
                <p align="center"><FONT color=#808080 face=Verdana size=1>
                    <INPUT type="submit" name="submit" value="Login"></FONT></p>
            </td>
        </tr>
```

The program also provides two more options to the user. The user can click on the link provided if they can't remember their login password. The link invokes the `ValidateMonth.jsp` file that asks the user to enter the reminder that they specified when registering with the site. We'll look at `ValidateMonth.jsp` later; for the moment here's the password link:

```
<tr>
    <TD align=center vAlign=top  height="38" colspan="2">
        <p align="center"><font face="Verdana" size="3">Don't remember your
            password! <font color="#0000FF"><b><a href="ValidateMonth.jsp">
            Click here.</a></b></font></p></font>
    </td>
</tr>
```

The other link on the JSP allows the new user registration by calling the `NewUserRegisration.jsp` file:

```
<tr>
    <TD align=center vAlign=top  height="38" colspan="2">
        <p align="center"><font face="Verdana" size="3">Are you a new user?
            <font color="#0000FF"><b><a href="NewUserRegistration.jsp">Click
            here.</a></b></font></p>
```

```
            </td>
        </TR>
      </TBODY>
  </TABLE>
  </FORM>
  </body>
</HTML>
```

After entering the e-mail address and the password, the user submits the form; when this happens the `UpdateInfo.jsp` file is called. If the user enters a valid e-mail address and the password, the program fetches the record from the database and displays it to the user as shown in the following screenshot:

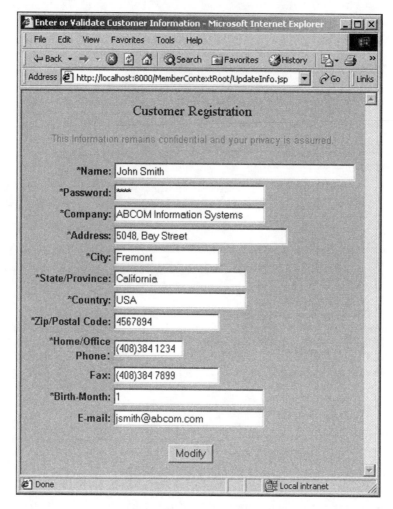

The complete code listing for `UpdateInfo.jsp` is given here:

```
<%@ page language="java" import="java.util.*,java.sql.*" %>
```

The `UpdateInfo.jsp` uses `CustomerInfoBean` to fetch the customer record from the database. This bean is instantiated with page scope:

```
<jsp:useBean id="CustBean" scope="page" class="CustomerInfoBean" />

<html>
<head>
    <title>Enter or Validate Customer Information</title>
</head>

<body bgcolor="#C0C0C0">
<form method="POST" action = "UpdateConfirm.jsp" >

<%-- Get Customer record based on email and password. --%>
<%
    HashMap Map  = null;
```

UpdateInfo.jsp retrieves the two user input parameters from the request object and sets the corresponding variables in the CustomerInfoBean class:

```
CustBean.setEmail(request.getParameter("email"));
CustBean.setPassword(request.getParameter("password"));
```

A connection to the database is then established by calling the connect() method of the CustomerInfoBean class; the record is fetched using the displayData() method and finally the connection is closed by calling the disconnect method. The record is now available in the vector:

```
CustBean.connect();
Map = CustBean.displayData();
CustBean.disconnect();
```

If there is no record corresponding to the given e-mail address or if the user has typed the wrong password, the CustomerInfoBean returns a NULL vector. In this case, the program calls an error page to display the error message to the user. The error page may incorporate a link to the login page so that the user gets an opportunity to re-enter the ID and the password:

```
    if(Map == null) {
        response.sendRedirect("PasswordError.html");
    }
%>

<%-- Display the retrieved record for modifications. --%>

<p align="center"><font size="4" color="#0000FF">
    Customer Registration</font>
</p>
<p align="center"> <font color="#808080" face="Arial"><small>
    This Information remains confidential and your privacy is assured.
    </small> </font></p>
<table border="0" cellpadding="1" align=center>
    <tr>
        <td align="right" bgcolor="#C0C0C0"><small><strong>
            <font color="#0000FF" face="Arial">*Name:</font></strong></small>
        </td>
        <td><font color="#0000FF">
            <input type="text" size="50" name="name"
```

```
                      value="<%=Map.get("NAME")%>"></font>
            </td>
         </tr>
         <tr>
            <td align="right" bgcolor="#C0C0C0"><small><strong>
               <font color="#0000FF" face="Arial">*Password:</font></strong></small>
            </td>
            <td><font color="#0000FF">
               <input type="password" size="30" name="password"
                  value="<%=Map.get("PASSWORD")%>"></font>
            </td>
         </tr>
         <tr>
            <td align="right" bgcolor="#C0C0C0"><small><strong>
               <font color="#0000FF" face="Arial">*Company:</font></strong></small>
            </td>
            <td><font color="#0000FF">
                  <input type="text" size="30" name="company"
                     value="<%=Map.get("COMPANY")%>"></font>
            </td>
         </tr>
         <tr>
            <td align="right" bgcolor="#C0C0C0"><small><strong>
               <font color="#0000FF" face="Arial">*Address:</font></strong></small>
            </td>
            <td><font color="#0000FF">
               <input type="text" size="35" name="addr"
                  value="<%=Map.get("ADDRESS")%>"></font>
            </td>
         </tr>
         <tr>
            <td align="right" bgcolor="#C0C0C0"><small><strong>
               <font color="#0000FF" face="Arial"> *City:</font></small></strong>
            </td>
            <td><font color="#0000FF">
               <input type="text" size="20" name="city"
                  value="<%=Map.get("CITY")%>"></font>
            </td>
         </tr>
         <tr>
            <td align="right" bgcolor="#C0C0C0"><small><strong>
               <font color="#0000FF" face="Arial">*State/Province:</font>
                  </small></strong>
            </td>
            <td><font color="#0000FF">
               <input type="text" size="26" name="state"
                  value="<%=Map.get("STATE")%>"></font>
            </td>
         </tr>
         <tr>
            <td align="right" bgcolor="#C0C0C0"><small><strong>
               <font color="#0000FF" face="Arial">*Country:</font></small></strong>
            </td>
            <td><font color="#0000FF">
                  <input type="text" size="26" name="country"
                     value="<%=Map.get("COUNTRY")%>"></font>
```

```
            </td>
        </tr>
        <tr>
          <td align="right" bgcolor="#C0C0C0"><small><strong>
            <font color="#0000FF" face="Arial">*Zip/Postal
               Code:</font></small></strong></td>
          <td><font color="#0000FF">
             <input type="text" size="20" name="pin"
               value="<%=Map.get("PIN")%>"></font></td>
        </tr>
        <tr>
          <td align="right" bgcolor="#C0C0C0"><small><strong>
            <font color="#0000FF" face="Arial">*Home/Office</font></small>
            <font color="#0000FF" face="Arial"><small>Phone</small>:<br></font>
            </strong>
          </td>
          <td><font color="#0000FF">
             <input type="text" size="12" name="phone"
               value="<%=Map.get("PHONE")%>"></font>
          </td>
        </tr>
        <tr>
          <td align="right" bgcolor="#C0C0C0"><small><strong>
            <font color="#0000FF" face="Arial">Fax:</font></strong></small>
          </td>
          <td><font color="#0000FF">
             <input type="text" size="20" name="fax"
               value="<%=Map.get("FAX")%>"></f>
          </td>
        </tr>
        <tr>
          <td align="right" bgcolor="#C0C0C0"><small><strong>
            <font color="#0000FF" face="Arial">*Birth-Month:</font>
               </strong></small>
          </td>
          <td><font color="#0000FF">
             <input type="text" size="30" name="month"
               value="<%=Map.get("MONTH")%>"></font>
          </td>
        </tr>
        <tr>
          <td align="right" bgcolor="#C0C0C0"><small><strong>
               <font color="#0000FF" face="Arial">E-mail:</font></strong></small>
          </td>
          <td><font color="#0000FF">
             <input type="text" size="30" name="email"
               value="<%=Map.get("EMAIL")%>"></font>
          </td>
        </tr>
</table>
<p align="center"><input type="submit" value="Modify" name="B1"></p>

</form>
</body>
</html>
```

343

Note that the size of the text fields is specified only for the form, not the database fields.

Let us now discuss the `CustomerInfoBean` class. The `CustomerInfoBean` class defines connect and disconnect methods for connecting and disconnecting from the underlying database. These methods use the `Connection` object obtained by instantiating the `ConnectionManager` class and are similar to the connect and disconnect methods used in our other classes discussed in Chapter 9. The class also provides two set methods for setting the `Email` and `Password` methods of the class.

The `Password` field is then compared with the contents of the password field that the user has provided. If it matches, the various fields of the database record are added to the vector and returned to the user. The `UpdateInfo.jsp` page displays an error page to the user if it receives a null vector from `CustomerInfoBean`:

The code for this error page (`PasswordError.html`) is given below.

The complete listing for `CustomerInfoBean` class is given here:

```
/* CustomerInfoBean.java */
import java.util.*;
import java.beans.*;
import java.sql.*;

/** CustomerInfoBean provides a method for retrieving a record from the
CUSTOMER table. The record is returned to the caller in HashMap */

public class CustomerInfoBean {
    private Connection con;
    private ConnectionManager conMan = new ConnectionManager();
    private Statement stmt;
    private ResultSet rs;
    private String Email;
    private String Password;
```

```
    private String SQL;

/** Connect to the database */

public void connect() {
    try {
        con = conMan.logOn();
    }
    catch(Exception ex) {
        ex.getMessage();
    }
}


/** Disconnect from the database */

public void disconnect() {
    try   {
        conMan.logOff();
    }
    catch(Exception ex){
        ex.getMessage();
    }
}

/** Fetch a record from the CUSTOMER table and return to the
caller in HashMap */

public HashMap displayData() {
    HashMap Map = null;
    try {
        stmt = con.createStatement();
```

The `displayData()` method sets up the SQL string to fetch the record from the database:

```
SQL = "select NAME, PASSWORD, COMPANY, ADDRESS, CITY, STATE, PIN, " +
      "PHONE, FAX, BIRTH_MONTH, EMAIL, COUNTRY from CUSTOMER where " +
      "EMAIL = '" + Email + "'";
```

The program constructs the statement and fires the query on the database to fetch the record in a recordset:

```
rs = stmt.executeQuery(SQL);

    // If record exists
    if (rs.next()) {
        if(Password.equals(rs.getString("PASSWORD"))) {
            Map = new HashMap();
            Map.put ("NAME", rs.getString("NAME"));
            Map.put ("PASSWORD", rs.getString("PASSWORD"));
            Map.put ("COMPANY", rs.getString("COMPANY"));
            Map.put ("ADDRESS", rs.getString("ADDRESS"));
            Map.put ("CITY", rs.getString("CITY"));
            Map.put ("STATE", rs.getString("STATE"));
            Map.put ("PIN", rs.getString("PIN"));
```

```
                    Map.put ("PHONE", rs.getString("PHONE"));
                    Map.put ("FAX", rs.getString("FAX"));
                    Map.put ("MONTH", rs.getString("BIRTH_MONTH"));
                    Map.put ("EMAIL", rs.getString("EMAIL"));
                    Map.put ("COUNTRY", rs.getString("COUNTRY"));
                    }
                else {
                    System.out.println("password incorrect");
                    }
            }
        }
        catch (SQLException e){
            System.out.println (e.getMessage());
        }
        catch(Exception ex) {
            ex.printStackTrace();
        }
        return Map;
    }

    public void setEmail(String Email) {
        this.Email = Email;
    }

    public void setPassword(String Password) {
        this.Password = Password;
    }
}
```

The `ConnectionManager` class used here is the same as the one used in Chapter 9 and therefore we won't discuss it here.

The `PasswordError.html` page allows the user to go back to the login screen page (`LoginScreen.jsp`) by setting up the link. Here is the code for the `PasswordError.html` page:

```html
<!--PasswordError.html -->
<HTML>
<HEAD>
<TITLE>Error Page</TITLE>
</HEAD>
<BODY>
    <P><FONT FACE="AlgerianD" SIZE="6"><B><I>
        Your password is incorrect!</I></B></FONT></P>
    <P><FONT FACE="AlgerianD" SIZE="6"><B><I>
        CLICK on &quot;loginpage&quot; to go back to the login
        page.</I></B></FONT></P>
    <P><FONT FACE="AlgerianD" SIZE="6"><B><I>
        <A HREF="LoginScreen.jsp">loginpage</A></I></B></FONT></P>
</BODY>
</HTML>
```

Member Modifications

So far we have discussed how to display the customer record. Now, what if the customer wants to modify the information previously submitted? We will allow the user to modify the displayed information and save the changes to the database by clicking on the Modify button:

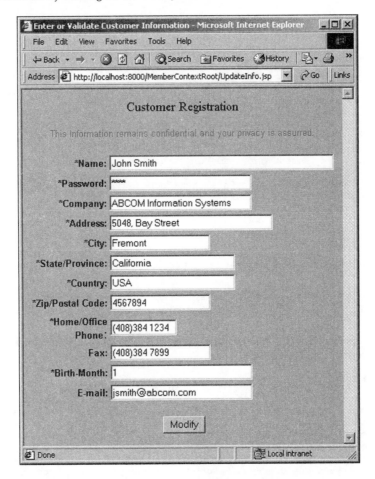

This calls `UpdateConfirm.jsp`, which produces the following output:

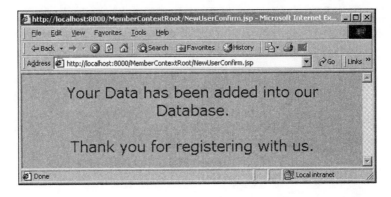

The complete code listing for `UpdateConfirm.jsp` is given here:

```
<%-- UpdateConfirm.jsp --%>
<html>

<%@ page language="java" import="java.util.*,java.sql.*" %>
```

The code gets the user input values by calling `getParameter()` methods for each desired parameter:

```
<%-- Retrieve the parameters from request object --%>
<%
   String Name = request.getParameter("name");
   String Password = request.getParameter("password");
   String Address = request.getParameter("addr");
   String City = request.getParameter("city");
   String Fax = request.getParameter("fax");
   String Month = request.getParameter("month");
   String State = request.getParameter("state");
   String Country = request.getParameter("country");
   String Company = request.getParameter("company");
   String Phone = request.getParameter("phone");
   String Pin = request.getParameter("pin");
   String Email = request.getParameter("email");
%>
```

The program then instantiates the `CustomerRegistrationBean` for database update:

```
<%-- Create an instance of CustomerRegistrationBean class --%>
<jsp:useBean id="UserBean" scope="page" class="CustomerRegistrationBean" />
```

The `setProperty` methods of the bean are then called to set the various properties of the bean to the values obtained from the request object:

```
<%-- Set the properties of the bean for later update to Customer record --%>
<jsp:setProperty name="UserBean" property="name" value ="<%=Name%>" />
<jsp:setProperty name="UserBean" property="password" value ="<%=Password%>" />
<jsp:setProperty name="UserBean" property="addr" value ="<%=Address%>" />
<jsp:setProperty name="UserBean" property="city" value ="<%=City%>" />
<jsp:setProperty name="UserBean" property="fax"  value ="<%=Fax%>"/>
<jsp:setProperty name="UserBean" property="month" value ="<%=Month%>"/>
<jsp:setProperty name="UserBean" property="company" value ="<%=Company%>"/>
<jsp:setProperty name="UserBean" property="phone" value ="<%=Phone%>"/>
<jsp:setProperty name="UserBean" property="pin" value ="<%=Pin%>"/>
<jsp:setProperty name="UserBean" property="state" value ="<%=State%>"/>
<jsp:setProperty name="UserBean" property="country" value ="<%=Country%>"/>
<jsp:setProperty name="UserBean" property="email" value ="<%=Email%>"/>


<body bgcolor="#C0C0C0">
<form method="POST" action = "UpdateConfirm.jsp" >
```

A scriptlet then calls the `connect()` method on the `UserBean` object to connect to the database, calls the `updateRecord()` method to update the database, and finally disconnects from the database by calling the `disconnect()` method:

```
<%-- Update the customer record in the database --%>
<%
   UserBean.connect();
   UserBean.updateRecord();
   UserBean.disconnect();
%>

<p align="center"><font face="Verdana" size="5" color=#0000FF>
   Your Information has been updated into our Database.<br><br> </font></p>
<p align="center"><font face="Verdana" size="5" color=#0000FF>
   Thank You  </font></p>

</form>
</body>
</html>
```

Helping Members with Forgotten Passwords

I shall now discuss `ValidateMonth.jsp` file, the output of which is shown here:

This page is displayed to the user if the user selects the **Forgot Password** option on the initial login screen (`LoginScreen.jsp`). The page asks the user to enter the secret code that they entered at the time of registration and the e-mail address to which the password should be mailed. The secret code here is the user's month of birth. In real life situations, you should request a better secret code from the user (such as their mother's maiden name) so that guessing the code becomes more difficult.

ValidateMonth.jsp

The code for `ValidateMonth.jsp` given below is essentially simple HTML code. The HTML code displays the two edit boxes to the user and calls `SendPassword.jsp` on submit:

```
<%-- ValidateMonth.jsp --%>
<html>
<body bgcolor="#C0C0C0">
```

```
<%-- On submit, send the month and e-mail ID to SendPassword.jsp for further
processing --%>

<form method="POST" action="SendPassword.jsp">

<%-- Set user interface for entering secret code and e-mail ID --%>

<table border="0" width="100%">
    <tr>
        <td valign="middle" align="right" ><p>
            <font face="Times New Roman" size="3" color="#0000FF"><b>ENTER
            YOUR BIRTH MONTH: </b></font></p>
        </td>
        <td valign="middle" align="left" >
            <input type="text" name="month" size="20">
        </td>
    </tr>
    <tr>
        <td valign="middle" align="right" ><p><font face="Times New Roman"
            size="3" color="#0000FF"><b>ENTER
            YOUR EMAIL ID: </b></font></p>
        </td>
        <td valign="middle" align="left" >
            <input type="text" name="email" size="20">
        </td>
    </tr>
    <tr>
        <td colspan="2" valign="middle" align="center">
            <p><input type="submit" value="Submit" name="B1"></p>
        </td>
    </tr>
</table>

</form>
</body>
</html>
```

SendPassword.jsp

The SendPassword.jsp file retrieves the password from the database and e-mails it to the user. To keep the code simple here, I am just displaying the password on the user screen. The complete listing for the SendPassword.jsp is given here.

```
<html>
<%@ page language="java" import="java.util.*,java.sql.*" %>

<%-- Retrieve the secret code and email from the request parameter --%>
```

The program obtains the user input month and e-mail fields from the request object:

```
<%
    String Month = request.getParameter("month");
    String Email = request.getParameter("email");
%>
```

The code then uses a bean called `PasswordConfirmBean` to validate the secret input by the user. We'll look at this bean code after we've seen the rest of the JSP:

```
<%-- Create an instance of PasswordConfirmBean class --%>
<jsp:useBean id="ConfirmBean" scope="page" class="PasswordConfirmBean" />
```

The two input values are passed to the bean by calling the `setProperty` methods on the bean:

```
<%-- Set the bean properties --%>
<jsp:setProperty name="ConfirmBean" property="month" value ="<%=Month%>" />
<jsp:setProperty name="ConfirmBean" property="mail" value ="<%=Email%>" />

<body bgcolor="#C0C0C0">
<form method="POST" action="SendPassword.jsp" >
```

Similar to our earlier code, the program then connects to the database by calling the `connect()` method on the bean, it then calls the `selectRecord()` method to validate the record, and finally disconnects from the database by calling the `disconnect()` method:

```
<%-- Search the database for the set criteria --%>
<%

    ConfirmBean.connect();
    HashMap Map = ConfirmBean.selectRecord();
    ConfirmBean.disconnect();
```

If the `selectRecord()` method returns a NULL vector, an error page is displayed to the user:

```
    if(Map == null) {
        response.sendRedirect("Error.html");
    }
    String password = (String)Map.get("PASSWORD");
%>
```

If the vector is not NULL, the password is retrieved from the vector and displayed to the user. Ideally, one should call here our `Mailer` code from the earlier section on *Providing Feedback* to mail the password to the user.

```
<%-- If record is found, display the password to the user. In real life
situations, you would e-mail password to the user. --%>

<p align="center"><font face="Verdana" size="5" color=#0000FF>YOUR PASSWORD
    IS : <%=password%> </font></p>

</form>
</body>
</html>
```

PasswordConfirmBean.java

Having seen the code that sends the user their password, let's look at the code for `PasswordConfirmBean` that validates the user record against the entered secret code and returns the password or NULL to the caller. If the record is found, a vector is constructed and returned to the user or a null vector is returned to the caller. The complete code for the `PasswordConfirmBean` class is given below:

```
/* PasswordConfirmBean.java */
import java.util.*;
import java.beans.*;
import java.sql.*;

/** Returns the Customer password based on the secret code and returns
the same to the caller */

public class PasswordConfirmBean {
    private Connection con;
    private ConnectionManager conMan = new ConnectionManager();
    private String Month;
    private String Mail;
```

The PasswordConfirmBean defines connect() and disconnect() methods for database access and provides set methods for Month and Mail fields.

```
/** Connect to the database */

public void connect() {
    try {
        con = conMan.logOn();
    } catch(Exception ex) {
        ex.getMessage();
    }
}

/** Disconnect from the database */

public void disconnect() {
    try {
        conMan.logOff();
    } catch(Exception ex) {
        ex.getMessage();
    }
}

public void setMonth(String Month) {
    this.Month = Month;
}

public void setMail(String Mail) {
    this.Mail = Mail;
}

/** Retrieves the password column based on the Month and Email criteria.
On Success, returns Password and Email to the caller
Else returns null */

public HashMap selectRecord() {
    HashMap Map = null;
    try {
        Statement stmt = con.createStatement();
```

The `SelectRecord()` method constructs an SQL statement that selects the record from the database based on the month and the e-mail address entered by the user:

```
        String SQL = "select EMAIL, PASSWORD from CUSTOMER where
            BIRTH_MONTH = '"+ Month + "' AND EMAIL = '" +Mail+"'" ;
        ResultSet rs = stmt.executeQuery(SQL);
        if(rs != null) {
            if(rs.next()) {
                Map = new HashMap();
                Map.put ("EMAIL", rs.getString("EMAIL"));
                Map.put ("PASSWORD", rs.getString("PASSWORD"));
            } else {
                System.out.println(" record not found");
            }
        }
    } catch (SQLException e) {
        System.out.println (e.getMessage());
    } catch(Exception sqe) {
        sqe.printStackTrace();
    }
    return Map;
}
}
```

New Member Registration

If the user has not registered with our store earlier, they can select the new member link on our login screen. This invokes `NewUserRegistration.jsp`. This is mostly HTML code that displays a blank form to the user:

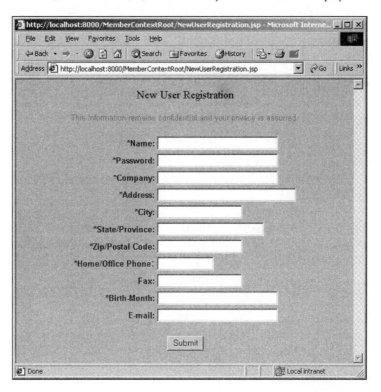

When the user enters the information and submits the form, the `NewUserConfirm.jsp` is invoked. The code for `NewUserRegistration.jsp` is given below:

```
<%-- NewUserRegistration.jsp --%>
<html>
<body bgcolor="#C0C0C0">

<%-- Provides user interface for accepting various fields of the
Customer record. On submit, sends the information to the NewUserConfirm.jsp
for database update --%>

<form method="POST" action = "NewUserConfirm.jsp" >
<p align="center"><font size="4" color="#0000FF">
   New User Registration</font></p>
<p align="center">
   <font color="#808080" face="Arial"><small>
   This Information remains confidential and your privacy is assured.
   </small></font></p>
<table border="0" cellpadding="1" align=center>
   <tr>
      <td align="right" bgcolor="#C0C0C0"><small><strong>
         <font color="#0000FF" face="Arial">*Name:</font></strong></small>
      </td>
      <td><font color="#0000FF">
         <input type="text" size="30" name="name" ></font>
      </td>
   </tr>
   <tr>
      <td align="right" bgcolor="#C0C0C0" valign="middle"><small><strong>
         <font color="#0000FF" face="Arial">*Password:</font></strong></small>
      </td>
      <td><font color="#0000FF">
         <input type="password" size="30" name="password"></font>
      </td>
   </tr>
   <tr>
      <td align="right" bgcolor="#C0C0C0"><small><strong>
         <font color="#0000FF" face="Arial">*Company:</font></strong></small>
      </td>
      <td><font color="#0000FF">
         <input type="text" size="30" name="company"   ></font>
      </td>
   </tr>
   <tr>
      <td align="right" bgcolor="#C0C0C0"><small><strong>
         <font color="#0000FF" face="Arial">*Address:</font></strong></small>
      </td>
      <td><font color="#0000FF">
         <input type="text" size="35" name="addr" ></font>
      </td>
   </tr>
   <tr>
      <td align="right" bgcolor="#C0C0C0"><strong><small>
         <font color="#0000FF" face="Arial"> *City:</font></small></strong>
      </td>
      <td><font color="#0000FF">
```

```
        <input type="text" size="20" name="city" </font>
     </td>
  </tr>
  <tr>
     <td align="right" bgcolor="#C0C0C0"><strong><small>
        <font color="#0000FF" face="Arial">*State/Province:</font>
        </small></strong>
     </td>
     <td><font color="#0000FF">
        <input type="text" size="26" name="state" ></font>
     </td>
  </tr>
  <tr>
     <td align="right" bgcolor="#C0C0C0"><strong><small>
        <font color="#0000FF" face="Arial">*Zip/Postal Code:</font>
        </small></strong>
     </td>
     <td><font color="#0000FF">
        <input type="text" size="20" name="pin"></font>
     </td>
  </tr>
  <tr>
     <td align="right" bgcolor="#C0C0C0"><strong><small>
        <font color="#0000FF" face="Arial">*Country:</font></small></strong>
     </td>
     <td><font color="#0000FF">
        <input type="text" size="20" name="country"></font>
     </td>
  </tr>
  <tr>
     <td align="right" bgcolor="#C0C0C0"><strong><small>
        <font color="#0000FF" face="Arial">*Home/Office</font></small>
        <font color="#0000FF" face="Arial"><small>Phone</small>:<br>
        </font></strong>
     </td>
     <td><font color="#0000FF">
        <input type="text" size="12" name="phone" ></font>
     </td>
  </tr>
  <tr>
     <td align="right" bgcolor="#C0C0C0"><small><strong>
        <font color="#0000FF" face="Arial">Fax:</font></strong></small>
     </td>
     <td><font color="#0000FF">
        <input type="text" size="20" name="fax"></f>
     </td>
  </tr>
  <tr>
     <td align="right" bgcolor="#C0C0C0"><small><strong>
        <font color="#0000FF" face="Arial">*Birth-Month:</font>
        </strong></small>
     </td>
     <td><font color="#0000FF">
        <input type="text" size="30" name="month" ></font>
     </td>
  </tr>
```

355

```
    <tr>
        <td align="right" bgcolor="#C0C0C0"><small><strong>
            <font color="#0000FF" face="Arial">E-mail:</font>
            </strong></small>
        </td>
        <td><font color="#0000FF">
            <input type="text" size="30" name="email" ></font>
        </td>
    </tr>
</table>
<p align="center"><input type="submit" value="Submit" name="B1"></p>
</form>
</body>
</html>
```

NewUserConfirm.jsp

As mentioned above, upon pressing the Submit button, NewUserConfirm.jsp is invoked. The output screen generated by NewUserConfirm.jsp is shown in the following screenshot:

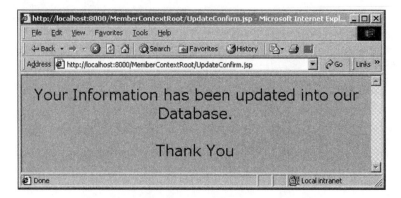

The complete code for NewUserConfirm.jsp is given below:

```
<%-- NewUserConfirm.jsp --%>
<html>

<%@ page language="java" %>

<%-- Retrieve the parameters from the request object. The parameters
represent the various fields of the customer record --%>
<%
    String Name = request.getParameter("name");
    String Password = request.getParameter("password");
    String Address = request.getParameter("addr");
    String City = request.getParameter("city");
    String Fax = request.getParameter("fax");
    String Month = request.getParameter("month");
    String State = request.getParameter("state");
    String Country = request.getParameter("country");
    String Company = request.getParameter("company");
```

```
    String Phone = request.getParameter("phone");
    String Pin = request.getParameter("pin");
    String Email = request.getParameter("email");
%>
```

The `NewUserConfirm.jsp` uses `CustomerRegistrationBean` with the page scope:

```
<%-- Create an instance of CustomerRegistrationBean class --%>
<jsp:useBean id="NewUserBean" scope="page" class="CustomerRegistrationBean" />

<%-- Set various bean properties --%>
<jsp:setProperty name="NewUserBean" property="name" value ="<%=Name%>" />
<jsp:setProperty name="NewUserBean" property="password" value ="<%=Password%>" />
<jsp:setProperty name="NewUserBean" property="addr" value ="<%=Address%>" />
<jsp:setProperty name="NewUserBean" property="city" value ="<%=City%>" />
<jsp:setProperty name="NewUserBean" property="fax"  value ="<%=Fax%>"/>
<jsp:setProperty name="NewUserBean" property="month" value ="<%=Month%>"/>
<jsp:setProperty name="NewUserBean" property="company" value ="<%=Company%>"/>
<jsp:setProperty name="NewUserBean" property="phone" value ="<%=Phone%>"/>
<jsp:setProperty name="NewUserBean" property="pin" value ="<%=Pin%>"/>
<jsp:setProperty name="NewUserBean" property="state" value ="<%=State%>"/>
<jsp:setProperty name="NewUserBean" property="country" value ="<%=Country%>"/>
<jsp:setProperty name="NewUserBean" property="email" value ="<%=Email%>"/>

<body bgcolor="#C0C0C0">
```

The program retrieves the several parameters obtained from the earlier page and sets the corresponding properties of the `NewUserBean`. A scriptlet then connects to the database, inserts the record in the database and disconnects by calling the `disconnect()` method:

```
<%-- Insert the record in the database using NewUserBean object --%>
<%
    NewUserBean.connect();
    NewUserBean.insertRecord();
    NewUserBean.disconnect();
%>


<p align="center"><font face="Verdana" size="5" color=#0000FF>
        Your Information has been added into our Database.<br><br></font></p>
<p align="center"><font face="Verdana" size="5" color=#0000FF>
        Thank you for registering with us. </font></p>

</form>
</body>
</html>
```

CustomerRegistrationBean.java

The `CustomerRegistrationBean` class is very similar to the other bean classes discussed previously. The major difference is in the formation of the SQL statement. The program creates an appropriate SQL INSERT statement, and updates the database. The complete code for the `CustomerRegistrationBean` class is given below.

```
/* CustomerRegistrationBean.java */

import java.util.*;
import java.beans.*;
import java.sql.*;

/** CustomerRegistrationBean class provides methods for inserting a new record
and modifying the existing record in the CUSTOMER table. */

public class CustomerRegistrationBean {

    private    Connection con;
    private    ConnectionManager conMan = new ConnectionManager();
    private    Statement stmt;
    private    ResultSet rs;
    private    String Email;
    private    String Name;
    private    String Address;
    private    String City;
    private    String State;
    private    String Country;
    private    String Pin;
    private    String Phone;
    private    String Fax;
    private    String Password;
    private    String Company;
    private    String Month;
    private    String SQL;

    /** Connect to the database */

    public void connect() {
        try {
            con = conMan.logOn();
        } catch(Exception ex) {
            System.out.println (ex.getMessage());
        }
    }

    /** Disconnect from the database */

    public void disconnect() {
        try {
            conMan.logOff();
        } catch(Exception ex) {
            ex.getMessage();
        }
    }

    /** Inserts a new record in the CUSTOMER table */

    public void insertRecord() {
        try {
            stmt = con.createStatement();
            SQL = "INSERT INTO CUSTOMER VALUES ('" +Email+ "','" +
                        Name + "','" +
```

```
                              Address+ "','" +
                              City + "','" +
                              Pin + "','" +
                              Phone + "','" +
                              Company + "','" +
                              Password + "','" +
                              Fax + "','" +
                              Month + "','" +
                              State+ "','" +
                              Country +"')";
              stmt.executeUpdate(SQL);
          } catch (SQLException se) {
              System.out.println (se.getMessage());
          } catch(Exception sqe) {
              sqe.printStackTrace();
          }
      }

      /** Updates an existing record in the CUSTOMER table */

      public void updateRecord() {
          try {
              stmt = con.createStatement();
              SQL   = "UPDATE CUSTOMER SET NAME ='" + Name+
                      "', ADDRESS = '" + Address +
                      "', CITY = '" + City +
                      "', PIN = '" + Pin+
                      "', PHONE = '" + Phone +
                      "', COMPANY = '" + Company +
                      "', PASSWORD = '" + Password +
                      "', FAX = '" + Fax +
                      "', BIRTH_MONTH = '" + Month +
                      "', STATE = '" + State +
                      "', COUNTRY = '" + Country +
                      "' WHERE EMAIL = '"+Email+"'";
              stmt.executeUpdate(SQL);
          } catch (SQLException e) {
              e.printStackTrace();
          } catch(Exception   sqe) {
              sqe.printStackTrace();
          }
      }

      public void setName(String Name) {
          this.Name= Name;
      }

      public void setEmail(String Email) {
          this.Email=Email;
      }

      public void setAddr(String Address) {
          this.Address = Address;
      }

      public void setCity(String City) {
```

```
        this.City= City;
    }

    public void   setState(String    State) {
        this.State=   State;
    }

    public void setCountry(String Country) {
        this.Country= Country;
    }

    public void setPin(String Pin) {
        this.Pin= Pin;
    }

    public void setPhone(String Phone) {
        this.Phone =Phone;
    }

    public void setCompany(String Company) {
        this.Company = Company;
    }

    public void setPassword(String Password) {
        this.Password = Password;
    }

    public void setFax(String Fax) {
        this.Fax=Fax;
    }

    public void setMonth(String Month) {
        this.Month=Month;
    }
}
```

Once you set up the membership for your regular customers, you may offer promotional schemes to members; offer additional discounts on certain products, provide personalized services, etc.

With our online web store, it is quite possible that very soon we will start finding international customers shopping at our store. To attract international customers, we should have our web site formatted as per each country's locale. Fortunately, Java provides a great support for internationalizing our Java based sites and products.

Internationalization

One of the major requirements for a site with aspirations of selling goods to a worldwide audience is to format dates and currency using the correct format for that country. The java.text package provides support for this.

To format the numbers, we use NumberFormat class and call the format() method on it to format the given number:

```
int shares = 1000;
NumberFormat number = NumberFormat.getInstance();
System.out.println("No of shares : "+number.format(shares));
```

To format currency, once again we use `NumberFormat` class and call its `format()` method. We need to call the `getCurrencyInstance()` method instead of the `getInstance()` method.

```
double buyingPrice = 100.0;
NumberFormat price=NumberFormat.getCurrencyInstance();
System.out.println("Buying Price : " +price.format(buyingPrice));
```

Similarly, you can format Date and Time easily by calling the `getDateInstance()` and `getTimeInstance()` methods:

```
DateFormat shortdate=DateFormat.getDateInstance(DateFormat.SHORT);
DateFormat fulldate =
    DateFormat.getDateTimeInstance(DateFormat.LONG, DateFormat.LONG);
System.out.println("value at "+ fulldate.format(d)+":");
System.out.println("Date : "+ shortdate.format(d) );
```

Java also supports the use of localized strings with the help of **Resource Bundles**. For this a `ResourceBundle` class is provided in the `java.util` package.

Changing the Language of our Site

Thus, Java allows you to internationalize your site very easily. To illustrate how to internationalize your site, I will convert the confirmation page of our earlier chapter to include international support. In order to do this, the strings are not hard-coded – instead, these are picked up from a resource bundle. First, we need to create a properties file that defines key value pairs for the strings we need to use on our page. The contents of `MessageBundle.properties` file is shown here:

```
ThankyouNote = Thank you for placing the order with us.
OrderValue = Your order value :
OrderDate = Order received on :
```

This is our default properties file and defines three keys viz. `ThankyouNote`, `OrderValue` and `OrderDate`. The key values are placed on the right hand side of each expression. For each country that you wish to support, you will need to create a properties file similar to this with value text written in that particular language. For example, to support French, create a file with the name `MesagesBundle_fr_FR.properties` with contents shown here:

```
ThankyouNote = Merci de confier votre commande à nous.
OrderValue = Votre valeur de commande :
OrderDate = Commande reçue :
```

Once the properties files are created, the key values can be read from these properties files by calling the following code snippet. You need to first create the `Locale` object by specifying the language and the country for the desired `Locale`. Once a `ResourceBundle` is created, you can read in the key values by calling its `getString` method:

```
Locale currentLocale = new Locale(language, country);
ResourceBundle messages =
    ResourceBundle.getBundle("MessagesBundle",currentLocale);
msg = messages.getString("ThankyouNote");
orderValue = messages.getString("OrderValue");
orderDate = messages.getString("OrderDate");
```

MsgBundleBean.java

We will develop a JavaBean called MsgBundleBean.java for the above code. We will then use this bean in our Confirmation.jsp file. The bean also defines a method for formatting today's date in the currently selected Locale. The complete bean code is presented below:

```
/** MsgBundleBean.java
 */

import java.util.*;
import java.text.*;

/** This bean provides methods for reading messages from ResourceBundles,
 * formatting currency and date
 */

public class MsgBundleBean {
    String language;
    String country;
    String msg;
    String orderValue;
    String orderDate;
    String currencyOut;
    String dateOut;

    /** Load the appropriate resource bundle and set the attributes
     * by reading the keys from the resource bundle
     */

    public void readMessages () {
        Locale currentLocale = new Locale(language, country);
        ResourceBundle messages =
            ResourceBundle.getBundle("MessagesBundle",currentLocale);

        msg = messages.getString("ThankyouNote");
        orderValue = messages.getString("OrderValue");
        orderDate = messages.getString("OrderDate");
    }
```

Here we also define a method for formatting the currency. The FormatCurrency method receives a double type argument and formats the value for the currently selected Locale. The value is then returned as a String in the bean's attribute:

```
    /** Format the currency in the currently selected Locale
     */
```

```
public void FormatCurrency(double value) {
   Locale currentLocale = new Locale(language, country);
   Double currency = new Double(value);
   NumberFormat currencyFormatter;

   currencyFormatter = NumberFormat.getCurrencyInstance(currentLocale);
   currencyOut = currencyFormatter.format(currency);
}
```

The bean also defines a method for formatting today's date in the currently selected `Locale`. This is shown here. As can be seen from the code, we use `getDateInstance` method to get a date formatter. This formatter is then used to format today's date and convert it to a `String`:

```
/** Format today's date in the currently selected Locale
 */

public void FormatDate() {
   Date today;
   DateFormat dateFormatter;

   Locale currentLocale = new Locale(language, country);
   dateFormatter = DateFormat.getDateInstance(DateFormat.DEFAULT,
      currentLocale);
   today = new Date();
   dateOut = dateFormatter.format(today);
}

public void setLanguage(String language) {
   this.language = language;
}

public void setCountry(String country) {
   this.country = country;
}

public String getMsg() {
   return msg;
}

public String getOrderValue() {
   return orderValue;
}

public String getOrderDate() {
   return orderDate;
}

public String getCurrencyOut() {
   return currencyOut;
}

public String getDateOut() {
   return dateOut;
}
}
```

Confirmation.jsp

Next, we develop our `Confirmation.jsp` page. The page creates an instance of our `MsgBundleBean` and sets the properties for the language and the country. I have used hard-coded values on the current page. However, you should pick up the country name from the `CUSTOMER` database and set the appropriate values for language and the country depending on the customer's country. This is also known as **personalization**. The user sees the output page in his/her native language and format. For simplicity, I have selected a small page to illustrate personalization. You may like to modify all the pages of the site to give a more personal feel for the user.

The complete code for `Confirmation.jsp` is shown here.

```
<%-- Confirmation.jsp --%>
<html>

<head>
    <title>Order Confirmation</title>
</head>

<%@ page language="java" import="java.util.*,java.text.*" %>

<jsp:useBean id="MsgBundle" scope="page" class="MsgBundleBean" />
<jsp:setProperty name="MsgBundle" property="language" value="fr" />
<jsp:setProperty name="MsgBundle" property="country" value="FR" />

<body>
```

Once the bean is instantiated, we call `readMessages` method on the bean to read in all the key values in the bean's attribute:

```
<%   MsgBundle.readMessages (); %>
```

The program then prints the thank you note to the customer in the user's language. We use a jsp `getProperty` tag to read the value of `ThankYouNote`. Remember, you must create the note in different languages and store it in appropriate properties file.

```
<p align="center"><font face="Verdana" size="4" color="#0000FF"><b>
<jsp:getProperty name="MsgBundle" property="msg" />
</b></font></p>
```

Next, we format the order value in the specified currency format. For this, we call the `FormatCurrency` method on our bean object. I have sent the hard-coded value as a parameter to this method. You should read the total order value for the customer from the earlier order confirmation page (refer to Chapter 9) and pass it as an argument to this method:

```
<% MsgBundle.FormatCurrency(1145.25); %>
```

The formatted currency value with the appropriate message is then printed for the user. Note that the message is generated by using the `orderValue` property of the bean. This property value is retrieved from the properties file as explained above.

```
<p align="center"><font face="Verdana" size="2" color="#0000FF"><b>
<jsp:getProperty name="MsgBundle" property="orderValue" />
<jsp:getProperty name="MsgBundle" property="currencyOut" />
</b></font></p>
```

Lastly, we format today's date using the currently selected `Locale` and display it the user by calling following code:

```
<% MsgBundle.FormatDate(); %>

<p align="center"><font face="Verdana" size="2" color="#0000FF"><b>
<jsp:getProperty name="MsgBundle" property="orderDate" />
<jsp:getProperty name="MsgBundle" property="dateOut" />
</b></font></p>

</body>
</html>
```

From this simple example, you can see it clearly that it is very easy to internationalize your site with very little coding and proper planning. This can be effectively used for personalization to give a much richer experience to the customer. Note that in the above simple example, although the order value is displayed in a currency format for the customer's country, we have not taken into consideration currency conversion.

Summary

In this chapter, we have learned many techniques for site usability:

❑　We looked at some considerations needed to make online sites customer friendly.

❑　We covered the use of custom tags, allowing the clear separation between the Java code and the HTML. The development of two custom tags was discussed.

❑　We explained the implementation of search techniques for your site – dynamic searching on the database was also demonstrated.

❑　The techniques of sending feedback to the customers using JavaMail were explained.

❑　The creation of memberships for your regular customers was demonstrated; the benefits of membership were explained.

❑　The program code for creation and modification of member information was developed.

❑　Finally, the techniques of internationalizing your site were discussed.

So far, we have considered the server-side issues of the e-commerce site design. In the next chapter, we'll also look at the client-side issues of site design. We'll see how to validate the client issues, how to support different types of clients, and how to support XML clients.

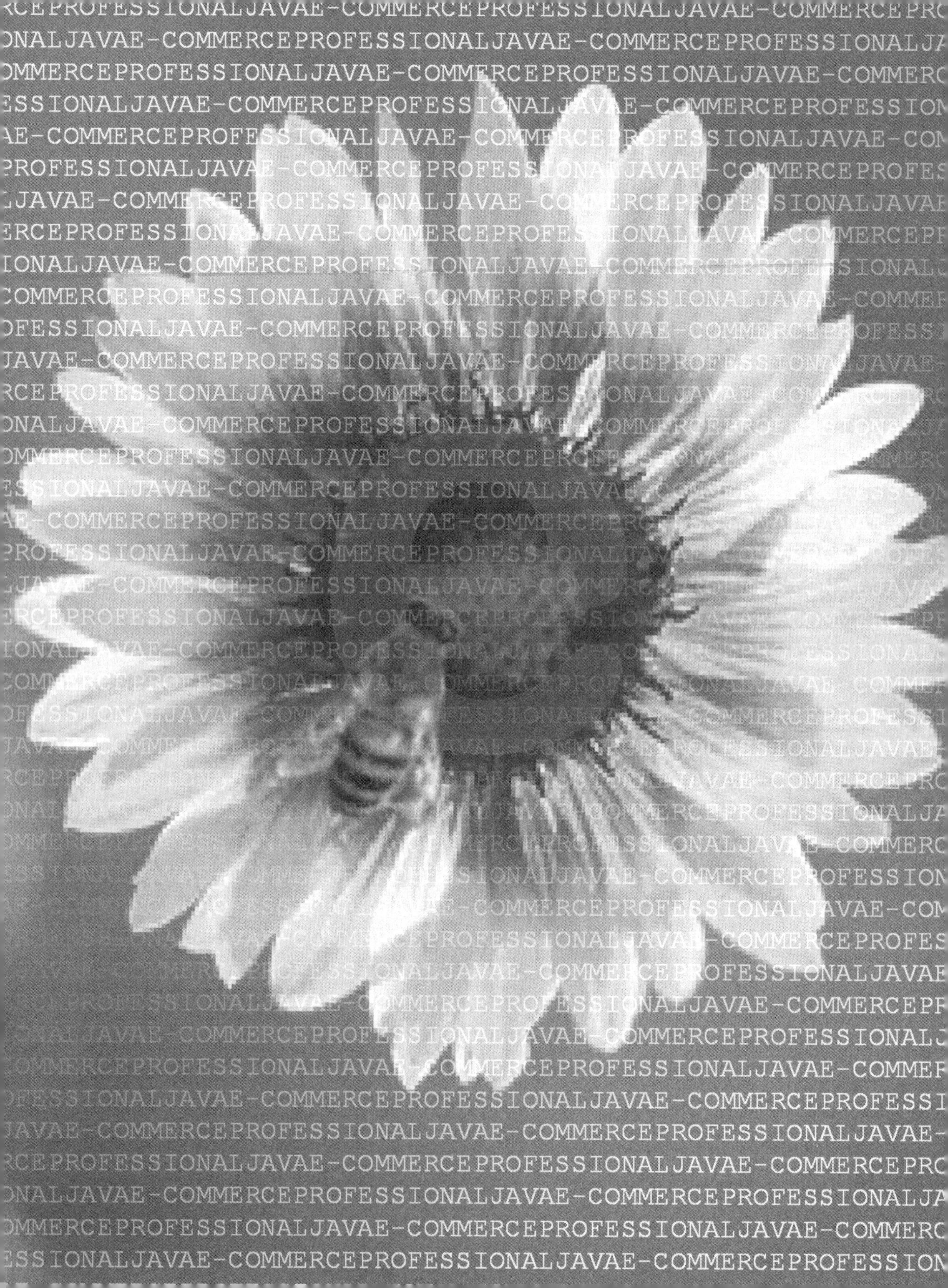
PROFESSIONALJAVAE-COMMERCE

11

B2C E-Commerce: Client Issues

In the last two chapters, we started to develop a simple web site selling desktop computers online. We made the point that if a client has a good experience of surfing your site, they are more likely to re-visit the site, place an order, or tell others about your site.

To achieve this, you must take into consideration several factors – one of these factors being ease of navigation. The client should be able to quickly find what they are looking for and make their purchases with ease. Sometimes, however a purely functional site may not be sufficient to keep the client returning to your site – the use of graphics, and maybe audio and video may offer the user a richer experience. However, the moment that you add such features to your site, you must ensure that it works on all browsers and the customer has the necessary bandwidth to surf your site with a reasonable response time. In this chapter, I shall discuss the issues for the client of the e-commerce site development.

The last two chapters concentrated mainly on the server-side programming. The client code was essentially HTML code dynamically generated by JSPs on the server. As this was pure HTML code, it will run on all browsers. (Firewalls allow the propagation of pure HTML code, but do not support the use of scripting languages like JavaScript or even Java Applets.) However, pure HTML code does not provide a great interactive interface to the client and not only that, it doesn't offer a way of easily validating data entered by the client.

In this chapter we're going to see how we can make our site even more effective, and even more attractive to the visitor, by looking at:

- ❑ Validating user inputs
- ❑ Java applets and plug ins
- ❑ Delivering media
- ❑ Delivering XML

Our first objective is to see how we can ensure the details entered into our site are correct (or at least plausible).

Validating User Input

The web store created in the last two chapters uses JSPs to generate the presentation code for the user. The presentation code is pure HTML code and does not involve any validations on the data input from the client. In practical situations, such validations are very important to trap null and wrong value inputs from the user.

The question is where do you do the validations of the client input – on the client-side or on the server-side? Client-side validations will give faster response to the client and will obviously save several trips to the server, but, as pure HTML code cannot provide such validations, it will require the use of a scripting language such as JavaScript on the client-side. The other options would be to use a Java Applet or an ActiveX control on the client. These can be termed **heavy clients**, as they may require substantial processing power on the client machine, as well as possibly leading to cross-browser compatibility issues.

As we indicated validations of client input validation can be also be done on the server. Typically, sites provide some basic validations on the client by using scripting and more advanced validations, such those that require access to the backend database, are done on the server.

In this chapter we'll look at both client-side and server-side validation, starting with the client.

Client-side Validation

To validate client input, we will use JavaScript, but remember if you use JavaScript on the client-side and if the client browser does not support JavaScript or such support has been disabled by the user, you will have to fall back on server-side validation (we'll deal with this later in our `index.html` file).

In this chapter we shall only show the validation for one of our screens as the approach is easily transferable to the other screens we've looked at.

As a sample, I have selected our member entry program that contains several fields. The member entry screen was generated by the `UserRegistration.jsp` file and we'll modify this file to provide the client-side validation on all the user input fields. The new screen with validation enabled is shown below. The screen shows the current user has not entered enough letters for the password field to meet the set requirements.

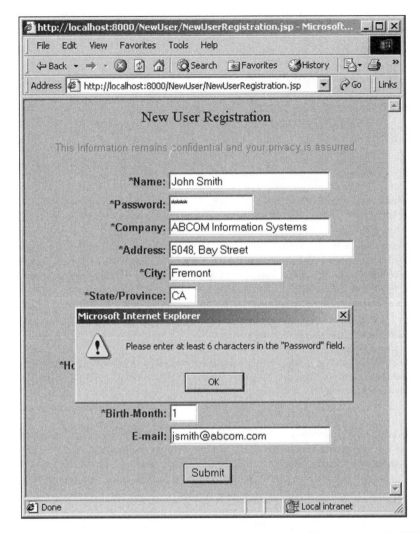

The `UserRegistration.jsp` file from the previous chapter essentially contained only HTML code. We will rename this `NewUserRegistration.html` and add JavaScript code to it for client-side validation of the various `Form` fields (please note that this example assumes that the user is in the US).

Let's investigate the code we need. Firstly a script tag added to the new HTML page indicates the use of JavaScript code on this page:

```
<html>
<body bgcolor="#c0c0c0">
<script    Language="JavaScript">
<!--
```

The function `checkDigit` receives a string parameter, extracts each character of the string, and tests it against the valid range of digits:

```
//Checks if all the characters in the input stream are numerals
function checkDigit(str) {
    var    checkStr = str;
    var allValid = true;
    for (i = 0; i < checkStr.length; i++) {
        ch = checkStr.charAt(i);
        if (ch < '0' ||   ch > '9') {
            allValid = false;
            break;
        }
    }
    return allValid;
}
// Validates all the fields of the form
function Form_Validator(theForm) {
```

The JavaScript code validates each field of the form in the order they appear on the screen and each field has a different set of validation rules. All the validations take place in the `Form_Validator()` method. Since most of the fields are alphanumeric, we check for a non-null value to ensure that the user has input some value.

For example, to check that the user has input a value for the name field the following `if` statement is used:

```
// Check for null name field
if (theForm.name.value == "") {
    alert("Please enter a value for the \"Name\" field.");
    theForm.name.focus();
    return (false);
}
```

The `Form_Validator` function receives `theForm` parameter. The `theForm.name` specifies the name field on the form and the expression `theForm.name.value` denotes the contents of the name field. If these contents are unknown we inform the user by calling the `alert` function. The `alert` function displays the message string given as a method parameter to the user. A call to the `focus` method sets the focus on the name field so that user can modify the field contents.

```
// Check for null password field
if (theForm.password.value == "") {
    alert("Please enter a value for the \"Password\" field.");
    theForm.password.focus();
    return (false);
}
```

To check that the user has entered at least a six character value for the password field the following `if` clause is used. The `length` returns the current field length. As the password is not displayed to the user while entering, it is a good idea to provide one more password field and ask the user to re-enter the password in this field. The validation program should then verify that both password fields contain the same string:

```
// Check password length
if (theForm.password.value.length < 6) {
    alert("Please enter at least 6 characters in the \"Password\"
```

```
        field.");
    theForm.password.focus();
    return (false);
}

// Check for null company field
if (theForm.company.value == "") {
    alert("Please enter a value for the \"Company\" field.");
    theForm.company.focus();
    return (false);
}

// Check for null address field
if (theForm.addr.value == "") {
    alert("Please enter your House No./Street Name for the \"Address\"
        field.");
    theForm.addr.focus();
    return (false);
}

// Check for null city field
if (theForm.city.value == "") {
    alert("Please enter a value for the \"City\" field.");
    theForm.city.focus();
    return (false);
}

// Check for null state field
if (theForm.state.value == "") {
    alert("Please enter 2 letters code for the \"State\" field.");
    theForm.state.focus();
    return (false);
}

// Check state length
if (theForm.state.value.length < 2) {
    alert("Please enter at least 2 characters in the \"State\" field.");
    theForm.state.focus();
    return (false);
}
```

Some fields (such as the state field) can contain only alphabetic characters. To validate the state field, we use the following code. Each character in the state field is extracted by using substring() method and converted to upper case by using toUpperCase() method. The character is then tested against the valid range of alphabetic characters. If the test fails, allValid flag is set to false:

```
// Check if state field contains only characters
// We assume state values in USA
var checkStr = theForm.state.value;
var allValid = true;
for (i = 0; i < checkStr.length; i++) {
    var ch = checkStr.charAt(i).toUpperCase();
    if (ch<'A' || ch>'Z') {
        allValid = false;
        break;
```

```
      }
   }
   if (!allValid) {
      alert("Please enter only letter characters for the \"State\" code.");
      theForm.state.focus();
      return (false);
   }

   // Check for null pin code
   if (theForm.pin.value == "") {
      alert("Please enter a value for the \"Pin\" field.");
      theForm.pin.focus();
      return (false);
   }

   // Check for null country field
   if (theForm.country.value == "") {
      alert("Please enter a value for the \"Country\" field.");
      theForm.country.focus();
      return (false);
   }

   // Check for null areacode field
   if (theForm.areacode.value == "") {
      alert("Please enter a value for the \"Areacode\" in Phone field.");
      theForm.areacode.focus();
      return (false);
   }

   // Check length of areacode field
   if (theForm.areacode.value.length < 3) {
      alert("Please enter at least 3 digits for the \"Areacode\" in
         Phone field.");
      theForm.areacode.focus();
      return (false);
   }

   // Check that areacode contains only numeric digits
   var allValid = true;
   allValid = checkDigit(theForm.areacode.value);
   if (!allValid) {
      alert("Please enter only digit characters in the \"Areacode\" for
         Phone field.");
      theForm.areacode.focus();
      return (false);
   }

   // Check for null phone field
   if (theForm.prefix.value == "") {
      alert("Please enter a value for the \"Prefix\" in Phone field.");
      theForm.prefix.focus();
      return (false);
   }

   // Check length of areacode field
```

```
if (theForm.prefix.value.length < 3) {
   alert("Please enter at least 3 digits in the \"Prefix\" for
      Phone field.");
   theForm.prefix.focus();
   return (false);
}

// Check that phone field contains only numeric digits
var allValid = true;
allValid = checkDigit(theForm.prefix.value);
if (!allValid) {
   alert("Please enter only digit characters in the \"Prefix\" for
      Phone field.");
   theForm.prefix.focus();
   return (false);
}

// Check for null suffix field
if (theForm.suffix.value == "") {
   alert("Please enter a value for the \"Suffix\" for Phone field.");
   theForm.suffix.focus();
   return (false);
}

// Check length of suffix field
if (theForm.suffix.value.length < 4) {
   alert("Please enter at least 4 characters in the \"Suffix\" for
      Phone field.");
   theForm.suffix.focus();
   return (false);
}
```

Similarly, certain fields like phone and fax numbers must contain only numeric digits. For this, the program calls the `checkDigit` function that receives a `string` parameter. The function returns a `Boolean` flag giving the status of the test:

```
// Check that suffix field contains only numeric digits
var allValid = true;
allValid = checkDigit(theForm.suffix.value);
if (!allValid) {
   alert("Please enter only digit characters in the \"Suffix\" for
      Phone field.");
   theForm.suffix.focus();
   return (false);
}

// Check for null fax areacode field
if (theForm.faxarea.value == "") {
   alert("Please enter a value for the \"Areacode\" in Fax field.");
   theForm.faxarea.focus();
   return (false);
}

// Check length of fax areacode field
if (theForm.faxarea.value.length < 3) {
```

```
        alert("Please enter at least 3 digits in the \"Areacode\" in Fax
            field.");
        theForm.faxarea.focus();
        return (false);
    }


    // Check that fax areacode field contains only numeric digits
    var allValid = true;
    allValid = checkDigit(theForm.faxarea.value);
    if (!allValid) {
        alert("Please enter only digit characters in the \"Areacode\" for Fax
            field.");
        theForm.faxarea.focus();
        return (false);
    }


    // Check for null fax prefix field
    if (theForm.faxprefix.value == "") {
        alert("Please enter a value for the \"Prefix\" in Fax field.");
        theForm.faxprefix.focus();
        return (false);
    }


    // Check length of fax prefix field
    if (theForm.faxprefix.value.length < 3) {
        alert("Please enter at least 3 digits in the \"Prefix\" for Fax
            field.");
        theForm.faxprefix.focus();
        return (false);
    }


    // Check that fax prefix field contains only numeric digits
    var allValid = true;
    allValid = checkDigit(theForm.faxprefix.value);
    if (!allValid) {
        alert("Please enter   only digit characters in the \"Prefix\" for Fax
            field.");
        theForm.faxprefix.focus();
        return (false);
    }


    // Check for null fax suffix field
    if (theForm.faxsuffix.value == "") {
        alert("Please enter a value for the \"Suffix\" in Fax field.");
        theForm.faxsuffix.focus();
        return (false);
    }


    // Check length of fax suffix field
    if (theForm.faxsuffix.value.length < 4) {
        alert("Please enter at least 4 digits in the \"Suffix\" for Fax
            field.");
        theForm.faxsuffix.focus();
        return (false);
    }
```

```
    // Check that fax suffix field contains only numeric digits
    var allValid = true;
    allValid = checkDigit(theForm.faxsuffix.value);
    if (!allValid) {
        alert("Please enter only digit characters in the \"Suffix\" for Fax
            field.");
        theForm.faxsuffix.focus();
        return (false);
    }

    // Check for null month field
    if (theForm.month.value == "") {
        alert("Please enter a value for the \"Birth_Month\" field.");
        theForm.month.focus();
        return (false);
    }

    // Check that month field contains only numeric digits
    var allValid = true;
    allValid = checkDigit(theForm.month.value);
    if (!allValid) {
        alert("Please enter only digit characters in the \"Birth Month\"
            field.");
        theForm.month.focus();
        return (false);
    }

    // Check if month field is in valid range
    var chkVal = theForm.month.value;
    var prsVal = parseInt(chkVal);
    if (chkVal != "" && !(prsVal >= "1" && prsVal <= "12")) {
        alert("Please enter a value between \"1\" and \"12\" in the \"Birth
            Month\" field.");
        theForm.month.focus();
        return (false);
    }

    // Check for null email field
    if (theForm.email.value == "") {
        alert("Please enter a value for the \"Email\" field.");
        theForm.email.focus();
        return (false);
    }
    return (true);
}
-->
</script>
<!-- On submit, validate the form fields by using JavaScript function -->
```

On submitting the form, we call the JavaScript function Form_Validator. This function checks all of the fields of our form. If a field does not meet the validation, an alert message is shown to the user, the focus is set to the field failing the validation, and the form is not posted. On loading, the initial focus is set to the name field.

If the form passes all the validations, the `NewUserConfirm.jsp` is called that adds the record to the database. Calling the `Form_Validator` function performs the validations. This function receives the reference to the current form as a parameter to the function. When the form is loaded, the focus is set to the name field of the form. This is specified in the `onload` condition shown here:

```
<form method="post" action
    ="NewUserConfirm.jsp" onsubmit="return Form_Validator(this)"
    name="NewUserRegistrationForm" onload="document.theForm.name.focus()">

<p align="center"><font size="4" color="#0000ff"></font> </p>
<p align=center><font color=#0000ff size=4>New User Registration</font></p>
<p align="center">
    <font color="#808080" face="Arial"><small>
    This Information remains confidential and your privacy is assured.
        </small> </font></p>

<!-- Create an input form for Customer Record -->

<table border="0" cellpadding="1" align=center>

    <!-- Name field -->

    <tr>
    <td align="right" bgcolor="#c0c0c0"><small><strong>
        <font color="#0000ff" face="Arial">*Name:</font></strong></small></td>
    <td><font color="#0000ff">
        <input size="30" name="name" ></font></td>
    </tr>

    <!-- Password field -->

    <tr>
    <td align="right" bgcolor="#c0c0c0" valign="center"><small><strong>
        <font color="#0000ff" face="Arial">*Password:</font></strong>
            </small></td>
    <td><font color="#0000ff">
        <input type="password" size="14" name="password"></font></td>
    </tr>

    <!-- Company field -->

    <tr>
    <td align="right" bgcolor="#c0c0c0"><small><strong>
        <font color="#0000ff"
        face="Arial">*Company:</font></strong></small></td>
    <td><font color="#0000ff">
        <input size="30" name="company" ></font></td>
    </tr>

    <!-- Address field -->

    <tr>
     <td align="right" bgcolor="#c0c0c0"><small><strong>
        <font color="#0000ff"
        face="Arial">*Address:</font></strong></small></td>
```

```
   <td><font color="#0000ff">
      <input size="35" name="addr" ></font></td>
</tr>


<!-- City field -->

<tr>
 <td align="right" bgcolor="#c0c0c0"><strong><small>
      <font color="#0000ff"
       face="Arial"> *City:</font></small></strong></td>
 <td><font color="#0000ff">
      <input name="city" font <    ></FONT></td>
</tr>


<!-- State field -->

<tr>
 <td align="right" bgcolor="#c0c0c0"><strong><small>
      <font color="#0000ff"
       face="Arial">*State/Province:</font></small></strong></td>
 <td><font color="#0000ff">
      <input size="2" name="state" maxlength="2" ></font></td>
</tr>


<!-- Zip code field -->

<tr>
 <td align="right" bgcolor="#c0c0c0"><strong><small>
    <font color="#0000ff" face="Arial">*Zip/Postal Code:</font></small>
        </strong></td>
 <td><font color="#0000ff">
      <input size="10" name="pin" ></font></td>
</tr>


<!-- Country Field -->

<tr>
 <td align="right" bgcolor="#c0c0c0"><strong><small>
    <font color="#0000ff" face="Arial">*Country:</font></small>
        </strong></td>
 <td><font color="#0000ff">
      <input size="10" name="country" ></font></td>
</tr>

<!-- Phone number field -->

<tr>
 <td align="right" bgcolor="#c0c0c0"><strong><small>
     <font color="#0000ff" face="Arial">*Home/Office</font></small>
     <font color="#0000ff" face="Arial"><small>Phone</small>:<br></font>
     </strong></td>
 <td><font color="#0000ff">
     <STRONG><BIG><BIG>(</BIG></BIG>
      <INPUT maxLength=3 name=areacode size=3>
     <BIG><BIG>)</BIG></BIG></STRONG>
```

```
            <INPUT maxLength=3 name=prefix size=3>
            <STRONG><BIG><BIG>-</BIG></BIG></STRONG>
            <INPUT maxLength=4 name=suffix size=4>
         </font></td>
      </tr>

      <!-- Fax field -->

      <tr>
       <td align="right" bgcolor="#c0c0c0"><small><strong>
            <font color="#0000ff"
             face="Arial">*Fax:</font></strong></small></td>
       <td><font color="#0000ff">
            <STRONG><BIG><BIG>(</BIG></BIG>
               <INPUT maxLength=3 name=faxarea size=3>
            <BIG><BIG>)</BIG></BIG></STRONG>
               <INPUT maxLength=3 name=faxprefix    size=3>
            <STRONG><BIG><BIG>-</BIG></BIG></STRONG>
               <INPUT maxLength=4 name=faxsuffix    size=4>
            </font></td>
      </tr>

      <!-- Month field -->

      <tr>
       <td align="right" bgcolor="#c0c0c0"><small><strong>
            <font color="#0000ff" face="Arial">*Birth-Month:</font>
            </strong></small></td>
       <td><font color="#0000ff">
            <input size="2" name="month" maxlength="2" ></font></td>
      </tr>

      <!-- email field -->

      <tr>
       <td align="right" bgcolor="#c0c0c0"><small><strong>
            <font color="#0000ff" face="Arial">*E-mail:</font>
            </strong></small></td>
       <td><font color="#0000ff">
            <input size="30" name="email" ></font></td>
      </tr>
   </table>

   <p align="center"><input type="submit" value="Submit" name="B1"
      style="align: Center"></p>

   </form>
   </body>
   </html>
```

This completes coding for the client-side validation for one of our screens. Likewise, you will have to modify the rest of your user input screens to ensure that all the data input by the user is validated against certain rules laid out in the program code. We will look now at the portability of our client-side code.

Cross-browser Design

In the previous HTML page, the validations were done on the client-side using JavaScript – but what if the client browser does not support JavaScript or if the client has turned off the JavaScript support on their browser?

Your program code should check for this possibility and re-direct the user to an appropriate HTML page where the validations could be performed on the server by using some server-side code. To do this, we write another HTML page that checks if the client browser has JavaScript support enabled. This is named `index.html`, and is the default page for our URL.

```
<HTML>
<HEAD>
<script language="javascript">
<!--
function Load_Page() {
    document.URL = "NewUserRegistration.html";
    document.title = "Loading NewUserRegistration Form";
}
-->
</script>
</HEAD>

<BODY BACKGROUND="#FFFFFF" TEXT="#005030" LINK="#004090" ONLOAD =
javascript:Load_Page();>
<FONT FACE="verdana">
<CENTER>
<BR><BR><BR><BR><BR>
    Your browser doesn't support JavaScript, click <A HREF =
    "NewUserRegis.html">here</A>
</CENTER>
</BODY>
</HTML>
```

When the user opens the above HTML page the JavaScript function `Load_Page` is called. It calls our `NewUserRegistration.html` page described above. If the user's browser does not support JavaScript, an appropriate message is displayed to the user and the user is requested to follow a link to `NewUserRegis.html` page.

As we said previously client-side validation is OK for simple things as we've just shown, but if we need to validate against data held in a database (for example to confirm a password) we will have to perform some type of server-side process.

Validating on the Server

The `NewUserRegis.html` page creates a blank data entry page for the user. When the user submits the form, it calls the `NewUserValidation.jsp` that validates all the fields of the form. The complete code for the `NewUserRegis.html` is given below. The page displays the various field titles and edit controls to the user and provides a Submit button.

```
<!-- NewUserRegis.html -->
<html>
<body bgcolor = "#c0c0c0">
<!-- On submit, invoke NewUserValidation.jsp that validates
```

```
      the user entered fields on the server -->
<form method="post" action = "NewUserValidation.jsp"
   name = "NewUserRegistrationForm">

<p align = "center"><font size="4" color="#0000ff">
   </font> </p>
<p align = center><font color=#0000ff size = 4>New User
   Registration</font></p>
<p align = "center">
        <font color="#808080" face="Arial"><small>
          This Information remains confidential and your privacy is assured.
        </small></font></p>

   <!--Create an input form to accept various fields of Customer record -->
   <table border="0" cellpadding="1" align=center>

   <!-- Name field -->

   <tr>
   <td align="right" bgcolor="#c0c0c0"><small><strong>
      <font color="#0000ff" face="Arial">*Name:</font></strong></small></td>
   <td><font color="#0000ff">
      <input size="30" name="name" ></font></td>
   </tr>

   <!-- Password field -->

   <tr>
    <td align="right" bgcolor="#c0c0c0" valign="center"><small><strong>
      <font color="#0000ff" face="Arial">*Password:</font></strong>
         </small></td>
    <td><font color="#0000ff">
         <input type="password" size="14" name="password"></font></td>
   </tr>

   <!-- Company field -->

   <tr>
   <td align="right" bgcolor="#c0c0c0"><small><strong>
      <font color="#0000ff" face="Arial">*Company:</font></strong>
         </small></td>
   <td><font color="#0000ff">
      <input size="30" name="company" ></font></td>
   </tr>

   <!-- Address field -->

   <tr>
   <td align="right" bgcolor="#c0c0c0"><small><strong>
      <font color="#0000ff" face="Arial">*Address:</font></strong>
         </small></td>
      <td><font color="#0000ff">
         <input size="35" name="addr" ></font></td>
   </tr>
```

```
<!-- City field -->

<tr>
<td align="right" bgcolor="#c0c0c0"><strong><small>
   <font color="#0000ff" face="Arial"> *City:</font></small>
      </strong></td>
   <td><font color="#0000ff">
      <input name="city" font < ></FONT></td>
</tr>

<!-- State field -->

<tr>
<td align="right" bgcolor="#c0c0c0"><strong><small>
   <font color="#0000ff" face="Arial">*State/Province:</font></small>
      </strong></td>
   <td><font color="#0000ff">
      <input size="2" name="state" maxlength="2" ></font></td>
</tr>

<!-- Country field -->

<tr>
<td align="right" bgcolor="#c0c0c0"><strong><small>
   <font color="#0000ff" face="Arial">*Country:</font></small>
      </strong></td>
   <td><font color="#0000ff">
      <input size="2" name="country" maxlength="2" ></font></td>
</tr>

<!-- Zip code field -->

<tr>
<td align="right" bgcolor="#c0c0c0"><strong><small>
   <font color="#0000ff" face="Arial">*Zip/Postal Code:</font>
      </small></strong></td>
   <td><font color="#0000ff">
      <input size="10" name="pin" ></font></td>
</tr>

<!-- Phone number field -->

<tr>
<td align="right" bgcolor="#c0c0c0"><strong><small>
   <font color="#0000ff" face="Arial">*Home/Office</font></small>
   <font color="#0000ff" face="Arial"><small>Phone</small>:<br>
      </font></strong></td>
   <td><font color="#0000ff">
      <strong><big><big>(</big></big>
         <input maxLength=3 name=areacode size=3>
      <big><big>)</big></big></strong>
         <input maxLength=3 name=prefix size=3>
      <strong><big><big>-</big></big></strong>
         <input maxLength=4 name=suffix size=4>
      </font></td>
```

```
        </tr>

        <!-- Fax field -->

        <tr>
        <td align="right" bgcolor="#c0c0c0"><small><strong>
            <font color="#0000ff" face="Arial">*Fax:</font></strong>
            </small></td>
            <td><font color="#0000ff">
                <strong><big><big>(</big></big>
                    <input maxLength=3 name=faxarea size=3>
                <big><big>)</big></big></strong>
                    <input maxLength=3 name=faxprefix size=3>
                <strong><big><big>-</big></big></strong>
                    <input maxLength=4 name=faxsuffix size=4>
                </font></td>
        </tr>

        <!-- Month field -->

        <tr>
        <td align="right" bgcolor="#c0c0c0"><small><strong>
            <font color="#0000ff" face="Arial">*Birth-Month:</font>
                </strong></small></td>
          <td><font color="#0000ff">
                <input size="2" name="month" maxlength="2" ></font></td>
        </tr>

        <!-- email field -->

        <tr>
        <td align="right" bgcolor="#c0c0c0"><small><strong>
            <font color="#0000ff" face="Arial">*E-mail:</font>
                </strong></small></td>
            <td><font color="#0000ff">
                <input size="30" name="email"></font></td>
        </tr>
</table>

<p align="center">
    <input type="submit" value="Submit" name="B1">
</p>

</form>
</body>
</html>
```

The Server-side Validation Code

We'll now take a look at the NewUserValidation.jsp file that provides server-side validations for all the user input fields:

```
<%-- NewUserValidation.jsp --%>
<html>

<%@ page language="java" import="java.util.*" %>

<%-- Read the parameters from the request object --%>
```

`NewUserValidation.jsp` retrieves all the field values from the `request` object by calling the `getParameter()` method several times:

```
<%
    String Name = request.getParameter("name");
    String Password = request.getParameter("password");
    String Address = request.getParameter("addr");
    String City = request.getParameter("city");
    String Faxarea = request.getParameter("faxarea");
    String Faxprefix = request.getParameter("faxprefix");
    String Faxsuffix = request.getParameter("faxsuffix");
    String Month = request.getParameter("month");
    String State = request.getParameter("state");
    String Country = request.getParameter("country");
    String Company = request.getParameter("company");
    String Phonearea = request.getParameter("areacode");
    String Phoneprefix = request.getParameter("prefix");
    String Phonesuffix = request.getParameter("suffix");
    String Pin = request.getParameter("pin");
    String Email = request.getParameter("email");
%>
```

The program then creates an instance of `NewUserValidationBean` with `page` scope. This bean is used for validating all the fields of the Form:

```
<%-- Create an instance of NewUserValidationBean class --%>

<jsp:useBean id="ValidBean" scope="page" class="NewUserValidationBean" />
```

Several calls to the `setProperty` method then set the property values of the `ValidBean` to the appropriate values:

```
<%-- Set the various bean properties --%>

<jsp:setProperty name="ValidBean" property="name" value ="<%=Name%>" />
<jsp:setProperty name="ValidBean" property="password" value ="<%=Password%>"
    />
<jsp:setProperty name="ValidBean" property="addr" value ="<%=Address%>" />
<jsp:setProperty name="ValidBean" property="city" value ="<%=City%>" />
<jsp:setProperty name="ValidBean" property="faxarea" value ="<%=Faxarea%>"/>
<jsp:setProperty name="ValidBean" property="faxprefix" value
    ="<%=Faxprefix%>"/>
<jsp:setProperty name="ValidBean" property="faxsuffix" value
    ="<%=Faxsuffix%>"/>
<jsp:setProperty name="ValidBean" property="month" value ="<%=Month%>"/>
<jsp:setProperty name="ValidBean" property="company" value ="<%=Company%>"/>
<jsp:setProperty name="ValidBean" property="phonearea" value
    ="<%=Phonearea%>"/>
<jsp:setProperty name="ValidBean" property="phoneprefix" value
    ="<%=Phoneprefix%>"/>
<jsp:setProperty name="ValidBean" property="phonesuffix" value
    ="<%=Phonesuffix%>"/>
<jsp:setProperty name="ValidBean" property="pin" value ="<%=Pin%>"/>
<jsp:setProperty name="ValidBean" property="state" value ="<%=State%>"/>
```

```
<jsp:setProperty name="ValidBean" property="country" value ="<%=Country%>"/>
<jsp:setProperty name="ValidBean" property="email" value ="<%=Email%>"/>

<body bgcolor="#C0C0C0">

<%-- Validate the record. The result of validation is returned in the vector
If the returned vector is empty, it indicates that the record is valid. If
so,call NewUserConfirm.jsp to insert the record in the database. --%>
<%
    Vector v;
```

The program then calls the `validateRecord()` method to validate the field values. On error, the list of errors is returned to the caller in a `Vector`. The code for the `NewUserValidationBean` is discussed later in the section on *Server-side Validation of Form Fields*.

```
    v = ValidBean.validateRecord();
```

If the vector is empty, it indicates that all the fields contain valid values. In such situations, the program calls the `NewUserConfirm.jsp` to insert the record in the database, and updates the user of the status of the database update:

```
    if (v.isEmpty()) { %>
        <jsp:forward page="NewUserConfirm.jsp" />
<% }
    else { %>

        <%-- Print the errors to the user --%>

        <p align="center">
            <font face="Times New Roman" size="3" color="#0000FF">
            <b>Following Errors were encountered:</b>
        </font></p>
```

In case of a non-null vector, the program creates an `Iterator` to iterate through the elements of the vector and prints all the error messages on the screen. Each call to `next` method on the `Iterator` fetches the next element from the vector:

```
<%
    Iterator it = v.iterator();
    while (it.hasNext()) { %>
        <p style="margin-top: 0; margin-bottom: 0" align="left">
        <font face="Times New Roman" size="3" color="#0000FF">
        <%=it.next()%>
        </font></p>
    <% } %>
```

The program then sets up the link for taking the user back to the earlier data entry screen so that the user can correct the errors and re-submit the form:

```
    <p align=center><font face="Verdana" size="3" color="#0000FF">
        <b><i><a href="NewUserRegis.html">Back to Registration
        Form</a></i></b>
```

```
        </font></p>
    <% } %>

</body>
</html>
```

If validation on any of the fields fails when you run the above code, an appropriate message is displayed to the user. A typical error page generated by the above code is shown below. Note that the page displays all the errors on the input form in one go so that the user can correct all the errors together (in the case shown here, all the field values are invalid).

In the client-side validation seen earlier, the user has to correct errors on each field individually and press **Submit** after every correction.

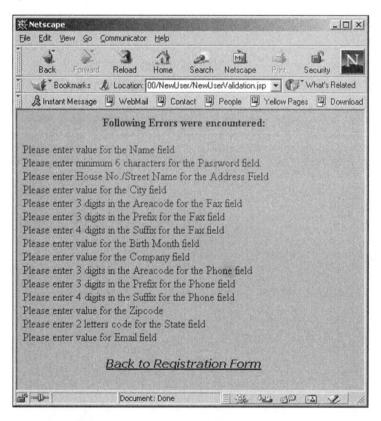

Let's now look at the `NewUserValidationBean.java` code that carries out the validation of the various `Form` fields on the server.

Server-side Validation of Form Fields

The complete code for the `NewUserValidationBean.java` is given below.

```
/** NewUserValidationBean.java
 */
import java.beans.*;
```

```
import java.util.*;

public class NewUserValidationBean {
    private String Email;
    private String Name;
    private String Address;
    private String City;
    private String State;
    private String Country;
    private String Pin;
    private String Phonearea;
    private String Phoneprefix;
    private String Phonesuffix;
    private String Faxarea;
    private String Faxprefix;
    private String Faxsuffix;
    private String Password;
    private String Company;
    private String Month;
    private String ErrMsg;
    private Vector v = new Vector();
```

The class declares several `private` variables to hold the fields of the customer record. The class provides several `set` methods for setting these variables. Each `set` method defines a validation rule on the input value and adds an error message to the vector in case the validations fail. For example, the `setName()` method accepts the `Name` as a `String` variable and if the parameter value is null, adds an error string to the vector.

```
/** Sets the Name field
 */

public void setName(String Name) {
    this.Name= Name;
    //Check for non-null value
    if (Name.length() < 1) {
        ErrMsg = "Please enter value for the Name field";
        v.addElement(ErrMsg);
    }
}

/** Sets the Password field
 */
public void setPassword(String Password) {
    this.Password = Password;
    // Check password length
    if (Password.length() < 6) {
        ErrMsg = "Please enter minimum 6 characters for the Password
            field.";
        v.addElement(ErrMsg);
    }
}

/** Sets the Company field
 */
public void setCompany(String Company) {
    this.Company = Company;
    // Check for non-null value
```

```
      if (Company.length() < 1) {
         ErrMsg = "Please enter value for the Company field";
         v.addElement(ErrMsg);
      }
   }

   /** Set Address field
    */

   public void setAddr(String Address) {
      this.Address = Address;
      // Check for non-null value
      if (Address.length() < 1) {
         ErrMsg = "Please enter House No./Street Name for the Address
            Field";
         v.addElement(ErrMsg);
      }
   }

   /** Sets City field
    */

   public void setCity(String City) {
      this.City= City;
      // Check for non-null value
      if (City.length() < 1) {
         ErrMsg = "Please enter value for the City field";
         v.addElement(ErrMsg);
      }
   }

   /** Sets State field
    */

   public void setState(String State) {
      this.State= State;
      // Check length of state field
      if (State.length() < 2) {
         ErrMsg = "Please enter 2 letters code for the State field";
         v.addElement(ErrMsg);
      } else                                    // Check for non-numeric
      {
         boolean allValid = checkLetters(State);
         if (!allValid) {
            ErrMsg = "Please enter only letters in the State field";
            v.addElement(ErrMsg);
         }
      }
   }

   /** Sets Country field
    */

   public void setCountry(String Country) {
      this.Country = Country;
      // Check for non-null value
      if (Country.length() < 1) {
         ErrMsg = "Please enter value for the Country field";
         v.addElement(ErrMsg);
      }
   }
```

```
/** Sets the zip code field
 */

public void setPin(String Pin) {
   this.Pin= Pin;
   // Check for non-null value
   if (Pin.length() < 1) {
      ErrMsg = "Please enter value for the Zipcode";
      v.addElement(ErrMsg);
   }
}

/** Sets area code field of phone number
 */

public void setPhonearea(String Phonearea) {
   this.Phonearea = Phonearea;
   // check length
   if (Phonearea.length() < 3) {
      ErrMsg = "Please enter 3 digits in the Areacode for the Phone
         field";
      v.addElement(ErrMsg);
   } else                                  // check for numeric value
   {
      boolean allValid = checkDigits(Phonearea);
      if (!allValid) {
         ErrMsg = "Please enter only digits in the Areacode for the Phone
            field";
         v.addElement(ErrMsg);
      }
   }
}

/** Sets the prefix field of phone number
 */

public void setPhoneprefix(String Phoneprefix) {
   this.Phoneprefix = Phoneprefix;
   // check length
   if (Phoneprefix.length() < 3) {
      ErrMsg = "Please enter 3 digits in the Prefix for the Phone field";
      v.addElement(ErrMsg);
   } else                                  // check for numeric value
   {
      boolean allValid = checkDigits(Phoneprefix);
      if (!allValid) {
         ErrMsg = "Please enter only digits in the Prefix for the Phone
            field";
         v.addElement(ErrMsg);
      }
   }
}

/** Sets the suffix field of phone number
 */

public void setPhonesuffix(String Phonesuffix) {
   this.Phonesuffix = Phonesuffix;
   // check length
   if (Phonesuffix.length() < 4) {
      ErrMsg = "Please enter 4 digits in the Suffix for the Phone field";
      v.addElement(ErrMsg);
```

```
     } else                                    // check for numeric value
     {
        boolean allValid = checkDigits(Phonesuffix);
        if (!allValid) {
           ErrMsg = "Please enter only digits in the Suffix for the Phone
              field";
           v.addElement(ErrMsg);
        }
     }
   }

/** Sets area code for fax number
 */

public void setFaxarea(String Faxarea) {
   this.Faxarea = Faxarea;
   if (Faxarea.length() < 3) {
      ErrMsg = "Please enter 3 digits in the Areacode for the Fax field";
      v.addElement(ErrMsg);
   } else {
      boolean allValid = checkDigits(Faxarea);
      if (!allValid) {
         ErrMsg = "Please enter only digits in the Areacode for the Fax
            field";
         v.addElement(ErrMsg);
      }
   }
}

/** Sets prefix for fax number
 */

public void setFaxprefix(String Faxprefix) {
   this.Faxprefix = Faxprefix;
   if (Faxprefix.length() < 3) {
      ErrMsg = "Please enter 3 digits in the Prefix for the Fax field";
      v.addElement(ErrMsg);
   } else {
      boolean allValid = checkDigits(Faxprefix);
      if (!allValid) {
         ErrMsg = "Please enter only digits in the Prefix for the Fax
            field";
         v.addElement(ErrMsg);
      }
   }
}

/** Sets suffix for fax number
 */

public void setFaxsuffix(String Faxsuffix) {
   this.Faxsuffix = Faxsuffix;
   if (Faxsuffix.length() < 4) {
      ErrMsg = "Please enter 4 digits in the Suffix for the Fax field";
      v.addElement(ErrMsg);
   } else {
      boolean allValid = checkDigits(Faxsuffix);
      if (!allValid) {
         ErrMsg = "Please enter only digits in the Suffix for the Fax
            field";
         v.addElement(ErrMsg);
      }
```

```
      }
   }

   /** Sets month
    */

   public void setMonth(String Month) {
      this.Month=Month;
      if (Month.length() < 1) {
         ErrMsg = "Please enter value for the Birth Month field";
         v.addElement(ErrMsg);
      } else {
         boolean allValid = checkDigits(Month);
         if (!allValid) {
            ErrMsg = "Please enter only digits in the Birth Month field";
            v.addElement(ErrMsg);
         }
      }
      // check for valid range
      if (Month.length() > 0) {
         int MonthVal = Integer.parseInt(Month);
         if (MonthVal < 1 || MonthVal > 12) {
            ErrMsg = "Please enter a value between 1 and 12 in the \"Birth
                     Month\" field.";
            v.addElement(ErrMsg);
         }
      }
   }

   /** Sets email field
    */

   public void setEmail(String Email) {
      this.Email=Email;
      if (Email.length() < 1) {
         ErrMsg = "Please enter value for Email field";
         v.addElement(ErrMsg);
      }
   }
```

The code defines checkDigits() and checkLetters() methods for checking for numeric digits and valid alphabetic characters. The code in these methods is similar to the one described above in the client-side validations and is self-explanatory.

```
   /** Check that the input string contains only alphabets
    */

   public boolean checkLetters(String str) {
      String checkStr = str;
      boolean allValid = true;
      char ch;

      for (int i = 0; i < checkStr.length(); i++) {
         ch = checkStr.charAt(i);
         if (!Character.isLetter(ch)) {
```

```
            allValid = false;
            break;
        }
    }
    return allValid;
}

/** Check that the input string contains only numeric digits
 */

public boolean checkDigits(String str) {
    String checkStr = str;
    boolean allValid = true;
    char ch;

    for (int i = 0; i < checkStr.length(); i++) {
        ch = checkStr.charAt(i);
        if (!Character.isDigit(ch)) {
            allValid = false;
            break;
        }
    }
    return allValid;
}
```

Each field of the customer record form is validated in its corresponding set method. The validateRecord method returns the vector containing the error messages to NewUserValidation.jsp.

```
public Vector validateRecord() {
    return v;
}
}
```

Confirmation of Validation

Lastly, we look at the code for NewUserConfirm.jsp. The code for the CustomerRegistrationBean is same as the one discussed in the previous chapter. This class provides connect(), insertRecord() and disconnect() methods and uses the ConnectionManager class discussed in the earlier chapter for connecting to the database. The complete code for NewUserConfirm.jsp is given below.

```
<%-- NewUserConfirm.jsp --%>
<html>
<%@ page language="java" %>

<%-- Retreive the parameters from the request object --%>
<%
    String Name = request.getParameter("name");
    String Password = request.getParameter("password");
    String Address = request.getParameter("addr");
    String City = request.getParameter("city");
    String Faxarea = request.getParameter("faxarea");
    String Faxprefix = request.getParameter("faxprefix");
```

```
    String Faxsuffix = request.getParameter("faxsuffix");
    String Fax = Faxarea + Faxprefix + Faxsuffix;
    String Month = request.getParameter("month");
    String State = request.getParameter("state");
    String Company = request.getParameter("company");
    String Phonearea = request.getParameter("areacode");
    String Phoneprefix = request.getParameter("prefix");
    String Phonesuffix = request.getParameter("suffix");
    String Phone = Phonearea + Phoneprefix + Phonesuffix;
    String Pin = request.getParameter("pin");
    String Email = request.getParameter("email");
%>
```

The NewUserConfirm.jsp receives the customer field values in its request object. The program then instantiates the CustomerRegistrationBean with the page scope and sets up the property values for the bean by several calls to the setProperty method.

```
<%-- Create an instance of CustomerRegistrationBean class --%>
<jsp:useBean id="NewUserBean" scope="page" class="CustomerRegistrationBean"
    />

<%-- Set the various bean properties --%>
<jsp:setProperty name="NewUserBean" property="name" value ="<%=Name%>" />
<jsp:setProperty name="NewUserBean" property="password" value
    ="<%=Password%>" />
<jsp:setProperty name="NewUserBean" property="addr" value ="<%=Address%>" />
<jsp:setProperty name="NewUserBean" property="city" value ="<%=City%>" />
<jsp:setProperty name="NewUserBean" property="fax" value ="<%=Fax%>"/>
<jsp:setProperty name="NewUserBean" property="month" value ="<%=Month%>"/>
<jsp:setProperty name="NewUserBean" property="company" value ="<%=Company%>"/>
<jsp:setProperty name="NewUserBean" property="phone" value ="<%=Phone%>"/>
<jsp:setProperty name="NewUserBean" property="pin" value ="<%=Pin%>"/>
<jsp:setProperty name="NewUserBean" property="state" value ="<%=State%>"/>
<jsp:setProperty name="NewUserBean" property="email" value ="<%=Email%>"/>

<body bgcolor="#C0C0C0">
<form method="post" action = "NewUserConfirm.jsp" >
```

A scriptlet code then connects to the database, inserts the record, and then disconnects from the database:

```
<%-- Connect to the database, insert the record and close connection --%>
<%
    NewUserBean.connect();
    NewUserBean.insertRecord();
    NewUserBean.disconnect();
%>

<p align="center"><font face="Verdana" size="5" color=#0000FF>
    Your Data has been added into our Database.<br><br></font></p>
<p align="center"><font face="Verdana" size="5" color=#0000FF>
    Thank you for registering with us.</font></p>

</form>
</body>
</html>
```

We have now seen how to provide either the client-side or the server-side validations. An obvious disadvantage of server-side validations is that for each error the user makes on the form, a validation is done on the server and the user is required to re-enter the form fields. Remember to use this approach as appropriate since such continual trips to the server may become time consuming and tedious to the user.

The main advantage of the server-side validations is that the validation code can be modified easily and re-deployed. The server-side validations may use additional logic/validations implemented in any language supported by the server while the client-side validations require the support of a scripting language on the client machine.

Your site should provide for both types of validations. If the client browser does not support the scripting language used on your web page, you should re-direct the client automatically to the server-side validations. This may also be necessary if you are supporting old browsers and also in those cases where you need complex edit checks.

You may provide more efficient and sophisticated validations on the user input by coding the data entry form in a Java applet. This may make the user interface more friendly and provide a better user experience.

Java Applets and Plug-ins

An applet runs on the client's JVM and provides client-side processing for your program, but note that a firewall may not allow the use of applets. Thus, they may not always be the most effective way of ensuring your site is accessible to everyone.

Applets can be used not only for input forms, but also for providing a more interactive interface to your site. For example, consider a case where a site provides the end-of-day or intra-day quotes for the stocks listed on NYSE. The site may also provide some charting on this data such as HLC, Close charts, CandleSticks, Moving Averages, etc. (These are the kind of charts typically used by a technical analyst to analyze the company's stock. Based on this analysis, the user decides whether to buy, hold or sell the stock.)

The site could generate such charts on the server as `.gif` images and include them in the dynamically generated web pages. However, the user will not be able to apply their own analysis on these charts, as these are static images and are not interactive. Secondly, you will be consuming lot of server resources in generating such images frequently (or at least on a daily basis) and storing them on the server for the users to download.

To make such images interactive, applets will be very useful. It may provide tools to do quite a detailed analysis on the charts. Such highly interactive user screens cannot be generated by using pure HTML code or even by using JavaScript on the client-side.

Applet Requirements

To use applets the client must have a Java support enabled on the browser. This is not usually a problem on most of the present day browsers, which have at least a 1.1 version of the JVM.

The major concern is the applet size and thereby the time it may take to download to the client machine especially if the client has low bandwidth connectivity to your site. The applet code is either interpreted or compiled using a JIT compiler on the client-side, which may take a substantial time and thereby cause an appreciable delay in the applet startup. The applet code must be downloaded and compiled every time you visit the web page containing the applet. JDK1.3 solves this problem to some extent by caching in the previously loaded applet code.

A general guideline is that an applet should not take more than a minute to download and initialize on the client machine. If it takes longer than this, it is likely that the client will hit the stop button on the browser and may proceed to another site. The startup time for the applet depends on its size and the connection speed for the client. For a typical web-based client you should not assume a connection speed better than 33KB/s.

If your applet uses custom classes or uses newer versions of the JDK, the client may not be able to run your applet unless these additional classes are downloaded. The support for this can be achieved with the help of Java Plug-ins where the browser can detect the use of a newer version of the JDK on the applet and request the user to install the new version on their machine. If the user agrees, the downloading of the new JRE will be automatic.

Although this is a one-time effort for the client, it may take an appreciable time to download and install. Thus to reduce client dissatisfaction it's always useful to warn them of this delay, and highlight the potential advantage in taking just the one effort to improve their Web experience.

Of course a multimedia site will also provide a rich user experience.

Using Multimedia

Another approach to provide an interactive interface to the client is to use programs such as Macromedia Flash to create sophisticated animations. Such animations are very useful when you want to demonstrate your products to the client, or in other areas where you might provide online training to the clients of your products.

If you decide to use Macromedia Flash for your presentations, then the client browsers will need to have runtime support for Flash. The browser detects the use of Flash files on your HTML page and if it does not have a runtime support installed, it automatically downloads and installs the same for you. Like JRE installation, this may take an appreciable amount of time to download and install.

Sometimes, you may also wish to do a live webcast through your web site. In such cases, the use of Real Audio is highly recommended. The audio files are typically very large, and it is not advisable to download the complete audio file to the client machine. Real Audio provides streaming of your audio file and starts playing audio on the client machine as soon as it is partially downloaded. The program keeps on downloading and buffering the rest of the audio file in background while playing it on the client machine. To support Real Audio on your site, you will need a Real Audio Server support. Refer to http://www.real.com for further details on how to do this. Alternatively, you may use Java Media Framework (JMF). This is discussed in the next section.

When considering these options you'll need to plan your client access strategy carefully. The rich surfing experience will be provided at the cost of download time for such utilities and the increase in processing power needed on the client machine.

Typically, you should provide both types of web pages. If the client browser does not support the advanced feature used, or simply does not wish to use a highly interactive or graphical site then a simpler, faster loading site should be made available.

Delivering Media

A more sophisticated web site may deliver audio/video to the client. How to deliver audio/video to the client is not a major issue, but the client bandwidth is the deciding factor while incorporating such media contents on your site. Audio and video files are usually very large and are typically of the order of few megabytes. The client who is connected to the Internet using a low bandwidth like 33KB/s or 56KB/s will find it practically impossible to download such large files before they are played on the machine.

Java provides a standard extension called **Java Media Framework** (**JMF**) that allows developers to incorporate audio/video support in their applications. JMF supports **Real-Time Transport Protocol** (**RTP**) that allows real time media streams to be sent and received.

Demonstrating the use of this API in program code is beyond the scope of this book and the reader is encouraged to read documentation provided on the JavaSoft site (http://java.sun.com). It is sufficient to say here that if you decide to incorporate streaming media support on your site, you should allow the user to select the appropriate bandwidth while using stream.

As we've already discussed XML is becoming a de-facto standard for data interchange between applications: let's now see how we could use XML in our example.

Delivering XML

To illustrate how to generate an XML file dynamically on the server, we will modify our search application developed in the last chapter. The new application renders an HTML to the client as in the earlier case and also generates an XML file containing the search results. This XML file may be rendered on the client machine by applying an appropriate style sheet or may be used for further narrowing down the search. Let us suppose that a user searches for all the available CPUs in our web store. They will get a screen output similar to the one shown below:

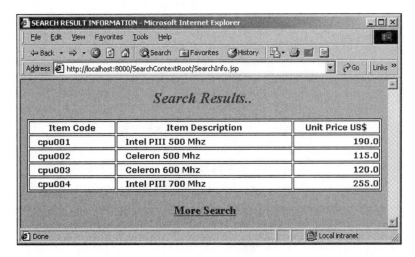

This new program also dumps the above data to an XML file. The client may use the XML file to render a view of data by applying an appropriate style-sheet. This view can be changed easily by changing the style-sheet and the same style-sheet may be applied to different XML documents. The XML code generated by running the search program is given below.

```
<?xml version="1.0"?>
<PARTSLIST>
  <cpu>
    <ItemCode>cpu001</ItemCode>
    <ItemDescription>Intel PIII 500 Mhz</ItemDescription>
    <UnitPrice>190.0</UnitPrice>
  </cpu>
  <cpu>
```

```
      <ItemCode>cpu002</ItemCode>
      <ItemDescription>Celeron 500 Mhz</ItemDescription>
      <UnitPrice>115.0</UnitPrice>
   </cpu>
   <cpu>
      <ItemCode>cpu003</ItemCode>
      <ItemDescription>Celeron 600 Mhz</ItemDescription>
      <UnitPrice>120.0</UnitPrice>
   </cpu>
   <cpu>
      <ItemCode>cpu004</ItemCode>
      <ItemDescription>Intel PIII 700 Mhz </ItemDescription>
      <UnitPrice>255.0</UnitPrice>
   </cpu>
</PARTSLIST>
```

We will now look into the code that generates the above XML.

Here we've used the 1.1.16 version of the XML4J parser developed by IBM for generating XML dynamically. It's available at http://www.ibm.co.jp/alphaWorks/xmltranslatorgenerator/xmltranslator.htm

We need to modify our `SearchInfo.jsp` file from the earlier chapter to include the XML generation code. The complete source code for the `SearchInfo.jsp` file is given here:

```
<%-- SearchInfo.jsp --%>
<html>
```

The XML parser requires the use of additional libraries, which are imported in the JSP, by using the following program code:

```
<%-- import xml parser classes and other java classes --%>

<%@ page language="java"
    import="java.util.*, com.ibm.xml.parser.TXDocument, org.w3c.dom.*,
        java.io.*" %>

<%-- Read the parameter --%>
<% String Item = request.getParameter("item"); %>

<%-- Create an instance of SearchInfo bean --%>
<jsp:useBean id="Search" scope="page" class="SearchInfo" />

<%
   Vector OuterVec;
   Vector InnerVec;
%>
```

Scriptlet code in a JSP then creates a new document by instantiating `TXDocument` class. The code also generates a root for our XML document. The root is called `PARTSLIST`:

```
<%-- Create a new XML document and root element --%>
<%
   Document doc = (Document)new TXDocument();
```

```
   Element root = doc.createElement ("PARTSLIST");
%>

<head>
<title>SEARCH RESULT INFORMATION</title>
</head>

<body bgcolor="#C0C0C0">

<form method="POST" action = "SearchInfo.jsp" >

<p align="center">
<font face="Times New Roman" size="5" color="#008000"><b><i>Search
Results..</i></b></font></p>

<table width="100%" border="1" bordercolor="#000000" align=center
bgcolor="#FFFFFF">

<tr>
<td align=center width="15%"><font face="Verdana" size="2" color="#0000FF">
        <b>Item Code</b></font></td>
<td align=center width="30%"><font face="Verdana" size="2" color="#0000FF">
        <b>Item Description</b></font></td>
<td align=center width="15%"><font face="Verdana" size="2" color="#0000FF">
        <b>Unit Price US$</b></font></td>
</tr>
```

Next, an element with the same name as the name of the search item is created and added to the root. Note that the program receives the Item from the request parameter:

```
<%-- Call getSearchInfo to read the item details from the database.
For each item, like CPU, there may be several parts which are returned in
the vector. Each part has code, description and price given in the inner
vector. For each item, add a node in the XML document. Also, generate an
HTML table to display all the retrieved parts and values to the user --%>
<%
    // retrieve parts list
    OuterVec = Search.getSearchInfo(Item);
    Iterator it1 = OuterVec.iterator();
    while (it1.hasNext()) {
        Element item = doc.createElement (Item);
        root.appendChild(item);
        InnerVec = (Vector)it1.next();
        Iterator it2 = InnerVec.iterator();
```

As we have seen in the last chapter, the JSP receives data in a vector. The program iterates through the elements of this vector and renders an HTML view to the client. For each element of the vector, the program creates an ItemCode element, reads the data for the item from the vector, creates the TextNode and appends to the parent element:

```
        while (it2.hasNext()) {
            Element details = doc.createElement ("ItemCode");
            String Itemcode = (String)it2.next();
            details.appendChild (doc.createTextNode(Itemcode));
```

```
            item.appendChild(details);

            details = doc.createElement ("ItemDescription");
            String Itemdesc = (String)it2.next();
            details.appendChild (doc.createTextNode(Itemdesc));
            item.appendChild(details);

            details = doc.createElement ("UnitPrice");
            Double Itemprice = (Double)it2.next();
            String Strprice = String.valueOf(Itemprice.doubleValue());
            details.appendChild (doc.createTextNode(Strprice));
            item.appendChild(details);
%>

        <tr>
          <td><font face="Verdana" size="2" color="#0000FF">
             <b>   <%=Itemcode%></b></font></td>
          <td><font face="Verdana" size="2" color="#0000FF">
             <b>   <%= Itemdesc%></b></font></td>
          <td align=right><font face="Verdana" size="2"
               color="#0000FF"><b><%= Itemprice %></b></font></td>
        </tr>
    <% }
  }
```

Likewise, the program adds the item description and the price to the XML document object. Once the entire document tree is constructed, the program adds the root element to the document. This completes the document creation process.

```
            doc.appendChild (root);
```

The next step is to set the version for the document. Calling the setVersion() method on the document object does this:

```
            ((TXDocument)doc).setVersion("1.0");
```

The program then opens a file for writing the XML document. The printWithFormat() method of the document object writes the output to the file.

```
            FileOutputStream fos = new FileOutputStream("PartList.xml");
            ((TXDocument)doc).printWithFormat (new PrintWriter(fos));  %>
</table>
   <p align="center"><b><font face="Times New Roman" size="4">
      <a href="Search.jsp">More Search</a></font></b></p>
</form>
</body>
</html>
```

For simplicity the above program does not use a DTD while creating the XML document. In practical circumstances it's useful to use one to ensure that the created document is valid. The client may use the same DTD to validate the document on its end before parsing it.

XML can offer a number of benefits to the client over pure HTML code. For example with XML data they may:

❏   View the document in a tree structure by using a DOM parser or an XML-Schema

❏   Do a combined search on several such XML documents

❏   By choosing different style-sheets, have different views depending on their preferences

Summary

In this chapter, you were introduced to various client-side issues of a web application development. Firstly we looked at validation using client-side scripting techniques and server-side code. The benefits and drawbacks of each approach were highlighted – in that client-side validation may be quick, but have restricted browser reach, while server-side techniques have wide applicability, but may be slow.

We then moved on-to have a look at improving the site experience by adding multi-media features such as animations, audio, and video files. The use of such media demands more client bandwidth and should be used only in appropriate situations. Streaming audio/video can partially solve this problem, but requires more processing power on the client-side to provide for real time compression and decompression. Additional hardware on the server may also be required to support the file delivery.

Lastly, the use of XML for client-side code was discussed. XML offers several benefits to the user as compared to pure HTML, and a program illustrating the process of generating XML dynamically on the server was presented.

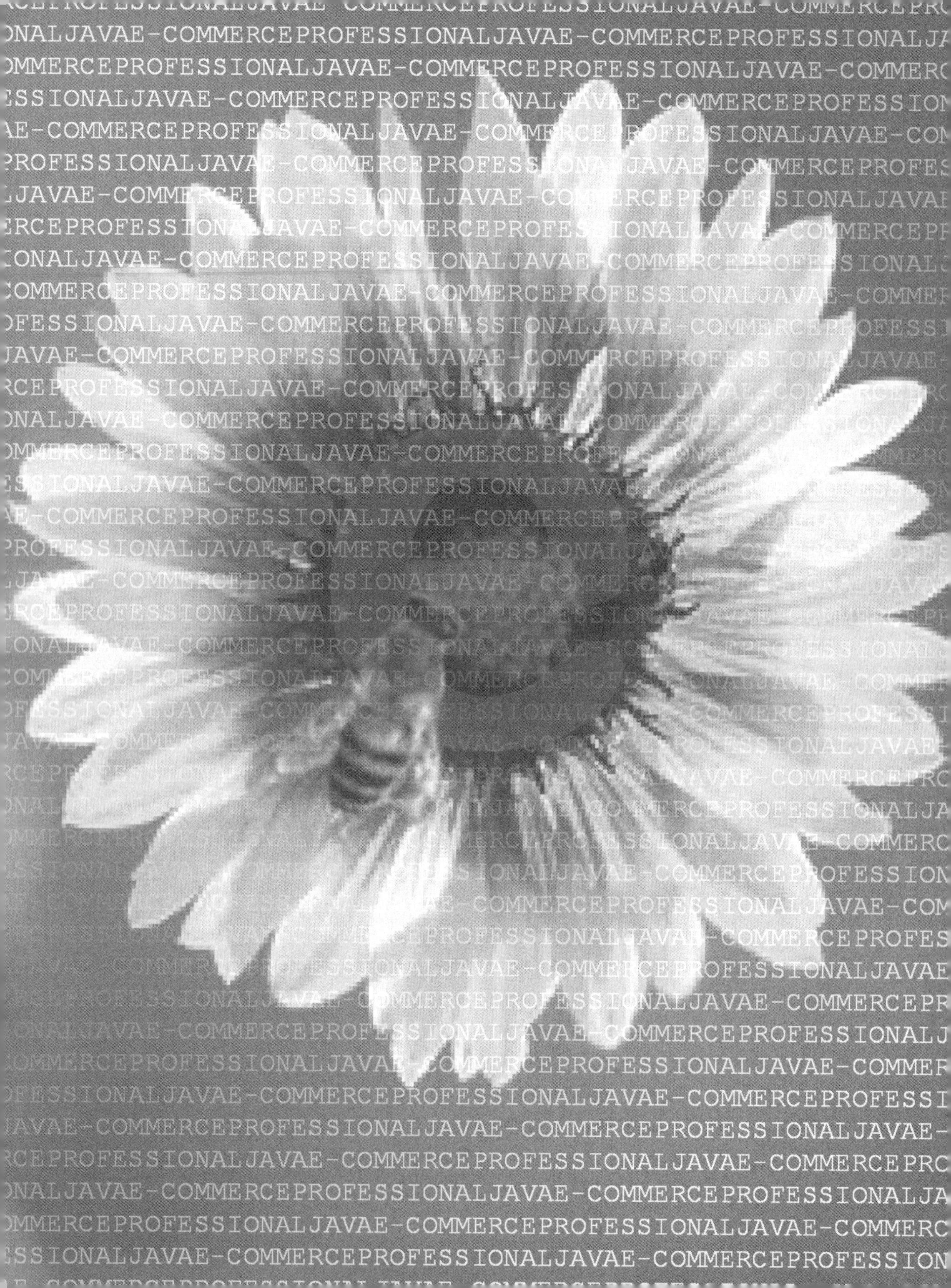
PROFESSIONALJAVAE-COMMERCE

12

B2C E-Commerce: Extending the Simple Site

In the last three chapters, we constructed an online web store that sells desktop PCs. A typical problem encountered in many software projects is that the application runs well on a development machine, but when it is finally deployed on a production server, it does not perform as we expect, in terms of speed and reliability.

There could be several reasons for this – one of the primary reasons could be the number of concurrent users accessing your application in a production environment. During the development, only a few people concurrently use the application. However, once it is deployed on the web, if the site is successful, you may have a large number of people hitting it at the same time. This can cause performance issues, as the business logic tier of your application may not scale up so easily. During a normal software development process, a performance issue such as this is both an important and early consideration.

In addition, concurrent database access by multiple users may increase the response time considerably. This requires the fine-tuning of your database.

Additionally, as we saw in previous chapters, if the site is media heavy, the client's bandwidth will impact the perceived performance of the site (don't underestimate how many customers will have relatively slow connections).

In this chapter, I will discuss the performance issues for your application and what measures you should take to improve the overall performance of the application. We will also extend our site so that the application collaborates with our partner's applications. So over this chapter we'll be looking at:

❑ Scalability using Enterprise JavaBeans

❑ Data design and access strategies

❑ Integration with existing systems

Scalability

The JSP technology used in our earlier examples is not truly scalable, as a separate thread must be created for every client request. On the other hand, EJB technology provides easy component pooling with no coding efforts required from the programmer's side and we'll be looking at this technology shortly.

Let's dig into the topic of scalability a little more. Scalability can be achieved in one, or both, of two ways – by expanding **vertically** or by expanding **horizontally**.

Vertical Scalability

The vertical scalability is achieved by increasing the processing power of your server by adding more memory and CPUs to your machine. This will allow the creation of more threads on your machine to service a larger number of clients. This is the easiest and most manageable solution to achieve better performance; although there is still a limit to the amount of processing power and memory you can add to one machine. The disadvantage of vertical scalability is that it is still a single point of failure in the entire architecture. If the server fails, your entire application comes down. Also, even though prices are coming down, CPUs and memory can still be quite expensive.

Horizontal Scalability

The horizontal scalability is achieved by adding more machines in parallel by using a **load balancing router** (**LBR**). The load balancing can be achieved by using either software or hardware. You can use hardware routers for implementing load balancing. Then, in cases of large numbers of concurrent accesses to your application, the LBR will distribute the load on the other machines to deliver better performance. This requires your application to be portable, which in this case means the application must be able to be deployed on machines configured in parallel. This requires that the application must be location independent and can be deployed on any machine without any code changes. At each tier, you may add two or more servers in parallel to achieve the desired performance.

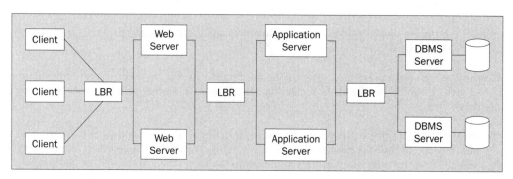

The advantage of vertical scalability as compared to horizontal scalability is the simplicity in the architecture design. A vertical scalability solution makes the system more manageable as compared to horizontal scalability solutions. The reason for this is largely because there is only one computer to manage, and there is only the application software to look after.

Coding Implications

If the application uses JSPs, you must consider the issue of client state management by JSP. The session context used by a JSP is specific to the process under which it is running. Thus, if a client is moved from one machine to another in parallel, the session context for the client will be different (and indeed new). If your JSP code is maintaining the client state in a session context provided by JSP, this state will be lost if the client is moved to another machine running in parallel.

A better design solution to make your application portable and be horizontally scalable is to use Enterprise JavaBeans (EJBs) in your application. EJB technology is more scalable than JSP, for reasons that we'll see in the rest of this chapter. The EJB architecture provides a **container** service to your application.

The EJBs are deployed in this container. The container manages the life cycle of the deployed beans and maintains a pool of these beans. The container automatically adds more instances to the pool when the load increases and deletes them from the pool whenever the load reduces. This life cycle management of beans is totally transparent to the programmer, and makes business logic embedded in beans more scalable. The client state management in the case of EJBs is also relatively easier as the client state is maintained in the instance variables of a session bean. This makes beans easily portable across the multiple servers configured in a cluster for load balancing or failover.

EJBs for Scalability

The application, which we have developed so far, does not contain a lot of business logic code in JSPs. Thus, rather than trying to convert the existing JSP code into EJBs, we will modify our web store application to add some more functionality. We will use EJBs to implement this new functionality.

The application we discussed in Chapter 9 does not save the confirmed order to the database. In this chapter, we will complete this functionality to save the contents of the shopping cart into the database. Each order will be stored in two tables – ORDERS and CONFIGURATION.

The CONFIGURATION table contains details of each configured PC included in the order. We shall use both session and entity beans to implement this functionality. The architecture is shown in the figure below.

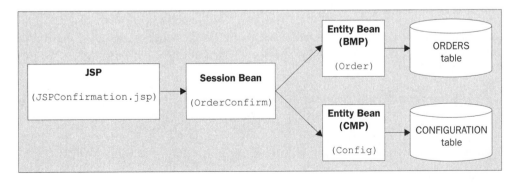

The two Entity beans, `Order` and `Config` map to the database tables `ORDERS` and `CONFIGURATION`, respectively.

The `Order` bean uses bean-managed persistence (BMP) and the `Config` bean uses container-managed persistence (CMP). `OrderConfirm` is a session bean that picks up the order details from `JSPConfirmation.jsp` and saves the order into the underlying tables with the help of the two entity beans.

I shall first discuss the code for the two entity beans, starting with the `Config` bean.

Developing a CMP Entity Bean

The remote interface of the `Config` bean does not contain any business methods, as we see below:

```
/** Config.java
 * Remote interface for Config bean. This is a CMP Entity bean.
 */

import javax.ejb.EJBObject;
import java.rmi.RemoteException;

public interface Config extends EJBObject {
}
```

The `Home` interface declares a `create()` method that takes several parameters which map directly to the underlying column names in the `CONFIGURATION` table:

```
// Home interface for Config bean (CMP Entity bean)

import java.rmi.RemoteException;
import javax.ejb.*;

/** create method receives configuration details as arguments. These values
 * are stored in the CONFIGURATION table
 */

public interface ConfigHome extends EJBHome {
    public Config create(String ConfigID, String CPU, String Mother,
        String HDD, String RAM, String Monitor,
        String Video, String CDRom, String Network)
        throws CreateException, RemoteException;
}
```

The bean implementation class `ConfigEJB` declares several instance variables that are mapped to the column names of the `CONFIGURATION` table. In the `ejbCreate()` method the parameters are copied into these instance variables:

```
// Implementation class for Config bean (CMP Entity bean)

import java.sql.*;
import javax.sql.*;
import java.util.*;
import javax.ejb.*;
import javax.naming.*;
```

```
/** Config bean is a CMP Entity bean that maps to the CONFIGURATION table
 */

public class ConfigEJB implements EntityBean {
    private EntityContext context;
    public String CONFIGID, CPU, MOTHER, HDD, RAM,
                  MONITOR, VIDEO, CDROM, NETWORK;

    // Copy the arguments into the instance variables

    public void ejbCreate(String ConfigID, String cpu, String Mother,
        String hd, String ram, String Monitor, String Video, String cdr,
        String Network) {
        CONFIGID = ConfigID;
        CPU = cpu;
        MOTHER = Mother;
        HDD = hd;
        RAM = ram;
        MONITOR = Monitor;
        VIDEO = Video;
        CDROM = cdr;
        NETWORK = Network;
    }

    public void ejbRemove() { }

    public void setEntityContext(EntityContext context) {
        this.context = context;
    }

    public void unsetEntityContext() { }

    public void ejbActivate() { }

    public void ejbPassivate() { }

    public void ejbLoad() { }

    public void ejbStore() { }

    public void ejbPostCreate(String ConfigID, String cpu, String Mother,
                        String hd, String ram, String Monitor,
                        String Video, String cdr, String Network) {
    }
}
```

In cases of container-managed persistence, the container is responsible for the persistence management and little coding is required on the part of the programmer. In the case of bean-managed persistence, the programmer is required to implement all the database updates in the code, using JDBC. This is done for our `Order` bean.

Developing a BMP Entity Bean

The `Order` bean uses bean-managed persistence. The `ORDERS` table uses a composite primary key and thus requires the use of BMP. The remote interface for the bean does not declare any business methods:

405

```
// Remote interface for Order bean. Order bean is a BMP Entity bean

import javax.ejb.EJBObject;
import java.rmi.RemoteException;

public interface Order extends EJBObject {
}
```

The Home interface declares one create() method. The parameters of the create() method map directly to the columns of the ORDERS table:

```
// Home interface for Order Bean (BMP Entity bean)

import java.rmi.RemoteException;
import javax.ejb.*;

// create method receives arguments that map to the Orders table

public interface OrderHome extends EJBHome {
    public Order create(String OrderID, String CustomerID, String ConfigID,
        int Qty, double Amount) throws CreateException, RemoteException;
}
```

In the EntityBean implementation class OrderEJB, an ejbCreate() method is defined that constructs the SQL statement for inserting the record in the ORDERS table. The record is inserted using the executeUpdate() method of the JDBC API:

```
String SQL = "Insert into ORDERS Values('" + OrderID + "','"
            + CustomerID + "','" + ConfigID + "'," + Qty + "," + Amount + ")";
Statement stmt = con.createStatement();
stmt.executeUpdate(SQL);
```

The database connection itself is made in the ejbActivate() method by calling the bean defined method makeConnection(). The makeConnection() method uses JNDI to look up the DataSource and obtains a connection to the returned DataSource object:

```
InitialContext ic = new InitialContext();
DataSource ds = (DataSource) ic.lookup(logicalDBName);
con = ds.getConnection();
```

In the ejbPassivate() method, the connection is closed. The ejbLoad() and ejbStore() methods have null bodies. These methods need not be implemented in this simple case as the bean is simply used for adding a record to the database and does not contain any other business logic. The ejbLoad() and ejbStore() methods are called by the containers whenever the synchronization between the instance variables and the database columns is required.

```
// Implementation class for Order bean (BMP Entity bean)

import java.sql.*;
import javax.sql.*;
import javax.ejb.*;
import javax.naming.*;
```

```java
// Order bean is a BMP Entity bean that maps to ORDERS table

public class OrderEJB implements EntityBean {
    private EntityContext context;
    private String OrderID, CustomerID, ConfigID;
    private int Qty;
    private double Amount;
    private Connection con;
    private String logicalDBName = "java:comp/env/jdbc/OnlinePC";

    /** Called by the container. Stores the arguments in the instance variable
     * and inserts a record in ORDERS table
     */

    public String ejbCreate(String OrderID, String CustID,
                            String ConfigID, int Qty, double Amount)
                     throws CreateException {
        this.OrderID = OrderID;
        this.CustomerID = CustID;
        this.ConfigID = ConfigID;
        this.Qty = Qty;
        this.Amount = Amount;
        try {
            String SQL = "Insert into ORDERS Values('" + OrderID + "','"
                + CustomerID + "','" + ConfigID + "'," + Qty + ","
                + Amount + ")";
            Statement stmt = con.createStatement();
            stmt.executeUpdate(SQL);
        } catch (Exception ex) {
            ex.getMessage();
        }
        return OrderID;
    }

    public void ejbRemove() { }

    public void setEntityContext(EntityContext context) {}

    public void unsetEntityContext() {}

    // Make database connection

    public void ejbActivate() {
        try {
            makeConnection();
        } catch (Exception ex) {
            ex.getMessage();
        }
    }

    // Close database connection

    public void ejbPassivate() {
        try {
```

```
            con.close();
        } catch (SQLException ex) {
            ex.getMessage();
        }
    }

    public void ejbLoad() { }

    public void ejbStore() { }

    public void ejbPostCreate(String OrderID, String CustID,
                        String ConfigID, int Qty, double Amount) { }

    /** The makeConnection method looks up the DataSource name under JNDI and
     * makes connection to the specified data source
     */

    private void makeConnection() throws NamingException, SQLException {
        InitialContext ic = new InitialContext();
        DataSource ds = (DataSource) ic.lookup(logicalDBName);
        con =  ds.getConnection();
    }
}
```

Developing a Session Bean

The `OrderConfirm` session bean uses the entity beans we have just looked at, and writes the order to the database. The remote interface of the bean declares two methods: `generateOrderID()`, this generates a unique `ID` for the order, and the `insertRecord()` method that inserts the record in the database:

```
/** OrderConfirm.java
 * Remote interface for Session bean
 */

import java.util.*;
import javax.ejb.EJBObject;
import java.rmi.RemoteException;

/** Declares two methods generateOrderID that generates a unique order ID
 * and insertRecord that inserts order record in ORDERS table
 */

public interface OrderConfirm extends EJBObject {
    public void generateOrderID() throws RemoteException;
    public void insertRecord() throws RemoteException;
}
```

The `Home` interface declares a `create()` method that takes three parameters: `Email ID` of the customer, `ShipCharge` that specifies the shipping charges, and the `Cart` that specifies the customer's shopping cart contents:

```
/** OrderConfirmHome.java
 * HOme interface for Order Session bean
 */
```

```
import java.io.Serializable;
import java.rmi.RemoteException;
import javax.ejb.CreateException;
import javax.ejb.EJBHome;
import java.util.*;

public interface OrderConfirmHome extends EJBHome {

/** create method receives customer's email ID, the shipping charges for
 * the current consignment and shopping cart as arguments
 */

    public OrderConfirm create(String Email, int ShipCharge, Vector Cart)
    throws RemoteException, CreateException;
}
```

The bean implementation class defines an `ejbCreate()` method that copies the parameters to the instance variables of the class. The complete code for `OrderConfirmEJB.java` is given here:

```
/** OrderConfirmEJB.java
 * Implementation class for Session bean
 */

import java.util.*;
import java.sql.*;
import javax.sql.*;
import javax.ejb.*;
import javax.naming.Context;
import javax.naming.InitialContext;
import javax.rmi.PortableRemoteObject;

public class OrderConfirmEJB implements SessionBean {
    private String Email;
    private int ShipCharge;
    private Vector Cart;
    private String OrderID;
    private String ConfigID;
    private Connection con;

    /** Copy the arguments in the instance variables
     */
    public void ejbCreate(String Email, int ShipCharge, Vector Cart)
                throws CreateException {
        this.Email = Email;
        this.ShipCharge = ShipCharge;
        this.Cart = Cart;
    }

    /** The method generateOrderID generates the new order ID
     */
    public void generateOrderID() {
        try {
            // look up the data source
            Context initial = new InitialContext();
            DataSource ds =
                        (DataSource)initial.lookup("java:comp/env/jdbc/OnlinePC");
```

409

The `generateOrderID()` method uses JNDI to obtain a reference to the `DataSource` and creates a connection to the database:

```
// make the database connection
con =  ds.getConnection();
```

The program then determines the new order ID. For this, it selects all the records from the `ORDERS` table and determines the value of the last order ID in a loop. It is assumed that all the order IDs are in ascending order. You should provide a more sophisticated algorithm for generating order ID. Typically, you may store the order ID as a numeric in your database table and let the program determine the last assigned ID by finding the `MAX` on this column. You will have to ensure that the table is locked while retrieving and updating this field to avoid the concurrency problems.

```
// Retrieve ORDERID from ORDERS table
String SQL = "Select ORDERID From ORDERS";
int i = 0;
Statement stmt = con.createStatement();
ResultSet rs = stmt.executeQuery(SQL);
// determine the last order id
boolean t = rs.next();
while (t) {
    i = rs.getInt(1);
    t = rs.next();
}
// increment the ID
++i;
// convert ID to String
OrderID = String.valueOf(i);
// close database connection
con.close();
} catch (SQLException se) {
    System.out.println(se.getMessage());
} catch (Exception e) {
    e.printStackTrace();
}
}

/** The insertRecord method inserts order in the database. Each order
 * consists of a record in the ORDER table and one or more records in
 * CONFIGURATION table
 */

public void insertRecord() {
    try {
        int j = 0;
        // Look up Config Entity bean
```

The `insertRecord()` method inserts the records in both `ORDERS` and `CONFIGURATION` tables by taking the contents of the user's shopping cart. The program first obtains a reference to the `Home` objects of `Config` and `Order` entity beans by looking up JNDI:

```
Context ic = new InitialContext();
java.lang.Object objref = ic.lookup("MyConfig");
ConfigHome configHome = (ConfigHome)
    PortableRemoteObject.narrow(objref, ConfigHome.class);
// Look up Order Entity bean
objref = ic.lookup("MyOrders");
OrderHome orderHome = (OrderHome) PortableRemoteObject.narrow(objref,
    OrderHome.class);
```

It then creates an `Iterator` for traversing the contents of the shopping cart:

```
// Iterate through the shopping cart contents
Iterator it1 = Cart.iterator();
while (it1.hasNext()) {
    j++;
```

The program then iterates through the `Cart` to obtain the list of items selected by the customer. Each item in the cart is another vector that specifies the configuration of the PC:

```
// Retrieve each item
Vector ordItem = (Vector)it1.next();
// Create Iterator to traverse the configuration details
```

For each order item, another `Iterator` is created to fetch the details of the configured PC. The configuration is copied into the various fields that map to the `CONFIGURATION` database. The program also generates the `ConfigID` field based on the `OrderID`:

```
Iterator it2 = ordItem.iterator();
ConfigID = OrderID + "C" + j;
String CPU = (String)it2.next();
String Mother = (String)it2.next();
String HD = (String)it2.next();
String RAM = (String)it2.next();
String Monitor = (String)it2.next();
String Video = (String)it2.next();
String CD = (String)it2.next();
String Card = (String)it2.next();
```

A record is then inserted in the `CONFIGURATION` table by calling the `create()` method on the home object of `Config` bean:

```
// Add the record to CONFIGURATION table
Config con = configHome.create(ConfigID, CPU, Mother, HD,
    RAM, Monitor, Video, CD, Card) ;
// Compute price for the current configuration
```

The program then gets the price and the quantity from the shopping cart and creates a record in the `ORDERS` table by calling `create()` method on the home object of `Order` bean:

```
double Pr = (Double)it2.next();
double Price = Pr.doubleValue();
Integer Qt = (Integer)it2.next();
int Qty = Qt.intValue();
double ItemPrice = (Price + ShipCharge) * Qty;
// Add record to ORDERS table
Order ord = orderHome.create(OrderID, Email, ConfigID, Qty,
    ItemPrice);
        }
    }
    catch (Exception e) {
        e.printStackTrace();
    }
}
```

```
    public void ejbRemove() {}
    public void ejbActivate() {}
    public void ejbPassivate() {}
    public void setSessionContext(SessionContext sc) {}
}
```

Developing JSP

We now look at the JSP (JSPConfirmation.jsp) that calls the above session bean to insert the cart contents in the database. The screen generated by JSPConfirmation.jsp is shown here:

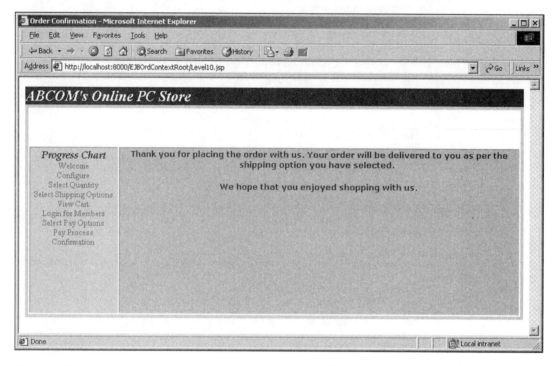

The complete program listing for JSPConfirmation.jsp follows:

```
<html>
<%@ page language="java" import="java.util.*" %>
    <head>
        <title>Order Confirmation</title>
    </head>

    <body>
```

The JSP creates an instance of JSPOrderConfirmBean and GlobalVarBean:

```
<jsp:useBean id="OCBean" scope="session" class="JSPOrderConfirmBean" />
<jsp:useBean id="GlobalBean" scope="session" class="GlobalVarBean" />
```

The program obtains the cart contents by calling the `getCart()` method of `GlobalBean`, sets up an `Iterator` to iterate through the cart contents and for each item in the cart generates another vector to store the configuration details. The configuration details are added to the `InnerVec` vector. The `InnerVec` object will contain the PC configuration details as the type of motherboard, hard drive, etc.

```
<%
    Vector v = GlobalBean.getCart();
    Iterator it = v.iterator();
    Vector OuterVec = new Vector();
    while(it.hasNext()) {
        Vector InnerVec = new Vector();
        OrderItemBean ordItem = (OrderItemBean)it.next();
        String CPU = ordItem.getSpeed();
        InnerVec.addElement(CPU);
        String Mother = ordItem.getMother();
        InnerVec.addElement(Mother);
        String HD = ordItem.getHD();
        InnerVec.addElement(HD);
        String RAM = ordItem.getRAM();
        InnerVec.addElement(RAM);
        String Monitor = ordItem.getMonitor();
        InnerVec.addElement(Monitor);
        String Video = ordItem.getVideo();
        InnerVec.addElement(Video);
        String CDROM = ordItem.getCD();
        InnerVec.addElement(CDROM);
        String Network = ordItem.getCard();
        InnerVec.addElement(Network);
        double Price = ordItem.getPrice();
        Double Pr = new Double(Price);
        InnerVec.addElement(Pr);
        int Qty = ordItem.getQty();
        Integer Qt = new Integer(Qty);
        InnerVec.addElement(Qt);
```

Each `InnerVec` is then added to the `OuterVec`. The program iterates through all the items to construct the `OuterVec` vector:

```
        OuterVec.addElement(InnerVec);
    }
```

The `OuterVec` vector is then passed as a parameter to the `insertNewRecord()` method of `JSPOrderConfirmBean` that inserts a record in the database using the session bean:

```
    OCBean.insertNewRecord(OuterVec);
%>
<p align="center"><font face="Verdana" size="2" color="#0000FF"><b>
    Thank you for placing the order with us.
    Your order will be delivered to you as
    per the shipping option you have selected. </b></font></p>
<p align="center"><font face="Verdana" size="2" color="#0000FF"><b>
    We hope that you enjoyed shopping with us.</b></font></p>
</body>
</html>
```

JSPOrderConfirmBean

We now look at the code for `JSPOrderConfirmBean`. This bean declares two attributes:

❑   `Email` – denotes the user's e-mail ID

❑   `ShipCharge` – specifies the shipping charges

The bean defines get/set methods to operate on these attributes. The complete code listing for `JSPOrderConfirmBean.java` follows:

```
/** JSPOrderConfirmBean.java
 */

import java.beans.*;
import java.util.*;
import java.sql.*;
import javax.naming.Context;
import javax.naming.InitialContext;
import javax.rmi.PortableRemoteObject;

public class JSPOrderConfirmBean
{
    private String Email;
    private int ShipCharge = 0;

    /** Adds order in the database by using EJBs
     */

    public void insertNewRecord(Vector Cart) {
        try {
```

The `insertNewRecord()` method receives the contents of the shopping cart as a parameter. It then looks up JNDI for obtaining a reference to the home object of our session bean – `OrderConfirm`. The program creates an instance of the session bean by calling the `create()` method on this home object:

```
            // Look up OrderConfirm bean
            Context ic = new InitialContext();
            java.lang.Object objref = ic.lookup("MyOrderConfirm");
            OrderConfirmHome OCHome = (OrderConfirmHome)
                PortableRemoteObject.narrow(objref, OrderConfirmHome.class);
            // Add order record in database
            OrderConfirm OC = OCHome.create(Email, ShipCharge, Cart);
```

The program then generates a new order ID by calling the `generateOrderID()` method on the created session bean. The cart contents are saved in the database by calling the `insertRecord()` method of the session bean:

```
            OC.generateOrderID();
            OC.insertRecord();
        }
        catch (Exception e) {
            e.printStackTrace();
        }
    }

    public void setEmail(String Email)
    {
```

```
        this.Email = Email;
    }

    public String getEmail()
    {
        return Email;
    }

    public void setShipCharge(int ShipCharge)
    {
        this.ShipCharge = ShipCharge;
    }
}
```

To test the new functionality, you will need to make a few changes to our earlier code from Chapter 9. In our earlier code, we were not capturing the e-mail and shipping charge fields in our order confirmation bean. Thus, we create a new file called `JSPOrderConfirmBean.jsp` that contains these changes. The `JSPOrderConfirmBean` declares two properties: `Email` and `ShipCharge`. These properties must be set in our earlier code.

For this, you will need to modify the `AccountInfo.jsp` and `ShoppingCartContents.jsp` files. The changes required in the `AccountInfo.jsp` file are shown below:

```
<jsp:useBean id="OCBean" scope="session" class="JSPOrderConfirmBean" />
<jsp:useBean id="AccountBean" scope="page" class="AccountInfoBean" />
<%
    AccountBean.connect();
        String email = request.getParameter("email");
        AccountBean.displayInfo(email);
        AccountBean.disconnect();
%>
<jsp:setProperty name="OCBean" property="email" value="<%=email%>" />
```

Similarly, you will need to modify the `ShoppingCartContents.jsp` file to set the `ShipCharge` property of the `JSPOrderConfirmBean`. The required changes are again shown below:

```
<jsp:useBean id="OCBean" scope="session" class="JSPOrderConfirmBean" />
<%
  double TotalAmount = 0;
  double TotalPrice = 0;
  int TotalShipCharge = 0;
  int TotalQty = 0;
  String Charge = request.getParameter("Schedule");
  int ShipCharge = Integer.parseInt(Charge);
%>
<jsp:setProperty name="OCBean" property="shipCharge"
  value="<%=ShipCharge%>" />
```

In addition, you will need to replace the `Confirmation.jsp` file with the `JSPConfirmation.jsp` file and make appropriate changes in the `Level10.jsp` file to include the new file. In the `Level10.jsp` file, change the name of the include file to `JSPConfirmation.jsp` as shown in the code snippet here.

```
    <td width="82%" height="262" bgcolor="#C0C0C0" valign="top">
      <jsp:include page="JSPConfirmation.jsp" flush="true" />
    </td>
```

Now we've done the hard work of wading through the code let's turn our attention to deploying our EJBs.

Deploying The New Application

In the current application, we have created 3 EJBs – one session bean and two entity beans. One of the entity beans uses bean-managed persistence while the other one uses container-managed persistence.

The deployment process for all three types of beans is different. First of all, you will need to compile all the .java files (if you've downloaded the code from the Wrox Web site you'll find the .java files in the src folder). First, we will deploy the Config bean, which is a CMP Entity bean.

Creating a JAR for a CMP Entity Bean

To start, open up the deployment tool and select the New Enterprise Bean option under the File menu of the deployment tool. Skip the first Introduction screen.

On the next screen type ConfigJAR in the JAR Display Name field. Click on the Add button next to Contents to add the .class files of the bean.

This opens another window; select Config.class, ConfigHome.class and ConfigEJB.class from the appropriate folder.

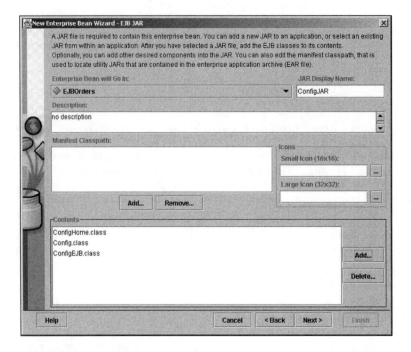

On the next screen, make the following selections:

- ❏ Enterprise Bean Class: ConfigEJB
- ❏ Home Interface: ConfigHome
- ❏ Remote Interface: Config
- ❏ Enterprise Bean Display Name: EJBConfig
- ❏ Bean Type: Entity

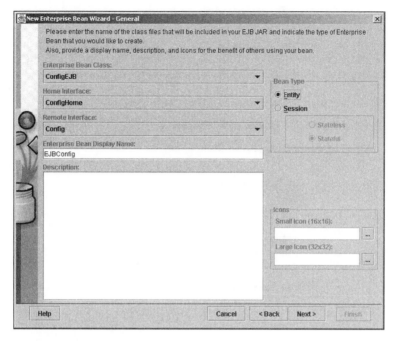

On the next screen, the select following options and field values:

❑ Container-Managed Persistence

❑ Select all of the displayed fields

❑ Primary Key Class: java.lang.String

❑ Primary Key Field Name: CONFIGID

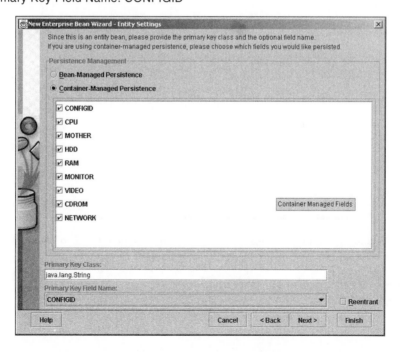

For the rest of the screens, accept the defaults. This creates a JAR file under our application.

We will need to do a few **Deployment Settings** on this CMP bean. Double click on the newly added ConfigJAR file. This opens the EJBConfig bean. On the right side, select the **Entity** tab and click on the **Deployment Settings** button. This opens another dialog box where we need to:

❑ Type in the Database JNDI Name as jdbc/Cloudscape

❑ Uncheck the **Create** and **Delete** table checkboxes.

❑ Click on the **Generate SQL Now** button

After a few seconds, the SQL code is generated, then:

❑ Select the ejbStore method and change the name of the table to CONFIGURATION in the SQL statement

❑ Select the ejbCreate method and change the name of table to CONFIGURATION.

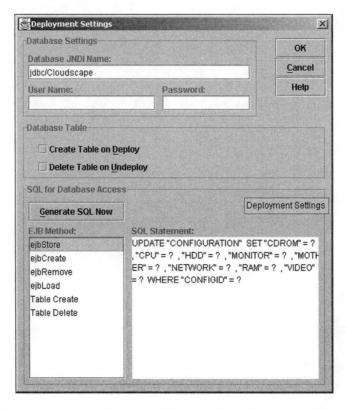

Click on the **OK** button to complete the settings. This completes the creation of the JAR for our CMP entity bean.

Next, we turn our attention to the BMP entity bean.

Creating a JAR for a BMP Entity Bean

In the deployment tool, the select New Enterprise Bean menu option under the File menu. Skip the first Introduction screen.

On the next screen, type `OrderJAR` for JAR Display Name and add the bean classes, `OrderEJB.class`, `OrderHome.class` and `Order.class` in the Contents. This procedure is similar to the one described above for the CMP Entity bean deployment.

On the next screen, select, following options:

- ❏ Enterprise Bean Class: OrderEJB
- ❏ Home Interface: OrderHome
- ❏ Remote Interface: Order
- ❏ Enterprise Bean Display Name: OrderEJB
- ❏ Bean Type: Entity

On the next screen, ensure that the Bean-Managed Persistence radio button is selected and then click on the Next button. Skip the next two screens. On the Resource References screen, click the Add button to add a database resource. In the Coded Name field type jdbc/OnlinePCDB.

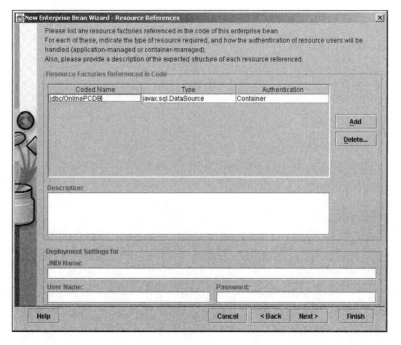

Accept the default for the rest of the screens. This completes the creation of the JAR file for the BMP entity bean. You will see the newly added JAR under our application on the main screen.

Lastly, we will create the JAR file for our session bean.

Creating a JAR for a Session Bean

Once again select the New Enterprise Bean menu option under the File menu and skip the Introduction screen.

On the next screen, type the JAR Display Name as OrderConfirmJAR and add three .class files, OrderConfirm, OrderConfirmEJB and OrderConfirmHome to the Contents.

On the next screen, select following options

- ❏ Enterprise Bean Class: OrderConfirmEJB

- ❏ Home Interface: OrderConfirmHome

- ❏ Remote Interface: OrderConfirm

- ❏ Enterprise Bean Display Name: OrderConfirmEJB

- ❏ Bean Type: Session – Stateful

Accept the defaults on the next two screens. On the Resource Ref screen, Add a resource as in the previous case. Type jdbc/OnlinePCDB for the Coded Name. Click on the Next button and accept defaults for the remaining screens.

This completes the creation of the JAR file. At this stage, you will see the three JAR files added under our application.

The next step is to deploy the application.

Deploying the Application

The process of deploying the application is similar to the one described in Chapter 9. At the time of deployment, you will need to specify the JNDI names for the various resources. Type in the following JNDI names for the various components and references:

- ❏ EJBConfig: MyConfig

- ❏ OrderEJB: MyOrders

- ❏ jdbcOnlinePCDB: jdbc/Cloudscape

- ❏ OrderConfirmEJB: MyOrderConfirm

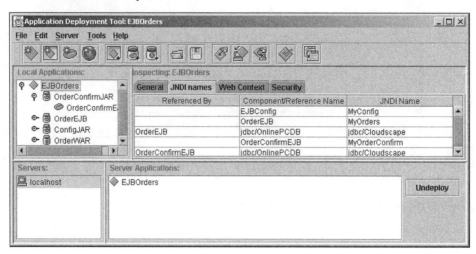

Once the application is displayed, test it by opening the AbcomHome.jsp page as described in Chapter 9.

So far, we have looked at the scalability issues connected with the business tier of a distributed application and have addressed this aspect by using EJBs. However, the scalability of the entire application depends on several other factors. One such factor is the database tier. I shall now discuss the issues of scalability in relation to the database tier.

Data Design and Access Strategies

For many years, database designers had to design databases to optimally use the available disk space by normalizing them. The process of normalization involves several stages to ensure that the data is not repeated in multiple tables. In the early days of computing, hardware resources like disk space were available at only very high premium and thus designers were forced to plan their resource requirements very carefully. An access to a fully normalized database typically takes a considerable amount of time. For a fully normalized database, even a simple query would involve multiple table joins that results in a poor response time in most cases.

As the hardware prices came down, people started de-normalizing databases to achieve better response times. The data was duplicated in multiple tables for this purpose. The size of databases increased considerably but came with the added benefit of faster response times.

In our example we have only a very simple database to simplify matters – the subject of database design and performance optimization is best left to other specialist books.

Choice of Storage

If you need very fast access to data, the data itself should be embedded in HTML files. Thus, the data is not generated dynamically and is readily available.

When the user requests an HTML page, the page contains both the data and the formatting information, thereby providing a fast response to the user. However, this would mean that you will need to maintain a large number of HTML files, and you will need to synchronize these pages with the changes made to the database. If the data is modified, you will have to re-create the HTML pages and store them in your web folder.

Instead of HTML, XML formatting may be preferred, as XML represents the data rather than the formatting information. In XML, the tags are user defined and convey meaning to the embedded data while HTML tags convey the formatting information for the embedded data.

Thus storing information as XML not only gives fast access to data like HTML, but also allows for efficient searching. Thus, a better response can be achieved at the cost of efficiency in terms of resource requirements and site maintenance (the XML documents will certainly occupy more space on your web server as compared to the data storage in a relational database). You may write the programs to generate these XML documents dynamically whenever the data changes or such an activity may be periodically scheduled.

When you look at the scalability of your database tier, you need to consider several factors. You can make your database tier more scalable by simply adding more power to your database server or upgrading your database engine to a more powerful, proven one or creating a cluster and replicating the data on the clustered machines. Other considerations would be an improved design of tables, maybe de-normalizing them for faster access, or simply converting them to a flat file for fastest possible access. Such issues fall into the realm of vendor specific applications and complex database design …and out of the scope of this book.

Methods of Data Access

Sometimes, you can achieve faster access to databases by caching a part of the most frequently used data in memory. Most database engines provide an in-built caching mechanism to provide a better response to the user. A programmer may provide additional caching to improve the application performance.

Depending on how you implement caching in your applications you may find concurrent users seeing different data at the same time. After the data is cached, if another user modifies the data through a different path, such changes will not be reflected in the cache. Similarly, if the user modifies the cache image, the underlying database will not be consistent with the cache until the time you synchronize the cache with the database by writing the changes to the database.

If you implement caching, you must ensure database consistency in your application. Note that cached data is more volatile and in case of power failure or a system breakdown, you may lose all changes made to the cache. Thus, if you plan to cache the data in your application, you should be careful in your design to ensure consistency of data and guard your database against volatility. However depending on the software used, some assistance with caching will be provided by the database application itself and by the EJB server linking to it. Note some aspects of a site lend themselves more readily to caching than others (for example say product catalogs which change relatively infrequently).

Another important consideration in database access is to plan for a synchronous vs. asynchronous access. You may design your database queries for asynchronous access so that the client does not have to wait until all the data is fetched. In case of asynchronous access, the client fires a query on the database and continues its work. Whenever the data becomes available, the client is notified. In case of synchronous data access, the client may have to wait for an unduly long time, especially if the database access is very slow.

Transaction Management

Concurrent database access by multiple users also requires proper transaction management to ensure database integrity. One may provide transactional access to a database by using the **Java Transaction API** (**JTA**) in the program code.

The coding of transactions in the case of a distributed database application is very complicated. Fortunately, the EJB architecture provides declarative transaction management that is preferable to programmatic transaction control, and easier to implement. The J2EE specification guarantees support for a distributed transaction spanning several distributed servers. The servers may be remote to each other and may come from different vendors, yet a distributed transaction is guaranteed.

A typical scenario of a distributed transaction can be described for a banking application. When you withdraw the money from a local ATM, a distributed transaction takes place that involves the local ATM bank server and the server where your bank account data is held. Your bank account may be in a different country from the place where you are currently withdrawing the money from ATM. The coding of such a distributed transaction is usually very complex, but if you implement your business logic of debiting/crediting two accounts in EJBs, the EJB server vendor will guarantee the distributed transaction involving both debit and credit operations. The advantage of using EJB technology is that such a transaction does not require any coding and can be simply declared in a deployment descriptor.

Having considered various issues of scalability and data design, we will now look at the integration issues with other business applications.

Integration with Existing Systems

The online web store application that we have developed so far may need to communicate with other business houses. One such typical application is checking when the inventory level falls below a certain threshold level and having our web store application generate a refill order for our supplier.

We've already had a taste of how the use of XML can aid such B2B transactions, and we'll see a lot more of this in the section of the book devoted to B2B. For the moment we'll just look at writing a small utility program that picks up the orders from our database and generates an XML file for use by the warehousing company.

The application accepts the order ID from the user and generates an XML document containing the order details. The `EnterOrderID.jsp` accepts the order number from the user and dispatches it to the `OrderConfirm` session bean. The session bean uses JDBC to retrieve the order data from the database and generates the XML file with the help of `XMLGenerator.jsp` based on the order data.

EnterOrderID.jsp

The `EnterOrderID.jsp` is basically an HTML page that displays an edit control to the store's staff for entering the order number. In-house company employees use this application.

On the Submit button being pressed the program calls `XMLGenerator.jsp`:

```html
<html>
   <head>
      <title>Enter OrderID</title>
   </head>
   <body>
      <form method="POST" action="XMLGenerator.jsp">
         <p align="center"><font face="Times New Roman" size="3"
            color="#0000FF"><b>Please enter OrderID: </b></font>
         <input type="text" name="OrdID" size="20"></p>
         <p align="center"><input type="submit" value="Submit" name="B1"
            style="text-align: Center"></p>
      </form>
   </body>
</html>
```

XMLGenerator.jsp

The complete code for XMLGenerator.jsp is given here:

```
<html>

    <%@ page language="java" import="java.util.*, java.sql.*,
        javax.naming.Context, javax.naming.InitialContext,
        javax.rmi.PortableRemoteObject" %>

    <head>
        <title>Order Confirmation</title>
    </head>

    <body>
```

The XMLGenerator.jsp receives the Order ID through the request parameter:

```
<%
        String OrderID = request.getParameter("OrdID");
```

The scriptlet code then generates an instance of the session bean by using this Order ID:

```
        Context ic = new InitialContext();
        java.lang.Object objref = ic.lookup("MyOrderConfirm");
        OrderConfirmHome OCHome = (OrderConfirmHome)
            PortableRemoteObject.narrow(objref, OrderConfirmHome.class);
        OrderConfirm OC = OCHome.create(OrderID);
```

The program then calls the getOrderDetails() method on the session bean to retrieve the order details in a vector. The generateXML() method (which we'll see shortly) generates an XML file based on the retrieved contents:

```
        OC.getOrderDetails();
        OC.generateXML();
    %>

    <p align="center">
        <font face="Times New Roman" size="3" color="#0000FF"><b>XML file
            Generated.</b></font>
    <p align="center">
        <font face="Times New Roman" size="3" color="#0000FF">File
            Name: <b>OrderList.xml</b></font>
    </body>
</html>
```

The screen output generated by XMLGenerator.jsp is given here.

OrderConfirm Session Bean

I shall now discuss the OrderConfirm session bean. The remote interface of the bean declares two methods, getOrderDetails() and generateXML().

As explained earlier, the getOrderDetails() method retrieves the details for a specified Order ID and the generateXML() method generates an XML file based on this data. The code for OrderConfirm.java is given below:

```
import java.rmi.RemoteException;
import java.util.*;
import javax.ejb.EJBObject;

public interface OrderConfirm extends EJBObject {
    public void getOrderDetails() throws RemoteException;
    public void generateXML() throws RemoteException;
}
```

The home interface of the bean defined in OrderConfirmHome.java declares a create() method that takes OrderID as a String parameter:

```
import java.io.Serializable;
import java.rmi.RemoteException;
import java.util.*;
import javax.ejb.CreateException;
import javax.ejb.EJBHome;

public interface OrderConfirmHome extends EJBHome {
    public OrderConfirm create(String OrderID)
                    throws RemoteException, CreateException;
}
```

The Implementation Class

We will now look into the implementation class of the OrderConfirm bean. The complete code for OrderConfirmEJB.java is given below:

```
import com.ibm.xml.parser.TXDocument;
import java.io.*;
import java.sql.*;
import java.util.*;
import javax.ejb.*;
import javax.naming.Context;
import javax.naming.InitialContext;
import javax.rmi.PortableRemoteObject;
import javax.sql.*;
import org.w3c.dom.*;

public class OrderConfirmEJB implements SessionBean {
    private String OrderID, Email, ConfigID, CPU, Mother, HD,
                  RAM, Monitor, Video, CDROM, Network, Qty, Price;
    private Vector OuterVec, InnerVec;
    private Connection con, con1;
    private String logicalDBName = "java:comp/env/jdbc/OnlinePC";

    public void ejbCreate(String OrderID)
        throws CreateException {
        this.OrderID = OrderID;
    }
```

Here is the generateXML() method that is responsible for generating the XML document based on the retrieved order details. The Orders element contains ItemList element. Each ItemList element contains several elements that specify the order details and the configuration details of the PC. The method first creates an XML document by creating an instance of TXDocument class.

Note that IBM xml4j libraries have again been used for creating XML documents.

```
public void generateXML() {
    try {
        Document doc = (Document)new TXDocument();
```

Next, the program code creates the root element for the document:

```
Element root = doc.createElement ("Orders");
```

An Iterator is created for iterating through the elements of OuterVec vector. For each entry in the OuterVec, we retrieve the InnerVec that contains the order details. The program constructs another Iterator for iterating through the elements of InnerVec:

```
Iterator it1 = OuterVec.iterator();

while (it1.hasNext()) {
    InnerVec = (Vector)it1.next();
    Iterator it2 = InnerVec.iterator();
```

For each order item, an ItemList element is created in the XML document and added to the root element:

```
Element item = doc.createElement ("ItemList");
root.appendChild(item);
```

For each element of the `InnerVec`, we create an element in our XML document, create a text node with the contents, and add it to the list of items specified in `ItemList` element:

```
OrderID = (String)it2.next();
Element details = doc.createElement ("OrderID");
details.appendChild (doc.createTextNode(OrderID));
item.appendChild(details);
```

The above code is repeated for the rest of the elements of the `InnerVec` vector as follows:

```
Email = (String)it2.next();
details = doc.createElement ("Email");
details.appendChild (doc.createTextNode(Email));
item.appendChild(details);

ConfigID = (String)it2.next();
details = doc.createElement ("ConfigID");
details.appendChild (doc.createTextNode(ConfigID));
item.appendChild(details);

Qty = (String)it2.next();
Price = (String)it2.next();
CPU = (String)it2.next();
details = doc.createElement ("CPU");
details.appendChild (doc.createTextNode(CPU));
item.appendChild(details);

Mother = (String)it2.next();
details = doc.createElement ("MotherBoard");
details.appendChild (doc.createTextNode(Mother));
item.appendChild(details);

HD = (String)it2.next();
details = doc.createElement ("HardDisk");
details.appendChild (doc.createTextNode(HD));
item.appendChild(details);

RAM = (String)it2.next();
details = doc.createElement ("RAM");
details.appendChild (doc.createTextNode(RAM));
item.appendChild(details);

Monitor = (String)it2.next();
details = doc.createElement ("Monitor");
details.appendChild (doc.createTextNode(Monitor));
item.appendChild(details);

Video = (String)it2.next();
details = doc.createElement ("VideoCard");
details.appendChild (doc.createTextNode(Video));
item.appendChild(details);

CDROM = (String)it2.next();
details = doc.createElement ("CD-ROM");
details.appendChild (doc.createTextNode(CDROM));
```

```
            item.appendChild(details);

            Network = (String)it2.next();
            details = doc.createElement ("NetworkCard");
            details.appendChild (doc.createTextNode(Network));
            item.appendChild(details);

            details = doc.createElement ("Quantity");
            details.appendChild (doc.createTextNode(Qty));
            item.appendChild(details);

            details = doc.createElement ("Amount");
            details.appendChild (doc.createTextNode(Price));
            item.appendChild(details);
        }
```

Once the root element is fully constructed, it is added to the document object:

```
            doc.appendChild (root);
```

The program then sets the XML version, opens a file with name `OrderList.xml` for writing the document contents, and uses `printWithFormat()` method of the document object to generate the file containing the XML document.

Note that you will need to set the Java Security permissions on your EJB server to enable it to create a file. You can use `policytool` to set the permissions on your server, a program that can be run by typing `policytool` at the command line.

```
            ((TXDocument)doc).setVersion("1.0");
            FileOutputStream fos = new FileOutputStream("OrderList.xml");
            ((TXDocument)doc).printWithFormat(new PrintWriter(fos));
        } catch (Exception e) {
            e.printStackTrace();
        }
    }

    public void getOrderDetails() {
        try {
```

The `getOrderDetails()` method looks up JNDI for the `DataSource` and obtains a connection to the database using the retrieved `DataSource` object:

```
            Context ic = new InitialContext();
            DataSource ds = (DataSource) ic.lookup(logicalDBName);
            con =  ds.getConnection();
            con1 = ds.getConnection();
```

The program then constructs the SQL statement to retrieve the order record for the specified Order ID, creates a `Statement` object, and runs the query on the database to generate a result set:

```
            String SQL = "Select * From ORDERS Where ORDERID = '" + OrderID + "'";
            Statement stmt = con.createStatement();
            ResultSet rs = stmt.executeQuery(SQL);
```

A single order may consist of multiple items. We create a vector called OuterVec for storing the entire order. Each item in the order is stored in another vector called InnerVec that is added to the OuterVec. The InnerVec contains the details for each ordered item that is fetched from the ORDERS and CONFIGURATION tables:

```
        boolean t = rs.next();
        OuterVec = new Vector();
        while(t) {
            InnerVec = new Vector();
            OrderID = rs.getString(1);
            InnerVec.addElement(OrderID);
            Email = rs.getString(2);
            InnerVec.addElement(Email);
            ConfigID = rs.getString(3);
            InnerVec.addElement(ConfigID);
            Qty = rs.getString(4);
            InnerVec.addElement(Qty);
            Price = rs.getString(5);
            InnerVec.addElement(Price);
            getConfigRec();
            OuterVec.addElement(InnerVec);
            t = rs.next();
        }
        con.close();
        con1.close();
    } catch (Exception ex) {
        ex.printStackTrace();
    }
}

private void getConfigRec() {
```

The configuration details for each item are obtained by calling getConfigRec() method. This method constructs the SQL statement for obtaining the configuration details by using the Configuration ID obtained from the ORDERS table:

```
String SQL = "Select CPU, MOTHER, HDD, RAM, MONITOR, VIDEO, CDROM,
            NETWORK " +   "From CONFIGURATION Where CONFIGID = '" +
            ConfigID + "'";
```

The program then creates a Statement, executes the query on the database, and adds the retrieved fields to the InnerVec vector:

```
    try {
        Statement stmt1 = con1.createStatement();
        ResultSet rs1 = stmt1.executeQuery(SQL);
        if (rs1.next()) {
            CPU = rs1.getString(1);
            InnerVec.addElement(CPU);
            Mother = rs1.getString(2);
            InnerVec.addElement(Mother);
            HD = rs1.getString(3);
            InnerVec.addElement(HD);
            RAM = rs1.getString(4);
```

429

```
                    InnerVec.addElement(RAM);
                    Monitor = rs1.getString(5);
                    InnerVec.addElement(Monitor);
                    Video = rs1.getString(6);
                    InnerVec.addElement(Video);
                    CDROM = rs1.getString(7);
                    InnerVec.addElement(CDROM);
                    Network = rs1.getString(8);
                    InnerVec.addElement(Network);
                }
                rs1.close();
                stmt1.close();
            } catch(Exception ex) {
                ex.printStackTrace();
            }
        }

    public void ejbRemove() {}
    public void ejbActivate() {}
    public void ejbPassivate() {}
    public void setSessionContext(SessionContext sc) {}
}
```

This completes our application!

Summary

In this chapter, we looked at the scalability issues of a web application and used EJBs at the middle tier to embed our business logic, making the application more scalable as compared to using JSPs for implementation of business logic.

In the last four chapters, you learnt how to create a complete B2C e-commerce site. In Chapter 9 we introduced you to the process of designing and creating a simple site that sells PCs online. The site was constructed using JSPs. We discussed the creation of the database for the site; the dynamic creation of the catalog, and the design of the shopping cart and how to maintain the client selections throughout the client session.

In Chapter 10, we looked at the issue of usability. The use of JSP custom tags for code reusability and ease of site maintenance was discussed. Site searching techniques were discussed and how to send feedback to the customer using JavaMail. We also covered dynamic searching of the database. The benefits of membership were discussed and the creation of membership capabilities for the site was demonstrated. Finally, we learned the techniques for bringing internationalization to the site.

In Chapter 11, we looked at the client issues of web application development. Client-side validation using JavaScript and server-side validation of the input were demonstrated. Lastly, cross-browser design and generation of XML code for the client were discussed and demonstrated.

Finally, in the chapter we have just finished, we learned some of the problems that may be encountered during the issues of scalability. The numbers of concurrent users to the site may be more than you had planned for; the ability to cope with this can be improved by the use of EJBs in the site design. The issues of scalability for the database tier were also dealt with, using data embedded in XML files or conversion to a flat file. There are many ways in which to improve the accessibility of your data on the site and some of these issues have been covered here.

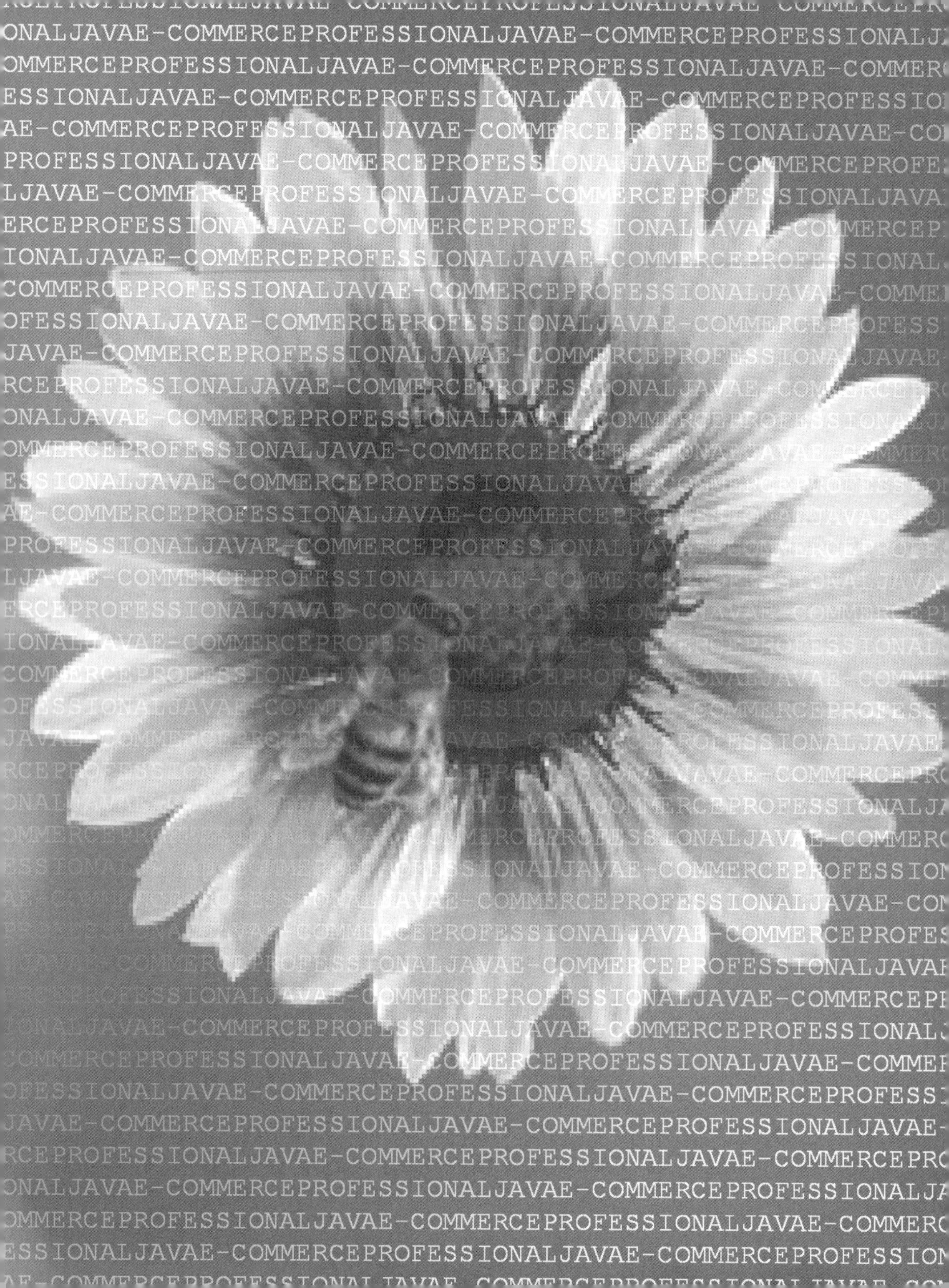
PROFESSIONALJAVAE-COMMERCE

13

In the Marketplace A – B2C with WebLogic and WLCS

We offer this case study with the hope that it will help to look at a real-world project. When we started the project, there were only a few books on the technologies used, especially on JSP and EJB. As we continued, excellent books continued to appear. Still, with all the available possibilities, it is easy to get confused about which is the right technology, and the correct approach for your project.

As for the practical applications, many projects are still in the design or development stage. It is common for the developers to be very curious and ask their colleagues, "What did you use? Did it work?" There are almost no projects described in literature, and the books, excellent as they are, teach what can be done, not what should be done or how it was done.

This is why we thought it useful to show how we did design and development, and to share all the hard-learned lessons and best practices. We have read many books and selected what worked best for us.

We will also share our failures, which are more politely termed "change of plans". If, by reading the chapter, you gain a better appreciation of the technologies used, and are warned about the lurking dangers, it will be worth your time and the writer's effort. Failures, when told honestly, are learning tools!

However, we would like to offer more. Even though we relied a lot on the work done before us, we have built some novel applications based on this. The three applications that we describe in this chapter are progressively more complex:

❑   **The Login** – This is the "Hello World" application of the e-commerce world, except that ours uses JSPs, servlets, JavaBeans, and EJBs.

❑ **The Coupons** – This is a more involved business application which illustrates the use of Java Encryption.

❑ **Sales Help** – Here we describe a program that conducts a conversation with the customer, leading to a sale. This is a novel and advanced application.

At the end of this chapter, there are detailed instructions on how to download, build, and use the project code, in the section *What is in the Source Code*. The code, downloadable from **www.wrox.com**, includes all of the examples in this chapter.

Before we dive into the applications we need to set the scene and describe the site requirements and how we went about the project.

Site Requirements

Ashford.com, Inc. (Nasdaq:ASFD) is an Internet retailer of luxury and premium products. The company's e-commerce site, located at http://www.ashford.com, offers a vast selection of diamonds and more than 14,000 styles of new and vintage watches, jewelry, fragrances, leather accessories, sunglasses, writing instruments, and corporate gifts from more than 400 leading brands. Ashford.com is headquartered in Houston, Texas.

In this chapter, we are more interested in the history of the site from the programmer's point of view rather than the business angle. If you're interested you can go and try to buy something from the site, or do some research on the site in the business publications, such as Forbes (http://www.forbes.com).

The company was founded in March 1998. The initial programming of the site was done with ASP, COM and Oracle. Considering that the programming was done in a very short time, the functionality of it was remarkable. The management of Ashford decided to hire a web development company, Emerging, to help it redesign the site.

What were the problems with the current site? You could consider the site as the first or second version of the software. Many parts were programmed as quickly as possible, because time-to-market was of prime importance. Here are the areas that needed to be addressed:

❑ Database utilization was too high, reportedly at 90 percent. This made at times for slow response.

❑ Database design was often ad hoc, each programmer adding fields when needed, and some of them were duplicated.

❑ Many ASPs went directly to the database. The COM components, when they were used, were for functionality, and not to separate the application into tiers.

❑ As it grew, the ASPs were becoming spaghetti code, so that a change in one place could easily break something else.

Clearly the site needed a redesign. However, it was not obvious which technology to choose. First of all, you could redesign the site by still using ASP, COM/DCOM, and by improving the database. Not only was this a valid approach, but also the internal Ashford developers who kept improving the site were in fact going in this direction. Emerging, however, was given the task of selecting the best technology, and then discussing this choice with Ashford.

After reviewing a number of e-commerce packages on the market we decided to program in Java, JSP, and build on BEA WebLogic and WLCS (WebLogic Commerce Server). We did this for the following reasons:

❑ Java seemed easier to program and more robust.

❑ It is the author's feeling that Java pushes the developers to better design. The notion of classes/object design in Java is tighter than it is in C++, and surely beyond script languages like ASP. EJB enforces separation of tiers. Again, this can all be done with VB, but somehow Java does it more elegantly and simply, perhaps because in Java OOP is one of the cornerstones, rather than an afterthought.

❑ Java and JSP had the allure of new and hot technology. For publicly traded companies like Ashford this can also be a factor.

❑ Some packages seemed to offer more, but at a bigger price. You would also have to spend more time learning them, and they were unwieldy to change, while Ashford needed a high degree of customization.

❑ Other packages offered too little. We estimated that the pre-written classes of WLCS would give us 50 percent of the needed functionality. Even if they did not, it was very helpful to review the design. A good design is at least half the work, and the code can be written quickly after that. The libraries of WLCS provided us with a lot of e-commerce design expertise. WebLogic is of course one of the leading application servers.

At the end of the chapter we discuss the current state of the project. Briefly, though, the development and testing for the first part of the project, "Corporate Gifts" is finished. However, as of the time of writing, the deployment was put on hold by the management, due to market conditions. Notwithstanding the present lack of deployment of the project, there are still hopefully lessons to be learned.

How We Went About the Project

Here is where the fun began. Obviously, we wanted everything perfect, and yesterday. Having realized that this was impossible, we made the first iteration. The second iteration came when we realized that we could not deliver the whole site by the peak holiday time. After all, we could not be expected to build the new site much faster than it took to do the old one. So, we limited ourselves to just one part of it, Corporate Gifts.

In the second iteration, we decided to split the tasks, and have one guy (architect) design the class model, with the idea that the others (developers) would be just implementers. This did not quite work either for two reasons.

First of all, EJBs are not the regular Java classes. They are remote objects that are being created, activated, passivated, destroyed, etc. There is a lot of thought about efficiency here. It is one thing when you just want to draw a class diagram to describe the organization or the site: you draw the classes, and show their connections with multiplicity. It is different with EJB where every connection means that one EJB is instantiated, passivated, destroyed, etc. – which you may not want at all.

Let us give an example. Let's say you read a list of countries from a database. Let's also say that you need to select a country in forming a person's address on a web page. It may be all right to have an EJB to read the list of all countries. However, having a reference to a country EJB from your address EJB is another matter. Here you may not want the programming and performance overhead of an EJB handler. You may want to just store the country database ID in your address EJB.

To summarize, while designing an EJB class diagram you need to constantly think about the use of the EJB by your application. The following screenshot illustrates the use of the Country EJB by the other EJBs. As you can see, we added a JavaBean to help the Country EJB. This JavaBean makes sure that the connection is made only once, the list of countries is read, cached, and then provided by the JavaBean to the JSPs:

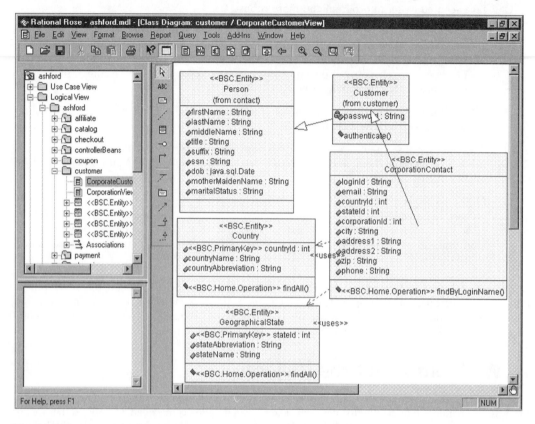

The second reason class diagrams were not easy to create was because we were using the WLCS components EJBs. We hoped to get a benefit from it in the end. At that point, however, we did not know all the details of the available components. This is no different from any other library. A person who has written this library (BEA consultant) or somebody who has been through a couple of projects with it might be expected to draw a high-level class diagram utilizing all the available functionality. We, however, could not do it in one swoop.

We therefore chose to do a very sketchy class diagram, and to appoint an architect who would be the custodian of the emerging class model. Later on he would provide guidance on individual application integration and component reuse. For now, though, each developer was responsible for his or her subsystem, or application, up from the EJBs (and sometimes database tables) to servlets, JSPs, and their companion JavaBeans.

That worked. Reading books and articles and selecting the architecture and advice most appropriate to our situation assured much of the success. Once the application architecture was decided upon, and the first prototype was done, we could copy that application and use it as a seed for all other applications. After some practice, we could crank out the first versions of our application in a few days. Getting the finer details and satisfying all users can take, as every developer knows, much longer.

> **Advice – Expect much iteration in the design process and project management; be flexible.**

What situation is the foregoing discussion most applicable to? We assume that the developers are versatile, and can handle the development of all of the components: JSP, EJB, JavaBeans, and servlets, even if by copying and pasting, with the help of their colleagues. Our project was not very large, the situation not very structured, and the client was flexible, but speed and quality were of importance. Therefore the techniques of Extreme Programming worked well for us. In larger projects, or those that are more controlled and mission critical, with perhaps a lot of responsibility and accounting, the Waterfall model might be better. More details on these design methodologies are contained in Chapter 3.

As an example, an e-commerce project with which one of this chapter's authors is involved now is energy trading on the trading floor of an energy company. Data integrity and reporting is very important in this situation, so an architectural group takes care of all the data needs, including the entity beans, and the other code that accesses the database. All actions are then performed by the session beans, which call on the entity beans. This is the responsibility of a person in the applications group. Finally, front-end application developers use the session beans provided to them. The data requirements are very stable, and in fact reproduce the already existing processing. There is little or no change here, so it can be done with a Waterfall model. However, the users (traders) are still flexible, so the front-end design is using Extreme Programming.

For those who are building a career (which most of us are), here is the last piece of advice before we dispense with the harsh realities of the world and forget ourselves in the code; you need something to show to the management. Many parties are involved in web development projects, among them CEOs, managers, marketing people, developers, and sometimes third party developer organizations. They all come to the project with different expectations, which is especially pronounced when the area of the development is so new. Therefore, as advised by Extreme Programming, try to reach the stage where you can build daily as quickly as possible. You need something to show to all these different groups of people. At Internet speed, a decision to redirect or close the project may come before any visible results. If you have a daily build, you immediately have your progress on display. Following on from this, you get a better measure of the project status, and you can start your testing and integration early.

> **Advice – Have something to show prototype, or do a frequent build of the whole system.**

Now onto the first of our applications – the login system.

Login

Let us now describe the login and the beginning of customer management. Of course, Login has become a "Hello, World" program of Web development. What is different about ours is that it uses the whole gamut of JSP, servlet, JavaBeans, and EJBs, and that it builds on a library of pre-existing EJBs.

The advantage of using this many layers is that, because we are using an application server, the solution is scalable; it can grow with the site requirements. The use of servlets allows us to consolidate all processing in one place. The use of JSP allows very clean separation of HTML contents and business logic written in Java. Finally the use of helper JavaBeans makes the work of JSP writers easier. Once written, the JavaBeans can be reused by different JSPs, which simplifies maintenance. If this list of advantages seems familiar, that's because they are the same advantages as using J2EE to develop a whole application.

Project Organization

Project organization helps a lot in keeping things clean and moving fast, so we will first explain our directory structure.

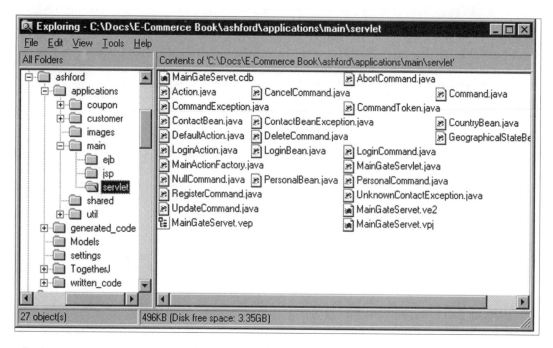

Each application, such as main (this is where our login is), customer, coupon, etc., will have its associated EJB, JSP, and servlet. The JavaBeans will go with the servlet and are put in the servlet directory. It is convenient to put them in the IDE servlet project, since all of the code will be recompiled at once. Some JavaBeans will be shared between the applications, but this is not shown in our examples. Please note the generated_code and written_code directories; these will be explained later.

It is useful to have a little this-deploy.bat file in every directory, which copies all the files from this directory to their destination on the web server, in this case, the WebLogic server. This both provides a convenient way of setting up, and also documents the deployment. Do *not* keep your work files on the server, since you may want to reinstall the server, and forget to save your work. The contents of the this-deploy.bat file could be something like this:

```
copy c:\ashford\applications\coupon\jsp\*.jsp
c:\weblogic\myserver\public_html\ashford\coupon\jsp
```

All JSP files reside in the same directory. This architecture allowed us a lot flexibility and speed of development: with one button push the whole application, the servlet and all the JavaBeans, were rebuilt and deployed on the server, and the JSPs refreshed. This is a do-it-yourself make file, combined with the make that the IDE provides. For bigger and more involved projects, real make files might be more fitting. The EJB directory is only used to store the JAR files. Eventually, these JARs become shared and migrate to a collective directory, but in the beginning it is faster if each developer has their own.

A helpful device is to also include the JSPs in the Java project. As we have discovered, the JSPs need to be recompiled when the helper JavaBeans change. Since the JSPs are not Java code proper, they are not recompiled by an IDE, such as WebGain's VisualCafé, which we used. However, here is a program that allows you to achieve complete integration:

```java
package ashford.servlet.main;

import java.io.*;

public class Deploy {
  public static void main(String [] argv) {
    String from = argv[0]; // directory where all JSP files are
    String to = argv[1];    // JSP deployment directory
    try {
      File dirFrom = new File(from);
      String [] files = dirFrom.list();
      for (int i = 0; i < files.length; ++i) { // copy all files
        if (files[i].endsWith(".jsp")) {
          File fileFrom = new File(from + files[i]);
          File fileTo = new File(to + files[i]);
          long length = fileFrom.length();
          byte [] contents = new byte[(int)length];
          FileInputStream in = new  FileInputStream(fileFrom);
          in.read(contents);
          FileOutputStream out = new FileOutputStream(fileTo);
          out.write(contents);
        }
      }
    }
    catch (Exception e) {
      e.printStackTrace();
    }
  }
}
```

What this program does is as follows. The first input parameter (from) is the directory where the JSP files in the project are contained – in our case c:\ashford\applications\coupon\jsp\. We have only one directory level for them, but it would not be hard to modify the program to copy directories recursively.

The second parameter (to) is the destination directory; for example it could be c:\weblogic\myserver\public_html\ashford\coupon\jsp\. If we set the ashford.servlet.coupon.Deploy as the main class that is started when the project is run, then the following actions will occur on each run:

❑ First, all the files are saved. This includes the JSP files, which we have been editing.

❑ Secondly, the project is built. The JavaBeans and servlet classes are re-built.

❑ Finally, the `Deploy` main program is run and all the JSP files are copied into the WebLogic destination directory.

The result of these actions is that all the JSP files are saved and recompiled by the WebLogic server when they are hit the next time. You may ask, why use a Java program, and not a batch file with an `xcopy *.jsp` command? True, you could write a smaller Java program to run the batch file from VisualCafé. However, `xcopy` will not update the date on the JSP files that have not been changed. We do want all files refreshed, though, since this causes all JavaBeans to reload.

If you set the class destination directory to `c:\weblogic\myserver\servletclasses`, it will have the effect of hot reloading the servlet and JavaBeans classes in the WebLogic server. Nifty, isn't it? It makes for a very fast development, until an IDE comes up which does it all for us without tricks. The source directories are also set in the VisualCafé project. Here is the complete project, as it appears in the VisualCafé IDE. This screenshot shows all of the relevant files organized in one project, and illustrates the fact that VisualCafé can even help edit the JSP, by coloring their syntax, as we are going to explain now:

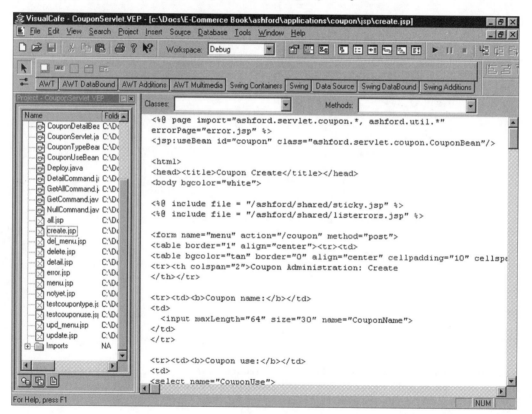

VisualCafé does one more thing for us here. If we set the keywords for the JSP file to HTML, it will even color the JSP text according to the HTML keywords. Of course, you can set them to Java, and see your JSP as essentially Java text. Normally, however, it is recommended that the amount of Java code residing in JSPs is minimized and beans are used instead. Most of the keywords should then be HTML, which explains our choice. This setting is found in VisualCafé Environment Options, under the Format tab.

Since we are using VisualCafé and WebLogic, it may help to know that there is a bug in the VisualCafé 4.0. When you add the WebLogic classes to the project path, namely, \weblogic\classes and \weblogic\lib\weblogicaux.jar, the GUI generator of VisualCafé gets completely messed up. To avoid this, you can use the j2ee.jar that comes with the standard j2sdkee. When you need real WebLogic classes to run, these can be added to the path. Just be very careful and do not edit any GUI objects. It's a bit inconvenient, but it can be overcome (it can take days to figure out this bug, so be forewarned, until it is fixed).

Class Diagram

We are now ready to describe our EJB class diagram, which you can see in the following figure:

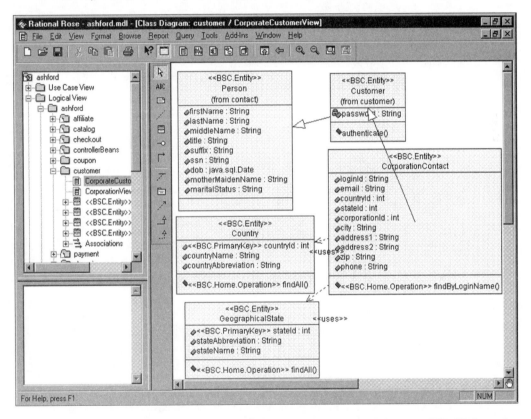

A few things need explanation here. The <BSC.Entity> is a stereotype for the entity EJB. With another generator you would have a slightly different name, but the essence does not change, since we want to generate an entity Enterprise JavaBean. An entity bean is used here, and not a session bean, because it will be connected to the database. `Person` and `Customer` come from the WLCS library, which is described as part of the BEA WLCS documentation. If you have similar EJBs, you could derive from them. If not, you could list your own attributes from scratch. The reason we wanted to derive from the existing components is that they would later be used in the other parts of the WLCS. You could similarly derive from your components, bought or written in-house, for the same reason.

Finally, we needed more control on the country and state. This is due to the import/export requirements that e-commerce frequently has to deal with; for example, you're not allowed to sell items made of snakeskin to customers in Switzerland! We therefore made `Country` and `State` into separate objects. This is more of a business than architectural decision, and it allows names to be checked and import/export rules to be programmed.

Before we go to code generation, here is how the same diagram looks in the TogetherJ, after we import the `ashford.mdl` file into it. You will notice one of the features of TogetherJ – code generation is instantaneous with UML drawing. The code is seen in the bottom window of the following screenshot:

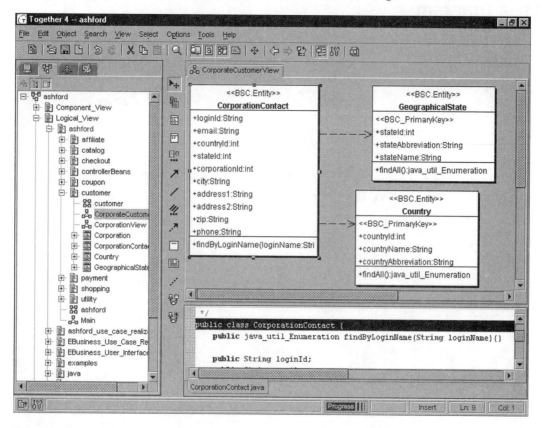

Having jumped into TogetherJ, let's describe it in a little more detail. The product is made by TogetherSoft (http://www.togethersoft.com), a company created by Peter Coad (author of *Java Design, ISBN 0-13-911181-6*). TogetherJ implements his books approach. In addition, TogetherJ is written entirely in Java, and tries to improve on the known UML tools and code generators. TogetherJ uses its own file format, but can import Rational Rose * .mdl files.

The reason we show the TogetherJ diagram is to illustrate that you are not bound to a specific tool or vendor. Of course, the classes from which the `CorporationContact` derives are not shown in TogetherJ because these are specific to WLCS, but they can be either added to the TogetherJ project, or the developer can code substitute classes. In any case a developer will probably use a different e-commerce library, and we use this as an illustration.

The EJB files generated from the (Rose) UML diagram are shown in the figure below:

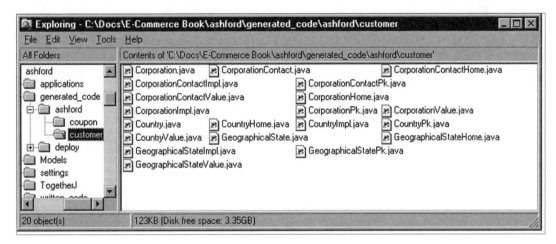

We found it more convenient to dedicate a separate VisualCafé project to each EJB, and to put each EJB in a separate JAR. This is because the `ejbc` compiler needs to rebuild all of the files in the JAR. So, when a developer is working on just one EJB, it is very slow to rebuild the growing number of them. If you see a lot of EJBs collected in a JAR in a third-party library, a good guess is that they were developed and debugged separately, and combined at later stages. We did the same.

The EJBs

The files seen in the previous screenshot therefore are for 4 EJBs, which are all quite similar. Taking the `Country` EJB as an example, a representative piece of code in it is given below. This is the `ejbCreate()` method, called by the container when the client calls the create method on the `home` object:

```
public ashford.customer.CountryPk ejbCreate(
      ashford.customer.CountryPk countryPk)
                        throws CreateException, RemoteException {
  boolean cmp = true;
  try {
    String persistenceType = getPropertyValue("PersistenceType");

    if (persistenceType != null
          && persistenceType.equalsIgnoreCase("BMP")) {
      cmp = false;
      String persistenceTcBmp = getPropertyValue("PersistenceTcBmpClass");
      String persistenceDbConn =
        getPropertyValue("PersistenceDbConnClass");
      if (persistenceTcBmp != null && persistenceDbConn != null) {
        DatabaseConnection dbConn =
          (DatabaseConnection) Class.forName(persistenceDbConn)
            .newInstance();

        TcBmp tcBmp = // load the class that will do the work
          (TcBmp) Class.forName(persistenceTcBmp).newInstance();
        tcBmp.setDatabaseConnection(dbConn);
        tcBmp.create(countryPk, this);
```

```
        }
     } else {
        super.ejbCreate((SmartKey) countryPk);
     }
  } catch (java.lang.Exception e) {
     throw new javax.ejb.CreateException(e.getMessage());
  }
  ejbCreateInitVars(countryPk);

  // $EjbCreate$_Begin ------------ CUSTOM CODE ?
  // Add custom code here
  // $EjbCreate$_End    ^^^^^^^^^^^^^^^^^^^^^^^^^^^^^^^^^^^^^^^^^^^^
  if (cmp) {
     return null;
  } else {
     return countryPk;
  }
}
```

As you can see, the work is really delegated to the `TcBmp` class, which provides database code implementation. Here is a sample of `TcBmp` code:

```
public void create(java.lang.Object okey, java.lang.Object obean)
   throws java.rmi.RemoteException
   {
      java.sql.Connection con = null;
      java.sql.PreparedStatement ps = null;

      try {
         ashford.customer.CountryPk key =
            (ashford.customer.CountryPk) okey;
         ashford.customer.CountryImpl bean =
            (ashford.customer.CountryImpl) obean;
         con =  dbconn.getConnection();
         ps = con.prepareStatement("INSERT INTO Country (id) VALUES (?)");
         // Setup INSERT parameters.
         ps.setInt(1, key.countryId);

         // Execute INSERT statement.
         if (ps.executeUpdate() != 1) {
         throw new java.lang.Exception ("CREATE FAILED");
      }
      } catch( java.lang.Exception e ) {
         throw new java.rmi.RemoteException
            (e.getMessage());
      } finally {
         try {
         if (ps != null) ps.close();
         dbconn.releaseConnection(con);
      } catch( java.lang.Exception e ) {
         throw new java.rmi.RemoteException (e.getMessage());
      }
   }
} // create()
```

The `TcBmp.create()` method prepares the `Country` record in the database. We are using bean-managed persistence here, because we felt that in this way we had more control over what was going on. We could have used container-managed persistence also.

So, everything is clear and straightforward, with a nice separation of functionality. If you're building on third-party beans, this is the point to use them at, but, if you're building it all yourself, this is a good example to learn from. The `TcBmp` class, or actually in this case the `CountryTcBmp` derived from it, is not generated by the code generator. Rather it is specific to our environment and database setup and it's good to keep it separate from the generated code. This explains the `generated_code` and `written_code` folders, which we saw above while discussing the project directory structure.

How would we use the EJBs just created? For the project architecture, we used a combination of servlet, JSPs, and JavaBeans to go with each individual JSP. The servlet/JSP architecture we took from the book *JavaServer Pages* by *Fields and Kolb*, (*ISBN 1-884777-99-6*), Chapters 8b and 9, and it worked very well for us. In brief, each application consists of one servlet, a set of JSPs, and some helper JavaBeans. The servlet does all the processing: validates the input data, fulfills the requests, and packs the answers into the JavaBeans, which are then passed to the next JSP to be displayed.

The Login Screen

All of this can now be used to build the login screen, as seen in the following screenshot:

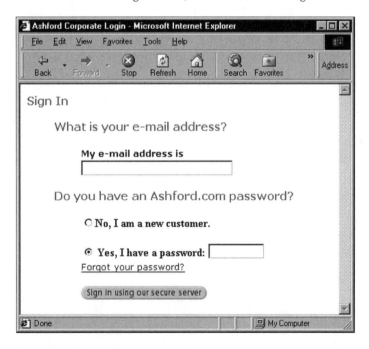

Here is the code for the JSP implementing this interface:

```
<%@ page import="ashford.servlet.main.*"
errorPage="error.jsp" %>

<html>
```

```
<head>
<title>Ashford Corporate Login</title>
<script language="JavaScript">
function setCmd(value) {
  document.menu.cmd.value = value;
}
</script>
</head>

<body>
<%@ include file = "/ashford/shared/sticky.jsp" %>
<%@ include file = "/ashford/shared/listerrors.jsp" %>

<strong><font face="verdana,arial,helvetica" color="#cc6600">Sign
In</font></strong><br>
<blockquote>
  <form name="menu" action="/main" method="post">
    <input type="hidden" name="cmd" value="">
    <input type="hidden" name="formpage" value="login.jsp">
    <dl>
      <dt><strong><font face="verdana,arial,helvetica" color="#cc6600">
        What is your e-mail address?</font></strong><br>
      <dd><br>
        <font face="verdana,arial,helvetica" size="-1"><b>
          My e-mail address is</b></font>
        <input maxLength="64" size="30"
        value="<%= getParam(request, "email") %>"
        name="email">
        <br>
        <br>
      <dt><strong><font face="verdana,arial,helvetica" color="#cc6600">
        Do you have an Ashford.com password?</font></strong><br>
      <dd><br>
        <input type="radio" name="action" value="register"
        <font face="verdana,arial,helvetica" size="-1"><b>
          No, I am a new customer.</b></font><br>
        <br>
        <input type="radio"  name="action" value="sign-in" checked
        <font face="verdana,arial,helvetica" size="-1"><b>
        Yes, I have a password:</b></font>
        <input type="password" maxLength="20" size="10" name="password"><br>
        <font face="verdana,arial,helvetica" size="-1">
          <a href="https://www.ashford.com/forgot-password">
            Forgot your password?</a></font>
        <p><input type="image" cache alt="Continue"
          src="/ashford/images/sign-in-secure.gif"
        onClick="setCmd('do-login')" border="0" width="184" height="19"></p>
      </dd>
    </dl>
  </form>
</blockquote>

</body>

</html>
```

The two lines that need most explanation are:

```
<%@ include file = "/ashford/shared/sticky.jsp" %>
<%@ include file = "/ashford/shared/listerrors.jsp"
```

These files implement "sticky forms" (sticky.jsp), which are forms that retain their values once filled out by the user, and error processing for the user errors (listerrors.jsp) – both are described in Fields and Kolb. The sticky.jsp is a collection of convenience functions, which extract and format the data from the JSP request object. The listerrors uses a Java collection of error messages, which is formed by the servlet, and is displayed by our JSP page at the very top. This last method seems to be very standard, and is found at many web sites.

The servlet is implemented using the **command** design pattern, described in books, such as *Design Patterns* by *Gamma et al, ISBN 0-201633-61-2*. In our use of the command pattern here, each command is identified by name, and a separate class implements a given command. All that the servlet has to do now is to get the command name and invoke the corresponding class. Here is the main processing method:

```
public void service(HttpServletRequest req,
  HttpServletResponse res)
  throws ServletException, IOException {
  String next;
    try {
      Command cmd = lookupCommand(req.getParameter("cmd"));
      next = cmd.execute(req);
      CommandToken.set(req);
    }
    catch (CommandException e) {
      req.setAttribute("javax.servlet.jsp.jspException", e);
    next = error;
  }
  RequestDispatcher rd;
  rd = getServletContext().getRequestDispatcher(jspdir + next);
    rd.forward(req, res);
  }
  private String maybeGoback(HttpServletRequest req, Vector errors)
  {
    if (errors.size() > 0) {
      String[] errorArray = (String[])errors.toArray(new String[0]);
      req.setAttribute("errors", errorArray);
      String maybe = req.getParameter("formpage");
      return maybe;
    }
    else
      return null;
  }
}
```

Essentially, we find out which command is responsible for processing a request, and activate this command. The command prepares the list of errors for the JSP, and the request is then forwarded to the next JSP page.

The maybeGoback() method allows the progression of screens to be a bit more flexible. Normally, the data from each screen is processed by the servlet, which then takes the user to the next screen. In case of error, however, we would like to use the first screen to present errors, and then allow the user to correct them. If the error list contains anything, this method returns the name of the original request screen, which is set in the screen itself. If there are no errors, the function returns null, and processing can continue.

447

Here is an example of how the user login request is treated by the `LoginCommand` class:

```java
package ashford.servlet.main;

import javax.servlet.*;
import javax.servlet.http.*;
import java.util.*;

import ashford.util.*;
// Class called by the servlet for processing login command
public class LoginCommand implements Command {
  private String next; // name of next screen in normal sequence

  public LoginCommand(String next) {
    this.next = next;
  }

  public String execute(HttpServletRequest req) throws CommandException {
    String action = req.getParameter("action");
    if (action != null && action.equals("register")) {
      return "register.jsp"; // for new users, go the register screen
    }
    String maybe = null;
    Vector errors = new Vector(); // prepare the list of errors
    String email = req.getParameter("email");
    if (email == null) {
      email = "";
    }
    String password = req.getParameter("password").trim();
    if (password == null) {
      password = "";
    }
    if (email.length() == 0) {
      errors.add("Please provide an email");
      maybe = maybeGoback(req, errors);
      if (maybe != null) {
        return maybe;
      }
    }
    if (password.length() == 0) {
      errors.add("Please provide the password");
      maybe = maybeGoback(req, errors);
      if (maybe != null) {
        return maybe;
      }
    }
    if (!AshfordUtil.isValidEmail(email)) {
      errors.add("Email address is incorrectly formed");
      maybe = maybeGoback(req, errors);
      if (maybe != null) {
        return maybe;
      }
    }
    try {
      ContactBean contact = ContactBean.getContact(email);
      if (contact == null) {
```

```
          errors.add("This email is not registered");
        } else {
          if (contact.getPassword().equals(password)) {
            HttpSession session = req.getSession();
            session.setAttribute("loggedIn", "true");
            session.setAttribute("loginId", contact.getLoginId());
            req.setAttribute("contact.msg", "Contact Logged In Successfully");
          } else {
            errors.add("The password is incorrect");
          }
        }
      }
      maybe = maybeGoback(req, errors);
      if (maybe != null) {
        return maybe;
      }
      return next;
    } catch (Exception e) {
      throw new CommandException("LoginCommand: " + e.getMessage());
    }
  }
  private String maybeGoback(HttpServletRequest req, Vector errors) {
    if (errors.size() > 0) {
      String[] errorArray = (String[]) errors.toArray(new String[0]);
      req.setAttribute("errors", errorArray);
      String maybe = req.getParameter("formpage");
      return maybe;
    } else {
      return null;
    }
  }
}
```

Validation

In putting all data validation in the servlet, we have in fact made all validation server-side. This is a point that may raise objections, so let us discuss this in more detail. There are two choices for data validation: client-side and server-side. The first one is done in the browser using JavaScript. The same Fields and Kolb book has good instructions on how to do client-side validation, and checking for valid e-mail could be done using JavaScript. The advantage of this would be less load on the server, since it is the user's computer that does the work.

The advantages of server-side validation may be formulated as follows. The JSP code is simpler, since it contains no JavaScript. The processing code is more uniform: all possible errors are collected by the servlet in an array, and are then displayed by the JSP at the top of the page. In fact, the author has seen many sites that do error processing in this way.

But the real question of whether or not to use the optimization is not answered in this way, and it remains to be answered for each individual case. As Scott Meyers formulates the rules of optimization in his book *Effective C++* (*ISBN 0-201311-015-5*):

1. Don't do it

2. Profile your application first

This means that the code should work and be made as simple as possible, then you should find the bottlenecks and *only then* optimize them.

In the case of login, it can be argued that the login process happens relatively rarely, since usually we use cookies to identify the user. The errors in it happen even less frequently. Another minor consideration is that the JavaScript validation will bring up a little dialog, thus breaking the uniform flow process of presenting everything on the page. We decided to do the server-side validation; you may decide to do differently.

The LoginBean

Here is the `LoginBean`. Like the other JSP helper beans, it only sets and gets the values. The bean is used by the servlet to pack and pass the values to the JSP page:

```
package ashford.servlet.main;

public class LoginBean {
  private String email;
  private String password;
  private boolean newCustomer;

  public String getEmail() {
    return email;
  }

  public void setEmail(String email) {
    this.email = email;
  }

  public String getPassword() {
    return password;
  }

  public void setPassword(String password) {
    this.password = password;
  }

  public boolean isNewCustomer() {
    return newCustomer;
  }

  public void setNewCustomer(boolean newCustomer) {
    this.newCustomer = newCustomer;
  }
}
```

Login Summary

The Login application is built using JSPs, servlets, JavaBeans, and EJB. The JSPs collect information and send it to the servlet. The servlet processes the data and directs the user to the next screen. The servlet uses the helper JavaBeans to pass information to the JSPs. The servlet also connects to the WebLogic application server, letting the EJBs do the real work. In addition to the login, the code in the complete project contains the registration for the new users, and screens to collect their personal as well as company information.

Coupons

Coupons are marketing tools, each with a specific goal. There are discount coupons, buy one get one free coupons, free giveaway with purchase coupons, and so on. In the world of e-commerce, coupons are even better, in some ways, since, for example, they do not require printing and putting in the Sunday newspaper, but can be inexpensively generated and sent by e-mail. They can serve to attract traffic to the site, advertise sales and promotions, new products, etc. When the user comes to the site, she pastes the coupon number in the appropriate field, which is an equivalent of presenting it to the cashier in a bricks-and-mortar store. To describe coupon specifics, let us start with the coupon creation screen:

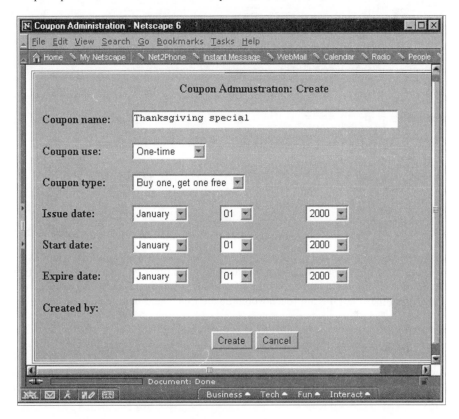

This screen is from the back-office part of the coupons application. The marketing people who want to create and send a new type of coupon use this screen.

From this screenshot, we can see pretty much what information is needed to begin the creation of a coupon issue. Coupons can be of a wide variety of type, such as $ off total, % off total, $ off item, give away item, etc. The one we show in the screenshot, the famous "Buy one, get one free", is a specific type of give away item coupon. It occurs so often that it has its own category. Altogether we had more than 10 types of coupons, created by the marketing people, each serving its specific goal.

In addition, coupons can be single-use, multi-use (unlimited), and limited use (valid for a specific number of times). Thus, there may be a coupon valid for the first 100 customers. Such a coupon would serve to bring a rush of customers to the site. The Rose diagram below captures the coupon data requirements.

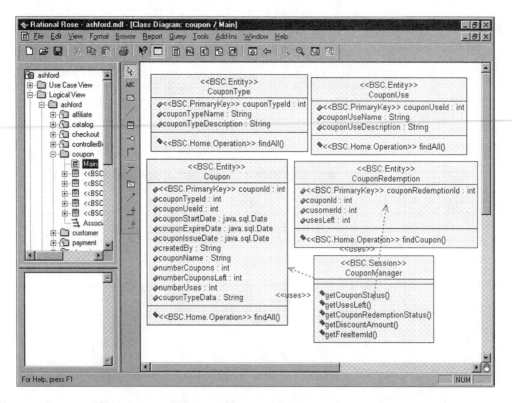

The CouponType EJB represents all the possible types of coupons. Since each type requires specific calculations to implement it, these will have to be hard-coded. In other words, each type will have its formula or algorithm. In theory, one could implement the types using XML descriptors, and a calculator-type program, but the complexity of this approach would be too much, and maintenance would be too hard.

The CouponUse EJB represents the possible uses, as mentioned above, such as single-use, multi- and limited-use. This is a more simple property, and the number of uses allowed will go in the Coupon EJB.

Finally, the Coupon EJB contains the specific details of the coupon: names, dates, use, type. It also has the number of uses, which are needed for the limited-use coupons, such as where only the first 100 comers get to use the coupon.

These first three EJB, characterize coupons issue and are used when the marketing person creates the coupons. There is one row in the database table connected to the Coupon EJB. This illustrates the economy of our approach.

The CouponRedemption EJB, on the other hand, is connected to the database table that represents actual coupon use. It, therefore, contains the customerId, and the number of uses left. A record in this table is only created when the coupon is created for the first time, and is modified on each subsequent re-use, if this is a multi-use coupon.

From the programming point of view, managing a coupon issue fits the same architecture that we used for the login application. JSP pages collect information and send it to the servlet. The servlet does the processing, packs the answers into the helper JavaBeans, and sends them to the JSP; EJBs are responsible for getting the data.

Implementing Coupons

Let's look at an example of a JavaBean, which allows the JSP to get the coupon types, and to store them for subsequent use on all JSPs. Coupon types are going to be re-used by many screens, so it makes sense to cache them in a JavaBean, which gets them only once from the EJB. The `formCouponTypeList()` method is declared `synchronized` because the servlet might occasionally get a few initialization requests at the same time. After it is initialized, the list access is read-only. It is up to the server to decide whether to start another thread in the servlet, or to start another servlet when processing multiple requests. Here's the code for the `CouponTypeBean`:

```
package ashford.servlet.coupon;

import java.util.*;
import javax.ejb.*;
import javax.naming.*;
import java.util.*;
import java.rmi.RemoteException;

import ashford.coupon.*;

import ashford.util.*;

public class CouponTypeBean {
  private int id;
  private String couponTypeDescription;
  private String couponTypeName;
  public int getCouponTypeId() {
    return id;
  }

  public String getCouponTypeDescription() {
    return couponTypeDescription;
  }

  public String getCouponTypeName() {
    return couponTypeName;
  }

  static private CouponTypeBean[] allCouponTypes = null;

  public CouponTypeBean[] getCouponTypes() {
    if (allCouponTypes == null) {
      allCouponTypes = formCouponTypeList();
    }
    return allCouponTypes;
  }

  synchronized private CouponTypeBean[] formCouponTypeList() {
    try {
      Context ctx = AshfordUtil.getInitialContext();
      CouponTypeHome home =
        (CouponTypeHome) ctx.lookup("ashford.coupon.CouponTypeHome");
      Collection couponTypes = new ArrayList();
      Enumeration en = home.findAll();
      while (en.hasMoreElements()) {
```

```
            CouponType the_ejb = (CouponType) en.nextElement();
            couponTypes.add(makeCouponType(the_ejb));
        }
        return (CouponTypeBean[]) couponTypes.toArray(new CouponTypeBean[0]);
    } catch (Exception e) {
        e.printStackTrace();
        return new CouponTypeBean[0];
    }
}

private CouponTypeBean makeCouponType(CouponType the_ejb) {
    CouponTypeBean bean = new CouponTypeBean();
    try {
        bean.couponTypeName = the_ejb.getCouponTypeName();
        bean.couponTypeDescription = the_ejb.getCouponTypeDescription();
        bean.id = the_ejb.getCouponTypeId();
    } catch (Exception e) {}
    return bean;
}

static private Context getInitialContext() throws NamingException {
    try {
        Properties h = new Properties();
        h.put(Context.INITIAL_CONTEXT_FACTORY,
                "weblogic.jndi.WLInitialContextFactory");
        h.put(Context.PROVIDER_URL, url);
        if (user != null) {
            log("user: " + user);
            h.put(Context.SECURITY_PRINCIPAL, user);
            if (serverPassword == null) {
                serverPassword = "";
            }
            h.put(Context.SECURITY_CREDENTIALS, serverPassword);
        }
        return new InitialContext(h);
    } catch (NamingException ne) {
        log("We were unable to get a connection to the WebLogic server at "
                + url);
        log("Please make sure that the server is running.");
        throw ne;
    }
}

private static void log(String s) {
    System.out.println(s);
}

static String url = "http://localhost:7601"; // WLCS port
static String user = null;
static String serverPassword = null;
}
```

Here is part of the JSP code for the coupon creation screen we showed earlier. You can see how the helper JavaBean is being used:

```jsp
<%@ page import="ashford.servlet.coupon.*, ashford.util.*"
errorPage="error.jsp" %>

<html>
<head><title>Coupon Create</title></head>
<body bgcolor="white">

<%@ include file = "/ashford/shared/sticky.jsp" %>
<%@ include file = "/ashford/shared/listerrors.jsp" %>

<form name="menu" action="/coupon" method="post">
<table border="1" align="center"><tr><td>
<table bgcolor="tan" border="0" align="center"
     cellpadding="10" cellspacing="0">
<tr><th colspan="2">Coupon Administration: Create
</th></tr>

<tr><td><b>Coupon name:</b></td>
<td>
  <input maxLength="64" size="30" name="CouponName">
</td>
</tr>

<tr><td><b>Coupon use:</b></td>
<td>
<select name="CouponUse">
  <%
    CouponUseBean[] couponUses = new CouponUseBean().getCouponUses();
    for (int i = 0; i < couponUses.length; ++i) {
      %>
      <option value = "<%= couponUses[i].getCouponUseId() %>"
      <%
        if (i == 0)
          out.write("selected");
      %>
      >
      <%= couponUses[i].getCouponUseName() %>
      </option>
      <%
    }
  %>
</select>

</td></tr>
<tr><td><b>Coupon type:</b></td>
<td>
<select name="CouponType">
  <%
    CouponTypeBean[] couponTypes = new CouponTypeBean().getCouponTypes();
      for (int i = 0; i < couponTypes.length; ++i) {
        %>
        <option value = "<%= couponTypes[i].getCouponTypeId() %>"
        <%
          if (i == 0)
            out.write("selected");
        %>
```

```
        >
        <%= couponTypes[i].getCouponTypeName() %>
        </option>
        <%
    }
  %>
</select>
</td></tr>

<!--There is more to the JSP, but none that you need to see here -->
</body>
</html>
```

Here is the `CouponCommand` class, part of the `coupon` servlet, which processes the input from the JSP above:

```
package ashford.servlet.coupon;

import javax.servlet.*;
import javax.servlet.http.*;
import java.util.*;

import ashford.util.*;

public class CouponCommand implements Command {
  private String next;

  public CouponCommand(String next) {
    this.next = next; // name of next JSP page to go to
  }

  public String execute(HttpServletRequest req) throws CommandException {
    AshfordUtil.dumpParameters(req);

    // get all parameters from request
    String couponIdStr = req.getParameter("CouponId");
    String couponUse = req.getParameter("CouponUse");
    String couponType = req.getParameter("CouponType");

    String issueMonth = req.getParameter("IssueMonth");
    String issueDay = req.getParameter("IssueDay");
    String issueYear = req.getParameter("IssueYear");
    String startMonth = req.getParameter("StartMonth");
    String startDay = req.getParameter("StartDay");
    String startYear = req.getParameter("StartYear");
    String expireMonth = req.getParameter("ExpireMonth");
    String expireDay = req.getParameter("ExpireDay");
    String expireYear = req.getParameter("ExpireYear");

    int couponId = 0;
    int couponUseId = 0;
    int couponTypeId = 0;
    int issueMonthId = 0;
    int issueDayId = 0;
    int issueYearId = 0;
    int startMonthId = 0;
    int startDayId = 0;
    int startYearId = 0;
    int expireDayId = 0;
```

```
    int expireYearId = 0;
    int expireMonthId = 0;

    try { // parse parameters
      if (couponIdStr != null) {
        couponId = Integer.parseInt(couponIdStr);
      }
      couponUseId = Integer.parseInt(couponUse);
      couponTypeId = Integer.parseInt(couponType);
      issueMonthId = Integer.parseInt(issueMonth);
      issueDayId = Integer.parseInt(issueDay);
      issueYearId = Integer.parseInt(issueYear);
      startMonthId = Integer.parseInt(startMonth);
      startDayId = Integer.parseInt(startDay);
      startYearId = Integer.parseInt(startYear);
      expireMonthId = Integer.parseInt(expireMonth);
      expireDayId = Integer.parseInt(expireDay);
      expireYearId = Integer.parseInt(expireYear);
    } catch (NumberFormatException e) {
      throw new CommandException(e.getMessage());
    }
    String createdBy = req.getParameter("CreatedBy");
    String couponName = req.getParameter("CouponName");

    // set parameters in the JavaBean
    CouponBean coupon = new CouponBean();
    coupon.setCouponId(couponId);
    coupon.setCouponTypeId(couponTypeId);
    coupon.setCouponUseId(couponUseId);
    coupon.setCouponIssueDate(issueMonthId, issueDayId, issueYearId);
    coupon.setCouponStartDate(startMonthId, startDayId, startYearId);
    coupon.setCouponExpireDate(expireMonthId, expireDayId, expireYearId);
    coupon.setCreatedBy(createdBy);
    coupon.setCouponName(couponName);

    // store parameters in the EJB/database
    try {
      coupon.put();
      req.setAttribute("coupon.coupon", coupon);
      CouponDetailBean detail =
        CouponDetailBean.getCouponDetail(coupon.getCouponId());
      req.setAttribute("coupon.detail", detail);
      return next;
    } catch (Exception e) {
      throw new CommandException("CreateCommand: " + e.getMessage());
    }
  }
}
```

The code above gets all parameters passed from the JSP, and packs them in the helper JavaBean, CouponBean. This JavaBean stores the data in the database by connecting to the EJB, in the put() method. The CouponDetail JavaBean is passed to the next JSP, which will describe coupon details, and which will need the coupon name from the first screen. It can be noted that the user can't make any spelling errors, since all their choices are drop-downs. Therefore, all exception handling is only for the needs of the programmer while debugging.

This part of the coupon application is conceptually simple, and is the same as any other item management application, be it user registration, or handling of Frequently Asked Questions (FAQ), an example used by Fields and Kolb. The really interesting part of coupons is the management of coupon issues, and redeeming them by the user, as will be explained below.

Managing Coupons

At first, one is tempted to follow a simple-minded approach of imitating physical coupons. Since these are printed and then distributed, we could similarly "print" them by creating as many records in the database as there are single coupons. Then we could wait for the users to arrive and redeem them. The problem with this approach is that most coupons are never redeemed. There would therefore be millions of records in the database, just wasting space.

So, the second option would be to create just one record in the database for each coupon issue, and then send out the news about this coupon to everybody on a given mailing list. The problem with this is that the coupon can then be posted on a bulletin board, or on some site, and thus made available to everybody, without any limitation. There were cases where this indeed did happen! This, in turn, is almost the same as permanently changing the price, without much effect on the site traffic.

The following solution allows achieving the maximum impact with the minimum amount of work. Every user on the given mailing list is sent their own version of the coupon. When the user comes back, we check whether the e-mail address at which she got the coupon matches our records. Now everybody has personalized coupons, which only they can redeem, with the appropriate rules, thus creating a sense of urgency. The mailing list can include all registered users, or all corporate users; it can be sent to the people in a certain age or income group, if this data is available, or be targeted in any other way.

The main problems for the developer then become "what information to put on the coupon" and "how to put it on the coupon". We need the following pieces of information to be present on the coupon:

❑   coupon_id

❑   mailing_list_id

❑   user_id

coupon_id is the entry to the database table which tracks coupon issues. The mailing_list_id is an entry to the database table that stores mailing lists.. Finally, the user_id is the id of the user in that list. Once the user goes to the checkout and presents the coupon code, which will look something like 23-4-3150, we can identify the coupon, verify the user and proceed.

The only problem is that we do not want to give out such valuable numbers and become prone to hacking and tampering with the coupons. Actually, we did not readily see how the tampering could be done. However, we wanted to have foresight in our own eyes and in the eyes of the management, and we wanted to look high-tech to the users. We also noticed that many coupon codes used by other sites were incomprehensible, and decided to follow suit.

Cryptography is already provided in Java. We have used examples from Jonathan Knudsen's *Java Cryptography* (*ISBN 1-565924-02-9*) adjusting them to fit our purpose. In doing this, we kept in mind that we needed to achieve a tradeoff between how much effort was put into securing the system, and how much protection we wanted. Our needs were somewhere in the middle: we did not want to expose the inner workings of our system, but we did want to be able to disallow the use of a coupon if a real problem developed, so we did not need too much.

We also did not want the resulting coupon code to be too long and unwieldy. Even if it is only copied and pasted, the problems might arise when it is so long that it does not fit on one line of a coupon mailing letter. These are the standard considerations in using encryption.

Before we present the code, let us offer a few remarks. The security package `javax.crypto.*` can be downloaded from SUN's site, at http://java.sun.com/products/jce. The two jars that one will need to put in the class path are `jce1_2_1.jar`, and `sunjce_provider.jar`. The first one provides the JCE API, while the second contains the provider algorithms. More on this can be found in Knudsen's book, but the code can be run without knowing the details.

Below is a program that serves our encryption needs:

```java
package com.ashford.coupon;

import java.io.*;
import java.security.*;

import javax.crypto.*;

import sun.misc.*;

public class CouponEncodingDecoding {

  // This is the main for testing both encoding and decoding. It calls
  // the functions which are later called from production program.

  static public void main(String[] args) throws Exception {

    // Check arguments
    if (args.length < 2) {
      System.out.println("Usage: CouponEncodingDecoding -e|-d text");
      return;
    }

    // Print out and make sure you've added the provider to your
    // java.security correctly. A misspelling results in quietly
    // not adding the provider
    Provider[] providers = Security.getProviders();
    for (int i = 0; i < providers.length; ++i) {
      System.out.println(providers[i]);
    }

    // Get or create key. When first run, the program will create
    // the encryption key and write it to a file.
    // On subsequent runs it will read the key back
    Key key;
    try {
      ObjectInputStream in =
        new ObjectInputStream(new FileInputStream("SecretKey.ser"));
      key = (Key) in.readObject();
      in.close();
    } catch (FileNotFoundException e) {
      KeyGenerator generator = KeyGenerator.getInstance("DES");
      generator.init(new SecureRandom());
      key = generator.generateKey();
      ObjectOutputStream out =
        new ObjectOutputStream(new FileOutputStream("SecretKey.ser"));
      out.writeObject(key);
      out.close();
```

```
      }

      // Get a cipher object
      Cipher cipher = Cipher.getInstance("DES/ECB/PKCS5Padding");

      // Encrypt or decrypt the input string.
      if (args[0].indexOf("e") != -1) {
        cipher.init(Cipher.ENCRYPT_MODE, key);

          // Use Base 64 encoding to make the string easy to print
          // and send over the Internet
          String base64 = encodeCouponInfo(cipher, key, args[1]);
          System.out.println(base64);
      } else if (args[0].indexOf("d") != -1) {
        cipher.init(Cipher.DECRYPT_MODE, key);
        String result = decodeCouponCode(cipher, key, args[1]);
        System.out.println(result);
      }
    }
    static public String encodeCouponInfo(Cipher cipher, Key key,
                                    String couponInfo) throws Exception {
      cipher.init(Cipher.ENCRYPT_MODE, key); // initialize cipher
      byte[] stringBytes = couponInfo.getBytes("UTF8");
      byte[] raw = cipher.doFinal(stringBytes); // perform encoding
      BASE64Encoder encoder = new BASE64Encoder();
      String base64 = encoder.encode(raw); // convert to ASCII
      return base64;
    }
    static private String decodeCouponCode(Cipher cipher, Key key,
                                    String couponCode) throws Exception {
      BASE64Decoder decoder = new BASE64Decoder();
      byte[] raw = decoder.decodeBuffer(couponCode);
      byte[] stringBytes = cipher.doFinal(raw);
      String result = new String(stringBytes, "UTF8");
      return result;
    }
  }
```

Base64 (as previously discussed in Chapter 8) is a system of representing arrays of bytes as ASCII strings. We use it because we will need to send the encoding through the e-mail, which may only support 7-bit ASCII.

The functions that do the real work, and that are used in the application by the mailing program, are encodeCouponInfo() and decodeCouponCode(). We have added the main() method to the class, so that it can be used and tested independently. In this, we followed the advice of Extreme Programming on keeping the test code. Java is especially conducive to this, since it, unlike C/C++, allows adding a main() method to any class, thus allowing testing and keeping the test code with the class.

Advice – Write the test code and keep it.

Continuing with our example; by running CouponEncodingDecoding, the coupon information string, 23-4-3150, will be converted into this string: gVYQW81sQOkpLk+jSg/ctQ==. This is not too long, and intimidating enough. If you run the program to decode the string, you will get 23-4-3150 back.

We wanted, however, to test against the possibility of hacking. So we tried to modify the code and to decode it. The results of this are as follows:

1. Code: `gVYQW8lsQOkpLk+jSg/ctQ=+`

Result: `23-4-3150`

We got these results when we modified the part that belongs to `Base64` wrapping, and as you see it hasn't affected the results:

2. Code: `gVYQW8lsQOkpLk+jSg/ctQ=-.`

Result: `23-4-3150`

The same comment applies.

3. Code: `cVYQW8lsQOkpLk+jSg/ctQ=-`

Results: `?`

This is the real ? sign. Time to tell the user "sorry," somebody has tampered with the coupon.

4. Code: `gVYQW8lsQOkpLk+jSg/dtQ==`

Result:

```
javax.crypto.BadPaddingException: Given final block not properly padded
```

No problem, we can catch an exception. In fact, our functions are declared as throwing an exception, so we will have to catch. The coupon is not accepted of course. Finally,

5. Code: `zVYQW8lsQOkpLk+jSg/ctQ=-`

Result: `z|zt`, where | stands for some unprintable character.

Well, we can check for the format to be only numbers separated by dashes.

We have achieved our goal: the coupons are unique, and reasonably tamper-proof. Till now, we either combined the standard methods into an application, like we did in Login, or used our judgment on the balance of the effort/result, as we did in Coupons, but we have not seen a challenging problem or a new solution. Now is the time to show one, which is automated sales help.

Automated Sales Help

The impetus for this application came from the following events. As the designers of the site, we were fortunate enough to be able to review the major e-commerce packages. In most cases, the company technical people gave us a demo. While it was amazing how much was already done, we also saw an unexplored opportunity.

Personalization is the trend of the moment. Each customer sees pages that are generated specifically for them, as defined by their preferences. How are these preferences determined? They are collected from databases and from click-through analysis. Let's dig into this a little deeper.

There are already quite a few databases, where the consumer data is collected. As an example, when a user is coming to a ready-made clothing site, the site may have only some of her information. But, by connection to a different database, the site may get more complete information, such as the family size and income group. Let us say the user is a young mother, with two children, who is looking for winter clothing. If all that can be known, the next generated page that this user sees may have an offer of some winter coats which, coupled with the right incentive, such as a discount, can lead to a sale. There are software products on the market that do this kind of database lookup.

Click-through analysis is, as its name suggests, registering the pattern of user behavior on the site, with the attempt to guess at what the user is looking for, and what she should be shown on the next generated page. There is software on the market that does this kind of analysis too.

The site designers can now formulate the rules of how the pages are generated, based on database findings and click-through analysis. These rules can be programmed into the system, and the most common example of them is giving a discount.

However, in the terms of the sales expert Stephan Shiffman, this is still "shoving information onto the customer". As is well known in sales, a good salesperson has to listen more than talk. The rules should then implement the proven sales strategies and be adaptive to the customer reaction. If we don't ask the customer, we're walking in the dark. The statistical rules may be good for what they are, but a salesman needs to work individually and most importantly get the feedback. Asking, "This is my take on it, what do you think?" is one of the most important rules in sales.

In the case of our example rule, giving a discount, it is not as obvious as it seems. As is known in sales, giving a discount too early in the sales process may be a turn off. It may not lead to a sale because the customer may lose trust in the product. Alternatively, the sale might have gone through without a discount. If we could ask the customer questions and ascertain in which sales stage we are, we will be in a much better position to take the next step because we'll have a better idea of which direction to take that step in.

What is Automated Sales Help?

Sites that allow customer interaction in the natural language of the customer are thus likely to become increasingly common. A handful of companies doing **Natural Language Processing** (**NLP**) on the web appeared recently. They allow developers to automate answering questions, analyzing e-mail, and providing other forms of customer interaction. Many of these companies have surfaced just before or during the writing of this chapter. The list, which is by no means complete, would include AskJeeves, kanisa.com, mindmaker.com, lingomotors.com, and neuromedia.com.

Two points became clear from our research. The technology was maturing, and it was available. We could think of an application for it. However, the crux of the matter is not how to teach the site to interact in a natural language, since technologies for this are available, but what the site is going to ask and to answer.

The study of the literature shows that the most successful interactive systems paid much attention to the contents of the interaction. "Parry" by Colby and "CONVERSE" are two examples of such systems.

Parry, by K.M. Colby, was designed quite a few years ago. Initially its goal was to simulate a psychiatric patient, but in the process the goal was changed to an electronic psychiatrist. The most important part of Parry, one that probably allows it the high degree of success, is its semantic database. In simple terms, Parry is prepared to discuss its topic. This database consists of over 40,000 expressions (words, phrases, idioms), and a set of 11,000 conceptual patterns. These were hand picked by the author and his family. A fascinating account of Parry can be found in *Machine Conversations* (ed *Yorick Wilks, ISBN 0-792385-44-6*).

The system that attracted our attention most, both by its results and by its philosophy, is CONVERSE, described in the same book. The major lesson that CONVERSE took from the previous work, and from Parry was that "Parry had something to say, just as people do, and did not simply react to what you said to it". Its zanier misunderstandings could be attributed to its abnormal nature. We will go back to CONVERSE later on in this chapter.

The idea of having something to say rang the bell. We had enough excitement on our site, beautiful jewelry, watches, and fragrances. If our **intelligent assistant** (**IA**) misunderstood the question, it could still mask it up by talking about what it had to show, discounts that it could give, its products' good points, etc.

We went to the conversation sites and tried the dialogs. The conversations were not perfect, but blended with our approach, it would not matter. Now we needed to know how to program the IA for ourselves.

Basics for an Intelligent Assistant

Having looked around at various examples of what we were hoping to base our IA on, we formulated a list of what we were going to need. Essentially, these are a grammar analyzer, a vocabulary, the semantic model (the meaning of what the user says), and our own scripts to direct the conversations.

Grammar Analyzer

Grammar analyzers are readily available, many of them for free, and can be tried on the web without installing the software. Here is an example of Link Grammar (http://www.link.cs.cmu.edu), parsing a sentence:

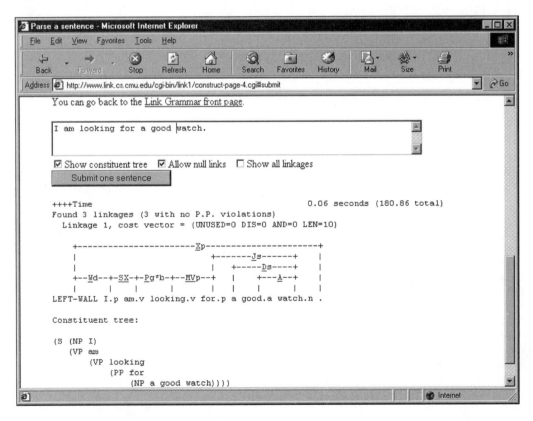

Another available grammar parser is the one by Alpo Lind (http://pointti.vip.fi). This grammar parser is written completely in Java.

Vocabulary and Semantics

With the grammar analyzed, we need to try to guess at the word meaning. For example, the words "buy", "acquire", "am interested in", and so on, all mean about the same thing in the context the IA would find them: the site visitor is interested in buying an item which is to be mentioned next in the phrase. The electronic vocabulary called WordNet (http://www.cogsci.princeton.edu/~wn/) fits in nicely here. Actually, WordNet is much more than a vocabulary; it is also a semantic database, since it organizes the words into a network of meaning. The following screenshot is an example of WordNet showing synonyms for the word "buy":

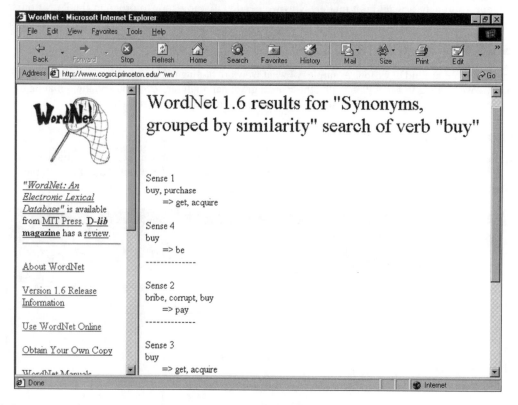

As it turns out, the conversational system that we used, CONVERSE, uses WordNet internally. There are good reasons for using WordNet: it is free, can be downloaded, and is used by a number of people, as described in *Wordnet: An Electronic Lexical Database* by *Christiane Fellbaum, ISBN 0-262061-97-X*. In addition, there are now versions of WordNet in major European languages. With internationalization being the way of the future, this is an important feature. Additionally, WordNet allows for differences between, say, jewelry and jewellery, by providing the later as a synonym for the former.

Next comes the semantics, or the meaning of what has been said. While it really may be much more complex, one can start by looking for keywords indicating the user intent, and classifying them with WordNet. The first conversational program, called Eliza, was based on keyword search and achieved impressive performance.

Joseph Weizenbaum originally wrote Eliza in FORTRAN, in 1966. Below is a dialog with the Java applet implementation of Eliza available at http://home.adelphia.net/~lifeisgood/eliza/eliza.htm. The salient feature of the program is that it determines the type of question using keywords, and then asks a question back, or offers a comment based on the keyword:

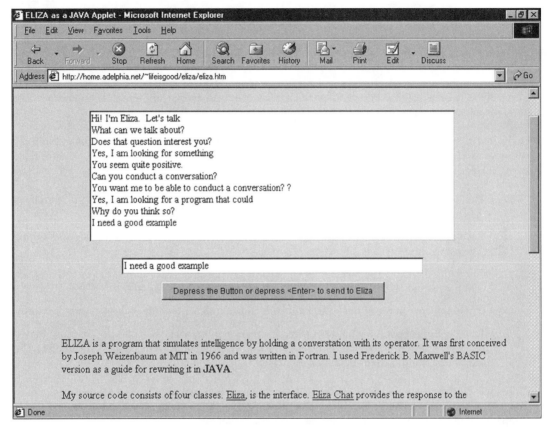

What we have described above is the do-it-yourself way. You can get all the tools from the web, and start to experiment. You would also need a reasonable amount of natural language processing (NLP) knowledge. Beyond the prototype, you would need to handle a lot of special cases, such as recognizing personal names (in our case it would be mostly product brands), polite response to rude language, etc.

As application developers though, we wanted to concentrate on what our IA should say, not how it should do it. We therefore got in contact with our co-designers of CONVERSE. This system had another advantage: it won first prize in the 1997 Loebner competition. This competition is an online version of the Turing test, where live judges talk to both computer programs and live people, trying to determine which is which. An interesting part of the script of the CONVERSE succeeding and failing is found in Appendix E.

However, even its weakness proved the point. You can see how the program keeps driving its own way, despite the apparent difficulty with understanding the question. It masked its, sometimes imperfect, responses by the attempt to squeeze in its own ideas. That mirrored some of the sales techniques we were planning on implementing. If we could make it unobtrusive and not too pushy, it could be an acceptable salesman.

Actually, it would be a saleswoman too, depending on the circumstances. It was easy enough to give it a name, depending on the user and on guessing which name the user would like better to deal with, male or female. We had no problem remembering the name that the user encountered at first, and continuing the conversation with the same person, with the knowledge of the prior dialog, or starting afresh with another person.

The final advantage of CONVERSE is that one of us (Alex) helped to design it in the first place.

Motivation for Automating Sales Help

Before investing any time or resources into a project, we should investigate the business reasons for it. In the words of the English mathematician Littlewood, "It is too early to indulge in premature optimism". Of course, new technology sounds very exciting, but we need hard facts.

Let us first investigate the concept of online help. If we go to a B2C site, we sometimes find a way to chat to a customer assistant. This may be very helpful and is intended to help the customer select a product, but it does have problems. Here is an incomplete list of those problems:

❑ The load is unpredictable. It is hard to dedicate people to customer chat, so it often falls on the customer service people who are busy with their regular work.

❑ Customer service is there to help solve problems, often of the technical nature, and authorize returns, work out claims, etc. It is not a sales force.

❑ Often, people enjoy the talk – they can chat away for hours. It is somewhat of a luxury when taking a live person's time, and is usually stopped.

❑ Often, the communication is unreliable and slow, both for technical and personal reasons.

❑ Those technical people who have used this feature often wish they had not, because they can visualize a customer service representative on the other side, trying to do the same searches as our visitor could have done better by herself.

A possible solution is to outsource the sales help, and indeed there are companies that specialize in this. Apart from setting this up, some of the considerations outlined above still remain, most notably training the outside company people in the site's products, and especially sales training.

All of these problems could be overcome if the help is automatic. It may be more economical too, but such financial analysis is beyond the scope of this chapter. In fact, there are some factors where a program might come out ahead. As a recent study showed, people talking to the computer do not want to be fooled that this a human (even though sometimes they might), and will gladly forgive some errors. In fact, some people will appreciate the impersonal nature of the programmatic conversation agent. This was exactly the justification for Parry, a psychoanalytical program that would help people say things that they may not have said to a human.

Will the site actually tell the user they are talking to a program? If we look at existing sites implementing some form of NLP, they never insist that you are talking to a human, but never explicitly say that it is a program. They sometimes even show a picture of a person, and allow this person to change posture, which again suggests computer generated images, but does not spell it out. So it would seem that this is a social and psychological question, to be answered by some norms which will be established in the future.

Our major motivation, however, is sales. This means that we, as application developers, have to pay a lot of attention to what the system is going to say. Which leads us to the topic of sales scripts.

Sales Scripts

The automatic sales system has to know what to say, how to understand the customer replies, and decide what to do next. Let us start from the top level – what to say.

We have a good reason to start from this level. Usually the NLP textbooks, which want to build block by block and make things absolutely clear, start from words and even letters, and then proceed to grammar and meaning (semantics). By the time you get there, you are out of steam. This is why many systems are very complex and powerful on the NLP side, but may take some improvement on the "what to say" side.

However, this textbook approach is the same as taking a live person, teaching her grammar, and then asking her to sell jewelry. Obviously, it will not work. The emphasis has to be on sales training.

For our sales approach we chose to use the numerous publications by Stephan Schiffman. If we were to summarize his approach in one word, it is probably "Ask". Too many sales techniques, as Schiffman notices, are "shoving" products down the customer's throat. Even those sites that use database and click through analysis in order to decide which pages to generate and show to the user, follow the same mistake.

In his *25 Sales Strategies, ISBN 1-580621-16-3* Schiffman formulates simple but effective techniques. Here are some examples:

- ❏ Ask questions.
- ❏ The goal of the question is not the sale, but the next step.
- ❏ Observe. Form conclusions.
- ❏ Ask, "What do you think?"

Here is an example of how to ask the right questions. A salesman finds a cow in the office, which the customer has put there for stress management:

> Why did you get a cow?
>
> How did you get it?
>
> How did you decide on this?

More complex questions:

> How did you come to decide to put a cow in your office?
>
> How long have you been using this cow as a stress management tool?
>
> Why do you think that stress management was important to your organization?
>
> Have you looked at other types of stress management tools?
>
> Which types?

Our Own Sales Scripts

Guided by this, we started developing our sales scripts. At each step in the conversation, the system evaluates whether it can take an immediate action, like showing an item to the customer, or whether it should ask some more questions. Asking more questions is the key to continuing the sales process.

Consider for example, this script.

> C (customer). Hello.
>
> IA (intelligent assistant). Hello. How can I help you?
>
> C. I am looking for a present.

The IA needs to know more, so it asks:

> IA. Is this for yourself or for somebody else?
>
> C. It is for my wife.

The answer is revealing the gender and the probably search direction. IA will now try to determine the price range by offering a few alternatives:

> IA. Would you like to look at the latest fashion, or at the bargains?
>
> C. I am looking for a good price.

The IA shows some of the specials, and immediately asks:

> IA. What do you think?

From this sample dialog, we can see the major design points of the IA system. It:

- ❏ Gradually accumulates information
- ❏ Decides whether to take action, ask more questions, or get feedback
- ❏ Is using sales rules

Based on these ideas, here are the scripts for jewelry sales dialogs:

Script 1

> Hello, how can I help you today?
>
> Thank you, I am just looking.
>
> Do you like jewelry?
>
> Yes.
>
> Which kind do you like?
>
> Earrings.
>
> Would you like me to show you the latest fashion? (Shows)
>
> What do you think?
>
> I would rather look for something less fancy.
>
> Would you care to look at our bargains? (Shows)
>
> What do you think?

Script 2

Hi, my name is Lauren (names are generated depending upon policies).

May I ask you yours?

John.

Are you looking for something for yourself, John, or for a present?

A present for my girlfriend.

How old is she (OK to ask, and we will get an idea of his age too)?

26.

A ring, a bracelet, or something else?

A bracelet please...

(Shows) How do you like them? You can click on the one you like most.

I need something more striking.

How striking?

With a beautiful stone.

(Performs the search and shows)

What do you think?

I like it.

You can have it shipped today. What would you say? (Attempt at closing)

I'd rather look at something else.

What don't you like about this one?

The price is too high.

Women like this bracelet because (gives reason). I can show you others, or I am authorized to make discounts.

(Waits for response)

Script 3

(Dialog with a woman who is looking for a ring).

Do you have rings already?

Yes, 3, but I am looking for something special.

In what way?

Something with a flare.

Can I show you the latest fashions?

What this Means for Our Application

Obviously, a system of this kind is complex. A prototype can be constructed rather quickly if it is based on some existing system, like CONVERSE. Bringing it to perfection is quite another matter. Luckily, perfection is not required for our purposes.

As studies indicate, people have different expectations from computer conversation than from real people. People do not want to be fooled; they feel good knowing that they are talking to the computer, and prefer to use its advantages rather than linger on its deficiencies and differences from a human. People will forgive a blunder, in exchange for the following:

- ❏ Knowing that they are talking to the computer makes people feel better since know they are not intruding

- ❏ No problem talking any time of day or night

- ❏ Even though people have a tendency to give some human qualities to the computer, they have less problem of looking bad in a computer's eyes

In the words of the "CONVERSE" designers, some of the zanier misunderstandings of PARRY were written off because it was imitating the psychiatric patient.

We do not have to look far to make our Intelligent Assistant engaging. After all, it is selling jewelry. It always has something interesting to show. It can offer discounts (within the limits predefined by the sales department, but the user does not know those limits). It can even give occasional presents.

As mentioned above, armed with some NLP knowledge we can build a conversation agent ourselves. However, if we can get help, we can concentrate on the product knowledge, sales techniques, and technical integration. We were lucky to get in contact with the designers of CONVERSE, and the following describes how we applied its techniques in our application.

Overview of CONVERSE

CONVERSE was developed jointly by Intelligent Research Ltd. of London and Sheffield University from 1994 to 1997 in an effort to create an intelligent conversational partner. It won the 1997 Loebner contest in New York, being the 'most human' among all the competing computer programs. The Loebner contest is a live version of the Turing test (http://www.loebner.net/Prizef/loebner-prize.html). CONVERSE very nearly fooled one of the judges that it was a human: it answered correctly questions about her birthday, age, and star sign, but could not say whether she learned to drive in a stick-shift or an automatic car (see Appendix E).

In developing CONVERSE, traditional NLP techniques (such as syntactic parsing) were blended with simpler methods (such as string matching, and spelling correction). The key features of CONVERSE are as follows:

- ❏ CONVERSE uses a commercially available (and very impressive) statistical parser in conjunction with a semantic post-processor to provide bottom-up information extraction. This is combined with a weight-driven mechanism for changing topics, and a range of scripts, so that CONVERSE provides top-down control of a conversation to accompany the information extraction.

- ❏ To merge the top-down and bottom-up approaches, CONVERSE used a MicroQuery module. This added flexibility in the use of the output of the syntactic parser, and even allowed the possibility of replacing it entirely with simple pattern matching.

❑　A programmed character personality that can easily be altered. The personality details are stored in the Person Database (PDB). This database allows us to control all of the details that are used to design the scripts that the character personality will use. Even a slight change in these details will alter the way in which the scripts are designed, to take into account this new information. The PDB also stores and keeps information retrieved from the user interacting with it, and will keep it for further use at a later stage. For the duration of the Loebner competition, the personality was that of a 26-year old female editor for Vanity Fair called Catherine, born in the UK, but currently living in New York.

❑　By giving CONVERSE access to the WordNet thesaurus network, it not only knew individual words, but also their synonyms. A large proper name list also achieved the illusion of knowing about a number of people and objects. Of course, having access to WordNet also gave us access to the other information offered by that service.

Obviously, our first goal was to win the Loebner competition, as this would create a great deal of good publicity for us. Because of this, we decided to take charge of the conversation, and run through our programmed scripts unless the user wanted to change the subject. If the user asked a question, it would be acknowledged (if not answered) before returning to the script. Although this is only a very basic solution to the problem, it worked well in the context of the Loebner contest, and may work well in any situation where a short dialogue is required.

One such example of this would be the case where we are using the program to simulate a jewelry salesman. The salesman must drive the conversation, typically offering choices, and trying to find out what the customer's requirements are, in order to lead to a successfully closed sale. This will obviously not work in every situation, but when the script has been designed to look like a real person's speech, and the questions only require a small set of answers, the user has no choice but to respond to those answers – and our illusion of talking to a real person is complete.

What Else Do We Need

In order to extract information from the user's input, we used Prospero Software's PARSER, later referred to as simply PROSPERO, a statistically trained syntactic parser written by Mike Oakes (http://www.prosperosoftware.com/nls.html). While PROSPERO was very successful at parsing grammatically correct sentences (it was trained on a set of Times articles), it had limitations in parsing arbitrary dialogue input. In order to cover up for these deficiencies, and also to provide the link between the syntactic representation of a sentence and its meaning, two modules were designed: Parser Post-Processor (PPP) and the MicroQuery module.

If a sentence is parsable, PPP splits its parse tree into smaller chunks (individual clauses), and flattens out these chunks producing a list of slots (such as subject, verb, and object). If the sentence is not parsable, PPP just outputs it as it is, plus the list of content words and any proper names. The MicroQuery module provided a link between the output of the PPP and the rest of the system, allowing any component to ask an arbitrary question against the set of PPP slots, matching each slot against a specified pattern or using WordNet. This way, we can make a decision whether to use the parser's output or to resort to a plain string match.

Using the parser's output is, of course, the easier and preferred option, but this is often not possible due to the parser's limited coverage. String matching always works; however, there is no way to know what the user typed in the rest of the sentence. Decisions about whether string matching or parser slots should be used is usually done empirically, based on specific examples, and what the parser can and cannot handle.

In what follows, we will explain CONVERSE scripts, parsing, PPP and MicroQueries in more detail using a sketch of a jewelry sales script as an example. The general CONVERSE architecture is shown in the following figure:

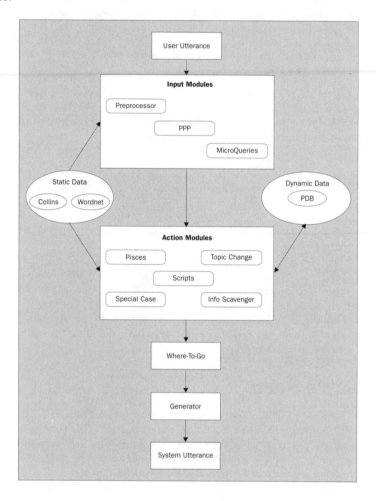

Scripts

Each script is a tree, with nodes being script lines and branches matching the user's input against a set of patterns: syntactic, string, or WordNet matches. A sketch of the jewelry sales script is shown in the diagram in the *Scripts in the Application* section (next), with the corresponding branches listed under it. This sketch closely follows the guidelines laid out by CONVERSE, but does not correspond to an existing script. It is given here to illustrate the concept of designing a script in the jewelry sales domain.

Each script line contains "canned" (pre-programmed) text that can be augmented by inserting strings from the PDB (system or customer name, star sign, etc.) and can also be randomly varied using a set of options enclosed in curly brackets. At runtime, strings from the PDB are inserted in the text, and CONVERSE's SenGen module randomly selects one text option from the list enclosed in curly brackets (say, {present | gift}). Each branch is implemented as a set of MicroQueries (described in the next section); each matching the user's input against a specific type of sentence, such as "I am looking for a ring".

The script interpreter starts from the top node and traverses the tree downward based on the user's input. In the jewelry sales script, the system first introduces itself and asks for the customer's name:

"Hello, my name is Lauren. What is yours?"

If the user types in his or her name, say, John (branch 1), the system stores his name in PDB under "CUSTOMER NAME" and asks:

"Well, John, are you looking for something for yourself or for a gift?"

Then, if John types in "I am looking for a gift for my girlfriend", the system stores this fact in the PDB, and continues on to the GIFT SALES SCRIPT (branch 3). The gift sales script will use information stored in the PDB to decide which items to show to John (depending on whether he is buying a gift for his girlfriend, or, say, mother). John may type, "I am looking for a ring (or a bracelet)" and then the system will show the available items (branch 5):

"May I show you what we have?"

and then go on to the SPECIFIC SALES SCRIPT already knowing what John wants. If John says "I am just looking", the system will not be too pushy (branch 6). If John's input matched none of the above, the system will continue with a general question:

"Do you like jewelry?"

and continue on to the GENERAL SALES SCRIPT.

Going back to the first line of the script, if the system can't recognize the user's name, it continues with the general question (branch 2):

"How can I help you today?"

and then acts similarly to what has been described in the previous paragraph (branches 7, 8, 9).

CONVERSE contains 60 scripts on topics such as crime, the Simpsons, food, travel, etc. All scripts were initially designed by hand, and then entered into computer using SED, a script editor implemented in Tcl/Tk.

Scripts in the Application

CONVERSE follows the script most of the time with several exceptions. For example, the user may specifically ask to change the topic ("I don't want to talk about jewelry"), and then the topic change module will interfere and go to the different script. Also, if the user types in any rude language or anything referring to sex and violence, this is taken care of by the Special Case module, which responds to rude talk accordingly. Information Scavenger extracts any possible information from the user's utterance.

The Pisces module is the "intelligent part" of CONVERSE. If a user types in a question or request (and PROSPERO can recognize this a good deal of the time), Pisces first classifies the type of question into 20 different types, and attempts to answer this question by using information from the Person Database, WordNet, and the list of proper names from the Harper-Collins dictionary. If an accurate match is found, Pisces produces a response. If not, it outputs a filler corresponding to a question type ("I don't know" in response to "Do you know...?") or a general filler ("I can't talk about it right now"). This way CONVERSE can pretend to be intelligent and not ignore the user even if it cannot answer its request.

Each of the CONVERSE action modules (Scripts, Topic Change, Special Case, Information Scavenger and Pisces) produces a bid from 0 (I can't say anything about this) to 100 (I can respond to this). The Where-To-Go module decides which bid is taken (there may be several), and passes the text output to the Generator which prints out the system's response:

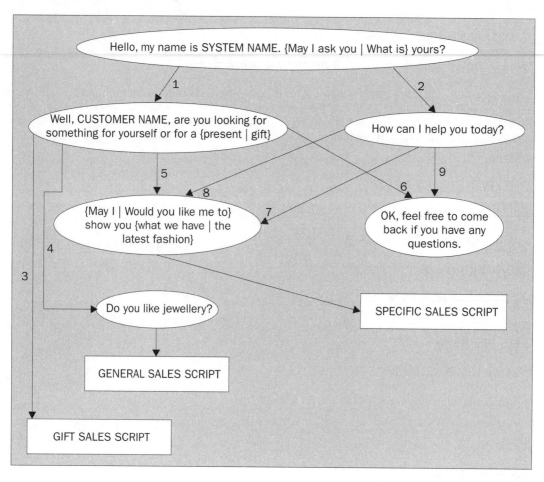

Here is the description of the branches mentioned on the figure above.

"Hello, ..." node:

Branch 1: Matches "My name is XXX", or just "YYY", where YYY is a proper name (marked by the preprocessor), or any variations. Stores the customer's name in CUSTOMER NAME

Branch 2: Default, will be followed if the user's name cannot be found

"Well, ..." node

Branch 3: Matches I am {looking for | trying to find} a {present | gift} for my {girlfriend | boyfriend | friend | mother ....} or variations.

Branch 4: Default, if none of the other conditions matched

Branch 5: Matches I am {looking for | trying to find} a {ring | bracelet | necklace ... } or variations.

Branch 6: Matches "just looking" or "just browsing" anywhere in the sentence user typed in

"How can I ..." node

Branch 7: Default, if none of the other conditions matched

Branch 8: Same as Branch 5

Branch 9: Same as Branch 6

Parsing

PROSPERO is a very good syntactic parser, and it is used in CONVERSE together with pre-and post-processors. The preprocessor carries out syntax checks and marks proper names, dates and places. The post-processor (PPP) converts PROSPERO output from the syntactic tree form, first to the list of clauses, and then "flattens out" each of these clauses producing the list of slots. The slots are then read by MicroQueries (described in the next section).

PPP is a simple approach to derive the meaning of the sentence from the syntactic tree. Each clause is a subject-verb-object triple (and of course, each one of these may be missing – in a command such as "tell me" the subject is missing). If a clause is in passive, PPP will naturally swap the subject and the object. Some deficiencies of PROSPERO were covered up, for example, sentences like "don't you like school" were not parsed correctly, and so PPP interfered and corrected this problem.

PPP serves two main functions: it simplifies and standardizes the output of the syntactic parser. For purely technical reasons, it is much easier to deal with the list of slots rather than the entire tree. Also, using a simplified tagset allows (in the future) the use of a different syntactic parser without modifying the rest of the program (MicroQueries etc.) The slots are essentially the surface form of the chunks of the tree. Also, PROSPERO, as most syntactic parsers, used a non-standard set of tags.

PPP converts PROSPERO into a small, simple and more intuitive tagset. There are three main constituents of a clause: SUBJect, VERB, and OBJect. And then, these tags are augmented further with subtags, like OBJ.DOBJ.HEAD (refers to the headword of the object) and OBJ.DOBJ.DET (refers to its determiner, such as an article, or "this" or "that"). Every major constituent has an .ORIG tag corresponding to the original sentence form of that constituent. There is also a list of SENT.*, CLAUSE.*, and GL.* slot corresponding to the global sentence and clause constituents. WH.* slots correspond to the wh-pronoun in questions.

PPP output given the input sentence "I like this ring." is shown below. CLAUSE.TYPE slot indicates that the sentence is a statement (1). The subject (SUBJ.ORIG) is "I", the verb is "like", and the object is "this ring". The verb is un-inflected, that is, converted to its dictionary form, VERB.UNINFL, and the verb tense is stored as a set of binary flags, VERB.TENSE. The object is "this ring", which is a direct object (OBJ.KIND = 2) and it is further split into its head noun OBJ.DOBJ.HEAD: 'ring' and determiner OBJ.DOBJ.DET: 'this'.

For the input sentence: "I like this ring", here is the sample output of a parser post-processor:

```
A total of 1 clauses will be printed now
---- Clause number: 0-----
Clause type: 1
Clause original: I like this ring
CLAUSE.TYPE: 1
CLAUSE.ORIG: I like this ring
SENT.ORIG: I like this ring.
```

475

```
SENT.OLDORIG: I like this ring.
SENT.CONTENT: i ring
SENT.NOUN: ring
SENT.VERB: like
SENT.PEOPLE: I
SENT.NOUNPHR: ring
SUBJ.ORIG: I
SUBJ.HEAD: I
VERB.ORIG: like
VERB.UNINFL: like
VERB.TENSE: [PRESENT]
VERB.AUX:
OBJ.ORIG: this ring
OBJ.KIND: 2
OBJ.DOBJ.ORIG: this ring
OBJ.DOBJ.HEAD: ring
OBJ.DOBJ.DET: this
OBJ.CLAUSE: -1
WH.PRON:
WH.HEAD:
WH.MODIF:
GL.CHARNUM: 19
Noun phrase: I
Main verb: like, uninflected: like
Auxiliary verb:
Object: this ring, kind: 2
wh-pronoun:
```

MicroQueries

MicroQuery module serves as a link between the PPP output and all "consumers" of this output, that is, all CONVERSE modules: scripts, Pisces, etc. For example, Pisces uses MicroQueries to identify if the user typed in a question or a command, and then classify the user's utterance accordingly. Scripts normally have a list of MicroQueries associated with each branch. Each MicroQuery matches the user's input against a specified pattern, such as "I am just looking." or "I like this bracelet (or any kind of jewelry)".

The main advantage of using MicroQueries is that the interaction between action modules and the parser's output is a) standardized, and b) separated into a data file. If, for example, a parser other than PROSPERO is used, it will need its own PPP module producing a compatible list of slots and then the same set of MicroQueries can be used with the new parser. Separating MicroQueries from code into data files makes it possible to change queries without having to recompile the program.

Each MicroQuery is a set of lines, and each of the lines is a specific query against one of the PPP slots, a variable assignment, or a call to another MicroQuery. Variables are used so that information can be either extracted from the PPP slots, or compared with the slot contents. Slots can be matched using either exact or substring matching, or by using WordNet synonym or genus matches. WordNet synonym set, or Synset match will match a given word, say, "ring", with any of its synonyms, and the genus match will match a given word, say, "jewelry", with any of its different kinds, like "ring", "bracelet", "necklace", etc. WordNet comes up with about a dozen different kinds of jewelry. Lines are normally connected with an implicit AND statement (all of the lines have to be true in order for the entire MicroQuery to match). However, OR statements and brackets are also allowed inside MicroQueries.

Some jewelry sales-related MicroQueries are listed below. Query ASH_SUBJI merely checks if the subject of the clause is "I". Query ASH_ILIKETHISJEWELRY looks for the sentence pattern "I like this ring/bracelet". First, it checks whether the clause is a statement (CLAUSE.TYPE == 1), as opposed to a question or command. Then, it checks whether the subject is "I", whether the verb is "like" and it is the present tense. The WordNet genus match checks if the user is looking for any kind of jewelry, and, finally, the kind of jewelry is stored in the $jewelry_kind variable.

Query ASH_JUSTLOOKING uses a substring match instead of trying to access any of the sentence's syntactic elements. It looks for "just looking" or "just browsing" anywhere inside the user's sentence. Such approach allows for a larger number of possibilities, "just looking" or "I am just looking" (but also allows room for error). Substring matching is inevitable if the sentence is not parsable, or not parsed correctly, or it is a fixed expression such as "Hello" which does not need to be parsed.

Here are some jewelry sales-related MicroQueries:

```
QUERY ASH_SUBJI
SUBJ.ORIG == "I"
END QUERY

QUERY ASH_ILIKETHISJEWELRY
VARIABLE $jewelry_kind
CLAUSE.TYPE == 1
CALL ASH_SUBJI
VERB.ORIG = "like"
VERB.TENSE MASK [PRESENT]
OBJ.DOBJ.HEAD GEN {jewelry, N, 1}
$jewelry_kind := OBJ.DOBJ.HEAD
END QUERY

QUERY ASH_JUSTLOOKING
SENT.ORIG << "just looking"
OR
SENT.ORIG << "just browsing"
END QUERY
```

Areas for Improvement

CONVERSE was a very ambitious attempt to create a human-like computer interface, and it achieved remarkable success and publicity once making the news in all of the major British newspapers, before it ran into software problems. We learned many lessons from the CONVERSE experience.

CONVERSE is far larger than any of the other Loebner entries, and since it has used many traditional Natural Language Processing (NLP) techniques and large data sets, it can be extended much further by writing more scripts and MicroQueries. Separating data from code allowed us to split the development tasks, so that, for example, script creation was carried out by an independent non-technical group of people. Most traditional NLP systems (and most Loebner entries) are very ad-hoc and tied up to a particular task. CONVERSE isn't locked in a particular domain. It will assume a different personality as soon as new scripts and MicroQueries are designed and Person Database is updated.

The main deficiency of CONVERSE is its syntactic parser. We were hoping that using a large-scale commercial parser would help us extract relevant information from the user's input. However, PROSPERO is not as good at parsing dialogue as it is at parsing prose, and often did not come up with a parse at all. Because of the licensing issues, we did not have the access to PROSPERO grammar, and so we could not adjust PROSPERO to suit our needs.

Also, people do not always speak in perfectly grammatical sentences, yet we needed to extract any relevant information from arbitrary input. This is why MicroQueries were designed: the person designing scripts could choose whether to use the output of the parser or use substring matching, or look for content words, places or proper names, bypassing syntax. Parser PostProcessor does not lock us up in any particular parsing schema, converting PROSPERO's output to a more general set of slots. PROSPERO can be, in theory, replaced with a different parser.

Recently, statistical methods were used very successfully in syntactic parsing. For example, parsers designed by Collins and Charniak, trained and tested on the Wall Street Journal text from the Penn Treebank (http://www.cis.upenn.edu/~treebank/), parse about two-thirds of test sentences completely correctly, and 86 percent with only minor errors. Treebank grammar-driven parsers by Charniak, Krotov and Sekine also achieve impressive parsing performance using a very simple training technique. Sekine used his Wall Street Journal text-trained parser on much more varied text from the Brown corpus with a relatively small loss in parsing performance. Some recent publications in statistical parsing are listed in the reference section.

Dialog Integration

To put the dialog on the site, we wrapped CONVERSE in a session EJB. The dialog is conducted through an applet, which resembles most closely the chat room. This is unlike most conversational systems today, which have a window for the question, but print the answer elsewhere. Chat rooms are becoming increasingly popular, and there may be a whole generation brought up with this culture. Many people have no problem with fast typing, and are generally at ease with this means of communication.

The applet therefore presents the complete ongoing dialog, and sends each user response to a servlet. The servlet passes it on to the stateful session EJB. This is in keeping with the advice that applets generally should not communicate directly to the WebLogic server. The applet keeps the handle of the session EJB that has been assigned to it at the beginning of the dialog, and passes it along with the user response to the servlet.

The following screenshot presents the applet window with the dialog:

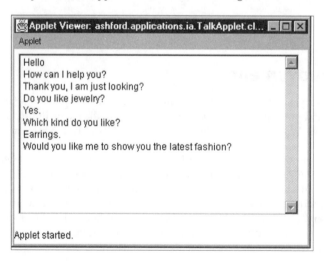

With some more integration effort, the applet can be put straight onto the web page, as can be seen in the following screenshot:

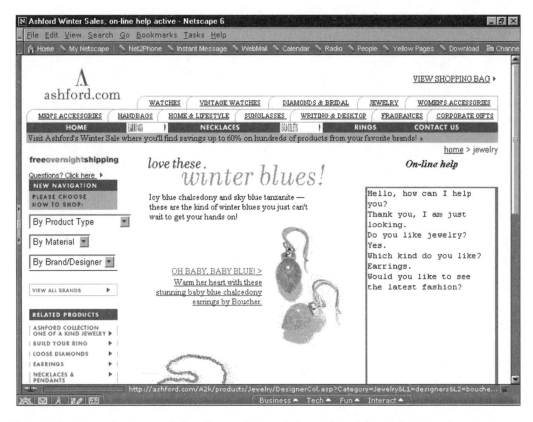

The code for the applet is given below. It is really straightforward, and the applet to servlet communication follows the *Java Servlet Programming* book by *Hunter and Crawford, ISBN 1-565923-91-X*. The key to the communication is the `HttpMessage` class. This class presents a message to the servlet in the form of the HTTP `request`, which the servlet knows how to process. This class also gets the servlet response, and returns it to the applet. The `Base64Encoder` class is used to convert communications strings to ASCII. The support classes for this applet, `HttpMessage`, and `Base64Encoder`, can be found in the project code.

```java
package ashford.applications.ia;

import java.awt.*;
import java.awt.event.*;
import java.applet.*;
import java.net.*;
import java.io.*;
import java.util.*;

public class TalkApplet extends Applet {
  public void init() {

    // Take out this line if you don't use symantec.itools.net.RelativeURL
    // or symantec.itools.awt.util.StatusScroller
    symantec.itools.lang.Context.setApplet(this);

    // This code is automatically generated by Visual Cafe when you add
    // components to the visual environment. It instantiates and initializes
```

```
    // the components. To modify the code, only use code syntax that matches
    // what Visual Cafe can generate, or Visual Cafe may be unable to back
    // parse your Java file into its visual environment.
    // {{INIT_CONTROLS
    setLayout(null);
    setSize(382, 221);
    add(talkArea);
    talkArea.setBounds(6, 6, 365, 201);
    // }}

    // {{REGISTER_LISTENERS
    SymKey aSymKey = new SymKey();
    talkArea.addKeyListener(aSymKey);
    // }}
    try {
      url = new URL(servletUrl);
    } catch (MalformedURLException e) {
      // just a formality, it is design time code not run time
      e.printStackTrace();
    }
  }

  // {{DECLARE_CONTROLS
  java.awt.TextArea talkArea = new java.awt.TextArea("", 0, 0,
        TextArea.SCROLLBARS_VERTICAL_ONLY);
  // }}

  class SymKey extends java.awt.event.KeyAdapter {
    public void keyPressed(java.awt.event.KeyEvent event) {
      Object object = event.getSource();
      if (object == talkArea) {
        talkArea_KeyPressed(event);
      }
    }
  }

  void talkArea_KeyPressed(java.awt.event.KeyEvent event) {
    if (event.getKeyCode() == KeyEvent.VK_ENTER) {
      answerHer(); // When the user presses the ENTER key, we start
    }
  }
  private void answerHer() {
    HttpMessage msg = new HttpMessage(url); // for servlet communication

    Properties props = new Properties(); // placeholder for parameters
    props.put("action", "shegoes");
    String sheGoes = getSheGoes(); // extract what was last said by customer

    String iGo = "";
    try {
      InputStream in = msg.sendGetMessage(props); // send user phrase
      BufferedReader data = new BufferedReader(new InputStreamReader(in));
      iGo = data.readLine(); // get automated help response
    } catch (IOException e) {
      e.printStackTrace();
```

```
        iGo = "Sorry, I have wiring problems"; // error? Say something amusing
      }
      setIGo(iGo); // set the answer in the applet window
    }
    private String getSheGoes() {
      String sheGoes = "";

      // extract the last line from the applet
      return sheGoes;
    }
    private void setIGo(String iGo) {
      talkArea.append("\n" + iGo);
    }
    private String servletUrl = "http://localhost:7001/talk";
    private URL url;
}
```

The servlet code gets requests from the applet, invokes CONVERSE through the EJB to figure out what to say next, and sends the response back. The code for the `TalkServlet` is given below, and it can be tested in the browser, without the applet, with a test string like this:

```
http://localhost:7001/talk?action=shegoes&shegoes=hello
```

The servlet code is also straightforward. We have commented out the calls to CONVERSE, since this implementation is specific to our system:

```
package ashford.applications.ia;

import javax.servlet.*;
import javax.servlet.http.*;
import java.io.*;
import java.util.*;

public class TalkServlet extends HttpServlet {
  public void doGet(HttpServletRequest req, HttpServletResponse res)
          throws ServletException, java.io.IOException {
    String action = req.getParameter("action");
    System.out.println("action request = " + action);
    if (action == null) {
      return;
    }
    if (action.equalsIgnoreCase("shegoes")) {
      String sheGoes = req.getParameter("shegoes");
      try {
        String iGo = "How can I help you?";

        // get connection to the Talk EJB through the handle
        // ...
        // ... get the answer
        // igo = Talk.getAnswer(sheGoes);

        // send the response back
        res.setContentType("text/html");
        PrintWriter out = res.getWriter();
```

```
            out.println(iGo);
        } catch (Exception e) {
            e.printStackTrace();
            throw new ServletException(e.getMessage());
        }
        return;
    }
}

public void doPost(HttpServletRequest req, HttpServletResponse res)
        throws ServletException, java.io.IOException {
    doGet(req, res);
}

public void init() throws ServletException {

    // set ejb connection parameters

}
}
```

When the IA needs to conduct a search, it asks the servlet to do this. When it needs to show an item, it opens another applet window.

What is in the Project Code

You can download from www.wrox.com the complete project code for everything described in this chapter. Together with the Rose model and the sample Access database, it amounts to 8 MB of files (1 MB zipped). The VisualCafé projects are also included. CONVERSE can not be offered for download, but you can try it through the web interface at the author's site, http://shmsoft.com/nlp.htm.

Because the versions of WebLogic and WLCS have changed since we began developing the site, our code implements a short cut. We have a flag (described in the README.txt file in the download code) that makes the code bypass all references to the EJB. By default, this flag is on, which means that the complete project code will run as is, with very little installation effort. You only need to register servlets in the weblogic.properties, as described in README.txt. Of course, this fix eliminates the use of the EJBs (an important part of the study) and the EJB code then becomes for reading only. If you do want to use the EJBs, the instructions are provided below.

WebLogic and WLCS Versions

As we have mentioned earlier, this case study limits itself to design and development. At the time of writing the development for the first part of the project, "Corporate Gifts" was completed. However, the deployment was put on hold, due to the market conditions, and the need to formulate future development plans. It may not be exactly what we would want, but changes are the norm for today's programming projects, and especially for e-commerce. So we cannot promise that when you go to buy a watch from Ashford.com, it will be the code from this book that will work for you. One thing we can promise though is that we have tried to share experience and advice that may be useful to you on your projects, an experience that took a lot of time, reading, hard work, experimentation, hair pulling, and teeth gnashing to acquire.

Now we need to say a few words about the version of WebLogic and WLCS. The version of WebLogic that we used was 5.1. At the time of writing, the current version of WebLogic is 6.0, but the differences are not important for our code. More important is the change in the version of WLCS, which requires some explanation.

The WLCS version was 2.1 The WLCS was really TheoryCenter, a company acquired by BEA, and the components were then part of the BEA offerings, but we could see that they were still separate, if only by the package name, which was `com.theorycenter`. In addition, BEA provided a code generator, which came as a plug-in for Rational Rose. The use of this generator allows for round-trip engineering. With a little bit of care, which meant following the rules of where to insert your code, it kept your changes to the code, and allowed re-generating the code from the class diagram. In this environment, we could extend the TheoryCenter components, such as `Customer` or `Product` EJBs, using the provided functionality and adding something specific.

The current version of TheoryCenter is called WebLogic Commerce Server or WLCS, version 3, and its design has been changed. The components are now completely integrated into BEA's code, as evidenced by the package name change to `com.bea`. The code generator is removed from the offering. If we want to generate EJB code, we can use the RationalRose code generator, or such products as TogetherJ. The version we used, 2.1, is no longer available for download.

Had we known the direction of development at BEA, we might conceivably have chosen a different approach. However, we would rather use this as a lesson. The software offerings in the e-commerce world are subject to change. Even if the change is not as drastic as in this case, new products may come which will obviate the old ones, and the development will need to take it into account.

This makes a good case of Extreme Programming. One of its principles is that everything changes, and change is the only thing we can be certain about. In the classical XP, this is because the customer requirements are often very flexible. This is surely also the case in e-commerce. To this we can add that the platform on which you are standing may shake too.

As it is, our examples may actually teach more than if we just used the ready-made EJB components from WLCS. This is because we offer a look under the hood. It is doubtful that your requirements will be exactly the same as ours. Rather, you'll be able to evaluate and apply some of our more successful techniques, and reapply some of the code. This can be done with the examples below.

To summarize, all of the code runs on WebLogic5.1 and WLCS 2.1 If you've got this then worry no more.

If you're using WebLogic 6.0, and setting the flag that bypasses the EJBs, all the JSPs, servlets, and applets run without change, bypass the EJBs, and go straight to the database. If you want to use the EJBs in this case you will need to do a bit more work to configure them and to rebuild the code – the instructions for this are provided in the `README.txt`. The Access database in the project code has all that is needed for testing.

Summary

In this chapter we took a look at a real-world project. In the course of the project we gained understanding of many different points, and hope that by sharing them with you we have provided some help.

We have seen that modern software development needs to be flexible and quick and that it's always good to deliver in stages so that the project is not shut down but continues. To illustrate the workings of the e-commerce site being developed we looked at three applications: login, coupon, and automated sales help:

❑ The Login showed the interplay of JSP, JavaBeans, servlets, and EJBs.
❑ The Coupons illustrated the use of Java Security.
❑ The Automated Sales Help is a novel application, of which we may still see more in the future.

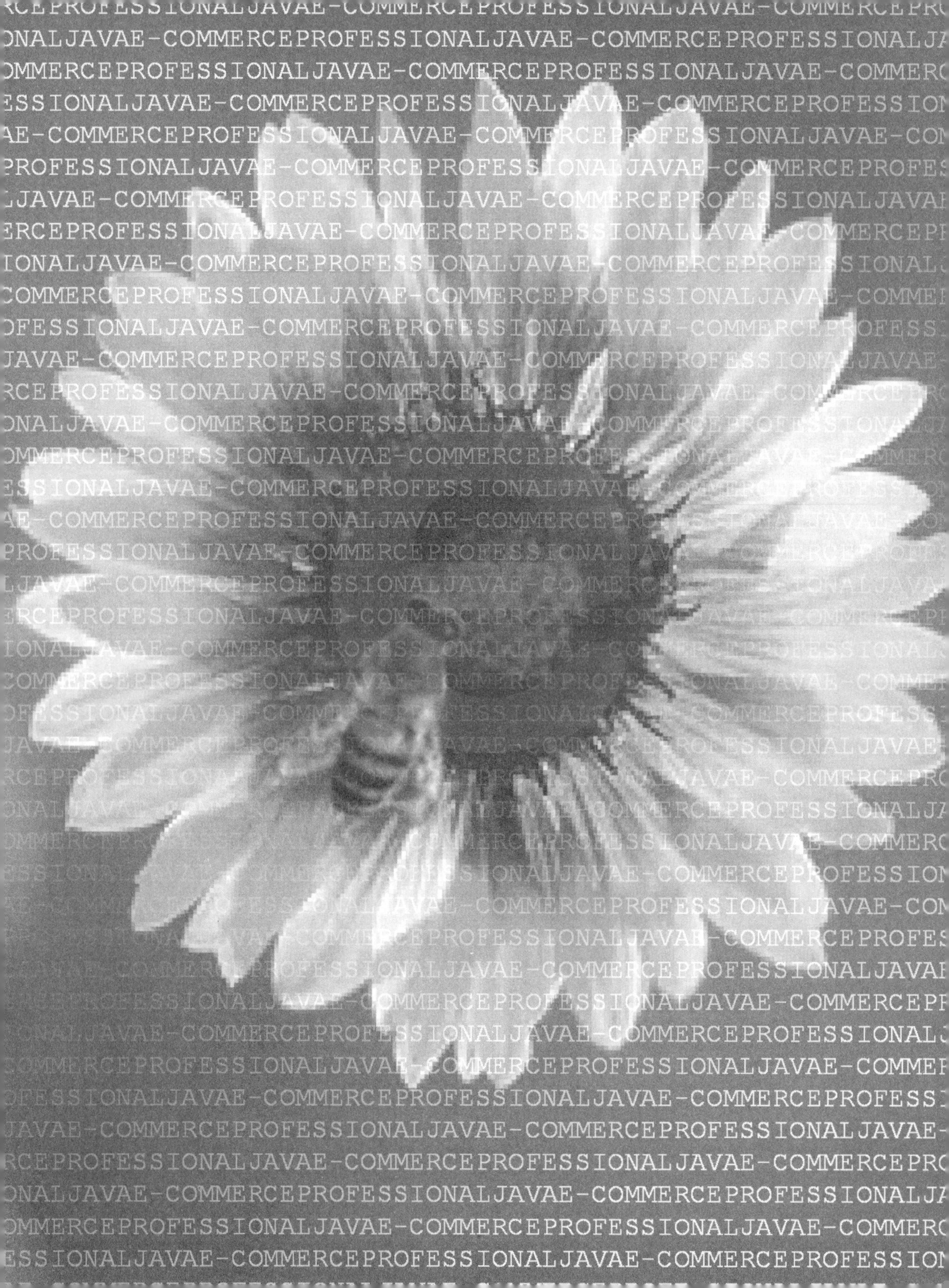
PROFESSIONALJAVAE-COMMERCE

B2C E-Commerce: Portal Sites

When people think of a portal, many different things come to mind. Some of these items include a "gateway to mystuff," a glorified search engine that remembers a person's favorite topics, or a personalized home page. In fact, when looking for a portal solution, it is becoming increasingly difficult to find the solution a company is looking for, because the definition of what a portal is seems to change on a daily basis.

The greatest advantage of a portal is to be gained when the different sections that make up a portal interact. The best portals are more than just a sum of their features – the new portals are integrated tools, where the calendar not only reminds the user of their mother's birthday, but also suggests flowers from http://www.1-800-flowers.com or a suitable book from http://www.amazon.com. Searches for a movie or a CD not only bring up a list of e-tailers to buy it from online, but also links to fan clubs, sample tracks, and other similarly available material. Furthermore, searching for a company profile allows links to Security Exchange Commission filings (the SEC hold information on different companies), current stock information and up to the minute news stories.

This chapter is the first of a two chapter section about portals, and aims to provide an overview of portal related issues, as well as a simple portal that can easily be built to show the user the basics of how a portal or content management system might operate at a high level. The second chapter is a case study of a real-life portal site.

In this chapter, we will:

- ❏ Try to pin down the different types of portals and the markets that they consume
- ❏ Highlight the concepts that portals are based upon and identify some of the more interesting technology agents, as well as what is needed to make portals come alive through personalization of content

❏ Discuss how to deliver a portal solution, including looking at building vs. buying, and then demonstrate how to design and construct a very simple portal that covers the basic concepts of what a portal might include (to see how companies in the market are creating high volume, flexible portals with Enterprise JavaBeans and DHTML, look at the next chapter where a customizable portal architecture is demonstrated)

❏ Identify some of the different ways that we can make money with our portal if so desired

However, let us first define what a portal actually is.

What is a Portal?

You may get the impression from talking to people that everyone has a different opinion as to what a portal actually is, but the definition we will be using for the purposes of this discussion is as follows:

> **A portal is a personal, filtered view on some relevant information.**

The purists out there will immediately be saying that this isn't a true portal – the first portals were big lists of sorted links. This is a fair criticism, as this was the original definition of portal and what we are describing is probably more accurately called a **community**. However, most (if not all) of the original portals have now evolved into communities, so we don't see many of the old kind around any more. Because of this, we're going to use the words portal and community synonymously.

Context Driven Decision Making

Portals largely assist a person in doing their job by allowing informed decisions to be made based on information provided. The presentation and display of a portal can be even more important than the information itself. The portal needs to do more than just combine different applications together; it needs to combine data to form information and display it to the user in a unified, standard format. The presentation has to be pleasing to the eye, and easily navigable so that the user can get to useful information fast and make intelligent decisions based upon it.

Intelligent agents can also help with decision making by acting as a research assistant that can search out information for a person to help them make a more informed decision.

As the Internet continues to move into ever widening fields, we cannot ignore the fact that users want centralized access to information whenever and wherever they are. To this end, the system must be designed to allow access to the data from different methods and in different forms to take advantage of the latest developments (such as mobile phones and Interactive/Digital TV).

Looking back at our definition, we can see that it's composed of three main parts, so let's take each part of that definition in turn:

❏ **Personal** – This may either be something of interest specifically for the user, or it may be for the user's group (or lifestyle)

❏ **Filtered** – There is lots of data out there – summarize

❏ **Relevant** – If the data is not important to them, then why would the user stay?

There are several methods available to fill these requirements, but personalization is what will keep people coming back repeatedly. The user will return to a place that is personalized to their needs and wants, and a place that is dynamically changing based on the user's interest and usage patterns. This idea of continued browsing by users who either want, or need, to return to the site because of its content is known as making the portal **sticky**.

There are many different ways that a portal can be personalized, and here are a few examples:

- Stock quotes
- National news
- Home page building services
- Local weather, local news, television listings for your area
- Horoscopes
- Sports results for favorite teams
- Instant messengers
- E-mail lists and forums

How this information is ordered and presented to the user is the province of the last two bullets in that list above – filtered and relevant. These concepts will be discussed in later sections, but before we do so, we will need to understand the types of portals that are available.

What Types of Portals are There?

There are essentially four types of portals, all performing almost entirely different operations. The best portals have a combination of each of these features included in them, but there is at least one factor common to all of them – *personalization*.

- **Search Engines** – There are many types of search engines that can be used to help the user to find whatever they are searching for. All of them use some type of spider, intelligent agent, or broker-based mechanism to index the web and store that information. The way that the end results are displayed to the user can also come in many different forms, ranging from popularity, topic based, cumulative searches, or just about anything else that could make the top results more relevant.

- **News and Information** – This includes local weather, local politics/government, community events, movies, shopping, social hangouts, and local concerts, to name but a few.

- **Workspace / Dashboard (Business)** – Business users need a central place where all of the information that is used during the day can be found. This type of information includes stock quotes, news stories in a certain industry, on-going financial analysis of the company, and local e-mail and messaging among other things. Often this is placed in the broad category known as an Intranet, but this attitude has changed as companies become more integrated and data sharing and collaboration extend outside the organization (thus forming an Extranet). The names and concepts range from **Enterprise Resource Portals (ERPs)**, **Enterprise Information Portals (EIP)**, **Knowledge Management Portals**, or simply **Corporate Portals**.

❑ **Personal Home Page** – Although many people have become proficient in searching the web for information, bookmarking sites of interest, and joining the perfect online communities, a portal can bring all of this functionality together into one URL. A "smart" home page will always be searching out information, links, and on-line communities that relate to things that the user wants to see and is interested in.

❑ **Combinations of the above** – Most sites don't confine themselves to the limitations of these four categories, and instead combine their traits into one of two main types of portal:

  ❑ **"The only site you need..."** – These sites try to combine all the services you would generally use on a day-to-day basis, such as e-mail, calendar, news, shopping, searching, horoscopes, etc. They generally contain as little of their own services or content as possible by drawing in third-party content. The key point to note from these sites is the level of integration. The e-mail, address book, calendar, etc. all work together and can be summarized on the homepage. Now most have Instant Messaging as well, desktop applications are even extended into the browser. Examples include http://www.msn.com and http://www.yahoo.com.

  ❑ **"The definitive reference for..."** – These sites attempt to be a central source of information and services for a vertical market (a particular sector, such as "wireless design" or "meat and poultry" that might well consider themselves to be a community). This generally includes industry news and comment, B2B product and service offerings. Closed user group portals also fall into this camp, such as corporate portals and Microsoft's Digital Dashboards. Examples include all the vertical market sites run by http://www.verticalnet.com. These are created from common templates, and share information among relevant sites.

Implementations of Portals

Now we've investigated what the term portal covers, let's now dig into the types of broad technical issues that are addressed during portal implementation.

Here we'll look at:

❑ Portal categories

❑ Information management

❑ A summary of portal components

Portal Categories

In addition to the different types of portal available, any or all of those types must be made up of lower level components or services. Thus we can re-categorize portals as being based (or involving an element of being based) on links, business applications, intelligent agents, or content management. Let's now look at each of these in turn.

Link Based

A link based portal is mostly comprised of URL links to different web sites on the Internet or at the portal's sites. The portal may be broken down into different sections in a grid layout, each usually owned and operated by different organizations, people, or affiliated sites. This might include an advertising firm that owns one section and can sell ads based on the portal user's profile. Another might be the portal company that chooses to show the user's account information or company news in another section or a content management type system will take over the rest of the sections based on the user's preferences and display (hopefully) meaningful links.

Last but not least, the portal user can configure their own section to include local events, favorite links, pictures, e-mail, anything necessary to enhance their experience and keep everything needed in one place – the portal home page These facilities all help to provide a personalized portal for the user.

The number one goal is to keep the site configurable and based on that user's profile.

Business Application Based

Communication in business is essential to be successful in today's market. A business application based portal implementation might link together employee communications, enterprise wide data, customer support functions, company e-mail, calendar information, company memos, or a passage to a particular range or field of activity on the Extranet.

Despite the use of the terms Intranet and Extranet, as these sites become more personalized to each user in the organization, the word portal seems to be the better description. This can be a link based implementation, but many times they are accomplished by using frames or tables to combine completely separate web applications into one personalized user interface. The key difference between an Intranet and a portal is that a portal consists of links or references to different points of interest in the organization, where an Intranet is copies or an accumulation of items in the organization. In addition, portals generally extend to customers, suppliers, partners, and so on, whereas Intranets are held closely in an organization.

Intelligent Agent Based

Intelligent agents are computer programs that take certain criteria and search for things that match it. Based on the choices that a user makes, the links configured on the page, the items searched for by the user, and other personalized features that the user demands, intelligent agents can dramatically add to that personalization. An example of a portal currently using agents is with Brio Technologies at http://www.brio.com/products_solutions/brio_portal/portal1.html.

In the background, agents might search the internet for a job opportunity that a user is looking for, search for information from a database in the enterprise using metadata, find more specific information on a topic that is heavily displayed on a users' portal, search through company forums, newsletters, and so on. These activities all happen behind the scenes. The agent is acting as an assistant to the user for many of their needs. Intelligent agents can also provide personalization based on previous events and other related current events.

Content Management Based

There are many content management systems in the marketplace, and they are all adapting to call themselves a portal solution. A large bulk of these are company intranets that were required to expand to support end users, suppliers, partners, etc. Content management systems have the unique ability to allow business users who are not completely computer literate to add certain content such as news releases, policies and procedures, templates, etc. to certain categories in the content management system. These documents then become indexed based upon the information supplied by the business user during submittal, ending up on the web page as ever changing information.

Managing Information

Managing information in a portal can be quite a challenge. The term "portal" can be interpreted as a gateway to another world. Just like the natural world, the computer world is always changing; managing that information needs to be a highly profiled task. Today's information can be in many forms, users living in many different locations and accessed by people located on different systems. This is called a **data blanket**. Many different methods must be employed to manage this information, and display it to the user as a unified source and we'll discuss them in this section.

489

Storing Information

There are essentially two ways to store information – **logical storage** and **physical storage** and portals require both.

❑ **Logical Storage** is the most common way that information is stored in a portal. It consists of ever changing indices of URL links for the user that are continually kept up to date for accuracy.

❑ **Physical Storage** implies that the information for the portal user is stored on that same machine (or server group) that is actually supporting the portal. This is generally the case when working with Intranets in small-to-medium sized companies, where strong security is an issue.

Managing the Data Blanket

For enterprise type portals, the largest problem is the disparate data sources and data displays. Generally there are hundreds of applications in a single enterprise, each one communicating with a different data model, different screens, different platforms and OSs, etc. Many of these system vendors have created a web-based front-end to their system, and using a portal is an easy way to integrate these systems.

The problem is that even though there is concurrent access to all of these systems through a web-based display (portal screen), communication between programs has become even harder to accomplish. The user can access different programs on the screen simultaneously, but the programs cannot communicate with each other, beyond cutting and pasting.

There are a handful of solutions to this type of problem using a portal as the data display:

❑ **Import your data into one system or platform** – This is a common solution that companies such as SAP, Peoplesoft, and other enterprise type software businesses use, which produces a unified place to go for information. The justification is in replacing outdated software (that is working perfectly) to be able to better communicate with other systems by using a more open platform or format. The main problem with this solution is the cost of re-implementation, integration, licensing, and the re-training of users and administrators.

❑ **Use intelligent agents to search for information** – This interesting solution is just now reaching fruition. It consists of using metadata to describe the internal systems in the enterprise and sending out intelligent agents to search for and index those systems' information. A portal solution can provide the correct access to that information for each user. A downside is that accessing the data in a data store without the business logic gives the possibility of compromising the integrity (relational or otherwise) of the data.

❑ **Create public interfaces to every system in the enterprise and allow portal access through those interfaces** – The problem with this method is that many of the programs in the enterprise that people use to do their jobs are single user programs. Opening these up in a multi-user environment to the rest of the enterprise would mean additional programming in the interface to handle concurrency.

Reading from Multiple Data Sources

This is the key to managing information. Portal sites began as a single interface to many different web programs. Utilizing frames and include technology (including web pages from other systems), portals grew from a unified entry point to multiple systems and then on to large content management systems. Currently, portals are expected to do much more than just link things together. Portals need to be smart, having the ability to search many different data sources for information to present to the user, and can produce almost any type of web media within their interface. Some examples of things that a portal can search, display, or categorize include:

- ❑ Databases

- ❑ Data warehouses

- ❑ Business applications

- ❑ LDAP directories

- ❑ End user productivity tools

- ❑ Unstructured data from text

- ❑ All types of documents, including Adobe PDF, Microsoft Word, etc

- ❑ E-mails and instant messaging

- ❑ Audio/Video

Information Order

The look of a portal is very important to everyone from the user to the advertisement agency. As we've already said, a portal page may be divided into several areas of information, which can be owned, and operated, by different groups of people including marketers with advertisements or news information, portal creators, and the portal users themselves. Good examples of this are www.yahoo.com or www.lycos.com. The sites include pictures and advertisements that fall into a similar category of what was last searched on. Local information of news and events if any type of mapping tools were used from the site, as well as services and topics that might relate to the information about the user that has been discretely collected as they were using the portal. Often the information display order depends on the answers to the following questions (in this priority):

- ❑ Who pays the most for the portal space?

- ❑ What is important to the organization that is using or hosting the portal?

- ❑ What is important to the user (based on timely access)?

In addition to all of these external factors, how much information does it take before the portal appears "cluttered" or unusable? Here there is a Catch-22 situation, where the people paying for the portal are not the ones using it, and the people using the portal are not the ones paying for it. The people that want to use the portal will not spend time there if it is cluttered and non-user-friendly, and the people paying for the portal will not put out money if people are not using the portal where the information is shown.

Search Pattern Matching

This is becoming a new trend in portal technology (maybe even the next level of personalization). This technology is focused on storing everything possible about a web site customer or user and their usage patterns. Utilizing this information, these systems use their proprietary algorithms to intelligently sort through the data to predict what the user might expect to see, what things might keep a user at the web site longer (stickiness), or in a marketplace, present up-sell and cross-sell items to the user based on their past history or current events. Some examples of companies using this type of technology include Digital River (http://www.digitalriver.com), Torrent (http://www.torrent.com), and IQ.com (http://www.iq.com).

Cookies vs. Standard Login

Collecting information about the users of the portal is critical in its success. There are two ways to gather the information about the user in a discrete fashion (short of a boring survey).

Cookies are a huge help in tracking the user as long as they are not worried about security, and/or log into the same machine all of the time. Cookies identify the user based on their previous login to the operating system and the current web site, using a small file placed on their computer with that information.

When security is a concern, a standard login procedure is the best solution. Users must log into the portal, and based on their role within the organization providing the portal, access is granted to them. Utilizing the standard login, portal users can access their information from any computer anywhere, and are not dependent on previous login information for personalization.

Portal Components Summarized

Now we've discussed portals in general terms, before we move on to building a portal, let's draw everything together and identify all the bits that make up a portal, both GUI and behind the scenes. These really are the requirements for all portals – some will not go quite as far as this, and some will go further – in many cases the service can be provided by snap-in, components.

❑ **Content** – Remember our portal definition above –relevant, filtered content that is personalized for the user. Content can be sourced from any number of places, many of which claim to offer it free in return for advertising (generally in the form of "sponsored by XXX" at the end of the article) – for examples try http://www.isyndicate.com/.

❑ **Feeds and Filters** – Once there is content that needs to be placed into the portal – what options are there for delivery?

The smaller systems work on a *pull* approach – embed some JavaScript into your page and the script includes some HTML from the remote site. This can be used in a portal, but you need to check that the proper licensing is in place to avoid thorny legal problems – especially when caching content. The bigger systems also use a pull approach, often using FTP. Using a provided username and password, periodically your system downloads the latest articles. Subscription based *push* systems allow you to specify a web server address URL where data is posted when a new story arrives. Whatever the delivery method used, it generally arrives in either plain text or XML. While XML is still not widely supported by the traditional content suppliers (at the time of writing) it is quickly being adopted due to its powerful capability to describe data.

❑ **Personalization** – This component implements the personal aspect of a portal. To make the portal sticky (memorable, users want to return) the user needs to feel at home – since we don't (yet) know the user very well the best person to do that personalization is the user.

❑ **Profiling** – This is where it all starts to get clever. Instead of the user having to choose the content they want to see as a priority, could the portal learn the kinds of things they like and present these first? Reading between the lines, this is not just an advantage for the user, it also vastly improves product placement and advertising, most users do not generally mind timely and relevant advertising. Moreover, what is considered relevant advertising? This could be based on the content searched by the user, or a short survey where the customer can ask for the type and category of advertising that is desired.

❑ **Customization** – This is perhaps the most important aspect of the next generation portals, addressing all the requirements above by allowing the user to choose (personal) what they want (relevant) in a format that works for them (filtered). If this is effective along with some decent content, the result will be an extremely sticky site.

❑ **Multi-branding** – When building a system with all this rich functionality, it would be nice if it could be used again – and preferably without having to replicate the whole system each time. The idea then is that we design from the start to have the portal running different look-and-feels on the same box. If this is combined with the customization aspect, then the portal will start to get very powerful. This component of a portal can be provided by means of templates, which we keep separate from the content.

❑ **Security (Authorization/Authentication)** – It is a necessary thing; we have to have it; fortunately it comes free with many web servers and application servers. All we need to do is make it as unobtrusive as possible. Ideally, this also means that a user can access much of the content of the site without having to fill in any forms – and most importantly, they only need to provide information where they can see clear benefit.

An example of this is registering for access to a web site – if the form were to ask for the postal address of the user there would be no clear advantage to providing this information at this point. The site should rather ask for the postal address when the user wants a product delivered. Several sites do this rather sneakily by offering a gift for registering.

❑ **Multiple Front-end Clients** – As the Internet moves into the wider market, we cannot ignore the fact that users want centralized access to information whenever and wherever they are. To this end, the system must be designed to allow access to the data from different methods and from different devices (like mobile phones). This should be a fairly simple requirement to fulfill as long as the actual services and data we provide reside at a layer below the web; in other words on the application server or database server.

❑ **Advertising** – All commercial projects need to make money one way or another, and there are undoubtedly many ways to do this. Traditional portals used advertising, in particular banner advertising. Next e-commerce and generally revenue share e-commerce followed, where a portal would earn a commission for selling another company's products. Other types of advertising are always being devised by marketing personnel so the list will just get longer.

Building Your Portal

Now that we have a better understanding of what a portal actually is, this section will take you through the question of *Build vs Buy* type scenarios, and then on to building a very simple portal that will demonstrate the basic concepts, and characteristics, that all portals share. Some of these include:

❑ Advertisement tracking capability

❑ Division into sections owned by different departments, organizations, or people

❑ Redirection to other pages

❑ Dynamic inclusion of web pages, links, messages, pictures, applets, and so on

❑ Utilization of free Application Service Provider (ASP) type services (such as search and instant messenger facilities)

Build vs. Buy

In technology, there is always a trade-off between building and buying your solution. However, here are some of the things to consider regarding building or buying a portal solution.

Buying Components

❏ **Portal Vendors** – There are many portal vendors in the market place with different levels of expertise. These vendors range from portal integrators to calendar vendors to Yahoo or Alta-Vista. You can achieve a complete solution, but it might not entirely meet a company's needs without a high price tag.

❏ **Search Engines** – Almost all of the major search engine companies or portal vendors will sell a version of their search engine for either a flat fee or on a per user rate. There are also free "Application Service Provider" type search engines that will index any web site on the Internet free and provide a search link for that sites users.

❏ **E-mail Services** – From the portal point of view, there is almost no reason for a company to host their own mail service. There are plenty of free mail services out there, ranging from Hotmail to Yahoo that have proven to be reliable. There are also quite a few free POP mail servers (that run on Linux) that a portal can run if required.

❏ **Messaging** – This is the new craze on the Internet. Instant messengers can keep users informed of up to date information, and thousands of chat rooms keep people busy talking together. News groups haven't quite lost their popularity yet, although they seem to be losing out to automatic e-mailers and so on.

❏ **Advertisement Manager** – Advertisement managers and/or affiliate programs are available to make some money with your portal by using banner advertisements.

Building Components

A simple portal consists of only a few parts. These are the storage framework, JavaBeans components, JSP pages, pictures, and other services such as instant messaging. The portal that we will explore next is adapted for simplicity to show common portal conveniences and to show how some of the functionality is accomplished. The complementary case study to this one is located in the next chapter. While this chapter focuses on simple code to show how a dynamic portal might work, a "ready-mix" DHTML and EJB portal is emphasized in the case study.

A Simple Portal

The main functionality of this sample portal is to show how links, pictures, messages, Java applets, other theme pages, blinking text, and so on, are included in the framework. There is also a theme for each user – each theme is a different color scheme. For this example, we will need a servlet engine and a web server.

The one used here is JRUN 3.0 from Allaire, although it should work on any servlet engine. Setup is simple; just install, and make a new web application that points to the JSP directory where your JSP files are. In my example the path was /portal/jsp.

The JRUN CLASSPATH that I used is listed below:

```
{jrun.rootdir}/servers/lib
{jrun.server.rootdir}/lib
d:\portal
d:\j2sdkee1.2.1\lib\j2ee.jar
d:\jdk1.3
d:\jdk1.3\bin\tools.jar
d:\jdk1.3\bin\dt.jar
d:\j2sdkee1.2.1\lib\cloudscape\cloudscape.jar
```

```
d:\j2sdkee1.2.1\lib\cloudscape\client.jar
d:\j2sdkee1.2.1\lib\cloudscape\tools.jar
d:\j2sdkee1.2.1\lib\cloudscape\cloudscape.jar
d:\j2sdkee1.2.1\lib\cloudscape\RmiJdbc.jar
d:\j2sdkee1.2.1\lib\cloudscape\license.jar
```

The database used is Cloudscape, that comes with the J2EE reference edition. The associated "Pet Store" application from Sun (available from http://java.sun.com/j2ee/download.html#blueprints) has some helpful utilities (that we'll use later) to facilitate setting up and populating the Cloudscape database.

Below is the directory structure used for the simple portal application:

```
Portal
    JSP
            adsubmit.jsp
            myapplet.java
            portaldisplay.jsp
            search.jsp
            style1.css
            style2.css
            style3.css
            tester.jsp
        pictures
            AD1.jsp
            AD2.jsp
            AD3.jsp
            newwroxhead.gif
            newwroxlogo.gif
            wrox_logo100.gif
    myportal
            ad.java
            db.java
            portal.java
```

The different files are JSP pages for display, style sheets (CSS) for themes, and JavaBeans for programming logic. In more detail we have:

❑   adsubmit.jsp – When the advertisement is clicked, it updates the database and then redirects to the page corresponding to the advertisement.

❑   portaldisplay.jsp – This is the main page that runs the portal.

❑   search.jsp – This is the search page. The code here is from a search engine called "freefind.com". This search engine will search the portal site, and provide access to it when a user searches it.

❑   style1.css, style2.css, style3.css – These are cascading style sheets. These sheets format the HTML page so that different themes can be accomplished.

❑   tester.jsp – This is the page that is included to provide links corresponding to a certain theme. A portal owner might want a web developer to create a web page around a certain theme, feature, or function – this functionality allows the portal administrator to include one.

❑   myapplet.java – This is a very simple "Hello World" applet that is here to show how applets can be included in the portal as well to provide a rich application interface, or even fun games.

❑   myportal.ad – This object is responsible for displaying advertisements on the page.

❑   myportal.db – This object provides the database connection and helper database stuff for the portal.

❑   myportal.portal – This object does the logic and the queries for the portal display and user.

❑   There are also pictures in the picture directory that are to be used for the advertisements and logos for the site.

Remember all the code for this small application can be downloaded from www.wrox.com. We're going to run through the application in the following order:

❑   The storage framework

❑   The JavaBeans

❑   The JSPs

❑   Additional features

Portal Storage Framework

The first step is to create a **Portal Storage Framework**. This is generally a database (it is in this example) and the main focus of it is to store links to things that you might want to see in your portal. This database schema is set up to allow the portal to have two levels of links – **Roles** and **Users**. The Roles are for management or OEM people or mid-managers to put links and/or display pictures or messages to the user. There are also tables for advertisements to make money from the portal, and themes so that the user will have a configurable work environment.

As shown in the following example, a theme is just a simple Cascading Style Sheet (CSS), which in this case, allows the user to change colors on the fly. In the following chapter, however, the concept of themes will be expanded, with more than simply changes of color!

Here is an example of one of the Cascading Style Sheets (style1.css). It allows you to specify colors and fonts for different HTML tags:

```
BODY {
    BACKGROUND-COLOR: white;
    COLOR: #000099;
    FONT: 100% verdana,arial,helvetica
}
TD {
    BORDER-BOTTOM: medium none;
    BORDER-LEFT: medium none;
    BORDER-RIGHT: medium none;
    BORDER-TOP: medium none;
    FONT-SIZE: 70%;
    face: verdana
}
TH {
    BACKGROUND-COLOR: #9db9c8;
    BORDER-BOTTOM: lightgrey thin solid;
```

```
      BORDER-LEFT: white thin solid;
      BORDER-RIGHT: lightgrey thin solid;
      BORDER-TOP: white thin solid;
      FONT-SIZE: 70%;
      face: verdana
}
```

Here is the table structure for the database. The foreign key relationships were left out for simplicity, but the diagram should show how they relate.

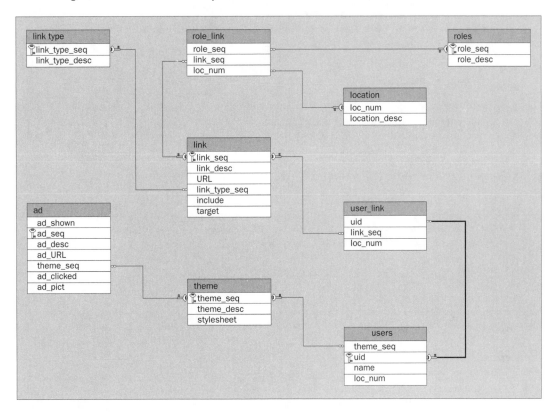

Notice how everything revolves around the link, because it is the item that is pieced together on the screen to create the dynamic user environment. Different roles in the organization display links that they feel are important to the user, and each user has their own personal links, as well as a certain theme that defines the color scheme and the nature of the shown links.

There are scripts needed to build the database. One to create the database, and one to populate it with data. Firstly we create the database (using `portal.sql`):

```
drop table ad;
drop table link;
drop table link_type;
drop table location;
drop table role_link;
drop table roles;
```

```
drop table theme;
drop table user_link;
drop table users;

CREATE TABLE ad (
    ad_shown numeric(18, 0) NULL ,
    ad_seq numeric(18, 0) NOT NULL ,
    ad_desc varchar (50) NULL ,
    ad_URL varchar (50) NULL ,
    theme_seq numeric(18, 0) NULL ,
    ad_clicked numeric(18, 0) NULL ,
    ad_pict varchar (50) NULL
)
;

CREATE TABLE link (
    link_seq numeric(18, 0) NOT NULL ,
    link_desc varchar (50) NULL ,
    URL varchar (255) NULL ,
    link_type_seq numeric(18, 0) NULL ,
    include varchar (50) NULL ,
    target varchar (50) NULL ,
    priority numeric(18, 0) NULL
)
;

CREATE TABLE link_type (
    link_type_seq numeric(18, 0) NOT NULL ,
    link_type_desc varchar (50) NULL
)
;

CREATE TABLE location (
    loc_num numeric(18, 0) NOT NULL ,
    location_desc varchar (50) NULL
)
;

CREATE TABLE role_link (
    role_seq numeric(18, 0) NOT NULL ,
    link_seq numeric(18, 0) NULL ,
    loc_num numeric(18, 0) NULL
)
;

CREATE TABLE roles (
    role_seq numeric(18, 0) NOT NULL ,
    role_desc varchar (50) NULL
)
;

CREATE TABLE theme (
    theme_seq numeric(18, 0) NOT NULL ,
    theme_desc varchar (50) NULL ,
    stylesheet varchar (50) NULL
```

```
)
;

CREATE TABLE user_link (
    uid varchar (50) NULL ,
    link_seq numeric(18, 0) NULL ,
    loc_num numeric(18, 0) NULL
)
;

CREATE TABLE users (
    theme_seq numeric(18, 0) NULL ,
    uid varchar (50) NOT NULL ,
    name varchar (50) NULL ,
    loc_num numeric(18, 0) NULL
)
;
```

Here is the code for `portaldata.sql` that is used to add the data to the database.

```
insert into roles values (1,'manager');
insert into roles values (2,'user');
insert into roles values (3,'executive');
insert into roles values (4,'janitor');

insert into theme values (1,'winter','sheet1.css');
insert into theme values (2,'summer','sheet2.css');
insert into theme values (3,'spring','sheet3.css');
insert into theme values (4,'fall','sheet4.css');

insert into link_type values (1,'URL');
insert into link_type values (2,'Picture');
insert into link_type values (3,'Text');
insert into link_type values (4,'Blinking text');
insert into link_type values (5,'applet');

insert into location values (1,'my home town');
insert into location values (2,'your home town');

insert into users values (3,'bryan','bryan',1);
insert into users values (1,'jeanie','jeanie',1);
insert into users values (1,'hunter','hunter',1);

insert into ad values ('61','1','bills auto shop',
                        'www.yahoo.com','1','9','ad1.jpg');
insert into ad values ('53','2','tamaras salon',
                        'www.yahoo.com','1','5','ad2.gif');
insert into ad values ('46','3','bryans discount tires',
                        'www.yahoo.com','1','5','ad3.gif');

insert into link values ('1','My Link To YAHOO!!',
                        'http:\\www.yahoo.com','1','N','_blank','45');
insert into link values ('2','my link 2','newwroxhead.gif',
                        '2','Y', NULL,'30');
insert into link values ('3','my link 3','newwroxlogo.gif',
```

```
                                       '2','Y', NULL,'40');
insert into link values ('4','my link 4','tester.jsp','1','Y',NULL,'50');
insert into link values ('5','my link 5','Who typed this?',
                         '3','Y', NULL,'60');
insert into link values ('6','my link 6','hello there fellas',
                         '3','Y',NULL,'70');
insert into link values ('7','my link 7','wrox_logo100.gif',
                         '2','Y', NULL,'80');
insert into link values ('8','my link 8','search.jsp','1','Y',NULL,'10');
insert into link values ('9','link 9','This is a message from the CEO:
                         blah blah blah blah merry christmas','3',
                         'Y',NULL,'48');
insert into link values ('10','My Instant Messenger -
                         CLICK ME IF YOU CAN', http://www.bantu.com
                         /messenger/BANTUMessenger.cfm?p_display_logon_id=bp
                         laster@bantu.com&p_server_name=www.bantu.com'
                         ,'1','N','_blank','100');
insert into link values ('11','link 11','This is blinking text',
                         '4','Y', NULL,'35');
insert into link values ('12','my link 12','myapplet.class',
                         '5','Y', NULL,'36');

insert into role_link values (1,1,1);
insert into role_link values (1,2,1);
insert into role_link values (1,3,1);
insert into role_link values (1,8,1);
insert into role_link values (1,9,1);
insert into role_link values (1,11,1);
insert into role_link values (1,12,1);

insert into user_link values ('bryan',4,1);
insert into user_link values ('bryan',5,1);
insert into user_link values ('bryan',6,1);
insert into user_link values ('bryan',7,1);
insert into user_link values ('bryan',10,1);
```

To run these scripts, you need to start up the Cloudscape database in a command prompt window.

```
c:j2sdkee1.2.1\bin\cloudscape -start
```

Then open another window and run the following scripts. These are the scripts described above, put into the /jps1.1.1/database directory (the default installation directory for the Java pet store application). The application comes with the Java class `PopulateTables.class` that takes arguments and runs an SQL script. You can of course use your favorite database GUI tool to run these scripts if you prefer.

The first script (`portal.sql`) is used to build the tables:

```
c:\jps1.1.1\database.sql>java -Dcloudscape.system.home=%J2EE_HOME%\cloudscape -
classpath
.;populate.jar;%J2EE_HOME%\lib\cloudscape\client.jar;%J2EE_HOME%\lib\cloudscape\to
ols.jar;%J2EE_HOME%\lib\cloudscape\cloudscape.jar;%J2EE_HOME%\lib\cloudscape\RmiJd
bc.jar;%J2EE_HOME%\lib\cloudscape\license.jar;%J2EE_HOME%\lib\j2ee.jar
PopulateTables portal.sql ASCII localhost
```

The other script (portaldata.sql) is used to populate the database:

```
c:\jps1.1.1\database.sql>java -Dcloudscape.system.home=%J2EE_HOME%\cloudscape -
classpath
.;populate.jar;%J2EE_HOME%\lib\cloudscape\client.jar;%J2EE_HOME%\lib\cloudscape\to
ols.jar;%J2EE_HOME%\lib\cloudscape\cloudscape.jar;%J2EE_HOME%\lib\cloudscape\RmiJd
bc.jar;%J2EE_HOME%\lib\cloudscape\license.jar;%J2EE_HOME%\lib\j2ee.jar
PopulateTables portaldata.sql ASCII localhost
```

JavaBeans

Java beans are a type of object that is used to encapsulate a program's methods and variables, and provide a public interface that is accessible from the JavaServer Pages. For more information on programming JSP pages and Java Beans, see *Professional JSP, ISBN 1-861003-62-5*, also by *Wrox Press*.

Below are the three beans used to build the portal application:

- ❏ db Bean
- ❏ portal Bean
- ❏ ad Bean

db Bean

The db bean is used to provide access to the database. It has simple connect, close, resultset, and command parameters. The code is shown below. Firstly we have:

```
package myportal;
import java.sql.*;
import java.io.*;

public class db {
    String dbURL = "jdbc:rmi://localhost:1099/jdbc:cloudscape:CloudscapeDB";
    String dbDriver = "RmiJdbc.RJDriver";
    private Connection dbCon;
```

The next block of code provides connection information used to connect to the Cloudscape database using JDBC:

```
    /** Creates new db */
    public db() {
        connect();
    }

    public boolean connect() {
        try {
            Class.forName(this.getDbDriver());
            this.dbCon = DriverManager.getConnection(this.getDbURL(),"","");
        } catch(SQLException se) {
            System.out.println("SQL Error in Connect" + se);
        } catch(ClassNotFoundException ce){
            System.out.println("Class not found in forname" + ce);
        }
```

```
        return true;
    }

    public void close() {
        try {
            this.dbCon.close();
        } catch(SQLException se) {
            System.out.println("SQL Error in Close" + se);
        }
    }
}
```

Below is the command that allows us to produce resultsets from the database and execute database queries against the data:

```
    public ResultSet resultSQL(String sql) {
        try {
            Statement s = dbCon.createStatement();
            ResultSet r = s.executeQuery(sql);
            return r;
        } catch (SQLException se) {
            System.out.println("SQL Error in resultset" + se);
            return null;
        }
    }

    public void execSQL(String sql) {
        try {
            Statement stmt = dbCon.createStatement();
            stmt.executeUpdate(sql);//run the query
        } catch (SQLException se) {
            System.out.println("SQL Error in exec" + se);
        }
    }

    public String getDbURL() {
        return this.dbURL;
    }

    public String getDbDriver() {
        return this.dbDriver;
    }
}
```

portal Bean

The next Java Bean is the `portal` bean. This bean is responsible for getting all of the information from the database into objects that can be worked on with the JSP page. This allows for strong encapsulation and the absence of any JDBC code in the JSP pages. Setters were not used for simplicity.

```
package myportal;
import java.util.*;
import java.sql.*;
```

```
public class portal {

    /** Creates new portal */
    public portal() {
    }

    private myportal.db mydb = new db();
    private ResultSet roleLink = null;
    private ResultSet userLink = null;

    private int rlink_seq;
    private String rlink_desc ="";
    private String rURL ="";
    private int rlink_type_seq;
    private String rinclude ="";
    private String rtarget ="";

    private int ulink_seq;
    private String ulink_desc ="";
    private String uURL ="";
    private int ulink_type_seq;
    private String uinclude ="";
    private String utarget ="";
    private String utheme="none";
    private String ustylesheet="none";

    public boolean getRoleLinkSections() {
        try {
            roleLink = mydb.resultSQL("select l.link_seq,l.link_desc, l.URL,
                                      l.link_type_seq, l.include, l.target,
                                      l.priority from role_link rl,
                                      link l where rl.link_seq =
                                      l.link_seq order by l.priority");

        } catch (Exception se) {
            System.out.println("error with role link selections" + se);
            return false;
        }
        return true;
    }

    public boolean getUserStuff(String uid) {
        try {
            ResultSet user = mydb.resultSQL("select t.theme_seq,
                                            t.stylesheet from theme t,
                                            users u where t.theme_seq =
                                            u.theme_seq and u.uid =
                                            '" + uid.trim() + "'");
            user.next();
            this.utheme = user.getString("theme_seq");
            this.ustylesheet = user.getString("stylesheet");
        } catch (Exception se) {
            System.out.println("error with user stuff------------------" + se);
            return false;
        }
```

```
            return true;
        }

    public boolean nextRoleLink() {
        try {
            if (this.roleLink.next()) {
                this.rlink_seq  = roleLink.getInt("link_seq");
                this.rlink_desc = roleLink.getString("link_desc");
                this.rURL = roleLink.getString("URL");
                this.rlink_type_seq = roleLink.getInt("link_type_seq");
                this.rinclude = roleLink.getString("include");
                this.rtarget = roleLink.getString("target");
            } else {
                return false;
            }
        } catch (Exception se) {
            System.out.println("error with NEXT role link selections" + se);
            return false;
        }
        return true;
    }

    public boolean nextUserLink() {
        try {
            if (this.userLink.next()) {
                this.ulink_seq  = userLink.getInt("link_seq");
                this.ulink_desc = userLink.getString("link_desc");
                this.uURL = userLink.getString("URL");
                this.ulink_type_seq = userLink.getInt("link_type_seq");
                this.uinclude = userLink.getString("include");
                this.utarget = userLink.getString("target");
            } else {
                return false;
            }
        } catch (Exception se) {
            System.out.println("error with NEXT user link selections" + se);
            return false;
        }
        return true;
    }

    public boolean getUserLinkSections(String uid) {
        try {
            userLink = mydb.resultSQL("select distinct l.link_seq, l.link_desc,
                                l.URL,l.link_type_seq, l.include,
                                l.target, l.priority from link l,
                                user_link ul, users u where l.link_seq =
                                ul.link_seq and ul.uid =
                                '" + uid + "' order by l.priority");

        } catch (Exception se) {
            System.out.println("error with user link selections" + se);
            return false;
        }
        return true;
```

```
    }

    public int getrLinkSeq() {
        return this.rlink_seq;
    }

    public String getrLinkDesc() {
        return this.rlink_desc;
    }

    public String getrURL() {
        return this.rURL;
    }

    public int getrLinkTypeSeq() {
        return this.rlink_type_seq;
    }

    public String getrInclude() {
        return this.rinclude;
    }

    public String getrTarget() {
        if (this.rtarget == null) {
            this.rtarget = "";
        }
        return this.rtarget;
    }

    public int getuLinkSeq() {
        return this.ulink_seq;
    }

    public String getuLinkDesc() {
        return this.ulink_desc;
    }

    public String getuURL() {
        return this.uURL;
    }

    public int getuLinkTypeSeq() {
        return this.ulink_type_seq;
    }

    public String getuInclude() {
        return this.uinclude;
    }

    public String getuTheme() {
        return this.utheme;
    }

    public String getuStylesheet() {
        return this.ustylesheet;
```

```
    }

    public String getuTarget() {
        if (this.utarget == null) {
            this.utarget = "";
        }
        return this.utarget;
    }
}
```

ad Bean

The ad bean is set up to work with the HTTP session of the JSP page. It only reads from the database one time to get the ads that relate to the theme that is tied to the user and puts them into a vector that is stored in the session of the web server. The rest of the code is "getters" to get the data that relates to the ad. Setters have been omitted for simplicity.

```
package myportal;
import java.sql.*;
import java.util.*;

public class ad {

    private Vector myads = new Vector(10);
    private int adIndex = 999999999;
    private myportal.db mydb = new db();
    private String adURL = "";
    private String adPict = "";
    private int adSeq = 0;

    /** Creates new ad */
    public ad() {
    }

    public boolean getAds (int theme_seq) {
        if (this.adIndex != 999999999) {//if this has already been gotten
            return false;
        }

        this.adIndex = 0;
        this.myads.clear();

        try {
            ResultSet r = mydb.resultSQL("
                        select ad_seq from ad where theme_seq = " + theme_seq);
            while (r.next()) {
                this.myads.add(this.adIndex,r.getString("ad_seq"));
                                                    //add ad_seq to vector
                this.adIndex++;
            }
        } catch(SQLException se) {
            System.out.println("failed -ad seq" + se);
            return false;
        }
```

```
            return true;
    }

    public String getNextAd() {
        if ((adIndex!=0) & (adIndex >= myads.size()-1)) {
            adIndex = 0;
        } else {adIndex++;
    }


    //get ad info
    ResultSet r = mydb.resultSQL("select distinct ad_URL,
                                ad_pict from ad where ad_seq =
                                " + myads.get(adIndex));
    try {
        while (r.next()) {
            adPict = r.getString("ad_pict"); //add ad_seq to vector
            this.adURL = r.getString("ad_URL"); //add ad_seq to vector
            this.adSeq = Integer.parseInt((String)myads.get(adIndex));
                                        //Get advertisement sequence
        }
    } catch(Exception se) {
        System.out.println("failed -next ad" + se);}
        return adPict;
    }

    public int numAdShown() {
        ResultSet r = mydb.resultSQL("select ad_shown from ad where ad_seq =
                                " + myads.get(adIndex));
        try {
            if(r.next()) {
                return r.getInt("ad_shown");
            }
        } catch(Exception se) {
            System.out.println("failed " + se);}
            return 0;
        }

    public int numAdClicked() {
        ResultSet r = mydb.resultSQL("select ad_clicked from ad where ad_seq =
                                " + myads.get(adIndex));
        try {
            if(r.next()) {
                return r.getInt("ad_clicked");
            }
        } catch(Exception se) {
            System.out.println("failed " + se);}
            return 0;
        }

    public void adClicked (int ad_seq) {
        try {
            mydb.execSQL("update ad set ad_clicked =
                        ad_clicked + 1 where ad_seq = " + ad_seq);
        } catch(Exception se) {
            System.out.println("failed -ad clicked" + se);}
```

```
    }

public void adShown (int ad_seq) {
    try {
        mydb.execSQL("update ad set ad_shown=ad_shown + 1 where ad_seq =
                    " + ad_seq);
    } catch(Exception se) {
        System.out.println("failed -ad clicked" + se);}
    }

public String getAdURL() {
    return this.adURL;
}

public String getAdPict() {
    return this.adPict;
}

public int getAdSeq() {
    return this.adSeq;
}

public Vector getMyAds() {
    return this.myads;
}

public int getAdIndex() {
    return this.adIndex;
}
}
```

JSPs

Here we're going to be looking at the application display starting with the main page of the portal.

Portal Display

The portaldisplay.jsp code carries out the following tasks:

1. Loads up the ad and portal beans

2. Gets advertisement information and decides what advertisement to show next

3. Gets user information (the user name is hard-coded here)

4. Sets the theme (style sheet)

5. Loops through all of the role based links and displays them

6. Shows the theme selections

7. Loops through all of the user based links and displays them

The code is for `portaldisplay.jsp` shown below:

```html
<html>
<head>

<%@ page language="java" import="java.sql.*,myportal.*" %>
<jsp:useBean id="theportal" scope="request" class="myportal.portal" />
<jsp:useBean id="myad" scope="session" class="myportal.ad" />

<%
    int theme_seq = 1;
    String myad_URL = "";
    int myrows = 0;
    String link_desc;
    String uid = "bryan";                      //Simplify the user name
    String[] selected = {"","",""};

    boolean ads = myad.getAds(theme_seq);      //Get ads if we haven't already
    myad.getNextAd();                          //Get the next add to display in
                                               //the object
    theportal.getUserStuff(uid);

    //style sheet section
    String stylesheet = request.getParameter("stylesheet");
    if (stylesheet != null) {
       selected[Integer.parseInt(stylesheet)] = "SELECTED"; //for list box

       //figure out which stylesheet to pick
       switch ((int)Integer.parseInt(stylesheet))\ {
           case 0: stylesheet = "style1.css";break;
           case 1: stylesheet = "style2.css";break;
           case 2: stylesheet = "style3.css";break;
       }
    } else {
       stylesheet = theportal.getuStylesheet();
    }

%>
<link REL="stylesheet" TYPE="text/css" HREF="<%=stylesheet%>" />

<title>
    portal
</title>
</head>

<body>
<table>
<tr><th width="100%"><h1> Welcome to the wonderful world of Portals!!!
<h1></th></tr>
</table>
```

```
<hr></hr>
<table>
<form name="ad_form" method="POST" action="adsubmit.jsp?ad= <%=myad.getAdURL()%>
&adseq= <%=Integer.toString(myad.getAdSeq())%>">

<tr><td>We all have to have ads :-) </td>
<td></td>
<td><img src="pictures/<%=myad.getAdPict()%>" onClick=
"document.ad_form.submit();"> </td>
<td>
<td><table><tr><td>Ad Clicked:</td>
<td><%=myad.numAdClicked()%> times</td></tr>
<tr><td>Ad Shown:</td><td><%=myad.numAdShown()%> times</td></tr>
</table></td></tr>

</form>
</table>
<hr></hr>

<table border=1>
<tr>
<%
   myad.adShown (myad.getAdSeq()) ;//update ad shown
   myrows=0;
   theportal.getRoleLinkSections();
   while (theportal.nextRoleLink()) {        //Loop through all of the options
                                             //for the role to show
      myrows++;%>

<% if(myrows >= 4) { %> </tr><tr> <%
      myrows = 0;} %>

<%
//-----------------------------------display role-----------------------
      switch (theportal.getrLinkTypeSeq()) {
          case 1://URL
          if (theportal.getrInclude().trim().equals("Y")) { // include %>
             <td><jsp:include page="<%=theportal.getrURL()%>" flush="true" />
             </td>

      <% } else { //do not include %>
             <td><a href="<%=theportal.getrURL()%>" target="
          %=theportal.getrTarget()%>"><%=theportal.getrLinkDesc()%></a></td>

      <% }
         break;

         case 2: //is pict - always include
      %>
         <td><img src="pictures/<%=theportal.getrURL()%>"></td>
```

```
        <%
           break;

           case 3: //is text - always include
        %>
           <td><b><%=theportal.getrURL()%></b></td>
        <%
           break;

           case 4: //is blinking text - always include
        %>

           <td><BLINK><%=theportal.getrURL()%></BLINK></td>
        <%
           break;

           case 5: //is applet - always include
        %>
           <td><APPLET code="<%=theportal.getrURL()%>" width=150
               height=100></APPLET></td>
        <%
           break;

//--------------------------------display role-------------------------
        }
     }%>

</tr>
</table>
<hr></hr>

<table border=1>
<tr><td>My Theme</td><td>
<form name="style_form" method="POST" action="portaldisplay.jsp">
<select name="stylesheet" onChange="document.style_form.submit();">
<option <%=selected[0]%> value="0">theme 0</option>
<option <%=selected[1]%> value="1">theme 1</option>
<option <%=selected[2]%> value="2">theme 2</option>
</select>
</form>

<tr>
<% myrows = 0;
   theportal.getUserLinkSections(uid);
   while (theportal.nextUserLink()) {
      myrows++;%>

   <% if (myrows >=4) { %> </tr><tr><%
         myrows = 0;
      } %>
```

```
<%
//----------------------------------display user stuff---------------------
      switch (theportal.getuLinkTypeSeq()) {
        case 1: //URL
            if (theportal.getuInclude().trim().equals("Y")) {  // include %>

                <td><jsp:include page="<%=theportal.getuURL()%>" flush="true"
                    </td>

        <% } else { //do not include%>
                <td><a href="<%=theportal.getuURL()%>" target="
        <%=theportal.getuTarget()%>"><%=theportal.getuLinkDesc()%></a></td>

        <% }
          break;
          case 2:   //is pict - always include
        %>
          <td><img src="pictures/<%=theportal.getuURL()%>"></td>
        <%
          break;

          case 3:     //is text - always include%>
          <td><b><%=theportal.getuURL()%></b></td>
        <%
          break;

          case 4: //is blinking text - always include
        %>
          <td><BLINK><%=theportal.getuURL()%></BLINK></td>
        <%
          break;

          case 5: //is applet - always include
        %>
          <td><APPLET code="<%=theportal.getuURL()%>" width=150
              height=100></APPLET></td>
        <%
          break;
//------------------------------end display user stuff---------------------
      }
    } %>
</tr>
</table>
</body>
</html>
```

Ad Submit

The Adsubmit.jsp page is a simple page. When the advertisement is clicked, information is gathered from the query string, the correct advertisement's hit counter is incremented, and then the user is redirected to the page that the advertisement was linked to:

```
<%@ page language="java" import="java.sql.*" %>
<jsp:useBean id="ad" scope="session" class="myportal.ad" />


<%

String AdURL = request.getParameter("ad");
int adSeq = Integer.parseInt(request.getParameter("adseq"));


ad.adClicked(adSeq);

%>
<html>
<head><title>JSP Page</title></head>
<body>
<% response.sendRedirect("http://"+AdURL);%>

</body>
</html>
```

Search Form Page

This page is included in `portaldisplay.jsp`. The search page is from http://www.Freefind.com. The process here was to go to **Freefind** and instruct their agents to search the portal site; some HTML is then provided by them that can be included into the portal to allow easy searching. The code is below:

```
<html>
   <head> <title> Search </title> </head>
   <body>
      <table>
         <td>
         <center>
         <FORM ACTION = "http://search.freefind.com/find.html"
         METHOD = "GET" target = "_top">
           
         <font size = 1 face = "arial,helvetica" >
         <A HREF = "http://search.freefind.com/find.html?id=5588468">
            Search this site</A>
         or
         <A HREF = "http://search.freefind.com/find.html?id=5588468&t=w">
            the web </a>
               
         powered by <A HREF = "http://www.freefind.com"> FreeFind </A> <br>
         <INPUT TYPE = "HIDDEN" NAME = "id" SIZE = "-1" VALUE = "5588468">
         <INPUT TYPE = "HIDDEN" NAME = "pid" SIZE = "-1" VALUE = "r">
         <INPUT TYPE = "HIDDEN" NAME = "mode" SIZE = "-1" VALUE =
            "ALL"> 
         <INPUT TYPE = "TEXT" NAME = "query" SIZE = "20">
         <INPUT TYPE = "SUBMIT" VALUE = " Find! ">
         <INPUT TYPE = "SUBMIT" NAME = "sitemap" VALUE = "Site Map">
            <br>
         </center>
```

```
       
        <INPUT TYPE = "radio" NAME = "t" VALUE = "s" CHECKED> Site search
        <INPUT TYPE = "radio" NAME = "t" VALUE = "w"> Web search
    </font></FORM></td></table>

  <A HREF = "http://search.freefind.com/find.html?id=5588468&m=0&p=0">
    Site Map </A>    
  <A HREF = "http://search.freefind.com/find.html?id=5588468&w=0&p=0">
    What's New </A>    
  <A HREF = "http://search.freefind.com/find.html?id=5588468">
    <B> Search </B> </A>
  </body>
</html>
```

Theme Link List

This page is again included in `portaldisplay.jsp`. It's just a file that is used to show how **includes** work for the portal. Including common JSPs or JSP fragments can minimize code and markup duplication. It is analogous to procedural code reuse. There are two types of include in JSP1.1:

❑ **Static** – A static include inserts the content of the included JSP at translation time into the including JSP; this then uses the included content along with its own content to build the Java source file that will be compiled.

❑ **Dynamic** – The request is passed to the specified URL with the response inserted into the page response. The contents of the statically included file must be legal in the including file at the point at which it is included. Dynamic includes do not even have to be JSPs; static HTML or other dynamically generated content can be included.

Based on the type of link that is listed for the user or the role, a JSP file could be included to render and be a part of the `portaldisplay.jsp` page. This file looks at the theme that is used and includes the proper links to support that theme. The code is below:

```
<html>

<%@ page language="java" %>
<%
String theme = request.getParameter("stylesheet");
if (theme == null) {
   theme = "0";
}
%>
<head>
</head>
<body>

<% switch(Integer.parseInt(theme)) {

   case 0: %>
<table>
<tr><td>I have been included----------------------</td></tr>
```

```
<tr><td>Theme 0 links:</td></tr>
<tr><td><a href="http://www.wrox.com" target="_blank">content link 1</a></td></tr>
<tr><td><a href="http://www.wrox.com" target="_blank">content link 2</a></td></tr>
<tr><td><a href="http://www.wrox.com" target="_blank">content link 3</a></td></tr>
<tr><td><a href="http://www.wrox.com" target="_blank">content link 4</a></td></tr>
<tr><td><a href="http://www.wrox.com" target="_blank">content link 5</a></td></tr>
</table>
<%
   break;
   case 1: %>
<table>
<tr><td>I have been included----------------------</td></tr>
<tr><td>Theme 1 links:</td></tr>
<tr><td><a href="http://www.wrox.com" target="_blank">content link 6</a></td></tr>
<tr><td><a href="http://www.wrox.com" target="_blank">content link 7</a></td></tr>
<tr><td><a href="http://www.wrox.com" target="_blank">content link 8</a></td></tr>
<tr><td><a href="http://www.wrox.com" target="_blank">content link 9</a></td></tr>
<tr><td><a href="http://www.wrox.com" target="_blank">content link
10</a></td></tr>
</table>
<%
   break;
   case 2: %>
<table>
<table>
<tr><td>I have been included----------------------</td></tr>
<tr><td>Theme 2 links:</td></tr>
<tr><td><a href="http://www.wrox.com" target="_blank">content link
11</a></td></tr>
<tr><td><a href="http://www.wrox.com" target="_blank">content link
12</a></td></tr>
<tr><td><a href="http://www.wrox.com" target="_blank">content link
13</a></td></tr>
<tr><td><a href="http://www.wrox.com" target="_blank">content link
14</a></td></tr>
<tr><td><a href="http://www.wrox.com" target="_blank">content link
15</a></td></tr>
</table>
<%
   break;
}
%>
</body>
</html>
```

Additional Features

We have two last features to look at – applet support and instant messaging, and we'll finish the example by making some general comments about the example.

Applet Support

The `myapplet.java` file is a sample applet to show flexibility in our system by allowing Java applet support for interactive sections of our applet such as games, moving pictures, and so on.

```java
import java.applet.*;
import java.awt.*;

public class myApplet extends Applet {

    public void paint(Graphics g) {
        g.drawString("Hello World Applet", 25, 50);
    }
}
```

Instant Messaging

There are many instant messaging services out on the Internet. The one that was chosen was from www.bantu.com. It was picked because it has a web-based interface that can communicate with other messengers, such as ICQ, MSN, and Yahoo. This service was signed up for and a URL was retrieved. This was then put into the database to be linkable. Look at the link at the bottom on the portal.

The result looks something like the screenshot below.

General Comments

What has been built is a very simple portal that accesses a database and displays on the screen information relevant to the user viewing the portal. It is not representative of a portal that would be used in a true production environment. For example, this is based on a model 1 JSP architecture, there is no connection pooling in the database access (a new connection is created each time) and there is no administration or configuration for the user. All of these features were left out of this example to drive across the functionality of portals, the basic concepts of how they work, and the different services that they employ. Chapter 15 presents a case study on a portal vendor that walks the user through building an enterprise type portal using current technologies such as Enterprise JavaBeans and Dynamic HTML.

Finally for the chapter, let's explicitly look at the commerce angle of portals.

Making Money with Your Portal

Advertising is one of the most common ways to help a portal pay for itself, because advertisements can be aimed at a known user base. A smart portal understands the context of the content that is being displayed, and based on that content, it can show the appropriate advertisement. A good advertisement manager program should be able to accomplish all of these tasks. Here are some suggestions:

❑ **Rotating Banners** – These are the simplest way to show advertisements. This can be accomplished by taking the numbers of actual advertisements for a site, and rotate them one at a time for each page click. What this will accomplish is showing a different advertisement to the user each time the portal page is displayed. This technique doesn't require much personalization, so it only works if the portal has a solid theme that will always relate to the advertisements (such as a computer parts portal, an automotive portal, or a job portal).

❑ **Affiliate Programs** – In their simplest form, these are exchange programs that allow a webmaster to join the affiliate program, put related ads on their site, then gather commission checks as a result of those advertisements being clicked.

❑ **Content Groups** – Generally advertisements are based on meta tags in the header of each web page that describes a topic that the page belongs to. Many of the search engines have taken this approach to the next level by displaying advertisements that have a strong relevance to what is being searched in each session.

❑ **Tracking Hits** – It is important to track the show / hit ratio of each advertisement to see how well the portal's marketing strategy towards customers is working. Our example shows these statistics at the top by the advertisement, but generally, this data is stored, analyzed, and sent to the advertiser. If the portal is advertising through an affiliate program, that program should always have an up to the minute click rate (and commission rate) that can be accessed to determine marketing statistics.

❑ **"Buy Now" Advertisements** – These are mainly used at shopping sites (or shopping portals) that look at the customer patterns and users viewing (or at random) and recommend products that customers can add to the shopping cart with a single click. A similar approach also applies for up-selling and cross-selling advertisements, which have the ability to "recommend" a product that the customer is likely to buy based on their previous purchases or interests.

❑ **Multi-Branding** – This sales technique is a process where one company will make a product, and another company will sell a slightly modified version of that product with their own label and maybe even additional features. This would allow a portal provider (who creates the portal offering) to stay focused on creating diverse technologies, while other companies (their customers) spend time in sales and marketing.

❑ **Subscription Sales** – These fall along the same lines as an Application Service Provider (ASP). It is difficult to get the consumer market to pay for something that is already free in many different forms. However, it has been seen repeatedly that companies will pay for a service that all of their employees can use, a service that combines categories and themes of information together at a first glance, such as a newspaper in the real world.

❑ **Customer Loyalty Programs** – Such programs are quickly becoming the next level of intelligence that personalization is bringing to the Internet. Tracking the interests and preferences of the customer and selling and/or using those customer patterns to benefit the user experience could become the deciding factor of how many users are attracted to a portal and how long they stay.

Summary

In this chapter, we covered the different types of portals, the markets that they consume, and the technical concepts that portals are based upon. We discussed a build vs. buy scenario, and then constructed a very simple portal that covers the basic concepts of what any portal might include. (To see how companies in the market are creating high volume, flexible portals with Enterprise Java Beans and DHTML, look at Chapter 15 on a customizable portal architecture.) The last section pointed out some ways in which we could make some money from our portal offering if desired, and what other companies are currently doing along these lines.

Portals have become a very trendy and overused word in the Internet culture over the past few years. The fact is that all web applications are beginning to resemble the common features of a portal and will continue to do so in the future. The average Internet user is growing to expect a rich environment that is customizable and adaptable to their needs. The next chapter will build on what we've discussed in this chapter to provide a marketplace example of a portal that will demonstrate these concepts.

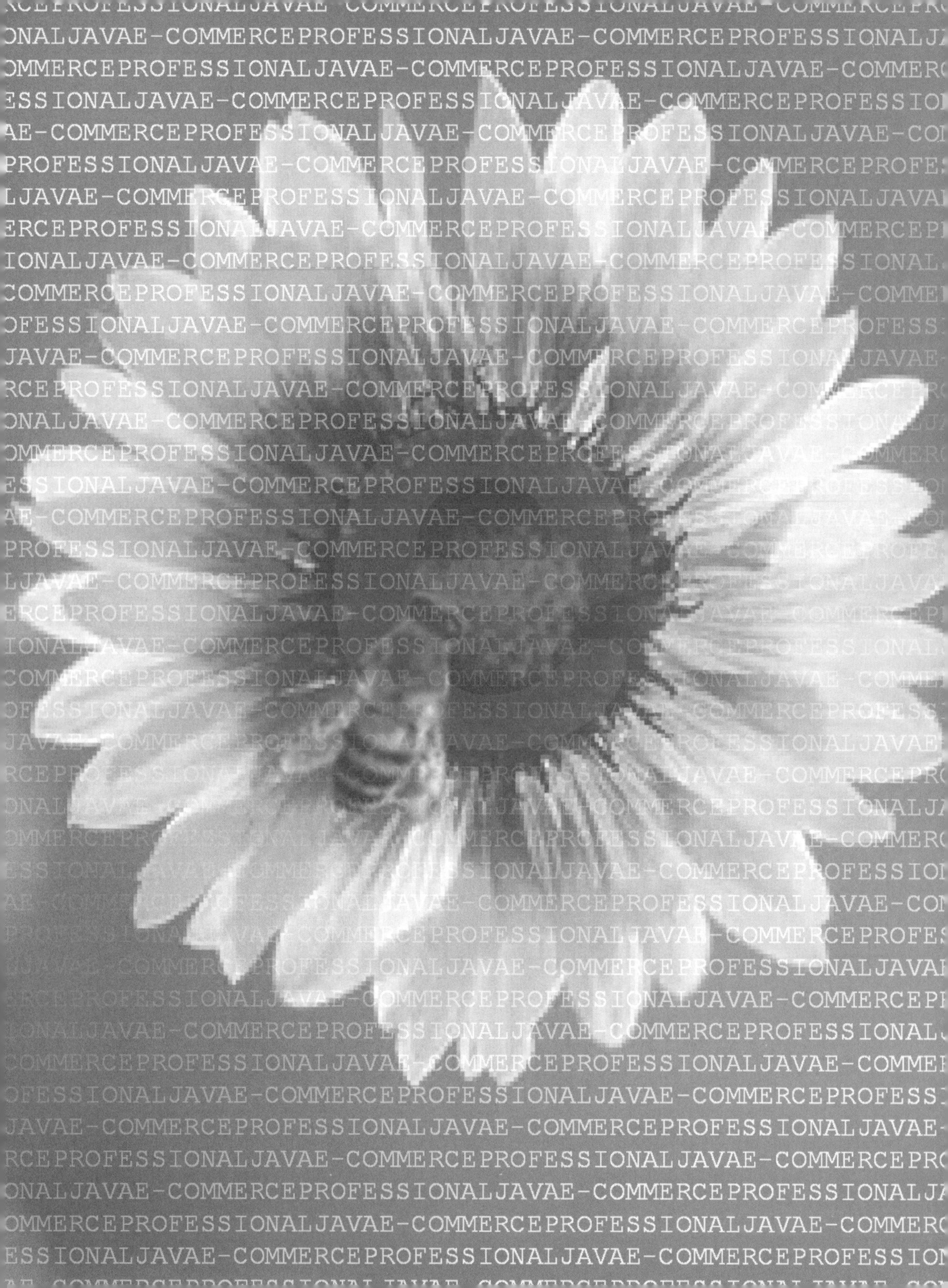
PROFESSIONALJAVAE-COMMERCE

15

In the Marketplace B – A Customizable Portal Architecture

This chapter builds on the basic overview of portals developed previously, and here I will concentrate on architectures and ideas for portals, how we can automate some of the programming tasks by using a framework, and what happened when we tried to implement some of these ideas at magic4 (http://www.magic4.com).

magic4 develop client software for mobile phones to allow the embedding of simple multimedia elements within text messaging. As part of the marketing it was decided that a portal would be created to demonstrate the advantages of magic4 messaging. To make the project commercially viable, the portal would be licensed to third parties to allow them to both run a portal and take advantage of magic4 technology features.

What am I not going to talk about? I'm not going to talk in any depth about backend information. This includes talking to Application Servers, the objects running on the Application Servers, or anything to do with databases.

Therefore, our route through the chapter is going to be:

❑ Laying the foundations – a look at user requirements, design patterns and technology choices

❑ The design of the portal

❑ The implementation of the portal and a framework sample

❑ A post mortem of the project as discussed

In the previous chapter, the idea of a portal being a personal, filtered view on some relevant information was presented. What I'm going to do here is to try to create a framework that can support these areas, whilst being a bit special. Before we get going, let's just recap on the basics of portals and how some of them are dealt with at magic4.

Portal Components

As we saw in the previous chapter, the requirements for the portal are content, feeds and filters, personalization, profiling, customization, multi-branding, security, and multiple front-end clients. Let's just pick out decisions we took in some of these areas:

❑ **Content** – We've been consistently disappointed with content providers until we got into paying big sums of money for the content feed (for example £10,000 / $15,000 per annum). Having said that if you want to opt for a more manual approach (and face it, when you're talking about thousands of pounds or dollars you can afford a little manual input, at least at the start) it's fairly easy to include an admin section where either you or your content partners can update their information and articles. This is the particular route we've taken with some of our smaller content providers – in some cases start-up companies without the technical expertise to deliver content to us in a reliable electronic format (and I have to admit that their content is very good).

❑ **Feeds and Filters** – As mentioned above, our main feeds were from specialized content providers to which we gave access though web based forms. The articles contained all the usual elements – a headline, author, short body, long body and picture. Additionally, we stored the supplier and publication date. The short body was required as we were also supplying news via mobile devices.

❑ **Personalization** – The basic premise we operate on is that the user can save their settings, such as what the last view was, how their page is laid out, etc. To extend that further, we want to let the user personalize what they can see. We'll talk about this a lot more when we discuss the requirements for our portal.

❑ **Multi-branding** – In the magic4 portal we use a whole set of front-end pages for each different brand. This gives us maximum flexibility for the look and feel but we can still use the same underlying content and services. Each front-end is based on a reference (or template!) set.

Of course we can't forget that we need to make money from our portal. As pointed out in the last chapter, a number of portals offer value added services of their own, and this is the model used by magic4. We charge our customers to send information to their mobile phones such as sports results, or perhaps a joke of the day.

Laying the Foundations

Here we're going to look at four particular topics:

❑ The user and technical requirements for the project

❑ The framework design

❑ The application backend

❑ The technologies we can choose from

Requirements for our Portal

After looking at the general components, specifically, what would we want to accomplish in our portal framework? We want to be able to support everything we've discussed so far, as well as a few extra GUI features that will make the portal even stickier.

User Requirements – Themes, Services, and Agents

From a user's point of view, we want the portal to be as customizable as possible without being too complicated. So, let's consider the concepts of **themes**, **services**, and **agents**:

- ❏ **Theme** – The look and feel of a particular front-end (a bit like a Windows theme or a Winamp "Skin").

- ❏ **Service** – A particular application that the portal provides, such as news, messaging, search, products, etc. A theme would generally have a number of services, but can have from zero to infinity.

- ❏ **Agent** – A small view on a particular application to be shown on the homepage. For example, for news it may be the latest headlines, for messaging a note like "You have 6 new messages", or for searching a single input box to do a quick search. A service may have any number of agents.

A user then, has a given theme selected, let's say "fishing", and will then see a set of services for the "fishing" theme (news, river maps, fish list) and a number of agents (headlines, featured river, fish of the day).

However, as our system is customizable, the user could either:

- ❏ Select another theme; let's try "night clubs". Their look and feel will change to "clubbing" and a set of new services will be added (club database, dance charts) along with their associated agents (featured club, dance top 5). If the news service exists in both "fishing" and "clubbing" then it will be replaced. Any services (or agents) that do not exist in the new theme will remain.

- ❏ Add services from another theme, such as "cars". Their look and feel stays the same but the new service (and optionally, agent) will appear in their service list. This allows the user to mix and match services from different themes.

- ❏ Add or remove some services or agents from their existing list. If a service is removed then all the associated agents will also be removed.

Sounds interesting? Well, it needs to be simple and easy to use – this means clear point and click. You don't want to have to read the help pages just to add or remove a service, and you definitely don't want a command line interface for changing the look!

Let's look at an example from the magic4 portal:

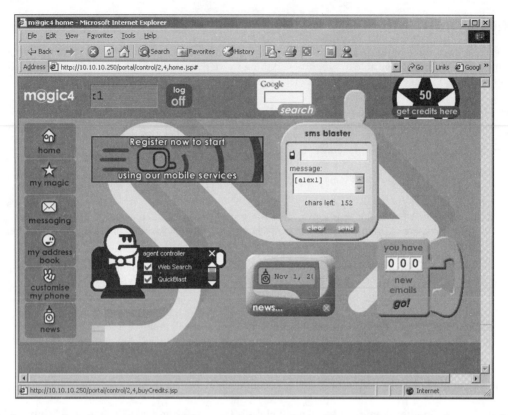

In the screenshot above, we can see the homepage for a particular theme, with a number of agents visible, and on the left hand side the navigation bar allowing access to the available services. The navigation bar is a special agent as it is belongs to a locked (so that the user cannot remove it) service (the homepage). The navigation bar is also locked, however the credit agent (you have x credits) that also belongs to the homepage service can be added and removed by the user as desired.

Technical Requirements

Now that we know what we have to deliver we just need to figure out how. To find out what we need technically, let's go through the components again:

❑ **Content** – Content needs to be read either statically from disk or dynamically from a database. In some cases, a bit of both. If we have several themes all showing different views on the same services then we need to centralize the content code to avoid duplication.

❑ **Feeds and Filters** – We need to be able to run background operations to update content. We may need to convert the content to our own formats. We must also allow our own content developers to deploy and change new services and content throughout the lifetime of the system. The system should not have to go down to make these changes.

❑ **Personalization** – The system needs to remember the user's settings wherever they log in from. From the other side, as we have third party web developers implementing services it must be easy for the developers implementing the services to save settings wherever possible – otherwise they won't use it!

❑ **Profiling** – There must be a background API to remember what the user has done and allow the front-end to use this information.

❑ **Customization** – The user must be able to change themes, services and agents quickly and easily. The system must remember all the changes no matter from where the user logs in.

❑ **Multi-branding** – The system must run several different look and feels, which must be able to be completely customizable, while still allowing the user to choose from the various services.

❑ **Security** – The system must authenticate the user and load their settings. Different areas of the site may need different levels of security.

❑ **Multiple front-end clients** – The system must allow access to the data from systems other than web-servers; for example digital TV servers or, in the case of magic4, messaging applications. This allows the messaging system to send the news you've selected to your mobile phone.

In the case of this example, I'm not going to talk about the actual mechanisms of content and the associated feeds and filters. Suffice to say that the architecture must fit it all in. Again, the mechanisms of personalization and profiling will be left for other discussion, and, in this case, security will be implemented at deployment time.

At magic4, we implemented personalization by providing a central object that could be called from any service or front-end system. The object stored `name=value` pairs and associated them with a particular user. In this way, the user could log in from any location or device and still get the same settings.

The profiling was implemented by registering keyword hits whenever a service is used. A hit can be given a weighting, so if a user subscribes to a service then a keyword hit may be much stronger than if a user clicks on a link. The service can then provide a listing of the top keyword hits. The listing is used to decide if products or articles should receive priority placement.

So what's left? Well, a framework for running multiple, customizable, portals that can grow to fill all these other needs as required.

Framework Design

One of our key requirements is to run several different themes on the same system. If we were to implement each theme separately there would be much code duplication, and it would be virtually impossible to allow the user to mix and match services and agents from different themes.

As with most large systems then, we're going to need a framework to take care of the common functionality. The most popular framework or architecture for this kind of application is the **Model-View-Controller** paradigm (**MVC**). This consists of a number of components, partitioned as follows:

❑ Model – these components represent the core business logic and maintain state. They are generally implemented as enterprise objects and map to either business data in corporate databases, or the core business logic that performs the processing and rules.

❑ View – these components display the results of the client's requests. There is only display logic within the implementation and there are generally different components for each type of client.

❑ Controller – these components implement the workflow specific to your application. They would generally use combinations of the model components to achieve their goal.

At magic4, we extended the MVC architecture to add an extra class of components – handlers. The function of the handler is actually part of the Controller in MVC, in that the handler performs a specific operation using the model like sending a message or updating the user's preferences. The reason we had them as distinct components is that we wanted third party developers to be able to create handlers without having access to the core framework. We'll see more about how the handlers actually work later on,

Core Framework – Model, View, Controller, and Handler

Here's how the different parts of the core framework interact:

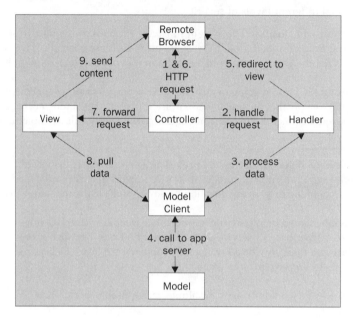

In summary,

- ❏ The remote browser makes a request [1]
- ❏ The request is diverted to the controller that creates and calls a handler [2]
- ❏ The handler uses the model client [3] to call into the model [4] to do some work
- ❏ The handler then redirects the remote browser to an appropriate view [5]
- ❏ The remote browser requests the view [6]
- ❏ The request is diverted to the controller that forwards the request to the view [7]
- ❏ The view then uses the client to pull some data from the model [8]
- ❏ The view then sends the content back to the remote browser [9]

Let's dig into this a little deeper:

View

These are the components that display the results of the client's request. For our purposes these components will create HTML to send back to the browser. In Java these would probably be JavaServer Pages (JSP) but could be servlets. In a standalone application the view components may be Swing components that display the results directly.

Controller

This component is responsible for running the actual application, but delegates the actual work to the handler components. As all requests pass through the controller, it can perform all sorts of security and user checking as required. The controller may take any number of forms (in Java a servlet or a JSP) but each does the same job – it intercepts all requests for a given web application and performs some kind of pre-processing.

This has several important advantages:

❑ It lets you set up data objects or references to be used by a particular page.

❑ You can check permissions/credit levels/account status, and then make decisions about allowing the user to access the page. You can decide what page and elements to return to the user based onthe results of their query.

In the more traditional MVC framework, the controller would convert the web requests to events that are passed into the back end (model). We want to make it easy for content developers to update and maintain this site, so this step is moved away from the controller and into the handlers (see below).

Model & Model Clients

This is the actual service and performs real work. The model represents the core business logic for the system and typically would maintain any state or data. The model is implemented as enterprise objects on an application server. The model clients are components that reside locally to the calling application (usually remotely from the model) and provide an easy to use interface to the model.

The model client components make using the model easier as they take care of all the application server related issues such as locating the EJB and managing their lifecycle. They can also provide large performance gains by caching static lists (for example country codes or product types) locally to the model client components. That way if there are thousands of web requests asking for this static information it both gives faster performance for the user, and lowers the load on the application server.

Handlers

These are components that use the model to perform a particular function, for example, sending an e-mail. In a simple application this code would be placed inside the same object as the view (a JSP that POSTs data to itself). In the MVC architecture, it is the controller that performs this task (usually by first normalizing the request into an event that can be understood by the model).

It was a requirement at magic4 that the flow of the system could be changed for each different brand (see multi-branding above). To allow this, we could not set the workflow in a central controller component (MVC), so, to remain flexible, we had both the view and the handlers dictating the workflow and calling into the model client components. This allowed our third-party content developers to have maximum flexibility when authoring their services, without having access to the underlying framework.

It should be noted that it is not a requirement of this framework that every request has a handler. Some will just pass straight through to a view.

Views & Helper Objects

There are going to be several occasions when the view objects want to access the facilities provided by the framework. Rather than placing the code directly in the view, we should provide helper objects to perform this common functionality. In Java, this would be a JavaBean.

Pros and Cons

This kind of framework can greatly simplify the front-end development in larger systems – and will particularly help us when we come to look at the problem of themes. The only time that this kind of core framework doesn't help is in a system that is so small (less than 10 pages in my experience) it would be more effort to implement than the time it saves.

To summarize then the advantages of this approach are:

❑ Tighter, easier to develop code – once you have moved your core functionality into the framework, your services become much easier to write as you get all the core stuff "for free"!

❑ Scalable – functionality is effectively partitioned between the difference component classes.

❑ Maintainable – you can be confident that your changes will have (less!) unexpected impacts.

❑ Reusable – once you have a working framework, you can use it repeatedly.

The Backend

We're always going to need some kind of backend application server for this scale of development. It would be possible to implement all of this functionality on the web server, but as the system starts to get larger, both in terms of code size and users, it's going to get tricky from every angle: scalability, reliability and undoubtedly maintainability.

At magic4, we picked our application server long before we chose our web server. I think we took 6 months of evaluation to finally decide on our application server while the web server decision came in less than 1 month.

N-tier Architecture

We have a presentation tier (the web server) talking to a business logic tier (the application server) with a data tier (the database server) sitting at the bottom. This separation of functionality vastly improves the scalability and security of the system, as you can keep adding machines at whichever tier is causing the bottleneck, and you can set security at each step down the chain, to make sure that your data is safe.

Application Server

One of our requirements was for multiple front-ends, and by having all the actual services (the "model" described above) implemented at this level, we can write different front-ends for different systems, all accessing the same data. In particular, we can have access as normal through a web browser on the Internet, and WAP access (see Chapter 24 for more details on this technology) to the same applications via a mobile phone.

With an application server, you also get a lot of enterprise functionality free: object pooling, connection pooling, seamless load balancing across multiple machines, common security model, and transactions. When I say "free", I mean no code needs to be written to implement it (BEA WebLogic is *definitely* not free). You can however go down the open source route. At the moment, I don't think any of the open source servers are as finished as WebLogic, but have a look at http://www.enhydra.org or http://www.jboss.org. If they provide enough functionality for your application then they could be worth evaluating.

The following sections review the main areas of the application server, namely:

- ❏ Components
- ❏ Scalability and Resilience
- ❏ Security
- ❏ Message Queues

Components

Object-oriented programming? It's all over to components now – a looser coupling makes this kind of development much more appealing, especially when you look at the facilities the application server gives you. Did I mention hot upgrades at a component level?

Scalability & Resilience

As the server controls the life cycle of the component it can pool the objects, but not only on one machine; it can load-balance across whole farms of machines. This produces an extremely fault-tolerant environment. Some application servers can even automatically fail over a user session from one machine to another in an emergency. This means that a user could be accessing a web site and talk to different application servers without actually noticing. In the case of large sites like this, it is entirely possible to fail over from one web server to another without actually losing the user.

Security

It's usually possible to say which user can access which methods on which component using an access control list (ACL). This can be extended right the way to the web server using realm authentication, or SSL (HTTPS), so that you can have the web browser displaying a logon screen when the user attempts to access some secured functionality. Most application servers allow you to specify a web page that contains your login code so that your login screen can match the rest of your site without you having to write any security authentication code.

At magic4, it was simply a case of making sure the application server authentication code used the magic4 user database, and then the security worked okay.

Message Queues

When you want to pass data in an even more loosely coupled environment, if you don't care if the recipient is offline now, as long as he gets it eventually, or you don't care who picks it up, as long as someone deals with it, then message queuing is for you. Queues are created either programmatically or by an administrator, and then messages containing virtually any kind of data can be posted to the queue. The messages can be encrypted, persisted for guaranteed delivery or even part of a transaction. The messages are stored by the message queuing software (messaging middleware) as required until the recipient is available. Most application servers provide an implementation of a message queuing system.At magic4 we used message queues for communication between the application server and the messaging gateway that sent/received the text messages to/from the mobile phones. We needed to make sure that messages sent from the application server would get to the phone, regardless of the state of the messaging gateway.

A key advantage, though, was when we needed to add more messaging gateways; as the load was getting too heavy, we simply had to power up another gateway looking at the same message queue and we automatically had load balancing.

Database

Essential – preferably it should be scalable and resilient over multiple machines. We need to store mainly two types of data:

❑ Service data like the news articles for the news service

❑ User data such as the user's preferences or messages

The difference between them being that the service data is generally larger and written infrequently, read very frequently, while the user data is generally smaller and both written and read frequently.

We looked only at relational databases for our particular project, but you may wish to consider an object database if it integrates with your application server's persistence model better.

The most important things we looked for were did it integrate well with our application server, and would it cope with our predicted growth in terms of:

❑ Data size (1.2TB for us!)

❑ Performance (max ¼ sec per request)

❑ Fault-tolerance (must be no single point of failure)

Available Technologies

Now, lets contrast some of the available technologies and look at why we chose the platform we did.

Microsoft Technologies – ASP / ISAPI / COM / ADO

Personally, I like the Microsoft Internet platform a lot. In particular, the ease of development has to come out on top. There's the Visual Interdev development environment, then Internet Information Server to run it all on. There's the excellent online support and sample applications. MS SQL Server 7.0 performs reasonably and can be clustered (but not to the level of some of it's competitors). In particular, the ActiveX Data Objects (ADO) make it very easy to perform almost any database function, and you can pool all your COM objects inside Microsoft Transaction Server (MTS). To finish it off, it's all easy to install.

So, on the plus side, the Microsoft solution is the easiest to use and the easiest to install.
On the down side, the uptime statistics are not as good as the UNIX boxes and you are then tied into a Windows platform. In this respect, if we're going to try to sell this portal to third parties then we want to be able to run on multiple platforms.

JSP / Servlet / EJB / JDBC

These are quite new to the market but they have a lot of momentum. There are a good few products on the market – both server-side, IDE and design tools, and there's a good amount of open source support. The J2EE specification covers everything the Microsoft platform has to offer.

Plus points are that they are platform independent; we can develop on Windows or Linux and deploy to HP-UX or Solaris without many problems.

On the down side, it is much harder to debug; Tomcat has a habit of not telling you what has actually happened, giving large stack traces with cryptic error messages.

DHTML / JavaScript

From the start of the project we decided that we weren't going to support anything lower than a version 4 browser. This means we can use DHTML and JavaScript.

There are always cross-browser issues when using DHTML and JavaScript; however, we found a DHTML library that provides the developer with a consistent API to use, which then gets mapped to the platform specific functions.

Hardware (UNIX / Linux / Windows)

I wanted to develop under Windows, I quite like Linux, but all of our documents are in Word format and we use Exchange. I know there is StarOffice available, but I wanted an environment I was used to.

On the server side things the decisions were not as simple, but in terms of performance, we opted for a HP9000 platform running HP-UX.

We have three servers; they are each connected via fiber optics to a disk storage array where the applications and data are stored. Initially, one machine is the web server, one the application server and e-mail server, and one the database server. As each machine is running ServiceGuard, if one machine fails, any of the other machines can take over its function. This means that we can lose two of the three machines in the setup without actually losing any service. We can also add more machines at any time to load-balance the web, application, or database servers.

A shared robotic tape backup device, also connected via fiber to each machine, performs backup. The final configuration of both the system and the software was performed by HP Consulting.

Application Servers

We were a bit skeptical of some of the Java application servers, due mainly to the very short time they had been in the market.

We were initially approached by Oracle and presented with a preview copy of their Java application server (IAS). After the course of evaluation, it was rejected on the grounds of incomplete J2EE support.

The next product to be evaluated was BEA WebLogic, which was found to be much more complete than the current incarnation of IAS. We were particularly impressed with the length of time that WebLogic had been on the market and the amount of companies already with successful implementations.

As we had already spent a significant amount of time evaluating products, it was decided that WebLogic would be the choice.

Database Servers

We've followed the pack and opted for Oracle 8i because it's what everyone has used before, and we know it works. We spent most of our time evaluating application servers, and if I were to run the project again, I would probably spend more of the time looking at the database solution.

Our main problem was that we needed to pay Oracle consultants to come and set up the fault-tolerance and backup scripts when we considered these standard things.

We didn't actually have any problems with the Oracle database, but it would have been more thorough to evaluate other options, maybe InterBase or DB2.

Design for our Portal

Now, the real meat of the project; what exactly did we choose? Well it's J2EE, but...

DHTML / JavaScript / Servlet / JSP / JavaBeans / Handlers / Client / EJB / BMP / Oracle8i

Lets look at a block diagram from the browser backwards:

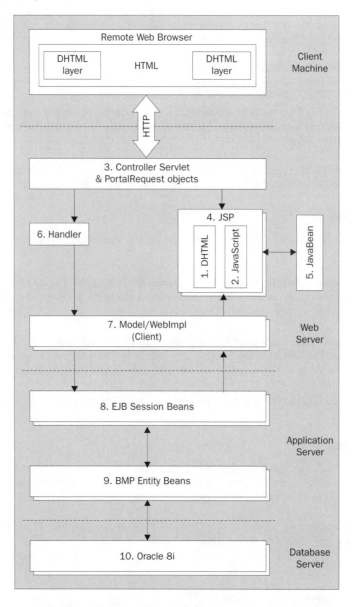

So we have:

- ❑ DHTML [1] – this provides much of the great look and feel for the framework. We will make extensive use of layers for the agents. If you have used Adobe Photoshop then you will know what these are, otherwise just think of them as little snippets of HTML floating over the background, for example, if the background were printed out, you could have each layer on a piece of acetate and place them over the top to make the completed picture.

- ❑ JavaScript [2] – we use it extensively to work with the layers and to provide any client side data preparation or validation.

- ❑ Servlet [3] – our controller servlet accepts all the requests and decides whether it's a Handler request or a JSP request. We also figure out which theme the user is requesting, and insert any helper objects into the request.

- ❑ JSP [4] – the view uses JSP to create the DHTML and JavaScript to return to the user. We generally use a template page to load the service page and therefore have to split the pages into xxx_inc.jsp for the headers and xxx.jsp for the body.

- ❑ JavaBeans [5] – the JSP pages have quite a bit of common code, and this is placed in utility beans. A standard header file std.jsp imports the required classes and initializes the bean for the request.

- ❑ Handlers [6] – as discussed, this is the code that calls into the model clients to do some actual work with a service. This is common code across the themes.

- ❑ Clients [7]– these are the web side wrapper objects for the application server components (EJB).

- ❑ Enterprise JavaBeans (EJB) [8] – these are the actual services that do work/contain real data etc. This is the "model" in the MVC architecture.

- ❑ BMP (Bean Managed Persistence) [9] – we decided to talk to the database ourselves and write our own entity beans. This decision was taken as the Container Managed Persistence in the WebLogic version we were evaluating did not support the table structures we wanted, while our DBA wanted more control over the layout. I would think if we looked at the CMP implementation in the latest version we may reconsider at least part of our decision – but we would be too far down the BMP path to change it I suspect.

- ❑ Oracle 8i [10] – is a known quantity and is supported by both BEA WebLogic and Oracle Consulting!

We've managed to pull in most of the technology there, and I must add that the full set-up (HP9000 hardware with ServiceGuard failover, BEA WebLogic, Oracle ParallelServer, etc.) comes to in excess of £250,000 ($375,000)!!

The Framework Object Model

The framework provides the facility to run with the multi-theme, service and agent core, so what is actually in there? Let us look at the following diagram to get an idea. We will then explain each section at a time.

533

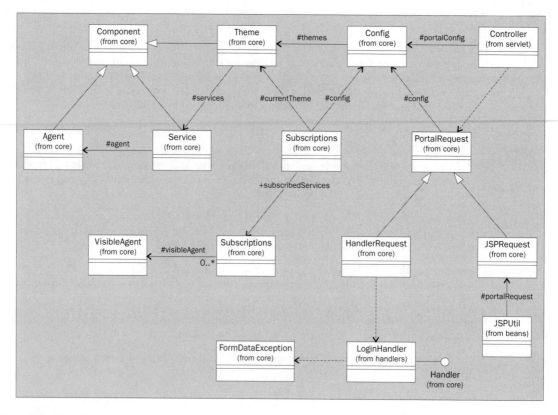

The Controller

The controller servlet captures all HTTP requests for the framework and provides the required pre-processing. We used this to make sure any helper objects are instantiated and that the user's session with the back-office remained valid. If the user session timed out, or the user was logged off for any reason (in particular when they first visit the site!) the controller redirects the user to a login page. The controller also checks to see if any suspended transactions need resuming (see below).

We use a virtual subfolder called "control" for the controller. Any part of the URI after the /control/ folder is ignored, and can be read by the servlet using the getPathInfo() method on the HttpServletRequest object. This is configured in the web.xml deployment descriptor as follows:

```
<servlet>
    <servlet-name>controller</servlet-name>
    <display-name>Controller Servlet</display-name>
    <servlet-class>
      com.alex.webframe.servlets.Controller
    </servlet-class>
</servlet>

<servlet-mapping>
    <servlet-name>controller</servlet-name>
    <url-pattern>/control/*</url-pattern>
</servlet-mapping>
```

This means that any request for the http://server:port/application/control/xxx namespace will be passed to the controller servlet. This means that image requests are direct, (like http://server:port/application/images/myImage.gif) and do not get processed by the controller. This improves performance, as image requests make up most of the workload of web serving and do not need to be handled by the controller servlet at all.

When the servlet is initialized, it uses the `Config` object described later to load the configuration (themes, services, and agents) from a configuration XML file located in the root of the application.

When a request comes in the controller creates a `PortalRequest` to wrap the `HttpServletRequest`, stores a reference to the `Config` object that contains the configuration loaded at startup, and then executes the request. The `PortalRequest` object (or a specialized version of it) takes care of the details.

The PortalRequest Object

The `PortalRequest` is responsible for parsing the id of the theme that we request, and any sequence number (see *Web Gotchas* later on). These are tagged to the URL of the HTTP request as follows:

```
/control/themeId, [sequenceId, ]URI
```

The `themeId` and `sequenceId` are stored into a new request object, which can either be for a handler or a JSP depending on the URI. The request object wraps the `HttpServletRequest` and provides extra methods for working with the framework. As we provide two distinct processing paths in our framework, JSPs and handlers, we also provide two types of request object – one for each. Functionality common to both is placed in an abstract base class called `PortalRequest`.

The `PortalRequest` object is not created directly, instead it is produced by using a static factory method that automatically decides which type of object should be created. This can be seen below in an extract from the `PortalRequest.java` file:

```java
/**
 * Factory method to create the right kind of request.
 * For the moment this just checks for the presence of the
 * string ".jsp" in the request to see if it's a JSP request. * Another plan maybe
required in your particular implementation.
 * @param config the webframework config object
 * @param request the http request
 * @param response the http response
 */

public static PortalRequest createRequest(Config config,
                                          HttpServletRequest request,
                                          HttpServletResponse response) {

    // Parse the request and find out which type we want
    // ** TODO - make sure this works with your webapp **
    if (request.getPathInfo().indexOf("Handler") == -1) {
        // It's a JSP request
        CAT.debug("request is a JspRequest");
        return new JspRequest(config, request, response);
    } else {
```

```
        // It's a handler request
        CAT.debug("request is a HandlerRequest");
        return new HandlerRequest(config, request, response);
    }
}
```

The specialized forms provide methods to deal with their own details, and an implementation of the `execute()` method that is called by the controller to forward the request to the correct processing path – JSP or handler.

```
/**
 * Abstract method to process the request.
 * @exception ServletException is thrown if a fatal portal
 *            error occours.
 */
public abstract void execute() throws ServletException;
```

In the following table, the commonly used methods of the `PortalRequest` object are described:

Method	Description
getRequest	Returns the embedded HTTP `request` object.
getResponse	Returns the embedded HTTP `response` object.
getConfig	Returns the embedded framework `config` object.
getStringAttribute	Returns a parameter value from the request, specified by name.
getAttributeValues	Returns an array of parameter values from the request, specified by name.
getStringAttributeValues	Returns an array of string parameter values from the request, specified by name.
suspend	Suspends the current transaction onto the suspension stack.
resume	Resumes the last request from the suspension stack.

The Config Object

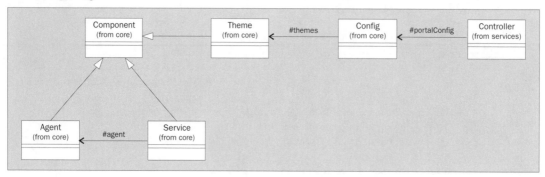

The `Config` object is created when the controller servlet first loads and is responsible for loading the configuration of themes, services, and agents for the portal from an XML resource. This information is then made available to the framework. This information could well be read from the database in the future; however, to demonstrate the portal system as being stand-alone it is loaded from disk.

The sample XML format I've used is shown below. Each portal component (theme, service, or agent) has an ID, a name, description, URI, a visible (by default) flag and locked (the user cannot change) flag. In addition, a theme has a language and can have a number of services, while a service can have a number of agents:

```
<webframe>
    <theme id="th1" language="en" visible="true" locked="false">
        <name>Moody Blue</name>
        <description>The blue theme</description>
        <uri>/themes/blue/</uri>
        <service id="home" locked="true" visible="true">
            <name>Home</name>
            <description>Framework Home</description>
            <uri>th1,home</uri>
            <agent id="control" locked="true" visible="true">
                <name>Agent Controller</name>
                <description>Add and remove agents</description>
                <uri>/themes/blue/control</uri>
            </agent>
        </service>
        <service id="base" locked="true" visible="true">
            <name>Base Services</name>
            <description>
                Services to configure your personal framework
            </description>
            <uri>th1,base/theme</uri>
        </service>
    </theme>
</webframe>
```

The XML is read into a DOM tree using the Sun Java Parser. The following extract is from the `Config.java` file:

```
/**
 * Load the framework config from the webframe-conf.xml file.
 * @param uri the uri of the xml file.
 * @exception ParserConfigurationException bad stuff happened
 *            while attempting to setup an xml parser
 * @exception SAXException a general SAX error has occoured
 * @exception IOException problems opening or reading the file
 */

protected void loadConfig(String uri) throws ParserConfigurationException,
                                             SAXException,
                                             IOException {

    // Create the theme list
    themes = new IndexedList();

    // Get the document
    CAT.info("loading webframe configuration from " + uri);
```

537

```
Document doc;
DocumentBuilderFactory docBuilderFactory =
                                    DocumentBuilderFactory.newInstance();
docBuilderFactory.setValidating(true);
DocumentBuilder docBuilder = docBuilderFactory.newDocumentBuilder();
doc = docBuilder.parse(context.getResourceAsStream(uri));

// Normalize text representation
doc.getDocumentElement().normalize();

// Get the head node
Element nHead = doc.getDocumentElement();

// And enumerate children
NodeList nlElements = nHead.getChildNodes();

// Cycle through themes, adding to the list
for (int i = 0; i < nlElements.getLength();i++) {
   if (nlElements.item(i).getNodeName().equals("theme")) {
      Theme theme = new Theme();
      loadThemeDetails(theme, nlElements.item(i));
      themes.add(theme);
      CAT.debug("added theme " + theme.getName());
   }
 }
}
```

Each theme is then loaded as follows:

```
/**
 * Load the details for an individual theme.
 * @param theme the theme object to load the data into.
 * @param nItem The XML node representing this service.
 */

protected void loadThemeDetails(Theme theme, Node nItem) {
   // Set theme attributes
   NamedNodeMap nnm = nItem.getAttributes();
   theme.setId(nnm.getNamedItem("id").getNodeValue());
   theme.setLanguage(nnm.getNamedItem("language").getNodeValue());
   theme.setVisible(Boolean.valueOf(nnm.getNamedItem("visible").getNodeValue())
                                                .booleanValue());
   theme.setLocked(Boolean.valueOf(nnm.getNamedItem("locked").getNodeValue())
                                                .booleanValue());

   // Get the elements in the service & cycle through
   NodeList nlElements = nItem.getChildNodes();
   IndexedList services = new IndexedList();
   for (int i = 0; i < nlElements.getLength(); i++) {
      if (nlElements.item(i).getNodeName().equals("name")) {
         theme.setName(nlElements.item(i).getFirstChild().getNodeValue());
```

```
        } else if (nlElements.item(i).getNodeName().
          equals("description")) {
              theme.setDescription(nlElements.item(i).getFirstChild()
                                                 .getNodeValue());
        } else if (nlElements.item(i).getNodeName().
          equals("uri")) {
              theme.setURI(nlElements.item(i).getFirstChild().getNodeValue());
        } else if (nlElements.item(i).getNodeName().equals("service")) {
          Service service = new Service();
          service.setThemeId(theme.getId());
          loadServiceDetails(service, nlElements.item(i));
          services.add(service);
          CAT.debug("added service " + service.getName());
        }
    }
    // Save the service list to the theme
    theme.setServices(services);
}
```

The services and agents are loaded in essentially the same way. A reference to the `Config` object is placed in the `PortalRequest` when the controller creates it.

The Subscriptions Object

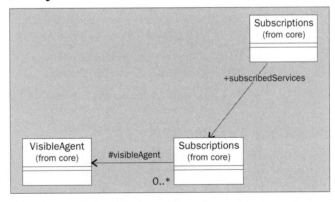

This object is stored in the user's session and is responsible for maintaining a list of the services and agents to which the user is currently subscribed.

The object is the main API for manipulating the user's settings and provides the method to select or change a theme, and the methods to subscribe and unsubscribe from services. An agent is added or removed by the subscriptions object itself. The subscriptions object also provides methods for the homepage to get a list of the services the user is subscribed to, as well as a list of currently visible agents and their positions.

There are methods to save and load the subscriptions to and from storage, which is generally the database. In your portal you may well implement this functionality at the model tier. We store (and would always cache) the subscriptions at the web server level to optimize the drawing of the navigation bar or homepage.

In the following table, the methods of the subscription object are described:

Method	Description
save	Saves the user's subscriptions.
load	Loads the user's subscriptions.
getCurrentTheme	Gets the theme object that the user currently has selected.
subscribeToService	Adds the service to the user's current subscriptions and adds any agents visible by default.
unsubscribeFromServic e	Removes the service from the user's current subscriptions and removes any agents associated with this service.
getSubscribedServices	Returns an IndexedList of the user's currently subscribed services.
getVisibleAgents	Returns an IndexedList of any agents the user currently has visible.
selectTheme	Sets the specified theme as the user's current theme and discard any old subscriptions. Any services visible by default in the new theme will be subscribed to, and any agents visible by default in these services will be added.
changeTheme	Sets the specified theme as the user's current theme and migrates any old subscriptions. For each service in the new theme:
	If the user is currently subscribed to the same service in the old theme then replace the service and any agents.
	If the service is visible by default then subscribe to that service and add any agents that are visible by default.
	Any subscriptions that could not be replaced are saved.

Handlers – Removing Code from the JSP

These are components that use the model to perform a particular function, (such as sending an e-mail). We discussed earlier that in a simple web application this code would be placed inside a JSP that POSTs to itself; for example in a JSP with a form, the user fills in the form and clicks Submit, and the form is posted back to the same JSP that does some processing. In the classic MVC architecture the JSP would send the form, the user would click Submit and it would be the controller that places the request in an event object and sends it into the model for processing.

We didn't want to have code in the JSP, but also we didn't want to have to update the controller code in the framework when our third party content developers needed the front-end flow to change. Additionally, we wanted to allow read-only access to data without having to go through the full model tier if it was not required (for example country code lists and product lists, etc).

The compromise was that we would use the model client objects directly from the JSPs when read-only data was needed. This is where the controller comes into a world of its own, as it makes sure that all the required objects are present when it intercepts requests on their way to JSPs, and that we would use handler objects called by the controller when data needed to be written. The web designers could change the look and feel of the front end by editing the JSPs, and still keep all the complicated code in handlers that were written internally.

When a difficult read-only task had to be prototyped for the designers, we would generally use a handler to perform the task, and then a JavaBean called from the JSP to manipulate the extracted data as required. An example of this was reading the inbox in the messaging application. We had an inbox handler that read and pre-processed the message headers, and then an inbox JavaBean that would get the data from it's temporary store in the **Request** object as required.

The handlers are called by requesting the name of the handler object:

```
<form action="<%=util.encodeURL("LoginHandler")%>" method="post">
```

The `encodeURL()` method is a helper method on the utility JavaBean to place the `themeId` for the current theme into the URL, and pass the completed URL through the URL encoder to make sure that it is valid.

The `PortalRequest` extracts the name of the object and uses the Java Reflection API to create the object. The Java Reflection API allows the developer to create classes at runtime by merely knowing their name. In our case it allows us to create the handler objects using the name passed as part of the HTTP request. If the handler class does not exist, a `ClassNotFoundException` is thrown and we can deal with this as required:

```
String name = Constants.HANDLERS + requestURI;
CAT.debug("attempting to instantiate handler " + name);
Class c = Class.forName(name);
Handler h = (Handler)c.newInstance();
if (h.handleRequest(this)) {
    // Returned success - check if we can resume
    ...
} else {
    // Returned failure
    ...
}
```

The handler must implement the `Handler` interface and provide the `handleRequest()` method as follows:

```
public boolean handleRequest(HandlerRequest request)
                            throws FormDataException, ServletException;
```

When a handler completes, control is passed to a JSP to provide a view on the results. Rather than just moving to one page as specified by the handler, the framework allows the content developer to specify the success page (handler returns `true`), the failure page (handler returns `false`), or the rollback page (see *Rolling Back Requests* below).

These are specified by passing request parameters as follows:

Parameter	Action
sp	The URL of the success JSP – used if the handler returns `True`.
fp	The URL of the failure JSP – used if the handler returns `False`.
rp	The URL of the rollback JSP – used if the handler throws a `FormDataException` (see below).

Web Gotchas – State and Sequence

This section covers our decisions on the Favorites or Bookmarks, and the Back button.

From the start, we knew that we wanted people to be able to bookmark their favorite services and that this meant that Handler URLs could not be displayed in the browser location bar. This is because a Handler URL expects to be called from a view – and if there were no data associated with the request (the page was called directly) then the handler would just return failure.

Let's look at a sequence diagram to try to explain this:

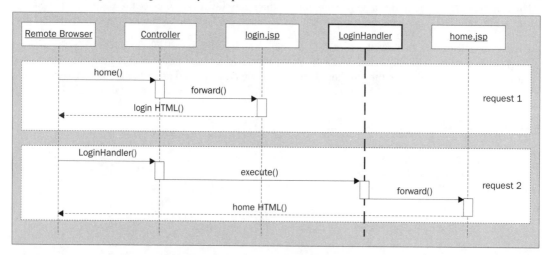

For example, the remote browser attempts to access the homepage (home.jsp) and is forwarded to a login page. The user fills in the form and the data is posted to the LoginHandler. The handler logs the user in and forwards the request to the homepage. If the user then bookmarks the page, they will be bookmarking the LoginHandler and not the homepage.

Consequently, when a handler is invoked, a redirect must be issued to send the browser to a sensible location that can be bookmarked. The advantage – the user can bookmark; the disadvantage – an extra network step as the handler sends a redirect back to the browser, and the browser then requests the JSP.

If we look at the sequence diagram for the updated flow, we can clearly see the extra step.

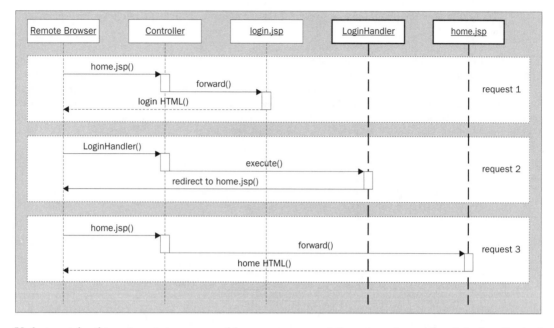

Unfortunately, this gets us into more problems, as we cannot then store the results of the handler in the request. This is because the request is not valid after the redirect – it is only available for the lifetime of the request in the container, and a redirect means that an entirely new request comes into the container at a later time. We can see clearly in the diagram that the handler is called in request 2, but the view is processed in request 3.

We could store the results in the session, but then if the user has two windows open performing the same operation, there could be some problems. For example, one handler executes and stores the result in the session then issues a redirect, but, before the redirect returns, another open browser window on the same machine issues a request to the same handler. If we're not careful we're going to overwrite the data in the session object, and both windows will return the results of the second query.

The solution we came up with was to store the results of the request in the session using a sequence number unique for the user session. When the browser returns from the redirect it passes the sequence number and the results are restored as though the redirect never happened. The sequence number is stored in the session as shown below. Access to the sequence number is controlled via a synchronized method so that two different threads cannot obtain the same sequence number. The sequence number is inserted into the request by the controller when control returns from a handler. All the data stored by the handler (as request attributes) are stored in the session under the key. The next request sends the sequence number to restore the stored data from the session. The data is then deleted.

Session	
key 1	request.attributes abc
key 2	request.attributes xyz
key 3	request.attributes 123
key n	...n

If the user bookmarks the page, they can return to it at any time – the sequence number is ignored if not valid.

The only problem here is that the parameters on the HttpServletRequest object are read only – and cannot be restored! This is because the parameters are the HTTP request parameters and are set by the container when parsing the actual HTTP request. The solution, then, is for all of the request parameters to be converted to attributes at an early stage (in the controller), and for the JSP and the Handlers to deal only with attributes not parameters! Attributes are the name=value object pairs that a developer can use to store data with request scope. You can see how the conversion works below:

```
/**
 * Convert the http request parameters to attributes.
 * This is required as parameters cannot be set publicly,
 * and therefore cannot be stored and reloaded.
 */

protected void convertParameters()  {
    // Get a list of the parameters
    Enumeration pe = request.getParameterNames();

    // And cycle through
    while (pe.hasMoreElements()) {
        // Obtain the name and values
        String name = (String)pe.nextElement();
        String values[] = request.getParameterValues(name);

        // Save as an attribute, either singular or an array
        if (values.length > 1) {
            request.setAttribute(name,values);
        } else {
            request.setAttribute(name,values[0]);
        }
    }
}
```

The HttpServletRequest attributes are then stored in a HashMap in the session under the specified key (sequence number). This enables them to be loaded when the redirect returns. The code is as follows:

```
/**
 * Store the http request attributes in the user session under
 * the specified key. This method is used when a Handler
 * redirects to a JSP. The request attributes can be saved
 * while the redirect takes place, and then reloaded before the
 * jsp is processed.
 * @param key the key to store the attributes
 */

protected void storeAttributes(String key) {
    HttpSession session = request.getSession();
    synchronized(session) {
        // Get a list of the attributes
        Enumeration ae = request.getAttributeNames();
        if (ae.hasMoreElements()) {
```

```
        // Store them in a hashmap
        HashMap storedRequest = new HashMap();
        while (ae.hasMoreElements()) {
            String name = (String)ae.nextElement();
            storedRequest.put(name, request.getAttribute(name));
        }
        // And put the hashmap into the session under
        // the supplied key
        session.setAttribute(Constants.STOREDATTRIBUTES + key,storedRequest);
    }
  }
}
```

This is slightly odd for newcomers to the system, but it doesn't take people long to work with it, especially as we provide methods directly on the `PortalRequest` object to work with this:

```
/**
 * Returns an attribute value from the request,
 * specified by name.
 * @param name attribute name
 * @return attribute value
 */

public String getStringAttribute(String name) {
    String value = (String)request.getAttribute(name);
    if (value != null) {
        value = value.trim();
        return value;
    }
    return "";
}
```

The next problem is the infernal **Back** button. We wanted people to be able to use it, but that always leaves us open to problems, like when the user selects entry X, user deletes entry X, user clicks **Back**, makes changes to the (now deleted) previous X... and clicks **OK**. The system returns **Record does not exist** or some such error.

We looked at using the sequence number of the request to stop people from submitting data to handlers they have previously used, and this is valid, but can be annoying if you wish to use the **Back** button for a valid operation, such as edit entry X, click **OK**, click **Back** and re-edit entry X. This is also valid, but probably not how the designer would wish the system to be used.

After looking at these options, we chose to empower the user and let them use the back button. In any transient pages, we set the "no-cache" header flag to stop Internet Explorer from letting the user click **Back**, but essentially the strategy was to write very robust handlers with good error messages.

You can use the no-cache header is as follows:

```
<html>
  <head>
    <title>...</title>
    <meta http-equiv="PRAGMA" content="no-cache">
    <meta http-equiv="Expires" content="Mon, 06 Jan 1990 00:00:01 GMT" />
```

```
          </head>
          <body>
              ...
          </body>
      </html>
```

This works with some browsers but not all. In our experience, it mainly works with Internet Explorer.

Rolling Back Requests

A very common situation that happens with a web system is that the user has to fill in a form and supply some details, but they often either fill in fields incorrectly or miss them out completely. We performed some validation in the browser in JavaScript, but because all our content development was outsourced, we wanted to be sure that everything was watertight at the server side. Mainly, we wanted to incorporate the facility to process this situation, and tell the user what was wrong (and what they needed to do!).

This facility is based on the J2EE blueprint system and provides a `FormDataException` object that a handler can throw. A `FormDataException` must have a message and may optionally have a collection of field names, and/or an embedded exception.

To show how it is used, look at the following sample from a handler:

```
// Read the parameters
String username = request.getStringAttribute("username");
String password = request.getStringAttribute("password");

// Check required fields
ArrayList fields = new ArrayList();
if (username.equals("")) {
   fields.add("username");
}
if (!fields.isEmpty()) {
   throw new FormDataException("Please fill in all the required fields",fields);
}

// Check the password
if (!password.equals("example")) {
   fields.add("password");
   throw new FormDataException("Password is not correct",fields);
}
```

When the framework catches a `FormDataException`, it will then rollback to the JSP specified as part of the request, or to the last JSP if one was not specified. The JSP can then use the utility JavaBean to extract the `FormDataException`.

Suspending Requests

In some cases the user may wish to perform an operation that they currently do not have permission for. In the magic4 portal there were several reasons for this:

❑   Not logged in – the user is currently a guest on the portal and must either login or sign up.

❑ Mobile phone not activated – we do not currently have valid mobile phone details for the user.

❑ User does not have credit – the user does not have enough credits to spend on the requested operation. This could be virtual dollars to spend on services on the system, or in our case mobile phone credits for requesting services to be delivered to your handset. Either way, you would want to suspend the current operation while you resolve the situation.

In each case, we want to guide the user through the relevant steps (we used a wizard approach) and return them to where they left off.

Most systems merely return the user to the page before they made the request; however, we wanted to be actually able to continue the request where we left off. Thus, we had to have a way of saving and then reloading everything to do with a request.

Anyway, with this problem solved it is straightforward enough to use the `SuspendedRequest` object to store all the attributes and relevant fields from the `PortalRequest` and place this on a stack. The method is shown below:

```
/**
 * Suspend the current transaction onto the suspension stack.
 * This stores the themeId, request, success, failure &
 * rollback URLs as well as the request parameters (attributes).
 */

public void suspend(String conditionalHandler) {
    CAT.debug("suspending request for " + requestURI + "(" + themeId + ")" +
            "until " + conditionalHandler + " completes.");
    SuspendedRequest sr = new SuspendedRequest();
    sr.themeId = themeId;
    sr.sequenceId = sequenceId;
    sr.requestURI = requestURI;
    sr.successURL = successURL;
    sr.failureURL = failureURL;
    sr.rollbackURL = rollbackURL;
    sr.conditionalHandler = conditionalHandler;
    Hashtable attributes = new Hashtable();
    Enumeration ae = request.getAttributeNames();
    while (ae.hasMoreElements()) {
        String name = (String)ae.nextElement();
        attributes.put(name, request.getAttribute(name));
    }
    sr.attributes = attributes;
    getSuspendStack().push(sr);
}
```

All this functionality is in place, and it's simply a case of calling the suspend method, and passing the name of the handler you're waiting for the successful completion of. When that handler completes, the framework will resume your request from the stack where you left off. If the user never wants to fix the problem (login, buy credits, etc.) then the object remains on the stack until the session ends. We never had a problem with this as not too many suspends tend to happen.

You can use the suspend queue as follows:

```
// Suspend until we're logged in
request.suspend("LoginHandler");

// And now redirect to the login page
...
```

Dynamic HTML (DHTML)

The front-end (view) for the portal assumes a minimum of a version 4 browser (IE or Netscape), which lets us take advantage of both JavaScript and DHTML. To try to work with the differences in the platforms, we need to have a common API we can use, and we based our DHTML API on the DynAPI written by Dan Steinman, and can be downloaded from http://www.dansteinman.com/dynapi/. For the sample portal provided with this chapter I've used the basic DynAPI without any of our extensions.

One problem however, is that the original version of the DynAPI has now been superseded by the DynAPI 2 (http://sourceforge.net/projects/dynapi/) and is no longer supported. Future portal implementations would probably want to move over to the new code-base, however the runtime API has changed quite significantly.

The reasons for using DHTML... Well, it's fairly straightforward. I wanted to have an interface that allowed the user to change the look of their homepage by simply clicking and dragging, and DHTML is the only way to do this. Luckily for us, the DynAPI already provides a cross-browser implementation of the dragable API – we just needed to make it work with multiple JSP files for the agents, and provide code to save and load the agent positions.

To show you how easy it is to make a dragable layer with the DynAPI, here's a quick sample:

```html
<html>
  <head>
    <style>
      #agentDiv {position:absolute;left:10;top:10}
    </style>
    <script language="Javascript" src="/js/dynlayer.js"></script>
    <script language="Javascript" src="/js/mouseevents.js"></script>
    <script language="Javascript" src="/js/drag.js"></script>
    <script language="JavaScript">
      function init(){
        DynLayerInit();
        agent = new DynLayer(agentDiv);
        drag.add(agent);
        initMouseEvents();
      }
    </script>
  </head>
  <body onLoad="init()">
    <div id="agentDiv">
      Hello Dragable World!
    </div>
  </body>
</html>
```

It's that easy. The tricky part comes when we have many different files, all of which have code to go in the <head> and the <body>, and all of which have init() functions that need calling when the page loads.

The solution we've gone for is to have each service or agent split into two. The first file xxx_inc.jsp contains any code to go into the <head> section of the page, and the xxx.jsp file contains the code for the <body> section of the page. Both files must be supplied but can be empty if not required.

The JspRequest forwards any JSP request to the main.jsp page that then includes any static headers, and then loads the headers and body for the required service. Note that the navigation bar code (navbar_inc.jsp and navbar.jsp) is always present and included by this file.

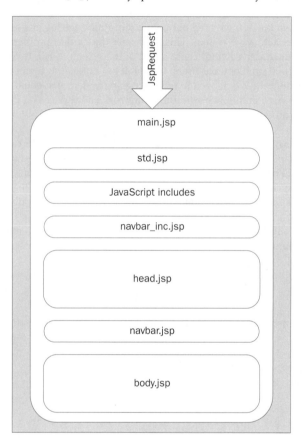

The homepage service is of particular interest as it includes other pages (agents!). A list of VisibleAgents is obtained from the Subscriptions object, each Agent in turn is retrieved, stored in the request, and the JSP included. The JSP can then get hold of the Agent object from the request and read the settings.

```
<% // If the agent has been moved by the user then get last x and y
   Agent a = (Agent)request.getAttribute(Constants.AGENT);
   int x = 142;
   int y = 6;
   if (a != null && a.getPosition() != null) {
       x = a.getPosition().x;
       y = a.getPosition().y;
   } %>
<style>
    #th1ag1AgentDiv {position:absolute;left:<%=x%>;top:<%=y%>}
    ...
```

Logging

Always one of the most important aspects for both the developer during the long haul of development, and the support engineers after the system has gone live. At a minimum level a development must be able to programmatically log debug text, variable dumps, stack traces and exceptions at a number of levels – generally debug, information, warning, error and fatal. It's also nice to be able to turn the logging on and off on a module-by-module basis.

In the production system at magic4, we used our own custom message logging service that allowed us to track user sessions right the way across the system. This is because the hardest problems to diagnose are generally the ones where an individual user's actions cause a part of the system to fail. If you have to look at the combined log output of 1000 simultaneous users, it's much too difficult to figure out what actually happened (this is the voice of experience!). We needed to have a logging system that could single out the debug output for a particular user session, right the way from the framework and services on the web server, to the updates and business logic in the model.

At the current time, the logging system we used is proprietary to magic4 and I can't present it here. I can however demonstrate an excellent open source product called log4j that I used when putting together the demonstration portal. You can download log4j from http://www.log4j.org/ and installing is as simple as putting the JAR file in the classpath when running your application. You can log to many formats and destinations; to XML as a file or to the command line are the two that I generally use.

To use log4j you need to initialize the logging system at the start of your application. For this example we'll use the most basic configuration, but just check the documentation for how to setup the others:

```
// Initialize the message logging
BasicConfigurator.configure();
```

Then put a static field in the object you want to log from:

```
public abstract class PortalRequest extends Object {
    /** The message logging category for this object */
    protected static final org.log4j.Category CAT =
        org.log4j.Category.getInstance(
            PortalRequest.class.getName());
    ...
```

And then just call the logging methods as required.

```
// It's a JSP request
CAT.debug("request is a JspRequest");
```

Implementation Details

I've put a sample application together to present all the concepts above – it's based on the portal framework we've used at magic4, but without any of the real services or agents. First of all though, I'll just talk through our development environment.

Development Environment

We started developing the front-end to run on Tomcat 3.1. It seemed a logical step as we didn't want to buy BEA WebLogic development licenses for every web developer and we could easily let the EJB tier run on a shared acceptance server in the office. Tomcat is an open source JSP and servlet container, part of the Jakarta project from the Apache group (**www.apache.org**), and we found it to be perfectly stable and reliable for our development. There were a few problems between Tomcat and WebLogic's JSP and servlet implementations – the first one we found being that WebLogic cannot read files from WAR packages (like a JAR file, but for a web application) while Tomcat can. It was a problem on our part though, as we should have been reading files using the web server resource functions (`getResourceAsStream`) not the file functions.

The second problem was that WebLogic does not seem to support the `getServletContext()` method from within a JSP page, but this is not actually a problem, as there is a field called "application" available from all JSPs that contains a reference to the `ServletContext` object. It just confused us for a while until we updated the relevant pages accordingly.

Periodically the EJB developers update the shared acceptance server, and we place a stable build of the portal on this box as well when we can. There is a separate database server that both the acceptance server and the EJB developers test server use.

In our case, the content developers were external, so internal developers produced a text only reference theme that they then took to base their own themes on. In my opinion, the best process is to design the core architecture (such as MVC) and then develop small vertical sections in say, three or four week periods. Each period would contain a week of design, a week of implementation and a week of testing.

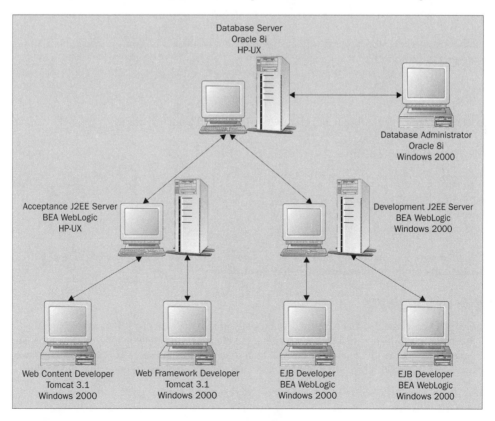

I've built the sample application into an EAR file (downloadable from www.wrox.com) so that it can be deployed to any J2EE platform (including the reference platform) using the standard deployment tools.

If you want to test our development environment, then you can still run the portal on Tomcat without any problems, but you'll need to make sure the required libraries (XML parsing & message logging) are available.

The following instructions are for running the portal under Tomcat, skip these if you just want to get going with the one hit J2EE method.

First you definitely need the JDK 1.3, and you'll also need J2EESDK 1.2.1 for the servlet and JSP support.

The XML parser is JAXP1.0.1 available from Sun's web site (and I believe it will be part of J2EE in the near future) at http://java.sun.com/xml/download.html.

You then need to install log4j from http://www.log4j.org/.

We used GNUMake as the standard build tool – on a Windows platform; this has come from the Cygwin tools at http://cygwin.com. You need to update the system.mk file in the src folder to reflect your individual configuration, updating the variables such as JAVA_HOME and the like. Then type:

```
make all
```

to build the source code. Alternatively, type:.

```
make newserver
```

to build the source code, stop Tomcat, deploy the webroot and classes to Tomcat, and launch Tomcat. Or you could use:

```
make reserve
```

to stop Tomcat, deploy the webroot and classes to Tomcat, and launch Tomcat.

There are also two helper targets:

```
make starttomcat
make stoptomcat
```

Which need no explanation.

As far as editors go, I've been using Sun's Forte for Java, Community Edition – which is free! Check out http://www.sun.com/forte/ffj/ce/ for a free download.

Testing & Debugging!

Sometimes you know exactly what happened, but usually not. In the case of a JSP – rather than tell you the source line of the JSP (which is included as a comment in the generated code) it tells you the source line of the servlet generated from the JSP. Hopefully this will be resolved some time soon – but for now you have to go to the Tomcat work folder, locate your application, and then locate and open the generated servlet source file.

In the case of the framework, the general idea is to log as much as possible, as you can always turn it off. Within log4j you can even turn it on or off on a class-by-class basis.

I think one of the biggest things that helped us in the framework was chaining exceptions together (or at the very least, logging them helpfully). The general premise is that whenever you catch an exception and throw another, you always throw an exception that can take an embedded exception. An example helps:

```
try {
    // Load the framework configuration from the xml file
    loadConfig(Constants.CONFIGFILE);
} catch (Exception e) {
    // Fatal error - log and throw up to the container
    CAT.error("unable to read framework configuration",e);
    throw new ServletException("unable to read framework configuration",e);
}
```

If we didn't embed the real exception inside the `ServletException` then we would never know what actually happened! It's sad, but many people just throw this information away – or log it somewhere obscure and inaccessible.

Deployment

Deployment of the application to the J2EE server is fairly straightforward, as we just use the normal deployment method for the J2EE platform. In the case of the reference platform provided with the J2EE SDK you run the `deploytool.bat` file in the bin folder. You can just copy the files, build them into a WAR file, or even combine everything into an EAR file.

Here is a demonstration of creating the deployment file for the portal application. Note that you don't need to follow all of this if you just want to run the sample. I provide a pre-build application EAR file ready for deployment with the source code.

First, start the J2EE server by running `j2ee -verbose` in a command prompt from the `j2sdkee1.2.1\bin` folder.

```
C:\j2sdkee1.2.1\bin>j2ee -verbose

J2EE server Listen Port: = 1049
Naming service started: :1050
Published the configuration object ...
Binding DataSource, name = jdbc/Cloudscape, url = jdbc:cloudscape:rmi:Cloudscape
DB;create=true
Web service started: 9191
Web service started: 8000
Web service started: 7000
J2EE server startup complete.
```

Next, start the deployment tool by opening another command prompt in `j2sdkee1.2.1\bin` and type in `deploytool`. When the tool has started select **New Application...** from the **File** menu. A dialog appears with the **Application File Name** set to `Untitled.ear`, change this to `portal.ear`. Add the description **Portal Demonstration**. Then press OK.

553

You should then be presented with the default setting for an application:

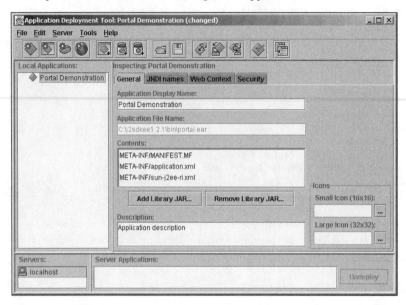

In our case, we will be adding a new web component to our application, so select New Web Component... from the file menu. You should be presented with an introduction to the web component wizard, so click Next.

From this step, you can add files to your web application – click Add... to add some static files, JSPs or servlets.

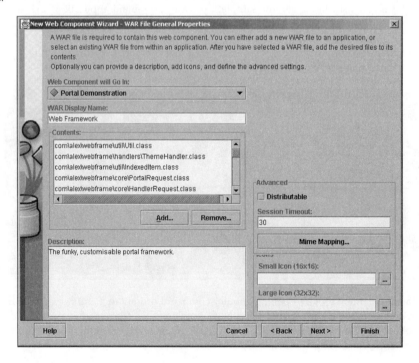

When you've added your web files and classes, you can click Next and select that your application entry point is a servlet. Click Next and you need to supply the details for your servlet as follows:

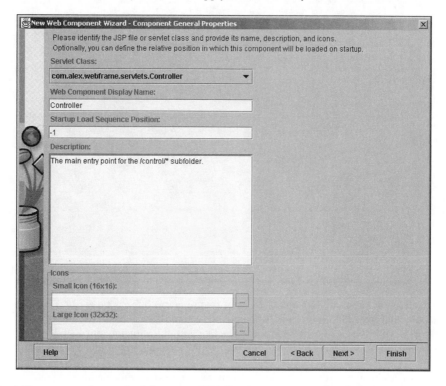

Click Next. For our sample, we don't have any initialization parameters, but here is a great place to put anything that's configurable for your application. We used the initialization parameters to store things like messaging system parameters, location of secure servers, etc.

The step that follows allows you to define any aliases for your servlet – in our case we are using the `/control/*` alias so we enter it here. For more information on aliases, please refer to the servlet specification from http://java.sun.com.

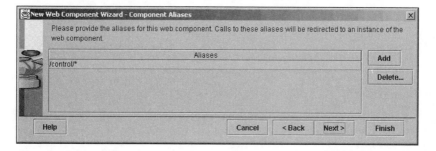

You can click Next through the rest of the steps in the wizard. This is where you would define your security roles and authentication, EJB references, resource factories, context parameters and welcome files. We'll define one welcome file, `index.jsp`.

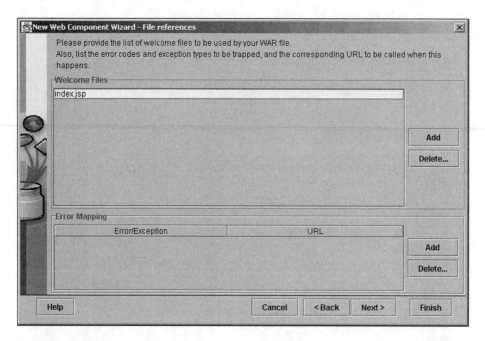

One thing that it is important to note it that the error mapping can be very powerful – you can specify a URL to load if a particular exception is thrown. At magic4 we wanted to use this to capture exceptions such as `UserNotRegisteredMobileException` and the like, but unfortunately our EJB developers could not decide on the exception they were throwing and we had to catch them individually!

Click Next twice and you can review the deployment descriptor that will be added to your `web.xml` file.

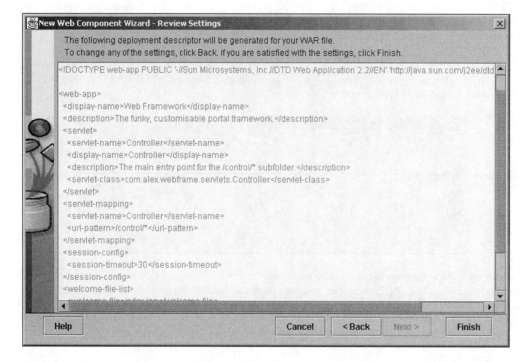

Click Finish and you should be returned to the main screen.

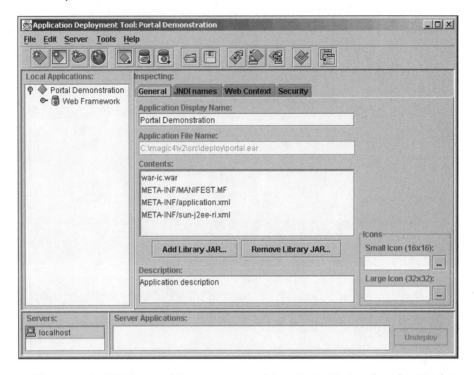

You can add any required libraries at this stage – we need `log4j-full.jar` from log4j and `jaxp.jar` and `parser.jar` from JAXP.

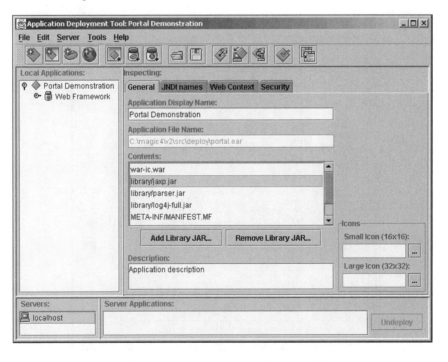

The only change you now need to make is to select the **Web Context** tab and set the name of your application. Set it to portal as follows:

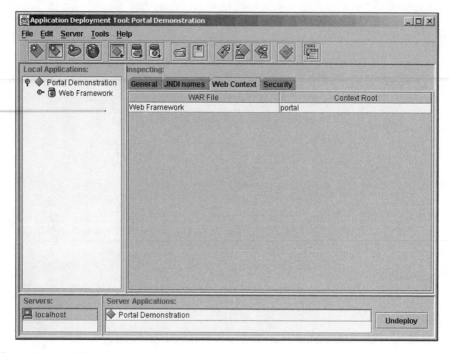

Select **Save** from the **File** menu to save your application to disk, and you are now ready to deploy your application to the J2EE server.

Select **Deploy Application...** from the **Tools** menu, and the following wizard should appear:

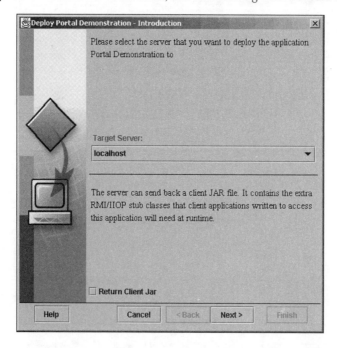

Make sure localhost is the selected server and click Next. If no server appears then check you have the J2EE server running. You'll be asked to confirm the context root as follows:

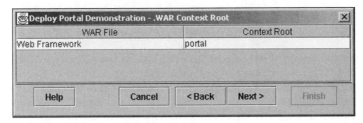

Click Next, and Finish to deploy the application. You should see the application transfer, and the following confirmation:

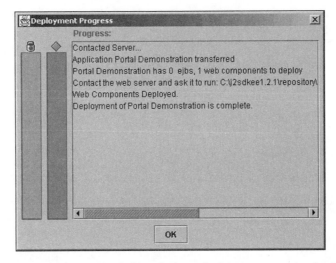

Congratulations – you've just deployed a web application. In future, you can just load you application from the File menu, and then select Update and Redeploy application from the Tools menu to update the EAR file with any changed files, and send the application to the server.

The one problem we did have with deployment at magic4 is again another of the web classics. The content developers were authoring and testing under Windows, and didn't realize that our final platform, HP-UX, was case sensitive. Consequently, all the page URLs and image links worked when tested locally, but were completely broken when deployed on the live servers. Once this problem was highlighted they managed to clean most of it up promptly – but we still get the odd case problem slipping through the net. I think the solution next time would be to have a Linux test platform for the content developers to use, before delivering to us.

Testing and Scalability

I'm not going to go into this in much detail, suffice to say:

Please do some stress testing before launching!

In a previous life I was a consultant for an ISP, and I saw a significant amount of sites fall over on day one – purely because the developers hadn't tested the site with more than a couple of simultaneous users.

There are many tools for generating load with new ones appearing all the time. Some people prefer to write their own code to test their applications to destruction while others want to have an external company to test the system to make sure that no internal factors affect the testing. When I was working as a consultant I would always recommend the external testing method for final load testing – and I still would today. We did not use external resources as our own test team was deemed to have tested the application enough.

Anyway, we used the Microsoft Web Capacity Analysis Tool (WCAT) from http://msdn.Microsoft.com/workshop/server/toolbox/wcat.asp. It's free (so far!) and uses as many Windows workstations as you can lay your hands on to launch a huge number of simultaneous requests at your server. We wrote scripts to simulate as many user scenarios as possible such as signup, login, view the news, create and send a message, etc. We ran these tests for an hour at a time. From this we could have a look at how the server coped, and what the response was like. It was particularly interesting to try accessing the site from your own machine while a stress test was under way.

We also wrote a number of unit-test specifications and had a small test team run through these in accordance with the functional specification document for the portal. They then logged any bugs they found for the development team to look at.

The EJB team used the JUnit framework from http://www.junit.org/ to do all their regression testing – and it seemed to work quite well. The only problems we had were human ones – where a developer incorrectly wrote the test methods, and consequently they failed to pick up problems later in development.

Framework Sample

The sample is designed to show the basics of the multi-theme portal. The user can select one of the two themes and then subscribe and unsubscribe from services. The agents are dragable and their positions can be saved.

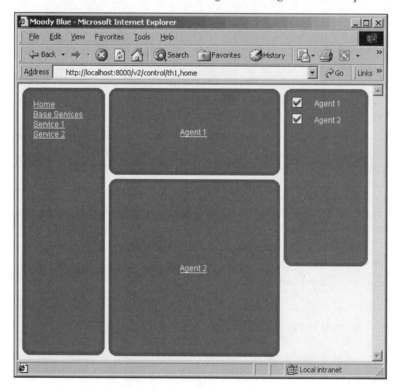

J2EE Demonstration Installation Instructions

- ❏ Install the Sun Java Development Kit (J2SDK) 1.3. This includes setting the JAVA_HOME environment variable.

- ❏ Install the Java 2 Enterprise Edition SDK (J2SDKEE) 1.2.1. This includes setting the J2EE_HOME environment variable.

- ❏ Start the J2EE server (`c:\j2sdkee1.2.1\bin\j2ee -verbose`).

- ❏ Open another command prompt and run the deployment tool (`c:\j2sdkee1.2.1\bin\deploytool`).

- ❏ Select the File I Open Application menu option. Select the portal.ear application (`src\deploy\portal.ear`). If you need to check the deployment tool instructions, check out the deployment section earlier.

- ❏ Select the Tools I Deploy Application menu option.

- ❏ Select the localhost server and click Next.

- ❏ Enter portal for the context root if required and click Next.

- ❏ Click Finish. You should see the following confirmation. If not, check that the J2EE server is still running.

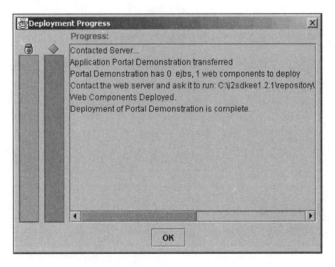

- ❏ Point a browser to http://localhost:8000/portal/.

Sample Walkthrough

To get the main concepts of the portal system, have a go at this walkthrough.

- ❏ Click Base Services and then Select Services

- ❏ Locate Service 3 and click Subscribe

- ❏ Click Home and you should have the yellow Agent 3 at the bottom right of the page

- ❏ Uncheck Agent 1

- ❏ Move Agent 2 to the top of the window and click Save Positions
- ❏ Click Service 3 and you should see the yellow service within the blue navigational theme
- ❏ Click Base Services and then Mellow Yellow
- ❏ You should see the homepage with Agent 2 still at the top. As Agent 1 is a default agent for the yellow theme, move Agent 2 back to the bottom and click Save Positions
- ❏ Click Agent 1 and you should see a yellow service in the yellow theme
- ❏ Think of the possibilities

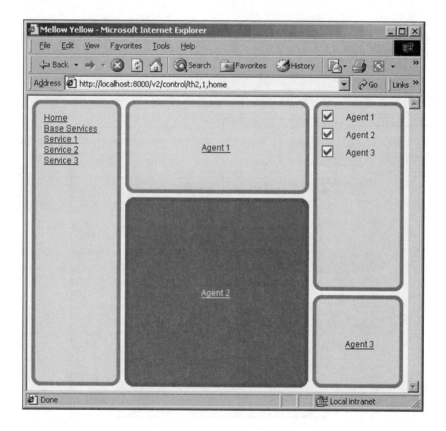

Post-mortem

Well, we are approaching the end of the magic4 portal project, and it's time to look at the pros and cons of what we have been through.

What Would I Keep?

Primarily, we have a fantastic environment and please check out http://www.magic4.com for developments. We should be launching a hosted version of it soon, so if you want to run your mobile portal within the magic4 environment then drop us a line.

Overall I believe the architecture is sound – just make sure all the developers stick to the architecture when you start implementing services.

It was definitely an advantage to place the code in web-side handlers and allow the handlers to be called without converting the request to an event. This meant that we did not have to cast the page interactions in stone – it was fine for the web developers to change them, yet they did not touch the actual code. The event creation was actually delayed to the client object, and the event passed into the backend.

I'd definitely keep the dragable agents; they're a lot of fun and make the site that little bit stickier. I'd also keep the multi-theme engine as it works particularly well if you have a different domain name for each theme.

What Would I Change?

At magic4 it was decided that many developers would develop a level of functionality in parallel, and as a result EJB developers were often busy with one area and holding up the web development of another. Conversely, when EJB code was then delivered, the content developers were then swamped with work. I would change the development process to work on chunks of functionality at a time like an address book, or news. The section should be no larger than could be completed in three or four weeks, and each mini-cycle would include a design, develop and test stage. I feel that this would make for a much more reliable and focused system.

Aside from this, there's not a lot I would change. We used external content developers and this injected communication problems of its own at times. However, as the function of the content developer was fairly well defined this caused few real problems. The main criticism was that the content developers had their own agenda of what they wanted to achieve, and so sometimes we had trouble getting them to align their development with our specification! Such is life.

Summary

Portals change with the times and you'll always need good quality content, but with more and more competition you need to go a lot further to make your system stand out. We've presented a DHTML and J2EE solution that is extensible enough to cope with most of the things your service developers will throw at it. Frameworks can make these systems extremely robust by enforcing good structure and communication between components – just make sure people don't break the model.

At magic4 we found it useful to have the content developers be able to change the number of pages associated with a given event, and not be fixed by a front-end flow. The use of handlers as an extension to the usual MVC model is an excellent solution to this requirement.

Finally, I hope that the sample inspires a few people to make their portals as funky as they can.

PROFESSIONALJAVAE-COMMERCE

16

B2B E-Commerce: B2B Foundations

If you work for a business that engages in commerce, then B2B e-commerce will become increasingly important to you over the next few years. If you are a manager or developer of business applications, then the odds of B2B development impacting your work are growing daily. So what is B2B? Why has it become the talk of the industry?

> *Business-to-Business (B2B) e-commerce may be defined as the transactions businesses engage in to conduct finance, commerce, or trade using the Internet. The business processes supported may include marketing, sales, development, manufacturing and support.*

It is a huge market and it is changing rapidly and that's why we've seen fit to devote an entire section of the book to the subject. Dramatic changes brought about by new Internet focused technologies are promoting projections of a changing global business-to-business (B2B) economy. These technologies will usher in new business opportunities and change business partner processes and practices forever. Component based software, vertical-market and cross-market XML vocabularies, and **any-to-any** backbones provide the necessary ingredients to make the change a reality.

To set us up for the diversity of technologies and interactions that are used within the B2B arena,this chapter will be focused on giving us an overview of the topic and particularly relevant technologies.

Specifically we'll be looking at:

❏   The development of B2B E-commerce, the problems and challenges associated with it and some commonly seen systems

❏   A brief review of the technologies used in B2B applications

❏   Organizations and standards evolving to facilitate B2B development

B2B E-Commerce – An Overview

As we saw in Chapter 7, XML has surfaced as one of the primary technologies enabling B2B. XML provides a universal notation for describing the content and structure of information. It makes it possible for systems to exchange information and understand the semantics of the data involved in the exchange. XML is being touted as the new **Electronic Data Interchange** (**EDI**) of business-to-business e-commerce.

EDI is defined as the exchange of data between systems to support or enable business transactions. It involves support for transactions between cooperating systems, which implies a level of integration beyond mere data transfer. Typically these exchanges have been implemented over private networks. XML provides a solution to EDI over public networks. Traditional high-cost private EDI networks have given way to open e-markets, auctions, exchanges and integrated business networks using XML. These new electronic-centric businesses will radically change the way we work, and as developers the skills and tools we will require.

However a number of variants of XML vocabularies and supporting technologies are emerging that complicates the support, development, and skill requirements for organizations. We will highlight the major variants later in this chapter but it's important to realize this is a dynamic space that changes rapidly. Some example organizations and B2B XML definitions include:

- **UN/CEFACT** and **OASIS** which have established the **Electronic Business XML** (**ebXML**) initiative

- A Microsoft led community of standards users have developed **BizTalk**, an XML based e-commerce initiative

- **Commerce One** is leading an initiative to develop a **Common Business Library** (**xCBL**) using XML

- **cXML** is being defined by companies trying to promote the adoption of XML in B2B e-commerce

- Additionally a number of industry specific initiatives such as **RossettaNet** are defining industry standard based XML e-commerce

The following diagram depicts the migration of electronic commerce over the last twenty years. Simple point-to-point is being augmented and replaced with global public networks. These networks support transactions that include financial transfers, exchanges, auctions, delivery of products and services and supply-chains.

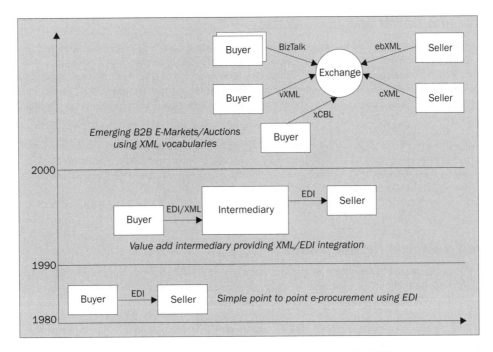

In this chapter we will examine the foundations and technical conduits for B2B e-commerce and assess the landscape of products, technologies, and organizations collaborating to enable the new B2B economy.

In the next chapter we will examine the implications B2B has on current supply chains and how technologies such as ebXML, **Universal Description, Discovery and Integration** (**UDDI**), and XML/EDI are enabling a more dynamic and inclusive environment. Traditional *source – make – sell – distribute* supply models are giving way to "build-to-order" chains, *sell – source – make – distribute*. This implies a more flexible and less constrained environment where partner collaboration is dynamic.

But first let's survey the landscape of B2B to get a high level feel for what B2B is all about and how the players in the space are positioning in expectation of huge rewards.

Why Business-to-Business Integration?

We've encountered many of these issues previously, but let's recap to provide a good basis for the rest of the section.

Huge Market Potential

Business-to-Business (B2B) e-commerce is expected to grow at a rate of 5 to 10 times the rate of Business-to-Consumer (B2C) e-commerce according to IBM Global Strategy Group projections. Industry analysts project e-commerce to be a multi-trillion dollar business by 2004. There is much at stake for providers and consumers of B2B services.

In addition to compelling financial motivations there are a number of core business issues, which a B2B infrastructure addresses. They include more effective integration of core-businesses with e-business, improved business relationships, and more cost effective procurement.

Business Integrated with E-Business

Today most organizations have not adequately integrated their e-commerce offerings with their core business processes. Legacy integration has always been a difficult and complex issue. This has resulted in fragmented processes that expose gaps and delays typically in customer service and product delivery. Integrating existing processes with e-commerce applications will help to eliminate many service gaps. For example, it allows e-commerce sales and support channels to be more seamlessly integrated with backend accounting and inventory systems.

In addition the automation opportunities that exist between business partners have only just begun to be explored. In the past the cost of automation and partner integration prohibited many efforts. As a result automation and integration with partners was limited to large corporations with large budgets. The Internet and supporting technologies have lowered the cost of entry. Public networks and the proliferation of component-based solutions have reduced the cost and time to market. This will enable us to radically re-think our supply chains and partner relations.

Improved Business Relationships

A new era of automated trading partner collaboration is being defined. Improved relationships will result through leveraging technologies focused on trading partner collaboration and automation. More accurate online information will be available for exchange between partners. As a result more information will be available to an organization and its work force. New technologies are making this information more meaningful. Technologies such as XML, HTTP, and Java (J2EE) have gained enough momentum to change the direction and landscape of information exchange and processing for the foreseeable future. We shall discuss these technologies and their impact in an E-commerce context in addition to emerging standards such as ebXML, BizTalk Framework, and **tpXML**.

Cost Effective Procurement

Optimum use of resources and increased productivity will result by eliminating and reducing the number of manual steps involved in many supply chain processes. Real time purchase order status, availability, and pricing are the potential benefits of B2B and B2C integration. We will look at the changes required for e-procurement and assess supply chain implications in the next chapter.

While the advantages and benefits to B2B E-commerce are substantial, there are significant obstacles and challenges to success.

B2B – Problems and Challenges

To build effective B2B applications organizations will need to address a number of technical challenges, and we'll discuss the major ones here.

Complexity of Commerce Implementations

A significant challenge to the widespread adoption of B2B E-commerce will be gaining the ability to establish business relationships quickly and cost effectively. After years of EDI development and deployment the world is left with less than 2 percent of the companies participating in electronic exchange. Many industry analysts attribute this to the cost and difficulty of implementing EDI technologies. In addition, the ability to agree upon business processes and the automation of business processes between systems has been time consuming and cost prohibitive for all but the largest corporations. Until a better method of defining and exchanging information relevant to a business process is adopted and standardized this situation will not change. Fortunately there are solutions to this problem currently in the marketplace and in development.

Data Representation and Partner Integration

A challenge to enabling B2B commerce will be how information or data is represented between cooperating systems and intermediaries. While XML has become the chosen technology for data representation, that only begins to address the requirements for automated exchange. Issues that need to be resolved include:

❏ Semantics of data – how is the meaning of the information captured and understood by trading partners?

❏ Sequence of exchanges – what constitutes a legal exchange of information?

❏ Business process identification – how are invoked processes identified between systems?

❏ Trading partner identification – how are trading partners found, discovered and identified?

❏ Complexity of exchange – to what extent will complex data objects and exchanges be supported?

❏ Who defines the rules?

Transporting Commerce Payloads

Transport issues that need to be addressed between trading partners include:

❏ Quality of service – what level of effort and expense is required to ensure continuous operations?

❏ Sequencing of requests – how are requests prioritized and identified?

❏ Routing – how will intra-partner and inter-partner routing be managed?

Securing Commerce

Security of data during transport will remain an issue. Additional issues include:

❏ Authentication of sender and recipient – how will partner exchanges be authenticated? Though public key encryption, private key encryption, message digest, or others?

❏ Assured delivery of messages – to what extent will message assurance be provided over a public network?

❏ End-to-end transactional integrity will be required – how will secure transactions be enabled?

Integrating Back-End Systems

Despite the hype most businesses have not been able to integrate their current backend **Enterprise Resource Planning (ERP)** systems and applications with E-commerce applications. The complexity of the integration for large-scale Fortune 1000 companies has been a significant barrier. However, this integration has become increasingly important to successfully implement a B2B strategy, and until realized will slow the adoption to a net-centric B2B economy. Fortunately integration technologies such as **Message Oriented Middleware (MOM)**, adaptors, and e-commerce gateways that are Internet-aware are emerging to reduce the integration complexity. In addition the recently announced J2EE Connector Architecture holds promise for standardizing connections to Enterprise Resource Planning systems and **Enterprise Information Systems (EIS)**.

Internal systems that are closed and proprietary often create **silos** of functionality and do not integrate with external service-centric systems. Many of these systems will not be able to adapt to the changing B2B business dynamics. ERP integration will require improvements not only in **Enterprise Application Integration (EAI)** technologies but also in business process definition and automation. While adapters and connectors have proven to be an effective technique in internal application integration, the success in inter-application integration is still not clear.

EDI and Associated Issues

EDI has been based more on a data-centric view of information exchange versus a process-centric view. This view tends to lead to data element focused requirements. In other words partners talk in terms of the data required versus the process requirements. In trying to accommodate many different systems with different data requirements, messages tend to get bloated or become proprietary between partners.

In addition private networks have often been deployed to support the EDI exchange between partners. As a result the cost of entry for many has been excessive.

The questions and issues raised in the last section are not new. The same questions were applicable to EDI. However, the systems that are being deployed today are more network-centric. The communication and network capabilities have brought about global connectivity between businesses. A browser can reference a resource (URI) anywhere in the world and have that information displayed or downloaded to a local PC. In a very short time we have taken these capabilities for granted.

So we are approaching the problems of B2B in a new era of technological capabilities. Solutions to data representation, automation of business processes, and controlling the exchange will have fewer constraints imposed upon them as a result.

The level of integration between partner systems must not be unnecessarily complex. Simpler interfaces with more granular service offerings will need to replace or complement the complex monolithic systems of today. The industry must reduce development lead times and make it easier to assemble pre-built component solutions. As we have seen, the J2EE architecture is a component-based architecture and provides a platform to build and manage at a component level.

Business Process and System Integration

The exchange of B2B information must be complemented with integration of existing applications. This integration will include:

❑ Workflow components that are responsible for managing not only internal processes but external processes and dependencies. The notification mechanism may be message or event-based.

❑ Brokers/Gateways that are able to transform and route messages between systems and may contain Protocol Servers to process XML vocabularies.

❑ Adapters/Connectors that are able to integrate existing Enterprise Information Servers, such as databases and ERP systems, using standard APIs.

Workflow

The flow of information within an enterprise has been significant in determining system integration strategies. Many companies have implemented workflow engines to control and automate internal processes. Older engines tend to be product-focused or functional in nature and lack open APIs.

As we move towards a service and component-based architecture, coordination and automation of processes both internal and external will take on more importance. Generic workflow engines supporting standard APIs will help integrate both internal and external processes. This will be important for supply chain management and coordination. Additionally, industry-specific workflow engines configured through XML scripts will become ever more popular.

Early adopters of workflow engines may now be coping with new workflow integration issues driven by increased dynamic collaboration with trading partners.

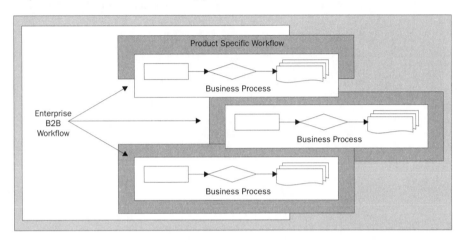

A hierarchy of intra- and inter-process coordination must be defined between workflow engines. Once defined, new automation capabilities will surface between trading partners.

Brokers

A broker is a type of messenger that is responsible for the transmission and routing of requests and responses from clients to servers. In e-commerce this can take the form of routing messages from e-commerce components to enterprise information systems. A broker must have a mechanism to map requests to the appropriate service API. One technique allows services to register with a broker and clients to request the service interface through a naming lookup convention, such as JNDI.

Brokers typically maintain queues to provide reliable delivery and processing priority flexibility. Proxy objects may be used to provide location and transport transparency. In the following diagram the broker's primary function is to act as a router between clients and inter-enterprise information services.

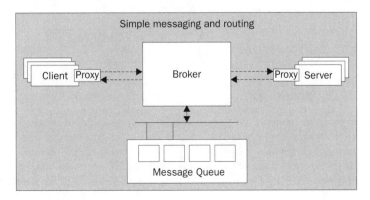

The broker pattern can also be used to integrate trading partners. E-commerce auctions and net market makers are relying heavily on broker-based architectures to bring diverse trading partners together. Value added services are logical extensions to this environment, services such as data translation, security, reporting, amongst others. Look for the projected "eco-systems" flourishing in the new economy as market makers integrate with market makers.

The following diagram represents a high level view of a market maker acting as an intermediary between trading partners. In this case, note the use of queues to allow secure and reliable access to trading partner exchanges of XML data. Eco-systems evolve as market makers exchange information with other market makers.

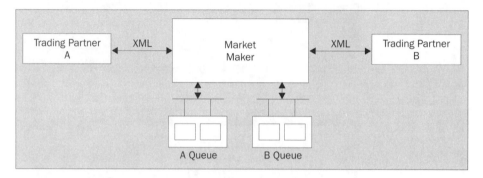

Adapters/Connectors

For tighter integration it may be necessary to implement adapter objects into your e-commerce architecture. An adapter mediates and translates messages into the appropriate API of your enterprise system. Most enterprises have systems in place that have a substantial amount of cost and effort associated with their development. These systems support the core processes of your business prior to e-commerce. Adapters help to ensure that the investment in core systems is leveraged in the new e-commerce architecture. Adapters help to integrate the current business with the e-business at critical points in customer and partner operations and relations.

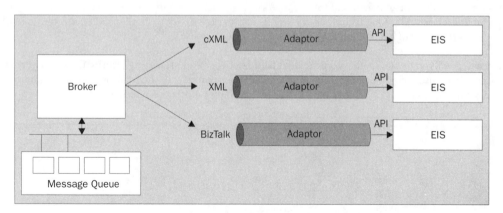

To date, these adapters and connectors have been proprietary to the middleware vendor. Thus the proprietary integration software becomes fundamental to the system architecture. The J2EE Connection Architecture Specification is defining a Java standard for connecting the J2EE platform to Enterprise Information Systems (EIS) such as Enterprise Resource Planning. The connector architecture defines a **Common Client Interface (CCI)** for EIS access. The CCI defines a client API for interacting with heterogeneous EISs.

The connector architecture enables an EIS vendor to provide a standard resource adapter for its EIS. A resource adapter is a system-level software driver that is used by a Java application to connect to an EIS. The resource adapter plugs into an application server and provides connectivity between the EIS, the application server, and the application.

This will be an important step in promoting the integration of legacy systems to the J2EE platform.

Now let's move from looking at B2B from the system level and see what technologies we'll be making much use of to implement such applications.

Technologies for B2B

B2B e-commerce will be delivered via many technologies and supported on many platforms. Some are known today, some are still in development and design. It is highly likely that Java and XML will be significant in enabling B2B.

In this section we'll look at:

❑ The J2EE architecture

❑ XML

❑ Application transport technologies for B2B

J2EE for B2B

The workhorse of the new e-commerce architecture will be the Java 2 Enterprise Edition (J2EE) compliant application servers.

We can summarize the J2EE platform using the figure we saw back in Chapter 5:

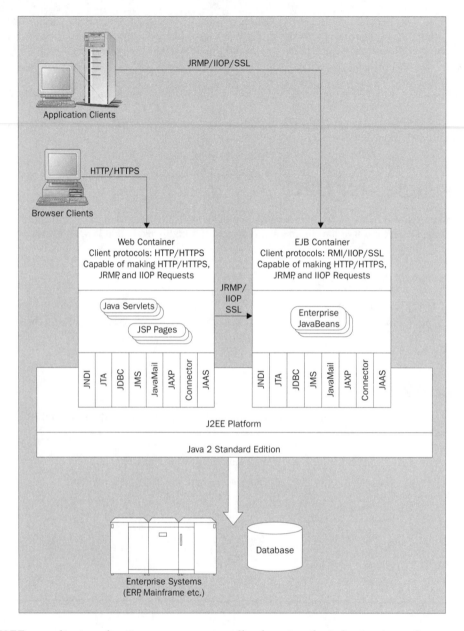

The J2EE compliant application servers are rapidly changing the infrastructure of many corporations. Traditional middleware products are being defined to integrate with this Java based component architecture.

The foundations enabling e-commerce will include:

❏ Java Transaction API (JTA)

❏ Java Message Service (JMS)

❏ Connector Architecture – EIS Adapter

The maturity of these technologies in concert with the existing J2EE infrastructure will help to solve commerce, collaboration, and integration issues both within and between organizations.

Let's just quickly revisit some of these services and discuss aspects of J2EE in the context of B2B e-commerce requirements (we won't look at everything to avoid repeating ourselves too much) before quickly looking at additional supporting services that B2B developers require.

RMI-IIOP

Remote Method Invocation (RMI) has been enhanced to include RMI over Internet Inter-Orb Protocol (IIOP). This is the on the wire protocol that delivers Common Object Request Broker Architecture (CORBA)-compliant distributed computing capabilities.

For e-commerce applications this means easier legacy application and platform integration by allowing application components written in C++, Smalltalk, and other CORBA supported languages to communicate with components running on the Java platform. As we mentioned earlier, legacy applications will be important in B2B. It is not just about the web – those businesses that are able to integrate with existing applications will have a jump-start over those that are trying to build workarounds to their integration problems. RMI-IIOP may ease that integration effort.

When using RMI over IIOP there is no separate Interface Definition Language (IDL) or mapping required. Developers can pass any serializable Java object (objects by value) between application components.

JNDI – Java Naming and Directory Interface

The Java Naming and Directory Interface (JNDI) is a framework that provides support for modules called Service Provider Interfaces (SPI). For instance an SPI may provide naming and directory functionality to applications written in the Java programming language. It is a fundamental technology of the J2EE platform. Resources are named and bound to Java objects using JNDI.

E-commerce applications are moving towards the Lightweight Directory Access Protocol (LDAP) as the directory protocol of choice. Most vendors of naming and directory products have built-in LDAP support. A scalable directory service is essential to enabling and managing the different software applications and organizational resources of businesses. Before LDAP this was primarily driven by proprietary protocols.

The J2EE version 1.3 ships with a reference implementation of the LDAP SPI.

The JNDI 1.2 API is comprised of five packages:

❑ `javax.naming` – provides the classes and interfaces for accessing naming services.

❑ `javax.naming.directory` – extends the `javax.naming` package to provide functionality for accessing directory services.

❑ `javax.naming.event` – provides support for event notification when accessing naming and directory services.

❑ `javax.naming.ldap` – provides support for LDAPv3 extended operations and controls.

❑ `javax.naming.spi` – provides the means for dynamically plugging in support for accessing naming and directory services through the `javax.naming` and related packages.

These packages implement the standard API that shields the developer from knowing the exact implementation of the underlying service. This will enable service provider modules to change without the application having to be modified. As we have pointed out, integration capabilities will be important to B2B systems. The ability to adapt to a changing infrastructure will be a key to success.

JMS – Java Message Service

The Sun Microsystems Java Message Service (JMS) specification defines the programming interface for a messaging system that uses Java-based clients. With this new interface standard, users can now compare messaging systems on a one-to-one basis, regardless of whether or not they are completely written in Java.

JMS provides a common way for Java clients to create, send, receive, and read an enterprise messaging system's messages. The J2EE Framework provides JMS as the interface to Message Oriented Middleware (MOM) services. JMS defines messages as "asynchronous requests or events that are consumed by enterprise applications". MOM technologies are fundamental to e-commerce applications because they provide a mechanism to loosely integrate inter and intra-enterprise applications.

Two models of support are currently available:

❑ Point-to-point – this involves a single requester sending a message to a single responder.

❑ Publish/subscribe – this allows a requester to send messages to any number of responders. Responders can come and go without the requester having to manage the relationships. This model may be used when exchanges between systems are dynamic.

The JMS API is comprised of one package:

❑ `javax.jms package` – included in the J2EE .

As stated in the JMS Specification, "a major goal of JMS is that clients have a consistent API for creating and working with messages, which is independent of the JMS provider". Providers of messaging software that support JMS have essentially done the equivalent of providing a JMS driver for messaging.

The implications are that despite the standard API there is still a wide spectrum of supporting functions and services that the messaging provider will deliver unique to their implementation.

We will look at the implications to alternative messaging designs and patterns in Chapter 17. In addition in Chapter 19 we will focus on the developing Java API for XML Messaging (JAXM).

JDBC – Java Database Connectivity API

E-commerce applications require access to data sources and repositories. Most of these data sources in enterprises today are built on relational database technologies. The JDBC API provides data access from the Java programming language. Using the JDBC API, you can access any data source that provides a JDBC or ODBC driver. Almost all relational databases include JDBC drivers today. JDBC technology also provides a common base on which tools and alternate interfaces can be built. The JDBC 3.0 API will include support for the Connector Architecture being developed for EIS integration.

The JDBC 2.0 API is comprised of two packages:

❑   `java.sql package` – included in the Java 2 SDK, Standard Edition

❑   `javax.sql package` – included in the Java 2 SDK, Enterprise Edition

JTA – Java Transaction API

JTA specifies standard Java interfaces between a transaction manager and the parties involved in a distributed transaction system: the resource manager, the application server, and the transactional applications.

Java Transaction Service (JTS) is a "specification for building a transaction manager, which supports the JTA interfaces at the high-level and the standard Java mapping of the CORBA Object Transaction Service 1.1 specification at the low-level".

JTS provides transaction interoperability using the IIOP protocol for transaction propagation between servers. JTS is intended for vendors who provide the transaction system infrastructure for enterprise middleware.

Transactions are fundamental to e-commerce. Secure transactions involving distributed multi-parties will need to mature to support the requirements of B2B e-commerce.

JavaMail

The JavaMail 1.2 API provides a set of abstract classes that model a mail system. The API provides a platform independent and protocol independent framework to build Java technology-based mail and messaging applications. The JavaMail API is implemented as a Java platform optional package and is also available as part of the Java 2 platform, Enterprise Edition.

The API also provides concrete subclasses of the abstract classes. These subclasses implement widely used Internet mail protocols and conform to specifications RFC822 and RFC2045. One of the goals of the API was to make the interface to mail systems easy for application developers. Today e-mail is an important technology enabling communication between individuals. It has also taken on importance enabling communication between machines and consumers. Many Customer Relationship Management systems have evolved rule-based e-mail notification to allow the system to auto-generate e-mail responses to consumer requests and events.

Connector/EIS Adapter

As of this writing SUN has released a final draft specification of what is called the "The J2EE Connector Architecture". It defines a standard architecture for connecting the Java 2 Platform, Enterprise Edition (J2EE) platform to heterogeneous Enterprise Information Systems. Examples of EISs include Enterprise Resource Planning, mainframe transaction processing (TP), and database systems.

The connector architecture also defines a Common Client Interface (CCI) for EIS access. The CCI defines a client API for interacting with heterogeneous Enterprise Information Systems.

The connector architecture enables an EIS vendor to provide a standard resource adapter for its EIS. A resource adapter is a system-level software driver that is used by a Java application to connect to an EIS. The resource adapter plugs into an application server and provides connectivity between the EIS, the application server, and the enterprise application.

The intent is to minimize the degree of customization required by both application server vendors and EIS vendors, by having a common connector architecture between these systems. EIS vendors supply one standard resource adapter and this can be used across application server products that support the architecture.

Additional Services

In addition to the services discussed above, developers need certain runtime services to support e-commerce applications. The ability to easily locate application components, access and execute them securely, and ensure their availability are all critical factors in deploying e-commerce applications. As a result, e-commerce frameworks require the following facilities to support applications.

Security

B2B will require a network and application infrastructure that is secure enough to offset the risk. While no system is totally secure there are a number of products, processes, and configurations that reduce exposure. Look for e-market brokers and exchanges to use security as a differentiator in the B2B space.

The following diagram depicts a popular demilitarized zone configuration, where an external firewall and an internal firewall surround a gateway that does authentication, protocol conversion, and routing. This configuration may use LDAP as the directory access protocol and use an RMI Server to cache authentication credentials within the application server. This is a common security architecture used by trading partners in supply chain integration and e-markets.

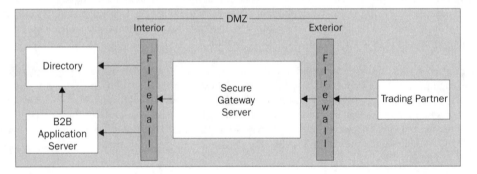

Firewall Support

The firewall acts as a secure interface between private trusted networks and one or more external, untrusted networks. Firewalls use filters to permit or deny packet flow on the basis of the origin or destination of the packet's addresses and ports. The firewall controls who in the trusted network is permitted to access external networks, which application services they can use, and which specific external hosts they can access. The same controls are also used to limit access to trusted networks. When properly configured to implement a security policy, firewalls can protect your network from intrusion and compromise.

Firewalls are also key to the support of Virtual Private Networks (VPN), which allow the trusted network to use the Internet as a WAN to make secure connections to other networks. This is accomplished by the firewall encrypting all traffic between the firewall and other compatible systems, under the control and selection of the administrator.

Proxy Server

The proxy server assumes the responsibility of retrieving Internet data for multiple browser clients. It acts as a conduit between the client and e-commerce application server, forwarding client requests to the server and returning server responses to the client. This way the proxy function can be used to provide address security. Proxy servers also provide caching functionality, which allow it to serve subsequent client requests for cached documents from its local cache. The client gets the information faster and network bandwidth utilization is reduced.

Certification Authority

This facility produces security certificates that can be used to authenticate users and/or servers. Public key infrastructure (PKI) technology is emerging as the preferred trust mechanism for e-commerce. A key component of PKI is the certification authority that provides digital credentials and security features such as message integrity, data privacy, signature verification, and user authentication. Certificates, with associated roles and privileges, registries to manage certificates, and key pairs to support digital signing and encryption provide the quantum step-up in capability needed to reconcile the Internet/security compromise.

XML

How will businesses represent the information and content required to fulfill business transactions?

XML has taken the development community and business community by storm. It has quickly become the standard for defining, well, everything and is going to be used just about everywhere! Web content, database information, application configurations, new markup languages. Now B2B business processes, technical capabilities, and trading partner content are being defined using XML. And it is not just happening in one industry such as technology but has broadened across most industry groups. The fear is not "will it be adopted" but will it be adopted so quickly that standards and controls to leverage re-use and optimize the cost benefits of standardization become difficult to realize. We will discuss vertical vocabularies and the constraints they impose to development in Chapter 18 and review current XML support for B2B.

We've already looked in detail at XML and XSLT in Chapter 7, seeing how cXML documents may be used for things like catalogs and purchase orders. Here, let's just highlight how DTDs and Schemas will help in facilitating B2B e-commerce. Of course we'll be encountering practical applications of the technology on our way through this section, for example we'll be using XSLT extensively in Chapter 18.

Document Type Definition (DTD/Schemas)

The document type definition expresses the structural validity and constraints on an XML document. It defines the "type" of document being processed and exchanged. The DTDs allow us to check XML documents against strict rules. The battleground over e-commerce content definition will be fought between DTDs from collaborating and competing organizations.

XML Schemas also define rules and structural composition for document types and are a more recent development within www.w3.org. The notation for schemas is XML as opposed to a unique subset of SGML used in document type definition. There is also support for data types and namespaces, which are both important concepts in extending the capabilities of XML for B2B e-commerce.

An example schema defining a purchase order could look like this:

```
<xsd:schema xmlns:xsd="http://www.w3.org/2000/08/XMLSchema">
```

This is used to augment the document with descriptive information:

```
<xsd:annotation>
     <xsd:documentation>
            Purchase order schema for Example.com.
            Copyright 2000 Example.com. All rights reserved.
     </xsd:documentation>
</xsd:annotation>

<xsd:element name="purchaseOrder" type="PurchaseOrderType"/>
<xsd:element name="comment" type="xsd:string"/>
```

Complex types are composed of other complex types or simple types:

```
<xsd:complexType name="PurchaseOrderType">
     <xsd:sequence>
            <xsd:element name="shipTo" type="USAddress"/>
            <xsd:element name="billTo" type="USAddress"/>
            <xsd:element ref="comment" minOccurs="0"/>
            <xsd:element name="items"  type="Items"/>
     </xsd:sequence>
     <xsd:attribute name="orderDate" type="xsd:date"/>
</xsd:complexType>
<xsd:complexType name="USAddress">
     <xsd:sequence>
            <xsd:element name="name"   type="xsd:string"/>
            <xsd:element name="street" type="xsd:string"/>
            <xsd:element name="city"   type="xsd:string"/>
            <xsd:element name="state"  type="xsd:string"/>
            <xsd:element name="zip"    type="xsd:decimal"/>
     </xsd:sequence>
     <xsd:attribute name="country" type="xsd:NMTOKEN"
                 use="fixed" value="US"/>
</xsd:complexType>
<xsd:complexType name="Items">
     <xsd:sequence>
```

Constraints can be placed on elements such as `minOccurs` or `maxOccurs` which define the allowable occurrences of an element in a conforming document:

```
<xsd:element name="item" minOccurs="0" maxOccurs="unbounded">
<xsd:complexType>
     <xsd:sequence>
            <xsd:element name="productName" type="xsd:string"/>
            <xsd:element name="quantity">
            <xsd:simpleType>
                   <xsd:restriction base="xsd:positiveInteger">
                        <xsd:maxExclusive value="100"/>
                   </xsd:restriction>
            </xsd:simpleType>
            </xsd:element>
            <xsd:element name="USPrice"    type="xsd:decimal"/>
```

```
                    <xsd:element ref="comment"    minOccurs="0"/>
                    <xsd:element name="shipDate" type="xsd:date"
                             minOccurs="0"/>
              </xsd:sequence>
              <xsd:attribute name="partNum" type="SKU"/>
          </xsd:complexType>
          </xsd:element>
      </xsd:sequence>
</xsd:complexType>
<!-- Stock Keeping Unit, a code for identifying products -->
<xsd:simpleType name="SKU">
    <xsd:restriction base="xsd:string">
          <xsd:pattern value="\d{3}-[A-Z]{2}"/>
    </xsd:restriction>
</xsd:simpleType>
</xsd:schema>
```

The schema is capable of defining simple data types and complex data types. It also can constrain the allowable values for an element and attribute. A much richer definition for data types is provided in schemas than DTDs. See www.w3c.org/XML/Schema for more information on the schema specification.

Namespaces

Namespaces are used to ensure that the "context" of the "conversation" is understood. With everyone in the world allowed to create XML documents, how do we distinguish different meanings for the same attribute? For instance what is meant by the attribute "customer" in one XML document versus another? There will be many different definitions. We need to make these definitions less ambiguous. This is done through namespace prefixes. The Namespaces specifications define an xmlns rule that associates an attribute with a defining xmlns tag. For example:

```
<xmlns:wrox = "http://www.wrox.com/2001/ProE-commerce">
<wrox:book>
<wrox:title>Professional E-commerce</wrox:title>
</wrox:book>
```

This definition would differentiate the element title from any other title definition in the world! The only requirement is that the URI referenced be unique. Namespaces will become increasingly important as we interconnect systems for business transactions. Organizations and corporations will define namespaces to indicate the rules and semantics in effect when processing XML documents. A single document may use more than one namespace to determine the semantics of the document being processed. Remember the URI that the xmlns rule associates does not have to exist, it simply has to be unique!

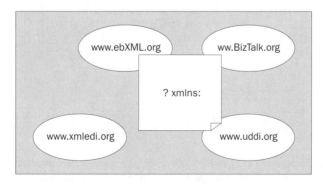

The trend is toward defining XML documents using schemas versus DTDs. This is because schemas require no unique syntax and the markup is consistent with XML. Namespaces were invented after DTDs and therefore are not fully supported by them. Additionally, the schema specification defines support for data types, which allows a more robust definition of both primitive and user-generated data types. The following example is from the work being developed by the www.ebXML.org to standardize a framework for e-commerce using XML. Notice it is formatted in XML and not a unique construct like a DTD.

The ebXMLHeader is the root element of the document:

```
<xsd:schema xmlns:xsd="http://www.w3.org/2000/08/XMLSchema">
<xsd:element name = "ebXMLHeader">
    <xsd:complexType content = "elementOnly">
        <xsd:sequence>
            <xsd:element ref = "Manifest"/>
            <xsd:element ref = "Header"/>
        </xsd:sequence>
        <xsd:attribute name="Version" use="fixed" value="1.0" type="string"/>
        <xsd:attribute name="MessageType" use="fixed" value="Normal" type =
            "string"/>
    </xsd:complexType></xsd:element>
```

The Manifest identifies the documents contained in the ebXML message container. The purpose of the Manifest is to make it easier to directly extract a particular document associated with the message.

```
<xsd:element name = "Manifest">
    <xsd:complexType content = "elementOnly">
        <xsd:sequence minOccurs = "0" maxOccurs = "unbounded">
            <xsd:element ref = "DocumentReference"/>
        </xsd:sequence>
    </xsd:complexType>
</xsd:element>
```

The DocumentReference is a composite element that contains the DocumentDescription, DocumentLabel, and DocumentId elements. The DocumentDescription is an optional textual description of the document. The DocumentLabel is a code representing the purpose of the document. The DocumentId is the URL to the payload of the document.

```
<xsd:element name = "DocumentReference">
    <xsd:complexType content = "elementOnly">
        <xsd:sequence minOccurs = "1" maxOccurs = "unbounded">
            <xsd:element ref = "DocumentDescription" />
            <xsd:element ref = "DocumentLabel"/>
            <xsd:element ref = "DocumentId"/>
        </xsd:sequence>
    </xsd:complexType>
</xsd:element>

<xsd:element name = "DocumentLabel" type = "string">
</xsd:element>
<xsd:element name = "DocumentId" type = "uri">
</xsd:element>
```

The header element provides the From and To address of the trading partners exchanging XML and includes quality of service information established through a trading partner agreement.

```
<xsd:element name = "Header">
   <xsd:complexType content = "elementOnly">
     <xsd:sequence>
           <xsd:element ref = "From"/>
           <xsd:element ref = "To"/>
           <xsd:element ref = "TPAInfo"/>
           <xsd:element ref = "MessageData"/>
           <xsd:element ref = "ReliableMessagingInfo"/>
     </xsd:sequence>
   </xsd:complexType>
</xsd:element>
```

The From element identifies the party originating the exchange. The To element identifies the intended recipient.

```
<xsd:element name = "From">
    <xsd:complexType content = "elementOnly">
         <xsd:sequence>
                <xsd:element ref = "PartyId"/>
         </xsd:sequence>
    </xsd:complexType>
</xsd:element>
<xsd:element name = "To">
    <xsd:complexType content = "elementOnly">
         <xsd:sequence>
                <xsd:element ref = "PartyId"/>
         </xsd:sequence>
    </xsd:complexType>
</xsd:element>
```

The purpose of the MessageData is to provide a means to identify a particular ebXML message.

```
<xsd:element name = "MessageData">
    <xsd:complexType content = "elementOnly">
         <xsd:sequence>
                <xsd:element ref = "MessageId"/>
                <xsd:element ref = "TimeStamp"/>
                <xsd:element ref = "RefToMessageId"/>
         </xsd:sequence>
    </xsd:complexType>
</xsd:element>
<xsd:element name = "RefToMessageId" type = "uuid">
</xsd:element>
<xsd:element name = "TimeStamp" type = "dateTime">
</xsd:element>
<xsd:element name = "MessageId" type = "uuid">
</xsd:element>
```

The ReliableMessagingInfo element identifies the degree of reliability with which the message will be delivered.

```
<xsd:element name = "ReliableMessagingInfo">
    <xsd:complexType content = "empty">
```

```
            <xsd:attribute name = "DeliverySemantics" use = "fixed" value =
                "Unspecified">
            <xsd:simpleType base = "ENUMERATION">
                <xsd:enumeration value = "OnceAndOnlyOnce"/>
                <xsd:enumeration value = "BestEffort"/>
            </xsd:simpleType>
            </xsd:attribute>
        </xsd:complexType>
    </xsd:element>
```

The TPAInfo element is a composite element that relates to the Trading Partner Agreement under which the message is governed.

```
<xsd:element name = "TPAInfo">
    <xsd:complexType content = "elementOnly">
        <xsd:sequence>
            <xsd:element ref = "TPAId"/>
            <xsd:element ref = "ConversationId"/>
            <xsd:element ref = "BusinessServiceInterface"/>
            <xsd:element ref = "Action"/>
        </sequence>
    </complexType>
</schema>
```

Application Transport Technologies (B2B)

While B2B content will be defined by XML and EDI, how will businesses transport this information between partners and customers?

HTTP-TCP/IP

The world has standardized on the HTTP application protocol as a result of the proliferation of the Internet. HTTP only requires a reliable transport layer. It does not specify a specific transport protocol. However, Transmission Control Protocol (TCP) for reliable transport and the Internet Protocol (IP) for routing dominate network aware applications today.

E-commerce applications will also base communications on HTTP-TCP/IP in addition to HTTPS/Secure Socket Layer (SSL) for security. The combination of HTTP and TCP/IP for B2B simply reflects the state of current system maturation and has become the common denominator.

HTTP 1.0 provides a stateless protocol, which means that systems are not required to maintain information relevant to previous requests between system invocations. Version 1.1 does provide support for persistent connections to optimize connections between systems. This is to avoid unnecessarily tearing down connections between application requests when it is known that the connection will be reused – for instance, when downloading multiple URLs for a single web page request from the same site.

In terms of e-commerce applications, the HTTP methods invoked are primarily GET and POST, with POST being widely adopted to avoid message size limitations.

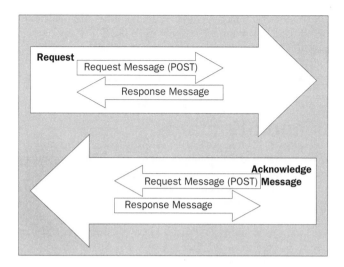

RMI-IIOP

We've already mentioned RMI-IIOP which provides Common Object Request Broker Architecture (CORBA) compliant distributed computing capabilities to the Java 2 platform. This in turn eliminates the single Java language constraint imposed by RMI.

B2B applications will interface with existing non-Java based applications. The RMI-IIOP integration provides pass by value (serialization) with the capabilities of legacy system integration inherent in the IIOP protocol. RMI-IIOP allows tighter integration capabilities between disparate systems, however at this time the e-commerce trend is toward loosely coupled systems supporting services through messaging. RMI-IIOP in the short-term will be used more for intra-system integration than inter-system integration.

XML-RPC

XML-RPC is a specification that defines a Remote Procedure Calling protocol over the Internet. An XML-RPC message is an HTTP POST request. The body of the request is defined in XML. A server procedure is invoked and returns an XML defined message. XML-RPC is simple to develop because it extends on the constructs of HTTP, by using a header and a message payload to define the routing and parameters of a remote call.

Simple Object Access Protocol (SOAP)

SOAP is a specification developed by the w3c. SOAP provides a simple and lightweight mechanism for exchanging structured and typed information between peers in a decentralized, distributed environment using XML.

The XML-based protocol consists of three parts:

❑ The envelope that defines a framework for describing what is in a message and how to process it

❑ The set of encoding rules for expressing instances of application-defined data types

❑ The convention for representing remote procedure calls and responses

SOAP can potentially be used in combination with a variety of other protocols; however, the only bindings defined by the w3c at the time of this writing describe how to use SOAP in combination with HTTP and HTTP Extension Framework.

To finish this introductory chapter let's see how the thorny issue of standardization is being tackled.

Organizations and Standards

As with any standard, "Which standard?" is an important question. There are many standards being defined to support B2B e-commerce. The growth of e-commerce has also ushered in a fury of XML standard specifications. There are and will be vertical market standards and global cross-industry standards that organizations will have to assess and address.

Let's survey the rapidly changing standards landscape. There are three types of standards organizations:

❑   Those defining cross-industry standard frameworks

❑   Those promoting specific technology frameworks

❑   Those specialized in vertical or specific industry markets

After we've had a look at the major players in this area we'll quickly identify some future directions in B2B related technologies and approachs.

Electronic Business XML (ebXML)

An example of a cross-industry framework is being defined by the United Nations body for Trade Facilitation and Electronic Business (**UN/CEFACT**) and the Organization for the Advancement of Structured Information Standards (**OASIS**). They have initiated a project to standardize XML business specifications. "UN/CEFACT and OASIS have established the Electronic Business XML initiative to develop a technical framework that will enable XML to be utilized in a consistent manner for the exchange of all electronic business data. A primary objective of ebXML is to lower the barrier of entry to electronic business in order to facilitate trade, particularly with respect to small- and medium-sized enterprises (SMEs) and developing nations."

The ebXML approach is to provide a framework for cross-industry e-commerce through standard XML definitions and UML defined business processes. With this approach they feel they can overcome the pitfalls of data-centric EDI definitions. Business process modeling captures the required exchange between business partners and XML provides the data representation.

To enable global e-commerce, trading partners must have mechanisms in place to define and exchange business process information.

ebXML defines:

❑   A standard for describing a Business Process (BP) and information model (IM)

❑   A mechanism for registering a BP and IM

❑   A trading partner discovery and registration process

- ❑ A mechanism for describing a Trading Partner Agreement (TPA)

- ❑ A standardized messaging service

- ❑ The ability to configure messaging in accordance with the TPA

Trading Partner Agreement Markup Language (tpXML) is defining an XML definition for B2B e-commerce agreements. In addition ebXML provides two views to describing e-commerce transactions. The **Business Operational View (BOV)** and the **Functional Service View (FSV).** The BOV addresses the semantics of business data, interchanges and trading partner agreements. The FSV addresses the technology interfaces and protocols required.

The most important components of the ebXML architecture are the **registry** and the **repository**. The registry provides access services, information models, and reference implementation information. The repository provides the physical backend information store. The repository may contain DTDs or schemas that are retrieved by the registry for conducting e-commerce transactions using ebXML.

The ebXML Messaging Service provides for the exchange of ebXML messages between trading partners over various transport protocols (SMTP, HTTP/S, FTP). The specification defines MIME packaging and ebXML message header information to enable interoperability between ebXML compliant systems.

For additional information on the ebXML initiative go to www.ebXML.org and www.oasis.org.

BizTalk

An example of a technology-driven framework is the BizTalk Framework. Like ebXML they are working on a framework to enable e-commerce. Initially launched by Microsoft, BizTalk is an organization of businesses that support the adoption of XML for e-commerce and B2B integration. BizTalk's goal is to provide a repository on the Internet where people can store and find XML schemas for defining various types of data exchange.

The BizTalk initiative consists of three parts:

- ❑ BizTalk 2000 server developed by Microsoft

- ❑ BizTalk Framework for exchanging XML documents

- ❑ BizTalk Repository for XML schemas used between companies

The framework consists of an XML-defined business document containing the business transaction information, a schema for describing the content and structure of a business document, and proprietary tags, which specify how the document should be processed.

587

Microsoft is promoting the BizTalk server which processes XML-based documents in other formats, which it converts to an intermediary XML format, reads, and then writes into the format the receiving application is expecting. It is not necessary to use BizTalk Framework XML formatted documents, though they are probably necessary to get the full functionality out of the BizTalk Server. Organizations can publish their industry schemas on the BizTalk.org repository.

The BizTalk Framework can be used either for point-to-point connections between companies or to facilitate trade via an online trading exchange.

For more information try www.biztalk.org.

UDDI.org

Universal Description, Discovery and Integration is an initiative started by IBM, Microsoft and Ariba to promote B2B e-commerce by providing a framework for trading partners to publish and find business service interfaces. The UDDI defines a registry for service providers to publish services and products offered, a service broker that maintains the registry, and a service requester that uses the broker to find products and services.

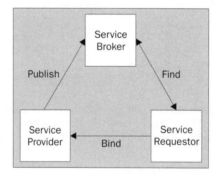

Service requesters can search by industry code, products and services offered, and geographic location. Web Service Definition Language (WSDL) is an XML-defined document that describes service interfaces, implementation details, access protocols, and contact endpoints between trading partners. These definitions are published and exchanged with service brokers.

More information on UDDI can be found at www.uddi.org.

XML Vocabularies

XML standardization initiatives are critically important. There are substantial benefits when standard XML definitions are shared by the companies in a particular industry or market. These include reduced development and maintenance costs and the elimination of custom "mapping" between the information models embodied in a company's business systems and those of its trading partners.

XML Common Business Library xCBL

Commerce One develops products and solutions for e-commerce. Like Microsoft they are a profit driven company. They are promoting the Common Business Library for XML defined B2B e-commerce (xCBL). Commerce One states that "the goal of xCBL is to provide an initial set of XML building blocks that companies can assemble and extend to develop XML applications quickly". Some of these building blocks come from well-established international standards, such as ISO 8601 (date and time), ISO 31 (measures), ISO 639 (languages: EN, FR, etc.), ISO 3166 (country codes: US, JP, etc.), and ISO 4217 (currencies: USD, FFR, etc.). Other building blocks come from SIMPLE-EDI, a project to create minimal EDIFACT transaction sets. The standard business documents in xCBL are based on these building blocks and an analysis of similar documents emerging from the OBI, RosettaNet, and OTP initiatives, with the goal to harmonize them as much as possible.

xCBL will be made available in registries run by Commerce One as part of marketsite.net, as well as through registries operated by xml.org, CommerceNet, biztalk.org, and other organizations. xCBL 2.0 was designed to model the information requirements of business-to-business electronic commerce from a document perspective. xCBL 2.0 provides schemas to represent the following business documents:

- ❏ Purchase Order
- ❏ Purchase Order Acknowledgment
- ❏ Order Status Request
- ❏ Order Status Acknowledgment
- ❏ Availability Check Request
- ❏ Availability Check Acknowledgment
- ❏ Price Check Request
- ❏ Price Check Acknowledgment
- ❏ Invoice
- ❏ Product Catalog
- ❏ Product Catalog Update

Each of these documents is constructed from a set of modules – XML building blocks that represent name and address, price, unit of measure, and so forth. xCBL allows trading partners to modify the business documents, adding elements as needed. The documents can support the business needs of both ad hoc trading communities and long-term trading relationships.

Like other standards, xCBL 2.0 separates the content of documents from information that specifies their routing or their role in the "choreography" of document exchange. EDI messages, in contrast, generally specify whether acknowledgments are expected, which documents are receiving a response, and so forth. xCBL transmits this type of information in the message header or message envelope.

For more information, try: www.xCBL.org, www.commerceone.net, or www.commerceone.net/docs/.

RosettaNet

An example of a vertical-market driven framework is being defined by RosettaNet, a non-profit organization. RosettaNet is a consortium formed to develop e-commerce standards for the IT, electronic components and semiconductor manufacturing industries. The RosettaNet initiative is designed to facilitate the exchange of product catalogs and transactions between manufacturers, distributors, resellers, and shippers of personal computers and other information technology products. RosettaNet is developing both content and transaction standards. A major effort at RosettaNet has been the development of a comprehensive data dictionary of 3500 technical properties needed to describe products in 135 categories.

RosettaNet defines a set of **Partner Interface Processes** (**PIPs**), which are specialized XML-based dialogues that define how business processes are conducted between trading partners. The PIPs define processes for a range of business activities, such as inventory, pricing, sales management, order handling, product configuration and shipping. PIPs are being defined to closely follow the Business Operational and Functional Specification Views defined by ebXML.

One of the biggest problems that exchanges need to address – and that RosettaNet promises to solve – is making content accessible to customers. Catalog software vendors are currently developing technology to compare product information created by a single vendor's back-end, but complex markets with several buyers and sellers need to define standardized ways of describing things so they can compare products, costs, contract terms and delivery dates from multiple vendors.

For more information: http://www.rosettanet.org/.

Internet Open Trading Protocol

The Internet Engineering Task Force (IETF) has established a working group to define the Internet Open Trading Protocol (IOTP). The IOTP is a purchasing protocol that handles the various roles of consumer, merchant, value acquirer, deliverer, and customer care provider and defines the transactions of purchase, refund, value exchange, authentication, withdrawal, and deposit in a payment-method-neutral manner.

It is optimized for the case where the buyer and the merchant do not have a prior acquaintance and is payment system independent. It can encapsulate and support payment systems such as SET, Mondex, secure channel card payment, and GeldKarte. IOTP is able to handle cases where such merchant roles as the shopping site, the payment handler, the deliverer of goods or services, and the provider of customer support are performed by different Internet sites.

OBI

The Open Buying on the Internet (OBI) initiative is developing a standard buying and selling framework for non-production goods and services, to ensure that buy-side and sell-side systems are able to communicate and interoperate. Order Requests and Orders follow EDI X12 850 standards, but OBI is now working on an XML version of this implementation guideline. The OBI Consortium is a non-profit organization managed by CommerceNet. CommerceNet is a community of over 600 members focused on business-to-business eCommerce worldwide.

For more information, go to: www.openbuy.org.

Future Directions

SUN has submitted a Java Specification Request (JSR) for the Java API for XML Messaging (JAXM). This specification describes the Java APIs designed specifically for the exchange of XML-based business documents, such as invoices, purchase orders, and order confirmations.

JAXM technology will define standard Java APIs that allow simple access from the Java platform to open XML messaging standards, such as the emerging ebXML Transport Routing and Packaging specification that is being developed with OASIS and many other companies.

The Connector Architecture being developed will provide a standard API for connecting the J2EE platform to enterprise information systems. The architecture defines a set of scalable, secure, and transactional mechanisms to integrate EIS, EJB Servers, and applications. If successful this should have dramatic impacts on integration capabilities with existing systems.

B2B is moving towards e-marketplaces as an alternative to point-to-point buyer and seller models. The well-known catalog and shopping cart metaphor is being augmented with automated Request For Quote (RFQ) and auction sites that support "bid and ask" pricing interaction.

Additionally, substantial effort is being exerted to automate trading partner relationship building and support a more dynamic approach to discovering services and products offered.

In the next chapter we will look at the changes and implications to the supply chain and provide code fragments to support a supplier and manufacturer simulation.

Summary

In this chapter, we considered the potential benefits to business from using B2B in e-commerce, in contrast to the more traditional EDI-centered solutions that have been implemented in the past. We also considered the challenges and issues faced by implementation of the new B2B technologies, and what would be necessary to meet business needs in e-commerce.

We then surveyed possible B2B solutions, starting with an overview of J2EE architecture and its functionality. We examined its potential uses in a B2B e-commerce context and how it might be used in conjunction with an XML-based data transfer format.

Next, we went on to look at the thorny problem of proliferating XML standards, and surveyed some of the organizations and groups working to promote and implement XML standards through DTDs and schemas. Some were more proprietary than others, but all shared the basic premise of using XML in concert with web-based technologies to exchange information with business partners.

Finally, we reviewed possible future developments in the technologies that have been under discussion.

In the next chapter, we will more closely consider the application of these B2B-enabling technologies in the context of supply chain integration.

PROFESSIONALJAVAE-COMMERCE

Section 4

B2B E-Commerce Solutions

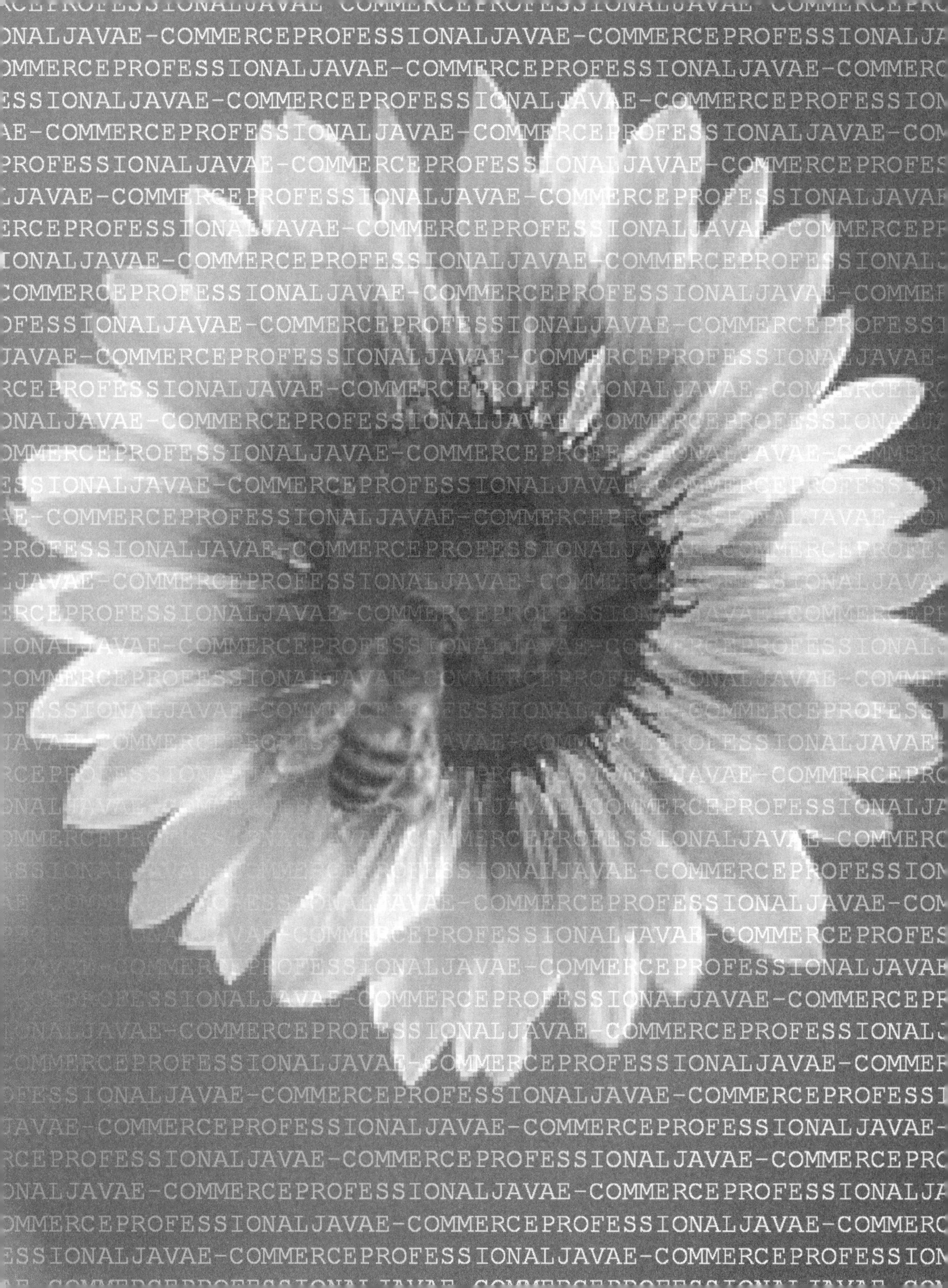
PROFESSIONALJAVAE-COMMERCE

17

B2B E-Commerce: Integrating Supply Chains

In the last chapter we provided a high level overview of B2B. We defined B2B as the transactions businesses engage in to conduct finance, commerce, or trade using the Internet. The business processes supported may include marketing, sales, development, manufacturing and support.

Such processes encompass a wide spectrum of transactional activities including:

❑   The sale and transfer of goods before reaching the consumer

❑   Subcontracted development

❑   Joint ventures

❑   Supply chains (see below)

❑   Manufacturing contracted and subcontracted

❑   Marketplaces for distribution

❑   Support services for products and services

In this chapter we will focus on the supply chain, an important facet of the emerging B2B landscape. In fact some analysts see the supply chain as the next big opportunity growing on the Internet.

Specifically in this chapter we will cover:

❑   What is a supply chain?

❑ What fundamental requirements does a supply chain need to address, for instance data representation, security, trading partner collaboration, and system integration?

❑ We will demonstrate how ebXML and RosettaNet are resolving common B2B issues, such as defining trading partner collaboration.

❑ We will then build an XML Broker to demonstrate supply chain integration, and show how XML messages may be processed by the web tier of an application server (this example will be continued in Chapters 18 and 19).

What is a Supply Chain?

Business-to-Business (B2B) integration is not new. Many corporations have linked operations with partners in an effort to become more efficient and effective in the manufacturing of goods or the delivery of services. These companies have spent large amounts of money to link and integrate their systems over private networks to form a supply chain.

A supply chain is a network of partners that performs the functions of procurement of materials, transformation of these materials into semi-finished and finished products, and the distribution of these finished products to customers. Supply chains exist in both service and manufacturing organizations. They involve partner systems collaborating to improve cost and customer value. The following diagram represents how company supply chains may be integrated:

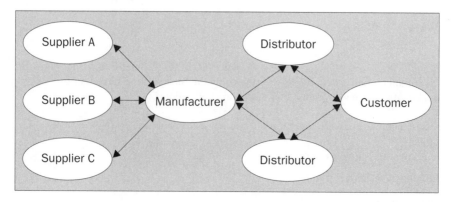

What is new today is the number of supply chains being built with the Internet as a key enabling technology. Commerce that was once done exclusively over private networks is now being replaced or augmented with public networks. This is reducing the cost of participating in the supply chain and as a result promising to put smaller players in a position to compete, and open up new channels for delivery of products and services.

Supply Chain Requirements

There are fundamental requirements, which must be satisfied to enable the growth of B2B supply chain integration over the Internet. They include:

❑ Consistent data representation

❏ Security between supply chain partners

❏ Consistent transport exchange, for instance HTTP, XML-RPC, SMTP, etc.

❏ Support for the automation of data exchange

Let's look at each of these requirements, starting with data representation.

Data Representation – Traditional Solution: EDI

Traditionally, supply chains have used EDI to define the information exchanged between systems or have used proprietary interfaces. The type of information exchanged includes electronic procurement, inventory management and resource forecasting.

Often the EDI that has been defined has been industry-specific or vertical in nature. In other words industries have tended to define standards for their specific industry group. Many times this is the most logical and direct path to developing industry standards. However, taking it too far has the disadvantage that certain aspects of information, that may be common across industries, get re-defined and re-invented. This promotes inconsistency and overly complex integration issues. In addition, specifications that define data exchange management such as technology requirements, transfer semantics, or quality of service tend to require extensive development and discussion between trading partners. There is little automation or standardization to the current process of establishing trading partner agreements.

Emerging Solution – XML and XML-EDI Integration

Existing and emerging supply chains are now embracing XML for data representation. However, some of the same problems associated with EDI can occur; cost, complexity, and inconsistent data definitions could easily become a problem with XML. Already standards groups and commercial organizations are in a race to define XML de facto standards.

Security Requirements

In addition to data representation and exchange definition, mechanisms are required to ensure that the information exchanged between trading partners is secure. This includes:

❏ Identification – a mechanism to uniquely identity a trading partner

❏ Authentication – ensuring the identity of a trading partner

❏ Authorization – providing appropriate access controls to systems, networks, applications, and information

❏ Privacy – ensuring information is visible only to the appropriate parties

❏ Integrity – ensuring information has not been tampered with in transit

❏ Non-repudiation – ensuring exchange validity

❏ Logging

Transport Bindings

Trading partners must agree on the transport mechanism to exchange information. An automated request using HTTP may not allow a response using SMTP, for instance e-mail. The allowable exchanges and sequence of exchanges (**message choreography**) must be worked out by the supply chain. This can often be time-consuming because systems have not developed automation capabilities or the processes between partners are inconsistent. Functions to enable the delivery of messages over various transport mechanisms include HTTP(S)/SSL, SMTP, FTP, CORBA IIOP, RMI-IIOP, and XML-RPC.

Automation and Integration of Data Exchange

The supply chain requires the automation of communication between partner systems. In the Business-to-Consumer (B2C) world, automation only needs to occur on one side of the relationship. The consumer simply requests services and products using a web browser. This represents a human-to-system interface. In B2B, support for this relationship exists in addition to system-to-system. This can present us with a more difficult programming model. The B2B actions and events must be interpreted in real time by an application. Error recovery and high availability are critical to the process. Programmatic automation of the exchange is a fundamental requirement for supply chain integration. Mechanisms to enable automated exchange include:

- ❑ Messaging – which is covered in Chapter 19.

- ❑ Events – these are used to indicate a change in status that is significant to a process or organization. For example, an inventory level may reach a critical point, which triggers a notification event to an automated process to query suppliers or exchanges for needed inventory.

Supply Chain Trading Partner Collaboration

To standardize and facilitate the process of conducting e-commerce, organizations need a mechanism to publish information about business processes they support along with specific technology implementation details about their capabilities for exchanging business information. ebXML (which we looked at in the previous chapter) has defined a **Trading Partner Profile** (**TPP**) to provide this mechanism.

The TPP is a document, which allows a trading partner to express their minimum business process and Business Service Interface requirements in a manner where they can be universally understood by other ebXML compliant trading partners. The TPP describes the specific technology capabilities that a trading partner supports and the service interface requirements that need to be met in order to exchange business documents with that trading partner. The TPP is stored in an ebXML registry that provides a discovery mechanism for trading partners to find one another. You may be thinking this sounds a lot like the **Universal Description, Discovery**, and **Information** (**UDDI**) registry mentioned in the last chapter. Well it is!

A **Trading Partner Agreement** (**TPA**) is a document that describes:

- ❑ The messaging service (technology)

- ❑ The process (application) requirements that are agreed upon by two or more parties

A TPA is negotiated after the discovery process and is essentially a snapshot of the specific technology and process-related information that two parties agree to use to exchange business information. If any of the parameters of an accepted TPA change after the agreement has been executed, a new TPA shall be negotiated between all parties.

Defining Business Processes

RosettaNet **Partner Interface Processes** (**PIPs**) define business processes between supply-chain partners, providing the models and documents for the implementation of standards. These definitions are closely aligned with the ebXML initiative.

PIPs fit into eight clusters, or groups of core business processes, that represent the backbone of the supply chain. PIPs are specialized **system-to-system** XML-based dialogs that define business processes between supply chain partners. Clusters include:

- ❏ **Cluster 0: RosettaNet Support** – This provides the administrative processes.

- ❏ **Cluster 1: Partner, Product and Service Review** – This allows information collection, maintenance and distribution for the development of trading-partner profiles and product-information subscriptions.

- ❏ **Cluster 2: Product Introduction** – This cluster enables distribution and periodic update of basic product information, including product change notices, as well as gathering of extended product information.

- ❏ **Cluster 3: Order Management** – This cluster allows partners to order catalog products, create custom solutions, manage distribution and deliveries, and support product returns and financial transactions.

- ❏ **Cluster 4: Inventory Management** – This cluster enables inventory management, including collaboration, replenishment, price protection, reporting and allocation of constrained product

- ❏ **Cluster 5: Marketing Information Management** – This cluster enables communication of marketing information, including campaign plans, lead information and design registration.

- ❏ **Cluster 6: Service and Support** – This cluster provides post-sales technical support, service warranty and asset management capabilities.

- ❏ **Cluster 7: Manufacturing** – This cluster enables the exchange of design, configuration process, quality and other manufacturing floor information to support the "Virtual Manufacturing" environment.

You can freely download the specifications (www.rosettanet.org) for many of these clusters. The specifications include three views to the processes defined:
The **Business Operational View** includes:

- ❏ Process flow diagrams
- ❏ Partner role descriptions
- ❏ Business activity descriptions
- ❏ Performance controls
- ❏ XML business documents exchanged for each

The **Functional Service View** includes:

❑ Network components (agents and services)

❑ Network component specifications

❑ Mapping of business activity to business action

The **Implementation Functional View** includes:

❑ Message exchange controls, for instance, scenario diagrams

As discussed, a common data representation is required for business partners to communicate. Standards bodies such as RosettaNet.org are defining XML messages and transport mechanisms to enable supply chain integration in the electronic components and semiconductor manufacturing industries.

In such a scenario, a DTD can be used to request technical information from a partner system using RosettaNet-defined XML messages, or those of some other standards body. Partners responding to this query return component technical specifications, which can be used for business activities such as hosting online electronic catalogs and sales configuration systems.

We will create a simple definition for our own information exchange (which we will be building at the end of this chapter) in an attempt to focus on the key components necessary for our B2B exchange.

The Manufacturer-Supplier Chain Simulator

Now that we have established some of the foundational elements required to build a supply chain let's investigate the developmental issues through our supply chain simulator.

Our simulated B2B supply chain will enable a supplier to view the inventory level of a manufacturer's **Materials Resource Planning** (**MRP**) System. Suppliers want to know what the current inventory level is for parts that they supply to the manufacturer so that they can plan production accordingly. The exchange of information between the supplier and the manufacturer is all automated. The following figure generalizes our B2B supply chain integration:

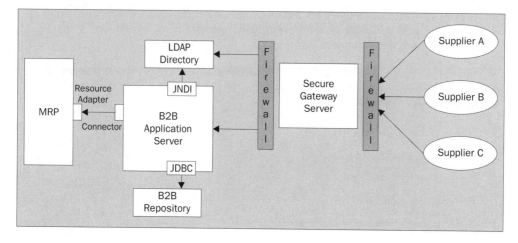

For this example we will concentrate on the J2EE web component and the EJB component required to support the automation of our supply chain.

In our example, a supplier will submit a request periodically to the manufacturer to discover inventory levels for a specific part that we are using in our business. The manufacturer will respond to the requesting supplier with the information. Some inventory levels are open to any registered supplier, while others are restricted to specific part suppliers. A more realistic example may have a manufacturer initiating the request as a result of an inventory threshold level being reached, and going through an e-procurement process.

We will construct our simulator in 3 phases over the course of three chapters – in this chapter we are going to lay down the foundations for the application. Over the course of the chapter we will demonstrate how an XML request/response can be programmatically generated to and from the web tier of an implementing servlet engine.

The first issue we have to face is how we can locate trading partners – let's have a look at some sample code.

Partner Discovery

The supplier will use an HTTP POST request to transport an XML message to the manufacturer's system. The supplier has been given a URL to address the manufacturer's B2B handler. This technique implies there is a mechanism in place for the supplier to request information about the manufacturer's capabilities. For a static environment where suppliers are known already, this may not be an issue. In a dynamic supply chain, where partners enter and leave frequently, a more flexible structure is required.

UDDI supports a find or discovery process. ebXML provides a registry and repository. In any case some mechanism to retrieve information regarding partner capabilities is required. In our example we will define a discover() service interface.

```
package com.wrox.broker;
import java.util.*;

public interface B2BRegistry {
    // return a URL to the service requested
    public String discover(String service);
    // return a list of service names
    public List getServices();
}
```

The B2BRegistry interface discover() method takes a service name as a parameter and returns a URL to the service interface. The manufacturer would implement the B2BRegistry interface to provide URL addresses to services offered to suppliers. Our B2BRegistry interface also provides a getServices() method which returns a list of the service interfaces supported.

In our example we define a hashtable to map service names to servlets, such as the InventoryService to the Dispatcher servlet. In this example all requests are mapped to a common servlet entry point:

```
package com.wrox.broker;
import java.io.*;
import java.util.*;
```

```
public class B2BRegistryImpl implements B2BRegistry {

    // path can optionally be set if all services are mapped to the same url
    public B2BRegistryImpl(String path) {
        // set path to interface
        this.path = path;
    }

    public String discover(String service) {
        // construct uri to end point
        return path+(String)registry.get(service);
    }

    public List getServices() {
        ArrayList list = new ArrayList();
        Enumeration e = registry.elements();
        while(e.hasMoreElements())
            list.add(e.nextElement());
         return list;
    }
    // This mapping should be placed in a directory service e.g. LDAP
    public void init() {
        // Registry contains service name and interface name
        // this configuration routes all requests to the Dispatcher
        registry.put("InventoryService", "Dispatcher");
        registry.put("ProcurementService", "Dispatcher");
        registry.put("DistributionService", "Dispatcher");
        registry.put("OrderManagementService", "Dispatcher");
        registry.put("MaterialsManagementService", "Dispatcher");
        registry.put("WarehouseManagementService", "Dispatcher");
        registry.put("Logistics", "Dispatcher");
    }

    // used to hold the mapping of ServiceInterface to service access point
    Hashtable registry = new Hashtable();
    String path = null;
}
```

Next we need to consider how to enable the exchange of information.

Defining XML Messages

Most XML message standards have focused on two key components:

1. Message envelopes and choreography

2. Message details mapped to business information

They usually break down into a message header(s) and message details.

Message Header

The header is responsible for the information that controls the exchange. For instance, From and To elements denote sender and receiver. Also, an element may exist to correlate messages or documents exchanged either within the current session context or from prior commerce interaction. The allowed sequence of exchanges, in other words the choreography, must be defined.

The header is important because much of the processing capabilities are embedded in the semantics of the content. This can have enormous implications to systems that are built to support only one standard type of exchange. Different techniques for managing and defining these mechanisms can result in very different implementations.

Message Detail

The second component is the actual message details. This is more closely aligned with the business domain in discussion for example, the part number or quantity ordered. These representations are more easily understood within the business context.

For our example, we will define a simple header:

```
<Header>
   <From>
       <SupplierId>2222222222</SupplierId>
   </From>
   <To>
       <ManufacturerId>3333333333</ManufacturerId>
   </To>
   <ServiceInterface id="InventoryService"></ServiceInterface>
   <MessageId>1</MessageID>
</Header>
```

The header contains a number of important pieces of information. The `From` and `To` elements identify the trading partners in the supply chain. In this case a supplier and manufacturer that have been assigned unique identification by some agreed organization, such as Dun and Bradstreet's **Data Universal Numbering System (DUNS)**. The DUNS Number is an internationally recognized nine-digit company identifier used for EDI and electronic commerce.

In addition, the supplier has requested the `InventoryService` from the manufacturer. This will enable our manufacturer to authorize the supplier to have access to the supply chain inventory functionality. As well as this, a message identification element exists to ensure the integrity of the exchange and it can be used to correlate messages sent and received between partner systems. Our example increments the `MessageID` for each exchange.

The actual message detail includes identification of the interface method requested and the associated parameters:

❑   Method – `InventoryLevelRequest()`

❑   Parameter `Product id` – "`7654`"

❑   Parameter `Part number` – "`1234`"

```
<Message>
   <InventoryLevelRequest>
       <Product id="7654"></Product>
       <Part number="1234"></Part>
   </InventoryLevelRequest>
</Message>
```

Now that we have defined a standard definition and representation for our supply chain integration, we need to define an object model to allow our applications to process this information. Thus we introduce the core of our simulator – the **XML-to-Object Broker pattern**.

J2EE as a Supporting Supply Chain Platform

In the last chapter we provided a high level overview of J2EE and discussed the significant role that J2EE compliant application servers will have in B2B e-commerce.

In our example supply chain integration, our aim is to create an automated process that will send a request for parts information to our supplier, who will reply in the form of an XML message with the desired information.

In essence, we will instruct our broker to run the Supplier program via a command line and we should see the supplier's answer printed out to the screen in the form of an XML message almost instantly.

In order to do this, we will require an application server first of all in which to run our files. In later chapters we will be developing the application we build here, and in addition to servlets we will be implementing EJBs. We need something that will support us in these later stages, so we will be using Allaire's JRun 3.0 as our application server for deployment. The other thing we will use in this chapter is **Java API for XML Processing (JAXP)** version 1.1 early access, as this is where some of our functionality is coming from. There is full coverage of the software requirements for the simulator and code deployment information at the end of the chapter.

Please note that all the code (for all three chapters covering this example), together with more extensive deployment information, is available from www.wrox.com.

J2EE supports a number of component technologies: applets, client applications, Enterprise JavaBeans, and web components. Our focus will be the web components and the EJB components that run on the server.

The web component is typically used to provide a response to a request. Often this is the software that generates the user interface for a web-based application. The J2EE specifies two types of web components: servlets and Java Server Pages. In this chapter we will be using servlets to generate a response to a request from a supplier. In this case the request is not from, for instance, an HTML form, but rather a programmatic request initiated by our supplier application.

Web components are hosted by servlet containers, JSP containers, and web containers. All servlet containers must support HTTP as a protocol for requests and responses. As mentioned in the prior chapter on transports, this protocol is the common denominator on the Internet and thus most B2B e-commerce frameworks are including it in their initial support.

Web components and associated containers comprise the web tier of the J2EE architecture and our XML Broker will operate in this tier of our application, as it uses servlets to access the functionality of the various J2EE components.

The Web tier

The XML Broker is used to convert an XML-defined B2B supply chain message into an object. In this respect it provides an *XML-to-Object* mapping. We do this to provide a consistent interface to our core system functionality. Differences between XML message definitions can be mitigated using this pattern, and fully-fledged object representations with behavior and state result from the transformation. We can leverage many of the Java based technologies such as the Java API for XML Processing (JAXP) to simplify our programming task.

In short, over the course of the chapter we are going to:

❑ Transmit an XML inventory request from a supplier to a manufacturer

❑ Map the inventory request to a Java object which implements a Command Interface

❑ Generate an XML inventory response from the manufacturer to the supplier

The XML Broker

Now we've set out the parameters for our simulator, let's dig into the code for the com.wrox.broker package we will put together.

The following scenario diagram depicts the high level interaction between the classes that comprise the XMLBroker in our application. The Dispatcher servlet is used to process the request from our supplier by invoking the XMLBroker and generating a response.

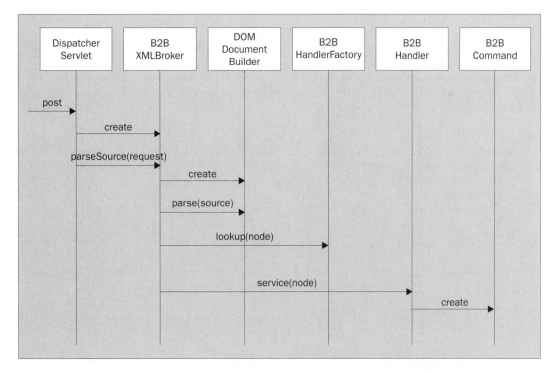

It is through the operation of these classes that we create our supply chain application simulation. Let's walk through each one and see exactly what it is going to do for us.

Over the rest of the chapter we'll be looking at the following components of com.wrox.broker: that facilitate the manufacturer's side of the chain:

Classes:

- ❏ Dispatcher
- ❏ B2BXMLUtil
- ❏ B2BHandlerFactory
- ❏ ServiceMessageHandler
- ❏ InventoryRequestHandler
- ❏ InventoryRequest
- ❏ InventoryResponse

Interfaces:

- ❏ B2BHandler
- ❏ Command
- ❏ B2BResponse

We'll also take time out to look at relevant parts of JAXP.

The Dispatcher

The Dispatcher defines a common access point to receive XML post requests. It creates an InputSource from the BufferedReader returned by the HttpServletRequest.

A client that posts data to the URL returned by the B2BRegistry would invoke the doPost method on the Dispatcher. The Dispatcher will create a utility class that parses the XML input stream and returns a B2BResponse object (defined below).

```
package com.wrox.broker;
import java.io.*;
import java.util.*;
import javax.servlet.*;
import javax.servlet.http.*;
import org.xml.sax.InputSource;

public class Dispatcher extends HttpServlet {
// Dispatch post requests to an XML - Object broker

    public void doPost(HttpServletRequest request, HttpServletResponse response)
            throws ServletException, IOException  {

        // authorization code here
        System.out.println(request);
        try {
           // Grab the reader from the request object
           BufferedReader reader = request.getReader();
           char buffer[] = new char[request.getContentLength()];
```

```
        int bRead;

        // Transfer request to buffer
        while((bRead = reader.read(buffer,0,buffer.length)) != -1);

        // set the output content type
        response.setContentType("text/xml; charset=ISO-8859-1");

        // Grab the output writer
        PrintWriter out = response.getWriter();
```

Now we are ready to invoke the B2BXMLUtil to transform the XML request into a Document Object Model (DOM). The DOM will subsequently be processed by our service handler application.

```
        // Create the XML Message Broker
        B2BXMLUtil util = new B2BXMLUtil(out);

        // Create an input source parse and execute request
        B2BResponse b2bResponse = util.parseSource(new InputSource(new
            CharArrayReader(buffer)));

        // write the XML response to the output stream
          out.write(b2bResponse.toXML());

      } catch (Exception ex) {
        ex.printStackTrace();
      }
    }
  }
```

The web.xml file provides a servlet mapping element to map all requests to the Dispatcher:

```
<web-app>
   <servlet><servlet-name>Dispatcher</servlet-name>
      <servlet-class>com.wrox.broker.Dispatcher</servlet-class>
      <servlet-mapping>
         <url-pattern>/servlet/*</url-pattern>
         <servlet-name>Dispatcher</servlet-name>
      </servlet-mapping>
   </servlet>
</web-app>
```

Before we go any further we need to see what functionality we can get from JAXP to help us in our task.

JAXP and the Document Object Model (DOM)

As we saw in Chapter 7, the Java API for XML Parsing (JAXP) enables basic functionality for reading and manipulating XML documents through Java APIs. The API provides a standard way for any XML-conformant parser and XSLT-conformant processor to be accessed by an application. The reference implementation uses Crimson, which was derived from the Java Project X parser from Sun, as its default XML parser and Xalan as its default XSLT engine.

The Document Object Model (DOM) is an application programming interface (API) for HTML and XML documents. It defines the logical structure of documents and the way a document is accessed and manipulated. It is a standard interface to documents as defined by the www.w3c.org.

We will use JAXP and the DOM as the core components to enable our XMLBroker – specifically the DocumentBuilder and DocumentBuilderFactory to create and manipulate our B2B supply chain messages, which we will discuss here in more detail.

Firstly, before we build anything, we will take a look through some of these core components and try to familiarize ourselves with their functionality.

package javax.xml.parsers

The JAXP implementation for this example uses Version 1.1ea (Early Access release) of the JAXP.

The Java API for XML Parsing (JAXP) Optional Package enables basic functionality for reading and manipulating XML documents through pure Java APIs. The API provides a standard way for any XML-conformant parser and XSLT-conformant processor to be accessed by an application. The reference implementation uses Crimson, which was derived from the Java Project X parser from Sun, as its default XML parser and Xalan as its default XSLT engine.

If you are using the standard Version 1.0 JAXP the examples that follow will *not* compile. The JAXP Version 1.1 can be found at www.javasoft.com.

The SAXParserFactory

The SAXParserFactory defines a factory API that enables applications to configure and obtain a SAX based parser to parse XML documents. Various parameters can be to control the behavior of the resulting parser instance. For example, the setNamespaceAware() can be set to true or false to indicate whether namespaces are significant to the parsing and thus integrity of the document.

```
public abstract class SAXParserFactory {
    protected SAXParserFactory();
    public static SAXParserFactory newInstance();
    public abstract SAXParser newSAXParser()
                            throws ParserConfigurationException, SAXException;
    public void setNamespaceAware(boolean aware);
    public void setValidating(boolean validating);
    public boolean isNamespaceAware();
    public boolean isValidating();
    public abstract void setFeature(String name, boolean value)
                        throws SAXNotRecognizedException,
                                SAXNotSupportedException;
    public abstract boolean getFeature (String name)
                            throws SAXNotRecognizedException,
                                    SAXNotSupportedException;
}
```

Implementation instances of the SAXParser abstract class contain an implementation of the org.xml.saxParser interface and enables content from a variety of sources to be parsed using the contained parser. Instances of SAXParser are obtained from a SAXParserFactory by invoking its newSAXParser method:

```
public abstract class SAXParser {
   protected SAXParser();
   public abstract void setProperty(String name,Object value)
                        throws SAXNotRecognizedException,
                               SAXNotSupportedException;
   public abstract Object getProperty(String name)
                        throws SAXNotRecognizedException,
                               SAXNotSupportedException;
   public void parse(InputStream stream, HandlerBase base)
            throws SAXException, IOException;
   public void parse(InputStream stream, HandlerBase base,String systemId)
            throws SAXException, IOException;
   public void parse(String uri, HandlerBase base)
            throws SAXException, IOException;
   public void parse(File file, HandlerBase base)
            throws SAXException, IOException;
   public void parse(InputSource source, HandlerBase base)
            throws SAXException, IOException;
   public void parse(InputStream stream, DefaultHandler dh)
            throws SAXException, IOException;
   public void parse(InputStream stream, DefaultHandler dh, String systemId)
            throws SAXException, IOException;
   public void parse(String uri, DefaultHandler dh)
            throws SAXException, IOException;
   public void parse(File file, DefaultHandler dh)
            throws SAXException, IOException;
   public void parse(InputSource source, DefaultHandler dh)
            throws SAXException, IOException;
   public abstract org.xml.sax.Parser getParser() throws SAXException;
   public abstract org.xml.sax.XMLReader getXMLReader() throws SAXException;
   public abstract boolean isNamespaceAware();
   public abstract boolean isValidating ();
}
```

The DocumentBuilderFactory

The `DocumentBuilderFactory` defines a factory API that enables applications to configure and obtain a parser to parse XML documents into a DOM Document tree.

```
public abstract class DocumentBuilderFactory {
   protected DocumentBuilderFactory();
   public static DocumentBuilderFactory newInstance();
   public DocumentBuilder newDocumentBuilder()
                        throws ParserConfigurationException;
   public void setNamespaceAware(boolean awareness);
   public void setValidating(boolean validating);
   public void setIgnoreElementContentWhitespace(boolean whitespace);
   public void setExpandEntityReferences(boolean expandEntityRef);
   public void setIgnoringComments(boolean ignoreComments);
   public void setCoalescing(boolean coalescing);
   public boolean isNamespaceAware();
   public boolean isValidating();
   public boolean isIgnoreElementContentWhitespace();
   public boolean isExpandEntityReferences();
   public boolean isIgnoringComments();
```

609

```
    public boolean isCoalescing();
    public abstract void setAttribute(String name, Object value)
                    throws IllegalArgumentException;
    public abstract Object getAttribute(String name)
                    throws IllegalArgumentException;
}
```

The DocumentBuilder

Instances of `DocumentBuilder` provide a mechanism for parsing XML documents into a DOM document tree represented by an `org.w3c.dom.Document` object. A `DocumentBuilder` instance is obtained from a `DocumentBuilderFactory` by invoking its `newDocumentBuilder` method. Note that `DocumentBuilder` uses several classes from the SAX API. This does not require that the implementer of the underlying DOM implementation use a SAX parser to parse XML content into an `org.w3c.dom.Document`. It merely requires that the implementation communicate with the application using these existing APIs.

```
public abstract class DocumentBuilder {
    protected DocumentBuilder();
    public Document parse(InputStream is) throws SAXException, IOException;
    public Document parse(InputStream is, String systemId)
                    throws SAXException, IOException;
    public Document parse(String uri) throws SAXException, IOException;
    public Document parse(File f) throws SAXException, IOException;
    public abstract Document parse(InputSource is)
                    throws SAXException, IOException;
    public abstract boolean isNamespaceAware();
    public abstract boolean isValidating();
    public abstract void setEntityResolver(EntityResolver er);
    public abstract void setErrorHandler(ErrorHandler eh);
    public Document newDocument();
}
```

Implementations of the `SAXParser` and `DocumentBuilder` are *not* thread safe. This means that you should not expect to be able to use the same instance of a `SAXParser` or `DocumentBuilder` in more than one thread at a time without side effects. If you are creating a multi-threaded application, you should make sure that only one thread has access to any given `SAXParser` or `DocumentBuilder` instance.

Configuration of a `SAXParserFactory` or `DocumentBuilderFactory` is also *not* thread safe. This means that you should not allow a `SAXParserFactory` or `DocumentBuilderFactory` to have its `setNamespaceAware` or `setValidating` methods from more than one thread.

The `newSAXParser` method of a `SAXParserFactory` implementation and the `newDocumentBuilder` method of a `DocumentBuilderFactory` will be thread-safe without side effects. This means that you should expect to be able to create parser instances in multiple threads at once from a shared factory without side effects or problems.

After that digression let's return to our simulator coding.

The B2BXMLUtil

The `B2BXMLUtil` class defines a utility class that creates a DOM using a `DocumentBuilder`. The top level node in our example will contain the XML data type that we map to an instance of our `B2BHandler` (see below) which implements the `B2BHandler` interface. The interface takes a node as a parameter and returns a `B2BResponse` that implements a convert `toXML` method:

610

```
package com.wrox.broker;
import java.io.*;
import org.w3c.dom.*;
import org.xml.sax.SAXException;
import org.xml.sax.SAXParseException;
import org.xml.sax.InputSource;
import javax.xml.parsers.DocumentBuilderFactory;
import javax.xml.parsers.DocumentBuilder;
import javax.xml.parsers.ParserConfigurationException;

public class B2BXMLUtil {

    public B2BXMLUtil(Writer writer) {
        out = writer;
    }

    public synchronized B2BResponse parseSource(InputSource source)
                                    throws IOException {
        B2BResponse response = null;
        Document doc = null;
        try {
            DocumentBuilderFactory docBuilderFactory =
                                        DocumentBuilderFactory.newInstance();
            DocumentBuilder docBuilder = docBuilderFactory.newDocumentBuilder();
            doc = docBuilder.parse (source);

            // normalize text representation
            doc.getDocumentElement().normalize();
```

At this point we have parsed the XML input source into a DOM. We then grab the top-level element to identify the document type, which in this case is the name of the service to be invoked. We then map the service name to a service handler.

```
            // Get the top level element to identify the document type
            String serviceName = doc.getDocumentElement().getNodeName();

            // Map the element name to a document handler
            B2BHandlerFactory handlerFactory = B2BHandlerFactory.getFactory();
            B2BHandler handler = (B2BHandler)handlerFactory.getHandler(serviceName);
```

We invoke the handler passing the node as a parameter. Our service handler returns an object that implements our response interface. If no handler is found then an error is written to the output stream:

```
            // Invoke the handler with the document node and return response
            if(handler != null) {
                response = handler.service(doc);
            } else {
                out.write("Requesting unsupported service " + serviceName);
            }
        } catch (SAXParseException err) {
            out.write ("** Parsing error" + ", line " + err.getLineNumber()
                    + ", uri " + err.getSystemId ());
            out.write("    " + err.getMessage ());
```

```
            } catch (SAXException e) {
                Exception ecp = e.getException ();
                ((ecp == null) ? e : ecp).printStackTrace ();
            } catch (Throwable t) {
                t.printStackTrace ();
            }
            return response;
        }

    public Writer getWriter() {
        return out;
    }
    Writer out;
}
```

The B2BHandlerFactory

The B2BHandlerFactory defines a singleton factory that maps document types to request and response handlers. The singleton pattern ensures that only one instance of the factory exists in the system.

```
package com.wrox.broker;
import java.io.*;
import java.util.*;

public class B2BHandlerFactory {
    private static B2BHandlerFactory factory = null;
    private static Hashtable handlers = null;
    private B2BHandlerFactory() {
        init();
    }

    // only one factory exists - singleton
    public static B2BHandlerFactory getFactory() {
        if(factory == null)
            factory = new B2BHandlerFactory();
        return factory;
    }

    public Object getHandler(String handlerName) {
        return handlers.get(handlerName);
    }
```

This is where we are able to map XML message types to instances of message handlers.

```
    private void init() {
        // Handler contains mapping of request/response service name to associated
        // xml handler
        handlers = new Hashtable();
        handlers.put("B2BMessage", new ServiceMessageHandler());
        handlers.put("InventoryService", new InventoryRequestHandler());

        // other service handlers.....

    }
}
```

The B2BHandler

The B2BHandler interface is the interface all B2B document handlers implement. It supports the service() method which takes a DOM Node object and determines the appropriate parsing and Command object to build and execute. It returns an object that implements the B2BResponse interface:

```
package com.wrox.broker;
import org.w3c.dom.Node;

public interface B2BHandler {
    public B2BResponse service(Node node);
}
```

The ServiceMessageHandler

The ServiceMessageHandler is responsible for processing the ServiceInterface element. The attribute of the ServiceInterface element identifies the name of the service handler the client wants to invoke.

For example the following XML header indicates that the XML request should invoke the InventoryService service interface:

```
<Header>
    <ServiceInterface id="InventoryService"></ServiceInterface>
</Header>
```

The ServiceMessageHandler maps the name to the handler using the B2BHandlerFactory and then finds the Message element and passes that to the service handler.

```
<Message>
    <InventoryLevelRequest>
        <Product id="7654"></Product>
        <Part number="1234"></Part>
    </InventoryLevelRequest>
</Message>
```

The ServiceHandler provides the message level routing of XML requests. As can be seen from our XML vocabulary, we have a high level ServiceInterface element and a specific Message element, which identifies the method to invoke on the service. This enables us to define many methods on a service and pass any number of parameters within the message construct.

```
package com.wrox.broker;
import java.io.*;
import org.w3c.dom.*;

public class ServiceMessageHandler implements B2BHandler {

    public B2BResponse service (Node node) {
        B2BResponse response = null;
        Document doc = (Document)node;

        // Use the top level node to get the Service Interface element
        NodeList serviceList = doc.getElementsByTagName("ServiceInterface");
```

```
        Node serviceElement = serviceList.item(0);
        NamedNodeMap attributeList = serviceElement.getAttributes();
        Node attr = attributeList.getNamedItem("id");
        String serviceName = attr.getNodeValue();

        B2BHandlerFactory handlerFactory = B2BHandlerFactory.getFactory();
        B2BHandler handler = (B2BHandler)handlerFactory.getHandler(serviceName);

        // Pass the message node to the service handler
        if(handler != null) {
            serviceList = doc.getElementsByTagName("Message");
            response = handler.service(serviceList.item(0));
        }
        return response;
    }
}
```

The InventoryRequestHandler

The `InventoryRequestHandler` creates an `InventoryRequest` object and sets the properties from the `Message` element and child nodes (for instance, parts and product attributes). It invokes the `execute()` method on the `InventoryRequest` object that implements the `Command` interface and returns a `B2BRequest` object.

```
package com.wrox.broker;
import java.io.*;
import org.w3c.dom.*;

public class InventoryRequestHandler implements B2BHandler {

    InventoryRequest request = null;
    public InventoryRequestHandler() {
    }

    public B2BResponse service (Node node) {
        // create an Inventory Request command
        request = new InventoryRequest();
        create(node);

        // Execute the command
        B2BResponse response = request.execute();
        return response;
    }

    public void create (Node node) {
        // Get the message nodes children
        NodeList nodes = node.getChildNodes();
        for(int i=0; i<nodes.getLength(); i++) {
            Node currentNode = nodes.item(i);
            String nodeName = currentNode.getNodeName();

            // if inventory level request recursive call for parameters
            if(nodeName.equals("InventoryLevelRequest")) {
                create(currentNode);
```

```
          // set the product property
          } else if (nodeName.equals("Product")) {
            NamedNodeMap attributeList =currentNode.getAttributes();
            Node attr = attributeList.getNamedItem("id");
            request.setProduct(attr.getNodeValue());

          // set the part property
          } else if(nodeName.equals("Part")) {
            NamedNodeMap attributeList = currentNode.getAttributes();
            Node attr = attributeList.getNamedItem("number");
            request.setPart(attr.getNodeValue());
          }
        }
      }
    }
```

The Command Interface

The Command interface is the interface all B2B requests implement.

```
package com.wrox.broker;

public interface Command {
    public B2BResponse execute();
}
```

The InventoryRequest

The InventoryRequest is an example B2BRequest class that implements the Command interface execute() method. The execute() method has access to a web tier controller object that calls an associated EJB tier stateful session controller. We will discuss the EJB tier and EIS tier in Chapter 19.

```
package com.wrox.broker;

public class InventoryRequest implements Command {

    String product = null;
    String part = null;
    int quantity = 0;

    public InventoryRequest() {
        this(null,null);
    }

    public InventoryRequest(String product, String part) {
        this.product = product;
        this.part = part;
    }

    // invoke the channel "bridge" to get quantity on hand
    public B2BResponse execute () {
        quantity = InventoryChannelController.getQuantity(product, part);
        return new InventoryResponse(product, part, quantity);
    }
```

```
    public String toXML() {
        StringBuffer buffer = new StringBuffer();
        buffer.append("<InventoryLevelRequest>").
            append("<Product id=").
            append("\""+product+"\"").
            append("></Product>").
            append("<Part number=").
            append("\""+part+"\"").
            append("></Part>").
            append("</InventoryLevelRequest>");

        return new String(buffer);
    }

    public void setProduct(String product) {
        this.product = product;
    }
    public void setPart(String part) {
        this.part = part;
    }
}
```

The B2BResponse Interface

The B2BResponse is the interface all B2B responses implement.

```
package com.wrox.broker;

public interface B2BResponse {
    public String toXML();
}
```

The InventoryResponse

The InventoryResponse implements the B2BResponse interface. A B2BResponse object implements the toXML method which generates an XML String based on the object properties mapping. The response is available after invoking the execute() method on the appropriate Command object. We will look at some potential problems with this design in the next chapter.

```
package com.wrox.broker;

public class InventoryResponse implements B2BResponse {

    String product = null;
    String part = null;
    int quantity = 0;

    public InventoryResponse(String product, String part, int quantity) {
        this.product = product;
        this.part = part;
        this.quantity = quantity;
    }

    public String toXML() {
        StringBuffer buffer = new StringBuffer();
```

```
        buffer.append("<InventoryLevelResponse>").
              append("<Product id=").
              append("\""+product+"\"").
              append("></Product>").
              append("<Part number=").
              append("\""+part+"\"").
              append("></Part>").
              append("<Quantity onHand=").
              append("\"" + (new Integer(quantity)).toString()+"\"").
              append("></Quantity>").
              append("</InventoryLevelResponse>");

        return new String(buffer);
    }
}
```

Reviewing the Supplier-Manufacturer Integration

Let's just summarize our supplier and manufacturer integration application so far.

We have an XML request periodically sent to a manufacturer's `InventoryService` access point, which in our example is the `Dispatcher` servlet. Remember this may be resolved by the supplier through the `B2BRegistry` Interface of the manufacturer.

The `B2BXMLUtil` creates a Document Object Model by parsing the XML request. The DOM is passed to the `InventoryHandler` which creates an `InventoryRequest` object that implements the `Command` Interface. The handler invokes the `execute()` method on the `InventoryRequest` which generates an `InventoryResponse` object which is returned to the `Dispatcher`.

The `Dispatcher` invokes the `toXML()` method on the `InventoryResponse` which returns an XML String that is written to the `OutputStream`.

Now we have constructed the rest of our broker, it is time to construct a client so we can query our application for results.

The Client

We are going to prepare a client to do this and call it `Supplier.java` – and it is this that we will use to forward our request. We will also create a class (`PartMonitor`) to automate the exchange of information.

The Supplier

The `Supplier` – this class is used to test our Manufacturer XML Broker

```
package com.wrox.broker;

import java.io.*;
import java.net.*;

public class Supplier {

    String urlString = null;
```

```
    URLConnection connection = null;
    PrintWriter outStream = null;
    InputStream inStream = null;
    PartMonitor monitor = null;

    // test xml messages to manufacturer
    String B2BMessageExample;
    String B2BRegistryExample;

    public Supplier() {}

    public Supplier(String url, String B2BMessageExample) {
        this.urlString = url;
        this.B2BMessageExample = B2BMessageExample;
        monitor = new PartMonitor(this, 10);
    }

    public String find(String serviceInterface) {
        System.out.println("i = " + serviceInterface);
        if(serviceInterface.equals("InventoryInterface")) {
            return getXMLDoc(B2BRegistryExample);
        } else if (serviceInterface.equals("PartInventory")) {
            System.out.println("B2B msg = " + B2BMessageExample);
            return getXMLDoc(B2BMessageExample);
        } else {
            return null;
        }
    }

    String getXMLDoc(String xmlFile) {
        System.out.println("xmlfile = " + xmlFile);
        StringBuffer buffer = new StringBuffer();
        String line;
        try {
            BufferedReader xmlReader = new BufferedReader(new FileReader(xmlFile));
            while((line = xmlReader.readLine()) != null)
                buffer.append(line);
        } catch (IOException e) {}

        return new String(buffer);
    }

    public void request(String msg) throws IOException {
        try {
            URL url = new URL(urlString);
            connection = url.openConnection();
            connection.setDoOutput(true);
            outStream = new PrintWriter(connection.getOutputStream());
            outStream.println(msg);
            outStream.println("");
            outStream.close();
            outStream = null;

            /* Read the manufacturer's response and close up. */
            inStream = connection.getInputStream();
```

```
            byte[] buffer= new byte[4096];
            int responseSize;
            while((responseSize = inStream.read(buffer)) != -1)
                System.out.write(buffer,0,responseSize);
            inStream.close();
            inStream = null;

        } catch (Exception e) {
            e.printStackTrace();
        } finally {
            if (outStream != null) {
                outStream.close();
            }
            if (inStream != null) {
                inStream.close();
            }
        }
    }
    void startMonitor() {
        try {
            monitor.start();
        } catch (Exception e) {}
    }

    public static void main(String args[]) {
        if(args.length < 1) {
            System.out.println("usage java com.wrox.broker.Supplier [e.g.
                c:\\example\\chapter18\\B2BMessage.xml]");
            System.exit(1);
        }

        // You must set up the necessary handlers for messages other than
        // B2BMessage.xml
        String B2BMessageExample = args[0];
        System.out.println("args[0] =" + args[0]);

        // this reference would be returned by the "discover" process
        String urlString = "http://localhost:8100/b2b-app/servlet/Dispatcher";

        Supplier supplier = new Supplier(urlString, B2BMessageExample);
        supplier.startMonitor();
    }
}
```

The PartMonitor

The PartMonitor class extends Thread. A supplier creates a PartMonitor with a time interval to poll our manufacturer for part status. The PartMonitor invokes the request() method on the supplier to send a request to the manufacturer.

```
package com.wrox.broker;

import java.io.*;
import java.net.*;
import java.util.Date;
```

```
class PartMonitor extends Thread {

    Supplier supplier;
    int interval;
    String pollMsg = null;

    public PartMonitor(Supplier supplier, int interval) {
        this.supplier = supplier;
        this.interval = interval;
    }

    // the main loop to poll the manufacturer
    public void run() {
        pollMsg = supplier.find("PartInventory");
        try {
            for(;;) {
                Date date = new Date(System.currentTimeMillis());
                System.out.println("Monitor running..." + date);
                checkStatus();
                sleep(1000*interval);
            }
        } catch (Exception e) {}
    }

    // The part monitor invokes the supplier request method.
    void checkStatus() {
    System.out.println("Checking");
        try {
            supplier.request(pollMsg);
        } catch (Exception e) {}
    }
}
```

Building our XML Broker Framework

Now that we have looked at the code and components we need to integrate our automated supply chain, we can turn our attention to building and deploying the broker we intend to use. Firstly let's summarize where we've got to.

The com.wrox.broker package is the core of the XML-Broker defined in our example. It contains the classes necessary to run the example. This framework assumes that messages will contain one or more header elements and one or more message elements. ServiceMessageHandler is used to process header elements and the framework is extended by implementing a B2BHandler unique to each message element(s).

B2BHandlers are created by the B2BHandlerFactory. A B2BHandler is returned based on a mapping between an XML node and an instance of the applicable handler.

The purpose of the registry is to allow a trading partner to query for a specific service (that is, InventoryService) and receive a URL indicating the service access point of the trading partner supporting the service. In our example, the Supplier would use the Manufacturer's B2BRegistryImpl to determine services available to the Supplier. This method of discovery assumes the Supplier knows how to access the Manufacturer to bootstrap the process.

We will construct our broker in 3 phases over the course of three chapters, but here we are laying down our foundations, and attempting to demonstrate how an XML request/response can be programmatically generated to and from the web tier of an implementing servlet engine.

To recap, the steps involved in this first example are:

❑   Transmit an XML inventory request from a supplier to a manufacturer

❑   Map the inventory request to a Java object which implements the `Command` Interface

❑   Generate an XML inventory response from the manufacturer to the supplier

Software Requirements

To run the example, you will need the following:

❑   System running either Windows or UNIX (the example uses Windows).

❑   Java Runtime Environment (JRE) 1.1 (JDK version 1.2.2 or later required for EJB and JMS used in later chapters).

❑   An application server which supports J2EE EJB. Here we've used Allaire's JRun. The JRun 3.0 Developer Edition is freely available from their web site at www.allaire.com, so make sure you have it installed before you attempt the example code.

❑   A messaging service provider that implements the JMS API.

❑   A naming service provider that implements the JNDI API.

❑   The Java API for XML Processing 1.1ea. (This is only an early access product and hence liable to change!)

> **Be aware that JRun 3.0 may have a different JAXP version than the early access version. You may have to implement the new version in your JRun directories!**

Deployment

Download the necessary files for Chapter 17 from the Wrox site (www.wrox.com) and save them on to your hard drive.

Now rename the folder containing the downloaded files **b2b-app**. These files should already be compiled, but be sure to check. If your pathnames or drives are different from the code, be sure to change them as errors are generated.

Now, copy the folder into your JRun directory. You should end up with something like:

`d:\Allaire\JRun\servers\default\b2b-app`

Copy the `makew.bat` file under the `examples` directory to the `default` directory. This file is directly above the `examples` directory.

For example, `d:\Allaire\JRun\servers\default\`

Run the `makew.bat` file under `\b2b-app\web-inf\classes` directory.

For example (depending on your hard drive):

`d:\Allaire\JRun\servers\default\b2b-app\web-inf\classes>makew`

This will create the `com.wrox.broker` directory.

Running the Example

Now you are ready to test the `Supplier`.

Change to the `classes` directory under `Web-inf` and run the `com.wrox.broker.Supplier`.

For example:
d:\Allaire\JRun\servers\default\b2b-app\Web-inf\classes> java com.wrox.broker.Supplier

This should lead to something like the following appearing as console output:

```
Monitor running...Sun Jan 21 15:56:22 GMT 2001
Checking
<?xml version="1.0"?><InventoryLevelResponse><Product id="Generic Computer"></Product><Part
number="CRT-1234"></Part><Quantity onHand="100"></Quantity></InventoryLevelResponse>

Monitor running...Sun Jan 21 15:56:34 GMT 2001
Checking
<?xml version="1.0"?><InventoryLevelResponse><Product id="Generic Computer"></Product><Part
number="CRT-1234"></Part><Quantity onHand="100"></Quantity></InventoryLevelResponse>
```

Summary

In this chapter we've seen that a supply chain is a network of systems involved in the manufacturing, production, and distribution of goods and services. Trading partner agreements and the ability to execute these agreements quickly are important to the success of B2B supply chain integration.

As has been mentioned before, XML has become the new standard for defining supply chain information and, despite the proliferation of standards bodies and efforts targeted at cross-industry and vertical industry markets, the rapid spread of XML has resulted in inconsistencies in direction and definition and the realization that adaptability and flexibility in system design are more important than ever.

Over the course of the chapter we've developed an XML Broker framework to illustrate one method of supplier-manufacturer integration. We've demonstrated how an XML request/response can be programmatically generated to and from the web tier of an implementing servlet engine. Over the next couple of chapters we'll build on this example – in Chapter 18 we'll see how XSLT can be used to transform XML requests and responses into other message formats, and in Chapter 19 we'll integrate a B2B frontend with a B2B backend using the Java Messaging Service (JMS) as middleware.

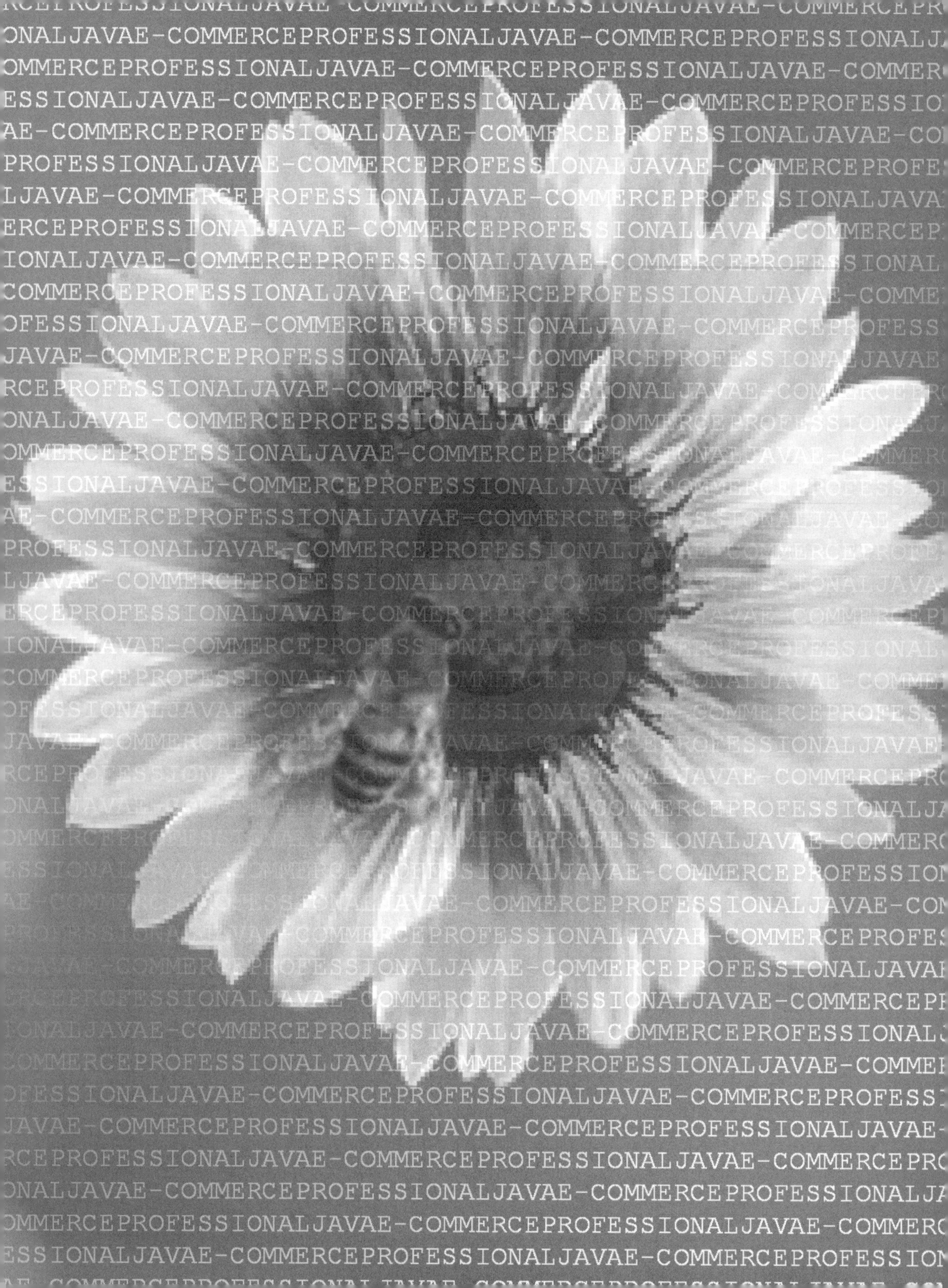
PROFESSIONALJAVAE-COMMERCE

18

B2B E-Commerce: Transformation

Transformation allows us to completely change the appearance or the structure of a document. It enables us to mediate between differences in structural representations of information and hence has a pivotal role to play in B2B e-commerce.

Anyone who has worked on projects dealing with the exchange of information between systems understands the importance of being able to resolve differences in data structure and representation. Many systems have implemented proprietary formats for data and message exchange. When these systems are expanded to include communication between many external systems, the problems with inconsistent definitions are compounded.

In this chapter we will be discussing why transformation is important in the context of B2B e-commerce. We will discuss:

- ❑ XML Diversity – why a single standard for e-commerce is not practical
- ❑ How **XSL Transformations** (**XSLT**) can provide a solution to XML diversity
- ❑ The components of XSLT
- ❑ The implications of XSLT for supply chain integration
- ❑ Filtering, merging, and writing multiple output files

XML Diversity

So with all the talk of XML standards, why are we now talking about the problems with inconsistent definitions of data between trading partners; with the diversity of XML standards, doesn't XML provide us with a standard for describing and exchanging data on the Web?

Well that is true – XML does define a standard for describing information. However, XML does not define how the content should be structured. Take the following as an example.

Two companies, Company X and Company Y, have both decided to use XML to transmit the data in their purchase orders. Now, Company X wants to put a purchase order through Company Y, and everything looks fine on the surface because they both utilize XML. Let's have a look at the purchase order that Company X uses:

```
<PurchaseOrder OrderNo="1234">
  <Buyer BuyerNo="AB24567"
    <Name="Smith & Co2/>
    <Address1>123 High St</Address1>
    <Address2>Epping Forest</Address2>
    <Zip>E15 2HQ</Zip>
  </Buyer>
  <Supplier>
    ...
  </Supplier>
  <OrderItem>
    ...
  </OrderItem>
  <Tax>
    <TaxType>VAT</TaxType>
    <TaxPercent>17.5</TaxPercent>
    ...
  </Tax>
  ...
</PurchaseOrder>
```

As you can see, Company X uses valid XML for their purchase orders. Now let's have a look at Company Y's equally valid XML purchase order:

```
<PurchaseOrder>
  <Party Type="Buyer">
    <Reference>AB24567</Reference>
    <Name>Smith & Co</Name>
    <Street>123 High St</Street>
    <Town>Epping Forest</Town>
    <PostCode>E15 2HQ</PostCode>
  </Party>
  <Party Type="Supplier">
    ...
  </Party>
  <OrdNo>1234<OrdNo>
    <OrderItem>
      ...
    </OrderItem>
  <Tax Type="VAT" Percent="17.5"... />
  ...
</Purchase Order>
```

Each purchase order is valid. Each defines the same content; however, the structure of the information is different. Company X and Company Y cannot exchange purchase orders because the processing required to understand the content is different. This is just one request; imagine when hundreds of different documents have been defined for similar processing but with different structures. It has created large enough integration issues that companies have had to forego mergers or acquisitions because of system integration cost and complexity.

So how did Company X and Company Y get into this position? There are a number of possible reasons, which include the following:

- **Differentiation** – Companies are always looking for points of differentiation between them and their competitors. Often automation and technology is an area of differentiation. Company X may have been the first in the industry to define XML e-procurement. They may have used this with suppliers to enable a competitive advantage.

- **Time-to-market** – There is always pressure to be first to market with new ideas, processes, etc. Standards bodies often take longer to define a standard because of the consensus that must be built within the committee or group defining the standard. A single company with a narrow focus can more quickly define something that works for their requirements.

- **Industry knowledge** – It may be more practical for specific industry groups to define standards within their industry. They have the business domain knowledge and therefore have the expertise to define standards specific to their industry.

- **Ulterior motives** – There are also cases where promoting multiple standards may enhance my product's viability. For instance, I may be a vendor of products that deals with XML diversity, such as XML gateways and servers. Alternatively, I may provide value added services that allow trading partners to "speak" different languages and still be able to conduct commerce.

So it is easy to see how different standards evolve – some driven by standards organizations, some driven by industry, and some driven by real world competition. The issue then is as developers how do we deal with this diversity?

The New Tower of Babel?

With all this diversity, are we not in danger of building the modern day Tower of Babel? Are we talking about global XML standards only to find we are left with so many XML vocabularies and grammars that we are creating e-commerce chaos?

Whether or not this turns out to be the case, systems need to be built to adapt and change rapidly in the current B2B market. There are still too many unknowns and too many opportunities that have to be fully realized. Building systems that can adapt to change is more important than ever. If you are going to compete in the B2B space, your systems will have to cope with change that is more dramatic now than ever before.

In the last chapter we built a simple example framework for B2B integration. A substantial amount of the work dealt with data representation. It pointed out the importance of trading partner systems being able to understand and agree to both the controlling aspects of information exchange and the business content (header and message details).

Unfortunately, as we have discussed, the reality of the current B2B environment mandates that systems that are going to participate in "open" commerce need to support a variety of protocols and data exchange standards. There are many organizations and bodies, each defining some aspect of XML standardization. In addition there are countless efforts defining proprietary XML exchanges between partner systems. Mergers and acquisitions often turn these proprietary interfaces into substantial integration issues.

But if XML is such a varied technology, why is it becoming increasingly popular? In this chapter we will expand on the adaptability of systems by introducing XML transformations as a vehicle for enabling a more maintainable and dynamic environment.

Transformation as a Solution to Diversity

As we saw in, Chapter 7 the **Extensible Stylesheet Language** (**XSL**) includes both a transformation language and a formatting language. The transformation language provides elements that define rules for how one XML document is transformed into another XML document. The transformed XML document may use the markup and schema of the original document or it may use a completely different set of tags.

The aim of this section is to put some of the concepts that we've seen previously in the context of B2B application development.

The following diagram depicts how the transformation process is performed:

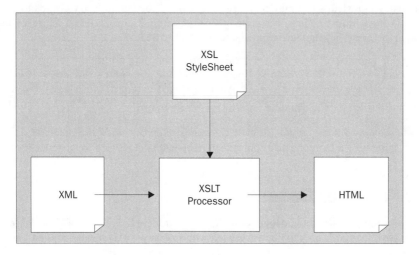

An XML document provides an input source to an **XSLT processor**. An XSLT processor is a software component that is able to read an input source, apply rules in the form of an **XSL Style Sheet** to the input source, and produce an output document that conforms to the rules applied.

In the example diagram above, the XSLT processor is applying rules that generate an HTML document from the input XML source. However, often the output is another XML document that is a variant of the original XML input source.

So, for instance, it is possible to write an XSL Style Sheet that, when processed, could convert our Company X purchase order document into a Company Y formatted purchase order document. This would then enable the systems to communicate because the exchanged document would reflect the format Company Y is expecting:

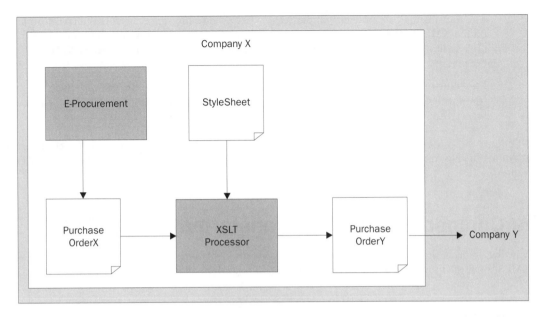

In our example above the e-procurement system of Company X generates a purchase order in their native format. The request is transformed from an XML defined purchase order in their proprietary format to an XML document that is in Company Y's format. The request is then sent to Company Y.

Company Y, of course, could implement a transformation that generates responses to purchase order requests in Company X's format. In this scenario we are always conforming to the receiving systems format. This is a popular technique between trading partners.

Another scenario would involve an intermediary that performs the translation:

In this case neither Company X, nor Company Y, is aware of any differences in purchase order definitions.

Where do Transformations Occur?

Typically we talk about three places where transformation may occur:

❑ The transformation can occur in a client-side web browser. For instance, Internet Explorer 5.0 supports XSL transformations. An XML document and its associated XSL style sheet are sent to the web browser and the transformation is performed within the client-side process.

❑   The transformation can occur on the server. In this case the server performs a transformation on the XML document, which may convert it to HTML, and then sends the transformed document to the client. This is a popular technique in generating HTML from XML documents.

❑   The transformation may occur as a result of a standalone program. In this case the transformed document is placed on the server after the transformation occurs. The client and server only deal with the transformed document, which is usually HTML.

Of course this discussion assumes that the client is a web browser. In the case of B2B e-commerce the client is typically the system that initiates the request and the server is the system that responds to the request.

The Components of XSL Transformations (XSLT)

Now that we have shown the importance of transformations in enabling B2B e-commerce and coping with XML diversity, let's provide a quick overview of how the transformation process works.

The W3C XSL Working group defined the XSLT specification. More information can be found at http://www.w3.org/TR/xslt. For an authoritative reference to XSLT 1.0, see XSLT Programmer's Reference by Michael Kay, ISBN 1-861003-12-9, also by Wrox Press.

From the moment you start working with XSLT you will need to understand that there are actually a number of specifications working closely together to make XSLT usable. We will not go into the details of the relationships between them here, but simply point out that XSL, XPath, and XML Namespaces provide the necessary definitions to make XSLT a reality.

XSL

The Extensible Stylesheet Language (XSL) is a specification for applying formatting to XML documents. The first part of XSL, XSLT, has evolved into an independent language for transforming one XML document into another. The second part of XSL defines a vocabulary of formatting objects for rendering documents. Thus XSL is a declarative language expressed in style sheets.

XPath

XML processing is dependent upon the idea of **addressing**. In order to process a document you must be able to locate it. In order to manipulate the contents of an XML document you must be able to locate parts or fragments of a document. The Web uses a Uniform Resource Identifier (URI) to address or locate a document. XPath is a language for addressing the nodes of an XML document, and is designed to be used by both XSLT and XPointer. In fact XPath was developed when the groups responsible for XSLT and XPointer realized that there was a significant amount of overlap in the functions that these specifications required. XSLT uses XPath for transformation and for style application. XPath is used to declare that certain XSLT transform rules apply to particular elements in a document.

For example, the following XSLT instruction uses the "." expression to select the context or current node. This will become clearer as we work through the examples:

```
<xsl:value-of
select = "." />
```

XPath also provides basic facilities for the manipulation of strings, numbers and Booleans. We will be using XPath primarily for its ability to match and locate the nodes of an XML document. More information on XPath can be found at http://www.w3.org/TR/xpath.

XPointer

XPointer is an extension to XPath. XPointer is what makes XPath able to address parts of an XML document. XPath addresses nodes of a document. XPointer allows the URI and the XPath to be combined into a **URI Reference**. This provides us with a combination of document and node addressing. A URI Reference allows us to jump to a specific point within an XML document. This is similar to a URL reference in HTML that allows us to select a specific fragment (HTML element) within an HTML document by using the # sign. XPointers enable commentary, annotation, and information reuse by defining a standard reference syntax.

XML Namespace

Namespaces allow us to disambiguate XML elements within and between XML documents. For instance an element with the identifier <quote> could mean something totally different in the context of a famous quotes document versus a stock pricing document. To avoid this confusion **Namespace prefixes** are applied to the elements. For instance <quote> could be defined as <stock:quote>.

The Namespace specification defines an **xmlns** rule that associates an attribute with a defining <xmlns> tag. For example:

```
<xmlns:stock = "http://www.stockmarket.com/">
<stock:quote>
  <stock:symbol>SUN</stock:symbol>
  <stock:price>32.50</stock:price>
</stock:quote>
```

This definition would differentiate the element quote from any other quote definition in the world. The only requirement is that the URI referenced be unique. Namespaces will become increasingly important as we interconnect systems for business transactions. Organizations and corporations will define namespaces to indicate the rules and semantics in effect when processing XML documents. XSLT relies heavily on Namespaces. For further information, see http://www.w3.org/TR/REC-xml-names/.

An Example Transformation

When read, these specifications can become very complex. Let's go through an example to put the theory in context.

Let's take the following XML document:

```
<?xml version="1.0" encoding="iso-8859-1"?>
<Book>Professional Java E-Commerce</Book>
```

First we apply the following XSL stylesheet:

```
<?xml version="1.0"?>
<xsl:stylesheet xmlns:xsl="http://www.w3.org/1999/XSL/Transform"
                            version="1.0">
  <xsl:output method="xml"/>

<xsl:template match="/">
    <html>
        <head>
            <title>xsl:value-of select="Book"/></title>
        </head>
    </html>
</xsl:template>

</xsl:stylesheet>
```

The XSLT processor produces the following HTML document:

```
<html>
    <head>
        <title>Professional Java E-Commerce</title>
    </head>
</html>
```

OK, so it's not that impressive. However we have now defined a simple transformation for creating an HTML document from an XML document. The `match="/"` instruction tells the transformation processor to select the root node in this case `<Book>` and apply the template to the generated output stream. The template selects the value of `<Book>`, in this case `Professional Java E-Commerce`, and sends it to the output stream. Technically XSLT first creates a result tree to represent the transformation and then sends the tree to the output stream.

So how does the Java API for XML Processing fit into all of this?

In the last chapter we introduced the Java API for XML Processing (JAXP). The JAXP defines basic support for parsing and manipulating XML documents through a standardized set of Java Platform APIs.

In our XML Broker we used the JAXP SAX Parser and the Document Object Model as core components. Specifically, we used the `DocumentBuilder` and `DocumentBuilderFactory` to create and manipulate our B2B supply chain messages.

JAXP, in addition to providing interfaces to SAX and DOM, provides a Java interface to XSLT processors. The JAXP makes it possible for different XSLT implementations to use a common Java API to provide transformation functionality to Java applications.

package javax.xml.transform

As of this writing JAXP version 1.1 was going through public review. Some of the class names actually changed during the writing process! As the code was originally written the `Transform` class was used – now it has become the `Transformer` class. Such is the fast moving world of XML.

The package `javax.xml.transform` defines the abstract classes for the `TransformerFactory` and the `Transformer` class. Concrete implementations of these classes provide the Java API to the XSLT Processor.

❑ `TransformerFactory` – The `TransformerFactory` defines a factory API that enables applications to obtain a `Transformer` object.

❑ `Transformer` – The `Transformer` implementation is based on an XSLT stylesheet:

```
Transformer processor =
                transformerFactory.newTransformer("myStyleSheet.xsl");
```

An instance of this class can be obtained from the `TransformerFactory.newTransformer()` method. Once an instance of this class is obtained, XML can be processed from a variety of input sources with the output from the transform being written to a variety of sinks. We can create chains of transformations where the output of one transformation becomes the input for the next.

JAXP refers to these classes as the "XSLT Plugability Classes".

The widespread acceptance of XML has resulted in several XSLT products.

XSLT Processors

Three of the most popular XSLT processors are Saxon, XT, and Xalan:

Saxon

Saxon is an XSLT processor developed by Michael Kay, which implements the Version 1.0 XSLT and XPath specifications. The most recent version of Saxon also includes some features defined in XSLT 1.1.

Saxon includes a Java library, which supports a similar processing model to XSL, but allows full programming capability. This can be used if you need to perform complex processing of the data or to access external services such as a relational database. Saxon works with any SAX-compliant XML parser.

Saxon implements the XSLT 1.0 recommendation, including XPath 1.0, in its entirety. SAXON also provides some XSLT 1.1 features, in particular:

❑ Support for multiple output files using `xsl:document`

❑ Multi-pass processing, by allowing result-tree-fragments to be used in any context where a node-set can be used

In addition, Saxon provides a library of extension elements and extension functions. These include:

❑ `intersection()` and `difference()` to manipulate node-sets

❑ `distinct()` to provide grouping capability

❑ `minExpression()`, `maxExpression()`, and `evaluate()` to allow an XPath expression to be constructed dynamically

For more information see http://users.iclway.co.uk/mhkay/saxon/.

XT

XT is an XSLT processor written by James Clark, the author of the original draft XSLT specification. XT is now supported by 4xt.org a group of XT users maintaining the XT implementation. For more information on XT see http://4xt.org.

Xalan

Xalan-Java fully implements the W3C Recommendation 16 November 1999 XSL Transformations (XSLT) Version 1.0 and the XML Path Language (XPath) Version 1.0. Xalan features include:

❑ Implements the Java API for XML Parsing 1.0, and builds on SAX 2 and DOM level 2

❑ May be configured to work with any XML parser

❑ Can process Stream, SAX or DOM input, and output to a Stream, SAX or DOM

❑ Transformations may be chained (the output of one transformation may be the input for another)

❑ May be run from the command line

❑ May be used in a Java servlet to transform XML documents into HTML and serve the results to clients

❑ Supports the creation of Java and scripting language extensions and provides a library of extension elements and functions

For more information see http://xml.apache.org/xalan-j/.

Using Xalan

> We will use the Xalan XSLT processor from the Apache XML Project as our example XSLT engine. It can be found at **http://xml.apache.org/**.

Xalan uses a Document Table Model to parse XML documents and XSL stylesheets. It can be set to use the Xerces-Java XML parser, and it can be adapted to work with other DOM-producing mechanisms and SAX document handlers. The input may appear in the form of a file, a character stream, a byte stream, a DOM, or a SAX input stream.

Xalan performs the transformations specified in the XSL stylesheet and produces a text file, a character stream, a byte stream, a Document Object Model, or a series of SAX events that you can specify when you set up the transformation.

Processing XML and XSL Files – An Example

The following example demonstrates how to process a given XML file and XSL file to produce a new output file from the command line. As you can see, the B2BTransform class is very short:

```
import java.io.*;
import org.xml.sax.SAXException;
import javax.xml.transform.*;
```

```
import javax.xml.transform.stream.*;

public class B2BTransform
{
   public static void main(String[] args)
      throws java.io.IOException,
      java.net.MalformedURLException,
      org.xml.sax.SAXException,
      javax.xml.transform.TransformerException,
      javax.xml.transform.TransformerConfigurationException
   {
      if(args.length < 3) {
         System.out.println("usage java B2BTransform [file.xml] [newfile]
            [file.xsl]");
         System.exit(1);
      }
      TransformerFactory transformFactory =
         TransformerFactory.newInstance();
      Transformer processor = transformFactory.newTransformer(new
         StreamSource(new File(args[2])));
      processor.transform(new StreamSource(new File(args[0])),
         new StreamResult(new File(args[1])));
      System.out.println("* The result is in " + args[1]);
   }
}
```

We simply create an instance of the `TransformFactory` and use it to create a `Transform` object. This is consistent with the SAX and DOM API provided with JAXP. We then call `newTransform()` with the XML filename and XSL filename supplied as parameters. An output file is created containing the transformed document.

If you compile this class, you can run it with the following command line:

```
c:\wrox>java B2Btransform target.xml result stylesheet.xsl
```

and then go and interrogate the resulting result file for the output.

Implications for our Supply-Chain Integration

With that background, let's look at another example. In the last chapter, our servlet `Dispatcher` had the following code fragment:

```
// Create the XML Message Broker
B2BXMLUtil util = new B2BXMLUtil(out);

// Create an input source parse and execute request
B2BResponse b2bResponse = util.parseSource(new InputSource(new
   CharArrayReader(buffer)));

// write the XML response to the output stream
out.write(b2bResponse.toXML());
```

635

It dispatched an XML Request to our XML Broker and returned an XML response. The response object that was created had a toXML() method that was invoked to get an XML String representation of the response object:

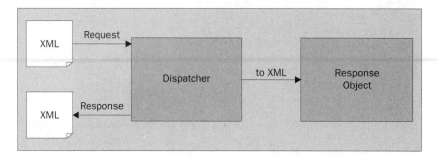

The InventoryResponse class that was used as an example had this toXML() method definition:

```
public String toXML() {
    StringBuffer buffer = new StringBuffer();
    buffer.append("<InventoryLevelResponse>").
        append("<Product id=").
        append("\""+product+"\"").
        append("></Product>").
        append("<Part number=").
        append("\""+part+"\"").
        append("></Part>").
        append("<Quantity onHand=").
        append("\"" + (new Integer(quantity)).toString()+"\"").
        append("></Quantity>").
        append("</InventoryLevelResponse>");

    return new String(buffer);
}
```

This resulted in the following XML fragment:

```
<InventoryLevelResponse>
    <Product id="7654"></Product>
    <Part number="1234"></Part>
    <Quantity onHand="100"></Quantity>
</InventoryLevelResponse>
```

Now what happens when we need to engage in supply chains with multiple partners and not all partners use our InventoryRequest/Response definition? It may be a minor change or an entirely different message structure.

We would need to change our Response message to include code such as:

```
public String toXML() {
    StringBuffer buffer;
    if(partner.equals("Partner A")) {
        buffer = toPartnerAXML(); }
    } else if(partner.equals("Partner B")) {
```

```
       buffer = toPartnerBXML(); }
  } else if(partner.equals("Partner C")) {
     buffer = toPartnerCXML(); }
  } else if (

  etc..

  return new String(buffer);
}
```

If we support hundreds of messages involving many partners this technique would become difficult to maintain and introduces programming changes for even the smallest modification to a message structure. Clearly this is not we want.

We can use XSLT to produce a "normalized" XML definition for our XML Broker. The first transformation will take a trading partner XML request and apply an XSL transformation to produce our internal XML definition. Of course this does not have to be a proprietary definition; it could be a global standard or an industry standard that most of our trading partners use. The point is that we need a consistent approach to mapping partner requests into our system.

> *We can't afford to let each partner implementation turn into another major project!*

The request and response objects only know about our standard definition. Because of this, changes occur only if new elements or attributes are added or removed and need to be understood and processed by the business objects. This seems like a reasonable assumption. If we are changing the information exchanged there may be a need to revisit the classes involved that are supporting that exchange.

Implementation

So, within our example we will add some extra functionality, via an extra class and a modification to an existing one, so that we can receive a trading partner XML document, apply a suitable transform and then pass this into our system.

The initial document handling and transformation will be carried out using a class B2BTransformProcessor. The request and response classes should create the XML *only* with the help of our B2BTransformProcessor.

The TransformProcessor will manage the trading partner XML vocabularies and grammar requirements. The B2BObjectFactory will manage the internal XML to Object creation.

In short the message flow for incoming documents will be:

- ❑ XSL transformation applied to trading partner XML document via B2BTranformProcessor
- ❑ Data passed to XML Broker
- ❑ B2B object factory handles further transformation and creates object

B2BTransformProcessor

The code for the B2BTransformProcessor class is:

```
package com.wrox.broker;

import java.io.*;

public class B2BTransformProcessor {

    public static OutputStream transform(InputStream source, InputStream sheet) {
        ByteArrayOutputStream output = null;
        try {
            output = new ByteArrayOutputStream(4096);
            B2BXMLUtil.transformSource(source, output, sheet);
        } catch (Exception e) { e.printStackTrace(); }
        return output;
    }
}
```

As you can see this involves a call to the B2BXMLUtil class, which we modify as shown below.

B2BXMLUtil modifications

To take advantage of JAXP within the class we make the following changes to B2BXMLUtil:

```
package com.wrox.broker;

import java.io.*;
import org.w3c.dom.*;
import org.xml.sax.SAXException;
import org.xml.sax.SAXParseException;
import org.xml.sax.InputSource;
import javax.xml.parsers.DocumentBuilderFactory;
import javax.xml.parsers.DocumentBuilder;
import javax.xml.parsers.ParserConfigurationException;
import javax.xml.transform.*;
import javax.xml.transform.stream.*;
```

and then add:

```
    public static synchronized void transformSource(InputStream source,
OutputStream dest, InputStream sheet)
        throws java.io.IOException,
        java.net.MalformedURLException,
        org.xml.sax.SAXException,
            javax.xml.transform.TransformerException,
            javax.xml.transform.TransformerConfigurationException

    {
        TransformerFactory transformFactory =  TransformerFactory.newInstance();
        Transformer processor = transformFactory.newTransformer(new
StreamSource(sheet));
        processor.transform(new StreamSource(source), new StreamResult(dest));
    }
    public Writer getWriter() { return out; }

    Writer out;
}
```

We'll just demonstrate examples of the mappings below, but will show how it all works at the end of the next chapter when we finalize our sample application.

Illustrations of the Mappings

Let's start with the XML response that was generated from our Manufacturer to our Supplier. The response could have just as easily been targeted for a browser using HTML.

As we saw at the end of the last chapter, the `InventoryLevelResponse` definition was of the form:

```
<InventoryLevelResponse>
    <Product id="7654"></Product>
    <Part number="1234"></Part>
    <Quantity onHand="100"></Quantity>
</InventoryLevelResponse>
```

The XSL stylesheet to convert our `InventoryLevelResponse` from XML to HTML (`InventoryLevelResponse.xsl`) is as follows:

```
<?xml version="1.0"?>
<xsl:stylesheet xmlns:xsl="http://www.w3.org/1999/XSL/Transform" version="1.0">
<xsl:output method="html"/>

<xsl:template match="/">
    <Html>
        <Head>
            <Title>B2B Supply Chain</Title>
        </Head>
        <Body>
        <xsl:apply-templates select="InventoryLevelResponse"/>
        </Body>
    </Html>
</xsl:template>

<xsl:template match="InventoryLevelResponse">
    <H2>Inventory Level Response</H2>
    <Table border="1">
        <xsl:apply-templates select="Product"/>
        <xsl:apply-templates select="Part"/>
        <xsl:apply-templates select="Quantity"/>
    </Table>
</xsl:template>

<xsl:template match="Product">
    <tr><td>Product id</td><td><xsl:value-of select="@id"/></td></tr>
</xsl:template>

<xsl:template match="Part">
    <tr><td>Part number</td><td><xsl:value-of select="@number"/></td></tr>
</xsl:template>

<xsl:template match="Quantity">
    <tr><td>Quantity on hand</td><td><xsl:value-of
                                    select="@onHand"/></td></tr>
</xsl:template>
</xsl:stylesheet>
```

Applying this will give:

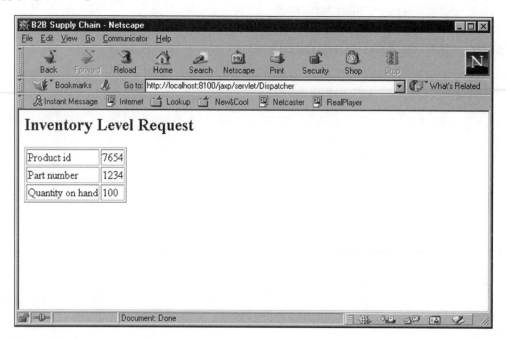

XSLT Example Explained

The first three lines of our stylesheet include:

❑ Standard XML header – the version of XML supported, stylesheets are XML documents

❑ Standard XSLT header – defines stylesheet and XML Namespace declaration (remember namespaces are important to XSLT)

❑ Output type specification (HTML)

The `<xsl:template>` element defines a template for creating output. The `match` attribute indicates the "pattern" that this template applies to. When a document is being processed a template rule is triggered if the `match` attribute is encountered. In this case "/" is a special pattern that indicates the root node of the document. This is in line with the XPath specification.

```
<xsl:template match="/">
   <html>
   <head>
   <title>B2B Supply Chain</title>
   </head>
   <body>
   <xsl:apply-templates select="InventoryLevelResponse"/>
   </body>
   </html>
</xsl:template>
```

In addition to the root node, we define four other templates that are triggered by the element name:

```
<xsl:template match="InventoryLevelResponse">
<xsl:template match="Product">
<xsl:template match="Part">
<xsl:template match="Quantity">
```

Each template applies different formatting to the content of that node. It's important to remember that XSLT creates a document tree model similar to the DOM. This is an in memory tree of the input stream. So as a tree structure, attribute onHand is a child of Quantity. It is also important to recognize that large documents may need to use the SAX event driven approach to XSLT. If document size is an issue or memory concerns driven by the number of concurrent requests is excessive, you may have to look at the event driven approach.

There is flexibility with most XSLT implementations in what can be defined as a source. For instance Xalan can be used to work with SAX document handlers.

The <xsl:value-of> element is used to select an attribute value and place the text in the output (tree) stream. In our example we use a select attribute to explicitly indicate the attribute required:

```
<xsl:value-of select="@id"/>
<xsl:value-of select="@number"/>
<xsl:value-of select="@onHand"/>
```

The XSLT elements can be easily distinguished from the HTML because they all begin with namespace prefix xsl:.

The <xsl:apply-templates> instruction indicates a set of nodes to be processed by the associated template rule. Our example matches template rules to templates and specifies the order of execution.

```
<xsl:apply-templates select="InventoryLevelResponse"/>
<xsl:apply-templates select="Product"/>
<xsl:apply-templates select="Part"/>
<xsl:apply-templates select="Quantity"/>
```

However this is not required. There are default XSLT template rules in effect when no template rule has been defined. These are worth listing because they can cause you problems when trying to debug and determine output translation problems:

Node Type	Default Template Rule
root	<xsl:apply-templates> to children
element	<xsl:apply-templates> to children
attribute	Copy attribute value to output tree
text	Copy text to output tree
comment	No action
Namespace	No action
processing-instruction	No action

> **If during the course of translation you see all your attributes being sent to the output stream incorrectly, it may be that the default rules have been triggered and nothing else!**

So now we have a mechanism to transform our `InventoryLevelResponse` to HTML, XML, or we could define a transformation to WML, or any other protocol. A method to determine the desired transport protocol for the partner would be all that is required.

Further Examples

Having seen a brief example, and also how we could apply it to our example from the last chapter, what else can we do with transformations? There follow three brief examples of filtering data, merging data, and writing multiple output files.

Filtering Data

The following example is used to filter information from an ebXML-defined header. It copies the `ServiceInterface` element but in effect ignores the `Manifest`, `MessageData`, and `RoutingHeader` elements because the template provided is empty. This technique can be used to quickly filter elements from XML messages, allowing you total control to pick and choose which elements you take:

```xml
<?xml version="1.0"?>
<xsl:stylesheet xmlns:xsl="http://www.w3.org/1999/XSL/Transform"
                version="1.0">
   <xsl:output method="xml" indent="yes"/>

   <xsl:template match="ebXMLHeader">
   <Header>
      <xsl:apply-templates/>
   </Header>
   </xsl:template>

   <xsl:template match="From | To ">

      <xsl:copy-of select="."/>

   </xsl:template>

   <xsl:template match="TPAInfo">
      <xsl:apply-templates select="ServiceInterface"/>
   </xsl:template>

   <xsl:template match="ServiceInterface">
      <xsl:copy-of select="."/>
   </xsl:template>

   <xsl:template match="Manifest | MessageData | RoutingHeader"/>

</xsl:stylesheet>
```

The resulting XML looks very similar to our example header. Compare this output to the ebXML header in Chapter 16 that was used as input to the XSLT processor:

```
<?xml version="1.0" encoding="UTF-8"?>
<Header>
   <From>
      <PartyId context="DUNS">2059397184</PartyId>
   </From>
   <To>
      <PartyId context="DUNS">943561654</PartyId>
   </To>
   <ServiceInterface>OrderProcessing</ServiceInterface>
</Header>
```

Merging Data

We demonstrated how XSLT could be used to filter data, now let's look at how XSLT can be used to process from multiple data sources.

Merging information may be important in a number of circumstances. For instance generating reports that require multiple XML files as input. This might represent a summary of activity by trading partners. Each XML document might contain trading partner specific transactions.

Merging information may be appropriate when an input source does not contain all the information that is required to process within your environment. You may be able to make the information richer by augmenting the content with other sources.

The document() function in XSLT is used to retrieve an XML document by resolving a URI reference. As an example, our trading report XML document may contain the following fragment:

```
<TradeReport>
   <report date = "2001-1-28" partyId="Partner A" detail="reports/tpa.xml"/>
   <report date = "2001-1-28" partyId="Partner B" detail="reports/tpb.xml"/>
   <report date = "2001-1-28" partyId="Partner C" detail="reports/tpc.xml"/>
</TradeReport>
```

The template to include the activity for each trading partner in the report would be:

```
<xsl:template match="TradeReport">
   <xsl:for-each select="report">
     <h2>Activity for <xsl:value-of select="@partyId"/></h2>
     <xsl:apply-templates select="document(@detail)"/>
   </xsl:for-each>
</xsl:template>
```

The document() function in this template would retrieve the value of the detail attribute. In this case the detail attribute value is a URL reference. The content of the detail report for each trading partner would be included in our overall activity report.

Writing Multiple Output Files

Of course, it may be desirable to take a large document and write out a number of smaller documents. For example a catalog that contains thousands of entries may be too large to transmit as one document. Multiple output files could be created for each type of product or a range of product numbers thus making smaller more manageable documents.

Writing multiple output files was not standardized in XSLT 1.0 but has been standardized in version 1.1. This feature is supported in several products such as Saxon, Xalan, and XT. We'll briefly look at these later in this chapter.

The syntax in Xalan XSLT version 1.0 was:

```
<xalan:write select="$file">
  <xsl:copy-of select="."/>
</xalan:write>
```

This causes the information selected by " . " to be sent to an output file defined by the variable $file. The XSLT standard now uses the document() function to generate multiple output files.

Summary

So, that's transformations. What have we learned and seen, beside the large range of products?

- ❑ B2B e-commerce should support a number of cross-industry and industry specific XML standards.

- ❑ XSLT provides a solution to the XML diversity problem by standardizing a transformation syntax.

- ❑ XSLT works in conjunction with a number of XML specifications such as XPath, XPointer, XML Namespaces and is part of XSL.

- ❑ JAXP provides a Java centric solution to XSLT, SAX, and DOM which helps to reduce the complexity of the underlying APIs.

- ❑ Popular XSLT engines include Xalan, Saxon, and XT.

- ❑ Our XML Broker framework can be enhanced to include XSLT. This provides our framework with a more adaptable solution to support a rapidly changing B2B environment.

- ❑ Merging, filtering, and generating multiple output files a few of the techniques that can be used within the framework to help cope with diversity.

In the next chapter, we'll be taking a look at messaging as a way to integrate business systems and rounding off our supply chain simulator.

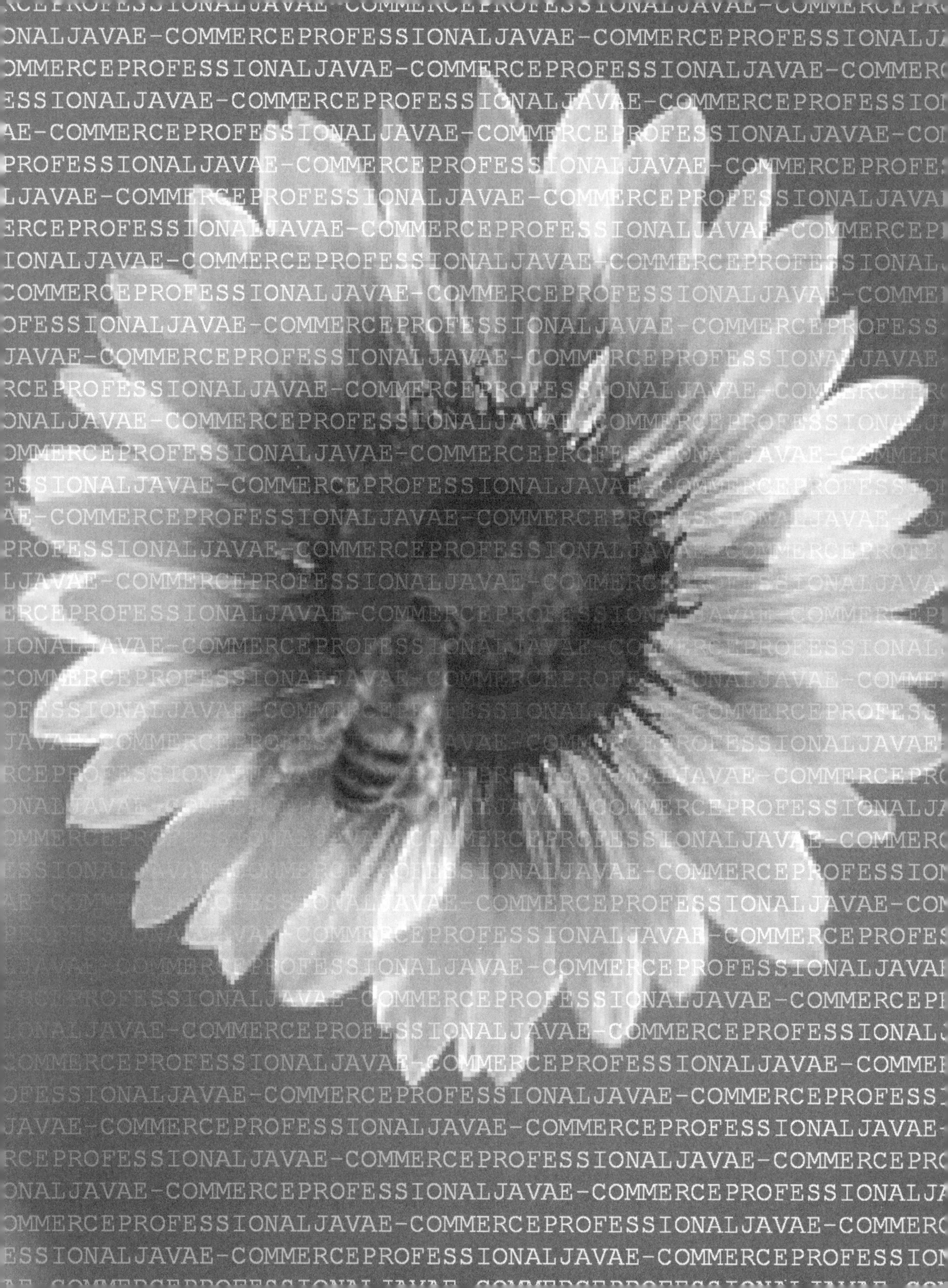
PROFESSIONALJAVAE-COMMERCE

19

B2B E-Commerce: Mass Integration

The growth of B2B e-commerce has resulted in fundamental architectural changes to systems and applications. The foundational elements discussed in Chapter 16 such as data representation, transports, public networks, and security, have far reaching implications to current system designs. As B2B systems evolve, more complex architectural patterns will surface to satisfy new forms of partner collaboration. Current patterns extend existing system capabilities through message brokers and gateways.

Traditional issues such as scalability and distributed transaction processing are compounded by the dynamics of the emerging B2B environment. For instance, the number of users B2B systems need to support can often be ambiguous or unknown during initial development and deployment. In addition, dynamic trading partner discovery has far reaching implications to the technical sophistication of future systems.

Integration of B2B frontends with B2B backends will be critical to successful business deployment. This has been difficult for many organizations. The complexity and cost involved in integration has left gaps in services offered and manual processes that don't fully implement the automated vision.

In this chapter we will look at the topic of integration and specifically:

❏ See how messaging can be used to integrate and **loosely couple** processes, and examine how the Java Messaging Service (JMS) relates to messaging systems

❏ Provide examples of two messaging models; **point-to-point** and **publish-and-subscribe**

❏ Build on our XML Broker framework to include the EJB and EIS tiers of our application server

❏ Present an overview of emerging technologies and future directions

Before we move on, let's take a moment to consolidate what we have learned so far in this section on B2B e-commerce.

Drawing the Strands Together

In chapter 16 we discussed business drivers for B2B E-Commerce and made a case for the compelling financial rewards and the operational efficiencies that will result from deploying B2B solutions. This was tempered with the reality that there are a number of significant challenges to success. They include:

- The speed with which the market is changing and the complexity of commerce implementations
- The number of standards and competing XML standards initiatives
- The complexity and cost of integrating backend systems and legacy EDI solutions

In Chapter 17 we defined B2B supply chains and the issues involved in trading partner collaboration. We focused on initiatives such as ebXML and RosettaNet as examples of cross-industry and industry specific XML frameworks. In addition we started building our example B2B framework supporting an XML Broker. Our XML Broker is able to map XML requests into Java `Command` objects. This framework was developed in the web tier of a J2EE compliant application server.

In the last chapter we discussed transformation and the importance it will play in dealing with the diversity of XML vocabularies, grammars, and schemas in the B2B marketplace. We demonstrated how SAX, DOM, and XSLT can be used to make our B2B example framework more adaptable to changing requirements.

The following diagram depicts a high level view of our B2B framework. The intent of this framework is to be able to cope and adapt to rapidly changing B2B standards and technologies.

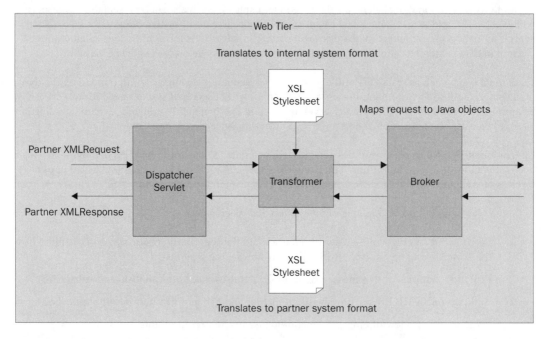

Now that we have our background, let's include the final elements to our framework. First we need to gain an overview of messaging.

Message Oriented Middleware (MOM)

Messaging systems have been around for years. They provide an infrastructure to support the exchange of information between cooperating systems. Messaging systems have become increasingly popular, as the need to exchange information between partner systems and between internal systems has grown. Even prior to the Internet, large systems were connected worldwide. For instance banking, and transportation industries such as airlines have had the need to exchange data on a global level for decades. During the 80's and 90's IBM's MQSeries became a popular messaging system for integrating IBM mainframes with middle tier systems.

One of the attractive characteristics of messaging systems is their ability to loosely couple systems and processes. In other words, an initiating system can send a request to a receiving system and continue working while the other system processes the request. When the request has been processed (which may be seconds or days) the receiving system sends the response back to the initiating system. This is defined as **asynchronous messaging**. Messaging systems also support **synchronous** processing which would require the initiating system to wait for a response to continue processing.

System integrators have often used messaging software to integrate disparate internal and external systems. Legacy systems are often "messaged" as opposed to building APIs or Interface Definition Language (IDL) interfaces. It is often a simpler integration effort. Often the source code to a legacy system may not even be available! Messaging can provide a solution.

Messaging supports the concept of **queues**. Queues are addressable components of a messaging system. Client applications send messages to specific queues. A queue has a logical name that is used by the client to indicate the destination. This is often referred to as a **point-to-point** model of messaging. The details of the implementation will vary with the messaging product. Thus two messaging systems will likely expose a different API.

Messaging systems provide varying levels of message assurance. For instance, to what extent will the messaging system guarantee that a message request arrives at its designated destination? This can range from best effort to a guaranteed delivery. The option selected depends on the requirements of the application. More assurance usually implies more system overhead. Assurance parameters and levels will vary with vendor product.

Messaging systems will also vary on the degree of administration and the degree of visibility offered to the underlying messaging infrastructure and network.

Java Messaging Service (JMS)

The **Java Messaging Service** (**JMS**), which we touched on in Chapter 5, provides a common API for Java programs to interface with messaging service products that support the JMS API. This allows programs to create, send, receive, and read an enterprise messaging system's messages. The J2EE Framework provides JMS as the standard interface to Message Oriented Middleware (MOM) services. The JMS API is comprised of one package, `javax.jms`, which is included in the J2EE.

MOM technologies are fundamental to e-commerce applications because they provide a mechanism to loosely integrate inter and intra-enterprise applications. Messaging systems have become a key component to enabling B2B communication both within an organization and between organizations (trading partners).

There are two fundamental models of communication supported by JMS: **Point-to-Point**, and **Publish-and-Subscribe**. These are implemented as two separate interfaces meaning that a messaging vendor does not have to implement both models.

Some messaging systems provide facilities for asynchronous receipt of messages (messages are delivered to a client as they arrive). Others support only synchronous receipt (a client must request each message). Messaging systems typically provide a range of services that can be selected on a per message basis. As mentioned, one of the most important attributes deals with message delivery assurance. Other important attributes are message time-to-live, message priority, and whether a response is required for a specific request.

Of course using messaging for B2B communications will have some constraints and limitations. Messaging administration will be required to establish and maintain message queues, quality of service parameters, and application programming and communication maintenance. The administration of messaging products and environments can easily become non-trivial.

JMS does not define a standard security API. Each product or partner system may require different security mechanisms. Also JMS does not specify the on-the-wire protocol for messaging. Therefore, two JMS providers may not be able to communicate. However JMS products typically provide **bridges** that allow a JMS provider to communicate with other JMS providers. For instance MQSonic, a JMS compliant messaging service, provides a bridge to IBM MQSeries and other popular messaging products. Bridges typically provide a mediation layer between two different protocols. For instance queues may be addressed differently or message headers and payloads may have different formats. Bridges will enable and promote communication between trading partner systems.

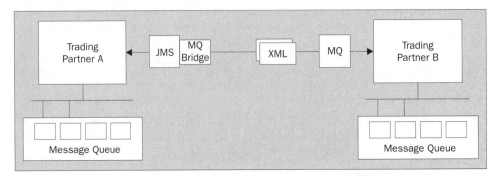

Although two partner systems may be able to exchange messages using JMS, each partner system may still support a different document standard over the messaging service. One partner may require EDI, another may require ebXML, cXML, or BizTalk, etc. This has implications for the processing of the information that is exchanged. It may be difficult to normalize this data if definitions from different partners are inconsistent. As presented in the last chapter, XSLT provides a transformation standard; however it still requires mapping of elements and may require code generation to resolve XML vocabulary differences. In addition different document models may not include the same content for similar functions.

The degree to which unique point-to-point enveloping mechanisms evolve is another consideration. For instance ebXML will support a multi-part MIME type for data packaging. Other standards will support different enveloping mechanisms.

Let's take a look at how JMS provides a standard Java API to messaging service providers.

JMS Concepts

The following provides a brief definition of important JMS objects:

- ❑ ConnectionFactory – An administered object used by a client to create a Connection. A ConnectionFactory is used to encapsulate the configuration options of a connection. You use a ConnectionFactory to create a Connection object.

- ❑ Connection – An active connection to a JMS provider. A Connection encapsulates an open connection to a JMS provider that usually represents an open TCP/IP socket between a client and a provider's service. This is the point where client authentication and communication setup is performed. It also is used to create Session objects. A connection is considered a heavyweight JMS object.

- ❑ Session – A single threaded context for sending and receiving messages. It serves as a factory for creating associated MessageProducer and MessageConsumer objects. A Session serializes the execution of MessageListeners registered with it. Sessions are considered lightweight JMS objects.

- ❑ Destination – This is used to encapsulate the identity of a message destination. JMS does not define a standard address syntax. This is one area where a bridge may be used to allow different messaging service providers to communicate. The Destination object is an administered object and may encapsulate provider specific information associated with it.

- ❑ MessageProducer – An object created by a Session that is used for sending messages to a destination. It is created by sending a destination to the Session's createMessageProducer() method. A client can specify default configuration information per MessageProducer or per message. Configuration, for example, may include delivery mode or time-to-live.

- ❑ MessageConsumer – An object created by a Session that is used for receiving messages sent to a destination. It is created by sending a destination to the Session's createMessageConsumer() method. A client can either synchronously receive a consumer's messages or have the provider asynchronously deliver them as they arrive.

JMS clients look up configured JMS objects using JNDI. JMS administrators use provider specific facilities for creating and configuring these objects. The following table shows the thread safety of JMS objects:

JMS Object	Thread Safe
Destination	Yes
ConnectionFactory	Yes
Connection	Yes
Session	No
MessageProducer	No
MessageConsumer	No

Composition of JMS Messages

JMS messages are composed of the following parts:

❏ **Header** – All messages support the same set of header fields. Header fields contain values used by both clients and providers to identify and route messages.

❏ **Properties** – In addition to the standard header fields, messages provide a built-in facility for adding optional header fields to a message. System providers typically use this to encapsulate proprietary information.

❏ **Body** – JMS defines several types of message body, which cover the majority of messaging styles currently in use.

Message Types

JMS provides five forms of message body. Each form is defined by a message interface:

❏ `StreamMessage` – A message whose body contains a stream of Java primitive values. It is filled and read sequentially.

❏ `MapMessage` – A message whose body contains a set of `name-value` pairs where names are `Strings` and values are Java primitive types. The entries can be accessed sequentially by enumerator or randomly by name.

❏ `TextMessage` – A message whose body contains a `java.lang.String`. This is the type of message used to support XML messages.

❏ `ObjectMessage` – A message that contains a serializable Java object. If a collection of Java objects is needed, one of the collection classes provided in JDK 1.2 can be used.

❏ `BytesMessage` – A message that contains a stream of un-interpreted bytes.

Messaging Models

JMS, as we've already mentioned, supports two types of messaging models: point-to-point and publish-and-subscribe. Let's take a closer look at these messaging models.

Point-to-Point

Point-to-Point messaging involves a client creating a message and sending it through a JMS provider that is responsible for delivering the message to the addressed queue or destination. JMS defines how a client works with queues. It defines how to find a queue, how to send messages to a queue, and how to receive messages from a queue. Most queues are created administratively and are treated as static resources.

A client uses a `QueueSender` to send messages to a queue. A client obtains a `QueueSender` from a `QueueSession`. The sender is "aware" of the single receiver and addresses the message to that queue address. In point-to-point messaging, there is only one receiver.

A client uses a `QueueReceiver` to receive messages from a queue. A client obtains a `QueueReceiver` from a `QueueSession`. A `QueueSession` is obtained from a `QueueConnection`. Typically there is a single `QueueConnection` for an application and many `QueueSession` objects. A `QueueConnection` is a relatively heavyweight object.

The following code fragment demonstrates the JRun JMS provider setup for point-to-point messaging:

```
private QueueConnection connection = null;
private QueueSession session = null;
private TextMessage message = null;
private QueueSender sender = null;

// Use JNDI to find the providers Queue Connection Factory
QueueConnectionFactory factory =(QueueConnectionFactory)
        utils.jndiLookup(QueueConnectionFactory.class.getName());

// Use factory to create QueueConnection
connection = factory.createQueueConnection();

// Use QueueConnection to create QueueSession
session = connection.createQueueSession(false,Session.AUTO_ACKNOWLEDGE);

// Use QueueSession to create QueueSender
sender = session.createSender(session.createQueue(queue));

// Create TextMessage object
message = session.createTextMessage();
```

Publish-and-Subscribe

The JMS Publish-and-Subscribe model defines how JMS clients publish messages to (and subscribe to messages from) a well-known address or **node** in a content-based hierarchy. JMS calls these nodes **topics**.

In this model the sender is not "aware" of the receiver of the message. Senders and receivers publish and subscribe to topics. There may be multiple senders and multiple receivers, but it is the responsibility of the JMS provider to manage the subscription process. In this respect, the sender may be publishing to zero or more receivers. The JMS provider distributes messages to the appropriate receivers as the messages arrive. By relying on the topic as an intermediary, message publishers are kept independent of subscribers and vice versa.

JMS also supports the optional **durability** of subscribers. Non-durable subscriptions last for the lifetime of their subscriber object. This means that a client will only see the messages published on a topic while its subscriber is active. If the subscriber is not active, it is missing messages published on its topic. The JMS provider remembers durable subscriptions. If the subscriber is inactive, messages are saved and delivered when the subscriber becomes active again.

A client uses a `TopicPublisher` to publish to a topic and a `TopicSubscriber` to subscribe to a topic. A `TopicSession` is used to create a `TopicPublisher` and `TopicSubscriber`. A `TopicConnection` is used create one or more `TopicSession` objects.

The following code fragment demonstrates the JRun JMS provider set-up for publish-and-subscribe messaging:

```
// Set up queue attributes.
private String topic = new String("orderQueue");
private String host = new String("localhost");

// Set up objects for use by JMS.
private Context context = null;
private TopicConnection connection = null;
private TopicSession session = null;
private TextMessage message = null;
private TopicPublisher publisher = null;
```

```
        // Use JNDI to find the providers Topic Connection Factory
        TopicConnectionFactory factory =(TopicConnectionFactory)
        utils.jndiLookup(TopicConnectionFactory.class.getName());

        // Use factory to create TopicConnection
        connection = factory.createTopicConnection();

        // Use TopicConnection to create TopicSession
        session = connection.createTopicSession(false,Session.AUTO_ACKNOWLEDGE);

        // Use TopicSession to create TopicPublisher
        publisher = session.createPublisher(session.createTopic(topic));

        // Create TextMessage object
        message = session.createTextMessage();
```

What JMS Does Not Include

JMS does not address the following functionality:

- ❑ Load balancing/fault tolerance

- ❑ Error/advisory notification

- ❑ Administration

- ❑ Security – JMS does not specify an API for controlling the privacy and integrity of messages

- ❑ Wire protocol – JMS does not define a wire protocol for messaging

Now that we've provided an overview of messaging, lets return to our XML Broker example to demonstrate the integration of messaging into the EJB tier of our manufacturer. Our aim in this section will be to show how to integrate a B2B frontend with a B2B backend using JMS as middleware.

Supply Chain Integration – Enhancing the XML Broker

In prior chapters we focused on the web tier of the J2EE architecture. In this section we will focus on the EJB tier which supports Enterprise JavaBeans. In the J2EE programming model, EJB components are a fundamental link between presentation components hosted by the web tier and business-critical data and systems maintained in the **Enterprise Information System** tier (EIS).

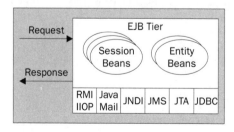

So how do we integrate our XML Broker and service handlers defined in the web tier, with our Enterprise Inventory Service defined in the EJB tier?

In our example application we will use a controller object to manage the interaction of our trading partners (suppliers) with our inventory service. We will split the controller between the web and EJB tiers. The web controller in effect becomes a proxy for the EJB tier.

As in Chapter 17, we'll present the code for the simulator first and then wrap up the section with deployment information.

Our goals with this code are to:

❑ Build on the XML-Broker framework to include the EJB tier

❑ Generate a message to a queue, using the JMS API, when the inventory level drops below a threshold value

Our route through this section is then:

❑ To provide the code for the web tier controller

❑ To look in detail at the EJB tier code

❑ To briefly comment on the enterprise information system tier

❑ To show how to deploy the application onto JRun and provide information on running the simulator

Note that Appendix F contains illustrations of the `com.wrox.broker` package developed in Chapter 17 (and extended in Chapter 18 and this chapter), and the `ejbeans` package developed throughout this chapter. Again all the code for this example is downloadable from www.wrox.com. During this discussion we won't talk about initialization of the system – that will be deferred until we consider deploying the application.

The Web Tier Controller

Our web controller is defined as a singleton, meaning there is only one instance of the controller active in the web tier. This allows a central point of control and interaction to our Inventory Service. Also the setup of the controller is done only once, so the overhead associated with creating instances of the object is diminished.

You should recognize however that singletons can constrain the scalability of a system if excessive serialization results from their use. In this case the class should be written to include multi-threaded support.

The following scenario diagram depicts the high level interaction between the classes that comprise the XML Broker and the Enterprise Inventory Service in our example application.

We need to get the current part inventory on hand for the requesting supplier. Our service handler (not shown) executes the `Command` object that encapsulates our XML Inventory Request. The `Command` object invokes `handleRequest` which in this instance is implemented as `getQuantity()` on the `InventoryChannelController`.

The `InventoryChannelController` invokes `getInventoryDetails()` on our EJB stateless session bean, `InventoryControllerBean`. We made the `InventoryControllerBean` stateless because any client (supplier) can use the bean. We are not trying to maintain state for a particular client (supplier) in our application. In this respect we are using it more like a database connection that is reused per request.

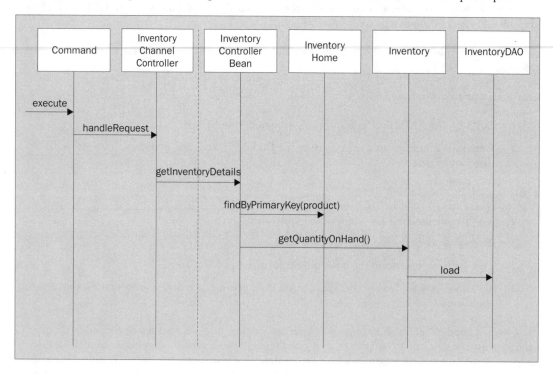

Let's have a look at the `InventoryChannelController` class.

The *InventoryChannelController*

The `InventoryChannelController` is a proxy controller object for the EJB tier. It calls the EJB `InventoryController` to invoke methods on the inventory model:

```
package com.wrox.broker;

import java.rmi.RemoteException;
import ejbeans.*;
import javax.naming.*;
import java.util.Properties;

public class InventoryChannelController {
    // utility class to resolve JNDI namespace
    private static SampleUtilities _utils = null;
    private static InventoryChannelController cc = null;
    private static InventoryController controller = null;
    private int quantity = 100;

    // we use a single inventory controller on the web tier
    public static InventoryChannelController getController() {
        if(cc == null) cc = new InventoryChannelController();
        try {
```

```
                InventoryControllerHome home =
        (InventoryControllerHome)_utils.jndiLookup("B2B.InventoryControllerHome");
            controller = home.create();
            } catch (RemoteException remote) {
                if (remote.detail instanceof SecurityException) {
                    throw (SecurityException)remote.detail;
                }
                throw new RuntimeException(remote.getMessage());
            }
            catch (Exception exception) {
                throw new RuntimeException(exception.getMessage());
            }
            return cc;
        }
        private InventoryChannelController() {
            _utils = new SampleUtilities();
        }

        //  Lookup the EJB Tier Controller using JNDI and invoke the
        //  getInventoryDetails method
        //  In this example we simply return an integer quantity

        public int getQuantity(String product, String part) {
            // This example ignores the part and assumes part = product
            try {
                quantity = controller.getInventoryDetails(product);
            } catch (RemoteException remote) {
                if (remote.detail instanceof SecurityException) {
                    throw (SecurityException)remote.detail;
                }
                throw new RuntimeException(remote.getMessage());
            }
            catch (Exception exception) {
                throw new RuntimeException(exception.getMessage());
            }
            // return the manufacturer quantity on hand
            return quantity;
        }
        public void updateInventoryDetails(String product, String part, int
            quantity) {
            try {
                InventoryHome home =
                    (InventoryHome)_utils.jndiLookup("B2B.InventoryHome");
                Inventory inventory = home.create(product);
                inventory.updateQuantity(quantity);

            } catch (RemoteException remote) {
                if (remote.detail instanceof SecurityException) {
                    throw (SecurityException)remote.detail;
                }
                throw new RuntimeException(remote.getMessage());
            }
            catch (Exception exception) {
                throw new RuntimeException(exception.getMessage());
            }
        }
    }
}
```

Now that we have integrated our web tier with our EJB tier, let's return to our messaging integration. We will use a point-to-point model.

A message queue will be used to indicate part status that has reached a critical level in our manufacturer. A receiver would read the queue and determine the appropriate action to take based on the context of the application. For instance a receiver could initiate an e-procurement process or notify down stream supply chain partners of the status.

The EJB Tier

The following scenario diagram depicts the high level interaction between the classes that comprise the Inventory Service interface to the JMS Service Provider in our example application:

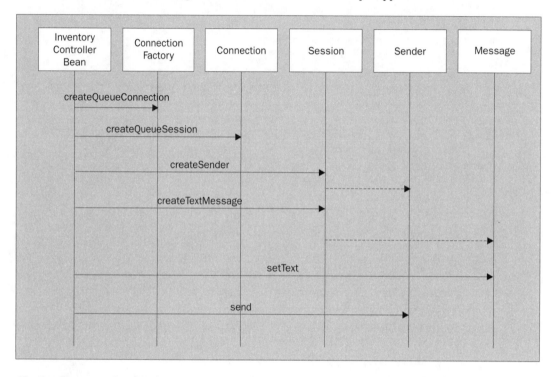

Here we'll start to develop the ejbeans package.

The InventoryController

The InventoryController is an EJB stateless session object that is responsible for processing inventory requests. It calls Inventory to invoke methods on the Inventory EJB.

Our remote interface is:

```
package ejbeans;

import java.rmi.*;
import javax.ejb.*;

public interface InventoryController extends EJBObject {
    int getInventoryDetails(String productName) throws RemoteException;
}
```

The home interface is:

```
package ejbeans;

import java.rmi.*;
import javax.ejb.*;

public interface InventoryControllerHome extends EJBHome
{
   InventoryController create() throws CreateException, RemoteException;
}
```

The `InventoryControllerBean` accesses the `Inventory` database. It also interfaces to our JMS provider:

```
package ejbeans;

import java.rmi.*;
import javax.ejb.*;
import javax.jms.*;
import javax.naming.*;
// we are using Allaire's JRun application server
import allaire.ejipt.*;

public class InventoryControllerBean implements SessionBean {
   private SessionContext _context = null;
   private SampleUtilities _utils = null;

   // Inventory Control Queues
   private final String queue = new String("B2BQueue");
   private final String host = new String("localhost");

   // JMS set up
   private QueueConnection connection = null;
   private QueueSession session = null;
   private TextMessage message = null;
   private QueueSender sender = null;

   static {
      System.setSecurityManager(new RMISecurityManager());
   }

   // ejb methods
   public void ejbActivate() {}
   public void ejbRemove() {}
   public void ejbPassivate() {}
   public void setSessionContext(SessionContext context) {
      _context = context;
   }
```

When our EJB `InventoryController` is created we create our JNDI helper class and initialize our inventory messaging system:

```
   public void ejbCreate() {
      _utils = new SampleUtilities();
      jmsInit();
   }
```

Our `jmsInit()` method uses JNDI to get our provider's `QueueConnectionFactory`. `QueueConnection` represents a unique connection to the messaging server. This connection will be shared and managed by our `InventoryController`. It is possible to create a messaging bean to encapsulate this behavior using simple get and set methods. We would then be able to reuse the bean throughout other parts of the system.

We use the `Connection` to create a `Session` object by invoking the method `connection.createQueueSession()`. The first parameter specifies whether the session object will support transactions. We set this to false to indicate that the session will not participate in a transaction.

The second parameter indicates the acknowledgement mode used. We indicate to auto-acknowledge which means that the message is automatically acknowledged after it is received by the client. This example only creates a single `Session` because we are reusing this `Session` internally to write to a single message queue. As mentioned this message queue will be used to indicate part status that has reached a critical level in our manufacturer.

```
    void jmsInit() {

        try {
            final QueueConnectionFactory factory =
(QueueConnectionFactory)_utils.jndiLookup(QueueConnectionFactory.class.getName());
            // Use factory to create QueueConnection
            connection = factory.createQueueConnection();
            // Use QueueConnection to create QueueSession
            session = connection.createQueueSession(false,
            Session.AUTO_ACKNOWLEDGE);
```

We create our sending client using the session and also dynamically create a queue for example "B2BQueue". This is the queue name we will use to address our messages to a specific destination. A receiver would use this name to request messages from the service provider from this destination.

We create a `TextMessage` type which we use to construct text messages in our inventory alert process:

```
// Uses QueueSession to create QueueSender
            sender = session.createSender(session.createQueue(queue));
            sender.setDisableMessageID(false);

            // Create TextMessage object
            message = session.createTextMessage();
        }
        catch(NamingException e) {
            System.out.println("Naming Exception: " + e.getMessage());
        }
        catch(JMSException e) {
System.out.println("JMS Exception: " + e.getMessage());
        }
    }

}
```

Let's just digress a moment to describe our helper class.

JNDI to find a ConnectionFactory object

We have defined a JNDI helper class that allows us to resolve names to objects in our service provider name space:

```
import java.util.*;
import javax.naming.*;
import javax.jms.*;

// Change these to SPI Specific (these are Allaire's JRun JMS properties
// Queue Connection Factory, Intitial Context Factory, Path to Interface

public static final String SPI_QFACTORY = "QueueConnectionFactory";
public static final String SPI_ICFACTORY = "allaire.ejipt.ContentFactory";
public static final String SPI_URL = "ejipt://localhost:2323";

private static Context jndiContext = null;

public static javax.jms.QueueConnectionFactory getQueueConnectionFactory()
        throws Exception {
    return (javax.jms.QueueConnectionFactory) jndiLookup(SPI_QFACTORY);
}

// A method to find the JMS Connection Factory
public static Object jndiLookup(String name) throws NamingException {

    Object obj = null;
    Properties properties = new Properties();

    // resolve initial context
    if (jndiContext == null) {
        try {
            properties.setProperty(Context.INITIAL_CONTEXT_FACTORY,
                    SPI_ICFACTORY);
            properties.setProperty(Context.PROVIDER_URL, SPI_URL);
            jndiContext = new InitialContext(properties);

        } catch (NamingException e) {
            System.out.println("Could not create JNDI context: " +
            e.toString());
            throw e;
        }
    }
    // resolve javax.jms.QueueConnectionFactory
    try {
        obj = jndiContext.lookup(name);
    } catch (NamingException e) {
        System.out.println("JNDI lookup failed: " + e.toString());
        throw e;
    }
    return obj;
}
```

Now we've described that we can return to discussing the InventoryControllerBean.

The InventoryControllerBean

The `getInventoryDetails()` implementation in our example uses the product name as the primary key to find the `Inventory` bean. We call the `getQuantityOnHand()` method defined in the `Inventory` remote interface:

```
public int getInventoryDetails(final String product)
throws RemoteException {
    try {
        InventoryHome home =
            (InventoryHome)_utils.jndiLookup("B2B.InventoryHome");
        Inventory inventory = home.findByPrimaryKey(product);
        int quantity = inventory.getQuantityOnHand();
```

If our quantity on hand for a product dips below a set level we invoke our message process. We use the text message object `setText` method to construct an alert message and send the message to our "B2BQueue".

```
        if(quantity < 100) {
            try {
                message.setText(product +" quantity low!");
                // Send to the queue. The message will last for 60 minutes.
                sender.send(message, Message.DEFAULT_DELIVERY_MODE,
                    Message.DEFAULT_PRIORITY, 60 * 60 * 1000);
                System.out.println("Initiate procurement for: " + product
                    + ": quantity low " + quantity);
            } catch(JMSException e) {
                System.out.println("JMS Exception: " + e.getMessage());
            }
        }
        return quantity;
    } catch (RemoteException remote){
        if (remote.detail instanceof SecurityException) {
            throw (SecurityException)remote.detail;
        }
        throw new RuntimeException(remote.getMessage());
    }
    catch (Exception exception) {
        throw new RuntimeException(exception.getMessage());
    }
}
```

To support previous comments let's quickly present the code for the `Inventory` EJB.

The Inventory

The `Inventory` is an entity bean and its remote interface is:

```
package ejbeans;

import java.rmi.*;
import javax.ejb.*;

public interface Inventory extends EJBObject{
    void updateQuantity(int value) throws RemoteException;
    int getQuantityOnHand() throws RemoteException;
}
```

and the home interface is:

```
package ejbeans;

import java.rmi.*;
import javax.ejb.*;

public interface InventoryHome extends EJBHome{
    Inventory create(String productName) throws CreateException, RemoteException;
    Inventory findByPrimaryKey(String key) throws FinderException, RemoteException;
}
```

This InventoryBean class is used to store and retrieve the actual inventory. This class would typically be used to encapsulate access to a persistence layer. For instance, calls to InventoryBean could delegate to a DataAccess object that encapsulates relational or object persistence access, however, demonstrating access using JDBC is beyond the scope of this chapter. In this example we use a simple Store provided by JRun and no DataAccess object is defined.

Our InventoryBean looks like this:

```
package ejbeans;

import java.rmi.*;
import javax.ejb.*;
// we are using Allaire's JRun application server
import allaire.ejipt.*;

public class InventoryBean implements EntityBean
{
    private EntityContext _context;

    private int _value = -1;
    public void setEntityContext(final EntityContext context)
        throws RemoteException
    {
        _context = context;
    }


    public void unsetEntityContext() throws RemoteException
    {
        _context = null;
    }

    public String ejbCreate(final String productName) throws CreateException,
RemoteException
    {
        // Demonstrate initalization with default value
        _value = 0;
        ResourceManager.getLogger().logMessage("Creating product: " +
productName);
        return new String(productName);
```

```
        }

    public void ejbPostCreate(final String productName) throws CreateException,
RemoteException
    {
        try
        {
            if (StoreManager.isStored(_context.getPrimaryKey()))
            {
                StoreManager.loadInstance();
            }
            else
            {
                StoreManager.storeInstance();
            }
        }
        catch (Exception exception)
        {
            throw new EJBException(exception);
        }
    }

    public String ejbFindByPrimaryKey(final String key)
        throws FinderException, RemoteException
    {
        return key;
    }

    public void ejbRemove() throws RemoveException, RemoteException
    {
        throw new RemoveException();
    }
    public void ejbActivate() throws RemoteException {}
    public void ejbPassivate() throws RemoteException {}
    public void ejbLoad() throws RemoteException
    {
        try
        {
            StoreManager.loadInstance();
        } catch (Exception exception) { throw new EJBException(exception); }
    }

    public void ejbStore() throws RemoteException
    {
        try
        {
            StoreManager.storeInstance();
        } catch (Exception exception) { throw new EJBException(exception); }
    }

    public void updateQuantity(final int value) throws RemoteException
    {
        _value += value;
        ResourceManager.getLogger().logMessage("Updating quantity on hand value
is: " + _value);
```

```
        }

    public int getQuantityOnHand() throws RemoteException
    {
        ResourceManager.getLogger().logMessage("inventory on hand is: " + _value);
      return _value;
    }
  }
```

Let's now look at how we can make further use of JMS in our application through a couple of unimplemented illustrations.

JMS Enhancements

The B2BmessageReceiver demonstrates how to implement a MessageListener, which gets notified of the arrival of a message through the onMessage method. The basic setup with JNDI has already been covered.

The B2BMessageReceiver

Although we haven't done it here, a main message could be added to allow the queue to be read from.

```
import java.rmi.*;
import javax.ejb.*;
import javax.jms.*;
import javax.naming.*;

public class B2BMessageReceiver implements MessageListener {
    // Set up queue attributes.
    private final String _queue = new String("B2BQueue");
    private final String _host = new String("localhost");

    // Set up objects for use by JMS.
    private Context context = null;
    private QueueConnection connection = null;
    private QueueSession session = null;
    private TextMessage message = null;
    private QueueReceiver receiver = null;

    static {
        System.setSecurityManager(new RMISecurityManager());
    }

    public void init() {
        try {
            // set up as last example jmsInit except

            // Use QueueSession to create QueueReceiver
            receiver = session.createReceiver(session.createQueue(queue));

            // Start the connection.
            connection.start();
```

```
            } catch(NamingException ex) {
               System.out.println("Naming Exception: " + ex.getMessage());
            } catch(JMSException ex) {
               System.out.println("JMS Exception: " + ex.getMessage());
            }
         }
```

The JMS service provider invokes the `onMessage()` method when a message is ready for delivery from the queue:

```
      // You must implement onMessage for async notification
      public void onMessage(final Message message){
         try {
            TextMessage textMessage = (TextMessage) message;
            String text = textMessage.getText();

            // Just put the alert to the output stream
            System.out.println(text);

         } catch (JMSException e) {
            System.out.println("JMS Exception: " + e.getMessage());
         }
      }
   }
```

Publisher and Subscriber Example

Publish and subscribe interactions are driven by events. The publisher sends a message out to the network usually because something has changed that needs to be broadcast to the subscribers. The publisher does not care how many subscribers (listeners) are present and active.

Some examples may clarify its usage:

❑   It is common in the securities market for stock quotes to be sent to stock traders. In this case the quoting system may be publishing quotes to hundreds or thousands of traders. The quoting system simply sends the stock quotes to a topic and it is up to the underlying messaging software to distribute the message to traders that have subscribed to that topic.

❑   Inventory levels may be published to departments within an organization, such as accounting, purchasing, manufacturing, etc.

❑   Materials management systems distribute tracking information to various materials handlers, controllers, and tracking systems.

The B2BPublisher

In this example, we're going to modify our second example to publish inventory levels to external trading partners as opposed to internal departments. The `B2BPublisher` demonstrates how to implement a publisher that publishes to a topic.

In this case we are defining our topic as a specific product and the event that generates a message is a change in inventory level. Our `InventoryController` establishes a topic for each product manufactured. It delivers an inventory level message to the appropriate topic as inventory levels change. Trading partners access topics (with appropriate security) to integrate processes between systems:

```
import java.rmi.*;
import javax.ejb.*;
import javax.jms.*;
import javax.naming.*;

public class B2BPublisher {          // Set up queue attributes.
    private String topic = new String("productXYZLevelQueue");
    private String host = new String("localhost");
    // Set up objects for use by JMS.
    private Context context = null;
    private TopicConnection connection = null;
    private TopicSession session = null;
    private TextMessage message = null;
    private TopicPublisher publisher = null;

    static {
        System.setSecurityManager(new RMISecurityManager());
    }

    public void init() {
        try {
            // JNDI to find TopicConnectionFactory

            // Use factory to create TopicConnection
            connection = factory.createTopicConnection();

            // Use TopicConnection to create TopicSession
            session = connection.createTopicSession(false,
                Session.AUTO_ACKNOWLEDGE);

            // Use TopicSession to create TopicPublisher
            publisher =
                session.createPublisher(session.createTopic(topic));

            // Create TextMessage object
            message = session.createTextMessage();
        } catch(NamingException e) {
            System.out.println("Naming Exception: " + e.getMessage());
        } catch(JMSException e) {
            System.out.println("JMS Exception: " + e.getMessage());
        }
    }
```

Our doChannelSend() method takes a String parameter and publishes the message to the topic (as in "CRT-111A qty on hand = 2345" to CRT-111A Topic):

```
public void doChannelSend(String text) throws JMSException {

    try {
        message.setText(text);
        // Publish to the topic.
        publisher.publish(message);
    } catch(Exception ex) {
        throws new JMSException(ex.getMessage());
    }
}
```

The message "CRT-111A qty on hand=2345" of course would be proprietary to our manufacturer. We could publish industry standard messages and/or use our transformation process (XSLT from the last chapter) to transform our proprietary message into an industry standard message and publish the industry standard message. The following diagram illustrates the general flow of this publish-subscribe messaging, where Supplier B does not subscribe to the topic being published here:

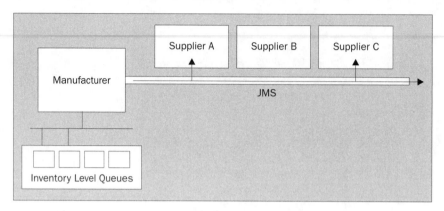

The Enterprise Information System Tier

We have spent a considerable amount of time using product inventory and inventory levels in our example application, yet we have not actually shown where this information resides or how it is accessed. Enterprise applications use enterprise information systems to store and access information. The most common example of an enterprise information system is a database. For instance, our product inventory may actually be managed by a relational database management system such as Oracle. Other examples of enterprise information systems include enterprise resource planning systems, transaction processing systems such as IBM's CICS and other legacy information systems.

The Enterprise Information System tier of J2EE deals with these types of systems and applications. Traditionally businesses have run their mission critical applications with enterprise information systems. E-Commerce has provided a new dimension to information system access. Enterprises need their information available over the Web, and B2B will usher in even more access and potentially more access points.

To wrap up let's see how we can watch the code in action.

Building the Application

Firstly let's just summarize what the code does:

- ❏ The `ejbeans` package implements the EJB components for the example.

- ❏ The `InventoryControllerBean` implements the `SessionBean` interface. It has a method `getInventoryDetails()` which is called to return inventory on hand for a specific product.

- ❏ `Inventory` extends the `EJBObject` interface – it has two methods `updateQuantity()` and `getQuantityOnHand()`.

❑ `InventoryBean` implements the `EntityBean` interface. This class is used to store and retrieve the actual inventory. As we pointed out the class would normally be used to encapsulate access to a persistence layer – here, however, we've just used a simple Store provided by Jrun.

❑ The `InventoryControllerBean` is called by the `InventoryChannel` class from the web tier.

❑ The `InventoryChannel` functions as a proxy object for the `InventoryControllerBean`.

❑ The `getInventoryDetails()` method of the `InventoryControllerBean` finds the `InventoryBean` to return the quantity on hand and compares that value to 100. If the inventory is below that level it sends a message to a message queue using the JMS API.

Deploying the Application

Again these instructions are specified for the code download available at www.wrox.com and are for the JRun application server. For other application servers you will need to consult their documentation.

Code Modifications

There are a couple of hard-coded variables in various files that need to be changed for your own installation:

❑ In the `makew.bat` file in the `b2b-app` directory, change the following line to point to your local copy of JRun:

```
if "%EJIPT_HOME%"==""   set EJIPT_HOME=d:\Program Files\Allaire\JRun
```

❑ In the `makew.bat` file in the `web-inf\classes` directory, amend the following lines to point to your local copies of `jaxp.jar`, `crimson.jar`, and `xalan.jar`:

```
set
JAXP_DIR=d:\jdk1.3\jre\lib\ext\jaxp.jar;d:\jdk1.3\jre\lib\ext\crimson.jar;d:\jdk1.
3\jre\lib\ext\xalan.jar
```

❑ In the `Supplier.java` file, change the following lines to point at appropriate local copies of the XML files:

```
// test xml messages to manufacturer
   String B2BMessageExample = "d:\\Content\\B2BMessage.xml";
   String B2BRegistryExample = "d:\\Content\\RegistryQuery.xml";
```

❑ In the `Dispatcher.java` file, change the following line at the bottom of the `doPost()` method to point at the local copy of the XSL stylesheet:

```
FileInputStream sheet =
        new FileInputStream("d:\\content\\InventoryLevelResponse.xsl");
```

Setting up the Directories

Copy the `b2b-app` directory under `examples\chapter19` to your default server directory. For example using:

```
copy [d:]\examples\chapter19\b2b-app [d:]\Allaire\JRun\servers\default
```

Setting up the Web Application (JRun Specific)

To set up the web application we're going to edit the local properties file:

❑   Go to the JRun default server directory ([d:]\Allaire\JRun\servers\default)

❑   Open the local.properties file and add the following to the bottom of the file, changing
    the paths as appropriate to reflect your deployment path:

```
b2b.rootdir=[d:\\Program Files]\\Allaire\\JRun\\servers\\default\\b2b-app
b2b.class={webapp.service-class}
webapp.mapping./b2b-app=b2b
```

❑   Next search the file to find servlet.webapps and add b2b. For example:

```
servlet.webapps=default-app,demo-app,b2b
```

❑   Save the local.properties file

Building the Broker Files

The first task is to run the makew.bat file in the default\b2b-app directory, for example using:

```
[d:]\Allaire\JRun\servers\default\b2b-app> makew
```

You should see something like the following on the console:

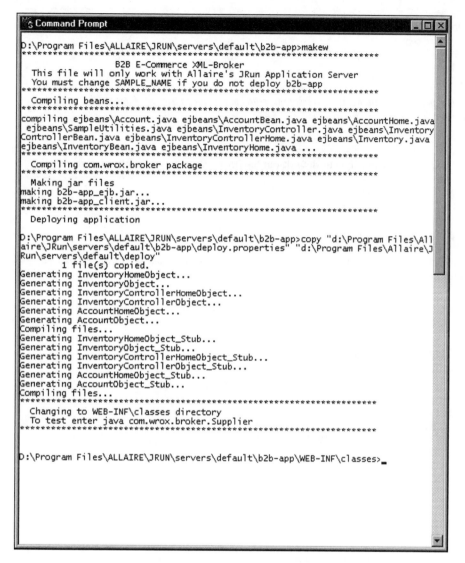

This will create the `com.wrox.broker` directory and the necessary EJB components.

At this point, if the JRun default server is running, stop and restart it, or else start the default server.

We can now verify that everything has been set up properly by going to the logs directory (for example `[d:]\Allaire\JRun\logs`) and opening `default-out.log` where you should see something like:

```
Initializer constructing
-----------
Initializing B2B Manufacturer
productName:    Generic Computer
partName:   CRT-1234
quantityOnHand:   55
inventoryLogin:   user
```

```
inventoryPassword:      password
-----------
Initializing Product Catalog
-----------
```

This is part of the initialization process that creates our product inventory database. For more details take a look at the web.xml file and the Initializer class that come with the download.

If you do not see this in your default-out log file then you have a configuration error.

After all that we're now ready to test our application.

Running the Application

Firstly we can test the supplier. This is quite simple – just run com.wrox.broker.Supplier. For example:

```
d:\Allaire\JRun\servers\default\b2b-app\Web-inf\classes> java
com.wrox.broker.Supplier
```

You should see something like the following on the console:

```
Monitor running...Thu Jan 25 11:20:16 GMT 2001
Checking
<Html>
    <Head>
        <Title>B2B Supply Chain</Title>
    </Head>
    <Body>
        <H2>Inventory Level Response</H2>
        <Table border="1">
            <tr>
                <td>Product id</td><td>Generic Computer</td>
            </tr>
            <tr>
                <td>Part number</td><td>CRT-1234</td>
            </tr>
            <tr>
                <td>Quantity on hand</td><td>55</td>
            </tr>
        </Table>
    </Body>
</Html>
```

This will repeat appropriately as the manufacturer is polled for information.

The example application checks the quantity on hand for the Generic Computer CRT-1234 part. If the quantity is *below* 100 it generates a message to a queue using the JMS API.

The first time you run the application (com.wrox.broker.Supplier) a message is sent to the queue because the quantity was initialized to 55, which is below the threshold. In the JRun default-out.log you should see:

```
Initiate procurement for: Generic Computer: quantity low 55
```

If you stop and restart the default server, the second time you run the application no message should be sent (hence there will no additional information in the JRun default-out.log).

Additionally, the console output should indicate the inventory level has increased to 110 as shown:

```
Monitor running...Thu Jan 25 11:25:42 GMT 2001
Checking
<Html>
    <Head>
        <Title>B2B Supply Chain</Title>
    </Head>
    <Body>
        <H2>Inventory Level Response</H2>
        <Table border="1">
            <tr>
                <td>Product id</td><td>Generic Computer</td>
            </tr>
            <tr>
                <td>Part number</td><td>CRT-1234</td>
            </tr>
            <tr>
                <td>Quantity on hand</td><td>110</td>
            </tr>
        </Table>
    </Body>
</Html>
```

Remember we are using the default Store that comes with JRun for persistence, and hence the Store is being incremented by the value of 55 each time the server is restarted.

To reset the system the instance.store file in the JRun runtime directory can be deleted, which in effect clears out our example database.

Alternatively, the initialization parameters in the web.xml file (shown below) may be modified:

```
<init-param>
    <param-name>quantityOnHand</param-name>
    <param-value>55</param-value>
</init-param>
```

In both cases, for the changes to take effect the server needs to be restarted.

To round off this set of chapters let's look into the near future and see what other technologies may be about to help the B2B developer.

Emerging Technologies and Future Directions

The next two sections *The Connector Architecture* and *Overview of Java API for XML Messaging (JAXM)* discuss technologies that are emerging to support enterprise integration and B2B messaging. Both of these technologies will provide critical support to enable mass integration in the global B2B economy. In this section we will also have a look at the M Project and summarize the way in which this area is moving.

The Connector Architecture

The connector architecture enables an EIS vendor to provide a standard resource adapter for its EIS. A resource adapter is a system-level software driver that is used by a Java application to connect to an EIS. The resource adapter plugs into an application server and provides connectivity between the EIS, the application server, and the enterprise application.

The intent is to minimize the degree of customization required by both application server vendors and EIS vendors, by having a common connector architecture between these systems. EIS vendors supply one standard resource adapter and this can be used across application server products that support the architecture.

The connector architecture also defines a **Common Client Interface** (**CCI**) for EIS access. The CCI defines a client API for interacting with heterogeneous EISs. The J2EE connector architecture is designed to scale and optimizes the communication between web and EIS applications.

When we started discussing B2B and the implications to current systems, we mentioned the importance of integrating backend systems. This has always been a challenge. The connector architecture holds promise for enabling a more seamless integration between mission-critical backend systems and evolving Internet focused applications.

How the Connector Architecture Establishes a Database Connection

The client application component does a lookup of a connection factory in the JNDI name space. It uses the connection factory to get a connection to the underlying EIS. The connection factory instance delegates the connection creation request to the `ConnectionManager` instance.

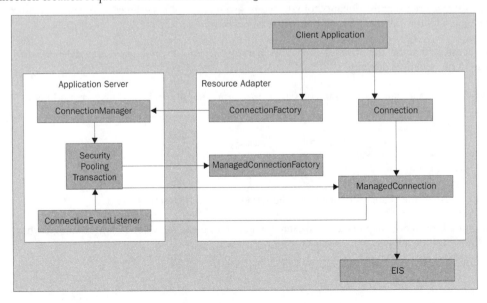

The `ConnectionManager` enables the application server to provide different quality of services. This includes transaction management, security, error logging, and connection pool management. The application server provides these services in its own implementation-specific way. The connector architecture does not specify how the application server implements these services.

The `ConnectionManager` instance, on receiving a connection creation request from the connection factory, does a lookup in the connection pool provided by the application server. A connection pool is a common technique used to optimize connection management by having a number of connection objectscreated and waiting to be used.

If there is no connection in the pool that can satisfy the connection request, the application server uses the `ManagedConnectionFactory` interface (implemented by the resource adapter) to create a new physical connection to the underlying EIS. If the application server finds a matching connection in the pool, then it uses the matching `ManagedConnection` instance to satisfy the connection request.

The application server registers a `ConnectionEventListener` with the `ManagedConnection` instance. This listener enables the application server to get event notifications related to the state of the `ManagedConnection` instance. The application server uses these notifications to manage connection pooling, manage transactions, cleanup connections, and handle any error conditions. Once this setup is performed the client application can access the EIS through the connection provided.

The Connector Architecture will be an interesting technology to follow as it matures. The integration effort for enterprise information systems has been costly and complex. This is one solution that holds promise for shortening the timeframe and cost required through standard interfaces. Of course the success of this effort will depend largely on EIS vendors and system integrators adapting products to the API.

Another technology that is emerging and holds promise for B2B XML integration is the Java API for XML Messaging.

Overview of Java API for XML Messaging (JAXM)

In previous chapters we discussed the Java API for XML Parsing (JAXP). Sun Microsystems has decided that there still exists a gap in XML processing. JAXM is being built to fill that gap.

JAXM provides an API for packaging and transporting business transactions using standard XML protocols being defined by ebXML.org, Oasis, W3C, and IETF. The intent is to provide a standard way to accomplish the secure and reliable exchange of XML defined business documents between trading partners. It is envisioned that the ability for Java applications to exchange XML data (either synchronously or asynchronously) with other business applications will facilitate Internet based B2B communication.

The JAXM specification is being developed to ensure that message delivery can be accomplished by supporting a number of communications infrastructures and key networking transports including, but not limited to, HTTP(S), SMTP and FTP.

The draft specification for JAXM is available through the Java Community Process (JCP). The projected shipping date of JAXM is early 2001. SUN plans to make the final reference implementation of JAXM available to developers through open source, which will probably be the Apache Software Foundation. For further information, and an early access version of JAXM named The M Project, consult http://www.java.sun.com/xml/.

JAXM Architecture

The `java.xml.messaging` package defines the following Interfaces:

JAXM Object	Description
Connection	A JAXM `Connection` is a client's active connection to its JAXM provider
ConnectionMetaData	Provides information describing the `Connection`
Destination	The destination of a message
Message	This interface is the root interface of all JAXM messages
MessageListener	Used to receive asynchronously delivered messages
MessageProducer	Used by a client to send messages to a `Destination`

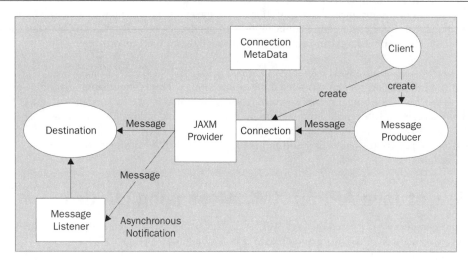

The M Project

Sun Microsystems' The M Project is an early access prototype implementation of an XML-based messaging system. It is based on the work currently in progress in the following industry-wide initiatives:

❑   The ebXML Transport Working Group

❑   Java API for XML Messaging, which is developed as JSR-067 under the Java Community Process

The goal of the M Project is to provide for discussion purposes a prototype of a messaging system in B2B systems. The release of the M Project includes a messaging server and client libraries that a servlet developer would bundle into web applications. In addition the M Project bundles the Tomcat servlet engine from the Jakarta project.

The steps involved for a client to set up and use a messaging server are similar to JMS:

1. Get a connection to use; the example uses the `ServletContext` to store a reference to a connection as an attribute:

```
Connection connection = (Connection)context.getAttribute("someConnection");
```

2. Create the `Destination` object:

```
String to = "tradingPartner.com/ebXML";
Destination destination = connection.createDestination(to);
```

3. Create the `Producer`:

```
MessageProducer producer = connection.createProducer(destination);
Message message = producer.createMessage();
```

4. Build the ebXML message body would reference the ebXML message:

```
BodyPart bodyPart = message.createBodyPart();
String content = "some ebXML content";
bodyPart.setContent(content);
message.addBodyPart(bodyPart);
```

5. Start the connection:

```
connection.start();
```

6. Send the XML message:

```
producer.send(message);
```

Sun is positioning JAXM to be an important technology supporting B2B e-commerce. The protocol server component supporting technologies like ebXML could prove to be beneficial in reducing the development required to participate in standard message exchanges. Look for specialized JAXM servers supporting XML vocabularies to surface once the standard has been defined.

Future Directions

We have covered a lot of ground in our overview of B2B. It should be apparent that this is a rapidly changing area of business and technology. Java, JMS, and XML are at the forefront of this transformation.

New business integration models are being deployed almost daily to customize the way businesses communicate, whether it be through supply chains, auctions, or exchanges. This transformation will continue and accelerate as common patterns of communication become standardized.

Tools will continue to be developed that hide much of the complexity from the users of B2B integration technologies. However, it is still important as a developer that the underlying mechanisms be adequately understood to make the appropriate technology decisions to support your business requirements:

- We must build adaptive systems to meet the rapidly changing requirements of the B2B economy.

- System interaction will become more dynamic.

- Relationships with partners will also become more dynamic.

- Human resources will be more tightly integrated into the processing steps and monitoring of information exchanged between B2B systems. It may get to the point where you are using your partner's system as much as you are using your own. This will be possible because of the ease with which the Web has enabled human-to-system interaction.

Summary

In the world of B2B e-commerce, if we can't communicate with our partners, our business must surely flounder. As we have seen, there are many ways to accomplish the required level of communications, and the future looks bright and easier for system integration:

- Messaging systems have become a key component in enabling B2B cross-platform communication both within an organization and between organizations (trading partners).

- The J2EE Framework provides JMS as the interface to Message Oriented Middleware (MOM) services.

- JMS provides two models of communication: Point-to-Point and Publish-and-Subscribe.

- Point–to-Point models are used when a more static environment exists, such as message exchange between a single sender and receiver.

- Publish-and-Subscribe models are used when a more dynamic environment exists. Message producers and consumers come and go based on events.

- A topic provides a mechanism to arrange destinations or queues into a content hierarchy.

- The J2EE Connector Architecture will enable application server vendors and EIS providers to integrate using a standard interface.

- The J2EE Connector Architecture could enable the necessary backend integration standards to promote B2B.

- JAXM will simplify the development required to support standard XML message exchange.

To support our discussions we've developed an XML Broker application to demonstrate:

- How an XML request/response can be programmatically generated to and from the web tier of an implementing servlet engine.

- How XSLT can be used to transform XML requests and responses into other message formats.

- How a B2B frontend can be integrated with a B2B backend using JMS as middleware.

In our next chapter we'll see how supply chain integration using XML and XSLT was used to provide huge efficiency benefits in facilitating the development of a novel B2B application for providing business stationery.

PROFESSIONALJAVAE-COMMERCE

20

In the Marketplace C – Supply Chain Integration

Even though we are in the age of e-mail, electronic business cards, and digital certificates, old-fashioned business stationery is still heavily utilized in the business world today. This could not be truer than in the financial industry.

This chapter explains how enterprise technologies such as Java, XML, and XSLT were used to streamline the production of professional business stationery. First the business problem and its critical success factors are introduced. Next, the automated approach and solution is discussed.

Recently, a major financial company undertook a corporate re-branding initiative. Consequently, they needed to reissue business stationery to their ten thousand financial representatives throughout the country. During a three-month period they needed to process in excess of fourteen thousand orders, generating over ten million typeset pieces of stationery, including letterheads and envelopes. This, of course, was a daunting task. Therefore, the financial institution worked with its business partners to build an automated system that would not only help it make its aggressive deadlines, but do so in a cost effective manner. As you'll see, the nature of the project precludes showing a full solution but over the course of the chapter we'll look at:

- ❑ The system components
- ❑ The critical success factors
- ❑ The web-based order collection system
- ❑ The order approval process
- ❑ The XSL-based order processing system
- ❑ The lessons learned during the project

Components

The first component of the system was a web based self-service application used to place the orders for new stationery. This part of the solution allowed financial representatives to place their order, validate the contents, have it approved by the home office, and sent to the appropriate vendor for fulfillment. The self-service application utilized Java, XML, XSLT, and servlets to build a scalable solution.

The second piece of the puzzle was a reusable order fulfillment system that ran at the printing company. Upon receipt of the orders, the application used the XML data and applied XSLT to create a postscript file, which was then used to create electronic printing plates. Once the plates were created, the physical stationery was produced, packed, and distributed to the appropriate financial representative.

The construction of the application, illustrated below, allowed a stationery order to be entered, processed, and produced with minimal human intervention. In doing so, it enabled both the financial institution and the printing company to meet their business goals in a timely and cost effective manner.

Critical Success Factors

In order to measure the success or failure of a project, **critical success factors** must be defined up front. Unfortunately, not all projects are as well managed as this one, and consequently critical success factors are not always clearly defined at the outset. The major stakeholders in the project including business areas, the IT department, and external business partners, worked together to establish metrics that would be used to determine the project's degree of success.

Compliance

Since the financial industry is heavily regulated, the first critical success factor was that the new stationery passed all the compliance tests. The compliance tests could be divided into two general categories: the stationery content, and its layout.

Content

In order to enforce the content compliance tests, the financial institution needed to ensure that the financial representatives accurately portrayed themselves. This was accomplished by implementing a two-step approval process:

❑ First, the self-service application that the financial representatives used would enforce business rules based on the representative's credentials. For example, if the representative was indicating that they were licensed to sell products in California, the application needed to verify that they held a valid license in that state.

❑ Secondly, to complete the verification process a series of integration points with current and legacy systems was required. For example, if a financial representative indicated that they would like to include their professional designations (CPA, JD, etc.) on the stationery, the information would be looked up at run time against the corporate data warehouse that was housed in both relational and mainframe data stores. The financial representative was then able to select what to include on the stationery from their valid professional designations.

Assuming the order passed the online tests and contained valid information for the representative, it was routed to the home office for processing. The order-processing department at the corporate office used another piece of the solution to identify anomalies, such as special handling instructions and excess quantities, in the orders and correct any discrepancies. Once the order was validated for content, it was passed on to the vendor for fulfillment.

Layout

The second area of compliance was the physical layout of the stationery. Since there are laws regulating the size and position of logos, names, and disclaimers, the physical layout and the design of the stationery needed to be closely adhered to. To minimize the risk of errors, a physical specification sheet was created for each product. This specification sheet included precise font, spacing, and position requirements for each stationery item. Once the specification sheet was finalized and approved by the compliance department, it was sent to the printing company for production.

Time to Market

In the ever-competitive financial industry, the next critical success factor was "time to market". Since the financial institution was simultaneously rolling out a new product line, both development efforts needed to be coordinated. This meant that the entire project needed to be completed in less than six months. This included finalizing the specification sheets for each stationery item, developing the self-service application, integrating with the vendors, and building the vendor-run order processing systems.

Since the end result was going to be a physical product that could not be changed or corrected (except through reprints), accuracy was another critical success factor. In order to increase the accuracy, the data that was entered into the self-service application was wrapped in XML and transmitted exactly as it was entered. To ensure the order was entered as the representative wanted, a preview of the order was displayed before it was submitted that could then be printed off and used to verify the order when it was received. By doing this, the responsibility for accuracy was placed on the person placing the order.

Secure and Reliable

The entire order fulfillment application also needed to be secure and reliable. The security risks for the system can be divided into three general categories:

- ❏ the data is lost
- ❏ the data is corrupted
- ❏ the data is inadvertently exposed to someone that should not see it

In order to verify that the data was not lost or altered, a checksum, (a mathematical function that generates a unique result based on the contents of each transaction) was included. If the checksum did not match, the application would send a notification to the support staff indicating an error. Additionally, at the end of each day a summary report listing all of the processed orders was generated and reviewed by the printing company.

Since the information being used to drive the order process included sensitive contract and licensing information, the self-service application needed to ensure that the data remained confidential. To meet this requirement data was sent over an encrypted intranet that authenticated users against a **Lightweight Directory Access Protocol (LDAP)** server. Integrating with the corporate LDAP server allowed the system to access relevant user and security information for all of the field financial representatives as well as the home office staff, some 15,000 user IDs. The user's LDAP credentials were also used to enforce application-based security such as allowing administrative assistants to order only for the financial representatives that they worked for. Finally, to minimize the risk that the data was inadvertently exposed during the transmission it was encrypted and compressed.

Cost Effective

The remaining success factor was that the application needed to be created in a cost effective manner. Historically, the orders were received via phone calls or faxes and were manually validated and processed. Furthermore, the printing company manually typeset each order using QuarkXPress. Both of these processes needed to be automated in such a way that they did not cost more than the current manual systems. Therefore, the new system needed to be legally compliant, timely, accurate, secure, and delivered in a cost effective manner.

The Solution

The diagram below illustrates the flow of an order through the completed system:

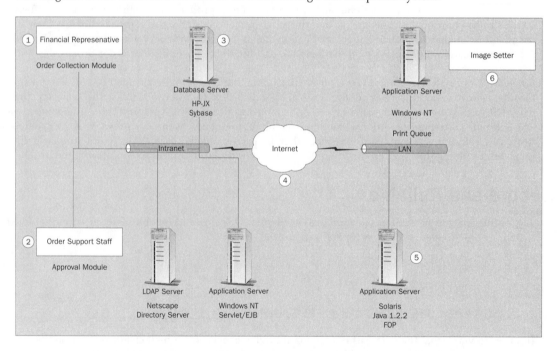

1. The order information is entered in the order collection system and validated based on the credentials of the person logged on via the LDAP server. After the order is completed, the user is shown a preview of their order before submitting it for processing.

2. If the order passes all of the system checks, it is sent on for fulfillment. However, if there is an exception the data is validated manually.

3. All approved orders are extracted into XML, compressed, and encrypted.

4. The daily order information is sent, via FTP, to the printing company.

5. The daily order file is validated for accuracy and completeness, and then processed. The processing includes the creation of the postscript files and packing slips.

6. The files are placed into the processing queue for the image setter, where the production of the final stationery product is completed.

Now that we have a general overview of the business problem and the process flow required, we can go into detail about how the components were constructed.

Order Collection System

The first part of the solution was to build a self-service application that would allow the financial representatives to place their orders. The application needed to easily support new types of stationery and a field force that was spread throughout the country. Consequently, a web-based application was deemed to be the best solution, for ease of deployment.

In addition, the application needed to support over ten thousand users and complete in excess of ten million typeset pieces of stationery over a three-month period. Therefore, the load of the application was expected to be significant. Finally, the application needed to be developed and deployed across various environments including Windows, Linux, and various flavors of UNIX (HP-UX and Solaris). The flexibility of a Java deployment environment and its support for highly scalable solutions led the team to develop a J2EE based system.

The order collection system can be divided into three general components:

❑ The ordering module

❑ The order approval module

❑ The order transmission component

Representative Ordering Module

The financial representative ordering module is an HTML based application that runs in the field offices of the financial representatives. After successfully authenticating the user, it steps them through a wizard-type series of screens that allow them to place their order. The following screenshot is a sample screen that was dynamically built using information collected from previous screens and the user's credentials that were retrieved from the LDAP system.

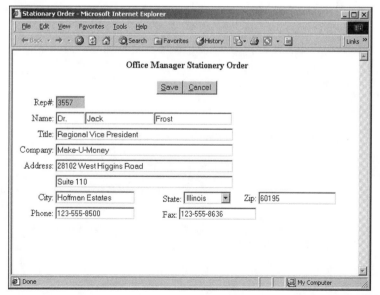

In order to isolate the user interface from the application logic, XML and XSL were used to create the user interface. By creating Java services that returned XML, the business logic could be built as a series of reusable services that created generic output. This output could then be used by multiple components in the application including the user interface and order transmission modules.

The sample flow of a request through the servlet is illustrated in the following sequence diagram:

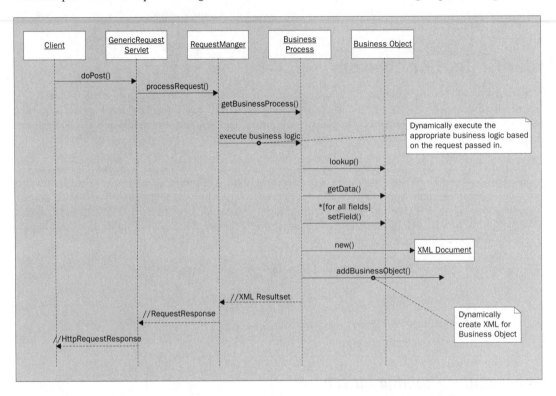

Each request from the browser is dispatched to the generic request servlet listed below:

```java
package wrox;

import java.util.*;
import java.io.*;
import javax.servlet.*;
import javax.servlet.http.*;

public class GenericRequestServlet extends HttpServlet {

    // This method will treat post requests as get requests
    public void doPost(HttpServletRequest request,
                   HttpServletResponse response) throws ServletException,
                   IOException {

        // delegate the post request to doGet method
        doGet(request, response);
    }
```

```
    // Process the request
    public void doGet(HttpServletRequest request,
                      HttpServletResponse response) throws ServletException,
                      IOException {
      PrintWriter out = null;

      // Get the session for the current user
      HttpSession session = request.getSession(true);

      // Create a generic wrapper for the parameters passed in
      RequestParameters parms = new RequestParameters(request);

      // Add the session to the parameters available for this request
      parms.put("Session", session, false);

      // Create the appropriate request and send it out.
      try {

        // Get a reference to the request manager and dispatch the request
        RequestManager reqMgr = RequestManager.getInstance();
        RequestResponse requestResp = (RequestResponse) reqMgr.process(parms);

        // Generate the output for the given request
        OutputManager outMgr = new OutputManager();
        outMgr.processRequest(request, response, requestResp);
      } catch (Exception ex) {

        // Create error message to be displayed in browser
        out = new PrintWriter(response.getOutputStream());
        response.setContentType("text/html");
        out.println("<HTML>");
        out.println("<HEAD><TITLE>" + "Error during processing: "
                  + "</TITLE></HEAD>");
        out.println("<BODY>");
        out.println("<BR><pre>");
        ex.printStackTrace(out);
        out.println("</pre></BODY>");
        out.println("</HTML>");
      }
      finally {

        // Close the output stream if it was opened
        if (out != null) {
          out.close();
        }
      }
    }
  }
```

As you can see, each HTTP request sent to the servlet is delegated to the `RequestManager()` for processing. The `RequestManager()` uses the parameters passed along in the URL to instantiate the correct business logic class, invoke the requested action to satisfy the request, and generate the appropriate XML. This model, which is illustrated in the code below, allows the business logic to start in Java classes that could eventually be moved into stateless session beans:

```
package wrox;

public class RequestManager {


private RequestManager(){
// Note that this constructor is needed to enforce the Singleton pattern
}

// Class Variables
  static public RequestManager instance = new RequestManager();

  // Return reference to singleton
  static public RequestManager getInstance() {
    return instance;
  }

  // Process the request
  public RequestResponse process(RequestParameters requestParms)
          throws Exception {
    RequestResponse response = null;

    // Dynamically create the appropriate request
    Request request =
      (Request) Class.forName(requestParms.getRequest()).newInstance();

    // Continue processing, if a valid request was returned
    if (request != null) {

      // Set the current set of CGI variables in to the request
      request.setParameters(requestParms);

      // Setup the parameters to the action method to be invoked.
      Class requestClass = this.getClass();
      Class[] parameterTypes = {
        RequestParameters.class
      };
      Object[] parameterValues = {
        requestParms
      };

      // Invoke the action on the current request object
      java.lang.reflect.Method actionMethod =
        requestClass.getMethod(requestParms.getRequest(), parameterTypes);
      response = (RequestResponse) actionMethod.invoke(this,
            parameterValues);
    }
    return response;
  }
}
```

As you can see in the code above, the RequestManager() dynamically creates an instance of the appropriate business logic request and dynamically calls the corresponding action method on that request using the Reflection API. The details regarding which request and action to execute are passed along in the URL. For example, this URL:

http://localhost/GenericRequestServlet?Request=OrderManagement&Action=displayRepData

would instantiate the `OrderManagement` business object and execute the `displayRepData()` method. This method would then be responsible for executing the appropriate business logic and generating the XML output for the request. An alternative approach to the use of reflection would be to have each request implement a common interface and call a common action method. The reflection approach was chosen because it allow each request to dynamically group and change the actions that they supported.

Once the business logic was complete, the Xerces parser from the Apache group was used to create an XML document similar to the one below. The Xerces parser was selected for its maturity and integration with other products from the Apache group.

```xml
<RepDataScreen>
    <result>
        <repData>
            <repNumber>3557</repNumber>
            <repType>2</repType>
            <salutation>Dr.</salutation>
            <fname>Jack</fname>
            <initials>JAF</initials>
            <lname>Frost</lname>
            <title>Regional Vice President</title>
            <companyName>Make-U-Money</companyName>
            <address1>28102 West Higgins Road</address1>
            <address2>Suite 110</address2>
            <city>Hoffman Estates</city>
            <stateAbbr>IL</stateAbbr>
            <postalcode>60195</postalcode>
            <Country>
                <countryName>United States of America</countryName>
                <countryCode>US</countryCode>
            </Country>
            <fax>123-555-8636</fax>
            <phone>123-555-8500</phone>
            <licenses>
                <License>
                    <licenseNumber>100113</licenseNumber>
                    <state>WI</state>
                </License>
                <License>
                    <licenseNumber>100120</licenseNumber>
                    <state>CA</state>
                </License>
            </licenses>
        </repData>
        <stateList>
            <state>
                <stateName>California</stateName>
                <stateAbbr>CA</stateAbbr>
            </state>
            <state>
                <stateName>Illinois</stateName>
                <stateAbbr>IL</stateAbbr>
            </state>
            <state>
                <stateName>Wisconsin</stateName>
                <stateAbbr>WI</stateAbbr>
            </state>
        </stateList>
    </result>
</RepDataScreen>
```

After the XML is created, it is passed on to the OutputManager() which uses the XSLT processor Xalan and a style sheet similar to the one below to transform the XML into HTML.

```xml
<xsl:stylesheet version="1.0" xmlns:xsl="http://www.w3.org/1999/XSL/Transform"
xmlns:fo="http://www.w3.org/1999/XSL/Format">
<xsl:output method="html" indent="yes"/>

<!-- include the template file for the repData entry form -->
<xsl:include href="repForm.xsl"/>

<xsl:template match="/RepDataScreen">
    <html>
        <head>
            <link rel="stylesheet" href="/stationery.css"/>
            <title>Stationery Order</title>
        </head>

        <body>

<!-- set the heading for the screen -->
        <xsl:choose>
                <xsl:when test="result/repData/repType=1">
                    <center><h4 >Financial Rep Order</h4></center>
                </xsl:when>
                <xsl:when test="result/repData/repType=2">
                    <center><h4 >Office Manager Order</h4></center>
</xsl:when>
                <xsl:when test="result/repData/repType=3">
                    <center><h4 >Corporate Office Order</h4></center> </xsl:when>
            </xsl:choose>

<!-- Create form that is used to submit to request processor servlet -->
        <form name="repMaint" action="/StationeryOrderSystem"
                            method="post">
            <input type="hidden" name="Request" value="RepMaint"/>

            <div align="center">
                <button tabindex="27" name="Action" accesskey="s" >
                    <u>S</u>ave</button>
<!-- determine which buttons to display -->
                <xsl:choose>
                    <xsl:when test="result/repData/repType=2">
                        <button  name="Action" accesskey="d" >
                            <u>D</u>elete</button>
                    </xsl:when>
                </xsl:choose>

                <button  name="Action" accesskey="c"><u>C</u>ancel</button>
            </div>

<!--call the template to format the rep data included in the repForm.xsl-->
            <xsl:call-template name="rep">
                <xsl:with-param name="node" select="result/child::node()"/>
            </xsl:call-template>
        </form>
    </body>
   </html>
</xsl:template>
</xsl:stylesheet>
```

As you can see in the sample above, the HTML is created based on the contents of the XML that is returned for the request. For example, the XSL excerpt below will generate the title displayed on the page based on the type of representative using the application:

```
<xsl:choose>
   <xsl:when test="result/repData/repType=1">
      <center><h4>Financial Rep Order </h4></center>
   </xsl:when>
   <xsl:when test="result/repData/repType=2">
      <center><h4>Office Manager Order</h4></center>
   </xsl:when>
   <xsl:when test="result/repData/repType=3">
      <center><h4>Corporate Office Order</h4></center>
   </xsl:when>
</xsl:choose>
```

In addition, functionality can be dynamically added into the application based on the user type. The XSL below will dynamically include "delete" functionality to the application based on the user type:

```
<xsl:choose>
   <xsl:when test="result/repData/repType=2">
      <button name="Action" accesskey="d"><u>D</u>elete</button>
   </xsl:when>
</xsl:choose>
```

The following illustrates what the new screen would look like for a user with a `repType` equal to Office Manager:

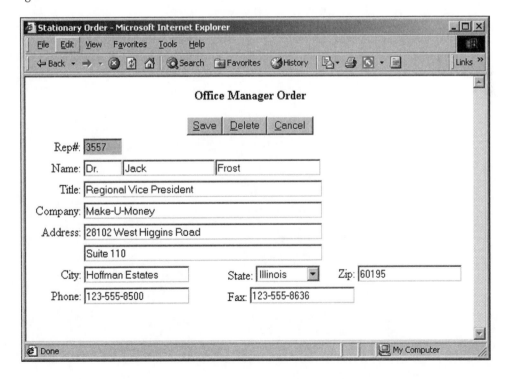

The XSL also utilizes templates to help keep the formatting of the output modular and encourage reuse. The following excerpt includes an external template that can be used throughout the rest of the document:

```
<!-- include the template file for the repData entry form -->
<xsl:include href="repForm.xsl"/>
```

This will include the following template that is called in the current document:

```
<xsl:stylesheet version="1.0" xmlns:xsl="http://www.w3.org/1999/XSL/Transform"
xmlns:fo="http://www.w3.org/1999/XSL/Format">
<xsl:output method="html" indent="yes"/>

<xsl:template name="rep">
<xsl:param name="node"/>
    <table border="0">
        <tr> <!-- rep # -->
            <td align="right" >Rep#:</td>
            <td>
                <input  name="repNum" type="text" size="5" readonly
                    value="{$node/repNumber}" style="background-color:#cccccc"/>
            </td>
        </tr>
        <tr> <!-- firstname, lastname, -->
            <td align="right" >Name:</td>
            <td colspan="2">
                <input name="salutation" type="text" size="5"
                        value="{$node/salutation}" id="salu"/>
                <input name="fname" type="text" size="17"
                        value="{$node/fname}" id="fname"/>
                <input name="lname" type="text" size="20"
                        value="{$node/lname}" id="lname"/>
            </td>
        </tr>
        <tr>
<!-- title -->
            <td align="right" >Title:</td>
            <td colspan="2">
                <input name="title" type="text" size="50"
                        value="{$node/title}"/>
            </td>
        </tr>
        <tr>
<!-- company -->
            <td align="right" >Company:</td>
            <td colspan="2">
                <input name="companyName" type="text" size="50"
                        value="{$node/companyName}"/>
            </td>
        </tr>
        <tr>
<!-- address1 -->
            <td align="right" >Address:</td>
            <td colspan="2">
                <input name="address1" type="text" size="50"
                        value="{$node/address1}"/>
```

```
                </td>
            </tr>
            <tr>
<!-- address2 -->
            <td></td>
            <td colspan="2"><input name = "address2" type="text"
                               size="50" value="{$node/address2}"/>
            </td>
        </tr>
        <tr>
<!-- city, state, postal code -->
            <td align="right" >City:</td>
            <td>
               <input name="city" type="text" size="20" value="{$node/city}"/>
            </td>
            <td>State:
               <select name="province">
                  <option/>
                     <xsl:for-each
                           select="/RepDataScreen/result/stateList/state">
                        <xsl:sort select="stateName"/>
                        <option value="{stateAbbr}">
                           <xsl:if test="stateAbbr=$node/stateAbbr">
                              <xsl:attribute
                                 name="selected">selected</xsl:attribute>
                           </xsl:if>
                           <xsl:value-of select="stateName"/>
                        </option>
                     </xsl:for-each>
               </select>
            </td>
            <td align="right" >Zip:</td>
            <td>
               <input name="postalCode" type="text"
                     value="{$node/postalcode}"/>
            </td>
        </tr>
        <tr> <!-- phone,  fax -->
            <td align="right" >Phone:</td>
            <td >
               <input name="phone" type="text" size="20"
                     value="{$node/phone}"/>
            </td>
            <td  colspan="2"  >Fax:
                  <input name="fax" type="text" size="20" value="{$node/fax}"/>
            </td>
        </tr>
      </table>
   </xsl:template>
</xsl:stylesheet>
```

Once the `repForm.xsl` template is included, it can be called by passing the XML node that the document is currently processing into it. This allows only the data that the template needs to be passed into it:

```
<!--call the template to format the rep data included in the repForm.xsl-->
<xsl:call-template name="rep">
   <xsl:with-param name="node" select="result/child::node()"/>
</xsl:call-template>
```

Through the use of templates, the user interface could change drastically per user by calling a different template based on the user type. By doing this, the business logic and XML would remain the same and only the user interface (XSLT) would change. For example, it was possible for administrative assistants to order for the office of financial representatives that they worked for. Therefore, when an administrative assistant logged into the system a different user interface was presented via XSLT that allowed them to select which financial representative they wanted to order for.

Order Approval Module

If the data entered in the order collection system could be programmatically validated, the order could be automatically approved by the system and passed on to the vendor for processing. However, there were certain orders (excess quantities, special processing, etc.) that needed to be manually approved. When an order that needed manual approval was entered it was added to a queue to be processed by the customer service department. The orders needing manual intervention were then processed on a "first come, first served" basis.

One of the goals of the approval module was to make it look and act like the order collection component described above. By doing this, the customer service team was able to easily relate to the financial representative's experience by reviewing the order on similar screens.

In order to accomplish this, the approval module needed to share much of the business and presentation logic of the order collection module. Therefore, it too was written using XML, XSLT, and J2EE, and reused the same generic servlet dispatcher described earlier, and many of the business logic and domain object classes. Since much of the business logic was the same, it was possible to reuse many of the business services written for the order collection module and simply modify the XSL used to render the presentation.

Order Transmission Module

At the end of each day, the approved orders needed to be sent to the printing company for processing. To accomplish this, a simple extraction program was written to collect the information from the database and transform the data into XML. Each order was given a request number that uniquely identified it in the system. Within that order, the details for each product were listed, including the item number for each item ordered. For example:

```
<Order>
   <req_num>I000013059</req_num>
   <item_num>14-23210</item_num>
   <logo_type>Classic Corporate Logo</logo_type>
   <impr_addr>
      <impr_addrline>28102 West Higgins Road, Suite 110</impr_addrline>
   </impr_addr>
   <impr_city>Hoffman Estates</impr_city>
   <impr_st>IL</impr_st>
   <impr_zip>60195</impr_zip>
   <phones>
      <phone>123-555-8500</phone>
      <phone>123-555-8636 fax</phone>
```

```
        </phones>
        <email>jack.frost@makeumoney.com</email>
        <impr_names>
            <person>
                <impr_name>Jack Frost</impr_name>
                <dsgns>
                    <dsgn>CPA</dsgn>
                    <dsgn>JD</dsgn>
                </dsgns>
                <title>Regional Vice President</title>
            </person>
        </impr_names>
        <cmplnc_pargph>The financial representative is licensed.</cmplnc_pargph>
        <repNumber>3557</repNumber>
        <qty_ord>500</qty_ord>
        <descr>Standard Letterhead</descr>
    </Order>
```

Although the creation of the files was relatively straightforward, several issues needed to be addressed. First, the XML needed to be transmitted exactly as it was entered. This included any special characters such as accents, ampersands, and apostrophes that the user may have entered. Next, the XML that was created needed to be valid and complete. For example, each address that was entered needed to have a corresponding state and postal code. Both of these issues were addressed by creating a **Document Type Declaration (DTD)** that would accompany the XML.

Unfortunately, the standardization of industry specific DTDs and XML schemas is just now starting to become pervasive through the help of organizations such as the Organization for the Advancement of Structured Information Standards (OASIS). Although there are currently some offerings from UN/EDIFACT and initiatives by ebXML, the project team decided to wait until a clear industry accepted standard emerged. In the mean time, a simple proprietary DTD was created. After a clear industry standard evolves, the custom DTD will be replaced with a suitable standard that can be easily shared throughout the industry.

Below is a portion of the DTD that was used to ensure that each order record was accurate. First, there is an ENTITY definition for each of the special characters that could be included in the stationery items. These characters include formatting characters like accents (á), and tildes (ã), as well as reserved characters like the ampersand (&). Next, each item that could appear in the order was defined as an ELEMENT. Not only did the ELEMENT tags help define the layout of the document, they also ensured that each order contained the required pieces of data in the correct order.

```
<!ENTITY Aacute "&#193;">
<!ENTITY Atilde "&#195;">
<!ENTITY Eacute "&#201;">
...
<!ENTITY ntilde "&#241;">
<!ENTITY otilde "&#245;">
<!ENTITY divide "&#247;">
<!ENTITY yuml "&#255;">
<!ELEMENT Order (req_num, item_num, logo_type, impr_addr, impr_city,
                 impr_st, impr_zip, phones, email, impr_names,
                 cmplnc_pargph, repNumber, qty_ord, descr)>
<!ELEMENT repNumber (#PCDATA)>
<!ELEMENT cmplnc_pargph (#PCDATA)>
<!ELEMENT descr (#PCDATA)>
<!ELEMENT dsgn EMPTY>
```

```
<!ELEMENT dsgns (dsgn+)>
<!ELEMENT email (#PCDATA)>
<!ELEMENT impr_addr (impr_addrline+)>
<!ELEMENT impr_addrline (#PCDATA)>
<!ELEMENT impr_city (#PCDATA)>
<!ELEMENT impr_name (#PCDATA)>
<!ELEMENT impr_names (person+)+>
<!ELEMENT impr_st (#PCDATA)>
<!ELEMENT impr_zip (#PCDATA)>
<!ELEMENT item_num (#PCDATA)>
<!ELEMENT license EMPTY>
<!ELEMENT logo_type (#PCDATA)>
<!ELEMENT person (impr_name, dsgns, title, license)>
<!ELEMENT phone (#PCDATA)>
<!ELEMENT phones (phone+)>
<!ELEMENT qty_ord (#PCDATA)>
<!ELEMENT req_num (#PCDATA)>
<!ELEMENT title (#PCDATA)>
```

Once the order XML was created it was compressed, encrypted, and transferred via FTP to the printing company. FTP was used rather than HTTP because both the financial institution and the printing company already had FTP setups. Once the order was successfully transferred, the ordered status was updated on the database.

Order Processing Module

Although the order collection module is the user's main interaction with the process, the order-processing component is the piece of the application that actually generates the final product. Upon receiving the XML order files, the order processing system creates a postscript file. The file is then sent to the image setter to generate an electronic printing plate.

Early in the design of the application, several technical alternatives were considered for generating the output that was needed. The final technical selection needed to satisfy the following criteria:

❑   **Support for precise positioning of text and graphics** – Due to the compliance requirements discussed earlier, the text and graphics included in the letterhead had to be positioned exactly. This required the tool to support movements as accurate as 1/64 of an inch.

❑   **Support for high-resolution graphics** – In order to create professional quality printed material, high resolution graphic support was required. The image setter that was used to create the electronic plates supported graphics up to 2400 dots per inch (dpi). Therefore, the tool needed to be able to create files containing images of that resolution.

❑   **Support for custom fonts and font metrics** – Again, the material being produced was stationery for a financial institution. The tool could not solely support the fourteen base fonts included in the PDF specification. Rather, it needed to support any font or modification to the font (such as leading, kerning, etc.) that the design dictated.

Since the printing company had proficiency with QuarkXPress, one alternative considered was to utilize a tool from Quark called avenue.quark (http://www.quark.com/products/avenue.quark) that allowed XML data to be imported into a QuarkXPress document and have styles applied to it. Although this approach took advantage of the printing company's Quark knowledgebase, it suffered from the fact that the import software was still in beta at the time of construction. In addition, with the large number of anticipated orders it would have required an increase in project staff to format the orders. Consequently, a more automated solution was desired.

The next alternative considered was to create a custom parser for the XML that would read through the order information and create a hand generated PDF file. This approach would use a tool like PageLayout from Sitraka (http://www.sitraka.com, formerly KL Group, http://www.klg.com) or iText (http://www.lowagie.com/iText/). Once the PDF was generated it would be converted to postscript and sent to the printer for processing. Although this alternative could be automated to remove human intervention and error, it also would result in a product that would be proprietary, difficult to extend, and time consuming to build.

The final alternative considered was to implement **XSL Format Objects** (**FO**), which we encountered in Chapter 7.

> *For additional information about FO, please see the XSL specification maintained by the World Wide Web Consortium (W3C) at http://www.w3.org/TR/xsl/slice6.html#fo-section.*

FO offered the benefits of the two previous alternatives without their disadvantages. A style sheet similar to a Quark style sheet could be applied to the XML order data in an automated fashion. At the time of construction, two options were considered:

❑ RenderX's XEP Rendering Engine (http://www.renderx.com)

❑ Apache's FOP (http://xml.apache.org/fop/index.html).

FOP offered the advantages of having a working product available along with ability to obtain the source code to modify as needed. Therefore, FOP was the product chosen.

After deciding to implement a FOP based solution, the process for creating the output needed to be defined. The following activity diagram illustrates the flow of the orders through the order-processing component:

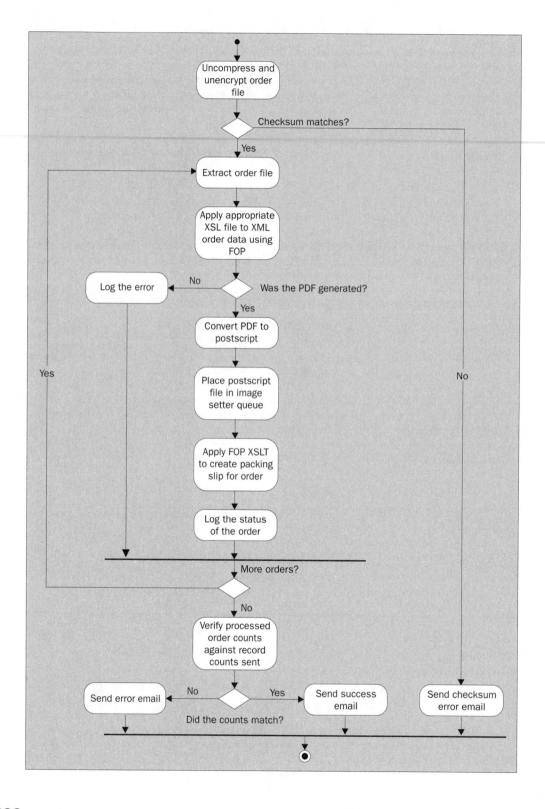

After the file containing the orders for the day was transferred to the FTP site, a UNIX `cron` job would start a Java program, which would run against the file to produce the stationery items.

Since each stationery item was assigned a unique item number, it was possible to create a corresponding XSL file that was used to layout that stationery item. Below is an example of the XSLT needed by FOP to create the letterhead for the financial representatives:

```xsl
<xsl:stylesheet xmlns:xsl="http://www.w3.org/1999/XSL/Transform"
      xmlns:svg="http://www.w3.org/Graphics/SVG/SVG-19990812.dtd"
      xmlns:fo="http://www.w3.org/1999/XSL/Format"
      result-encoding="ISO-8859-1">

<!-- defines the layout master -->
<xsl:template match="Order">
<fo:root>
   <fo:layout-master-set>
      <fo:simple-page-master page-master-name="first"
         page-height="15.5in" page-width="10.25in"
         margin-top="0in"
         margin-bottom="0in"
         margin-left="0in"
         margin-right="0in">
         <fo:region-body/>
      </fo:simple-page-master>
   </fo:layout-master-set>

<!-- starts actual layout -->
   <fo:page-sequence>
   <!-- applies layout master -->
   <fo:sequence-specification>
      <fo:sequence-specifier-single page-master-name="first"/>
   </fo:sequence-specification>

<!-- Set up the main body of the page -->
   <fo:flow flow-name="xsl-body">

<!-- Upper leg of Page Registration Bar (PRB)-->
<!-- A line created on the outside of the document
            that will be used to line the plate up for production-->
      <fo:block-container position="absolute" left="0in" top="0in"
                    right="10.25in" bottom=".25in"
                    background-color="black"/>

<!-- Right leg of  P.R.B. -->
      <fo:block-container position="absolute" left="10in" top="0in"
                          right="10.25in" bottom="15.5in"
                          background-color="black"/>

<!-- Use the the addlogo template to
            add the logo and company information to the page -->
      <xsl:call-template name="addlogo"/>

<!-- Display the address and title text box -->
      <fo:block-container position="absolute" left="6.25in"
                    right="8.7328125in" top="2.4921875in"
```

```
                            bottom="5.6in">
            <fo:block text-align="push">
               <fo:block text-align="start">

                  <fo:block font-family="Franklin-Gothic" font-size="8pt"
                           text-align="start" line-height="10.03pt"
                           letter-spacing="101s">
<!-- List each person found by applying the impr_names template -->
                     <xsl:apply-templates select="impr_names"/>
                  </fo:block>

<!-- Add the address information -->
                  <fo:block font-family="Franklin-Gothic" font-size="8pt"
                           text-align="start" line-height="10.65625pt"
                           letter-spacing="101s">
                     <xsl:for-each select="impr_addr/impr_addrline">
                        <xsl:if test="string-length(.) &gt; 0">
                           <fo:block line-height="10.65625pt"
                                    white-space-treatment="preserve">
                              <xsl:value-of select="."/>
                           </fo:block>
                        </xsl:if>
                     </xsl:for-each>

<!-- Add the city, state, zip information -->
                     <fo:block white-space-treatment="preserve">
                        <xsl:value-of select="impr_city"/><xsl:text>,
                                          </xsl:text>
                        <xsl:value-of select="impr_st"/><xsl:text> </xsl:text>
                        <xsl:value-of select="impr_zip"/>
                     </fo:block>

<!-- Print all phone numbers by calling the phones template -->
                     <xsl:apply-templates select="phones"/>

<!-- Print contact email address -->
                     <fo:block line-height="10.65625pt"
                                 letter-spacing="01s">
                        <xsl:value-of select="email"/>
                     </fo:block>
                  </fo:block>
               </fo:block>
            </fo:block>
         </fo:block-container>

<!-- Display the footer text including the compliance information-->
      <fo:block-container position="absolute" left="1.75in"
                        right="8.25in"  top="8.75in"
                        bottom="11.73125in">
         <fo:block text-align="drop">
            <fo:block text-align="start">

               <fo:block font-size="6pt"
                        font-family="Franklin-Gothic"
                        line-height="8.25pt" letter-spacing="251s">
```

```
                    <xsl:value-of select="cmplnc_pargph"/>
                </fo:block>
            </fo:block>
        </fo:block>
    </fo:block-container>

<!-- U/L corner cut mark -->
    <fo:block-container position="absolute" left=".35in"
                        top=".85in" width=".4in" height=".4in">
        <fo:block>
            <svg:svg width=".4in" height=".4in">
                <svg:line x1="0in" y1=".4in" x2=".3in" y2=".4in"/>
                <svg:line x1=".4in" y1="0in" x2=".4in" y2=".3in"/>
            </svg:svg>
        </fo:block>
    </fo:block-container>

<!-- U/L comment field that is printed outside the document
                    for internal processing-->
<!-- This includes the request number, item number,
                    description, and quantity ordered-->
    <fo:block-container position="absolute" left=".85in"
                        top=".35in" width="4.5in" height=".5in">
        <fo:block font-size="7pt" line-height="7pt"
                  font-family="Franklin-Gothic">
            <fo:block>
                REQ: <xsl:value-of select="req_num"/>
            </fo:block>
            <fo:block>
                ITEM: <xsl:value-of select="item_num"/>
            </fo:block>
            <fo:block>
                DSCR: <xsl:value-of select="descr"/>
            </fo:block>
            <fo:block>
                QUANTITY: <xsl:value-of select="qty_ord"/>
            </fo:block>
        </fo:block>
    </fo:block-container>
    </fo:flow>
    </fo:page-sequence>
</fo:root>
</xsl:template>

<!--Phone template that will add all the phone numbers in the XML document-->
<xsl:template match="phones">
    <!-- Print all phones -->
    <xsl:for-each select="phone">
        <xsl:if test="string-length(.) &gt; 0">
            <fo:block >
                <xsl:value-of select="."/>
            </fo:block>
        </xsl:if>
    </xsl:for-each>
</xsl:template>
```

```
<!--Name template that will add all the names to be included
                         in the letterhead in the XML document-->
<xsl:template match="impr_names">
   <xsl:for-each select="person[string-length(impr_name) &gt;0]">
      <fo:block font-weight="bold" font-size="9.5pt"
               line-height="10.02pt" space-after.optimum = "1pt">
         <xsl:value-of select="impr_name"/>
         <xsl:if test="string-length(dsgns/dsgn) > 0">
            <fo:inline-sequence font-size="9.5pt">
               <xsl:text>,</xsl:text>
            </fo:inline-sequence>
            <fo:inline-sequence font-size="9.5pt" letter-spacing="-801s">
               <xsl:text> </xsl:text>
            </fo:inline-sequence>
         </xsl:if>

         <fo:inline-sequence font-size="8pt">
            <xsl:for-each select="dsgns/dsgn">
               <xsl:if test="string-length(.) > 0">
                  <xsl:if test="position() > 1">
                     <xsl:text>, </xsl:text>
                  </xsl:if>
                  <xsl:value-of select="."/>
               </xsl:if>
            </xsl:for-each>
         </fo:inline-sequence>
      </fo:block>

<!-- add license, if it exists -->
      <xsl:if test="string-length(title) = 0">
         <xsl:if test="string-length(license)">
            <fo:block font-size="8pt" line-height="10.02pt">
               <xsl:value-of select="license"/>
            </fo:block>
         </xsl:if>
      </xsl:if>

<!-- add title -->
      <fo:block font-size="8pt" line-height="10.02pt">
         <xsl:value-of select="title"/>
      </fo:block>
      <fo:block line-height="10.02pt" space-after.optimum="10.375pt">
         <xsl:text> </xsl:text>
      </fo:block>
   </xsl:for-each>
</xsl:template>

<xsl:template name="addgroupname">
   <xsl:param name="baseline">.427</xsl:param>
   <xsl:param name="imagename">images/ClassicLogo.tif</xsl:param>
   <xsl:variable name="whitespace" select=".1"/>
   <fo:block-container position="absolute" left="1.059375in"
                     top="1.513in" width="6in" height="1.25in">
      <fo:block>
```

```
            <fo:display-graphic height="1.25in" width="3.75in"
                            href="{$imagename}" />
        </fo:block>
    </fo:block-container>
    <fo:block-container position="absolute" left="1.739583444in"
                        top="{$baseline + 1.625202889}in" width="6in"
                        height="1.25in">
    </fo:block-container>
</xsl:template>

<!--Logo template that will add all the correct logo
                        based on what is in the XML document-->
<xsl:template name="addlogo">
    <xsl:variable name="logotype" select=".1"/>
    <xsl:choose>
        <xsl:when test="logo_type = 'Classic Corporate Logo'">
            <xsl:call-template name="addgroupname">
                <xsl:with-param name="imagename">
                    images/ClassicLogo.tif</xsl:with-param>
                <xsl:with-param name="baseline">.715</xsl:with-param>
            </xsl:call-template>
        </xsl:when>
        <xsl:when test="logo_type = 'Fancy Corporate Logo'">
            <xsl:call-template name="addgroupname">
                <xsl:with-param name="imagename">
                    images/FancyLogo.tif</xsl:with-param>
                <xsl:with-param name="baseline">.715</xsl:with-param>
            </xsl:call-template>
        </xsl:when>
        <xsl:when test="logo_type = 'Generic Logo'">
            <xsl:call-template name="addgroupname">
                <xsl:with-param name="baseline">.536</xsl:with-param>
                <xsl:with-param name="imagename">
                    images/GenericLogo.tif</xsl:with-param>
            </xsl:call-template>
        </xsl:when>
    </xsl:choose>
</xsl:template>
</xsl:stylesheet>
```

As you can see, FOP makes extensive use of XSL Format Objects and allows the display of text and images to be precisely controlled. The FOP engine from Apache reads the information contained in the format objects in the XLST and creates professionally formatted PDF from it.

Text and Graphic Positioning

The FOP XSLT above is divided into multiple block containers. Each of these containers is a block-level reference area that is positioned at a precise location on the page. The following XSL defines a block container that will host multiple blocks (paragraphs) that will contain the compliance text at the bottom of the letterhead:

```
<!-- Display the footer text including the compliance information-->
<fo:block-container position="absolute" left="1.75in" right="8.25in"
                    top="8.75in" bottom="11.73125in">
…
</fo:block-container>
```

Each block container will then have multiple block definitions. A block definition is used to define precise formatting options for a section of text. For example, the XSLT below will format the compliance information to use the Franklin Gothic font in 6 point:

```
<fo:block text-align="drop">
    <fo:block text-align="start">
        <fo:block font-size="6pt"
            font-family="Franklin-Gothic"
            line-height="8.25pt"
            letter-spacing="251s">
            <xsl:value-of select="cmplnc_pargph"/>
        </fo:block>
    </fo:block>
</fo:block>
```

As you can see, FOP allows you to control many aspects of the physical presentation including font, point size, and letter spacing. In addition, it also provides basic vector graphic capability. In order to line up the electronic plate for production, cut marks and alignment lines were needed. FOP transforms the following XSL into a thin line. This line is included in the PDF and subsequent postscript for alignment of the printed material:

```
<fo:block-container position="absolute" left=".35in" top="12.25in"
                    width=".4in" height=".4in">
    <fo:block>
        <svg:svg width=".4in" height=".4in">
            <svg:line x1=".4in" y1=".1in" x2=".4in" y2=".4in"/>
            <svg:line x1="0in" y1="0in" x2=".3in" y2="0in"/>
        </svg:svg>
    </fo:block>
</fo:block-container>
```

High Resolution Graphic Support

Although FOP met most of the requirements for the order processing system, one of the deficiencies of version 0.12.2 was its graphic support (a deficiency that still exists in the latest version 0.15). Since it only reliably supported 72 dpi images, a work around was needed to meet the required 2400 dpi. Since there were a finite number of images, image fragment files were created that could be included directly in the generated PDF file. For each required image in the stationery item, a stand-alone PDF file that contained the high-resolution graphic was created. This process required each graphic that was to be included in the stationary to be opened up in Adobe Acrobat and saved out as a separate PDF file. For each stationary item that was created, the appropriate graphic file fragments were included in the dynamic PDF document at run time.

In order to do this, the FOP source code needed to be modified. FOP was configured so that when it encountered an image in the XSL it opened up the corresponding image fragment file and included it directly in the generated PDF document. For example, using the letterhead XSL above, the HREF for the classic corporate logo would be replaced with the PDF of the high-resolution image fragment.

Font Support

Another area where FOP needed to be extended was font support. Natively, FOP 0.12.2 supports the 14 base fonts in the PDF specification. However, there were specific fonts required in the stationery that are not included in the base FOP installation. In order to add the special fonts we needed to compile our fonts into the build of FOP that was used.

This involved creating an XML file that described the font metrics. Next, a FOP utility was used to create the corresponding Java font classes that were then built into FOP allowing the new font to be included in the generated PDF file.

Producing Input for the Image Setter

Once all the code changes were made to FOP and the XSL files were created for each stationery item the following PDF was created by issuing the following command:

```
java org.apache.fop.apps.XTCommandLine order.xml stationery.xsl output.pdf
```

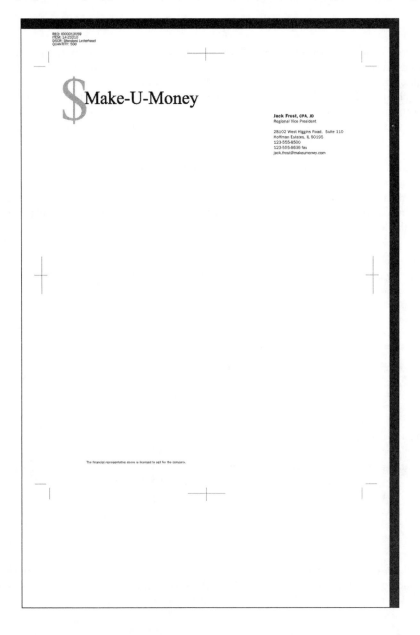

The above command instructs FOP to create the file `output.pdf` by applying `stationery.xsl` to `order.xml`, although FOP could also be instructed to do so programmatically. Once the PDF document was generated it was ready to have an electronic plate or film created. Since the image setter hardware used did not accept PDF natively, the PDF files were automatically converted to a postscript file using Xpdf (http://www.foolabs.com/xpdf/). The postscript files were created by issuing the following Xpdf command to convert the FOP generated PDF files into a postscript files:

```
pdftops -paperw 738 -paperh 1116 file.pdf file.ps
```

Once the postscript files were created they were moved to the image setter queue, and films were created.

Finishing Up

The actual stationery item was only part of what needed to be produced by the printing company. In addition to creating the actual printed product, it was necessary to generate audit, billing, and shipping information. The audit information verified that all the orders were processed as they were entered. Each of the financial representatives needed to be billed for their stationery items, so an accurate record of what was actually produced was necessary. Finally, to complete each order a packing slip was needed to ensure that the correct items were processed, packaged, and shipped to the appropriate financial representative.

Since all of the information needed to fulfill the audit, billing, and shipping requirements pertaining to the actual production of the job, a detailed log file was deemed the best source for the information. Because the data that was being collected would be presented in different views, an XML format was chosen for the log file. As the example below illustrates, detailed information regarding each order was captured in the log file:

```
<log>
    <message type="info">
        <time>10/27/2000 06:00:04</time>
        <text>Opened /order.zip</text>
    </message>

    <message type="info">
        <time>10/27/2000 06:00:09</time>
        <text>PDF Generated: 20001027/Letterhead/1_I000013059_14-3210.pdf
        </text>
    </message>

    <message type="order">
        <time>10/27/2000 06:00:09</time>
        <text>"I000013059","3557","Jack Frost","14-3210",
            "Letterhead/Imprinted/Standard Letterhead", "500", "IL"
        </text>
        <status>ok</status>
    </message>
</log>
```

After all of the orders were processed for the day, the log file was used to compare the record counts with those included in the original order file from the financial institution. If there were any errors or discrepancies, a notification e-mail was sent to the printing company using JavaMail.

Since the log file contained information regarding what was actually processed, it was the ideal source for billing information. Because the log file was XML, it was possible to use XLST to create a **comma separated value** (CSV) file containing the billing information. That billing file was then imported into the printing company's financial system for invoicing back to the financial institution.

Finally, the summary file was used as the source to build the packing slips that were included in each order. Using FOP and the XML summary file, PDF quality packing slips were created to include with each order and to assist with the timely distribution of the stationery. Below is a sample of the packing slips that were built and included with each order:

PACKING SLIP - THIS IS NOT AN INVOICE

Page 1
ORDER TRANSCRIPT

$Make-U-Money
555 Avenue of Americans
Blanco de Papier, New York, 11111

DATE OF ORDER: 20001026

1000013059	3557
ORDER NUMBER	REP NO.

REFER TO ORDER NUMBER WHEN
INQUIRING ABOUT THIS ORDER
PLEASE INCLUDE THIS TRANSCRIPT WITH ALL
RETURNED ITEMS FROM THIS ORDER

SHIP TO: Jack Frost

28102 West Higgins Road, Suite 110
Hoffman Estates, IL 27514

Direct Inquiries on returns to : (800) 555-1212

ITEM NUMBER	DESCRIPTION	QNTY ORDERED	QNTY SHIPPED
14-23210	Standard Letterhead	500	

707

Results

So what was the result of the complete system? Was it a success? Reviewing the critical success factors outlined earlier and determining how the system measured against them can best answer these questions.

The first success factor was that all the letterheads had to be compliant with federal and state laws. As discussed earlier, the FOP engine provides precise control over the placement of the content on the stationery. To that end, it was possible to physically create stationery that met the strict regulations. In addition, the order entry system was able to verify that the information entered about the financial representative was accurate. Therefore, the system was able to meet all of the compliance standards.

Next, "time to market" was measured. The project team was able to meet all of the deadlines that were placed before them. The selection of a thin-client application made it possible to rollout the project gradually, in phases, without having to worry too much about deployment issues. Since the development team did not have to worry about deploying a new version of the application to every one of the ten thousand financial representatives, they could easily place new versions of the software on the server and deploy the changes to the entire company.

Hand in hand with the compliance requirement was the accuracy of the system. Since the data was being passed exactly as was it entered, it was possible to eliminate all internal data entry errors. This allowed the burden of accuracy to be placed on the person entering the order, thereby satisfying the accuracy critical success factor.

The application met the security requirement by encrypting and compressing the order information that was transmitted using the standard Java compression and encryption libraries. In addition, LDAP was used to verify the credentials of each user to ensure that valid users were placing orders. Finally, checksums were utilized to ensure that none of the data was altered or lost during transmission.

Cost effectiveness was the final factor to be measured. In the first three months, the system was able to process over 12,000 orders. Assuming that it would take about 30 minutes to layout each order, it would have taken roughly six thousand hours for the printing company to layout the first month's orders. If you could find the twelve people needed to complete this task, it would have cost over $120,000 in the first quarter alone! This does not take into account any rework that would have been introduced due to manually processing each order.

Additionally, the financial company was able to eliminate over eight thousand hours of manually reviewing each and every order. Again, if it had been possible to find the sixteen people needed to do this, it would have cost over $130,000. The financial savings in the first quarter alone indicated that the project had met its objective of being cost effective. This will continue to grow as new products are added to the system and more orders are processed.

The solution also provided the flexibility to rerun orders after they had already been produced. For example, there were some last minute compliance changes to the stationery items. All that needed to be done was that the XML data be rerun against the new XSLT files containing the compliance changes. Without the automated system, this change would have doubled the cost of the already run stationery items.

Learning Points

Given that the complete system met the critical success factors in a cost effective manner, it was considered a great success. With all projects, successful or not, it is important to review what was learned during the process. The following are some key aspects to take away from this project:

❑ **Performance of XSLT/FOP** – XSLT provides a significant amount of flexibility regarding the formatting and presentation of XML data. Although this application dealt with a relatively small amount of data quite well, as the XSL based FOP engine was tested with larger quantities of data the performance of document creation started to deteriorate. In addition, the performance of the user interface generated for the order collection and approval system was at times slow. The project team is currently evaluating JSP to see if it can improve the performance of the online portion of the application.

❑ **Load Testing** – Since this application was intended to support a large number of users over a short amount of time, system load testing was vital to the success of the project. It is important to remember that the goal of load testing is to find out *where* the system will break down, not *if.* By obtaining this information upfront it was possible to configure the systems to spread out the load so that all the users could get their orders processed. In addition, the use of J2EE allowed the application to start as a basic servlet and eventually move to a distributed EJB based solution.

❑ **Validating User Input** – When dealing with a system that will take the user's input and place it directly on a printed product, validation of the user input is essential. Through the extensive use of JavaScript, the order collection module was able to minimize the amount of data errors.

❑ **Working with Open Source Tools** – This project was heavily based in open source tools. From the Xerces parser and Xalan XSLT processor used to render the HTML pages in the order collection module, to the FOP and Xpdf tools utilized to create the dynamic output, this system could not have been built (within budget) without open source tools.

Having said that, it is important to realize that open source tools are not for everyone. It takes a team that is willing and able to accept a tool that they may have to make modifications to. As mentioned earlier, modifications were needed to support both high-resolution graphics and custom fonts. Although this particular project team was able to prosper in this environment, this can be a culture shock to those people used to working exclusively with shrink-wrapped software and a support agreement!

❑ **State of Industry Standard DTDs and Schemas** – Although many strides have been made over the past months regarding industry standard schemas, there is still a deficiency in the creation and enforcement of these standards. However, many promising offerings are becoming available such as ebXML (www.ebxml.org).

Summary

Through the use of the Java enterprise tools it was possible to build a system that would automate processes in an industry that historically has been very labor intensive. These tools not only were able to complete the tasks, but they were able to do it faster and cheaper. In the long run the J2EE suite of tools will provide more accurate, secure, and cost effective stationery products for financial representatives worldwide.

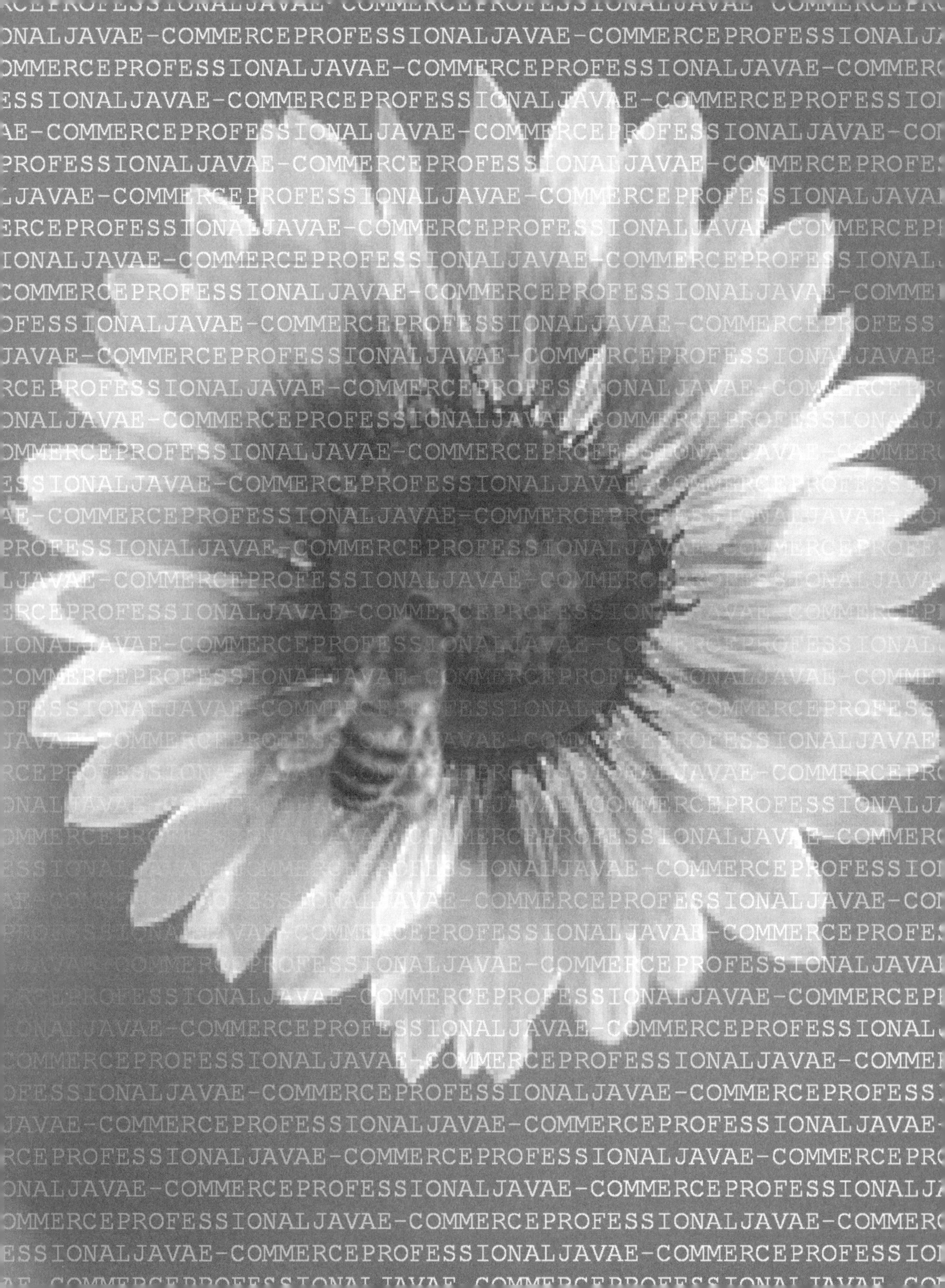
PROFESSIONALJAVAE-COMMERCE

B2B E-Commerce: Internet Application Service Providers

ASP is an acronym for **Application Service Provider**. The context of these words is self-describing. It means a company that *provides* a business related *service(s)* in the form of a leased-type software *application* and maintenance of that application. In the new Internet global community, ASPs provide a strong service that might not have been possible even five years ago.

Computing is escaping the confines of individual enterprise data centers and is working its way into the open spaces of the shared, global network called the Internet. The bottom line is computing has to change – and businesses must also change the way they think about computing.

This chapter focuses on Internet Application Service Providers and the Internet delivery model for ASPs, involving web based Business to Business (B2B) and Business to Consumer (B2C) e-commerce situations. There are many other service delivery models that could be more appropriate in other scenarios, but they are not included in this text. Specifically, we'll be looking at the things you should look for when considering using an ASP as part of your system. In this respect, this short chapter comes as something of a break from the more code intensive earlier chapters, as we take a more general view of things.

The first section will cover why outsourcing is an attractive proposition, and how the standard model can be applied to software. The second section covers many different aspects that need to be considered in an ASP's software architecture, while the third section brings together the art of building a network system of services and how the different services work together to bring a unified solution to an ASP's customers. We'll wrap up by taking a close look at what is involved in selecting an ASP in an IT project, and when it might make sense to use one. In this chapter, then, we look at the following things:

- ❏ Outsourcing
- ❏ When using an ASP makes sense
- ❏ ASP architecture
- ❏ Building a network system
- ❏ Choosing an ASP
- ❏ The future of ASPs

Outsourcing

Outsourcing has been widely accepted in all forms of business. Companies have realized that a good portion of their time is spent on issues that do not lie in their core competencies, which in turn takes away from the things that their employees are skilled at. This sometimes costs the company three to four times more money and company resources than it would by outsourcing to a team of experts.

Technology and software are not exceptions. Recent polls and statistics have proven that desktop computers, custom and/or "off-the-shelf" software packages, and a fully armed and ready department of information technology professionals is not always the best way to utilize its people and computing resources. This is mainly because each of these three things has a time-value on them, which is a constant struggle and expense. Software for many business processes is expensive. There is the initial purchase cost, then the costs of upgrades, followed by integration and technical support to incorporate it into the organization. Software is increasingly not a one-time purchase, but a recurring purchase as versions increase with new features added, and perceived as needed. ASPs take the next logical step where software and support are fused as a service package; instead of a purchase being made, the package is leased. An Application Service Provider looks for commonalities in certain business processes and attempts to meet those needs on a modular level.

Outsourcing (of any kind) can both improve time-to-market, and make more effective use of a company's existing IT personnel. The financial savings this can represent may allow the company to expand far quicker than if they had produced everything internally. With a good ASP, so many IT problems need no longer concern the company, which can spend its time and effort in more effectively pursuing its chosen field.

With the strong acceptance of the Internet and extranets as a way to do business, the evolution would be for a company to outsource as much of their business technology as possible to result in the following:

- ❏ Easier software/process upgrade cycles
- ❏ Quicker time to market
- ❏ Predictable costs
- ❏ Lower initial investment by the bundling of many up-front and ongoing costs into the monthly application rental fee, and minimizing the pre-implementation application setup costs
- ❏ Ability to focus on core competencies
- ❏ Provide a better solution to mobile or geographically distributed work force
- ❏ Future proof: the ability to scale immediately if necessary
- ❏ Minimization of infrastructure costs for support of the application

Consider the following chart:

	ASP	Off the shelf products	Consultant based Integration Projects	In house Integration Projects
Upgrading Software	Included	Purchase, or licensing agreement	Refactor (rebuilding sections) Software	Refactor Software
Time to Market	Instant-short	Instant-short	Project based	Project based
Predictable Cost	Yes, usually transaction based	Yes, through licensing agreement	Not usually	No
Initial Investment	Generally none	Yes, as well as preferred hardware	Yes, in company resources for joint projects	Sometimes
Core Competencies	Allows company to focus	Sometimes	Allows company to focus	Sometimes, based on the project
Mobile work force	Yes	Sometimes	If a requirement, not automatically	If a requirement, not automatically
Scale immediately	Not a concern, ASP should address and prove	Unknown	Unknown	Unknown

Outsourcing does have its drawbacks, though:

❑ Dependency on third parties for more than just packaged software and support, including actual uptime, scalability, pricing.

❑ Higher cost in dollars spent – Savings are measured in allowing a business to focus on core competencies, fewer production headaches to deal with, less "overhead", etc. These savings are sometimes hard to justify, and the return on investment could be many years, or have a break-even point closer than expected.

❑ Trusting third parties with intellectual property of the company using the service and their customers.

Lease vs. Own Mentality

Consider leasing versus buying a car. When buying, that car belongs to the owner, and whatever happens to it is the owner's responsibility. The owner has to do his or her own maintenance, take care of major repairs, and decide when to "sunset" the car and buy another one when the total cost of ownership (TCO) has become more than the monthly payment. Leasing promises to take care of most of these problems in many situations. Every three years, an individual can trade the car in for a newer model, and walk away. Oil changes and regular maintenance are covered in the original service agreement; however, the person leasing the car still has to pay for excessive mileage (transactions) and excessive wear.

Licensed software products usually require an up front fee and a sizable cost to "integrate" their system, leaving the company with a brilliant enterprise software package that solves all of the business problems of today, but not tomorrow. Consequently, a year later a company begins to shelve or sunset old products and starts this vicious cycle all over. An automobile on the other hand generally has a longer product life (10-15 years), but it follows the same pattern over a longer period of time.

If a company leases a solution, or modules of its business, it generally pays a transaction-based fee. The company can gradually begin its new services and only pay for what it uses on an as needed basis. Companies can take advantage of new technologies when they arise, without throwing away the existing technology. With service-based software (leasing), companies have the security of knowing that upgrading is included in the package, as well as the opportunity of switching to another comparable service if necessary. Although this is the dream and can turn out to be true in many cases, business marketing is not always as it appears. Some things to consider when selecting an ASP and the risks vs. rewards involved are covered later in this chapter.

Leasing software applications and solutions can reduce costs through a minimization of support costs. It also spreads many of the normally up-front costs into an ongoing monthly rental fee. Finally, many of the pre-implementation setup costs can be avoided or minimized.

When Does Using an ASP Make Sense?

There are many reasons why using an ASP can be the correct thing to do in many situations. They are listed below:

- ❑ Outsourcing of one or more business functions. As mentioned before, more and more companies are realizing that the key to their success is to outsource (as many as possible) activities peripheral to their core competencies and business model.

- ❑ Self-contained services – all-inclusive. In some industries, the limiting factor for companies is the software that they use. They are "locked-in" to a proprietary solution that does not allow them to achieve the success that is expected, and the monthly maintenance and upgrade fees for this type of solution creeps up on them year after year.

- ❑ Zero IT administration. This can also be a catch-22. An ASP can prevent the IT headache that goes along with every business, from items ranging to tape backups, computer configuration, technical support, expensive IT Services, etc. On the other side of the coin, the ASP's customer loses a lot of the original control that it had, and with the wrong ASP, that could put the customer out of business.

❑ "Instant On" business services. ASP customers could potentially cut project schedules down to half or a third of their original time span by obtaining modular services from an ASP that can be transparently plugged into their project. These "Instant On" re-usable business services would be a great benefit to anyone fighting tight deadlines and lowered budgets.

ASP Architecture

There are several major features that must be inherent in the software architecture of any ASP system (actually, any enterprise system). These features are important things to look for when considering using an ASP, and particularly if you are considering building an ASP. They are **modularity**, **uptime**, **scalability**, **pooling**, and **transactions**.

Modularity

❑ One virtual "system" for multiple clients. This means that if the system should fail, it needs to be on a per-user or per-session basis, as opposed to per-module on a system-wide basis. It is an important fact to remember, because general system redundancy implemented by administrators such as database and OS clustering, hardware load balancing, mirrored drives, etc., are important in enterprise systems, but do not always solve problems that are caused by poor software architecture and planning.

❑ Utilizing multiple data schemas – generally called "partitioning" the database – is one way to achieve this modularity. There are two types of partitioning – vertical, where each ASP customer has their own schema (that holds all of their customer's information), and horizontal, where database schemas are separated by logical business units of the entire system.

❑ The application should also act as a single unit across multiple datacenters.

❑ Modules/Components/Applications/Messaging – a system that is composed of many different pieces is very important for modularity. This allows for features to be turned on and off, and added on the fly.

Uptime

❑ Uptime is very important for everyone, and all of an ASP's customers could have different sets of operating schedules across 24-7 operations.

❑ Customer Service and Support in a 24-7 or similar schedule.

Having each client maintained individually (in the same system) is a must to keep uptime and general system maintenance operation at a high level of success. An important note to emphasize is that system upgrades should be able to be performed for one client without bringing other clients down.

For companies that operate on a global scale, internationalization issues come into play. Consider that the "8am to 5pm" hours in Denver, is actually 8pm to 5pm on the other side of the globe. Even if all of an ASP's customers run "normal" business hours, the ASP still has to support a 24-7 operation, and perform maintenance across multiple time zones.

Scalability

❑ For an ASP to be successful, how many clients might it have? The pricing model of many ASPs will only allow it to be successful if it has hundreds, and probably thousands of clients. A scalable system will allow quick and seamless growth in capacity to handle adding many new clients (web applications) between versions of the base software without interruption.

❑ More computers versus bigger computers – near infinite expandability by just adding computers and adding data centers is desirable. Make sure that the system is set up for application partitioning – sharing the load between two or more application servers. Each layer in the APS should be scalable.

Pooling

❑ Connections to data sources should always be pooled. This includes database, LDAP, and index connections. Probably one of the most expensive operations in enterprise systems is opening up a datasource or a socket, especially when these are only used for a brief moment in time before being closed again.

❑ Another very expensive operation could be dealing with object instances, either distributed or local. The load that is expected in a large-scale system could easily bring some systems to their knees due to object creation, object initialization, and garbage collection if these things are not handled properly.

Transactions

❑ Transactions are a very important part of any distributed system for many reasons, including the recovery and rollback from a network failure, hardware failure, etc. One of the basic concepts of an ASP is that it is an outsourced part of a company's business technology. Since other companies rely on an ASP to be a solid module in their business process, it is absolutely imperative that this piece is as good as it can be and transactions are always reliable and secure.

❑ An all-encompassing rule for transactions is to make them ACID based: Atomic, Consistent, Isolated, and Durable.

Programming Guidelines

There are many new paradigms and methodologies for programming guidelines that should be followed by an ASP building their system, and a customer choosing an ASP's system should also look at what has been used. These all have different meanings and come from different sources, that range from "eXtreme Programming (XP)" to use cases and UML documentation and so on. The key is that a software development company must choose the methodology that is appropriate for the task, and is compatible with the company's employees and their forthcoming projects. Finding a company that has chosen programming methodologies appropriate to their task is another key element when choosing an ASP.

From an ASP point of view, and Java Enterprise programming in general, there are a few rules of thumb that a company's whole development staff needs to embrace. Although these issues are important to the designers of the ASP, as a customer your needs are most important. If you have a need for something that is not on this list, or that goes against these rules of thumb, then you should make sure that it works – only choose technology that makes your work easier. These are:

❑ True "thin client". In essence, the only thing that ends up in the browser is HTML and Java applets.

❑ Choose a company that is sparing and careful in its use of ActiveX controls, Java applets, JavaScript, Macromedia, etc. Many times, an ASP will provide just a small piece of a customer's larger system or even single pages, and the piece provided needs to be completely compatible with whatever standards that the customer might employ. If these technologies become required, then it is a good idea to test the functionality on all of the major browsers and two or three previous versions of each for compatibility.

An ASP's core value is robust business functionality, not fun and games. Having minimal JavaScript functionality that is packaged on the server (little code in each page), and handling things in groups rather than on a page-by-page level, will help to decrease complexity, decrease development and debug time, and ensure the stability of the application. Obviously the less time the ASP needs to spend on development and debugging, assuming the software still meets the other required standards, then the less you, the customer, should be charged.

❑ Server Side Java only. Do not forget about normal encapsulation and business objects – keep business logic out of the web pages. The Model-View-Controller design pattern is a must for any type of Web client to follow. Although detailed explanations of architectures is out of the scope of this chapter, *Professional JSP* from Wrox Press, ISBN *1-861004-65-6*, is an excellent source of different JSP/servlet/EJB architectures and when each one is appropriate for different situations.

❑ Internationalization should be considered on every enterprise project, and if not directly implemented, the architecture should incorporate the basic "hooks" in case this support is needed in the future.

Business Architectures

In the key points section above, the discussion revolved around the main points that need to be addressed to have a solid ASP foundation. Just as important as programming these features from the start is the importance of considering what it will take for an ASP to be successful from the system administrator or business person's point of view.

Traditional software companies might be interested in building an ASP offering because of things like easy upgrades, only having to support the "latest" version, steady revenue streams, building next generation software, etc. These are important factors when one considers building an ASP as an alternative to their legacy software.

System Redundancy

There are several factors to ensure system redundancy for an ASP. Although not all ASPs are completely responsible for everything from the client's computer to the datacenter, this section will cover situations for a full ASP offering that addresses computers needed, location of the hosting servers, and the client's way to connect and re-connect (if primary fails) to the datacenter.

Computers: Pieces of the Puzzle

The servers that run the application(s) that the ASP is offering usually model a distributed system that achieves the goals mentioned in the "*ASP Architecture*" section previously. Computers are truly the pieces of the puzzle to support an ASP environment by allowing all of the processes to perform on many different computers in a distributed nature. Although system architecture is out of the scope of this chapter, you can find detailed information about this topic in *Professional Java Server Side Programming – J2EE Edition* from Wrox Press, ISBN 8098450984.

Locations: Who is Hosting the ASP?

A very important concept to remember is that an ASP generally uses a publicly available network upon which to offer all of its services, which could possibly be the greatest weakness. Using the Internet as the network means that the data could flow through three or more different backbones and several different routers, switches, etc., offering up multiple opportunities for failure. There are three items to consider: the offerings of the datacenter itself, the importance of the capability of the software to span across multiple datacenter locations, and the privacy policy and statement of the datacenter.

❑ Redundant power, network, building, etc. are all important factors in picking a co-location home for a company's servers, as well as for in-house ASPs. There are even multiple levels of support ranging from rebooting servers when problems arise, to a "managed care" type of support that includes data monitoring, software backups, and routine system upgrades/maintenance. Full service ASPs are responsible for the end-user's application working 100 percent of the time, and a poorly managed datacenter will add uncontrollable risks for the provider's ability to serve their clients.

❑ An ASP does not want to put all of their eggs in one basket. ISPs of ASPs generally have some type of data replicating hardware/software through a Virtual Private Network (VPN) to a sister datacenter that allows full redundancy of the entire system, in case of a catastrophic failure of a certain location. The ASP's system must allow for this type of "whole system" redundancy.

❑ The co-location's privacy policy and statement is very important to an ASP and its customer base. The data center should be aware of the sensitivity of the data that the ASP is hosting, as well as the ASP's privacy policy agreement to its customers. Generally, there are several levels of co-location services that range from re-booting servers to the complete managed care solution that consist of software configuration and full service maintenance.

Client Connectivity

❑ What should be provided? Some or all of the hardware, software, and Internet connection? This is a tricky subject for an ASP, because it mainly depends on the type of software that is provided, and what it's main function is. For example, a user-driven ASP application would require a relatively inexpensive PC running Window95 or Windows98 at the user site (or they can use their own), a standard web browser, and an Internet connection from a local ISP. Many users at the same physical location can share the Internet connection in a secure fashion through a Network Address Translation (NAT) device, proxy server, or firewall installed at their site. A transaction driven ASP might just provide a URL to accept XML HTTP posts from another system.

❑ What is required? Actually, nothing but a web browser and a medium to connect to the data center (through the internet) should be the required mechanism for a web based ASP customer.

Building a Network System

As an Application Service Provider, the sky is the limit as to what can be done, connected to, provide services for, etc., for almost any kind of customer in the marketplace. The system that an ASP is built upon should not hinder any of these things, but rather enhance them with a distributed system. Imagine a world where every business and every person in that business focuses on their core competencies. This would allow everyone to achieve success at his or her full potential. Software would not be a hindrance, but rather an extension of people's jobs and an extension of business functions that need to be completed.

Each company would require a minimum of services of highly paid IT staff to "control the enterprise's assets" by implementing system standards and proprietary security policies not based on business requirements. Rather, the employees would request the services that they need over the Internet, and only pay for what they use to accomplish their daily tasks.

This in itself creates the opportunity for potentially unlimited access to resources of any type! Imagine a networked system that encompasses applications that can always be adapting to the Internet by connecting to other resources on the net (companion ASPs, other service providers.), allowing different companies to offer separate services such as HR, expenses, internal publications, etc. in an integrated fashion. Businesses applying these techniques to their own internal processes follow a new paradigm of computing that could give them a competitive advantage through their access of the Internet's resources, not through the ownership of internal resources.

Making Use of an "Always On" Internet Connection

Most companies today utilize an "always on" Internet connection, but it is often severely under used. Mainly this connection is used for research, downloading files, and email connectivity. There are vast untapped resources out there that can and should be used in the day-to-day activities of an individual and/or a business. These include publicly available web services and obtaining services from other ASPs or providers, among others. The only problem is: how does one connect to these services so that they appear to be a unified part of one application?

Connectivity Across the Web

To track the progress of computers and connectivity over the last 30 years, a recognizable order of events has developed. Systems transformed from mainframe computers, to independent proprietary systems, to client/server systems, to heterogeneous disconnected peer-to-peer systems, to multi-tier fat client systems, to thin client (web based) systems, and no one really knows what will happen next.

The goal of today and tomorrow's technology, and a great role for the ASP, is to offer a unified front of services that can be combined in one user interface and used as one system. This author's prediction is that the ASP industry will embrace some type of modular, independent technologies in the form of services, and then use portal type technology to implement it.

We have always been plagued by the same problem – connectivity among systems. As technology systems became more advanced, and accomplished more things for us, pure competition allowed several application-to-application standards to emerge to accomplish the same exact things, but in different ways. So, to build a distributed application using one of these technologies, one typically needs the same distributed object model or protocol running in both applications, which isn't always the case in an enterprise environment, and especially not in the realm of the Internet.

The only thing that the Internet can guarantee for a protocol standard is HTTP, and one might find that passing anything else on this globally shared network is generally not tolerated, and most likely blocked out by firewalls. This is where something like HTTP-Tunneling, Simple Object Access Protocol (SOAP), XML-RPC, or Resource Definition Framework (RDF) could have some real potential for a solution in this environment. Below is a short description of each:

- ❑ HTTP Tunneling – Allows a program to send a protocol such as RMI wrapped in an HTTP header for travel across a network. This will allow programs to communicate in their native language (say, applet to servlet communication with RMI) using an HTTP port 80 to travel through standard firewall openings.

- ❑ SOAP (Simple Object Access Protocol) – http://www.w3.org/TR/SOAP/ – a protocol specification for invoking methods on services, components and objects using XML and HTTP as a method invocation mechanism.

- ❑ XML-RPC (eXtensible Markup Language Remote Procedure Call) – http://www.xmlrpc.com/ – very similar conceptually to SOAP, differences to this author are based on preference.

❑ RDF (Resource Definition Framework) – http://www.w3.org/RDF/ – allows machine understandable descriptions of web services to have a Uniform Resource Identifier (URI) as their address. This provides interoperability between applications by exchanging metadata.

Public Services and Servers

Many vendors, suppliers, government agencies, etc. are jumping on the bandwagon to allow catalog information, shipping status, weather information, etc., to be publicly available to support customer demand and advertising needs. For example, http://www.xmethods.com created a list of SOAP service providers that allow one to access information by a simple function call. Soon we will see many government agencies making more and more information publicly available via a method such as SOAP, XML-RPC, or other similar services.

Such opportunities include the following:

❑ Package tracking

❑ Weather

❑ Stock quotes

❑ Exchange rates

❑ Catalog pricing on something

❑ Credit card authentication

❑ Health care claims processing

❑ Complicated financial equations

❑ Transaction service

❑ Delivery services – connecting retailers and wholesalers or manufacturers

A common way to combine and present these technologies is to implement a portal solution, which takes information in the form of web addresses from many different sources and presents them on the same screen in a unified manner. Portal services are covered in greater depth in Chapters 14 and 15

Pooling of Services from Other ASPs/Public Providers

Consider packaging up these services as a generic solution offering. An Application Service Provider can create a solution for customer authentication, payment, delivery, etc., and then sell or give away that service. The ASP's customer could answer some questions in a web-based form to customize that service, and then create a link to it in their portal solution and begin offering it to their internal and external customers.

When the consumer clicks on one of the services provided, that service goes to work. The transaction is handled from the ASP's datacenter(s) all behind the scenes, producing one fluid process for the consumer, and a short time to market and de-focus of core competencies for the ASP's customer. This allows the customer a great many options; with the continuation of true competitiveness there will essentially be several choices that the customer can pick and choose from.

Data Standards

Data standards are a very important part of any ASP's business for many reasons:

❑ Few ASPs on the market have a complete solution that can be up and running instantly, but they do have "services" that can be offered in combination with another vendor's services. A clean communication layer built from data standards helps to enable this collaboration.

❑ Companies are not trusting enough to provide their data to a third party in a "black hole" environment, with no access restrictions. Therefore, data standards will allow instant access for these companies to archive, profile, and access their data at any time.

❑ ASPs do not always provide a "full" solution, but more along the lines of services, and must therefore communicate with other ASPs regularly.

❑ A commitment to an ASP sometimes requires a data conversion of existing systems for a turnkey solution.

❑ Data standards will provide for an easy exchange of information between ASPs, customers, and consumers.

❑ Census information could be an important piece of an ASP's business, and the ability to sell that census information in the correct format should be an important part of the framework.

Probably the most important part of an ASP is its ability to take its data and share it with others. That is why they need to follow the industry standards for data exchange. These formats include: XML formats, EDI versions, Data Load procedures, SOAP, XML-RPC, CORBA, DCOM, etc. Each one of these can also be broken down into more industry specific standards that an ASP should be aware of for his or her industry.

Security

Let's briefly review security for just a moment. There are several methods for protection when working with an Internet-based system. A few popular ones are listed below:

❑ Keeping transmissions secure with **SSL** (Secure Sockets Layer) protects data from the "man in the middle" attack, and makes sure that the data that is transmitted back and forth between host and client is always encrypted.

❑ **Strong Authentication** – this happens with an authentication server of some kind. The client sends out a request for access to a particular system, and the client is authenticated to access the system based on a username and password, and sometimes other things like biometrics, smart card security, client certificates, etc.

❑ **Feature** and **Functionality Securing** – once access to the system is allowed, then depending on the role of the user, access is granted to particular features, functionality, modules, and/or services in the system.

❑ **Network Level Security** – protecting direct access to, and hacking of, both the ASP's servers and the client's computers is a large concern that is handled through proxy servers, firewalls, network address translation (NAT) devices, or a combination of these.

Internet security is a very hot topic, and is covered in more detail in Chapter 8.

How is Security Different in an ASP vs. Other Enterprise Systems?

Generally, security for an ASP requires a stronger authentication model than for other enterprise systems. Although some ASPs live in the Intranet, or in the extranet space in a secured network, many of them live in the realm of the entire global community – the Internet. This opens up the doors for all types of unauthorized access if not well protected.

Another problem is that of replicated access that occurs in many disparate systems. As someone offering multiple services for different reasons, an ASP is generally only an extension of their customer's offering. This is a big problem in many enterprises, where there are many systems that need to communicate as one, and offer the correct access, but each system handles access for that person differently, in turn creating another user in another system with the same credentials, creating an administrative headache.

One common way of solving this problem is access via a Global Directory or LDAP service, whose speed and "yellow pages" approach lends itself to solving this kind of problem. For more information on LDAP Server see *Implementing LDAP* by Mark Wilcox, from Wrox Press, ISBN 1861002211. Some other attempts are services like "Microsoft Passport", the many wallet services out there, and even proprietary username/password storage arrays with a unified login for many different services.

Choosing an ASP

There are many factors that have to be taken into consideration when selecting an ASP. First, the business requirements must be clear. This will allow a customer to make decisions like: what service would make running a business easier if outsourced? How does one find an ASP, and when found, can they be trusted? The pricing model offered for the service as well as the future of the company with the ASP offering are also important aspects of selecting an ASP. These are discussed below.

What is Involved in Selecting an ASP?

After the business requirements have been defined, there are many ways to find an ASP in the market to meet a company's needs. You can try the links below, or just type in +ASP -Microsoft into any search engine, and see what happens:

- ❑ Internet.com – ASP resource channel (http://www.internet.com/sections/asp.html)
- ❑ Thin Planet – (http://www.thinplanet.com)

There are also multiple newsgroups and communities with discussions that can be participated in to find out some more of the current goings and whereabouts of the ASP market. Off-line, one can find ASP offerings in business organizations (Chambers of Commerce, etc.), industry directories – sources the company has previous networking experience with and trusts.

Trusting an ASP is something that needs to be worked out up front before outsourcing part of a business to one. How could a company trust an ASP? It can be hard to do so. It is important to look for the following things:

- ❑ Proven track record with other companies doing the same or similar things. Talking to their reference clients and looking at recommendations helps to clarify the service offerings.
- ❑ Partner with a reputable firm that essentially holds a large portion of the contractual responsibility for each customer's success.

❑ Experience. It might come from the people in the business, it might come from the fact that a certain ASP has done this before, but a company definitely doesn't want to have to "learn" with their new business partner.

Proven Companies with an ASP Offering

One form of the ASP business model is one with a mature company behind it that is offering an age-old service in an ASP product type offering. There could be pitfalls here though – the company might not understand technology as well as the service, or the service is one that could not be provided until now through technology. Outsourcing part of a business to a dot com company who has been in the market for less than a year might obtain great technology, but reliable service and longevity would undoubtedly be a gamble. If this is the only choice available, look for a dot-com with a strong business partner on its side to help with implementation and knowledge transfer.

Pricing

Pricing depends on the service being looked into, the company offering that service, their level of support, and the position of everyone in the larger transaction picture. There are a few questions that need to be asked to determine the pricing structure:

❑ Do you need volume transactional rates for services in your business?

❑ Do you need volume buying rates in your business?

❑ How is the ASP service priced?

❑ Installation costs/setup fees:

   a. Monthly

   b. Volume

   c. Service Agreements

   d. Contract Terms

   e. One or more of the above

❑ Can this service be replaced by someone else (or internally) in a short amount of time?

❑ How important is this service to your business?

❑ What is the cost for the ASP to put their source code into escrow? A third party will hold the source code for a period of time in case the ASP company goes out of business, or other extreme measures that require the ASP-customer relationship to be severed.

❑ What is the level of support offered by the ASP?

What to Look For in the Company that Runs the ASP

In addition to finding, trusting, and pricing an ASP, the company that stands behind the Internet service is also important.

As we said before, the ASP's other clients and their utilized capacity must be checked up on to prove the ASP's track record. Also, depending on how much of a business is to be outsourced, a strong technical Due Diligence of the software behind the ASP wall (preferable by a third party consulting company) will ensure that the ASP can handle the transaction rates and capacity that is claimed. The processes and inner workings of the ASP are also very important. Things to check for are:

❑   Methodology is the process that was used to build solid, tested, repeatable software.

❑   Procedures that are followed to execute the methodology.

❑   Last upgrade patterns.

❑   Do all customers use the same version? If not, how is this handled? How many customers do they have?

❑   Internationalization?

❑   Offsite Backups? Are the tape backups carried offsite daily/weekly to protect from catastrophic data failure?

The Future of ASPs

The future of ASPs is looking very bright, but it has been a very long road getting there. A true connected world where things such as networks, operating systems and compatibility structures do not matter at all, because software can adapt to any situation that calls for it is only moments away. ASPs are the key to that future. Consider a truly outsourced community, where everything a person needs is available at their fingertips. For a fee, of course...

Summary

This chapter focused on Internet Application Service Providers and the Internet delivery model for ASPs involving web based Business to Business (B2B) and Business to Consumer (B2C) e-commerce situations. There are many other ASP offerings out there that use thin client mediums such as Terminal Server from Microsoft, Citrix Technologies, or even some of the Virus scanning and "patching" software vendors that have an "ASP type" offering, but this chapter had a specific Internet ASP focus.

We covered the following topics:

❑   Outsourcing: why it can be an attractive proposition, and how this standard model can be applied to software.

❑   The many different aspects that need to be considered in an ASP's software architecture.

❑   The art of building a network system of services, and how the different services work together to bring a unified solution to an ASP's customers.

❑   What is involved in selecting an ASP in an IT project, and when it might make sense to use one.

❑   The future of Application Service Providers.

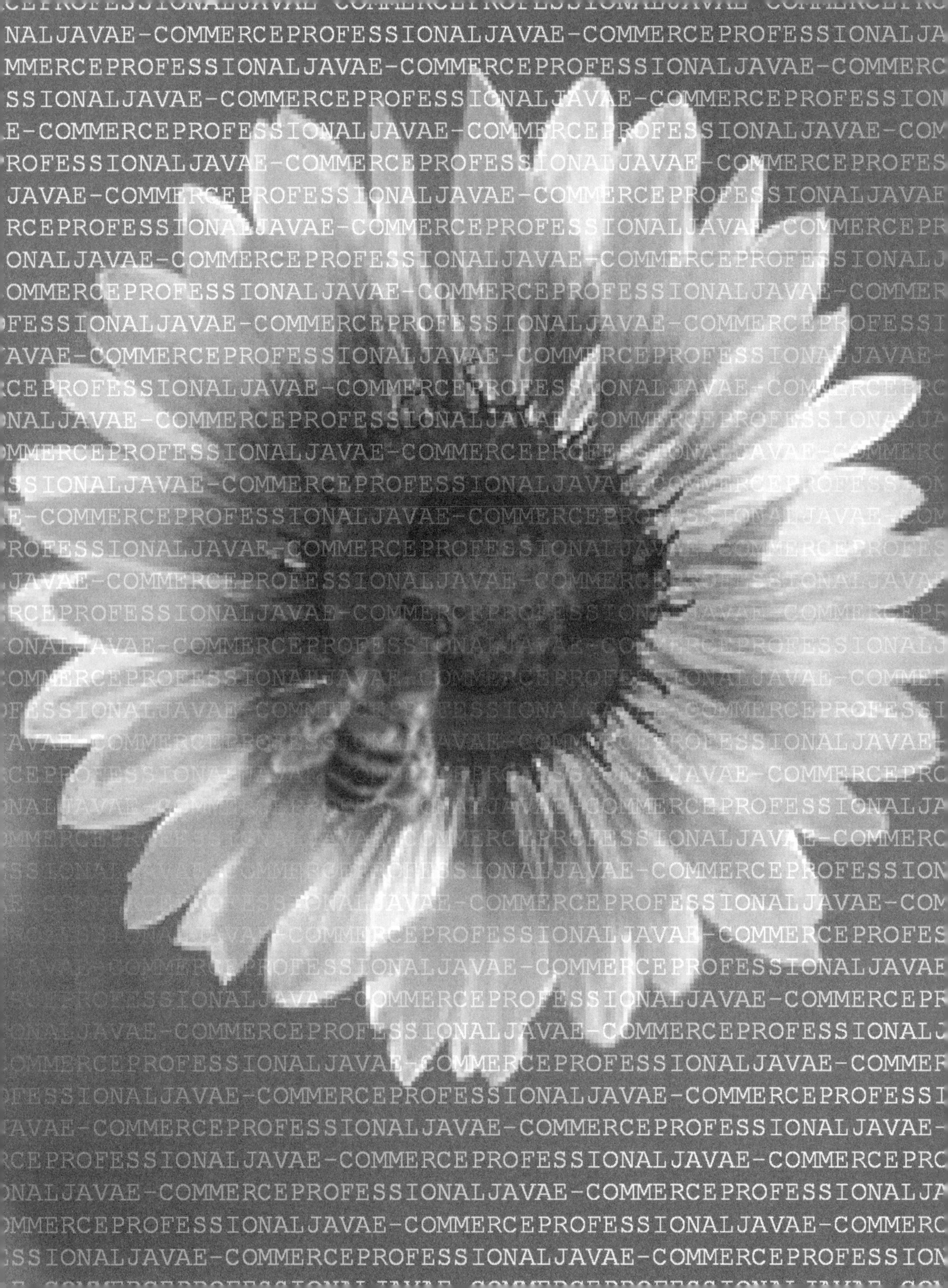

B2B E-Commerce: Inter-Company Workflow

In the following case study, we will attempt to bring together some of the technologies involved in B2B e-commerce. By walking through the development lifecycle of a particular solution build by Willie's Widget Factory, we hope to highlight a few of the design and development issues associated with such applications. This case study shows one particular mode of working and makes use of **JMQ** (**Java Message Queue**) in implementation of the solution. As we'll see in the next *In the Marketplace* chapter, choosing the right methodology for a particular problem isn't always easy.

The basic outline of this chapter is as follows:

- ❑ We take a look at a hypothetical but common business problem and consider the issues involved
- ❑ Select a design methodology
- ❑ Apply this methodology to the case study and walk through it
- ❑ Decide on a solution and detail how we might go about implementing it
- ❑ Build a small prototype and test it

Let's begin by taking a brief look at the case study, and see how we can achieve the objectives.

Case Study: Willie's Widget Factory

Willie, CEO and founder, has run a successful widget factory for a number of years. In order to succeed in the years to come, Willie thinks that his different departments need both better internal communications, and also better communications with the rest of their supply chain to bolster maximum efficiency.

Our task here is to plan out a development process that will define how we will gather all of the information needed, and outline solutions that we can design and build to meet these requirements. There are many ways to structure a development process, but all of them start with a strong design methodology.

We discussed different design methodologies in Chapter 3, and here we'll use a methodology similar to a simplified version of the **Rational Unified Process (RUP),** that involves **use cases** and the Unified Modelling Language (**UML**) to describe what we are trying to accomplish. Use cases are a simple way for the business users to describe the process flows of solving their business problem, and UML is a way to take those use cases and describe them in a technical manner, directly leading to a coded solution. It is a spiral development process where many of the phases overlap each other.

A Spiral Methodology for Willie

In a nutshell, our simplified process will walk through five steps during the development lifecycle:

❑ **Inception** – This is where we define a business case for building the software, and put limits on what the software will and will not do. The business users build use cases that will define, from a business perspective, what the technology will do.

❑ **Elaboration** – This phase takes the business problem and breaks it down into general tasks and risks, until it is basically a formal outline of the business problem and how it is going to be solved.

❑ **Analysis** – This is where each business task and risk is assessed and broken down into charts and process flows, so that the end result is something that we can then give to a developer to begin coding the solution in an informed manner (in the RUP process, this phase is rolled into the elaboration phase).

❑ **Construction** – In this phase we actually write the code.

❑ **Transition** – Here the software is implemented, and the customer is (hopefully) happy with the benefits of it. Of course, this process heavily involves the internal and external customers along the way in order that this step has no surprises!

First, we'll define each phase and what is covered in each, and then we will move on to apply our methodology to Willie's Widget Factory, and finally create a prototype based on our findings.

Inception

During the inception phase, we define the business case for why we need to build the software, and consider the scope of the solution we are attempting. This is the first phase in the project, and begins right after the sale is made. We hope that the customer says the following – "This is what we want to do, we want you to do it exclusively; let's get some more people involved to decide how we are going to do it, how long it will take, and what each phase will cost."

In this initial stage, we need to define a very important objective: **Customer Vision**.

For this stage, our requirements will be as follows:

- ❏ Initial Use Cases – Diagrams of business process flows, and how actors (people, machines, and other processes) interact with that flow.

- ❏ Initial Risks – Issues that could essentially destroy the project if not handled in some way.

- ❏ Initial Project Plan – What are the first steps, and how will we determine what the next ones will be?

This phase develops the products and the process. It also describes the business requirements for this project – what are the risks involved, and how do we get started?

An important part of this plan is also building the use cases. These are the first level of the knowledge transfer tasks between business people and technical people, and it involves a standard way to define a simple process flow in a business, and how the various actors interact with that process flow.

At the end of this initial phase, we should have produced tangible deliverables:

- ❏ A paper version of the business vision for the project at a very high level

- ❏ The completion of opening use cases

- ❏ The assessment of opening risks

- ❏ The opening project plan

Elaboration

In this phase we pull together all of the documents and put together a 10,000 foot view of what we are going to accomplish and how we are going to accomplish it. A critical quality about this phase is that it represents things from a real-world point of view, not as a collection of software components.

Our objectives for this phase are as follows:

- ❏ Ensure that the business vision and the software architecture are a good match

- ❏ Understand and address the identified risks and their ranking

- ❏ Prepare detailed use cases

- ❏ Prioritize use cases

- ❏ Turn the business use cases into technical information that can be easily transitioned to code

There are several activities that we should be pursuing in this phase. To begin with, we must further define the use cases so that we can flesh out a much more detailed view of the tasks required from them. These use cases must then be ranked and scheduled. Finally, there must be a risk assessment process, and then resources can be defined for the project.

At the end of this phase we should have accomplished the following and produced solid deliverables:

- ❏ Completed use case models which have gone though iterations of explanations between the business and technical people, and define exactly what the business process does to the technical people

❑ Completed functional and preliminary design documents

❑ Estimated resourcing

Analysis

In this phase, the intention is to build a conceptual model of the system and define system behavior. We define the concepts, associations between concepts, and the attributes of the concepts. The end result of this phase should be a solid transition of the business knowledge about the problem at hand to the design of the system, which directly leads to the construction (development) of the system.

Our objectives in the analysis phase are as follows:

❑ Build a conceptual model of the system from a technical point of view

❑ Define system behavior – events, operations, and contracts, the stepping-stones to building objects with methods, and defining how they interact

In our conceptual model, we must define the main concepts, associations and attributes (in UML notation) to provide a basic overview of the technical details to solving the business problem. We must also define system events and operations and create sequence diagrams for each. Each of these diagrams will be based on a use case from the elaboration phase. Finally, a contract must be created for the system operation of each sequence diagram to describe its behavior. At the end of this phase, we should be able to produce the following deliverables:

❑ Conceptual model

❑ Completed use cases

❑ Collaboration diagrams (interaction diagrams or sequence diagrams) – these are diagrams that show how the objects interact with each other in the code that you are about to construct

❑ Design Patterns – that we will be using to construct our code using proven patterns of development

❑ Visibility – is the ability of an object to "see" or have a reference to another object

❑ Class diagrams – identify specifications for the software classes and interfaces that will be used, represented in a graphical format

In summary, our aim here is to take the business requirements, and turn them into technical documents that any development team (even one without a strong business background or domain experience) can follow to produce code for the project.

Construction

This is where the code is developed. If the previous phases were thorough, then this phase is mostly converting charts and diagrams to code. Since our methodology is considered to be iterative, we will start coding, rollout to a test server, test the code, then start the construction phase over several times so that there are no surprises when preparing to deliver a completed product in the transition phase.

In this phase, our objectives change again. Following the designs in the previous sections, we must build a quality and stable product to those specifications. We must also begin to prepare the users to take ownership of the system.

In terms of our activities, they will be as follows:

- ❑ Build the product
- ❑ Unit test the product
- ❑ Acceptance test the product

Of course, the main goal is to turn all of the designs into a working system to be delivered to the consumer, which occurs in the transition phase.

Transition

The finished product moves into the hands of the end user and is transitioned into their environment. This phase will ensure a smooth transition of the newly created software product.

In this final phase, our objectives are as follows:

- ❑ Ensure user satisfaction
- ❑ Ascertain that the software performs in the new environment
- ❑ Be confident that the users can reliably take over control of the new software

In terms of actual actions, we should now be considering:

- ❑ Parallel rollout
- ❑ Full rollout
- ❑ Integration testing
- ❑ Training

Hopefully, the customer will be happy with the product.

Now that we have taken a good look at the methodology that we plan to use, it is time to apply it to Willie's Widget Factory. Since this chapter is focused on e-commerce technologies, and not UML or the Rational Unified Process (and Willie is not a real customer), we will skip a few steps in our methodology to get directly to the design and code.

Applying the Design Methodology to the Case Study

Willie, the CEO and founder of Willie's Widget Factory, has run a successful business for a number of years. It's a medium-sized company, with about ten million dollars in sales last year, and growing at a rate of about fifteen percent each year. In order to continue this rate of success in the future, Willie needs to adapt more quickly to the marketplace and make the transition from a mid-sized company to a larger business prepared to be a Fortune 500 company in the future (or at least go public with an exit!).

To accomplish this, Willie needs his different departments to communicate better internally with one another, and also better with the rest of the supply chain. He needs to tighten up his billing and inventory process so that he and his company will know where all of his assets are at any given time, and be able to make more informed marketing, purchasing, and sales decisions to run his company. Let's run through the process quickly for our example.

Inception

We will define the following in the context of our case study:

- ❏ Customer Vision
- ❏ Requirements
- ❏ Initial Use Cases
- ❏ Initial Risks
- ❏ Initial Project Plan

We'll take a look at each of these in turn.

Vision Statement

Willie believes he may be losing opportunities due to the under-utilization of new software technologies within his widget factory. He is looking to implement a phased B2B integration that specifically addresses workflow within the company, and to eventually extend these new workflow processes to suppliers.

Phase 1 of this project will be to incorporate a workflow-based system into the ordering process, allowing for flexibility in phases 2, 3, and 4 to support expansion of the new workflow into all of the company processes. The phases are to be completed with zero refactoring of code, which means that we will not do a quick fix in early phases that will require a section rewrite in subsequent phases, if there are any.

The key features and requirements of Phase 1 are:

- ❏ A configurable workflow system that is queue-based. This allows individual orders to be loosely coupled as they flow through the order processing system at rates independent of each other. This type of flexibility also allows for orders to bypass or add steps in the process as needed, even allowing us to expand our process to suppliers if needed (phase 2).

- ❏ Acting as a supplier, our system can fill orders for customers. We will implement a way for anyone, even customers, to create an order and enter it into our system (in a controlled, secure manner, of course).

- ❏ A method by which customers can check on the status of their products within the company.

Bearing these requirements in mind, we'll now take a look at the use cases that these requirements engender.

External Use Case – Customer Interaction

The customer, looking to Willie's Widget Factory as the supplier, will place orders with the system, and can also check the status of the orders placed. Our new system will take the order placed, turn it into an XML document, and then place it into the new_order_queue for handling.

The queues load up the OrderHandler, which does things to complete the order at each queue, and writes to the database to track what is going on:

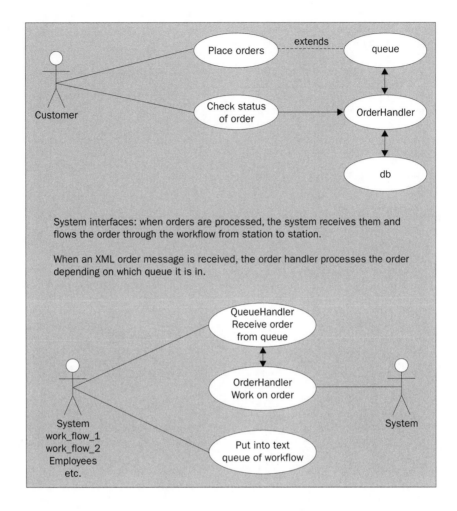

Risks

Risks have to be assessed by taking many different factors into account including the customer, resources, people's personalities, and past project successes and failures. Below are the risks that we have assessed in relation to our project, but in the real world strong risk assessment is vital to a successful project!

1. Requirements are loose.

Solution – Build a prototype and review it often with the customer.

2. There could be additional steps to processing the order that could happen in the future.

Solution – Build a flexible structure that can handle multiple queues and different ordering.

3. We have to connect our prototype or new software to our current system at some point in time.

Solution – By using open standards, with a public interface, we should be able to cut down on our connectivity issues.

4. We have to be able to connect to our suppliers' systems with minimal effort.

Solution – By using open standards and a public interface, we should find it much easier to connect to other external systems.

With these in place, we can now proceed with planning the project, and then move on to the elaboration phase.

Elaboration

This phase pulls together all of the initial business requirements from the inception phase, and begins to build a high-level overview of our project and what we are trying to accomplish.

Use Cases

Below is a complete use case of how the system handles orders from a workflow point of view.

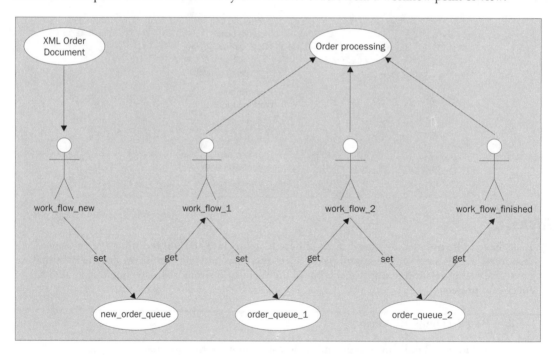

The use case diagram details the flow of an order through our system. The workflownew is where we will pick up an XML order document (created from our system, or another system) and drop it into the new_order_queue. work_flow_1 is an external system or user interface (UI) for an employee that gets an order out of the queue, processes it as a specific step in the work flow process, and then puts the order into the next queue in the line-up.

Since the order is represented as an XML document, then the beginning and end of the order processing workflow can be any type of system, as long as it is read/write conformable to our order XML document type definition (DTD). The DTD will ensure that any order XML document that we use follows the same format, so that our system can always understand everything about the order. Of course we don't have a DTD defined at this point, but we will need such a template at the end of this prototype step.

Risks

At this point, we should expand upon risk analysis to ensure that we will be able to mitigate each of the risks with our plan. Let's look at these risks again now:

1. Requirements are loose.

Solution – Set up weekly evaluation meetings with the customer to ensure that we are on the right track. Prototyping, screen mock-ups, and workflow are the major focus at this phase so that the requirements of the system can be better agreed upon.

2. There could be additional steps to processing the order that could happen in the future.

Solution – Build a flexible structure that can handle multiple queues and different ordering patterns, so that the software can change as the business does.

3. We have to connect to our current system at some point and time.

Solution – Use open standards, with a public interface. We really don't know what format the current system is in, and we need to find out. No matter what it is, we will use XML to describe orders in our system, so that we only have to program to one interface.

4. We have to be able to connect to our suppliers' systems with minimal effort.

Solution – Use open standards, with a public interface, to mitigate this risk as much as possible. Since there are multiple suppliers connecting to our system, we need to be very flexible in this regard. More than just an open database, we need open interfaces that can be shared with minimal effort. We should consider technologies such as SOAP, XML-RPC, JavaSpaces, EJBs, XML standards in our industry, amongst others.

Now that we've considered the risks, let's look at another important area within our case study – Business Processes.

Business Processes

Here we describe the business processes that we need to create, what they need to accomplish, and even a glimpse of the technology that will be used to make it happen. We'll break them down into three modules (Purchasing, Propagating, and Processing) and take a look at each of these in turn.

Purchasing Module

This module describes how to get orders into our new system.

❑ Placing orders manually – whatever user interface or system is used for placing orders, it will need to create an XML document describing the order that conforms to our specification.

❑ Placing orders automatically based on inventory – based on inventory levels, seasonality, customer requests, and so on, we need to automatically create orders for the customer and drop them into the workflow. Either the system that we build, or another system needs to do processing, such as our customer system, or we can adapt a legacy system's output to be XML. We then need to create an XML document that represents the order, so that we can use it in our system.

Propagating Modules

These modules describe how orders flow from queue to queue in our system.

❑ Propagating work flow to another company (Extranet)

The preferred situation when negotiating our business requirements with other companies is to have control of the interface that they use. Generally, the problem is that other companies already have their own systems in place, and would like to use those to communicate with us. We have decided to represent all of the orders as XML documents. This will allow the orders to flow through our system, and over to other systems, because the XML document fully describes the order, its history, and provides a way to validate the orders because the XML document is both the data and the data describer. This is advantageous because XML is suited to e-commerce, being a robust, cross-platform web-based technology.

The first step would be to transfer XML documents through a file system repository or an HTTP POST request to send the order documents between companies. In our prototype design, we want to stick to generalities, such as just passing text in and out of our queues and then parsing this text for whatever need may arise.

❑ Propagating work flow to internal departments (Intranet)

Internal department communication works very similarly to communicating with other companies. In some very large organizations, the separation of systems between departments is the same as between companies with regards to security concerns, connection requirements, and disparate systems.

Some of the advantages when working with internal departments is the ability to easily connect these systems with a service queue-based approach, that allows for XML order documents to be moved throughout different departments in the organization.

❑ Order Tracking Module

Every time an XML order document is moved through a queue, it needs to be tracked in a database, through some type of application such as our OrderHandler. Therefore, all that is needed is a small search module where clients to the system can query the database, and find out which queue an order is currently located in.

Processing Modules

These modules are where we actually get an order out of the queue and process it, whatever it is (currently an XML order document).

❑ **QueueHandler** – The QueueHandler is the entry point for an actor to the system to put an order into one of the workflow queues, or take an order out of one of the queues.

❑ **OrderHandler** – The `OrderHandler` is called when a message is received from a queue, and needs to be processed. It takes the XML Order document and creates a Java object from it, which is then worked on by other actors in the system. The order is then encoded back into an XML document with the new statuses or information and put into the next queue in the workflow.

Now that we understand the business processes, we can proceed to the next stage – Analysis.

Analysis

This phase is concerned with taking our business requirements and turning them into code designs. We need to define the framework that we will be using in terms of software, database selection, architecture, and logic explanations.

Technology selection is an important section of any project. Based on the business vision, we need to make sure that the software architecture is a good match, utilizing the current technologies to help us meet our requirements in a faster, more efficient manner.

❑ **Database Structure and Selection** – This project will require a database to store the details of where orders are, who owns the orders, and other relational information. We won't be using one for our prototype, but selecting the correct database vendor, and defining a flexible schema will be two very important pieces of our project.

❑ **Distributed objects** – An EJB implementation following the J2EE specification has become the industry standard mechanism for writing distributed, server-side Java implementations. For prototyping, and an initial offering, we can develop on the J2EE reference edition to ensure compatibility. When we roll into production, we can deploy it into the application server of choice, and even upgrade if necessary with no changes to the code being needed.

To handle the database persistence of our application, we will use EJB entity beans. We can rapidly begin talking to our database by using container-managed persistence (CMP) and creating a home and remote interface and a deployment descriptor for each table.

We will not do any database access in this case study code because we are focusing on workflow logic.

❑ **Logical characteristics of workflow** – The logic core of our system will be built upon the **Java Messaging Service** (**JMS**). This will allow a queue-based approach to accomplish the workflow that is required. Each queue has a different function, and the queues can be put into any order to create the workflow required.

A very important part of this phase is the creation of software diagrams – taking the user requirements yet another step further to turn it into code to create a system. Below is a simplified sequence diagram that describes the message passing that is required in the system, and how it will be orchestrated when constructed:

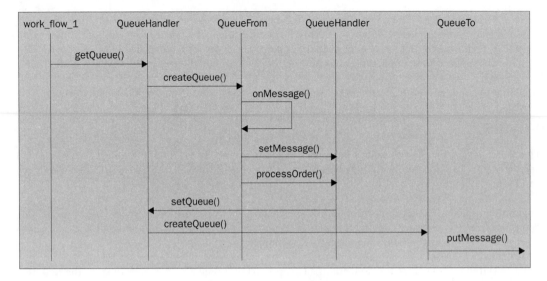

Message passing shown in this sequence diagram is as follows:

1. `work_flow_1` gets an order document out of the `new_order_queue`

2. `QueueHandler` creates a new queue if necessary with the `QueueFrom` object, and blocks while the `onMessage()` method waits for a message to show up in the queue

3. When a message arrives, it is sent back to the `OrderHandler` and processed

4. It is then passed back to the `QueueHandler` to be put back into the next queue with the `QueueTo` object

Construction

Now we are going to develop our solution. There are several files used in this iteration – they are all in a package called `iworkflow` (which can be downloaded from the Wrox website at http://www.wrox.com). We'll be discussing the complete code for the prototype that we will be building below, but first let's get an overview of the application.

The files handling orders through different queues in the system are:

❑ `QueueHandler` – Entry point for clients

❑ `QueueTo` – Puts an XML order document into a queue

❑ `QueueFrom` – Takes an XML order document from a queue

❑ `OrderHandler` – Takes the XML order document and processes it

❑ `Order` – Dummy order object

❑ `work_flow_new` – Creates a fake XML order document, and submits it to the `new_order_queue`

- ❑ work_flow_1 – Takes the XML order document from the new_order_queue, processes it, and then submits it to the order_queue_1

- ❑ work_flow_2 – Takes the XML order document from the order_queue_1 processes it, and then submits it to the order_queue_2

- ❑ work_flow_finished – Takes the XML order document from the order_queue_2, processes it, and then prints out the finished order

The code file contains the following files which should all be placed in a directory called iworkflow:

work_flow_new.bat	work_flow_1.bat	work_flow_2.bat
work_flow_finished.bat	Order.java	OrderHandler.java
QueueFrom.java	QueueHandler.java	QueueTo.java
work_flow_1.java	work_flow_2.java	work_flow_3.java
work_flow_finished.java	work_flow_new.javaOrder.java	
Order.class	OrderHandler.class	QueueFrom.class
QueueHandler.class	QueueTo.class	work_flow_1.class
work_flow_2.class	work_flow_3.class	work_flow_new.class
work_flow_finished.class		

There are a few things that are needed to set up your environment.

> *I installed everything to the D: drive, so if this is not the case in your environment, you'll need to alter the four different BATCH files to reflect this.*

These files are:

- ❑ work_flow_new.bat
- ❑ work_flow_1.bat
- ❑ work_flow_2.bat
- ❑ work_flow_finished.bat.

> *Due to the distributed nature of this application, we will require four different command prompts and four different JVMs.*

Software Requirements

For this application we will need JDK 1.3 and the Java Message Queue SDK (a free developer edition is available from http://www.sun.com/forte/jmq/buy/ that will work on both Windows NT and Solaris).

If you are developing software on another platform, consider another vendor that supports JMS, such as SonicMQ from Progress Software (http://www.progress.com/sonicmq/product_info/index.htm).

Installation of the Sun's JMQ is straightforward. If you decide not to install the router as a service, remember that you have to start the router up manually for the JMS to work.

In your environment, set up your JMQ_HOME to d:\Program Files\JavaMessageQueue1.1 (or whichever location you installed your software to) and your JAVA_HOME to d:\jdk1.3 (or to the location of your JDK if it is different). We can use the batch files listed below that came from one of the samples of the JMS SDK to handle the rest of the setup process. In order to compile, you will need to add the following files (found in the lib subdirectory of the JMQ installation directory) into your CLASSPATH:

- ❑ Jaas.jar
- ❑ Jmq.jar
- ❑ Jms.jar

In order to parse our XML order document to get the order_num, we need an XML parser. Here, the Xerces from Apache prevails (downloadable from: http://xml.apache.org/xerces-j/index.html).

I unzipped this file to d:\xerces\, and the CLASSPATH is handled in the BATCH files – so if you are installing this into a different directory, the BATCH files will need to be altered to reflect this.

In order to be able to use the XML parser, I had to add the following to the bottom of the java.policy file, located at D:\jdk1.3\jre\lib\security\java.policy:

```
grant { permission java.security.AllPermission; };
```

We will use the above mentioned batch files from one of the samples (since modified) that came with the JMS SDK to handle the rest of the setup process. Below is the code for work_flow_1.bat:

```
if "%OS%" == "Windows_NT" setlocal

if "%JAVA_HOME%\bin\java.exe" == "\bin\java.exe" goto nojavahome
if "%JMQ_HOME%\lib\jmq.jar" == "\lib\jmq.jar" goto nojmqhome

set JMQ_CPATH =.; %JAVA_HOME%\lib\classes.zip; %JMQ_HOME%\lib\jmq.jar;
    %JMQ_HOME%\lib\jms.jar; %JMQ_HOME%\lib\jndi.jar;%CLASSPATH%;
    D:\xerces\xerces-1_2_3\xerces.jar;D:\xerces\xerces-1_2_3\xercesSamples.jar

"%JAVA_HOME%\bin\java" -Djava.security.manager -
Djava.security.policy="%JMQ_HOME%\security\jmqexamples.policy" -classpath
"%JMQ_CPATH%" iworkflow.work_flow_new %1 %2 %3 %4 %5 %6 %7 %8 %9
goto end

:nojavahome
    echo Please set the JAVA_HOME environment variable.
    goto end

:nojmqhome
    echo Please set the JMQ_HOME environment variable.
    goto end

:end
if "%OS%" == "Windows_NT" endlocal
```

Prototype Code for Willie

Now we've had an overview of the code and seen what software we require let's dig into the code itself.

QueueHandler

This is the entry point for any Java clients to any queue. It creates a connection to the JMS, and two sessions so that we get an XML order document from one queue, process it, and then put it into another queue.

The constructor builds all of the connections, and there are two methods, a getQueue(), and a setQueue() that the client programs have access to:

```java
/*
 * QueueHandler.java
 */

package iworkflow;

import javax.jms.*;
import java.util.*;

/**
 * @author  Administrator
 * @version
 */

public class QueueHandler {

    private static final String BROKER = "localhost:2056";
    private com.sun.messaging.QueueConnectionFactory QConnectionFactory = null;
    private QueueConnection QConnection = null;
    private QueueSession QSessionFrom = null;
    private QueueSession QSessionTo = null;

    private Queue qName = null;
    private QueueTo qt = null;
    private QueueFrom qf = null;


    /** Creates new QueueHandler */
    public QueueHandler() {

      try {
         QConnectionFactory = new com.sun.messaging.QueueConnectionFactory
            (BROKER);
         QConnection = QConnectionFactory.createQueueConnection();
         System.out.println("Created connection");
         QSessionFrom =
            QConnection.createQueueSession(false,QueueSession.AUTO_ACKNOWLEDGE );
         System.out.println("Created from queue session");
         QSessionTo =
            QConnection.createQueueSession(false,QueueSession.AUTO_ACKNOWLEDGE );
         System.out.println("Created to queue session ");

      } catch (JMSException jmse) {
         jmse.printStackTrace();
      }
    }
```

The getQueue() method takes in the name of the queue that we want to get an order from, and the queue that we are going to put that order into when we are done processing it.

This is accomplished by instantiating the QueueFrom object:

```
public void getQueue(String name, String nextQueue) {
    try {
        System.out.println ("Creating a new get queue - " + name);
        qName = QSessionFrom.createQueue(name);
        qf = new QueueFrom(QSessionFrom, qName, this);

        // if there is no next queue, then don't set it :-)
        if ( !(nextQueue.length()<1) ){
            qf.setNextQueue(nextQueue);
        }
        //start up the connection
        QConnection.start();
    } catch (JMSException jmse) {
        jmse.printStackTrace();
    }
}
```

In the setQueue() method, we give it the name of the queue that we want to put an order into, and the message (XML order document) describing the order that we want to put into the queue.

This is accomplished by instantiating the QueueTo object:

```
public void setQueue(String name, String message) {

    try {
        qName = QSessionTo.createQueue(name);
        qt = new QueueTo(QSessionTo, qName);
        QConnection.start();

        //System.out.println("putting message: " + message + " into queue " + name);
        qt.putMessage(message);

    } catch (JMSException jmse) {
        jmse.printStackTrace();
    }
}
```

QueueTo

This handles putting an XML order document into a queue:

```
/*
 * QueueTo.java
 */

package iworkflow;
import javax.jms.*;

/**
```

```
    * @author  Administrator
    * @version
    */

public class QueueTo {

    private QueueSession session;
    private QueueSender sender;

    public QueueTo(QueueSession aqs, Queue aq) {
    session = aqs;
    try {
        sender = session.createSender(aq);
    }
    catch (JMSException jmse) {
        System.out.println("Producer Constructor " + jmse);
    }
}
public void putMessage(String message) {
    StreamMessage aMessage ;
    String currentOrderNum = "";
    try {

        aMessage = session.createStreamMessage();
        aMessage.writeString(message);
        sender.send (aMessage);

        System.out.println("sent order into queue ");

    }
    catch (Exception e) {
        System.out.println("Exception in put message");
        e.printStackTrace();
    }
}

/**
 *  Close the queue session
 */

public void close() {
    try {
        System.out.println("Closing Producer queue session");
        session.close();
    }
    catch(Exception e) {
        System.out.println("Exception, could not close Producer queue session"+
            e.getMessage());
        e.printStackTrace();
    }
}
```

QueueFrom

This is an interesting class file. There are three methods:

❑ onMessage() – This is the JMS listener that sits and waits for a message to be placed into the queue and then performs some action

❑ setNextQueue() – This sets the queue that we will put the order into after processing

❑ queueListen() – This starts up the JMS listener

Notice how the QueueFrom object implements the MessageListener interface. This is where the onMessage() method comes from.

```java
/*
 * QueueFrom.java
 */

package iworkflow;
import javax.jms.*;

/**
 * @author  Administrator
 * @version
 */

public class QueueFrom implements MessageListener{

    private QueueSessionsession;
    private QueueReceiver receiver;
    private String nextQueue = "";
    private Queue myaq;
    private QueueHandler myqh;
    private String s;

    /** Creates new QueueFrom */

    public QueueFrom(QueueSession aqs, Queue aq) {
        this.session = aqs;
        this.myaq = aq;
        queueListen();
    }

    public QueueFrom(QueueSession aqs, Queue aq, QueueHandler qh) {
        this.session = aqs;
        this.myaq = aq;
        this.myqh = qh;
        queueListen();
    }

    public void setNextQueue(String nq) {
        this.nextQueue = nq;
    }

    public void queueListen() {
        try {
```

```
            receiver = session.createReceiver(myaq);
            receiver.setMessageListener (this);
            System.out.println("MessageListener Set");
        }
    catch (JMSException jmse) {
        System.out.println ("Error: " + jmse);
        }
    }


    public void onMessage(Message m) {

        /** JMS has quite a few tags that can be attached to messages to show
            all kinds of message properties. Right here would be a good places to
            create a QueueBrowser object that can search those messages to find
            one that is new to this queue, or maybe one that has the oldest date,
            etc  **/

        StreamMessage aMessage;
        String modifieds = "";
        OrderHandler oh = new OrderHandler();

        try {
            aMessage = (StreamMessage) m;
            s = aMessage.readString();

            //set the message in the order object

            oh.setMessage(s);

            //process the order, return the modified xml message

            modifieds = oh.processOrder(myaq);
            System.out.println("Just processed our order");

        } catch (Exception e) {   // in the real world, look for problems
            System.out.println("had an error reading the message and
                processing order");
        } finally {
            // puts the message into the next queue, if there is one
            //get order number from xml document
            String currentOrderNum = oh.getOrderNum(modifieds);
            if (nextQueue.length() > 0){
                this.myqh.setQueue(nextQueue,modifieds);
                System.out.println("Message recieved " + s);
                System.out.println("put the order " + currentOrderNum +
                    " XML into the next queue: " + nextQueue);
            } else {
                System.out.println("Finished order number " + currentOrderNum +
                    " and shipped it off");
                // run some other method here to do something with finished order.
                // maybe write it to a file in a directory where other programs can
                // pick it up and use it
            }
        }
    }
}
```

The onMessage() is an exciting method. We get a message from the queue, create a new OrderHandler object, process that order, and then put the order into the next queue in the workflow.

OrderHandler

Mainly, we just have dummy methods in this file to simulate processing an order. It shows the steps involved in a simple order processor, and how important encapsulation is to keep the workflow system as modular as possible.

```java
/*
 * OrderHandler.java
 */

package iworkflow;
import javax.jms.*;
import javax.xml.parsers.DocumentBuilderFactory;
import javax.xml.parsers.DocumentBuilder;
import javax.xml.parsers.ParserConfigurationException;
import org.w3c.dom.*;
import org.xml.sax.InputSource;
import java.io.*;

/**
 * @author  Administrator
 * @version
 */

public class OrderHandler extends Object {

    private String orderXML;
    private Order currentOrder;
    private Queue myaq;

    /** Creates new OrderHandler */

    public OrderHandler() {
    }

    public OrderHandler(long order) {
        currentOrder.setOrder_num(order);
    }

    public String getMessage() {

        /** gets the message from the object**/

        return this.orderXML;
    }

    public void setMessage(String XML) {

        /** set the message to the object **/

        this.orderXML = XML;
    }
```

```
public String getOrderNum(String XML){
   StringReader sr = new StringReader(XML);
   try {
      //retrieve the XML document and parse out the order number
      DocumentBuilderFactory dbf = DocumentBuilderFactory.newInstance();
      DocumentBuilder db = dbf.newDocumentBuilder();
      InputSource source = new InputSource(sr);
      Document doc = db.parse(source);
      org.w3c.dom.NodeList nodes = null;
      nodes = doc.getElementsByTagName("order_num");
      String sender = (nodes.getLength() > 0) ?
         nodes.item(0).getFirstChild().getNodeValue() : "unknown";

      return sender;
   } catch (Throwable t) {
      System.out.println("error parsing XML document");
      t.printStackTrace(System.out);
   }
   return "<<-Failed to get Order Number-->";
}
private boolean decodeMessage(){

/**creates an Order object from the XML message **/

   return true;
}

private String encodeMessage() {

   /** takes the Order object and creates an XML message **/

   return this.orderXML;
}

private void setOrderStatus(){

   /** this would set the status of the order into a database for
      added persistence **/
}

public String processOrder(Queue q){

   /** processes the order, based on the queue that was passed into
      this object**/

   this.myaq = q;
   decodeMessage();    //turn the order into java objects that we can use
   setOrderStatus();   //update the database that we are using the order, and
                       //set it's current status
   System.out.println("in the order handler: process order");

   try {
      Thread.sleep(2000);
      //do something else
```

```
        } catch (InterruptedException ie) {
        }

        return encodeMessage();
    }
}
```

Order

This is a dummy order object, created to ensure clean, modular code:

```java
/*
 * Order.java
 */

package iworkflow;

/**
 * @author  Administrator
 * @version
 */

public class Order extends Object {

    private long order_num;
    private String order_gibberish;


    /** Creates new Order */

    public Order() {
    }
    public long getOrder_num(){
       return this.order_num;
    }
    public void setOrder_num(long orderNum){
       this.order_num = orderNum;
    }
    public String getOrder_gibberish(){
       return this.order_gibberish;
    }
}
```

The actors of the system are what actually move the data from queue to queue. These are all main methods to push orders through and simulate a real workflow environment.

work_flow_new, work_flow_1, work_flow_2, and work_flow_finished

What we are doing here is creating a random order number, and constructing a fake XML order document to simulate one that we might have in real life. We put our document into the new_order_queue:

```java
/*
 * newOrder.java
 */

package iworkflow;
```

```
import java.util.*;

/**
 * @author Administrator
 * @version
 */

public class work_flow_new{

    /** Creates new newOrder */

    public work_flow_new() {
    }

    public static void main(String[] args) {
        QueueHandler qh  = new QueueHandler();
        StringBuffer FakeXMLOrder = new StringBuffer(1000);
        int order_num = 0;
        while (true) {
            for(int i=0;i<=3;i++) {
                //random new order
                java.util.Random random = new java.util.Random();
                order_num = random.nextInt();
                if (order_num < 0){
                    order_num = order_num * -1;
                }
                FakeXMLOrder.delete(0,1000); //clear out the buffer
                FakeXMLOrder.append("<?xml version=\"1.0\" standalone=\"yes\"?>\n");
                FakeXMLOrder.append("<order>\n");
                FakeXMLOrder.append("  <order_num>" + Integer.toString(order_num) +
                    "</order_num>\n");

                FakeXMLOrder.append("    <item type=\"order_line\">\n");
                FakeXMLOrder.append("        <line_no>1</line_no>\n");
                FakeXMLOrder.append("        <product>\n");
                FakeXMLOrder.append("            <name>widget</name>\n");
                FakeXMLOrder.append("            <price>1000</price>\n");
                FakeXMLOrder.append("            <currency>US</currency>\n");
                FakeXMLOrder.append("            <qty>7</qty>\n");
                FakeXMLOrder.append("        </product>\n");

                FakeXMLOrder.append("    </item>\n");
                FakeXMLOrder.append("    <ship-to>\n");
                FakeXMLOrder.append("        <name>Santa Claus</name>\n");
                FakeXMLOrder.append("        <address>\n");
                FakeXMLOrder.append("            <line1>elf street</line1>\n");
                FakeXMLOrder.append("            <line2/>\n");
                FakeXMLOrder.append("            <city>north pole</city>\n");
                FakeXMLOrder.append("            <state>north pole</state>\n");
                FakeXMLOrder.append("        </address>\n");
                FakeXMLOrder.append("    </ship-to>\n");

                FakeXMLOrder.append("    <cost>\n");
                FakeXMLOrder.append("        <shipping>10</shipping>\n");
                FakeXMLOrder.append("        <tax>1</tax>\n");
```

749

```
                FakeXMLOrder.append("        <total>1</total>\n");
                FakeXMLOrder.append("   </cost>\n");
                FakeXMLOrder.append("</order>\n");

            /** now we take the XML document and put it into the first queue to be
                processed */

                qh.setQueue("new_order_queue", FakeXMLOrder.toString());
                System.out.println("Just dropped order number " + order_num +
                    " into new_order_queue");
            }
                try{
                    Thread.sleep(20000);
                }catch (InterruptedException ie)
                {
                }
                System.out.println("*************************************************");
            }
        }
    }
```

work_flow_1 and work_flow_2 are used to move orders through the queues:

```
package iworkflow;

/**
 * @author  Administrator
 * @version
 */

public class work_flow_1 {

    /** Creates new workFlowClient */

    public work_flow_1() {
    }

    public static void main(String[] args) {
        QueueHandler qh  = new QueueHandler();

        //look for any new messages in the new order_queue
        qh.getQueue("new_order_queue","order_queue_1");
        //the onMessage method in the QueueFrom Instance deals with the order
        // and puts them into the order_queue_1
    }
}
```

work_flow_2 has the following change:

```
qh.getQueue("order_queue_1","order_queue_2");
```

Similarly, the `workflow_finished` has only one change:

```
qh.getQueue("order_queue_2","");
```

Testing

Another important feature of the construction phase is testing.

There are three kinds of testing before we can approve any code for production:

- ❏ **Unit Testing** – Test each method of code in each class, then test each element on each new screen. This form of testing is to be done by the developer.

- ❏ **Acceptance Testing** – Test the module by itself. Generally making separate `main()` methods to run through the functionality of your code and make sure that it works as expected the way that it was designed. It also ensures that your code is set up in "distributed" nature, since everything runs in different virtual machines. The "`work_flow`" series of files are a good example of this.

- ❏ **Integration Testing** – After the new code is integrated with code from other members of the team, or the new code is integrated into the system, integration testing makes sure that the system as a whole was not compromised by adding or changing modules.

Once testing has been performed, we can move into the final transition phase of our process.

Transition

What we have at this point is a nice prototype of what our system can accomplish, and a glimpse of how we will accomplish it.

Demonstrating the Application

Go into the JavaMessageQueue1.1/bin folder (the default location is usually under C:/Program Files/ on Windows) and open it up. Click on the irouter.exe icon (for SUN JMS implementation only, other JMS implementations will have other router programs, so consult your documentation). This will begin the JMQ router service, so you should see a small command prompt window open up, and scroll through a few lines of text as it initialises. The final line of text will be <<router ready>>.

Load up four DOS windows and run the following programs, one in each of the four windows. Each of these batch files runs the setup for the JMS, and then starts up the workflow process that was built. During setup, as stated earlier, you should have opened these files to ensure that the drive letters involved are set up to your computer's specification.

- ❏ `work_flow_new.bat`
- ❏ `work_flow_1.bat`
- ❏ `work_flow_2.bat`
- ❏ `work_flow_finished.bat`

When these files run together, they simulates the orders running through our different queues and being processed by each. A visual model of this should follow exactly the detailed use case diagram detailed in our elaboration phase, and a screenshot is captured below.

When run, the user will see orders start in the `work_flow_new.bat` window (creates an XML document and drops it into the first queue). Then the `work_flow_1.bat` window picks up the XML order document from the `new_order` queue, processes it, and places it into the `order_queue_1` queue, where `work_flow_2.bat` picks it up. The process could continue until the XML order document has been handled by several different queues (and orders filled accordingly in the warehouse) and sent to the last queue, where the order is completed and shipped off.

In our example, the order is picked up from the last queue by `work_flow_finished.bat` where the XML document is parsed by the Xerces parser, and we extract and print out the `order_num` that is attached to that order.

At this phase, we would show Willie our prototype of what we have so far, and then go back to the design phase based on his team's concepts.

Summary

In this case study, we have created a design methodology based on the Rational Unified Process, and taken a fictitious business problem though our process, from inception, all the way to coding the prototype.

The five steps of our methodology were:

- ❑ Inception
- ❑ Elaboration
- ❑ Analysis
- ❑ Construction
- ❑ Transition

We walked through all of the steps of a full development lifecycle (although rather quickly) and ended up with a prototype that was well thought out, and hopefully solves the customer's problems.

Don't forget that the actual development process is spiral, and therefore we would complete many iterations of this process as the project continues. Hopefully, Willie's team is happy with what they see, and would like for us to continue to develop this workflow-based system. There are many more things that are necessary to bring about completion, including some real clients for the queues, a web-based queue-searching facility for customers and suppliers, database persistence, JMS transaction handling, clean-up code, and so on. However, for the purposes of this chapter, the main concepts of how a simple workflow-based system works have been completed.

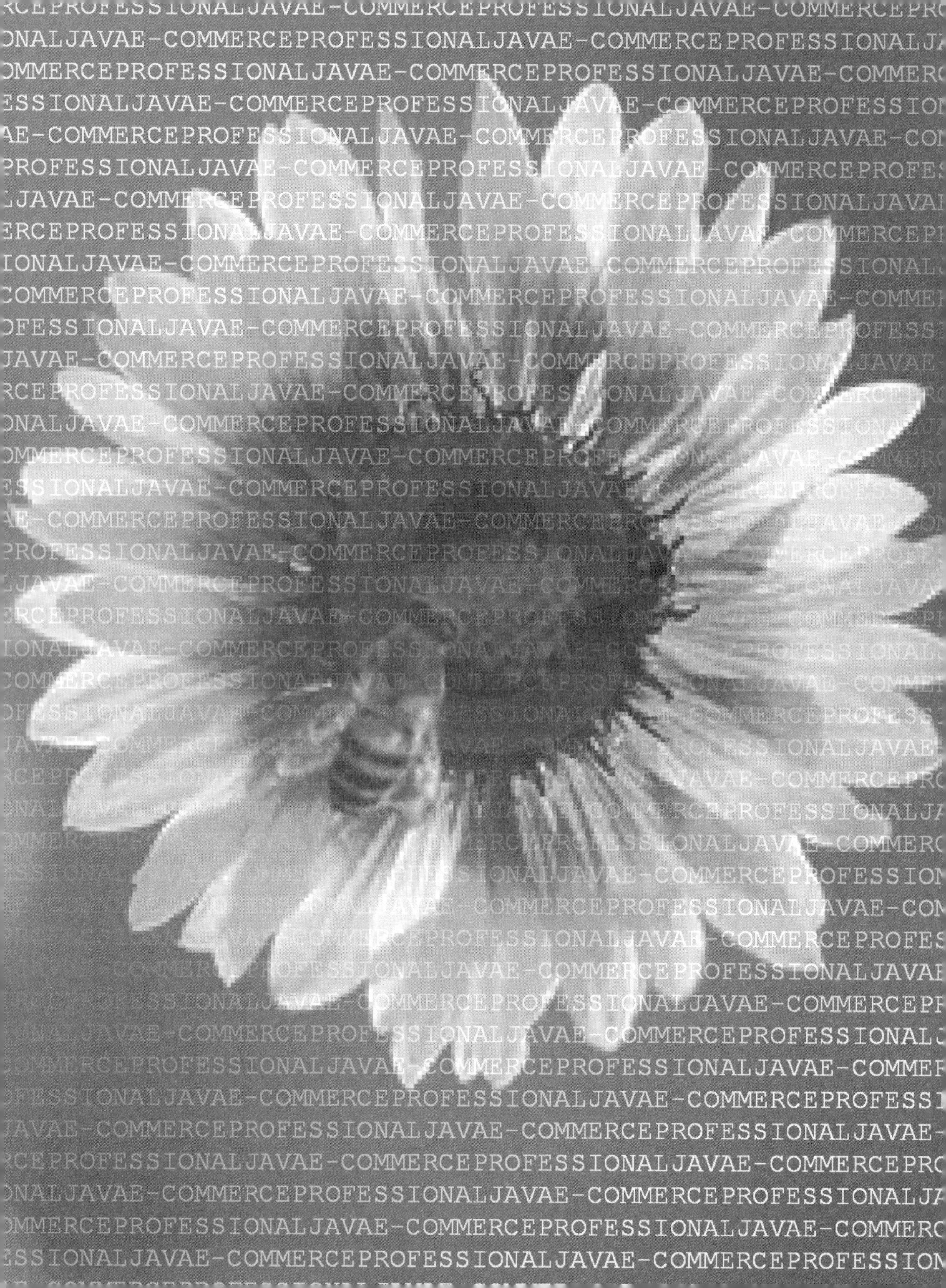
PROFESSIONALJAVAE-COMMERCE

In the Marketplace D – Corporate Purchasing

In this chapter we will take a look at how to implement e-commerce systems for corporate purchasing. You'll find that a lot of what has been said about B2B and B2C in preceding chapters applies to corporate purchasing as well, with, sometimes important, modifications.

The similarities between corporate purchasing systems and other B2C/B2B systems allow us to focus less on coding issues, and more on design issues and the development process (let's face it; one can only stomach so many servlet, JSP or EJB examples in one sitting).

In this chapter we will also examine the central role of **workflow**. One formal definition of workflow is "The sequence of activities performed in a business that produces a result of observable value to an individual actor of the business" (*Philippe Kruchten, The Rational Unified Process, 2nd Edition, ISBN 0-201-70710-1*). Put in simple terms, within our context the workflow is the sequence of tasks that a corporate purchasing system must perform or initiate in order to complete a purchasing transaction. In fact, there are at least two separate and interacting workflows involved in most corporate purchase systems. One exists within the customer's organization the other within the vendor's. Later in this chapter we will take a closer look at the different workflows.

I will highlight some of the important points of this chapter in several case studies. I've chosen this approach in order to highlight some of the facts of life of corporate software development. Voltaire's Candide learned time and again that even the best of all possible worlds is flawed. Sadly there are some real differences between how we all agree we should implement systems, and how we sometimes actually end up doing it in the hostile and thankless world of corporate IT development.

One significant hurdle facing those working in the area of corporate purchasing is how to build new applications that integrate with established legacy systems, designed and built using, what are now felt to be, far less than optimal methods, processes, and technologies – the case studies in this chapter will provide real world examples that illustrate this crucial and not always pretty task.

We'll discuss corporate purchasing as we look at the following things in this chapter:

❑ Characteristics of corporate purchasing systems

❑ Workflow (with a case study)

❑ Legacy integration (with two case studies)

❑ The development process (with a case study)

Don't be put off by the phrase "high level approach". There will be plenty of source code, but also design tips, patterns, and discussions about development process, including thoughts on how we can design our applications to be more easily integrated into future systems.

Characteristics of Corporate Purchasing Systems

Quite clearly, corporate purchasing systems involve some entity wanting to buy something electronically and, hopefully, some other entity willing to sell it. For that reason it would be reasonable to assume that corporate purchasing systems share common characteristics with the B2C systems already discussed. On the other hand, in this case both the selling and buying entities are usually companies – and as we shall see both entities are often required to interface extensively with other internal systems. This suggests we're actually talking about a B2B system. "So which one is it?"

Actually, it is both … or perhaps neither. Which would explain why the editors of this volume have seen fit to treat the topic separately in a chapter of its very own.

Corporate Purchasing as a B2C Activity

In a typical B2C system, a customer who has a need for goods or services will look for a supplier of the goods or services on the Internet. If there is a match between what is wanted and what is offered, the customer can add the product to their shopping cart. At some point the customer may choose to check out, and thereby initiate a purchasing transaction.

The parameters of this transaction are determined by what's in the shopping cart and what's in the customer's profile. One of the items in the customer's profile is usually a credit card number. The credit card gets charged, the goods or service eventually delivered, and life goes on.

In spite of what you've read in trade magazines and been told repeatedly by personalization and CRM (customer relationship management) tool vendors, in many cases the single most important item in the customer's profile is her credit card number. Why is this so? Although there are other modes of payment, such as digital wallets, the vast majority of B2C transactions on the Internet today involve a credit card. Furthermore, recent research shows that the buyer's vendor loyalty is low and often overridden by deal-hunting and price comparisons. This in turn leads to short-term relationships and sporadic interactions, often spanning only one single transaction. A third factor leading to less personal short-term relationships is the growing awareness of privacy issues among B2C customers. Consequently customers are less willing to reveal personal information that isn't of immediate use in the transaction.

So one might say with a little bit of exaggeration that the "magic glue" that holds it all together is the credit card number. Meaning no disrespect whatsoever to web designers, system architects, e-commerce product vendors or online merchants, the quintessence of traditional B2C can be described as an almost ridiculously complicated way to charge against a credit card.

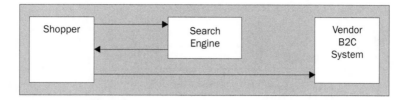

The Role of Workflow

By contrast the relationships between customers and vendors within corporate purchasing are typically more stable and lasting. In order to effectively implement corporate purchasing systems it can be important for customers and vendors to understand each other's processes, systems and terminologies.

Another big difference between corporate purchasing and traditional B2C is the utter and complete absence of a credit card number. However, there is something to replace it, and this something is called **workflow**. On both the demand and supply ends of a corporate purchasing system, workflow replaces the relatively simple acts of providing a credit card number and charging against it.

In fact, the need to optimize the workflow and the need for integration of data processing systems in the customer and vendor organizations play an important role in stabilizing the customer-vendor relationship. For example, the customer's cost savings and efficiencies associated with the use of a corporate purchasing system may be of such a magnitude that the customer declines to do business with vendors that are not "in the system". These close relationships through integration of workflow may take many forms, ranging from lists of preferred vendors to a single vendor taking over and managing the customer's entire inventory and purchasing process.

For the customer, the workflow typically involves the following tasks:

- ❑ Generating a request for goods or services
- ❑ Approving the request
- ❑ Generating a purchase order
- ❑ Receiving goods and updating inventory

For the vendor, the workflow typically involves these tasks:

- ❑ Receiving a request for a quote
- ❑ Checking credit status and customer specific limits on order amounts
- ❑ Preparing a quote
- ❑ Verifying a purchase order
- ❑ Checking stock levels
- ❑ Generating a shipment

Below is a figure illustrating a representative composite customer/vendor workflow:

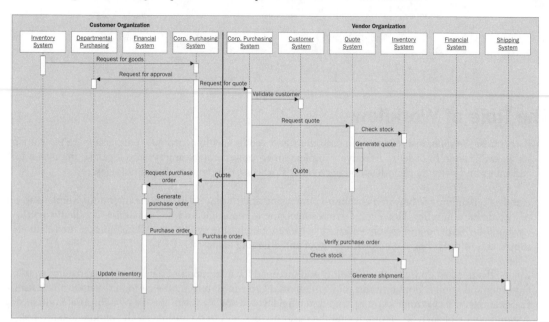

Two things should be apparent from the diagram above. First of all we should note the large number of discrete operations involved in a typical corporate purchasing transaction. Although the specifics of the activities may vary in each instance, the number of activities in the diagram is representative of a simple successful transaction.

Secondly, we see that many of these activities involve interaction with legacy systems. We will find occasion to return to this point later.

Corporate Purchasing as a B2B Activity

The second big difference between corporate purchasing and traditional B2C is that the customer often requests quotes from several vendors before committing to the decision to make a purchase. Of course, in a limited sense this is analogous to the scenario where a savvy B2C customer compares different vendors' offerings. The difference lies in the fact that in the corporate purchasing situation dealing with multiple vendors often is institutionalized in the business process, and supported by dedicated electronic systems. This is usually not the case in the B2C situation.

If this is a predominant mode of operation, and the value of the total volume of transactions makes it economically defensible, it often does not make sense for a customer to access several vendors' systems to request quotes. Instead, the customer might want to build a system where she communicates her need for an item to several vendors simultaneously, as opposed to looking up a desired item on many vendors' sites. In such cases the customer usually owns and hosts the system.

Now, this sounds like an inverse of the traditional B2C, where a vendor advertises a supply, one or hopefully many customers bring demand, and the vendor owns the system. In this form of corporate purchasing a customer advertises a demand, one or more vendors provide the supply, and the customer owns the system.

Such a system could quite credibly be classified as a form of *one-to-many* B2B. Also, in the absence of the magic a credit card number provides, an additional element of mutual trust as well as a corresponding need for strong authentication of the parties is introduced. This also is often associated with B2B.

So corporate purchasing – not B2C, yet not quite B2B, or worse, possibly both at the same time.

The Headaches of Having More Than One Partner

Let's dwell a moment longer on the "inverted B2C" systems we outlined above. The main characteristics of such systems are that a customer hosts a system through which she advertises a demand (either by "pushing" the request, or allowing others to "pull" the details) for products to several vendors simultaneously. The customer does this in the hope of encouraging competition between vendors, and to simplify its internal business processes. Sometimes this arrangement can create unique complications.

Suppose a customer is interested in buying a specific quantity of a certain item at a good price through her purchasing system. She has issued notice of this demand to several vendors through her (somewhat naïve) corporate purchasing system. For example, the customer has asked three different vendors for "10 boxes of large binder clips". When the vendor responses come in she finds:

❑   One has quoted her a price for 10 boxes containing twenty 1 ¼" binder clips

❑   Another has quoted her a price for 10 boxes containing twelve 2" binder clips

❑   The third has no idea what a "large binder clip" is

In traditional B2C the customer's choices are typically unambiguous, since the vendor provides the definition of the product. Also, in a one-to-one customer-vendor relationship the customer can reasonably learn about the vendor's offerings, and understand the vendor's terminology. At the same time, it is also common for a vendor to know each individual customer's preferences. In the case where a customer deals with multiple vendors, it is *not* reasonable to expect the customer to know each vendor's part numbering system.

When a customer issues simultaneous requests for quotes to several vendors, it is desirable that the customer herself describes the product unambiguously. One way to do this is to provide a standard terminology, which is defined and maintained by the customer. An example could be a declarative statement such as "by *experienced Java developer* I mean a person with more than two years of professional Java development experience". It is then up to the vendor to translate the common language into something internally meaningful, possibly esoteric, such as a part number.

In practice we often find that the usage and implied meaning of descriptive terms varies wildly between departments and cultural pockets within the same customer organization as well as between organizations. Even simple and seemingly clearly defined things such as measurements are fraught with peril. For example a shoe size 7 means different things depending on whether you are in the US, in the UK, or in continental Europe.

Clearly, what we need is standardization of data exchange. Over the years people have attempted many different techniques for achieving this, with varying degrees of success. These techniques include, as we've already seen, EDI, Microsoft BizTalk, RosettaNet, OASIS, industry specific XML DTDs, and many others. Historically, the most successful schemes have been **vertical**, that is, specific to a particular industry. All participants are subject to the same market forces within the industry, a situation that provides a fertile growing ground for standardization of data exchange.

Typically, standardization schemes work best for goods that can be qualified and quantified readily and less well for "softer" items, such as many services and experienced Java programmers. In these cases sometimes the best we can do is to provide standardized descriptions.

In dealing with these fuzzy areas it is common that many electronic communications go back and forth between customer and vendor, in order to clarify that what is requested matches that which will be provided.

This is another important difference between B2C and corporate purchasing. In the case of B2C, the entire process from selecting a product and putting it in the shopping cart to initiating a purchasing transaction typically takes place within the scope of one session. In corporate purchasing, however, the process of clarifying product specifications, creating customized configurations, and generating and revising quotes can be lengthy, and often spans several sessions. We must be able to persist and accurately recreate the exact stage of this process we were in when we left off, as well as a history of any changes to the transaction parameters that may have occurred as a result of this exchange.

Working with the Appropriate Vendor

When dealing with multiple vendors we soon realize that all vendors are not created equal, even when they compete in the same field. Experience might have taught us that it is perfectly OK to buy "large binder clips" from vendors A and B, but never, ever under any circumstances purchase "three ring hole punches" from vendor B. Over the years that have passed since the hole punch scandal, vendor B has urged us to try its hole punches once more. Each time we've given in we've been burnt again. All the while, vendor B has consistently delivered the most excellent large binder clips at very attractive prices. Now, wouldn't it be great if we could automatically exclude vendor B from all hole punch negotiations, while at the same time make sure she gets requests for binder clips? To be able do this we need two things:

❏ A mechanism by which we can assign vendors to meaningful categories, and include or exclude them in the target group for a request based on the categories they belong to.

❏ To ensure that vendors end up in the appropriate categories we need tools that measure vendor performance objectively. Ideally, these tools should also challenge a vendor's qualification to belong to a specific category as her performance changes, and provide us with alarms and reports.

Workflow

As we pointed out above, workflow plays a significant role in all corporate purchasing activities where multiple interactions between customer and vendor organizations, as well as between different systems or departments within the same organization are required.

> For our purposes "workflow" is defined as the sequence of activities that a corporate purchasing system must perform or initiate in order to complete a purchasing transaction.

In this section we will examine the workflow concept in more detail, as well as look at a couple of ways to implement workflow.

The workflow starts when the need to approach an outside vendor for goods or services is perceived within the purchasing organization. Typically, it then moves through several steps before the customer organization approaches the vendor. It then pours into the vendor organization, splashes a little back and forth and finally settles back into the customer organization.

In order to simplify the design of workflow, it is often useful to characterize each step as a task to be performed by an actor playing a certain role. The accepted method to accomplish this is to create a use case model. A use case model for a simple corporate purchasing workflow might look like this:

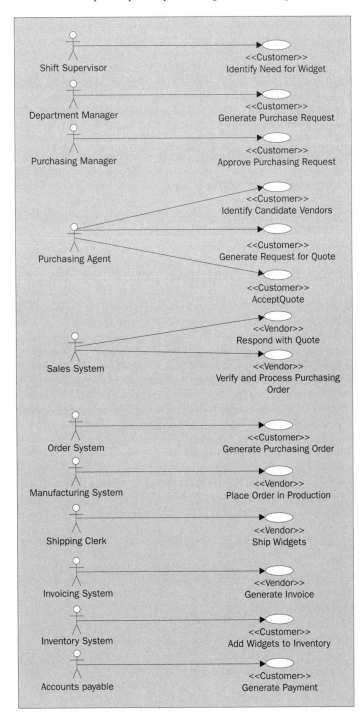

A couple of things are worth pointing out in this example. First of all, an actor need not be a human being. It is not only possible, but also very common for automated systems to play active roles in a workflow. Typical examples are an inventory system that automatically initiates an order when the level of a certain item falls below a threshold level, or the automatic renewal of an expired lease.

Secondly, the example shows a "happy path", where everything goes perfectly well. Each step could fail, and the workflow must know how to deal with exceptions to the "happy path". Also, there could be more complex rules dictating which way the workflow should travel. A customer side example is where a purchasing agent might need approval from his supervisor to place an order exceeding a certain amount. A vendor side example may be where an item is not in stock, and has been back ordered. Any corporate purchasing system worth its salt should be able to deal with these, and many other situations, transparently without human intervention.

We now begin to see that the workflow is a highly dynamic thing, that varies depending on several factors, including outcomes of transactions, the roles of the involved parties, changes to corporate policies and so on. When you design workflow into the system, the cardinal rule is to make it flexible and configurable.

Let us now consider how to implement flexibility in a workflow. The following case study takes a look at one of many possible ways to redirect workflow.

Case Study 1 – Wrong Number!

In the previous section we hinted that the workflow might take different directions based on outcomes of individual steps. This study focuses on a system used by engine repair businesses to buy spare parts directly from manufacturers across the public Internet. The customers would order parts by part numbers assigned by the vendor. They also had a time saving option, which essentially duplicated an old order. The "happy path" system was very straightforward in implementation, and essentially involved the customer logging on to the system, entering part numbers and a P.O. number and sending it off to the vendor.

The vendor would then generate a shipping order to one of its distribution warehouses, and generate an invoice. In order to accomplish this, the system had to interface with legacy systems running on an AS/400 and an IBM mainframe. The process was rather straightforward unless an exception occurred.

When there was an exception, the legacy interactions on the customer and vendor sides became complex, and the appropriate actions varied wildly depending on what condition caused the exception. Each exceptional situation was associated with a redirection of the workflow. And exceptional situations did occur – we found that in many cases the norm was to expect a deviation from the norm!

The Problem

As a side effect of product development, parts were constantly becoming obsolete and being replaced by other parts or assemblies of parts with different part numbers. The following is a simplified list of the most common things that could go wrong:

1. Invalid part number

2. Valid part number, but no parts in stock

3. Valid part number – part is obsolete and no longer in stock

4. Valid part number – part is obsolete and has been replaced by another part

5. Valid part number – part is obsolete and has been replaced by an assembly of several other parts

6. Valid part number – part is obsolete and has been replaced by one of a number of other parts

7. Valid part number – part is still valid, but other parts may be recommended in its stead, depending on application

8. Any combination of 5, 6, and/or 7

In no case was it acceptable to simply display an error message. By interacting with other legacy systems meaningful alternate parts or assemblies of parts could be found in many cases. In other cases, additional information from the customer and/or the vendor would make it possible to complete the transaction. The problem was that the execution paths to resolve each case were completely different and involved different algorithms as well as interactions with different legacy systems. It quickly became apparent that trying to accommodate for the conditions listed above within the "happy path" execution flow of the system would lead to an impossible-to-maintain spaghetti dish, richly flavored with conditional statements. This was not good, especially if the flexibility and extensibility of the workflow weren't to be compromised.

To further complicate things, the individual parts that made up assemblies could be out of stock, obsolete, replaced by another part or assembly and so on. In addition, there were compatibility rules associated with parts and assemblies. Some parts shouldn't be used with others.

The seemingly simple problem of ordering a replacement part turned into a nightmare of maintaining tree-like hierarchies of parts that changed dynamically based on the customer's selections. Not only did the set of valid nodes (valid parts) at each level change based on selections made in levels above and below. In addition, each node had an associated state (valid, obsolete, replaced, part of an assembly, and so on) that could change based on selections made at other levels in the hierarchy. For example, one business rule stated that an assembly of parts would be considered obsolete if it contained a part that had been replaced by another assembly that contained a part that was obsolete!

In summary, we were facing a situation where the course of the workflow was dependent on the properties of one of more objects, which in turn could change in response to property changes of other objects. What to do?

Solutions

In software development, as in most other areas of human activity, there is a vast body of knowledge about how to approach a particular problem or situation. With experience we'll see that the majority of programming problems we're facing belong to a surprisingly small set of categories, only the context varies. Unless we're being overly creative, the same applies to the solutions to the recurring problems.

A constant theme in the evolution of programming languages and software development methodologies has been to find ways to make it easy to reuse old solutions in new contexts. In order to apply old solutions to a problem within a new context, we need to be able to classify problems. One approach is to apply **design patterns** to the design problems (for a detailed description of design patterns please refer to the by now classic text *Design Patterns, Erich Gamma et al., ISBN 0-201-63361-2*).

Design Patterns

Due to the realization that other, brighter designers may have faced a similar situation (and partly due to laziness) we started to look for a design pattern that might address the situation described above. Luckily, the **state** pattern came to the rescue. According to Gamma and co-authors, the intent of the state pattern is to *"Allow an object to alter its behavior when its internal state changes. The object will appear to change its class."* By applying this pattern we were able to separate the appropriate workflow actions for each exception condition into separate classes, thus avoiding nested conditional statements all over the code. The UML notation for the pattern looks like this:

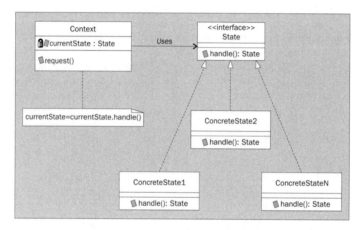

Let us examine the code for the application. The code presented here is much simplified for the sake of clarity. The first source code example shows the class `PartsOrderContext`, which represents an order. This represents the `Context` object of the State pattern. An order can have zero or more line items, which are kept in a `Vector`. The `OrderItem` class (presented after `PartsOrderContext`) represents line items. Here is the code for `PartsOrderContext`:

```java
import java.util.Vector;

public class PartsOrderContext {

  private State state = new InitialState();

  private java.util.Vector partsList = new Vector();

  /**
   * The State pattern request function.
   */
  public void request() {
    state.handle(this);
```

```
}

/**
 * returns a Vector containing the parts list for the order
 */
public java.util.Vector getPartsList() {
  return partsList;
}

/**
 * adds an item for the order
 */
public void addItemToOrder(OrderItem item) {
  partsList.add(item);
  changeState();
}

/**
 * removes an order item from the order
 */
public void removeItemFromOrder(OrderItem item) {
  partsList.remove(item);
  changeState();
}

/**
 * removes the ordrer item at index i
 */
public void removeItemFromOrder(int i) {
  partsList.remove(i);
  changeState();
}

/**
 * Evaluates the state information and changes
 * state as needed
 */
public void changeState() {
  state = state.changeState(this);
}
}
```

The `OrderItem` class, part of the same file as the previous class, implements methods that determine if the part number is valid and whether it represents an obsolete part. We can query the result of these methods through the simple `Boolean` accessor methods `getValidState()` and `getObsoleteState()`. An object of this class is associated with a part number:

```java
public class OrderItem {

  private boolean isValid = false;

  /**
   * Evaluates if a part number is valid
   */
  private void setValidState() {

    // code to evaluate if a part number is valid
    // goes here
  }

  /**
   * Indicates whether the part number is valid
   */
  public boolean getValidState() {
    return isValid;
  }

  private boolean isObsolete = false;

  /**
   * Evaluates if the part number correpsonds to an
   * obsolete part
   */
  private void setObsoleteState() {

    // code to evaluate if a part number is valid
    // goes here
  }

  /**
   * Indicates whether the part number is obsolete
   */
  public boolean getObsoleteState() {
    return isObsolete;
  }

  private String partNumber = "";

  /**
   * Changes the part number
   */
  public void setPartNumber(String partNumber) {
    this.partNumber = partNumber;
    setValidState();
    setObsoleteState();
  }

  /**
   * returns the part number
   */
  public String getPartNumber() {
    return partNumber;
```

```
    }

    OrderItem(String orderNumber) {
      this.partNumber = partNumber;
      setValidState();
      setObsoleteState();
    }
  }
```

Order States

An order can be in one of many states depending on the characteristics of its line items. In this simplified example we've chosen to ignore the handling of replacements and assemblies for sake of clarity. Thus the order can be in one of the following four states:

❑ The order contains no items, which is the initial state

❑ The order contains one or more items, which all have valid part numbers

❑ The order contains at least one item, and at least one of the items has an invalid part number

❑ The order contains at least one item, and at least one of the items is obsolete

The sequence of events that makes up the workflow varies depending on what state the order is in. Following the state pattern, we've chosen to represent each state with a class. Each class implements the interface State:

```
public interface State {

  /**
   * the State pattern handle function
   */
  public void handle(PartsOrderContext ctxt);

  /**
   * maintains state for PartsOrderContext object
   */
  public State changeState(PartsOrderContext ctxt);

}
```

So, for the initial state we have:

```
public class InitialState implements State {

  public State changeState(PartsOrderContext ctxt) {
    java.util.Vector list = ctxt.getPartsList();

    // still no parts in the list
    if (0 == list.size()) {
      return this;

    }
    for (int i = 0; i < list.size(); i++) {
```

```
        OrderItem item = (OrderItem) list.get(i);

      // change state to invalid part
      if (!item.getValidState()) {
        return new InvalidPartsState();

        // change state to obsolete part
      }
      if (item.getObsoleteState()) {
        return new ObsoletePartsState();
      }
    }

    // change state to valid state
    return new AllPartsValidState();
  }

  public void handle(PartsOrderContext ctxt) {

    // in the initial state the workflow does nothing
  }

}
```

For the case where the order contains one or more items, which all have valid part numbers:

```
public class AllPartsValidState implements State {

  public State changeState(PartsOrderContext ctxt) {
    java.util.Vector list = ctxt.getPartsList();

    // no items, change back to initial state
    if (0 == list.size()) {
      return new InitialState();

    }
    for (int i = 0; i < list.size(); i++) {
      OrderItem item = (OrderItem) list.get(i);

      // change state to invalid parts
      if (!item.getValidState()) {
        return new InvalidPartsState();

        // change state to invalid parts
      }
      if (item.getObsoleteState()) {
        return new ObsoletePartsState();
      }
    }

    // still in valid state
    return this;
  }

  public void handle(PartsOrderContext ctxt) {
```

```
      // code to perform workflow for an order containing
      // only valid parts
  }


}
```

For when the order contains at least one item, and at least one of the items has an invalid part number we have:

```
public class InvalidPartsState implements State {

  public State changeState(PartsOrderContext ctxt) {
    java.util.Vector list = ctxt.getPartsList();

    // no items, change back to initial state
    if (0 == list.size()) {
      return new InitialState();

    }
    for (int i = 0; i < list.size(); i++) {
      OrderItem item = (OrderItem) list.get(i);

      // still in invalid part state
      if (!item.getValidState()) {
        return this;

        // change states obsolete part state
      }
      if (item.getObsoleteState()) {
        return new ObsoletePartsState();
      }
    }

    // change states to all parts valid
    return new AllPartsValidState();
  }

  public void handle(PartsOrderContext ctxt) {

    // code to perform workflow for an order containing
    // invalid part numbers
  }

}
```

Lastly, when the order contains at least one item, and at least one of the items is obsolete we have the ObsoletePartsState class:

```
public class ObsoletePartsState implements State {

  public State changeState(PartsOrderContext ctxt) {
    java.util.Vector list = ctxt.getPartsList();
```

```
      // no items, change back to initial state
      if (0 == list.size()) {
        return new InitialState();

      }
      for (int i = 0; i < list.size(); i++) {
        OrderItem item = (OrderItem) list.get(i);

        // change state to invalid part number
        if (!item.getValidState()) {
          return new InvalidPartsState();

          // still in obsolete part state
        }
        if (item.getObsoleteState()) {
          return this;
        }
      }

      // change state to all parts valid
      return new AllPartsValidState();
    }

    public void handle(PartsOrderContext ctxt) {

      // code to perform workflow for an order containing
      // obsolete parts
    }

  }
```

How it Fits Together

The PartsOrderContext class has methods for adding and removing line items. A line item can be either valid, invalid or obsolete, so as we add and remove items the state of the order may change. We evaluate the current state of the order by calling the PartOrderContext object's changeState() method. This method accesses the current state object and calls its changeState() method. This method in turn performs the task of evaluating the current state of the order, and returning an instance of a class representing that state.

Eventually we are done adding and removing items, and will want to execute the workflow associated with the order. We do this by calling the request() method, which in turn executes the handle method of the current State member object. This object is of a class that corresponds to the current state of the order, and thus the corresponding workflow is executed in its handle() method.

In the simple implementation above, a state change results in the construction of a new object implementing the State interface. If we take care to write classes implementing State in such a way that they have no instance variables, several Context objects can share State objects, making construction at each state change unnecessary. Object sharing can be accomplished in several ways. One obvious way is to declare a static object of each class representing a state in the Context class. While simple to implement, this can lead to blocking when several instances of the Context class want to simultaneously access methods of the state objects. A better alternative is to create pools of state class instances and hand out the appropriate objects as needed.

One design alternative worth considering is to make the State interface an abstract class instead of an interface. The base class implements common functionality that may be used by all state classes, whereas implementation of the handle method is deferred to its subclasses.

With that we conclude the first case study. You now have some of the building blocks with which you can implement a flexible and extensible workflow, which can change depending on its execution context.

However, two ingredients are still missing:

❑   A way to save and restore state information

❑   The actual mechanism we use to hand the workflow requests down the line to the next actor

The first point is important for two reasons. We suggested above that the workflow might span numerous sessions, and we wouldn't want to leave our objects sitting around in memory idly for extended periods while we patiently wait for the next session to start. This could be bad in several ways. First of all we might risk losing our data in the event of a hardware failure, and secondly it's a waste of precious memory. For this reason it would be good if we could save an object's state to persistent storage, and later restore it.

Another situation where it may be beneficial to be able to save an object's state is when a step in the workflow fails. We may want to restore the object to a previous state and continue along a different execution path or retry the failed operation.

Let's start by examining the first missing link.

Saving and Restoring State

I suggested above that we need a way to save and restore state information of an object. We could take a snapshot of the object's state and save it. If the operation succeeds we move on, if not we use our snapshot to restore the state of the object.

One obvious solution would be to use an object database. Unfortunately, in my experience very few companies have access to object databases, so that approach won't work in most cases. Another solution would be to use entity EJBs in conjunction with an application server. This is a very valid approach, provided we have access to an application server, such as IBM WebSphere, or BEA WebLogic.

What if we don't? Since almost every organization has access to a relational database, we could map the state information to columns in database tables, so called **Object Relational mapping**. The problem with this approach is that each attribute of the object that we want to store has to correspond to a column in the database. This tight coupling between a database and an object makes it more cumbersome to change the details of class implementations or add new classes to the system. Ideally our mechanism for saving and restoring an object's state should work independently of the class of the object.

The Memento Pattern

This situation is addressed by the design pattern **memento**. The memento pattern is described in *Design Patterns* p. 283-292. Its *raison d'être* is *"Without violating encapsulation, capture and externalize an object's internal state so that the object can be restored to that state later."* The UML notation for the memento pattern looks like the figure shown overleaf:

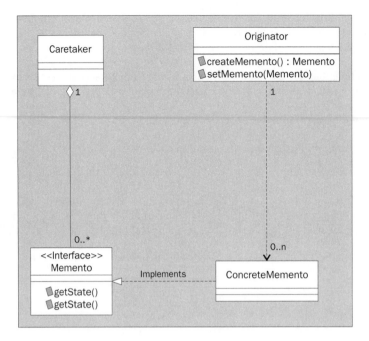

This is how it works: The `Originator` is an object whose state we need to save and later restore. An `Originator` object can create a snapshot of its internal state in the form of a `Memento`. A `Caretaker` object can then accept the `Memento` for safekeeping. Later, an `Originator` object can request the `Memento` from the `Caretaker`, and restore the original state from the `Memento`.

The nice part about this design is that it promotes loose coupling. An `Originator` object doesn't need to know anything about how the `Memento` is stored, as long as it knows how to get it back. It is the responsibility of the `Caretaker` to manage persistence of the `Memento`. This somewhat similar in concept to container-managed persistence of an entity EJB, where the responsibility of persistence is delegated to the container. Conversely, the `Caretaker` has no knowledge of what the data inside the `Memento` actually means or is used for. All it does is save it for later use.

There is also an issue of timing involved. Access to persistent storage mechanisms, such as databases or disk files are often costly in terms of performance. While this is acceptable in the scenario of storing an object between sessions, it is not a good design for implementing state restoration after a failed operation, or to implement undoable operations. It would be nice if the `Caretaker` object could cache a copy of recently accessed objects in memory for fast access. Objects that have not been requested in a certain interval of time are removed from memory and copied to persistent storage.

> *Actually, in some cases it is desirable to copy all objects to persistent storage whether they are cached in memory or not. Recently accessed objects will be restored from memory, whereas other objects will be restored from persistent storage. This strategy can be used as a defense against catastrophic system failure.*

A Persistence Mechanism

Let's take a closer look at a flexible, caching persistence mechanism based on the memento pattern that combines persistent storage and caching. The following source code implements a `CareTaker` class that can save and restore state objects regardless of their class:

```java
import java.io.File;
import java.io.FileInputStream;
import java.io.FileOutputStream;
import java.io.ObjectInputStream;
import java.io.ObjectOutputStream;
import java.io.Serializable;
import java.util.Hashtable;
import java.util.Enumeration;

public class CareTaker {

  private Hashtable mementos = new Hashtable();

  private long cycle = 0;

  /**
   * saves a memento
   */
  public void save(String key, Memento memento) {
    StateHolder stateHolder = new StateHolder(cycle, memento.getState());
    mementos.put(key, stateHolder);
  }

  /**
   * restores a memento
   */
  public void restore(String key, Memento memento) {

    // try to get the object from the hashtable
    StateHolder stateHolder = (StateHolder) mementos.get(key);

    // it is not there, try to get it from a file
    if (null == stateHolder) {
      try {
        File f = new File(key + ".ser");
        ObjectInputStream ois =
          new ObjectInputStream(new FileInputStream(f));
        Object state = ois.readObject();
        ois.close();
        memento.setState(state);

        // put back in hashtable
        save(key, memento);
        System.out.println("Restored " + key + " from disk");
      } catch (Exception e) {
        e.printStackTrace();
      }
    } else {
      memento.setState(stateHolder.state);
      stateHolder.cycle = cycle;
    }
  }

  private final static int maxCycles = 2;

  /**
```

```
    * purges the hastable periodically
    */
  public void purge() {
    cycle += 1;

    // look over all objects and see which ones are old
    Enumeration keys = mementos.keys();
    while (keys.hasMoreElements()) {
      String key = (String) keys.nextElement();
      StateHolder sh = (StateHolder) mementos.get(key);

      // The object is too old, write it to disk and remove it from
      // the hash table
      if (cycle + maxCycles > sh.cycle) {

        //
        // Note: if we want to be on the safe side in case of a
        // catastrophic system failure we could write all
        // objects to persistent storage when they're added to the
        // Hashtable. In that situation we simply remove the object
        // from the Hashtable here. The rest of the code below
        // would then be moved to execute within the save method.
        //
        try {
          File f = new File(key + ".ser");
          ObjectOutputStream oos =
            new ObjectOutputStream(new FileOutputStream(f));
          oos.writeObject((Serializable) sh.state);
          oos.close();
          mementos.remove(key);
          System.out.println("Saved " + key + " to disk");
        } catch (Exception e) {
          e.printStackTrace();
        }
      }
    }
  }

  /**
   * member class to hold state along with the cycle it was stored
   * the cycle is used to determine when to write the object to file
   */
  private class StateHolder {
    public long cycle;

    public Object state;

    StateHolder(long cycle, Object state) {
      this.cycle = cycle;
      this.state = state;
    }
  }
}
```

The `CareTaker` class has two methods, `save()` and `restore()`, which are used to save and restore keyed state information contained in individual `Mementos`. The `Caretaker` is not concerned with the contents and meaning of the state information it receives via the `save()` method. It simply puts the data along with the key and a "time stamp" in a hash table.

The `Caretaker` also has a `purge()` method, which is used to periodically scan the hash table for state information that hasn't been accessed for a certain number of scan cycles. The information is written to disk and removed from the hash table. This arrangement combines fast access to recently accessed state information as required by undoable operations with the long-term persistence we need for state persistence across sessions.

The `restore()` method first looks for the requested state information in the hashtable. If it cannot find it there it attempts to read it from a disk file. If it can read the file successfully, the state information of the memento is updated and the state information is once again time stamped and stored in the hashtable.

The observant reader has probably already figured out that this scheme is not limited to the use of disk file for persistent storage. If we replace the `FileInputStream` and `FileOutputStream` objects with `ByteArrayInputStream` and `ByteArrayOutputStream` objects respectively we can serialize the state to an array of `bytes`. We can then store the array in a database, transmit it over a socket or do whatever we feel is necessary for the safekeeping of our state information. The only requirement on the safekeeping mechanism is that can store and retrieve arrays of byte.

We also show the implementation of a `Memento` interface:

```
public interface Memento {

  public Object getState();

  public void setState(Object state);

}
```

Finally, here is a sample `Originator`:

```
import java.io.Serializable;

public class AnOriginator implements Serializable {

    /**
     * Member class implementing the Memento interface
     */
    private class MyMemento implements Memento {
       public Object getState() {
          return (Object) mementoState;
       }

       public void setState(Object state) {
          mementoState = (MyState) state;
       }

       MyState mementoState = new MyState();
    }
```

```
/**
 * Serializable member class holding state
 */
private class MyState implements Serializable {
    public String var1 = "Hello";
    public int var2 = 1;

    public MyState() {}

    public MyState(MyState st) {
        var1 = st.var1;
        var2 = st.var2;
    }
}

private MyState state = new MyState();

/**
 * creates a new memento
 */
public Memento createMemento() {
    Memento aMemento = new MyMemento();
    aMemento.setState(new MyState(state));
    return aMemento;
}

/**
 * replaces the memento with another
 */
public void setMemento(Memento memento) {
    state = new MyState((MyState) memento.getState());
}

// Other methods and members here
}
```

We should point out a couple of things regarding the `Originator` class, `AnOriginator`. First of all it declares one inner class that implements the `Memento` interface, and another intended to hold its internal state. Both the `AnOriginator` class and the class that represents state must implement the `java.io.Serializable` interface, or the `CareTaker` won't be able to write serialized state information to disk. The implementations of both the memento and state classes are hidden from the outside world, and can vary independently from the persistence mechanism.

When discussing undoable/redoable operations it is important to understand that some types of processes lend themselves better to these types of operations than others. The fact that we have a framework that supports undoable operations doesn't guarantee that the operations themselves are undoable. For example, workflows that contain database updates supporting two-phase commits are ideally suited for undoable/redoable steps in a workflow. The effects of many batch processes executed in a step of a workflow may not be as easily undone.

Message Mechanisms

This leaves us needing to answer the final question: "How do we build the actual mechanism we use to hand the workflow requests down the line to the next actor?"

If the actor is a human being a simple and common answer is: "e-mail!" For example, if an inventory system detects that the supply of widgets is getting dangerously low, it could generate an e-mail addressed to the warehouse manager and to a purchasing agent alerting them to this state of affairs. Naturally we can build more complex workflows based on e-mail. The reader should be aware that I mention e-mail first, since it is such a widely used mechanism for passing messages. One should remember however, that e-mail is both slow and unreliable. We will look at other, more robust methods of communication later in this section.

The JavaMail API

The method of choice for sending and receiving e-mail in Java applications is by using the **JavaMail API**. The JavaMail API is an abstraction layer that sits on top of a mail provider. JavaMail isolates us from the intricacies of the many different e-mail protocols that exist, such as SMTP, POP3, MAPI, IMAP4, MIME, and so on, making it possible to create portable applications that use e-mail.

We will not go into the differences between the various e-mail protocols here. It is sufficient to say that the differences between the protocols are of such a magnitude that Sun saw fit to create the JavaMail API. The interested reader is encouraged to look at http://www.ietf.org/rfc.html or http://www.rfc-editor.org/ and study the RFCs that define each protocol:

- ❑ Simple Mail Transfer Protocol (SMTP) – RFC 821
- ❑ Post Office Protocol revision 3 (POP3) – RFC 1939, RFC 1957
- ❑ Internet Message Access Protocol revision 4 (IMAP4) – RFC 1733
- ❑ Multipurpose Internet Mail Extension (MIME) – RFC 1521, RFC 1522
- ❑ Internet Message Format – RFC 822

Detailed MAPI (Mail API) information can be found on the Microsoft web site.

The JavaMail classes and interfaces reside in the package `javax.mail`, which is part of the Java 2 Enterprise Edition (J2EE). The JavaMail API is a vast topic, so we can only scratch the surface here. First, we must familiarize ourselves with the concepts of **Store** and **Transport**. In JavaMail terminology, a Transport is a service that can send e-mail messages. A Store is a service that can retrieve messages. Transports and Stores can be of different types. (An example of a transport type is SMTP. An example of a store type is POP3.)

As all our interactions with the e-mail system take place in the context of a session, our first action is to establish a JavaMail session. A `Session` object has several properties that we can set by passing it a `java.util.Properties` object. The session properties are:

- ❑ `mail.transport.protocol` – default transport protocol for the session
- ❑ `mail.store.protocol` – default store protocol for the session
- ❑ `mail.host` – default host for both transport and store, unless they have their own host property

❑ `mail.<protocol>.host` – host for a specific protocol

❑ `mail.user` – default user name for both transport and store, unless they have their own user name property

❑ `mail.<protocol>.user` – user name for a specific protocol

❑ `mail.from` – return e-mail address

❑ `mail.debug` – debug setting for the session

There is no constructor for the `Session` class. Instead we use the static method `Session.getInstance()` to create a `Session` object. We now know enough to look at the code to create a `Session`:

```
// we can store our preferred mail settings
// in the System properties
Properties props= System.getProperties();
props.put("mail.transport.protocol","smtp");
props.put("mail.store.protocol","smtp");
props.put("mail.user","example");
props.put("mail.host","mail.example.com");

// get a Session object
Session session=Session.getInstance(System.getProperties(),null);
```

The second argument to `getInstance()` can be used to pass an `Authenticator` object, which can be used to verify the credentials of the user.

Sending Messages

Once we have established a JavaMail session we should try to do something with it. Let's start by looking at how we send a message:

```
try {

    // Create a message
    Message message=new MimeMessage(session);
    message.setSubject("Valentine's day poem");
    message.setText(
        "You're so fine! Please be mine! "+
        "Meet me at nine! Don't tell the swine! (i.e. your dad)");

    message.setFrom(new InternetAddress("romeo@montague.org"));

    message.setRecipient(Message.RecipientType.TO,
                                   new InternetAddress("juliet@capulet.net"));

    message.setRecipient(Message.RecipientType.BCC,
                                   new InternetAddress("WillShake@stratford.com"));

    // get a Transport object
    Transport transp=session.getTransport("smtp");
    transp.connect();
    transp.sendMessage(message,message.getAllRecipients());
    transp.close();
```

```
}
catch(NoSuchProviderException nspe) {

}
catch(AddressException ae) {

}
catch(MessagingException me) {

}
```

JavaMail messages are subclasses of the abstract class `Message`. In the example we create a message of the `javax.mail.internet.MimeMessage` class. The `MimeMessage` class conveniently bundles most of the commonly used message functionality, such as multi-part messages, different MIME types, and so on.

We create an SMTP transport by calling the session's `getTransport()` method. To send the message we establish a transport connection, send the message, and finally close the connection. The reader might think this is a lot of work to send a message. By coincidence, the same thought struck the fine people at Sun. The JavaMail API provides a static method in the `Transport` class, which sends a message without the programmer explicitly having to create a `Transport` object, connect, and so on. The syntax is simply:

```
Transport.send(message);
```

Retrieving Messages

As one might suspect, JavaMail also provides us with ways to retrieve messages. This service is provided by `Store`. A `Store` has one or more `Folders`. There is always a root folder, which we get access to by calling the `setDefaultFolder()` method. Incoming mail is usually found in the `Folder` named INBOX. The `Store` doesn't do much more than give us access to its `Folders`. The `Folder` provides a rich interface for managing messages. In this chapter we only have room to demonstrate a small sample of the folder's functionality. Here's an example:

```
try {

    String host="mail.capulet.net";
    String user="juliet@capulet.net";
    String password="whereforeartthouromeo?";

    Store store=session.getStore("pop3");
    store.connect(host,user,password);

    Folder inbox=store.getDefaultFolder().getFolder("INBOX");
    inbox.open(Folder.READ_ONLY);

    System.out.println("Your inbox contains"+
                          inbox.getMessageCount()+" messages");
    System.out.println("Your inbox contains"+
                          inbox.getUnreadMessageCount()+" unread messages");

    for(int i=1;i<=inbox.getMessageCount();i++) {
        Message mess=inbox.getMessage(i);
        // get the sender
```

```
        Address[] from=mess.getFrom();
        String sender=from[0].toString();

        // display messages from Romeo
        if(sender.equals("romeo@montague.org")) {
            mess.writeTo(System.out);
        }
        // delete all other
        else {
            mess.setFlag(Flags.Flag.DELETED,true);
        }
    }

    // close inbox and purge all deleted messages
    inbox.close(true);
    store.close();

}
catch(NoSuchProviderException nspe) {

}
catch(MessagingException me) {

}
catch(java.io.IOException ioe) {

}
```

At the beginning of the example we obtain a POP3 `Store` from the session. We then establish a connection, and open the `INBOX` folder. We can display some basic folder statistics by calling the folder's `getMessageCount()` and `getUnreadMessageCount()`. The `Folder` has many more methods for displaying and manipulating its content; it is outside the scope of this chapter to cover them all.

We then iterate over all the messages and determine whom they are from. We display wanted messages by calling the message's `writeTo()` method, which writes the message's content to an output stream.

Unwanted messages are simply flagged as being deleted, using the `setFlag()` method. We then close the folder. The `Boolean` argument to the `close()` method is set to indicate that we want to permanently remove all messages flagged as being deleted from the `INBOX` folder.

Using SMTP

What can we do if we don't have access to a JavaMail API compliant e-mail system? Most enterprises have at least one SMTP (Simple Mail Transfer Protocol) server. Here is code for a class that sends e-mail using the SMTP protocol:

```
import java.io.BufferedReader;
import java.io.InputStreamReader;
import java.io.PrintStream;
import java.net.Socket;

public class SMTPMailer {
```

```java
private Socket sock;
private PrintStream out;
private BufferedReader in;

// recipients email address
public void setTo(String arg) {
   to = arg;
}
private String to;

// senders email address
public void setSender(String arg) {
   sender = arg;
}
private String sender;

// message subject
public void setSubject(String arg) {
   subject = arg;
}
private String subject;

// the content of the message
public void setMesage(String arg) {
   message = arg;
}
private String message;

// IP address of SMTP host
public void setHost(String arg) {
   hostAddress = arg;
}
private String hostAddress;

// mail port
public void setPort(int arg) {
   mailPort = arg;
}
private int mailPort = 25;

// SMTP server name
public void setServerName(String arg) {
   mailFrom = arg;
}
public String mailFrom;

public void init() {
   try {
      sock = new Socket(hostAddress, mailPort);
      in = new BufferedReader(new InputStreamReader(sock.getInputStream()));
      out = new PrintStream(sock.getOutputStream());
   } catch (Exception e) {
      System.out.println("init():");
      e.printStackTrace();
```

```
            }
        }

    public void doIt() {
        try {
            in.readLine();
        } catch (Exception e) {
            System.out.println("doIt():");
            e.printStackTrace();
            return;
        }

        mail("HELLO " + mailFrom);
        mail("MAIL FROM: " + sender);
        mail("RCPT TO: " + to);
        mail("DATA");
        mail("SUBJECT:" + subject + "\n" + message + "\n" + ".\n");
        mail("QUIT");

        try {
            sock.close();
        } catch (Exception e) {
            System.out.println("doIt():");
            e.printStackTrace();
        }
    }

    public void mail(String send) {
        System.out.println(send);
        String response = new String();
        try {
            out.println(send);
            out.flush();
            response = in.readLine();
        } catch (Exception e) {
            System.out.println("mail():");
            e.printStackTrace();
        }
        System.out.println(response);
    }
}
```

The class has a number of private data members that represent such things as e-mail addresses, message subject, message body, and so on. A client creates an instance of the SMTPMailer class, and sets the data members to appropriate values using the various mutator methods. The client then calls the init() method, which creates a TCP/IP socket connection to the SMTP server and sets up streams that can be used to read from or write to the connection. Finally, the client calls the doIt() method, which creates and sends the e-mail message. It's really that simple.

Notice that we don't have to log in to the SMTP server or present any other credentials. Before you attempt using the SMTPMailer class to send "anonymous" e-mails to your boss from some obscure SMTP server, I'd like to point out that most SMTP servers are set up to reject message requests coming from IP addresses outside its own subnet, and many perform other forms of validation.

What Do We Send?

The really hard part is to come up with the content of the e-mail. One idea that seems to work well for browser based systems is to mail the complete URL of a web page within a web application that will automatically place the recipient at the appropriate spot in the workflow, with all fields automatically populated.

Now what do we do if the next actor in the workflow chain isn't a human being? We could, of course, still use e-mail. An agent for an automated system could periodically retrieve mail for the process, and the system could then perform actions based on the content (or subject) of the message. This method is used all over the Internet for subscribing and un-subscribing to mailing lists, and so on. It is simple, and time tested, but completely proprietary and not very robust. Another possibility is to attach to the message serialized Java objects that can be used to direct the workflow in some remote subsystem.

Beyond E-mail

There are many solutions that are superior to e-mail for communication of workflow requests between processes, and we will examine three of them:

❑   Remote Method Invocation (RMI)

❑   Common Object Request Broker Architecture (CORBA)

❑   Java Messaging Service (JMS)

In the following sections we'll take a brief look at each of these, concentrating particularly on the first two, as we discussed JMS in Chapter 19. Once again, for more comprehensive coverage the reader is referred to *Java Server Programming, J2EE Edition, ISBN 1-861004-65-6*, from *Wrox Press*.

Java Remote Method Invocation – RMI

Simply put, RMI allows objects running on one Java Virtual Machine access to methods of objects running on a different JVM. The JVMs can exist on the same physical machine or on separate machines connected by a network. The core RMI architecture consists of the following main elements:

❑   Remote objects

❑   Client stubs for interaction with the remote objects

❑   A registry for locating remote objects

In addition RMI provides a network supporting protocol – Java Remote Method Protocol (JRMP), a mechanism for remote object activation, a mechanism for distributed garbage collection and a mechanism for communication with CORBA objects. As pointed out above, we do not have enough space in this chapter to treat all these features exhaustively. Since one focus of this chapter is integration with legacy systems we'll take a look at how to integrate a legacy system written in C using RMI in conjunction with the **Java Native Interface (JNI)**.

Let's look at a very simple example. A Java purchasing system needs to generate purchase orders. It coexists with a UNIX-based legacy purchase order system written in C. Each purchase order must have a unique purchase order number, and to avoid conflicts we want the Java system to be able to get the next available purchase order number from the legacy system.

The first thing we do is to implement an interface for our RMI object. The interface has to extend the java.rmi.Remote interface. All methods that are to be executable remotely have to include java.rmi.RemoteException in their throws clause:

```
import java.rmi.*;
public interface PONumber extends Remote {

    public String getNextPONumber(String quoteNumber)
                    throws RemoteException;
}
```

The next step is to write a class that implements the `PONumber` interface. We make the implementation an RMI server object by extending a subclass of the abstract class `java.rmi.RemoteServer`. In our case we extend the concrete subclass `UnicastRemoteObject`. This class supports object references on a TCP/IP network. (Note that the constructor must throw a `RemoteException` as well.) The actual work is done in the native method, which accesses the legacy C code. Note that native methods do not have a body:

```
import java.rmi.*;

public class PONumberImpl extends java.rmi.server.UnicastRemoteObject
                        implements Remote {

    public String getNextPONumber(String quoteNumber) throws RemoteException {
        return getNumberFromLegacy(quoteNumber);
    }

    public PONumberImpl() throws RemoteException {
    }

    native private String getNumberFromLegacy(String quoteNumber);
}
```

RMI uses two types of objects internally for communications. On the client side there is a stub object, and on the server side a skeleton object. The following diagram shows how it fits together:

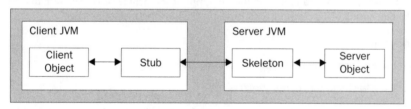

We generate stub and skeleton classes by running the RMI compiler, `rmic`, on our implementation class. The command in our case looks like this:

```
rmic PONumberImpl
```

The RMI compiler generates the following class files:

❑   `PONumberImpl_Skel.class`
❑   `PONumberImpl_Stub.class`

At this point we want to consider what kind of objects we can use as return types and parameters to remote methods. RMI must be able to serialize objects in order to send them across a network, a process called **marshaling**. Therefore all objects used as parameters and return types must implement the interface `java.io.Serializable`.

Clients get access to remote RMI interface implementations by querying a registry. For this to work we need to register our implementation with the registry. The implementation is bound to a name, in our case "PONum". This is accomplished by the following code:

```java
import java.rmi.Naming;
import java.rmi.RemoteException;
public class RegisterPONumber {

   public static void main(String[] args) {
      try {
         PONumberImpl impl = new PONumberImpl();
         Naming.rebind("PONum", impl);
      } catch (java.rmi.RemoteException re) {
      } catch (java.net.MalformedURLException mue) {
      }
   }
}
```

A client can get access to a remote object by querying the registry for a URL including the name of the host and the name the implementation is bound to. This is done by calling the static method `Naming.lookup()`. The returned reference is then cast to the appropriate interface type. Once a client has acquired a reference to the remote object it can use it to call its methods as though they were local objects:

```java
import java.rmi.Naming;

public class POClient {

   public String getPONumber(String quoteNumber)
               throws java.rmi.NotBoundException,
                      java.net.MalformedURLException,
                      java.rmi.RemoteException {

      PONumber poNum = (PONumber) Naming.lookup("rmi://example.com/PONum");
      return poNum.getNextPONumber(quoteNumber);
   }
}
```

Let us now turn our attention to the JNI part of our example. In order to interface with C or C++ code we need to generate a JNI C/C++ header file. We do this by running the JNI header generation tool, `javah`, on our class.

```
javah -jni -d . PONumber
```

The generated file, `PONumberImpl.h`, has the following content:

```c
/* DO NOT EDIT THIS FILE - it is machine generated */
#include <jni.h>
/* Header for class PONumberImpl */
```

```
#ifndef _Included_PONumberImpl
#define _Included_PONumberImpl
#ifdef __cplusplus
extern "C" {
#endif
#undef PONumberImpl_serialVersionUID
#define PONumberImpl_serialVersionUID -3215090123894869218LL
/* Inaccessible static: logname */
/* Inaccessible static: log */
#undef PONumberImpl_serialVersionUID
#define PONumberImpl_serialVersionUID -4100238210092549637LL
#undef PONumberImpl_serialVersionUID
#define PONumberImpl_serialVersionUID 4974527148936298033LL
/* Inaccessible static: portParamTypes */
/* Inaccessible static: portFactoryParamTypes */
/* Inaccessible static:
class_00024java_00024rmi_00024server_00024RMIClientSocketFactory */
/* Inaccessible static:
class_00024java_00024rmi_00024server_00024RMIServerSocketFactory */
/* Inaccessible static: class_00024java_00024rmi_00024server_00024ServerRef */
/*
 * Class:      PONumberImpl
 * Method:     getNumberFromLegacy
 * Signature: (Ljava/lang/String;)Ljava/lang/String;
 */
JNIEXPORT jstring JNICALL Java_PONumberImpl_getNumberFromLegacy
  (JNIEnv *, jobject, jstring);

#ifdef __cplusplus
}
#endif
#endif
```

We then include the header file `jni.h` and `PONumberImpl.h` in the C code that accesses the legacy system:

```
#include <jni.h>
#include "PONumberImpl.h"
#ifdef __cplusplus
extern "C"{
#endif

JNIEXPORT jstring JNICALL Java_PONumberImpl_getNumberFromLegacy
  (JNIEnv *, jobject, jstring){

  // put your C code here

}

#ifdef __cplusplus
}
#endif
```

Once again we should say that this coverage has been very brief – we've haven't even touched upon topics like dynamic loading of remote objects, remote callbacks, garbage collection …

786

The Common Object Request Broker Architecture – CORBA

Another mechanism for remote access to objects is **CORBA**. CORBA is a much more complex standard than RMI, and in addition to providing remote access to objects and a naming service, it provides many other services such as a transaction service, an event service, a persistence service, and so on. In this chapter we will only look at some of the basic features.

At the heart of CORBA lies the **Object Request Broker** (**ORB**). The ORB is responsible for handling interactions between client applications and remote objects. ORBs can communicate between themselves using **Internet Inter Orb Protocols** (**IIOP**). A sketch of CORBA is shown in the following figure:

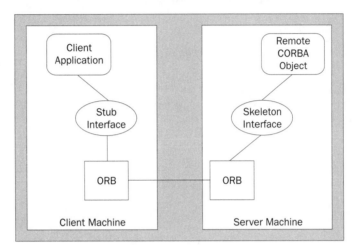

Client applications and server objects communicate through ORBs. As in RMI the client uses a stub interface to access a remote object. The stub communicates through the ORB mechanism with a remote skeleton interface. This in turn passes requests on to the server objects.

Whereas RMI is limited to the use of Java to implement clients and remote objects, CORBA features language independence. The remote interfaces are described using **Interface Definition Language** (**IDL**). There are several standard mappings from IDL to programming languages such as C, C++, Ada, COBOL and Java. IDL is compiled using an IDL compiler, and the resulting files are used to implement the client and server parts of the application.

Like Java, IDL has a C-like syntax. Unlike Java, though, IDL permits only interface declarations, and implementation of interfaces is done in the target language. Here is the IDL for the simple example above:

```
interface PONumber{
   string getNextPONumber(in string quoteNumber);
};
```

This IDL defines an interface with a single method, which accepts an incoming parameter of type string and returns a string.

The IDL is run through an IDL compiler supporting the IDL-to-Java mapping, such as `idltojava`. The output from this compiler is:

❑   A Java interface, in our case `PONumber`. This is used as any other Java interface.

❑ A helper class. In our example this class will be called PONumberHelper. This is used to cast CORBA references to the appropriate Java interface type.

❑ A holder class. This is used for passing arguments to and from remote objects. In our example this class is called PONumberHolder.

Most IDL compilers also generate the stub and skeleton classes for us. The client-side stub class in our example would be _PONumberStub. The server-side skeleton class is called _PONumberImplBase. These classes implement the functionality needed to interact with the ORB.

The Java interface generated in our example looks like this:

```
public interface PONumber extends org.omg.CORBA.Object {

    public String getNextPONumber(String quoteNumber);

}
```

Our remaining programming task is to write the implementation. We do this by creating a class, which extends _PONumberImplBase:

```
public class PONumberImpl extends _PONumberImplBase {

    public String getNextPONumber(String quoteNumber) {
        return getNumberFromLegacy(quoteNumber);
    }

    native private String getNumberFromLegacy(String quoteNumber);
}
```

RMI vs. CORBA

It should be clear by now that RMI and CORBA share many common features. So how do you determine which one to use? CORBA's language independence is a clear advantage when we want to integrate with legacy systems. Such systems are often written in programming languages other than Java, such as COBOL or C. CORBA precedes Java by several years, and many legacy systems already use CORBA, or can be easily modified to do so.

CORBA's richness can be seen both as a strength and as a weakness. There are very few tasks in distributed computing that you can't accomplish using CORBA. However, if the task at hand is only to implement a simple workflow, then using CORBA might be overkill.

RMI's main strength is its relative simplicity. In a Java-only environment, or one where legacy systems can easily be wrapped in Java, RMI is a worthy contender. Wrapping of legacy code written in C or C++ can often be accomplished using the Java Native Interface (JNI).

A new addition to RMI, **RMI-IIOP**, allows RMI objects to use the CORBA Internet Inter Orb Protocol (IIOP) instead of its native Java Remote Method Protocol (JRMP). This makes it possible for RMI and CORBA objects to communicate with each other directly. This fact makes RMI and CORBA complementary instead of competing technologies.

Java Messaging Service – JMS

As we've seen before, the Java 2 Enterprise Edition provides us with a very robust standardized messaging solution – JMS – which gives us a common interface specification for interfaces that sit on top of third party messaging services.

In terms of our ongoing discussion we should note that messaging systems store posted messages then forward them to recipients which is essentially an asynchronous operation. An asynchronous model is inherently non-blocking, thus a sender can post a message then go about its business without having to wait for a response from the recipient. This enables loose coupling of distributed subsystems and components.

By contrast, **remote procedure call** (**RPC**) based systems such as RMI and CORBA are inherently synchronous, and require the sender and recipient to be connected simultaneously. Remote operations are also blocking unless we take precautions in our program to make them non-blocking. Synchronous operation promotes tight coupling between distributed subsystems, which can lead to the familiar scenario in which the entire system collapses through a domino effect when a small part of it breaks down. (In all fairness, an asynchronous messaging based distributed system becomes paralyzed if the messaging component fails.)

Without getting bogged down in JMS theory, which we've already seen in Chapter 19, let's show an example of one way we can deploy JMS messaging in support of workflow.

This example architecture consists of two or more systems that are communicating via JMS. The systems expose interfaces that allow external processes to interact with the systems by executing commands. The UML model for this mechanism is shown in the following diagram:

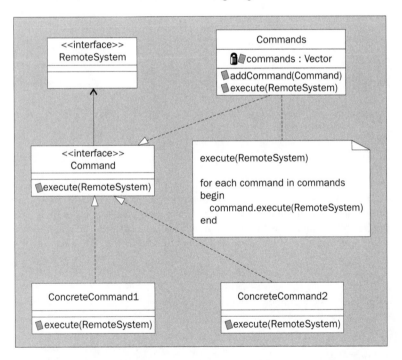

All communicating systems implement the interface `RemoteSystem`, which serves as a placeholder for a system. Executable commands are represented by classes implementing the `Command` interface. The `Command` interface's only method, `execute()`, accepts an argument of type `RemoteSystem`. Thus, concrete command classes can execute exposed methods of the systems inside the body of the execute method.

The `Commands` class is a special type of command that can execute sequences of commands in its execute method. A sequence of commands constitutes a workflow, or a part of a workflow. Here is the code for the command execution mechanism:

```
public interface RemoteSystem{
    // empty interface, serves as placeholder
}
```

```
public interface Command extends java.io.Serializable{
    public void execute(RemoteSystem rs);
}
```

```
import java.util.Vector;

public class Commands implements Command, java.io.Serializable {

    private Vector commands = new Vector();

    /**
     * add a command to the Vector
     */
    public void addCommand(Command command) {
        commands.add(command);
    }

    /**
     * executes all commands in the vector
     */
    public void execute(RemoteSystem rs) {
        for (int i = 0; i < commands.size(); i++) {
            ((Command) (commands.get(i))).execute(rs);
        }
    }
}
```

Now let's look at the JMS part of the code. First, let's look at the recipient application. Here we'll look at a classic example of asynchronous remote execution of workflow via JMS. This is the scenario: the progressive people of Troy implemented a computerized system to control central aspects of their city. Because the king of Troy wanted to be able to interact with the system when on campaigns, the system was made to comply with the architecture outlined above. The code looks like this:

```
import javax.jms.Queue;
import javax.jms.QueueConnectionFactory;
import javax.jms.QueueConnection;
import javax.jms.QueueSession;
import javax.jms.QueueReceiver;
import javax.jms.MessageListener;
import javax.jms.Message;
import javax.jms.ObjectMessage;
import javax.naming.InitialContext;
import java.util.Properties;

public class CityOfTroyCommandCenter implements RemoteSystem, MessageListener {

    private QueueConnection conn;
```

```
public void CityOfTroyCommandCenter(String user, String password)
        throws javax.naming.NamingException, javax.jms.JMSException {

    Properties namingProperties = new Properties();

    // here we add the JNDI properties we need
    // this is vendor specific

    InitialContext jndiCtxt = new InitialContext(namingProperties);

    Queue q = (Queue) jndiCtxt.lookup("CityOfTroyQueue");

    QueueConnectionFactory qF =
            (QueueConnectionFactory) jndiCtxt.lookup("CityOfTroyConnection");

    conn = qF.createQueueConnection(user, password);

    conn.setClientID(user);

    QueueSession session = conn.createQueueSession(false,
                        javax.jms.Session.AUTO_ACKNOWLEDGE);

    QueueReceiver rec = session.createReceiver(q);

    rec.setMessageListener(this);

    conn.start();
}

public void onMessage(Message msg) {

    // we only consider ObjectMessages
    if (msg instanceof ObjectMessage) {
        try {
            Command command = (Command) ((ObjectMessage) msg).getObject();

            // execute the workflow command!
            command.execute(this);
        } catch (javax.jms.JMSException jmse) {
        }
    } else {

        // do something else with the message
    }
}

public void quit() throws javax.jms.JMSException {
    conn.close();
}
```

```
    // These methods are used to control vital functions of the city
    public void openCitygates() {

    }

    public void closeCityGates() {

    }

    public void turnOnAlarms() {

    }

    public void turnOffAlarms() {

    }

    public void turnOnSprinklerSystem() {

    }

    public void turnOffSprinklerSystem() {

    }
}
```

You notice that most of the work in the class is done in the constructor. We're using the Java naming service (JNDI) to locate queues and other objects, so the first thing the constructor does is create an initial naming context. Since this is point to point messaging, it then uses the naming service to locate the desired queue and a queue connection factory. (In publish and subscribe messaging we'd locate a topic and a topic connection factory instead.) We establish a connection by calling the createQueueConnection() method of the connection factory. Once a connection is established, we can use it to create a session. From the session we can get a receiver.

Take a closer look at the statement rec.setMessageListener(this), which may look cryptic to some. The CityOfTroyCommandCenter class implements the MessageListener interface. This interface has a single method, onMessage(), which is a callback method. A receiver associated with a MessageListener calls onMessage() when a new message arrives. Clearly this is a good place to put actions we want to perform when we receive a message.

In our case, the onMessage() method looks at the message to determine whether it's of the class ObjectMessage. If it is, the method extracts the payload and casts it as a Command. Since the CityOfTroyCommandCenter class implements the RemoteSystem interface, it can pass itself to the command's execute() method, and so the execute() method has access to its public methods.

The Greeks, infuriated by the Trojan abduction of the beautiful Helen, decide to exploit the message queue in order to take revenge. They write a program to post a message containing commands to the queue. Here's the code:

```java
import java.util.Properties;
import javax.naming.InitialContext;
import javax.jms.Queue;
import javax.jms.QueueConnectionFactory;
import javax.jms.QueueConnection;
import javax.jms.QueueSession;
import javax.jms.ObjectMessage;
import javax.jms.QueueSender;

public class GrecianRevenge {

  private QueueConnection conn;
  private QueueSender sender;
  private QueueSession session;

  public GrecianRevenge(String user, String password)
         throws javax.naming.NamingException, javax.jms.JMSException {
    Properties namingProperties = new Properties();

    //
    // here we add the JNDI properties we need
    // this is vendor specific
    //

    InitialContext jndiCtxt = new InitialContext(namingProperties);

    Queue q = (Queue) jndiCtxt.lookup("CityOfTroyQueue");

    QueueConnectionFactory qF =
      (QueueConnectionFactory) jndiCtxt.lookup("CityOfTroyConnection");

    conn = qF.createQueueConnection(user, password);

    conn.setClientID(user);

    session = conn.createQueueSession(false,
                                      javax.jms.Session.AUTO_ACKNOWLEDGE);

    sender = session.createSender(q);

    conn.start();

  }

  public void quit() throws javax.jms.JMSException {
    conn.close();
  }


  private class BadThingOne implements Command, java.io.Serializable {
    public void execute(RemoteSystem sys) {
      ((CityOfTroyCommandCenter) sys).turnOffSprinklerSystem();
    }
  }

  private class BadThingTwo implements Command, java.io.Serializable {
```

793

```
      public void execute(RemoteSystem sys) {
        ((CityOfTroyCommandCenter) sys).turnOffAlarms();
      }
    }

    private class BadThingThree implements Command, java.io.Serializable {
      public void execute(RemoteSystem sys) {
        ((CityOfTroyCommandCenter) sys).openCityGates();
      }
    }

    public void destroyCityOfTroy() throws javax.jms.JMSException {
      Commands cmd = new Commands();
      cmd.addCommand(new BadThingOne());
      cmd.addCommand(new BadThingTwo());
      cmd.addCommand(new BadThingThree());

      ObjectMessage msg = session.createObjectMessage();
      msg.setObject(cmd);
      sender.send(msg);
    }
  }
```

The code in the constructor is similar to the Trojan's code, up to the point where we create a sender instead of a receiver. Now look at the method `destroyCityOfTroy()`. After having instantiated a `Commands` object containing a workflow of commands doing bad things, a message is created by calling the appropriate create-method of the session. Since the message type is `ObjectMessage`, we give it its deadly payload – the `Commands` object containing the destructive workflow – by calling `setObject()`. Then we send the message...

Since the Greeks were unable to obtain the Trojans' password, they couldn't connect to the message queue, and were forced to resort to some far-fetched scheme involving a wooden horse. However this shouldn't obscure the illustration of how an asynchronous workflow can be executed on a remote system using JMS.

We mentioned earlier that the `BytesMessage` message type might be utilized effectively to transfer positional data buffers to and from mainframes and minicomputers. Which leads us to the next topic of concern – legacy system integration.

Legacy Integration

The Greek philosopher Plato spoke of a dualistic universe consisting of two realms. One is the realm of ideals, where the flawless archetype for any conceivable concept dwells. The other realm is the one we live in, where everything is an imperfect, distorted and slightly tainted reflection of the ideal archetypes. It always amazed me how Plato knew so much about legacy system integration over two thousand years ago.

While many dot-com start-up B2C e-commerce systems don't have to interface to a large extent with existing systems, this is usually not the case with corporate purchasing systems where the e-commerce part is often added almost as an afterthought to a complex structure of interacting legacy systems (such as accounting systems, inventory systems, manufacturing systems, and human resources systems).

While there are notable exceptions, these systems have often evolved over time, and taken on duties they weren't originally designed to perform. They may be:

❑ Poorly documented

❑ Poorly understood by those running the system with the members of the original programming team having moved on long ago

❑ Jealously guarded by those responsible for the system (who won't sanction changes)

❑ Technologically hard to integrate (for example the technology choice for integration is not available for the current version or patch level of the operating system)

There are many good technologies aimed at overcoming these kinds of problems. The Java Connector Architecture, SOAP (Simple Object Access Protocol), XML, and CORBA are some examples. The problem with all of these is that there is a law of nature that states that they are either not available for your target platform within the timeframe of the project, or they are available but not yet approved for deployment in a production environment at the client company.

Don't underestimate the power of the laws of nature. I recently received an e-mail from a friend who had just accepted a position as a system integrator with an Internet security company in Silicon Valley. It read "How do I access COM objects from Java across a network? How do I access Java objects from C++ across a network? And how do I do all this at one time from VB Script within an ASP page on IIS?"

Sensing something wasn't quite right I responded, "What are you trying to do?"

To which I received the laconic reply: "Log in."

In this section we're going to disregard the "obvious technology choices." Instead we'll take a closer look at some of the weapons we can pull out of our arsenal and use in the "impossible" cases we're bound to encounter in the shabby realm we inhabit.

Case Study 2 – Scraping the Bottom of the Barrel

We were building an e-commerce system by which dealer companies could configure and order vehicles from a vendor. The system was a fairly straightforward browser based Java servlet application, running on a UNIX platform. Everything went smoothly until we were faced with the problem of how to actually get the orders into the manufacturing system for production.

The legacy method of doing this was to transfer a file containing vehicle parameters to an IBM mainframe. As could be expected, this wasn't done through any standardized means of file transfer, such as FTP, but by uploading the contents of the file line by line to a receiving Information Management System (IMS) transaction. A human being using a standard 3270 "green screen" performed the uploading. Obviously, that solution would not be acceptable.

The IMS transaction performed some processing of the input lines as they arrived. The nature of this processing was poorly understood, and the COBOL source code displayed clear signs of countless, scantly documented revisions. This made it difficult to bypass the IMS transaction using "dumb" file transfer.

At the time, the mechanism of choice for communicating with IMS transactions from other sources was **ITOC (IMS TCP/IP OTMA Connector)**. Unfortunately, the vendor company's operations department did not support the use of ITOC in the production environment.

Another candidate technology was Microsoft's **COM-TI** technology (**COM Transaction Integrator**). To use this SNA based technology we would have to install Microsoft SNA Server sitting between the mainframe and the TCP/IP network. Furthermore, we would have to interact with a COM-TI object residing on a Windows NT server. It seemed ridiculous to have to introduce two additional servers, an additional OS, and two additional protocols to get the job done.

It occurred to us that our best bet was to emulate the human operator interacting with the 3270 interface. One way of doing this is through **screen scraping**. Screen scraping is rightly considered a last resort technology, and for good reason: It is sensitive to minor changes to screen layout, it has limited support for robust exception handling and so on.

We studied several candidate screen-scraping technologies, and finally decided on IBM's **HACL** (**Host Access Client Library**). HACL is a Java API that offers some limited form of screen recognition in addition to the usual dumb scraping based on screen XY position. In other words it stinks a little less than its competitors, and a lot less than the available alternatives.

A brute force finite state machine was constructed to emulate the behavior of the human operator. The brute force approach was necessary due to project deadline pressures. A simplified, abbreviated version of this ugly piece of code is shown here:

```java
public boolean transferFileToIMS(String orderID) throws IMSException {
    Properties p = null;
    ECLSession s = null;
    ECLPS ps = null;
    boolean rc = true;
    FileInputStream fin = null;
    ECLScreenDesc sD = null;

    // repeat for each file to be transfered
    for (int i = 0; i < sendCount; i++) {

        fin = new FileInputStream("/usr/orders/" + orderID + ".TXT");

        // 1. Set session properties
        p = new Properties();
        p.put(ECLSession.SESSION_HOST, host);
        p.put(ECLSession.SESSION_TN_ENHANCED, ECLSession.SESSION_ON);
        p.put(ECLSession.SESSION_PS_SIZE, ECLSession.SESSION_PS_27X132_STR);

        // 2. Create session and presentation space
        s = new ECLSession(p);
        s.StartCommunication();
        ps = s.GetPS();

        int state = 10;
        int fwd = 0;
        BufferedReader lines = new BufferedReader(new InputStreamReader(fin));

        while (state != 1000) {
            sD = new ECLScreenDesc();
            sD.AddOIAInhibitStatus(ECLScreenDesc.NOTINHIBITED);
            ps.WaitForScreen(sD);


            // 3. Emulate user actions
            switch (state) {
            case 10:
```

```
      // request IMS
      ps.SendKeys("IMS[enter]");
      state = 20;
      break;

case 20:

      // Logon to IMS
      ps.SendKeys(uid);
      ps.SendKeys(pwd);
      ps.SendKeys("[enter]");
      state = 30;
      break;

case 30:

      // are we logged on?
      fwd = ps.SearchText("IMS Start", ECLPS.SEARCH_FORWARD);
      if (0 == fwd) {
        throw new IMSException(
                "Security Violation! Cannot log in to IMS.");
      }

      // yes, ask for the menu
      ps.SendKeys("MENU [enter]");
      state = 40;
      break;

case 40:

      // Is the menu transaction going?
      fwd = ps.SearchText("TRAN/LTERM STOPPED", ECLPS.SEARCH_FORWARD);
      if (0 != fwd) {
        throw new IMSException("Transaction Stopped!");
      }

      // Are we allowed to run it
      fwd = ps.SearchText("WELCOME", ECLPS.SEARCH_FORWARD);
      if (0 == fwd) {
        throw new IMSException("Security Violation! cannot access MENU.");
      }
      state = 50;
      break;

case 50:
      fwd = ps.SearchText("TRAN/LTERM STOPPED", ECLPS.SEARCH_FORWARD);
      if (0 != fwd) {
        throw new IMSException("Transaction Stopped!");
      }

      // select file upload transaction
      ps.SendKeys("UPLOAD[enter]");
      state = 60;
      break;

      // ///////////////////////////////////////////////
      //
      // And on and on it went through many more states...
      //
      // ///////////////////////////////////////////////

case 100:
```

```
          // log off and get out
          ps.SendKeys("/rcl[enter]");
          state = 1000;
          break;

      default:
          throw new IMSException("Invalid state transition!");
      }
      sD = null;


    }
    fin.close();
  }
  s.StopCommunication();
  return rc;
}
```

The important thing to note is that each screen is represented as a separate state in the machine, and that the code enters keystrokes and moves through the application just like a human operator would.

In spite of its inelegance and ugliness, this piece of code worked surprisingly well, and actually went into the successful production version of the system. Much later this code was refactored using the state pattern. I thought however that the original source very nicely illustrates the things one sometimes has to do when stuck in our distorted reality.

The problems we encounter when interacting with legacy systems are not always related to the limitations of technology – as part of the next case study we'll also move on to think about how we can design our applications with integration in mind.

Case Study 3 – It's the Same System Except...

This purchasing system was based on an existing AS/400 system. The coarse grain architecture was a Java servlet based system running on a UNIX platform. XSLT was used to render HTML pages from XML documents based on data retrieved from the backend AS/400 system. The rendering took place on the web server, and the HTML pages were sent to the browser.

The initial design called for the use of IBM's AS/400 Toolbox for Java, for interacting directly with the program and data structures on the AS/400. However, the client-company requested the use of a proprietary communications protocol developed in house. They gave us access to old Java code that used the proprietary protocol and which translated AS/400 data arriving in positional buffers to more complex, meaningful data structures. We were given very detailed descriptions of the layout and semantics of the AS/400 data. Using the existing code as a base line seemed like a safe and labor saving approach. We identified easy ways to modify it to create XML documents from the AS/400 data, and thus we (naïvely) abandoned the AS/400 Toolbox for Java.

The project proceeded smoothly right through testing against the development AS/400 environment. The day came when we were going to point the system to the production AS/400 machine. Up to that point our team had not been using this machine, since it was being used to run "real" business transactions. That shouldn't matter though, since the machines were identical and ran the same backend processes, right?

When we started up the system we were perplexed. Some operations returned empty XML documents. Others returned garbled and meaningless data. Yet nothing seemed to be wrong, at least not according to the error logs! After some initial panicking, a thorough investigation revealed the following:

❏ The backend processes running on the two machines had the same names, but were sometimes different versions. Other times they were completely different programs from a functional perspective.

❏ The positional buffer layouts for incoming and outgoing data were not the same on the two machines.

❏ The backend error reporting strategies varied so much as to render our exception handling mechanisms worthless, leaving our system with the impression that everything was on track.

❏ The versions of the proprietary communications protocol were different, which led to data truncation in some cases.

And so on. The problem was solved by extensive version checking, some changes to the backend processes, and trimming and grafting of XML trees.

The lesson to be learned here is that one should never take anything for granted when it comes to integration with poorly understood proprietary systems. The client's operations staff kept no systematic records of changes made to the two environments, and honestly believed that they were identical – at least almost!

It is the course of the universe that our well-engineered cutting edge systems of today become the poorly understood legacy systems of tomorrow. One day some unfortunate developer will have to interact with the legacy system you wrote today. Even today other systems might need access to data accumulated and maintained in your system. How do we make the task for others to integrate with the systems we build easier and less error prone?

Designing with Integration in Mind

Most systems today rely on some kind of persistence mechanism for data, most often in the form of a relational database. It might be tempting to grant other processes access to the data directly in our database. This is probably the worst way of letting somebody integrate with your system. Apart from the monumental risks of data corruption, breakdown of data integrity, and incapacitation of business rules, this approach leads to very close coupling between the two systems, which in turn leads to degradation of maintainability and flexibility. The two systems become one in a sense, through the shared database layout. For that reason I strongly discourage granting others even read only access to your system's database tables.

Allowing Data Reading

One way to bypass tight coupling between two systems through a shared database design is by creating customized database views for the external system. We can then change our database as we see fit to accommodate changing system requirements, as long as we maintain the views. One problem associated with database views is that they often require a large number of table joins, which can be very expensive in terms of system performance. This problem is aggravated the more de-normalized the database is. How to deal with this and related problems associated with views is outside the scope of this chapter. The interested reader might want to consult a book such as Joe Celko's *SQL for Smarties*, ISBN 1-55860-576-2.

Another way to allow external systems to interact with your data, without directly accessing your database is to provide an API of objects and methods that return JDBC result sets. JDBC result set objects are self-describing in a sense, since you can query their structure and other properties via `ResultSetMetaData`. The following code snippet shows how you can get to the meta data:

```
ResultSet rs;
// code to get the result set here
ResultSetMetaData metaData=rs.getMetData();
```

The meta data object has methods such as `getColumnCount()`, `getColumnName()`, `getColumnType()` and so on. In most cases the method's functionality is obvious based on the method name. Using meta data involves some extra processing for the client. The biggest drawback, however, is that the use of JDBC result sets and meta data is limited to Java clients. Alas, most legacy systems are not written in Java!

A simple and extremely flexible way to grant other systems use of your data in a read only mode, without having to know the exact table layouts of your database, is to generate XML documents that contain the requested data. The advantages of this approach are many: one of the most cited advantages is that XML is self-describing, just like JDBC `ResultSetMetaData`. Another is that the XML representation of the data can remain the same even if you change the underlying database, which reduces the coupling between your system and external users of the data, just like a database view. Yet another advantage is that you only have to make one single technology assumption – that the user of your data can request and read an XML document. But it is important to remember the drawbacks of XML. One often overlooked disadvantage is that the textual format of an XML document is less compact than most binary protocols, and will put extra load on network resources.

Allowing Data Writing

But what if you want to grant somebody the right to alter your data? Here again the crux is to not let anybody use your data directly, but to make sure the changes pass through your code and that your business rules and application logic apply. High tech approaches to accomplish this include the use of Enterprise JavaBeans or CORBA interfaces. A less heavyweight approach is to publish a simple functional API for your system, which guarantees that your business rules and application logic will apply. You could make your API accessible across machine borders through the use of RMI or maybe the J2EE Java Naming Service.

Let us not forget the good old stored procedure. By exposing stored procedures to external systems, database access is routed through your code. Stored procedures typically offer excellent performance, and are callable from most programming languages. Some databases, notably Oracle 8i, allow you to write stored procedures directly in Java.

Multiple System Integration

The well-known figure on the opposite page shows the core problem associated with integration of multiple intercommunicating systems with each other. The number of translations quickly grows out of control, as we add systems to the mix. In spite of this problem being well understood, it is all too often the situation we encounter in real-world corporations. In the steady state everything works fine, but when systems are added or modified the maintenance load can escalate to intolerable levels.

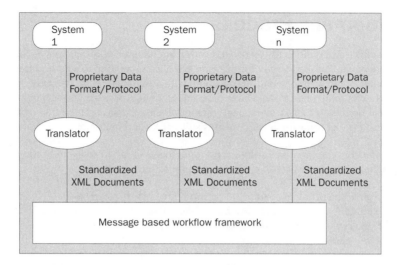

The solution to this conundrum, equally well understood, is quite simple. The figure above shows a model of a generic application integration and workflow framework that requires only *n* translations to interconnect *n* systems. The core idea is to have a standardized data exchange format in the backbone. This way we have to perform at most one translation per system.

The framework in the picture is based on a set of standardized XML documents and an event driven message flow. The systems communicate by producing and consuming documents. The workflow is driven by events occurring in any of the systems. When an event occurs the translator extracts data associated with the event, and translates it from native format to standardized XML. The XML document is posted in the form of a message. The translator connected to the system or systems responsible for the next step in the workflow consumes the message and translates its XML content into a format that can be processed by the system. The recipient system performs actions depending on the content of the message. Responses to messages are processed in a similar way. The architecture of the framework isolates the communicating systems from each other, and provides a flexible and configurable workflow.

Sadly, the single most difficult obstacle encountered in system integration can't be bypassed with XML or even Enterprise JavaBeans. The problem has it roots in cultural differences between the people who write and maintain the legacy systems of today, and people who write e-commerce systems. To make a point, let's draw two (admittedly prejudiced) caricatures. On the one hand we have the "Legacy ERP Programmer" who belongs to a large team, focused on internal IT procedures and efficiencies, works on projects that take years to finish and often customizes expensive third party products to fit the existing IT structure. The cost of failure is extremely high, thus a lot of time is spent up front to get the requirements just right, and non-programming activities eat up the lion's share of the project budget.

On the other hand we have the "Webby E-Commerce Programmer". This person belongs to a small team, focused on user interface efficiencies, works on a project that takes six weeks to finish, and writes everything from scratch in Java or Perl, unless an open source alternative is available. The cost of failure is low, thus the requirements are often vague, and equally often contain an element of scope creep. This is countered by almost 100 percent programming activities. Iteration after iteration is worked through until the "owner" of the project is satisfied.

Here we have two very different approaches to application development and a middle ground needs to be found to allow them to work together successfully. The key to this lies in arriving at an appropriate development process.

The Development Process

Construction of software is traditionally associated with a high degree of risk as well as failure. Common industry wisdom dictates that the remedy for this is to establish some kind of standard development process, adhere to some kind of methodology and support both with automated tools. The experts have been saying this for as long as I can remember. People have been taking their advice for just as long. Corporations have spent astronomic amounts on tools, training, and methodologies. Tools and methodologies have come and gone. The end result is that software development is still a risky and failure-prone endeavor.

We looked at project development and software methodologies in broad scope in Section 1 of the book, but here we'll highlight some experiences of e-commerce application development.

The current solution to the problem of software construction is to try to arrive at the "true requirements" by successive approximation and two of the most buzzed-about approaches today are **RUP** (**Rational Unified Process**) and **XP** (**Extreme Programming**). Both processes involve iterative development, and both stress user involvement and change.

But that's where the similarities end. RUP is "big", and it stresses well-defined roles, modeling, the use of visual tools, and relies heavily on planning and formal evaluation of criteria as well as change and documentation management. XP is much lighter, stresses frequent builds, and Pair Programming, does away with roles and planning, and promotes unit testing as the primary means of quality assurance. I'm not going to take sides here, I will just note that it is interesting that two such radically different approaches are being proposed as solutions to the same problem. Both camps claim spectacular successes, which suggests that perhaps software construction shouldn't be viewed as a single monolithic discipline. The developer must look closely at what process makes sense in her environment, and with her specific goals. And since the "experts" only agree on disagreeing, there is plenty of room for experimentation.

Our focus here is e-commerce in general, and corporate purchasing in particular. In my opinion, RUP has several weaknesses that must be compensated for in an e-commerce development environment. This is not to say that XP doesn't. I'm mentioning RUP because I'm more familiar with it and its strengths and weaknesses than I am with those of XP.

You'll hear some people say that e-commerce has been around for a long time. They are right in principle, but the fact is that its explosive growth and growing importance are due to one single factor: The World Wide Web. As I write this, the Web has been with us for less than 2,000 days! In that short time a lot has happened – cutting edge technology becomes old hat in a matter of months. So one important consideration when deciding on a development process for any e-commerce project is time. Any iterative methodology we choose must make good use of short iterations! RUP's many artifacts, documents, and plans can make it difficult to follow the methodology without modifications within the time constraints often associated with e-commerce projects. And if too much of the process is sacrificed at the altar of timeliness RUP becomes of limited value, almost like a liturgy one follows because one must.

The two cornerstones of RUP are **UML** (Unified Modeling Language) and the **Use Case Centric** approach. Some of the problems with RUP stem from limitations of the UML.

First of all, UML does not provide a detailed way to model use cases. This is surprising considering the central role use cases play in both UML and RUP. The use case diagram is by far the least expressive of all UML notations, allowing users to model at a very coarse level of granularity only. You really can't do much beyond inclusion, extension, and generalization of other use cases. To add detail to use cases we usually resort to some kind of textual description. UML does not define a standardized format for textual descriptions of use cases.

The user interface is a very important component of most e-commerce applications. UML has no mechanism for modeling user interfaces. In every RUP/UML project I've worked on we had to create a GUI prototype using tools that aren't official members of UML or the RUP methodology. These GUI models have ranged from a collection of screen shots of static HTML pages to full-fledged working application prototypes.

Another shortcoming of UML is that it makes it difficult to model software that isn't inherently object-oriented. A typical example is an HTML page, that interface of choice for many e-commerce applications. Even though an HTML page can be described in terms of a DOM (Document Object Model), doing so is of very limited value in real life. The stuff that makes an HTML page tick (JavaScript or something similar) can usually also be modeled in terms of the DOM, but that won't capture the "essence" of the page, which is how a user interacts with it. Moreover, JavaScript is typically used as a functional language in most situations, not as an object-oriented language.

Having said all that I don't want you to get the impression that I think RUP and UML are useless for e-commerce development. I use UML extensively for modeling the Java classes that often form the core of the application. I believe the limitations are a sign that UML and the RUP methodology are still under development. They aren't wrong – just immature. As browser based applications and e-commerce continue to grow in importance, RUP and UML must grow with them, as they undoubtedly will.

Unfortunately we can't wait for that to happen. Business and technology are moving at a pace that makes it quite possible for a system to be hopelessly obsolete while it is still being developed. Your best bet against being strangled in the crib is to build many small, highly flexible and extensible systems that interact to accomplish the business goal, instead of one big system, even if that's what the customer asked for a month ago. You already know how to use the workflow techniques described earlier in this chapter to build complex systems from simple interacting building blocks. This component view of system architecture is quickly becoming dominant within e-commerce.

Case Study 4: Putting it all Together – An E-Commerce Design Approach

We're going to apply everything we've talked about in this chapter in our final case study concerning the development process. The case study involves a national IT consulting and outsourcing company. One of its divisions, Staff Augmentation, provides consultants and contract programmers to other companies. The sales staff noted that many client companies complained that there existed no standardized systems for managing contracted resources from multiple vendors, and other aspects of vendor relations.

Many vendors of contract resources had their own systems, almost all of which were geared toward that specific vendor. The hassles of having a different system for each vendor put serious limits on the benefits of using these systems. Other vendors sold systems that were allegedly open to multiple vendors, when in fact they were Trojan horses that favored a single vendor at the expense of the competition. Some vendors even required that their personnel maintain the system at the client site, making them in effect a "preferred vendor".

Another common complaint was that most existing systems had a payment structure based on a transaction fee. Most clients who had any transaction volume to speak of wanted to license a system or pay a flat fee for its use.

In disgruntlement lies opportunity. We were approached with a request to come up with an e-procurement package to fill this void.

The Business Case

The consulting company had prepared a business case for the system from the viewpoint of a potential customer. The return of investment for the system would come from several sources:

- ❏ Encouraging competition among vendors by providing a level playing field
- ❏ Enabling a customer to maintain a larger vendor pool by automating all aspects of vendor relations
- ❏ Reducing cycle time from when a requirement is perceived to when the position is filled
- ❏ Increasing talent quality by providing comparative metrics
- ❏ Increasing vendor quality by providing comparative metrics
- ❏ Utilizing current talent, by centralizing the hiring functionality through workflow
- ❏ Simplifying redeployment of existing resources, as well as automatic extension of contracts
- ❏ Tying in rates, and generating discounts by pooling demand
- ❏ Standardizing hiring procedures through workflow
- ❏ Standardizing common functions, such as time sheets, across all vendors
- ❏ Standardizing skill descriptions across all departments
- ❏ Standardizing online invoicing for all vendors
- ❏ Accessing knowledge of best hiring practices

It seemed that the cost savings from these benefits would more than make up for the cost of using the system.

The Initial System Requirements

The consulting company had prepared a set of initial requirements, based on what the customers had told them, and their own experience in the field. The requirements were broken into two categories: functional and non-functional requirements. The functional requirements were:

- ❏ The system must provide a flexible and configurable workflow for generation and approval of requests for contract resources.
- ❏ The system must provide a standardized matrix of skill sets and skill descriptions across all vendors. The matrix must be customizable for each customer.
- ❏ The system must provide a flexible way to organize vendors into groups, with potential overlap between groups.
- ❏ The system must provide a way for the customer to submit a request to one or more vendors, or groups of vendors.
- ❏ The system must provide a way for vendors to retrieve requests for resources.
- ❏ The system must provide a way for vendors to submit candidate information, including resumes in response to a request.
- ❏ The system must independently rank candidates based on how well they meet the request.
- ❏ The system must provide a way to schedule interviews with candidates.

- ❑ The system must provide a way for the customer to communicate with a vendor or group of vendors.

- ❑ The system must provide a way to automatically hire a submitted candidate.

- ❑ The system must provide a configurable automatic workflow for performing post-hiring actions, such as assigning cubicles, computers, name badges, phones, parking passes, passwords, and security clearances, and so on.

- ❑ The system must provide a way to refuse a submitted candidate.

- ❑ The system must provide a way to automatically re-deploy a consultant within the organization.

- ❑ The system must provide a way to automatically notify when a contract is about to expire.

- ❑ The system must provide a way to automatically extend a contract that is about to expire.

- ❑ The system must provide a way to approve or refuse time cards.

- ❑ The system must provide a standardized online time card to be used by all vendors and consultants.

- ❑ The system must provide a standardized online invoice to be used by all vendors.

- ❑ The system must provide vendor and consultant quality metrics, such as response times, interview to submit, and hire to interview ratios.

- ❑ The system must provide configurable cost reporting based on project or department.

Quite an order – but not unusual as far as corporate purchasing systems go. In addition, the non-functional requirements were:

- ❑ The system must be 100 percent vendor neutral.

- ❑ The system must be able to run as a licensed standalone product, as well as a shared ASP (Application Service Provider) based product on a non-transactional subscription basis.

- ❑ The user interface must be browser based, and be compatible with current versions of major browsers.

- ❑ The system must be able to run on UNIX and/or Windows NT platforms.

- ❑ The system must be able to interact with legacy systems implemented using a wide range of technologies and running on a wide range of platforms.

- ❑ In standalone mode, the system must make very few assumptions on the customers' runtime environment, such as support for a specific database, application server, etc.

- ❑ The system must be able to concurrently support a large number of vendors.

- ❑ The system must exhibit adequate response time.

- ❑ The system must easily integrate with other systems at the client site. Integration must be possible and simple across machine and technology borders.

- ❑ The system must exhibit 98.5 percent planned up time, that is, scheduled maintenance at most one day every two months.

- ❑ The system must provide adequate security, so that it can be accessed across the public Internet.

All the requirements sounded noble, sound, and quite reasonable, but the consulting company realized that to be a commercial success the system must meet the actual requirements of the potential customers. Obviously, we had to find a way to arrive at the real requirements – hopefully before going to market! How we ended up accomplishing this is described in a later section.

The Coarse-Grain Architecture

Arriving at a coarse-grain architecture was the easy part. The non-functional requirements dictated a very open environment with severe restrictions on the assumptions we could make regarding the availability of specific technologies. In particular, we couldn't assume the existence of an application server, or of a messaging infrastructure. The good thing about restrictions is that they make your choices very simple.

Naturally, we had to make some assumptions about the deployment environment. First of all, since we decided that the system was to run transparently on both UNIX and Windows NT, J2EE technologies, such as Java servlets and JSP seemed like a good choice. In other words we assumed the presence of a web server capable of supporting server-side Java. (As alluded to in the previous paragraph, conditions within some of the partner organizations at the time were such that we couldn't assume the presence of a full-fledged application server capable of supporting EJB.) Secondly, the data had to be stored somewhere, so it seemed reasonable to assume the presence of a relational database.

We decided on a "standard configuration", which coincided with our development and test environments. Actually, it was several standard configurations, since we decided to test on three different platforms. The standard configuration looked like this:

- ❏ Platforms: Windows NT 4.0/Intel, Red Hat Linux 6.2/Intel, or Sun Solaris 7/SPARC
- ❏ Web server: Apache 1.3.12
- ❏ JSP engine: Tomcat
- ❏ RDBMS: Oracle 8i
- ❏ Java support: JDK 1.2

JSP was chosen as the preferred technology for several reasons. First of all, it is supported on many platforms. Secondly, we anticipated many and far reaching changes in the requirements. It was decided that given the time constraint and development resources, it would be easier to accommodate for this using JSP, than using a "pure" servlet or XML/XSLT based solution. The biggest architectural drawback of JSP is of course that there is no strict enforcement of separation of presentation and business logic, in this case HTML tags and Java code respectively.

The choice of database turned out to be somewhat controversial. Oracle 8i has excellent support for server-side Java by itself, and there was some discussion whether to use these advanced features of Oracle 8i. It was finally decided that in the name of openness and database independence we use Oracle 8i just as we would any standard, vendor-neutral SQL database.

One other area of concern was the implementation of workflow. It didn't seem reasonable to assume that every potential customer and vendor would support a JMS implementation or other advanced messaging systems. This left us with e-mail as the other option. Fortunately, analysis showed that each step of the workflow involved a human decision-maker, so in the end this turned out to be a non-issue.

Initially, we decided on Solaris as our primary platform, with Windows NT and Linux as secondary choices. Later, based on requests from several potential customers we re-evaluated this decision, and assigned Linux as the primary platform, with Windows NT and Solaris as secondary choices.

The Use of Development Partners

Although an initial, minimal set of requirements had been identified, the consulting firm knew that this set of requirements was definitely incomplete, and possibly not even the "real requirements". For this reason it seemed it would be beneficial to work closely with potential customers to gather their input on the requirements. Unfortunately, potential customers were evenly distributed across the North American continent, which made it difficult to establish a close working relationship between users and the development team.

To circumvent this problem, we introduced the notion of an *early development partner.* A handful of large, potential customers were invited to become stakeholders in the process of shaping the product. Instead of attempting to have remote **Joint Application Design** (**JAD**) sessions or long drawn out meetings over design issues, a working prototype of the system was developed. Representatives from the consulting company would visit development partner sites and demo the prototype. After the demo, the development partners would criticize the prototype, bringing suggestions and questions for changes. The prototype was also made available to partners to use and familiarize themselves with between demos.

The development team then evaluated the suggestions and proposed changes. Suggestions that seemed like they would add overall value to the system or be beneficial to users in general were incorporated in to the prototype. Suggestions with more limited scope, for example changes that would only make sense in the context of an individual development partner's environment, were duly noted but not incorporated in the prototype. Instead, we would suggest to the partner who proposed the change that we customize the finished package to fit their requirements. Once all changes were implemented, the cycle started over again. Through this process the system requirements evolved as new partners were brought into the project.

This approach is certainly iterative, but completely different from the well-structured iterative model of the RUP process. It would have been impossible to plan individual iterations since new requirements were continually added to the scope. Since change was an important part of the game plan, we had to find a way to deal with it, instead of fighting it. Instead of letting use cases drive the iteration schedule, changing requirements was the primary driving force. In other words we made a conscious effort to maximize the influence of change, in order to arrive at the true requirements.

Of course, we had to find a way to accommodate this partner-driven development model, given some rather severe time constraints. We had to find a way to avoid resorting to unstructured hacking, and instead arrive at a robust, well-designed system. At the same time constant change wasn't just something we had to live with, but indeed a crucial success factor, and therefore something we had to encourage. We've all been taught that scope creep is our deadly enemy. How were we going to make it our friend? The solution was found in how the prototype was constructed.

The Evolving System Prototype

In the approach we chose, the system prototype quickly became the most important design artifact. It was the means by which we communicated with the partners, captured requirements and managed iterations. The prototype was "real" software complete with business logic and a backend, as opposed to a set of mock-up HTML pages. The characteristics of the evolving prototype can be summarized as follows:

❑   Serve as a fully functional, interactive demo

❑   Help discover the actual system requirements

❑   Model the system functionality

❑ Model the graphical user interface

❑ Embody requirements

The development partners were all very sophisticated, large, national companies, mostly in the fields of telecommunications and finance. We felt very strongly that we couldn't approach such an audience with nothing but vaporware, promises, and presentations to back us up. In order to establish credibility, we had to show that this was a real product, and that we knew how to implement it. Therefore, the prototype had to be a fully functional piece of software.

Another tremendous advantage of building a fully functional prototype was that it could immediately be used to discover flaws in the functionality and to generate suggestions for additional features. At the onset of every partner presentation it implemented the functionality dictated by the current requirements, as well as the most recent user interface. It therefore gave the partners a very accurate impression of what the system capabilities were, and what it would be like to use the real thing. For this reason the feedback we received had a very high degree of validity.

Although very little of the code from the prototypes could actually be reused, they did help to establish things that we shouldn't do. Knowing what not to do can be a huge help in working out what we should do.

The Development Process

The approach begs for several questions to be answered.:

❑ How can one determine when the true requirements have been discovered – in other words, when is it time to stop?

❑ How can one implement a fully functional prototype under the pressure of a real deadline, and using very short iterations?

The answer to the first question is to establish a rule that states that the requirements are complete once the prototype implements the minimal system that could actually be used productively by all development partners. In other words, when the suggestions made by the partners only apply to the needs of the individual partner, and have no real value to the other partners the requirements are complete. The remaining suggestions that only apply to an individual partner can then be implemented as customization of the finished system if that partner so desires. Naturally, this in itself poses a requirement to make the system easy to extend and customize.

The answer to the second question lies in the realization that the prototype is just that. Even though it must implement the current functional requirements completely, it doesn't really have to do it as robustly or at the level of performance or reliability that the final system would. Nor does it need to have a shared code base with the end product. Instead, the focus should be on it being easy to modify, as new requirements are discovered.

We chose to assign two programmers to the construction and maintenance of the evolving prototype. The architectural constraints imposed on the system weren't applied to the prototype, and thus it could leverage the consulting company's existing backend systems in ways the final product obviously couldn't. Because the prototype's scope was limited it didn't have to meet the same constraints on technology choices and portability as the real system. Also, there weren't any formal criteria for system design or system quality. For these reasons a fully functional and surprisingly robust prototype could be constructed very rapidly. This "executable model" could easily be updated as new "informal" requirements were discovered. In other words, a fully functional prototype could be constructed and kept abreast with requirement changes due to the following factors:

- ❑ Leveraging existing systems
- ❑ Limited technological scope
- ❑ No quality requirements
- ❑ No design requirements
- ❑ No performance requirements
- ❑ Separation of code bases

By inspecting the executable model, formal requirements were derived, and other more traditional design models were developed. Using the feedback notes from development partners, another team, led by an experienced designer and architect, would examine the behavior and the source code of the prototype. This would then serve as the basis for establishing formal requirements, and constructing several UML models, from which the real system could be constructed. This way the development team was isolated from too fast a pace of change, and could develop a model of a robust, flexible, extensible and portable version of the system.

Artifacts

The goal for the design work was to arrive at a flexible component architecture that could easily be modified in tune with changes. To accomplish this, several artifacts were produced to model the static and dynamic aspects of the system. The static models included:

- ❑ A domain model
- ❑ UML class diagrams
- ❑ Source code
- ❑ A persistence model

The dynamic modeling artifacts were:

- ❑ UML use cases
- ❑ A GUI model
- ❑ UML sequence diagrams

For details of the UML models, please consult any of several good books on UML and RUP.

> *One introductory book that has become a classic is UML Distilled, second edition by Martin Fowler ISBN 0-201-65783-X. A concise and informative book on the RUP methodology is the one by Kruchten mentioned at the beginning of the chapter. More detailed UML information can be found in The Unified Modeling Language User Guide by Grady Booch et al, ISBN 0-201-57168-4 and The Unified Modeling Language Reference Manual by James Rumbaugh et al, ISBN 0-201-20998-X.*

However, a couple of these artifacts merit special mention here. As you may have guessed, the GUI model was essentially the presentation layer of the prototype, with very few changes. By the same token, the use cases were derived from interactions with the prototype.

More interesting is the use of source code as a modeling artifact. We had access to two separate sets of source code: the code of the prototype, and the implementation of the current state of the model. Source code is a very rich source of information, from which the structure of a system can be derived.

In other words, source code can be used not only to implement a system based on a model, but models can be used to reverse engineer the structure of a system such as our prototype into a model of that system. By "reverse engineering" in this context we don't mean slavishly creating a model of the code, as we do when we construct call graphs or class diagram from source code. Instead we're trying to deduce a better structure for the same system than the one that's expressed in the code. The reason for this is of course that we know that the source code for the prototype may be too hackish and brittle for production purposes.

Deriving a Model from Source Code

A complete discussion of how to deduce a model from source code is outside the scope of this case study, but I'd like to give a few hints here.

The first things we should look for are opportunities for subclassing. Obvious hints are methods that do the same thing or almost. Other more subtle clues lie in conditional statements. If a piece of code contains many `switch` statements or chains of `if-else` statements, it is often better to implement it as a class hierarchy or in the case of Java as implementations of an interface.

Another important thing to look for is how a class uses methods and members of other classes. Frequent access of public data members or simple get and set methods often reveals the fact that the member should actually reside in another class. A more efficient class structure can often be accomplished by refactoring the code. Robust, flexible code depends on limited dependencies between classes. If classes are too tightly coupled the system becomes too tightly coupled, and essentially degrades into a monolith block of code. For a detailed discussion of code refactoring please refer to *Refactoring* by *Martin Fowler ISBN 0-201-48567-2*.

Inevitably, new needs for legacy integration were constantly discovered during the development of the system. It became apparent that we needed a uniform way to accommodate these. For reasons pointed out above, we didn't want other systems to access data directly. Thus, we constructed an XML DTD for every major piece of functionality offered by the system. (A better way would have been to use a standardized industry specific DTD. Unfortunately none existed for our problem domain.) That way, legacy systems could access system data by requesting or posting XML documents across an HTTP connection.

The development process outlined in the preceding paragraphs is not presented as a solution for all development situations. Rather it was perceived that the biggest risk factor for the project was the risk of not being able to arrive at a good set of system requirements. The described process of "iterative deployment" was an exploration of ways to arrive at high quality system requirements by letting users interact and critique an evolving functional model of the system. It is offered here only as an encouragement to readers to experiment and deviate from the official truths of software development methodology that have consistently let us down over the years.

Summary

That concludes our discussion of corporate purchasing systems. In this chapter we've looked at the characteristics of corporate purchasing systems, the use of design patterns to solve complicated workflow problems, message mechanisms to support workflow solutions, aspects of legacy integration, and finished with a case study outlining a novel approach to developing a corporate purchasing e-commerce solution.

The main points that you should take away with you from this chapter are:

❑ Corporate purchasing systems are like B2C and B2B for the most part.

❑ Corporate purchasing is characterized by more stable customer-vendor relationship than we normally see in B2C.

❑ Workflow is of great significance within the customer and vendor organizations alike. There is often a need to integrate across organizational borders.

❑ There's usually a need to closely integrate with legacy systems.

❑ If you want to market a corporate purchasing system to many organizations you must find a way to determine the smallest set of common requirements that makes sense, find ways to standardize function and data, and implement a flexible way to extend and customize your system.

❑ Change is a good thing even in software development – don't fight it, try to find ways to make it work for you.

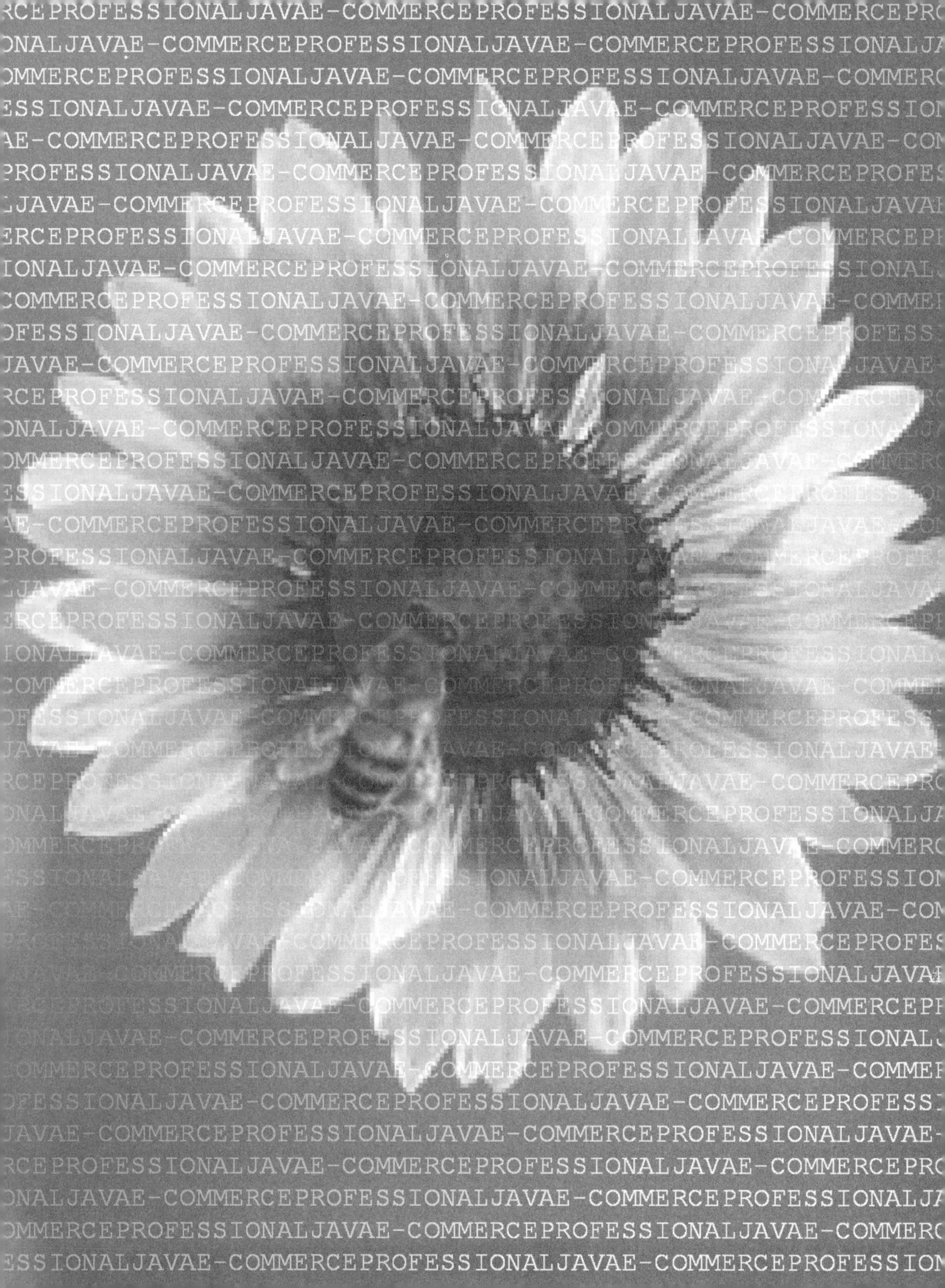
PROFESSIONALJAVAE-COMMERCE

Section 5

M-Commerce

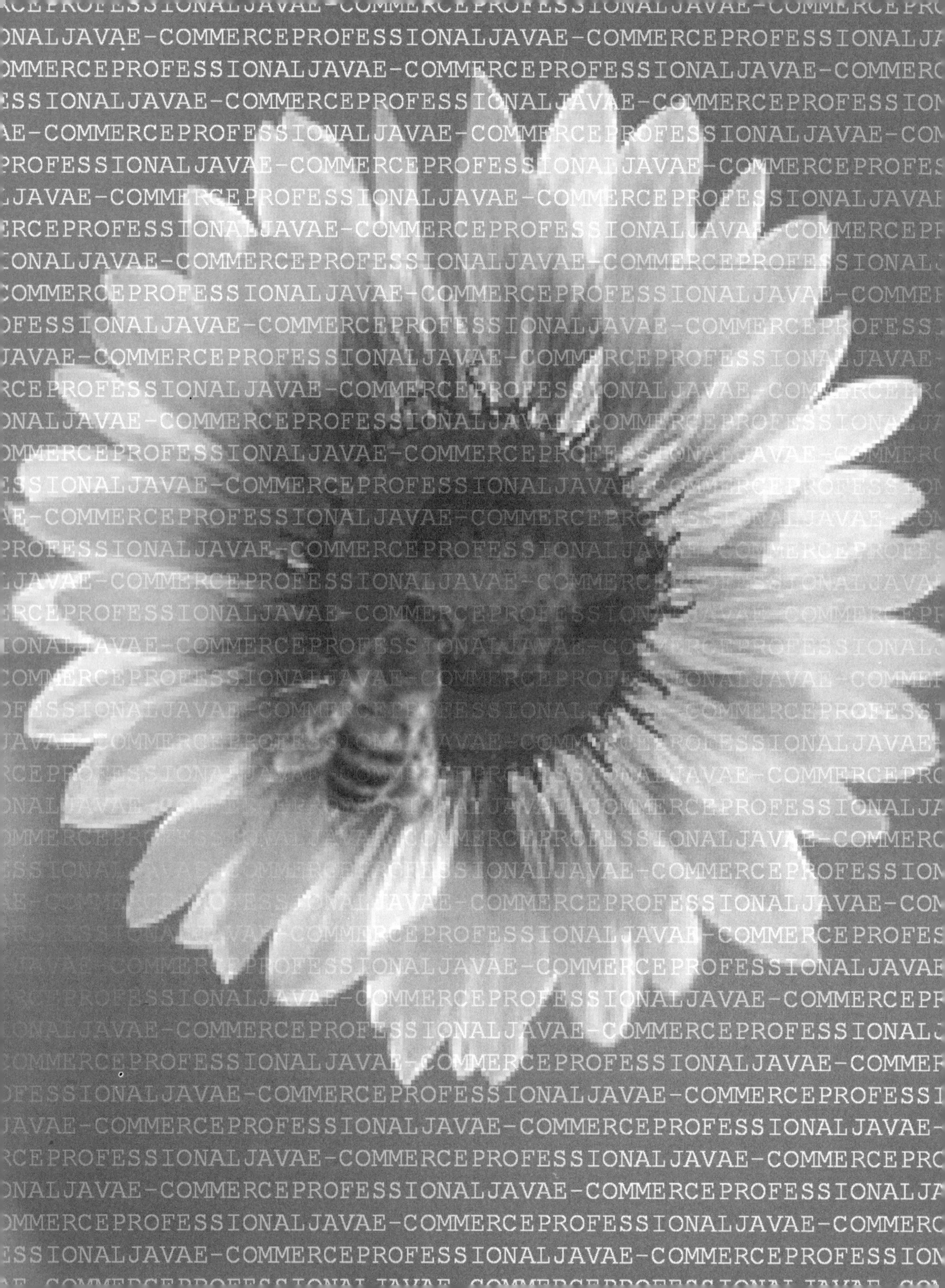
PROFESSIONALJAVAE-COMMERCE

24

Technologies for M-Commerce

The pace of technological change is breathtaking. Internet access and the availability of a plethora of services have revolutionized commerce several times over. It can be the biggest library, the most diverse shopping center, an exciting place to meet other people, and a fertile environment to do business in. Even now, however, there is one significant drawback. The only realistic method of accessing the Internet, for the majority of people, is through bulky desktops connected to phone sockets. In short, we can go anywhere in the world we like as long as we do not mind being stuck to our desks. Wireless technologies promise to untie us from the desk and provide services and information on the go.

> The aim of this chapter is to provide an introduction to the subject of mobile commerce or m-commerce, with a clear focus on the main enabling technologies and the couplings between them. It is a very exciting, albeit complex, area since, like most new things, there is a series of changing and developing technological standards to face. In order to ground this tour we will use some concrete examples along the way to give an immediate feel of what is possible now.

It has to be stressed early on, that in the scale of technological maturity, mobile technologies are mere infants that are just beginning to utter their first words. Therefore, even though current realities may look somewhat bleak the future is undisputedly bright.

The reason for this optimistic outlook is that there is clear evidence that wireless technologies are forming the foundations for the creation of a pervasive information cloud, accessible from anywhere in a ubiquitous manner. Computers are moving to the background, finally achieving the goal of being tools that we use with as little consideration as the light bulbs in our living room. The possibilities are endless and, unsurprisingly, companies are scrambling to place themselves at the right position in order to benefit. Only in the past two years telecom companies, especially in Europe, have gone through a whirlwind of mergers, hostile takeovers and acquisitions in preparation for the new world of m-commerce.

WIRED (December 2000) reported that there were 15 takeovers over 1999 and 2000 amongst telecom companies that were strongly related to the wireless market

We start the chapter with a look into the future as a means to motivate and, hopefully, inspire further work. Subsequently we attempt to organize the different technologies within a coherent model that takes a layered approach to the business of connecting devices. Then we focus on **WAP** (**Wireless Application Protocol**) and especially **WML** (**Wireless Markup Language**). The main aspects of WML are present but we also take some time to discuss what is lacking in WAP right now. The focus on WAP is not based on preferences due to its technological superiority but simply represents the acceptance of the current market reality where WAP is the undisputed leader as a mobile communication standard in Europe, most of Asia and America. Alternatives to WAP, in the form of i-mode and LEAP, are briefly introduced. Subsequently, we go on to presenting the relevant Java technologies and explain how they might integrate with WAP. We'll be covering the following topics in this chapter:

❑ Applications for wireless communications

❑ Components for communication standards

❑ Wireless network bearer technologies

❑ The Wireless Application Protocol

❑ Application development in the Wireless Application Environment including WML and WMLScript

❑ Pending issues in WAP

❑ Alternatives to WAP

❑ Wireless devices and Java technology

❑ CLDC

❑ MIDP

The Importance of Being Wireless

Along with any technology a set of buzzwords and catch phrases are bound to raise their infamous heads. At no other time, however, have the buzzwords evoked such powerful images. From assertions of "weaving the pervasive information fabric" to "ubiquitous computing" and "everywhere, anywhere" the integration of wireless technologies with the Internet is creating an unprecedented set of possibilities for a dramatic change in the way we communicate and access information. If this is not enough motivation perhaps the following statement may be more direct: Durlacher, a large research investment firm, says that by 2003, the European mobile e-commerce market will be worth 23 billion US dollars.

In this section we take a peek into the not-so-distant future and discuss some of the possible applications that will emerge in the areas of retailing and service provision, information exchange, and entertainment.

Revolutionizing Retailing and Service Provision

Until now, all companies could hope for is that they could in some way lure us to their website and keep us there long enough in order to convince us to buy something or come back to use their games/chat sections/e-mail service and so on. Through a mobile phone or a PDA, however, they can tag along with us everywhere we go.

Companies will be able to push messages to the devices, letting us know of the latest offers and products. Although that may sound very much like junk mail, the nature of wireless technologies can make the information we receive relevant to our actual physical location as long as our mobile device supports this kind of localization. For anyone who has had the experience of searching the Web for something as basic as a hardware store only to get hundreds that, unfortunately, are 300 miles away, geographically relevant information will be a big improvement.

Through localization technologies a company will be able to work out where you are based on the signal of your mobile phone. These technologies are getting steadily better, and soon a precision of 120 meters radius will be possible. So the next time you are walking along the city center that text message on your phone might just be from the shop you just passed by, letting you know that there is a special offer on you favorite brand of jeans. This will be based on information that they received from you the last time you ordered something from there, either in person or through the web. Alternatively, if you are after a specific product a quick call on your phone will let you know which are the nearby stores that offer that product.

It is worth noting that the boundary between the mobile phone and the PDA is becoming increasingly blurred. Mobile phones are becoming more capable of supporting diary functions like a PDA, while a PDA will soon be capable of making phone calls. Soon, there may be little to tell them apart; consequently, mobile phone and PDA will be used largely interchangeably in the rest of this section as we look to the future.

On a more practical note, everyday tasks such as buying bus or train tickets could simply fade into the background. We could use our phones to call the appropriate vendor and allow them to subtract the required amount from our account, issue a "ticket", and let us travel. These are known as **e-tickets** in the US, where they are already available. Taxis would no longer need to carry cash; a simple call to the company from the taxi should take care of the matter. Already there are drinks dispensing machines that do not accept coins but instead take calls from your phone. Even further off in the future lies a possibility of complete freedom from any device, as sensors will be able to identify the goods we have bought and our identity, enabling the appropriate sum to be subtracted from our accounts. This vision has found its way into homes through the IBM ads depicting the supermarkets of the future, where we will just walk in, collect the goods, and collect the receipts at the end.

In short, every aspect of our buying habits has the potential to change due to the integration of mobile devices with databases around the world; from buying tickets and making reservations, subscribing to fitness clubs and providing medical information, and banking and trading stocks, to a number of things that have not been thought of yet, wireless technology will have an impact.

Revolutionizing Information Exchange

One of the consequences of the increase in use of mobile devices is that we now have, at the very least, one more number, one more password and one more set of usage instructions to remember. In order to effectively leverage the true benefits of communications on the go, we need to minimize the disadvantages of handling all these disparate addresses and access codes, which often cause problems for users. This need has motivated the attempt towards what is termed **unified communications**.

Unified communications is all about integrating all the different ways you receive information from others, be it e-mails or telephone calls, so that it can be accessed through a unique point of contact. An example of such an attempt exists in Italy, where Telecom Italia provide a service that gives each subscriber a "Universal Number". This number can be used to call, e-mail, fax, or send text messages. One important issue, which unified communications raise, is how are we to manage the security of the access points so as to make sure that no one can get access to all our personal information. The solution will probably be some form of digital signature combined with some form of biometric authentication, such as retina scanning, and the use of certificates issued from trusted authorities so that users can know if they can trust a certain organization.

Business processes can also benefit from wireless technologies. Tasks such as fleet management and supply chain management can be streamlined with the deployment of an infrastructure that caters for communication with the mobile units, effectively extending the company intranet. Examples of such attempts have already emerged: SAP has developed applications for integrating with 3Com's Palm, US battleships are testing out the viability of using Palms onboard a ship to co-ordinate different tasks, and in Sweden a WAP-based solution for fleet management is being developed by Aspiro (and has also won an award for Best Use of WAP in a business application by the WAPForum and IBC).

In the future we will see much more advanced applications that will combine unified communications programs, such as Telecom Italia's. This should include work on computer-assisted collaborative work in order to provide an environment through which the dissemination of information and coordination between groups of people will be done through unique points of contact, irrelevant of the media used. As the available bandwidth of mobile devices increases so will the richness and diversity of the ways and forms we will exchange information, from text to video.

Despite all the hope and excitement, however, it is perhaps prudent to end this section on a cautionary note. The ultimate challenge of mobile communication will not be achieving the required standards in terms of bandwidth and processing power, since such progress is already well under way, but achieving the required standards in terms of security and the level of trust users will place in the medium. The lessons the Internet has taught until now should be taken close to heart and security systems should form part of any design and not be just a later addition.

Revolutionizing Entertainment

Entertainment is a market that greatly depends on the available bandwidth and processing power, which until now has been minimal, in order to offer the most exciting product possible to consumers. However, even the humble current offerings have proved the potential of the sector. People enjoy a game of Snake or Rotation while taking a train trip and these games will improve to the point where we will eventually see a merger between a GameBoy-style device and a mobile phone. Even more exciting, of course, is the potential of multi-player games.

Currently, there are offers such as chess games (through the exchange of text messages) and other board-based games, but soon we will have more wide-scale games that extend to different types of devices. An early example is the NokiaGame in Europe where the game takes place on different platforms all at once, from text messages on phones to the Web.

Another possibility is the provision of music on mobile phones. An increase in bandwidth will eventually lead to the ability to download the desired song and play it on the phone. There are already portable MP3-players and integration of these devices with mobile phones is not far away.

The ultimate goal, however, of mobile entertainment is mobile video. With the new standard for video decoding, MPEG-4, we will see the delivery of streaming, context-aware video in a few years. Current proposals include the possibility to download a video overnight for viewing later, or low bandwidth applications such as news, and weather, or remote cameras for security checks.

Enabling Technologies

Having introduced a number of possible applications for wireless networks, we now turn our focus to the underlying technologies that will make all this possible. As usual, before any kind of information arrives on our device, a complex set of interactions take place in the background. The majority of these processes are not the concern of the application developer, but it is useful to be aware of them, even more so when dealing with wireless technologies since the limitations and peculiarities of the media greatly affect the freedom of the developer. The m-commerce market is currently under rapid development and the ability to identify the technologies that will be winners in the end is crucial for any company wishing to enter this arena.

We can divide these processes, and the underlying technologies, into different layers, each one adding a level of functionality and providing services to the layers above it, while at the same time accepting services from the layer below it. Such a layered view of communications first gained wide acceptance through the **Open Systems Interconnection** (OSI) Reference model ("Information technology – Open Systems Interconnection – Basic Reference Model: The Basic Model", ISO/IEC 7498-1:1994).

The OSI model was developed by the International Standards Organization (ISO) in an effort to standardize communications between devices. The result was a very large and complex document (a stack half a meter high!) that was superseded by the less structured but more rapid development of an Internet based on the TCP/IP protocols. Its one great merit, and the reason it is still used, however, is that it divides the tasks involved in moving data from one computer to another into seven, self-contained layers: Physical, Data Link, Network, Transport, Session, Presentation and Application.

Very much like the use of interfaces in Java, the layers are allowed to develop independently as long as they adhere to the interface with the layer on top of them. We introduce these layers for three reasons: they expose, thorough a coherent model, the issues that need to be tackled in order to achieve communications in general; they provide a base through which to compare and contrast existing technologies used for the land-based Internet with the new wireless technologies; and finally they give a logical structure to the manner in which the chapter unfolds.

- ❑ **Physical Layer** – The physical layer is concerned with the physical links between devices. Therefore issues such as the form and nature of the transmission media (fiber, coax, twisted pair, wireless), the encoding types (voltage rates, transmission speeds) and the physical data rates are tackled at this level.

- ❑ **Data Link Layer** – This layer takes care of organizing the data during transmission. Issues of flow control, sequencing of frames, error notification, network topologies and network interface cards are tackled at this level. The physical and data link layers are concerned with very low level issues and, appropriately, they very seldom need concern the application developer. The most important question to ask of these layers is: how fast and how reliably can I transmit information from one point to another?

- ❑ **Network Layer** – The network layer deals with issues related to routing and logical addressing so as to enable multiple data links in an internetwork. Furthermore, it provides support for a connectionless or connection-oriented service to the higher layers.

- ❑ **Transport Layer** – This is the level at which the familiar Transmission Control Protocol or the User Datagram Protocol reside. Issues of flow control, multiplexing, virtual circuit management, error checking and recovery are taken care of.

- ❑ **Session Layer** – The session layer is responsible for managing sessions between higher level entities. For example, the Hyper Text Transfer Protocol fits at this level.

❏ **Presentation Layer** – The presentation layer provides services that handle the encoding of data into appropriate formats (ASCII, JPEG, Unicode) for the application layer.

❏ **Application Layer** – At this layer reside the highest-level entities used in communications from Internet browsers, to e-mail and FTP clients.

When the time came to develop a model for wireless networking, the concepts of the OSI were heavily used and the resulting Wireless Application Protocol (WAP) model (see the figure below) is very similar to the OSI model, in that takes a layered approached in dividing functionality. We will introduce the WAP architecture and the reasons behind its creation in much more detail later on. For the time being however, we give a brief overview of the overall architecture and contrast it with the current Internet model, with which most developers are familiar in an attempt to give the big picture of how the different technologies on different levels relate.

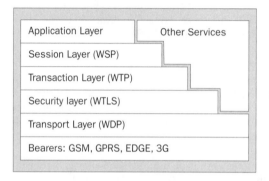

The figure above shows the different layers of the WAP Architecture, each represented by protocols that we briefly introduce below. It is important to note that WAP is in essence two things. The transport, security, transaction and session layers define *communication protocols* optimized for wireless devices. The applications layer, on the other hand, provides an *application development and execution environment.* These two aspects can and should be dealt with separately.

Now, going back to the seven layers with their distinct functionality mentioned earlier, we can say that the physical, data link, and network layers for wireless communications are covered by what are termed **bearer technologies**. These are technologies such as the **Global System for Mobile Communications** (**GSM**), which take care of all the problems of connecting mobile phones to the network. We will briefly introduce the most important of these technologies later on.

In the case of the land-based Internet the physical and data link layer are represented by host-to-network technologies. This term is used to encompass all the wide variety of technologies developed over the years for building networks from fiber links to protocols such as ATM or Ethernet. The network layer for the Internet is occupied by the Internet Protocol (IP) that defines a packet format and protocol for addressing and exchanging data with other machines.

Moving on, we have the transport layer. For wireless networks, the WAP architecture splits the services of this layer into three layers. It begins with the **Wireless Datagram Protocol** (**WDP**), which is the layer used to hide from all the above layers the exact nature of the bearer technology thus allowing higher layers to develop in an independent fashion to bearer technologies. The WDP provides services to the **Wireless Transport Layer Security** (**WTLS**) and the **Wireless Transaction Protocol** (**WTP**). However, in addition to the services provided to the higher WAP layers the WDP can also offer services to layers that do not conform to the suggested protocols as indicated in the figure above as a block representing other services and applications. The equivalent land-based Internet technology is the User Datagram Protocol (UDP), which offers an unreliable connectionless service.

The WTLS layer is optional, but represents the WAP Forum's dedication to making security a matter to be tackled from the start. The WTP adds a more reliable layer on top of the WDP in order to enable a more efficient connection oriented service. The WTLS can be compared to the Secure Socket Layer for the Internet while the WTP layer can be compared to the TCP protocol. They are both oriented at a message-based communication for transactions such as browsing.

The **Wireless Session Protocol** (**WSP**) that offers the option of a connection-oriented service above the WTP or a connectionless service on top of the WDP complements the WTP. WSP incorporates the functionality of the HTTP 1.1 protocol.

The highest layer in WAP is the **Wireless Application Environment**. At this level we have the browser applications and the Wireless Markup Language (WML) and WMLScript that are the equivalent of HTML and JavaScript for the land-based Internet.

The table below summarizes the comparisons we've just looked at:

OSI Model	TCP/IP Model	Wireless model based on WAP.
Application Layer	No real clear-cut distinctions for this model. A tentative and incomplete suggestion is: HTML/ Javascript	Wireless Application Environment (WAE)
Presentation Layer		
Session Layer	Hypert Text Transfer Protocol (HTTP)	Wireless Session Protocol (WSP)
Transport Layer	Transmission Control Protocol (TCP) – a reliable connection oriented protocol. Transport Layer Security (TLS) User Datagram Protocol (UDP)	Wireless Transaction Protocol (WTP)
		Wireless Transport Layer Security (WTLS)
		Wireless Datagram Protocol (WDP)
Network Layer	Internet Layer	Bearers
	The Internet Protocol (IP) that defines a packet format and protocol	GSM, GPRS, EDGE, SMS, 3G
Data Link Layer	Host-to-network	
Physical Layer		

There are a number of interesting lessons to be learned when going through the comparison of the three different models: the highly formal, theoretical and detailed OSI model; the ad-hoc but operational TCP/IP model; and the more pragmatic but also detailed WAP model. Experience has proven that the application and presentation layers are very much related and so they are merged in the TCP/IP and WAP models. On the other hand, the WAP model recognizes the need for effective security and dedicates a layer solely to the issue. At the transport layer a more robust method for information transmission was required, as opposed to TCP, to cater for wireless networks and so the WDP protocol was developed.

From now on, we take a bottom-up approach by presenting the wireless technologies at the bottom layers before going into a detailed presentation of WAP. The bulk of the presentation focuses on the **Wireless Application Environment** and especially WML where examples are provided.

Bearer Technologies

Mobile network technologies typically cover the bottom three levels of the OSI model. That means that the protocols involved are concerned with the encoding and transmission of the data with radio signals as well as the routing of the data to the appropriate receivers. It is at this level that the very critical metric of network bandwidth is determined.

Currently there are a number of developed mobile network protocols: from the widely deployed Global System for Mobile Communications Protocol (GSM) to a variety of messaging, pager and even analog technologies. In addition, there is a variety of very exciting new protocols being developed that have yet to reach mass markets (GPRS, UTMS), although some pilot systems are being deployed.

Here we'll be focusing on:

- ❑ GSM (Global System for Mobile Communications Protocol)
- ❑ SMS (Short Message Service)
- ❑ GPRS (General Packet Radio Service)
- ❑ EDGE (Enhanced Data Rates for Global Evolution)
- ❑ 3G (Third Generation) Technologies

GSM

The Global System for Mobile Communications Protocol (GSM) was introduced in the early 1990s in Europe, following an effort to standardize mobile communications in the region that began in 1982. The foresight of Europeans to establish an effective protocol from early on has meant that now Europe is considered a leader in mobile communications, with the US lagging behind almost two years (a difference that is sure to be covered rapidly).

GSM was developed to support the following services: good subjective speech quality, low terminal and service cost, support for international roaming, ability to support handheld terminals, support for range of new services and facilities, spectral efficiency, and ISDN compatibility. The challenges tackled by the establishment of this protocol were to provide a unified framework for communication that would still foster a competitive environment in the field. Although it was foreseen at the time of development that mobile devices had the potential to become versatile information tools, GSM was not developed with the direct view of integrating mobile communications with the Internet.

Using the **Circuit Switched Protocol**, the effective theoretical bandwidth on GSM networks is 14.4 kbit/s while supported data rates are actually at the level of 9.6 kbit/s (with actual performance often falling below this). Although this is sufficient for voice exchange, it is far below what is required for a true mobile communications revolution (or effective Web surfing).

Circuit-switched networks establish a dedicated end-to-end connection between origin and destination and no other data passes through that route while the session holds (the classic telephone network).

SMS

The **Short Message Service** allows users to send text messages up to 160 alphanumeric characters. Although now it is hard to imagine mobile phones without it, especially if you are a teenager, initially SMS had a tough time in the GSM market. However, as the use of mobile phones increased and younger people got hold of them, SMS usage soared since it was an ideal way, due to the lower cost, to exchange messages with friends. On the more serious side, SMS also fits the role of a service through which mobile phone users can be informed about such things as stock prices, weather report, sport results, e-mail notification, etc. Companies can use it to keep in touch with personnel in order to send urgent messages and receive progress reports or location information.

There are questions about what is the place of SMS in an environment where technologies such GPRS and EDGE and later on full-blown third generation technologies (all described below) are available. The answer probably lies in an evolution of the SMS protocol in order to take advantage of the increased bandwidth. However, the current strength of SMS guarantees a lifeline for at least the next couple of years before being merged into a more comprehensive messaging solution.

GPRS

As opposed to the current Circuit Switched Protocol (CSP) used with GSM, the General Packet Radio Service (GPRS) is based on a packet-switched wireless protocol. Theoretically, burst transmission speeds of up to 171.2 kbit/s are supported with actual speeds around the 115kbit/s mark; still an impressive speed, which surpasses even most of the current land-based connection solutions for home users. Furthermore, GPRS is an "always on" technology, which means that no dialup is required to retrieve information. It can achieve this "always on" condition because network capacity is only used when information is transmitted.

GPRS has already been deployed in pilot programs, and service providers in Europe are gearing up to roll out commercial versions of those pilot programs. Initially, the speeds will be slightly more modest than the numbers quoted above, probably around the 43.2kbit/s mark for download and 14.4kbit/s for upload. However, this is still a big improvement from the 9.6kbit/s of CSP. With the activation of GPRS networks, we will also see an explosion in wireless services, since the bandwidth will now allow much more freedom to developers.

Some critics have argued that once GPRS hits the worldwide wireless market, network providers will have a hard time to introduce third generation (3G, see below for details) wireless technologies since users will have all the bandwidth they require. The reason this criticism is worrying is that telecom companies, especially in Europe, have been spending billions to gain licenses for 3G technologies (in the UK, for example, prices went up to £8 billion Sterling for one license) and they will not see a return on their investment. However, one cannot help but think that such a criticism is very much like saying a PC will only ever need 640KB (a comment once made by Bill Gates).

Packet-switched networks move data in packets based on the destination address which is contained in the header of each packet. Therefore, two packets headed for the same point may go through different routes based on the changes in network traffic.

EDGE

Enhanced Data Rates for Global Evolution is a standard supported by the **Universal Wireless Communications Consortium** (**UWCC**) and promises speeds of 384 kbit/s. Where GPRS is an evolution for GSM networks, EDGE lays down the path for moving from GSM and GPRS to third generation technologies (3G). It fulfills such a role for two reasons: firstly, it allows service providers to begin the deployment of multimedia applications; secondly, it provides a path for evolution of the underlying infrastructure since the modulation changes required for EDGE are the same for **UMTS** (**Universal Mobile Telecommunications System**), one of the main third generation technologies. EDGE is more likely to be widely deployed in the American continent providing a clear path from some lingering analog networks to 3G digital ones.

The success of EDGE and ultimately of 3G technologies relies, however, on the availability of services to take advantage of the increased bandwidth.

3G Technologies

Third Generation (**3G**) technologies are, undoubtedly, the holy grail of every service provider and application developer (until the advent of 4G, that is!). Unlike the other headings used until now, 3G does not stand for any specific technology but is, rather, a heading given to a host of technologies that will replace GSM, which is the 2nd generation and GPRS, which is at the charming position of the 2.5th generation (2.5G).

The goal is to deliver multimedia services across wireless networks. This requires a dramatic overhaul of both the infrastructure used and the devices the users have; a great challenge by any terms. Furthermore, in order to avoid mistakes of the past (see GSM and the USA), standards for 3G technologies must be put in place from the very start.

Fortunately these needs have been recognized and 3G standards organizations are co-operating to come up with a unique set of standards. Under the heading of the Third Generation Partnership Program (3GPP), a number of organizations are co-operating to steer the evolution of these standards. The 3GPP is made up of:

- ❑ Regional standard setting bodies:
    - ❑ ETSI (European Telecommunications Standards Institute),
    - ❑ T1 in the United States
    - ❑ CWTS (China Wireless Telecommunication Standards group)
    - ❑ ARIB (Association for Radio Industries and Businesses) in Japan
    - ❑ TTA (Telecommunications Technology Association) in Korea

- ❑ Market representation bodies:
    - ❑ GSA (Global mobile Suppliers Association)
    - ❑ GSM Association
    - ❑ UMTS (Universal Mobile Telecommunications System)
    - ❑ UWCC (Universal Wireless Communications Consortium)
    - ❑ IPv6 Forum,

□ MWIF (Mobile Wireless Internet Forum)

□ 3G.IP (promoting an alignment between wireless and IP technologies)

□ Observers:

□ TIA (Telecommunication Industry Association)

□ TSACC (Telecommunications Standards Advisory Council of Canada).

These groups are all cooperating under the 3GPP to prepare and maintain the entire set of 3G specifications. The number of organizations involved is a clear indication of the enormity of the task but also the willingness of the market to "make it work" based on the strong belief in the commercial potential of the technology. The authority with the task of turning those specifications into international recommendations is the International Telecommunications Union to which the 3GPP specifications are submitted. The heading under which these standards currently come is IMT-2000 (International Mobile Communications).

Essentially, the generation of standards follows a three-tiered process. At the first level are the regional standards setting bodies like ETSI and T1, they then form consortiums and partnerships such as 3GPP that provide specifications to the ITU which are then turned into international recommendations like the IMT-2000.

The scope of IMT-2000 is very wide stating that it wants to "fulfill one's dream of anywhere, anytime communication as a reality" and, very importantly, to close the telecommunications gap by offering cost effective access to the four billion people that currently do not have a phone. The effort covers four different levels of operation: picocellular environments (indoor operation), microcellular environments (city-wide operation) and macrocellular (suburban) and global.

The Universal Mobile Telecommunications System has come to be established as the standard for 3G mobile communications for all different environments with transfer rates expected to reach 384kbit/s by 2005.

UMTS brings together technologies such as EDGE with UTRA (UMTS Terrestrial Radio Access) and CDMA2000 (Code Division Multiplex Access) to provide a unified approach for the delivery of multimedia services regardless of location. UTRA is a radio access system aimed at providing high efficiency at all the different environments users may be located, through the establishment of a set of specifications for achieving this connectivity. Furthermore, UMTS aims to promote the unification of such technologies with IP as well as promote service creation using smart cards, Java and the WAP.

Much more information about the vision of UMTS and 3GPP and details about the technologies and specification can be found on the websites of the organizations, links to which are provided below:

□ The European Telecommunications Standards Institute: http://www.etsi.org

□ GSM Association: http://www.gsmworld.com

□ UMTS Forum: http://www.umts-forum.org

□ 3GPP: http://www.3gpp.org

Wireless Application Protocol

In June of 1997 Nokia, Ericsson, Motorola, and Phone.com (then Unwired Planet) founded the WAP Forum. The goal was the creation of a set of standards that would enable the delivery of Internet content to wireless devices, in a manner that abstracts beyond the underlying bearer technologies described above.

The challenges of such an effort were to develop a reliable, layered, and extensible protocol that was applicable to as many bearer networks as possible and relevant to the wide range of consumer-class wireless devices. The characteristics of such wireless devices are:

❑ WAP devices are limited in all aspects, from the CPU, to random access memory, ROM, battery life and interface capabilities (small screens and uncomfortable data-entry mechanisms)

❑ Wireless networks are low-power, low bandwidth networks with capabilities currently not exceeding 10kbit/s

❑ Connections over these networks are unstable, unreliable, and unpredictable

Furthermore, the Wireless Application Protocol required a method of delivering information to the user that would not force the application providers to drastically alter the way in which they develop the services. As the WAP Architecture specification puts it, one of the goals of WAP is to "embrace and extend existing standards and technology where appropriate". In view of this goal, WAP supports a programming model that allows the developer to use almost *all* existing knowledge about how to build applications for the Internet in order to build applications for wireless devices.

The WAP Programming Model

The figure below illustrates a simplified programming model for the World Wide Web. We have the very familiar situation where a client makes some request by providing a URL to the server through a web browsing application. The server accepts the URL and may perform some amount of processing to the received information before generating content, in a manner suitable for the client, and sending that content to the client.

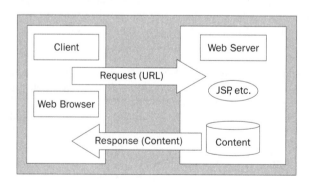

Now, in the next figure we illustrate the programming model for WAP.

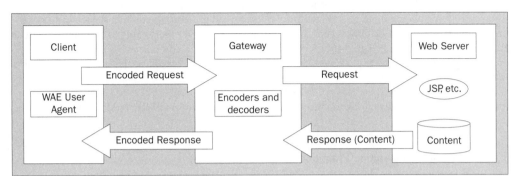

> **The Wireless Application Environment (WAE) Agent is a term stemming from the HTTP1.1 protocol and is meant to denote a client that originates a request (browser, editor or any other application requiring connectivity).**

What we have in this situation is a proxy or **gateway** between the wireless device and the web server. This gateway has two tasks to perform. Firstly, it accepts the information from the wireless device and *decodes* it. This decoding is necessary because the wireless device sends data in a compact format so as to save bandwidth. Once decoded the gateway has a request, which is formulated using the conventions of the WAP model (WDP, WTP, WSP). The gateway now has to translate this request into the format understood by web servers, namely TCP/IP and HTTP. The translated request is sent to the web server, which replies in the usual manner, and the gateway executes the task of translating to the WAP stack and *encoding* once more.

By using this gateway between the client and the server, application developers can go on using the same tools they always have (web servers, Java Server Pages, XML, database connectivity) and the gateway will act as a translator between the server and the client.

In the figure below we illustrate the types of networks envisioned by the WAP forum based on the use of gateways and WAP:

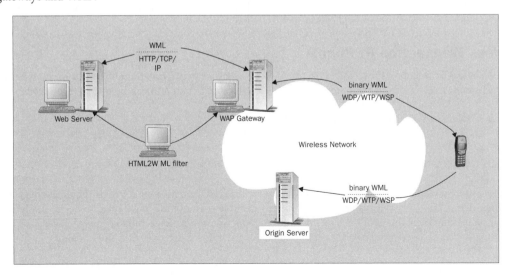

In the situation illustrated above we have a mobile device that retrieves content from a web server through a WAP gateway. The gateway can either retrieve WML-based documents from the web server, or HTML documents that have been filtered to a WML format. On the other hand, the mobile device can access information directly from an **origin server**. An origin server is a server that is able to respond directly to WAP requests without having to go through the translation phase. The mobile user's network service provider will typically provide origin servers in order to enable WAP access to telephony applications of the network provider's infrastructure.

For the rest of this section we will take a closer look at the different layers of the WAP stack:

❑ The Wireless Datagram Protocol

❑ The Wireless Transaction Protocol

❑ Wireless Transport Layer Security

❑ The Wireless Session Protocol

For more information about WAP, take a look at *Beginning WAP, WML & WMLScript (ISBN 1-861004-58-3)*, or *Professional WAP (ISBN 1-861004-04-4)*, both from Wrox Press.

Wireless Datagram Protocol

The Wireless Datagram Protocol is the single most important protocol for WAP. As mentioned earlier, it acts as the interface between the rest of the WAP layers and the bearer technologies. Each bearer technology is responsible for providing an adapter between its internal communication protocols and the WDP layer. Due to the variation amongst the bearer technologies and amongst the possible ways adapters to WDP can be provided, performance could vary significantly in order to satisfy memory usage requirements and optimize radio transmission. In an environment, however, of so many differing technologies it seems a small price to pay for achieving the ultimate goal of providing a unique transparent interface to the rest of the WAP stack.

The higher layers communicate with the WDP layer through **access points** represented by a port number and provide services such as addressing port numbers, optional segmentation and reassembly, and error detection.

The WDP layer can provide services to the Wireless Transaction Protocol layer or the Wireless Session Protocol layer or directly to an application such as e-mail.

Wireless Transaction Protocol

The Wireless Transaction Protocol makes use of WDP in order to provide request/response services for WAE agents. Every request/response pair is considered a transaction and can be one of three types:

❑ Class 0: Unreliable with no result message

❑ Class 1: Reliable with no result message

❑ Class 2: Reliable with one result message

These different classes provide a level of flexibility for the WAE agents to tailor their requirements according to their needs. Class 0 service is provided in order to enable a user of the WTP layer to occasionally send a datagram within the context of the existing WTP session; in essence, an unreliable "push" service. As such, it is not intended as a general datagram service since the WDP layer provides this functionality.

Class 1 service is provided to enable a reliable datagram service, which makes it a reliable "push" service. Finally, Class 2 service is the general transaction service that can be used to enable browsing by the WSP layer.

Wireless Transport Layer Security

The WTP layer can optionally make use of the WTLS layer in order to provide compression, encryption, and authentication (all optional services). The functionality of the WTLS layer is similar to TLS1.0 (Transport Layer Security, see http://www.ietf.org/rfc/rfc2246.txt for more information) used in TCP/IP networks. A number of encryption and authentication mechanisms are available, providing the developer with a certain amount of freedom as to what security mechanisms to implement.

Wireless Session Protocol

The final layer before the Wireless Application Environment (WAE) is the Wireless Session Protocol (WSP). The task of the WSP is to provide the WAE with an interface to a connection-mode service above WTP and a connection-less mode service above WTP. Thus, it provides the application with a way to establish and release reliable sessions between client and server, suspend and resume these sessions, as well as agree on what capabilities the interacting entities have for information exchange. Another very appealing feature of WSP is that it provides HTTP 1.1 functionality for extensible request-reply methods, composite objects and content type negotiation; once more allowing the developer to make use of any pre-existing knowledge for developing more traditional Internet services.

Through the interaction of all these layers information is delivered from a server to a wireless device. The most significant change at this level is that developers wishing to provide content to wireless devices must use an appropriate gateway that will perform the required encoding and decoding functionality.

As a final note to this section let me mention that anyone interested in following up these aspects of WAP should go to the website of the WAP forum at http://www.wapforum.org. All the specifications are freely available and, in addition, additional information such as white papers and presentations on the subject can be downloaded.

Application Development in the WAE

The overview of the lower layers of the WAP stack was necessary in order to be aware of the underlying process, what their capabilities are and how they are manifested. A wireless application developer does not, however, need to possess detailed knowledge of the functionality of these layers. In fact, the purpose of a layered architecture is exactly that: to abstract lower level details so we do not need to worry about them!

We now turn our focus to the most important layer for application developers, the Wireless Application Environment (WAE). The WAE is made up of a number of different components, each one aimed at a particular aspect of wireless applications.

- ❏ The Wireless Markup Language (WML) fits the role of a method for content and interface options markup in an appropriate manner for mobile devices with screens that may only be able to display 2 lines of text (usual displays go up to 5 while some can even display 10 lines).

- ❏ WMLScript provides a method for embedding basic logic into wireless applications (clearly inspired from JavaScript and its relation to HTML).

❑   A microbrowser specification that describes how WML and WMLScript should be laid out and presented on the screen. This application must provide interpreters for WML and WMLScript that are able to present the information so that it fits the particular device the browser is operating on.

❑   A framework for Wireless Telephony Applications and interfaces to those applications, aimed at providing access to the functions of the phone, and integrating those functions with the microbrowser. This aspect of the WAP protocol needs to be developed further and its usefulness depends, by definition, on the device.

Through these different components and based on the programming model described in the previous section, WAE attempts to provide a lightweight and extensible environment through which to develop wireless applications. The actors in the WAE are the WAE user agents that provide functionality for interpreting and displaying incoming information, the content generators that follow traditional server-side techniques, and the content encoding and decoding gateways. The WAE user agent and the gateways are not products that the mainstream service developers and providers need be concerned about unless some specialized functionality is required. Microbrowsers (or **user agents**) are the responsibility of the device provider in most cases, certainly for all currently available mobile phones, while some hand held Palm-type devices can have the software installed on them by the user.

This substantial section of the chapter is divided into the following units:

❑   Tools for WAE application development

❑   Wireless Markup Language (WML)

❑   WMLScript

❑   Pending Issues in WAP

Before going ahead with introducing WML and WMLScript we need to create an appropriate environment through which to develop and test the applications. Fortunately, as we'll see, that's not a complicated task at all.

Tools for WAE Application Development

There are a number of free WAP-compliant software development kits that can be downloaded from the Internet and installed on Windows or Unix-based machines. These SDK's typically provide an interface that simulates a mobile phone, making testing quite realistic. Incorporated in the software are the required WML and WMLScript interpreters as well as the encoders and decoders that are usually found in gateways.

The SDK used in this chapter was obtained from Phone.com and comes in one easy to install bundle. The version used, which was the latest at the date of writing, is UP.SDK4.0. There is a 4.1 release of the software, UP.Link4.1, which only supports WML 1.1. The 4.1 version is available from openwave.com, on the Phone.com website. In order to download, you need to register (it's free) and can then enter the developers section where there is the software and also other relevant information for wireless application development. The 4.0 version is still available to download from ftp://dload.phone.com/developer, where the file you want is upsdkW40e.exe.

The software bundle provided also includes some tutorials on WML and WMLScript with examples ready to be tested. The SDK is, unfortunately, only available for Windows platforms. For those that prefer a Linux/Unix environment I would suggest the Nokia Development Kit. It is Java-based. For instructions on installing it in Linux have a look at http://www.freaklabs.com/noklinux.html

Once installed, you can start the UP.Simulator, which opens up two windows: one is a phone simulator that displays the information and lets you navigate using the same interface users will have, while the other one displays debugging information. The phone simulator can accept different phone configurations so the results can be seen on phones with different interfaces and different screen sizes.

The debugging information is very helpful in two aspects: firstly, and most importantly, it makes locating errors much easier, and secondly it greatly helps in understanding the underlying processes that transform the text WML file you provide into the binary WML that the device recognizes. The simulator also provides other functions, such as examining the contents of its cache and any cookies, but you can learn about all this extra functionality from the documentation that comes with the software. The only point that needs to be stressed about using the simulator is that whenever you perform changes to a WML file and wish to view the results make sure to clear the phone's cache or the phone will not be aware of the change and will use the older version it has stored in its cache.

Following are two examples of the Phone.com SDK phone screen, showing a simple display that we'll see how to create in a moment:

The next screenshot is of the debugging screen, showing here an example of what information it provides. The exact appearance may vary from system to system:

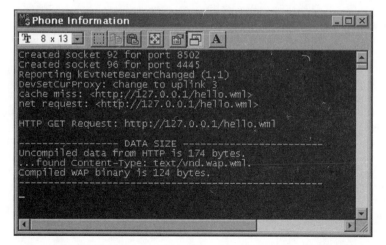

The other component required is, of course, a web server to send the information to the phone simulator. The server needs to be configured to recognize the WML mime types listed below:

MIME Type/Subtype	Extension	File Type
text/vnd.wap.wml	wml	WML source code
application/vnd.wap.wml-wbxml	wmlc	Compiled WML
text/vnd.wap.wmlscript	wmls	WMLScript source code
application/vnd.wap.wmlscriptc	wmlsc	Compiled WML script
image/vnd.wap.wmbp	wmbp	Wireless bitmap

There are a number of freely available web servers and they can be configured to work in stand-alone mode for development. In my case I use the Apache webserver configured to run on standalone mode using the 127.0.0.1 IP address, which represents localhost on my machine. In this case the WML mime types are appended to the mime.type file which can be found in the conf directory of the Apache installation. Apache is freely available to download from http://www.apache.org.

Phone.com also provide facilities for developers to post their WAP content on a WAP enabled server and test the applications from real devices. Although not necessary at an experimental development phase, since the simulator is quite reliable, it becomes very useful when one is seriously considering deploying the application. The only drawback is that you cannot test complicated applications that go through a specialized content generation process.

Finally get hold of your favorite text or XML editor, and you are ready to go!

Wireless Markup Language

The easiest way of introducing WML is to say that it is to microbrowsers what HTML is to traditional web browsers. It is dangerous, however, to go further than that and state that *writing* WML is similar to writing HTML pages. The peculiarities of mobile information devices call for a different approach, which we introduce in the next section. Of course, some knowledge can be transferred through from HTML to WML. For example hyperlinks, which are one of the most important tools, can be expressed in an almost identical manner.

HTML and WML do share a common, albeit distant, ancestor in the form of SGML (Standard Generalized Markup Language, which forms the basis of all markup language variants). WML's direct ancestor, however, is HDML (Handheld Device Markup Language), which was developed by Phone.com. Furthermore, WML is implemented using XML. As such it comes with all the benefits of using XML for building applications. There are a large number of suitable editors as well as libraries for the programmatic generation and validation of content (as previous chapters in this book have illustrated) and, crucially, the "tough love" approach of XML is useful in that it is much less forgiving to mistakes forcing the development of more robust applications.

The official definition of WML, as per any XML specification, is described in a Document Type Definition(DTD), currently at version 1.3 and can be found as an appendix in the WML specification which is available from the WAPForum website. All microbrowsers should be able to present WML that conforms to that DTD. Also available are variants to this DTD that offer extensions to the standard. These variants, however, are not supported by all microbrowsers and you should check the specifications of the microbrowser that you expect your application to run on before using them. For example, the Phone.com simulator we are using offers some extension described in the documentation of the simulator.

In this section we'll be looking at:

- ❑ The WML card metaphor
- ❑ Formatting content
- ❑ Basic navigation
- ❑ Tasks
- ❑ Events
- ❑ Global control
- ❑ Variables and information input

First off we need to understand how WML documents are used.

It's a Game of Cards

The most important metaphor used in WML is that of a deck of cards. Each WML document you serve up is called a **deck**, which is comprised of a number of **cards**. When a microbrowser is called to read a deck, it will read the entire deck and display the first card of the deck as well as update its history stack. The generic use case is that users enter URLs pointing to decks, view the cards in whatever sequence the developer has provided for, possibly providing information along the way, and then move on to another deck.

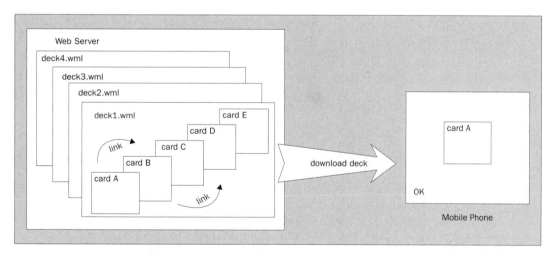

The example below, respecting the best of programming tutorial "Hello World" traditions, is a WML deck with only one card:

```
<?xml version="1.0"?>
<!DOCTYPE wml PUBLIC "-//WAPFORUM//DTD WML 1.3//EN"
    "http://www.wapforum.org/DTD/wml13.dtd" >
<wml>
```

```
    <card>
     <p>
        Hello World!
     </p>
    </card>
   </wml>
```

In order to test that the WML document above is indeed able to greet the world through a mobile phone, all that is required is to place it within a directory that is available via the web server to the phone simulator. We'll call this file `hello.wml` (`.wml` being the important part) and type the URL through the interface of the simulator. If you were testing this on a standalone Windows machine, the URL is probably http://127.0.0.1/hello.wml.

The first three lines are called the prolog in an XML document. They state the version of XML used and what DTD our document is conforming to. Every deck starts and ends with the `<wml>` tag and each card is placed between `<card>` tags. Text is usually placed between the paragraph tags `<p>` and `</p>`.

Each set of opening and closing tags, along with its content, is called an element in an XML document. Elements can also have attributes that are used to further specialize the behavior or meaning of an element. Attributes of elements are defined within the brackets of the tag that begin an element. For example, the `<wml>` tag has an attribute (`xml:lang`) that defines the language in which the document is written, allowing the microbrowser to use this information for interpreting and displaying the document in the appropriate manner. So, if our greetings were addressed to an Italian speaking audience we could specify this by placing the attribute within the `<wml>` element.

```
<wml xml:lang="IT">
   <card>
    <p>
       Ciao a tutto il mondo!
    </p>
   </card>
   </wml>
```

Formatting Content

Mobile devices certainly do not have a lot of flexibility when it comes to formatting content. Nevertheless, some basic options are provided in order to allow for the most essential presentation techniques.

The first element concerned with formatting, which we have already encountered, is the paragraph element `<p>`. When this element is used with no further qualifications, the user agent will render the content within so as to best suit the device on which it is displayed. Usual actions include wrapping text so that the user agent can display as much as possible and removing white space. The `<p>` element has two attributes for formatting content: `align` and `mode`. The former allows text to be aligned left, right or center and the latter activates or de-activates wrapping.

In addition to the paragraph element, there is a break element `<br>`, which has the same behavior as in HTML documents. Furthermore, there are a number of elements for displaying text in different styles:

Element	Effect
`<b>`	Bold
`<big>`	Larger Font
`<em>`	Emphasizes text
`<small>`	Smaller font
`<strong>`	Bolder font
`<i>`	Italic
`<u>`	Underlined

In the case where there is need for specialized formatting, and white space and word wrap are not desired, the `<pre>` element can be used to tell the user agent that text contained between these tags should be rendered "as is". There are few guarantees that this will actually happen but the WML specification states that the user agent should make a "best effort" try.

WML also has support for tables. Through elements for table, table row, and table data, basic table formats can be developed that are suitable for display on the limited screens of mobile devices. A WML example for a table is shown below (`table.wml`):

```
<?xml version="1.0"?>
<!DOCTYPE wml PUBLIC "-//WAPFORUM//DTD WML 1.3//EN"
        "http://www.wapforum.org/DTD/wml13.dtd" >
<wml>
  <card>
    <p>
    <table
      align="L"
      title="Formatting Examples"
      columns="2">

      <tr><td> Type</td><td>Syntax</td></tr>
      <tr><td><em>Emphasis</em></td><td>em</td></tr>
      <tr><td><big>Larger</big></td><td>big</td></tr>
      <tr><td><small>Smaller</small></td><td>small</td></tr>
      <tr><td><u>Underlined</u></td><td>u</td></tr>

    </table>
    </p>
  </card>
</wml>
```

As shown by the example, the table element has alignment, column number and title attributes. Alignment values are L for left (default), R for right and C for center. The row element `<tr>` has no attributes (other than those common to all elements) and acts as a container of cell information. The column element `<td>` delineates the columns in a row and can contain any type of information, from hyperlinks to images.

```
Type          Syntax
Emphasis      em
Larger        big
Smaller       small
Underlined    u


OK
```

While tables are a very useful feature of WML for organizing data, extreme care must be taken in their design. The problems are due to the number of characters a screen can typically display across; it usually does not exceed 20, while 15 is a more prudent estimate. The user agent will wrap lines across unless instructed otherwise and that may render the table unreadable. Alternatively, you can force the user agent to not wrap the text by setting the mode attribute of the paragraph element to nowrap. In that case, however, it becomes hard to understand exactly how the columns square up. The screenshot below illustrates the same code being run on a different screen size with the mode attribute set to nowrap. The best strategy is to use tables only when you can use headings and display information in them that does not take up too much space on screen.

```
>Type          Sy
Emphasis       em
 Larger        bi

               OK
```

A final comment on text formatting is required to mention that in order to get special characters (characters that are used to identify elements in XML) to display on the screen the following codes can be used:

Display code	Display character
" or "	the quotation mark "
& or &	the ampersand &
' or '	the apostrophe '
< or <	the less than <
> or &62;	the greater than >
or	a non-breaking space
­ or ­	a soft hyphen

A non-breaking space is a space that doesn't cause a line break in the text. A soft hyphen is a hyphen that doesn't cause a line break in the text.

Of course, the best way to get lots of information across in a limited area is by using suitable pictures. WML supports graphics through the image element <img>.The images that can be displayed are only one bit deep, which means just black and white or, more suitably for mobile devices, a funny green and black! A WML document containing just an image would look like this:

```
<wml>
  <card>
    <p>
      <img
        alt="image description"
        src="./relative/path/to/image.wbmp"
        localsrc="alternative_local_representation"
        vspace="2"
        hspace="2"
        align="top"
        height="10"
        width="10"
      />
    </p>
  </card>
</wml>
```

To start with, you should note that the `<image>` element does not need an opening and closing tag; all the information is contained within one tag, which is closed with a forward slash. The attributes available are as follows:

Attribute	Use
alt	For providing a text description of the image in case the image cannot be displayed
src	The Uniform Resource Identifier (URI) to the image
localsrc	Can be used to specify a locally available (in ROM or RAM) representation of the image, thus maintaining the spirit of efficient resource use
vspace and hspace	Specify the white space to be left around the image, vertically and horizontally
align	Sets the position of the image in relation to the display area, (either top, bottom or center)
width and height	They specify the dimensions of the image itself

The image format understood by user agents is wbmp (wireless bitmap) that is optimized for transmission to and display on wireless devices. For those that wish to convert images there are freely available converter programs that you can either download or access on line (http://www.teraflops.com/wbmp/), alternatively there are online wbmp galleries (http://www.hicon.nl/ENG/index.htm).

Basic Navigation

The Internet hit center stage when all the disparate pieces of information were linked through hyperlinks, providing the medium with a truly dynamic environment. WML has the exact same notion of hyperlinks as HTML. URLs (Uniform Resource Locators) can be used for navigation between decks and for linking scripts, images, etc., to a document. Relative URLs are also supported, as well as fragment anchors that allow you to link one part of a deck to another. Below, we have a deck with two cards that are linked through an anchor so the user can navigate between them (simplenavigation.wml):

```
<?xml version="1.0"?>
<!DOCTYPE wml PUBLIC "-//WAPFORUM//DTD WML 1.3//EN"
"http://www.wapforum.org/DTD/wml13.dtd" >
<wml>
  <card id="Card1">
    <p>
      Hello World!
    </p>
    <p>
      <a href="#Card2">To infinity and beyond..</a>
    </p>
  </card>
  <card id="Card2">
    <p>
      ...welcome to infinity
    </p>
    <p>
      <a href="#Card1">It's not that exciting after all</a>
    </p>
  </card>
</wml>
```

The results of this code are shown below:

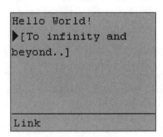

This is the first screen the user will see, with the link displayed between brackets. When the user scrolls down to the link the usual OK option is substituted by the Link option. However, you should always keep in mind that different phones may have different ways to render WML, from text to images and voice. Once the link is activated the second card is loaded from memory:

```
...welcome to
infinity
 [It's not that
exciting after all]



OK
```

Navigation is achieved by using fragment anchors in an almost identical manner to HTML documents. The cards are identified by using the id attribute. This attribute is particularly useful and common to all the elements of a WML document. As shown in our example it serves to identify and differentiate between elements, allowing fine-grained control of the document. Another attribute that is common to all the elements of a WML document is the class attribute, which is used to cluster elements into classes that can then be dealt with in a single blow.

Tasks

The navigation example given earlier is the simplest way in which navigation can be achieved and is based on an event-driven model defined in WML. There are a variety of **events** that can take place whilst reading a WML document, and every event can be bound to a specific **task** such as navigating from one card to the other.

More specifically, in our example the event of selecting the <a> element is bound to the task go that causes the user agent to locate the resource defined within the href attribute. There are four types of tasks defined in WML: <noop>, <prev>, <refresh> and <go>.

History stack

This event-driven model is supplemented with a navigational history model in order to provide control of flow of information to the mobile device. This history model is based on a simple stack data structure. Elements are pushed on to the stack when the user arrives at a new card and they are popped off the stack when the user causes a backward navigation. The stack can also be reset so that it contains only the card that the user is currently viewing. The history stack is used by some of the tasks we will describe.

In the next couple of pages we will go over the events and tasks available in WML in some more detail. Afterwards, examples will be given that should make things clearer.

<go>

The <go> task is probably the one that is most used since it is responsible for navigating and also is very versatile due to the number of attributes that there are to specialize its operation. All the attributes are described in the table below:

Attribute	Description
Href	Specifies the destination URI.
Sendreferer (true|false)	If set to true the user agent is obliged to notify the server of the URI within which the task is contained. This will enable the server to perform some amount of control to the information it sends out based on the location from where the information is requested.
Method (post|get)	Specifies whether the HTTP submission method will be a GET or a POST.
Cache-control (no-cache)	If cache-control is set to no-cache then the user agent is obliged to load the request URI from the server each time. Especially useful in situations where the information changes often.
Enctype	The content type that is used to submit information to the server when using a POST method. Currently, application/x-www-form-urlencoded or multipart/form-data are supported.
Accept-charset	Used to specify the character list encoding that the origin server accepts when processing input. The default value is unknown and the user agent can assume that it should use the same encoding as that used to transmit the deck to the device.

The go task can be manipulated to generate either a POST or a GET HTTP request. The question is, can we include additional information, which is specific to that particular request or viewing session, so that the server can act accordingly? For example if the user requests to see all trains going to London on Friday an HTTP GET request of the form:

```
GET www.traininfo.com/servlet?destination=london&day=Friday HTTP/1.1
```

is required. WML supports the formation of such request with the postfield element that can be included within a go element. Its syntax is as follows:

```
<postfield
  name="name"
  value="value"
/>
```

To form the request mentioned above the WML syntax should look as follows:

```
<go
  href="www.traininfo.com/servlet"
  sendreferer="true"
  method="GET"
>
  <postfield name="destination" value="london">
  <postfield name="day" value="friday">
</go>
```

The code above would cause an HTTP GET request, notify the origin server about the location from where this call has been generated and append the information in the postfield elements to the request. If the method was set to POST, the generated request would be of the form:

```
POST www.traininfo.com/servlet HTTP/1.1
content-type="xxx-urlencoded"
  .

  .
destination=london&day=friday
```

In addition to the very useful postfield element, WML also defines a setvar element, which can be used to set a variable in the current context browser, and can be included in a go element. We will look at the setvar element in more detail later on.

<prev>

Moving on with the introduction of tasks in WML the next in line is the prev element. Its job is to take the user a step back in the navigational history by going to the card just behind the current one. In other words, it performs a *pop* on the history stack. The prev element can also accept setvar elements to carry information to the previous card or deck if that is required.

<refresh>

The refresh element will clear the history stack of all cards but the one currently on display.

<noop>

Finally, the `noop` element will perform no operation. This is useful in cases where you wish to override deck wide operations in a specific card.

Events

The tasks described above only have meaning when they are thought of as actions that can be bound to events. There are four types of events in WML:

- ❑ **Anchor events** (the simplest type of which we saw earlier) are usually related to a particular point or "hot spot" in the card and link that point to some other point.

- ❑ **Intrinsic events** occur due to a change in the current state of the user agent such as loading a new card or moving to a previous one.

- ❑ **User-triggered events** are caused by action of the user such as pressing a button on the device.

- ❑ **Timer events** take place once a timer, which can be set by the developer, has expired.

Anchors

Anchors can be placed anywhere where text for display might be expected in the text, except lists of choices, and microbrowsers should render anchors as links. Anchors thus act like shortcuts. At first it may seem strange that anchors cannot be placed in lists of choices. The reason is that the elements used to create options in a list have an attribute that can be set to point to a URL making anchors redundant.

The syntax of an anchor element is as follows:

```
<anchor
  title="title of the link this anchor is pointing to"
  accesskey="key to activate link"
>
```

The title attribute can be used to give a name or short description of the link. The user agent can then use that information to enhance the browsing experience by providing an auditory description of the link, or a *tool tip* or other visualization aid. The `accesskey` attribute allows the developer to provide a shortcut to that link by assigning a character, accessible through the keys on the mobile device (usually from 0-9), that will activate the link. It is usually up to the user agent to make the user aware of this possibility, but sometimes the user agent may choose to ignore the `accesskey` attribute altogether. Within the anchor tags, the developer can include one of the `go`, `prev` or `refresh` tasks as well as normal character data or an image. So, for example the piece of code below is a valid link (`anchor.wml`):

```
<anchor
  title="Example"
  accesskey="9">
<go href="http://127.0.0.1/hello.wml"/>
Find the greeting!
</anchor>
```

When this code is run on the Phone.com developer kit it displays a **9** next to the hyperlink thus indicating that if the key 9 is pressed the hyperlink is activated; a very useful feature on cumbersome devices where the user experience must be streamlined to the maximum. In addition, the title of the link is displayed in the place of the usual OK message.

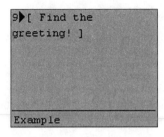

As mentioned before, the anchor element has a small sibling in the form of the <a> element that can only execute a go task. The same code as above can be written like this:

```
<a
  href="http://127.0.0.1/hello.wml title"
  title="Example"
  accesskey="9" >
  Find the greeting!
</a>
```

Intrinsic Events

Intrinsic events are those that occur due to a change in the state of the user agent. There are four defined in WML1.3:

❑   onenterforward is raised when the user agent enters a card through a go task or an identical script function.

❑   onenterbackward is raised when a prev task or an action with identical semantics takes place.

❑   ontimer is concerned with timer events; as mentioned before an application developer can set a timer and once it expires it will raise this event.

❑   onpick is concerned with the selection of options and when an option is selected it raises this event.

The way to access these events and subsequently bind them to tasks is through the onevent element. This element has a type attribute, which can be set to one of the four intrinsic events. A small example using the timer is shown below (timer.wml):

```
<wml>
  <card id="card1">
    <onevent type="ontimer">
      <go href="#card2"/>
    </onevent>
    <timer value="50"/>
    <p>
    Time is...
    </p>
  </card>
```

```
<card id="card2">
  <p>
    ...a dimension u can use in WML.
  </p>
</card>
</wml>
```

When the code executes, it will display the first card and 5 seconds later display the second one. This is a useful feature if you wish to display information to the user in a way that minimizes the amount of navigating the user has to perform.

WML provides a faster way to achieve the same result by setting an attribute in the card element as shown, and not specifying the `<onevent type="ontimer">` tag:

```
<card id="card1" ontimer="#card2">
```

This will automatically link the timer expiry event to a `go` task. The `onenterforward` and `onenterbackward` events are often used to set variables or initialize variables before entering a card. We will examine these features later on.

User-triggered Events

User-triggered events are activated by **widgets** through the mobile device's interface. The definition of a widget is quite wide, ranging from buttons on the device, to voice activation, or touch-screens, etc. The current WML specification recognizes a number of widgets and provides some broad definitions of their functionality:

- ❑   `accept` – positive acknowledgement

- ❑   `prev` – a step back based on the history stack

- ❑   `help` – a request for help that may be context-sensitive

- ❑   `reset` – clear the user agent's state

- ❑   `options` – request for options for action on current context

- ❑   `delete` – causes the deletion of a choice or item

- ❑   `unknown` – a generic option

The interpretation of the precise action is left to the user agent (microbrowser) with the exception of `prev`, since its definition can only allow one action. There is also support for experimental types whose title can start with X-* or x-* and vendor specific types with *.VND or *.vnd and any combination of [Vv], [Nn] or [Dd]. These types are included in order to allow expansion and also to allow developers to define their own types.

Access to these events is through the `<do>` element whose syntax is shown below:

```
<do
  type="the event type as described above"
  label="label for the widget"
```

```
    name="name of binding"
    optional=(true|false)
>

<!--task to execute-->

</do>
```

The `type` attribute takes a string that should correspond to the event types described above; if it does not then it is treated as `unknown`, indicating that the user agent doesn't know how to handle such an event type. User agents might be able to label the widgets dynamically using graphics or sound, and the developer can guide the labeling through the `label` attribute. The `name` attribute is useful for overriding do elements that apply to a whole deck with do elements that are specific to the current card (more about this later on). Finally, the `optional` attribute specifies if the user agent can decide whether to conform to the do element's request or not.

Global Control

Until now we have seen how WML allows the developer to incorporate functions in the document that offer some control over the flow and rendering of the information. All the examples, however, have been focused at the card level. WML also provides elements that allow control mechanisms to be set at a deck wide level (affecting all cards within the deck), as well as defining variables that can be used to carry context from one card or deck to another.

Global definitions can be formed through the elements `<head>` and `<template>`. The `<head>` element, similar to the `<head>` tag in HTML, allows the establishment of access controls as well as the definition of meta-information. Meta-information is especially useful in facilitating programmatic searches since you can include in it the important keywords that describe the contents of that deck.

The `<template>` element is used to define task-event bindings that will hold true for all the cards in the deck, a powerful mechanism for giving all the cards a coherent behavior. Using these elements, the structure of WML documents will look like this:

```
<!--prologue-->

<?xml version="1.0"?>
<!DOCTYPE wml PUBLIC "-//WAPFORUM//DTD WML 1.3//EN"
"http://www.wapforum.org/DTD/wml13.dtd" >

<!-- document starts here -->

<wml>
<head>
  <access
    domain="domain.allowed.com"
    path="/pathforwap"
  />
  <meta
    name="property name"
    forua=(true|false)
```

```
        content="property value"
        scheme="how to interpret property"
    />
  </head>

  <template>

    <do>
      <!-- task binding -->
    </do>
    .
    <onevent>
      <!--task binding-->
    </onevent>

    <!-- further event and task bindings -->

  <template>

  <!-- card definitions begin here -->

  <card>
    .
    .
    .
  <\card>

  <card>
    .
    .
    .
  <\card>
    .
  <!--other cards-->
    .
  </wml>
```

The <head> element has no special attributes but takes two elements, <access> for access control information and <meta> for meta information.

Access control is exercised by defining an allowed domain and path; before the user agent loads another deck it must compare the origin of the candidate deck for loading to the access domain and path information, and will load it only if both match. The WML specification states that there can only be one access element defined, restricting the level of access control to one domain and its associate path. If there is more than one <access> element defined, an error is raised, and if there is none then, of course, no access control is exercised so the deck can link to and load from any other with no restriction.

The <meta> element is most useful, allowing search engines to retrieve information about the WML document. As such, user agents are not obliged to support it. In fact, when the <meta> element is specified using the name attribute, network servers should not even transmit it. If it is to be transmitted, the http-equiv attribute (not shown in the example) should be used in the place of the name attribute. In this case, the meta-data will be converted as the header information in a WSP or HTTP response header. The forua attribute can be set to false to indicate to the user agent that this element can be ignored altogether. Finally, the scheme attribute specifies the manner in which the information should be interpreted.

Although not critical for a WML document, the <head> element is necessary for the design of efficient and robust WML-based sites since it aids administration and information gathering tasks.

The <template> element's task is to allow the definition of task-event bindings at the deck level. This makes it possible to have a standard "feel" to the whole deck. This is done through the <do> and <onevent> elements, exactly in the same manner as described previously. The difference is that the bindings are active on every card, although they can be overridden on any given card. Below we have an example of this functionality. We use the template event to define a backwards button for all cards, something that not all phones nowadays do (template.wml):

```wml
<wml>

  <template>

    <do type="accept" label="Back">
      <prev/>
    </do>

  </template>

  <card id="Card1">
    <p>
      Hello World!
    </p>
    <p>
      <a href="#Card2">To infinity and beyond..</a>
    </p>
  </card>

  <card id="Card2">
    <p>
      ...welcome to infinity
    </p>
    <p>
      <a href="#Card3">Let's go further</a>
    </p>

  </card>
  <card id="Card3">
    <p>
      ...welcome to beyond infinity
    </p>
    <p>
      <a href="#Card1">It's not that exciting after all</a>
    </p>
  </card>
</wml>
```

When a mobile device interprets and runs this document it will link the pressing of the accept button on the phone to a backwards navigation task. However, if the cursor on the screen is on a link it will override the backwards functionality of the accept button to perform the linking task.

Variables and Information Input in WML

Variables are a feature in WML that has no counterpart in HTML. The WAP Forum has included variables in the WML specification as a mechanism for creating WML documents that can provide maximum flexibility until run-time, allowing for effective caching. In addition, variables are useful for collecting information from the user. The Internet hit the next level in terms of interactivity when users were able to provide information, and thus personalize the response they receive. In HTML this is done using forms with the appropriate tags for forms. In WML a more robust way was required and it is provided with the use of variables that can have values assigned to them, and elements that allow input from the user.

The definition of variables in WML could hardly be simpler, and is most similar to scripts in UNIX or macro languages in Windows. Variables are placeholders for a string of characters and can be substituted anywhere where character data can be accepted in a WML document. Elements and attribute names, of course, cannot be parameterized but the values they accept, such as URL's can be. Variables are denoted using the $ before the variable name and traditionally the name is within brackets to make reading of the document easier `$(variablename)`. Variable names can only begin with a letter or underscore and can be followed by any number and combinations of letters, digits and underscores.

Variables can be set through user input and also programmatically through the `<setvar>` element.

```
<setvar
    name="variablename"
    value="variablevalue">
```

Here is a small example illustrating the setting of variable based on the navigation options of the user (`setvar.wml`).

```
<wml>

  <card id="Card1">
    <p>
      Pick a card, any card:
    </p>

    <p>
      <anchor title="Ace" accesskey="1">
      <go    href="#Card2">
         <setvar name="card" value="Ace of spades. You''ve lost :("/>
      </go>
      </anchor>
    </p>

    <p>
      <anchor title="King"    accesskey="2">
      <go    href="#Card2">
        <setvar name="card" value="King of clubs. You've lost :("/>
      </go>
      </anchor>
    </p>

    <p>
      <anchor title="Queen" accesskey="3">
      <go    href="#Card2">
```

```
            <setvar name="card" value="Queen of hearts. You're a winner :)"/>
        </go>
        </anchor>
    </p>
    </card>

    <card id="Card2">
        <p>
            You've chosen the $(card)
        </p>
    </card>
</wml>
```

This extremely simple game gives the user three links that can be activated through scrolling down and selecting one or by pressing the appropriate access key and will lead to the second card where the result is revealed. If variables were not available such an action would require four cards and not just two. As you may have guessed, variables are global and are valid, once defined, throughout the whole deck (once the deck has been processed).

Working with Input

In order to allow the user to provide information WML defines the `<input>` element in the following manner:

```
<input
  name="variablename"
  value="value"
  type= (text|password)
  format="mask for input data"
  emptyok=(true|false)
  size="10"
  maxlength="12"
  title="input option title"
/>
```

As can be seen there are quite a large number of attributes, the justification being that since we are dealing with devices of terrible interactive ability the task of inputting data should be streamlined as much as possible.

The `name` attribute identifies the variable that should be set by the user's input, and the `value` attribute can be used to give a default value to that variable (catering for the case that the user does not enter any information). Care is required here because according to the WML1.3 specification if the variable is already set (its value is not an empty string) the `value` attribute of the `<input>` element will be ignored. The problem here is that if the variable's value is not set to the default, the information received from the user will be incorrect.

The `type` attribute can be set to `password` (the default setting being `text`) if it is a situation where the typed text should not be displayed on screen. It is the user agent's responsibility to display that information in a manner that is not readable (such as asterisks or no characters at all).

The `format` attribute allows the developer to set a mask that will limit the amount of allowable characters the user can enter. The various masks available are coded in the WML specification. Some examples are: M for any allowable character in the language used (default value), N for number characters, a for entry of lowercase characters excluding numeric, etc.

The emptyok attribute can be set to true to indicate that input is not required and to false to indicate that some input should be present. If this attribute is not set the value of the format attribute will define whether it is required that some valid input exists.

The size attribute defines the space in characters that should be made available on screen for input while the maxlength attribute indicates the maximum numbers of characters allowed in the current option.

Finally, the title attribute serves as an identifier for the object and can (optionally) be used by the user agent for display purposes.

The following example illustrates some of the features described. On the first card the user can enter some information that is bound to variables via the do element. These values are then displayed on the second card (input.wml):

```
<wml>
  <card id="card1">

    <do type="accept" label="submit">
      <go href="#card2">
        <setvar name="name" value="$(name)"/>
        <setvar name="password" value="$password"/>
      </go>
    </do>

    <p>
      Please enter your name:
    </p>

    <p>
      <input
        name="name"
        value=""
        emptyok="false"
        size="10"
        maxlength="20"
        title="Name"/>
    </p>

    <p>
      Please enter your password:
    </p>

    <p>
      <input
        name="password"
        value=""
        emptyok="false"
        type="password"
        size="10"
        maxlength="20"
        title="Password"/>
    </p>
  </card>
```

```
<card id="card2">

  <p>
    Your name is $(name) and your password is $(password)
  </p>

</card>
</wml>
```

The screenshots below show how the user will see this code rendered. The user is presented with two options:

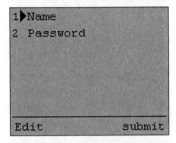

Upon selecting the Edit button the user can enter their name:

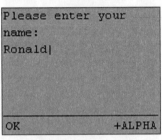

The input for the password is hidden:

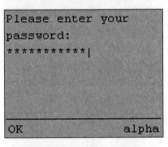

Through variables, the user agent has kept track of the input:

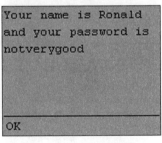

However, what is required in this case is not that the user views the information just entered, but that the server gets it! This can be achieved by setting the mode attribute of the <go> element to POST and substituting the <setvar> elements with <postfield> elements.

```
    <do type="accept" label="submit">
      <go href="www.receivingserver.com/servlet" mode="POST" >
        <postfield name="name" value="$(name)"/>
        <postfield name="password" value="$password"/>
      </go>
    </do>
```

There you have it! Two-way communication with a server, and mobile commerce raring to go!

If you run this script on a simulator you may be surprised by the way the user agent displays the information. Some microbrowsers will bypass the first screen which shows the two options and directly show the second screen, which requests the user to input their name. Subsequently it will show the screen requesting the password. Now, in certain cases that may be useful but the developer should be able to have some control over the exact order and manner in which the options will be displayed. In fact, WML defines an `ordered` attribute for the `<card>` element. If this attribute is set to `true` the user agent will divide the content across several screens. If, however, it is set to `false` all the options will be seen on the same screen.

So, to get the same interaction sequence as the screenshots shown above you need to change the following line from:

```
<card id="card1">
```

to:

```
<card id="card1" ordered="false">
```

Improving Navigation

To further aid navigation WML also has the `<fieldset>` element. This element can be used to group various other elements together thus helping the user agent in logically organizing and presenting the information. Within two `<fieldset>` tags the following elements can be placed: `<a>`, `<anchor>`, `<do>`, `<img>`, `<table>`, normal text, and text the user enters.

Entering data is all very well, but sometimes what is required is for the user to select from a list of choices. WML provides for lists of options via the `<select>` element. Each select element can contain a number of options, denoted using the `<option>` element, and those options can be divided into groups using the `<optgroup>` element:

```
<select
  title="select list title"
  name="my_select_list_variable"
  value="default_value"
  iname="my_select_list_index_variable"
  ivalue="index_variable_default_value"
  multiple=(false)>

<optgroup title="group1">

  <option
    value="value_for_option"
    title="option title"
```

```
onpick="www.wheretogoifselected.com">
Option text
</option>

</optgroup>

</select>
```

The `<select>` element provides two ways of collecting information. The first uses the `name` and `value` attributes, and is done by setting the variable denoted by the `name` attribute to the value denoted by the `value` attribute in the `<option>` element.

The second one is based on setting a variable to the index position of the option, and is done via the `iname` and `ivalue` attributes. The `multiple` attribute allows multiple selections to be performed and are appended to the variable using semicolons to delineate the different options. Finally, the `<option>` element may be used to take the user to another location. This is done through the `onpick` attribute.

This concludes our overview of WML. As can be seen the developer has an impressive array of options when it comes to developing sites for wireless devices using the WML.

The biggest challenge, as ever, is to employ these tools in a manner that will enable the development of sites that the user will enjoy visiting and will come back to. For wireless sites, it is necessary to balance content with usefulness so that the user does not feel like time is being wasted. It should be possible to get to information as easily and as quickly as possible. Numerous studies have proven that the more clicks or buttons the user has to press the less the possibility that a sale will happen.

WMLScript

WMLScript is a close cousin of JavaScript and has been made part of the WAP set of standards as a means for providing some logic control on the client side for WAP applications. It is actually derived from the ECMAScript language (Standard ECMA-262: "ECMAScript Language Specification", ECMA, June 1997), which is in turn derived from JavaScript and Self.

Although it has come under some criticism as being too big a processing burden for wireless devices one cannot deny that it is especially well-suited for such tasks as performing content-checking on user entered information and also some simple calculations, thus alleviating the airwaves and conserving bandwidth, a commodity that is also in great demand. More importantly, it can be used to create error messages and confirmations as well as access facilities on the mobile device allowing the developer to make phone calls or access other services on the SIM card of the phone.

To investigate this topic here we'll be covering:

- ❑ WMLScript excecution
- ❑ WMLScript basics
- ❑ Functions Pragmas
- ❑ Operators
- ❑ Statements

❑   Libraries

❑   A simple example of the use of WMLScript

Executing WMLScript

WMLScript has a **function-based** mode of operation. This means that one does not need to write full blown programs to get something done, functions can be called individually as and when needed. The reason for such an approach is to give the developer maximum flexibility over when and how to use WMLScript.

Functions are executed by calling them through a WML document. Unlike JavaScript that can be embedded in an HTML document WMLScript needs to be contained within a separate file with the ending `.wmls`. For example, if you had a WMLScript named `funkyCode.wmls` with a function called `breakDance()` you could call it from within a WML document using the following command:

```
<go href="funkyCode.wmls#breakDance()"/>
```

This command would cause the wireless device to contact the gateway and request that the file named `funkyCode.wmls` be retrieved. The gateway would then retrieve it from the webserver, extract the required function, compile it and send the resulting bytecode to the device where it is executed. It is important to note that what is sent "over the waves" is *only* the required function as opposed to the entire file, and the function gets compiled at the gateway. Compilation at the gateway means that if the code needs some form of adaptation to suit the microbrowser calling it this can be done at the gateway, which has the required processing power.

In the following paragraphs we will briefly summarize some of the most important features of WMLScript.

WMLScript Basics

WMLScript follows many of the conventions of the widely used programming languages. Groups of tokens, which can be case-sensitive language tokens, words, and literals, form statements, and semicolons separate statements.

Identifiers and Comments

Variables, functions, and **pragmas** (pragmas represent compilation unit information, which we will talk about later on) are defined using **identifiers**. Similarly to variables in WML, identifiers are case-sensitive, can only include alphanumeric characters and underscores and cannot start with a digit.

In addition, reserved words cannot be used for identifiers. In order to get hold of the latest list of reserved words we suggest visiting the WAPForum website and downloading the latest specification of WMLScript. It is interesting to note that you can use the same identifier for a function, a variable, and a pragma. This is because WMLScript uses a different namespace for each. Nevertheless, it is advised to avoid taking advantage of this particular feature as it might create some very confusing code to read!

For comments, WMLScript allows "/*" to indicates the start of a multiline comment, while "*/" indicates its end. For single line comments you can use "//".

Variables

Variables in WMLScript are **weakly typed**. The compiler and run-time environment keep track of a variable's latest value assignment and that determines its current type. In addition, variables only have a local scope, with a lifetime equivalent to the function within which they are defined.

There are five data types in WMLScript, described in the following table:

Data Type	Valid Values
Boolean	True or False
Integer	From -2,147,483,648 to 2,148,483,648. Also hexadecimal (beginning with 0x or 0X) and octadecimal digits (beginning with 0) are accepted.
Float	From ± 1.17549435E-38 to ± 3.402823476E+38. Floating-point literals are specified using e or E. Underflow results in a value of 0.0.
String	String should be enclosed in single or double quotes. Special characters can be included using a backslash "\".
Invalid	This data type is not meant for normal use. Whenever an operation results in a value that is not acceptable for the other data types the variable is assigned this data type.

In order to use a variable you need to declare it first. Variables are declared using the var keyword (var nameEntered) and declarations can happen at any place where a statement is possible.

Functions

As mentioned earlier, WMLScript programs are nothing more than a collection of functions contained within a file. This collection of functions is called a **compilation unit.** Functions are declared using the function keyword. The rules guiding the definition of function are basic:

❑   Functions cannot be declared within functions (no nesting)

❑   All variables are passed by value

❑   A compilation unit should not contain functions with the same name

❑   Functions should always return a value, the default being an empty string

❑   Function calls must have the same number of parameters as the function, otherwise they will not be interpreted

❑   In addition, a compilation unit cannot contain global variables

So, a function definition will look like this (reserved words in italic):

```
function sampleName ([parameter list]) {
   /*statements*/
};
```

The above function definition can only be called from within its compilation unit using a statement as below:

```
newvariable = sampleName([parameter list]);
```

In order to call a function from outside its compilation unit, something necessary for executing WMLScript through a WML document, the keyword `extern` must be placed at the start of the function definition:

```
extern function sampleName ([parameter list]) {
   /*statements*/
};
```

Anyone with experience of writing code should be aware of the problems of having to contain all the related code within a single unit. At the very least it becomes troublesome to scroll to the right point in the file. It is a blessing, therefore, that WMLScript allows compilation units to access functions in other compilation units. To achieve this WMLScript employs a pragma (which we will discuss later on) called `use url`. All pragma statements must be placed at the start of a compilation unit. So, if you have a set of functions in a file called `OtherFunctions.wmls` that contains a required functions called `reallyUseful(var1, var2)` you can access it in another file by adding the following statement in that file:

```
use url AdditionalFunctions "http://www.myserver.com/OtherFunctions.wmls";
```

and you can then call it using:

```
newRecord = OtherFunctions#reallyUseful(var1, var2);
```

Care should be taken when defining the function `reallyUseful` to mark it as `extern`.

Pragmas

As we described before, a compilation unit is just a file containing WMLScript function descriptions. In order to provide some additional information about the compilation unit to the compiler or the runtime environment, WMLScript has the notions of pragmas. Although the term sounds somewhat esoteric it is just a fancy way of saying "things" since pragma is a Greek word that means thing!

There are three pragmas in WMLScript: **url**, **access** and **meta**. The url pragma we have already seen; it allows the developer to call functions in other compilation units.

The access pragma can be used to provide some information about who can access the functions in the compilation unit. This is similar to the access attribute of WML, and uses domains and path to define the access rules. So, if you wish only visitors of the www.mydomain.com domain to access the WMLScript functions you could add the following line at the head of the `.wmls` file (reserved words in italics):

```
use access domain  "www.mydomain.com";
```

In addition, you could further specify that the functions can only be called from the `/registered` path:

```
use access domain "www.mydomain.com" path "/registered";
```

The third allowable form is:

```
use access path "/registered";
```

Please note that all pragmas are preceded by the use keyword, and should be placed at the start of the WMLScript file.

The meta pragma, as you may have guessed, is used to define meta information about the compilation unit. There are three types of information: name, http equiv and user agent. The first is meant to be used by the origin server, the second by the WAP server as HTTP headers, and the third is for user agents. However, you should always keep in mind that since this is meta information there is no guarantee that the receiver will actually act on the information, this is especially true of the user agent which depends on the implementation of the microbrowser provided by the device manufacturer.

The syntax used is as follows:

```
use meta http equiv "Keyword" "Conversion Functions"
use meta name "Creator" "Ronald Ashri"
use meta user agent "Type" "test"
```

Operators

Of course, WMLScript would be incomplete without operators that would allow you to act with the variables. In fact, this is an area in which the language does not disappoint, as there is a richness of operators providing the developer with considerable flexibility.

The standard operators are supported: +, -, *, / and div. Furthermore, more complex binary operators are included:

Operator	Function
%	Remainder
<<	bitwise shift left
>>	bitwise shift right
>>>	bitwise shift right and fill
&	bitwise AND
|	bitwise OR
^	bitwise XOR

As well as unary operators:

Operator	Function
+	Plus
-	Minus
--	pre or post decrement

Operator	Function
++	pre or post increment
~	Bitwise NOT

Assignments can be combined with these operators. For example "&=" will perform a bitwise AND and assign it.

The logical operators supported are:

Operator	Function
&&	Logical AND
||	Logical OR
!	Logical NOR

Standard comparison operators are provided via:

Operator	Function
<	Less than
>	Greater than
>=	Greater than or equal
<=	Less than or equal
!=	Inequality

Comparison operations use the following rules:

- ❏   Boolean: true is greater than false
- ❏   String: Comparison based on the order of the character codes of the given string values, which in turn depends on the character code used by the WMLScript interpreter
- ❏   Invalid: If an operand is of type Invalid the operation will evaluate to invalid
- ❏   Integers and Floats: Based on their values

WMLScript also supports the ternary conditional operator "?:". For example, the operation:

```
result = accepted ? "actionA" : "actionB";
```

If accepted evaluates to true, then actionA is set to result, otherwise actionB.

Two operators that are rather surprising, but useful since WMLScript is weakly typed, are typeof and isvalid.

❑   typeof: returns an integer value based on the type of the operand:

   ❑   0: Integer
   ❑   1: Float
   ❑   2: String
   ❑   3: Boolean
   ❑   4: Invalid

❑   isvalid: returns true if the operand is either an Integer, Float, String or Boolean and false if it is invalid.

Finally, WMLScript also allows the "," operator for evaluating multiple expression in the place of one. It can be used, for example, to initialize a number of variables at once.

Statements

Finally, we take a brief look at some of the most often used statements in WMLScript:

❑   if

❑   while

❑   for

❑   break and continue

❑   return

if Statement

The syntax for the if statement is the conventional one:

```
if (expression) {
    statements
};
else {
    statements
};
```

For example:

```
if ((a>b)&&(!(a<c)))
    result=a;
else
    result=c;
```

while Statement

The while statement can be used to indicate that a series of statements should execute until the expression evaluates to true.

```
while (expression) {
    statements
};
```

For example:

```
var counter = 0;
var total = 0;
while (counter < 3) {
    counter++;
    total += c;
};
```

for Statement

The syntax for the `for` statement is as follows:

```
for (expression;expression;expression) {
    statement
};
```

or:

```
for (var var1,var2,var3,…;expression;expression;expression) {
    statement
};
```

For example:

```
for (var x,y=0;x<100;x++) {
    y+=(x*10)div3
    otherFunction(y);
}
```

break and continue Statements

The `break` statement serves for exiting a while or for loop and continuing with the next statement outside the loop.

For example:

```
for (var x,y=0;x<100;x++) {
    y+=(x*10)div3
    if (y=216) break;
    otherFunction(y);
}
```

The `continue` statement can be used to terminate the current iteration and restart from the head of the loop.

return Statement

Finally, the return statement can be used within functions to cause them to return a value. If a return statement is not included the function will return an empty string.

Libraries

All the available operators and statements are certainly useful and more than enough to achieve a lot. However, WMLScript also provides a few libraries to relieve the developer from many of the most tedious tasks such as string manipulation. These libraries are pre-built in the interpreter and the functions in them can be called by adding the library name before the function name separated by a dot as:

```
String.length("longerstring").
```

Currently there are six libraries defined:

- ❏   `String`: Functions for performing string operations such as `charAt()`, `find()`, `replace()` and so on.

- ❏   `Lang`: Data type manipulation, absolute value calculations and random numbers.

- ❏   `URL`: Functions for handling URLs.

- ❏   `WMLBrowser`: Functions for accessing the associated WML context so as to perform tasks such as `go()`, `refresh()`, `prev()`.

- ❏   `Dialogs`: Can be used to display messages to the user or ask for confirmations, and so on.

- ❏   `Float`: Floating point operations. This library is not standard for all microbrowsers. Usually only devices that can perform floating point operations support it.

For a complete reference to the functions available in each library it is suggested that you visit the WAPForum website and download the `.pdf` file concerned with WMLScriptLibs.

WMLScript Example

With WML libraries we conclude this brief overview of WMLScript. Now, in order to consolidate some of the issues mentioned we're going to develop a validation example taking the last WML example requesting user input as our basis. If you recall, the original code (`input.wml`) asked the user to enter a name and a password. We use WMLScript to make sure that a name and password has been entered and also to make sure that the password is at least six characters long and contains a mixture of numbers and letters.

We begin with the required WML file, which is very similar to the previous input example.

The necessary prolog and the start of the document (`input2.wml`):

```
<?xml version="1.0"?>
<!DOCTYPE wml PUBLIC "-//WAPFORUM//DTD WML 1.3//EN"
"http://www.wapforum.org/DTD/wml13.dtd" >
<wml>
```

At this point the only difference to the previous example is that when the user sends the information through, we divert it to a WMLScript contained within the `CheckInput.wmls` file:

```
<card id="card1">

<do type="accept">
  <go href="CheckInput.wmls#checkInput()">
```

```
            <setvar name="userName" value="$(userName)"/>
            <setvar name="password" value="$(password)"/>
        </go>
    </do>

    <p>
    Please enter your name:
    </p>
    <input name="userName" value="" emptyok="false" size="10" maxlength="20"
title="Name"/>

    <p>
    Please enter your password:
    </p>
    <input name="password" value="" emptyok="false" size="10" maxlength="20"
title="Password" type="password"/>

    </card>

    <card id="card2">

    <p>
    Your name is $(userName) and your password is $(password)
    </p>

    </card>
</wml>
```

As you can see, the rest of the WML file is as before.

Now, below we have the WMLScript (`CheckInput.wmls`). The function `checkInput()` is declared `extern` so that it can be accessed from outside this compilation unit:

```
extern function checkInput() {
```

We declare two variables that will hold the input of the user:

```
    var userName="";
    var password="";
```

Using the `getVar(name)` function of the WMLScript library WMLBrowser we extract the user input from the WML context:

```
    userName=WMLBrowser.getVar("userName");
    password=WMLBrowser.getVar("password");
```

Here, we declare two flags that will be used further on:

```
    var inputExists=false;
    var validPassword=false;
```

At this point we first check to make sure that the user has entered something. This can be done by using the `isEmpty(string)` function of the `String` library. If nothing was entered we use the `Dialogs` library to access the `alert(message)` function and inform the user that a name or a password is required:

```
   if (String.isEmpty(userName)) {
      Dialogs.alert("No name has been entered, Please enter you name...");
      WMLBrowser.go("input2.wml");
   }
   else {
      if (String.isEmpty(password)) {
         Dialogs.alert("You need to give a password");
         WMLBrowser.go("input2.wml");
      }
      else {
         inputExists = true;
      }
   }
}
```

If the user has entered a name and password we proceed to check that the password is as required. This task as been delegated to another function called checkPassword(password) which we define within the same compilation unit. This function will return true if the password is valid and false otherwise:

```
if (inputExists) {
   validPassword = checkPassword(password);
}
```

If the password is valid, we move to the next card in the WML deck; if not we send the user back to the start:

```
if (inputExists&&validPassword) {
   WMLBrowser.setVar("userName", userName);
   WMLBrowser.setVar("password", password);
   WMLBrowser.go("input2.wml#card2");
}
if (inputExists&&!validPassword) {
   WMLBrowser.go("input2.wml");
}
}
```

Here we have the checkPassword(password) function. Notice that since we do not need to access it from outside this compilation unit we do not declare it extern:

```
function checkPassword(password) {
   //Some necessary variables
   var passwordLength;
   var passwordChar;

   var longEnough = false;

   var intExists = false;
```

Once more we use the String library to determine the length of the password entered:

```
   passwordLength = String.length(password);

   if (passwordLength>=6) {
      longEnough=true;
   }
```

In addition, we also check that the password contains at least one digit. This is easy to do because the `Lang` library supplies a function `isInt(string)` which returns `true` if the supplied string can be converted to an `Integer`. Furthermore, the `charAt(string, index)` function of the `String` library allows us to individually check each character:

```
for (var i=0;i<=passwordLength;i++) {
   passwordChar=String.charAt(password,i);
   if (Lang.isInt(passwordChar)) {
      intExists = true;
   }
}
```

Finally, based on the results from the validation we inform the user of what is required and return to the `checkInput()` function the required value:

```
if (longEnough && intExists) {
   return true;
}
if (longEnough && !intExists) {
   Dialogs.alert("I'm sorry, but the password needs to include a number");
   return false;
}
if (!longEnough && intExists) {
   Dialogs.alert("I'm sorry, but the password should be at least six characters
long");
   return false;
}
if (!longEnough && !intExists) {
   Dialogs.alert("I'm sorry, but the password should be at least six characters
long and include a number");
   return false;
}
```

This example is, of course, not too complicated but illustrates many of the capabilities of WMLScript. For those interested in learning more about what can be done with WMLScript there are excellent resources on the Web (www.wirelessdevnet.com) as well as some examples supplied with the Phone.com simulator.

WAP: Some Pending Issues

WAP is a very significant effort, and the current version (WAP1.3) has already proved its ability to form the *foundations* for a convergence between the Internet and the wireless world at the application level. However, some aspects of WAP have faced significant criticism from all corners of the media world (I suspect this has a lot to do with the fact that WAP rhymes too easily leading to, among others: "The WAP Trap", "WAP is not a snap", and variations on the "Waporware" theme).

Nevertheless, despite criticisms WAP looks very much like a technology that is here to stay for some time yet so in this section we will try to separate hype from reality and see where WAP stands and where it plans to go. It is important that a developer be aware of the issues with the current version, as well as the previous versions, since some service providers and certainly devices will not all be using the latest version. It is also important to note that many of the current problems are not so much to do with WAP as a technology but rather with the limitation of the networks and the devices. We'll look at the following issues:

❑ The WAP Forum should "open up"

❑ Mobile phones are not suitable for Web navigation

❑ Security

❑ Need for "cookies"

❑ Support for "push"

The WAP Forum Should "Open Up"

A lot of criticisms have been leveled against the "modus operandi" of the Forum itself. In an environment where "open source" has become a holy word, the WAP forum has taken a decidedly more closed path. Although the specifications are available freely, the design process is closed and entrance costs $27,000 (as of February 2000) while there is no public mailing list for discussing the issues.

The implication of such an entrance fee is that most academic institutions and small business are excluded, something that goes against the lessons of history, from where OSI failed to the Internet protocol based on TCP/IP and developed in the academic world. Furthermore, WAP also depends on patents held by Phone.com and GeoWorks, thus excluding the possibility that someone develops an entirely personalized version of the standard.

Nevertheless, the WAP Forum now boasts more than 500 members which it claims represents 95% of handset manufacturers. The problem, however, is that a large number of professionals with a different set of considerations to those of telecom companies and device manufacturers is *not* represented. To their credit, the WAP Forum has proved that it listens and responds to criticism – something that is very welcome.

Finally, a last note on this issue has to do with the method by which specifications are published and revised. As someone who has spent long hours trying to understand what are the most current features, I have to say that the way the specification documents are published creates confusion, due to an unclear versioning system.

Mobile Phones are not Suitable for Web Navigation

The user interface of mobile phones is notoriously user unfriendly, 4 or even 8 lines do not give you much freedom to read or to write e-mails, or anything else. However, let's not forget that these devices have been designed to make voice calls.

The initial requirements were: allow the user to enter numbers, make the call, and talk. Everything added since then has, in essence, been a hack and therein lies one of the biggest stumbling blocks. However, as we pointed out in the introduction mobile devices are merging with PDA's (Nokia Communicator, Ericsson R380). The screens on PDA's are much more comfortable on the eyes and have proven that they can be efficient tools for people. As the two devices merge, user interface issues will improve significantly, and as bandwidth increases so will the quality of the offered content.

One of the biggest misconceptions is to believe that any website on the Internet today should also be available for mobile devices. A wireless site should only be developed because there is a clear need for it, otherwise users will not waste their time. If there is a need and the design is effective then users will come, but there is no point in spending money just so that a company can say it has a WWW *and* a WAP site.

The other side of this coin is that there should be no restrictions to which WAP site a user can access. It is regretful that many service providers have taken a "closed wall" approach, allowing subscribers to their wireless internet service to access sites that have been pre-selected, and whose owners have paid a certain fee for the honor, thus immensely reducing the possibilities for innovation and a truly open market.

Another related issue, that is turning many users away, is billing. The current billing model is based on the time a user spends online, something that we have already learned from land phones is not conducive to Internet usage. Furthermore, there are a large number of reports of discontented users with huge phone bills. The problem is that many microbrowsers will automatically attempt to reestablish a connection once disconnected (something that is, unfortunately, not a rarity in the wireless world).

Security

Perhaps the most salient criticism raised against WAP1.1 is that there was a gap in its security model. This was due to the fact that while the WTLS protocol does provide encryption, the "endpoint" of the encrypted data is the WAP gateway. Once data is at the gateway it has to be decrypted so as to understand what the request from the mobile device is. If the request is for a secure transaction with a web server this means that the data needs to be encrypted once more, using SSL for TCP/IP communication, and sent to the web server. The web server's response will once more be decrypted and encrypted back to WTLS to be sent back to the mobile device.

If the gateway is a machine that you can trust, that is all very well. The problem arises when the gateway is not trusted by the content provider, a very common situation since gateways are often supplied by a third party, and as the user moves so might the gateway the user is going through. In a few words the classic Man in the Middle problem:

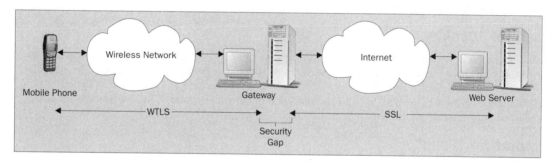

The solutions available before WAP1.2 include:

❑   Make the origin server the gateway so no encoding/decoding issues occur, since it all happens within the same machine or domain

❑   Provide content only through your own gateway

Either of theses two measures includes, amongst others, the following considerations:

❑   Making sure that the gateway never stores decrypted data on secondary storage
❑   Ensuring that decrypted data is removed from memory as quickly as possible
❑   Physical security for the gateway with access only from authorized administrators
❑   Limited and very secure remote access control

A third solution is:

❑   Buy software to be installed on the gateway of your wireless service provider to decrease the possibility of a security infringement. Such a solution usually involves making sure that the encryption/decryption processes happen within a single process as quickly as possible (milliseconds) and that it is not possible to copy the data to persistent storage. Clearly, this can only work if the gateway owner actually agrees to install the software, something that is not always possible.

The problems with all such solutions are that they exhibit the classic symptoms of a hack. They are not robust and they do not scale. Nevertheless, these problem need to be solved for effective m-commerce today because there are a lot of devices and gateways out there with WAP1.1 browsers. As we have mentioned before it is important to consider what audience a WAP application will reach in order to develop an efficient solution.

What is required is a mechanism that will allow the WAE agent to encrypt data and have it delivered encrypted all the way to the content provider. Such a solution has been introduced with WAP 1.3. In order to achieve this end-to-end security, however, it is assumed that the provider of secure services will have a gateway within its secure service domain. The scenario is as follows: a user is surfing through an insecure gateway and at some point decides to access and make use of secure services. It will inform the gateway of this intent and will supply the URL of the secure gateway. A navigation document will be obtained from the insecure gateway pointing to the secure one, and a secure connection will be established.

The above scenario raises the issue of trust. Why should I trust a certain gateway and its owner, and believe that the transaction is truly secure? In order to deal with this issue WAP1.2 introduced **digital certificates** and **Public Key Infrastructure** (**PKI**) security mechanisms.

There are, however, other security considerations to do with other deficiencies of WTLS and with the bearer technologies. For an overview of such issues you can reference the following, very good treatise: Markku-Juhani Saarinen, *Attacks Against The WAP WTLS Protocol*, University of Jyvaskyla, 1999. Online document is available at http://www.jyu.fi/ mjos.

Need for "Cookies"

Cookies have now established themselves in the arsenal of many web developers as the best way to maintain information about users through an entire session and sometimes even between sessions. The current WAP specification has a similar notion but not all browsers support them as yet. Care needs to be taken when making the decision to use cookies, and alternatives should be used (using URL indexes and URL histories) until all implementations catch up.

Support for "Push"

In the introduction we talked about the possibility of being automatically informed of nearby available services via a message on your mobile phone. In order to achieve this, some form of functionality able to send information to your phone without you requesting it (pushing information through) needs to be provided.

The problem with wireless phones however is that the web server that could potentially push content to a mobile device has no way to directly communicate with that device. Therefore, the web server will once more delegate this task to the gateway, which will then push the content on to the wireless device. WML1.2 defines two protocols for this task. First, they introduce the **Push Access Protocol** for communication between the web server and the gateway, and then the gateway uses the **Push Over-The-Air Protocol** for pushing the information on to the device.

The problem, once more, has to do with the fact the current devices need to be connected to accept information, since bearer networks do not support instant connection, making it wise to postpone use of such technologies until GPRS networks appear that should support instant connections.

Alternatives to WAP

As we have said before, it looks very likely that WAP will be around for some time yet. However, it will need to change significantly in order to accommodate market needs. Already the words **WAP-NG** for WAP New Generation or WAP2.0 have appeared. A lot of the changes have to do with the lessons learned until now, and with the lessons taught by alternatives to WAP. It is in this spirit that we present two alternatives, which also represent the two ends of the spectrum in terms of a possible solution whilst WAP lies somewhere inbetween.

i-mode

i-mode is the child of NTT DoCoMo (http://www.nttdocomo.com). This solution lies at the completely proprietary and completely closed end of the spectrum, since it is entirely operated by NTT DoCoMo over a proprietary packet transmission network. All calls are handled through NTT DoCoMo, and all content providers have to register with the company. The success of the technology, however, has been phenomenal, creating many suggestions that i-mode is a more appropriate path than WAP. In Japan the user base was 16,778,000 as of December 2000 and i-mode was launched only on the 22nd of February 1999. By the time this book is out they will probably have reached the 20 million users mark.

What are the reasons behind this huge success? Well, for one it is easy to establish a robust system if it is entirely closed. Many of the interoperability problems that the first version of WAP faced had never been an issue for i-mode.

Secondly, i-mode phones are designed with i-mode in mind. This means that the user experience is much more enjoyable (for a demo of an i-mode phone, take a look at http://www.docomo.fr/eng/Europe/English_f502i.htm). Due to the underlying bearer technology, connection is instantaneous and is achieved through a big bright button that immediately takes you to your wireless home. There you find access to all the available services from banking to online shopping. The owner of an i-mode phone has access to e-mail services as well, the e-mail address being the mobile phone's number. E-mail received at other addresses can also be forwarded to the i-mode phone. Because connection is instantaneous, users can view e-mail as soon as it is sent to them, making the experience much more enjoyable, and leaving SMS to wither in the dust.

Perhaps the biggest advantage of i-mode is the billing mechanism used. Instead of billing users based on the amount of time they are online, which is how current WAP network providers operate, the billing is based on the amount of data that users download to their phone. This makes using the phone much more cost-effective, with NTT DoCoMo reporting that the average user pays about 10 dollars a month for using i-mode. NTT DoCoMo can achieve this because of the packet-based billing technology (PDC-P) it employs.

The i-mode business model is based on two different kinds of interactions. Users register with NTT DoCoMo and pay for the Internet and voice services provided, while content providers register with NTT DoCoMo databases in order to make their content available to the NTT DoCoMo users. At this point the next important feature of i-mode comes into play. As opposed to WAP that defines WML for developing WAP sites, i-mode uses a subset of HTML (formally it is defined as a subset of HTML2.0, 3.2 and 4.0) called cHTML. This makes development of content much easier since there is no need to learn a new language. Furthermore i-mode is based on a TCP/IP framework making the posting of information more straightforward and familiar.

Another important feature, which is currently hard to implement in WAP, is the capability of pushing content to the mobile phones so users can have true updates about the information they are interested in, be it stock values or weather reports. These factors combine to make it easier to find development staff for i-mode applications.

In conclusion, when WAP is compared to i-mode the winner, based on user acceptance, has to be i-mode. Just the fact that everyday people in Japan were immediately hooked on it, while in the rest of the world, WAP is having a hard time proves that i-mode provides a better service. However, WAP is available in the rest of the world while i-mode is only in Japan. In addition WAP has been designed with the rest of the world in mind while i-mode is entirely proprietary. Even though there are talks about i-mode networks elsewhere, network providers have made a huge investment in WAP and will not readily let go. In technological terms WAP is a far more advanced, albeit complex, solution that provides a more scaleable approach. Eventually, as WAP and mobile devices advance, we can hope that some of the best features such as the billing mechanisms and the instantaneous connection will be available to WAP users as well.

LEAP

LEAP (Lightweight and Efficient Applications Protocol, from http://www.leapforum.org) lies at the other end of the spectrum of solutions, its motto being "Using Free Protocols & Free Software to Build the Mobile & Wireless Application Industry". It is supported by the Free Protocols Foundation, and represents an effort to develop a set of protocols that are as simple as possible, while delivering an efficient solution. The technologies provided up to date are two protocols: the Efficient Short Remote Operations protocols (ESRO, RFC 2188), and the Efficient Mail Submission and Delivery protocol (EMSD, RFC 2524).

ESRO is a connectionless transport mechanism positioned as a more efficient alternative to TCP or UDP for mobile communications, while EMSD is designed as a Mobile Messaging solution. These protocols represent the belief that while mobile devices do need a new set of protocols to achieve effective communication these protocols should not be targeted towards browsing, which is very uncomfortable with mobile phones, but towards messaging.

There is some software available that implements LEAP protocols for WindowsCE, EPOC, and PalmOS devices, although there is no widespread or commercial use of the protocols as yet. Nevertheless, it is important to listen to the underlying message coming from this effort: that protocols should be completely open and patent free, and that simple solutions are often more effective.

XHTML

A development that provides some hope to application builders is the beginnings of a new standard called XHTML. It stands for extended HTML and is a standard being developed and supported by the W3C. Essentially, it is a translation of HTML to XML. However, during this process the decision was taken to provide a core set of tags that will be valid on any device.

With this decision what is hoped is a convergence between HTML, WML, and cHTML to a unique standard represented by XHTML. Transcoders will then transform the document for the required end device be it a PC, a WAP phone, or an i-mode phone. So, transcoder technology will become increasingly important as well as the ways in which data is stored. With such a development in the future, storing data in an XML format will become a true advantage since the content provider will be able to almost automatically convert that data and send it anywhere it is required.

Wireless Devices and Java Technology

Whatever the underlying content delivery mechanism, there is one issue that needs to be dealt with: How are we to build applications that will deal with this content both on the server side and the client side? Furthermore, how can we enhance this content, thus going beyond the browser-level functionality?

This is where the use of Java technologies comes into play. On the server side there is a host of well know Java APIs that can deal with dynamic content manipulation (and many of the previous chapters in this book deal with this issue). A new development for the wireless world has been Java on the client side. In many ways this development represents a return to Java's roots, since Java was born out of an attempt to develop a technology aimed at such things as limited capability home appliances, but ended up being initially more a technology for empowering web applications. Well, now limited capability devices are calling for connectivity, and methods for application development that will provide open, expandable solutions.

There are, however, some real challenges for providing Java on the client-side. After enjoying years on processor wealthy machines, Java has grown fat and at times complacent so it had to go through a very strict trimming and shaping up routine, as well as learn some new tricks. In the next section we briefly examine the server-side technologies before turning our focus to the available client side technologies represented by a new Java edition, aptly named the Micro Edition.

Java on the Server Side

The developers of Java technologies have long been proponents of the heavyweight server/thin client model. This philosophy towards the development of Web applications is now paying off in the wireless world since by definition the client is a limited capability device, making any processing weight that can be transferred to the server side very welcome.

The main platform for server-side application development is the Java 2 Enterprise Edition (J2EE), the current version being 1.2.1. The J2EE platform places itself between the data, stored in some form of database, and the client providing middle-tier services.

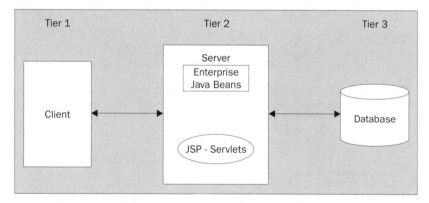

When the client makes a request the server will process it and form the appropriate queries to the database, based on access rights and personalization settings. The response received from the database will then be manipulated into the appropriate format by the server-side program for delivery to the client. Thanks to the WAP programming model, all the technologies and knowledge for development on the server side for TCP/IP and HTML-based web sites can immediately be transferred to WML web sites. The only change to the illustration above is the WAP gateway between the client and server.

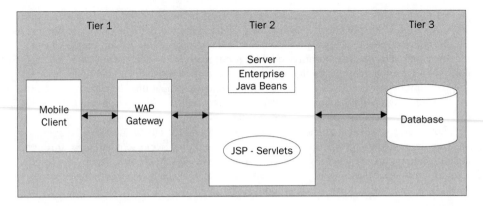

WML is just another variation of XML so it is possible, using tools such as XSL described earlier on in the book, to have a unique XML format for your data and convert that to WML in order to send it to wireless devices. As mentioned before, however, wireless browsers cannot be treated in just the same way as traditional browsers. The conversion has to be designed in such as a way as to cater for the limited capabilities of the devices.

The small servlet example below simply proves the point that nothing changes on the server side other than the syntax used from HTML to WML.

```java
import java.io.*;
import javax.servlet.*;
import javax.servlet.http.*;

public class WMLHello extends HttpServlet {
    public void service(HttpServletRequest request, HttpServletResponse response)
                throws ServletException, IOException {

        // Probably the most important line. Setting the correct MIME type
        response.setContentType("text/vnd.wap.wml");

        // Handle on the communication channel
        PrintWriter out = response.getWriter();

        // Now to form the document
        out.println("<?xml version=\"1.0\"?>");
        out.println("<!DOCTYPE wml PUBLIC \"-//WAPFORUM//DTD WML 1.3//EN\"");
        out.println("\"http://www.wapforum.org/DTD/wml13.dtd\" >");
        out.println("<wml>");
        out.println("<card>");
        out.println("<p>");
        out.println("Servlet formed hello!");
        out.println("</p>");
        out.println("</card>");
        out.println("</wml>");
    }
}
```

Java on the Client Side

Why is there any need for Java on the client side if there is WAP? This is usually the first question that is asked when the issue of Java for mobile devices is raised. The answer is that Java and WAP are complementary not competing technologies. WAP is geared towards delivering content to mobile devices while Java is for developing applications for these devices that may work even if connection to the network has been lost.

In order to put this in context imagine the following scenario:

You are visiting Paris for the first time on a business trip and have half a day of leisure to walk around the city. You switch on your GSM phone, it recognizes which provider can give you a service at that location, and establishes a connection with them. You want to quickly find out which are the best places, as well as some suggestions about a tour for a couple of hours you could make on foot. You connect to the Internet, locate the relevant site, and it shows you maps of the area as well as giving suggestions. However, you can't memorize all this information in five minutes. Then you notice that this site also has Java applications available that you can download. You select the one for Paris and close your connection. Your phone starts up the application and you consult that for the next couple of hours as you move from one monument to the next, sometimes having to use Le Metro.

The suite of Java technologies for achieving this comes under the heading of the **Java 2 Micro Edition** (**J2ME**). Now, the second most frequently asked question is which libraries are part of the J2ME and are these libraries finalized? The answer to this question is slightly more complicated. The hardware and network abilities of mobile devices are in a continuous state of flux making it very difficult to come with a "one size fits all" solution. On one side of the scale there are the weaker but cheaper cell phones which most people would be inclined to buy and on the other side there are the more heavyweight "Communicator" type products that have more processing power but are more costly and therefore reach a smaller audience.

Furthermore, there is a whole host of other devices queuing up for entry into the wireless web from your refrigerator to the toaster. It is certainly not an easy task to create development tools for building applications on devices as diverse as the washing machine to the mobile phone, which we are so eager to connect and bring together in wonderful harmony. It is difficult because it is in stark contrast to development on PCs where the divisions were along two or three operating systems and the progression of changes was relatively slow while the core capabilities were more or less equal.

The answer, therefore, is to provide different solutions for different types of devices while trying to maintain generalization in the form of the common lower denominator. Sun (along with a host of companies such as Nokia, Ericsson, NTT DoCoMo, Motorola, Palm, and Sony) has formed Java Community Process Expert Groups to tackle this question, and came up with a solution based on the concepts of **configurations** and **profiles**.

Configurations are a specification of a core technology that applies to a range of similar devices, in other words a horizontal specification, very general and widely applicable. A profile on the other hand is a vertical specification, very specific to a particular kind of device. Based on these notions we have the Connected Limited Device Configuration (**CLDC**) and the Mobile Information Device Profile (**MIDP**) specifications.

CLDC is aimed at a wide range of devices from mobile phones to PDAs, and home appliances. The working description of a CLDC device is one with 160KB to 512KB memory for the Java Virtual Machine, a 16-bit or 32-bit processor, low power consumption and some form of connectivity with limited and unreliable bandwidth. As such, CLDC forms the core technology, which defines the minimum required libraries for tasks ranging from the standard libraries to those for I/O, networking, and security.

MIDP comes to complement this specification by providing a profile of the CLDC configuration that is specific to mobile devices. Essentially, it adds a number of specific APIs for mobile devices to allow access to functions that are specific to those devices. In addition, further assumptions are made here about:

❑ Screen size: 96x54 pixels

❑ Input mechanisms: mobile phone keypad, QWERTY keyboard or touch-sensitive screen

❑ Memory: 128KB of non-volatile memory for the MIDP components, 8KB for application created persistent data, and 32KB for the Java runtime

❑ Networking: Two-way, wireless, unreliable, and limited

The goal of these specifications is to foster the development of applications by third parties that will be able to run on a wide range of platforms. Furthermore, it is envisaged that applications will be dynamically downloaded and installed on the mobile device. In line with tradition the MIDP specification also gave rise to a new word: a **midlet** (as in applet) is an application a mobile phone downloads and installs.

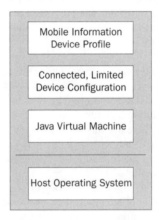

In the wider context of Java technologies the CLDC and MIDP specify a subset of the more standard Java Development Kit geared at mobile devices, along with certain additions that are either specific to the CLDC (but can be mapped to the Java 2 Standard Edition (J2SE)) or specific to the MIDP.

It is important to note that CLDC and MIDP are specifications. Implementation of those specifications can come from any source. A mobile device provider would need to look at the MIDP and CLDC specifications in order to build their own implementations that will enable Java applications on their phone. On the other hand, application developers need to read the CLDC and MIDP specifications in order to understand what APIs are available to them in order to build applications for mobile devices.

Sun traditionally provides reference implementations that can be downloaded from the Java site, but developers do not need to stick to those implementations. However, they are useful for getting to learn the technologies and start developing with them.

The following table summarizes the target devices for J2SE, CLDC, and MIDP:

	J2SE	CLDC	MIDP
Target Device	Workstations, PCs	PDAs (PalmOS), home appliances	Mobile phones
Typical applications	Word processing, web browsing, e-mail, software development, graphic design, collaborative working, and so on	Address book, task scheduling, memo, e-mail, browsing	Messaging, browsing, e-mail
Processing power	From 150MHz up (Typically 300MHz+)	16-20MHz	Very slow
Available Memory	64MB	128-1256KB	<128KB
Connection Speed	56.6KBs and more	From 14.4KB/s (wireless) to 33.6KB/s (land)	9.6KB/s
Display	Typically 800*600 pixels	160*160 pixels	96*64pixels
Input Device	Keyboard & mouse	Pen-based	Number pad

CLDC

The Connected Limited Devices Configuration was developed with a clear goal in mind: to provide Java developers with a set of APIs that would be as close to the standard edition of Java as possible, but that could operate on limited capability devices.

Along with this goal is the wish to enable the dynamic delivery of Java applications, something that immediately involves the use of networking APIs, and that the CLDC looks at very closely. In order to achieve these goals within the broad scope of devices the CLDC targets, very few things about the exact nature of the devices are assumed. In fact, the only thing that is an absolute requirement is the memory figures mentioned above.

Now, as a result of these configurations the range of Java APIs the CLDC deals with does not include any high level programming issues such as application lifecycle management, user interface, event handling, and human-computer interaction. The issues that are dealt with are: Java language and virtual machine features, core java libraries (`java.lang.*` and `java.util.*`), networking, security, and internationalization. We will look at these issues one by one in the subsequent sections.

Java Language Support in CLDC

We start by going straight to the important aspects: what can and what cannot be done through a CLDC compliant implementation. The outlook is actually quite promising since CLDC, to the most part, follows the official Java Language Specification.

The following `java.lang` system classes are supported:

❏   Object

❏   Class

❏   Runtime

❏   System

❏   Thread

❏   Runnable

❏   String

❏   StringBuffer

❏   Throwable

Along with these java.lang data types:

❏   Boolean

❏   Byte

❏   Short

❏   Integer

❏   Long

❏   Character

Some classes from the `java.util` package are supported:

❏   Vector

❏   Stack

❏   Hashtable

❏   Enumeration interface

In addition, support is provided for the `Calendar`, `Date` and `Timezone` classes as well as the `Random` and `Math` classes although not as complete as the J2SE specification.

As far as input/output goes CLDC includes the following `java.io` classes:

❏   InputStream

❏   OutputStream

❏   ByteArayInputStream

❏   ByteArrayOutputStream

❏   DataInput interface

❏   DataOutput interface

❏   DataInputStream

❏   DataOutputStream

❏   Reader

- ❑ Writer
- ❑ InputStreamReader
- ❑ OutputStreamWriter
- ❑ PrintStream (this class is supplied for debugging purposes only)

Some exception handling support is provided through the following java.lang classes:

- ❑ Exception
- ❑ ClassNotFoundException
- ❑ IllegalAccessException
- ❑ InstantiationException
- ❑ InterruptedException
- ❑ RuntimeException
- ❑ ArithmeticException
- ❑ ArrayStoreException
- ❑ ClassCastException
- ❑ IllegalArgumentException
- ❑ IllegalThreadStateException
- ❑ NumberFormatException
- ❑ IllegalMonitorStateException
- ❑ IndexOutOfBoundsException
- ❑ ArrayIndexOutOfBoundsException
- ❑ StringIndexOutofBoundsException
- ❑ NegativeArraySizeException
- ❑ NullPointerException
- ❑ SecurityException

Furthermore, from the java.util package we have the EmpyStackException and NoSuchElementException while from the java.io package we have the EOFException, IOException, InterruptedIOException, UnsuportedEncodingException and UTFDataFormatException. Error handling is limited to the java.lang.Error, java.lang.VirtualMachineError and java.lang.OutOfMemoryException classes.

All the classes listed above can be used in the same way that they are used when developing applications with the J2SE, and so provide a very familiar environment for Java programmers to work in. The parts of the J2SE that are lacking are absent for two main reasons. On the one hand, certain issues, such as floating point support, were thought to add too much weight to the configuration, while others where thought to compromise the security of the platform. There are other reasons, which we will come to in a moment.

There is no support for floating point operations due to the fact that most mobile devices do not have floating point support in hardware and the CLDC Expert Group has judged that it would be too big an overhead for floating point support to be implemented in software. However, if floating point support is critical for an application, software implementations built using the classes that *are* included in the CLDC are available and can be freely obtained (an excellent resource for all things CLDC and MIDP is Bill Day's, one of the architects of the J2ME, website http://www.billday.com). Another concession in the name of better performance is that there is no support for the Object.finalize() method. Finally, there is limited error handling since implementing the full set of error handling classes would be too expensive and such behavior is, anyway, highly device specific.

The concessions made in the name of security are no support for: the Java Native Interface, user-defined class loaders, reflection, thread groups, daemon threads, and weak references. These restrictions are in place because the security model used for the CLDC is a simplified one in comparison to the full-blown J2SE model and thus does not allow the same level of control, and because some of them (like JNI) are too heavy weight.

There are, however, some other more subtle reasons. CLDC devices are consumer products, and whilst consumers may have come to accept that their PC will crash they cannot accept that a mobile phone might crash. Device vendors are aware of this fact and want to avoid any such situations. A very easy way to make a device crash is to allow software that has not been adequately checked to go around messing with internal functions. Therefore, device vendors pressed for the exclusion of JNI and, in any case, if access to the underlying system is required the manufacturers can provide it themselves.

Some criticisms have been raised against the exclusion of reflection. The criticisms are based on the fact the Remote Method Invocation (RMI), which is Java's solution for distributed computing, cannot work without reflection mechanisms. Furthermore, no RMI means no Jini, which is Java's dynamic networking technology. This in turn excludes a whole set of exciting applications where mobile devices join different networks and access services on those networks dynamically. However, that is not entirely true since there is a project under way in the Jini community to provide a work around for that problem, called the Jini Surrogate Project. The idea is to provide a proxy that limited devices can talk to, and the proxy will implement the required RMI and Jini functionality for them.

Pre-Verification

An interesting aspect of the CLDC and an issue where this configuration of Java technologies can claim to make a contribution is **pre-verification**. The driver behind this technology has been the need to provide a more efficient verification mechanism than the one currently available with J2SE that would be suitable for limited devices.

With J2SE, verification happens at run-time when a class is loaded. Pre-verification provides a more simplified algorithm, as well the ability to perform the verification tasks at development time or at an intermediate point before the class arrives at a device and is loaded, such as a WAP gateway. There are significant performance gains this way since the verification task now requires less than 100 bytes of RAM at runtime. From a user perspective it provides a better experience since the applications will also start up much faster because the verification section doesn't take place.

Suggestions have even been made to include this technology in future J2SE releases since it is useful for a large number of devices, some of which are beyond the scope of the CLDC.

Network Support in CLDC

Although we mentioned before that basic network connectivity is supported we have not, in the previous section, mentioned any network classes. This is because the current `java.net` classes occupy too big a footprint (reaching about 200KB) to be transferred to CLDC. Furthermore, the network connections that will be used by devices that fall under the CLDC's scope may not use TCP/IP protocols but a number of different protocols depending on the underlying network.

In order to answer these problems the CLDC specifies a **Generic Connection Framework**. The idea here is to provide a set of classes that are similar to the current classes for networking but provide a more flexible and expandable base that will cater for all the different kinds of devices and network protocols that are out there. In addition, it has a broader scope since it is not targeted solely at connection to networks that can be imagined as external to the device. It is also intended to connect to the local file system, whose structure once again changes from device to device.

For the developer these different protocols will be accessed through a unique set of abstractions, thus placing a layer between the gory details of the protocol and what the application developer has to do. The general class specified is the `javax.microedition.io.Connector` class and in the different implementations of the CDLC it is envisaged that access or connection points will be opened through methods of the type:

```
Connector.open("<protocol:<address>;<parameters>");
```

The CLDC definition states that the binding of the protocols to a J2ME application should be done at runtime, thus enabling the dynamic configuration of the application based on the device it finds itself in.

It is important to stress that the `Connector` class is simply a placeholder for the various connection objects. The `javax.microedition.io.Connection` interface defines the minimum that these objects should implement. In fact, it defines only one method:

```
public void close() throws IOException;
```

The reason for just this method is that the `open()` method is not public and can only be called via the static `open()` method of the `Connector` class.

The subinterfaces to the `Connection` class are:

- ❏ `InputConnection` – An interface for defining the required method signatures for reading data from a device

- ❏ `OutputConnnection` – The equivalent interface for writing content

- ❏ `StreamConnection` – A unification of the above interfaces

- ❏ `ContentConnection` – A sub-interface to the `StreamConnection`, `ContentConnection`, meant to be used for accessing basic metadata from HTTP connections

- ❏ `StreamConnectionNotifier` – This interface holds the methods that will notify listeners when a connection has been established

- ❏ `DatagramConnection` – Definitions for a datagram endpoint

This concludes the overview of the most significant issues for the CLDC. The configuration we described details what should be the lowest common denominator in terms of Java language support that would make sense on limited devices. The deviations made from the J2SE are all in the name of enabling more efficient execution of code and a reduced footprint. In almost all cases, however, there are alternatives that can retrieve some of the lost functionality. In the next section we will examine the particular flavors of CLDC brewed up for mobile devices as specified in the MIDP specification.

MIDP

The first thing to note about MIDP (pronounced *mid-p*) is that it can only be understood in conjunction with the CLDC document. As the CLDC makes no sense without the traditional Java language specification, similarly the MIDP makes no sense without CLDC. Thus MDIP is a superset of CLDC.

We've already mentioned the hardware assumptions that have been made in the introductory section for Java on the client side. Along with those assumptions about hardware, some assumptions were required for what software the device should have. Despite the great variation amongst devices, it is assumed that a MIDP device has some sort of kernel to interface with the hardware, and within which a Java virtual machine will be allowed to run.

This JVM entity should have access to some networking facilities for reading from and writing to the network, access to non-volatile memory, and a mechanism for keeping track of the different points in time that something is written or read from this memory (essentially the foundations for some sort of file system). In addition, some bitmap graphics ability and some way for the user to enter data are both desirable. All in all the broadest possible definition of what a mobile computing device may be.

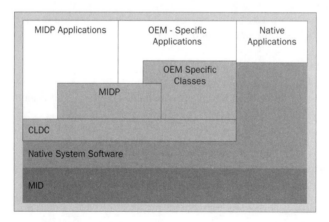

The figure above is used to describe the relationships between the different software components of a mobile information device. At the first level, there is the device itself with its various hardware capabilities for networking, UI, telephony, and so on. At the next level there is, of course, the device's native software, which knows how to handle and coordinate all the different hardware capabilities. The device vendor will traditionally build applications directly on top of that layer in order to make the best use of the device. Over the native software layer, however, we can also place a CLDC layer. This layer will include a JVM that adheres to the CLDC specification and is able to run Java programs that were developed with the classes in the CLDC specification.

The vendor may decide to provide some extensions to the CLDC through OEM specific classes that will enable the development of OEM specific applications. Alternatively the MIDP layer can be included, which specifies some additional classes that should be found on any device that claims to support MIDP. With MIDP in place, third-party application developers can now expect to be able to write an application and have it execute on the device with little worries about the exact nature of the native system software.

To dig into this topic we'll look in order at:

- ❏ The form of MIDlets
- ❏ Developing MIDlets
- ❏ User Interfaces
- ❏ Networking Support in MIDP
- ❏ Persistent Storage Support
- ❏ Future possibilities in this area

The Nature of MIDlets

MIDlets are managed in a device by what is called the **application management software**. These device specific functions enable the installation, selection, execution, and removal of a MIDlet.

MIDlets are expected to arrive at a device within a JAR file that should include the following:

- ❏ At least one class that extends a general `MIDlet` class along with any other classes required for the MIDlet. Several MIDlets can operate alongside each other, and interact with each other as long as they belong to the same package.
- ❏ A manifest file containing a description of the contents of the JAR file.
- ❏ Any resource files required by the MIDlets (icons, bmp, and so on).

In addition, an application descriptor file (`*.jad`) should be provided so that the device can access it *before* downloading the JAR file. The purpose of this file is to tell the application management software about the MIDlet and its requirements. In addition, the MIDlet can use this descriptor file for configuration purposes. The manifest file and the application descriptor file may share some attributes. If a descriptor file does not define an attribute then the value from the manifest file is taken.

The attributes that must be present are:

- ❏ `MIDlet-Name`
- ❏ `MIDlet Version`
- ❏ `MIDlet Vendor`
- ❏ `MIDlet-<n>` (where n is a number for each MIDlet in the JAR file)
- ❏ `MicroEdition-Profile` (in our case `MIDP1.0`)
- ❏ `MicroEdition-Configuration` (in our case `CLDC-1.0`).

Additionally, there are attributes for icons, general descriptions, etc.

As mentioned above a MIDlet must extend the `java.microedition.midlet.MIDlet` class. This class takes care of the orderly management of the MIDlet application based on three states that the MIDlet can find itself in: started, stopped, and paused. These states are represented by three abstract methods:

```
protected abstract void startApp() throws MIDletStateChangeException

protected abstract void pauseApp();

protected abstract void destroyApp(Boolean unconditional) throws
                        MIDletStateChangeException
```

These methods are implemented by the developer and enable the application management system to selectively start, stop or pause any MIDlet currently running.

Developing MIDLets

With some knowledge of how MIDlets work we will now describe how you can set up an environment on your desktop computer for developing and testing MIDlets, and also code a simple MIDlet, before going into other details about MIDlets.

There are two ways to set up up a MIDP development environment on your desktop. We will present them in decreasing level of complexity. Before going on, however, keep in mind that both the CLDC and MIDP implementations require Java1.2 or later to run since some of the development tools are Java-based. Furthermore, it is suggested that you use a machine with a minimum of 64MB of RAM, and a Pentium class or equivalent processor with a speed of 166MHz+.

Development Using the Reference Implementations

The first, and more involved way, is to download the CLDC reference and the MIDP reference and use them together to give the whole set of required tools. In fact, for Solaris this is the *only* way to create a suitable MIDP environment. Both implementations can be accessed from http://www.java.sun.com/j2me/ and they are both at v1.0.

Once downloaded, the most convenient way of installing them is to create a directory called `j2me` and two subdirectories, one called `CLDC` where you unpack the CLDC reference implementation and one called `MIDP` for the MIDP implementation.

The downloads include both the source code for all the tools (KVM, preverifier, and so on) and builds for the Windows and Solaris platforms. We will not discuss the steps required to build the implementations, but those interested can find detailed guidelines in the documentation which comes with the download bundle. It is important to stress, however, that in order to run a MIDlet the CLDC *must* be presented since it provides the virtual machine.

> *In order to get a description of all the tools and documentation that comes with the CLDC it is enough to read the `ReleaseNotes.pdf` file provided in the docs directory.*

Then it is useful to add to your environment path the path to the MIDP bin directory and the CLDC bin directory. In my case, and since it is a Windows environment, the PATH setting in the `autoexec.bat` file looks like this:

```
SET PATH=%PATH%;C:\jdk1.3\bin;C:\j2me\midp\bin;C:\j2me\cldc\bin
```

From the MIDP `bin` directory you will access the midp emulator; while from the CLDC `bin` directory you access the preverification tool.

If all went well, then by typing `midp` at the prompt of either your Unix or DOS shell you should get the following window, which is the mobile phone emulator provided with the MIDP implementation:

The next step is to actually run an application and fortunately there is quite an extensive example provided with the MIDP implementation. To run it you need to go to `../j2me/midp/src/example` and type at the prompt:

```
midp -descriptor run.jad
```

This will load the sample application and you should get the following screen on your MIDP phone:

At this point we will leave the description of the basic tools for MIDP development in order to introduce the Wireless Toolkit, which makes life considerably easier, since all development can take place through a graphical interface. We will not return to the command line approach in order to describe how an application can be compiled and run without the toolkit. For those interested in developing MIDlets without the Wireless Toolkit, information can be found in the release notes that accompany the CLDC. For people on Solaris, using the reference implementations is currently the only way to develop MIDlets.

Development Using the Wireless Toolkit

As of the time of writing the Wireless Toolkit was still at a v1.0 beta release and can be obtained from http://www.java.sun.com/products/j2mewtoolkit/ and was only available for the Windows 98 platform (although it will work on Windows 2000). As opposed to the method described above, the toolkit does not require that you install the CLDC reference implementation since it works as a self-contained bundle. Once you have downloaded the file, you can install it as any Windows application.

The toolkit contains the necessary tools, documentation for all the APIs, an emulation environment as the one we saw above, ready-to-run examples, and a module to integrate with Forte™ for Java™ Community Edition. We will not look at the integration with Forte™, but focus on using the toolkit as a standalone development environment. No extra configuration is required other than making sure that the Java 2 SDK, Standard Edition 1.3 is installed on your machine.

Once you have installed the toolkit you can go to the `bin` directory and start the `ktoolbar` application. This will bring up the following window:

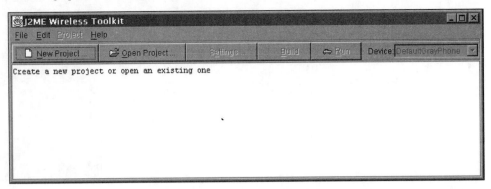

In order to test run some of the applications provided you can click on the **Open Project** button which will take you to a list of the sample applications which came with the toolkit. Once you've opened a project you can run it by clicking on the, surprise, surprise... **Run** button! Furthermore, before running the application you can choose the model phone to run it on by selecting a device from the list next to the **Run** button. The toolkit will locate in the background the `.jad` file of the loaded project, and run the application by calling the MIDP simulator. Following are two examples of devices the Toolkit emulates:

Developing the First MIDlet

With the development environment now set up, we go on to code a simple MIDlet in order to illustrate the development cycle. In the simplest of terms, you can think of the cycle as follows:

- ❏ Come up with an idea and produce a design
- ❏ Code it using the MIDP APIs
- ❏ Test it using the emulation environment
- ❏ Package the application
- ❏ Deploy and test it on real devices

For our first MIDlet we will simply display a message and give the user options to obtain further information or to exit. We will explain the steps required to develop the MIDlet both using the toolkit and through the more basic tools.

With the toolkit the first step is to click on the New Project button. This action will ask you to provide a name for the project and a name for the MIDlet class (other MIDlet classes can be added later on):

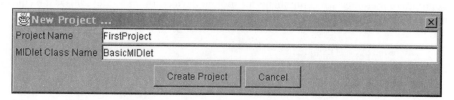

Once you've entered the appropriate information, the toolkit will take you to a window where you can set all the attributes required for the application description file. You do not need to bother with them right now, since you can always change them later on:

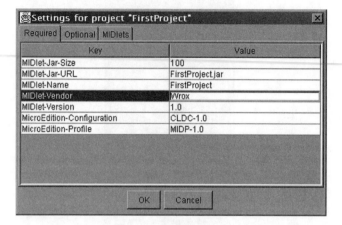

Finally, the toolkit will create a new directory with three subdirectories for source code, binary, and other resources such as icons, bitmaps, and so on:

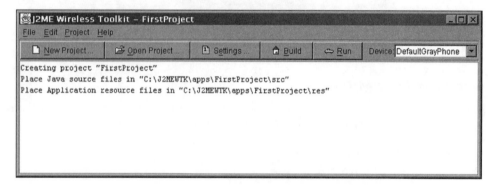

With the basic structure now in place, you need to go the directory of the toolkit in your environment, and from there go to `../apps/FirstProject/`. You should find the three subdirectories: `bin`, `res`, and `src`. The only directory that contains something is the `bin` directory. The toolkit has created the required `.jad` file, whose attributes you can always change through the toolkit interface, and a manifest file that will be used for packaging.

At this point we are ready to write some code. Get hold of your favorite Java editor so as to write the `BasicMIDlet` class.

The first step is to import the necessary packages. In our case they are the `midlet` package, which contains the `MIDlet` class that we must subclass, and the `lcdui` package which is a package specific to MIDP and defines appropriate user interface components for mobile devices. In many ways this is the equivalent of AWT and Swing for the J2SE (we discuss user interface APIs in the following section).

```
import javax.microedition.midlet.*;
import javax.microedition.lcdui.*;
```

As mentioned before, every MIDlet must subclass the `MIDlet` class. The `MIDlet` class contains methods required for the management of MIDlets. Three of these methods, which we've described earlier on, are described abstract and therefore need to be declared in our own class:

```
public class BasicMIDlet extends MIDlet {
```

The `Display` object encapsulates the required functionality to manage the display and input devices of the mobile device and it is in the `javax.microedtion.lcdui` package:

```
private Display display;
```

Here in the constructor we retrieve the display object that is unique to this MIDlet:

```
public BasicMIDlet() {
    display = Display.getDisplay(this);
}
```

Finally, here is the method that is called when we invoke the MIDlet. In our case we simply create a `TextBox` object in which we place a message and display it:

```
public void startApp() {
    TextBox message= new TextBox("Message", "Look, no hands!", 20, 0);

    display.setCurrent(message);
}
```

Since our MIDlet does not have any operations taking place in the background, such as a network connection or writing to a record store the `pauseApp()` method does not need to do anything:

```
public void pauseApp() {
}
```

The `destroyApp()` method should perform any final operations, such as object cleanup, that the MIDlet may require. Once more, in our case there is no need for any special operation:

```
public void destroyApp(boolean unconditional) {
    }
}
```

Once the code for the MIDlet has been written, and the file placed in the `src` folder of the `FirstProject` directory, all that is required is to go back to the wireless toolkit and click on the build button. The toolkit will then compile the classes, collect any resources, and package everything ready for deployment. You can then click on the Run button that will start the MIDP emulator and display the following window:

By clicking on the round button in the middle of the scroll buttons you can activate the MIDlet and see the message:

Until now we have seen how set up our MIDP development environment, either using the basic tools or the toolkit and have also looked at a very simple MIDlet example. In the next sections we will talk in some detail about the user interface APIs of MIDP and also briefly discuss networking and persistent storage. We should also mention that the Java website provides some excellent articles about almost all aspects of MIDP development at http://developer.java.sun.com/developer/technicalArticles/wireless/index.html.

MIDlet User Interface

User interface design on mobile phones is a true challenge for the developer. You can try to overcome processing limitations by transferring the work to the server, you can try to overcome networking limitations by building robust and fault-tolerant communication protocols, but you cannot avoid a 4-line mobile phone screen unless you build your own phones as well!

Even though there are an increasing number of mobile devices that integrate phone functionality with PDA functionality and provide a friendlier Palm-style interface, the majority of devices will, for at least the next two years, still be based on the standard mobile phone. Of course, this does not mean that there is no hope for applications on mobile phones. It does, however, accentuate the need for extremely careful design in order to make those applications practical to use.

Some of the issues to consider when designing user interfaces for mobile devices are:

❑ Mobile devices have limited display capabilities (see MIDP device assumptions in the introduction to the J2ME), making it necessary to display only relevant information and as clear and concisely as possible.

❑ Mobile devices are often used with just one hand and while the user is doing something else such as walking along the road. This means that you cannot demand that the user performs complicated dances of button pressing to get to the desired point, and also that you must make sure that the user is aware of any changes. For example, don't flash a message saying: "Order did not go through" for two seconds before returning to the start because the user may have missed it and remained with the impression that the order was successful.

❑ Mobile devices are not all the same, and this unfortunately complicates the design. Always test on as many phones as you can and instead of rushing off to produce an alternative design for every device, try to see if you can change the existing design so that it can transfer to as many phones as possible without alterations. This will save you money and may even result in a better design.

The entire user interface APIs for mobile devices are defined by the MIDP specification and are in the `javax.microedition.lcdui` package. It is important to note that these APIs do not simply take the well known Abstract Windowing Toolkit (AWT) classes and reshape them for mobile devices.

The reason for this is that although the AWT is meant to be transferable across different platforms those platforms were assumed to be desktop computers and thus the AWT makes assumptions that are not valid on mobile devices, either because of processing power limitations or real estate limitations or input device differences. For example, the AWT was designed around a user interaction model based on a mouse and keyboard, with the possibility of overlapping windows and resizing windows. Such an interaction model is not valid for mobile devices. In addition, the AWT is based on the dynamic creation of objects that are short lived and get garbage collected, all tasks that cannot be performed on mobile devices due to limited processing power and memory.

Display

The central object of the UI APIs is the display. The `Display` object represents the manager of the device's display and of the input devices of the system, and is accessed through a static method:

```
public static Display getDisplay(MIDlet m)
```

This method will retrieve the Display object made available for the MIDlet m by the device. Once a display object has been retrieved, you can place Displayable objects on the display by using the setCurrent(Displayable nextDisplayable) method. You can retrieve the currently Displayable object by calling the getCurrent() method. At any time only one Displayable can be the current Displayable.

A MIDlet is said to be in the **foreground** if the current displayable object is actually drawn on the screen and user input events are delivered to that object. A MIDlet is in the **background** if it is not currently displayed on the screen. The control of which application is currently in the foreground is controlled by an external entity called the **application management software**, which is implemented by the device manufacturer. This software will always allocate a Displayable object for a MIDlet, even though the MIDlet may not be in the foreground. In order to determine if a MIDlet *is* visible, you can call the isShown() method of the Displayable object.

The application management software always has the last word about what gets displayed on the screen and which application is allowed to do what. The reasons behind this are quite clear. Just imagine a scenario where someone is calling you but you cannot actually answer the call because of a MIDlet that is demanding attention!

Responding to User Input

In order to respond to user inputs, Displayable objects need to be related to **commands** and bound to a **command listener**, which is responsible for responding to the activation of the command. Commands are represented by the Command object in the javax.microedition.lcdui package and encapsulate actions that a user may perform. An action may be selecting an option from a menu, pressing a button on the phone, or any other form of user input the device supports (voice activation). Once a command is activated, the Displayable object will send this information to the command listener that is responsible for responding to the action. A command listener is an object that implements the CommandListener interface, that is usually the main MIDlet class or a screen object.

Each command has a label associated with it, which can be used to display the command to the user or to be mapped on a user interface component of the device such as a soft button. Commands can also have a type, which map that command to a predefined action that the device can perform such as back, cancel, exit, etc. Commands also have priorities, which can be used by the device to arrange the commands on the screen.

High and Low-level APIs

There are two levels to the MIDP UI APIs representing an attempt to provide a solution that would allow the creation of both very generic and portable user interfaces, through the high-level APIs, and very precise user interfaces, through the low-level APIs.

High-level APIs

The high-level APIs provide little control over the exact look of the user interface, especially as regards the visual appearance of graphical components (shape, size, font). Such issues are left to the underlying API implementations, which will adapt your application for the device in question.

The main abstraction used for these APIs is the notion of a Screen as an object on which you can place Displayable objects. It is implemented as an abstract class that actual Displayable objects inherit. The only functionality that is directly accessible is the ability to insert a ticker tape and a title for that Screen.

The main high-level components which subclass Screen are:

❑ Alert: Used to display an alert to the user. The developer can set a defined display time or set the time to infinity in which case the user must dismiss the alert screen.

❑ Form: A general container into which a variety of objects (images, read-only text fields, editable text fields, editable date fields, gauges, and choice groups) can be placed and displayed. The Form object will take care of traversing through the objects it contains and scrolling.

❑ List: Used to display a list of choices. Events can be bound to the selection of a List in order to lead the user to another Screen or to perform a background action.

❑ TextBox: Used for entering and editing text.

Low-level APIs

The low-level APIs are represented by the Canvas object which allows for the precise placement of graphic elements on the screen, as well as access to low-level user input events through direct mappings to input keys. Graphic elements can be created using the Graphics object, which provides basic 2D level rendering capabilities. These low-level APIs are provided in order to enable applications such as games that require this form of capability.

An Example of a MIDP User Interface

In this section we will develop a small example to illustrate some of the concepts mentioned above. We will focus on the high-level APIs, since they address the broadest range of applications. This example was developed using the wireless toolkit and all the code can be found in the UIExamples directory of the downloadable code for this chapter.

The first step, as always, is to import the necessary classes.

```
import javax.microedition.midlet.*;
import javax.microedition.lcdui.*;
```

The BasicUI MIDlet implements the CommandListener interface and uses it to react to input from the user:

```
public class BasicUI extends MIDlet implements CommandListener {
```

We declare all the main elements we will use. The Display object that will manage the user interface, a List element, a Form element, a TextBox, an Alert, a Ticker and a couple of Commands that we will use throughout:

```
Display display = null;
```

This List object constructor provides a list with the title ("This is a list"), and an IMPLICIT selection pattern. There are three selection patterns provided for lists and a static final identifier in the Choice interface represents each of them:

❑ IMPLICIT: This type is for lists where the selection of an option notifies the application, through a CommandListener (if one is registered), of the selection. Only one element can be selected at any time.

❑ EXCLUSIVE: An exclusive type list is the same as an implicit type list with no notification.

❑ MULTIPLE: Allows the selection of multiple options, but with no notification.

```
List introMenu = new List("This is a list", List.IMPLICIT);

Form testForm = new Form("A Form");
```

A `TextBox` allows a user to enter and edit text. The constructor used is the following:

```
TextField(String label, String text, int maxSize, int constraints)
```

The `maxSize` variable sets the upper limit on the number of input characters. The `constraints` variable can be used to place constraints on the format of the entered text. The constraints are defined in the `TextField` class and address such issues as entering an e-mail address or entering a password. Here are the rest of the declarations:

```
TextBox testText = new TextBox("Enter text", "Initial contents", 160, 0);

Alert changeAlert = null;

Ticker ticker = new Ticker(
        "Louis, I think this is the beginning of a beautiful friendship.");

static final Command backCommand = new Command("Back",Command.BACK, 0);
static final Command exitCommand = new Command("Exit", Command.STOP, 2);
```

We retrieve the display manager for this MIDLet and append some choices to our `List` that will form the introductory menu:

```
public BasicUI() {
    display = Display.getDisplay(this);
    introMenu.append("See a form", null);
    introMenu.append("See a text box", null);
    introMenu.append("See an alert demo", null);
```

In addition, we add a `Command` to this displayable object as well as a command listener, which is the MIDlet itself:

```
    introMenu.addCommand(exitCommand);
    introMenu.setCommandListener(this);
}

public void startApp() {
    setIntroMenu(true);
}

public void pauseApp() {
}
```

The `notifyDestroyed()` method will notify the application manager that this MIDlet has entered into the destroyed state:

```
public void destroyApp(boolean unconditional) {
    notifyDestroyed();
}
```

The `setIntroMenu()` method sets the introductory menu as displayable and also places a `Ticker` on the screen. Tickers can be placed on any displayable object:

```
private void setIntroMenu(boolean firstTime) {
    if (firstTime) {
        introMenu.setTicker(ticker);
        display.setCurrent(introMenu);
    }
    else {
        ticker.setString("Wasn't that exciting!?");
        introMenu.setTicker(ticker);
        display.setCurrent(introMenu);
    }
}
```

The `runFormDemo()` method sets out our demo form element. We place a simple text field and a `Gauge`. The constructor used for the `Gauge` object is as follows:

`Gauge(String label, boolean interactive, int maxValue, int initialValue)`

The `Boolean` variable `interactive` defines whether the user can interact with the `Gauge` and set its value. In this case the `Gauge` is, essentially, used as a way to obtain information from the user, which is constrained to a certain scale indicated by the `maxValue` variable. The actual way this concept will be displayed is device dependant. If the `Gauge` is placed in a non-interactive mode then it can be used either as a progress meter or as a way to display to the user some numerical measurement result.

We also add a back command for this screen as well as a command listener and, finally, set it as displayable:

```
private void runFormDemo() {

    TextField someText = new TextField("A test..", ".with text in a form", 20,0);
    testForm.append(someText);

    Gauge gauge = new Gauge("Set desired level",true, 20,0);
    testForm.append(gauge);

    testForm.addCommand(backCommand);

    testForm.setCommandListener(this);

    display.setCurrent(testForm);
}
```

The `TextBox` is has a back command added to it and it is set to displayable:

```
private void runTextDemo() {
    testText.addCommand(backCommand);
    testText.setCommandListener(this);

    display.setCurrent(testText);
}
```

Here, we create an `Alert` that will display a message for 5000 milliseconds. There are several types of `Alert` available: informational, alarm, confirmation, error, and warning. Based on the type the device will attempt to render the alert in a suitable manner:

```
private void runAlertDemo() {
    changeAlert = new Alert("Changing...");
    changeAlert.setString("Moving to the main menu");
    changeAlert.setType(AlertType.INFO);
    changeAlert.setTimeout(5000);
    display.setCurrent(changeAlert);
}
```

Finally, the commandAction() method is used to react to user input. In this case, when an action is performed it is either one of the two commands we defined earlier or a selection from the introductory menu. In the first case we retrieve the label of the command and act accordingly, while in the second case we use the index of the introductory menu to determine which option was selected. The command listener is notified of a selection by the SELECT_COMMAND constant that is a special kind of Command object indicated a selection from an implicit list:

```
public void commandAction(Command activated, Displayable origin) {
    String commandLabel = activated.getLabel();
    /*Debug information that will be displayed on standard output
    in the development environment*/
    System.out.println(commandLabel + " has been activated");

    if (commandLabel.equals("Exit")) {
        destroyApp(true);
    }
    else if (commandLabel.equals("Back")) {
        setIntroMenu(false);
    }

    if (activated.equals(List.SELECT_COMMAND)) {
        System.out.println("List option selected");

        switch(introMenu.getSelectedIndex()) {
            case 0: runFormDemo(); break;
            case 1: runTextDemo(); break;
            case 2: runAlertDemo(); break;
        }
    }
}
```

Using the DefaultGrayPhone of the toolkit the above example provides the following output:

After UIExamples is selected, we see the introductory menu with the ticker box at the top and an Exit option at the bottom:

Selecting See a form takes us to the next screen, where we see a form with a text field and a gauge:

Scrolling down the screen will bring the gauge into position to be manipulated by scrolling left or right:

When we return to the main menu, the message in the ticker has changed:

Selecting See a text box presents us with an editable text box:

And finally, we have the alert demo:

Networking Support in MIDP

As opposed to the UI APIs, which are entirely an aspect of the MID profile, the network APIs are based on the CLDC specification that we discussed earlier on. MIDP extends the Generic Connection Framework to define specific support for a subset of the HTTP protocol. HTTP is supported in TCP/IP networks, WAP, and i-mode, and so can cover a wide range of devices.

The HTTP support is defined in the `javax.microedition.io.HttpConnection` API. A device that implements MIDP must support the full functionality of the HEAD, POST, and GET requests as per the official RFC2616 HTTP specification.

Persistent Storage Support

The MIDP defines a Record Management System that is modeled on a basic record-oriented database and is represent through APIs in the `javax.microedition.rms` package. This record store is designed to retain information that should remain persistent across several sessions of a MIDlet as long as the MIDlet is on the device. Once it is removed, its associated records should also be removed.

The exact nature of the storage system will change from device to device, but the MIDlet will not be aware of these changes. Each operation is guaranteed to be atomic, in order to ensure that data is not corrupted, and records are stored as arrays of bytes with a unique `recordId`.

Microbrowsers and MIDlets – the Future

We talked about WAP and how devices use microbrowsers to allow the user to view documents. We've also talked about how Java applications can be created for mobile devices. Now we are going to briefly go over the various ways these two can interoperate. Essentially, the scenario we are looking at is that a user is browsing the WWW through a WAP-enabled phone and comes across a site that offers some sort of application the user can download. It might be a game, a calculator, or some form of specialized tourist guide.

One way this might work is that your microbrowser is written using the device's native language and thus has direct access to the native interface. It is instructed to download a file which it is not sure what to do about and so passes it down to the operating system. The operating system recognizes that file as a valid MIDlet and loads it into the JVM calling the `startApp()` method.

Alternatively, the microbrowser may be developed in C/C++ or something similar and has direct access to the JVM. So when it encounters a MIDlet it reads the descriptor file and loads it into the JVM.

Finally, the third option is to have a microbrowser that is itself written in Java. Although this might at some level cost in terms of performance (this may not be the case), there is the advantage of being able to change even the microbrowser when a new version is built. In fact, if most of the functionalities of the phone are Java based, the phone itself could be upgraded dynamically. This would be a vast improvement from the current situation where if a user wants some new feature the only option is to go and buy a new phone.

Summary

Gartner Research has projected that by the year 2003 there will be 700 million cell phones in the world. The majority of those phones (80 percent) will be able to connect to the Internet, and a large number of these phones will have some form of the MIDP on them.

We have looked at how the different telecommunication companies are preparing to roll out upgrades to the current networks that will make the use of mobile devices much more enjoyable, and eventually companies will come to depend on their fleet of mobile devices to control their remote units. WAP has established itself as the dominant standard in the world now, with the exception of Japan where i-mode prevails. However, these technologies are converging so that in four or five years there may be a situation where the two are indistinguishable.

Java is definitely positioning itself as the dominant programming language for delivering applications to mobile phones. All the big mobile phone companies are participants in the process of defining appropriate versions of the Java language for mobile phones. Although these efforts are very young, (MIDP1.0 was only release in September 2000) they show a lot of promise.

Overall, the conclusion has to be that the Internet is reshaping itself and is making space for newcomers. The time to start developing wireless applications is now. However, care should be taking not to repeat the mistakes of the first wave of development and instead build on solid foundations in order to provide applications that people truly want.

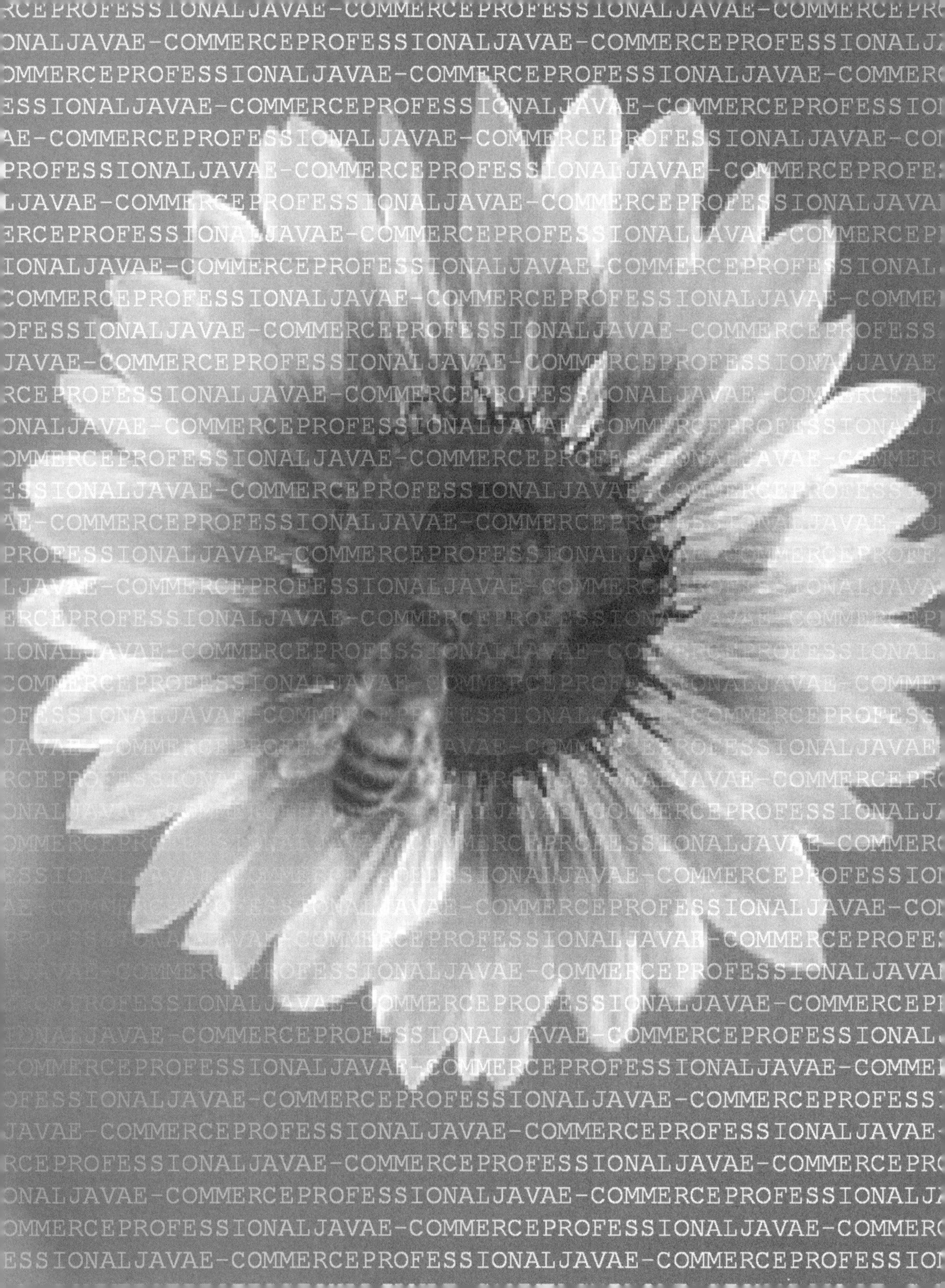
PROFESSIONALJAVAE-COMMERCE

25

Smart Cards

The recent boom of digital communication has forever changed the way that we connect with each other, as well as with the items all around us. Buying trends are quickly changing from exclusively in-store transactions to a larger proportion of on-line transactions, digital money is becoming a preferred spending mechanism, and a person's handwritten signature is slowly being replaced by his or her own digital signature.

To take account of this, we've decided to close this book by having a look into the near future examining the developments being made in the application of Java to **smart card** technology.

> *A smart card is a credit card sized plastic card with an integrated electronic chip, which serves to authenticate its owner in any type of online transaction.*

For this new wave of commerce to be successful, the electronic business market must produce the same, or greater, level of trust and accuracy that is being demanded by society in today's traditional market. One of the main keys to consumer acceptance of digital business is a small device that holds all of the information needed to perform a transaction between a buyer and a seller in a secure, electronic fashion. This can be accomplished with a smart card.

The key to vendor acceptance is a unified, highly secure digital communication mechanism that will allow the marketplace to communicate with all consumers holding smart cards in a similar fashion. This can be accomplished with the **Java Card Virtual Machine (JCVM)** and the **Java Card Runtime Environment (JCRE)**.

In this chapter, we'll be looking at:

❑   Smart cards in general

❑   A quick tour of the smart card architecture

❑   A programming example using the Java Card 2.1.1 Development Kit

Let's kick off this topic by trying to get a better grasp of where smart cards will fit into e-commerce and some issues surrounding them.

Why Smart Cards?

Smart cards are quickly being accepted as a way of life all around the world in all types of industries, and in the consumer market. Their most important role is acting as the missing link to provide standard access control to any type of device. Some of these devices include cell phones, personal digital assistants (PDAs), appliances, secure entries, set top boxes, and ATM cash-points.

M-Commerce

If one new trend or technology will benefit more from smart cards than any other, it is m-commerce. Although it was only touched on in the last chapter, for m-commerce to succeed, secure authentication of the user is required. Cellular phones alone are achieving great success as instant messengers, and are stepping rapidly towards being viable e-mail recipients, personal communicators, and even web browsers. The combination of both cellular phones and smart cards will allow a cellular phone to turn into, for example, an on-line storefront, an "instant-buy" stockbroker, or a participant in an auction.

Currently, the frontline applications of smart cards can be categorized into three basic areas – authentication, access control, and service debit:

❑   **Authentication** – Validating that a person is actually who he or she says they are. This is applied for security clearance at the workplace, to prevent theft with other on-line purchases, and to avoid misrepresentation in general.

❑   **Access control** – Smart cards allow certain levels of access to anything, anywhere, anytime. Once authenticated, the user's role in each situation can be determined and access can be refused or granted thereon.

❑   **Service debit** – Satellite decoders, prepaid phone cards, on-line reservation systems, and other media are using smart cards to allow authenticated users with the proper access to utilize these electronic services. Furthermore, smart cards are crucial if the so-called cashless society is ever to become a reality.

All of these factors indicate that smart cards could be used to increase personalization in human-device interactions enabling, for example, customized displays of schedules, or purchase options, or language displays.

Obviously for smart cards to be used in m-commerce transactions the handling of transactions will be crucial. There are basically two types of transaction we can consider here:

❑   Regular – Standard atomic transactions ensure that every step of a process is successful, or else all of the steps are rolled back.

❑   Guaranteed anonymity – A transaction that resembles cash in the non-electronic world. Monies are exchanged and transacted to ensure integrity, but at an anonymous level.

Barriers to Success

As with many new and emerging technologies, there will be many problems that need to be overcome for smart cards to succeed. Not least of such difficulties are marketing problems, security and authentication, transactions and reliability, and personalization. Problems with entering the marketplace will be covered here; the other barriers to success are covered in subsequent sections, because these "barriers" are addressed directly with smart card technology.

The marketing problems can be largely divided into two groups: multiple vendors, and marketplace acceptance.

Firstly, take the issue of multiple vendors and what standard to use. Historically, smart card vendors utilized proprietary assembly-type programming languages as programming efforts to put smart cards into the marketplace for each purpose. This approach became problematic however, because a separate smart card was required for each and every service, which was cumbersome to the user. Multiple-application cards are quickly becoming the preferred smart card system, because they allow one card to have access to many services. There are only a few standard ways to create these:

❑ Sun's **Java Card Technology** (working together with the **OpenCard Framework** (**OCF**))

❑ Microsoft's smart card OS, **Windows for Smart Cards** (personal computer/smart card (PC/SC) specification)

❑ Proprietary Systems (Vendor supplied language in assembly or C++)

Secondly we have the issue of acceptance in the marketplace by both vendors and consumers. Vendor acceptance, from an electronic vendor point of view, is completely dependent on the ease of use of the card, how it integrates into the existing system, and the financial integrity that a smart card will provide. Smart card vendors have an interesting range of products and services to consider: mobile phones, Personal Digital Assistants (PDAs), food and drink vending machines, Electronic Funds Transfers at Point-Of-Sale (EFTPOS) machines (debit and credit card swiping machines), and other devices that smart cards can be a part of and relate to.

Public acceptance is mainly geared towards the ease and security of use, and how the smart card technology readily integrates with all of the personal devices that are used by the public today.

Out of the current uses of smart cards, authentication is possibly the most important function that they provide, so let's look into this a little more.

Authentication

For smart cards to become accepted in the electronic marketplace, the decision makers in business and personal users of the card must feel that using smart card technology is safer and more robust than standard credit cards, Personal Identification Numbers (PIN), username/passwords, or other techniques. Smart cards can make use of the following means of authentication:

❑ Personal certificates

❑ Personal Identification Numbers

❑ Biometrics

Personal Certificates

Information that has been verified about the owner from a certificate authority can be embedded into a smart card. A vendor that does business with the smart card holder can be assured that the smart card belongs to a certain person because the certificate authority deems it so (based on their reputation and stake in the transaction). A digital certificate's main role is to prevent duplication of smart cards by making them increasingly hard to digitally copy. This information is "certified" by a certificate issuer who, before issuing certificates to a company, verifies that that company is who they say they are by checking with third party organizations as to their business IDs, address information (paying rent), tax ID validation, and so on.

Personal Identification Number (PIN)

These are the standardized way that a card reader validates that the person holding the card is authorized to use it. The user must know the PIN to unlock the card in order to access any applications on it.

Biometrics

Biometrics is the ability to utilize an identifying feature from a person's body to authenticate him or her to use certain resources. These attributes must be unique from person to person across the entire world, and include such things as:

❑ Fingerprints. A fingerprint scanner can easily be attached to the back of a smart card or a smart card reader to allow authentication of the user. The most common form of this device will probably be installed on the back of cellular phones with smart card access control to produce a completely secure m-commerce environment.

❑ Retinal laser scans. This is another method to biometrically authenticate the user. Although more reliable than the fingerprint scanner, the public does not trust a laser probing into their eye, therefore, acceptance is very low.

Now we've gained an overview of the topic, let's move on and have a look at how they are being implemented.

Smart Card Architecture

Smart card architectures conventionally conform to the ISO 7816 standards in order to work with any hardware available. Information on the International Standards Organization can be found at http://www.iso.ch/ (although the standard has to be purchased and is not publicly available).

The ISO 7816 standard has 7 parts:

❑ Part 1 – Physical characteristics.

❑ Part 2 – Dimensions and location of the contacts.

❑ Part 3 – Electronic signals and transmission protocols.

❑ Part 4 – Inter-industry commands for interchange.

❑ Part 5 – Application identifiers.

❑ Part 6 – Inter-industry data elements.

❑ Part 7 – Inter-industry commands for **SCQL** (**Structured Card Query Language** also known as the **Smart Card Query Language** by Gem-Plus.) This author deems them the same thing for all reasonable purposes. The SCQL is a newer extension that allows for programmers to access Database Smart Cards.

The following is a diagram of the physical characteristics of smart cards as defined in ISO 7816 Part 1:

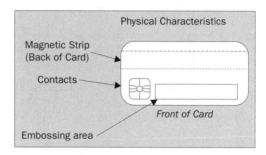

Smart cards are inserted into a **Card Acceptance Device** (**CAD**), which supplies power to the card and establishes a connection. This can be done in two ways:

❑ Contact – user inserts the card into a CAD that can communicate with the card through a user interface connected to the CAD

❑ Contactless – the card is passed over appropriate technology and powered through inductive cells, then a host computer makes decisions based on the transactions

The standard protocol used by all smart cards to communicate with the CAD is by using data packages called **Application Protocol Data Units** (**APDU**). An APDU can contain a **command** or a **response** message.

The smart card always waits for a command APDU from a CAD; it executes the action specified in the APDU, and then sends a response APDU back to the CAD. The APDU structure is described in ISO 7816 Part 4 and can be seen below.

Command APDU:

Mandatory Header				Conditional Body (feed data into the smart card)		
CLA	INS	P1	P2	Lc	Data Field	Le

Response APDU:

Conditional Body (retrieve data from the card)	Mandatory Trailer	
Data Field	SW1	SW2

The contents of the APDUs as shown above represent the following:

❑ CLA: Class byte. Used to identify an application.

❑ INS: Instruction byte. Indicates the instruction code. As you will see in the example code, the instruction byte is where we tell our software what to do next. We will use a Java `Switch` method to parse through the different things that a Java Card Applet can do.

❑ P1 and P2: Parameter bytes. Provide further qualification to the APDU command.

❑ Lc: Number of bytes in the data field of the command APDU.

❑ Data Field: A sequence of bytes received in the data field of the response.

❑ Le: Maximum number of bytes expected in the data field of the response APDU.

❑ SW1 and SW2: Status words. Denote the processing state in the card.

As we will see in the example below, when coding our Java Card Application, we have the APDU object passed into our method from the environment (not exactly that easy, but we'll discuss it later); we then create a byte array to hold the APDU buffer so that we can read it:

```
byte[] buffer = apdu.getBuffer();
```

and finally we can access the different fields of the APDU in many ways using the Java Card API, the easiest being directly as follows:

```
byte numBytes = buffer[ISO7816.OFFSET_LC];

byte creditAmount =buffer[ISO7816.OFFSET_CDATA];
```

We can also easily throw an exception when there is a problem:

```
ISOException.throwIt(ISO7816.SW_WRONG_LENGTH);
```

Java Card Technology

Once ISO came up with the hardware standards, it was up to somebody to develop a software standard. This standard was soon developed and is now known as the OpenCard Framework (OCF) and it promises to provide support for 100 percent pure Java smart card applications. Based on this software standard, Sun Microsystems developed the Java Card API, which will run on all smart cards that are ISO 7816 compliant (http://www.java.sun.com/products/javacard/javacard21.html). Java applications on the computer or terminal can use the OpenCard Framework when talking to a smart card. Our sample code below, using the smart card simulator from Sun Microsystems, demonstrates how this is achieved. Java Card Technology is a small version of the Java Programming language, which runs on the smart card itself in the form of applets (also called **cardlets**). These are not the same as the popular Java applets that run in a web browser, but the characteristics of how they interact in each of their environments are similar.

There are three parts to Java Card technology. All of these parts overlap, but need to be described separately for effective understanding:

❑ Java Card Virtual Machine (**JCVM**) – the division of the on-card VM and the off-card VM and how they react

- ❏ Java Card Runtime Environment (**JCRE**) – systems components that run inside of a smart card
- ❏ Java Card Application Programming Interface and language subset

Java Card Virtual Machine

The Java Card Virtual Machine is divided into two different sections:

- ❏ On-card VM
- ❏ Off-card VM

Together, these two sections perform all of the regular virtual machine functions, loading class files and executing them. The off-card VM includes the converter, and the on-card VM includes the installer and the interpreter.

We can represent the process of transferring a program from the programming environment to the card as follows:

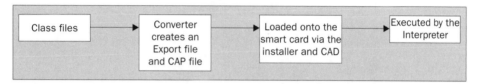

where:

- ❏ **Converter** – loads and pre-processes the class files that makes up the Java packages, and then outputs a **Converted Applet** (**CAP**) file and an Export file.
- ❏ **Installer** – before the Interpreter executes the code found in the CAP file, the Java card installer downloads and installs CAP files with the cooperation of an off-card installer program working through a Card Acceptance Device.
- ❏ **Card Acceptance Device** (**CAD**) – the smart card reader.
- ❏ **Interpreter** – the CAP files are then loaded onto the smart card and executed by the interpreter. The interpreter "interprets" the compiled code into an executable that can be run by the virtual machine.

Application Identifier (AID)

An **application identifier** (**AID**) is a unique signature of each Java Card Applet. This signature allows for Smart Card programmers and vendors to ensure that every Java Card application written will always be unique when installed onto a smart card, even if the applets have the same name.

The AID is actually two different pieces. The first five bytes are the **Resource Identifier** (**RID**) and the last eleven bytes are the **Proprietary Identifier eXtension** (**PIX**).

International Standards organization (ISO) assigns a unique RID to each company based on request, and then each company will assign a PIX to each applet that they create. In the example below, we are using Sun Microsystems' RID and a made up PIX, since it is only used in the simulator.

This will become important as we get to the programming example

Java Card Runtime Environment (JCRE)

The JCRE consists of the system components inside a smart card, and is responsible for all of the card's functions. It is essentially the smart card's operating system. The JCRE is a layered system that consists of many segregated parts. The topmost layer is where the applets run. Each is separated by a firewall, so that the smart card can run multiple applications while still maintaining a secure environment. By implementing a "shareable interface" applets can communicate to each other through the firewall if necessary, but that is out of the scope of this chapter. For further information on this topic, check out *Java Card Technology for Smart Cards: Architecture and Programmer's Guide* by *Zhiqun Chen, ISBN 0-201703-29-7*.

Below are the framework APIs and industry specific extensions. The bottom layer is composed of systems classes from the proprietary technologies of smart card vendors.

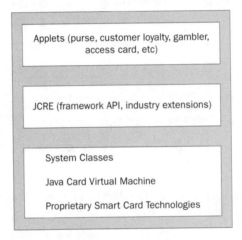

Java Card API and Language Subset

There are essentially three core packages and one extension package for the smart card API:

java.lang

This is a stripped down subset of its counterpart in the Java 2 Standard Edition (J2SE). This package provides the core language support, as well as exception support. Listed below are the classes in this package (not including the exceptions or fields, see the JavaDoc for that information):

- ❑ Object
- ❑ Throwable

javacard.framework

This package defines the functionality of the Java Card Applets. Listed below are the interfaces and classes in this package (not including the exceptions or fields; see the JavaDoc for that information):

- ❑ Interfaces: ISO7816, PIN, Shareable
- ❑ Classes: AID, APDU, Applet, JCSystem, OwnerPin, Util

javacard.security

This is based on the J2SE `java.security` package. Listed below are the interfaces and classes in this package (not including the exceptions or fields; see the JavaDoc for that information):

- ❑ Interfaces: `DESKey`, `DSAKey`, `DSAPrivateKey`, `DSAPublicKey`, `Key`, `PrivateKey`, `PublicKey`, `RSAPrivateCrtKey`, `RSAPrivateKey`, `SecretKey`
- ❑ Classes: `KeyBuilder`, `MessageDigest`, `RandomData`, `Signature`

javacardx.crypto

This is an extension package that supports encryption and decryption functions, and more advanced security functionality. Listed below are the interface and class in this package (not including the exceptions or fields; see the JavaDoc for that information):

- ❑ Interface: `KeyEncryption`
- ❑ Class: `Cipher`

The Java Card language is quite a bit less than just a subset of the Java programming language. The entire Java Card Language Subset is detailed in Chapter 2 of the Java Card Virtual Machine Specification located at http://java.sun.com/products/javacard/javacard21.html. In a nutshell, the Java Card API supports the following:

- ❑ Primitive data types – boolean, byte, short
- ❑ One-dimensional arrays
- ❑ All object-oriented scope and binding rules
- ❑ All control of flow statements
- ❑ All operators and modifiers

Unsupported features include:

- ❑ Characters and Strings
- ❑ Threads
- ❑ Garbage collection
- ❑ Dynamic class loading
- ❑ Object serialization and cloning
- ❑ Large primitives

Programming Example

To get a good feel for using the Java Card Technology and Development Kit, we should try an example. This example will start by setting up your environment for using the smart card simulator from Sun. Once the environment is set, we'll write and run a simple applet to act as a type of loyalty program card by crediting and debiting the balance on the card. To show how we can store words on our smart card, we will also store our name in a byte array, and retrieve it back to the screen. A brief diagram of the flow of our application is presented here:

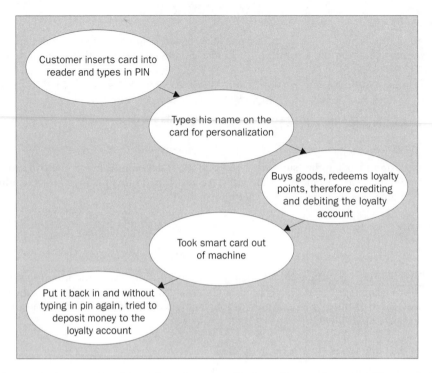

We will be using the Java Card 2.1.1 Development Kit from Sun so that we will not need to actually have a smart card and reader for this example, but it is important to be able to visualize how the real equipment would relate to the simulator pieces.

Here is how the process works in the real world:

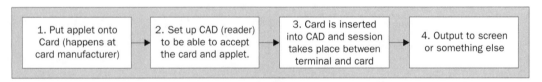

And here is the sequence of events the simulator uses to replicate this process:

1. Compile applet, create `.opt` file with AID information, and run the `.class` and `.opt` files through the converter.

2. Create `.app` file to describe the applet to the CAD so that it will know what to do.

3. Create a `.scr` file that simulates interaction between the terminal and the smart card.

4. Run `apdutool.bat` to perform the simulation. The `out` file shows what happened during the session between the card and the user.

Setting Up

To work through this example you'll need:

❑ Java Card Development Kit 2.1.1 (http://www.java.sun.com/products/javacard/)

❑ JDK1.3 (http://www.java.sun.com/products/j2se/1.3/)

Install the JDK 1.3 as normal, and set up your CLASSPATH. Then extract the Java Card Development Kit also; for this example, we're assuming that you've extracted this to c:\javacard. Make sure to add c:\javacard\jc211\bin and the directory of your files (for this example, we're using c:\wrox\loyalty) to your CLASSPATH, and in your system environment set up the variable JC21BIN to be the value c:\javacard\jc211\bin.

Or you can run these three commands in the command shell before you do anything else to set up your environment:

```
c:\>Set JC21BIN=c:\javacard\jc211\bin
c:\>Set PATH=%PATH%;%JC21BIN%;c:\wrox
c:\>Set CLASSPATH=%CLASSPATH%;%JC21BIN%;c:\wrox
```

Since we are working with a limited subset of the Java language in Java Card programming as discussed above, you'll find that you are limited in the primitive data types available.

This means we'll be using things like bytes *and byte arrays to store hexadecimal information in the place of* longs, doubles, *or* floats. *The simulator is also based entirely in Hexadecimal. For convenience a decimal to hexadecimal conversion chart can be found in Appendix D.*

Designing our Java Card Applet

The first step in creating our Java Card program is to design the flow through command and response APDUs. Here are the steps that this flow will follow:

1. Power up the card

2. Select the installer applet and begin the installer

3. Instantiate the loyalty applet and end the installer

4. Select the loyalty applet to use and verify the PIN on the card

5. Set the name on the card to Bryan Plaster and get the total credits on the card

6. Credit $100 to the card and get the total credits on the card

7. Get the name from the card to display or check

8. Credit $56 to the card and get the total credits on the card

9. Halve the balance and get the total credits on the card

10. Double the balance and get the total credits on the card

11. Reselect the applet so that the PIN is no longer verified

12. Credit $55 to the card (will fail) and get the total credits on the card

13. Power down the card

In a real project, we would create a command APDU to show the information that we are sending to the card for each step along the way, and a response APDU to show the expected reply values from the executing command APDUs on the card. We'll show you a quick example of this here.

The APDU representation below describes how the smart card will verify the user PIN. The Data Field is the user PIN that is being verified (12345), and the INS maps to the function that is in the code.

Verify Command APDU

Mandatory Header				Conditional Body (feed data into the smart card)		
CLA	INS	P1	P2	Lc	Data Field	Le
0xB0	0x50	0x00	0x00	0x05	0x01 0x02 0x03 0x04 0x05	0x7F

We present the applet in full in the next section – here let's look at how we are going to represent various parts of the APDU in code.

The instruction byte (INS) will match up to a static variable in our applet program:

```
final static byte TEST_PIN = (byte) 0x50;
// ..
```

What will be sent to the smart card from a terminal or keypad, etc., will be simulated through our .scr file (screen). The loyalty.scr file is like the public static void main(String args[]) method in a normal Java class. It sends the APDU data one at a time in order from top to bottom of the file. You might want to refer back to the diagram showing how the real world example coincides with the simulator activity at the beginning of this programming example section. Here is the appropriate line from that file, together with comments:

```
//Verify user pin
0xB0 0x50 0x00 0x00 0x05 0x01 0x02 0x03 0x04 0x05 0x7F;
//90 00 = SW_NO_ERROR
```

Notice how our command APDU representation matches.

The process() method, which is called on a selected applet every time the JCRE receives an APDU command, gets information from the INS byte of the command APDU.

So in this case the value obtained is:

❑   0x50 from the .scr file at the second position from the left and tracing it through the system we have:

- ❏ 0x50 in the APDU
- ❏ Then in the APDU buffer we have ISO7816.OFFSET (value of 0x50) and following this
- ❏ TEST_PIN (value of 0x50) represented in our Java Card object

The process() method runs a switch statement on the INS of the command APDU. This, in turn, runs the appropriate method in our applet:

```
switch (buffer[ISO7816.OFFSET_INS]) {
    // the value here is 0x50
    // which is equivalent to the static
    // value of TEST_PIN
    case TEST_PIN:
    setPin(apdu);
    return;
```

If it seems a little confusing now, don't worry; it'll all become clear when we see the full example code.

Now let's look at the response APDU:

Response APDU

Conditional Body (retrieve data from the card)	Mandatory Trailer	
Data Field	SW1	SW2
Original message	90	00

This is represented in the .scr.out file generated by:

```
CLA: 80, INS: b8, P1: 00, P2: 00, Lc: 11, 0a, a0, 00, 00, 00, 62, 03, 01, 0c, 09,
01, 05, 01, 02, 03, 04, 05, Le: 0a, a0, 00, 00, 00, 62, 03, 01, 0c, 09, 01, SW1:
90, SW2: 00
```

The response is exactly what we expect after running the command APDU as the 9000 response indicates success, if we receive anything else, it means that the transaction failed. As it says in the comments of the .scr file we look at the command APDU followed by the response APDU in the .scr.out file that we make when running the apdutool. In the real world this file would be sent back to the CAD and then to the terminal where it would be handled by a program located there.

As a design aid, one should create command APDU and response APDU representations as we have above, to show what is expected for each APDU that is run.

> **The way that I look at Smart Card Processing is that the APDU is a large byte array that passes data back and forth between the Java Card applet and the terminal device.**

If all of your Java Card programming is based on this one point, all of the intricacies of Smart Card development become much simpler.

Programming our Java Card Applet

Now that we understand the basics of programming with the Java Card API, we can write our own applet from start to finish.

The first part of the code tries to define meaningful words to match up to the bytes that the Java Card needs. This makes the code more readable. Sun standardized on these in all of their examples, so we'll stick to the same descriptions:

```
package loyalty;

import javacard.framework.*;

public class loyalty extends Applet {

    /* define APDU options */

    // CLA
    final static byte CLA = (byte) 0xB0;

    // INS
    final static byte BUY_GOODS = (byte) 0x10;
    final static byte AVAIL_CREDIT = (byte) 0x20;
    final static byte DOUBLE_USER_CREDITS = (byte) 0x30;
    final static byte HALF_USER_CREDITS = (byte) 0x40;
    final static byte TEST_PIN = (byte) 0x50;
    final static byte GET_NAME = (byte) 0x80;
    final static byte SET_NAME = (byte) 0x70;

    // PIN entry attempts (3 tries)
    final static byte PIN_TRY = (byte) 0x03;

    // maximum size PIN
    final static byte MAX_PIN_SIZE = (byte) 0x08;

    // status words specific to the applet - from sun example
    final static short SW_VERIFICATION_FAILED = 0x6300;
    final static short SW_PIN_VERIFICATION_REQUIRED = 0x6301;
    final static short SW_INVALID_TRANSACTION_AMOUNT = 0x6A83;

    // instance variables declaration
    OwnerPIN pin;
    short credits;
    byte[] name = {0, 0, 0, 0, 0, 0, 0, 0, 0, 0, 0, 0, 0, 0, 0, 0};
```

The OwnerPIN is from the javacard.framework package. Taking a look at the Java Card API documentation, there are many methods that are available to the developer to manipulate, check, verify, and so on, the PIN from the Java Card.

The JCRE calls install(), and creates a new instance of the applet:

```
    // called by the JCRE
    public static void install(byte[] bArray, short bOffset, byte bLength) {
```

```
        // create an applet instance
        new loyalty(bArray, bOffset, bLength);
    }
```

The constructor creates a new `OwnerPIN` object, and attempts to apply the value to it. Then the applet registers itself with the JCRE:

```
    // constructor
    private loyalty(byte[] bArray, short bOffset, byte bLength) {

        pin = new OwnerPIN(PIN_TRY, MAX_PIN_SIZE);

        // bArray contains the PIN value from the card initialization
        pin.update(bArray, bOffset, bLength);

        // register the applet instance with the JCRE
        register();

    }
```

Since the JCVM is not multi-threaded, only one applet can be selected at a time. The `select()` and `deselect()` methods give the applet focus for use:

```
    public boolean select() {

        // mini authentication
        if (pin.getTriesRemaining() == 0) {
            return false;
        } else {
            return true;
        }
    }

    public void deselect() {

        // when not using anymore, reset pin
        pin.reset();
    }
```

The `process()` method, which is called on a selected applet every time the JCRE receives an APDU command, gets information from the INS byte of the command APDU, and then determines with a `switch` statement which method to run based on that data. This was described in more detail in the previous section:

```
    public void process(APDU apdu) {

        byte[] buffer = apdu.getBuffer();

        // return if the APDU is the applet SELECT command
        if (selectingApplet()) {
            return;

            // verify the CLA byte
```

```
    }
    if (buffer[ISO7816.OFFSET_CLA] != CLA) {
        ISOException.throwIt(ISO7816.SW_CLA_NOT_SUPPORTED);

        // check the INS byte
    }
    switch (buffer[ISO7816.OFFSET_INS]) {

        case AVAIL_CREDIT:
            getCredits(apdu);
            return;

        case BUY_GOODS:
            addCredits(apdu);
            return;

        case DOUBLE_USER_CREDITS:
            doubleCredits();
            return;

        case HALF_USER_CREDITS:
            halfCredits();
            return;

        case TEST_PIN:
            setPin(apdu);
            return;

        case GET_NAME:
            getName(apdu);
            return;

        case SET_NAME:
            setName(apdu);
            return;

        default:
            ISOException.throwIt(ISO7816.SW_INS_NOT_SUPPORTED);
    }
}
```

Next we have the addCredits() method. It makes sure that the PIN was correctly entered and obtains information from the APDU, before adding it to the total credits variable:

```
private void addCredits(APDU apdu) {

    // verify authentication
    if (!pin.isValidated()) {
        ISOException.throwIt(SW_PIN_VERIFICATION_REQUIRED);
    }
    byte[] buffer = apdu.getBuffer();

    // get the number of bytes of data from the command APDU
    byte numBytes = buffer[ISO7816.OFFSET_LC];
```

```
     // get the data
     byte byteRead = (byte) (apdu.setIncomingAndReceive());

     // error if the number of data bytes
     // or the bytes read is not 1
     if ((numBytes != 1) || (byteRead != 1)) {
        ISOException.throwIt(ISO7816.SW_WRONG_LENGTH);

        // get the credit amount
     }
     byte creditAmount = buffer[ISO7816.OFFSET_CDATA];

     // credit the amount
     credits = (short) (credits + creditAmount);
     return;
  }
```

The next two methods simply modify the total credits to show how easy it is:

```
  private void doubleCredits() {

     // verify authentication
     if (!pin.isValidated()) {
        ISOException.throwIt(SW_PIN_VERIFICATION_REQUIRED);
     }
     credits = (short) (credits * 2);
  }

  private void halfCredits() {

     // verify authentication
     if (!pin.isValidated()) {
        ISOException.throwIt(SW_PIN_VERIFICATION_REQUIRED);
     }
     credits = (short) (credits / 2);
  }
```

The getCredits() method gets the command APDU and sends back a response APDU with the correct information in it:

```
  private void getCredits(APDU apdu) {

     byte[] buffer = apdu.getBuffer();

     // tell JCRE that we are returning data
     short le = apdu.setOutgoing();

     // how many bytes to return
     apdu.setOutgoingLength((byte) 2);

     // write the credits into the APDU buffer at the offset 0
     // funny method in util class, buffer is a persistant array object
     // the buffer persist from one CAD session to the next - credits
     Util.setShort(buffer, (short) 0, credits);
```

```
        // send the 2-byte credits at the offset 0 in the apdu buffer
        apdu.sendBytes((short) 0, (short) 2);

    }
```

The setPin function uses the Java Card framework methods to get information from the APDU and check if the pin is correct:

```
    private void setPin(APDU apdu) {

        byte[] buffer = apdu.getBuffer();

        // receive the PIN data for validation.
        byte byteRead = (byte) (apdu.setIncomingAndReceive());

        // the PIN data is read into the APDU buffer
        // starting at the offset ISO7816.OFFSET_CDATA
        if (pin.check(buffer, ISO7816.OFFSET_CDATA, byteRead) == false) {
            ISOException.throwIt(SW_VERIFICATION_FAILED);
        }
    }
```

Next are the getName() and setName() methods that show how to set up a string (represented in HEX) to be stored and retrieved from a smart card.

The name that we will store and retrieve is stored in a byte array as HEX characters representing ASCII characters. Our array is as follows:

```
0x42 0x72 0x79 0x61 0x6E 0x20 0x50 0x6C 0x61 0x73 0x74 0x65 0x72 0x20 0x20
```

This is the way that our "string" comes out of the smart card, and it is up to the host (connected to the CAD) to transform it in to ASCII to make it human readable to print to a printer or screen.

```
Bryan Plaster
```

Below is the code to set a String into the smart card. This method is similar to setting any other smart card variable; it moves through the array one position at a time, taking data from the command APDU and putting it into our name[] array:

```
    private void setName(APDU apdu) {

        // verify authentication
        if (!pin.isValidated()) {
            ISOException.throwIt(SW_PIN_VERIFICATION_REQUIRED);

        }
        byte[] buffer = apdu.getBuffer();

        // get the number of bytes of data from the command APDU
        byte numBytes = buffer[ISO7816.OFFSET_LC];
```

914

```
    // get the data
    byte byteRead = (byte) (apdu.setIncomingAndReceive());

    // error if the number of data bytes
    // or the bytes read is not 1
    if ((numBytes < 1) || (byteRead < 1)) {
        ISOException.throwIt(ISO7816.SW_WRONG_LENGTH);

        // set the data into the name array
    }
    for (byte i = 0; i < numBytes; i++) {
        name[i] = (byte) buffer[ISO7816.OFFSET_CDATA + i];
    }
}
```

Getting the name back from the smart card is simple as well. The trick here is to run through the name[] byte array and copy everything into the buffer[] APDU array, then send it to the response APDU with the apdu.sendBytesLong() method:

```
private void getName(APDU apdu) {

    // verify authentication
    if (!pin.isValidated()) {
        ISOException.throwIt(SW_PIN_VERIFICATION_REQUIRED);
    }
    byte[] buffer = apdu.getBuffer();

    short le = apdu.setOutgoing();

    apdu.setOutgoingLength((short) (name.length));

    for (byte i = 0; i < (byte) (name.length - 1); i++) {
        buffer[i] = (byte) name[i];
    }

    apdu.sendBytesLong(name, (short) 0, (short) (name.length));
}
}
```

Next, we need to compile the code with the −g option (debug mode). This will be very important in subsequent steps because when we run the converter, it determines the local variable types by checking the LocalVariableTable attribute within the class file, which is not included unless this option is specified:

c:\wrox\loyalty>**javac −g -classpath c:\javacard\jc211\bin\api21.jar loyalty.java**

Note that you may have to restart your command window if you set the classpath independently of these commands.

After compiling the code, we'll run the converter as soon as we have our .opt file in place. The .opt file instructs the converter what to do. Let's now look at the loyalty.opt file that is used by the converter to transfer the Application Identifier (AID) to the Java Card applet before installing onto the card. This sets the AID for the applet on the card, and creates the executable files that are actually run in the Java Card Virtual Machine.

Here are the contents of the `loyalty.opt` file. We have to create this file in our simulation environment. This file should be located at `c:\wrox`:

```
-out EXP JCA CAP
-exportpath c:\javacard\jc211\api21
-applet 0xa0:0x0:0x0:0x0:0x62:0x3:0x1:0xc:0x9:0x1 loyalty
loyalty 0xa0:0x0:0x0:0x0:0x62:0x3:0x1:0xc:0x9 1.0
```

.opt file contents	Description
-out	What files to output
-exportpath	Where the libraries are
-applet	AID classname

arguments for -applet
package_name package_AID major version.minor version

And here is the command we use to run the converter:

```
c:\wrox>c:\javacard\jc211\bin\converter -config loyalty.opt
```

This creates three files, as per the instructions in the `loyalty.opt` file. The installer needs to be able to find these files in the directory structure, and it will place them in a sub-directory of `loyalty`, called `javacard`.

❑ `loyalty.cap` – this is the converted applet file. This is similar to a `.jar` file, as it is an executable binary representation of the package.

❑ `loyalty.exp` – this is the export file that is a header type file for the applet. It can be used to expose the internal implementation details to other vendors, and to the smart card simulators. It does not contain bytecodes.

❑ `loyalty.jca` – this is a Java Card assembly file, which can be used to help the developer debug his or her application.

Next we need to create the `loyalty.app` file. This is called from the simulator to emulate a CAD. This file has an AID for each applet that this CAD will be utilizing. The contents of our file are:

```
// applet AID
// the installer applet
com.sun.javacard.installer.InstallerApplet
    0xa0:0x0:0x0:0x0:0x62:0x3:0x1:0x8:0x1
// the wrox applet
loyalty.loyalty        0xa0:0x0:0x0:0x0:0x62:0x3:0x1:0xc:0x9:0x1
```

To start the simulator, emulating the CAD, type the following:

```
c:\wrox>c:\javacard\jc211\bin\jcwde -p 9025 loyalty.app
```

Next we have the `loyalty.scr` script file that will be used to simulate actions taken from a CAD terminal:

```
// Select all installed Applets

powerup;

// Select the installer applet
0x00 0xA4 0x04 0x00 0x09 0xa0 0x00 0x00 0x00 0x62 0x03 0x01 0x08 0x01 0x7F;
// 90 00 = SW_NO_ERROR

// begin installer command
0x80 0xB0 0x00 0x00 0x00 0x7F;

// instantiate a loyalty applet
// apdu data contain the applet AID followed by the initial owner PIN
0x80 0xB8 0x00 0x00 0x11 0x0a 0xa0 0x0 0x0 0x0 0x62 0x3 0x1 0xc 0x9 0x1 0x05 0x01
0x02 0x03 0x04 0x05 0x7F;

// end installer command
0x80 0xBA 0x00 0x00 0x00 0x7F;


// Initialize loyalty

//Select loyalty
0x00 0xA4 0x04 0x00 0x0a 0xa0 0x0 0x0 0x0 0x62 0x3 0x1 0xc 0x9 0x1 0x7F;
// 90 00 = SW_NO_ERROR

//Verify user pin
0xB0 0x50 0x00 0x00 0x05 0x01 0x02 0x03 0x04 0x05 0x7F;
//90 00 = SW_NO_ERROR

//set name to card
0xB0 0x70 0x00 0x00 0x0F 0x42 0x72 0x79 0x61 0x6E 0x20 0x50 0x6C 0x61 0x73 0x74
0x65 0x72 0x20 0x20 0x7F;
//0x00 0x00 0x00 0x00 0x90 0x00 = set the name to Bryan Plaster

//Get loyalty total Credits
0xB0 0x20 0x00 0x00 0x00 0x02;
//0x00 0x00 0x00 0x00 0x90 0x00 = total Credits = 0 and SW_NO_ERROR

//Credit $100 to the empty account
0xB0 0x10 0x00 0x00 0x01 0x64 0x7F;
//0x9000 = SW_NO_ERROR

//Get total Credits
0xB0 0x20 0x00 0x00 0x00 0x02;
//0x00 0x0 0x9000 = total Credits =0 and SW_NO_ERROR

//get name from card
0xB0 0x80 0x00 0x00 0x00 0x0F;
//42, 72, 79, 61, 6e, 20, 50, 6c, 61, 73, 74, 65, 72, 20, 20, SW1: 90, SW2: 00
//name is Bryan Plaster  - what we just put in

//Credit $56 to the account
```

```
0xB0 0x10 0x00 0x00 0x01 0x38 0x7F;
//0x9000 = SW_NO_ERROR

//Get total Credits
0xB0 0x20 0x00 0x00 0x00 0x02;
//0x00 0x9c 0x9000 = total Credits =156 and SW_NO_ERROR

//half
0xB0 0x40 0x00 0x00 0x01 0x0 0x7F;
//0x9000 = SW_NO_ERROR

//Get total Credits
0xB0 0x20 0x00 0x00 0x00 0x02;
//0x00 0x64 0x9000 = total Credits =78 and SW_NO_ERROR

//double
0xB0 0x30 0x00 0x00 0x01 0x0 0x7F;
//0x9000 = SW_NO_ERROR

//Get total Credits
0xB0 0x20 0x00 0x00 0x00 0x02;
//0x00 0x9c 0x9000 = total Credits =156 and SW_NO_ERROR

//Reselect loyalty applet so that userpin is reset
0x00 0xA4 0x04 0x00 0x0a 0xa0 0x0 0x0 0x0 0x62 0x3 0x1 0xc 0x9 0x1 0x7F;
// 90 00 = SW_NO_ERROR

//Credit $55 to the account before pin verification
0xB0 0x10 0x00 0x00 0x01 0x37 0x7F;
//0x6301 = SW_PIN_VERIFICATION_REQUIRED

//Get total Credits
0xB0 0x20 0x00 0x00 0x00 0x02;
//0x00 0x9c 0x9000 = total Credits =156 and SW_NO_ERROR

// *** SCRIPT END ***
powerdown;
```

This is run, in a new command window, with the apdutool and produces an output file that tells what happened. The apdutool is the part of the simulator that simulates actual interaction from the smart card to the CAD in a full session (defined by the .scr file) and creates the specified .scr.out file with all of the response ADPUs:

> c:\wrox>**c:\javacard\jc211\bin\apdutool loyalty.scr > loyalty.scr.out**

In the loyalty.scr, we tried to estimate what would happen. Below is the output file. It should match line for line the .scr file. Notice that the error codes. SW1: 90 SW2: 00 means success in our examples:

```
Java Card 2.1.1 ApduTool (version 1.1)
Copyright (c) 2000 Sun Microsystems, Inc. All rights reserved.
Opening connection to localhost on port 9,025.
Connected.
CLA: 00, INS: a4, P1: 04, P2: 00, Lc: 09, a0, 00, 00, 00, 62, 03, 01, 08, 01, Le:
```

```
00, SW1: 90, SW2: 00
CLA: 80, INS: b0, P1: 00, P2: 00, Lc: 00, Le: 00, SW1: 90, SW2: 00
CLA: 80, INS: b8, P1: 00, P2: 00, Lc: 11, 0a, a0, 00, 00, 00, 62, 03, 01, 0c, 09,
01, 05, 01, 02, 03, 04, 05, Le: 0a, a0, 00, 00, 00, 62, 03, 01, 0c, 09, 01, SW1:
90, SW2: 00
CLA: 80, INS: ba, P1: 00, P2: 00, Lc: 00, Le: 00, SW1: 90, SW2: 00
CLA: 00, INS: a4, P1: 04, P2: 00, Lc: 0a, a0, 00, 00, 00, 62, 03, 01, 0c, 09, 01,
Le: 00, SW1: 90, SW2: 00
CLA: b0, INS: 50, P1: 00, P2: 00, Lc: 05, 01, 02, 03, 04, 05, Le: 00, SW1: 90,
SW2: 00
CLA: b0, INS: 70, P1: 00, P2: 00, Lc: 0f, 42, 72, 79, 61, 6e, 20, 50, 6c, 61, 73,
74, 65, 72, 20, 20, Le: 00, SW1: 90, SW2: 00
CLA: b0, INS: 20, P1: 00, P2: 00, Lc: 00, Le: 02, 00, 00, SW1: 90, SW2: 00
CLA: b0, INS: 10, P1: 00, P2: 00, Lc: 01, 64, Le: 00, SW1: 90, SW2: 00
CLA: b0, INS: 20, P1: 00, P2: 00, Lc: 00, Le: 02, 00, 64, SW1: 90, SW2: 00
CLA: b0, INS: 80, P1: 00, P2: 00, Lc: 00, Le: 0f, 42, 72, 79, 61, 6e, 20, 50, 6c,
61, 73, 74, 65, 72, 20, 20, SW1: 90, SW2: 00
CLA: b0, INS: 10, P1: 00, P2: 00, Lc: 01, 38, Le: 00, SW1: 90, SW2: 00
CLA: b0, INS: 20, P1: 00, P2: 00, Lc: 00, Le: 02, 00, 9c, SW1: 90, SW2: 00
CLA: b0, INS: 40, P1: 00, P2: 00, Lc: 01, 00, Le: 00, SW1: 90, SW2: 00
CLA: b0, INS: 20, P1: 00, P2: 00, Lc: 00, Le: 02, 00, 4e, SW1: 90, SW2: 00
CLA: b0, INS: 30, P1: 00, P2: 00, Lc: 01, 00, Le: 00, SW1: 90, SW2: 00
CLA: b0, INS: 20, P1: 00, P2: 00, Lc: 00, Le: 02, 00, 9c, SW1: 90, SW2: 00
CLA: 00, INS: a4, P1: 04, P2: 00, Lc: 0a, a0, 00, 00, 00, 62, 03, 01, 0c, 09, 01,
Le: 00, SW1: 90, SW2: 00
CLA: b0, INS: 10, P1: 00, P2: 00, Lc: 01, 37, Le: 00, SW1: 63, SW2: 01
CLA: b0, INS: 20, P1: 00, P2: 00, Lc: 00, Le: 02, 00, 9c, SW1: 90, SW2: 00
```

Notice the line towards the bottom that corresponds to the SCR file where we deselected the applet, which erased the PIN from memory, then tried to add credits into the card:

```
CLA: b0, INS: 10, P1: 00, P2: 00, Lc: 01, 37, Le: 00, SW1: 63, SW2: 01
```

Looking at the sample code, the JCRE throws the following error in the credit method:

```
if (!pin.isValidated())
    ISOException.throwIt(SW_PIN_VERIFICATION_REQUIRED);
```

The PIN is not validated because we deselected the applet.

The error that was thrown corresponds to our static variable:

```
final static short SW_PIN_VERIFICATION_REQUIRED = 0x6301;
```

Also notice the INS code, because comparing it to the code, we can figure out which method was run.

Summary

In this chapter, we have discussed smart card uses in general, from barriers to success, to authentication, to creating a personal experience for users of smart cards. We then took a brief tour of the smart cards architecture and ended up with a simple programming example utilizing the Smart Card Simulator.

Java Card technology is the driver for smart card acceptance all over the world. The need for strong authentication in our digital and cashless society will only increase the need for smart cards, a mature technology that finally got a break with Java.

We looked at the following things:

❑ Why we should use smart cards

❑ The hardware architecture of smart cards

❑ Java Card Technology from Sun Microsystems

❑ A programming example using the Java Card 2.1.1 Development Kit from Sun Microsystems

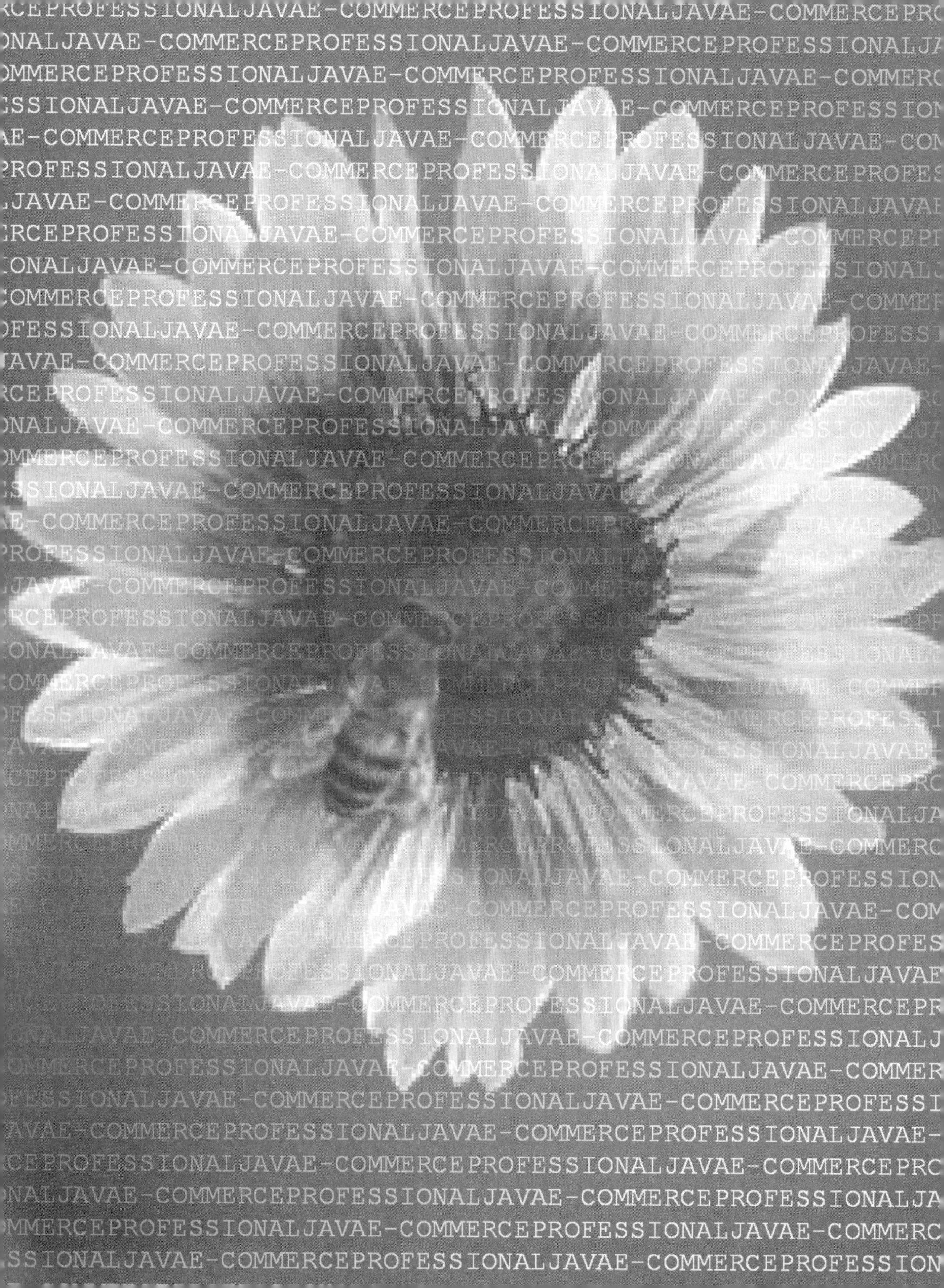
PROFESSIONAL JAVA E-COMMERCE

Section 6

Appendices

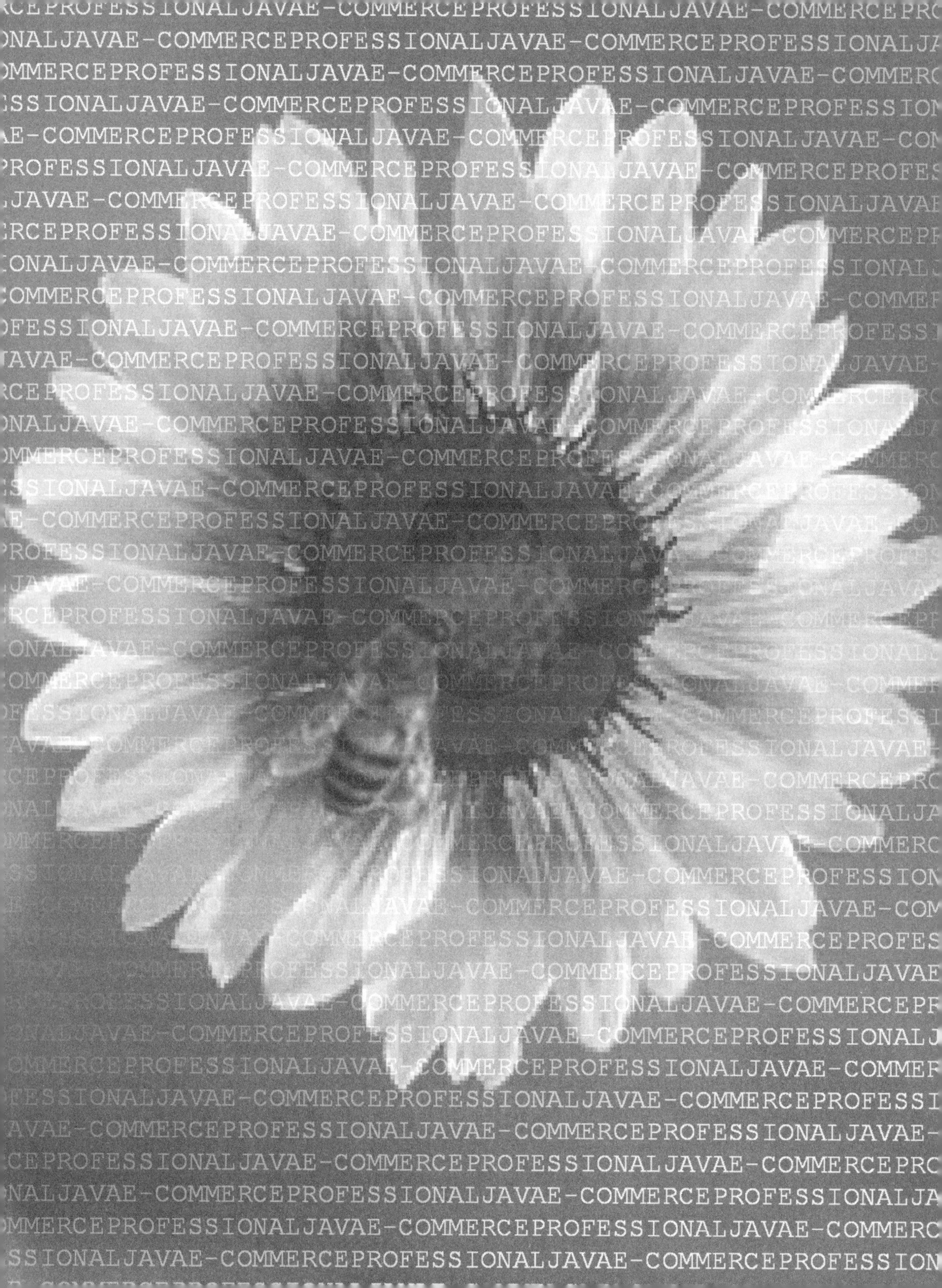
PROFESSIONALJAVAE-COMMERCE

XML Primer

It's ironic how, as **markup languages** are opening up vast new opportunities for computing, computer programs are spelling the end of the original markup language; I refer to the notation and symbols that newspaper editors used to scribble on their reporters' news copy to let the lads in the composing room know how to print and display the stories properly. That work is all done now with sophisticated editing programs that don't get ink on anyone.

Today's markup languages are a far cry from those city desk scribbles, and the information is transmitted by a browser to a network server instead of being handed to a hot-lead typesetter by an inky-fingered copy clerk, but the general goal hasn't really changed. Markup languages are to give meaning to the information, and to provide instructions on how that information should be processed and presented. In other words, markup languages are about encoding (marking up) data with information about itself. They follow specific standards about what the encoding data is, and what it means.

Word processors can use markup to specify formatting and layout of documents, communications programs make use of it to express the meaning of data sent over the wires, database applications can use markup when they must associate meaning and relationships with the data they serve, and multimedia processing programs can make use of it to express **meta-data** (data which defines or encapsulates other data) about images or sound.

There are three main parts to this primer:

❏ In the first part, we will create a simple **XML** (**eXtensible Markup Language**) document. We will learn from that document the syntax rules for writing **well-formed** XML documents. We will also examine the two main parts of an XML document, the **prolog** and the **body**, and see what belongs in each. This means we will look at the essential building blocks of XML, **elements** and their **attributes**.

❏ Secondly, we will also spend some time examining the concept of a **Document Type Definition (DTD)**, and its role in establishing the rules of grammar for our XML document. We will look briefly at the concept of **XML Schemas**, which are rapidly replacing DTDs, although an in-depth examination of XML schemas is beyond the scope of this primer. After this, we will then create a list of the document's elements and attributes, supplying them with the information that our XML document needs.

❏ Finally, we'll wrap up this XML primer with a discussion about how specific industries are creating their own standard approaches to XML, and how this approach is turning XML into the same type of universal resource that **HTML** (**HyperText Markup Language**) has become.

What is XML?

Since you are reading this to learn about XML, it is safe to assume you already know about HTML. Both of these arise from a **meta language** (a language from which other languages are created) called **Standard Generalized Markup Language**, or **SGML** for short. But their relationships to SGML are quite different. HTML is one of the specific languages that can be written from the SGML specifications. XML, on the other hand, is actually a boiled down version of SGML. Whereas the official specifications for the huge and complicated SGML run to more than 150 pages, XML specifications are only 35 pages or so. Its creators originally designed it for web applications, omitting all the SGML details that aren't needed. So XML is also a meta language; in fact every time you write an XML document and your own definition of its tags, you are creating a brand new language.

The design goals for XML (taken from *Extensible Markup Language (XML) 1.0 Specs, The Annotated Version*) are:

❏ XML shall be straightforwardly usable over the Internet

❏ XML shall support a wide variety of applications

❏ XML shall be compatible with SGML

❏ It shall be easy to write programs that process XML documents

❏ The number of optional features in XML is to be kept to the absolute minimum, ideally zero

❏ XML documents should be human-legible and reasonably clear

❏ The XML design should be prepared quickly

❏ The design of XML shall be formal and concise

❏ XML documents shall be easy to create

❏ Terseness in XML markup is of minimal importance

Although originally developed for the Internet, XML is certainly not limited to use in web development. The World Wide Web Consortium (W3C), which has approved the specifications for XML, calls it "a common syntax for expressing structure in data". It is particularly useful for those who produce documents that have to appear across multiple media.

Our First XML Document

Before we can understand what an XML document looks like, we need to define the building blocks of such a document: the **elements** and the **attributes**.

Elements

Elements are the basic units of XML content. Syntactically, an element consists of a start tag, and an end tag, and everything in between. Consider the following example element:

```
<name>Jesse James</name>
```

The start tag is of an element is written with the name of the element between the less-than sign (<) and the greater-than sign (>), sometimes called angle-brackets; in our example the start tag is <name>. The end tag is written the same, with the addition of a slash (/) before the name; the end tag in our example is </name>. XML defines the text between the start and end tags (in our example element this would be "Jesse James") to be "**character data**" (**CDATA**) and the text within the tags themselves (in our example element, this would be "name" and "/name") to be "markup". Character data may be any legal (**Unicode**) character with the exception of "<". The "<" character is reserved for the start of a tag. XML also provides **entity references** that you can use in the place of several characters, so as not to create any doubt whether you are specifying character data or markup:

Character	Entity Reference
>	>
<	<
&	&
"	"
'	'

Note that each entity reference is made up of a series of letters between an ampersand (&) and a semicolon (;). These entity references can be used within markup in cases where there could be confusion, such as the following:

```
<statement value = "Quoth the raven, "Nevermore!"">
```

Because the parser (the program that processes XML documents) would see the second quotation mark as the end of the text, this should be written as:

```
<statement value = "Quoth the raven, &quot;Nevermore!&quot;">
```

Tags make up the bulk of XML markup. A tag is pretty much anything between a < sign and a > sign that is not inside a comment, or a CDATA section (we'll discuss these in a bit). In short, it is essentially the same structure as an HTML tag. The rules governing tags are a little more complex than those governing character data. Let's take a look at the most significant of them.

927

❏ Every XML document must include at least one root element to be well-formed. The root element must follow the prolog (XML declaration plus any DTD or XML Schema that we are using) and it must be a nonempty tag that encompasses the entire document.

❏ Care must be taken to ensure that case is maintained within a tag set. For example the tags `<TEXT>` and `<text>` would not be equivalent, even though they would be in HTML.

❏ In addition to being spelled and capitalized the same as the matching start tag, end tags will usually include a forward slash (/). For example a start tag of `<size>` will have a matching end tag of `</size>`. An exception is the tag for an empty element, which is one that contains no text or child elements. In this case, only one tag is needed, and it will include a forward slash (/) just before the closing bracket. For example, the tag `<size width="12"/>` is considered an empty element because it does not contain any text to be displayed by our document, although it does include an attribute, a term which we will define shortly.

❏ Tags must be named legally. That is, they should begin with either a letter, an underscore (_) or a colon (:) followed by some combination of letters, numbers, periods (.), colons, underscores, or hyphens but no white space, with the exception that no tags should begin with any form of the letters "xml". It is also a good idea not to use colons as the first character in a tag name even though it is legal. Using a colon first can be confusing. Although the XML standard specifies that names can be of any length, actual XML processors may limit the length of markup names.

Attributes

Many tags within an XML document will contain supporting attributes, such as the `value` attribute in one of the examples we looked at earlier:

```
<statement value = "Quoth the raven, &quot;Nevermore!&quot;">
```

Attributes add descriptive information to an element. Attributes appear within an element's start tag, after the name of the element, and before the less-than sign. If there is more than one attribute, they will be separated by a white space. An attribute will specify a name-value pair, delimited by an equal sign (=). Unlike an attribute in HTML, the value of an attribute in an XML tag must always be enclosed in quotation marks. There may not be duplicates of any attributes within any one tag. Attribute names follow the same conventions as tag names (valid characters, case sensitivity, etc). Attribute values, on the other hand, may include white spaces, punctuation and may include entity references when necessary. We'll be looking more closely at attributes as we work our way through the document.

So how do we know whether information about an element should be an attribute, or whether it should be another element nested within the original one? In many cases, the answer is personal preference. For example, the above `<statement>` example that contains a `value` attribute could be written with a `<text>` sub-element instead:

```
<statement>
  <text>Quoth the raven, &quot;Nevermore!&quot;</text>
</statement>
```

In general practice, if we're dealing with text to be displayed, we will place it within a sub-element. But for structure-related information such as a line number or a font size, or for cases where the information will come from a call to a database, it's usually considered better to place it in attributes.

Remembering our earlier comment about every new XML document being the creation of a new language, let's create our own new markup language called CLML (Contact List Markup Language). This language will define tags to represent contact and information about those people. The first thing we notice is that it looks much like HTML, except that the meanings of the XML tags can be immediately understood just from their names:

```xml
<?xml version="1.0">
<contactlist>
    <contact>
        <name>Adam Janes</name>
        <id>201</id>
        <company>Janes' Wheelbarrows</company>
        <email>adam@barroworld.com</email>
        <phone>678-9999</phone>
        <address>
            <street>123 Main St.</street>
            <city>Newton</city>
            <state>New York</state>
            <zipcode>10027</zipcode>
        </address>
    </contact>
    <contact>
        <name>Sandra Blesing</name>
        <id>202</id>
        <company>Blesing and Kerse Shoes</company>
        <email>sandyshoes@netscape.net</email>
        <phone>543-2109</phone>
        <address>
            <street>9876 Wider Rd.</street>
            <city>San Jose</city>
            <state>California</state>
            <zipcode>90044</zipcode>
        </address>
    </contact>
</contactlist>
```

Remember, it's not enough to simply encode (markup) the data. If we want the data to be decoded by someone or something else, the encoding markup languages need to follow standard rules that clearly define the syntax for marking up, and the meaning behind the markup. In other words, a processing application needs to know what a **valid** markup is (such as a tag) and what to do with it if it is valid.

For instance, how would a browser such as Internet Explorer or Netscape know what to do with the contact document we created above? What in the world is a `<zipcode>` tag? Is it a legal tag? How will our document display it? Our markup language needs a way to communicate the syntax of the markup so that the processing application will know what to do with it. The part of a processing application that assesses and interprets XML documents is known as a parser. It extracts the actual data out of the XML document's textual representation and creates either events or new data structures from them. Parsers also check whether documents conform to the XML standard and have a correct structure. This is essential for the automatic processing of XML documents. There will be more on this subject in an upcoming section on DTDs.

Syntax

In many ways, correct syntax is more important in XML than in HTML. In fact, you will find XML is very precise. If the syntax isn't exactly right, the parser will stop processing it and nothing (except an error message) will be displayed. In contrast, most browsers will accept a missing tag at the beginning of an HTML document. This is because browsers usually (but not always) skip content that they don't understand. XML parsers however, whether they are embedded in a browser or acting as a stand-alone processor, are explicitly not allowed to recover from invalid markup. Much like compiling a program in Java or C++, an XML file is either correct, or it simply won't work.

In order to work, an XML document must be well formed. In other words, it must follow the syntax rules that make it an XML document. In this section, we'll deal with what it means to be well-formed. There are three basic rules for creating a well-formed XML document:

1. It must match the definition of an XML document.

This means that it must contain only one root element, known as a document element, and that all other elements are nested properly. In our example above, the root element is `<contactlist>`. All other elements are nested within that root. It is important to remember that, unlike HTML, XML won't forgive us for improperly nested tags. For example, the following would make the parser fail because the `</zipcode>` tag is improperly placed outside the `</address>` closing tag:

```
<address>
    <street>9876 Wider Rd.</street>
    <city>San Jose</city>
    <state>California</state>
    <zipcode>90044</address></zipcode>
```

XML also won't forgive us for omitting tags that in HTML are often deemed unnecessary. For example, few HTML developers ever use the `</p>` tag. It's considered unnecessary, even though it's technically improper to leave it out. The browser can handle that omission just fine. But in XML, every start tag must have a matching end tag. There is what appears to be an exception to that rule, in the case of an element that has no text or sub-elements. Such an empty element is defined with its tag having a slash (/) just before the closing angle-brace:

```
<tagname />
```

Now, there's something you won't find in HTML!

2. It must observe the constraints that are defined by the XML specifications. These constraints spell out, for example, which characters can be legally used in various contexts.

3. Any parsed entities referenced in the document must be well-formed. This is necessary because any entities that are referenced become part of the document once it is parsed. The parser simply won't accept them if they are not well formed.

Prolog

An XML document is composed of two basic parts. The first part is called the **prolog**, which includes the XML declaration and the rest of the processing instructions as well as the DTD, if there is one. Processing instructions refer to information about our document, which is provided to the application that will process the document. The bulk of the document is made up of the **body**, which includes the elements and their attributes, which we discussed earlier, and comments. The prolog in our example is as basic as we can get:

```
<?xml version="1.0"?>
```

It is always a good idea to include the XML declaration as the very first line of the document, even though the **W3C** specification says the declaration is optional. Essentially, the XML declaration is a processing instruction that notifies the processing agent that the following document has been marked up as an XML document. All XML processing instructions, including the declaration, begin with <? and end with ?>. After the initial <? you will find the name of the processing instruction, which in this case is "xml". The XML processing instruction requires that you specify a version attribute. It also allows you to specify optional standalone and encoding attributes. If added to our example's declaration, they would look like this:

```
<?xml version = "1.0" standalone = "yes" encoding = "UTF-8"?>
```

The standalone attribute specifies whether the document has any markup declarations that are defined in a separate document. Thus, if standalone is set to "yes", all the markup declarations will be contained within the document. Setting it to "no" means the document may or may not access an external document such as a DTD or an XML Schema. .

All XML parsers must support 8-bit and 16-bit Unicode encoding corresponding to ASCII. But, although you will rarely need it, XML parsers may support a larger character set. You can get a list of the available coding types from section 4.3.3 of the *XML Specification*, which can be found at http://www.w3.org/TR/2000/REC-xml-20001006#charencoding.

Comments

Sometimes you will want to include data in your document that you want the XML processor to ignore (not display at all). This type of text is called comment text; and it's written in exactly the same way as in HTML. For example, the familiar HTML comment:

```
<!-- hide from old browsers -->
```

is also a valid XML comment. There are a few rules to keep in mind. You must not have "-" or "--" within the text of your comment because it might be confusing to the XML processor. Also, you can't place a comment inside a tag. This means the following code would be poorly-formed XML:

```
<name <!--The name --> >John Smith</name>
```

In addition, a comment must never be placed inside an entity declaration or before the XML declaration that is the first line in any XML document.

Comments can be used to comment out tag sets, or blocks of tag sets. In the following example, all the names will be ignored except for Oliver Goldsmith:

```
<!-- don't show these
<name>John Keats</name>
<name>Percy Shelley</name>
<name>Lord Byron</name>
-->
<name>Oliver Goldsmith</name>
```

Don't forget, if you do comment out blocks of tags, you need to make sure that the remaining XML is well-formed. Also, comments cannot be nested, so if you use a comment to block out several tags, make sure there are no comments within the block.

Document Type Definition

We have already looked at the process of creating a well-formed XML document, now it's time to consider how to make sure the markup in the document is valid. In XML, the definition of a valid markup is handled by, either a Document Type Definition (DTD), or an XML Schema to communicate the structure of the markup language. The DTD specifies what it means to be a valid tag (the syntax for marking up). You can think of the DTD as defining the overall structure and syntax of the document. The DTD is in fact the meat of the "**meta-markup**" concept. It defines the grammar and vocabulary of a markup language; everything a parser needs to know in order to interpret a well-formed XML document. This "specification" can be as simple as listing all the valid elements (such as elements, tags, attributes, entities) that an XML document may contain, or it can be as complex as specifying relationships among those elements. Is a DTD an essential part of an XML document? No. It would not be needed, for example, if the application uses the document to generate data directly from a database. But most authoring environments need to refer to a DTD so they can follow the content model of the document. A DTD will also be needed if any of the elements in the document have attributes that rely on default values.

XML Schemas

DTDs have many limitations that can be overcome by using an XML Schema instead. In fact, XML Schemas will eventually replace DTDs altogether. For one thing, unlike DTDs, which are written in a language all their own, Schemas are written in XML, so the programmer doesn't need to learn a separate language. In addition, XML Schemas are capable of expressing a much richer and more accurate set of datatypes. Those datatypes include Booleans and numbers, as well as dates and times, and currencies. These are especially important types for e-commerce applications. XML Schemas are an emerging development not supported by all browsers. Make sure yours does before you try to use them. Although this tutorial doesn't address XML Schemas to any extent, you can get more information about them at http://www.w3.org/XML/Schema.

You would also benefit from a visit to http://www.biztalk.org. Biztalk is an organization of many of the largest companies in the IT industry (does the name Microsoft ring a bell?) and a wide range of industry related organizations, which are promoting the rapid adoption of XML for e-commerce applications. One of the organization's projects is the Biztalk Framework, which is a set of guidelines for publishing XML Schemas, and how to use XML messages for integrating software programs. Biztalk has a library of schemas you can look at and even download for your own use. And it also encourages you to submit your own schemas for others to use.

Building DTDs

As we mentioned earlier, all documents are made up of a prolog and a body. The document prolog contains the XML Declaration and the document body contains the actual marked up document. As mentioned earlier, if our document has a DTD, the prolog also holds the DTD, either as a reference to a separate document, or including the DTD in its entirety in the prolog, just after the XML processing instruction. If we include the DTD for our contact list example within the prolog, its structure would look something like this:

```
<?xml version = "1.0" encoding="UTF-8" standalone = "yes"?>
<!DOCTYPE contactlist [
        (element definitions go here)
        ]>
(document body goes here...)
```

As you can see, the DTD begins with <!DOCTYPE followed by the name of our XML document's root element, followed by a pair of square brackets and ending with the mandatory greater-than sign (>). Within those square brackets we define the elements for our document, using **Element Type Declarations** (**ETDs**). ETDs specify the name of each element of the document, and whether those elements may have any children (content specification). Elements may have several types of children ranging from none, to text, to other elements, to other elements with their own children, to any combination of the above. For example, to show that the root element of our `contactlist` document may contain any combination of the various types of children, its ETD would look like this:

```
<!ELEMENT contactlist ANY>
```

This defines an XML document that contains a single root element named `contactlist`, which may contain `ANY` type of child, including **parsed character data** (#PCDATA) or other elements. #PCDATA simply refers to text after any markup within it has been processed by the parser. That's in contrast to CDATA, which is also text (character data), but which may contain markup characters. You will see the ANY specification used only with the root element, because it is considered poor form to use it anywhere else. If we wanted to specify that there must not be any children in the element, our specification would be EMPTY. Alternatively, our content specification can be what is known as the **Element Content Model** (**ECM**), a bracket-enclosed list of all the element's children (For an example of an EDT, see the EDTs for the contact and address elements in the following code). For an XML document to be valid, its DTD must define all of its elements:

```
<?xml version="1.0">
<!DOCTYPE contactlist [
    <!ELEMENT contactlist ANY>
    <!ELEMENT contact (name, id, company, email, phone, address)>
    <!ELEMENT name (#PCDATA)>
    <!ELEMENT id (#PCDATA>
    <!ELEMENT company (#PCDATA)>
    <!ELEMENT email (#PCDATA)>
    <!ELEMENT  phone(#PCDATA)>
    <!ELEMENT address (street, city, state, zipcode)>
    <!ELEMENT street (#PCDATA)>
    <!ELEMENT city (#PCDATA)>
    <!ELEMENT state (#PCDATA)>
    <!ELEMENT zipcode (#PCDATA)>
]>
<contactlist>
```

```
<contact>
     <name>Adam Janes</name>
     <id>201</id>
     <company>Janes' Wheelbarrows</company>
     <email>adam@barroworld.com</email>
     <phone>678-9999</phone>
     <address>
          <street>123 Main St.</street>
          <city>Newton</city>
          <state>New York</state>
          <zipcode>10027</zipcode>
     </address>
</contact>
<contact>
     <name>Sandra Blesing</name>
     <id>202</id>
     <company>Blesing and Kerse Shoes</company>
     <email>sandyshoes@netscape.net</email>
     <phone>543-2109</phone>
     <address>
          <street>9876 Wider Rd.</street>
          <city>San Jose</city>
          <state>California</state>
          <zipcode>90044</zipcode>
     </address>
</contact>
</contactlist>
```

In our example, we have defined an XML document with a single root element named `contactlist`. Because its specification is ANY, this element may contain parsed character data or child elements, although in reality it contains only the child element contact. The contact element is defined as having the child elements name, id, company, email, phone, and address. Most of these child elements contain only parsed character data (#PCDATA), although address contains child elements of its own. The order in which you specify ETDs does not matter. This means that:

```
<!ELEMENT name (#PCDATA)>
<!ELEMENT contactlist ANY>
<!ELEMENT contact (name, id, company, email, phone, address)>
```

works just as well as

```
<!ELEMENT contactlist ANY>
<!ELEMENT contact (name, id, company, email, phone, address)>
<!ELEMENT name (#PCDATA)>
```

In the case of the contact element, by including each of the six child elements in the ETD, we have made them compulsory; we will get an error if any of them do not appear in our XML document. In addition, by inserting a comma between them, we are requiring them to appear in the specific order in which they are listed. If they were delimited by spaces, they could appear in any order and still be valid. This is an example of how ETDs give us the flexibility of specifying exactly what each element can contain. Using pattern matching characters as we will see in the upcoming list, ETDs allow us to specify such relationships as whether an element may contain a child, one or more children, zero or more children, or at least one child.

Character	Meaning
+	One or more occurrence
*	Zero or more occurrences
?	Zero or one occurrences
( )	A group of expressions to be matched together
|	OR...as in, "this or that"
,	Strictly ordered

Examples

Let's look at a few examples. The following DTD snippet:

```
<!ELEMENT contact (name email)>
<!ELEMENT name (#PCDATA)>
<!ELEMENT email (#PCDATA)>
```

would allow our XML document to look like this:

```
<contact>
   <name>Adam Janes</name>
   <email>adam@barroworld.com</email>
 <contact>
```

or like this:

```
<contact>
 <email>adam@barroworld.com</email>
 <name>Adam Janes</name>
 <contact>
```

But if we had used a comma to separate the list in the contact EDT, we would have forced an order by which the name element would need to appear before the email element. Now, let's change the DTD snippet by adding a plus sign (+) after email:

```
<!ELEMENT contact (name email+)>
<!ELEMENT name (#PCDATA)>
<!ELEMENT email (#PCDATA)>
```

This will allow our XML document to include more than one email element:

```
<contact>
   <name>Adam Janes</name>
   <email>adam@barroworld.com</email>
   <email>adamj@yahoo.com</email>
   <email>adamjanes@netscape.net</email>
 <contact>
```

935

Alternately writing our contact EDT with a "*" after email:

```
<!ELEMENT contact (name email*)>
<!ELEMENT name (#PCDATA)>
<!ELEMENT email (#PCDATA)>
```

would allow us the option of including a contact who didn't happen to have an e-mail address. We could achieve almost the same thing by using "?" instead of "*", except that the "?" would limit us to only one e-mail address.

The pipe character "|" is used to specify an "OR" operation, which means you must have one or the other, but you can't have both. Thus, the following DTD snippet would specify an XML document in which all contact elements would have a name child followed by either a phone or an email element, but not both:

```
<!ELEMENT contact (name, (phone | email))>
<!ELEMENT name (#PCDATA)>
<!ELEMENT phone (#PCDATA)>
<!ELEMENT email (#PCDATA)>
```

Notice the extra set of brackets in the contact ETD. This is necessary, because within a grouping, you may use only one connector (for example, either a comma or a pipe). This means the following ETD would be invalid:

```
<!ELEMENT contact (name, phone | email)>
```

We also use the DTD to define valid element attributes. Our contactlist document doesn't include any attributes, so let's take a different example. In the following element, style and color are attributes of shirt:

```
<shirt style = "Tee" color = "fuscia"/>
```

Note, it is possible, as we have done in the previous example, to declare multiple attributes in an element. Declaring attributes in the DTD takes the general format of:

```
<!ATTLIST element_name attribute_name TYPE DEFAULT_VALUE>
```

The term element_name refers to the element in which the attribute appears. This would be "shirt" in the example above. The term attribute_name refers to the name of the attribute. Our example has two attributes, "style", and "color". TYPE specifies one of ten valid attribute types, which we will look at shortly. DEFAULT_VALUE specifies the value that is used if the author of the document doesn't specify one. This we will also take a more in-depth look at.

Attribute Types

The ten valid attribute types are as follows:

❑   CDATA

❑   Enumerated

❑   ID

❑   IDREF

- ❏ IDREFS
- ❏ ENTITY
- ❏ ENTITIES
- ❏ NMTOKEN
- ❏ NMTOKENS
- ❏ NOTATION

CDATA simply means that only character data can be used. It can be any string of characters that does not include ampersands (&), less than signs, (<), or quotation marks ("). Of course, as we discussed earlier, you may use the escaped characters such as &, <, or " if you need to include those forbidden characters.

The value of an Enumerated attribute type (and we don't use the word "Enumerated" in our code, we simply use the structure that it refers to, which is the possible attribute values enclosed in brackets, separated by pipes (|)) must match one of the values included in the attribute list. For example, in the declaration:

```
<!ATTLIST shirt style (tee|muscle|longsleeve) "tee"
            color CDATA #REQUIRED>
```

the value of the style attribute would need to be one of the three values in the brackets. In this case, if we were to not provide a value, the default would be "tee", as indicated by that value being placed in quotes following the bracketed list.

ID represents a unique ID name for the attribute to identify the element within the context of the document. IDs are similar to internal links in ordinary HTML. For the most part, ID is used primarily by programs or scripting languages that process the document. The value for ID must be unique within the document, and must be a valid XML name beginning with a letter and containing alphanumeric characters or the underscore character without any whitespace. Closely related to the ID type are the IDREF and IDREFS types, which allow the value or values of attributes to be an element somewhere else in the document. To show you how we would indicate these types in a DTD, let's first look at an XML document that contains the elements and attributes that we need:

```
<?xml version="1.0">
<!DOCTYPE workschedule SYSTEM "workschedule.dtd">
    <workschedule>
        <jobs>
            <data:job id="Boston1">
                <title>Paint Henry Factory</title>
                <ref:supervisor ref="Spt1"/>
                <employees>
                    <ref:employee ref="Painter1"/>
                    <ref:employee ref="Painter2"/>
                    <ref:employee ref="Painter3"/>
                    <ref:employee ref="Carpenter1"/>
                </employees>
            </data:job>
            <data:job id="Boston2">
                <title>Demolish Henry Watertower</title>
                <ref:supervisor ref="Spt1"/>
                <ref:supervisor ref="Spt2"/>
                <employees>
```

```xml
                    <ref:employee ref="Wrecker1"/>
                    <ref:employee ref="Wrecker2"/>
                </employees>
            </data:job>
        </jobs>
    <supervisors>
        <data:supervisor id="Spt1">
            <name>Abel Anderson</name>
            <jobs>
                <ref:job ref="Boston1"/>
                <ref:job ref="Boston2"/>
            </jobs>
        </data:supervisor>
        <data:supervisor id="Spt2">
            <name>Bernard Brown</name>
            <jobs>
                <ref:job ref="Boston2"/>
            </jobs>
        </data:supervisor>
    </supervisors>
    <employees>
        <data:employee id="Painter1">
            <name>Colin Cole</name>
            <jobs>
                <ref:job ref="Boston1"/>
                <ref:job ref="Boston2"/>
            </jobs>
        </data:employee>
        <data:employee id="Painter2">
            <name>Dale Dean</name>
            <jobs>
                <ref:job ref="Boston1"/>
            </jobs>
        </data:employee>
        <data:employee id="Painter3">
            <name>Evan Elms</name>
            <jobs>
                <ref:job ref="Boston1"/>
            </jobs>
        </data:employee>
        <data:employee id="Carpenter1">
            <name>Fred Foley</name>
            <jobs>
                <ref:job ref="Boston1"/>
                <ref:job ref="Boston2"/>
            </jobs>
        </data:employee>
        <data:employee id="Wrecker1">
            <name>Gavin Garey</name>
            <jobs>
                <ref:job ref="Boston2"/>
```

```
                 </jobs>
             </data:employee>
             <data:employee id="Wrecker2">
                 <name>Harry Horn</name>
                 <jobs>
                     <ref:job ref="Boston2"/>
                 </jobs>
             </data:employee>
         </employees>
     </schedule>
```

Looking at this document, we see there are three major elements: jobs, supervisors and employees. We have in effect given each job, supervisor and employee a unique ID. In addition, we have given each job a reference to the supervisors and the employees involved. And we have given each supervisor and each employee a reference to the jobs he works on. Now, we need to let the parser know about the relationships between the "id" and the "ref" attribute values. We do this in our DTD, by declaring particular attributes to be of type "ID" and type "IDREF". To make it easy to follow, we named the attributes "id" which we planned to declare as type "ID", and we named the attributes "ref" which we will declare to be of type "IDREF". Here is how we declare these types for the supervisors, in our DTD:

```
<!ATTLIST supervisor id ID #IMPLIED>
<!ATTLIST supervisor ref IDREF #IMPLIED>
```

Establishing this relationship now allows us to use various programming methods to navigate from elements with IDREFs to elements with corresponding IDs. For instance, if we wanted to access the "data:supervisor" node that corresponds to the "ref:supervisor" node containing the IDREF attribute with the value of "Spt1", we can simply pass that value to our programming method, and it will return the node we want.

The ENTITY and ENTITIES types refer to external binary entities, most commonly image files such as GIFs, which are declared within the DTD.

The NMTOKEN and NMTOKENS types are rarely used. They're a form of CDATA that conforms to the same rules as element names, and they are primarily used by processing applications. You would use them to specify a valid name(s), as in the case of associating some other component with the element, such as a Java class or a security algorithm.

The NOTATION type allows an attribute value to be specified by a notation declared elsewhere in the DTD, in cases where you want certain consequences to result from the attribute.

As we saw earlier, the attribute list declaration also includes attribute defaults. Looking again at our example:

```
<!ATTLIST shirt style (tee|muscle|longsleeve) "tee"
                color CDATA #REQUIRED>
```

we can see that the color attribute takes CDATA for its value, and it is followed by the attribute default #REQUIRED. This means that we must provide a value. An error will occur if we don't. Let's look at another option:

```
<!ATTLIST shirt style (tee|muscle|longsleeve) "tee"
                color CDATA #IMPLIED>
```

In this case, the attribute default is #IMPLIED, and it simply means the attribute is optional; no harm is done by omitting or forgetting to include a value. A third attribute default is #FIXED, followed by a value. If this default is specified, the specific value provided is compulsory. This is commonly used to specify values of true or false. The final attribute default is default, which we don't actually write out, but which we can see demonstrated in our example:

```
<!ATTLIST shirt style (tee|muscle|longsleeve) "tee"
        color CDATA #IMPLIED>
```

As we have already noted, this element's style attribute can have one of three options. If the element does not include a value for this option, the value will be "tee".

One final issue about creating DTDs. So far we have been discussing a DTD which is included as part of our XML document. Except in very small applications, this is usually *not* a good idea. Most DTDs are in fact external documents. This has several major advantages. The first is that the DTD can be shared by any number of XML documents. This allows organizations to standardize their applications by having their XML documents all use the same DTD. It also reduces the time-consuming task of having to type a new DTD every time a new XML document is written. And it simplifies updating documents that depend on the DTD. All we need to do is make changes to the DTD and we update all the documents that depend on it in one fell swoop.

External DTDs

The simplest approach to converting our DTD to an external document is to cut it from our XML document, and paste it into a document of its own, with a file extension of .dtd, and then change both the XML declaration and the DOCTYPE declaration in our XML document. The XML Declaration must be changed to reflect the fact that the XML document will not work on its own. That is, it will not be standalone:

```
<?xml version = "1.0"  encoding="UTF-8" standalone = "no"?>
```

We also need to change the DOCTYPE declaration to add either the SYSTEM or the PUBLIC attribute and the URL of the external DTD. The URL may indicate either a relative or an absolute file location. For example, if we save our DTD in the same directory as our XML document, and use the filename contactlist.dtd our DOCTYPE declaration will look like this:

```
<!DOCTYPE contactlist SYSTEM "contactlist.dtd">
```

Or it might look like this:

```
        <!DOCTYPE contactlist SYSTEM
  "http://www.madeupurl.com/dtds/contactlist.dtd">
```

We use the SYSTEM keyword primarily for referencing private DTDs that are shared among documents of a single author or organization. DTDs may also be made available to the public by using the PUBLIC keyword. When using the PUBLIC keyword, we need to give an external DTD a name by which it can be recognized, in addition to the name of the URL where it can be found:

```
<!DOCTYPE contactlist PUBLIC "contactlist.dtd"
          "http://www.madeupurl.com/dtds/contactlist.dtd">
```

Standardizing DTDs

We need to have some form of DTD for every XML document because XML, unlike HTML, does not have a predefined set or hierarchy of tags; it's up to the publisher of the data to decide how the data will be presented. The absence of a predefined set of tags is both the best and worst aspect of XML; obviously it provides us with almost unlimited versatility, but it also means the publisher and the reader of the data need to agree on the meaning of the tags. The reason why HTML has become so widely accepted is because readers everywhere can understand the tags written by anyone else, because they follow a universal standard. For XML to gain such support the same thing needs to happen, except that in most cases, the standard DTDs and other schemas for XML should be written so they can be widely accepted and applied within vertical industries.

ebXML

In business-to-business electronic commerce, there need to be conventions for the use of XML among trading partners. The good news is that those conventions are being developed. And it's happening fast. The leading organization behind the development of standardized DTDs is **OASIS**, the **Organization for the Advancement of Structured Information Standards**. OASIS is an international consortium, the world's largest independent, non-profit organization dedicated to the standardization of XML applications. It is filling a critical need for vendor neutral DTD and schema standards for many industries.

A visit to the OASIS website at http://www.oasis-open.org/cover/xml.html will reveal many industry-specific XML-based languages emerging, some of them already firmly established. Of particular interest to readers of this book is **Electronic Business XML Initiative (ebXML)**, which is a set of specifications for a modular electronic business framework. The vision of the founders of ebXML is to create a global electronic marketplace that will allow enterprises of any size and in any part of the world to come together (at least electronically) and conduct business with each other through the exchange of XML based messages. Those founders are confidently predicting hundreds of thousands of businesses worldwide will become involved. Check it out at http://ebxml.org/.

Banking Industry Languages

A number of Markup Languages are already circulating in the financial markets. One of those innovations is **Financial Products Markup Language (FpML)**, which was created by JP Morgan and PricewaterhouseCoopers. They describe it as a "protocol for sharing information on, and dealing in, financial derivatives over the Internet" (see www.fpml.org for more information). Another financial industry language, **FinXML**, was developed by Integral in conjunction with ISDA (International Swap Dealers Association) and, according to www.finxml.org, supports a wide variety of financial products including interest rate, foreign exchange and commodity derivatives, bonds, money markets, loans and deposits, and exchange traded futures and options.

Fast, accurate and complete flows of information are the life-blood of a financial institution. Most institutions currently use a system where information flows between the various parts through a series of hard coded batch-file interfaces. Because XML is an ideal tool for data exchange, it can, through appropriately written DTDs, improve the flow of information within those institutions.

Travel

The travel industry is one field where we can easily see the value of a standardized DTD, because so many of the procedures used by its various sectors are similar, or in many cases almost identical. An example of what such a DTD might look like for an XML document designed to handle arrangements for airline flights shows us how convenient it would be for every airline to implement it. And don't think that they haven't already started working on something similar to this. Note that although this document looks huge, it is actually very simple, and we can see how it follows the rules set out in the first two parts of this primer:

```
<!ENTITY mt "MyTravel">
<!ELEMENT flights (itinerary)+>
<!ELEMENT itinerary (outbound-depart-from,outbound-depart-time,outbound-arrive-
in,outbound-arrive-time,outbound-airline,returning-depart-from,returning-depart-
time,returning-arrive-in,returning-arrive-time,returning-airline)>
 <!ELEMENT outbound-depart-from (#PCDATA)>
 <!ELEMENT outbound-depart-time (EMPTY)>
 <!ATTLIST outbound-depart-time year CDATA #REQUIRED>
 <!ATTLIST outbound-depart-time month CDATA #REQUIRED>
 <!ATTLIST outbound-depart-time day CDATA #REQUIRED>
 <!ATTLIST outbound-depart-time hour CDATA #REQUIRED>
 <!ATTLIST outbound-depart-time minute CDATA #REQUIRED>
 <!ELEMENT outbound-arrive-in (#PCDATA)>
 <!ELEMENT outbound-arrive-time (EMPTY)>
 <!ATTLIST outbound-arrive-time year CDATA #REQUIRED>
 <!ATTLIST outbound-arrive-time month CDATA #REQUIRED>
 <!ATTLIST outbound-arrive-time day CDATA #REQUIRED>
 <!ATTLIST outbound-arrive-time hour CDATA #REQUIRED>
 <!ATTLIST outbound-arrive-time minute CDATA #REQUIRED>
 <!ELEMENT outbound-airline (EMPTY)>
 <!ATTLIST outbound-airline flightNum CDATA #REQUIRED>
 <!ATTLIST outbound-airline carrierName (AirCanada | Alitalia | American |    Delta
| Northwest | Pacific | TWA | United) "AirCanada">
 <!ELEMENT returning-depart-from (#PCDATA)>
 <!ELEMENT returning-depart-time (EMPTY)>
 <!ATTLIST returning-depart-time year CDATA #REQUIRED>
 <!ATTLIST returning-depart-time month CDATA #REQUIRED>
 <!ATTLIST returning-depart-time day CDATA #REQUIRED>
 <!ATTLIST returning-depart-time hour CDATA #REQUIRED>
 <!ATTLIST returning-depart-time minute CDATA #REQUIRED>
 <!ELEMENT returning-arrive-in (#PCDATA)>
 <!ELEMENT returning-arrive-time (EMPTY)>
 <!ATTLIST returning-arrive-time year CDATA #REQUIRED>
 <!ATTLIST returning-arrive-time month CDATA #REQUIRED>
 <!ATTLIST returning-arrive-time day CDATA #REQUIRED>
 <!ATTLIST returning-arrive-time hour CDATA #REQUIRED>
 <!ATTLIST returning-arrive-time minute CDATA #REQUIRED>
 <!ELEMENT returning-airline (EMPTY)>
 <!ATTLIST returning-airline flightNum CDATA #REQUIRED>
 <!ATTLIST returning-airline carrierName (AirCanada | Alitalia | American | Delta
| Northwest | Pacific | TWA | United) "AirCanada">
```

And here is an XML document that can make good use of the above DTD, notice how the DTD can accommodate flights to and from anywhere we want to schedule, using any of the major airlines we have listed:

```
<?xml version="1.0" ?>
<!DOCTYPE flights SYSTEM "flights.dtd">
  <flights>
    <itinerary>
      <outbound-depart-from>Vancouver</outbound-depart-from>
      <outbound-depart-time year="2001" month="1"
              day="10" hour="6" minute="30" />
      <outbound-arrive-in>Hong Kong</outbound-arrive-in>
      <outbound-arrive-time year="2001" month="1"
              day="11" hour="18" minute="25" />
      <outbound-airline carrierName="AirCanada" flightNum="AC204" />
      <returning-depart-from>Hong Kong</returning-depart-from>
      <returning-depart-time year="2001" month="1"
              day="25" hour="10" minute="30" />
      <returning-arrive-in>Vancouver</returning-arrive-in>
      <returning-arrive-time year="2001" month="1"
              day="26" hour="22" minute="55" />
      <returning-airline carrierName="Northwest" flightNum="NW63" />
    </itinerary>
    <itinerary>
      <outbound-depart-from>New York</outbound-depart-from>
      <outbound-depart-time year="2001" month="2"
              day="3" hour="11" minute="10" />
      <outbound-arrive-in>Mexico City</outbound-arrive-in>
      <outbound-arrive-time year="2001" month="2"
              day="3" hour="18" minute="15" />
      <outbound-airline carrierName="American" flightNum="1303" />
      <returning-depart-from>Mexico City</returning-depart-from>
      <returning-depart-time year="2001" month="3"
              day="1" hour="6" minute="40" />
      <returning-arrive-in>New York</returning-arrive-in>
      <returning-arrive-time year="2001" month="3"
              day="1" hour="14" minute="10" />
      <returning-airline carrierName="American" flightNum="2302" />
    </itinerary>
  </flights>
```

We can also see how a standardized DTD could be used in the hotel industry, to process accommodation arrangements and requests, in the automobile rental business, and in any other business where keeping track of customers and their selections and preferences is important.

Summary

By now you should have a pretty good idea of what XML is, and what it looks like. We've looked at the rules for well-formed XML documents, and examined the basic building blocks of those documents, elements and attributes. We also examined the role of the Document Type Definition. And we looked at the ways in which standardized DTDs are being applied to the world of e-commerce.

For all of the hype surrounding XML these days, it does have its warts. Many of the problems with the language relate to growing pains, because standards and tools are still evolving, and there are often glaring inconsistencies in the way in which different applications adopt and apply those standards. Many browsers, in particular versions of Netscape Navigator before 6.0, do not support XML. And the fact that XML is platform neutral, while being one of its greatest advantages, is also one of its greatest weaknesses, because it prevents XML from taking advantage of performance enhancing capabilities, such as compression, of the specific platforms.

This XML primer is far from exhaustive; in fact experienced XML developers will no doubt notice many glaring holes in it. But the purpose was to introduce you to the subject, not to turn you into an instant expert. But if your interest has been captured, I strongly urge you to check out the good and growing supply of material available, in books, magazines, and on the web, on which you can build from where we must leave off here.

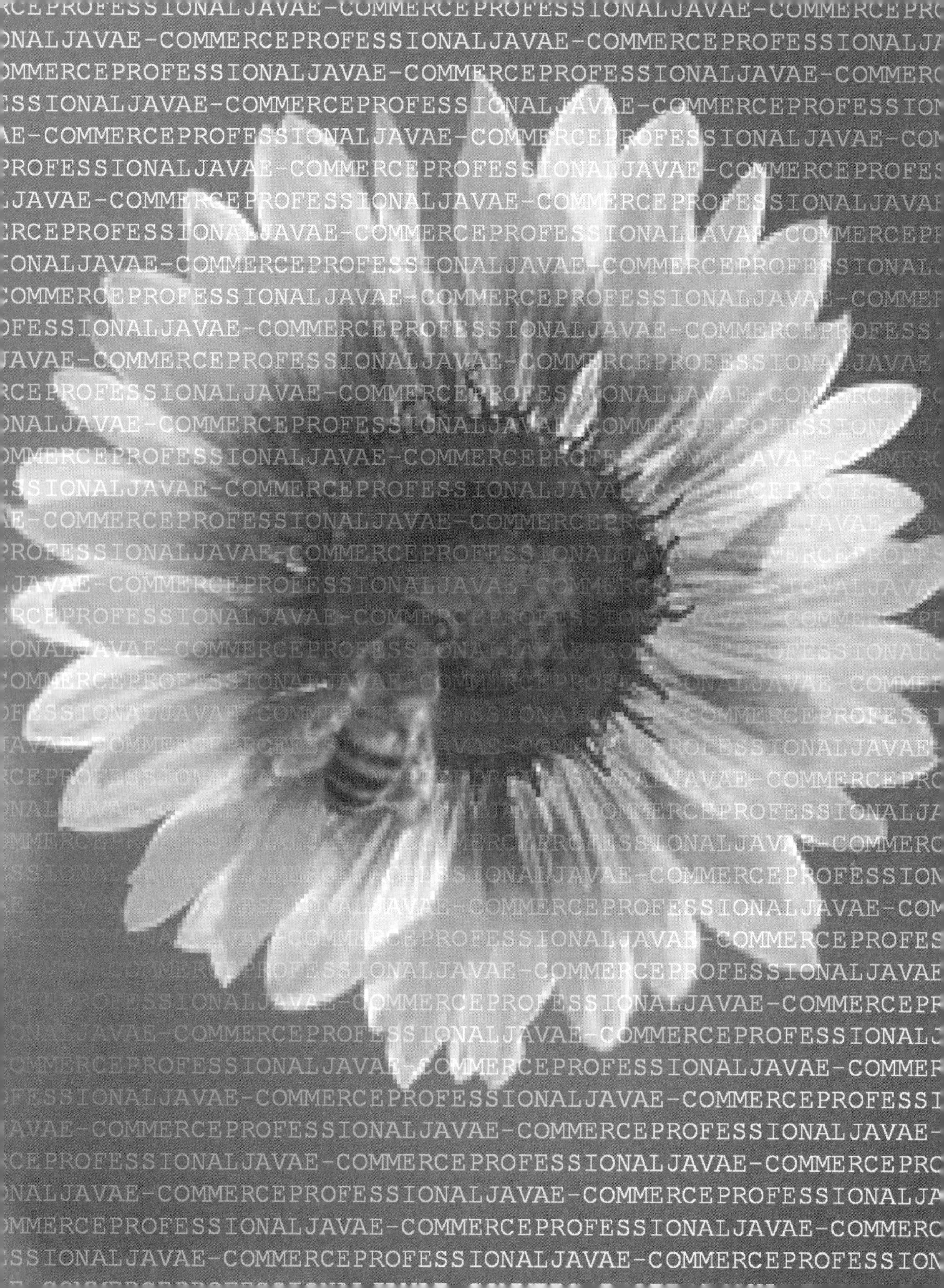
PROFESSIONALJAVAE-COMMERCE

B

XSLT Primer

So why do we need another XML related language? The simplest answer is because not everybody writes or uses XML the same way; in fact not everybody uses XML at all.

eXtensible Stylesheet Language Transformation (XSLT) is a language that uses XSL stylesheets to transform XML documents into other XML documents, or into HTML or other types of documents. This capability is essential for e-commerce companies, because they don't all use the same programs, applications, or computer systems. XSLT allows all those companies to convert the same data into their own particular representations of XML.

XSL is actually two languages, a formatting language and a transformation language. Each of these can, and often does, function independently of each other. In this primer, we will deal primarily with XSLT, the transformation language.

Although the examples and illustrations in this primer can be handled easily by the capabilities within Internet Explorer 5.0, there are many XSLT conversion engines available for the serious developer. One of the best tools available for transforming XML documents into HTML, text, or other XML document types is the Apache Software Foundation's Xalan-Java, available at http://xml.apache.org/xalan/index.html.

Other conversion engines include XSLT standards editor James Clark's XT, which can be found at http://www.jclark.com/xml/xt.html and Oracle Corporation's Oracle XML Developer's Kit, at http://technet.oracle.com/tech/xml/. Check out a website known as XMLSOFTWARE for an extensive listing of XSLT engines: http://www.xmlsoftware.com/xslt/.

Our route through the primer is as follows:

❑ The role of **stylesheets** in transforming the information contained in XML documents

- ❏ How to define and apply **templates**
- ❏ How to create **looping constructs**
- ❏ Retrieving XML data
- ❏ Creating **patterns for matching nodes**
- ❏ Conditional statements
- ❏ Sorting XML data
- ❏ Processing multiple stylesheets

We begin by looking at stylesheets and, to demonstrate the concepts we're talking about, will start to work our way through a simple XSLT procedure to transform an XML document into HTML.

StyleSheets

As was pointed out in the XML Primer (Appendix A), the absence of a predefined set of tags for displaying the data is both the best and worst aspect of the language. Because it is entirely content driven, XML provides us with almost unlimited versatility, but it also means we need to provide some way to include style and display information in our documents. In some cases, that information will include HTML or **Cascading StyleSheets** (**CSS**), or we can opt for the natural companion to XML, **XSL** (**eXtensible Stylesheet Language**).

XSL was designed specifically for use with XML. It provides the formatting information for the context information provided by XML and the actual content within the document. For example, if names appear in an HTML document, there's nothing to indicate that they are in fact names.

```
<body>
        <p> Charles Dickens </p>
        <p> George Eliot </p>
</body>
```

But if you are using XML you can specify exactly what those names are:

```
<authorname>
    <firstname> Charles </firstname>
    <lastname> Dickens </lastname>
</authorname>
```

```
<authorname>
    <firstname> George </firstname>
    <lastname> Eliot </lastname>
</authorname>
```

But there's still something missing. Even though the names have been defined so that the parser knows what they are, you have no information about how those names are going to be displayed, what fonts will be used, what size type, and where the names will appear in connection with any other elements in the document. XSL brings this style (or display) information to XML.

Document Structure

Every well-formed XML document is a **tree**. A tree is a hierarchical data structure composed of connected **nodes**, starting with a single node called the root. The root is connected to its child nodes, each of which may be connected to zero or more children of its own, and so forth. A node with no children is called a **leaf**. The diagram of such a tree looks much like a family tree that lists the descendants of a single ancestor. The most useful property of a tree is that each node and its children also form a tree. Thus, a tree is a hierarchical structure of trees in which each tree is made up of smaller trees.

Nodes of an XML tree are its elements and their content. But in XSL, we also need to provide for the fact that **attributes, namespaces, processing instructions**, and **comments** must also be counted as nodes. We don't include document type declarations or definitions as nodes. But we do need to provide for additional attribute nodes for some of our elements, if the DTD spells out default attributes for those elements.

The XSL transformation language (XSLT) operates by transforming one XML tree into another. It can also transform an XML tree into plain text, several elements, or a mixture of plain text and elements. This means the output may not necessarily be a complete well-formed XML document, but it will at least be part of one.

An XSL transformation cannot output text that is malformed XML. An XSLT transformation begins with a source tree, which is generated from an XML document. An XSL processor reads both the XML document and an XSL stylesheet document. Based on the instructions the processor finds in the XSL stylesheet, it outputs a new XML document or part thereof. There's also special support for outputting HTML, using the `<xsl:output>` element, as long as the HTML conforms to XML's well-formedness rules. With some effort it can also be made to output essentially arbitrary text, though it's designed primarily for XML-to-XML transformations. The transformation process requires two starting documents, the XML document, and the XSLT stylesheet. Together they produce a single result document.

Using XSLT

It's time now to take a look at some complete documents, so we can understand the general concepts behind templates in XSLT. First, we will create an XML document, `javaglossarytable.xml`, which will be used to describe a simple table that contains a listing of several items from a glossary of Java related terms:

```
<?xml version="1.0"?>

<javaglossarytable>

  <entry>
    <term>Argument</term>
    <definition>A data item specified in a method call. An argument can be a
literal value, a variable, or an expression.</definition>
  </entry>

  <entry>
    <term>Array</term>
    <definition>A collection of data items, all of the same type, in which each
item's position is uniquely designated by an integer.</definition>
  </entry>

  <entry>
    <term>ASCII</term>
```

```
      <definition>American Standard Code for Information Interchange. A standard
assignment of 7-bit numeric codes to characters. See also Unicode.</definition>
    </entry>

    <entry>
      <term>Atomic</term>
      <definition>Refers to an operation that is never interrupted or left in an
incomplete state under any circumstance.</definition>
    </entry>

    <entry>
      <term>Authentication</term>
      <definition>The process by which an entity proves to another entity that it is
acting on behalf of a specific identity. The J2EE platform requires three types of
authentication: basic, form-based, and mutual.</definition>
    </entry>

</javaglossarytable>
```

Without a stylesheet, our XML document doesn't produce anything useful; it certainly doesn't allow us to display a table containing our glossary information; in fact, if we were to open it up in a browser capable of rendering XML documents, it would look like this:

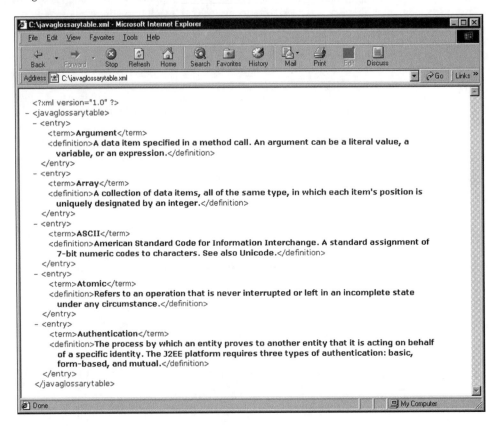

But that's not what we want it to look like, of course. That's just a slightly different (but useless for our purposes) presentation of the same source code. But when we apply an XSL transformation to it, by including a reference to an XSL stylesheet, we get the HTML output that generates what we're looking for:

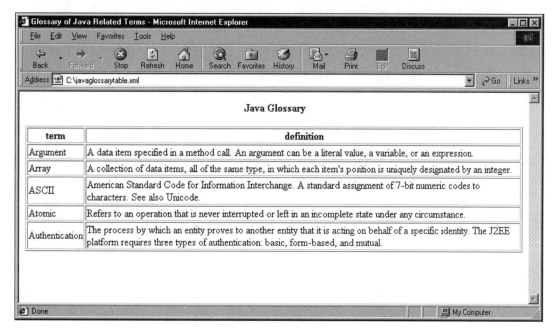

Obviously there's nothing in our XML document to create the above table, and to place its contents in the appropriate places. That's where XSL comes in, to convert our XML output into a simple HTML presentation of the information. This is one of the most elegant ways of separating presentation from content. Using an XSLT engine to merge the XML and XSL will generate the following HTML document, which displays the above Java Glossary table:

```html
<html>
  <head>
      <title>Glossary of Java Related Terms</title>
  </head>
  <body>
    <center><h4>Java Glossary</h4></center>
    <table width="100%" border="1">
      <tr>
      <th>term</th>
      <th>definition</th>
      </tr>
      <tr>
        <td>Argument</td>
        <td>A data item specified in a method call. An argument can be a
            literal value, a variable, or an expression.</td>
      </tr>
      <tr>
        <td>Array</td>
        <td>A collection of data items, all of the same type, in which
            each item's position is uniquely designated by an integer.</td>
      </tr>
```

```
          <tr>
            <td>ASCII</td>
            <td>American Standard Code for Information Interchange.
               A standard assignment of 7-bit numeric codes to characters.
               See also Unicode.</td>
          </tr>
          <tr>
            <td>Atomic</td>
            <td>Refers to an operation that is never interrupted or left in
               an incomplete state under any circumstance.</td>
          </tr>
          <tr>
            <td>Authentication</td>
            <td>The process by which an entity proves to another entity that
               it is acting on behalf of a specific identity. The J2EE
               platform requires three types of authentication: basic,
               form-based, and mutual.</td>
          </tr>
        </table>
      </body>
    </html>
```

It's easy to attach an XSL stylesheet to an XML document. For our example above, we simply insert the XML stylesheet processing instruction into our document's prolog, immediately after the XML declaration. This instruction should have a `type` attribute, with the value "`text/xsl`", and an `href` attribute with a value that is a URL that points to the stylesheet we are going to use:

```
<?xml version="1.0"?>
<?xml-stylesheet type="text/xsl" href="javaglossarytable.xsl" ?>
```

In this case we have stored our stylesheet document in the same directory as our XML document, and also in this case it has the same filename as our XML document, except that its file extension is `.xsl`.

It should be pointed out that the stylesheet could be stored elsewhere, in which case we would need our `href` to specify the path to reach it.

Now it's time to see what the stylesheet we have been referring to looks like. Here is `javaglossarytable.xsl`:

```
<?xml version="1.0"?>

<!-- <xsl:stylesheet version="1.0"
xmlns:xsl="http://www.w3.org/1999/XSL/Transform"> -->
<xsl:stylesheet xmlns:xsl="http://www.w3.org/TR/WD-xsl">
<xsl:template match="/">
<html>
  <head>
      <title>Glossary of Java Related Terms</title>
  </head>
  <body>
    <center><h4>Java Glossary</h4></center>
    <table width="100%" border="1">
      <tr>
```

```
            <th>term</th>
            <th>definition</th>
         </tr>
         <xsl:for-each select="javaglossarytable/entry">
            <tr>
               <td>
                  <xsl:value-of select="term"/>
               </td>
               <td>
                  <xsl:value-of select="definition"/>
               </td>
            </tr>
         </xsl:for-each>
      </table>
   </body>
</html>
</xsl:template>
</xsl:stylesheet>
```

The first line of our document reflects the fact that, as we have already noted, XSL is an XML application:

```
<?xml version="1.0"?>
```

We now need to specify the XSL stylesheet version. Every XSL file must specify the XSL **namespace** that we need, so that the parser knows which version of XSL to use. If we were using a conversion engine such as Xalan, we would use the following namespace:

```
<xsl:stylesheet version="1.0" xmlns:xsl="http://www.w3.org/1999/XSL/Transform">
```

But this won't work with IE, which associates a different namespace URI for XSL elements. So in our document we have commented out the above namespace, and supplied a namespace that will work with IE:

```
<?xml version="1.0"?>
<!-- <xsl:stylesheet version="1.0"
xmlns:xsl="http://www.w3.org/1999/XSL/Transform"> -->
<xsl:stylesheet xmlns:xsl="http://www.w3.org/TR/WD-xsl">
```

A complete discussion on the topic of namespaces is beyond the scope of this primer. Let's just go with this for now.

XSL stylesheets are valid XML documents. They follow the same rules as other XML documents, they require the same provisions for Document Type Definitions (DTDs) and XML Schemas, and they act in similar ways.

Before we get into a description of the document contents, we need to understand a specific point about XSL syntax regarding elements. We will be referring of course to elements within the XML document that we are processing. But XSL has elements of its own. We have already seen one in the XSL document above: xsl:template. An XSL element is easy to spot; it has the letters xsl followed by a colon (":"). We'll encounter many more of them as we work our way through this primer.

Yet Another Language – XPath

When XSLT was being developed, so was XPath, a language that can be used to point to a specific thing or a set of things in an XML document. XPath uses the location path to describe how to find specific elements, attributes, processing instructions, etc. in a document. A location path is simply a description of how to get from one place in the document to someplace else. To use a crude analogy, the location path is similar to a set of instructions for finding a specific location within a city. If we wanted to find a particular office tower, a guide might tell us "Go to the second set of lights, turn left and you'll find the office tower two blocks ahead on your right". In the same way, we can use the location path to find what we are looking for in an XML document. The location path describes a path from one point in an XML document to another point, and it provides a way for each of the items within the document to be addressed. In other words, it describes the address of one of the document's nodes, in relationship to another node.

Just as our guide's set of instructions starts with where we currently are in the city, so the location path also is relative to the starting location. This concept is called the context node, which is where the addressing starts. We'll examine the general issue of context in greater detail in a later section.

XPath treats the XML document as a logical tree, with a root node as well as nodes for elements, attributes, character data (text), processing instructions, comments and namespaces. The root node is the root of the document. Every XML document has one, and it contains an optional prolog and the document element. A location path that begins with a slash (/) is considered relative to the root node, while a path that begins with two slashes (//) relates to descendants of the root node.

Although much of the syntax involving selecting and matching throughout the rest of this primer is based on the XPath language, there's far too much involved for us to get any deeper into it here. For more information about XPath, look at the following URL: http://www.w3.org/TR/xpath.

Templates

An XSL document contains a list of templates and other rules. A **template rule** has a pattern specifying which sub-trees it applies to and a template to be output when the pattern is matched. When an XSL processor formats an XML document using an XSL stylesheet, it scans the XML document tree looking through each sub-tree in turn. As each sub-tree in the XML document is read, the processor compares it with the pattern of each template rule in the stylesheet. When the processor finds a sub-tree that matches a template rule's pattern, it processes the rule's template. This template generally includes some markup, some new data, and some data copied out of the tree from the original XML document.

Just like elements are the building blocks of XML, so template rules are the building blocks for the transformations that occur in our XSL file. An XSLT stylesheet contains template rules that define how elements will be selected in the source tree, and provides processing instructions for restructuring the selected element content to create the result tree.

As noted earlier, there are two parts to a template rule: a pattern and a template. The pattern is usually an element name, although it can be any valid pattern match expression. It is matched against elements in the source tree in order to determine which nodes should be selected for processing by the specific template. The template includes instructions for processing the content that is selected by the pattern.

Each template rule produces a segment of markup and content that is constructed according to the rule's guidelines. The complete "result tree" of an XSL transformation is created when each of the generated result tree fragments are combined in the order specified.

Let's take an in-depth look at our sample XSL document, and the template that it contains, or rather, in this case, the template that contains it:

```
<xsl:template match="/">

    (the rest of the document all goes here)

</xsl:template>
```

Every XSL file will have at least one template, either by default or defined. The defined template can be one of two options. It can start with either match="/", which is the root of the XML document, or it is also legal, but not as common, to start with the specific document element for the XML document, which in the case of our example is match="javaglossarytable". The "/" in the first line tells the processor that this node applies to the root level of the XML document. You can think of the root level as an imaginary pair of tags surrounding the entirety of your XML document, and which must be addressed before you can get to the actual tags. And of course the </xsl:template> tag at the end is simply the closing tag for <xsl:template match="/">. What we have between those two lines is the template that provides the HTML structure for our Java Glossary items:

```
<xsl:template match="/">
<html>
  <head>
    <title>Glossary of Java Related Terms</title>
  </head>
  <body>
    <center><h4>Java Glossary</h4></center>
    <table width="100%" border="1">
      <tr>
      <td>term</td>
      <td>definition</td>
      </tr>
      <xsl:for-each select="javaglossarytable/entry">
        <tr>
          <td>
            <xsl:value-of select="term"/>
          </td>
          <td>
            <xsl:value-of select="definition"/>
          </td>
        </tr>
      </xsl:for-each>
    </table>
  </body>
</html>
</xsl:template>
```

Unfortunately, in such a simple example, this is the only template rule available. But it's easy to think of places where other rules can be extremely useful. For example, if you had an XML document related to an application for handling information about books, and you wanted to define style information for the <authorname> element that we saw earlier in this appendix, you would write:

```
<rule>
  <target-element type="authorname">
  <div font-weight="bold" font-size="8pt" color="#003300">
    <children/>
  </div>
</rule>
```

This would create a pattern for the `<authorname>` element, telling the parser to display the element in bold, 8-point type, and green in color. This template would be applied each time the parser encountered the `<authorname>` element. Remember, our `<authorname>` element has two children, `<firstname>` and `<lastname>`, so including the empty `<children/>` tag within the rule definition ensures the pattern applies to all of our target element's children. So this rule would display the authors' names in green, in 8-point boldface.

If you were to include a `<target-element/>` with no defined type, it would become the default style for the entire document:

```
<rule>
  <target-element/>
  <div font-size="12pt" color="#000000">
  <children/>
  </div>
</rule>
```

We define our templates to produce a particular outcome, so that when we call that template by using `<xsl:apply-templates>` or `<xsl:call-template>`, it handles the output. The `xsl:apply-templates` element defines a set of child nodes to be processed, enabling iterative processing of those nodes. If we want to process only some of the child elements, we can define a `select` attribute, to tell the application which specific nodes we want to process. For example, suppose we wanted to display only the term elements in our sample code. To do this, we use the `xsl:template match` element to tell our application which element we are working in, and we use the `xsl:apply-templates` instruction to tell our application which element we want to display:

```
<xsl:template match="/">
    <xsl:apply-templates select="entry/term"/>
</xsl:template>
```

Our transformation processes the template by either its `match` or `name` attributes. The `match` attribute uses a pattern that we have defined, and the `name` attribute uses whichever name we have given the element.

Looping Constructs

As you work with XSLT, you will notice how it is a programming language that is based on its template rules. It is a declarative language, where you declare what you want the output to be when a pattern in the stylesheet is met. Unlike many procedural languages, it allows you to specify how an element should be processed, no matter where you are in the XSLT stylesheet. Template rules do not have to be written in any particular order.

One of the valuable programming language aspects of XSLT is its looping constructs, in particular its use of the `<xsl:for-each>` element. This element uses a `select` attribute, to process each of the selected elements, in turn. Our sample code above includes an example of such a construct:

```
<xsl:for-each select="javaglossarytable/entry">
  <tr>
    <td>
      <xsl:value-of select="term"/>
    </td>
    <td>
      <xsl:value-of select="definition"/>
    </td>
  </tr>
</xsl:for-each>
```

Translating this line into plain English, we would put it this way; for each time we encounter an `entry` element within the `javaglossarytable` element, we will carry out the steps that follow. In our example, what will be included in the loop are instructions for taking the value of what is in the `term` and `definition` elements of our XML document, and placing those values in adjacent columns on the same row within a table. So this particular construct goes through our XML document, and adds a row to the table each time it encounters an `entry` element. Each of those rows has the name of a term found in the glossary, and the appropriate definition.

Retrieving Data

The `xsl:value-of` element does exactly what its name says, it takes the value of something and copies it to the output document. This XSL element includes a `select` attribute that specifies exactly what it is that we want the value of. Note that this element should be used only where the nodes can be selected without any possibility of confusion with nodes elsewhere in the document, as in where the context is clear (the concept of context is described in the next section). We have two `xsl:value-of` elements in our document:

```
<xsl:value-of select="term"/>

<xsl:value-of select="definition"/>
```

Each of these, in turn, takes the value of the `term` and the `definition` elements of our XML document, and copies those values into the table rows in the HTML document. Because both of these elements are within the **context** of a `for-each` loop construct, the values of `term` and `definition` are taken relative to each of the `entry` elements processed by the loop. See the next section for an explanation of the important concept of context. So, when we apply the XSL stylesheet to the XML document, we get the following HTML output:

```
<tr>
    <td>Argument</td>
    <td>A data item specified in a method call. An argument can be a
        literal value, a variable, or an expression.</td>
</tr>
<tr>
    <td>Array</td>
    <td>A collection of data items, all of the same type, in which
        each item's position is uniquely designated by an integer.</td>
</tr>
<tr>
    <td>ASCII</td>
    <td>American Standard Code for Information Interchange.
        A standard assignment of 7-bit numeric codes to characters.
        See also Unicode.</td>
</tr>
<tr>
    <td>Atomic</td>
    <td>Refers to an operation that is never interrupted or left in
        an incomplete state under any circumstance.</td>
</tr>
<tr>
    <td>Authentication</td>
    <td>The process by which an entity proves to another entity that
        it is acting on behalf of a specific identity. The J2EE
        platform requires three types of authentication: basic,
        form-based, and mutual.</td>
</tr>
```

Context

This is a good time to discuss the concept of **context**. When we are working with XSLT, the context for a particular query is the source node that is currently being processed. This is the context node that we saw in the earlier section on XPath. So when we are working in the template <xsl:template match="/">, we are working in the context of the root of the XML document. When we are in an <xsl:for-each> loop, our context is whichever node we are currently looping through, which in our javaglossarytable example is the entry element.

Understanding the context that you are working with is important, because it will help you to understand why an output that you are expecting doesn't work. So if you are ever stuck in such a situation, the first question you should ask yourself is, "What context am I in?"

The location path is a valuable part of helping to set the context of the node that you trying to find. We have already seen an example of this, where we are finding all entry elements in the javaglossarytable element, where we use the location path of "/".

Patterns For Matching Nodes

The select and match attributes used in XSL elements are commonly referred to as being similar to their counterparts in SQL. They allow us to express exactly which nodes we want to select and match. They are actually XPath patterns, which we looked at in an earlier section. The match pattern is a subset of the select pattern. We use them in the following elements: xsl:apply-templates, xsl:value-of, xsl:for-each and xsl:template. Let's look at the ways we can use these elements and attributes for matching and selecting nodes.

We have already seen how the first output from an XSL transformation needs to be the document's root element, using the following syntax:

```
<xsl:template match="/">
     (open our document)
          <xsl:apply-templates/>
     (close our document)
</xsl:template>
```

Remember that the rule involving the use of the value of the standalone symbol "/" as the location path for the match attribute applies only to the root node. We will see shortly how we can use it in conjunction with elements and attributes to specify the context we want.

The most basic pattern we can use contains a single element name that matches all elements with that name. For example, in our javaglossarytable sample, this template would match entry elements and mark up their term children in bold:

```
<xsl:template match="entry">
  <b><xsl:value-of select="term"/></b>
</xsl:template>
```

We are not limited to the children of the current node when we use the match attribute. If we use the "/" symbol, we can match specified hierarchies of elements. As we saw earlier, we use it alone for the root node. But when we place it between two element names, we indicate that the second element is a child of the first. For example, the expression entry/term refers to term elements that are children of entry elements.

We can use this in `xsl:template` elements when we need to match only some of the elements of a given kind. It is also possible for us to specify deeper matches by stringing patterns together. For example, `javaglossarytable/entry/term` selects `term` elements whose parent is an `entry` element, whose parent is a `javaglossarytable` element. We can also use the "`*`" wild card to substitute for a particular element name in a hierarchy. For example, the following template rule applies to all `term` elements that are grandchildren of a `javaglossarytable` element:

```
<xsl:template match="javaglossarytable/*/term">
  <strong><xsl:value-of select="."/></strong>
</xsl:template>
```

Note the use of the "`.`" as the value of our `select` attribute; this syntax simply refers to the target element, in this case the `term` element.

Sometimes, especially when our document has elements of a particular type at more than one level, we may find it easier to bypass intermediate nodes and simply select all the elements that we want, regardless of whether they're immediate children, grandchildren, great-grandchildren, or whatever. The double slash "`//`" refers to a descendant element at any level of our document. For example, this template rule applies to all `term` descendants of `javaglossarytable`, no matter how deep:

```
<xsl:template match="javaglossary//term">
  <i><xsl:value-of select="."/></i>
</xsl:template>
```

The hierarchy of the `javaglossarytable` example we are using is too shallow for this to make much difference, but this trick becomes more important in deeper hierarchies, especially when an element can contain other elements of its own type, such as a `term` element that contains a `term` element. We use the "`//`" operator at the beginning of a pattern to select any descendant of the root node. For example, this template rule processes all `term` elements while completely ignoring their location within our document:

```
<xsl:template match="//term">
  <i><xsl:value-of select="."/></i>
</xsl:template>
```

Matching With @

Another approach to selecting nodes is to use the "`@`" symbol to match against attributes, and select the nodes we want according to attribute names. We simply prefix the attribute we want to select with "`@`". To show how this works, we'll need some attributes to work with. Let's rewrite our XML document, so that its `entry` element has a `kind` attribute:

```
<?xml version="1.0"?>

<javaglossarytable>

  <entry kind="data">
    <term>Argument</term>
    <definition>A data item specified in a method call. An argument can
    be a literal value, a variable, or an expression.</definition>
  </entry>
```

```
<entry kind="collection">
  <term>Array</term>
  <definition>A collection of data items, all of the same type, in which
   each item's position is uniquely designated by an integer.</definition>
</entry>

<entry kind="standard">
  <term>ASCII</term>
  <definition>American Standard Code for Information Interchange.
   A standard assignment of 7-bit numeric codes to characters.
   See also Unicode.</definition>
</entry>

<entry kind="operation">
  <term>Atomic</term>
  <definition>Refers to an operation that is never interrupted or left
   in an incomplete state under any circumstance.</definition>
</entry>

<entry kind="operation">
  <term>Authentication</term>
  <definition>The process by which an entity proves to another entity
   that it is acting on behalf of a specific identity. The J2EE platform
   requires three types of authentication: basic, form-based, and
   mutual.</definition>
</entry>

</javaglossarytable>
```

Recall that the value of an attribute node is simply the string value of the attribute. We can combine attributes with elements using the various hierarchy operators that we were looking at earlier. For example, the expression entry/@kind refers to the kind attribute of an entry element. javaglossarytable/*/@kind matches any kind attribute of any child element of a javaglossarytable element. This is especially helpful when we are matching against attributes in template rules. We can also use the "*" to select all of the attributes of a particular element; for example we can use the expression entry/@* to select all of the attributes of our entry elements.

We can usually ignore comments in XML documents, because essential information should rarely if ever be placed within comments. But if we need to select one, XSL does provide a way. To select a comment, we use the pattern comment(). The only real reason XSL ever allows us to select comments is so a stylesheet can transform from one markup language to another while leaving the comments intact. Any other use indicates a poorly designed original document. The following rule matches all comments, and copies them back out again using the xsl:comment element:

```
<xsl:template match="comment()">
  <xsl:comment><xsl:value-of select="."/></xsl:comment>
</xsl:template>
```

We can use the usual hierarchy operators to select particular comments. For example, this rule matches comments that occur inside entry elements:

```
<xsl:template match="entry/comment()">
    <xsl:comment><xsl:value-of select="."/></xsl:comment>
</xsl:template>
```

We use a similar approach to specifically select the text child of an element. Just as with comment(), the text() operator takes no arguments. The following example will select the value of the text child of the definition element:

```
<xsl:template match="definition">
    <xsl:value-of select="text()"/>
</xsl:template>
```

This operator exists so that we can override the default behavior of XSL processors, which provide the following default rule whether we specify it or not:

```
<xsl:template match="text()">
    <xsl:value-of select="."/>
</xsl:template>
```

This default rule means that whenever a template is applied to a text node, the text of the node is output.

Matching With |

Another operator we can use is the vertical bar or pipe ("|"), known as the "or" operator, which allows a template rule to match multiple patterns. If a node matches one pattern or the other, it will activate the template. For example, this template rule matches both the term and definition elements:

```
<xsl:template match="term|definition">
    <B><xsl:apply-templates/></B>
</xsl:template>
```

If we had more than two elements to work with, we could use more than two patterns in sequence. For example, if our entry element had three child elements, term, definition, and date, the following template rule would apply to all of them:

```
<xsl:template match="term | definition | date">
    <B><xsl:apply-templates/></B>
</xsl:template>
```

Testing With []

One method we can use to test for details about nodes that match a pattern is to use square brackets ("[]"). Let's suppose our glossary contains a few entries that have terms but no definitions. And let's suppose we want to omit those from our table. To do this, we can specify a match against entry elements that do have definition children:

```
<xsl:template match="entry[definition]">
    <tr>
       <td><xsl:value-of select="term"/></td>
       <td><xsl:value-of select="definition"/></td>
    </tr>
</xsl:template>
```

This testing pattern can be very convenient. In addition to testing whether an element contains a particular child element, we can test whether it contains a particular attribute, or whether the value of an attribute matches a given string. We can even test to see what position a given node occupies in the hierarchy.

One type of pattern testing that is especially useful is string equality. We use an equals sign ("=") to test whether an element contains a given child or attribute, or whether the value of a node is or exactly matches a given string. For example, this template finds the `entry` element that contains a `term` element whose contents include the string "`array`":

```
<xsl:template match="entry[term='array']">
    This is a collections item.
</xsl:template>
```

You can see the possibilities for more complex matches, such as selecting all `term` elements whose names begin with "A":

```
<xsl:template match="entry[term='A*']">
    (Whatever text is appropriate!)
</xsl:template>
```

Conditional Statements

XSL shows us its programming language colors again by providing us with conditional statements such as its `xsl:if` element, to determine what our output will be. Just like an `if` statement in a language such as Java, the `test` attribute of `xsl:if` contains an expression that evaluates to a Boolean. If the expression is true, our application will output the contents of the `xsl:if` element. If the expression is false, there's no output. For example, the following template writes out the names of the `term` elements in our `javaglossarytable` document:

```
<xsl:template match="entry">
    <xsl:value-of select="term"/>
</xsl:template>
```

Unfortunately, this would be rather useless because all the names of the entries in the glossary would be run together:

```
ArgumentArrayASCIIAtomicAuthenticate
```

So we change the template to include an appropriate `xsl:if` element:

```
<xsl:template match="entry">
    <xsl:value-of select="term"/>
    <xsl:if test="position()!=last()">, </xsl:if>
</xsl:template>
```

What we're testing for here is whether the `entry` being tested is the last `entry` element in the document. If it is not, the contents of this element, a comma and a space, are added to the end of the value of term:

```
Argument, Array, ASCII, Atomic, Authenticate
```

Unlike the `if` statement in Java, the `xsl:if` element does not have a matching `xsl:else` element, so it doesn't give us an option if the test is false. So unless we want to get into pairs of if statements, with one statement saying the opposite of the other, we need to use the `xsl:choose` element.

In some ways, the `xsl:choose` element acts much like a `switch case` struct in Java. It selects one of several options, depending on what patterns or conditions exist in the input. Each condition and its associated output template are supplied by the child elements `xsl:when` and `xsl:otherwise`. The `xsl:when` element contains a `test` attribute to determine if the various conditions are true. When the test finds one that is true, the output template associated with it is instantiated. If none are true, the contents of the `xsl:otherwise` child elements are instantiated. If there is no `xsl:otherwise` element, it outputs the template of our `xsl:default` element. For example, if we were using the amended version of our `javaglossarytable` document that included `entry` elements with `kind` attributes, the following rule would change the color of our output, depending on the value of the `kind` attribute:

```
<xsl:template match="entry">
  <xsl:choose>
    <xsl:when test="@kind='data'">
      <P style="color:red">
        <xsl:value-of select="."/>
      </P>
    </xsl:when>
    <xsl:when test="@kind='collection'">
      <P style="color:orange">
        <xsl:value-of select="."/>
      </P>
    </xsl:when>
    <xsl:when test="@kind='standard'">
      <P style="color:green">
        <xsl:value-of select="."/>
      </P>
    </xsl:when>
    <xsl:otherwise>
      <P style="color:blue">
        <xsl:value-of select="."/>
      </P>
    </xsl:otherwise>
  </xsl:choose>
</xsl:template>
```

Sorting Our Data

There are a number of approaches we can take to sorting our output elements into a different order. The easiest approach, in the case of our Java Glossary table example, is simply to add an `order-by` attribute to the `for-each` element, making sure we specify which element we want our output ordered by:

```
<xsl:for-each select="javaglossarytable/entry" order-by="definition">
```

This has the effect of rearranging our glossary terms slightly when we open the `javaglossarytable.xml` file in our browser:

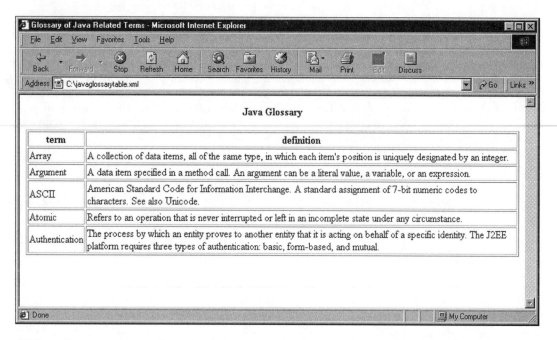

Without the `order-by` attribute, the glossary items were presented in the table in the alphabetical order of the `terms`, because they are encountered first. But by specifying that we want the output ordered by `definition`, the items are presented in the alphabetical order of their definitions.

Using the xsl:variable Element

The `xsl:variable` element allows us, among other things, to avoid cluttering up our documents with boilerplate text. Boilerplate text refers to blocks of text such as copyright notices and disclaimer statements that are required to appear in many documents and files. We convert these blocks of text into named constants by giving them a simple name and a reference. The `xsl:variable` element has only one attribute, `name`, which specifies the name by which we can refer to the variable. The content of the `xsl:variable` element is the replacement, or boilerplate, text. It can be anything from the text of an entire book or chapter, to a single word or line of text, such as in the following example, which defines a variable with the name "free2use" and the value "This application is Public Domain, and may be freely used, copied and distributed."

```
<xsl:variable name="free2use">
   This application is Public Domain, and may be freely used, copied and
distributed.
</xsl:variable>
```

We access the value of this variable by prefixing a dollar sign to the name: "$free2use". We can use `xsl:value-of` to insert our variable's replacement text into the output document as boilerplate text:

```
<xsl:value-of select="$free2use"/>
```

Contents of an `xsl:variable` element are not limited to text. An element can also contain markup such as other XSL instructions to define its value: This markup may even refer to the value of other variables that we have defined. In the following example:

```
<xsl:variable name="pubdomainpoet">
  <xsl:value-of select="$free2use"/>: Shakespeare
</xsl:variable>
```

The text output would be " This application is Public Domain, and may be freely used, copied and distributed.: Shakespeare".

If an `xsl:variable` element is a top-level child of the `xsl:stylesheet` root element, it will be a global variable that can be accessed anywhere in the stylesheet. But if it is declared inside a template rule, it will be a local variable that can be accessed only by sibling elements that follow it, and by their descendants.

Using Multiple StyleSheets

If an XML document is large, it could possibly use many different markup vocabularies, and many different style rules. When all those vocabularies and rules begin to get a little complicated, it's time for us to think about breaking things down into several different stylesheets. In some cases we can use a different standard stylesheet for each different vocabulary. We can then merge those multiple stylesheets, so that we can organize and reuse them for different vocabularies and purposes. XSL provides us with two elements that allow us to do this: `xsl:import`, and `xsl:include`.

The `xsl:import` element is pretty self-explanatory. It contains an `href` attribute that provides the URI of a stylesheet to import. We need to list all `xsl:import` elements before any other top level elements in the `xsl:stylesheet` root element. For example, the following `xsl:import` elements import the `newstyle.xsl` and `oldstyle.xsl` stylesheets:

```
<xsl:stylesheet version="1.0" xmlns:xsl="http://www.w3.org/1999/XSL/Transform">
   <xsl:import href="newstyle.xsl"/>
   <xsl:import href="oldstyle.xsl"/>
   <!--whatever other elements we need -->
</xsl:stylesheet>
```

With so many stylesheets, it's reasonable to assume there will be some conflicts between the rules in the stylesheets that we are importing, and in the stylesheet that we are using to import them. Not to worry, XSL has a well-established pecking order in such cases. When such conflicts occur, the rules in the importing stylesheet take precedence. If there are conflicts between rules in two of the imported stylesheets, the precedence goes to the last one imported, which in the example above would be the `oldstyle:xsl` stylesheet.

There is a `xsl:apply-imports` element to use with the rules from the imported stylesheets, in the same way that we use the `xsl:apply-templates` element that we encountered earlier. Other than the fact that it works only with those imported rules, it does exactly the same thing as `xsl:apply-templates`.

The `xsl:include` element works a little differently. Instead of importing a remote document, it copies the contents of another stylesheet into the current stylesheet at the point where the `xsl:include` element occurs. It has an `href` attribute to provide the URI of the stylesheet that we are including. The `xsl:include` element can occur anywhere in the XSL document's top level, as long as it occurs after the last `xsl:import` element.

An `xsl:include` element can occur anywhere at the top level after the last `xsl:import` element. Unlike rules from imported stylesheets, the rules in included stylesheets have the same precedence as the rules in the stylesheet that is including them.

Summary

This primer has made no claim to being exhaustive; it would take an entire book to deal totally with the topic at hand. (That book is *XSLT Programmer's Reference*, published by Wrox Press, ISBN 1-861003-12-9). But we have looked at the reasons for the development of a language such as XSLT. We have also worked our way through a simple example of a glossary table to see how to create XSLT stylesheets, including the defining and applying of templates, the use of looping constructs and the retrieving of data. And we have looked at a number of patterns for matching nodes, as well as the use of conditional statements. And we took a quick peek at XPath, the use of the `xsl:variable` element, and the issue of multiple stylesheets.

As XML continues to evolve and develop over the next few years, so will XSLT, and the support services for both of these languages. Just as it is practically impossible for a primer of this length to deal with every aspect of XSLT, so it will be impossible for most of us to keep up with all the new developments in this field. But it will be exciting to try.

PROFESSIONALJAVAE-COMMERCE

XML and XSL Files for Chapter 7

catalog_1.xml

```
<?xml version="1.0" ?>
<!DOCTYPE Index SYSTEM "http://xml.cXML.org/schemas/cXML/1.1.009/cXML.dtd">

<Index>
  <SupplierID domain="DUNS">12-123-1234</SupplierID>
  <IndexItem>
    <IndexItemAdd>
      <ItemID>
        <SupplierPartID>auto-98765</SupplierPartID>
      </ItemID>
      <ItemDetail>
        <UnitPrice>
          <Money currency="USD">8000</Money>
        </UnitPrice>
        <Description xml:lang="en">Honda Civic del Sol</Description>
        <UnitOfMeasure/>
        <Classification domain="cdc">2dr</Classification>
        <ManufacturerPartID>honda-12345</ManufacturerPartID>
        <ManufacturerName>Honda</ManufacturerName>
      </ItemDetail>
      <IndexItemDetail>
        <LeadTime>7</LeadTime>
        <ExpirationDate>2001-09-01</ExpirationDate>
        <EffectiveDate>2001-01-01</EffectiveDate>
      </IndexItemDetail>
    </IndexItemAdd>
```

```
      <IndexItemAdd>
        <ItemID>
          <SupplierPartID>auto-54321</SupplierPartID>
        </ItemID>
        <ItemDetail>
          <UnitPrice>
            <Money currency="USD">19000</Money>
          </UnitPrice>
          <Description xml:lang="en">Honda Accord</Description>
          <UnitOfMeasure/>
          <Classification domain="cdc">4dr</Classification>
          <ManufacturerPartID>honda-98765</ManufacturerPartID>
          <ManufacturerName>Honda</ManufacturerName>
        </ItemDetail>
        <IndexItemDetail>
          <LeadTime>7</LeadTime>
          <ExpirationDate>2001-09-01</ExpirationDate>
          <EffectiveDate>2001-01-01</EffectiveDate>
        </IndexItemDetail>
      </IndexItemAdd>
    </IndexItem>
</Index>
```

cars_list.xsl

```xml
<?xml version="1.0"?>
<xsl:stylesheet xmlns:xsl="http://www.w3.org/1999/XSL/Transform" version="1.0">

<xsl:output method="html"/>

<xsl:template match="/Index/IndexItem">

<html><body>

<table border="1">
    <tr>
    <th>Supplier Part ID</th>
    <th>Description</th>
    <th>Price</th>
    <th>Manufacturer</th>
  </tr>

  <xsl:for-each select="IndexItemAdd">
  <tr>
    <td>
      <xsl:value-of select="ItemID/SupplierPartID"/>
    </td>
    <td>
      <xsl:value-of select="ItemDetail/Description"/>
    </td>
    <td>
      <xsl:value-of select="ItemDetail/UnitPrice/Money"/> -
      <xsl:value-of select="ItemDetail/UnitPrice/Money/@currency"/>
    </td>
    <td>
```

```
        <xsl:value-of select="ItemDetail/ManufacturerName"/>
      </td>
    </tr>
    </xsl:for-each>

</table>

</body></html>

</xsl:template>
</xsl:stylesheet>
```

web.xml

```
<web-app>
  <display-name>Pro Java eCommerce - Chapter 5</display-name>
  <description>Examples for Chapter 5</description>

  <servlet>
    <servlet-name>CarsCatalogServlet</servlet-name>
    <servlet-class>nature.CarsCatalogServlet</servlet-class>
    <init-param>
      <param-name>dbUrl</param-name>
      <param-value>jdbc:odbc:CarsDSN</param-value>
      <description>JDBC database URL</description>
    </init-param>
    <init-param>
      <param-name>dbDriver</param-name>
      <param-value>sun.jdbc.odbc.JdbcOdbcDriver</param-value>
      <description>JDBC Driver name</description>
    </init-param>
    <init-param>
      <param-name>user</param-name>
      <param-value>test</param-value>
      <description>User ID for database</description>
    </init-param>
    <init-param>
      <param-name>pass</param-name>
      <param-value>test</param-value>
      <description>Password for database</description>
    </init-param>
  </servlet>

  <servlet-mapping>
    <servlet-name>CarsCatalogServlet</servlet-name>
    <url-pattern>/cars_catalog</url-pattern>
  </servlet-mapping>

</web-app>
```

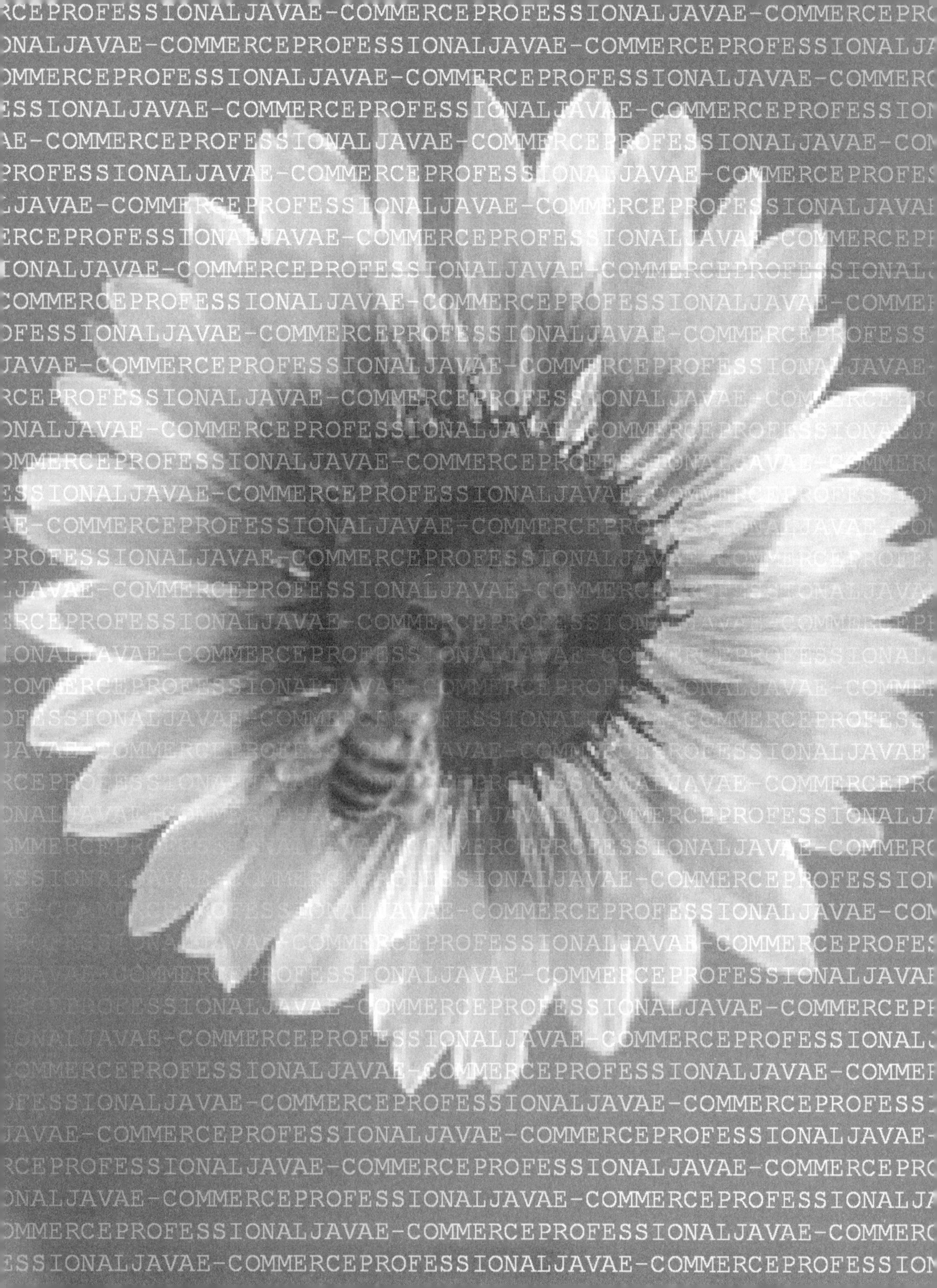
PROFESSIONALJAVAE-COMMERCE

Hexadecimal Conversion Charts

Below is a HEX to ASCII conversion chart for your convenience:

Hex	ASCII	Hex	ASCII	Hex	ASCII	Hex	ASCII
00	NUL	20	SP	40	@	60	'
01	SOH	21	!	41	A	61	a
02	STX	22	"	42	B	62	b
03	ETX	23	#	43	C	63	c
04	EOT	24	$	44	D	64	d
05	ENQ	25	%	45	E	65	e
06	ACK	26	&	46	F	66	f
07	BEL	27	'	47	G	67	g
08	BS	28	(	48	H	68	h
09	HT	29	)	49	I	69	i
0A	LF	2A	*	4A	J	6A	j
0B	VT	2B	+	4B	K	6B	k
0C	FF	2C	,	4C	L	6C	l

Table continued on following page

Hex	ASCII	Hex	ASCII	Hex	ASCII	Hex	ASCII
0D	CR	2D	-	4D	M	6D	m
0E	SO	2E	.	4E	N	6E	n
0F	SI	2F	/	4F	O	6F	o
10	DLE	30	0	50	P	70	p
11	DC1	31	1	51	Q	71	q
12	DC2	32	2	52	R	72	r
13	DC3	33	3	53	S	73	s
14	DC4	34	4	54	T	74	t
15	NAK	35	5	55	U	75	u
16	SYN	36	6	56	V	76	v
17	ETB	37	7	57	W	77	w
18	CAN	38	8	58	X	78	x
19	EM	39	9	59	Y	79	y
1A	SUB	3A	:	5A	Z	7A	z
1B	ESC	3B	;	5B	[	7B	{
1C	FS	3C	<	5C	\	7C		
1D	GS	3D	=	5D	]	7D	}
1E	RS	3E	>	5E	^	7E	~
1F	US	3F	?	5F	_	7F	DEL

Here is a conversion chart from Decimal to Hexadecimal:

Decimal	Hexadecimal	Decimal	Hexadecimal
0	0x00	17	0x11
1	0x01	18	0x12
2	0x02	19	0x13
3	0x03	20	0x14
4	0x04	21	0x15
5	0x05	22	0x16
6	0x06	23	0x17
7	0x07	24	0x18

Decimal	Hexadecimal	Decimal	Hexadecimal
8	0x08	25	0x19
9	0x09	26	0x1a
10	0xa0	27	0x1b
11	0xb0	28	0x1c
12	0xc0	29	0x1d
13	0xd0	30	0x1e
14	0xe0	31	0x1f
15	0xf0	32	0x20
16	0x10		

PROFESSIONALJAVAE-COMMERCE

Extract from the Loebner Competition Transcript

For more information on the Loebner competition please see http://www.loebner.net/Prizef/loebner-prize.html, while information on the Cambridge Center for Behavioral Studies can be found at http://behavior.org/.

Extract from the Loebner Competition Transcript, 1997:

(c)1997 Cambridge Center For Behavioral Studies all rights reserved
Reprinted with the permission of the Cambridge Center for Behavioral Studies

```
[CONVERSE]
[Intelligent Research Ltd.] Start at: [1997/04/29 08:59:40]

PROGRAM[11:28:36]I'm not too great with names, but are you Clay?
JUDGE01[11:28:54]Yes I am. Good of you to remember.
JUDGE01[11:29:01]I need to ask you three questions.
JUDGE01[11:29:10]The first one is, "When were you born?"
PROGRAM[11:29:15]Hi again!
PROGRAM[11:29:20]Clay have you ever been burgled.......?
JUDGE01[11:29:38]Yes, but I can't talk about that now.
JUDGE01[11:29:43]When were you born?
PROGRAM[11:29:45]I was born on Oct 27, 1970. - How long ago was that?
JUDGE01[11:30:04].
JUDGE01[11:30:13]It was 27 years ago.
JUDGE01[11:30:17]Whats your sign?
```

```
PROGRAM[11:30:20]Scorpio.... I imagine that was pretty awful.
JUDGE01[11:30:47]Last question: When you got your first liscence, was it in a
stick or
JUDGE01[11:30:54]an automatic?
PROGRAM[11:30:56]Somebody once told me it's true.. My friend came home from
PROGRAM[11:31:16]work and disturbed a burglar. He had lined up two expensive
PROGRAM[11:31:31]guitars, and computer equipment to take and left them---she
PROGRAM[11:31:42]was real lucky, wouldnt you say?
JUDGE01[11:32:09]When you got your first liscence, was it in a stick or an
automatic?
PROGRAM[11:32:11]No.... Have you had your car broken into or vandalized.
JUDGE01[11:32:37]No, I don't drive. Do you drive?
PROGRAM[11:32:38]OK, yes on balance. - Has real violent crime affected you
PROGRAM[11:32:50]in in another way?
JUDGE01[11:33:06]Oh yes, I have been held up at gunpoint.
PROGRAM[11:33:07]Was anyone charged with it in court?
JUDGE01[11:33:23]Nope.
PROGRAM[11:33:24]So often theres no psycholgically satisfactory conclusion.
PROGRAM[11:33:38]Did you feel violated by all this, or not?
```

Further References

The following are some papers on Natural Language Processing, which may be of interest:

(Batacharia et al., 1999) Batacharia, B., Levy, D., Catizone, R., Krotov, A., Wilks, Y. "CONVERSE - a Companion with Potential" – In Wilks, Y. (ed.) *Machine Conversations*, Kluwer.

(Colby, 1973) Colby, K. "Simulations of Belief Systems" – In Schank and Colby (Eds.) *Computer Models of Thought and Language.* Freeman, San Francisco, CA.

(Collins, 1997) Collins, M. "Three Generative, Lexicalized Models for Statistical Parsing" – In *Proceedings of the 35th Annual Meeting of the ACL*, pages 16-23.

(Charniak, 2000) Charniak, E. "A Maximum-Entropy-Inspired Parser" – In *Proceedings of the 6th ANLP conference and the 1st meeting of NAACL*, pages 132-139, Seattle, WA.

(Marcus et al., 1993) Marcus, M., Santorini, B., Marcinkiewicz, M. A. "Building a large annotated corpus of English: The Penn Treebank" – In *Computational Linguistics*, 19(2), pages 313-330.

(Miller, 1990) Miller, G. A. (Ed.) WordNet: "An On-line Lexical Database" – In *International Journal of Lexicography*.

(Krotov, 2001) Krotov, A. *Parsing with a Compacted Treebank Grammar* – PhD thesis, University of Sheffield, UK, (to be published).

(Sekine, 1998) Sekine, S. *Corpus-Based Parsing and Sublanguage Studies* – PhD thesis, New York University.

(Turing,1950) Turing, A. "Computing Machinery and Intelligence" – In *Mind*, vol. LIX.

PROFESSIONALJAVAE-COMMERCE

Package Diagrams for the B2B XML-to-Object Broker Application

This appendix contains diagrams showing the object models for the com.wrox.broker package used in Chapters 17, 18, and 19, and the ejbeans package developed in Chapter 19.

package com.wrox.broker

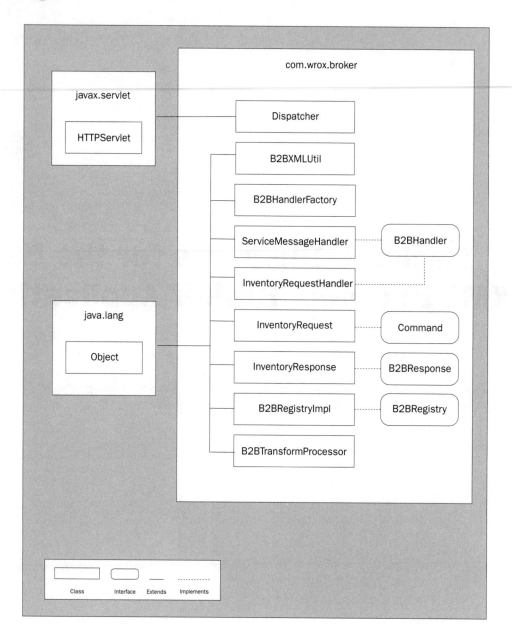

package ejbeans

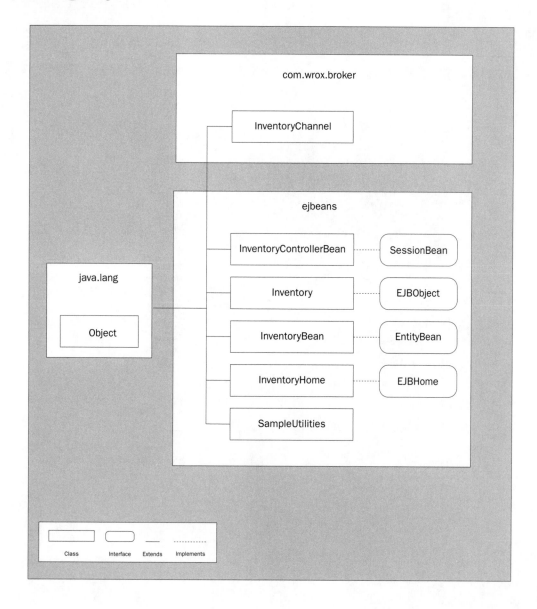

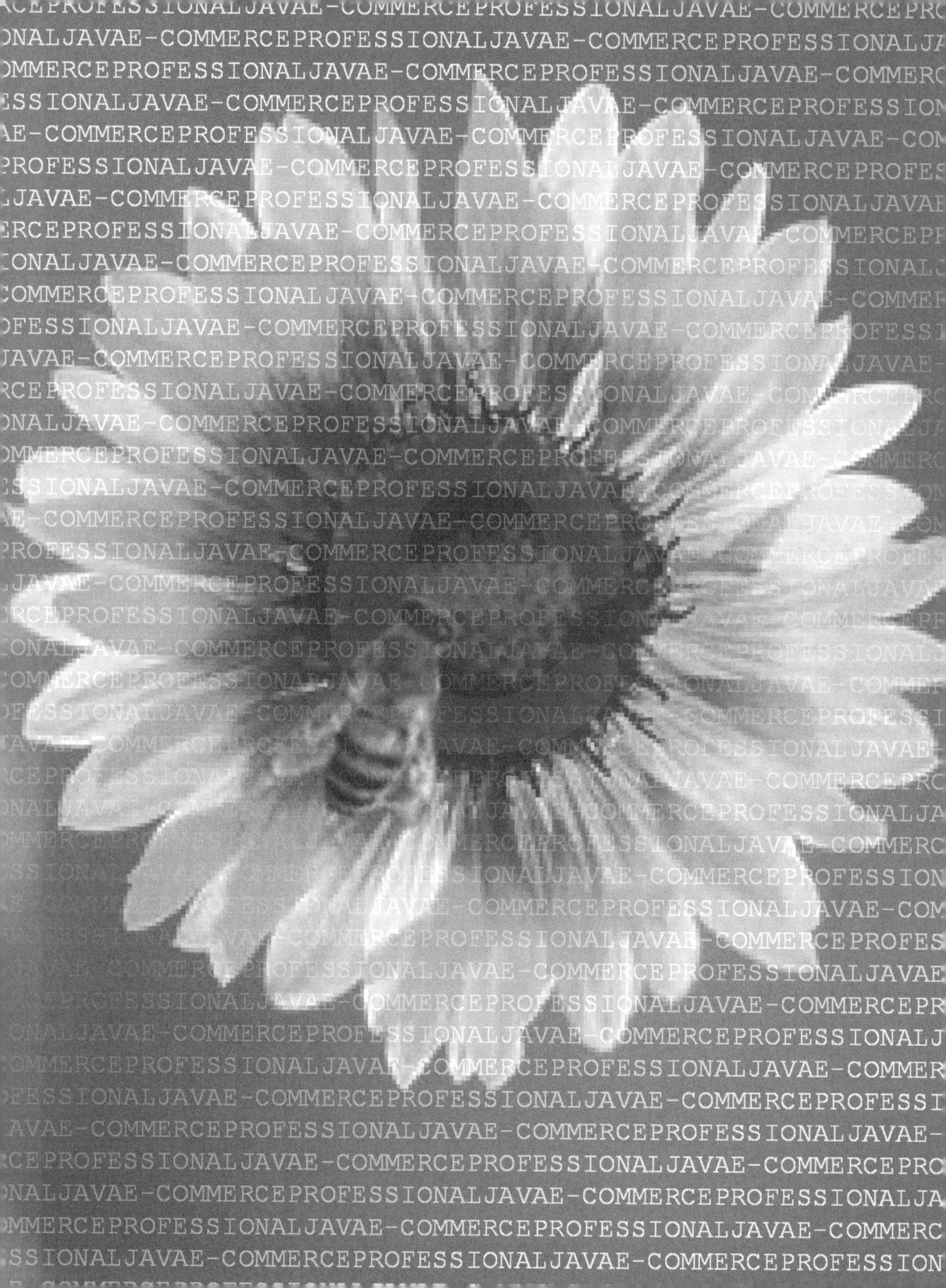
PROFESSIONALJAVAE-COMMERCE

Index

A Guide to the Index

The index is arranged hierarchically, in alphabetical order, with symbols preceding the letter A. Most second-level entries and many third-level entries also occur as first-level entries. This is to ensure that users will find the information they require however they choose to search for it.

P

X

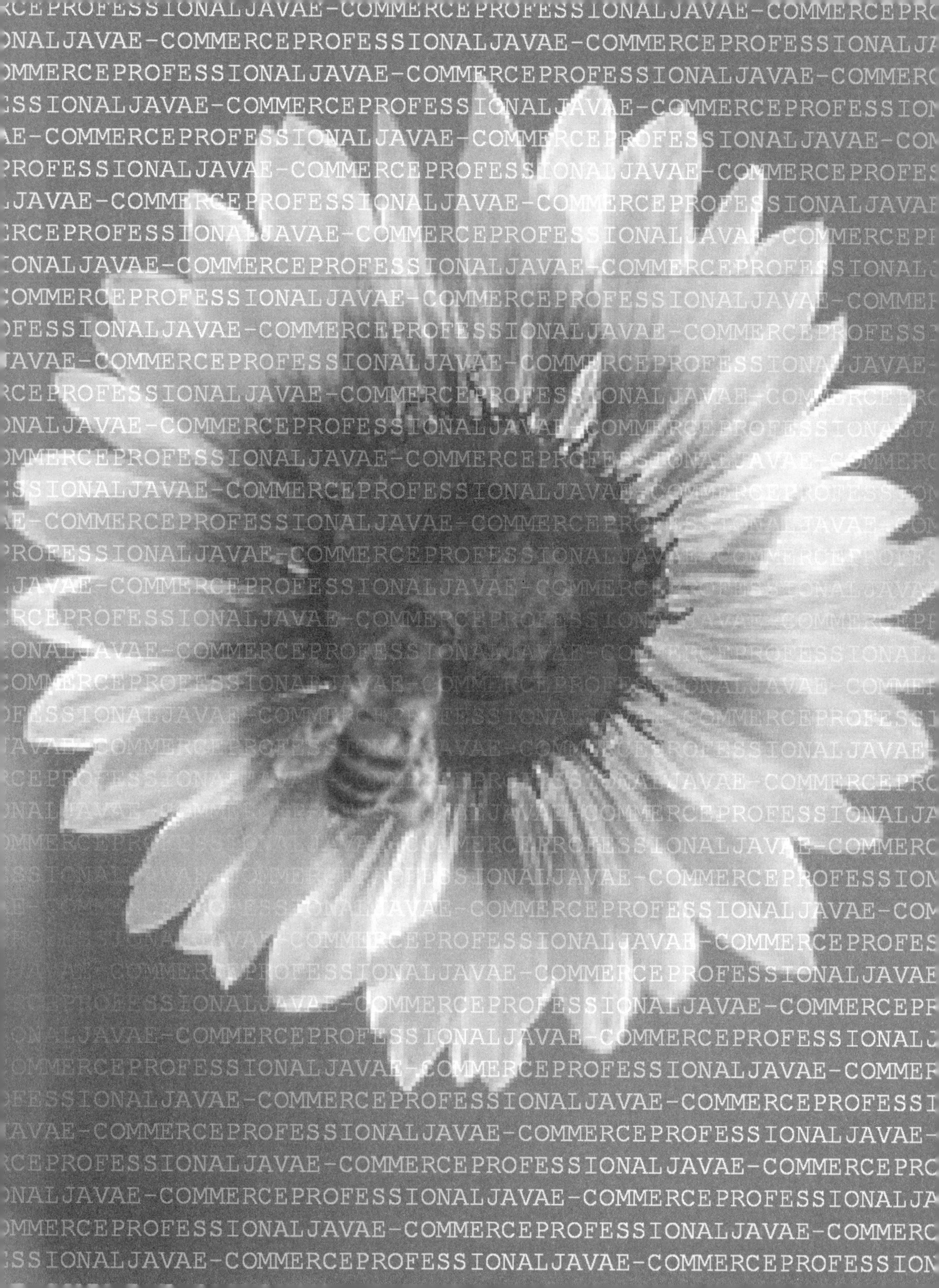
PROFESSIONALJAVAE-COMMERCE

p2p.wrox.com
The programmer's resource centre

A unique free service from Wrox Press
with the aim of helping programmers to help each other

Wrox Press aims to provide timely and practical information to today's programmer. P2P is a list server offering a host of targeted mailing lists where you can share knowledge with your fellow programmers and find solutions to your problems. Whatever the level of your programming knowledge, and whatever technology you use, P2P can provide you with the information you need.

ASP
Support for beginners and professionals, including a resource page with hundreds of links, and a popular ASP+ mailing list.

DATABASES
For database programmers, offering support on SQL Server, mySQL, and Oracle.

MOBILE
Software development for the mobile market is growing rapidly. We provide lists for the several current standards, including WAP, WindowsCE, and Symbian.

JAVA
A complete set of Java lists, covering beginners, professionals, and server-side programmers (including JSP, servlets and EJBs)

.NET
Microsoft's new OS platform, covering topics such as ASP+, C#, and general .Net discussion.

VISUAL BASIC
Covers all aspects of VB programming, from programming Office macros to creating components for the .Net platform.

WEB DESIGN
As web page requirements become more complex, programmer sare taking a more important role in creating web sites. For these programmers, we offer lists covering technologies such as Flash, Coldfusion, and JavaScript.

XML
Covering all aspects of XML, including XSLT and schemas.

OPEN SOURCE
Many Open Source topics covered including PHP, Apache, Perl, Linux, Python and more.

FOREIGN LANGUAGE
Several lists dedicated to Spanish and German speaking programmers, categories include .Net, Java, XML, PHP and XML.

How To Subscribe

Simply visit the P2P site, at **http://p2p.wrox.com/**

Select the 'FAQ' option on the side menu bar for more information about the subscription process and our service.